Magruder's

American Government

Allyn and Bacon, Inc.

Boston   Rockleigh, N. J.   Atlanta   Dallas   Belmont, Calif.

Magruder's

American Government

Revised by

William A. McClenaghan

DEPARTMENT OF POLITICAL SCIENCE
OREGON STATE UNIVERSITY

✤ ✤

AMERICAN GOVERNMENT, first published in 1917, celebrates its fifty-fourth annual revision with the publication of this edition. It is an enduring symbol of the author's faith in American ideals and American institutions. The life of Frank Abbott Magruder (1882–1949) was an outstanding example of Americanism at its very best. His career as a teacher, author, and tireless worker in civic and religious undertakings remains an inspiring memory to all who knew him.

✤ ✤

Graphic material and maps prepared by: Visual Services, Inc.

Library of Congress Catalog Card Number: 17–13472

PREFACE

The first edition of *American Government* was published more than a half-century ago, in 1917. This book, *American Government, 1971,* is the fifty-fourth annual revision of the original text. As were each of its fifty-three predecessors, this edition is based upon the conviction that it is absolutely essential that *all* Americans know and understand the nature of the American system of government. Throughout its pages it emphasizes the supreme and fundamental characteristic of that system: the fact that government at *every* level in the United States is government *of* the people, *by* the people, and *for* the people. It treats the origins, development, principles, organization, powers, functions, and actual workings of American government as matters so closely related to one another that they must be studied as an integrated whole rather than as separate and unrelated subjects.

American Government, 1971, is a carefully and thoroughly revised successor to previous editions. Much new material has been included, because government in the United States is far from static — it is dynamic and continually changing and developing. While its basic principles and the core of its organization and powers remain constant from decade to decade, many of its other aspects change from year to year and even from day to day.

All of the changes incorporated in this edition reflect the dynamic character of our governmental system. Some of the more important of them may

be cited here to illustrate the point: President Nixon's difficulties in filling of a Supreme Court vacancy in 1969 and 1970, and Harry Blackmun's final appointment to the High Court is treated. Information on the anticipated gains and losses in the apportionment of House seats on the basis of the 1970 Census, as well as updated maps, charts, and graphs reflecting results of the 1970 gubernatorial and Congressional elections are also included. New, expanded material is presented on immigration and the quota system, detailing how visas are allocated on a "first-qualified, first-served" basis. The significance of minor political parties and their role as critic and innovator on the political scene is discussed in expanded terms. Such other matters as the creation in 1970 of the long-sought post in the House of District Delegate for the District of Columbia and the creation of the United States Postal Service by Congress under the Postal Reorganization Act of 1970 are accounted for. A highly significant Supreme Court decision, further defining the "one-man, one vote" decision in the *Kirkpatrick* v. *Preisler* case is discussed. The Senate filibuster in 1970, killing the measure to provide for direct popular vote in Presidential elections, is dealt with. Changes in judicial administration are discussed, as is the new post of United States Magistrate, which replaces that of United States Commissioners. The 1970 federal budget, the new ceiling on the public debt and the borrowing power, higher interest rates on Treasury bonds and Savings Bonds (Type E) are discussed in revised terms. Other matters as new salary arrangements and recent changes in voting requirements and other aspects of state election law are also treated. A vast amount of other material has been added to the book and some additional reorganizations have been made — all too numerous to cite here. The wealth of statistical data included is the latest available and has been drawn from primary sources wherever possible. All recent developments at the local, national, and international levels with an important bearing on the governmental system have been interwoven into the body of the text. Several "last-minute" matters have been noted in a three-page section, Stop the Presses, at the end of the text.

American Government, 1971, offers a strong selection of graphic and tabular material — including a four-color, two-page, political and physical map of the United States; full-page spreads of graphic art to complement the discussions on the National Economy, Foreign Affairs, Voting Behavior, Education, Health, Welfare, and Housing; plus numerous maps, graphs, charts, diagrams, and tables to illustrate trends, concepts, principles, and facts.

Newly added to this edition of *American Government* are preview inquiry questions at the opening of each chapter and case studies. The preview inquiry questions are "open-ended" and are intended to motivate the student to seek out in the chapters information needed to apply to the query posed. Each of the "case studies" raises a problem or presents conflicting points of view related to government, and the associated questions provoke students to discuss the issues raised.

The end-of-chapter matter has been reset in a new format. The problems, projects, and suggested readings are designed to stimulate student participation in order to make the course in American government as challenging and stimulating as possible. The suggested readings, pointed toward recently published materials and composed very largely of citations to readily-available periodicals, are in-depth studies to complement the chapter; additional bibliographical material is included in the *Teacher's Manual.* The review questions for each chapter and the supplementary materials — *Our Government at Work* and *Tests for American Government* — are also designed to broaden both the text and the course.

Both the original author, the late Frank Abbott Magruder, and the present author have sought to make each new edition of *American Government* as accurate, objective, and up-to-date as possible. Over the years we have received much valuable help in that effort from the many teachers and students actually using the book in classrooms across the nation. A special word of thanks is gratefully given to all those teachers throughout the country who have generously contributed their suggestions and ideas for the fifty-fourth annual revision.

This edition, like each of its predecessors, is intended for use as a basic tool in the learning process — but it is *not* presented as the last and ultimate word on its subject. Rather, it is offered as a point of departure for the study of American government. Some criticize textbooks because, they claim, they are "too large" and "too factual," and they sometimes argue that textbooks should be "more interpretive." *This* textbook includes that material which, in the author's judgment, is necessary to a basic knowledge of the American governmental system. If it is a "large" one, it is because its subject is a large and an important one.

As you use this book, remember that today our nation faces the gravest threat we have ever known. Our aims and ideals and the very existence of our system of government are challenged by the tyranny and totalitarian ideology of international communism, irrevocably dedicated to the destruction of all that we cherish. It is more vital now than ever before that all Americans possess a thorough knowledge and understanding of the American governmental system — and, too, that all Americans work to help in making that system work as effectively as it can.

WILLIAM A. McCLENAGHAN

CONTENTS

Part One

FOUNDATIONS AND PRINCIPLES OF AMERICAN GOVERNMENT   1

Part Two
NATIONAL GOVERNMENT 198

Part Three

STATE AND LOCAL GOVERNMENTS 600

CASE STUDIES

125°

· Seattle
Olympia · WASHINGTON
Spokane ·

CANADA

INTERNATIONAL PEACE PARK

GLACIER NATL PARK

CEDED BY GREAT BRITAIN – 1818

45°

Grand Coulee Dam

Mt. Rainier 14,410

CONTINENTAL

Missouri River

NORTH DAKOTA

Bismarck ⊛

Portland · Mt. Hood 11,245
Salem ·

Lewiston ·

MONTANA

Helena ·

Yellowstone River

Billings ·

SOUTH DAKOTA

Pierre
Columbia River

CASCADE RANGES

OREGON

IDAHO

Boise ⊛

PLATEAU

ROCKY

Grand Teton 13,766

DIVIDE

YELLOWSTONE NATL PARK

Bighorn River

BLACK HILLS

Little Missouri River

LOUISIANA PURCHASE – 1803

OREGON TREATY 1846

Snake River

MTS.

WYOMING

UINTA MTS.

North Platte River

Cheyenne ⊛

NEBRASKA

COAST RANGES

Reno ·

Carson City ·

NEVADA

GREAT

Great Salt Lake

Salt Lake City ⊛

Ely ·

UTAH

Green River

COLORADO

Denver ·

Platte River

San Francisco

Sacramento ⊛

Oakland

San Jose ·

BASIN

MEXICAN CESSION – 1848

ROCKY

P L A

KANSAS

Salina ·

Monterey ·

SIERRA NEVADA

CENTRAL VALLEY

Mt. Whitney 14,495

DEATH VALLEY –282

CALIFORNIA

Lake Mead

ZION NATL PARK

Colorado River

COLORADO

PLATEAU

MTS.

CONTINENTAL DIVIDE

Arkansas River

Dodge City ·

Wichita ·

35°

PACIFIC

Santa Barbara ·

LOS ANGELES ·

Hoover Dam

GRAND CANYON NATL PARK

Santa Fe ⊛

Albuquerque ·

OK

Oklahoma City ·

San Diego ·

ARIZONA

Phoenix ⊛

Colorado River

Gila River

GADSDEN PURCHASE – 1853

Tucson ·

NEW MEXICO

Rio Grande

Pecos River

TEXAS ANNEXATION – 1845

Fort Worth

Red River

120°

OCEAN

30°

El Paso ·

MEXICO

TEXAS

EDWARDS PLATEAU

Austin ·

San Antonio ·

Rio Grande

0   300   600
Scale 600 miles to one inch

POINT BARROW · Barrow
70°

BROOKS RANGE

ARCTIC CIRCLE

Fort Yukon

Nome ·

Tanana ·
Tanana River
Yukon River

ALASKA

Mt. McKinley 20,320

ALASKA RA.

CANADA

Bering Sea

Anchorage ·

Seward ·

Juneau ⊛

ALEUTIAN ISLANDS

60°

ALASKA PURCHASE – 1867

160°   150°   140°   130°

0   100   200
Scale 200 miles to one inch

NIIHAU

KAUAI

HAWAII

OAHU

Pearl Harbor ⊛

Honolulu ·

MOLOKAI

MAUI

LANAI

KAHOOLAWE

Mauna Kea 13,796

20°

HAWAII ANNEXATION – 1898

HAWAII

· Hilo

160°   155°

THE UNITED STATES

0   100   200

Scale 200 miles to one inch

Lambert Conformal Conic Projection

THE AMERICAN'S CREED

I believe in the United States of America as a government
of the people, by the people, for the people,
whose just powers are derived
from the consent of the governed;
a democracy in a republic,
a sovereign Nation of many sovereign States;
a perfect union, one and inseparable,
established upon those principles of
freedom, equality, justice, and humanity
for which American patriots
sacrificed their lives and fortunes.

I therefore believe it is my duty to my country
to love it, to support its Constitution,
to obey its laws, to respect its flag,
and to defend it against all enemies.

William Tyler Page

Part One

FOUNDATIONS AND PRINCIPLES OF AMERICAN GOVERNMENT

This is a book about government. More particularly, of course, it is a book about government in the United States. Over the course of its pages, we shall consider the ways in which the American governmental system is organized, the ways in which it is controlled by the people, and the ways in which it functions.

You will soon see that the American governmental system is almost certainly the most complicated of the more than 130 such systems which now exist in the world. You will soon see, too, that our governmental system is a democratic one – one in which government may be conducted *only* on the basis of the consent of the governed. And you will see, as well, that in this country government is an all-pervading social force; there is literally *no* moment in our daily lives when government does not play a meaningful part in our existence.

Before we become involved in the details of our subject, however, a few preliminary words are in order.

The American Heritage. Our governmental system rests upon two mighty pillars: the Declaration of Independence and the Constitution of the United States of America. This nation was born with the bold words of the Declaration. Its very heart is in these hallowed lines:

> *We hold these truths to be self-evident: that all men are created equal; that they are endowed by their Creator with certain unalienable Rights; that among these are Life, Liberty, and the pursuit of Happiness.*

The Union was created by the lofty phrases of the Constitution. Its very first words are among the most important in all of the document:

> *We, the People of the United States, in order to form a more perfect union, establish justice, insure domestic tranquillity, provide for the common defence, promote the general welfare, and secure the blessings of liberty to ourselves and our posterity, do ordain and establish this Constitution for the United States of America.*

These two passages are brief, yes; and their words are simple. Yet, they are of deep and lasting significance. In them is to be found the fundamental expression of the American heritage—a deep and abiding faith in individualism, in freedom, and in equality.

It is this faith that has made us the greatest of nations the world has ever known. Look about you: the things that show our greatness can be seen on every hand. There are huge cities, bustling towns, fertile farms, thriving stores, and busy factories. Our roads and highways teem with traffic; railroads and airlines span the continent. There are millions of telephones, radios, and television sets, clothes dryers, dishwashers, and other conveniences. We have harnessed mighty rivers, split the atom, and are probing outer space. The list is well-nigh endless.

But these things are only the *material* evidence of our greatness. They may *show* that we are a great nation; but in themselves they do not *make* us great. We are a great nation and a mighty people because we were born with and we strive to live by the faith that is our American heritage.

Will America remain a great nation? Will it continue to become, as it has throughout its history, an even greater one? It will if *you* believe in and live by our heritage. The future of the nation rests with you. That future is secure if *you* and *all* of your generation dedicate yourselves to the high purpose of carrying that great heritage forward.

You will find that many things are indispensable as you prepare yourself to meet that high purpose—and, certainly, not the least of them is the thing that this book hopes to further: a knowledge and understanding of the nature and workings of the American system of government.

The Basic Tasks of Government. The nature of our governmental system can be better understood if we look at the basic tasks it performs. They are—as they have been from our beginnings—the great purposes set forth in the Preamble to the Constitution: to "form a more perfect union," "insure domestic tranquillity," "provide for the common defense," "promote the general welfare," and "secure the blessings of liberty."

A More Perfect Union. We are a highly heterogeneous and, at the same time, a homogeneous people. We are compounded of many stocks — English, Irish, Spanish, French, German, Italian, Polish, Jewish, Scandinavian, Indian, Black, Oriental, and many others. The more than 45,000,000 immigrants who followed in the wake of our earliest settlers came from widely varied places and backgrounds. They brought with them many different languages, customs, and religious, political, economic, and social ideas. America has, indeed, been the "melting pot" of the world.

Out of the many, we have forged one mighty and united people. Regardless of ancestry, place of birth, religious and political views, and other differences among us, we share the same basic ideals, a common language, similar customs, and a single nationality. We are all Americans.

We have shown the rest of the world that independent states can unite through peaceful agreement. Our struggle for an ever-closer Union has not always been an easy one. Occasionally, political strife and sometimes physical violence have marred our progress. Yet, these growing pains have not kept us from rising to the pinnacle we occupy today.

Establish Justice. We have said that the American heritage is a faith in individualism, in freedom, and in equality. It is a belief in the fundamental worth and dignity of each and every human being. The men who framed the Constitution recognized that an ordered system of justice is essential to the maintenance of this belief. They agreed with Thomas Jefferson that the establishing and maintaining of justice is "the most sacred of the duties of government."

Insure Domestic Tranquillity. Order is essential to the well-being of any society, and keeping the peace at home has always been one of the major functions of government. In fact, it is quite likely the oldest of all governmental functions.

Government maintains order in several different ways. Essentially, however, it does so through the making of rules (laws) for the regulation of human behavior and by providing the machinery through which those rules can be enforced. Thus government makes it possible for disputes between or among its citizens to be settled by peaceful means, without resort to violence.

Provide for the Common Defense. Just as government must keep the peace at home it must also defend the homeland and its people against foreign attack. Today, the task of providing for the common defense is the most demanding and costly of the functions of the National Government. Two World Wars, the Korean War, the continuing Cold War, the hot war in Viet Nam, and the constant threat of World War III all have emphasized its importance.

As a people, we hate and deplore war. We know that wars and national defense are extremely costly in terms of dollars and natural resources — and terribly and incalculably more so in terms of human lives. But we also know that, in a world as unsettled as this one, we must be prepared for any eventuality. We hope, pray, and work for peace — but we keep our powder dry.

Promote the General Welfare. Over the centuries, government—especially in democratic countries such as the United States—has become the *servant* as well as the protector of the people. Few Americans fully realize the many and varied ways in which government in this country—at all levels, National, State, and local—provides us with services we could hardly live without. From the very instant he is born (usually in a government-regulated hospital under the care of a government-licensed doctor) until he dies and is buried (after proper legal certification of his death and in a government-regulated cemetery), each American citizen is in constant contact, and in myriad ways, with the agencies and services of government—that is, with government serving the people to "promote the general welfare."

Secure the Blessings of Liberty. One need not look far—into history nor in the contemporary world—to discover that government can be and often has been the mortal enemy of human freedom. For us, however, this has not been so. The United States was founded by men who loved liberty and prized it above all earthly possessions. For it they pledged their lives, their fortune, and their sacred honor. They declared "life, liberty, and the pursuit of happiness" to be the inalienable rights of all men. They *also* declared "that to *secure* these rights *governments* are instituted among men." For us, then, one of government's prime tasks today is, as it has always been, that of protecting and promoting freedom for the individual—that of securing "the blessings of liberty" to each and to all Americans.

At the beginning of this introductory comment we noted that in this book we shall consider the ways in which our governmental system is organized, the ways in which it is controlled, and the ways in which it functions. We shall, in fact, be concerned with those matters throughout *all* of the book. In this first part of it, however—over its first ten chapters—we shall be concerned with them in a basic sense. That is, we shall consider what may be called the foundations of the American system of government. We shall look at its origins and development, the fundamental principles upon which it is laid, and the primary means by which it is limited and made to do the bidding of the people. In Part Two we shall turn more specifically to the organization and functions of the National Government, and in Part Three to the governmental structure and operations of the fifty States and their local governments.

He who considers things in their first growth, whether a state or anything else, will obtain the clearest view of them.

ARISTOTLE

❖❖❖Was John Adams correct when he observed: "If men were angels no government would be necessary"? Explain.

❖❖❖Why do people regularly accept the authority and abide by the decisions of government? Should government always be obeyed?

❖❖❖Is the will of the majority always obeyed in a democracy? Should it be?

"We, the People of the United States . . ." With these words the Constitution of the United States begins, and no other words in all of that momentous document are more important. For here, in this short phrase, is to be found the very essence of the American system of government.

As Americans, we take great and justifiable pride in that system. We are proud of the fact that it is a system of self-government under law. We are proud of the fact that it is a system in which "We, the People" are all-powerful and in which government exists *only* to do our bidding.

We are proud, too, that our system of government is, and has been for generations, the envy of other peoples the world over. While other nations have experimented with governments not unlike our own, none of them has lasted for so long a time nor been developed on such a scale.

As we take pride, however, it seems wise to recall that we have learned from and we owe much to some of those other systems. Our debt to ancient Athens and to not-so-ancient England is especially large. And it seems wise to recall another fact: systems of self-government have been exceedingly rare in the history of man. Ours, now nearly 200 years old, has existed for a longer time than any other. Authoritarian systems, on the other hand — whether known as despotisms or tyrannies or, more recently, as dictatorships — have been much more numerous and far more durable.

Viewed against this backdrop, and against the backdrop of the conflict-ridden world of today, it also seems quite wise to begin a study of the American system of government with a brief examination of the governmental systems to be found in the world today. We live in a world in which much of what exists and many of the things that occur in even the most remote corners of the globe have an immediate and a vital effect upon our daily lives and even upon the very future of our existence as a nation.

GOVERNMENTS IN THE WORLD TODAY

When, more than 2300 years ago, Aristotle observed that "man is by nature a political animal," he was recording a fact which has been apparent for many thousands of years. At some point, lost in the ages of antiquity, man realized that he could not live with his fellow men without some form of government. That is, he realized that he could not live without some kind of organization vested with authority over himself and his neighbors.

The State. Over the long course of man's political evolution, the *state* has become the dominant political unit in the world. It may be defined as a body of people, occupying a defined territory and organized politically with the power to make and enforce law without the consent of any higher authority.

There are more than 130 states in the world today.[1] They vary greatly in terms of size and importance, but each possesses the four characteristics in the preceding definition: population, territory, sovereignty, and government.

Population. Obviously there must be people. The size of the population is not essential to the existence of a state, however. The smallest, in terms of population, is San Marino. Nestled in the Apennines and bounded on all sides by Italy, it contains only some 18,000 people. Communist China's population is the largest, some 730,000,000 — so many that, if they were all to line up in single file, they could encircle the globe nearly ten times.

Territory. Just as there must be people, there must also be territory with definite and known boundaries. In terms of territory, as well as population, San Marino is the smallest state in the world, with an area of only some 23 square miles. The largest, the Soviet Union, contains some 8,650,000 square miles and covers approximately one-sixth of all of the land surface of the earth. The total area of the United States is 3,615,211 square miles.

Sovereignty. Every state is sovereign. That is, every state has supreme and absolute power to chart its own courses of action, both foreign and domestic. It is not responsible to any higher authority. Hence, as a sovereign state, the United States is free to determine its own form of government, its economic system, its foreign policy, and all other matters for itself.[2]

The *location* of sovereignty within a state — that is, who holds and exercises the sovereign power — is of immense importance. Its location determines whether the government of the state is democratic or dictatorial in form. If the people are sovereign, then the governmental system is a democratic one. If, on the other hand, one person or a small group holds the power, a dictatorship exists.

Government. Every state is politically organized. That is, every state has a *government*. Although sovereignty is the distinctive characteristic of a state, the nature of its government is also a matter of paramount importance.

Origin of the State. For centuries historians, political scientists, philosophers, and others have pondered the question of the origin

---

[1] The Vatican is not cited here primarily because the United States does not recognize its existence as a sovereign state; it is recognized by fifty-six other states, however. Vatican City has a population of about 900 and is a roughly triangular area of approximately 109 acres wholly surrounded by Rome. Nor is the Principality of Monaco cited; its several legal ties to France deny it the status of sovereignty. Monaco, bounded on three sides by France and by the Mediterranean Sea on the south, contains 370 acres and a population of about 23,000.

[2] The States within the United States are not sovereign and thus not states in the international legal sense. A superior force, the Constitution of the United States, stands above them. Neither do the various dependent areas of the world (*e.g.,* Puerto Rico and Hong Kong) qualify as states.

of the state. How did it arise? What factor or set of circumstances first brought it into being? Although many theories have been advanced, there is no general agreement among authorities, nor is there sufficient historical evidence in support of any one of them.

The Force Theory. Many scholars have long argued that the state was born of force. They hold that it developed because one man — or perhaps a small group of men — claimed control over an area and forced all within it to submit to his — or their — rule. When that rule was established, they argue, all of the basic elements of the state — population, territory, sovereignty, and government — were present.

The Evolutionary Theory. Others claim that the state developed naturally and gradually out of the early family. They maintain that the primitive family, of which the father was the head and thus the "government," was the first stage in man's political development. Over countless years the original family became a network of closely related families; that is, it became a clan. Eventually the clan became a tribe. When the tribe first turned to settled agriculture — when it abandoned its nomadic ways and first tied itself to the land — the state was born.

The Divine Right Theory. Some theorists have argued that the state arose as the result of the "divine right of kings." According to this view, God granted to those of royal birth the right to rule other men. Of course, the theory seems to most of us today to be a patently ridiculous one. But it was widely accepted in the seventeenth and eighteenth centuries; and much of the thought upon which present-day democratic government was built was first developed as an argument against the theory.

The Social Contract Theory. In terms of our political system, the most significant of the various theories concerning the origin of the state is that of the social contract. It was developed in the seventeenth and eighteenth centuries by such philosophers as John Locke, John Harrington, and Thomas Hobbes in England and Jean Jacques Rousseau in France.

The theory holds that in his earliest history man lived in unbridled freedom, in a "state of nature." No government existed; no man was subject to any power superior to that of his own will. Each man could do as he pleased and in whatever manner he chose, at least to the extent that he was physically capable of so doing. That which he could take by force was his, and for as long as he could hold it. But all men were similarly free. Thus, each man was only as secure as his own physical prowess and watchfulness could make him. His life in the state of nature, wrote Hobbes, was "nasty, brutish, and short."

Men overcame their unpleasant condition, says the theory, by agreeing with one another to create a state. By contract, men within a given area joined together, each surrendering to the state as much power to control his own behavior as was necessary to promote the safety and well-being of all. And again, by contract (through a constitution), the members of the state created a government to exercise the powers they had granted to the state.

In short, the social contract theory argues that the state arose as the result of a voluntary act of free men. It holds that the state exists only to serve the will of the people, that the people are the sole source of political power, and that the people are free to grant or withhold that power as they choose. Although the theory seems to many of us far-fetched today, the great concepts it fostered — popular sovereignty, limited government, and individual rights — were, as we shall see, immensely important to the shaping of our own governmental system.[3]

---

[3] The Declaration of Independence (see pages 748–750) laid its justification for revolution on the social contract theory, arguing that the British Government had violated the contract. Indeed, its principal author, Thomas Jefferson, described the document as "pure Locke."

Definition of Government. Government is the institution through which public policy is made and the affairs of the state are conducted. To put the definition another way, government is the agency through which the state exerts its will and accomplishes its ends. It consists of the machinery and the personnel by which the state is ruled (governed). In effect, government may be likened to the engine which makes the machine (the state) move.

Forms of Government. No two governments are exactly alike, and there are vast differences among many of them. Obviously this must be so since governments are the products of human needs and human experiences and are shaped by many other factors, including: geography, climate, history, customs, resources, and the capacities of the people. But each governmental system may be *classified* in terms of one or more of its basic features. Political scientists have developed numerous classifications, and three of them are especially useful here—those made according to: (1) the geographic distribution of governmental powers, (2) the relationship of the executive to the legislative branch, and (3) the number of individuals who may participate in the governing process.

Geographic Distribution. In every government the power to rule is located in one or more places, geographically. Viewing governments from this standpoint, three basic forms may be identified: *unitary, federal,* and *confederate.*

Unitary. A unitary government is one in which all of the powers which government possesses are concentrated in the hands of a single central agency. Although local governmental units do exist in the typical unitary system, they do so only as administrative creatures of the central government. They are created by and for the convenience of the central government and derive such powers as they have from the central government.

The governments of most states in the world today are unitary in form. Great Britain affords an outstanding example: all of the power that British government possesses is held by one central organ, Parliament. Local governments exist to relieve Parliament of a burden it could perform only with extreme difficulty and inconvenience. If Parliament so desired, it could actually abolish all agencies of local government in Great Britain.

Be careful *not* to confuse a unitary government with a dictatorship. In the unitary form *all of the powers government possesses* are concentrated in the central government. But government might *not* possess *all* power. In Great Britain, for example, the powers of government are strictly limited.

Federal. A federal government is one in which the powers of government are divided between a central and several local governments. This *division of power* is made, on a geographic basis, by a power superior to both levels of government, and cannot be changed by either acting alone.

In the United States, for example, certain powers are possessed by the National Government and others by the States. The sovereign people have made this division of powers through the Constitution of the United States —which stands above both levels of government and which cannot be altered unless the people, acting through both the National Government and the States, approve such a change. Australia, Canada, Mexico, New Zealand, and Switzerland are a few of the other states which utilize the federal form. (Note that the government of each of the fifty States in the American Union is unitary, not federal, in form.)

Confederate. A confederation is an alliance of independent states with a central organ (the confederate government) possessing the power to handle only those matters of common concern which the member states have delegated to it. Typically, confederate governments have possessed limited powers in such fields as defense and foreign commerce. There are no confederations in the world today. But, in our own history, the United States

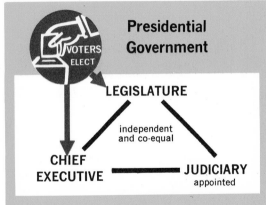

Most governments in the world today are parliamentary in form. Note that the chief executive is subordinate to, rather than co-equal with, the legislature in that form.

under the Articles of Confederation (1781–1789) and the Confederate States (1861–1865) afford examples of the form.

Legislative-Executive Relationship. Governments may also be classified on the basis of the relationship that exists between its legislative (law-making) and executive (law-administering) branches.

Presidential. The presidential form of government is characterized by a chief executive (president) chosen by the voters for a fixed term of office. Hence, the executive is independent of the legislature; the legislature does not select him and cannot remove him, except perhaps by a difficult and cumbersome process such as impeachment. Usually, as in the United States and each of the fifty States, a written constitution provides for a *separation of powers* among the executive, legislative, and judicial (law-interpreting) branches. Although each branch is given its own distinct powers, all three are co-equal and must work together to provide effective government.

Parliamentary. Under the parliamentary form of government the executive is composed of the prime minister (or premier) and his cabinet, and they are themselves members of the legislative branch (parliament). The prime minister is the leader of the majority party in

parliament and is chosen to his office by that body. With its approval, he selects the members of his cabinet from among the members of parliament. The executive is thus chosen by the legislative branch and is subject to its direct control.

The prime minister and his cabinet — usually referred to as "the government" — remain in office only as long as their policies and administration retain the confidence and support of a majority in parliament. If they are defeated on an important matter (if they do not receive a "vote of confidence"), they must resign from office. Then a new "government" must be formed. Either parliament chooses a new prime minister or, as often happens, a general election is held in which all of the seats in parliament go before the voters. The British, most European, and a majority of all other governments in the world today are parliamentary in form.

Number Who May Participate. What is probably the most meaningful of classifications of government is that based upon the number of individuals who may participate in the governmental process. Formal legal institutions are important to the mechanical operations of government, but the degree of popular participation is the vital heart of the

The prime example of modern dictators was Adolf Hitler, who led Nazi Germany (1933–1945) into World War II and to her downfall. (Prudential Insurance Co.)

matter. Here we consider *dictatorship* and *democracy*.

Dictatorship. Where the power to govern is exercised by one person or by a small group, a dictatorship exists. It is probably the oldest form of government known to man.

All dictatorships are *authoritarian* in character. That is, they are governmental systems in which the ruling power is not limited but is supreme and unchallengeable. Modern dictatorships have tended to be *totalitarian* in character, as well. That is, they exercise dictatorial (authoritarian) power with regard to virtually every aspect of man's affairs; their power embraces all (the *totality* of) matters of human concern.

The prime examples of dictatorship in the twentieth century are those which existed in Nazi Germany (1933–1945) and in Fascist Italy (1922–1943) and those which continue to flourish in the Soviet Union (since 1917) and Communist China (since 1949).

One-man dictatorships are relatively uncommon, especially today. Much more frequently, dictatorial regimes are dominated by the will of a small, tight-knit group. For example, although the premier of the Soviet Union may be properly described as a dictator, he is, in fact, powerless to act without the support and approval of the potent *politburo* (executive council) of the Communist Party of the Soviet Union.

The primary characteristic of any dictatorship is that *it is not responsible to the people and cannot be limited by them*. It is not accountable to any higher authority for its actions or for the manner in which they are taken.

Dictatorships often present the outward appearance of control by the people. Thus, popular elections are usually held; but they are rigidly controlled and, typically, the voter is offered the candidates of only one political party. An elected legislative body often exists; but it is a sham, a puppet to rubberstamp the policies and programs of the dictator.

Public support for the regime is mobilized through massive propaganda and absolute control of the educational system. Opposition is suppressed, often ruthlessly by the secret police. Only one political party, highly organized and rigidly disciplined, is permitted. Freedom of speech, thought, and association — so vital in a democracy — are not tolerated. And, typically, the government engages in a vast amount of activity intended to promote economic and social welfare or to enhance the nation's military power and prestige.

Benito Mussolini stated the basic philosophy of the modern totalitarian dictatorship when he proclaimed: "All is in the state and for the state, nothing outside the state, nothing against the state."

Democracy. In the democratic form of government supreme political authority rests with the people. The people are sovereign, the people govern themselves. Put another way, democratic government is government conducted by and with the consent of the governed.

Abraham Lincoln gave immortality to the definition of democracy in his Gettysburg Address: "government of the people, by the people, for the people." Nowhere is there a better, more concise definition of the term. But notice that it is the *second* of Lincoln's three phrases which distinguishes a democracy from any other form of government. All governments are *of* the people—that is, over the people. Even a dictatorship may function *for* the people. But only a democracy is of, for, *and by* the people.

A democracy may be either *direct* or *indirect* in form. A *direct* (or *pure*) democracy exists where the will of the people is translated into public policy (law) directly by the people themselves in mass meetings. Obviously, such a system is practicable only in very small communities where it is physically possible for the citizenry to assemble in a given place and where the problems of government are few and simple. Direct democracy does not exist at the national level anywhere in the world today, but the old New England town meeting and the *Landsgemeinde* in a few of the smaller Swiss cantons are excellent examples of direct democracy in action.[4]

In the United States we are more familiar with *indirect* (or *representative*) democracy. In a representative democracy the popular will is formulated and expressed through a relatively small group of persons chosen by the people to act as their representatives. These representatives are responsible for the day-to-day conduct of government; and they are held accountable to the people for the manner in which they execute that responsibility, especially through periodic elections.

There are some who insist that the United States is a *republic* rather than a democracy, for in a republic the sovereign power is held by the electorate and is exercised by representatives chosen by and held responsible to the electorate. To these people, a democracy may be defined only in terms of direct democracy. Of course, they are entitled to their view. To most Americans, however, the terms democracy, republic, representative democracy, and republican form of government generally mean the same thing.

Regardless of the terms used, remember that above all else in a democracy the people are sovereign, the people are the only source for any and all governmental power, the people rule. Today, most of the states of the Western World are representative democracies—although, certainly, some are more democratic than others.

Basic Concepts of Democracy. There is nothing inevitable about democracy. It does not exist in the United States simply because we regard it as the best of all possible political systems.[5] Nor will it continue to exist for that reason. Rather, democracy exists in this country because, as a people, we believe in the concepts upon which it is based. It will continue to exist and be perfected in practice only for so long as we continue to subscribe to—and *seriously attempt to practice*—those concepts.

---

[4] The *Landsgemeinde,* like the original New England town meeting, is an assembly open to all local citizens qualified to vote. In a more limited sense, lawmaking by initiative petition is also an example of direct democracy; see page 631.

[5] The late Sir Winston Churchill once argued for democracy in these terms: "Many forms of government have been tried in this world of sin and woe. No one pretends that democracy is perfect or all-wise. Indeed, it has been said that democracy is the worst form of government except all of those other forms which have been tried from time to time. . . ."

The basic concepts of democracy—especially as we understand and apply the term in the United States—are:

(1) A recognition of the fundamental worth and dignity of each and every individual.
(2) A respect for the equality of all men.
(3) A faith in majority rule and an insistence upon minority rights.
(4) An acceptance of the necessity of compromise.
(5) An insistence upon the widest possible area of individual freedom.

Of course, these ideas may be, and often are, phrased in many other ways. No matter what the phrasing, however, any formulation of the basic concepts of democracy must include the five presented here. They form the very *minimum* that must be subscribed to by anyone who professes to believe in democracy. Some people argue that other concepts belong in such a listing; for example, the right of each person to at least a certain minimum level of economic security. But the point here is that, no matter what else might be included, at least those cited *must* be.

Fundamental Worth of the Individual. Democracy is firmly based upon a belief in the fundamental importance of the individual. Each and every individual, no matter what his station in life may be, is a separate and distinct being. Democracy insists that the worth and dignity of each person must be recognized and respected by society and by all other individuals at all times.

This concept of the sanctity of the individual is of overriding importance in democratic thought. It is the *central concept* from which all else in democracy flows. Anything and everything a democratic society does must and should be done within the limits of this great concept.

It is true that the welfare of one or a few individuals is sometimes subordinated to the interests of the many in a democracy. For example, an individual may be forced to pay taxes to support the functions of government, whether he wants to or not. He may be required to serve in the Armed Forces, be prohibited from constructing a building in a certain location, or even be forced to give up his home for some public purpose, such as a new highway. When these or similar things are done, a democratic society is serving the interests of the many. But it is *not* serving them simply as the interests of a mass of people who happen to outnumber the few. Rather, it is serving the many who, *as individuals*, altogether, make up the society.

The distinction we are trying to make here—between *an* individual and *all* individuals—may be a very fine one. It is, however, a most important one to a true understanding of the meaning of democracy.

Equality of All Men. Hand-in-hand with the belief in the sanctity of the individual, democracy stresses the equality of all individuals. It holds, with Jefferson, that "all men are created equal."

Obviously, the democratic concept of equality does not claim that all men are born with the same mental or physical abilities. Nor does democracy argue that all men are entitled to an equal share of worldly goods. It does insist, however, that all men are entitled to: (1) *equality of opportunity* and (2) *equality before the law.* That is, the democratic concept of equality holds that no man should be held back for any such artificial or arbitrary reasons as those based on race, color, religion, or economic or social status; that each man should be free to develop himself as fully as he can (or he cares to); and that each man should be treated as the equal of all others under the law.

Majority Rule and Minority Rights. In a democracy public questions are decided in accord with the will of the people. The people often disagree among themselves in public matters, however. There must, therefore, be some method, some device, for discovering the popular will—for finding the "right" answers to public questions. The only satisfactory device we know is that of *majority rule.*

Democracy is firmly committed to the proposition that the majority of the people will be right more often than they will be wrong. It is also committed to the belief that the majority will be right far more often than will any one man or small group.

A democracy cannot function without the principle of majority rule. Unchecked, however, the majority could readily become a tyranny. It could easily destroy its opposition (the minority) and, in the process, destroy democracy, too. Thus, democracy insists on majority rule *restrained by minority rights.* The majority must always recognize the right of any minority to become, if it can, by fair and lawful means, itself the majority. The majority must always be ready to listen to a minority argument, to hear its objections, to hear its criticisms, and to welcome its suggestions. Anything less contradicts the very meaning of democracy.

Necessity of Compromise. In a democracy public decision-making is very largely a process of give-and-take, of accommodating competing views and interests with one another. That is, it is very largely a matter of *compromise,* the process of blending and adjusting in order to find the particular position most acceptable to the largest number.

Compromise is an essential part of the democratic process for two major reasons. First, democracy exalts the individual and insists that each man is the equal of all others. It is only natural, then, that a democratic society is composed of individuals and groups with widely varying opinions and interests which must be reconciled. Secondly, few public questions have only "two" sides. Most can be answered in any one of several ways.[6] As a simple illustration, take the problem of how a

city should finance the paving of a particular street. Should it charge the costs to those who own property along the street? Or should all of the city's residents pay the costs from the city's general treasury? Or should the city and the adjacent property owners share the costs? What of those who use the street but do not own adjoining property? Or those who use the street but do not live within the city? Should they be charged a toll to help defray the costs?

It would be impossible for the people in a democratic society to decide most public questions without the element of compromise. Remember, however, that compromise is a *process,* a way of achieving majority agreement. It is never an end in itself. Not all compromises are good, and not all are necessary. There are some things — the sanctity of the individual, for example — that can never be and should never be the subject of compromise if democracy is to survive.

Individual Freedom. From all that has been said to this point, it should be clear that democracy can thrive only in an atmosphere of individual freedom. But democracy *does not* and *cannot* insist upon complete freedom for the individual. No man can be absolutely free to do as he pleases, for this would ultimately mean that no man would be free. Absolute freedom can only exist in a state of anarchy; and anarchy can only lead, inevitably and quickly, to rule by the strong.

Democracy does insist, however, that each man must be as free to do as he pleases as the freedom of all will permit. In other words, each man's liberty is relative to and dependent upon the liberties of all men.

Drawing the line between what an individual may or may not do is an extremely difficult

---

[6] The people are often asked to make a public decision by electing one candidate or another to a particular office. In a two-party system, such as ours, the voter is thus faced with a "yes-or-no" — that is, a two-sided — question. Even here, however, the process of compromise is important, especially at the nominating stage in the election process.

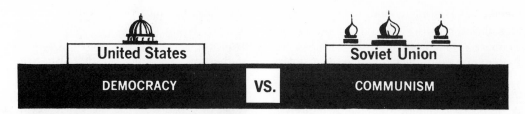

United States		Soviet Union
DEMOCRACY	**VS.**	**COMMUNISM**

POLITICAL INSTITUTIONS	**POLITICAL INSTITUTIONS**
1. Presidential and Federal System	1. Parliament mere form; actual control of government by Communist Party
2. Two-party system; free elections	2. Single party; uncontested elections
3. Government responsible to people	3. Government neither responsible to nor limited by people
4. Civil Liberties (e.g., freedom of speech, press) guaranteed in Constitution	4. Civil Liberties exist only in accordance with the will of the Party
ECONOMIC CONDITIONS	**ECONOMIC CONDITIONS**
1. Free Enterprise; limited government regulation	1. State Ownership; all activity planned and directed by Government
2. High standards of living with full employment and economic security as goals	2. Full employment (including conscript labor) operated to serve the ends of a controlled state
SOCIAL CONDITIONS	**SOCIAL CONDITIONS**
1. Emphasis on worth and dignity of individual	1. Individual exists to benefit the communist state

task. Abraham Lincoln once posed this democratic dilemma in these words:

> Must a government of necessity be too *strong* for the liberties of its own people, or too *weak* to maintain its own existence?

The problem goes to the very heart of democracy. Men desire both liberty and authority. Democratic government must strike the balance between the two. The authority of government must be adequate to the needs of society, but never so great as to restrict the individual beyond the point of necessity.

Democracy regards all civil rights as vital, but it places its highest value on those guarantees necessary to the free exchange of ideas: on *freedom of expression* and *freedom of thought*. Several years ago, the President's Committee on Civil Rights made the point this way:

In a free society there is faith in the ability of the people to make sound, rational judgments. But such judgments are possible only when the people have access to all relevant facts and to all prevailing interpretations of the facts. How can such judgments be formed on a sound basis if arguments, viewpoints, or opinions are arbitrarily suppressed? How can the concept of the marketplace of thought in which truth ultimately prevails retain its validity if the thought of certain individuals is denied the right of circulation?

CAPITALISM, SOCIALISM, COMMUNISM

What are the functions which, whatever its form, a government ought to undertake? What should it have the power to do? What should it not be permitted to do? Certainly these questions may be, and often are, posed with reference to virtually all areas of human activity; but they are raised most often, and most significantly, in the realm of economic affairs.

Questions of politics and of economics are, in fact, inseparable. What, for example, should be the nature of the relationship between labor and management in a nation's economy? On what basis should goods and services be distributed and exchanged within a nation? What provisions, if any, ought to be made for the well-being of a nation's elderly? What role, if any, should government play in these and similar matters? Clearly these are crucial economic questions. Just as clearly they are crucial political questions, as well.

Capitalism. The American economic system is based upon private ownership, individual initiative, profit, and competition and is known as *capitalism*. It is often described, as well, as the *free enterprise* or *private enterprise* system.

Basic Nature of the Capitalistic System. In the capitalistic system the means by which goods and services are produced are held, very largely, as the private property of individuals or of companies formed, owned, and controlled by one, a few, or many individuals. That is, the instruments of production, of distribution, and of exchange (factories, mines, stores, farms, railroads, airlines, banks, and the like) are privately owned and managed.

Those who own these means hire labor and *compete* with one another to produce goods and services at a *profit*. Competition is the lifeblood of the system, and in its purest form involves the providing of the best possible product at the lowest possible price. Profit is the motive power of the system. The profits

CASE STUDY
The Declaration of Independence was proclaimed to the world on July 4, 1776. For nearly 200 years this remarkable document has stood as an inspiration to millions upon millions of persons, here and abroad.

One of the Declaration's basic purposes was, of course, the proclamation of the independence of the United States of America. Another and equally vital purpose was the setting out of the basic theses upon which the American governmental system would be built. This latter purpose was accomplished in two crucial sentences in the second paragraph of the document:

We hold these truths to be self-evident, that all men are created equal, that they are endowed by their Creator with certain unalienable Rights, that among these are Life, Liberty and the pursuit of Happiness. That to secure these rights, Governments are instituted among Men, deriving their just powers from the consent of the governed; That whenever any Form of Government becomes destructive of these ends it is the Right of the People to alter or to abolish it, and to institute new Government, laying its foundation on such principles and organizing its powers in such form, as to them shall seem most likely to effect their Safety and Happiness.

What basic principles of government are here proclaimed? Did the promulgation of the Declaration amount to: American commitment to democratic government? Why, according to the Declaration, do governments exist? Does the Declaration of Independence proclaim a right of revolution?

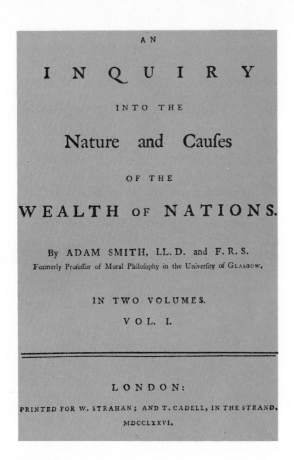

AN

INQUIRY

INTO THE

Nature and Caufes

OF THE

WEALTH OF NATIONS.

By ADAM SMITH, LL. D. and F. R. S.

Formerly Profeffor of Moral Philofophy in the Univerfity of GLASGOW.

IN TWO VOLUMES.

VOL. I.

LONDON:

PRINTED FOR W. STRAHAN; AND T. CADELL, IN THE STRAND.

MDCCLXXVI.

The writings of Adam Smith were an important contribution to the field of political economy, and had much influence on the developing philosophy of capitalism. (The Bettmann Archive)

of an enterprise are its earnings, the excess of income over expenditures; that is, the returns realized by the owners over and above the costs of doing business. Put another way, profits represent the rewards received for the risks taken and the initiative shown.

Generally speaking, anyone may start an enterprise — attempt to produce or sell goods or offer services — and the risks and rewards are his. Most of the larger and many of the smaller businesses in the United States today are actually owned by large numbers of persons — by stockholders who own shares in them.

The American Telephone and Telegraph Company, the world's largest private utility, for example, is owned by more than 3,100,000 stockholders. Altogether, some 27,000,000 persons in the United States own shares in American business today.

Typically, a portion of the profits earned by an enterprise is paid out as *dividends* (interest) and a portion is reinvested in the business. Thus, the investor receives a return on his investment, the business expands, more jobs are created, individual purchasing power increases, and a still higher standard of living results.

Laissez-Faire Theory. American capitalism as we know it today bears only a distant resemblance to classical capitalistic economics. The origins of capitalism are laid in the concepts of *laissez-faire,* a doctrine developed in the late eighteenth and early nineteenth centuries.[7]

According to *laissez-faire* theory, government's proper role in society is a very limited one, confined to three essential areas: (1) the conduct of foreign relations and national defense, (2) the maintenance of police and courts to protect private property and the health, safety, and morals of the people, and (3) the performance of certain necessary functions which cannot be provided by private enterprise at a profit.

The theory was given its classic expression by Adam Smith in *The Wealth of Nations,* first published in London in 1776. Its basic assumption was well summarized in Thomas Jefferson's often quoted remark: "That government is best which governs least." Its proponents opposed any governmental activity which tended to hamper free enterprise. They insisted that government's place in economic affairs ought to be limited to those functions designed to protect and promote the free play of competi-

---

[7] The term *laissez-faire* comes from a French idiom meaning "to let alone." Translated literally, it means "allow to act."

tion and the operation of the law of supply and demand.

The theory of *laissez-faire* economics never operated in fact in this country, even in the earliest days of the Republic. Government at both the National and the State levels has played a meaningful role in economic affairs throughout our history. Even so, it is obvious that the concepts of *laissez-faire* had, and continue to have, a profound effect upon the nature of our economic system. Most business enterprises in the United States are private in character. They are owned by private persons, not by government; they are financed with private capital, not with public funds; they are managed by private citizens, not by public officials.

A "Mixed Economy." While the American economic system is essentially private in character, government has always played a considerable and a steadily increasing role. Indeed, our system may be properly described as a "mixed economy." That is, it is one in which private enterprise is combined with and supported by governmental regulation and promotion. It is one in which there is a substantial amount of governmental activity and control designed to protect the public interest and to preserve private enterprise. To put the point another way, in the development of our economy we have recognized that unregulated capitalism would result in a system of injustice and selfishness, a system in which the cruel philosophy of "dog-eat-dog" would prevail.

A vast amount of economic regulation and promotion occurs at all levels of government in the United States — National, State, and local. Thus, to cite only a few of an almost unlimited number of examples, economic activity is regulated by government through antitrust laws, pure food and drug laws, labor-management relations statutes, zoning ordinances, building codes, agricultural marketing regulations, minimum wage laws, and the policing of investment practices. Similarly, the nation's economic life is promoted in a myriad of public ways; for example, through direct subsidies, public roads

and highways, such services as the postal system and weather reports, research programs at State universities, a variety of loan programs for a multitude of purposes, advisory information to farmers, and public housing.

Our economy is also "mixed" in the sense that some enterprises and functions which might be conducted privately are, in fact, operated by government. Public education, the postal system, the monetary system, and road-building are familiar examples of long standing.

To what extent should government participate, regulate and promote, police and serve? Many of our most heated political debates revolve about the question. In the constant search for answers, we tend to follow the general rule expressed by Abraham Lincoln:

> The legitimate object of government is to do for the community of people whatever they need to have done, but cannot do so well for themselves, in their separate and individual capacities.

One needs only to look at the great achievements and the standard of living of the American people to see the advantages of our economic system. We view the trends toward nationalization and socialism in other countries with grave misgivings. We believe that a well-regulated capitalistic system — one of free choice, individual incentive, private enterprise — is the best guarantee of the better life for all mankind.

Socialism. Socialism is a philosophy of economic collectivism. It advocates the collective — that is, the social, public — ownership of the instruments of production, distribution, and exchange. It insists that the means by which goods and services are produced should be publicly owned and managed.

Socialism argues that the economic order should be designed and operated in behalf of all, for the use and benefit of all. It thus rejects the concepts of private ownership, competition, and profit which lie at the heart of capitalist thought and practice.

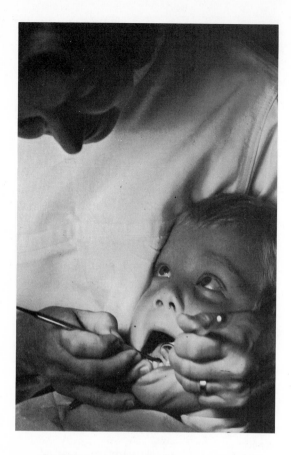

Socialism, generally speaking, advocates the public ownership and control of the major instruments of production, distribution, and exchange. In practice, however, institutions other than key industries (steel, coal, electricity, and railroads) — for example, dental services in Sweden — come under the control of the government. (Swedish Information Services)

The roots of socialism lie deep in recorded history. Almost from the beginning there have been those who have dreamed and planned for a society built upon socialist doctrine. Most of the earlier socialists foresaw a collective economy arising out of and managed by voluntary private action. With few exceptions, they considered governmental action unnecessary to the realization of their goals. Thus, early socialist doctrine is often referred to as "private socialism."

Socialism in its modern form — that is, *state socialism* — has emerged only over the course of the past 100 years or so. Only since the middle of the last century have most socialists argued that the reaching of their goal is too big a task for private action alone, that the power of the state must be used to bring about that end.

The most extreme form of socialism today is *communism,* to which we shall turn in a moment. Most socialists outside the Soviet and Chinese orbits are *evolutionary socialists,* or as they are often called *social democrats.* They believe that socialism can best be achieved gradually and peaceably, by lawful means, and by working within the established framework of government. They believe that, even after they have won control of government, the new order should be introduced only in stages, beginning with the *nationalization* (socialization) of a few key enterprises, such as banking, transportation, and the steel industry.

Evolutionary socialists argue that political democracy, with its emphasis upon popular participation in government, is incomplete. True democracy can exist, they claim, only when the people share in the management of their economic destinies as well. The British Labor Party and the major socialist parties of Western Europe and the Scandinavian countries are prime examples of evolutionary socialism in action.[8]

---

[8] Although socialism and communism are often identified with each other, the socialists of the non-communist world (the evolutionary socialists) are usually bitter foes of the communists. They share many of the ideas supported by the Russian, Chinese, and other Marxists; but most of them reject the theory of the class struggle, the necessity of violent revolution, and the dictatorship of the proletariat — all fundamental to Marxian communism.

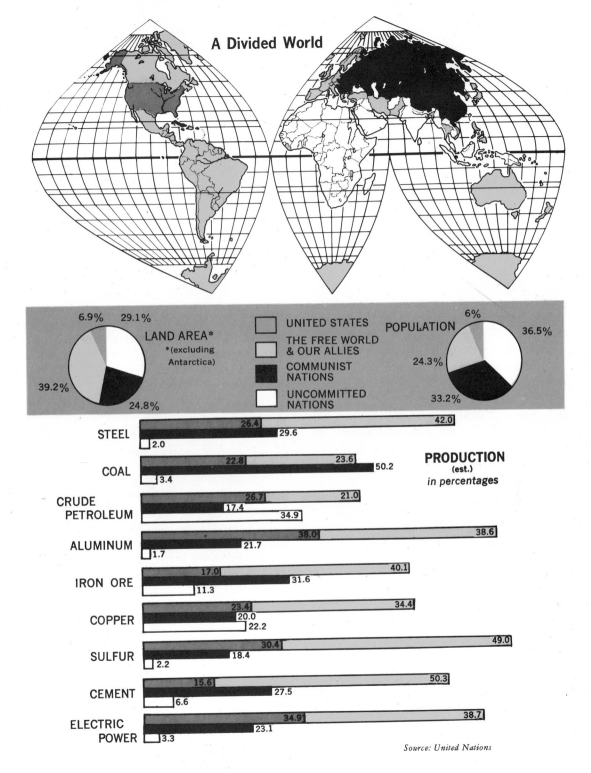

A Divided World

LAND AREA*
*(excluding Antarctica)

6.9% 29.1%
39.2%
24.8%

UNITED STATES
THE FREE WORLD & OUR ALLIES
COMMUNIST NATIONS
UNCOMMITTED NATIONS

POPULATION

6%
36.5%
24.3%
33.2%

PRODUCTION
(est.)
in percentages

STEEL 26.4 42.0 / 29.6 / 2.0

COAL 22.8 23.6 50.2 / 3.4

CRUDE PETROLEUM 26.7 21.0 / 17.4 / 34.9

ALUMINUM 38.0 38.6 / 21.7 / 1.7

IRON ORE 17.0 40.1 / 31.6 / 11.3

COPPER 23.4 34.4 / 20.0 / 22.2

SULFUR 30.4 49.0 / 18.4 / 2.2

CEMENT 15.6 50.3 / 27.5 / 6.6

ELECTRIC POWER 34.9 38.7 / 23.1 / 3.3

Source: United Nations

To the socialist, the philosophy of socialism is just because it aims at a more equitable distribution of wealth and opportunity among men. Man's economic affairs should be organized and managed, says the socialist, for the good of the entire community.

Opponents of socialism condemn it because they believe that it stifles individual initiative and denies to the capable and the industrious the justifiable rewards of their efforts. Many also argue that the increased governmental regulation necessary to socialism would inevitably lead to a communist dictatorship.

The complexities of modern society have led to vast expansion of governmental functions in most countries, including the United States. Many of the activities undertaken by government in this country in the past four decades or so have been attacked by opponents who insist that they are "socialistic" and thus ill-advised and a threat to the nation and its future.

Communism. As we know it today, communism was born in 1848 with the publication of *The Communist Manifesto,* a brief, inflammatory pamphlet written by Karl Marx with the aid of his close colleague, Friedrich Engels. In *The Communist Manifesto* and his later and very extensive writings Marx laid down the cardinal premises of *scientific socialism,* or communism.[9]

From the death of Marx in 1883, and that of Engels in 1895, communism has been interpreted and expanded by his followers. The most important of the latter-day "high priests of communism" have been Vladimir Ilyich Lenin, Josef Stalin, and Nikita Khrushchev in the Soviet Union, and Mao Tse-tung in Communist China. The doctrine they have developed is distinctly both political and economic in nature.[10]

Communist Theory. The four central features of communist theory are: (1) its theory of history, (2) the labor theory of value, (3) its theory of the nature of the state, and (4) the dictatorship of the proletariat.

The Communist Theory of History. According to Marx, all of man's history has been a story of the "class struggle." The communists say that there have always been two opposing classes in society—one an oppressor (dominating) class and the other an oppressed (dominated) class. In feudal times the two classes were the nobility and the serfs. Today, say the communists, the capitalists (the *bourgeoisie*) keep the workers (the *proletariat*) in subjugation. Workers in capitalistic countries are described as "wage slaves" who are paid barely enough to permit them to eke out a starvation living as they continue to toil for their masters.

The communists contend that the class struggle has become so bitter and the divisions between the classes so sharp that the situation cannot continue. They claim that a revolt of the masses and the destruction of the bourgeoisie are inevitable. They see their function as that of speeding up the "natural" course of history, by violence if necessary.

The Labor Theory of Value. According to communist theory, the value of any commodity is determined by the labor necessary to produce it. In other words, a suit of clothes is worth so much because it takes so much labor to produce it. Because the laborer

---

[9] The term *scientific socialism* was used to distinguish Marxian thought from the older and less extreme forms of socialism. In later years, Marx and his followers came to prefer the term *communism.*

[10] Capitalism is also a political and an economic doctrine, but in a much more limited sense. To the capitalist, the proper role of government is that of stimulator, servant, and regulator or referee. Socialism is much more a political as well as an economic theory than is capitalism, but it is not nearly so distinctly political as is communism.

Our system of free enterprise, based on healthy competition, has given us the highest standard of living in the world. The Communist prophecy of the collapse of capitalism has proved both false and foolish. (Ray Justus, Minneapolis Star)

produced the suit and thus created its value, the communists claim that he should receive that value in full. They maintain that all income should come from work. They are vehemently opposed to the free enterprise profit system and condemn profits as "surplus value" which should go to the worker.

The Communist Theory of the Nature of the State. To the communists, the state is the instrument or "tool" of the dominating class—a tool with which the bourgeoisie keeps the proletariat in bondage. Because the bourgeoisie is so firmly entrenched in its control of the state and its power, said Lenin, it is only through a "violent and bloody revolution" that the situation can be altered. (The communists also claim that other institutions are used as "tools" as well. Thus, Marx described religion as "the opiate of the people"—a drug fed to the people as a hoax through which they are

led to tolerate their supposed harsh lot in this life in order to gain a "fictional afterlife.")

The Dictatorship of the Proletariat. The communists do not foresee a proletariat able to govern themselves after a revolution. Rather, the proletariat would need "guidance and education"—from the communist party, of course. Hence, the dogma calls for a *dictatorship of the proletariat,* a totalitarian regime to lead the people to the theoretical goal of communism: a "free classless society." As that goal is realized, it is claimed, the state would "wither away." The cardinal principle of the new society would be: "From each according to his ability, to each according to his need."

Evaluation of Communism. The Soviet Union presents the outstanding example of communism in action. Strictly speaking, the Russians do not practice pure communism today, but

In elections conducted in the Soviet Union, only those candidates approved by the Communist Party appear on the ballot. (SOVFOTO)

an extreme form of socialism.[11] Their system stems from the October Revolution of 1917 when Lenin and his followers came to power.[12] Immediately, Lenin attempted to establish a communist system. But the attempt failed. The inefficient and the lazy received as much as the efficient and the industrious. Workers and peasants rebelled. The government took severe reprisals; many thousands were executed. Finally, the Soviet leaders modified their approach, turning to an advanced form of socialism. The Soviets now claim to be working *toward* the eventual establishment of pure communism.

---

[11] According to Marx, the guiding principle in a communist society should be: "From each according to his ability, to each according to his need." But compare this with Article 12 of the Soviet Constitution of 1936: "Work in the USSR is a duty and a matter of honor for every able-bodied citizen, in accordance with the principle: 'He who does not work, neither shall he eat.' The principle applied in the USSR is that of socialism: 'From each according to his ability, to each according to his work.'"

[12] The revolution occurred on October 25, 1917, by the calendar then in use in Russia. By the Western calendar, now also used in the Soviet Union, the date was November 7. The communists did not, as is often supposed, revolt against the czarist regime. Rather, they overthrew the fledgling democratic government headed by Alexander Kerensky. The Kerensky government had been created as a consequence of a revolution in March of 1917. It was in this earlier, non-communist revolt that the czarist tyranny had been deposed.

More than a century of Marxist theory and a half-century of Soviet communism have exposed many of the fallacies of communist doctrine. We note the major ones here.

Marx argued that the divisions between the bourgeoise and the proletariat would continue to deepen, ultimately reaching a point where capitalism would collapse under its own weight. He claimed the struggle between the bourgeoisie and the proletariat would grind the middle class down into the ranks of the proletariat. Quite the contrary has actually happened. The economic gap between workers and owners has narrowed almost to the point of extinction, especially in the United States. Marx and his followers failed to foresee the tremendous growth of the middle class. The poor have not become poorer; they have, in fact, become much, much richer.

Communist theory makes no place for individual initiative and incentive, so vital in our own economic system. One of the basic differences between our system and the communists' is that where we strive to promote *equality of opportunity,* the communists argue for *equality of condition.* Experience has forced the communists to recognize the importance of incentive, however. The labor theory of value has been very largely ignored in communist practice. Income in the Soviet Union today is based largely on the amount or the importance of the work one does. Thus, scientists, managers, administrators, teachers, and others in the professions receive much larger incomes and are granted many more privileges than those available to the masses of others in the working class.

The state has not been the tool of the dominant class in the non-communist world. Rather, the state — acting through government controlled by and responsive to the will of the people — has become one of the chief agents through which the people have made great strides in social progress.

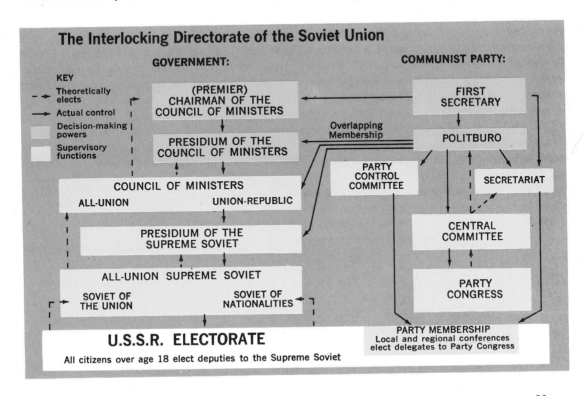

Benito Mussolini founded the Fascist movement. As dictator of Italy he made that nation into a totalitarian state. (Wide World Photos)

Marx predicted that the emergence of communism would promote peace among the nations of the world. Obviously, quite the opposite has occurred. Further, he and his followers confidently expected communism to appeal to workers throughout the world, regardless of nationality. *The Communist Manifesto* closed with the cry: "Workingmen of all countries, unite!" But, in fact, communism has failed to eliminate nationalistic sentiments, as the continuing disputes between the Soviet Union and Communist China so aptly demonstrate.

The state in the Soviet Union, Communist China, and other communist countries shows no sign of "withering away." Indeed, under communism the power of the state has been drastically *increased*. The dictatorships established in these countries have become the most totalitarian the world has ever seen. All forms of opposition are ruthlessly suppressed. Basic freedoms are not permitted, lest the people examine and question the policies of the state. Fear is a weapon in the hands of the ruling few. And, certainly, there is no guarantee that the

dictatorship will ever end — not, at least, of its own accord. With all power in the hands of the ruling clique, nothing prevents it from perpetuating its rule.

But man is independent and creative by nature. By suppressing these traits, communism has almost certainly forecast its own demise.

Fascism. Clearly, the Soviet and Chinese communist dictatorships pose the gravest of threats to the security of the United States and that of the other free nations of the world. Although recognizing this fact, we should not overlook still another serious challenge: *fascism*. Despite the democratization of West Germany and of Italy following World War II, fascist doctrine still exists and remains a potential danger to the free world.

Essentially, fascism rests upon two tenets utterly contrary to those of democracy: (1) the *Führer prinzip* (the leadership principle) and (2) *etatism* (statism). Under the *Führer prinzip*, supreme and unchallengeable power is held by the leader, an absolute dictator whom all must obey. *Etatism* is the extreme expression of totalitarianism: the state embodies everything; absolutely nothing exists outside the sphere of its domination and control. In fascist doctrine, then, *all* matters — political, social, economic — are subject to the state, and the state and its powers are personified in the leader.

Both fascist and communist regimes operate in strikingly similar fashion. Force and terror are combined with massive propaganda to further the interests of the state, which, of course, are defined by the dictatorship and override all other interests. In both, the outward forms of representative government are maintained, but only in terms of form and of no real consequence. All matters of public policy are determined by the regime.

In fascist, as in communist, states only the political party of the ruling elite is allowed. No form of dissent is tolerated, and a highly developed secret police and informer system is used to ferret out and eliminate all opposition.

Key Concepts

A knowledge of the governmental and economic systems which exist today is essential in our conflict-ridden world.

The *state,* the dominant political unit in the world today, is a body of people occupying a defined territory and organized politically with the power to make and enforce law without the consent of any higher authority. Every state possesses four essential characteristics: (1) population, (2) territory, (3) sovereignty, (4) government.

While no two governments are identical, each may be classified in various ways on the basis of certain factors. A *unitary* government is one in which all of the powers possessed by the government are lodged in a single central organ, as in Great Britain. A *federal* government is one in which governmental powers are distributed on a geographic basis between a central and several local governments, as in the United States. A *confederate* government is an alliance of independent states with a weak central government with some powers over matters of common concern.

A *presidential* government is one in which the executive (president) is independent of and co-equal with the legislature, as in the United States. In a *parliamentary* government the executive (prime minister and cabinet) is a part of and subordinate to the legislature, as in Great Britain.

A *dictatorship* exists where the power to govern is held by one person or, as is typically the case, a small group. All dictatorships are authoritarian in character, and modern distatorships have tended to be totalitarian, as well. The primary characteristic of a dictatorship is that it is not responsible to and cannot be limited by the people.

A *democracy* exists where the power to govern is held by the people themselves, where government is conducted by and with the consent of the people. Modern democracies are indirect—that is, representative democracies—rather than direct (or pure) in form. Democratic thought insists upon belief in: (1) the fundamental worth of every individual, (2) the equality of all men, (3) majority rule and minority rights, (4) the necessity of compromise, and (5) individual freedom.

Capitalism is an economic doctrine based upon private ownership of the means by which goods and services are produced and upon individual initiative, profit, and competition.

Socialism is a philosophy of economic collectivism, advocating public ownership of the major instruments of production, distribution, and exchange. *Evolutionary* socialists are to be distinguished from *revolutionary* socialists, most of whom are communists.

Communism is an extreme form of socialism. As founded by Karl Marx in 1848, its four central concepts are: (1) its theory of the nature of history, (2) the labor theory of value, (3) its theory of the nature of the state, and (4) the dictatorship of the proletariat.

Facism, like communism, is a totalitarian political philosophy. It rests upon two basic concepts: (1) the *Führer prinzip* and (2) *etatism.*

Important Terms

authoritarian	dictatorship	*laissez-faire*	representative democracy
capitalism	equality	majority rule	republic
communism	*etatism*	minority rights	socialism
competition	fascism	"mixed economy"	sovereignty
compromise	federalism	parliamentary government	state-State
confederation	*Führer prinzip*	presidential government	totalitarian
democracy	government	profit	unitary government

Questions for Inquiry and Review

1. What is a *state?* What are its four essential characteristics?

2. What is the difference between state and government?

3. Why is the location of sovereignty within a state of such vital importance?

4. On what particular basis can a unitary government be distinguished from a federal one? Presidential from parliamentary? Dictatorial from democratic?

5. With what particular form of democracy are we most familiar in the United States?

6. What are the five basic concepts of democracy?

7. According to *laissez-faire* theory, what is the proper role of government in a society?

8. Why may the American economic system be properly described as a "mixed economy"?

9. What is the general rule we tend to follow in determining the proper role of government in the nation's economy?

10. Why is modern socialism often referred to as "state socialism"?

11. What are the essential differences between evolutionary socialists and communists?

12. Who founded modern communism? When?

13. What is the communist theory of history? The labor theory of value? The communist theory of the nature of the state? The dictatorship of the proletariat?

14. What are five major fallacies or shortcomings of communist doctrine?

15. Why may it be said that fascist and communist regimes operate in strikingly similar fashion?

For Further Inquiry

1. In 1733 Alexander Pope penned these lines in his "Essay on Man":

> For forms of government let fools contest;
> Whate'er is best administer'd is best.

Do you agree or disagree with Pope's view?

2. Of the various forms of government, why has democracy been practiced in only a comparatively few places and for only relatively brief periods of time?

3. Do you agree with James Bryce's observation that: "No government demands so much from the citizens as democracy and none gives back so much."? Why?

4. How would you expand upon this observation by Adlai Stevenson: "America has

made socialism obsolete and has shown communism to be a stagnant pool of violence and reaction."

5. Democracy has been described as "a never-ending search for truth." How apt is this description? Why must the search be a never-ending one?

6. Why do such terms as "democracy," "republic," and "people" appear so often in communist propaganda slogans?

7. Karl Marx predicted that successful communist revolutions would occur first in the more highly industrialized nations, particularly in Germany and England and then in the United States. But history has shown this to be another of his false prophecies. Communist revolutions have occurred, instead, in underdeveloped and predominantly agrarian countries. Can you give any reasons for this?

Suggested Activities

1. Examine the governmental systems of selected foreign states and present a class report based upon your research.

2. Make a list of: (a) examples of the ways in which economic activities are regulated by the National, State, and local governments in your area, (b) examples of the ways in which the three levels of government aid the economy in your community, or (c) the publicly conducted enterprises in your community.

3. Invite a local businessman to give a talk to your class on the various ways in which government regulates and aids his business.

4. Prepare a series of posters or displays to illustrate the basic concepts of democracy.

5. Stage a debate or class forum on the following: (a) *Resolved,* That the United States may be described properly as both a republic and a democracy; (b) *Resolved,* That it is more desirable that government strive to promote equal opportunity for all than to strive to promote an equality of condition for all.

6. Construct a glossary of key words and phrases in American politics. The "Important Terms" section at the end of each of the chapters could be used as a basis for such a project. Each term could be defined or described on a separate card or sheet of paper, filed alphabetically, and improved throughout the year.

Suggested Reading

ALDRIDGE, JOHN W., "In the Country of the Young," *Harper's,* October & November, 1969.

BRAINE, JOHN, "Why One British Socialist Turned Conservative," *New York Times Magazine,* March 2, 1969.

"China's Two Decades of Communism," *Time,* October 3, 1969.

EISENHOWER, DWIGHT D., "We *Must* Avoid the Perils of Extremism," *Reader's Digest,* April, 1969.

FISHER, ALLAN C., "The Investiture of Great Britain's Prince of Wales," *National Geographic,* November, 1969.

"Good Life: Where Russia Lags," *U.S. News,* November 24, 1969.

HARRINGTON, MICHAEL, "Whatever Happened to Socialism?" *Harper's,* January, 1970.

KING, CORETTA S., "He Had a Dream," *Life,* September 12 and 19, 1969.

KUZNETSOV, ANATOLY, "Why I Left Russia," *Reader's Digest,* November, 1969.

MACHIZ, MARC and ROBERTSON, JAMES L. "One Generation Speaks to Another," *U.S. News,* July 7, 1969.

"Report From Black America," *Newsweek,* June 30, 1969.

"Revolution," *Life,* October 10 and 17, 1969.

2
THE HERITAGE OF AMERICAN GOVERNMENT

***Out of what historical setting did the American Constitutional System emerge?

***How and why did the Constitution, written in 1787, differ so markedly from the Declaration of Independence, written only eleven years earlier?

***Why may it be argued that the words "We, the People" are the most important in all of the Constitution?

We hold these truths to be self-evident: that all men are created equal; that they are endowed by their Creator with certain unalienable rights; that among these are Life, Liberty, and the pursuit of Happiness.

THE DECLARATION OF INDEPENDENCE

The American system of government did not suddenly spring into being, at the wave of some political magician's wand. Nor was it pulled out of thin air by the Founding Fathers at Philadelphia in the summer of 1787. Rather, its roots reach deep into the past. Indeed, its origins may be traced back to the very beginnings of Western civilization. It has developed through centuries of experience, tradition, thought, and deed. We review here the major aspects of that development.

THE COLONIAL PERIOD

Our English Heritage. Although the French, the Dutch, the Spanish, the Swedes, and many others settled in many parts of what was to become the United States, it was the English who came in the largest numbers. It was also the English who came to control the thirteen colonies that stretched for some 1300 miles along the Atlantic seaboard.

The early pioneers who cleared the wilderness and fought off the Indians had to hack out their own economic future in the New World. But they came here in search of greater freedom, and they brought much of their political future with them, ready-made. They brought with them the knowledge of a governmental system that had been working and developing in England for centuries. They brought three political concepts which especially were to loom large in the shaping of government in the United States.

Concept of Ordered Government. The early colonists recognized the necessity for government and quickly created local governments based upon those they had known in England. Many of the offices and units they established are still to be found in American local government: sheriff, coroner, justice of the peace, county, and borough, for example.

Concept of Limited Government. The early colonists brought with them, too, the idea that government is limited. That is, that govern-

The history of democratic government can be traced through those great documents which are the landmarks of its development. Notable among them are the Magna Carta, wrung from King John at Runnymede in 1215, and the Mayflower Compact of 1620, which served as the basis of civil government in Massachusetts until 1691. (The Library of Congress)

ment is *not* all-powerful, that it is limited in what it may do, and, especially, that it is limited in the sense that each man has certain rights that government cannot injure or take away. The concept of limited government was deeply embedded in English practice by the time the first colonists reached the New World, and it was enshrined there in such historic documents as the Magna Carta of 1215, the Petition of Right of 1628, and the Bill of Rights and the Act of Toleration of 1689.

Concept of Representative Government. A third and profoundly important concept brought to America by English settlers was that of representative government. For centuries there had been developing in England the idea that government exists to serve the people and that the people should have a voice in shaping the poli-

cies of government. As with the concept of limited government, representative government found fertile soil in America and flourished quickly.

While we have changed, developed, and added to the institutions and ideas which came to us from England, there is much in the American governmental system that bears the stamp of our English heritage. Certainly, this is not so strange when we recall that the Colonial Period of American history lasted for 168 years (1607–1775) and that the United States has existed as a nation for only a slightly longer time.

Government in the Colonies. The first permanent English settlement in America was made at Jamestown, Virginia, in 1607. The other twelve English colonies were established over the next century and a quarter, the last being Georgia in 1732.

The colony of Virginia was founded by a group of settlers sent out from England by a commercial corporation, the London Company. The company, acting under a royal charter, founded the colony as a money-making venture.

At first there was little local government in Virginia; a governor and council were set up, but tight control was held by the company in London. In 1619 the London Company did permit the creation of a legislature of burgesses[1] elected from each settlement. This assembly, the first representative legislature to meet in America, met on July 30, 1619, in the chancel of the church at Jamestown. In its first session it passed laws to aid the farmers of the colony and to curb idleness, gambling, improper dress, and drunkenness.

Because the London Company had failed to create a prosperous colony, the king (James I) withdrew its charter in 1624. From then until it became an independent State, Virginia was a *royal colony.*

Types of Colonies. According to the form of government in each—particularly the way in which the governor was chosen—there were three types of colonies: *royal, proprietary,* and *charter.*

Royal Colonies. The royal colonies were the most numerous. By the beginning of the American Revolution they included: New Hampshire, New York, New Jersey, Virginia, North Carolina, South Carolina, Georgia, and Massachusetts. For each of these colonies a royal governor and a council (or "upper house")

was appointed by the king, and a popular assembly (or "lower house") was elected in the colony. The governor, together with his council and the assembly, ruled the colony according to written instructions issued from time to time by the crown. The royal governors most often ruled with a stern hand, and much of the resentment that finally led to the American Revolution originated in these royal colonies.

Proprietary Colonies. The proprietary colonies were Pennsylvania, Delaware, and Maryland. The name "proprietary" came from the term "proprietor." The *proprietor* was an individual to whom the king had made a grant of land which could be settled and governed as the proprietor (owner) saw fit, subject only to the general supervision of the crown. The proprietor appointed the governor and established a legislature, court system, and local governments. He was, in effect, a "little king." The *Frame of Government* (a constitution) that William Penn first drew for Pennsylvania in 1682 was, for that day and age, exceedingly democratic.

Charter Colonies. The charter colonies were Rhode Island and Connecticut. In each of these colonies the king granted a charter to the colonists themselves, as a group. The charter was a written document outlining certain rights of self-government which could be withdrawn by the king if he chose to do so. The governor was elected annually by the freemen of the colony; and although the king's approval was required, it was seldom asked. The council and assembly were elected annually, and the governor had no veto over the assembly's acts.

The Rhode Island and Connecticut charters were so liberal that, after independence, they continued to serve as State constitutions until 1818 and 1842, respectively.

The Colonies and England. The colonists were British subjects, and they owed allegiance to the crown. In the minds of the king and his ministers, the colonies existed as handmaids to

---

[1] The term "burgesses" was used because it was expected that the settlements would develop into *boroughs* (towns). After 1634 the burgesses represented counties, and in 1776 the name was changed to "assemblymen." Virginia called the lower house of its colonial legislature "House of Burgesses"; South Carolina, "House of Commons"; Massachusetts, "House of Representatives."

serve the mother country. They were regarded as sources of raw materials and as markets for finished products. They were far-off territories to be held and ruled for the benefit of England.

In *theory*, the colonies were controlled in all important matters from London. But London was 3000 miles away. It took almost two months to sail from England to America. So, in *practice,* the colonists became quite accustomed to doing much as they pleased. They made their own laws, and the few regulations imposed by Parliament, concerned largely with trade, were generally ignored.

In the early 1760's matters changed, however. When George III ascended the throne, England began to deal more firmly with its American colonies. The king's ministers felt that the time had come to enforce and expand the restrictive trading acts; and they felt, too, that the colonists should be required to pay a larger share for the support of British troops stationed in America.

Many colonists took strong exception to these moves. They saw no need for the troops — the power of the French had been broken in the French and Indian War (1754–1763). They objected to taxes they had no part in levying—it was "taxation without representation." They recognized the sovereignty of the king, but they flatly refused to recognize any right of Parliament to control affairs within the colonies. In short, the colonists maintained that they possessed the same rights as Englishmen at home and that they had the right to manage their own local affairs as they saw fit.

The king's ministers were poorly informed and stubborn. They pushed ahead with their plans despite the resentment their policies stirred in America. Within a very few years the colonists found themselves faced with a fateful choice — to submit or to revolt.

The Colonies Unite. Long before the 1770's attempts had been made to bring the colonies together for collective action.

Early Attempts. In 1643 the Massachusetts Bay, Plymouth, Connecticut, and New Haven

The Capitol at Williamsburg, Virginia, was the seat of the House of Burgesses, the first representative assembly in America. (Colonial Williamsburg Photograph)

settlements had joined in the New England Confederation, a "league of friendship" for defense against Indian hostility. But as the Indian danger passed and frictions developed, the confederation lost importance and finally died in 1684. William Penn, in 1696, proposed an elaborate plan for colonial cooperation, especially in trade and criminal matters, but nothing came of it.

The Albany Plan, 1754. In 1754 the Lords of Trade called a conference of seven of the northern colonies[2] at Albany to consider the problems of colonial trade and the threat of French and Indian attacks. Here Benjamin Franklin proposed what came to be known as his Albany Plan of Union.

Franklin would have created an annual *congress* (conference) consisting of one delegate from each of the thirteen colonies. This body would have power to raise military and naval forces, make war and peace with the Indians,

---

[2] New Hampshire, Massachusetts, Rhode Island, Connecticut, New York, Pennsylvania, and Maryland.

regulate trade with the Indians, and collect customs and levy taxes.

Franklin's plan was ahead of its time, but it was to be remembered later when independence came. Although it was adopted by the Albany meeting, it was rejected by each of the colonies as a *surrender of too much* local power. At the same time, it was opposed in London as a *grant of too much* power to the colonies.

The Stamp Act Congress, 1765. As we know, the harsh tax and trade policies of the 1760's fanned colonial resentment. A series of new laws had been passed by Parliament, among them the Stamp Act of 1765. This law required a stamp tax to be paid on all legal documents and agreements and on newspapers circulating in America.

Immediately, a Stamp Act Congress met in New York City. Delegates from nine of the colonies[3] drafted a Declaration of Rights and Grievances protesting the stamp tax and other stern policies of the king's ministers. The meeting was the first occasion on which a significant number of the colonies joined together to oppose the mother country.

Parliament repealed the Stamp Act, but events were moving rapidly toward the final break. Resentment and anger were expressed in wholesale evasion of the laws; mob violence took place at the ports; English goods were boycotted; and such outbreaks as the Boston Tea Party of December 16, 1773, occurred. Organized resistance was carried on through Committees of Correspondence which had grown out of a group formed in 1772 by Samuel Adams in Boston. By 1773 committees were to be found throughout the colonies, providing a network for cooperation and the exchange of information among the patriots. In many places the committees even took over the management of public affairs.

The First Continental Congress, 1774. In the spring of 1774 Parliament passed another set

of laws, this time intended to punish the colonists for the disturbances in Boston and elsewhere. The "Intolerable Acts," as they were called in the colonies, prompted the Massachusetts and Virginia assemblies to call a general meeting of the colonies.

Fifty-six delegates, from every colony except Georgia, assembled in Philadelphia on September 5, 1774. Many of the leaders of the day were there—men such as Patrick Henry, Samuel Adams, Richard Henry Lee, and George Washington. For nearly two months the members of this First Continental Congress debated the strained and critical situation with England.

A Declaration of Rights protesting the British attitude was drafted and sent to George III. The delegates also urged each of the colonies to refuse to trade with England. They called for the creation of local committees to enforce the boycott and to take stern action against anyone who bought, sold, or consumed English goods. Before they adjourned on October 26, the delegates called for a second congress to convene the following May if conditions had not improved. Later, the assemblies in each of the colonies, including Georgia, approved the actions of the First Continental Congress.

INDEPENDENCE

Events moved swiftly in the months following the adjournment of the First Continental Congress. The British, instead of compromising to pacify the colonists, applied even stricter measures. Then it happened. On April 19, 1775, at Lexington and Concord, open and armed conflict occurred. The "shot heard round the world" was fired just three weeks before the Second Continental Congress assembled.

The Second Continental Congress, 1775. All thirteen colonies sent delegates to the Second Continental Congress which convened on

---

[3] All *except* New Hampshire, Virginia, North Carolina, and Georgia.

Much praise has been heaped upon the men who drafted the Constitution of the United States. Thus, Thomas Jefferson, writing from Paris, described the framers as "an assembly of demi-gods." A French diplomat, reporting to his government, wrote: ". . . if all the delegates named for this Philadelphia Convention are present, one will never have seen, even in Europe, an assembly more respectable for talents, knowledge, disinterestedness and patriotism than those who will compose it."

Well over a century later the historian Charles Beard was to write of that "truly remarkable assembly of men" that ". . . never in the history of assemblies has there been a convention of men richer in political experience and in practical knowledge, or endowed with a profounder insight into the springs of human action and in intimate essence of government." *(The Supreme Court and the Constitution,* 1912, pages 86–87.)

But another noted constitutional scholar, Max Farrand has concluded that:

Great men here and there, it is true, but the convention as a whole was comprised of such as would be appointed to a similar gathering at the present time: professional men, businessmen, and gentlemen of leisure; patriotic statesmen and clever, scheming politicians; some trained by experience and study for the task before them, and others utterly unfit. It was essentially a representative body, taking possibly a somewhat higher tone from the social conditions of the time, the seriousness of the crisis, and the character of the leaders. *(The Framing of the Constitution of the United States,* 1940, pages 40–41.)

Which of these views of the Founding Fathers do you think is the more likely or accurate? Do you think that a "similar gathering at the present time" could, in fact, be had? Explain.

May 10, 1775, in Independence Hall in Philadelphia. Most of the delegates who had attended the First Continental Congress were again present. Especially notable among the new members were Benjamin Franklin and John Hancock.

Hancock was chosen president of the Second Continental Congress.[4] Almost immediately a "continental army" was organized, and George Washington was appointed its commander in chief. Washington accepted and took formal command of the army at Cambridge, Massachusetts, on July 3, 1775; and Thomas Jefferson then replaced him as one of the delegates from Virginia.

---

[4] Peyton Randolph, who had also served as President of the First Continental Congress, was originally chosen to the office. He resigned on May 24, however, because the Virginia Assembly, of which he was the Speaker, had been called into session. Hancock was then chosen to succeed him.

The Second Continental Congress became, by force of circumstance, our first national government. Although it rested upon no constitutional basis, it served as the first government of the United States for nearly five years; that is, from the signing of the Declaration of Independence in July 1776, until the Articles of Confederation went into effect on March 1, 1781. It raised armies and a navy, borrowed, purchased supplies, created a monetary system, negotiated treaties with foreign powers, and performed the other functions any government would have had to under the circumstances.

The Second Continental Congress exercised both legislative and executive functions. In legislative matters each colonial delegation (later State delegation) had one vote. Executive functions were performed by the delegates through committees.

The Declaration of Independence. On June 7, 1776, over a year after open rebellion had broken out in the colonies, Richard Henry

Lee of Virginia proposed to the Second Continental Congress:

> *Resolved,* That these United Colonies are, and of right ought to be, free and independent States, that they are absolved from all allegiance to the British Crown, and that all political connection between them and the state of Great Britain is, and ought to be, totally dissolved.

A committee of five of the ablest men in the Second Continental Congress—Benjamin Franklin, John Adams, Roger Sherman, Robert Livingston, and Thomas Jefferson—was appointed to draft a statement to proclaim independence. Their momentous product, the Declaration of Independence,[5] was almost wholly the work of the young and brilliant Jefferson.

On July 2 the final break came. By unanimous vote the delegates adopted Lee's resolution. Two days later, on July 4, the Declaration of Independence itself was adopted and announced to the world.

What the Declaration Says. Most of the great document deals with the grievances the colonists felt toward England and George III. Its real heart, the lines which have made it our most precious charter, are found in the second paragraph:

> We hold these truths to be self-evident: that all men are created equal; that they are endowed by their Creator with certain unalienable Rights; that among these are Life, Liberty, and the pursuit of Happiness. That to secure these rights, Governments are instituted among Men, deriving their just powers from the consent of the governed; That whenever any Form of Government becomes destructive of these ends it is the Right of the People to alter or to abolish it, and to institute new Government, laying its foundations on such principles and organizing its powers in such form, as to them shall seem

most likely to effect their Safety and Happiness.

With these brave words the United States of America was born. The thirteen former colonies were now free and independent States. The fifty-six men who gave birth to the new nation sealed the Declaration of Independence with this final sentence:

> And for the support of this Declaration, with a firm reliance in the Protection of a divine Providence, we mutually pledge to each other our Lives, our Fortunes, and our sacred Honor.

THE FIRST STATE GOVERNMENTS

In January 1776, New Hampshire adopted a constitution to replace royal control. Within two months South Carolina did the same. Then, on May 10, 1776, nearly two months before the Declaration of Independence, the Second Continental Congress urged each colony to adopt:

> such governments as shall, in the opinion of the representatives of the people, best conduce to the happiness and safety of their constituents.

Most of the States adopted written constitutions in 1776 and 1777. With minor changes, Connecticut and Rhode Island transformed their colonial charters into State constitutions. Assemblies or conventions were commonly used to draft and approve the new documents. Massachusetts set a lasting precedent when it submitted its new fundamental law to the voters for approval. The Massachusetts constitution of 1780, still in force, is the oldest of the present-day State constitutions.[6] In fact, it is the oldest written constitution in force in the world today.

---

[5] The full text of the Declaration of Independence appears at pages 748–750.

[6] From independence until the adoption of its constitution in 1780 Massachusetts relied on the charter in force prior to 1691 as its fundamental law.

State Constitutions. Although the new State constitutions differed widely in detail, they had many important features in common. Four of these features should be noted, especially since these documents within a few years were to have a marked effect on the drafting of the Constitution of the United States.

Popular Sovereignty. The people were recognized as the *sole* source of governmental authority. All power held by government could come from one, and *only* one, fountain: the people themselves.

Limited Government. Government could exercise *only* those powers granted to it by the people. Because of the oppression experienced by the people in the colonies under British rule, the new State constitutions granted powers very sparingly.

Civil Liberties. Seven of the new State constitutions [7] began with a bill of rights containing the "unalienable rights" of the people. In every State it was made clear that the sovereign people had rights that government must at all times respect.

Separation of Powers and Checks and Balances. The powers that were given to the new State governments were purposely divided among three distinct branches—the legislative, the executive, and the judicial.

Each branch of the government was given powers with which to "check" the other branches of the government.

The first State constitutions were very short compared to those of today. Since the memory of royal governors was fresh in the minds of the people, the new State governors were given little real power. Most of the authority granted to each State was vested in its legislature. The right to vote was limited to those adult males who could meet high property ownership and other rigid suffrage qualifications.

THE CONFEDERATION AND THE CRITICAL PERIOD

Our First National Constitution. The First and Second Continental Congresses rested on no legal base. They were called in haste to meet an emergency, and they were intended to be temporary. Something more regular and permanent was clearly needed.

When Richard Henry Lee introduced his resolution which led to the Declaration of Independence, he also called for a "plan of confederation." Off and on for seventeen months the Second Continental Congress debated and considered a scheme to unite the States. Then, on November 15, 1777, the Articles of Confederation were approved.[8]

The Articles of Confederation did not go into effect immediately, however. The ratifications of all thirteen States were required. Eleven States approved the Articles of Confederation within the year following their proposal. Delaware added its approval in mid-1779. But Maryland did not ratify until February 27, 1781. The Second Continental Congress then set March 1, 1781, as the date upon which the Articles of Confederation were to become effective.

The Articles of Confederation established "a firm league of friendship" among the States. Each State retained "its sovereignty, freedom, and independence, and every 'power, jurisdiction, and right . . . not . . . expressly delegated to the United States, in Congress assembled." The States came together "for their common defense, the security of their liberties, and their mutual and general welfare."

The government established by the Articles of Confederation was exceedingly simple. A Congress, composed of delegates appointed annually by the States in whatever manner their legislatures might direct, was the single organ created. Each State had one vote in the

---

[7] Delaware, Maryland, Massachusetts, New Hampshire, North Carolina, Pennsylvania, Virginia.

[8] The text of the Articles of Confederation appears at pages 751-754.

Congress, regardless of its population or wealth. Neither an executive nor a judicial branch was provided. These functions were to be handled by committees of the Congress, and civil officers (postmasters, for example) were to be appointed by the Congress.

The powers of the Congress appear, at first glance, to have been considerable. Its more important powers included those to make war and peace, send and receive ambassadors, enter into treaties, borrow money, raise and equip a navy, maintain an army by requesting troops from the States, request funds from the States to meet the costs of government, regulate Indian affairs, fix standards of weights and measures, and establish post offices.

Several important powers were *not* granted to the Congress, however. The lack of them, together with other weaknesses in the Articles of Confederation, soon proved the document inadequate to the pressing needs of the times.

The Congress was not given the power to tax. It could raise needed funds in only two ways: by borrowing and by requesting money from the States. Heavy borrowing had been necessary to finance the American Revolution, and many of those debts had not been repaid. At best, then, this source for funds was none too good. And throughout the period the Articles of Confederation were in force not one of the States came close to meeting the financial requests made by the Congress.

The Congress also had no power to regulate trade between the States. It could not even levy duties on imports or exports.

Still worse, the Congress had no power to force either the States or the people to obey the Articles of Confederation or its own laws. All that the Congress could do was to *advise* and *request* the States to do this or to do that. In effect, all it could do was to say "please" and wait with hat in hand—often in vain.

Finally, most of the important powers that the Congress did have could be exercised only with the consent of the delegates from *nine* of the thirteen States. No changes could be made in the Articles of Confederation unless *all* of the States agreed.[9] The result of these weaknesses, as we shall see, was chaos.

The Critical Period, 1781–1787. On October 19, 1781, a British band played the old tune, "The World Turned Upside Down," as Lord Cornwallis formally surrendered his army to General Washington at Yorktown. Victory had come to the United States, and it was confirmed by the Treaty of Paris in 1783.

The coming of peace brought the political, social, and economic difficulties of the new nation into sharp focus. With a central government powerless to act, the States bickered among themselves and became increasingly jealous of one another. They levied tariffs on

---

[9] To get all thirteen jealous and increasingly unfriendly States to agree on anything seemed hopeless. In 1785 Congress made a final attempt to solve its financial problems by proposing an amendment to the Articles of Confederation to provide for import duties. But New York was reaping a handsome return from its own tax on imports and so refused to approve the proposal; thus, the measure died.

one another's goods and even banned some trade. They negotiated directly with foreign governments, even though this was forbidden in the Articles of Confederation. They often refused to obey laws and treaties made by the Congress. Most States even raised their own armies and navies. They printed their own money, often supporting it with little backing. Prices soared sky-high. Debts, public and private, went unpaid. Sound credit vanished. National respect began to disintegrate, since the States refused to support the central government, financially and in almost every other way.

George Washington was moved to complain:

> We are one nation today and thirteen tomorrow. Who will treat with us on such terms?

James Madison wrote of the situation:

> New Jersey, placed between Philadelphia and New York, was likened to a cask tapped at both ends; North Carolina, between Virginia and South Carolina, to a patient bleeding at both arms.

John Fiske thus described existing commercial conditions:

> The city of New York, with its population of 30,000 souls, had long been supplied with firewood from Connecticut, and with butter and cheese, chickens and garden vegetables from the thrifty farms of New Jersey. This trade, it was observed, carried thousands of dollars out of the city and into the pockets of the detested Yankees and despised Jerseymen. "It was ruinous to domestic industry," said the men of New York. "It must be stopped by ... a navigation act and a protective tariff." Acts were accordingly passed, obliging every Yankee sloop which came down through Hell Gate, and every Jersey market boat which was rowed across from Paulus Hook to Cortlandt Street, to pay entrance fees and obtain clearances at the custom

State money, like this note (left) issued by Rhode Island, had insufficient backing and was often not negotiable. The refusal of paper money in payment led to many court complaints and was one of the prime factors in the economic chaos of the 1780's. The Founding Fathers were convinced that the National Government must have the exclusive power "to coin money and regulate the value thereof." (New York Public Library)

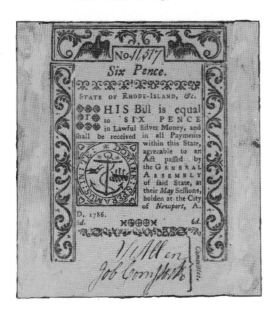

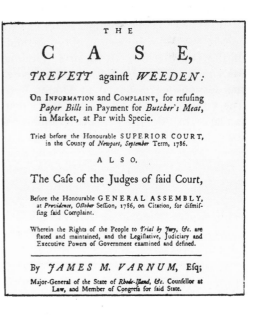

house, just as was done by ships from London and Hamburg; and not a cartload of Connecticut firewood could be delivered at the back door of a country house in Beekman Street until it should have paid a heavy duty. Great and just was the wrath of the farmers and lumbermen. The New Jersey legislature made up its mind to retaliate. The city of New York had lately bought a small patch of ground on Sandy Hook, and had built a lighthouse there. This lighthouse was the one weak spot in the heel of Achilles where a hostile arrow could strike, and New Jersey gave vent to her indignation by laying a tax of $1800 a year on it. Connecticut was equally prompt. At a great meeting of businessmen, held at New London, it was unanimously agreed to suspend all commercial intercourse with New York. Every merchant signed an agreement, under a penalty of $250 for the first offence, not to send any goods whatever into the hated State for a period of twelve months.[10]

Such distressing conditions as these led many, especially merchants and creditors, to yearn for a stronger central government better able to cope with the situation.

The Conventions at Mount Vernon and Annapolis. Several disputes between Maryland and Virginia, most of them centering on the navigation of the Potomac River and Chesapeake Bay, led to a meeting of representatives of the two States at Alexandria, Virginia, in March of 1785. At Washington's invitation the sessions were moved to Mount Vernon. The conference proved so successful that on January 21, 1786, the Virginia Assembly called for a "joint meeting of . . . the States to recommend a federal plan for regulating commerce."

When this convention met at Annapolis, Maryland, in September 1786, only five States were represented—New York, New Jersey, Pennsylvania, Delaware, and Virginia. Discouraged, but not completely, the delegates to the Annapolis Convention proposed another meeting of the States:

> . . . at Philadelphia on the second Monday in May next . . . to devise such further provisions as shall appear to them necessary to render the constitution of the Federal Government adequate to the exigencies of the Union . . .

By February 1787, seven of the States[11] had named delegates to convene at Philadelphia. Then on February 21, the Congress, which had been hesitating, also called upon the States to send delegates to the Philadelphia meeting:

> . . . for the sole and express purpose of revising the Articles of Confederation and reporting to Congress and the several legislatures such alterations and provisions therein as shall when agreed to in Congress and confirmed by the States render the [Articles of Confederation] adequate to the exigencies of Government and the preservation of the Union.

THE CONSTITUTIONAL CONVENTION

The Constitutional Convention began its work on Friday, May 25, 1787.[12] In all, twelve States were represented; only Rhode Island did not participate.[13]

The Founding Fathers. Seventy-four men were chosen as delegates by the various State legislatures but, in fact, only fifty-five attended

---

[10] John Fiske, *The Critical Period of American History.* Boston: Houghton Mifflin, 1888, page 146.

[11] Delaware, Georgia, New Hampshire, New Jersey, North Carolina, Pennsylvania, Virginia.

[12] Not enough States were represented on the original date, Monday, May 14. Those delegates who were present met and adjourned each day until May 25, when a majority of the States was on hand.

[13] The Rhode Island legislature was controlled by the so-called "soft money" group—mainly debtors and farmers who benefited by inflation and were thus against the creation of a stronger central government. New Hampshire's delegation, delayed especially by a lack of funds, did not reach Philadelphia until late in July.

sessions of the Constitutional Convention. Never before, or since, has so remarkable a group of men met under one roof. George Washington, James Madison, and Edmund Randolph came from Virginia; Benjamin Franklin, Gouverneur Morris, and James Wilson from Pennsylvania; Alexander Hamilton from New York; William Livingston and William Paterson from New Jersey; Elbridge Gerry and Rufus King from Massachusetts; Luther Martin from Maryland; Oliver Ellsworth and Roger Sherman from Connecticut; John Dickinson from Delaware; and John Rutledge and the two Pinckneys from South Carolina.

These were men of wide knowledge and public experience, men of wealth and prestige. Many of them had served in the American Revolution. Thirty-nine had served in the Continental Congresses or the Congress of the Confederation or both, eight in constitutional conventions in their own States, and seven had been State governors. Thirty-one of the delegates had college educations, and their number included two college presidents and three professors. Eight had signed the Declaration of Independence. Two were to become Presidents of the United States, and one a Vice President. Seventeen were later to serve in the Senate and eleven in the House of Representatives.

Is it any wonder that the product of such a gathering was described by the English statesman, William E. Gladstone, nearly a century later as: "the most wonderful work ever struck off at a given time by the brain and purpose of man"?

Remarkably, the average age of the Founding Fathers was only forty-two, and half of them were only in their thirties. Indeed, most of the real leaders were all in that age bracket — Madison was thirty-six, Gouverneur Morris thirty-five, Randolph thirty-four, and Hamilton thirty-two. Franklin, at eighty-one the oldest member, was failing and unable to attend many of the sessions. Washington, at fifty-five, was one of the few older members who played a leading part in the making of the Constitution.

By and large, the Framers of the Constitution represented a new generation in American politics. Many of the prominent leaders of the American Revolution were notable by their absence. Patrick Henry said that he "smelt a rat" and refused to attend. Samuel Adams, John Hancock, and Richard Henry Lee were not selected as delegates by their respective States. Thomas Jefferson was our minister to France, and John Adams was serving in a similar capacity to England and Holland at the time.

Organization and Procedure. The Constitutional Convention met in Independence Hall, very likely in a room immediately above the one in which the Declaration of Independence had been signed. Of the fifty-five delegates who reached Philadelphia, some attended only a part of the time. The attendance at a typical daily session ran to about thirty.

When the Constitutional Convention organized itself on May 25, George Washington was the unanimous choice to preside. It was decided that each State should have one vote on all questions and that a simple majority of the votes cast would carry any proposal.

The meeting naturally attracted much public attention. Thus, to ensure free and unrestrained debate, and to protect themselves as much as possible from outside pressures, the delegates pledged themselves to the strictest secrecy concerning their proceedings. The pledge was kept in remarkable fashion.

A secretary (William Jackson) was appointed, and a *Journal* was kept. The official record, however, was little more than a bare listing of formal motions and votes, and it was not always accurate, at that. Fortunately, some of the delegates — most notably James Madison — kept private accounts of the proceedings. Most of what we know today of the work of the Constitutional Convention comes from Madison's careful and voluminous *Notes*. His brilliance and vast knowledge led his colleagues to hold him in profound respect. He was, in effect, the floor leader at the Constitutional Convention and contributed more to the Constitution than did any of the others—and, still, he was able to keep such a close record. There is little doubt that he deserves the title history has given him: "The Father of the Constitution."

The relatively small number of delegates made it possible for them to do most of their work on the convention floor. Some matters were dealt with by committees, but all questions were ultimately settled by the full body. Daily sessions usually began at 10 A.M. and adjourned about 3 P.M.

The Great Agreement. Almost at once the delegates agreed that they were meeting to create a *national* government:

> *Resolved,* . . . that a national government ought to be established consisting of a Supreme Legislative, Executive, and Judiciary.

The delegates had been appointed to "recommend revisions" in the Articles of Confederation. But, with this decision, they set about writing a whole new constitution. This meant the creation of a vastly expanded government with extensive new powers—a government with powers supreme over the States.

The debates were often bitter, and at times the Constitutional Convention even seemed to be on the verge of collapse. Once the Great Agreement was reached, however, the determination of the majority never wavered.

The Virginia Plan. No State had been more responsible for the calling of the Constitutional Convention than Virginia. It was natural, then, that its delegates should present the first plan for a new constitution. On May 29 the Virginia Plan, fifteen separate resolutions drafted largely by Madison, was presented by Edmund Randolph.

The Virginia Plan called for a new government to be composed of three branches—legislative, executive, and judicial. The legislature (Congress) would consist of two houses (be, then, *bicameral*). Representation in each house was to be based upon either each State's population or the amount of money it contributed to the central government. The members of the lower house (the House of Representatives) were to be elected popularly and those of the upper house (the Senate) were to be chosen by the lower house from candidates nominated by the State legislatures. Congress was to be given all the powers it held under the Articles of Confederation. In addition, it was to have the power to legislate "in all cases in which the States are incompetent" to act, the power to veto any State law in conflict with national law, and the power to use the armed forces to compel a State to obey national law.

The Virginia Plan also called for a "national executive" and a "national judiciary" to be chosen by Congress. Together, these two branches would compose a "council of revision" with the power to veto acts of Congress, but such an action could be overridden by a vote of the two houses. It further provided that all State officers should take an oath to support the Union, that each State should be guaranteed a republican form of government, and that new States might be admitted to the Union by a majority vote of Congress.

The Virginia Plan, then, proposed a *thorough* revision of the Articles of Confederation—the creation of a *national* government with vastly expanded powers and, importantly, with the power to enforce its decisions.

Although the Virginia Plan served as a model for discussion through the remainder of the Constitutional Convention, some of the delegates—especially those from the smaller States of Delaware, Maryland, and New Jersey and from New York [14]—considered its proposals

---

[14] The Virginia Plan's major support came from the delegations of the three largest States: Virginia, Pennsylvania, and Massachusetts. New York was then only the fifth largest. Alexander Hamilton, the Constitutional Convention's most outspoken champion of a stronger central government, was regularly out-voted by his fellow delegates from New York.

too radical and far-reaching. In the course of discussions of the Virginia Plan, they developed their counter-proposals. On June 15, William Paterson of New Jersey presented them to the convention.

The New Jersey Plan. Paterson and his colleagues proposed amendments to the Articles of Confederation, but not nearly so thorough a revision as that offered by the Virginia Plan. The New Jersey Plan would have retained the unicameral Congress of the Confederation, with each of the States equally represented. To the existing powers of the Congress would be added a limited power to tax and the power to regulate interstate commerce. It also called for a "federal executive" and a "federal judiciary" to be elected by the Congress.

The major point of difference between the two rival plans concerned representation in Congress. Should the States be represented on the basis of their populations (or financial contributions) or should they each be represented equally? For weeks the delegates returned to this conflict, debating it again and again. The lines were sharply drawn. Several delegates on both sides threatened to withdraw. But, finally and fortunately, a compromise was reached—one of the truly great compromises of the Constitutional Convention.

The Great Compromises. The Constitution, as it was drafted at Philadelphia, has often been described as a "bundle of compromises." The description is an apt one—*if* it is properly understood.

By no means all, or even most, of what went into the document resulted from compromises among the delegates. The Founding Fathers were, in fact, in close agreement on many of the basic issues they faced. Virtually all of them were convinced that a *new* central government was essential and that the government had to have the powers necessary to cope with the nation's economic and social problems. They were dedicated, too, to the concepts of popular sovereignty and of limited government. None of them questioned for a moment the wisdom of representative government. The principles of separation of powers and of checks and balances—woven into the Constitution to prevent the new government from abusing its powers—were accepted by the delegates almost as a matter of course.

There were differences of opinion among the delegates, of course, and often very important ones. Matters could hardly have been otherwise. After all, the delegates came from twelve different States which were, in 1787, widely separated in both geographic and economic terms; and, quite naturally, the delegates tended to reflect the interests of their respective States.

Many disputes did occur, and the compromises by which they were resolved often were reached only after hours and days or even weeks of intense debate. But the point here is that the differences were *not* over the *most fundamental* of questions. Rather, the differences were over such vital but lesser questions as the details of the composition of Congress, the manner by which the President should be chosen, and the specific limitations that should be placed upon such grants as the taxing power and the commerce power.

The Connecticut Compromise. The most famous of the disputes was that between the large and the small States over representation in Congress. The former expected to dominate the new government, and the latter feared that they would be unable to protect their interests. The conflict between the rival Virginia and New Jersey Plans was finally settled by a compromise first suggested by Roger Sherman of Connecticut. It was agreed that Congress should be composed of two houses, a Senate and a House of Representatives. In the smaller Senate the States would be represented equally. In the House representation would be in accordance with population. Thus, by combining basic features of both the Virginia and New Jersey Plans, the Convention's most serious conflict was resolved.

The Three-Fifths Compromise. Once it had been agreed that representation in the lower house would be based on population, another question arose. Should the Southern States be permitted to count their slaves in determining their populations? Again, the arguments were fierce. But, finally, the delegates agreed that all "free persons" would be counted and so, too, would "three-fifths of all other persons." The "three-fifths" won by the Southern States was balanced by the fact that it was to be used *not only* for setting each State's quota of seats in the House of Representatives *but also* its quota of money to be raised under any direct tax levied by Congress. Of course, this curious compromise disappeared with the adoption of the Thirteenth Amendment in 1865.

James Madison, the "Father of the Constitution" and our first true political scientist, kept careful and exhaustive notes on the work of the Constitutional Convention. His notes are the most reliable source as to what took place there.

The Commerce and Slave Trade Compromise. Much of the agitation that had led to the calling of the Constitutional Convention came from those who were most interested in diminishing, if not eliminating, the economic chaos of the times—especially through national regulation of interstate and foreign trade. But if the National Government controlled commerce, Southerners were afraid that Northerners, in control of Congress, might tax their flourishing agricultural trade with England. They were particularly fearful that their cotton trade might be forced to the less profitable markets in the North.

Again, compromise was reached. Congress was given the power to regulate interstate and foreign commerce. But it was expressly forbidden the power to tax exports or to favor one port over another in the regulation of trade; and it was also prohibited from interfering with the slave trade, except by a small head tax, until at least 1808.

Other Compromises. Several other compromises went into the making of the Constitution. For example, several methods for selecting the President were proposed, including election by the people, by Congress, and by the State legislatures. Twice the delegates approved election by Congress. Opponents of that scheme argued that it would inevitably lead to legislative domination of the executive branch and would thus destroy the concept of separation of powers. They finally won their point in the closing weeks, and the Electoral College system was devised as a compromise among the various alternatives.

The President's four-year term and his eligibility for re-election came from a compromise between those who favored a longer term and those who feared that long tenure in office was a threat to liberty. The question of who could vote in national as well as State elections was left to each of the States as a compromise of the arguments of those who favored a small, aristocratic electorate and those who wanted to broaden the suffrage.

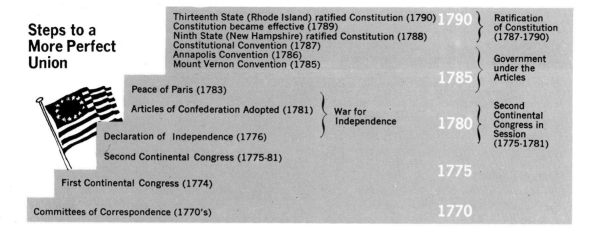

Steps to a More Perfect Union

Thirteenth State (Rhode Island) ratified Constitution (1790)
Constitution became effective (1789)
Ninth State (New Hampshire) ratified Constitution (1788)
Constitutional Convention (1787)
Annapolis Convention (1786)
Mount Vernon Convention (1785)

} 1790 Ratification of Constitution (1787-1790)

} 1785 Government under the Articles

Peace of Paris (1783)
Articles of Confederation Adopted (1781)
Declaration of Independence (1776)
Second Continental Congress (1775-81)

} War for Independence

} 1780 Second Continental Congress in Session (1775-1781)

First Continental Congress (1774)

1775

Committees of Correspondence (1770's)

1770

The achieving of a strong national Union took numerous "building steps," covering a construction period of approximately 150 years. The Constitution was the end result of much experience in the ways of government.

The method of choosing Senators, the manner of selecting judges and the status of the judicial branch, the admission of new States, the amendment process—these and many other topics provoked debate and painstaking consideration. As Benjamin Franklin put it, the Constitutional Convention spent much time "sawing boards to make them fit."

Sources of the Constitution. As we noted, the Framers of the Constitution were, by and large, well-educated men. In drafting the Constitution they drew upon their knowledge of history and of governments of antiquity and of contemporary England and Europe. They were familiar with the political writings of their time—especially with Blackstone's *Commentaries on the Laws of England*, Montesquieu's *Spirit of Laws*, Rousseau's *Social Contract*, and John Locke's *Two Treatises on Government*. As one writer has put it, they were "saturated with the revolutionary literature that some of their contemporaries, including some of those at the Convention, helped write and disseminate."

More immediately, the Framers of the Constitution drew upon their experience with and the records of the Second Continental Congress, the Articles of Confederation, and their respective State governments. Thus, much that went into the Constitution came directly—sometimes word for word—from the Articles of Confederation and from various State constitutions.

The Convention Completes Its Work. By the end of July the delegates had tailored a series of resolutions into an organized text. The next several weeks were spent in analyzing, debating, and perfecting their handiwork. On September 8, a Committee on Style was named to "revise the style and arrange the articles which had been agreed to by the house." This group, headed by Gouverneur Morris, put the Constitution in its final clear, concise form. At last, on September 17, thirty-nine names were signed to the finished document.[15]

---

[15] Three of the forty-one delegates present refused to sign: Edmund Randolph of Virginia, who later did support ratification and then served as Attorney General and Secretary of State in the Washington administration; Elbridge Gerry of Massachusetts, who later became Vice President under Madison; and George Mason of Virginia. George Read of Delaware signed both for himself and for his absent colleague, John Dickinson.

Perhaps none of the Founding Fathers was *completely* satisfied with their work, but Benjamin Franklin spoke for most of them when he said:

I agree to this Constitution, with all its faults, if they are such; . . . I doubt whether any other Convention we can obtain may be able to make a better Constitution. For when you assemble a number of men to have the advantage of their joint wisdom, you inevitably assemble with those men all their prejudices, their passions, their errors of opinion, their local interests, and their selfish views. From such an assembly can a perfect production be expected? It therefore astonishes me, Sir, to find this sytem approaching so near to perfection as it does; and I think it will astonish our enemies . . .

While the Constitution was being signed, Madison tells us:

Doct^r Franklin looking toward the President's Chair, at the back of which a rising sun happened to be painted, observed to a few members near him, that Painters had found it diffi-

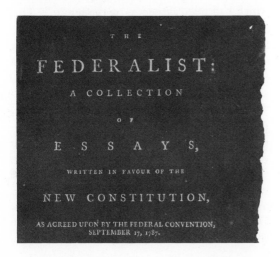

Written by Hamilton, Madison, and Jay as an argument for ratification of the Constitution, The Federalist, a series of remarkable essays, remains one of the best commentaries on the Constitution. (Culver Pictures, Inc.)

cult to distinguish in their art a rising from a setting sun. I have, said he, often and often in the course of the Session . . . looked at that behind the President without being able to tell whether it was rising or setting: But now at length I have the happiness to know that it is a rising and not a setting sun.

Ratification. The new Constitution was intended to replace the Articles of Confederation. The Articles of Confederation provided that changes could be made *only* with the approval of *all* of the States. But the Founding Fathers had seen how crippling this requirement had been. Thus, the new Constitution provided (Article VII) that the ratifications "of nine States shall be sufficient for the establishment of this Constitution between the States so ratifying the same." The Congress of the Confederation agreed to this irregular procedure when it sent the new document on to the States on September 28, 1787.

Federalists and Anti-Federalists. The proposed Constitution was printed, circulated, and debated throughout the country. Two factions quickly emerged in each of the States: the *Federalists*, who supported ratification, and the *Anti-Federalists*, who opposed it.

The Federalists were led in the main by many of the men who had attended the Constitutional Convention. Among them, the most active and the most effective were James Madison and Alexander Hamilton. Their opposition was headed by such respected Revolutionary War figures as Patrick Henry, Richard Henry Lee, John Hancock, and Samuel Adams.

In arguing their case, the Federalists emphasized the weaknesses of the Articles of Confederation. They insisted that the many difficulties facing the Republic could be overcome only by replacing the existing governmental system with a new one founded upon the proposed Constitution.

The Anti-Federalists attacked nearly every feature of the new document. Many objected to the fact that they had either to accept or to reject it as it stood, without an opportunity to amend it before a final decision was made. Some complained that nowhere did it specifically recognize the existence of God. Others criticized the Framers for providing a method of ratification contrary to that required by the Articles of Confederation. Still others, especially debtors, were vehemently opposed to the denial to the States of the power to print money.

The largest amount of criticism focused upon two aspects of the Constitution, however: (1) the vast increases it provided in the powers of the central government and (2) its lack of a bill of rights proclaiming such fundamental liberties as freedom of speech, press, and religion and guarantees of fair trial. Patrick Henry expressed the view of many when he declared:

> I look upon that paper as the most fatal plan that could possibly be conceived to enslave a free people.

Success. Although the struggle for ratification was a bitter one in many States, the Federalists ultimately prevailed in all of them. The Constitution was ratified by the convention in each State on the date and by the vote shown in the following table:

RATIFICATION OF THE CONSTITUTION

State	Date	Vote
1. Delaware	Dec. 7, 1787	30–0
2. Pennsylvania	Dec. 12, 1787	46–23
3. New Jersey	Dec. 19, 1787	38–0
4. Georgia	Jan. 2, 1788	26–0
5. Connecticut	Jan. 9, 1788	128–40
6. Massachusetts	Feb. 6, 1788	187–168
7. Maryland	Apr. 28, 1788	63–11
8. South Carolina	May 23, 1788	149–73
9. New Hampshire	June 21, 1788	57–46
10. Virginia	June 25, 1788	89–79
11. New York	July 26, 1788	30–27
12. North Carolina *	Nov. 21, 1789	184–77
13. Rhode Island	May 29, 1790	34–32

* Second vote. Ratification was originally defeated on Aug. 4, 1788, by a vote of 184–84.

On June 21, 1788, New Hampshire brought the number of ratifying States to nine. According to Article VII, its action should have brought the Constitution into effect. But, in fact, it did not. Neither Virginia nor New York had yet ratified, and without either of them the new government could not hope to succeed.

Virginia. Virginia's ratification followed New Hampshire's by a scant four days. The debates in its convention were intense and brilliant, and they were followed closely throughout the State. The Federalist cause was led by Madison, the young John Marshall, and Governor Edmund Randolph (even though, recall, he had refused to sign the Constitution at Philadelphia). Patrick Henry was the leader of the opposition and was joined by such outstanding Virginians as James Monroe, Richard Henry Lee, and George Mason (another of the non-signers).

Although George Washington was not a delegate, his strong support for ratification proved a vital factor in persuading the convention. Together with Madison, he was able to convince a reluctant Jefferson to agree. Had Jefferson fought as did other Anti-Federalists, Virginia might never have ratified.

New York. A narrow vote in the New York convention brought the number of ratifying States to eleven on July 26, 1788. Clearly, New York's approval was very largely the result of the appearance of *The Federalist*—a remarkable series of eighty-five essays discussing the Constitution virtually line by line and defending it against its critics. These "papers," written by Hamilton, Madison, and John Jay, were first published in various newspapers of the State and shortly thereafter in book form. They remain today an excellent commentary on the Constitution and continue to rank among the very best of all political writings in the English language.

Inauguration of the New Government. On September 13, 1788, with eleven of the thirteen States "under the federal roof," the

Congress of the Confederation paved the way for its successor. It chose New York City as the temporary capital, provided for the selection of presidential electors in the States, set the first Wednesday in February as the day on which they would vote, and decided that the new government should be inaugurated on March 4, 1789.

The new Congress met on March 4, 1789, in Federal Hall on Wall Street. Because a *quorum* (enough members to conduct business) was lacking, this First Session of the First Congress did not count the electoral vote until April 6. Then on April 30, after a memorable trip from his home in Mount Vernon, Virginia, to New York City, George Washington, the unanimous choice of the electors (and the only person ever accorded this honor), was sworn in as the first President of the United States of America.

❖❖❖❖❖❖❖❖❖❖ CONCEPT BUILDING ❖❖❖❖❖❖❖❖❖❖

Key Concepts

Government in the United States did not suddenly spring into being. It is the product of centuries of development.

The English, who settled the thirteen colonies, contributed much to the shaping of our governmental system: particularly, the pattern of early government in America and the concepts of limited government and of representative government.

Beginning with the founding of Jamestown, Virginia, in 1607, all thirteen colonies were established by 1732. Three types of colonies existed: royal, proprietary, and charter. The eight royal colonies were ruled by a royal governor under the king. The three proprietary colonies were governed under a proprietor who was, in turn, responsible to the king. The two charter colonies, the most democratic, governed themselves much as they saw fit.

England's control over its colonies was tightened in the 1760's, and the resentment this created led to the American Revolution. England looked on the colonies as handmaids to serve the mother country; the colonists demanded the right to manage their own affairs. The colonists did attempt to head off the break, especially in the First Continental Congress in 1774.

By the meeting of the Second Continental Congress in 1775, the American Revolution had actually begun. This body functioned as our first national government. It proclaimed the Declaration of Independence on July 4, 1776, and drew up our first national constitution, the Articles of Confederation, which went into effect in March, 1781.

The government set up under the Articles of Confederation proved too weak for the times. The chaos of the Critical Period led to the meeting of the Constitutional Convention.

From May 25 to September 17, 1787, the Founding Fathers worked to produce the Constitution. It replaced the Articles of Confederation in 1789 when George Washington was inaugurated as the First President of the United States of America.

Important Terms

Albany Plan of Union
Anti-Federalists
Articles of Confederation
charter colonies
Critical Period
Declaration of Independence

Federalists
First Continental Congress
Founding Fathers
limited government
New Jersey Plan
popular sovereignty

proprietary colonies
ratification
royal colonies
Second Continental Congress
The Federalist
Virginia Plan

Questions for Inquiry and Review

1. What were the major political concepts the early English settlers brought to America?

2. What distinguished the three major types of colonies from each other?

3. What was the English attitude toward the colonies? What was the colonial attitude toward the relationship with England, particularly after 1763?

4. What body became our first national government? How?

5. The Declaration of Independence was drafted by whom?

6. Which portion of the Declaration of Independence is the most important? Why?

7. What, in brief, was the nature of the first State governments?

8. What were the Articles of Confederation? When and by whom were they framed? When did they become effective?

9. What was the structure of the government created by the Articles of Confederation?

10. What were the major powers of the Congress under the Articles of Confederation? What were the document's major weaknesses?

11. When and where was the Constitution framed?

12. Who were the outstanding members of the Constitutional Convention?

13. What momentous decision did the Founding Fathers make at the outset of the Constitutional Convention?

14. Who is called the "Father of the Constitution"?

15. What were the similarities and the differences between the Virginia Plan and the New Jersey Plan?

16. What were the three major compromises made at the Constitutional Convention?

17. In what sense was the Constitution a "bundle of compromises"?

18. From what sources did the Framers of the Constitution draw in drafting the Constitution?

19. What were the major objections raised against the new Constitution?

20. When did the new government begin functioning?

For Further Inquiry

1. On the first day, May 25, 1787, the delegates to the Constitutional Convention unanimously elected George Washington the presiding officer. Why was this action so significant? What was Washington's status with the people of the day? Could the fact that he presided at the Convention have had any effect in the ratification controversy?

2. Why has it been said that the fact that such men as Patrick Henry, Samuel Adams, and John Hancock were not delegates to the Constitutional Convention was a fortunate thing? Could it have been unfortunate?

3. In what ways did the Constitution provide for "a more perfect Union" than the Articles of Confederation?

4. The Preamble of the Constitution declares that the document was ordained and established by "We, the People of the United States." Yet, in fact, it was drafted by fifty-five delegates at Philadelphia and was subsequently ratified by conventions in the thirteen States. How can one reconcile the apparent contradiction here?

5. It has been said that the Declaration of Independence was a radical and revolutionary document but that the Constitution was not. Do you agree?

6. Do you agree with Jefferson's thought: "Each generation . . . has a right to choose for itself the form of government it believes most promotive of its own happiness"?

Suggested Activities

1. Make a brief outline of the Articles of Confederation and of the Constitution (see pages 751–754 and 755–768).

2. Prepare short biographical sketches of such outstanding Revolutionary War leaders and of the Founding Fathers as George Washington, Benjamin Franklin, Thomas Jefferson, Alexander Hamilton, Samuel Adams, Patrick Henry, James Madison, John Hancock, Richard Henry Lee, Gouverneur Morris.

3. Stage a debate or class forum on the following: (a) *Resolved,* That the thirteen colonies should have remained within the British Empire; (b) *Resolved,* That the Framers of the Constitution should have provided for a unicameral Congress in which each State would have been equally represented; (c) *Resolved,* That the States should have rejected the Constitution proposed by the Philadelphia Convention and that the governmental arrangements provided by the Articles of Confederation should have been continued.

4. Prepare a wall chart or bulletin board display depicting the major steps and events leading finally to the Constitution and its ratification.

5. Compare the organization, length, and contents of the Constitution of the United States and the constitution of your State. (If a copy of the latter is not available in the school or other local library, one can usually be obtained from the office of the Secretary of State in the State capital.)

6. Prepare a wall chart or bulletin board display depicting the major weaknesses of the Articles of Confederation and the manner in which these weaknesses were corrected in the Constitution.

Suggested Reading

ADRIAN, CHARLES R. and PRESS, CHARLES, *The American Political Process.* McGraw-Hill, 1969. Chapter 4.

BLACKMORE, CHARLES P. and YESELSON, ABRAHAM (eds.), *The Fabric of American Democracy.* Van Nostrand, 1969. Chapter 1.

BURNS, JAMES M. and PELTASON, J. W., *Government By the People.* Prentice-Hall, 1969. Chapter 2.

FLEMING, THOMAS J., "One Flag Out of Many," *Reader's Digest,* September, 1969.

LEVY, LEONARD W. (ed.), *Essays on the Making of the Constitution.* Oxford, 1969.

ODEGARD, PETER H., *et al., The American Republic.* Harper & Row, 1969. Chapter 4.

PRITCHETT, C. HERMAN, *The American Constitution.* McGraw-Hill, 1968. Chapters 1, 2.

REDFORD, EMMETTE S., *et al., Government and Politics in the United States.* Harcourt, Brace, and World, 1968. Chapter 2.

SCOTT, ANDREW M. and WALLACE, EARLE (eds.), *Politics, U.S.A.: Cases on the American Democratic Process.* Macmillan, 1969. Ch. 2.

WOOD, GORDON S., *The Creation of the American Republic 1776–1787.* University of North Carolina Press, 1969.

THE CONSTITUTION: BASIC PRINCIPLES AND DEVELOPMENT

All men are born equally free and independent; therefore, all government of right originates from the people, is founded in consent, and instituted for the general good.

ARTICLE I, CONSTITUTION OF
NEW HAMPSHIRE, 1784

✳✳✳Did the founding Fathers in fact produce (as John Marshall later described it) "a Constitution intended to endure for years to come"?

✳✳✳Why may it be said that the Constitution of the United States today is and at the time is not the document that was written in 1787?

✳✳✳Is the Constitution too easily amended—either formally or informally?

The Constitution of the United States is the nation's fundamental law. It embodies the principles upon which government in the United States was established. It prescribes the basic organization and procedures by which, and the limits within which, government must operate.

Even with its twenty-five amendments, the Constitution of the United States is quite brief. It contains only some 7000 words and may be read in a leisurely half hour. It is especially concerned with fundamental principles rather than with specific and detailed matters of governmental procedure and organization.

In this chapter we consider six basic principles of the American constitutional system: popular sovereignty, limited government, separation of powers, checks and balances, judicial review, and federalism. In a real sense, this entire text is devoted to these principles because they lie at the very heart of any discussion of American government.

THE BASIC PRINCIPLES

Popular Sovereignty. *All* political power in the United States belongs to the people. The people are sovereign. From them *must* flow any and all authority for *any* governmental action. In the United States it is the people who rule. Government at any level may be conducted *only* with the consent of the governed. The principle of popular sovereignty is most clearly spelled out in the Preamble to the Constitution:

We, the People of the United States, . . . do ordain and establish this Constitution for the United States of America.

In our political theory it is through the Constitution that the people have delegated (granted) powers to the National Government. It is through the Constitution of the United States and the State's constitution that each of the fifty States has received its powers from the people.

49

Limited Government. The principle of limited government holds that governments in the United States may exercise *only* those powers which the *sovereign* (the people) have seen fit to vest in them. In effect, this is the other side of the coin of popular sovereignty. All governments in the United States are limited to the powers granted to them by the people. None can exercise any other powers. And none of the powers a government does possess may be exercised in an arbitrary or unfair manner.

The Constitution of the United States contains several provisions specifically prohibiting the National Government and the States the power to do several things. For example, neither the National Government nor the States may levy any duties on exports.[1] The National Government may not force any person accused of a crime to testify against himself.[2] Nor may a State deprive any person of the right to vote on account of sex.[3]

The great constitutional guarantees of personal freedom (civil rights) flow from the principle of limited government. Thus, the rights of freedom of speech, press, religion, assembly, and petition all are enshrined in the 1st Amendment, which begins with the words: "Congress shall make no law . . ."

Separation of Powers. When we discussed the presidential and parliamentary forms of government (see page 9), we noted this fact: The basic powers of government—legislative, executive, and judicial—may all be held by a single supreme agency *or* may be divided (separated) among three distinct branches. In a parliamentary system, like Great Britain's, for example, these powers are concentrated in the Parliament. In the presidential system, like that of the United States, these powers are separated among three branches.

---

[1] Article I, Section 9, Clause 5 and Article I, Section 10, Clause 2.

[2] The 5th Amendment.

[3] The 19th Amendment.

The Constitution distributes the powers of the National Government among the Congress (the legislative branch), the President (the executive branch) and the courts (the judicial branch). Article I, Section 1 provides: "All legislative powers herein granted shall be vested in a Congress of the United States . . ." Article II, Section 1 provides: "The executive power shall be vested in a President of the United States of America." Article III, Section 1 provides: "The judicial power of the United States shall be vested in one Supreme Court, and in such inferior courts as the Congress may from time to time ordain and establish."

In defense of this arrangement James Madison wrote:

> The accumulation of all powers, legislative, executive, and judiciary, in the same hands, whether of one, a few, or many, and whether hereditary, self-appointed, or elective, may justly be pronounced the very definition of tyranny.

The Congress exercises *legislative* (law-making) powers. It cannot authorize any other agency or person to make laws in its stead. But it can, and often does, pass acts which outline general policies and set certain standards while leaving the actual details of day-to-day administration to some agency under the President. For instance, Congress has provided for the regulation of air transportation and has set out the standards to be followed in this respect. The actual details of regulation—involving such complex matters as the setting of passenger and freight rates, air traffic control, safety requirements, and pilot licensing—are handled by various agencies within the Department of Transportation.

The President possesses *executive* (law-executing, law-enforcing, law-administering) powers. Of course, he is assisted by all of the several departments, agencies, officers, and employees in the vast executive branch. But he alone is personally and finally responsible for executive actions.

The Major Features of the American System of Checks and Balances

EXECUTIVE BRANCH
THE PRESIDENT

President may veto legislation, call special sessions, recommend legislation, appeal to the people.

President appoints federal judges.

Congress creates agencies and programs, appropriates funds, may override veto, may remove President through impeachment; Senate approves treaties and presidential appointments.

Judges, appointed for life, are free from executive control; courts may declare executive actions to be unconstitutional.

Courts may declare acts of Congress to be unconstitutional.

Congress creates lower courts, may remove judges through impeachment; Senate approves appointment of judges.

LEGISLATIVE BRANCH
THE CONGRESS

JUDICIAL BRANCH
THE SUPREME COURT
and other Federal Courts

The balance of power among the three branches is maintained through the system of constitutional checks which keep the National Government on an even keel.

The courts, and most importantly the Supreme Court, exercise the *judicial* (law-interpreting, law-applying) powers. The courts exercise their powers in actual disputes as the disputes are brought before them by government or by private parties.

The early State constitutions had provided for a separation of powers. Mistrust and suspicion of *any* government was common in the United States of the late 1700's. Thus, separation of powers was both natural and inevitable in the writing of the Constitution.

Checks and Balances. While there are three *separate* and *distinct* branches of the National Government, these branches are *not* completely independent of each other. Each branch has its own field of powers, but it is also subject to a series of constitutional *checks* (restraints) which either of the other two branches may exercise against it.

The Constitution interlaces the three branches with several of these checks. For example, Congress has the power to make laws; but the President may veto an act of Congress; and Congress may pass legislation over a President's veto by a two-thirds vote in each house. Congress may refuse to appropriate funds requested by the President, or the Senate may refuse to approve appointments or treaties the President has made. The President has the power to appoint all federal judges. The courts have the power to determine the constitutionality of acts of Congress or actions of the President and his subordinates.

Head-on clashes between the branches seldom occur. The check and balance system, however, operates constantly, in almost routine fashion. The very existence of the system shapes much that happens in the National Government. Consider two common examples of this fact: In making an important appointment to a post in his administration, the President must always bear in mind that whomever he appoints must be acceptable to the Senate. In framing legislation, Congress must always keep in mind the President's veto power and the power of the courts to declare an act unconstitutional.

Of course, spectacular clashes, dramatic applications of the check and balance system, do happen occasionally. Thus, Mr. Nixon's difficulties with the filling of a Supreme Court vacancy in 1969 and 1970 afford an example. The Senate rejected first one and then another of his nominees before finally agreeing to the President's appointment of Justice Harry Blackmun to the High Court. Such occurences are quite rare, however; both Congress and the President regularly take particular pains to avoid them.

The Founding Fathers intended the check and balance system to prevent "an unjust combination of the majority." On the whole, the system has worked well. But the people have learned that while mistakes or evil designs of one branch may be checked by another, so too can well-planned, honest policies be checked for political reasons.

When both houses of Congress are controlled by the President's supporters, the system works well. But when the opposing party controls one or both houses, it is sometimes quite difficult for the National Government to operate smoothly. In such instances the National Government does not fail completely, of course, but it is often stalled over vital policy decisions.

The check and balance system makes compromises necessary, and compromise *is* of the essence in a democratic system. Dictatorships are based on the seizure and possession of power by one man or a small group. The many checks with which each branch may *balance* (restrain) either or both of the others makes such an occurrence virtually impossible in our system of government.

Judicial Review. Judicial review may be defined as the power of a court to determine the constitutionality of a governmental action and to *void* (declare unconstitutional) any governmental action found to be in conflict with some provision of the Constitution. The power is held by all federal courts and by most State courts, as well.[4]

The Constitution does not provide for the power of judicial review *in so many words*. But, clearly, the Founding Fathers intended that the federal courts, and especially the Supreme Court, should possess the power. They felt that its existence was clearly implied in the words of the Constitution.[5] In *The Federalist* (Number 78) Alexander Hamilton wrote:

> The interpretation of the laws is the proper and peculiar province of the courts. A constitution is, in fact, and must be regarded by the judges, as a fundamental law. It therefore belongs to them to ascertain its meaning, as well as the meaning of any particular act proceeding from the legislative body. If there should happen to be an irreconcilable conflict between the two, that which has the superior obligation and validity ought, of course, to be preferred; or, in other words, the Constitution ought to be preferred to the statute, the intention of the people to the intention of their agents.

The Supreme Court first exercised the power of judicial review in *Marbury* v. *Madison* (1803).[6] By 1971 it had declared more than 100 acts or portions of acts of Congress unconstitutional. It has also voided many presidential actions, and held hundreds of actions of

---

[4] Generally, it is held by all State courts which are *courts of record;* that is, courts which keep a record of proceedings and have the power to punish for contempt of court. Only the lowest of State courts (for example, justice of the peace and municipal courts) are not usually courts of record.

[5] See Article III, Section 2 and Article VI, Section 2.

[6] See pages 58, 68–69.

the States and their local governments unconstitutional, including some 1000 State laws.

Federalism. When we discussed various forms of government in Chapter 1, we learned that governments may be classified in several ways. Among these classifications is that based on the geographic distribution of the powers of government. From this standpoint, governments may be *unitary, confederate,* or *federal* in form.

As we know, the Government of the United States is a federal government. That is, the powers of government are distributed between the National Government on the one hand and the fifty States on the other.

None of the basic principles of the American constitutional system was a more natural result of the birth of the United States than federalism. The colonists had rebelled against the harsh rule of a powerful central government. They had rebelled because, they insisted, they had the right to handle their own local affairs without meddling and dictation from the king's ministers. Surely, they would not have permitted the creation of another such government at Philadelphia.

Even so, it was obvious that a National Government much stronger than the weak Congress under the Articles of Confederation was necessary. The economic and political chaos of the 1780's had more than proved that fact. The solution to the problem was found in federalism—a compromise between the system of nearly-independent States loosely tied to one another in the Confederation and a much-dreaded, too-powerful central government.

The nature of American federalism is explored at length in Chapter 4, The Federal System.

OUR CHANGING CONSTITUTION

The Constitution of the United States has now been in force for more than 180 years—longer by far than the written constitution of any other nation in the world.[7]

In the eighteen decades since the Constitution was drafted great changes have taken place. In 1787 the young Republic was a small agricultural nation of less than 4,000,000 people scattered for some 1300 miles along the eastern edge of the continent. The original thirteen States, joined to one another only by horses and sailing ships, struggled to stay alive in an essentially hostile world.

Today, however, the United States has grown to a population of more than 205,000,000. The now fifty States span the continent and beyond, and the nation has many far-flung dependencies and commitments. This nation is the most powerful one on earth, and our modern, highly industrialized and technological society enjoys the highest standard of living ever known to man.

How has the Constitution, written in 1787, managed to endure, to keep pace with this astounding change and growth? The answer to that question is to be found in the fact that the Constitution today, at one and the same time, *is and is not* the document of 1787. Many of the words are the same; and much of their meaning remains the same, too. But some words have been changed, some have been eliminated, and some have been added. Meanings have been modified through eighteen decades, too.

This process of constitutional change and growth has come about in two basic ways: by *formal amendment* and by *informal amendment.*

Formal Amendment. The Founding Fathers were well aware that even the wisest of constitution-makers cannot hope to build for

---

[7] The British constitution dates from well before the Norman Conquest of 1066, but it is not a single, written document, as is the Constitution of the United States. Rather, it is an "unwritten constitution," a collection of principles, customs, traditions, and significant parliamentary acts which guide British government.

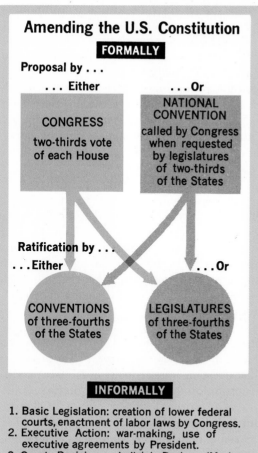

Amending the U.S. Constitution

FORMALLY

Proposal by . . .

. . . Either

CONGRESS
two-thirds vote
of each House

. . . Or

NATIONAL CONVENTION
called by Congress
when requested
by legislatures
of two-thirds
of the States

Ratification by . . .

. . . Either

CONVENTIONS
of three-fourths
of the States

. . . Or

LEGISLATURES
of three-fourths
of the States

INFORMALLY

1. Basic Legislation: creation of lower federal courts, enactment of labor laws by Congress.
2. Executive Action: war-making, use of executive agreements by President.
3. Court Decisions: Judicial Review (Marbury v. Madison).
4. Party Practices: national conventions to nominate presidential, vice-presidential candidates.
5. Custom: Cabinet, senatorial courtesy.

ratified by three-fourths of the State legislatures. Twenty-four of the twenty-five amendments have been adopted in this manner.

Second, an amendment may be proposed by a two-thirds vote in each house of Congress and ratified by conventions in three-fourths of the States. Only the 21st Amendment, ratified in 1933, was adopted in this way. Under this method there is only one opportunity in each State for ratification; if a convention rejects an amendment, it is quite unlikely that another convention would be held. Under the first method, however, if a legislature refuses to ratify at one session, a later one might do so.[8] The 21st Amendment was ratified by the convention method because Congress felt that the people (who chose the delegates to the conventions) would be more favorable to it than the State legislators.[9]

Third, an amendment may be proposed by a national convention, called by Congress at the request of two-thirds of the State legislatures, and ratified by the legislatures of three-fourths of the States. To date, Congress has never had occasion to call such a convention.

Fourth, an amendment may be proposed by a national convention, called by Congress at the request of two-thirds of the State legislatures, and ratified by conventions in three-fourths of the States. The Constitution itself was originally adopted in a manner quite similar to this.

Notice that the federal nature of our governmental system is demonstrated by the amendment process: Proposal of amendments is a *national* function and ratification is a *State* matter. In our political theory, the adoption of an amendment represents an expression of the people's sovereign will.

---

[8] The Supreme Court has held that even though a State has rejected an amendment it may always reconsider that action; but once a State does ratify, it can never rescind that action.

[9] Congress determines whether an amendment is to be considered by the State legislatures or by State conventions.

all time. Thus, they included within the Constitution provision for its amendment.

Article V sets out the ways in which the Constitution may be amended. Two methods of proposal and two methods of ratification are provided. By combining one or the other method of proposal with one or the other method of ratification, there are four different means of amendment.

First, an amendment may be proposed by a two-thirds vote in each house of Congress and

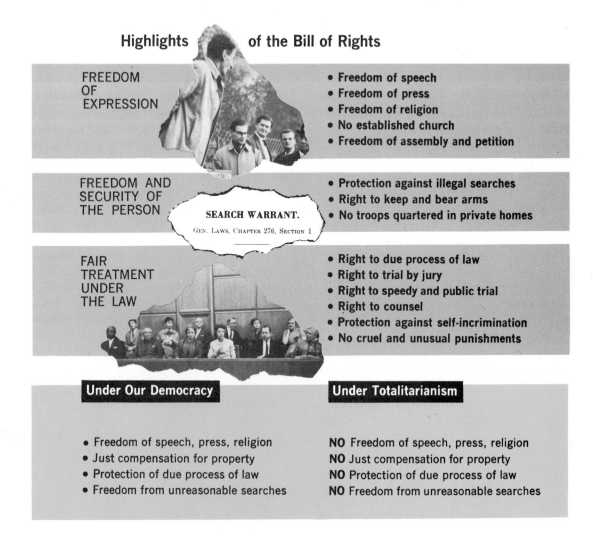

Highlights of the Bill of Rights

FREEDOM OF EXPRESSION
- Freedom of speech
- Freedom of press
- Freedom of religion
- No established church
- Freedom of assembly and petition

FREEDOM AND SECURITY OF THE PERSON

SEARCH WARRANT.
GEN. LAWS, CHAPTER 276, SECTION 1

- Protection against illegal searches
- Right to keep and bear arms
- No troops quartered in private homes

FAIR TREATMENT UNDER THE LAW
- Right to due process of law
- Right to trial by jury
- Right to speedy and public trial
- Right to counsel
- Protection against self-incrimination
- No cruel and unusual punishments

Under Our Democracy
- Freedom of speech, press, religion
- Just compensation for property
- Protection of due process of law
- Freedom from unreasonable searches

Under Totalitarianism
- NO Freedom of speech, press, religion
- NO Just compensation for property
- NO Protection of due process of law
- NO Freedom from unreasonable searches

When Congress passes a joint resolution proposing an amendment, the resolution is not sent to the President for his signature or veto — despite the fact that the Constitution would seem to require it.[10] In proposing an amendment Congress is not *legislating* (making law); and, too, the vote required to propose an amendment is the same as the vote necessary to override a presidential veto.

[10] See Article I, Section 7, Clause 3.

The wording of Article V is quite specific. No State may require for itself additional steps in the ratification process. If it could, that State would, in effect, be amending the Constitution for its own purposes. Thus, in 1920 the Supreme Court held that Ohio (or any other State) could not require that a proposed amendment to the Constitution of the United States be approved by the people by a referendum before it could be ratified by the State legislature. Of course, a legislature could be influenced (but not bound) by an *advisory* vote of the people.

Only one constitutional restriction is placed on the subjects with which a proposed amendment may deal. Article V provides that the amendment process cannot be used to deprive any State "without its consent, ... its equal suffrage in the Senate." [11]

Some 4000 joint resolutions proposing amendments have been introduced in Congress since the Constitution became effective in 1789. Thus far (1971), Congress has approved and sent on to the States only thirty. And, of these, only twenty-five have become a part of the Constitution.[12] The amendments, the year in which each was adopted, and the period of time required for the ratification of each is shown in the table on page 57.

Informal Amendments. Important as they are, the formal amendments have *not* been especially responsible for the Constitution's amazing vitality. Rather, the *informal* amendments have been and are most responsible. That is, as the United States has changed and grown through the years, the Constitution has kept pace through changes (*informal*

---

[11] Like the House of Representatives, the Senate possesses the power to refuse to seat a member-elect or to expel one of its members (Article I, Section 5, Clauses 1 and 2). Whenever it takes such an action, however, only the Senator or Senator-elect involved, not the State, is denied the seat.

[12] To date, five amendments have been proposed but not ratified. Two of them were proposed in 1789 together with the ten which became the Bill of Rights; one dealt with the apportionment of the House of Representatives, the other with the compensation of members of Congress. A third, proposed in 1810, would have voided the citizenship of any person accepting a foreign title or other honor. A fourth, proposed in 1861, would have prohibited the adoption of any amendment relating to slavery. A fifth, proposed in 1924, would have given Congress the expressed power to regulate child labor.

amendments) which have *not* involved additions or deletions in its actual wording. These changes have come through the day-to-day, year-to-year experiences of government under the Constitution.

Certainly, the Founding Fathers did not intend to place future generations in a constitutional straitjacket. Rather, they recognized that, inevitably, the future would call for changes in what they had done. As George Washington put it in a letter written during the campaign for ratification:

I do not think we are more inspired, have more wisdom, or possess more virtue than those who will come after us.

Thomas Jefferson made the point thus:

I am certainly not an advocate for frequent and untried changes in laws and constitutions. I think moderate imperfections had better be borne with; because, when once known, we accommodate ourselves to them, and find practical means of correcting their ill effects.

But I know also, that laws and institutions must go hand in hand with the progress of the human mind. As that becomes more developed, more enlightened, as new discoveries are made, new truths disclosed, and manners and opinions change with the change of circumstances, institutions must advance also, and keep pace with the times. We might as well require a man to wear still the coat which fitted him when a boy, as civilized society to remain even under the regimen of their barbarous ancestors.

In order to gain a true understanding of the nature of our constitutional system as it exists today, we must consider five methods by which the Constitution has changed and developed aside from the process of formal amendment.

Basic Legislation. Many portions of the Constitution are vague and skeletal. The Founding Fathers purposely left it to Congress to fill in the details as circumstances required. In so doing, Congress has spelled out many of the Constitution's provisions. For example,

AMENDMENTS TO THE CONSTITUTION

Amendments	Subject	Year Adopted	Time Required For Ratification
1st–10th	The Bill of Rights	1791	2 years, 2 months, 20 days
11th	Immunity of States from certain suits	1795	5 months, 2 days
12th	Changes in Electoral College procedure	1804	7 months, 15 days
13th	Prohibition of slavery	1865	10 months, 5 days
14th	Citizenship, due process, and equal protection	1868	2 years, 23 days
15th	No denial of vote because of race, color, or previous condition of servitude	1870	11 months, 7 days
16th	Power of Congress to tax incomes	1913	3 years, 6 months, 22 days
17th	Direct election of U.S. Senators	1913	10 months, 26 days
18th	National (liquor) prohibition	1919	1 year, 1 month, 2 days
19th	Woman suffrage	1920	1 year, 2 months, 14 days
20th	Change of dates for congressional and presidential terms	1933	10 months, 21 days
21st	Repeal of 18th Amendment	1933	9 months, 15 days
22nd	Limit on presidential tenure	1951	3 years, 11 months, 7 days
23rd	District of Columbia electoral vote	1961	9 months, 12 days
24th	Prohibition of tax payment as a qualification to vote in federal elections	1964	1 year, 4 months, 26 days
25th	Procedure for determining presidential disability and for filling vacancy in the Vice Presidency	1967	1 year, 7 months, 4 days

the entire federal court system, except for the Supreme Court itself, has been created by acts of Congress. So have all of the numerous departments, agencies, and offices in the executive branch, except the offices of President and Vice President.

Then, too, Congress has added to the Constitution by the manner in which it has exercised its various powers. For example, Congress is given the expressed power to regulate interstate commerce.[13] But *what is* interstate commerce? The Constitution does not say. In passing literally thousands of statutes under the Commerce Clause, Congress has, in effect, done much to define its meaning; and it has, in the process, then, informally amended the document.

Executive Action. The manner in which the various Presidents have exercised their power has contributed to the informal amendment process. This has been especially true of the stronger Presidents: George Washington, Thomas Jefferson, Andrew Jackson, Abraham Lincoln, Grover Cleveland, Theodore Roosevelt, Woodrow Wilson, Franklin D. Roosevelt, and Harry S. Truman.

For example, only Congress may declare war,[14] but the President is made Commander in Chief of the Armed Forces.[15] Acting as Commander in Chief, various Presidents have used the Armed Forces for military action abroad — *without a declaration of war* — on no fewer than 150 separate occasions.

[13] Article I, Section 8, Clause 3.

[14] Article I, Section 8, Clause 11.
[15] Article II, Section 2, Clause 1.

President Richard Nixon escorts Indonesian President Suharto and his wife to a state dinner in his honor. In meetings with heads of foreign states, the President sometimes makes executive agreements which are binding on the nation. (AP Wirephoto)

Among the many other examples, the device of "executive agreements" is typical. Recent Presidents have made many such agreements instead of using the process of treaty-making outlined in the Constitution.[16] Executive agreements are agreements made personally between the President and the head of a foreign state (or his subordinates). Though they do not require Senate approval, the courts consider executive agreements legally binding.

Court Decisions. Under the principle of judicial review, as we have seen, the courts have the power to interpret and apply the law in cases which come before them. The ultimate exercise of the power rests with the highest court in the land, the Supreme Court of the United States.

We have already referred to some instances of constitutional interpretation (that is, informal amendment) by the Supreme Court — most notably *Marbury* v. *Madison* (1803) — and we shall refer to many more elsewhere in the text. But in short, the Court may be viewed in the words of the late Chief Justice Charles Evans Hughes as "a continuous constitutional convention." As the Chief Justice also said, "The Constitution means what the judges say it means."

In expanding the Constitution through judicial interpretation, the Supreme Court has leaned most heavily on the Necessary and Proper Clause, the Commerce Power, and the Taxing Power, all in Article I, Section 8.

Party Practices. Political parties have also contributed to the informal amendment process. Parties themselves have developed *extraconstitutionally*. Not only does the Constitution not even mention parties, but most of the Founding Fathers were opposed to their growth. In his Farewell Address in 1796 George Washington warned the people against "the baneful effects of the spirit of party."

Yet, in many ways today, government in the United States is government by party. For example, the Electoral College system has become a "rubber stamp" for party action. The national convention system for selecting party candidates for the Presidency is not provided for in the Constitution; the device was originated by the parties.[17] Both houses of Congress are organized and conduct much of their business on the basis of party. The President makes appointments to major federal offices with an eye to party politics.

Custom. Unwritten custom may be as strong as written law. For example, on each of the eight occasions when Presidents have died in office, the Vice President then became President. Yet, the Constitution did *not* provide

---

[16] Article II, Section 2, Clause 2.

[17] The first to hold a national convention to nominate a presidential candidate was the Anti-Masonic party in 1831. See page 163.

for the succession of the Vice President *until* the adoption of the 25th Amendment in 1967. Until then, it provided only that *the powers and duties of the office* of President should devolve on the Vice President.[18]

It is a well-established custom for the Senate to reject a presidential appointment if it is opposed by a Senator of the majority party from the State where the appointee is to serve. This practice, known as *senatorial courtesy,* practically shifts the power to appoint many federal officers from the President to members of the Senate.

The strength and importance of unwritten customs is well illustrated by the rare instance in which one of them was nullified. From the time George Washington refused a third term as President in 1796, there had existed the so-called "no-third-term tradition." In 1940, and again in 1944, Franklin D. Roosevelt broke with tradition, however, by seeking and winning a third, and then a fourth, term. As a direct result, the 22nd Amendment was added to the Constitution in 1951—making what had been an unwritten custom a part of the written law of the land.

_____

[18] Read carefully the *exact* wording of Article II, Section 1, Clause 6, and then note the wording of Section 1 of the 25th Amendment.

❊❊❊❊❊❊❊❊❊❊ CONCEPT BUILDING ❊❊❊❊❊❊❊❊❊❊

Key Concepts

The Constitution of the United States is the nation's fundamental law. It contains the basic principles of our governmental system and sets forth the basic organization and procedures by which, and the limits within which, government in the United States must operate. The six basic principles are:

(1) Popular Sovereignty—that the people are the only source for *any* and *all* governmental authority.

(2) Limited Government—that government is not all-powerful, that it may do *only* what the *sovereign* (the people) permit it to do.

(3) Separation of Powers—that the legislative, executive, and judicial powers are separated among three independent branches of government.

(4) Checks and Balances—that the three branches are tied together through a series of *checks* (restraints) that each may exercise against the others.

(5) Judicial Review—that the courts possess the power to review executive and legislative actions in the light of their constitutionality.

(6) Federalism—that the powers of government are distributed on a territorial basis between the National Government on the one hand and the States on the other.

The amendment process clearly demonstrates the federal nature of our governmental system—proposal being a *national* function and ratification a *State* matter. With two methods of proposal and two of ratification, there are four ways in which the Constitution may be amended. To date, however, only two of them have been used. Twenty-five formal amendments have been added to the Constitution since it was drawn up in 1787.

In addition to the formal amendments, the Constitution has been changed and has kept pace with the changing times by "informal amendment." The change and development has come about in five ways—by (1) basic acts of Congress, (2) precedent-setting actions of various Presidents, (3) significant decisions of the Supreme Court, (4) political party practices, and (5) custom.

Important Terms

amendment	executive agreement	*Marbury* v. *Madison*	separation of powers
checks and balances	federal system	Preamble	sovereign
Constitution	informal amendment	ratification	unconstitutional
delegated	judicial review	review	

Questions for Inquiry and Review

1. What, in general terms, is the Constitution?

2. What are the six basic principles of the American constitutional system?

3. Why is the wording of the Preamble so important?

4. How do people delegate to governments in the United States the powers those governments possess?

5. What are the three great branches of the National Government, and what basic powers does each possess?

6. Why does each branch possess powers with which it can restrain the others?

7. What is the power of judicial review? Is it provided for in the Constitution (explain)?

8. Why was a federal system a natural outgrowth of our earlier system?

9. Why did the Founding Fathers make specific provisions for constitutional amendment?

10. In what particular ways may the Constitution be amended formally? Which of these have actually been used?

11. How many formal amendments have thus far been added to the Constitution?

12. How has the Constitution been changed and developed otherwise?

13. What are the five methods by which this change and development has been accomplished?

For Further Inquiry

1. Select a particular provision of the Constitution which illustrates one of the basic principles of our constitutional system (for example, the President's veto power which illustrates the principle of checks and balances). Why was the particular provision included in the Constitution? What arguments for and against its inclusion would you have made as a member of the Constitutional Convention?

2. Many view the Constitution as a document that should not be changed. Jefferson expressed the contrary view in these words:

Some men ascribe to the men of the preceding age a wisdom more than human, and suppose what they did to be beyond amendment. I knew that age [of the late 1700's] well. I belonged to it and labored with it. It deserved well of its country. It was very like the present, but without the experience of the present; and forty years of experience is worth a century of book reading; and this they would say themselves were they to arise from the dead.

Do you agree or disagree with Jefferson's viewpoint? Are these words more or less valid today than when they were written?

3. On several occasions Congress has refused to approve proposals which would permit constitutional amendments to be proposed by a simple majority in each house and ratified by a majority vote of the people at a national election. Do you think that Congress has acted wisely in this matter?

4. What prompted the proposal and ratification of each of the Constitution's twenty-five amendments?

5. In what particular terms, if any, do you feel the Constitution should be further amended?

6. What restrictions, if any, are there on the lengths to which the process of informal amendment may be carried?

7. The Constitution is often described as a "living document." What do you think is meant by that phrase?

Suggested Activities

1. Ask a prominent local attorney or judge to speak to the class on the place of the judiciary in the American system of government.

2. Prepare a large poster display illustrating: (a) the principles of separation of powers and checks and balances, and (b) the constitutional amendment process.

3. Write a report on the historical background of one of the twenty-five formal amendments.

4. From current newspapers and periodicals make a bulletin board display of examples of the informal amendment process in action.

5. Stage a debate or class forum on the following: (a) *Resolved,* That in today's world a unitary system of government is more practical than a federal system; (b) *Resolved,* That in today's world it is more practical for the basic powers of government to be concentrated in one supreme agency than to be divided among three distinct branches.

6. Compare the methods by which the Constitution of the United States may be amended with the amendment procedures prescribed in the constitution of your State.

Suggested Reading

ADRIAN, CHARLES R. and PRESS, CHARLES, *The American Political Process,* McGraw-Hill, 1969. Chapter 4.

BURNS, JAMES M. and PELTASON, J. W., *Government By the People.* Prentice-Hall, 1969. Chapter 3.

DYE, THOMAS R., *et al., American Government: Theory, Structure, and Process.* Wadsworth, 1969. Chapter 3.

HEATHCOCK, CLAUDE L., *The United States Constitution In Perspective.* Allyn and Bacon, 1968.

HOLCOMBE, ARTHUR N., *The American Constitutional System.* Scott, Foresman, 1969.

LEACH, RICHARD H., *Governing the American Nation.* Allyn and Bacon, 1967. Chapter 4.

MAGRATH, C. PETER, *et al., The American Democracy.* Macmillan, 1969. Chapter 2.

NIMMO, DAN and UNGS, THOMAS D., *American Political Patterns.* Little, Brown, 1969. Chapter 4.

ODEGARD, PETER H., *et al., The American Republic.* Harper & Row, 1969. Chapters 4, 5.

PRITCHETT, C. HERMAN, *The American Constitution.* McGraw-Hill, 1968. Chapters 3, 4.

SCOTT, ANDREW M. and WALLACE, EARLE (eds.), *Politics, U.S.A.: Cases on the American Democratic Process.* Macmillan, 1969. Chapter 2.

SIDEY, HUGH, "Thoughts on a Stroll Through Williamsburg," *Life,* November 8, 1968.

4
THE FEDERAL SYSTEM

***Why has the United States a federal rather than a unitary system of government?

***Should a State be permitted to withdraw from the Union if it chooses to do so?

***What factors account for the marked growth of the functions performed by the National Government in recent years?

The Constitution, in all its provisions, looks to an indestructible Union, composed of indestructible States.

CHIEF JUSTICE SALMON P. CHASE,
Texas v. *White* (1868)

The Founding Fathers faced many difficult and perplexing problems as they drafted a new Constitution for the United States in the summer of 1787. Among the most difficult—and most crucial—of those problems was: How were they to provide a national government of real authority and, yet, preserve the already existing States?

Few, if any, of the Founding Fathers favored the creation of a strong centralized (unitary) government in the British pattern. They knew how stoutly the people had fought to retain their rights of local self-government, and they knew how much the people would distrust a strongly centralized National Government. Still, they knew that they had to create a government with sufficient power to meet the country's needs. The solution they found was *federalism.*

Federalism Defined. A federal system is one in which a constitution divides the powers of government on a territorial basis, between a central and several local governments. Each level exercises its own distinct field of powers and neither, acting alone, can alter the division the constitution makes between them. In the United States, of course, the central government is the National Government and the local governments are those of the fifty States.

Federalism's major strength lies in the fact that it permits *local* action in matters of primarily local concern and, at the same time, *national* action in matters of wider concern. Local needs and desires may vary from one State to another, and federalism allows for this fact. Illustrations of the point are nearly limitless. Thus, most forms of gambling are legal in Nevada but are outlawed in most other States; New Jersey provides free bus transportation for private as well as public school students but most other States do not; a third of the States regulate the liquor business via a public monopoly, but in most of them private enterprise holds sway.

While federalism permits and encourages local preferences in many matters, it also pro-

The constitutional validity of the concept of implied powers was first tested in the Supreme Court in the landmark case *McCulloch* v. *Maryland,* 1819. The state of Maryland, defending its view of the federal division of powers, had challenged the constitutionality of the creation by Congress of the Bank of the United States. The Court unanimously upheld the establishment of the Bank as a necessary and proper means for carrying into execution such expressed powers as those to tax, to borrow, and to coin money and regulate its value. Declared Chief Justice John Marshall:

> We admit, as all must admit, that the powers of the government are limited, and that its limits are not to be transcended. But we think the sound construction of the Constitution must allow to the national legislature that discretion, with respect to the means by which the powers it confers are to be carried into execution, which will enable that body to perform the high duties assigned to it, in the manner most beneficial to the people. Let the end be legitimate, let it be within the scope of the Constitution, and all means which are appropriate, which are plainly adapted to the end, which are not prohibited, but consist with the letter and spirit of the Constitution, are constitutional.

Why do you think the Supreme Court provided so broad and sweeping a definition to the powers of Congress? Should the Court have done so? Explain.

vides for the strength that comes from union. Thus, if a natural disaster, such as a severe flood or earthquake, or some other crisis should occur in a State or region of the nation, the resources of the entire Union are available to aid the stricken area.

The terms *federalism* and *democracy* are not synonymous. Remember, federalism refers to a territorial division of powers, while democracy refers to the role of the people in the governing process. Still, it is almost impossible to imagine a democratic system operating over any large area in which there is not also a very large degree of local self-government.

THE CONSTITUTIONAL DIVISION OF POWERS

The Constitution sets out the basic scheme of the American federal system. It provides for a *division of powers* between the National Government on the one hand and the States on the other.[1] This division is most clearly stated in the 10th Amendment to the Constitution:

> The powers not delegated to the United States by the Constitution, nor prohibited by it to the States, are reserved to the States respectively, or to the people.

The National Government, One of Delegated Powers. The National Government possesses only those powers which are *delegated* (granted) to it by the Constitution. That is, it is a government of *delegated powers.* There are *three* types of delegated powers: *expressed, implied,* and *inherent.*

The Expressed Powers. The expressed powers are those provided in so many words in the Constitution. Most, but not all of them, are

----
[1] The charts on pages 66 and 67 present the division of powers in graphic form.

Because of the huge costs, usually only the National Government can finance the building of gigantic power dams—a function reasonably implied from the expressed power to regulate interstate commerce. (Library of Congress)

contained in Article I, Section 8. They include, among others, the power to:

Declare war and make peace
Maintain armed forces
Make treaties and otherwise conduct foreign relations
Regulate foreign and interstate commerce
Levy and collect taxes
Establish post offices and post roads
Coin money and regulate its value
Fix uniform standards of weights and measures
Borrow on the credit of the United States
Grant patents and copyrights
Establish a federal court system
Regulate bankruptcy
Regulate naturalization
Do those things "necessary and proper for carrying into execution" the various expressed powers

The Implied Powers. The implied powers are those which are not specifically stated in the Constitution but which may be reasonably *implied* from the expressed powers. The constitutional basis for the existence of the implied powers is to be found in Article I, Section 8, Clause 18, the Necessary and Proper Clause. It reads:

> Congress shall have power ... to make all laws which shall be necessary and proper for carrying into execution the foregoing powers, and all other powers vested by this Constitution in the Government of the United States, or in any department or officer thereof.

The Necessary and Proper Clause is sometimes known as the Elastic Clause; through congressional and court interpretation, the words "necessary and proper" have come to mean, in effect, "convenient and useful." To cite but a few of the literally hundreds of illustrations of the exercise of the implied powers, note: Congress has provided for the regulation of labor-management relations; for the building of hydro-electric power dams; river and harbor improvements; punishment for such federal crimes as transporting stolen goods across a State line. All these, and many other acts, may be reasonably implied from the expressed power to regulate interstate commerce.[2]

The Inherent Powers. The inherent powers are those which belong to the National Government by virtue of the fact that *it is* the national government of a sovereign state. They are not specifically mentioned in the Constitution, but they have been possessed by national governments since time immemorial. It is only logical to assume that the Founding Fathers—since they were creating the government of a nation—assumed that these powers would be exercised by the National Government.

The inherent powers are few in number. The chief ones include: the powers to regulate immigration, deport aliens, acquire territory, extend diplomatic recognition, and protect the

[2] See pages 266–270.

nation against rebellion and internal subversion.

Actually, each of the inherent powers might also be classed as an implied power. For example, it is relatively easy to imply the power to regulate immigration from the expressed power to regulate foreign commerce, or the power to acquire territory from the treaty-making and war powers.

Powers Denied the National Government. While the Constitution delegates certain powers to the National Government, it also *denies* certain powers to it. It does so in three particular ways.

First, some powers are denied to the National Government *in so many words* in the Constitution;[3] for example, the powers to levy export duties, grant titles of nobility, or deny freedom of speech, press, and religion.

Secondly, some powers are denied to the National Government because of the Constitution's *silence* concerning them. Remember, the National Government is *a government of delegated powers;* it has *only* those powers delegated to it by the Constitution. Many powers are *not* granted to the National Government; for example, the powers to create a national system of public schools, enact a national marriage and divorce law, set a uniform voting age, or establish units of local government.

Thirdly, some powers are denied to the National Government because of the very nature of the federal system. That is, the National Government is not permitted to do certain things because to do so would be to strike at the existence of the States. Thus, the National Government cannot tax the governmental functions of a State (for example, public education, road building, law enforcement).

State Governments, Ones of Reserved Powers. The Constitution *reserves* (leaves) to the States those powers which are not granted to the National Government and are not at the same time denied to the States. Read again the words of the 10th Amendment.

Thus, Alabama (or any other State) may require police consent for the holding of religious services in public parks or buildings. It may forbid persons under twenty-one to marry or purchase liquor; may prohibit the carrying, or even owning, of firearms; and may charter and regulate corporations doing business in the State. It may also establish public school systems and units of local government and may set the conditions under which divorces may be granted. The sphere of State power is vast, indeed. Alabama can do all of these things and more because there is nothing in the Constitution of the United States which prohibits it from doing so. The National Government cannot do these things because it has not been delegated the power to do so. The power to do these things has been *reserved* to the States.

Powers Denied the States. The Constitution prohibits the States from doing several things. Some powers are denied to the States in so many words in the Constitution.[4] For example, no State may enter into any treaty, alliance, or confederation; nor may it coin money, make any law impairing the obligations of a contract, grant titles of nobility, nor deprive any person of life, liberty, or property without due process of law.

Some powers are also denied to the States because of the very nature of the federal system. Thus, the States are not permitted to tax the agencies or functions of the National Government.

Then, too, note each State has its own constitution which contains many prohibitions of power to the State, as we shall see when we consider State constitutions at length in Chapter 35.

Exclusive Powers. The exclusive powers are those which, in our federal system, may be exercised *only* by the National Government.

---

[3] Most of these are found in Article I, Section 9 and in Amendments 1–8.

[4] Most of these are found in Article I, Section 10 and in Amendments 13, 14, 15, 19, and 24.

THE DIVISION OF POWERS IN THE AMERICAN FEDERAL SYSTEM

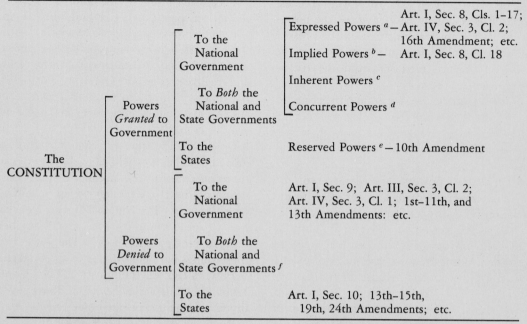

The CONSTITUTION

Powers *Granted* to Government
- To the National Government
  - Expressed Powers [a] — Art. I, Sec. 8, Cls. 1–17; Art. IV, Sec. 3, Cl. 2; 16th Amendment; etc.
  - Implied Powers [b] — Art. I, Sec. 8, Cl. 18
  - Inherent Powers [c]
- To *Both* the National and State Governments
  - Concurrent Powers [d]
- To the States
  - Reserved Powers [e] — 10th Amendment

Powers *Denied* to Government
- To the National Government
  - Art. I, Sec. 9; Art. III, Sec. 3, Cl. 2; Art. IV, Sec. 3, Cl. 1; 1st–11th, and 13th Amendments: etc.
- To *Both* the National and State Governments [f]
- To the States
  - Art. I, Sec. 10; 13th–15th, 19th, 24th Amendments; etc.

[a] Those powers *expressly* (explicitly) granted to the National Government in the Constitution.

[b] Those powers which may be *reasonably implied* from the expressed powers — *e.g.,* to aid States in highway construction, provide for federal crimes, regulate labor-management relations.

[c] Those powers, although not explicitly granted, which are possessed by virtue of the fact that the National Government is the *national* government of a sovereign state — *e.g.,* the power to regulate immigration.

[d] Those powers which may be exercised by *both* National and State Governments. Some powers of the National Government are of such nature as to be "exclusive powers" — *e.g.,* to declare war.

[e] Those powers not granted to the National Government and not denied to the States by the Constitution — *e.g.,* to create local government and to provide public schools.

[f] *E.g.,* to pass *ex post facto* laws or bills of attainder (Art. I, Secs. 9 and 10) or deprive any persons of life, liberty, or property without due process (5th and 14th Amendments). The National Government is denied powers by: (1) several expressed prohibitions in the Constitution; (2) the Constitution's silence on many subjects; (3) the fact that the exercise of certain powers (*e.g.,* taxing governmental functions of the States) could endanger the federal system itself. The States are denied powers by: (1) several expressed prohibitions in the Constitution; (2) many provisions in their own constitutions; (3) the fact that the exercise of certain powers (*e.g.,* taxing the National Government) could endanger the federal system itself.

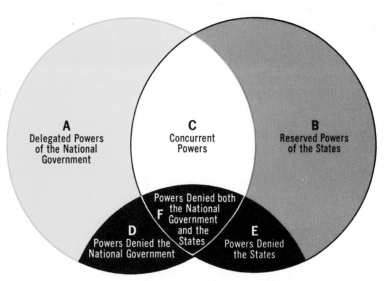

The Division of Powers between the National Government and the States

A Delegated Powers of the National Government

C Concurrent Powers

B Reserved Powers of the States

F Powers Denied both the National Government and the States

D Powers Denied the National Government

E Powers Denied the States

Some of the powers delegated to the National Government are expressly denied to the States. For example, the powers to coin money, make treaties, and levy import duties are expressly granted to the National Government, and they are expressly denied to the States. Thus, these powers belong exclusively to—are among the *exclusive powers* of—the National Government.

Some of the powers which are delegated to the National Government but which are *not expressly* denied to the States are also among the exclusive powers of the National Government. This is so because of the nature of the particular powers involved. For example, the States are not expressly denied the power to regulate interstate commerce; but, if they were

to be permitted to do so, chaos would result.[5]

Concurrent Powers. The concurrent powers are those powers which belong to and are exercised by *both* the National Government and the States. For example, both levels of government possess the powers to lay and collect taxes, to define and punish crimes, and to condemn private property for public use.

THE SUPREME LAW OF THE LAND

The division of powers between the National Government and the States is a complicated arrangement, as we have just seen. It produces what has been called a "dual system of government." That is, it produces a system in which

[5] The States may not regulate interstate commerce as such. But in the exercise of their various powers they inevitably *affect* it. For example, in regulating highway speeds, the States regulate vehicles operating not only within the State (that is, in intrastate commerce) but also those operating from State to State, as well. The general rule here is that the States, in exercising their powers, may affect interstate commerce—but only as long as they do not impose an unreasonable burden upon it. See pages 276–277.

two basic levels of government operate over the same territory and the same people at one and the same time.

In such an arrangement there are bound to be conflicts between the two levels, conflicts between national law on the one hand and State law on the other. Anticipating this, the Founding Fathers wrote the Supremacy Clause into the Constitution. Article VI, Section 2 provides:

> This Constitution, and the laws of the United States which shall be made in pursuance thereof, and all treaties made or which shall be made under the authority of the United States, shall be the supreme law of the land; ...

And, significantly, the provision adds:

> ... and the judges in every State shall be bound thereby, anything in the Constitution or laws of any State to the contrary notwithstanding.

This section, then, makes the Constitution and the acts and treaties of the United States the highest forms of law. The Constitution stands at the top; immediately beneath it are the acts and treaties of the United States.[6]

No form of State law may conflict with *any* form of national law. As an illustration, when Oregon entered the Union in 1859, its constitution prohibited voting by any person of Chinese descent. When the 15th Amendment was added to the United States Constitution in 1870 prohibiting any State to deny any person the right to vote on account of either race or color, the provision in the Oregon constitution ceased to be effective.

In effect, the Supremacy Clause creates a "ladder of laws" in the United States. The Constitution occupies the topmost rung. Immediately beneath it stand acts of Congress and treaties of the United States. Each State's constitution—supreme over all other forms of *a State's law*—stands beneath *all* forms of federal law. At the base of the ladder are those other forms of State law—statutes, city and county charters and ordinances, etc.

The Supreme Court as Referee in the Federal System. The final authority on questions of constitutionality is the Supreme Court of the United States.[7] Several examples of the Court acting in this role have already been cited. It should be noted, however, that more often than not when a State or national law is challenged as unconstitutional it is found in fact to be *valid* (constitutional).

Judicial Review. When the Court is acting to determine constitutionality of a governmental action, it is exercising its power of judicial review. As noted on page 52, the Constitution does not provide for judicial review in so many words. It is, however, clearly intended in the Constitution.

Marbury v. *Madison* (1803). The Supreme Court did not have occasion to declare an act

---

[6] Acts of Congress and treaties stand on an equal plane with each other beneath the Constitution. Neither may conflict with a provision of the Constitution. In cases of conflict between the provisions of an Act and the provisions of a treaty, the one more recently made takes precedence—the reasoning here being that it is the later expression of the public will.

[7] Of course, Congress or a State's legislature could amend a statute voided by court action and thus remove the conflicts; or a State or the National Constitution could be amended to that end. For example, in 1895 the Supreme Court voided an income tax law enacted by Congress the year before; it held that since the income tax was a direct tax, the statute violated the Constitution's limitation on the power of Congress to levy direct taxes (Article I, Section 2, Clause 3.) The 16th Amendment, ratified in 1913, in effect erased the Court's decision.

of Congress unconstitutional until 1803.[8] Quite late on the night of March 3, 1801, President John Adams had signed the commissions of office for several newly-appointed federal judges.[9] On the next day, Thomas Jefferson was inaugurated. He immediately ordered his new Secretary of State, James Madison, not to deliver the commissions.

One of the appointees, William Marbury, then applied to the Supreme Court for a *writ of mandamus* (a court order) to force Madison to make delivery. Marbury based his request on a provision in the Judiciary Act of 1789 which empowered the Court to hear such cases in its original jurisdiction, not on appeal from a lower court.

In a unanimous opinion written by Chief Justice John Marshall, the Supreme Court refused the request. The Court refused because it held that the section of the Judiciary Act empowering it to issue the writ was unconstitutional. Article III of the Constitution sets out the original jurisdiction of the Supreme Court and does not provide for cases such as Marbury's. Congress was, in effect, attempting to amend the Constitution by a mere act. If Congress could amend the Constitution by simply passing a law, of what use are the amendment procedures provided in Article V? Indeed, if Congress could so change the Constitution, of what use is the Constitution itself?

Since 1803 the Supreme Court has exercised its power of judicial review literally thousands of times—usually upholding, but sometimes denying, the constitutionality of federal and State actions.

Upholding the doctrines of national supremacy and liberal interpretation of the Constitution, John Marshall established the Supreme Court as a powerful institution in our governmental system of checks and balances.

THE NATIONAL GOVERNMENT'S OBLIGATIONS TO THE STATES

The Constitution imposes several obligations on the National Government for the benefit of the States. Most of these are found in Article IV.

Guarantee of a Republican Form of Government. The National Government is required to "guarantee to every State in this

---

[8] A State law was first held unconstitutional in 1810, in *Fletcher* v. *Peck,* in which a Georgia law was voided. The case involved the Contract Clause in the Constitution. The Court held an act of the legislature in which a grant of land had been made was a valid contract between Georgia and the grantee; the legislature's later attempt to rescind the contract was an unconstitutional violation of Article I, Section 10, Clause 1: "No State shall . . . pass any . . . law impairing the obligation of contracts."

[9] Because Adams signed the commissions so late on the night before he left office, these men are known in history as the "midnight justices."

Union a republican form of government."[10] Although the phrase "republican form of government" is not defined in the Constitution, and has never been defined by the courts, it is generally understood to mean a representative democracy.

President John Tyler acted under this constitutional guarantee when he moved to put down Dorr's Rebellion in Rhode Island (1841–1842). The followers of Thomas Dorr attempted to force the conservative ruling group in the State to adopt a new constitution and ease the voting laws. They proclaimed a new constitution and named Dorr governor. When Dorr attempted to put his new government into operation, however, the legally elected governor appealed to President Tyler for help. When the President took steps to put down the rebellion, it collapsed.

In a case growing out of this incident, the Supreme Court held in 1849 that the question of whether or not a State has a republican form of government is a *political* and not a *judicial* issue and is to be decided by the political branches of the National Government (the President and Congress).

In 1912 the Court repeated this holding in the only other case which has arisen under the provision. An Oregon corporation had refused to pay a tax enacted by the voters of the State. The company claimed that the use of the initiative and referendum, "direct legislation" by which voters propose and enact laws at the polls, meant that Oregon lacked a *republican* (representative) government.

Protection against Invasion and Domestic Violence. The National Government is also required to ". . . protect each of them against invasion; and on application of the legislature, or the executive (when the legislature cannot be convened), against domestic violence."[11]

---

[10] Article IV, Section 4.

[11] Article IV, Section 4. Recall, the States themselves cannot maintain armies or navies (Article I, Section 10, Clause 3).

Foreign Invasion. It is clear beyond any question today that an invasion of any one of the fifty States would be met as an attack upon the United States itself. Hence, the fact that the Constitution obligates the National Government to protect each of the States against foreign invasion is, in this day and age, a matter of little practical significance. But, recall, such was *not* the case in 1787. Then it was not at all clear that all thirteen of the States would stand together in the face of an invasion of one of them. Before any of the original States would agree to abandon its own warmaking and defense powers, each insisted upon an absolute pledge that an attack upon any one of them would be met as an attack upon all.

Domestic Violence. The federal system assumes that each of the fifty States will maintain the peace within its own borders. Thus, the primary responsibility for curbing insurrection, riot, and other internal disorder rests upon the individual States. However, the Constitution does recognize the possibility that, on occasion, a State may find itself unable to control a particular situation—hence, the guarantee of protection against domestic violence.

Historically, the use of federal force to restore order within a State has been a rare event. The latest uses have occurred quite recently, however. When racial unrest exploded into violence in Detroit in the midst of the "long, hot summer" of 1967, President Johnson ordered Regular Army units into the city. He acted at the request of Governor George Romney, and only after local police and firemen, supported by Michigan State Police and National Guard units, found themselves unable to cope with widespread rioting, arson, looting, and other pillage in the city's ghetto areas. In 1968, again at the request of the governors involved, the President sent federal troops into Chicago and Baltimore to help State and local forces quell the violence in those cities following the assassination of Dr. Martin Luther King.

Normally, a President has sent troops into a State only in response to a request from its governor (or legislature). But when national laws are being violated, or national functions interfered with, or national property endangered, a President need not wait for such a request.[12]

The ravages of nature can be far more destructive than man-made violence. Here, too, the Government stands ready to and regularly does come to the aid of stricken areas.

Respect for Geographic Identity. The National Government is also constitutionally bound to respect the geographic identity or integrity of each of the States. Thus, Congress may not create a new State from territory belonging to one or more of the existing States unless it first has the consent of the legislature or legislatures of the State or States involved.[13] Nor may a State be denied its equal representation in the Senate without its own consent.[14]

FEDERAL–STATE COOPERATION

As we have said, the American federal system is one in which there exists a division of powers between the National Government and the States. All too often, however, the system is viewed *only* in these terms — as one of *separate* spheres of power and of conflict between the two levels of government. Emphasis should also be given to the vast, and constantly growing, areas of *cooperation* between them.

Federal Grants-in-Aid. Perhaps the best-known example of this cooperation is the system of federal grants-in-aid to the States (and, increasingly in recent years, to their local units, as well.)

Federal aid to the States dates back to 1785. In that year the Congress under the Articles of Confederation directed lands in the Northwest Territory be set aside for the support of public schools. Today the National Government grants to the States well over $20,000,000,000 annually for the support of literally dozens of different programs.

The funds go to the States (and their local governments) for such programs as highway construction and maintenance, aid to dependent children, school lunch programs, unemployment insurance, public health work, aid to the needy aged, wildlife conservation, urban renewal and slum clearance, aid to education, hospital construction, forest fire fighting and prevention, civil defense, airport construction, better mass transportation services and many, many more.

The constitutional basis for the grant-in-aid program is found in the Taxing Power. Article I, Section 8, Clause 1 gives to Congress the power to tax in order

> ... to pay the debts and provide for the common defense and general welfare of the United States.

In providing for the grants, Congress normally attaches conditions which the States

---

[12] President Cleveland sent federal troops to restore order in the Chicago railyards during the Pullman Strike of 1894, *acting over the express objections* of Governor Altgeld of Illinois. The Supreme Court upheld his action in 1896 because rioters had threatened federal property and impeded the mails and interstate commerce. Several Presidents since have acted without a request; most recently, Mr. Eisenhower at Little Rock in 1957, and Mr. Kennedy at the University of Mississippi in 1962 and again at the University of Alabama in 1963 to halt the unlawful obstruction of school integration orders issued by federal courts.

[13] Article IV, Section 3, Clause 1.

[14] Article V.

must meet in accepting them. These usually require a State to: (1) use the grant only for the purpose specified, (2) make a matching appropriation (ordinarily an amount equal to that provided in federal funds, but occasionally much less), (3) create a suitable agency to administer the program, and (4) meet certain standards set for the project for which the aid is furnished.

Grants-in-Aid: Pro and Con. Some object to the grants-in-aid system because, they insist, it forces States to undertake programs for which many of them have neither the desire nor money. In theory, each State is free to accept or reject the federal funds; in practice, however, and even with the "strings" attached, they prove politically irresistible.

Another ground for criticism is that the arrangement enables the National Government to participate in activities in which it would otherwise have no constitutional authority (for example, public education and urban renewal). Critics also contend that, because the funds involved come from those who pay federal taxes, the residents of the wealthier States bear an unjust burden.

Supporters of the system insist that grants-in-aid have encouraged the States to undertake worthwhile activities they would not have otherwise performed. They argue that minimum standards are necessary to insure proper use of funds and success for programs. They also claim the various programs supported by grants are of national concern and importance; and, they add, what benefits one State or section of the nation, in effect, benefits all.

Whatever the merit of the arguments that rage over the matter, it is clear that the grants-in-aid device *does* extend federal authority into areas from which the Constitution otherwise excludes it. But, notice in this connection, that the grants-in-aid arrangement is in fact simply an aspect of the doctrine of implied powers. (See page 64.)

Other Forms of Federal Aid. The National Government furnishes aid to the States in a number of other ways. Thus, it shares revenues from some activities; for example, from the sale of timber from national forests, mineral leases on public lands, migratory bird hunting licenses, and leases of power sites on federal lands. It also makes some direct payments to local governments in areas where there are large federal landholdings. These payments are made in lieu of the property taxes the local governments cannot collect (and are, then, known as "lulu payments").

There are many other ways in which the National Government renders aid to the States. For example, the FBI assists State and local police in criminal law enforcement. The Census Bureau makes its studies available to State and local school systems to help them plan for the future. The Army and Air Force equip and train each State's National Guard units. Congress has prohibited, as federal crimes, the movement of certain persons (such as escaped prisoners) and goods (such as those stolen) across State lines. A listing of this sort may be carried on and on; numerous other illustrations appear throughout the remainder of this book.

State Aid to the National Government. Federal-State cooperation is distinctly a two-way street. The States and their local units also aid the National Government in a variety of ways. For example, national elections are conducted in each State by State and local elections officials, financed by State and local funds, and regulated very largely by State laws.

Among many other illustrations of the point: State and local draft boards administer the Selective Service System. Civil defense depends very largely on State and local personnel. Fugitives from federal justice are often apprehended by State and local police, and federal prisoners are regularly lodged in local jails while awaiting trial in federal courts and later while awaiting transportation to federal penitentiaries. Again, numerous other illustrations of Federal-State cooperation appear throughout this book.

INTERSTATE RELATIONS

The rivalries, jealousies, and disputes among the States under the Articles of Confederation furnished one of the reasons for drafting the National Constitution in 1787. The fact that the new Constitution strengthened the hand of the National Government eliminated many of these interstate frictions. The States were restrained even more closely by certain constitutional provisions dealing with interstate relations as such.

States Legally Separated. *Each State is legally separate* from every other State in the Union. When the States are acting within the sphere of their reserved powers, they stand toward one another as independent and wholly separate. Put the other way around, each State has no jurisdiction outside its own boundaries.[15]

Obviously, the States must have dealings with one another. These interstate relationships are covered by the Constitution in several important respects.

Interstate Compacts. As we have seen, no State may enter into any treaty, alliance, or confederation. The States may, with the consent of Congress, enter into *compacts* or agreements among themselves and with foreign states, however.[16]

Little use was made of interstate compacts until relatively recently. In fact, to 1900 Congress had approved only nineteen of them, and each of those involved the settlement of boundary disputes. In this century, however, and particularly since the mid-1930's, their use has increased considerably. New Jersey and New York led the way in 1921 when, by compact, they created the Port of New York Authority to manage and develop the harbor facilities of that great metropolis.

Well over 200 compacts exist today, and many of them involve several States. One, the Interstate Parole and Probation Compact, now involves all fifty States; in it, each has agreed to a uniform system for the supervision of parolees and probationers from other States. Other compacts, many with multi-State membership, cover a widening range of subjects; for example, the development and conservation of such natural resources as water, oil, wildlife, and fish; forest fire protection; regional cooperation in the use of higher education facilities; stream pollution; and the coordination of civil defense programs.

Most compacts deal with the common use of natural resources. The Colorado River (Hoover Dam) Compact of 1928, involving the States of the Colorado River Basin, was the

---

[15] This statement must be qualified slightly. Various States now cooperate with one another in some common programs, usually through interstate compacts. For example, several States now have "hot-pursuit agreements" with neighboring States. These States permit police officers from an adjoining State to pursue a lawbreaker across the State line; when a fugitive is captured in such circumstances, however, he must be turned over to local authorities. In effect, the "hot-pursuit agreements" make a police officer of one State temporarily an officer of another State.

[16] Article I, Section 10, Clause 3. The Supreme Court has held that congressional consent need not be obtained for compacts which do not "tend to increase the political power of the States"; but because it is often difficult to determine whether a particular agreement is "political" or "non-political" in nature, most interstate agreements are submitted to Congress as a matter of course. Increasingly in recent years Congress has given consent to the making of compacts in certain areas *in advance* of the actual concluding of the agreements; for example, compacts providing for cooperation in such fields as forest fire prevention, nuclear research, and higher education.

first great attempt to bring several of the States together for the development, control, and management of a regional river; and it has benefited each of them.

Full Faith and Credit. The Constitution requires each State to give "full faith and credit . . . to the public acts, records, and judicial proceedings of every other State." [17] The words "public acts, records, and judicial proceedings" as used here refer to State laws and local ordinances; records of births and marriages, deeds and contracts, licenses to drive, to practice law or medicine, or to hunt and fish; and to judgments and decrees.

Suppose that a man dies in Baltimore and his will disposes of property in Chicago. In regard to that property Illinois must give *full faith and credit* (recognize the validity of) to the *probating* (proving) of that will as a judicial proceeding of the State of Maryland. One may prove age, marital status, title to property, or similar facts by obtaining the necessary certificate or certificates from the State where the record was made.

Exceptions. The Full Faith and Credit Clause normally operates as a routine matter among the States. Two exceptions to the rule must be noted, however. First, it applies only to *civil matters;* that is, one State will not enforce another State's criminal law. Second, for now at least, full faith and credit need not be given to certain divorces granted by one State to the residents of another State.

This confusing situation in the matter of "interstate divorces" resulted from a 1945 Supreme Court decision. The case, *Williams* v. *North Carolina,* involved a couple (Mr. Williams and Mrs. Hendrix) who had gone from North Carolina to Nevada to obtain divorces in order that they could marry one another. After residing in Las Vegas for six weeks (the minimum residence period Nevada

requires under its divorce laws), they obtained divorces, immediately married one another, and returned to North Carolina as husband and wife. North Carolina refused to recognize their Nevada divorces. They were convicted in North Carolina on the charge of bigamous cohabitation.

The Supreme Court upheld North Carolina's refusal to grant full faith and credit to the Nevada divorces involved here. It held that the couple had not established *bona fide* (good faith) residence in Nevada, and thus Nevada had no jurisdiction to grant the divorces to the couple from North Carolina.

A Nevada divorce granted to a *bona fide* resident of Nevada must be given full faith and credit by all other States, of course. But to become a legal resident of a State, a person must intend to reside there permanently, or at least indefinitely. In the *Williams* case, the Supreme Court held that Nevada residence had not been established, that Mr. Williams and Mrs. Hendrix were, in fact, North Carolina residents and had remained so. This decision, and several since, has cast a dark cloud of doubt over the validity of thousands of interstate ("quickie") divorces.

Extradition. The Constitution provides:

> A person charged in any State with treason, felony, or other crime, who shall flee from justice, and be found in another State, shall, on demand of the executive authority of the State from which he fled, be delivered up, to be removed to the State having jurisdiction of the crime.[18]

The return of a fugitive is usually a routine matter. The governor of the State from which a fugitive fled is informed that he has been found. The governor then makes formal appli-

---

[17] Article IV, Section 1. The provision was taken practically intact from Article IV of the Articles of Confederation. See page 751.

[18] Article IV, Section 2. Extradition has been carried on between sovereign states from early times. The word *extradition* has been the popular term used in the United States for what is technically known in the law as *interstate rendition.*

cation to the governor of the second State, and the accused is "delivered up."

Occasionally, however, a governor will refuse to surrender a wanted man. Constitutional custom, backed by Supreme Court decisions dating from 1861, has made the word "shall" actually read "may" in the Extradition Clause. There is no way in which a governor may be forced to act; the matter lies within his discretion. When one governor refuses the request of a governor from another State, whether the reasons be good, bad, or indifferent, there the matter ends.

Instances of a governor's refusal are not common, but they are not rare, either. Some years ago, the governor of Oregon refused a West Virginia request based on a crime committed in 1903. He did so because the wanted man had lived as a respected member of his Oregon community for nearly half a century and because, in the governor's opinion, the man had long since paid for his crime in his conscience.

Privileges and Immunities. The Constitution provides:

> The citizens of each State shall be entitled to all privileges and immunities of citizens in the several States.[19]

Essentially, this provision means that a resident of one State will not be discriminated against *unreasonably* by another State.

The courts have never given a complete list of the privileges and immunities of "interstate citizenship," but these are some of them: the right to pass through or reside in any other State for the purpose of trade, agriculture, professional pursuits, or otherwise; to demand the writ of *habeas corpus;* to sue in court; to make contracts; to buy, sell, and hold property; to pay no higher taxes than the residents of the State; to marry.

Of course, the provision does not mean that a resident of one State need not obey the laws of another State while he is in that State. Nor does it mean that a State may not make *reasonable* discrimination against residents of other States. For example, a State is not required to grant *public* or *political* privileges to nonresidents. It may require (and all States do) that one live in the State for a certain period before being eligible to vote or to hold public office. It may require a period of residence within the State before it grants one a license to practice medicine or dentistry, and it may restrict the practice of law to residents of the State.[20]

Wild fish and game are the common property of the people of a State. Therefore, a nonresident may be compelled to pay a higher fee for a hunting or fishing license than a resident who pays taxes to maintain game, provide fish hatcheries, and the like. By the same token, State colleges and universities usually charge higher tuition to students from other States than to its own residents.[21]

THE ADMISSION OF NEW STATES

Only Congress has the power to admit new States to the Union. The Constitution places only one restriction on the power: A new State may not be created by taking territory from one or more of the existing States with-

---

[19] Article IV, Section 2, Clause 1. This provision is reinforced in the 14th Amendment.

[20] Each State has the right to take time to observe the moral character of a person who desires to enter an occupation of great importance to the general public.

[21] A corporation is not regarded as a citizen under the Privileges and Immunities Clause. Thus, a State may refuse a corporation chartered in another State the privilege of conducting business within its borders; but, in doing so, it cannot impose an unreasonable burden on interstate commerce.

out the consent of the State legislatures involved.[22]

Congress has admitted thirty-seven States since the original thirteen formed the Union. Although North Carolina (November 21, 1789) and Rhode Island (May 29, 1790) ratified the Constitution after the new Government had been organized (March 4, 1789), they are, of course, included among the original thirteen. Five States—Vermont, Kentucky, Tennessee, Maine, and West Virginia—were created from parts of already existing States. Texas was an independent republic before admission. California was admitted after being ceded by Mexico. Each of the other thirty States was admitted only after a period as an organized territory.

The table on page 77 indicates the sources of lands comprising the fifty States, the dates on which thirty of them were organized as territories before admission, and the date upon which each joined the Union.

Admission Procedure. The usual process of admission is relatively simple. The area desiring Statehood first *petitions* (applies to) Congress for admission. If and when it is favorably disposed, Congress passes an *enabling act* which directs the framing of a proposed State constitution. After that document has been drafted by a convention and approved by a popular vote, it is submitted to Congress. If Congress is still agreeable to Statehood, it then passes an *act of admission.*

The two newest States, Alaska and Hawaii, abbreviated the usual process. Each adopted a proposed constitution without waiting for an enabling act: Alaska in 1956 and Hawaii in 1950.

Conditions for Admission. Before finally admitting a new State, Congress has often imposed certain conditions. When Ohio entered the Union in 1803, it was forbidden to tax for five years any public lands sold within its borders by the United States. In 1896 Utah was admitted on condition that its constitution outlaw polygamy.[23] In the act admitting Alaska in 1959 the State was forever prohibited from claiming title to any lands legally held by an Indian, Eskimo, or Aleut.

Each State enters the Union on an equal footing with each of the other States. Thus, although it is possible for Congress to impose conditions like those just mentioned, it *cannot* impose conditions of a political nature. For example, when Oklahoma was admitted in 1907, Congress forbade the State to remove its capitol from Guthrie to any other place prior to 1913. In 1910, however, the legislature moved the capitol to Oklahoma City. When this step was challenged, the Supreme Court held that Congress may impose conditions for admission as it pleases *but* the conditions cannot be enforced when they compromise the independence of a State to manage its own internal affairs.

Arizona provides another example of the kind of condition that may be imposed but not enforced. President Taft vetoed a resolution admitting Arizona in 1911. He objected because Arizona's proposed constitution provided that judges might be recalled from office

---

[22] Article IV, Section 3, Clause 1. It is sometimes argued that this restriction was violated regarding the admission of West Virginia in 1863. That State was formed out of the forty western counties which broke away from Virginia over the issue of secession from the Union. The consent required by the Constitution was given by a minority of the members of the Virginia legislature—those representing the forty western counties. Congress accepted their action on the ground that they were the only group legally capable of acting as the Virginia legislature at the time.

[23] Utah, or any other State, could legalize polygamous marriages today, if it chose to do so; the matter is one that is within the reserved powers of the States.

ORIGIN AND ADMISSION OF THE 50 STATES

Order Of Admission	Sources Of State Lands	Organized As Territory	Admitted As State
Delaware	Swedish Charter, 1638; English Charter, 1683	...	7 Dec. 1787 *
Pennsylvania	English Grant, 1680	...	12 Dec. 1787 *
New Jersey	Dutch Settlement, 1623; English Charter, 1664	...	18 Dec. 1787 *
Georgia	English Charter, 1732	...	2 Jan. 1788 *
Connecticut	English Charter, 1662	...	9 Jan. 1788 *
Massachusetts	English Charter, 1629	...	6 Feb. 1788 *
Maryland	English Charter, 1632	...	28 Apr. 1788 *
South Carolina	English Charter, 1663	...	23 May 1788 *
New Hampshire	English Charter, 1622 and 1629	...	21 June 1788 *
Virginia	English Charter, 1609	...	25 June 1788 *
New York	Dutch Settlement, 1623; English Control, 1664	...	26 July 1788 *
North Carolina	English Charter, 1663	...	21 Nov. 1789 *
Rhode Island	English Charter, 1663	...	29 May 1790 *
Vermont	Lands of New York and New Hampshire	**	4 Mar. 1791
Kentucky	Lands of Virginia	**	1 June 1792
Tennessee	Lands of North Carolina	**	1 June 1796
Ohio	Lands of Virginia; Northwest Territory, 1787	13 July 1787	1 Mar. 1803
Louisiana	Louisiana Purchase, 1803	24 Mar. 1804	30 Apr. 1812
Indiana	Lands of Virginia; Northwest Territory, 1787	7 May 1800	11 Dec. 1816
Mississippi	Lands of Georgia and South Carolina	17 Apr. 1798	10 Dec. 1817
Illinois	Lands of Virginia; Northwest Territory, 1787	3 Feb. 1809	3 Dec. 1818
Alabama	Lands of Georgia and South Carolina	3 Mar. 1817	14 Dec. 1819
Maine	Lands of Massachusetts	**	15 Mar. 1820
Missouri	Louisiana Purchase, 1803	4 June 1812	10 Aug. 1821
Arkansas	Louisiana Purchase, 1803	2 Mar. 1819	15 June 1836
Michigan	Lands from Virginia; Northwest Territory, 1787	11 Jan. 1805	26 Jan. 1837
Florida	Ceded by Spain, 1819	30 Mar. 1822	3 Mar. 1845
Texas	Republic of Texas, 1845	**	29 Dec. 1845
Iowa	Louisiana Purchase, 1803	12 June 1838	28 Dec. 1846
Wisconsin	Lands of Michigan; Northwest Territory, 1787	20 Apr. 1836	29 May 1848
California	Ceded by Mexico, 1848	**	9 Sept. 1850
Minnesota	Northwest Territory, 1787; and Louisiana Purchase, 1803	3 Mar. 1849	11 May 1858
Oregon	Louisiana Purchase, 1803; Treaty with Spain, 1819; and Treaty with Great Britain, 1846	14 Aug. 1848	14 Feb. 1859
Kansas	Louisiana Purchase, 1803; and lands from Texas	30 May 1854	29 Jan. 1861
West Virginia	Part of Virginia to 1863	**	20 June 1863
Nevada	Ceded by Mexico, 1848	2 Mar. 1861	31 Oct. 1864
Nebraska	Louisiana Purchase, 1803	30 May 1854	1 Mar. 1867
Colorado	Louisiana Purchase, 1803	28 Feb. 1861	1 Aug. 1876
South Dakota	Louisiana Purchase, 1803	2 Mar. 1861	2 Nov. 1889
North Dakota	Louisiana Purchase, 1803	2 Mar. 1861	2 Nov. 1889
Montana	Louisiana Purchase, 1803	26 May 1864	8 Nov. 1889
Washington	Louisiana Purchase, 1803; and Treaty with Great Britain, 1846	2 Mar. 1853	11 Nov. 1889
Idaho	Louisiana Purchase, 1803; and Oregon Territory	3 Mar. 1863	3 July 1890
Wyoming	Louisiana Purchase, 1803	25 July 1868	10 July 1890
Utah	Ceded by Mexico, 1848	9 Sept. 1850	4 Jan. 1896
Oklahoma	Louisiana Purchase, 1803	2 May 1890	16 Nov. 1907
New Mexico	Ceded by Mexico, 1848	9 Sept. 1850	6 Jan. 1912
Arizona	Ceded by Mexico, 1848; Gadsden Purchase, 1853	24 Feb. 1863	14 Feb. 1912
Alaska	Territory, Purchase from Russia, 1867	24 Aug. 1912	3 Jan. 1959
Hawaii	Territory, Annexed 1898	14 June 1900	21 Aug. 1959

* Date of ratification of U.S. Constitution.   ** No territorial status before admission to the Union.

by a vote of the people. To President Taft this meant that a judge would have to keep one eye on the law and the other on public opinion. The offending section was removed. The next year he signed a new act of admission under which Arizona became the forty-eighth State in the Union. Almost immediately thereafter the voters in Arizona amended the State constitution by adding the popular recall of judges provision.

❈❈❈❈❈❈❈❈❈❈❈❈ CONCEPT BUILDING ❈❈❈❈❈❈❈❈❈❈

Key Concepts

A *federal system* is one in which the powers of government are divided on a territorial basis between a central and several local governments, with each level exercising its own distinct field of powers. The Founding Fathers created the American federal system to satisfy the need for a stronger national government and, at the same time, to preserve the rights of local self-government.

Our federal system's chief advantage is that it permits local problems to be dealt with in accord with local needs and desires while matters of wider concern may be handled on a national basis. It also provides for the strength of union. *Federalism* and *democracy* are not synonymous terms, but it is extremely difficult to conceive of a democracy involving a large area in which federalism is not also present.

The Constitution establishes a *division of powers* between the National Government and the States. The National Government possesses *only* those powers *delegated* to it in the Constitution. The *delegated powers* are of three kinds: (1) the *expressed powers*—those delegated in so many words in the Constitution, (2) the *implied powers*—those that may be reasonably implied from the expressed powers, and (3) the *inherent powers*—those that belong to (inhere in) the National Government because it is a *national* government. The Constitution also *denies* certain powers to the National Government—in so many words, through the silence of the Constitution, and as a result of the existence of a federal system.

The States possess the *reserved powers*—those powers not delegated to the National Government and not denied to the States by the Constitution. The States are also *denied* certain powers—in so many words in the Constitution, as a result of the existence of a federal system, and by their own constitutions.

The *exclusive powers* are those that belong *only* to the National Government. The *concurrent powers* are those that may be exercised by *both* the National Government and the States.

The Constitution is the "supreme law of the land." Immediately under it are acts of Congress and treaties of the United States. No provisions in State constitutions or State and local laws may conflict.

The Supreme Court of the United States is the "referee" in the federal system. It is the final interpreter of the Constitution. The power of *judicial review,* first exercised in 1803, is the power of a court to determine the constitutionality of any governmental action.

The National Government has certain obligations toward the States under the Constitution. It must guarantee to each State a republican form of government, protect each State against foreign invasion and domestic violence, and respect the geographic integrity of every State in the Union.

The States and the National Government cooperate with one another in many ways, from the grants-in-aid programs to the selective service system.

Each of the States is legally separate from all the others. The Constitution does require the States to cooperate with one another through the Full Faith and Credit Clause, the Extradition Clause, and the Privileges and Immunities Clause. The States may, with the consent of Congress, enter into Compacts among themselves.

New States may *only* be admitted by Congress, and Congress often imposes requirements on States as they come into the Union. Each State enters the Union on an equal footing with the other States.

Important Terms

concurrent powers
delegated powers
division of powers
exclusive powers

expressed powers
extradition
full faith and credit
grants-in-aid

implied powers
inherent powers
interstate compacts
privileges and immunities

republican form of government
reserved powers
Supremacy Clause

Questions for Inquiry and Review

1. Why did the Founding Fathers provide for a federal system?

2. What is *federalism?*

3. What is the chief advantage of a federal system?

4. What is meant by the term *division of powers?*

5. Why is the National Government properly described as a government of *delegated powers?*

6. What are the *expressed powers?* The *implied powers?* The *inherent powers?*

7. Why are the States properly described as governments of *reserved powers?*

8. What are the *exclusive powers?* The *concurrent powers?*

9. If the provisions of a State law conflict with those of a national law, which must yield? Why?

10. Why is the Court's decision in *Marbury v. Madison* so important?

11. What are the three obligations which the Constitution imposes upon the National Government with regard to the States?

12. What is the phrase "a republican form of government" generally understood to mean?

13. What is probably the best known example of federal aid to the States? On what grounds is the arrangement sometimes criticized? On what grounds is the arrangement sometimes defended?

14. In what other ways is federal aid extended?

15. In what ways do the States aid the National Government?

16. What agreements are the States constitutionally forbidden to make? What agreements may they make?

17. What, in brief, does the Full Faith and Credit Clause provide? The Extradition Clause? The Privileges and Immunities Clause?

For Further Inquiry

1. What do you think conditions might be like in what is now the United States if no federal system had been created and the thirteen States had attempted to continue under the Articles of Confederation?

2. Why are the powers to declare war, to conduct foreign relations, and to regulate foreign and interstate commerce exclusive powers of the National Government?

3. The Constitution (Article I, Section 10, Clause 3) forbids the States to "engage in war." Why is this prohibition qualified?

4. In 1954 the Supreme Court held that racial segregation in the public schools violates the Equal Protection Clause of the 14th Amendment. Why has it been said that the aftermath of this decision poses the most serious problem to face American federalism since 1865?

5. As a delegate to a convention to "modernize" the Constitution, what changes in the federal system, if any, would you support?

6. What factors have been most responsible for the growth of national power in the federal system?

7. Speaking of the role of the Supreme Court in the American governmental system, Justice Oliver Wendell Holmes once remarked: "I do not think the United States would come to an end if we lost our power to declare an act of Congress void. I do think the Union would be imperiled if we could not make that declaration as to the laws of the several States." Do you agree or disagree with his view?

Suggested Activities

1. Using current newspapers and periodicals, find examples of each of the types of power and denials of power shown in the chart on page 66.

2. Invite your local chief of police to speak to the class on the ways in which the National Government cooperates with him in his work.

3. Stage a debate or class forum on the question: *Resolved,* That the grants-in-aid system undermines American federalism and reduces the power and importance of the States.

4. Prepare a class report on the history of the admission of your State to the Union.

Suggested Reading

BECKER, THEODORE L. (ed.), *The Impact of Supreme Court Decisions.* Oxford, 1969.

BLACKMORE, CHARLES P. and YESELON, ABRAHAM, *The Fabric of Democracy.* Van Nostrand, 1969. Chapter 2.

BURNS, JAMES M. and PELTASON, J. W., *Government By the People.* Prentice-Hall, 1969. Chapters 4, 5.

"Comeback of the States," *U.S. News,* October 27, 1969.

DYE, THOMAS R., *et al., American Government: Theory, Structure, and Process.* Wadsworth, 1969. Chapter 4.

"FBI's Computer War Against Crime," *U.S. News,* October 20, 1969.

KUTLER, STANLEY L., *The Supreme Court and the Constitution: Readings in American Constitutional History.* Houghton Mifflin, 1969.

RIKER, WILLIAM H., *Federalism: Origin, Operation, Significance.* Little, Brown, 1967.

SCOTT, ANDREW M. and WALLACE EARLE (eds.) *Politics, U.S.A.: Cases on the American Democratic Process.* Macmillan, 1969. Chapters 2, 3.

"The 50th State: Still Soaring, But...," *U.S. News,* November 10, 1969.

*"Keep ancient lands, your storied
    pomp!" cries she
With silent lips. "Give me your
    tired, your poor,
Your huddled masses yearning to
    breathe free,
The wretched refuse of your teeming
    shore.
Send these, the homeless, tempest-tost
    to me,
I lift my lamp beside the golden
    door!"*

EMMA LAZARUS,
from the poem *The New Colossus*

❦❦❦Is it either fair or reasonable for the law to draw distinctions between aliens and citizens?

❦❦❦What responsibilities should accompany the possession of American citizenship?

❦❦❦Is American citizenship (either native-born or naturalized) now too easily obtained?

IMMIGRATION

We are a nation of immigrants. Except for the American Indians—and even they are descendants of earlier immigrants—all of us have come here from abroad or are descended from those who did.

Power to Regulate Immigration. In international law every sovereign state possesses the power to regulate the crossing of its borders. In our law this power, although not expressed in the Constitution, is an inherent and an exclusive power of the National Government.

In a long series of cases, dating from 1849, the Supreme Court has held that, in addition

to its status as an inherent power, the power to regulate immigration is also implied from the powers to regulate foreign commerce and to conduct foreign relations.

Our Population Growth. There were only some 2,500,000 persons living in the United States when independence was declared in 1776. In the years since, the nation's population has increased over eighty-fold and now totals more than 205,000,000.

This tremendous growth has come, of course, from two principal sources: (1) the natural increase in population and (2) immigration.

Only 3,929,214 residents were counted in the First Census in 1790. The unsettled and seemingly unlimited expanse of the country, with its vast and untapped natural wealth,

---

[1] Recall, too, that the United States was founded in part as a haven for the oppressed. One of the complaints listed in the Declaration of Independence against George III had been that "he has endeavored to prevent the population of these States; for that purpose obstructing the Laws for the Naturalization of Foreigners; refusing to pass others to encourage their migration hither, . . ."

81

IMMIGRATION AND OUR NATIONAL POPULATION
1790–1970

Census Year	National Population	Since Preceding Census			
		Immigration	Natural Increase	Percentage of Increase Due to Immigration	Percentage of Total Increase
1790	3,929,214	....	....	...	...
1800	5,308,483	(1,379,269) *		...	35.1
1810	7,239,881	(1,931,398) *		...	36.4
1820	9,638,453	(2,398,572) *		...	33.1
1830	12,866,020	151,824	3,075,743	4.7	33.5
1840	17,069,453	599,125	3,604,308	14.3	32.7
1850	23,191,876	1,713,251	4,409,172	28.0	35.3
1860	31,443,321	2,598,214	5,653,211	31.5	35.5
1870	38,558,371	2,314,824	4,800,226	32.5	22.6
1880	50,155,783	2,812,191	8,785,221	24.2	30.1
1890	62,947,714	5,246,613	7,545,318	41.0	25.5
1900	75,994,575	3,687,564	9,359,297	28.3	20.7
1910	91,972,266	8,795,386	7,182,305	55.0	21.0
1920	105,710,620	5,735,811	8,002,543	41.8	14.9
1930	122,775,046	4,107,209	12,957,217	24.1	16.1
1940	131,669,275	528,431	8,315,798	5.9	7.2
1950	150,697,361	1,035,039	17,993,047	5.4	14.5
1960	179,323,175	2,515,479	26,110,335	8.8	18.5
1970 (est.)	204,800,000	?	?	?	14.2

* Immigration figures were not recorded until the 1820 Census. These figures represent the *total* population increase over the ten-year periods.

As you can see from the foregoing table, our population grew by about one-third from decade to decade until the 1860's. From then until the 1940's, the rate of growth dropped steadily. That is, although the total number of persons in the United States continued to increase from census to census, the total did not increase as rapidly after 1860 as it had before. The rate of growth fell to an all-time low of one-fourteenth during the depression years of the 1930's, but it climbed sharply in the 1940's and 1950's. The rate steadied at about the one-fifth level into the early 1960's but has dropped sharply since then.[2] By the time of the 1970 census (April 1), the population had almost reached 205,000,000.

Since 1820, when such figures were first recorded, more than 45,000,000 immigrants have entered the United States. Our population today is the result of that immigration.

Early Immigration Restrictions. The United States made no serious attempt to regulate immigration for more than a century after independence. Indeed, Congress did not enact its first statute in the field until 1819, when it provided only for the collection of immigration statistics and for the regulation of the carriage of steerage passengers. As long as land was plentiful and rapidly expanding indus-

---

[2] The recent decline has been caused by a sharp drop in the nation's birth rate over the past decade. In 1960 it stood at 23.7 live births per 1000 population. It fell to a record low of 17.8 in 1967 and has continued to drop since then, falling below 17.0 in 1970.

try demanded more and still more laborers, immigration was actively encouraged.

By 1890, however, the open frontier had become a thing of the past, and labor was no longer in critically short supply. Then, too, the major source of immigration had shifted. Until the 1880's most immigrants had come from the countries of Northern and Western Europe; the "new immigration" from the 1880's onward came chiefly from Southern and Central Europe.

Each of these factors—the closing of the frontier, a more abundant labor supply, and the shift in the major source of newcomers—combined to bring changes in our traditional policy of encouragement, ultimately reversing it.

Oriental and Personal Exclusion Policies. Congress placed the first major restrictions on immigration with the passage of the Chinese Exclusion Act in 1882.[3] At the same time it barred the entry of convicts, lunatics, paupers, and others likely to become public charges. Over the next several years a long list of "undesirables" was composed; for example, contract laborers were excluded in 1885, immoral persons and anarchists in 1903, and illiterates in 1917.[4] By 1920 more than thirty groups were listed as ineligible on grounds of personal characteristics.

But, despite the growing restrictions, the tide of immigration mounted. In the ten years from 1905 through 1914, an average of more than 1,000,000 persons came to the United States annually. World War I slowed the tide to a mere trickle; but with the end of the war, it rose rapidly again.

National Origins. By 1921 Congress had become convinced that broader restrictions were necessary. Immigration was nearing the million-a-year level once more. Ellis Island, the major immigration facility in New York Harbor, was swamped; thousands of potential entrants were forced to wait there for months while the administrative machinery determined their admissibility. Patriotic societies and labor unions were alarmed. Thus, Congress enacted the Immigration Act of 1921.

This law placed a *quantitative* restriction on immigration. That is, to the exclusion policies based upon race and upon personal characteristics, Congress now added a numerical restriction. The maximum number of persons (the "quota") to be admitted from each country in Europe was fixed at three per cent of the natives of that country residing within the United States in 1910. This set a total maximum on European immigration at about 355,000 per year.

The 1921 law was intended as a stop-gap measure. It was replaced by a more comprehensive and restrictive law, the Immigration (Johnson) Act of 1924. Under the 1924 statute, the quota admissible from each European country was reduced to two per cent of those residing within the United States in 1890 (a total of approximately 165,000). By pushing the base back to the 1890 census, im-

---

[3] The law was intended to stem the flow of "coolie labor" to the Pacific Coast; the Chinese could and did work for far less than white laborers, especially in the mines and on the railroads. By 1924 *all* Orientals had been excluded except for temporary visits. The policy was relaxed somewhat during World War II when provision was made for the admission of limited numbers of Chinese, Filipinos, and natives of India. Since 1952, immigration from each independent country in the Far East has been regulated by the quota system.

[4] Congress had originally provided for the barring of those who could neither read nor write in 1897, but President Cleveland vetoed the bill. He held that literacy was much more a gauge of one's opportunities than of intelligence or other worthy qualifications. President Taft vetoed a similar bill in 1913 on the same basis, and the 1917 law was passed only over a veto by President Wilson.

migration from Northern and Western Europe was purposefully favored over that from Southern and Central Europe.[5]

The 1924 law was refined by the National Origins Act of 1929 which set the basic pattern for our system of immigration control until 1965. It established an overall quota of 150,000 and changed the base for quota calculation to 1920.

Present Immigration Policy. Present immigration policy is set out in two basic statutes: the Immigration and Nationality (McCarran-Walter) Act of 1952 and the Immigration Reform Act of 1965. The latter act made significant modifications in the 1952 law, but both statutes are direct descendants of the legislation of the 1920's. Major responsibility for their enforcement is lodged in the Immigration and Naturalization Service in the Department of Justice.

Immigration is rigidly controlled under both of these statutes — and in terms of both *quantity* and *quality*. That is, only a *limited number* of those persons who possess certain *satisfactory personal characteristics* can be admitted as immigrants to the United States.

Personal Qualifications. The list of "undesirable aliens" barred today takes up five pages in the *United States Code.* It includes among many others: mentally retarded or insane persons, chronic alcoholics, drug addicts, vagrants, beggars, stowaways, paupers, those with any dangerous contagious disease, criminals, immoral persons, polygamists, adults unable to read and understand any language or dialect, advocates of forcible overthrow of our government, present or former members of communist or other totalitarian groups, and those who advocate in any way world communism or other forms of totalitarian dictatorship.[6] No person ineligible to become a citizen can enter the United States as an immigrant.

The Quota System. The Immigration Reform Act of 1965 made extensive changes in the *numerical* limits which are placed upon immigration to this country. The McCarran-Walter Act had continued the national origins quota system begun in the 1920's; and, in only slightly modified form, it also continued the favor shown to immigration from Northern and Western Europe.

Under the 1952 law each nation outside the Western Hemisphere was assigned an annual quota. Each nation's quota was equal to one-sixth of one per cent of the number of persons in the United States in 1920 who had been born in or were descended from those who had been born in that country, except that no nation was given a quota of less than 100.

Altogether, by 1965 a total of 158,561 *quota immigrants* could be admitted to this country each year. Of that total, by far the largest share was that assigned to Great Britain (including Northern Ireland), 65,361; and most of the remainder was allocated to other European countries. The total annual quota immigration allowed from *all* of the rest of the world — that is, from all nations other than those

---

[5] Recall that the largest proportion of immigration prior to 1890 had come from Northern and Western Europe. The Johnson Act also broadened the Oriental exclusion policy. It expressly prohibited immigration from Japan (which, in fact, had been virtually eliminated by the Gentleman's Agreement of 1907 which President Theodore Roosevelt had made with the Japanese government). The Oriental exclusion policy was finally abandoned in 1952; see page 83, note 3.

[6] An alien who can prove that his membership in or support of a communist or other totalitarian group was unknowing, involuntary, or based on economic necessity or that he has honestly reformed may be admitted. The Attorney General may allow the admission of or deny entry to any alien whenever he finds such action to be in the best interests of the United States.

in Europe and this hemisphere—amounted to only 8,864 persons.

The 1965 law made sweeping changes in the quota system. It eliminated the old national origins (country-by-country) basis for the quota system. Now 170,000 quota immigrants may be admitted each year, and that total is allocated among several "preference classes" composed of applicants for admission who are granted *visas* (entry permits) on a "first-qualified, first-served" basis.[7]

The preference classes, in the order of their priority, and the percentages allocated to each are:

(1) Unmarried adult sons and daughters of American citizens—the first 20% of the total of 170,000.

(2) Spouses and unmarried sons and daughters of resident aliens—20% of the total plus any unused portion of class 1.

(3) Members of the professions, such as lawyers, doctors, and teachers, and others with special talents or education—10% of the total quota.

(4) Married sons and daughters of citizens—10% of the total plus any unused portion of the first three classes.

(5) Brothers and sisters of citizens—24% of the total plus any unused portion of the first four classes.

(6) Skilled and unskilled persons to fill specified labor needs in the United States—10% of the total quota.

(7) Refugees from communist domination, from the Middle East, and from natural calamities—6% of the total quota.

If all of the higher preference slots are filled, no places would be available in the seventh class and only a few would be open in the sixth. If, after the allocation of all preferences, there is any unused portion of the total quota, it is available to other qualified (but non-preference) applicants on a "first-come, first-served" basis.[8]

Special Immigrants. As we have just seen, not more than 170,000 immigrants may enter this country each year under the new quota system. But thousands of others—*special immigrants*—may be and are admitted each year.

These special immigrants—persons who are admissible without regard to any numerical restrictions—include such individuals as the alien wives, husbands, unmarried minor children, and parents of American citizens; resident aliens returning from abroad; certain former citizens; and ministers who intend to preach in this country.

Until recently, persons born in any independent country in the Western Hemisphere could also enter the United States without regard to numbers. But the 1965 law provided that, beginning July 1, 1968, a total of not more than 120,000 such persons can be admitted in any one year.

Congress occasionally relaxes the bars for certain groups, as it did for 415,744 refugees from war-torn Europe in the Displaced Persons Acts of 1948 and 1950. It also allowed the admission of another 214,000 refugees, mostly from "iron-curtain" countries, between 1953 and 1956. Nearly 40,000 who fled their homeland after the Hungarian Revolt in 1957 and several thousand who fled starvation and oppression in Communist China in 1962 were also permitted special entry. The thousands of Cuban refugees who fled to this country prior to mid-1968 entered without numerical limit, as persons born in this hemisphere.

Each year Congress also enacts a number of "private laws" to permit the entry of certain persons without regard to the quota system.

---

[7] This ceiling does not include the various classes of *special immigrants,* as we shall see in a moment. The 1965 law provided for the phasing out of the old quota system over a three-year period.

[8] Except that a limit is imposed upon the number of immigrants who may be admitted from any one country in any one year: 20,000, not counting the parents, spouses, and unmarried minor children of American citizens.

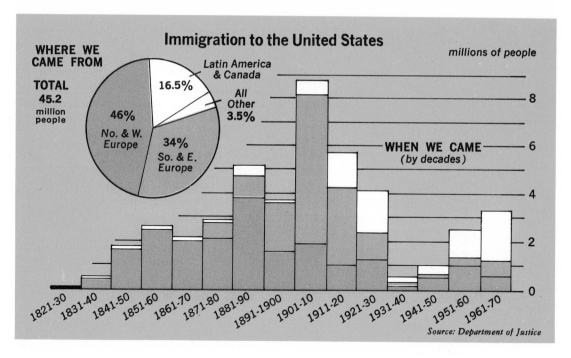

Immigration to the United States

WHERE WE CAME FROM

TOTAL 45.2 million people

- 46% No. & W. Europe
- 34% So. & E. Europe
- 16.5% Latin America & Canada
- All Other 3.5%

millions of people

WHEN WE CAME (by decades)

8 — 6 — 4 — 2 — 0

1821-30, 1831-40, 1841-50, 1851-60, 1861-70, 1871-80, 1881-90, 1891-1900, 1901-10, 1911-20, 1921-30, 1931-40, 1941-50, 1951-60, 1961-70

Source: Department of Justice

These laws usually allow the entry of "hardship" or "humanitarian" cases—for example, an alien child an American family plans to adopt.

Nonimmigrants. Many thousands of persons come to the United States each year as nonimmigrants; that is, for *temporary* purposes. This group includes such visitors as students, newspapermen, tourists, businessmen, touring entertainers, and athletes

Aliens in the United States. Some 3,500,-000 aliens now (1971) live in the United States. More than 350,000 immigrants and 2,000,000 nonimmigrants now arrive each year.

In many respects aliens enjoy the same privileges and benefits held by citizens. Most of the great constitutional guarantees of freedom are written in terms of "persons" rather than "citizens"; thus, they apply to aliens. Generally, aliens may attend public schools, make contracts, use the courts, own property, and engage in most businesses. In short, aliens may do most of the things any citizen may do.

There are several disadvantages to the status, however. Contrary to a widespread impression, aliens must shoulder most of the responsibilities imposed upon citizens. They must obey the law and pay taxes. In some circumstances, aliens may even be drafted for military service. Of course, they cannot vote, nor may they hold most public offices. Many jobs in defense work are denied them. In many States they cannot enter certain professions such as law, medicine, or dentistry. In a few States their right to own property is severely restricted. In some States they cannot own firearms. Several States also deny them unemployment compensation and various other welfare benefits available to citizens. When and if an alien does become a citizen, these disadvantages evaporate, and he assumes all of the rights and privileges of that cherished status.

How Immigrants Enter the United States. Every immigrant seeking to enter the United States must go before an American consul and obtain from the consul a *visa* (a permit to enter)

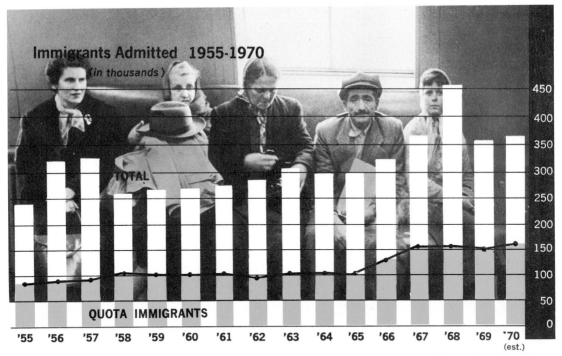

Immigrants Admitted 1955-1970
(in thousands)

TOTAL

QUOTA IMMIGRANTS

	450
	400
	350
	300
	250
	200
	150
	100
	50
	0

'55 '56 '57 '58 '59 '60 '61 '62 '63 '64 '65 '66 '67 '68 '69 '70
(est.)

establishing his apparent right to enter the United States, subject to a further examination at the port of entry. Consuls deny visas to aliens who are legally inadmissible to the United States. Some immigrants are turned back on arrival at our ports of entry by immigration officials.

A steamship or airline which knowingly or carelessly brings an alien who is not admissible is required to return the alien to the port where he boarded. In one instance, an alien from Brazil was rejected for insanity. Since he was not a Brazilian, however, Brazil refused to take him back. The ship, therefore, was forced to carry him back and forth for years until his condition improved.

Deportation. A citizen cannot be deported. An alien may be forced to leave the country for a variety of reasons, however. Illegal entry is the most common cause. Aliens who enter with falsified passports, attempt to sneak in by airplane or ship, or attempt to cross the border at night are usually persons of low moral code. Having entered illegally, they are considered a menace and are deported. In times like these, immigration and other federal officers are especially alert to prevent the entry of espionage agents.

Any alien who commits a crime involving moral turpitude, violates narcotics laws, or commits practically any other felony may be deported. In recent years, a sizable number of aliens with gambling, narcotics, and similar records have been deported.

Finally, any alien may be deported who teaches or advocates the forcible overthrow of the Government of the United States, or who belongs to an organization which does (the communist party, for example). We have no use for those who would come here to enjoy our liberties while working at the same time to destroy them.

The Alien Record a Good One. Through the years, the record of the alien population has been quite good. According to FBI records, for example, the crime rate for aliens is well below that for citizens. Because those who are admitted must meet the high standards set by law, many times they become among the very best of our citizens.

AMERICAN CITIZENSHIP

Every person living in the United States or in any of its territories falls into one of three classes. Most are citizens of the United States, a few are nationals of the United States, and the others are aliens. *Citizens* are full-fledged members of the political community. They are entitled to all the privileges of citizenship, including the protection of the National Government while traveling or residing abroad. They owe full allegiance to the United States and, with their fellow citizens, must bear the responsibilities of government.

Nationals are not full-fledged citizens. They do owe full allegiance to the United States, and they are entitled to its protection.[9] They enjoy many, but not all, of the rights of citizenship.[10] The few nationals of the United States are chiefly the natives of the smaller outlying possessions.

Aliens are those persons within the United States or any of its possessions, either temporarily or permanently, who are neither citizens nor nationals.

The Constitution and Citizenship. As it was originally written, the Constitution contained no definition of citizenship. It mentioned both "citizens of the United States" and "citizens of the States." [11] Until the 1860's it was generally agreed that national citizenship followed that of the States; that is, any person recognized as a citizen of one of the States was

recognized as a citizen of the United States, as well.

Actually, the question was of little importance before the 1860's. Much of the population was the product of recent immigration, and little distinction was made between citizens and aliens. The Civil War and the subsequent adoption of the 13th Amendment raised the need for a constitutional definition, however.[12]

Section I of the 14th Amendment, adopted in 1868, laid down the basic statement of national citizenship. The provision reads:

> All persons born or naturalized in the United States, and subject to the jurisdiction thereof, are citizens of the United States and of the State wherein they reside.

As the chart on page 91 demonstrates, the 14th Amendment thus provides for two ways in which one may acquire citizenship: (1) by birth, and (2) by naturalization.

Citizenship by Birth. Most Americans have acquired their citizenship because they were born in the United States. It is possible, however, to be a native-born citizen even though one was actually born abroad. Two basic rules are applied in determining citizenship by birth: (1) *jus soli*—the law of the soil, *where* born, and (2) *jus sanguinis*—the law of the blood, *to whom* born.

Jus Soli. According to the 14th Amendment, any person born in the United States and subject to its jurisdiction automatically becomes an American citizen at birth. That is, he becomes a native-born citizen because of the *location* of his birth. Thus, any person born in any of the fifty States, the District of Columbia, or the organized territories of Guam, Puerto Rico, and the Virgin Islands is a citizen at birth. So, too, is any person born in an

---

[9] The term *national* is also used in international law to identify any person, citizen or not, who owes allegiance to and is entitled to the protection of a particular state.

[10] For example, they do not possess political rights (that is, the rights to vote and to hold elective office).

[11] Article I, Section 8, Clause 4 gives Congress power "to establish a uniform rule of naturalization."

---

[12] In the famous Dred Scott Case *(Dred Scott* v. *Sanford)* in 1857, the Supreme Court had ruled that neither the States nor the National Government had the power to confer national citizenship on Negroes, slave or free.

1969 ALIEN ADDRESS REPORT

COMPLETE ALL ITEMS ON BOTH
SIDES OF THIS CARD --- PRINT
OR TYPE ANSWERS.

DO NOT MAIL

WHEN COMPLETED--HAND CARD
TO CLERK IN ANY U.S. POST
OFFICE.

(1) MY NAME IS:

(FAMILY) (FIRST) (MIDDLE)

(2) COPY NUMBER FROM ALIEN CARD

(3) MY ADDRESS IS: (SHOW U.S. ADDRESS, EXCEPT COMMUTERS AND SEASONAL WORKERS SHOW ADDRESS IN MEXICO OR CANADA, SEE ITEM 9.)

(IN CARE OF) (APARTMENT OR HOUSE NO.) (STREET OR RURAL ROUTE)

(CITY) (COUNTY) (STATE) (ZIP CODE)

(4) MY SEX IS:

☐ MALE ☐ FEMALE

(5) I WAS BORN IN:

(COUNTRY OF BIRTH)

(6) MY DATE OF BIRTH IS:

(DAY) (MONTH) (YEAR)

(7) I AM A CITIZEN OF:

(COUNTRY OF CITIZENSHIP)

(8) I ENTERED THE UNITED STATES

AT:

(PLACE OR PORT)

ON:

(DAY) (MONTH) (YEAR)

(9) I AM IN THE UNITED STATES AS: (CHECK APPROPRIATE BLOCK)

1 ☐ IMMIGRANT-U.S. RESIDENT

2 ☐ IMMIGRANT-COMMUTER WORKER (CHECK THIS BLOCK IF YOU
ENTER U.S. DAILY OR AT LEAST TWICE A WEEK.)

3 ☐ IMMIGRANT - SEASONAL WORKER (CHECK THIS BLOCK IF YOU
REMAIN IN U.S. DURING ALL PERIODS OF EMPLOYMENT AND
USUALLY RETURN TO CANADA OR MEXICO WHEN NOT EMPLOYED.)

4 ☐ VISITOR   7 ☐ EXCHANGE ALIEN

5 ☐ CREWMAN   8 ☐ CONDITIONAL ENTRANT

6 ☐ STUDENT   9 ☐ OTHER (SPECIFY)

BE SURE YOU HAVE
COMPLETED THE OTHER
SIDE.

FORM I-53 (REV. 1-1-69)

(10) I CERTIFY THAT MY STATEMENTS ON THIS CARD ARE TRUE TO THE BEST OF MY KNOWLEDGE.

(YOUR SIGNATURE, OR IF UNDER 14 YEARS OLD, SIGNATURE OF PARENT OR GUARDIAN)   (DATE) IBM D92200

All aliens residing in the United States must register with the Immigration and
Naturalization Service during January of each year.

American embassy or legation in any foreign country or an American public vessel anywhere in the world.[13]

Just how broad the 14th Amendment's statement of *jus soli* is can be seen from one of the leading cases in the law of citizenship, *United States* v. *Wong Kim Ark* (1898). Wong Kim Ark had been born in the United States to parents who were citizens of China. After an extended visit to China, he was refused entry to the United States by immigration officials at San Francisco. They insisted the 14th Amendment should not be applied so literally as to mean that he was a citizen. They held that as an alien he was prohibited from entry by the Chinese Exclusion Act of 1882. The Supreme Court, however, ruled that under the clear words of the 14th Amendment Wong Kim Ark was, indeed, a native-born citizen and that the Chinese Exclusion Act could not be applied to him.

A very small number of persons who are born *physically* in the United States do not become citizens at birth. They are the few who are born not "subject to the jurisdiction of the United States." These few include children born to foreign diplomatic officials and children born on foreign public vessels in American waters.[14]

Jus Sanguinis. A child born abroad to parents, at least one of whom is an American citizen and who has at some time resided in the United States, also becomes an American citizen at birth. That is, he becomes a native-born citizen on the basis of the parents to *whom* he is born.

Although the 14th Amendment does not specifically provide for *jus sanguinis,* Congress has recognized it by law since 1790. The constitutionality of the arrangement has never been challenged. If it were to be today, it

---

[13] Under international law, United States embassies and legations are, in effect, parts of the United States. A *public vessel* is any vessel (warship, cutter, lightship, and so forth) operated by an agency of the National Government.

[14] Until 1924 Indians born to tribal members living on reservations were not considered citizens, but *wards* (persons legally held to be under the guardianship of the government). In that year Congress conferred citizenship on all Indians not already possessing it.

Handling the problems of immigration requires the skills of a variety of specialists. Inspectors also extend official welcome to the United States to all new arrivals and returning citizens. (U.S. Immigration and Naturalization Service)

would almost certainly be upheld—if for no other reason than the longstanding nature of the practice.

When both parents of a child born abroad are citizens, the law requires only that one of them must have lived in the United States or one of the outlying possessions at one time in order that the child may become a citizen at birth. If one parent is a citizen and the other a national, the citizen-parent must have resided in the United States or an outlying possession for at least one year; otherwise the child does not become a citizen under the principle of *jus sanguinus*. If one of the parents is a citizen and the other is an alien, the citizen-parent must have lived in the United States or one of the possessions for at least ten years, five of them after age fourteen, for the child to become a citizen at birth.

When a child is born abroad to an American parent or parents, his birth is usually registered with the nearest American consulate. If one of the parents is an alien, then the child must later live in the United States for at least five continuous years between the ages of fourteen and twenty-eight to retain his citizenship.

Citizenship by Naturalization. *Naturalization* is the legal process by which a person acquires a new citizenship at some time after birth. Congress has the *exclusive* power to provide for naturalization; no State may do so.[15] The naturalization process usually involves individual persons. On occasion, however, it has involved particular groups. Thus, naturalization may be accomplished *individually* or *collectively*.

Collective Naturalization. At various times in our history it has seemed desirable for Congress to provide for the naturalization *en masse* of a number of persons at one time. This has usually happened when the United States has acquired new territory. The residents of the areas involved were naturalized by the terms of treaties, by acts, or by joint resolutions as indicated in the chart on page 91. All noncitizen Indians were collectively naturalized by law in 1924.

Individual Naturalization. Naturalization is much more commonly an individual process. Generally, any person eligible to enter the United States as an immigrant is eligible to become a naturalized citizen. The naturalization of both parents automatically naturalizes any of their children under age sixteen.[16] The naturalization of a husband or wife, however, does not automatically naturalize the other.

Congress has provided that one may be naturalized by any United States District Court or in any State or territorial court of

---

[15] Article I, Section 8, Clause 4.

[16] Such children must be living in the United States at the time of naturalization. The naturalization of one parent is sufficient if the other has died or in the case of divorce.

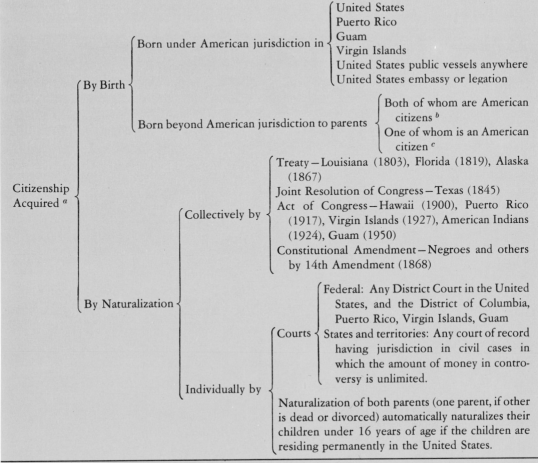

Citizenship Acquired [a]

By Birth
- Born under American jurisdiction in
  - United States
  - Puerto Rico
  - Guam
  - Virgin Islands
  - United States public vessels anywhere
  - United States embassy or legation
- Born beyond American jurisdiction to parents
  - Both of whom are American citizens [b]
  - One of whom is an American citizen [c]

By Naturalization
- Collectively by
  - Treaty — Louisiana (1803), Florida (1819), Alaska (1867)
  - Joint Resolution of Congress — Texas (1845)
  - Act of Congress — Hawaii (1900), Puerto Rico (1917), Virgin Islands (1927), American Indians (1924), Guam (1950)
  - Constitutional Amendment — Negroes and others by 14th Amendment (1868)
- Individually by
  - Courts
    - Federal: Any District Court in the United States, and the District of Columbia, Puerto Rico, Virgin Islands, Guam
    - States and territories: Any court of record having jurisdiction in civil cases in which the amount of money in controversy is unlimited.
  - Naturalization of both parents (one parent, if other is dead or divorced) automatically naturalizes their children under 16 years of age if the children are residing permanently in the United States.

[a] See 14th Amendment. [b] At least one of the citizen parents must have resided in the United States or an outlying possession at some time. [c] The citizen parent must have resided in the United States or an outlying possession for at least 10 years, 5 of them after age 14. Such a child must live in the United States continuously for at least 5 years between ages 14 and 28.

record having jurisdiction in civil cases in which the amount of money in controversy is unlimited.

According to the McCarran-Walter Act, an applicant for naturalization must meet the following conditions:[17]

---

[17] Except that some of the requirements are eased for the spouses or children of citizens and for those serving or who have served in the Armed Forces; for example, a citizen's alien wife need reside in the United States for only three years (from date of marriage) rather than the five years normally required before the filing of a naturalization petition.

(1) He must have entered the United States legally, have resided here continuously for at least five years (including six months in the State in which he files his petition for naturalization), and be at least eighteen years old.

(2) He must be of "good moral character," be "attached to the principles of the Constitution of the United States," and be "well disposed to the good order and happiness of the United States."

(3) He must be able to read, write, speak, and understand words in ordinary usage in the English language (unless he is over fifty years of age and has lived in this country for twenty years), and he must demonstrate "a knowledge and understanding of the fundamentals of the history, and of the principles and form of government, of the United States."

(4) He must not, within ten years prior to filing his petition, have advocated opposition to organized government *(anarchism)* or the overthrow of government by force or violence, or belonged to an organization advocating either of these ends (unless he can show that his membership was unknowing, involuntary, or based upon economic necessity). Of course, these stipulations are aimed specifically at communists.

(5) He must take an oath (or affirmation) in which he renounces allegiance to any foreign state or ruler, pledges that he will support and defend the Constitution and laws of the United

Naturalization Process

DECLARATION
OF INTENTION (Optional)
Filed with clerk of court; petitioner must be at least 18 years of age; states intention to renounce allegiance to former country.

PETITION
Filed with clerk of court after 5 years of residence (3 if married to an American citizen); renounces allegiance to former country and declares not opposed to organized government nor a polygamist.

PETITION ATTESTED
2 American citizens (witnesses) verify petitioner's 5 years of continuous residence, good moral character, and belief in principles of the Constitution in sworn statement to clerk of court.

EXAMINATION
By judge, or appointee who reports findings and makes recommendations to judge.

CITIZENSHIP GRANTED
Not less than 30 days after filing of petition; judge administers oath of allegiance and signs certificate of citizenship.

States against all enemies foreign and domestic, and agrees to take up arms in defense of this country or to perform noncombat service if called upon to do so by law.

The major steps to naturalization are outlined in the chart on page 92. Examiners from the Immigration and Naturalization Service usually play a very significant role in the process. They examine applicants, often very closely, to ensure that the applicants meet the conditions that have just been outlined. The final decision to grant or to deny citizenship is made by the federal or State judge in whose court the petition has been filed, but the decision almost always follows the recommendation made to the judge by the examiner.

In 1963 Congress enacted a statute directing the President to proclaim Sir Winston Churchill an "honorary citizen" of the United States. Lafayette was made an honorary citizen of two States during the American Revolution, but the honor accorded Great Britain's late wartime Prime Minister is unique in our history.

Loss of Citizenship. Under present law, one may lose his citizenship in one of three ways: (1) as punishment for certain federal crimes, (2) by expatriation, or (3) by denaturalization.

Punishment for Crime. Despite the popular impression, a person *cannot* lose his citizenship upon being convicted of *most* federal or *any* State crimes. Some of the *privileges* of citizenship, especially the right to vote, are often denied to felons in various States. But under *no* circumstances may a State deprive a person of his citizenship.

Any citizen, whether naturalized or native-

Refugees from the totalitarian dictatorship of Castro's Cuba have been admitted to our country without numerical limits. (Wide World Photos)

born, may be stripped of his citizenship upon conviction of such specific federal crimes as treason or advocating or attempting overthrow of the government by force.[18]

Expatriation. One may *expatriate* himself (renounce his citizenship) in a variety of ways;

---

[18] Until recently, desertion from the Armed Forces in wartime and flight from the country to avoid wartime service also were punished with the loss of citizenship. However, the Supreme Court in 1958 held the desertion provision to be unconstitutional as a violation of the 8th Amendment's ban of cruel and unusual punishment; and in 1963 it struck down the draft-evasion provision as a bill of attainder. (See page 115.)

and he may do so either voluntarily or involuntarily. For example, expatriation may occur if one takes an oath of allegiance to or is naturalized by a foreign State.[19] A child is expatriated if his parents become naturalized citizens of another country. Any American citizen may renounce his or her citizenship by making a formal declaration to that effect to a representative of the Attorney General or to an American diplomatic or consular officer abroad.[20]

Denaturalization. The process by which a naturalized citizen may be stripped of his citizenship is that of denaturalization. It is far easier for a naturalized citizen to lose his citizenship than it is for a native-born citizen. He can lose it on any of the grounds upon which a native-born citizen can, of course.

In addition, he may be denaturalized if he joins a communist organization or other group, membership in which would have barred his naturalization, within five years after becoming a citizen; or, if at any time within ten years he refuses to testify before a congressional committee concerning alleged subversive activities; or, if it is shown that he obtained his citizenship by fraud or took the oath of allegiance with mental reservations.[21]

---

[19] Until recently the law provided that one automatically forfeited his citizenship by voting in a foreign election. The Supreme Court declared the provision to be unconstitutional in 1967, however. It held, 5–4, that the 14th Amendment's definition of citizenship in effect forbids to Congress the power to provide for the revocation of any person's citizenship without his consent. Although the case (*Afroyim* v. *Rusk*) involved only the matter of voting in a foreign election, the Court's opinion appears to say, quite clearly, that one may lose his citizenship *only* as a result of a *voluntary* renunciation of it.

[20] American citizenship is neither lost nor acquired by marriage today. The only significant effect marriage has on the subject now is to shorten the time required for naturalization in the case of one who marries an American citizen.

[21] Until recently the law also provided that if a naturalized citizen returned to his former country and resided there for a period of three years he would thereby be denaturalized. However, the Supreme Court held the provision unconstitutional in 1964. It held, 5–3, that, as the Constitution draws no distinctions between naturalized and native-born citizens (except in eligibility to the Presidency), Congress has no authority to do so.

✳✳✳✳✳✳✳✳✳✳ CONCEPT BUILDING ✳✳✳✳✳✳✳✳✳✳

Key Concepts

We are a nation of immigrants. More than 45,000,000 have come to this country since 1820. While immigration was encouraged for more than a century, the closing of the frontier by 1890, a lessening demand for new labor, and a shift in the main source of immigration brought a change in that policy.

The power to regulate immigration is an exclusive power of the National Government. The first major restrictions on admission came when Congress enacted the Chinese Exclusion Act of 1882. This was followed by the exclusion of several classes of undesirables.   A continuing flood of immigration finally brought restrictions in the form of national quotas in the 1920's.

Today under the Immigration and Nationality (McCarran-Walter) Act of 1952 and the Immigration Reform Act of 1965 immigration is rigidly controlled in terms of *both* quality and quantity.   Immigrants must meet high personal qualifications.   Under the quota system, only 170,000 quota immigrants may be admitted from countries outside the Western Hemisphere and only 120,000 from within this hemisphere each year.   Many special immigrants are admitted, however, as are many nonimmigrants.

All persons living in the United States or its possessions are *citizens, nationals,* or *aliens*.   The original Constitution contained no definition of citizenship;   the 14th Amendment added one in 1868.   Citizenship may be acquired either by birth or by naturalization.   A person may become a native-born citizen by being born in the United States (*jus soli*) or by being born abroad to parents possessing American citizenship (*jus sanguinis*).   Naturalization may be either individual or collective.

Citizenship imposes some duties and accords some privileges not extended to aliens.   Over all, the alien record in the United States is quite good.   One may be stripped of his citizenship *only* by the National Government, *never* by a State.   Citizenship is lost as a result of punishment for a few specific federal crimes, by expatriation, or by denaturalization.

Important Terms

alien	denaturalization	*jus sanguinis*	Oriental exclusion policy
citizen	expatriation	*jus soli*	quota immigrant
citizenship	immigration	McCarran-Walter Act	quota system
collective natural-	Immigration Re-	national	special immigrant
ization	form Act	naturalization	visa

Questions for Inquiry and Review

1. On what grounds does the United States Congress possess the power to regulate immigration?

2. What two factors have been especially responsible for our tremendous population growth?

3. How many immigrants have come to the United States since such records were first kept?

4. What factors were chiefly responsible for our original policy of encouraging immigration?

5. What factors brought a change in this policy?

6. What and when was the first major attempt made to restrict immigration?

7. What act of Congress set the basic pattern for our present system of immigration control?

8. What are the two major statutes under which immigration is regulated today?

9. May a person ineligible to become a citizen nonetheless enter as an immigrant?

10. Immigration is rigidly controlled today on the basis of what two factors?

11. What area of the world was favored by the former quota system?

12. What are special immigrants? Non-immigrants?

13. Approximately how many aliens now live in the United States? Approximately how many immigrants come here each year?

14. On what two broad bases may one acquire citizenship?

15. What is the differences between *jus soli* and *jus sanguinis?*

16. Who may become a naturalized citizen?

17. May a State grant citizenship? May it deprive citizenship?

18. On what grounds may one be expatriated? Denaturalized?

For Further Inquiry

1. Arguing against passage of the Immigration Reform Act of 1965, Senator Spessard L. Holland of Florida asked on the Senate floor: "Why, for the first time, are the emerging nations of Africa to be placed on the same basis as our mother countries, Britain, Germany, . . .?" Do you agree with the position implied by Senator Holland's question? If so, why? If not, why?

2. Many argue that because the personal qualifications an alien must meet are so high we could well afford to raise the number of quota immigrants admissible in any one year. Do you agree? Why?

3. Do you think that aliens should be permitted to vote? Do you think they should be permitted to practice law or medicine? If not, why not? If so, under what conditions?

4. In what ways can a nation's immigration history and its present policies have important consequences for its foreign relations?

5. For the alien about to be naturalized, the court ceremony involved is a unique, solemn, and significant occasion. Most judges regard it in this light and arrange proceedings in a fitting manner. A few judges do not, however; they seem to view the matter as an unwelcome interruption. If you were a judge, what steps would you take to insure that the courtroom ceremony matched the importance of the occasion?

Suggested Activities

1. Invite a naturalized citizen to speak to the class on his or her experiences in obtaining citizenship.

2. Arrange a class trip to attend a naturalization ceremony.

3. Stage a debate or class forum on the question: *Resolved,* That the present immigration policies of the United States are, in many particulars, much too restrictive.

4. Prepare a wall chart or bulletin board display presenting the material contained in the table on page 82 or the chart on page 91.

Suggested Reading

FERGUSON, JOHN H. and MCHENRY, DEAN E., *The American System of Government.* McGraw-Hill, 1968. Chapter 9.

KRISTOL, IRVING, "Today's Negroes — Better Off than Yesterday's Immigrants?" *U.S. News,* November 27, 1967.

LEACH, RICHARD H., *Governing the American Nation.* Allyn and Bacon, 1967. Chapter 12.

MAGRATH, C. PETER, *et al., The American Democracy.* Macmillan, 1969. Chapter 5.

PRITCHETT, C. HERMAN, *The American Constitution.* McGraw-Hill, 1968. Chapter 35.

U.S. Immigration and Naturalization Service, *U.S. Immigration and Naturalization Laws,* Washington, D.C. Annual.

The God who gave us life, gave us liberty at the same time.

THOMAS JEFFERSON

***Why is the relationship between liberty and authority so critical in a free society?

***Should all of the civil rights guarantees in the Constitution be available to <u>all</u> persons in the United States?

***Which should be the principle concern in criminal justice: that the innocent be protected or that the guilty be punished?

The United States was born out of a struggle for freedom. The men who founded this nation loved liberty above all earthly possessions. For them, freedom for their country and freedom for the individual were the greatest of the blessings Providence could bestow. In proclaiming the independence of the United States from England on July 4, 1776, they declared:

We hold these truths to be self-evident: that all men are created equal; that they are endowed by their Creator with certain unalienable rights; that among these are Life, Liberty, and the pursuit of Happiness.

And, significantly, in the very next line of the Declaration of Independence they added:

That to secure these rights, Governments are instituted among Men, deriving their just powers from the consent of the governed; . . .

The Founding Fathers repeated this justification for the existence of government in the Preamble to the Constitution:

We, the People of the United States, in Order to. . .secure the Blessings of Liberty to ourselves and our Posterity, do ordain and establish this Constitution for the United States of America.

Civil Rights and Limited Government. Government in the United States is firmly based upon the concept of *limited government* — on the principle that government is not all-powerful, that it has *only* those powers the sovereign people have given to it. This fact is nowhere better illustrated than in the field of civil rights. The Constitution is literally studded with guarantees of personal freedom; that is, with prohibitions of governmental action.

All governments exercise authority over individuals. The crucial difference between democracies and dictatorships lies in the *extent* of that authority. In a dictatorship that authority is practically unlimited. In the Soviet Union, for example, opposition to the dictatorship is ruthlessly suppressed. Even such forms

97

(handwritten British document reproduced)

British writs of assistance—general search warrants (note the screened words)— were bitterly resented. Today the Constitution guarantees that the people shall be secure against unreasonable search and seizure. (The Archives of the Supreme Judicial Court of Massachusetts)

of expression as art, music, and literature must glorify the state. In the United States, on the other hand, governmental authority is severely limited. Peaceable opposition to the government is not only tolerated, it is actively encouraged. The late Justice Robert H. Jackson put it well:

> If there is any fixed star in our constitutional constellation, it is that no official, high or petty, can prescribe what shall be orthodox in politics, nationalism, religion, or other matters of opinion or force citizens to confess by word or act their faith therein.[1]

---

[1] *West Virginia Board of Education* v. *Barnette*, 1943; see page 109.

Historical Background. As we noted in Chapter 2, our system of civil rights is one of those valuable legacies which came to us from England and which proved so important to the shaping of government in the United States. Over a period of several centuries, Englishmen had waged a continuing struggle to establish individual liberties. The early colonists brought a dedication to that cause with them to the New World.

The concept of civil rights took root and flourished in the fertile soil of America. The Revolutionary War was fought to maintain and expand the rights of the individual against government. The very first State constitutions contained long lists of rights held by the people.

The National Constitution, as it was drafted at Philadelphia in 1787, contained several civil rights guarantees.[2] But it did not contain a bill of rights, a general listing of the people's liberties. The outcry this omission raised was so marked that several of the States ratified the original Constitution only on the condition that a Bill of Rights be added immediately. The very first session of Congress in 1789 proposed a series of amendments. Ten of these, the Bill of Rights, were ratified and became a part of the Constitution on December 15, 1791. Later Amendments, especially the 13th and 14th, have added to the freedoms guaranteed by the Constitution.

The Courts and Civil Rights. In the United States the courts, especially the Supreme Court of the United States, stand as the principal guardian of individual liberties. The executive and legislative branches of the National and State Governments are also responsible for safeguarding the people's rights, of course. But it is the courts which must *interpret* and *apply* the constitutional guarantees whenever an individual claims that govern-

---

[2] Especially in Article I, Sections 9 and 10 and in Article III.

ment (or another individual) has infringed upon his liberty.

The fact that the courts do stand as guardians does *not* mean that the citizen can sit back in assured safety. Nor does the fact that the National Constitution and the State constitutions contain lists of basic rights mean that our forefathers bought and paid for them and that they are ours forever. To preserve and protect those liberties, each generation must learn and understand them anew, and be willing to fight for their preservation. Learned Hand, one of the nation's great jurists, put it this way:

> I often wonder whether we do not rest our hopes too much upon constitutions, upon laws and upon courts. These are false hopes; believe me, these are false hopes. Liberty lies in the hearts of men and women; when it dies there, no constitution, no law, no court can even do much to help it. While it lies there it needs no constitution, no law, no court to save it.[3]

Civil Rights Are Relative, Not Absolute. Even though basic civil rights are guaranteed to *everyone* in the United States, *no one* has the right to do whatever he pleases. Each person has a right to do as he pleases *as long as* he does not interfere with the rights of others. That is, each person's rights are *relative* to the rights of all others. For example, each person in the United States enjoys the right of free speech. But no person has *absolute* freedom of speech. Thus, a man who uses obscene language may be punished by a court for committing a crime; or one who damages another by what he says may be sued for slander. The great Justice Oliver Wendell Holmes made the point in this oft-quoted passage:

> The most stringent protection of free speech would not protect a man in falsely shouting fire in a theatre and causing a panic.[4]

---

[3] Quoted in Irving Dillard (ed.), *The Spirit of Liberty: Papers and Addresses of Learned Hand;* Knopf; 2nd edition, © 1953; pages 189–190.

[4] *Schenck* v. *United States,* 1919; see page 111.

Persons to Whom Rights Are Guaranteed. Most of the civil rights guaranteed in the Constitution are extended to *all persons.* The Supreme Court has often held that the word "persons" includes aliens in the United States as well as citizens.

Not *all* rights are extended to aliens, however. For example, the 2nd Amendment forbids the National Government from interfering with the "right to keep and bear arms." Aliens, however, may be and are restricted in this connection.

In 1942, shortly after the beginning of World War II, all Japanese living on the West Coast were evacuated inland. Some 120,000 persons, at least two-thirds of whom were *native-born American citizens,* were involved. These people were interned in "war relocation camps" operated by the Government. The relocation program caused severe economic and personal hardship for many. In 1944, however, in *Korematsu* v. *United States* the Supreme Court held that the evacuation program was legal as a wartime emergency measure. The action has been severely criticized ever since. Japanese-Americans fought heroically in the armed forces in World War II, and not a single case of *Nisei* (American-born Japanese) disloyalty has ever been found.

Federalism Complicates Our System of Civil Rights. We have, as you well know, a federal system of government in the United States. Federalism affects our system of civil rights in these several ways:

(1) There are some civil rights which are enjoyed against the National Government only.

(2) There are some civil rights which are enjoyed against the States (and their local governments) only.

(3) There are some—a great many—which are enjoyed against both the National Government and the States.

(4) Some of the civil rights enjoyed against a State arise from the National Constitution whereas others arise from the particular State constitution.

As we shall see in a moment, the Supreme Court has lessened the complicated effects of federalism on our system of civil rights through a broadening interpretation of the Due Process Clause in the 14th Amendment.

The Bill of Rights Restricts the National Government Only. The several guarantees contained in the Bill of Rights were originally intended to be, and still are, restrictions upon the National Government, *not the States*.[5] To illustrate the point, take the 2nd Amendment. It reads:

> A well-regulated militia being necessary to the security of a free state, the right of the people to keep and bear arms shall not be infringed.

The restriction in the 2nd Amendment applies *only* to the National Government. The States may, and very often do, restrict the right to keep and bear arms. (As a matter of fact, the Amendment does not impose a significant limit on the National Government, either — as we shall note shortly, on page 106.)

Modifying Effect of the 14th Amendment. Again, the provisions of the Bill of Rights apply only against the National Government. *But* notice that the Due Process Clause of the 14th Amendment provides:

> ... nor shall any State deprive any person of life, liberty, or property, without due process of law, ...

In performing its task of interpreting and applying the Constitution, the Supreme Court has held that this clause guarantees to all persons *all* of those rights which are "basic or essential to the American concept of liberty."

In a long series of cases the Court has held that a number of the specific guarantees in the Bill of Rights are *also contained* in the 14th Amendment's Due Process Clause. For example, in 1925 it declared freedom of speech and press — protected against the National Government in the 1st Amendment — to be "among the fundamental personal rights and liberties protected by the Due Process Clause in the 14th Amendment from impairment by the States."[6] Soon the other 1st Amendment guarantees — of religious freedom and of the right of assembly and petition — were held to be within the meaning of the 14th Amendment.

In recent years the Court has enlarged the scope of the 14th Amendment's Due Process Clause still further. In 1961 it held that the clause prohibits unreasonable searches and seizures by State and local authorities — just as the 4th Amendment bans such action by federal officers. In 1962 it gave the same coverage to the 8th Amendment's prohibition of cruel and unusual punishments, in 1963 to the 6th Amendment's guarantee of the assistance of counsel for persons accused of a crime, in 1964 to the 5th Amendment's ban on self-incrimination, in 1965 to the 6th Amendment's guarantee to those accused of crime the right to confront witnesses against them, in 1967 to the 6th Amendment's guarantees to the accused of the right to compulsory process for obtaining witnesses in their favor and to speedy trials, in 1968 to the 6th Amendment's guarantee of the right to trial by jury (in all cases involving serious crimes, at least), and in 1969 the 5th Amendment's bar to double jeopardy.

In effect, the Supreme Court has "nationalized" these basic rights. By declaring them to exist against *the States* through the 14th

---

[5] Recall that Amendments 1–10 were added (in 1791) to meet one of the major objections raised during the struggle for ratification of the Constitution; see page 45. The Supreme Court held the amendments to apply only against the National Government in the first case in which the point was raised, *Barron* v. *Baltimore,* decided in 1833; it has followed that holding ever since.

[6] The case, *Gitlow* v. *New York,* involved a communist who had been convicted of the crime of criminal anarchy in New York. He had published a subversive pamphlet. In upholding his conviction the Court also sustained the constitutionality of the New York law under which he had been tried.

Concurring in *Whitney* v. *California,* 1927, Justice Louis Brandeis wrote:

> Fear of serious injury alone cannot justify suppression of free speech and assembly. Men feared witches and burnt women. It is the function of speech to free men from the bondage of irrational fears. To justify suppression of free speech there must be reasonable ground to fear that serious evil will result if free speech is practiced. There must be reasonable ground to believe that the danger apprehended is imminent. There must be reasonable ground to believe that the evil to be prevented is a serious one. . . . The wide difference between advocacy and incitement, between preparation and attempt, between assembling and conspiracy, must be borne in mind. In order to support a finding of clear and present danger it must be shown either that immediate serious violence was to be expected or was advocated, or that the past conduct furnished reason to believe that such advocacy was then contemplated.
>
> Those who won our independence by revolution were not cowards. They did not fear political change. They did not exalt order at the cost of liberty. To courageous, self-reliant men, with confidence in the power of free and fearless reasoning applied through the processes of popular government, no danger flowing from speech can be deemed clear and present, unless the incidence of the evil apprehended is so imminent that it may befall before there is opportunity for full discussion.

Do you agree with this restatement of the "clear and present danger" rule? Does it have any application to the civil rights problems of today? How? Can you discover the facts and the decision in the case cited here? Why has it been said that what Justice Brandeis was propounding here was not a "clear and present danger" rule but, rather, an "is there yet time to call the cops?" rule.

Amendment, *as well as* against the National Government through the Bill of Rights, it has made their meaning and application uniform throughout the nation. In the process, much of the effect that federalism has upon our civil rights system has been very sharply reduced. But, notice, the 14th Amendment's Due Process Clause *does not* cover other rights provided in the Bill of Rights; it covers *only* those the Supreme Court has found to be "basic or essential to the American concept of liberty."

No Complete Listing of Rights. In neither the United States nor the various State constitutions—indeed, nowhere—is there a full and complete catalogue of the rights held by the American people.

Most of the guarantees contained in the National Constitution are in Amendments 1–8. Others are found in Article I, Sections 9 and 10; Article III, Sections 2 and 3; and the 13th and 14th Amendments. But the 9th Amendment declares:

> The enumeration in the Constitution of certain rights shall not be construed to deny or disparage other rights retained by the people.

What are these "other rights retained by the people"? It is impossible to say. As early as 1873 the Supreme Court noted that discovering them must be a "gradual process of judicial inclusion and exclusion."

THE TWO DUE PROCESS CLAUSES

The Constitution contains two Due Process of Law Clauses. In the 5th Amendment the National Government is forbidden the power to deprive any person of "life, liberty, and property, without due process of law." As we have just seen, the 14th Amendment places the same restriction on the States.

Double Meaning of Due Process. The phrase "due process of law" naturally makes one think of due procedures (that is, fair, proper procedures) employed by government. This is what the constitutional phrase originally meant. It still means that; but it has come to mean much more, as well.

The 14th Amendment was designed to guarantee that the States would not use unfair, arbitrary procedures in their dealings with any person [7]—and especially with newly freed Negroes. Fair *procedures* were of little value, however, if those procedures were employed to carry out unfair *laws*. Because of this, the Supreme Court soon held that the guarantee of due process requires that *both* the procedures followed and the laws under which they are followed be *fair*. That is to say, due process of law has come to have two meanings—one *procedural* and the other *substantive*. It may be said that procedural due process involves the *how* and substantive due process involves the *what* of governmental action.

Procedural Due Process. From the procedural standpoint, then, due process requires that in dealing with people government must *act fairly*. A California case furnishes a good illustration of procedural due process.

A man named Rochin was suspected of selling narcotics in Los Angeles. Acting on a tip, three deputy sheriffs went to his rooming house. Finding the outside door open, they entered and then forced open the door to Rochin's room. They found him sitting on the side of a bed. Two capsules were lying on a night stand beside the bed. When asked "Whose stuff is this?" Rochin seized the capsules and put them in his mouth. The officers jumped on him, but he managed to swallow the capsules.

Rochin was handcuffed and taken to a hospital where his stomach was pumped. The two capsules were found to contain morphine. Rochin was convicted of violating the State's narcotics laws. The capsules proved to be the chief evidence against him, and he was sentenced to sixty days.

The Supreme Court reversed his conviction in 1952, holding the deputies had violated the 14th Amendment's guarantee of procedural due process. Said the Court:

> This is conduct that shocks the conscience. Illegally breaking into the privacy of the petitioner, the struggle to open his mouth and remove what was there, the forcible extraction of his stomach's contents—this course of proceeding by agents of government to obtain evidence is bound to offend even hardened sensibilities. They are methods too close to the rack and the screw. . .

Substantive Due Process. Substantive due process requires that in dealing with people government must *proceed under fair laws*. A case from Oregon provides a good illustration of this form of due process.

At the 1922 election the voters of the State adopted a law requiring that all children between the ages of eight and sixteen who had not completed the eighth grade had to attend *public* schools. Under the law private schools were practically abolished.

A Roman Catholic order challenged the constitutionality of the act. In 1925 in *Pierce* v. *Society of Sisters* the Supreme Court unanimously decided that the law violated substantive due process as guaranteed in the 14th Amendment. The Court held that it "unreasonably interferes with the liberty of parents to direct the upbringing and education of children under their control." It also held that the law denied private schoolteachers and administrators their liberty to practice a vocation "long regarded as useful and meritorious."

Due Process Versus the Police Power. Each of the States has among its reserved

---

[7] Also corporations, as the Supreme Court has held that they are "persons" within the meaning of the 14th Amendment.

CIVIL RIGHTS GUARANTEED IN THE FEDERAL CONSTITUTION

Against the National Government

1. Writ of habeas corpus not to be suspended except in rebellion or invasion. *Art. I, Sec. 9, Cl. 2.*

2. No bill of attainder. *Art. I, Sec. 9, Cl. 3.*

3. No *ex post facto* laws. *Art. I, Sec. 9, Cl. 3.*

4. Treason specifically defined and punishment limited. *Art. III, Sec. 3.*

5. No establishment of religion. *1st Amendment.*

6. No interference with religious belief. *1st Amendment.*

7. No abridging of freedom of speech and press. *1st Amendment.*

8. No interference with right of peaceable assembly and petition. *1st Amendment.*

9. No interference with right of people to keep and bear arms. *2nd Amendment.*

10. No quartering of soldiers in private homes without owners' consent. *3rd Amendment.*

11. No unreasonable searches and seizures; no warrants issued but upon probable cause. *4th Amendment.*

12. No criminal prosecution but upon grand jury action. *5th Amendment.*

13. No double jeopardy. *5th Amendment.*

14. No compulsory self-incrimination. *5th Amendment.*

15. No persons to be deprived of life, liberty, property, without due process of law. *5th Amendment.*

16. Speedy and public trial. *6th Amendment.*

17. Trial of crimes by impartial jury. *Art. III, Sec. 2, Cl. 3; 6th Amendment.*

18. Persons accused of crimes must be informed of charges, confronted with witnesses, have power to call witnesses, have assistance of counsel. *6th Amendment.*

19. Jury trial of civil suits involving more than $20. *7th Amendment.*

20. No excessive bail or fines. *8th Amendment.*

21. No cruel and unusual punishments. *8th Amendment.*

22. No slavery or involuntary servitude. *13th Amendment.*

Against the States and Their Local Governments

1. No bills of attainder. *Art. I, Sec. 10, Cl. 1.*

2. No *ex post facto* laws. *Art. I, Sec. 10, Cl. 1.*

3. No slavery or involuntary servitude. *13th Amendment.*

4. No denial of privileges and immunities of citizens of other States. *Art. IV, Sec. 2, Cl. 1; 14th Amendment, Sec. 1.*

5. No denial of equal protection of the laws. *14th Amendment, Sec. 1.*

6. No person to be deprived of life, liberty, property, without due process of law. *14th Amendment, Sec. 1.*

7. Guarantees of freedom of religion, speech, and press and the right of peaceable assembly and petition. *Through Due Process Clause in 14th Amendment.*

8. No unreasonable searches and seizures; no warrants issued but upon probable cause. *Through Due Process Clause in 14th Amendment.*

9. No cruel and unusual punishments. *Through Due Process Clause in 14th Amendment.*

10. Right of the accused to counsel. *Through Due Process Clause in 14th Amendment.*

11. No compulsory self-incrimination. *Through Due Process Clause in 14th Amendment.*

12. Right of the accused to confront witnesses against him. *Through Due Process Clause in 14th Amendment.*

13. Right of the accused to call witnesses in his favor. *Through Due Process Clause in 14th Amendment.*

14. Right of the accused to a speedy trial. *Through Due Process Clause in 14th Amendment.*

15. Right of the accused to trial by jury in serious criminal cases. *Through Due Process Clause in 14th Amendment.*

16. Prohibition of double jeopardy. *Through Due Process Clause in 14th Amendment.*

17. Guarantee of all freedoms "basic or essential to the American concepts of liberty." *Through Due Process Clause in 14th Amendment.*

★ ★ ★

That to secure these rights, Governments are instituted among Men. . . . July 4, 1776.

powers what is known as the *police power*. A State's police power is its power to regulate in the interest of public health, public safety, public welfare, or public morals.

When an action of a State (or one of its local governments) is challenged as a violation of the 14th Amendment's Due Process Clause, the defense almost invariably argues for it as a valid exercise of the police power. If the courts can be convinced that this is so, the action will be upheld as constitutional. A Kansas case of several years ago illustrates the situation.

In 1881 Kansas outlawed the manufacture or sale of intoxicating liquor, except for medicinal purposes. A man named Mugler was convicted of making and selling beer in violation of the law. His attorneys argued that he had invested his money in a brewing business when such activity was lawful in Kansas. Thus, to deny him the right to operate his business, they said, would be to deprive him of both liberty and property without due process of law. The Supreme Court refused to accept this argument. In 1887 it ruled that prohibition fell within the State's right to regulate in order to promote the public health, safety, welfare, and morals.

One liberty after another has been restricted because legislators and the courts have held health, safety, welfare, and morals to be of overriding importance. For example:

To promote health, States have been permitted to forbid or restrict the sale of intoxicants and opiates, forbid the practice of medicine or dentistry without a license, quarantine communicable diseases, require residences to be connected to sewers, and permit officers to seize food products that are unfit for human consumption.

To promote safety, States have been permitted to forbid the carrying of concealed weapons, require snow to be shoveled from sidewalks, require weeds to be removed from city lots, and require accident insurance for motor vehicles using the public highways.

To promote welfare, States have been permitted to restrict reasonably the hours of labor, set reasonable minimum wages, restrict public utilities to reasonable profits, forbid oil and gas wells to be operated in a wasteful manner, and require cedar trees to be cut to protect orchards from cedar rust.

To promote morals, States have been permitted to forbid gambling or the sale of lottery tickets, confiscate vehicles used in violating liquor laws, forbid the sale of obscene literature, and forbid taverns in certain places.

Again, note the fact that though States can restrict or regulate many things through the valid exercise of their police power, they *cannot* use their police power in an unreasonable or unfair manner. Thus, States cannot establish arbitrary licensing qualifications, discriminate against one class unfairly in regulating certain practices, nor require such things as compulsory church attendance.

THE RIGHT TO FREEDOM AND SECURITY OF THE PERSON

Every law-abiding person has a right to be free from physical restraint, secure in his person, and secure in his home.

Slavery and Involuntary Servitude. The 13th Amendment, added to the Constitution in 1865, prohibits "slavery and involuntary servitude." Even today—a full century later—there are still rare but occasional cases of it. Not long ago a man and woman were convicted in a United States District Court in Los Angeles for holding a Negro woman and her child in slavery.

The 13th Amendment prohibits more than slavery, however. *Peonage* [8] is also forbidden. Thus, a sharecropper cannot be forced to work on the land until he works out a debt to the

------

[8] Peonage is a condition of servitude in which a person is bound to perform a personal service on account of debt.

owner or to a company store. Although a person may quit a job whenever he wishes,[9] he may be sued for money damages if he breaks a contract.

The 13th Amendment does *not* forbid certain forms of involuntary labor, however. There is a distinction between "servitude" and "duty." Thus, in 1918 the Supreme Court held that selective service (the draft) does not violate the 13th Amendment's prohibition; nor does imprisonment for a crime, as the amendment itself declares.

"A Man's Home Is His Castle." In addition to the right to physical freedom, each individual enjoys the right to be secure in his home and in his person against arbitrary actions by government.

The 3rd Amendment forbids the quartering of soldiers in private homes in peacetime. It also prohibits the practice in time of war except "in a manner to be prescribed by law." The guarantee was added to the Constitution to prevent what had been British practice in colonial days. It has had little real importance in our national history.

The 4th Amendment also grew out of colonial practice. It was designed to prevent the use of *writs of assistance,* blanket search warrants with which customs officials had invaded private homes in the search for smuggled goods. Unlike the 3rd Amendment, however, the 4th Amendment has proved to be a highly significant guarantee.

The carefully worded 4th Amendment reads:

> The right of the people to be secure in their persons, houses, papers, and effects, against unreasonable searches and seizures, shall not be violated, and no warrants shall issue, but upon probable cause, supported by oath or affirmation, and particularly describing the place to be searched, and the persons or things to be seized.

---

[9] Except that the courts have held that seamen, train crews, firemen, policemen, and the like may be punished for quitting a job under circumstances which endanger the public.

Each of the State constitutions contains a similar guarantee.

Notice that only *unreasonable* searches and seizures are prohibited. A basic purpose of the guarantee is to prevent "fishing expeditions" in which officers of the law cast about with either a vaguely worded warrant or no warrant at all in hope of uncovering evidence of a crime. But there are many situations in which *reasonable* searches or seizures may occur *without* a warrant. For example, no warrant is needed if an officer is in "hot pursuit" of a fugitive. Nor does an officer need a warrant when a crime is committed in his presence, or to search a boat, a car, an airplane, or other "movable scene of crime" which might vanish while he sought a warrant.

The real heart of the search and seizure guarantee lies in the answer to this question: *If* an unlawful search and seizure *does* occur, what use may be made of the evidence thus obtained? If it might be used in court, the 4th Amendment's guarantee would provide no real protection for one accused of a crime. The officers who had committed the illegal act might be punished, but this would provide no particular help to the person being tried on the basis of the evidence they had turned up.

The Weeks Doctrine. To make the guarantee truly effective, the federal courts have, since 1914, followed what is known as the Weeks Doctrine. Under this rule any evidence obtained from an unlawful search or seizure by federal agents cannot be used in a federal court. For example, federal officers searched a Chinese laundry, with a warrant describing the laundry and specifying illegal liquor as the object of the search. No liquor was found; but, in a living room off the laundry, dope was found in a baby's crib. When the laundryman was brought to trial, the charges against him were dismissed; the warrant had described the laundry and liquor, not the living room and narcotics.

Until 1960, however, the federal courts did admit evidence illegally gained by State or local police and then handed to federal agents, as "on a silver platter." The Supreme Court finally outlawed the Silver Platter Doctrine in 1960.

Then, in a historic decision in 1961 (*Mapp* v. *Ohio*), it extended the Weeks Doctrine to its full limits. It held that the 14th Amendment's Due Process Clause forbids unreasonable searches and seizures by State and local officers, just as the 4th Amendment bars such actions by federal officers; *and* it held as well that the fruits of an illegal search or seizure cannot be used in a *State* court.

In the case Cleveland policemen had gone to a woman's home to search for gambling materials. They entered without a warrant and searched the house. They found no gambling materials but they did find some obscene books, the possession of which Ohio law prohibits. The woman was convicted for possession of the books and sentenced to prison. On appeal, the Supreme Court reversed her conviction because of the absence of a search warrant.

Until 1961 the courts of twenty-four States admitted evidence regardless of the nature of the search or seizure by which it had been obtained. But, today, the 4th and the 14th Amendments forbid the use of any evidence secured by unlawful search and seizure in *any* court in the land.

Right to Keep and Bear Arms. The 2nd Amendment, quoted on page 100, is a widely misunderstood part of the Bill of Rights. It was added to the Constitution *solely* to protect the right of the States to maintain and equip a militia. It was intended to preserve the concept of the citizen-soldier — the "minuteman," as its text clearly indicates. It does *not* guarantee to any person the "right to keep and bear arms" free from restriction by the National Government — nor was it ever intended to do so.

The Amendment has little real significance today. The courts have held that it applies only to the ordinary arms carried by a soldier at the time the 2nd Amendment was adopted, not to such weapons as sawed-off shotguns, submachine guns, blackjacks, and the like.

Congress enacted the most far-reaching gun-control law in our history in 1968. Generally, the measure bans the mail-order or other interstate retail sale of firearms and ammunition. It also generally prohibits the across-the-counter sale of guns or ammunition to persons who do not live in a dealer's State. The law further forbids the sale of rifles, shotguns, and their ammunition to persons under age eighteen and the sale of handguns and ammunition to persons under age twenty-one; and it prohibits the importing of foreign-made surplus military weapons.

The law does not require registration of all privately-owned firearms; but certain guns — for example, all machine guns — must be registered with the Justice Department.

As a provision in the Bill of Rights, the 2nd Amendment has no application against the States, of course. They may, and very often do, limit the right to keep and bear arms. Thus, it is a crime in most States to own various automatic weapons or to carry a concealed weapon without a proper license.

THE RIGHT TO FREEDOM OF EXPRESSION

The right to freedom of expression is basic to the very existence of a free society. As we noted on page 14, it lies at the very heart of the democratic philosophy. It is enshrined in our constitutional system in the guarantee of freedom of religion, speech, press, assembly, and petition.

The 1st Amendment protects these fundamental freedoms against the National Government, and the 14th Amendment's Due Process Clause extends them against the States and their local governments.

Freedom of Religion. The 1st and 14th Amendments guarantee that: (1) there shall be no "establishment of religion" in the United

States, and (2) there shall be no governmental restriction of personal religious belief.[10]

Separation of Church and State. The Establishment Clause creates, in Thomas Jefferson's phrase, a "wall of separation between church and state." But that wall is not infinitely high, nor is it impenetrable. That is to say, church and state, while constitutionally separated, are not enemies in the United States. Nor are they strangers to one another. In fact, their relationship is a friendly one.

Government has done much to encourage churches and religion in this country. For example, nearly all church-owned property and contributions to churches and religious sects are exempted from federal, State, and local taxation. Chaplains serve with each branch of the Armed Forces. Most public officials take an oath of office in the name of God. Sessions of Congress and of most State legislatures and city councils are opened with prayer. Even the nation's anthem and its coins and currency contain references to God.

The content of the Establishment Clause cannot be described in precise terms, and the nature of the "wall of separation" remains a matter of continuing and often heated controversy. Only a few cases involving the clause have thus far been decided by the Supreme Court. In fact, the Court did not rule upon the meaning of the provision until as recently as 1947. A few earlier cases did bear on the problem, but each of them was decided without a direct consideration of the nature of the "wall of separation."

In 1925, in *Pierce* v. *Society of Sisters,* the Supreme Court voided an Oregon compulsory school attendance law requiring that all persons between the ages of eight and sixteen attend

Jews come to worship before the Holy Ark in the Synagogue. The 1st Amendment guarantees their freedom of religion. (A. Devaney, Inc., N.Y.)

public schools. The statute was purposely designed to eliminate the private (especially the parochial) schools in the State. The Court held the law to be a deprivation of liberty and of property in violation of the 14th Amendment.

In 1930, in *Cochran* v. *Louisiana,* the Supreme Court upheld a Louisiana law authorizing the use of public funds to supply "schoolbooks to the school children of the State." Under that law, textbooks were furnished to pupils in both public *and* private schools, including those attending parochial schools. Said the Court: "The school children and the State alone are the beneficiaries" of the law, and not the particular schools they attend.

---

[10] Also, Article VI, Section 3 provides that ". . . no religious test shall ever be required as a qualification to any office of trust or profit under the United States." In 1961 the Supreme Court in *Torcaso* v. *Watkins* held that the 14th Amendment applies the same ban upon the States when it unanimously invalidated a provision in the Maryland constitution requiring all public officeholders to declare a belief in the existence of God.

In 1934, in *Hamilton* v. *Board of Regents,* the Supreme Court also upheld a suspension by the University of California of two students who refused to take part in a compulsory ROTC program. The students had refused to do so on religious grounds, arguing that the university's requirement deprived them of their liberty as guaranteed by the 14th Amendment. The Court was not sympathetic to their position. It held that although the Constitution undoubtedly protects the right to object to such training on religious grounds, "California has not drafted or called them to attend the University."

The first clear-cut ruling on the meaning of "an establishment of religion" came in *Everson* v. *Board of Education,* decided in 1947. In that case the Court upheld a New Jersey law permitting public (tax-provided) school bus transportation for parochial school students. The Court ruled, 5–4, that the law was not an aid to religion but, rather, a safety measure intended to benefit school children no matter what particular school they might attend. Said the Court:

> The "establishment of religion" clause of the 1st Amendment means at least this: Neither a State nor the Federal Government can set up a church. Neither can pass laws which aid one religion, aid all religions, or prefer one religion over another.... No tax in any amount, large or small, can be levied to support any religious activities or institutions, whatever they may be called, or whatever form they may adopt to teach or practice religion. Neither a State nor the Federal Government can, openly or secretly, participate in the affairs of any religious organizations or groups and *vice versa.*

Only five major Establishment Clause cases have been decided by the Court since 1947. In two of them the justices were faced with the question of the constitutionality of State "released time" laws. These laws, now found in most States, provide for the "release" of students on school time if they wish to attend classes in religious instruction.

In *McCollum* v. *Board of Education* (1948) the Supreme Court struck down, 8–1, an Illinois law because it permitted the use of public school classrooms and other tax-supported facilities for religious purposes.

In *Zorach* v. *Clauson* (1952), however, New York's law was upheld, 6–3. The chief distinction between the two statutes lay in the fact that New York requires the holding of the religious classes in some place away from school grounds.

The other decisions have involved the recitation of prayers and Bible-reading in the public schools. In *Engel* v. *Vitale* (1962) the reading of "official prayers" in the public schools was barred. In a 6–1 decision, the Supreme Court outlawed the use, even on a voluntary basis, of a nondenominational prayer written by the New York State Board of Regents. The Court found that:

> ...the constitutional prohibition against laws respecting an establishment of religion must at least mean that in this country it is no part of the business of government to compose official prayers for any group of the American people to recite as part of a religious program carried on by government.

To those who insisted that the Board of Regents' prayer posed no real threat of religious establishment, the Court quoted the author of the 1st Amendment, James Madison:

> ...It is proper to take alarm at the first experiment on our liberties.... Who does not see that the same authority which can establish Christianity, in exclusion of all other Religions, may establish with the same ease any particular sect of Christians, in exclusion of all other Sects? That the same authority which can force a citizen to contribute three pence only of his property for the support of any one establishment, may force him to conform to any other establishment in all cases whatsoever?

The most recent major rulings were made in 1963; two cases, from Pennsylvania and from Maryland, were combined for decision. In *Abington Township* v. *Schempp* reading from the Bible, as required by State law, and reciting the Lord's Prayer at the beginning of each school day was challenged. In *Murray* v. *Baltimore School Board* a board rule that required each day to open with "reading, without comment, a chapter in the Holy Bible and/or the use of the Lord's Prayer" was also challenged.

By an 8–1 majority, the Supreme Court held that both cases involved violation of "the command of the 1st Amendment that the government maintain strict neutrality, neither aiding nor opposing religion." And it added:

> ...The place of religion in our society is an exalted one, achieved through a long tradition of reliance on the home, the church, and the inviolable citadel of the individual heart and mind. We have come to recognize through bitter experience that it is not within the power of government to invade that citadel whether its purpose or effect be to aid or oppose, to advance or retard.

Freedom of Religious Belief. Everyone has the right to believe whatever he pleases in regard to religion. If he chooses to believe nothing, that is his right, too.

All civil rights are relative, however. Thus, no one has a right to commit a crime in the name of religion. The Supreme Court upheld the fraud conviction of a man who took money from the sick and promised a supernatural cure. It has ruled that polygamy may be outlawed, that one with religious objections to service may nonetheless be drafted, and that such articles as snakes may be banned from use in church services.

In recent years several cases have been taken to the Supreme Court by the Jehovah's Witnesses, a sect active in promoting their beliefs through such devices as handbills, door-to-door campaigning, and phonograph records. In various cases it has been held that "such peddlers of religious thought" cannot be required to buy peddlers' licenses, be discriminated against in the use of public halls or parks, or be punished as "nuisances" for playing phonograph records on public streets.

In one of the most important cases involving the Jehovah's Witnesses *(West Virginia Board of Education* v. *Barnette),* the Supreme Court ruled in 1943 that no State may require a school child to salute the American flag if such an action is contrary to his religious beliefs. The Court said:

> A person gets from a symbol the meaning he puts into it, and what is one man's comfort and inspiration is another's jest and scorn.

Freedom of Speech and Press. The protection of freedom of speech and freedom of the press by the 1st and the 14th Amendments serves two basic purposes: (1) to guarantee to *each individual* the right to express himself freely, in both the spoken and the written word, and (2) to guarantee to *all persons* an adequate and unrestricted discussion of public affairs.

The freedoms of speech and press are most often thought of in terms of the first purpose; that is, in terms of the right of each individual to express his views. But the second purpose is just as vital as the first. It is because our system of government rests upon a faith in the ability of the people to make sound, reasoned judgments. Clearly, such judgments can best be made only where the people have the widest possible access to any and all of the facts in a given matter; and they can best be made, too, only where the people have the widest possible access to any and all interpretations of those facts.

The late Justice Oliver Wendell Holmes once put the point in these words:

> Persecution for the expression of opinions seems to me perfectly logical. If you have no doubt of your premises or your power and want a certain result with all your heart, you naturally express your wishes in law and sweep

Freedom of expression is absolutely indispensable to the existence of a free society. (Talburt, <u>New York World-Telegram</u>)

Notice that these guarantees are *especially* intended to protect the expression of unpopular views. The opinions and ideas which are held by the majority need, after all, little or no constitutional protection. Again in Justice Holmes words, the guarantees are purposefully designed to insure "freedom for the thought that we hate"; or, in Justice Robert H. Jackson's words, "freedom to differ on things that go to the heart of the matter."

Rights Relative, Not Absolute. The 1st and 14th Amendments do *not* provide for unbridled freedom of speech and press, however. Many reasonable restrictions may be and are imposed. For example, no man has a right to *libel* or *slander* [12] another. The use of profanity, the printing of pornography, or using words to incite a riot may be and are prohibited by law.

Drawing the line between those expressions which are protected by the Constitution and those which are not is an extraordinarily difficult task. Where is the line between, on the one hand, the right of the individual to express himself and, on the other, the right of society to protect itself?

<u>Prior Censorship Forbidden</u>. Government may punish certain utterances, *but* it may *not* censor ideas *before* they are expressed. [13] Thus, a paper or magazine may be punished if it prints obscene articles and might even be denied use of the mails; but it cannot be forbidden to publish.

<u>"Clear and Present Danger."</u> When a con-

away all opposition.... But when men have realized that time has upset many fighting faiths, they may come to believe even more than they believe the very foundations of their own conduct that the ultimate good desired is better reached by free trade in ideas—that the best test of truth is the power of the thought to get itself accepted in the competition of the market, and that truth is the only ground upon which their wishes safely can be carried out. That at any rate is the theory of our Constitution. [11]

---

[11] *Abrams* v. *United States* (1919); see also pages 13–14.

[12] *Libel* (the printed word) and *slander* (the spoken word) involve the use of words *maliciously* (with vicious purpose) to injure one's character or reputation or expose him to public contempt, ridicule, or hatred. Truth is usually an absolute defense. The law is less restrictive concerning criticism of public officials, however. In 1964 the Supreme Court held that a public official may not recover damages for criticism, even if it is exaggerated or false, unless "the statement was made with actual malice—that is, with knowledge that it was false or with reckless disregard of whether it was false or not."

[13] Except in time of war when a considerable measure of censorship may be imposed. During World War II, however, the National Government chose to rely chiefly (and successfully) on a system of voluntary censorship.

flict between free expression and the demands of public safety occurs, the courts usually rely on the Clear and Present Danger Rule. This standard, formulated by Justice Holmes, was first laid down by the Supreme Court in its decision in *Schenck* v. *United States* (1919).

Schenck, a Socialist, had been convicted of attempting to obstruct the war effort in violation of the Espionage Act of 1917. He had sent some 15,000 leaflets to men who had been called to military service, urging them to resist the draft. In upholding both the law and the conviction, the Supreme Court said:

> Words can be weapons.... The question in every case is whether the words used are used in such circumstances and are of such a nature as to create a clear and present danger that they will bring about the [actions] that Congress has a right to prevent.

What constitutes a clear and present danger? This question can be answered only on the basis of the facts in each particular case.

Internal Security and Freedom. For the past several years the major conflicts between freedom of expression and public safety have centered around communists and their activities in this country. Congress has attempted to meet the internal communist threat in several statutes, especially: the Alien Registration (Smith) Act of 1940, the Internal Security (McCarran) Act of 1950, and the Communist Control Act of 1954. In their most pertinent provisions:

The Smith Act makes it unlawful for any person to teach or advocate the violent overthrow of government in the United States or to organize or knowingly to be a member of any group with such an aim. It also forbids any person to conspire with others to accomplish these ends.

The McCarran Act requires all "communist-front" and "communist-action" organizations to register with the Attorney General. They must report annually, filing complete membership lists, the names of their officers, and the details of their financing.[14] The act created the Subversive Activities Control Board (SACB) to determine which groups are in fact subject to the law. It also forbids members of communist organizations to hold any federal office or to serve as officers or employees of labor unions.[15]

The Communist Control Act declares the Communist party in this country to be "a conspiracy to overthrow the Government of the United States" and that "its role as the agency of a hostile power" makes it "a clear, present, and continuing danger" to the nation's security. The act denies to the party any of the rights or privileges commonly held by political parties in either federal or State law.[16]

The Supreme Court first upheld the constitutionality of the Smith Act in *Dennis* v. *United States* (1951). Eleven of the Communist party's top leaders had been convicted of teaching and advocating violent overthrow. They appealed to the Court, arguing that the Smith Act violates the 1st Amendment's speech and press guarantees and that no act of theirs posed a clear and present danger to this country. The Court disagreed, declaring:

> An attempt to overthrow the government by force, even though doomed from the outset because of inadequate numbers or power of the revolutionists, is a sufficient evil for

[14] The law also provided that the SACB could order individual members of communist action groups to register. But the Court voided the provision in *Albertson* v. *SACB,* 1965, as a violation of the 5th Amendment's guarantee against self-incrimination.

[15] The act also forbade communists to obtain or use passports, but the Court held the provision unconstitutional in *Aptheker* v. *Rusk,* 1964; it found the section too broadly and vaguely worded and thus violative of the 5th Amendment's Due Process Clause. In *United States* v. *Robel,* 1968, it also struck down the act's ban on the employment of communist organization members in defense plants; it found the section so loosely drawn as to be "an unconstitutional abridgment of the right of association protected by the 1st Amendment."

[16] Several States have similar statutes.

Congress to prevent.... We reject any principle of governmental helplessness in the face of preparation for revolution, which principle, carried to its logical conclusion, must lead to anarchy.

Merely to urge one to *believe* something, in contrast to urging him to *do* something, however, cannot be made illegal. It was for this reason that, in *Yates* v. *United States* (1957), the Supreme Court upset the Smith Act convictions of fourteen subordinate Communist party leaders.

The "knowing membership" clause of the Smith Act was upheld by the Supreme Court in *Scales* v. *United States* (1961). In that case the Court held that it was those who are active, not passive, within the Communist party and those with a clear and specific intent to overthrow the Government of the United States that the Smith Act intends to punish.

The McCarran Act's requirement that communist-action organizations register when ordered to do so by the SACB was upheld in *Communist Party* v. *Subversive Activities Control Board* in 1961. The SACB had first ordered the party to register in 1953, and the Supreme Court's 5–4 decision came only after a lengthy legal battle in which the Communist party argued that the act deprived it and its members of freedom of expression.

In spite of the Court's 1961 decision, the party has continued to refuse to register as the law requires. And, at least thus far (1970), the government has been unable to force it to do so. Its defiance has led to two convictions in federal district courts, in 1962 and again in 1965. Both of these convictions have been upset on appeal, however.

The 1962 verdict was overturned by a court of appeals decision that it was in conflict with the 5th Amendment's ban on self-incrimination. The appellate court ruled that the person (a party officer) who would have to file the papers required by the McCarran Act would, in doing so, lay himself open to prosecution under the Smith Act. In *United States* v. *Communist Party* (1964), the Supreme Court refused to review the case; it thus upheld the reversal of the original conviction.

The 1965 conviction came to grief on the same grounds. The court of appeals noted that there is "very much indeed" that the Congress might do to force subversive organizations to disclose information about themselves; but it held that Congress cannot do so by forcing individuals to incriminate themselves. This time (1967) the Justice Department elected not to appeal the decision to the United States Supreme Court.

It seems clear today that the net effect of the various court decisions has been to leave the McCarran Act a hollow and largely meaningless shell. This result was far from unexpected. Indeed, the grounds upon which the courts have acted were the very ones stressed by President Truman in his veto message which Congress overrode when it enacted the law two decades ago.

No portion of the Communist Control Act has as yet (1970) been tested in the courts. But, since its enactment, and despite the lack of success under the McCarran Act, the party has all but disappeared as an active and open political movement in this country. It has all but abandoned the nomination of candidates for office; in fact, in 1968 it nominated its first presidential candidate since the elections of 1940. The FBI continues to keep the party under very close surveillance and places its current membership at no more than 10,000 persons.

Picketing. Peaceful picketing involves an expression of opinion and is protected by the 1st and 14th Amendments. The Supreme Court has said:

> In the circumstances of our times, the dissemination of information concerning the facts of a labor dispute must be regarded as within the area of free discussion that is guaranteed by the Constitution.

Thus, peaceful picketing is regarded as lawful, but picketing which is "set in a background of violence" may be prevented. A State may not prohibit the use of pickets who are not themselves employees or former employees of the picketed establishment. A labor union may not picket one employer not a party to a labor dispute to force him to bring pressure upon a second employer who *is* involved in a dispute.

Motion Pictures and Freedom of Expression. Motion pictures did not exist, of course, when the 1st and the 14th Amendments were written. The question of whether the movies are protected by the guarantees of freedom of expression first came before the Supreme Court early in motion picture history. In *Mutual Film Corporation* v. *Ohio* (1915) the Court upheld an Ohio statute which prohibited the showing of films not of "a moral, educational, or amusing and harmless character."

At that time the Court viewed the showing of motion picutres as "a business pure and simple, originated and conducted for profit like other spectacles, not to be regarded . . . as part of the press of the country or as organs of public opinion." Nearly all of the States and thousands of local communities then established strong movie censorship programs.

In 1952, however, the Supreme Court expressly overruled its 1915 decision. In *Burstyn* v. *Wilson,* involving movie censorship in New York, the Court held that the "liberty of expression by means of motion pictures is guaranteed by the 1st and 14th Amendments."

Movie censorship as such, however, is *not* unconstitutional today. The Supreme Court has struck down State and local censorship of films in several recent cases, but it has done so only when that censorship has conflicted with the principle of freedom of expression.

Freedom of Assembly and Petition. The 1st Amendment also guarantees:

> . . . the right of the people peaceably to assemble, and to petition the government for a redress of grievances.

Of course, the 14th Amendment's Due Process Clause extends this provision against the States.

The rights to assemble and to petition the government are just as essential to the existence of a free society as are the freedoms of speech, press, and religion. Under the 1st and the 14th Amendments the right to assemble and discuss public questions is assured. So, too, is the right to organize to secure action, as in political parties and in pressure groups. The people are also guaranteed the right to express their opinions, favorable and unfavorable, to public officials by such means as formal petitions, letters, lobbying, and the like.

Peaceful picketing is constitutionally protected as a lawful expression of opinion. Here we see pickets countering each other's demonstration. (Frank Aleksandrowicz, from Black Star)

Like other civil rights, the rights of assembly and petition must be exercised with regard to the rights of others. Notice that it is "the right of the people *peaceably* to assemble" that is guaranteed. Thus, mass meetings which become riots may be dispersed by local police. Naturally, no group has a right to assemble to commit a crime.

The right of assembly is further limited, particularly in the interests of safety. Thus, no group has the right to assemble in a way which will interfere with traffic, create a fire hazard, or otherwise endanger lives or property. What is protected by the assembly and petition guarantees is the free, lawful, public exchange of opinions and ideas.

THE RIGHT TO FAIR TREATMENT UNDER THE LAW

Democracy cannot succeed *except* where all people are entitled to fair treatment under the law. Here the individual's basic rights fall into one of two classes: (1) those which guarantee fair and impartial treatment to those accused of a crime and (2) those which guarantee that the law will not discriminate unreasonably against *any* person or group.

Fair Treatment for Those Accused of Crime. Both the Constitution of the United States and the various State constitutions contain numerous guarantees of fair treatment for those accused of a crime. As noted earlier, the 14th Amendment reinforces the guarantees against unfair treatment by the States. Each of these rights springs from the ancient concept that one is presumed innocent until proven guilty.

Writ of Habeas Corpus. The *writ of habeas corpus* — sometimes called the "writ of liberty" — is designed to prevent arbitrary arrest and unlawful imprisonment. It is a court order directed to any person holding another. It requires that the person being held be brought before the court and that those detaining him show cause why he should not be released. If sufficient cause cannot be shown, the court will then order the person freed.

The right to the writ of habeas corpus is guaranteed against the National Government in Article I, Section 9 of the Constitution. It is guaranteed against each of the States in their own constitutions.

The right to the writ may not be suspended, says the Constitution, "unless when in cases of rebellion or invasion the public safety may require it." But the Constitution does not make clear whether the right may be suspended *only* in those areas immediately involved in the rebellion or invasion. Nor does it indicate which branch of the National Government — Congress, the President, or the courts — possesses the power of suspension.[17]

The right to the writ has been suspended only once over the past century — in Hawaii

---

[17] President Lincoln, acting without congressional authorization, suspended the writ in 1861 in various parts of the country, including areas in which war was not then being waged. Chief Justice Roger B. Taney, sitting as a circuit judge, held Lincoln's action unconstitutional in *Ex parte Merryman,* 1861; he declared that the power to suspend the writ was vested exclusively in Congress. Congress then passed the Habeas Corpus Act of 1863, specifically authorizing the President to suspend the writ whenever and wherever, in his judgment, such action was necessary. Whether the writ may be suspended in areas not the scene of actual fighting, or not in serious danger of becoming so, was considered by the Supreme Court in *Ex parte Milligan,* 1866. The full Court agreed that the President could not do so, and a majority of five of the justices also held that even Congress did not have such power.

during World War II. And the United States Supreme Court held in 1946 that action to have been illegal.[18]

The writ of habeas corpus may be used against private persons as well as against public officers. It has been used by a husband to secure the return of his wife who was taken home by her parents and by a mother to recover her baby mistakenly exchanged for the child of another woman.

Bills of Attainder. A *bill of attainder* is a legislative act which provides for punishment without judicial trial. Both Congress and the State legislatures are forbidden to pass such bills.[19]

The ban on bills of attainder was included in the original Constitution because the British Parliament had passed many during the colonial period. They have been quite rare in our own history.

Even so, the Supreme Court in 1963 found a part of the Immigration and Nationality Act of 1952 unconstitutional as a bill of attainder. The offending section ordered the automatic and involuntary expatriation of any person who fled the country to evade the draft in wartime (see page 93). In 1965 the Court struck down the provision in the Landrum-Griffin Act barring communists from holding office in a labor union on the same ground (see page 479).

Ex Post Facto Laws. An *ex post facto* law is a *criminal law* which is applied to an act committed *before* the passage of the law and which works to the *disadvantage* of the accused. Neither Congress nor the State legislatures may pass such a law.[20]

This means, for example, that a State law making it a crime to sell liquor cannot be applied to a man who sold liquor *before* the act was passed, but that it can be applied for selling liquor *after* the law was passed. Nor could a law increasing the penalty for murder from life imprisonment to death be applied to a man convicted of a murder committed prior to the increasing of the penalty; it could be applied only to one committing a murder after the act was passed.

Notice that for a law to be *ex post facto* — and hence unconstitutional — it must meet *all* three requirements previously mentioned; that is, it must be (1) a criminal law, (2) applied to an act committed before enactment of the law, and (3) disadvantageous to the accused. Thus, a retroactive *civil law* is not forbidden. For example, an income tax law enacted in November can impose a tax upon one's income for the entire year, including the preceding ten months.

Right to a Fair Trial. The Bill of Rights contains several guarantees relating to fair trial in the federal courts.[21] A fair trial is

---

[18] The Hawaiian Islands were placed under martial law by order of the territorial governor immediately after the attack on Pearl Harbor, December 7, 1941. His order, issued with the approval of President Roosevelt, not only suspended the writ of habeas corpus but also provided for the supplanting of the civil courts by military tribunals. Martial law was not ended, by presidential proclamation, until 1944 — long after the danger of invasion had passed. While it was in force, civilians were tried for crimes before military courts without benefit of jury or similar processes. In 1946, in *Duncan* v. *Kohanamoku*, the Supreme Court held that the governor's order had been too sweeping in character. Its decision was not based upon the constitutional provision, however; rather, it found that in the Hawaiian Organic Act of 1900, under which the governor had acted, Congress had not intended to authorize so drastic a subordination of civil to military authority.

[19] Article I, Sections 9 and 10.   [20] Article I, Sections 9 and 10.

[21] See the 5th, 6th, 7th, and 8th Amendments and also Article III, Section 2, Clause 3. The practice of excluding evidence obtained in violation of the 4th Amendment (see page 105) is also intended to guarantee a fair trial.

guaranteed in the State courts through a State's own constitution and through the Due Process Clause in the 14th Amendment.

No Double Jeopardy. The 5th Amendment says, in part, that no person shall be "twice put in jeopardy of life or limb." In ancient times a man could be penalized by taking his life or by cutting off his arm, leg, ear, or some other "limb." Hence the old English phrase "life or limb" was carried into our Constitution.

Today the provision means, in plain language, that once a man has been tried for a crime he may *not* be tried again for that same crime. This requires some elaboration, however.

A single act may violate both a national and a State law, for example, selling liquor without a license or peddling narcotics. The accused may be tried for the federal crime in a federal court and for the State crime in a State court.

A single act may also result in the commission of several different crimes. If a man breaks into a store at night, steals liquor, and later resells it, he can be tried for at least three separate offenses—illegal entry, theft, and selling liquor without a license.

In a trial in which a jury cannot agree, there is no "jeopardy." It is as though no trial had been held, and the accused may be retried. Nor is double jeopardy involved when a case is appealed by the defendant to a higher court.

Recall that in 1969 the Court held the 5th Amendment's ban on double jeopardy applies against the States through the 14th Amendment.

Indictment by Grand Jury. The 5th Amendment further provides that in a case involving a "capital or otherwise infamous crime" (one punishable by imprisonment) a person may be tried only after indictment by a grand jury.[22]

A federal grand jury is a body of from sixteen to twenty-three persons. The Supreme Court has held that no person may be barred from grand jury service on grounds of race or color.

But "blue-ribbon" juries, composed of those whose reputations indicate them to be responsible citizens, are legal.

An *indictment* is a written accusation and is brought against a person only when a grand jury feels that there is sufficient evidence to warrant a trial.[23] Most States also provide for the grand jury; but as early as 1884 the Supreme Court held that the 14th Amendment does not *require* a State to provide for this method of accusation.

Speedy and Public Trial. The 6th Amendment guarantees a "speedy and public trial." This guarantee is intended to provide a trial within a reasonable time and to prevent one accused of a crime from languishing in jail while awaiting trial. The trial, though, must not be so speedy that one does not have time to prepare a defense nor so public that mob rule prevents a fair trial.

The Supreme Court has thrown out several State convictions where the trials have been *too* speedy or public—as in conflict with the 14th Amendment's guarantee of procedural due process. In 1967 the Court specifically held that the 6th Amendment's guarantee of a speedy trial is extended against the States through the 14th Amendment (see page 100.)

Trial by Jury. A trial by an *impartial* jury is guaranteed in all federal criminal cases[24] and in civil cases involving $20 or more.[25] Under the common law, a trial jury (known as a *petit* jury) consists of twelve persons. In federal cases the jurors must be drawn "from the State and district wherein the crime shall have been committed."[26]

As we noted earlier (page 100), the Supreme

---

[22] One may waive (put aside) his right to grand jury if he chooses to do so.

---

[23] An indictment is drawn up and laid before a federal grand jury by a United States prosecuting attorney. The 5th Amendment also permits a *presentment:* a formal accusation made by a grand jury on its own motion.

[24] Article III, Section 2, Clause 3; and 6th Amendment.

[25] 7th Amendment.

[26] 6th Amendment.

Court held in 1968 that the 14th Amendment's Due Process Clause requires that a State provide for trial by jury (at least in all cases involving serious crime). A State may not exclude anyone from jury service on grounds of race or color.

Right to an Adequate Defense. The 6th Amendment guarantees four particular rights to enable an accused person to present the best possible defense *in a federal court:*

> In all criminal prosecutions, the accused shall enjoy the right. . .to be informed of the nature and cause of the accusation; to be confronted with the witnesses against him; to have compulsory process for the obtaining of witnesses in his favor; and to have the assistance of counsel for his defense.

If a *State* fails to provide any of these safeguards *in its own courts,* one may appeal a conviction on the ground that the 14th Amendment's Due Process Clause has been violated. Recall that the Supreme Court has specifically held that the 6th Amendment's guarantees of the rights to counsel, of confrontation, and to compel witnesses are assured in State courts through the 14th Amendment (see page 100.)

Self-Incrimination. According to the 5th Amendment, no person accused of a crime may be forced to testify against himself. Thus, a prosecutor cannot force an accused to take the stand to convict himself. The prosecution must prove its charges against the defendant. Freedom from self-incrimination also extends to the husband or wife of the accused; that is, a husband or wife cannot be forced to testify against his or her spouse. They may testify if they so choose, however.[27]

A person may maintain the privilege against self-incrimination in *any* proceeding where

---

[27] Evidence gained by wiretapping or other electronic eavesdropping was not admissible in federal cases until 1968; but now Congress has authorized gathering and use of such evidence in circumstances closely controlled by court orders and in some other "emergency" situations.

testimony is legally required. It has been used many times before congressional investigating committees. If one carries the plea of self-incrimination too far, however, he may be held in *contempt;* that is, he may be punished by a court for obstructing the lawful processes of government. Many people have been found in contempt for refusing to answer proper questions of congressional committees.

The protection against self-incrimination is also provided in most State constitutions; and, in 1964, the Supreme Court held that it is one of the "basic rights" covered by the 14th Amendment. Of course, confessions obtained by "third degree" methods have always been outlawed by the Due Process Clauses.

But the gulf between what the Constitution decrees and what does in fact occur in some local police stations can be a broad one. As a result, the Supreme Court has in recent years borne down hard in cases involving the protection against self-incrimination and the closely related right to counsel. In a series of decisions it has insisted upon the strictest police compliance with the commands of the Constitution. In the most notable of these, it has held that: (1) a confession cannot be used against a person if it was obtained by police who did not permit him to see an attorney and did not advise him of his right to refuse to answer their questions (*Escobedo* v. *Illinois,* 1964); and (2) prior to any police questioning a suspect must be warned that anything he might say can be used against him and he must be advised that he has the right to remain silent and the right to the presence of an attorney — court-appointed if he cannot afford one (*Miranda* v. *Arizona,* 1966).

Excessive Bail and Fines. The 8th Amendment declares that "excessive bail shall not be required," although what constitutes "excessive" has never been clearly defined. *Bail* usually monetary, is the assurance that an accused person gives that he will appear in court at the proper time. Failure to appear is ground for forfeiture. Bail is almost never allowed persons accused of capital crimes.

The 8th Amendment also prohibits "excessive fines," and the States are similarly restricted by their constitutions. A fine must fit the crime for which it is imposed. For most crimes the fines are prescribed by law.

Cruel and Unusual Punishment. The 8th Amendment further prohibits "cruel and unusual punishment." What is prohibited are the barbaric and bloody penalties fancied a few centuries ago — burning at the stake, drawing and quartering, dismemberment, and the like. A punishment must not be unreasonably severe in relation to the offense being dealt with. For example, starvation is not permissible, but solitary confinement is. So is execution by hanging, electrocution, lethal gas, or firing squad.

The State constitutions and the 14th Amendment also prohibit cruel and unusual punishments. In 1879 the Supreme Court upheld the Utah practice of execution by firing squad. It also has upheld flogging of prisoners as cruel *but not unusual* punishment. Thus, for a punishment to be considered unconstitutional it must be *both* cruel and unusual.

Treason. The crime of treason is the *only* crime which is defined in the Constitution. The Founding Fathers provided a specific definition because they knew that the charge of treason is a favorite weapon tyrants use against political opponents. Examples of its unjust use in recent times are easy to find — in Nazi Germany, Fascist Italy, Castro's Cuba, and in the communist nations of Europe and Asia.

Treason, says Article III, Section 3, can include but two things: (1) levying war against the United States or (2) "adhering to their enemies, giving them aid and comfort." The Constitution also adds that no one may be convicted of treason "unless on the testimony of two witnesses to the same overt act, or on confession in open court." A penalty for treason can be imposed only on the traitor, not on his family or descendants.

The death penalty was not imposed for treason against the United States until as recently as 1942, when four German-born American citizens were sentenced to be hanged for aiding a group of saboteurs who had been landed on the East Coast from a Nazi submarine.[28]

Most State constitutions also provide for treason. John Brown, hanged as a traitor to Virginia after his raid on Harpers Ferry in 1859, is believed to be the only one ever executed for treason against a State.

Equality before the Law. The various rights we have just listed, those guaranteed to persons accused of a crime, are a necessary part of the broad right of fair treatment under the law. As we noted on page 114, the right to fair treatment includes, as well, another basic category of individual rights: those designed to insure the equal status of all persons before the law — that is, those which guarantee that government will not discriminate unreasonably against any person or group.

The Equal Protection Clause. The equality of all men — so prominently asserted in the Declaration of Independence — is nowhere proclaimed in so many words by the Constitution. Even so, the entire document is permeated by the concept.

The closest approach to a statement of the concept is to be found in the 14th Amendment's Equal Protection Clause. It forbids any State the power to:

> deny to any person within its jurisdiction the equal protection of the laws.

This clause prohibits a State (and its local governments, of course) from making *unreasonable* distinctions between different classes of persons. *Reasonable* classifications are not only permitted; they are absolutely necessary. If government were unable to classify (draw

---

[28] The sentences were in fact never carried out. The sentence of one was commuted to life in prison; he was later denaturalized and then deported. The other three appealed their convictions and won new trials. One of them was again convicted of treason, but this time sentenced to life imprisonment; the other two pleaded guilty to reduced charges and received five-year prison sentences.

distinctions between, discriminate among, certain persons and groups), it would be impossible for it to regulate any aspect of human behavior.

That is to say, the States may and do discriminate, and often. Thus, those who rob banks fall into a special class and are subject to special treatment by the law. This sort of distinction between classes or groups of persons is obviously a reasonable one. A State may legally prohibit marriage by those under a certain age or who are currently married to another person. It may impose a tax on the purchase of cigarettes, and thus tax smokers but not non-smokers. But a tax could not be levied only upon *blonde* smokers; nor could a State, for example, prohibit all price-fixing "except by farmers."

The Equal Protection Clause applies to *all* persons, aliens as well as citizens. In 1914 Arizona enacted a statute requiring that not less than eighty per cent of the employees of any firm hiring five or more workers had to be either qualified voters or native-born citizens. The next year, in *Truax* v. *Raich,* the Supreme Court held the law to be an invalid discrimination against aliens, depriving them of the equal protection of Arizona's laws.

Beginning in the latter 1800's, nearly half of the States adopted racial segregation laws. The statutes were aimed primarily at Negroes, but they often affected such other groups as those of Oriental or Mexican descent and American Indians. In the main, they provided for the compulsory segregation of races in the use of both public and private facilities in such areas as transportation, education, housing, recreation, and the service of meals.

The Supreme Court provided a constitutional basis for racial segregation—the "separate-but-equal" doctrine—in 1896. It did so in the famous case, *Plessy* v. *Ferguson,* in which it upheld a Louisiana law requiring the segregation of Negroes and whites in rail coaches. It held that the required segregation did *not* violate the Equal Protection Clause as long as the

separate facilities for Negroes were *equal* to those provided for others.

Segregation in Education. The "separate-but-equal" doctrine was soon extended to other fields as a constitutional justification for racial segregation. The doctrine stood for nearly sixty years. Indeed, until the late 1930's, little serious attempt was made by the courts—or by any other arm of government—to insist even that the separate facilities were, in fact, equal ones.

Then, in 1938, the Supreme Court began to "chip away" at the rule laid down in *Plessy* v. *Ferguson.* In *Missouri ex rel. Gaines* v. *Canada* it required that Missouri either admit Gaines, a qualified Negro, to the law school at the State university or make provision for his legal training within the State (that is, establish a separate but equal law school for Negroes). Over the next several years the Court adopted an increasingly stern attitude toward the requirement of equal facilities.

Finally, in a historic decision in 1954, the Supreme Court reversed itself. In *Brown* v. *Topeka Board of Education* it struck down laws in four States (Kansas, Delaware, South Carolina, and Virginia) requiring or permitting separate elementary and high schools for white and Negro students. Holding segregation of the races in public education to be unconstitutional, Chief Justice Warren said for a unanimous Court:

Today, education is perhaps the most important function of State and local governments. Compulsory school attendance laws and the great expenditures for education both demonstrate our recognition of the importance of education to our democratic society .... Such an opportunity, where the State has undertaken to provide it, is a right which must be made available to all on equal terms.

... Does segregation of children in public schools solely on the basis of race, even though the physical facilities and other "tangible" factors may be equal, deprive the children of the minority group of equal educational opportunities? We believe that it does.

> ... To separate them from others of similar age and qualifications solely because of their race generates a feeling of inferiority as to their status in the community that may affect their hearts and minds in a way unlikely ever to be undone. ... We conclude that in the field of public education the doctrine of "separate but equal" has no place. Separate educational facilities are inherently unequal.

The Court recognized that enforcing its decision presented a "problem of considerable complexity." [29] Therefore, in a *second* opinion in the *Brown Case,* in 1955, it directed the States to make "a prompt and reasonable start toward full compliance" with its 1954 decision and to end segregation "with all deliberate speed." Local federal district courts were ordered to supervise the process.

Desegregation proceeded much more rapidly in the border States than in the deep South. But the pace was quickened considerably in the latter area under the terms of the Civil Rights Act of 1964, which forbids the use of federal funds to aid any State or local activity in which segregation is practiced.

And the pace was further accelerated when, in 1969, the Supreme Court ruled that time had finally run out on the doctrine of "all deliberate speed." In a case from Mississippi, *Alexander* v. *Holmes County Board of Education,*

---

[29] At the time of the Court's decision (May 17, 1954), segregation was required by law in seventeen States: Alabama, Arkansas, Delaware, Florida, Georgia, Kentucky, Louisiana, Maryland, Mississippi, Missouri, Oklahoma, North Carolina, South Carolina, Tennessee, Texas, West Virginia, and Virginia. It was also permitted by local option in four others: Arizona, New Mexico, Kansas, and Wyoming (where it had never been exercised). The Court held segregation in the District of Columbia to violate the 5th Amendment's Due Process Clause in *Bolling* v. *Sharpe,* 1954.

it unanimously held that "the continued operation of segregated schools under a standard allowing for 'all deliberate speed' ... is no longer constitutionally permissible."

Civil Rights Legislation. The Civil Rights Acts of 1957, 1960, 1964, and 1968 were enacted by Congress to implement the Constitution's insistence upon equality before the law. The Civil Rights Acts of 1957 and 1960 deal very largely with the right to vote. Together with related provisions of the Civil Rights Act of 1964 and the Voting Rights Act of 1965, they are discussed on pages 152–154. The 1968 law on civil rights deals very largely with "open housing"; see pages 275, 514.

The Civil Rights Act of 1964 is much broader than the other statutes; it also:

(1) Provides that no person may be denied access to, or service in, various public establishments—most restaurants, hotels, motels, and the like—on grounds of race, color, religion, or national origin. See page 275.

(2) Directs the Justice Department to bring suits to force the desegregation of public facilities (that is, those owned, operated, or managed by States or local governments) such as schools, playgrounds, golf courses, libraries, and the like. But such suits may be brought only at the request of private persons who cannot do so themselves because of financial limitations, fear of reprisal, or similar reasons.

(3) Authorizes the Office of Education to give advice and financial assistance to public school systems planning or undergoing the process of desegregation.

(4) Extended the life of the Civil Rights Commission to 1968 (later extended to 1971.) The Commission, originally established in the Civil Rights Act of 1957, is composed of six members appointed by the President and Senate. It oversees the operation of the three Civil Rights Acts, investigates instances of alleged discrimination, and reports its recommendations to the President and Congress.

(5) Prohibits discrimination on grounds of race, color, religion, national origin, or sex

against any person under any program or activity which receives federal financial assistance.

(6) Outlaws various practices by management and labor—especially in hiring and union membership—which result in discrimination based upon race, color, religion, national origin, or sex.

(7) Created a Community Relations Service to aid communities to resolve disputes relating to discrimination. See page 410.

✦✦✦✦✦✦✦✦✦✦ CONCEPT BUILDING ✦✦✦✦✦✦✦✦✦✦

Key Concepts

Because ours is a democratic government, it is limited, not all-powerful. It is most severely limited in power and in action in the area of civil rights.

Our individual liberties come down to us through centuries of English and American history. Today, the courts stand as the principal guardian of them, but these rights cannot exist unless we know them and are willing to fight for them when they are endangered.

All civil rights are *relative*, not absolute. No one has an absolute right to do as he pleases; he must respect the rights of others. With minor exceptions, aliens are entitled to the same civil rights as citizens.

The fact that we have a federal system complicates our system of civil rights somewhat, but the effects of this complication have been lessened by the Due Process Clause of the 14th Amendment.

The provisions of the Bill of Rights apply *only* against the National Government. But the Court has held that the 1st and 4th Amendments, the 5th Amendment's ban on self-incrimination and double jeopardy, the 6th Amendment's guarantees of the right to counsel, of confrontation, to compel witnesses, to jury trial, and to a speedy trial, and the 8th Amendment's ban against cruel and unusual punishment are extended against the States through the Due Process Clause of the 14th Amendment.

Due process has a double meaning: *procedural due process* guarantees fair procedures by government; *substantive due process* guarantees that government will act under fair laws. Corporations as well as persons are protected by the Due Process Clause.

A State law which can be justified as a valid exercise of the *police power* does not violate the 14th Amendment's Due Process Clause.

No all-inclusive listing of civil rights is possible, but they involve: (1) *The right to freedom and security of the person,* which includes freedom from slavery and involuntary servitude, from the quartering of soldiers in private homes, from unreasonable searches and seizures, and the right to keep and bear arms (with certain restrictions by the States). (2) *The right to freedom of expression,* which includes freedom of religion, speech, press, assembly, and petition. Freedom of religion includes both the right to freedom of belief and a ban on the establishment of religion. (3) *The right to fair treatment under the law,* which includes guarantees to those accused of a crime (such as, the writ of habeas corpus; prohibitions against bills of attainder, *ex post facto* laws, double jeopardy, self-incrimination, excessive bail and fines, and cruel and unusual punishments; guarantees of grand jury indictment, trial by jury, speedy and public trial, and an adequate defense; and a specific definition of the crime of treason, and guarantees of equality before the law in the Equal Protection Clause.

Important Terms

Bill of Rights
clear and present
  danger
double jeopardy
due process of law
Equal Protection
  Clause

establishment of
  religion
involuntary servitude
libel
peonage
police power

procedural due
  process
"released time" laws
segregation
self-incrimination
"separate-but-equal"
  doctrine

slander
substantive due
  process
treason
writ of habeas
  corpus

Questions for Inquiry and Review

1. How do civil rights guarantees illustrate the concept of limited government?

2. Why do the courts stand as the principal guardian of our individual liberties?

3. Why does no one possess an absolute right to do as he pleases in this country?

4. In what ways does federalism complicate our system of civil rights?

5. Why does the 2nd Amendment not prevent the States from regulating the keeping and bearing of arms?

6. In what sense have certain rights been "nationalized" by the Supreme Court?

7. What is the *police power* of the State?

8. How is *peonage* distinguished from slavery?

9. Will the federal courts admit evidence obtained by an unlawful search and seizure? The State courts? Why?

10. What are the two basic purposes of the guarantee of freedom of expression?

11. What are some of the restrictions on the freedoms of speech, press, and religion?

12. In what situations do courts employ the "clear and present danger" doctrine?

13. When can the writ of habeas corpus be suspended?

14. What requirements must be met for a law to be *ex post facto?*

15. Can one be tried twice without being placed in double jeopardy? Explain.

16. Why is an accused person entitled to a speedy and public trial?

17. What are some of the specific provisions of the guarantee of the right to an adequate defense?

18. The ban on self-incrimination includes who else but one's self?

19. Why is treason strictly defined in the Constitution? How is it defined?

20. Does the Equal Protection Clause of the 14th Amendment forbid a State to make *any* distinctions between persons? Explain.

21. What was the "separate-but-equal" doctrine?

For Further Inquiry

1. The Constitution contains a Bill of Rights but no "Bill of Obligations." If it did, what would you have it include?

2. In an article written for a London newspaper in 1958 an Englishman confessed to a particularly brutal murder committed eight years earlier. He had been tried at that time and acquitted by the jury. As in our law,

double jeopardy is prohibited in English law. Thus, a confessed murderer cheated the law. Do you think it should be possible to retry him?

3. Woodrow Wilson once wrote:

> We have learned that it is pent-up feelings that are dangerous, whispered purposes that are revolutionary, covert follies that warp and poison the mind; that the wisest thing to do with a fool is to encourage him to hire a hall and discourse to his fellow citizens. Nothing chills folly like exposure to the air; nothing dispels folly like its publication; nothing so eases the machine as the safety valve.

Do you agree with Wilson's thoughts? Why?

4. Explain the statement: "One man's liberty ends where the next man's liberty begins."

5. Throughout this chapter the phrases "civil rights" and "civil liberties" are used interchangeably to mean the same thing, and they are customarily used in this manner. Some authorities, however, insist on drawing a distinction between them. On what basis do you think they do so?

6. Do you agree with the statement: "It is better that the law allows one hundred guilty persons to go free than that it punishes one innocent man."

7. Why couldn't the legislature of your State legally provide that no farmhand work more than five hours a day?

Suggested Activities

1. Invite a judge, attorney, or newspaper editor to address the class on the importance of civil rights.

2. Obtain a copy of the Report of the President's Committee on Civil Rights, *To Secure These Rights,* to use as the basis for a written report on civil rights.

3. Give a class talk on one of the provisions of the Bill of Rights.

4. For two or more of the civil rights guaranteed in the Constitution, draw up three hypothetical cases in which you think the Supreme Court would hold that a person's civil rights have been violated.

5. Write a report tracing the recent history of the Civil Rights movement.

6. Stage a debate or class forum on: (a) *Resolved,* That discrimination in any form should be illegal; (b) *Resolved,* That all civil rights are privileges, since none are absolute.

Suggested Reading

BURNS, JAMES M. and PELTASON, J. W., *Government By the People.* Prentice-Hall, 1969. Chapters 6, 7, 8.

"'Desegregate Now'-But How to Do It?" *U.S. News,* November 10, 1969.

"Does TV Tell It Straight?" *Newsweek,* November 24, 1969.

DUNBAR, ERNEST, "Seven Dobbs Against the Odds," *Look,* December 2, 1969.

"How Militants Try to Destroy a Court," *U.S. News,* November 17, 1969.

KING, CORETTA S., "He Had a Dream," *Life,* September 12 and 19, 1969.

KUTLER, STANLEY L., *The Supreme Court and the Constitution.* Houghton Mifflin, 1969.

LEWIS, ANTHONY, "A Talk With Warren," *New York Times Magazine,* October 19, 1969.

MARSHALL, JUSTICE THURGOOD, "A Supreme Court Justice's Warning to Fellow Negroes," *U.S. News,* May 19, 1969.

RITTER, JESSE P., "Nightmare in a California Jail," *Life,* August 15, 1969.

RODELL, FRED, "Can Nixon's Justices Reverse the Warren Court?" *Look,* December 2, 1969.

STENNIS, SENATOR JOHN C., "Why Not Desegregate in the North?" *U.S. News,* November 3, 1969.

WILSON, JAMES Q. and VORENBURG, JAMES, "Is the Court Handcuffing the Cops?" *New York Times Magazine,* May 11, 1969.

7
POLITICAL PARTIES

❖❖❖ Are political parties indispensable to democratic government?

❖❖❖ Should our two-party system be reorganized to provide two new major parties—one distinctively liberal and the other distinctively conservative?

❖❖❖ Which of these adjectives may be properly applied to our two major parties today: pragmatic, non-ideological, decentralized, fragmented, factionalized? Why?

Party divisions, whether on the whole operating for good or evil, are things indispensable from free governments.

EDMUND BURKE

Politics is the term we use to describe the conduct of public affairs. It embraces *all* of the aspects of the governing process: the making of public policies, the execution of those policies, the selection of those who make and of those who execute those policies, and all else involved in the art and science of government.

There are those who regard politics as a "dirty business"—something unsavory, something in which "good people" should not take part. Only a moment's thought should be sufficient to realize the sheer nonsense of this attitude.

Government cannot possibly exist without politics. It is the very core of *any* government, no matter its form. It is true that at times in some places in the United States the quality of politics is not all it might be. It is also true, however, that *at all times* and *in all places* in the United States the people themselves are responsible for the nature of politics. It is this that Elihu Root—distinguished statesman, Cabinet officer, Senator, and winner of the Nobel

Prize for Peace—had in mind when he remarked:

> Politics is the practical exercise of the art of self-government, and somebody must attend to it if we are to have self-government.... The principle ground for reproach against any American citizen should be that he is not a politician.

NATURE OF POLITICAL PARTIES

Definition of Party. With *particular reference* to the two major parties in American politics, a political party may be defined as a *voluntary association* of voters which seeks to *control government* through the winning of elections and the holding of public office.

A somewhat more specific definition may be applied to *other* parties, here and elsewhere: an organization of voters joined together on the basis of certain common principles for the purpose of controlling government and securing the adoption of the party's program.[1] Such a definition, with its emphasis upon basic principles as the cement which binds the party's membership, is *not* an accurate description of the two major parties in the United States, however. Indeed, attempts to define and describe our major parties in terms of "principles" and "issues" distort their true nature.

Certainly, it is true that nearly all of the members of each of our two major parties *do* share with one another a dedication to *certain* basic principles—for example, popular sovereignty, limited government, federalism, and the like. But, notice, *not only* are Republicans united with Republicans and Democrats with Democrats on these matters, Republicans and Democrats are *also* united with one another in support of them.

At the same time, however, many Republicans *and* many Democrats find that they have little in common with many other members of *their own* party on many questions. Thus, Republicans often disagree with other Republicans, and Democrats with Democrats, on such important matters as taxes, foreign policy, defense issues, civil rights, welfare legislation, and numerous other vital questions of public policy.

Clearly, there is much disagreement on public questions within both major parties. But *all,* or at least *nearly* all, of the members of each party *are* united with their fellow party members by their desire to win elections and control government.

If everyone agreed with everyone else on most public issues, there would be little or no need for political parties. If, on the other hand, no one could agree with anyone else, political parties would be impossible. Actually, our political parties are composed of a great many persons who, broadly speaking, hold *somewhat similar* views on various public questions.[2]

Functions of Parties. We know from our own history, and from that of other peoples, as well, that political parties are absolutely essential to the successful operation of the democratic process. It is the *party* which provides the link between government and the people in a democracy—the link through which the public will is made known to government and through which government is held responsible for its actions. The pivotal place of party in a democratic system can be seen most clearly by examining the major functions that parties perform.

Nomination of Candidates. A party's *major* function and, indeed, its chief reason for existence is to nominate candidates and present them to the electorate. There must be some device for finding and sifting the candidates for public office; and there must be some device for concentrating strength (votes) behind those candidates, especially when we insist on majority rule. Parties are the best device we have yet found for these purposes. In fact, parties are generally the only groups which make nominations in American politics.[3]

Informer and Stimulator. A party helps to inform the people and to stimulate their interest in public affairs in a variety of ways: by campaigning for its candidates, by taking stands on certain issues, and by criticizing the stands

---

[1] The famous English statesman Edmund Burke (1729–1797) provided a classic definition of a party nearly 200 years ago. Many definitions given today are simply variations of his. A political party, wrote Burke, is "a body of men united, for promoting by their joint endeavors the national interest, upon some particular principle in which they are all agreed."

[2] Note that the discussion here is chiefly concerned with the *major* parties in the United States. The various *minor* parties in American politics are considered on pages 132–133. State election laws commonly define political parties, but these legal definitions are very narrow and are intended only to identify the objects to which laws regulating political party activities apply.

[3] Except in non-partisan elections and in those infrequent situations in which an independent candidate enters a partisan election.

and candidates of its opposition. Of course, each party attempts to inform the voters in the way it thinks they should be informed—to the party's advantage. This "educational" process is carried on in several ways: through pamphlets, signs, and newspaper advertisements, by speeches on radio, on television, and in person at rallies and conventions, and by virtually every other means available.

By taking at least some kind of stand on various public issues, parties and their candidates offer the voters alternatives from which to choose. But the major parties usually do not take *too* firm a stand on controversial issues. Recall, each party's primary aim is that of winning elections; it attempts to do this by attracting as many voters as possible while, at the same time, offending as few as possible.

MUSICAL CHAIRS. To win control of Congress both parties must appeal to as many groups as possible. Thus, their differences are ones of degree, not kind. (Reg Manning, McNaught Syndicate, Inc.)

Bonding Agent. A party acts as a "bonding agent" to insure the good performance of its candidates. A party must stand behind its candidates and officeholders. In choosing its candidates, a party attempts to see that they are persons who are both qualified and of good character or, at least, that they have no serious blemishes on their records. It also attempts to see that its candidates elected to office "toe the line." When it fails to do these things, the party runs the serious risk that it and its candidates will suffer in future elections. (Remember, unscrupulous political machines and incompetent officeholders exist only where the voters are not doing *their* work properly.)

Watchdog. Parties act as "watchdogs" over the conduct of public business. Primarily, this is the function of the party out of power. Its criticisms of the party in power are intended to convince the voters that the "outs" should become the "ins." Its attacks also make the "ins" a little more careful of their public charge and more responsive to the wishes of the voters. In effect, it is the function of the "out" party to serve as the "loyal opposition."

Conduct of Government. Parties provide a basis for the conduct of government. In many ways government in the United States is government by party. For example, Congress and the State legislatures are organized and conduct their business on the basis of party, and appointments to executive offices are generally made on a party basis. Under the American system of separation of powers the party is usually the agent through which the legislative and executive branches cooperate with one another.

THE TWO-PARTY SYSTEM

Ours is basically a two-party system. That is, in the typical election in the United States only the candidates of the Republican and Democratic Parties have a realistic chance of winning public office. There have been and

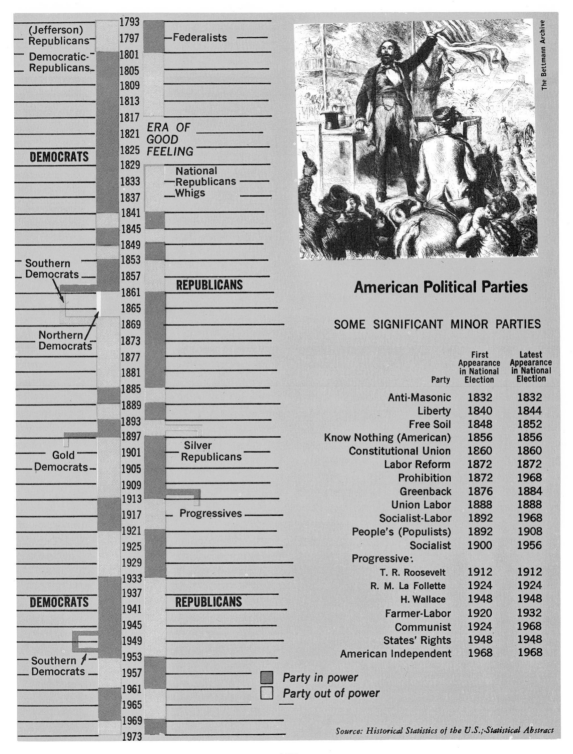

The Bettmann Archive

American Political Parties

SOME SIGNIFICANT MINOR PARTIES

Timeline (left side):

(Jefferson) Republicans
Democratic-Republicans
DEMOCRATS
Southern Democrats
Northern Democrats
Gold Democrats
DEMOCRATS
Southern Democrats

Years: 1793, 1797, 1801, 1805, 1809, 1813, 1817, 1821, 1825, 1829, 1833, 1837, 1841, 1845, 1849, 1853, 1857, 1861, 1865, 1869, 1873, 1877, 1881, 1885, 1889, 1893, 1897, 1901, 1905, 1909, 1913, 1917, 1921, 1925, 1929, 1933, 1937, 1941, 1945, 1949, 1953, 1957, 1961, 1965, 1969, 1973

Federalists
ERA OF GOOD FEELING
National Republicans
Whigs
REPUBLICANS
Silver Republicans
Progressives
REPUBLICANS

Party	First Appearance in National Election	Latest Appearance in National Election
Anti-Masonic	1832	1832
Liberty	1840	1844
Free Soil	1848	1852
Know Nothing (American)	1856	1856
Constitutional Union	1860	1860
Labor Reform	1872	1872
Prohibition	1872	1968
Greenback	1876	1884
Union Labor	1888	1888
Socialist-Labor	1892	1968
People's (Populists)	1892	1908
Socialist	1900	1956
Progressive:		
T. R. Roosevelt	1912	1912
R. M. La Follette	1924	1924
H. Wallace	1948	1948
Farmer-Labor	1920	1932
Communist	1924	1968
States' Rights	1948	1948
American Independent	1968	1968

■ Party in power
□ Party out of power

Source: Historical Statistics of the U.S.; Statistical Abstract

127

are other parties—*minor* or *third parties*—in American politics, of course; we shall consider them shortly. But they usually do not make serious bids for power or contest only a handful of offices in particular locales. Their existence does not offset the basic fact that the American party system is dominated by two major parties.

Historical Basis. Our two-party system is rooted in the formation of the country. The Founding Fathers were opposed to political parties and hoped to discourage their development. As noted in Chapter 2 (page 44), their hope was a futile one, however. The debates over the ratification of the Constitution itself saw the beginnings of our first two parties—the Federalists led by Alexander Hamilton and the Anti-Federalists (later the Democratic-Republicans) led by Thomas Jefferson.

These first two groupings set the pattern for our party system, and the force of historical tradition has played a part in maintaining it as such. Although parties are not mentioned in the Constitution, they have been vitally significant in the development of our constitutional system—and have themselves been prime examples of it.

Single-Member Districts. Most elections in the United States, from the presidential election to those at the local level, are *single-member district* elections. That is, in most elections only *one* candidate is elected to each of the offices on the ballot. The victorious candidate is the one who receives a *plurality* (the largest number)[4] of the votes cast for the office he seeks.[5]

Where there are only two candidates for an office—as is usually the case in American politics—one or the other is bound to win a majority vote. Thus, from a very practical standpoint, it has seemed wise to us to limit election contests to two major contenders.

The single-member district system rather obviously tends to discourage third parties. Because only one winner is possible in each contest, the voter has, really, only two practical choices: to vote for the candidate of the party which holds the office or for the candidate of the party with the best chance to replace him. A vote for a third party's candidate is, in effect, a "wasted" one.

Similarity of the Two Parties. The fact that ours is a two-party system necessarily forces each of the major parties to be moderate rather than extreme in outlook. This is so because each of them, in trying to attract a majority vote, must appeal to as many individuals and groups as possible.

Each must also direct its appeal to essentially the same great mass of voters. Neither can long afford to concentrate its chief efforts on any one particular group such as farmers, businessmen, or labor union members. Neither can long afford to ignore any such group, either.

The fact that it is often difficult to distinguish one party from the other except by name is regarded by many as a weakness in our political system. Actually, it is but a reflection of the nature of the American people. We are, in most respects, a homogeneous people. We are not plagued by sharp cleavages based upon

---

[4] A candidate who wins a plurality of the votes wins more than does any other candidate. A candidate who wins a *majority* of the votes wins more than half of all the votes cast in the election. Thus, a majority is always a plurality, but a plurality is *not* necessarily a majority.

[5] A relatively few *multi-member district* elections are held in the United States, notably for some seats in various State legislatures. But the principal offices—*especially* the Presidency, which is the "grand prize" of American politics, and also all of the seats in both houses of Congress, each of the governorships, and most of the seats in the State legislatures—are filled from single-member districts.

economic, geographic, religious, nationality, or ideological factors. That is, those conditions which would encourage sharp distinctions between the two parties—and very likely prompt the existence of a multi-party system—do not exist in this country. The late Adlai Stevenson had this very much in mind when, congratulating Dwight D. Eisenhower on election night in 1952, he said:

> It is traditional for Americans to fight hard before an election. It is tradition also to close ranks after an election. We vote as many, but we pray as one.

The Power to Govern. As was pointed out in the discussion of party functions on page 126, the two-party system means that the power to govern is placed in the hands of one party or the other. The voters are thus able to fix the blame or to give credit for the nature of that conduct at election time. Although they may not be presented with sharp alternatives in the form of policies, they are presented with the very significant alternative of the "out" party's bid for power.

Multi-Party Systems. There are some who argue that our two-party system should be scrapped in favor of a multi-party arrangement. In such a system several major and a number of lesser parties would exist, each based upon a particular ideological or class position, as in many European countries. It is claimed that such an arrangement would give the voters truly meaningful choices among candidates and policies.

The practical effects of two particular factors previously cited—the single-member district system and the homogeneity of our population—seem to make such an arrangement an impossibility, however. Also, we know that a multi-party system tends to promote instability in government. One party is seldom able to win the support of a majority of the voters, and the power to govern must therefore be shared by several parties. France and Italy, two of the leading multi-party nations of

Europe, furnish excellent illustrations of the point: since the end of World War II, both of these democracies have been plagued by governmental crises and with frequent shifts in party control.[6]

One-Party Systems. In dictatorships, such as the Soviet Union and Communist China, opposition to the regime is not tolerated. Only one party, that of the ruling clique, is allowed to exist. To all practical purposes, it would be just as accurate to describe such systems as "no-party systems."

THE TWO MAJOR PARTIES

The Democratic Party. The Democratic Party, one of the oldest political parties in the world, is now some 175 years old. It began to develop during George Washington's administration and was originally known as the Anti-Federalist Party. For a brief time it was called the Republican, then the Democratic-Republican, before finally being named the Democratic Party in 1825.

In its early years the party was dominated by Thomas Jefferson. Originally, it championed a strict construction of the Constitution, argued that "that government is best which governs least," and stressed the importance of individual liberties.

Its early opposition, the Federalist Party, died out by 1816, and it was unopposed in national politics during the Era of Good Feeling. By the 1830's, however, during Andrew Jackson's Presidency, a new and powerful Whig Party arose to challenge it.

---

[6] The French nation achieved a semblance of political stability with the return to power of General Charles de Gaulle and the creation of the Fifth Republic in 1958. Until then, France had had 25 changes of government since the end of World War II. De Gaulle resigned the Presidency in 1969, and this likely means a return to the former pattern in French politics.

The Democratic Party was so sharply divided by the issues of slavery and union that, from 1860 through 1932, only two of its presidential candidates, Grover Cleveland and Woodrow Wilson, were elected to the office. The Republicans controlled the Presidency and both houses of Congress, as well, through most of that period.

The Depression brought the Democrats back into power in 1932, however, and Franklin D. Roosevelt won four consecutive terms in the White House. President Roosevelt's death in 1945 elevated Vice President Harry S Truman. He completed Roosevelt's fourth term and won a full term of his own in an upset victory over the Republican nominee, Thomas E. Dewey, in 1948. But the Democratic nominee in 1952, Adlai Stevenson, was defeated in the landslide election of Dwight D. Eisenhower in that year.

Except for the years, 1947–1948, the Democrats controlled both houses of Congress for the twenty years after 1932. They regained that control in 1954, retained it despite the second Eisenhower landslide victory over Stevenson in 1956, and have kept it ever since.

The party recaptured the Presidency with John F. Kennedy's razor-thin victory over Richard Nixon in 1960. Lyndon Johnson became President upon Mr. Kennedy's death in 1963 and won a full term by a landslide vote in 1964. The Democrats lost the White House in 1968, however; their nominee, Vice President Hubert Humphrey, could not withstand Mr. Nixon's second bid for the office.

The Republican Party. The Republican Party of today was born in 1854. It nominated its first presidential candidate, John C. Frémont, in 1856 and elected its first President, Abraham Lincoln, in 1860. It is the only party in the history of American politics to have managed the vault from minor to major party status.

The GOP is the descendant of two earlier parties. In the nation's earliest years, the *Federalists* advocated a broad construction of the Constitution, a strong National Government, and governmental aid to business and commerce. Its successor, which rose in the 1830's in opposition to Jacksonian Democracy, first called itself the National Republican and then the Whig Party. It was the *Whig Party* which gave way to the Republicans in the latter 1850's.

The Republicans dominated the national scene until the elections of 1930 and 1932. Except for a victory in the congressional elections of 1946, the Republican Party served as the opposition party from 1933 to 1953. In 1952 and again in 1956 General Eisenhower was the party's presidential nominee, and he won by large majorities in both elections. Although the Eisenhower victory in 1952 brought with it Republican majorities in both houses of Congress, Republican control of the legislative branch was short-lived. It lost the congressional elections of 1954 and has been the minority party in Congress ever since.

The GOP also lost the Presidency in the close Nixon-Kennedy race in 1960, and its 1964 nominee, Barry Goldwater, suffered a massive loss. It regained the White House with Mr. Nixon's victory in 1968, however.

Party Membership. The general similarity of—the lack of sharp distinctions between—our two major parties is clearly reflected in the composition of each of them. Each is a cross-section of the population. Protestants, Catholics, and Jews; whites and Negroes; professional men, farmers, employers, and union members; the young, the middle-aged, and the elderly; city-dwellers, suburbanites, and small-town and rural residents—members of these and of all of the many other groupings which make up American society are to be found in both the Republican and the Democratic Parties. It is true that, for brief periods, the members of certain groups tend to align themselves more solidly with one party than the other; but these alignments are seldom permanent or even relatively long-lasting.

Membership in either party is purely voluntary. A person is a Democrat or a Republican, or a member of a minor party or an indepen-

Congressional Elections of 1970

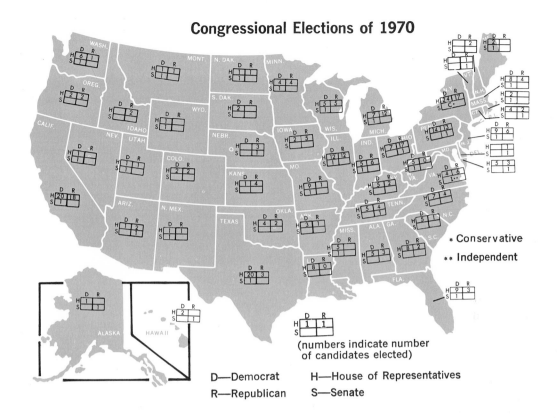

* Conservative
** Independent

(numbers indicate number of candidates elected)

D—Democrat   H—House of Representatives
R—Republican S—Senate

dent, simply because he chooses to regard himself in such terms.[7] There are no dues to be paid; party membership costs nothing, unless one chooses to contribute to his party's coffers. There are no chores a party member must perform—though, of course, he may work for the party and its candidates if he so chooses.

A variety of factors may cause one to say that he is a Republican or a Democrat. The most important is that of family tradition. Approximately two out of every three voters

follow the party allegiance of their parents. Better than nine out of ten married couples share the same party preference and vote alike, usually in the belief that to do otherwise would cancel out the effect of their votes.

The second most important influence on party choice is economic status. As a general rule, those with higher incomes tend to regard themselves as Republicans and those with lower incomes usually think of themselves as being Democrats. The section of the country in which one lives—for example, the South—often has an effect on party membership and voting behavior, too. National origin is sometimes a consideration; as a general rule, descendants of Northern Europeans tend to vote Republican, whereas those of Southern and Eastern European extraction tend to vote

---

[7] In order to participate in the primaries in several States, a voter must indicate his party preference—or, as it is often put, "declare his party membership"—when he registers to vote; but this requirement is a mechanical one and wholly a matter of individual choice. See pages 164–165.

Democratic. While the effect of religious affiliation is a highly debatable one, it is true that there is a higher proportion of Protestants within the Republican Party than the Democratic Party.

Again, notice, the comments just made are *generalizations*. Various of these and other factors may very well conflict with one another in the case of a particular individual—and, indeed, they often do. For example, a young man from a strongly Democratic family in a Southern State may move to a high-income suburb near a large Northern city and, sooner or later, switch his allegiance to the Republican Party. For a more specific discussion of political preferences and voting behavior of various groups see pages 156–158.

MINOR PARTIES

The Republican and Democratic Parties have dominated the American political scene for well over a century now. But that fact should not blind us either to the existence or the importance of the *minor* or *third* parties. A large number of them have flashed across that scene over the years. Only a few have achieved any degree of permanence—for example, the Prohibition Party founded in 1869; but their collective imprint has been a large one.

Types of Minor Parties. The number and variety of these parties makes it somewhat difficult to classify them. Thus, some of them have limited their activities to a particular locale, others to a particular State, some to a particular region of the country, and still others have sought support throughout the nation. As we've already noted, most minor parties are shortlived but some have existed for decades. Then, too, most minor parties have lived mothlike around the flame of a single issue or idea while others have had a broader and more practical base.

No method of classifying these parties is altogether satisfactory; but most of them do fall fairly neatly into one of two categories: They have either been parties of "the great idea" or parties of "the great personality." For example, such groups as the Prohibition, Socialist, Socialist-Labor, Greenback, Vegetarian, and Populist Parties were each built upon a special set of concepts or issues. So, too, is the American Independent Party of today. The Progressive Parties of 1912 and of 1924, on the other hand, were each founded and lived upon the appeal of a single dominant personality—*i.e.,* Theodore Roosevelt and Robert M. LaFollette, respectively.

The "great idea" parties have regularly collapsed or faded to impotence as either: (1) their central theme has failed to appeal to any significant portion of the electorate or (2) one or both of the major parties have adopted their stands on the key issues. Similarly, the "great personality" parties have passed into the limbo of the history books when their leaders have stepped aside—as, for example, did the Bull Moose Progressive Party when TR returned to the Republican fold after the election of 1912.

The Republican Party was originally one of the "great idea" parties. It was born in the cause of antislavery in 1854. When the Whig Party failed to embrace the new party's burning issue, it passed into oblivion as the Republican Party became the major party in opposition to the Democrats.

Some minor parties have been—and even are today—successful at the State or local level. They have, at times, elected a few members of Congress and occasionally gained some electoral votes; but none has ever captured the Presidency.

Importance of Minor Parties. Despite the general unwillingness of most Americans to support them, minor parties have had a very significant effect upon our political history and upon the major parties. Thus, it was a minor party, the Anti-Masons in 1831, that introduced the national convention as a device for nominating presidential candidates; the Democrats and the Whigs each seized upon the method for the elections of 1832, and it has been the means by which the major parties have picked their presidential candidates ever since.

A strong third-party candidacy *can* play a decisive role in an election contest. This is true at any level in our politics, national, State, or local—and it is especially true when the two major parties compete on roughly equal terms. The point was dramatically illustrated in the presidential election of 1912. A split in the Republican Party and the resulting third-party candidacy of Theodore Roosevelt that year produced these results:

Party and Candidate	Popular Vote	%	Electoral Vote
Democrat— Woodrow Wilson	6,301,254	41.8	435
Progressive— Theodore Roosevelt	4,127,788	27.4	88
Republican— William H. Taft	3,485,831	23.1	8
Socialist— Eugene V. Debs	901,255	6.0	—
Prohibition— Eugene Chafin	209,644	1.4	—

Historically, the most important roles the minor parties have played have been those of critic and of innovator. Unlike the major parties, most of them have been ready, willing, and able to take quite specific stands on difficult issue questions. In doing so they have often drawn attention to controversial issues the major parties have preferred to ignore or straddle.

Many of the more important issues in American politics over the years—for example, the progressive income tax, prohibition, woman suffrage, railroad and banking regulation, old-age pensions, farm relief—were first brought to prominence by a minor party. But this very important function of minor parties has also been a major source of their frustrations.

When their proposals have gained any significant public support, one and then shortly both of the major parties have adopted and presented them as their own. The late Norman Thomas, six times the Socialist Party nominee for President, often complained that "the major parties are stealing from my platform"; and he was speaking for many of his third-party colleagues as he did so.

Most often, American third parties have been more "liberal" or "radical" than have the older and established major parties—but this has not always been the case, of course. Occasionally one of them becomes a vehicle for deception, as did the Progressive Party of 1948; its presidential candidate, Henry A. Wallace, did not himself then recognize the influence exerted by communists in his party.

The presidential candidates of a number of minor parties were carried on the ballots of various of the States in 1968, including those of the Prohibition, Socialist-Worker, Socialist-Labor, Peace and Freedom, and Constitution Parties—and, of course, the Wallace-LeMay ticket of the American Independent Party was on the ballot in all fifty of the States. More than 100 third party candidates sought seats in Congress from the various States, as well, in 1968; and approximately half that number ran for the Senate and House in the 1970 elections.

PARTY ORGANIZATION

To accomplish its goal—the control of government through the winning of elections—a party must have effective organization. Lord Bryce once underscored this fact:

Organization is essential to the accomplishment of any purpose. To attempt to govern a country by the votes of the masses left without control would be like attempting to . . . lay the course of a sailing ship by the votes of the passengers.

More than half a century ago Lord Bryce reported that:

> . . . an eminent journalist remarked to me in 1908 that the two great parties in the United States were like two bottles. Each bore a different label denoting the kind of liquor it contained, but each was empty. *(The American Commonwealth,* rev. ed., 1911, Vol. II, page 29.)

More recently another perceptive Englishman remarked that:

> In contemplating American parties as they were and are, it is necessary to dismiss from our minds the ideal party of Burke's imagination or of the old-fashioned textbooks. American parties have never been bodies of men united on some general principles of government and united to put these principles into concrete legislation and by administration. There have been moments when parties have looked like that, but they have been brief moments, and even in those moments, appearances have usually been deceptive. (D. W. Brogan, *Politics in America,* 1954, pages 45–46.)

Accepting the Republican presidential nomination at San Francisco in 1964, Senator Barry Goldwater called upon the GOP to unify itself, binding the party to his conservative views. He climaxed his acceptance speech with an invitation to liberals to leave the party:

> Anyone who joins us in all sincerity, we welcome. Those who do not care for our cause we don't expect to enter our ranks in any case. And let our Republicanism, so focused and so dedicated, not be made fuzzy and futile by unthinking and stupid labels. We would remind you that extremism in the defense of liberty is no vice. And let me remind you also that moderation in the pursuit of justice is no virtue.

Do these comments present an accurate picture of the nature of two major parties in American politics? Which, if any of them, portrays what you think *should* be the nature of our two major parties?

Both of our major parties are organized in much the same fashion. Before we turn to their structure, however, a note of caution must be added: it is misleading to conceive of them in terms of a consistent organizational pattern.

Although it is convenient to think of party organization in terms of a pyramid, with a "chain of command" running from the national through the State down to the local level, in neither party is this the case. Both parties are highly *decentralized;* they are best described as federations. Each of the State party organizations is only loosely tied to the party's national structure, and local party organs are often quite independent of their State organizations.

The President's party is normally much more solidly unified than is the opposition. The President is, automatically, the leader of his party; and he has available a number of weapons with which he can assert that leadership—

including, for example, his personal popularity and his power to make appointments to federal office. The party out of power has within its ranks no one in any even roughly comparable position. Indeed, it is virtually impossible to find anyone in the opposition party who can properly be called the party's leader.[8]

National Party Machinery. There are four main elements at the national level in the hierarchy of both parties.

The National Convention. The national convention is often described as the party's national voice. It meets in the summer of every fourth year to select the party's candidate for

---

[8] Except the party's presidential candidate from the time of his nomination until the election is held. The defeated presidential candidate is often called his party's "titular leader"—an apt label, for he is the party's leader in title, by custom, but not in fact.

President and for Vice President and to pro-claim the party's platform. Beyond these functions it has little or no authority, however. It has literally no control over such matters as the nomination of candidates for other offices and cannot force anyone to pledge support to the party platform. We shall return to the national convention later, when we consider the subject of presidential selection in Chapter 16.

The National Committee. In the lengthy period between national conventions the party's affairs are managed, at least in theory, by the national committee and the national chairman. The national committee consists of one man and one woman from each of the States and several of the territories. Since 1952 the Republican National Committee also has included the State chairman from each State that went Republican at the most recent presidential election or that has a Republican governor or a Republican majority in its congressional delegation.

The national committeemen and committeewomen are chosen in various ways among the fifty States. In most States they are selected by the State convention, but in some they are chosen by the party's national convention delegation, by the State central committee, or by the party's voters at the primaries.

On paper the national committee appears to be a powerful organ within each party — though, in fact, it is not. It is chiefly concerned with the problems involved in staging the national convention every fourth year.

The national committeemen and committeewomen *themselves* are usually powerful political figures within their own States. They serve as the major links between State and national party organization; and, when their party is in power nationally, they have a large voice in federal *patronage* matters within their State. That is, they have much to say about the making of appointments to such federal offices as postmasters, customs collectors, and marshals, as well as the dispensing of other "favors."

The National Chairman. The head of the national committee is the national chairman. In formal terms, he is appointed by the national committee. In actual practice, however, he is selected by the party's presidential nominee. His major election-year tasks are to act as the national campaign manager and fund-raiser. He directs the work of the party's national headquarters in Washington, D.C., and has a small staff to assist him in such matters as publicity, research, fund-raising, and the special problems of attracting the votes of such groups as women, veterans, labor, new voters, farmers, racial and national origin minorities, and the like.

Between campaigns the national chairman

WE CAN GET IT FOR YOU WHOLESALE. Each of the major parties seems willing to promise even the moon in its effort to attract the voters in an election year. (White, Akron Beacon Journal)

and the national committee attempt to strengthen the party and its machinery by raising funds, recruiting new voters, and keeping its political fences mended.

The Congressional Campaign Committee. Congressional Campaign Committees are organized for both the House of Representatives and the Senate. In the House the Republican Congressional Campaign Committee consists of one Representative from each State with party representation, and this member is chosen by the Republican Representatives from his State (unless he is the sole Representative, of course). The Democratic Congressional Campaign Committee includes a Representative from each State and a member for each of several territories.[9] Women who are not members of Congress are often appointed to each party's Congressional Campaign Committee on the suggestion of a member. The Senatorial Campaign Committee of each party consists of a dozen or so members, who are appointed for two-year terms by the party's leaders in the Senate.

These committees are very active, especially in the "off-year" elections, and are assisted by a party staff. They have no official connection with the other party groups but work with them to secure the election of the party's candidates for seats in Congress.

State and Local Party Machinery. National party organization is largely the result of custom and of the rules adopted by each quadrennial national convention. The State and local party structure, however, is largely determined by State law.

The State Central Committee. A State central committee, headed by a State chairman, supervises the party's machinery in each of the fifty States. It varies in composition and powers rather widely across the country. Its members are chosen from congressional or legislative districts or counties within the State, and by a variety of methods: by a State convention, in the primaries, or by the local units.

The State chairman is elected by the State central committee. Occasionally he is an important political figure in his own right; much more often, however, he fronts for the governor, a Senator, or some other potent leader or faction in the party. With the members of the State central committee, he works to promote his party and its fortunes—especially by maintaining an effective State organization, promoting party harmony, raising campaign funds, and assisting candidates in their bids for office.

Local Units. Local party structure varies so widely among the States that it almost defies brief description. The typical organization usually follows the lines of the electoral districts. That is, there is usually a party committee for each congressional and legislative district and county, town, borough, precinct, and ward in the State. In the more populous cities party organization is also broken down by residential blocks and even apartment buildings.

It is in the local party units that party workers often come into the closest contact with the voters themselves. Most young people who are interested in going into politics frequently begin at this level, gaining valuable experience "laboring in the party's vineyards." These mostly voluntary and unpaid workers are really the lifeblood of the party. Without their dedication and enthusiasm neither party could hope for much, if any, success for their respective candidates on election day.

PARTY FINANCE

Election campaigns cost money—and very often a great deal of it. No one knows just how much is spent in any election year. But

---

[9] States not represented in the House by a Democrat, as well as the several territories, have a member chosen for them by the chairman of the Democratic Congressional Campaign Committee.

we do know that elections are becoming more and more expensive. Reliable estimates indicate that some $250,000,000 was spent on all elections in 1968. In other words, about $3.00 for every voter who cast a ballot.

Radio and television time, paper, printing, billboards, office furniture, newspaper advertising, paid workers, campaign pins and stickers, and travel expenses—these and a host of other items account for party expenditures. To cite one example of the astronomical costs involved: a single half-hour of network television time can run to $180,000; it is conservatively estimated that for 1968 the Republicans and the Democrats bought more than $20,000,000 of prime television time.

Sources of Funds. From where does the money come? Unlike many European parties, our major parties do not collect dues from their members. Instead, they depend upon "voluntary" contributions from well-wishers who are interested in the party and the success of its candidates and programs and from those who expect "favors" in return.

The major sources of campaign funds today are: (1) individual and family contributors, (2) officeholders and office-seekers, (3) non-party groups such as COPE (AFL–CIO's Committee on Public Education), (4) temporary committees formed for the purposes of a campaign such as the Citizens for Nixon-Agnew and Independents for Humphrey-Muskie, and (5) party social-electioneering functions such as the Jefferson, Jackson, and Lincoln Day Dinners, rallies, and testimonials.

Regulation of Finances. Congress has attempted to regulate the use of money in any election at which federal officers are chosen.[10] It has done so because of the importance of the electoral process, because of the power money obviously has in politics, and because

---

[10] Every State also has enacted laws to regulate campaign finances and check corrupt practices. Like the federal statutes, however, they contain many loopholes which make them easy to evade.

The campaign trail often leads into a camp of the opponent's supporters. (Wide World Photos)

the line between a political contribution and a bribe can be an exceedingly narrow one.

Federal campaign finance laws deal with three major aspects of the problem. They: (1) require financial reports, (2) limit contributions and expenditures, and (3) prohibit contributions from certain sources.

Financial Reports. Congress first began to require the reporting of political finances in 1910. Today any political committee which seeks to influence federal elections in two or more States must make public the contributions it receives and the expenditures it makes. Any such body must file the required financial reports with the Clerk of the House of Representatives quarterly, yearly, and twice just before an election. These reports must contain detailed accounts of all income, total expenditures, an itemization of any expenditure over $10, and the names and addresses of all persons who contribute more than $100 to such groups.

A candidate for any federal office must file financial reports twice — just before and just after an election. His reports must show the amount and sources of all contributions and the amounts spent for certain, but not all, campaign purposes.[11] A candidate need not report the amounts taken in and spent by others in his behalf, unless he has explicitly authorized them to work for him.

Any individual who contributes more than $50 to federal candidates in two or more States must report the details of these transactions, unless he makes his contributions to a political committee required to report.

Limits on Campaign Expenditures. The Hatch Act of 1940 limits the national committees to the spending of not more than $3,000,000 in any one campaign. Since 1940 the national committees have stayed within that figure. Other party committees have simply stepped into the breach. Many millions of dollars that otherwise would be spent by the national committees are now spent by the Congressional and Senatorial Campaign Committees, the State party organizations, and various temporary party groups created for the purpose.

The Corrupt Practices Act of 1925 limits the expenditures that may be made by congressional candidates. A candidate for the Senate is limited either to a maximum of $10,000 or to 3¢ per voter up to a maximum of $25,000. A candidate for the House of Representatives is limited to a flat $2500 or to 3¢ per voter up to a maximum of $5000. Other persons and groups can, and do, spend in behalf of congressional candidates, however.

The Hatch Act also provides that no individual may contribute more than $5000 to a candidate or committee. An individual can, and many do, contribute $5000 or less to each

---

[11] The law specifically exempts outlays he makes for travel, subsistence, stationery, postage, circulars, telegraph and telephone service, and "personal" items.

of several candidates and committees, however. Then, too, members of the same family can make contributions, all to the same candidate or committee.

Prohibited Sources. Since 1907 corporations, and since 1943 labor unions, have been prohibited from contributing funds to a federal campaign. But, of course, the officers of a corporation and the members of a union can contribute their own funds if they choose. Corporations often make indirect contributions by using their national advertising programs to support or oppose some matter especially identified with one party or the other. Many labor unions have created "political action committees" to work with funds contributed by union members. Neither of these practices is illegal.

No person or business firm having a contract with any federal agency can make or promise a contribution to any candidate or party, nor may any person knowingly solicit such funds from them.

Other Regulations. No federal employee, and no State or local government worker whose job is financed in whole or in part with federal funds, can be forced to make a political contribution. Nor may these persons offer governmental favors as a reward, or threaten dismissal as a penalty, for a vote or for other political activity, nor otherwise use their official positions to influence the outcome of an election.

Newspaper advertisements, circulars, radio and television programs, and the like relating to any federal candidate must name the persons or groups sponsoring them.

That we have not solved the many problems created by the power of money in politics is obvious. That these problems must be met, and soon, is also obvious. Otherwise, we may very well have to resign ourselves to accepting certain unnecessary restrictions on the successful operation of the democratic process. For example, we may have to accept as commonplace the fact that in many elections the wealthier candidate or the one with the heavier financial backing will win largely because of the money available to him.

Clearly, much can be done to update and tighten existing laws, both federal and State. The major reform proposals today center on requirements for more publicity on contributions and spending and on attempts to attract more contributions from the average voter. The publicity suggestions are based on the assumption that the power of money in politics will be lessened if the average voter knows more about where the funds of a candidate come from and where they go. The proposals to broaden the base of contributors are founded on the hope that, if more small contributors support the party and candidates of their choice, the large contributors would not be so necessary to either party and thus would have less influence.

The President's Commission on Campaign Costs. The late President Kennedy appointed a nine-member commission to study and make specific proposals to ease the problem of party finance. Its report, made in 1962, stresses the need for more adequate publicity and for increasing the number of smaller contributors.

Its chief recommendation calls for an income tax credit as an incentive to spur a large number of smaller gifts to each party.[12] The commission also asks for a stricter enforcement of federal and State laws now on the books, for more effective fund-raising efforts by the parties themselves, and for a continuing study of campaign finance problems. Then, too, it proposes the outright repeal of the present $3,000,000 limit on spending by national committees and the $5000 limit on contri-

---

[12] A provision to allow taxpayers to deduct up to $50 for campaign contributions was approved by the Senate but finally eliminated from the House-Senate compromise version of what became the Revenue Act of 1964. Congressional approval of some form of the commission's proposal seems likely in the near future.

"WE COULD GET IN PRETTY DEEP, COULDN'T WE?" Both major political parties continually face the critical problem of raising enough funds to meet their ever-mounting campaign costs. (Art Bimrose, The Portland Oregonian)

butions by individuals, calling them both unrealistic and unenforceable.

Some other proposed reforms also are advocated by various persons and groups. Most of these proposals are aimed at reducing the candidates' and the parties' total campaign bill. They include suggestions that: (1) radio and television stations be required to give free air time to major candidates, (2) a "voter's pamphlet" containing factual information and partisan views be published and distributed at public expense, (3) campaigns and other party activities be financed in whole or in part with public funds, (4) campaign funds be raised in large part by a non-partisan group and distributed by it among the parties and candidates.

Key Concepts

The term *politics* describes the whole process by which public policies are determined and public affairs conducted. Government without politics is impossible.

With particular reference to our two major parties, a political party may be defined as a voluntary association of voters seeking to control government through winning elections and holding public office.

Parties perform five vital functions; they: (1) nominate candidates and present them to the voters, (2) inform the voters and stimulate interest in public affairs, (3) act as a "bonding agent" to insure the good performance of their candidates, (4) act as a "watchdog" over the conduct of public business, and (5) provide a basis for the conduct of government.

Our two-party system developed out of the contest over the ratification of the Constitution. It is made practically necessary by the single-member district system of most American elections. Because both major parties must appeal to exactly the same mass of voters, compromise is an essential ingredient in each. The lack of sharp distinctions between our two major parties is essentially a reflection of the homogeneous character of the American people.

The Democratic Party of today traces its origins directly to Thomas Jefferson and the Anti-Federalists. A little less directly, the Republican Party traces its origins to Alexander Hamilton and the Federalists.

In the United States party membership is voluntary. A person is a Republican or a Democrat simply because he chooses to be, although he must register by party in several States. Family background, place of residence, economic status, and similar factors influence party choice.

Minor, or third, parties are one of two kinds: parties of the "great idea" or of the "great personality." They are valuable forces in American politics, especially in prompting the major parties to action.

Each major party is organized on the national, State, and local level. The national convention stands at the top of the national machinery, but meets only once every fourth year. The national committee and the national chairman conduct the party's business between conventions. The Congressional Campaign Committees concentrate their efforts in congressional elections. State and local organization is organized on a geographic basis.

The already high and increasing cost of elections poses problems for democratic government. The major sources for campaign funds are: (1) individual contributors, (2) officeholders and office-seekers, (3) non-party groups, (4) temporary campaign committees, and (5) party fund-raising social functions.

Congress and the States attempt, but rather ineffectively, to control campaign financing by requiring statements of contributions received and expenditures made, limiting expenditures and contributions, and prohibiting certain contributions.

Important Terms

campaign
Congressional Campaign Committees
Corrupt Practices Act
Hatch Act
major parties

majority vote
minor parties
multi-party system
national chairman
national committee
national convention

one-party system
plurality vote
political party
single-member district
State central committee
two-party system

Questions for Inquiry and Review

1. To what does *politics* refer?

2. Why is a definition emphasizing principle and issue inappropriate to our two major parties?

3. What are the five major functions performed by a political party?

4. What is the historical basis for our two-party system?

5. Why is the single-member district factor important as a significant reason for our two-party system?

6. Why are the two major parties not sharply different from one another?

7. Why can neither major party long neglect any major group of the electorate?

8. Why might a one-party system be described as a "no-party" system?

9. What is the chief factor which determines party preference?

10. What are the two basic types of minor parties in American politics?

11. Of what particular value have minor parties been in our system?

12. Why is it misleading to describe party organization in terms of a national-down-to-local pyramid?

13. What are the four major elements of national party organization?

14. Who heads each party's national committee? How is he selected?

15. On the basis of what particular factor is the typical State party organization built?

16. Why does it seem necessary that campaign finances be regulated by law?

17. What are the five major sources for campaign funds?

18. Along what three principal lines are campaign finances regulated?

For Further Inquiry

1. What advice would you give to a person who wanted to make politics his or her career?

2. In Great Britain the party out of power is known as Her Majesty's Loyal Opposition and its leader is paid an official salary. Why has it been said that the phrase "Her Majesty's Loyal Opposition" is "one of the most illustrative terms in the democratic dictionary"? Do you think the leader of the party out of power in the United States should be paid an official salary?

3. After his defeat for the Presidency in 1940, Wendell Willkie said:

A vital element in the balanced operation of a democracy is a strong, alert, and watchful opposition. Ours must not be an opposition against—it must be an opposition for—an opposition for a strong America, a productive America. For only the productive can be strong and only the strong can be free.

How would you phrase Mr. Willkie's thought in your own words? How would you compare Mr. Willkie's comments with those of Mr. Stevenson quoted on page 129.

4. Which of the following proposals do you consider to be the most important? (a) Pay

the costs of political campaigns from public funds. (b) Outlaw party organizations. (c) Encourage the growth of a third party. (d) Compel all citizens to vote in elections. (e) Reduce the number of elective offices in the United States. Why?

Suggested Activities

1. Invite local political party officials and public officeholders to class to discuss their conceptions of a political party.

2. Stage a debate or class forum on the question: *Resolved,* That the two major parties should be completely reorganized so that each one truly reflects sharp differences of opinion in American society.

3. Secure copies of the most recent platforms of the Republican and Democratic Parties. Hold a panel discussion on how they differ from one another, in what ways they are quite similar, and in what ways they are more vague than specific.

4. Write a report on one of the following topics: (a) party organization in your State, (b) the history of one of the "great idea" parties, (c) campaigning for local office.

5. Prepare a bulletin board display depicting eventful happenings in the history of each of our two major parties.

Suggested Reading

ADRIAN, CHARLES R. and PRESS, CHARLES, *The American Political Process.* McGraw-Hill, 1969. Chapter 9.

BLACKMORE, CHARLES P. and YESELSON, ABRAHAM (eds.), *The Fabric of American Democracy.* Van Nostrand, 1969. Chapter 5.

BURNS, JAMES M. and PELTASON, J. W., *Government By the People.* Prentice-Hall, 1969. Chapter 12.

COTTER, CORNELIUS P. (ed.), *Practical Politics in the United States.* Allyn and Bacon, 1969.

"Democratic Platform, 1968," *U.S. News,* September 9, 1968.

DYE, THOMAS R., *et al., American Government: Theory, Structure, and Process.* Wadsworth, 1969. Chapter 8.

HUMPHREY, HUBERT H., "Political Power and the Middle Class in the '70s," *U.S. News,* November 24, 1969.

JAMES JUDSON L., *American Political Parties.* Pegasus, 1969.

JONAS, FRANK H. (ed.), *Politics in the American West.* University of Utah Press, 1969.

LARNER, JEREMY, "Inside the McCarthy Campaign," *Harper's,* April and May, 1969.

LOWI, THEODORE J., *The End of Liberalism.* Norton, 1969.

MCBEE, SUSANNA, "The Wallace Clout," *Life,* August 2, 1968.

MCGOVERN, SENATOR GEORGE, "Politics and the Presidency," *Harper's,* January, 1970.

PORTER, KIRK H. and JOHNSON, DONALD B., *National Party Platforms, 1840–1968.* University of Illinois Press, 1969.

"Real Story of the '68 Election," *U.S. News,* October 27, 1969.

REDFORD, EMMETTE S., *et al., Government and Politics in the United States.* Harcourt, Brace and World, 1968. Chapters 5, 6.

REID, REPRESENTATIVE OGDEN R., "Do Republicans Have the Courage to Become the Majority Party?" *Look,* May 13, 1969.

"Republican Strategy for '70 Election," *U.S. News,* November 24, 1969.

RIBICOFF, ABRAHAM and NEWMAN, JON O., *Politics: The American Way.* Allyn and Bacon, 1969.

SCOTT, ANDREW M. and WALLACE, EARLE (eds.), *Politics, U.S.A.: Cases on the American Democratic Process.* Macmillan, 1969. Chapter 6.

Why should there not be a patient confidence in the ultimate justice of the people? Is there any better or equal hope in the world?

ABRAHAM LINCOLN

❉❉❉ Is the "right to vote" most properly viewed as a right, a privilege, or a duty?

❉❉❉ Should there be a single, national set of voter qualifications applicable to all elections in the United States?

❉❉❉ Can one in fact express a position in an election even though he fails (whether purposefully or not) to vote in that election?

Our governmental system, we know, is a representative democracy, a republic; that is, it is a system in which public policies are determined and expressed by the elected representatives of the people. These representatives are responsible to the people for the day-to-day conduct of the government, and they are held accountable for their actions at periodic elections. It is at these elections, through the exercise of the *suffrage* [1] — the right to vote, that the typical citizen can most directly affect the course of public events. Clearly, then, no right can be more precious to an American citizen than his right to vote. It is, as the famous poet Oliver Wendell Holmes wrote, "the vote that shakes the turret of the land."

Suffrage a Political Right. The use of the word "right" in the phrase "right to vote" must be clearly understood. No one possesses the right to vote in the same sense in which he possesses the right to free speech, a fair trial,

or any of the other *civil* rights guaranteed by the Constitution. The right to vote is *not* a civil right — one belonging to all persons. Rather, it is a *political right* — one belonging only to those who can meet certain requirements set by law.

The right to vote is sometimes described as a privilege — and it is, in the sense that it is one of the privileges we enjoy as a result of the nature of our governmental system. But it most certainly is *not* a privilege in the sense that it is a favor that government may grant to or withhold from particular individuals as it pleases. If voting is to be described as a privilege, then it must be noted that it is a privilege which democracy demands must be made available to all persons on the same terms.

SUFFRAGE AND THE CONSTITUTION

The Constitution of the United States does *not* grant to the National Government the

---

[1] The term came from the Latin *suffragium* — literally, "a vote."

power to establish suffrage qualifications. Rather, that power—the power to determine who may vote—is left very largely to the States.

THE POWER TO ESTABLISH SUFFRAGE QUALIFICATIONS

With the enactment of the Voting Rights Act amendments of 1970 Congress passed a statute designed to extend the life of the Voting Rights Act of 1965 for an additional five years, to 1975; see pages 152–154. IN ADDITION, the new law also:

(1) Provides that, effective January 1, 1971, the minimum voting age in *all* States for *all* elections shall be eighteen years of age.

(2) Suspends the use by *any* State of *any* literacy test or similar device as a voting qualification for a period of five years, to 1975.

(3) Requires *each* State to permit any person to vote in a presidential election if that person has resided in the local precinct (or similar unit) for thirty days immediately prior to the presidential election and is otherwise qualified to vote in that State.

These latter provisions raise serious constitutional questions: Does Congress in fact possess the power to enact such provisions? Or are these matters, instead, properly within the reserve powers of the States?

As this book went to press, the Supreme Court had not decided any of several pending cases challenging the new law. The reader should discover the Court's disposition of those cases and read the materials presented in this chapter in light of those actions.

But, while the States have the primary responsibility for the fixing of suffrage qualifications, the Constitution *does* place four specific restrictions upon them in their exercise of that power. It provides that:

(1) Any person whom a State permits to vote for members of the "most numerous branch" (the larger house) of its own legislature must also be permitted to vote for Representatives and Senators in Congress.[2] This restriction is of little, if any, real significance today. With only minor exceptions, each of the States commonly permits the same voters to vote in *all* elections within the State.

(2) No State may deny any person the right to vote on account of race, color, or previous condition of servitude.[3]

(3) No State may deny any person the right to vote on account of sex.[4] Wyoming, while still a federal territory, first provided for "woman suffrage" in 1869. By the time this restriction became a part of the Constitution in 1920, women had been granted the right to vote in some or all elections in over one-half of the States.

(4) No State may require the payment of a poll tax or of any other tax as a condition for participation in the nomination or election of *any* federal official—that is, in any process held in connection with the selection of the President, Vice President, or members of Congress.[5]

The Supreme Court has held that a poll tax cannot be imposed as a qualification for voting in State or local elections, either—as we shall see on page 152. But the States may impose other taxpaying qualifications if they choose.

---

[2] Article I, Section 2, Clause 1; 17th Amendment.

[3] 15th Amendment. Note that the amendment does *not* guarantee the right to vote to Negroes, or to anyone else. Instead, it provides that the States may not discriminate against any person because of race, color, or previous condition of servitude in setting suffrage qualifications.

[4] 19th Amendment. Note that this amendment does *not* guarantee the right to vote to females, as such. Rather, it is cast in terms of *sex* and, technically, prohibits a State from discriminating against either males *or* females in setting suffrage qualifications.

[5] 24th Amendment.

In addition to these four specific restrictions, of course, no State may violate any other provision in the Constitution in the setting of suffrage qualifications. Thus, no State could draw its election code in such manner as to exclude some persons or groups from the suffrage on arbitrary or unreasonable grounds. Thus, in 1969 the Supreme Court voided a New York law permitting only parents of school children and property owners or renters to vote in school district elections. The Court held the law contrary to the 14th Amendment's Equal Protection Clause. But—as long as a State does not violate the Constitution of the United States—it is free to set suffrage qualifications as it sees fit.

SUFFRAGE QUALIFICATIONS AMONG THE STATES

Qualifications Imposed by All States. Each of the fifty States requires that all voters meet three particular qualifications: (1) United States citizenship, (2) a minimum period of residence within the State, and (3) a minimum age.

Citizenship. No alien may vote in any public election held anywhere in the United States. Nothing in the Constitution prohibits voting by aliens, and any State could permit them to do so if it chose. Many States, especially in the West, did so in the nineteenth century; but Arkansas, the last State in which it was possible, prohibited voting by aliens in 1926.[6]

To qualify to vote today in three States — California, Minnesota, and Utah — naturalized citizens must have been citizens for at least ninety days; Pennsylvania requires thirty days. The other States draw no such distinction between native-born and naturalized citizens.

In actual practice a few aliens do vote — though in what number no one knows, of course. Those who do either mistakenly believe that they are citizens or purposefully and unlawfully pose as citizens.

Residence. Each State requires that a potential voter live within the State for a minimum period in order to: (1) prevent an unscrupulous machine from importing a group of voters, called *floaters,* to swing a particular election and (2) guarantee that every voter has at least had an opportunity to become familiar with the candidates and issues in an election.

As the table on page 147 indicates, the actual period required varies considerably — from three months in two States, to six months in fifteen others, and one year in the remaining thirty-three. All but one of the States (Oregon) also require a period of *local* residence — in the county, city, town, ward, or precinct.[7] For example, Nebraska requires a voter to have resided in the State for at least six months, in the county for at least forty days, and in the precinct for at least ten days; Texas requires one year in the State and at least six months in the county. Typically among the States, the qualification is one year in the State, sixty or ninety days in the county, and thirty days in the precinct.

Nearly all of the States prohibit *transients,* persons who are within the State only for a limited time for a specific purpose, from acquiring legal residence. Thus, such groups as members of the Armed Forces and out-of-State college students usually find it impossible to

---

[6] At one time about one-fourth of the States permitted those aliens who had applied for naturalization to cast ballots. Typically, western States followed the practice in the hope of attracting settlers; in those eastern States where large numbers of the foreign born were concentrated, the opposite attitude prevailed.

[7] The *precinct* is the basic, smallest unit of election administration; for each precinct there is a polling place. It is also the basic unit in party organization; see pages 135–136. The *ward* is a unit into which cities are often divided for the election of city councilmen.

qualify to vote in the State in which they have a *physical* residence.

In recent years—beginning with California in 1958—several States have relaxed their residence rules to permit new residents to vote in presidential elections. Two considerations have prompted the trend. First, the fact that the major justification for a residence requirement—time in which voters may become familiar with candidates and issues—has no real application to presidential elections. A voter may be just as well- or ill-informed in such an election no matter where he lives or how long he has lived there. Secondly, the fact that our population is a highly mobile one. On the basis of Census Bureau figures, an estimated 6,000,000 persons who *might* have voted in the last presidential election could not do so because of recent changes in residence.

To date (1971), thirty States[8] have set a reduced residence period for newcomers—but *only* for voting in presidential elections, and *only* if they are otherwise qualified, of course. Several other States will undoubtedly make such changes in the next few years, too.

Age. Age twenty-one has generally been accepted by the States as the legal age of majority—the age at which a person is legally entitled to the full management of his own affairs. Until 1943 that age was also accepted by all States as the minimum age for voting purposes.

Georgia lowered the voting age to eighteen in 1943. Eight other States have since taken similar steps: The voting age is now also eighteen in Alaska and Kentucky, nineteen in Massachusetts, Minnesota, and Montana, and twenty in Hawaii, Maine, and Nebraska.[9]

Although there must be *some* minimum age for voting, age twenty-one has no special magic. In recent years many, including Presidents Eisenhower, Johnson, and Nixon, have urged that the voting age be lowered in all States; and most would set it at eighteen. Those who favor the move usually argue that a person who is old enough to be drafted and asked to fight for his country is old enough to have a voice in his country's affairs. They also contend that today most young people are more mature and better prepared than were their ancestors at twenty-one.[10]

---

[8] California requires at least 54 days in the State; Delaware 90 days; Arizona, Idaho, Missouri, North Carolina, Texas, Washington 60 days; Ohio 40 days; Massachusetts and Colorado 32 days; Florida, Georgia, Maine, Minnesota, New Hampshire 30 days. Connecticut 60 days in the town; Illinois 60 days in the precinct; Kansas 45 days in the township; Maryland 45 days in the ward or election district; New Jersey 40 days in the county; Michigan 30 days in the city or township. Alaska, Hawaii, Louisiana, Nebraska, North Dakota, Oklahoma, Oregon, Wisconsin set no minimum period. Most of these and a few other States also allow voting by *former* residents unable to meet their new residence requirements.

[9] It is also legally possible for some persons who are less than twenty-one to vote in four other States—but only a comparative handful are involved in each instance. Thus, in Pennsylvania the election code provides that one becomes of age for voting purposes on the day *before* his twenty-first birthday. In North Carolina, Kansas, and West Virginia a minor may vote in the primary if he will be of age before the general election in November.

[10] Some sophisticated proponents also note that the poorest record of voter participation by age-group is among those twenty-one to thirty. They claim that this is caused by the fact that most young people, having just completed their formal education, are forced to wait three or four years—until the first election after their twenty-first birthday—to vote. They contend that this waiting period causes a loss of interest, and that the poor turnout could be reversed by reducing the voting age. Of course, some opponents cite the same data to support their view.

STATE SUFFRAGE QUALIFICATIONS

State	Minimum Age	U.S. Citizen	State	County	Residence City, Town	Ward, Precinct	Literacy
Alabama	21	Yes	1 year	6 months	—	3 months	Yes
Alaska	18	Yes	1 year *a*	—	—	30 days	Yes
Arizona	21	Yes	1 year *a*	30 days	—	30 days	Yes
Arkansas	21	Yes	1 year	6 months	—	30 days	—
California	21	90 days	1 year *a*	90 days	—	54 days	Yes
Colorado	21	Yes	1 year *a*	—	—	32 days	—
Connecticut	21	Yes	6 months *a*	—	6 months	—	Yes
Delaware	21	Yes	1 year *a*	3 months	—	30 days	Yes
Florida	21	Yes	1 year *a*	6 months	—	—	—
Georgia	18	Yes	1 year *a*	6 months	—	—	Yes
Hawaii	20	Yes	1 year *a*	3 months *f*	—	—	—
Idaho	21	Yes	6 months *a*	30 days	—	—	—
Illinois	21	Yes	1 year *a*	90 days	—	30 days	—
Indiana	21	Yes	6 months	60 days	—	30 days	—
Iowa	21	Yes	6 months	60 days	—	—	—
Kansas	21 *b*	Yes	6 months *a*	—	—	30 days	—
Kentucky	18	Yes	1 year	6 months	—	60 days	—
Louisiana	21	Yes	1 year *a*	6 months	—	3 months	Yes
Maine	20	Yes	6 months *a*	—	3 months	—	Yes
Maryland	21	Yes	1 year *a*	6 months	—	—	—
Massachusetts	19	Yes	1 year *a*	—	6 months	—	Yes
Michigan	21	Yes	6 months *a*	—	33 days	—	—
Minnesota	19	90 days	6 months *a*	—	—	30 days	—
Mississippi	21	Yes	1 year	1 year	6 months	6 months	Yes
Missouri	21	Yes	1 year *a*	60 days	—	—	—
Montana	19	Yes	1 year	30 days	—	—	—
Nebraska	20	Yes	6 months *a*	40 days	—	10 days	—
Nevada	21	Yes	6 months	30 days	—	10 days	—
New Hampshire	21	Yes	6 months *a*	—	6 months	—	Yes
New Jersey	21	Yes	6 months *a*	40 days	—	—	—
New Mexico	21	Yes	1 year	90 days	—	30 days	—
New York	21	Yes	3 months	3 months	3 months	—	Yes
North Carolina	21 *b*	Yes	1 year *a*	—	—	30 days	Yes
North Dakota	21	Yes	1 year *a*	90 days	—	30 days	—
Ohio	21	Yes	1 year *a*	40 days	—	40 days	—
Oklahoma	21	Yes	6 months *a*	2 months	—	20 days	—
Oregon	21	Yes	6 months *a*	—	—	—	Yes
Pennsylvania	21 *b*	30 days	90 days	—	—	60 days	—
Rhode Island	21	Yes	1 year	—	6 months	—	—
South Carolina	21	Yes	1 year *c*	6 months	—	3 months	Yes *d*
South Dakota	21	Yes	1 year *e*	90 days	—	30 days	—
Tennessee	21 *b*	Yes	1 year	3 months	—	—	—
Texas	21	Yes	1 year *a*	6 months	—	—	—
Utah	21	90 days	1 year	4 months	—	60 days	—
Vermont	21	Yes	1 year	—	90 days	—	—
Virginia	21	Yes	1 year	6 months	—	30 days	Yes
Washington	21	Yes	1 year *a*	90 days	—	30 days	Yes
West Virginia	21 *b*	Yes	1 year	60 days	—	—	—
Wisconsin	21	Yes	6 months *a*	—	—	10 days	—
Wyoming	21	Yes	1 year	60 days	—	10 days	Yes

a These States allow new residents to vote in presidential elections after shorter residence periods; see page 146. *b* Minor exceptions to the 21-year age rule exist in these States; see page 146. *c* Only 6 months for ministers, public school teachers, and their wives. *d* Property ownership is an alternative to literacy. *e* Must have resided in the United States for at least 5 years. *f* Residence in legislative district.

Those who oppose lowering the voting age question the maturity and experience of the average person at eighteen. They also counter the "old-enough-to-fight, old-enough-to-vote" argument by noting that there is no logical correlation between one's *physical* fitness as a soldier and his *mental* fitness as a voter. They also argue that slightly more than one-half of the approximately 11,000,000 persons in the affected age-group will *never* be old enough to fight—because they are female.

Over the past several years Congress and most of the State legislatures have considered proposals to reduce the voting age—with the relatively scant results already indicated. Long-established usage, conformity with other age requirements, and inertia all seem to suggest that twenty-one will continue to be the age in most States. Neither Congress nor any of the State legislatures have seriously considered the setting of a *maximum* age for those qualified to vote—nor are they likely to do so.

Qualifications Imposed by Some States. A few other suffrage requirements are found in several of the States—notably those based upon registration, literacy, and tax-payment.

Registration. Forty-nine States—all except the State of North Dakota—today (1971) require that all, or at least most, voters be *registered.*[11] Registration is simply a device intended to provide election officials with a list of those persons who are, in fact, entitled to vote in an election. That is, registration is designed to prevent fraudulent voting.[12]

---

[11] Two States have added a registration qualification in recent years—Arkansas (1964) and Texas (1966). Each did so after abandoning its poll tax (page 152); as only eligible voters were liable for the tax, it served the same end (*i.e.,* voter identification) as a registration system.

[12] Several States also use their registration systems to identify voters in terms of party preference and, hence, eligibility to participate in closed primaries; see page 165. In a few States—Colorado, Illinois, Indiana, Iowa, and Utah, for example—registration is not required for *all* elections.

Without a registration system, it is often difficult to determine whether a person who claims to be eligible is actually entitled to vote. It may have been true that in earlier times election officials commonly knew most of the residents of their local areas; but obviously a much different situation prevails today.

Most States require *all* voters to register; but in a few States—for example, in Iowa—it is demanded only of those who reside in urban areas. Typically, a prospective voter must "register" his name, age, place of birth, present address, length of residence, and similar pertinent facts with a local registration officer.[13]

Registration systems are generally of two types. Most States now use the *permanent* system. Under it, a voter once registered remains registered unless something occurs to void his registration. Typically, a voter remains registered unless or until he moves, dies, is convicted of a crime, is committed to a mental institution, or fails to vote within a certain number of years or elections. For example, in Oregon if a voter fails to vote in any two-year period in an election at least countywide in scope, he must re-register in order to vote again.

Seven States still use the older *periodic* registration system. Under it, a person must re-register at stated intervals in order to remain a qualified voter. In South Carolina he must re-register every ten years, in Vermont before every election, and in Texas annually. In some areas in three of the States—Iowa, Louisiana, and Missouri—registration is required quadrennially; in the other parts of these States the permanent system is now used.

Most authorities recommend the permanent system, of course. It is much more convenient for both election officials and voters. But if

---

[13] Most often with an officer known as the *registrar of elections,* or with the county clerk. In some States party officials and even candidates are allowed to register new voters.

the permanent registration lists are not kept current and accurately, a large amount of "deadwood" can accumulate; and, of course, the chances for fraud are magnified. Whichever system is used, the integrity of the process must be preserved to prevent such practices as *ghost voting,* voting in the name of one who has died or moved away, or voting by *repeaters,* those who have already voted in the election.

Literacy. A literacy requirement is now found in some form in eighteen States, as the table on page 147 indicates. In some States it is merely the ability to read that is required; in other States, to read and write; and in still other States, to read, write, and "understand" a passage from the State constitution or the Constitution of the United States.

The first literacy test was adopted by Connecticut in 1855 during the "Know-Nothing" agitation against foreign immigration. Massachusetts followed in 1857, Wyoming in 1889, Mississippi in 1890, and Maine in 1891. Since then, most of the Southern States have adopted literacy tests, usually with an "understanding clause." [14] Outside the South, in addition to the States already listed, California (1894), Washington (1896), New Hampshire (1902), Arizona (1913), New York (1921), Oregon (1924), and Alaska (1959) also now have a literacy qualification of some type. North Dakota's constitution was amended in 1898 to permit a literacy test, but the necessary legislation has not been enacted to date.

In South Carolina any person who owns and has paid the taxes on property assessed at $300 or more need not satisfy the State's literacy requirement.

California's literacy test is rather typical. Each voter is required to be able to "read the Constitution in the English language and write his or her name." Usually the voter's word is taken as proof of literacy, but, unless he is physically handicapped, he must be able to sign his name when he registers.

New York has the most comprehensive literacy test. The State constitution provides that:

> ... no person shall become entitled to vote by attaining majority, by naturalization or otherwise, unless such person is also able, except for physical disability, to read and write English.

Because local election officials did not always administer the law impartially, the New York legislature gave the power to determine literacy to the Board of Regents (the State board of education). Under the New York arrangement, a new voter must be able to prove that he has had at least an eighth-grade education or he must present a certificate of literacy issued by the Board of Regents. For those who do not have the necessary formal education, the Board of Regents determines literacy by examinations which are prepared by testing experts and given annually by local school superintendents.

The literacy requirement can be—and in some places is—administered unfairly to prevent certain groups from voting. Legitimately, however, it is intended to guarantee that any qualified voter has at least some capacity to cast an intelligent or informed ballot. In recent years Congress has attempted to destroy the unfair use of the literacy requirement.

---

[14] A "grandfather clause" was added to the Louisiana constitution in 1895, and six other States (Alabama, Georgia, Maryland, North Carolina, Oklahoma, and Virginia) soon followed suit. These clauses provided that any person, or his male descendants, who had voted in the State at some time prior to the adoption of the 15th Amendment (1870) could become a legal voter without regard to a literacy or tax-paying qualification. The basic purpose was to enfranchise those whites who were otherwise disqualified by such requirements. The Supreme Court found the Oklahoma provision, the last to be adopted (1910), in conflict with the 15th Amendment in *Guinn* v. *Oklahoma* in 1915.

Selected Presidential Elections

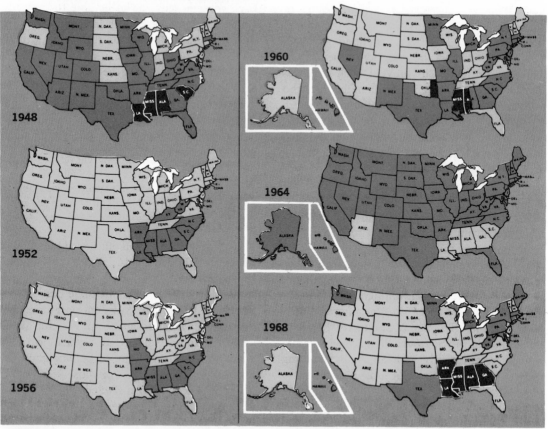

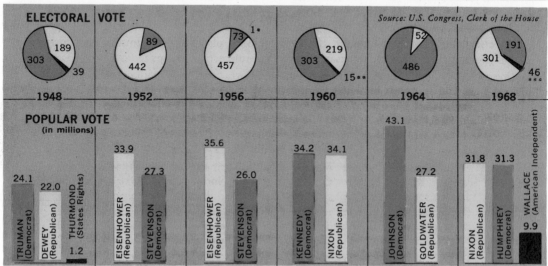

ELECTORAL VOTE

Source: U.S. Congress, Clerk of the House

- 1948: 303 / 189 / 39
- 1952: 442 / 89
- 1956: 457 / 73 / 1*
- 1960: 303 / 219 / 15**
- 1964: 486 / 52
- 1968: 301 / 191 / 46***

POPULAR VOTE
(in millions)

- 1948: TRUMAN (Democrat) 24.1 / DEWEY (Republican) 22.0 / THURMOND (States Rights) 1.2
- 1952: EISENHOWER (Republican) 33.9 / STEVENSON (Democrat) 27.3
- 1956: EISENHOWER (Republican) 35.6 / STEVENSON (Democrat) 26.0
- 1960: KENNEDY (Democrat) 34.2 / NIXON (Republican) 34.1
- 1964: JOHNSON (Democrat) 43.1 / GOLDWATER (Republican) 27.2
- 1968: NIXON (Republican) 31.8 / HUMPHREY (Democrat) 31.3 / WALLACE (American Independent) 9.9

*Cast for Walter B. Jones by an elector from Alabama

**Cast for Harry F. Byrd by 6 unpledged Alabama Democrats, 8 unpledged Mississippi Democrats, and 1 Oklahoma Republican

***One Republican elector from North Carolina cast his ballot for Wallace

American Voting Records

millions

per cent

NUMBER VOTING
IN PRESIDENTIAL
ELECTION YEARS

-125

ELIGIBLE TO VOTE

-100

DID NOT VOTE

-75

VOTED

-50

-25

1920　'28　'36　'44　'52　'60　'68

PER CENT VOTING
FOR PRESIDENT

-70

-60

-50

FOR CONGRESSMEN IN
NON-PRESIDENTIAL
ELECTION YEARS

-40

-30

-20

-10

-0

1920　'30　'40　'50　'60　'70

Source: Bureau of the Census

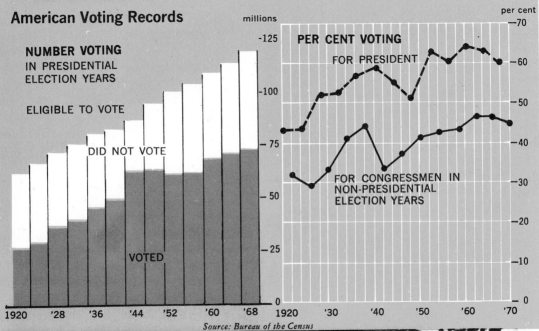

151

Tax Payment. Property ownership—as evidenced by the payment of property taxes—was once a common suffrage requirement among the States, but it has now all but disappeared.[15] Only six States—Michigan, Montana, Nevada, New Mexico, Texas, and Utah—impose a property tax qualification today; and in each of them it is used only as a qualification for voting on bond issues or special assessments. And in South Carolina, as we know, property ownership as a qualification for voting is used as an alternative to the literacy requirement.

The *poll tax,* once found throughout the South, has now disappeared altogether as a suffrage qualification.[16] Beginning with Florida in 1889, each of the eleven Southern States had by 1902 provided for it as a part of the concerted effort to disfranchise the Negro. The device proved to be of only limited effect, however; and that fact, combined with opposition to its use—from within the South as well as elsewhere in the country—led to its abandonment by most of those States. By 1966—the final year in the life of the poll tax as a suffrage qualification—it was still being used by but four States: Alabama, Mississippi, Texas, and Virginia.[17]

The 24th Amendment, ratified in 1964, prohibits the use of the poll tax—or, indeed, of *any* tax—as a qualification for participation in any aspect of the selection of federal office-holders, as we have seen.

The Supreme Court wrote *finis* to the poll tax as a qualification for participation in *any* election—State or local as well as federal—in 1966. In *Harper* v. *Virginia State Board of Elections* the Court held the Virginia tax to be

in conflict with the Equal Protection Clause of the 14th Amendment. Said the Court:

> . . . once the franchise has been granted to the electorate, lines may not be drawn which are inconsistent with the Equal Protection Clause . . . Voter qualifications have no relation to wealth nor to paying or not paying this or any other tax. Wealth, like race, creed, or color, is not germane to one's ability to participate intelligently in the electoral process.

Suffrage Disqualifications. Every State bars certain groups from voting. Most States, for example, exclude the mentally incompetent and those who have been convicted of a felony. Some States bar only those convicted of such serious crimes as murder or robbery, but in many States those guilty of such election offenses as bribery or ballot-box stuffing are also disqualified. A few States do not allow voting by anyone dishonorably discharged from the armed forces, and in some States paupers and vagrants are also disqualified.

The Civil Rights Acts of 1957, 1960, 1964, and 1968; the Voting Rights Act of 1965. The five major civil rights laws enacted by Congress in recent years [18] contains provisions designed to protect citizens in the exercise of the right to vote. Especially, they seek to implement the 15th Amendment's guarantee against denial of the suffrage on grounds of race or color.

The 1957 Civil Rights Act. This act directs the Civil Rights Commission to investigate and report to Congress on those situations in which it is claimed that suffrage has been denied, or otherwise interfered with, because of race or color. The act prohibits any person,

---

[15] The once common religious test has completely disappeared from American elections; no State has imposed such a qualification since 1810.

[16] A few States still levy a poll tax—a head or capitation tax—today; but they do so as a revenue-raising measure, *not* as a suffrage qualification. See page 690.

[17] Seven States had abandoned the poll tax several years earlier: North Carolina in 1920, Louisiana in 1934, Florida in 1937, Georgia in 1945, South Carolina in 1950, Tennessee in 1951, and Arkansas in 1964 (shortly after the ratification of the 24th Amendment).

[18] See also pages 120–121.

whether a public official or a private citizen, from intimidating or coercing another person in the exercise of his right to participate in *any* aspect of the federal election process. The Attorney General is empowered to seek injunctions in United States District Courts to prevent such practices; and any person who refuses to obey such a court order may be punished for contempt of court.

The 1960 Civil Rights Act. This act further safeguards the right to vote in federal elections. It provides that whenever a United States District Court finds that "a pattern or practice" of denial of the right to vote exists in a local area, the judge may appoint one or more *voting referees* to ascertain the facts and report to the court. The judge may then issue *certificates of eligibility* to vote to those persons he finds to be qualified. These certificates must be honored by local election officials, else such officials can be held for contempt.

The 1964 Civil Rights Act. This act is a much more extensive civil rights law than either of the earlier ones. Four of its provisions are expressly designed to protect the right to vote in federal elections without regard to race or color, and these provisions are specifically aimed at methods which have been commonly used in voter discrimination. The law provides that:

(1) No State or local registration requirement may be applied in any discriminatory manner.

(2) Minor errors in registration forms will not void a person's registration or attempt to register as a voter.

(3) All literacy tests must be given in written form, except where the Attorney General agrees that such tests are, in fact, administered fairly.

(4) Any person with a sixth-grade education shall be deemed to be literate, unless it can be shown otherwise, regardless of any provision in a State's literacy requirement.

The 1965 Voting Rights Act. This act added new strength to the drive to implement the 15th Amendment. Unlike the three earlier statutes, it deals exclusively with the right to vote, and it applies to the election process at *all* levels—State and local as well as federal. The provisions of the Voting Rights Act build and expand upon those statutes and, as the 1964 law, are aimed directly at the principal legal barriers to Negro suffrage: registration and literacy requirements.

The law provides for the appointment of a number of *voting examiners* by the United States Civil Service Commission. These federal officers are given the power to register those voters whom they find to be qualified in any State, or in any country or other local unit, in which a United States District Court has found that the vote is, in fact, denied on grounds of race or color.

Voting examiners may also be appointed to serve in any State or locale in which the Attorney General makes three findings: (1) that voter discrimination exists, (2) that a literacy test or similar device was used as a suffrage qualification as of November 1, 1964, and (3) that less than fifty per cent of the population of voting age was registered to vote on November 1, 1964, or actually did vote in the presidential election of 1964.

In any State or locale in which the Attorney General makes these three findings, the law further provides that the State's literacy test shall be suspended—and that it shall not become effective again unless the federal courts are satisfied that voter discrimination is no longer practiced in that State or locale.[19]

The constitutionality of the Voting Rights Act was upheld by the Supreme Court in 1966.

---

[19] The law also declares that no person may be denied the right to vote because of an inability to read and write in English if that person has completed the sixth grade in a school taught under the American flag but in which some language other than English was used. The provision was expressly designed to enfranchise thousands of Puerto Ricans in New York despite that State's literacy requirement; see page 149.

In its unanimous decision, in *South Carolina* v. *Katzenbach,* the Court ruled that Congress had chosen both "rational and appropriate" means for carrying out the purpose of the 15th Amendment. Said the Court:

> After enduring nearly a century of widespread resistance to the 15th Amendment, Congress has marshalled an array of potent weapons against the evil, with authority in the Attorney General to employ them effectively. We here hold that the portions of the Voting Rights Act properly before us are a valid means for carrying out the commands of the 15th Amendment. Hopefully, millions of non-white Americans will now be able to participate for the first time on an equal basis in the government under which they live.

The Civil Rights Act of 1968. Most of the provisions of this statute deal with the matter of "open housing," as we noted on page 120. It does include a section adding still more federal protection to the exercise of the right to vote, however. The 1968 law makes it a federal crime for any person to injure, intimidate, or interfere with—or attempt to injure, intimidate, or interfere with—any other person as that person votes or campaigns as a candidate in *any* public election anywhere in the United States.

NON-VOTING

We began this chapter with a comment on the critical relationship between the suffrage and democratic government—and observed that "clearly, . . . no right can be more precious to an American citizen than his right to vote." But, despite the obvious truth of this remark, there are literally millions of *non-voters* in this country—literally millions of Americans who rarely, if ever, exercise that precious right.

Scope of the Problem. The table on page 155 illustrates the major features of the non-voter problem in American elections. Notice, for example, that in 1968 there were an esti-

mated 120,006,000 persons of voting age in the United States on general election day; yet, only 73,211,562 persons—61.0 per cent—actually voted in the presidential election of 1968. That is to say, some 46,800,000 persons of voting age—nearly two out of every five—did not vote in the most recent presidential election.

Also, in 1968 only some 66,109,209 votes—55.1 per cent—were cast in the election held across the country to fill the 435 seats in the House of Representatives. That is, *more* than two out of every five persons of voting age did not vote in the congressional elections that year.[20]

Little-Recognized Aspects of the Problem. The fact that we do have a non-voter problem of considerable size in this country is widely recognized, of course. The figures just presented—and those in the table on page 155—simply detail the fact. But there are several aspects of the problem which are not widely recognized at all. For example, very few people realize that there are literally millions of non-voters *among those who vote.* Take another look at the 1968 figures: more than 7,000,000 persons who *did* vote in the presidential election did *not* vote, at the same election, for a candidate for the House of Representatives!

The "non-voting voter" aspect of the problem is not confined to federal elections, of course. In fact, the problem is a much larger one at the State and local levels. As a general rule, the further down the ballot an office is the lesser the number of votes that will be cast for it. As a quick illustration of the point: more votes are regularly cast in the presidential

---

[20] Except for the District of Columbia, the 435 congressional districts altogether occupy the same geographic area and involve the same voters as does the presidential election. As only 170,578 votes were cast in the District of Columbia in the 1968 presidential election, the fact that its voters do not elect a representative does not affect the accuracy of the comparisons here.

VOTER TURNOUT, 1920–1970

Year	Population of Voting Age [a] (Estimated)	Vote Cast For Presidential Electors		Vote Cast For U.S. Representatives	
		Number	Percent	Number	Percent
1920	61,495,000	26,748,000	43.5	25,080,000	40.8
1922	63,598,000	–	–	20,409,000	32.1
1924	66,195,000	29,086,000	43.9	26,884,000	40.6
1926	68,550,000	–	–	20,435,000	29.8
1928	70,993,000	36,812,000	51.9	33,906,000	47.8
1930	73,521,000	–	–	24,777,000	33.7
1932	75,671,000	39,732,000	52.5	37,657,000	49.8
1934	77,898,000	–	–	32,256,000	41.4
1936	80,055,000	45,643,000	57.0	42,886,000	53.6
1938	82,225,000	–	–	36,236,000	44.1
1940	84,319,000	49,891,000	59.2	46,951,000	55.7
1942	85,759,000	–	–	28,074,000	32.7
1944	90,599,000	47,969,000	52.9	45,103,000	49.8
1946	92,018,000	–	–	34,398,000	37.4
1948	94,877,000	48,691,000	51.3	45,933,000	48.4
1950	97,058,000	–	–	40,342,000	41.6
1952	98,279,000	61,551,000	62.6	57,571,000	58.6
1954	100,475,000	–	–	42,580,000	42.4
1956	103,166,000	62,027,000	60.1	58,426,000	56.6
1958	105,455,000 [b]	–	–	45,818,000 [b]	43.4
1960	107,597,000	68,839,000	64.0	64,133,000	59.6
1962	109,687,000	–	–	51,261,000	46.7
1964	112,184,000	70,644,000	63.0	65,886,000	58.7
1966	114,377,000	–	–	52,902,000	46.3
1968	120,006,000	73,211,562	61.0	66,109,209	55.1
1970 (est.)	124,018,000	–	–	56,100,000	45.1

[a] Population 18 years and over in Georgia since 1944; 18 years and over in Kentucky since 1956; 19 years and over in Alaska; 20 years and over in Hawaii.

[b] Includes Alaska which voted for a Representative in November, 1958, but did not become a State until January 3, 1959; also includes Hawaii and vote cast for Representative in July election just prior to Statehood, August 21, 1959.

than in the gubernatorial election in every State; more votes are usually cast for the governorship than for such other Statewide offices as lieutenant-governor and attorney general; more votes are cast in a county for the governorship and for other Statewide offices than for such county offices as coroner or sheriff; and so on.

There are other little-recognized facets of the non-voter problem, too. Notice from the table shown above the fact that more voters turn out for presidential elections than for the "off-year" congressional elections. The same pattern holds true among the States in terms of primary, special, and general elections. More voters regularly participate in general elections than in either primaries or special elections; and, typically, more vote in the primaries than in special elections.

Reasons for Non-Voting. Why do we have so many non-voters? Why, even in a presidential election year, do nearly four of every ten potential voters stay away from the polls?

There are many reasons. Of the approximately 46,800,000 persons of voting age who did not vote in 1968, some 5,000,000 were ill or otherwise physically handicapped on election day. Another very large group – an esti-

NO TIME FOR APATHY. Good citizens take an active interest in elections. (S. J. Ray, Kansas City Star)

Several thousand persons—perhaps 100,000 or more—have religious scruples against voting. There are others who do not vote because they are opposed to *all* candidates on the ballot, and some who are quite serious, or at least think they are, when they insist that it makes no difference to them who holds public office and makes public policy. And there are some who do not vote in some elections because of such factors as the absence of a real contest or of meaningful issues, cumbersome election procedures, a long ballot, or over-crowding at the polls.

Even with all of the reasons we've just listed, the *chief cause* for non-voting—the reason why over 20,000,000 persons did not vote in 1968 —is a quite simple one: a *lack of interest*.[21]

Those people who lack sufficient interest to vote—who are indifferent and apathetic, who just cannot be bothered—are usually uninformed. They are often unaware of even the basic and relatively simple facts concerning an election and ignorant of the precious significance of the right to vote. The fact that such persons often do stay away from the polls might well be counted among our blessings—for, surely, elections are not intended to be polls of the indifferent, the lazy, or the ignorant.

VOTER BEHAVIOR

Although many millions of potential voters do *not* go to the polls, many millions more quite obviously *do*. *How* do those who do vote tend to cast their ballots? *Why* do they vote as they do? That is, what factors tend to prompt some voters to cast their ballots most often for Republican candidates, and what factors tend to

mated 6,000,000—had recently moved and so were unable to meet local residence requirements. Another 2,500,000 million or so were travelling away from home on business or pleasure at election time. About the same number were barred from the polls as aliens, and approximately 1,000,000 persons could not vote in 1968 because of illiteracy.

Then, too, as many as 5,000,000 persons were disenfranchised by suffrage qualifications purposely drawn and administered to discriminate against them, or by "informal" local pressures designed to the same end. Another 550,000 were confined in mental institutions and 250,000 in prisons and thus could not vote.

---

[21] Studies of voter behavior indicate that sex, economic status, education, age, and place of residence all are significant influences affecting voter participation. Thus, men tend to vote more often than women, persons with higher incomes more often than those with lower incomes, persons with more education more often than those with less, persons over age thirty more often than those younger, and urban residents more often than those who live in rural areas.

prompt other voters to support Democratic candidates?

While these questions cannot be answered categorically, extensive studies of voter behavior have produced a mass of information relating to the *how* and the *why* of voting.[22] Thus, a vast amount of factual data concerning *how* voters have cast their ballots can be and has been discovered through the careful study of election returns. For example, an analysis of the votes cast in areas populated very largely by blacks or by Catholics or by high income families will show how those particular groups have voted. The reasons *why* particular groups voted as they did can be sought by interviewing representative cross-sections (samples) of voters.

Party Preference and Voter Behavior. However it may have been acquired, a person's party preference appears to be the most significant factor among the many factors which prompt people to vote as they do. As was pointed out on page 131, approximately two out of every three voters inherit their choice of party; that is, they adopt the party label worn by their parents. Then, too, better than nine out of ten married couples share the same party preference. But, as we noted earlier, many other factors — such as economic status, sectionalism, and religion — also affect party choice. So it is with voting: Family influence plays a significant role, but several other forces also shape the manner in which people vote.

Demographic Factors. Among these several other forces, various *demographic factors* — that is, population characteristics — are quite important. In summary form, the leading studies of voter behavior indicate that in gen-

eral people *tend* to vote for one party or the other in terms of certain characteristics. The following table points up the relationship of these characteristics to voting behavior:

Demographic Factors	Voting Tendency	
	Republican	Democratic
Sex		
Male		x
Female	x	
Race		
White	x	
Black		x
Religion		
Protestant	x	
Catholic		x
Jewish		x
Age		
Under 35		x
Over 55	x	
Education		
Grade school		x
High school		x
College	x	
Income		
Low		x
High	x	
Occupation		
Business, professional	x	
Other white collar	x	
Skilled, semi-skilled		x
Unskilled		x
Farm operator	x	
Type of Community		
Urban, metropolitan		x
Rural, small town	x	
Labor Union Affiliation		
Member		x
Non-member	x	

Note that the table indicates that various groups *tend* to vote in certain ways. It would be a serious mistake to assume that any given election can be predicted on the basis of the findings it summarizes. Many of the factors it includes are closely interrelated, and frequently they act in combination with one another to affect voting. For example, women tend to vote Republican — but, of course, many women do not. In fact, *black* women and *Catholic* women tend to vote more often for

[22] The systematic study of political behavior is still a distinctly infant science. Much research and considerable refinement of techniques remain to be done before questions such as these can be answered in other than generalized and highly qualified terms. A major share of the most useful work on voter behavior has been done by the Survey Research Center at the University of Michigan.

Democratic than for Republican candidates, and so do the majority of women *under* age 35. Then, too, most residents of urban areas tend to vote Democratic—but again many do not. Businessmen who live in cities usually support Republican candidates. These illustrations can be multiplied several times, which indicates that the demographic factors reported in the table cannot be regarded as mutually exclusive in their effect.

Other Factors. Any one or more of a considerable number of other factors may—and often do—exert a determining influence on voter behavior. Included among the many other factors are such things as the personalities of the opposing candidates, economic conditions at the time, local, national, or international events, sensational campaign charges, the ability of a candidate to use television as an effective campaign device, and even the marital status of a candidate. These examples can be multiplied many times, too. But to illustrate the point: Franklin D. Roosevelt's election to the Presidency in 1932 was decisively influenced by the Great Depression which plagued the nation at the time, and Dwight D. Eisenhower's election in 1952 was strongly influenced by his role as a military hero.

✳✳✳✳✳✳✳✳✳✳ CONCEPT BUILDING ✳✳✳✳✳✳✳✳✳✳

Key Concepts

No right is more precious to an American than his right to vote—the suffrage. It is not, however, a civil right, one belonging to all persons. It is, rather, a political right, one belonging to those persons who meet the qualifications set by law.

Suffrage qualifications are set by each State, subject to four specific restrictions imposed by the Constitution of the United States: the "most numerous branch" provisions and the prohibitions against denying any person the right to vote on grounds of race, color, or previous condition of servitude; on ground of sex; or, in federal elections, on ground of failure to pay a poll or other tax.

All States now have suffrage qualifications based upon three factors: United States citizenship, a minimum period of residence, and a minimum age. In the United States no alien can vote, but any State *could* permit aliens to vote if it chose to do so. In recent years over half of the States have relaxed their residence requirements to facilitate voting in presidential elections. Forty-one States set the minimum voting age at twenty-one; Georgia, Kentucky, and Alaska put it at eighteen, Massachusetts, Minnesota and Montana at nineteen, and Hawaii, Maine, and Nebraska at twenty.

Today, all except one of the fifty States—North Dakota—have registration systems to prevent fraudulent voting. Eighteen States impose a literacy qualification. The once-common property requirement has all but disappeared; and in 1966 the Supreme Court declared the imposition of a poll tax as a qualification for voting in State or local elections to be unconstitutional. Mental incompetents, convicts, and others are commonly barred from voting by the States.

Congress has passed five significant statutes in recent years—the Civil Rights Acts of 1957, 1960, 1964, and 1968 and the Voting Rights Act of 1965—to implement the guarantees of the 15th Amendment.

Millions of non-voters—persons who are or could be qualified to vote—fail to vote for a variety of reasons, but chiefly out of a lack of interest. Among the millions who *do* vote, party preference exerts a strong influence upon the way in which they do vote. But a large number of other factors also shape voter behavior.

Important Terms

Civil Rights Acts	literacy test	precinct	suffrage
demographic factors	non-voter	political right	voter behavior
floaters	periodic registration	poll tax	Voting Rights Act
ghost voting	permanent registration	repeaters	ward

Questions for Inquiry and Review

1. What is the distinction between a *civil* and a *political* right?

2. Are the terms *citizenship* and *suffrage* synonymous?

3. Does the Constitution guarantee the right to vote to any group?

4. What four specific restrictions does the Constitution place upon the States in the setting of suffrage qualifications?

5. What three bases for suffrage qualifications are common to all fifty States?

6. In what manner do a few States distinguish between native-born and naturalized citizens in terms of suffrage?

7. What is the basic justification for a residence requirement?

8. Why have several States relaxed the residence qualifications in recent years?

9. Which nine States have set the minimum voting age at less than twenty-one? What is the age in each of them?

10. On what major grounds do many persons favor reducing the voting age in all States? On what major grounds do others oppose such a move?

11. What is the essential purpose of a registration system?

12. Why do most authorities favor the permanent rather than the periodic registration system?

13. What is the legitimate purpose of a literacy requirement?

14. Why may the States not impose a poll tax as a suffrage qualification in federal elections?

15. Why may the States not impose a poll tax as a suffrage qualification in State or local elections today?

16. What groups are excluded from the suffrage by most States?

17. What is the principal purpose of the voting provisions in the recent civil rights statutes enacted by Congress?

18. Approximately how many persons voted in the last presidential election? Approximately how many persons of voting age did not vote?

19. What is the major cause for non-voting in American elections?

20. Why might the fact that many fail to vote be counted as a blessing?

21. What appears to be the most significant factor in prompting people to vote as they do in elections?

For Further Inquiry

1. Does your State have an absentee voting law? If not, do you think one should be enacted? If your State has such a law, what are its provisions?

2. What are the suffrage qualifications imposed in your State? What qualifications, if any, should be added? What qualifications should be omitted? Should any of the existing ones be modified?

3. Should suffrage be viewed as a right, a privilege, or a duty?

4. Why would you favor or oppose the enactment of a compulsory voting law in your State?

5. What do you think the late historian and novelist, H. G. Wells, meant by the following statement? "Until a man has an education, a vote is a useless and dangerous thing for him to possess." Do you agree?

6. Some people criticize the American election system for putting too much emphasis upon the *quantity* as opposed to the *quality* of the electorate. Do you think this is a just criticism?

Suggested Activities

1. Invite the registrar, county clerk, or other local election official to discuss in class your State's suffrage requirements and registration system.

2. Stage a debate or class forum on one of the following questions: (a) *Resolved,* That the voting age in all States should be set at eighteen; (b) *Resolved,* That a maximum age for voting should be set in this State; (c) *Resolved,* That voting qualifications should be uniform throughout the United States.

3. Present to the class a report on voting behavior in your State at the most recent election, giving the reasons for non-voting and your recommendations on how more people might be encouraged to vote and to vote intelligently.

4. Write a report on one of the following topics: (a) voter apathy, (b) the history of the suffrage in the United States, and (c) methods of disenfranchisement of various minority groups.

Suggested Reading

BURNS, JAMES M. and PELTASON, J. W., *Government By the People.* Prentice-Hall, 1969. Chapter 10.

"End to Literacy Tests in U.S.?" *U.S. News,* July 7, 1969.

"47 Million Will Not Vote—Why?" *U.S. News,* November 4, 1968.

HACKER, ANDREW, "If the 18-Year-Olds Get the Vote," *New York Times Magazine,* July 7, 1968.

HUMPHREY, HUBERT H., "Political Power and the Middle Class in the '70s," *U.S. News,* November 24, 1969.

MAGRATH, C. PETER, *et al., The American Democracy.* Macmillan, 1969. Chapter 7.

"Negro Voting Power: How Strong?" *U.S. News,* September 29, 1969.

ODEGARD, PETER H., *et al., The American Republic.* Harper & Row, 1969. Chapter 7.

"Pro and Con: Controversy Over the Federal Voting Rights Act," *Congressional Digest,* November, 1969.

RIBICOFF, ABRAHAM and NEWMAN, JON O., *Politics: The American Way.* Allyn and Bacon, 1969.

SORAUF, FRANK J., *Party Politics in America.* Little, Brown, 1968. Chapters 6–8.

"What If You Don't Vote?" *Time,* November 1, 1968.

NOMINATIONS AND ELECTIONS

The right of popular government is incomplete unless it includes the right of the voters not merely to choose between candidates when they have been nominated but also the right to determine who these candidates shall be.

THEODORE ROOSEVELT

✳✳✳Which is the more critically important point in the selection of public officials—nomination or final election?

✳✳✳How does the potentially divisive character of the nominating process affect the nature of our two-party system?

✳✳✳Is there an adequate alternative to popular election for choosing public policymakers in a democracy?

In a representative democracy there must be some method by which the people are able to select those who represent them. There must be some method by which those who govern with the consent of the people may be held accountable to the people. The only process we know which satisfies these needs is that of a popular election.

The popular election process is composed of two basic steps: (1) the nomination of candidates for office and (2) the selection of office-holders from among the candidates who have been nominated.

THE NOMINATING PROCESS

The importance of the first step, the nominating process, cannot be overstated. It is as fundamental to the fabric of democracy as is the final election itself. The making of nominations is the selection of those who will run for office. It provides the answer to the question:

Between or among whom are the voters to be permitted to choose?

The fact that ours is a two-party system means that in the typical election in this country the voters must choose between *two* candidates for a given office. Clearly, those who make nominations thereby place very drastic limits upon the practical exercise of the right to vote. In those areas in which one party regularly wins elections, the nominating stage is the only point at which there is usually any real contest for office.

Dictatorial systems provide abundant proof of the crucial importance of nominations. In the Soviet Union, for example, general elections are conducted in much the same manner as in the United States. The comparison is only a superficial one, however; for in the Soviet Union, as in most other dictatorships, only those candidates *acceptable* to the ruling party are *nominated*. Most often only one candidate (the Communist Party nominee) is permitted to run for each office on the ballot.

It is hardly surprising that in such a system the successful candidates usually win with majorities of ninety-eight or even ninety-nine per cent.

No single method is used for the making of all nominations in American politics. Rather, a variety of different ones is found across the country. In broad terms, these various methods can be grouped into five classifications: (1) self-announcement, (2) the caucus, (3) the delegate convention, (4) the direct primary, and (5) petition.

Self-Announcement. Sometimes called "self-nomination," self-announcement is the oldest form of the nominating process in American politics. It was first used in colonial times and is still quite common today for local offices in small towns and rural areas.

The method is a simple one: a person who desires to run for a particular office simply announces that fact. Modesty or local custom may dictate the announcement of his candidacy by someone else, but still the process is essentially the same.

Self-announcement is sometimes used by a candidate who sought but failed to secure a regular party nomination, or by a person who is otherwise dissatisfied with the nominee his party has chosen. Notice that whenever a "write-in" candidate appears in an election the process of self-announcement has been used.

The Caucus. As a nominating device,[1] a caucus is a group of like-minded persons who meet to select—that is, nominate—the candidates they will support in an upcoming election. The first caucus nominations were made during

---

[1] The term *caucus* as used here should not be confused with a caucus in a legislative body. The latter is a meeting of a party's members in the legislature to decide upon such questions as legislative organization, committee assignments, the party's position on pending bills, and the like. See page 223. The term probably comes from the Algonquin Indian word *kaw-kaw-was,* meaning "to talk over."

latter colonial times, in informal meetings of influential citizens. One of the earliest descriptions of a caucus can be found in an entry in John Adams' diary for February 1763.

> This day learned that the caucus club meets at certain times in the garret of Tom Dawes.... He has a large house, and he has a movable partition of his garret, which he takes down, and the whole club meets in one room. There they smoke tobacco till you cannot see from one end of the room to the other. There they drink flip, I suppose, and there they choose a moderator who puts questions to the vote regularly; and selectmen, assessors, collectors, firewards, and representatives are regularly chosen before they are chosen in the town.

In its early form the caucus was an informal, private meeting, attended only by a select and influential few. The growth of party organization tended to regularize it and to break down its closed character.

Independence brought with it the need to make nominations for offices above the local level. The *legislative caucus,* a meeting of a party's members in the legislature to nominate candidates for the governorship and other State offices, developed quickly and rather naturally out of the local caucus system. By 1800 both the Federalists and the Democratic-Republicans were selecting their presidential candidates in *congressional caucuses.*

The legislative and congressional caucuses were quite practical devices in their day. Transportation and communication were difficult at best, and legislators were regularly assembled at a central place. The growth of democracy produced increasing criticism of their use, however. They were widely condemned, especially in the newer States on the frontier, as closed, unrepresentative gatherings in which only a very few could participate.

Opposition to "King Caucus" reached its peak in the early 1820's. The supporters of the three leading Democratic-Republican contenders for the Presidency in the election of 1824—Andrew Jackson, Henry Clay, and

CASE STUDY

A large slice of the American electorate—and probably a majority of it—professes to believe that one "should always vote for the man, not for the party." In fact, many voters—again, probably a majority—express disdain for those who admit to "voting a straight party ticket." But a host of studies of voting behavior contradict these claims. They show instead that the single most significant, durable, and predictable factor in determining the partisan character of a vote cast by a typical voter in an American election is his party preference. Put another way, these studies show quite conclusively that the typical voter who regards himself as a Republican (or a Democrat) is *for that very reason* strongly inclined to and regularly does vote for the Republican (or Democratic) candidate. Various other factors may influence his partisan choice, of course—including such factors as the issues involved in the election, candidate personalities, the campaigns waged by the respective candidates, incumbency, name familiarity, and so on; but, again, *the* dominant factor in the typical voter's partisan choice is his party preference.

On what grounds can one build an argument in support of the "man, not party" view? On what grounds can one defend the "straight-ticket voter"? Why do you think it is true that party preference is the typically dominant factor in the making of partisan choices by the "typical" voter in American elections?

John Quincy Adams—boycotted their party's congressional caucus. In fact, Jackson and his supporters made the use of the device a leading campaign issue. The other major aspirant, William H. Crawford of Georgia, was the caucus nominee. He ran a poor third in the electoral college balloting, and the reign of "King Caucus" at the national level was ended. The caucus system died out at the State level in a very short time, as well, to be replaced by the delegate convention. Caucuses are still used to make local nominations in some parts of the country, especially in the New England States, where they are open to all party members and bear only a faint resemblance to the original device.

The Delegate Convention. As the caucus method collapsed, it gave way to the delegate convention system. The first national convention to select a presidential candidate was held by a minor party, the Anti-Masons, in Baltimore

in 1831. Both the Democrats and the Whigs picked up the practice in 1832, and all major party presidential nominees have been chosen in conventions since that time. By 1840 the delegate convention system had come into use for nearly all nominations in American politics.

On paper the system seems ideally suited to representative government. Under it, a party's members meet in a local caucus to pick candidates for local office and, at the same time, to select delegates to represent them at a county convention.[2] At the county convention the delegates choose candidates for the various county offices and also select delegates to the next rung in the convention ladder, usually the

---

[2] The local meetings in the convention system are sometimes called the *primary* (that is, first meeting), but this term should not be confused with the *direct primary* (see page 164).

State convention. At the State convention the delegates selected at the county conventions nominate the party's candidates for State office and also select delegates to the national convention. At the national convention the State delegates pick the party's presidential and vice presidential candidates.

In the theory of the convention system, the will of the party's rank and file membership is supposed to be channeled upward through each of its levels. Actual practice soon demonstrated the shortcomings of the theory, however. The system easily proved to be subject to control by party bosses. By manipulating the selection of delegates, especially in county conventions, they were able to control the system quite handily.

The caliber of conventions at all levels deteriorated, especially in the late 1800's. The depths to which some declined is shown by this description of the delegates to a Cook County convention held in Chicago in 1896:

> Of the delegates those who had been on trial for murder numbered 17; sentenced to the penitentiary for murder or manslaughter and served sentence, 7; served terms in the penitentiary for burglary, 36; served terms in the penitentiary for picking pockets, 2; served terms in the penitentiary for arson, 1; ... keepers of gambling houses, 7; keepers of houses of ill fame, 2; convicted of mayhem, 3; ex-prize fighters, 11; poolroom proprietors, 2; saloon keepers, 265; [public officeholders, 148;] ... total delegates, 723.

The delegate convention system, originally hailed as a vast improvement on the caucus, proved to be a poor substitute. Its evils were a major target of the great reform movement which swept the country at the turn of the century, and it was soon replaced by the direct primary as the principal nominating method.

Although the system has been practically abandoned for the making of congressional, State, and local nominations, no adequate substitute for it has been found at the presidential level; and it is still used in some States.

The Direct Primary. The direct primary is the most widely used method for the making of nominations in American politics today. It is an intra-party nominating election; that is, it is an election at which the party's candidates are chosen by a vote of the party's membership.

The origins of the primary are obscure, but the first one was apparently held by the Democratic Party in Crawford County, Pennsylvania, in 1842. Its use spread gradually to various other locales. Wisconsin enacted the first Statewide direct primary law in 1903, and several other States promptly followed its lead.

All fifty States now provide for its use for the selection of candidates for some or all State and local offices. In most States it is the device required by law for the choice of congressional candidates, as well.[3]

Although the primary is a party nominating election, it is closely regulated by law in most States. The State usually sets the date upon which the parties hold their primaries, commonly in May or June before the general election in November. The State usually conducts the primary, too, providing the ballots, paying the election officials, using its official registration lists, and otherwise policing the process.

Two basic forms of the direct primary are in use today: the *closed* and the *open* primary.

The Closed Primary. Now found in forty States,[4] the closed primary is a nominating election in which *only* those who are actually members of the party may participate. It is *closed* to all other persons.

---

[3] The convention system is still used to select congressional candidates in Delaware, Indiana, and Connecticut. In Connecticut, however, any aspirant who receives at least one-fifth of a convention's vote may demand a primary to make the final selection of a candidate for the office he has sought. In New York, *all* candidates for Statewide office are nominated by each party's State central committee; but any aspirant with at least one-fourth of the vote of his party's committee may demand a primary.

[4] In all States *except* those cited in footnote 5.

In most of the closed primary States party membership is established by registration (see page 148). When the voter appears at the polls on primary election day, his registration is checked, and he is then handed the ballot of the party in which he is registered.

In some States, especially those of the South, party membership is established through the use of the "challenge system." Under this scheme any voter who doubts the party loyalty of another may challenge the latter's right to vote in the party's primary. The challenged voter is then required to pledge his intention to support the party's candidate at the upcoming general election.

In any of the closed primary States a person who does not wish to disclose his party preference may nonetheless register to vote. But he cannot vote in the primaries; they are *party* nominating elections. He may vote in the general election and any special elections, of course.

The Open Primary. Although it was the original form of the direct primary, the open primary is now used in only nine States.[5] It is a nominating election in which *any* qualified voter may participate. No voter is required to declare his party preference at registration or at any other time. When the voter appears at the polling place on primary election day, he is handed the ballots of *all* parties holding primaries (usually there are only two, the Republican and the Democratic parties). In the privacy of the voting booth the voter then picks the party in whose primary he wants to participate and marks its ballot.

A unique and interesting variation of the open primary is used in the State of Washington, where it is known as the "wide-open" or "blanket" primary. There, the voter is handed only one ballot, but it contains the names of *all* those who are seeking nominations in *each* party. The voter may vote in a single party's

Party primary contests are sometimes as hotly waged as any election between parties. Candidates spend much time campaigning throughout the State in their efforts to persuade the voters that they be chosen the party's nominee. (Steve Schapiro, Black Star)

primary, or he may switch back and forth office to office among the parties. For example, he may vote to nominate a candidate for governor in the Republican primary, then a candidate for the United States Senate in the Democratic primary, and so on down the ballot.

The Pros and Cons of the Two Primaries. Those who favor the closed rather than the open form of the direct primary do so because, they argue, the closed primary: (1) prevents the members of one party from "raiding" the other's primary in the hope of nominating weak candidates,[6] (2) tends to make a candidate more responsible to his party's members, and (3) tends to make one more conscious of his role as a voter because he must choose between the parties in order to participate in the primaries.

---

[5] Alaska, Idaho, Michigan, Minnesota, Montana, North Dakota, Utah, Vermont, Washington, and Wisconsin.

[6] The practice of "raiding" became so common in the early years of the direct primary that the closed form was developed to prevent it.

Those who prefer the open primary usually do so because they believe that it: (1) provides greater protection for the secrecy of the ballot since no one need divulge his party preference and (2) permits independents to participate in the nominating process.

The Run-Off Primary. In most States a candidate needs only a plurality of the votes cast in the primary in order to be nominated.[7] In ten States,[8] however, a majority is required. If no one receives a majority in a particular race, a second or "run-off" primary is held a few weeks later. In the run-off primary the top two contestants face one another, and the winner becomes the party's nominee.

Cross-Filing. In a few States one may "cross-file"; that is, he may seek (file for) a primary nomination by more than one party. Although seldom used today, the practice makes it possible for a candidate to run in the general election as the nominee of both major parties—in effect, to run unopposed.

Nonpartisan Primaries. In most States such officials as the State Superintendent of Public Instruction, other school officials, judges, and city and town officers are elected on a nonpartisan ballot.

The nominations for such officials are also made on a nonpartisan basis. Those who seek nonpartisan offices gain a place on the primary ballot by submitting petitions, paying fees, or both. If one of the contenders for a particular office gains a clear majority in the primary, his name usually appears unopposed on the general election ballot—but is subject to write-in opposition, of course. If there is no majority winner in the primary, the names of the top two contenders for an office are then placed on the general election ballot.

Evaluation of the Direct Primary. The direct primary, open or closed, is a *party nominating election.* It is intended to give the party members themselves a direct voice in the selection of the party's candidates for office. Although it has not proved a panacea for all of the ills of the convention system, it does offer the party voters an *opportunity* to defeat a conspicuously unfit candidate or to nominate a conspicuously well-qualified one. No primary or general election machinery, however, can take the place of intelligence and public spirit. The direct primary places much of the responsibility for good government squarely upon the shoulders of the voter.

Only a very few people seriously advocate abolishing the direct primary. But the device does have some weaknesses. For example, it often costs a party's candidate a great deal of money to run first in the primary and again in the general election. The primary also adds to the voter's burden. Some primary ballots are so long that the voter faces a frightful task.

The Presidential Primary. Some form of the presidential primary is now provided for in nineteen States[9] and in the District of Columbia. In essence, this device is one which permits each party's voters to elect some or all of the party's delegates to the party's national convention.

---

[7] Iowa and South Dakota require a candidate to win at least thirty-five per cent of the votes cast in his primary contest; if no aspirant wins that many votes in a given race, the party must then nominate a candidate for that office by convention.

[8] Alabama, Arkansas, Florida, Georgia, Louisiana, Mississippi, North Carolina, Oklahoma, South Carolina, and Texas. In Virginia a run-off primary is held only if the second highest person asks for one. A run-off primary is held in Tennessee only in cases of ties.

[9] Alabama, California, Florida, Illinois, Indiana, Massachusetts, Nebraska, New Hampshire, New Jersey, New York, Ohio, Oregon, Pennsylvania, South Dakota, West Virginia, and Wisconsin. Maryland, New Mexico, and Rhode Island have since provided for them in 1972. See page 294.

Oregon adopted the first presidential primary law in 1910. By 1916 nearly half of the States had provided for its use, but several States have abandoned it in the years since then.

The specific details of the presidential primary vary greatly among the States in which it is used—even in the matter of dates, for example. Thus, New Hampshire slated the first one in 1968 (March 12); the others were held over the next three months, with Illinois holding the final one on June 11.

Thirteen States [10] provide a separate vote— a *presidential preference primary*—to enable voters to express a preference among the contenders for their party's presidential nomination. To illustrate: In 1968 Oregon's Republican voters indicated a preference for Richard Nixon, and all of the eighteen delegates they also selected were bound to support him at the Republican National Convention. At the same time the State's Democratic voters expressed their preference for Eugene McCarthy, and thirty-three delegates to the Democratic National Convention were pledged to him.

In four of the States [11] the voter is not able to indicate his preference among the presidential hopefuls in a separate balloting. But, in each of them, the candidates for delegates may indicate on the ballot whom *they* support as the party's presidential nominee. Thus, although no *preference* primary is held in these States, the voter still can indicate his choice for the presidential nomination by voting for those delegates who prefer his choice.

---

[10] Illinois, Indiana, Maryland, Massachusetts, Nebraska, New Hampshire, New Jersey, New Mexico, Oregon, Pennsylvania, Rhode Island, West Virginia, Wisconsin. Indiana and New Mexico hold only a preference primary; the delegates are actually chosen at the parties' State conventions. Wisconsin is the only one of these States in which the presidential primary is an *open* one (see page 165); Wisconsin and New Mexico permit voters to cast a "no" vote in the preference poll to indicate that they prefer *none* of a party's presidential aspirants.

[11] California, Florida, Ohio, and South Dakota.

In the remaining two States (Alabama and New York) and the District of Columbia neither the presidential aspirants' names nor the preferences of the candidates for delegate are included on the ballot. Even so, it is commonly known which candidate for delegate favors which presidential aspirant.

In several of these States *only some* of the delegates to the national conventions are selected in the primaries. The rest are chosen by the parties at their State conventions or through their State central committees. For example, in Illinois two delegates are chosen in the primaries held in each of the twenty-four congressional districts in the State, and whatever additional delegates there may be are selected by each party at its State convention. In New York and Pennsylvania district delegates are picked in the primaries held in the States' congressional districts and at-large delegates by the State central committees.

Many urge the choosing of *all* delegates to the national conventions in presidential primaries. Some would abolish the national conventions altogether, or keep them only to draft party platforms. These people favor nominating each party's presidential and vice-presidential candidates at a nationwide presidential primary. As matters now stand, not quite half of all delegates to each party's national convention are chosen in presidential primaries.

Those who oppose the presidential primary device do so for two major reasons. First, they argue that campaigning for a State's delegates and preference vote balloons the already high costs of a presidential campaign. Secondly, they claim that primary fights often inflict party wounds that are difficult to heal in time for the general election campaign against the other party. Another argument, although seldom put into words by the opponents, is that the presidential primary tends to take the choice of the party's nominee out of the hands of the party's leaders.

Four States—Maryland, Nebraska, Oregon, and Wisconsin—require that the names of *all* leading contenders for a party's presidential nomination appear on the ballot. In the other States a candidate may or may not enter the primary, depending on whether or not he thinks he has a chance to win. Because of this situation, the value of the presidential preference vote is considerably reduced.

Nomination by Petition. One other general method for making nominations is in use: the nomination of candidates by petitions signed by a specified number of qualified voters in the election district involved. The details of the method vary widely from State to State, but in most States this is the method provided for the nomination of independent and minor party candidates. It is also being used more and more for local offices, especially in nonpartisan elections.

THE ELECTION PROCESS

Once candidates have been nominated, they must face their opposition and the voters at the general election. In most areas in the South, and in some northern States such as New Hampshire and Vermont, however, the real contest *usually* comes in the primaries; the dominant party's nominees are almost always certain to win in the general election.[12]

Extent of Federal Control. Nearly all elections in the United States are held to choose officers in approximately 80,000 units of State and local government. It is quite natural, then, that most of the laws regulating the election process are State laws.

The Constitution, however, does give Congress the power to fix the "time, places, and manner of holding elections" of members of Congress.[13] Congress also has the power "to determine the time of choosing" presidential electors and to set the date for the casting of their electoral ballots.[14]

Congress has set the date for congressional elections as the first Tuesday following the first Monday in November of every even-numbered year. It has set the same date every fourth year for the holding of presidential elections. Thus, in 1972 the congressional and presidential elections are set for November 7, and the congressional elections in 1970 were held on November 3.[15]

Congress has also required the use of secret ballots and permitted the use of voting machines in federal elections. It has prohibited various corrupt practices, regulated campaign financing, and provided for the protection of the right to vote in any primary or general election involved in the selection of federal officeholders (see pages 137–139, 152–154).

---

[12] This is not always true, of course. One-party domination tends to be more complete at the local than at the State or, especially, at the national level. For example, despite the traditional voting pattern in the South, the Republicans carried four States in the South (Florida, North Carolina, South Carolina, and Virginia) in the 1968 presidential election, and a number of Southern Republicans now (1971) hold seats in Congress. Similarly, both New Hampshire and Vermont went to the Democrats in the 1964 presidential election, and the Democrats held the governorship in each of these States from 1963 to 1969.

[13] Article I, Section 4, Clause 1.

[14] Article II, Section 1, Clause 4.

[15] Congress has made an exception for Alaska which may, if it chooses, elect its congressional delegation and cast its presidential vote on a different date. Thus far, however, Alaska has followed the regular November date. Up to 1960 Maine was also allowed to hold its congressional elections on another date, early in September; the practice gave rise to the often-quoted, but not-too-often accurate, saying: "As Maine goes, so goes the nation." See page 205.

All other matters concerning procedures in national elections, and the entire system of choosing the more than 500,000 elective State and local officials, are dealt with in the laws of the individual States.

When Elections Are Held. Most States hold their elections for State offices on the same date Congress has set for national elections—in November of each even-numbered year. Some States, however, have chosen other dates. For example, Kentucky, Mississippi, New Jersey, and Virginia hold their State elections in November of the odd-numbered years. In Louisiana State elections are held on the Tuesday after the third Monday in April of every fourth year. Alaska's constitution permits the legislature to fix the date at its discretion. City and other local election dates differ from State to State. Commonly they are held in the spring.

When State and local elections are held on some date other than that set for national elections, many feel that the voters will pay more attention to State and local candidates and issues. Their votes are not so liable to be influenced by their Republican or Democratic choices for national office.

How Elections Are Held. For each voting district or precinct into which the county or city is divided, the clerk, board of election commissioners, or some other designated official provides a polling place, equipped with voting booths, a ballot box or voting machines, and poll books listing the voters. On election day the polls are open during certain hours—commonly from 8 A.M. until 8 P.M.

Each polling place is in the charge of judges of election who pass upon a voter's qualifications. The judges are assisted by clerks. They open and close the polls, count the ballots, and certify the results to the proper officials (usually the clerk or board of elections).

A "watcher" from each party is permitted to be present at the polling place. He may challenge any person whom he does not believe to be qualified to vote, checks to be sure that

Richard Nixon shunned debates with his opponents in the 1968 presidential campaign, but made good use of his many appearances on television to reach large numbers of voters throughout the nation. (M. S. Stern, Black Star)

as many as possible of his own party members get to the polls, and watches to see that the votes cast are counted fairly.

How Ballots Are Cast. When the voter enters the polling place, he finds himself in a room in which no one else is allowed except election officers, party watchers, perhaps a policeman, and other voters. The voter gives his name; if it is found in the poll book, he is then handed a ballot. This he carries into an enclosed booth. After marking it, he folds the ballot, leaves the booth, and goes to the ballot box to deposit his ballot for counting.

In most States the ballot has two perforated stubs at the top, each containing the ballot's number. When the voter is handed his ballot, one of the stubs is torn off. Then, after the voter has marked his ballot but before he deposits it in the ballot box, the second stub is torn off. By comparing the two stubs, the election judges can be certain that the voter is casting the same ballot he was handed.

The use of the ballot stubs prevents the working of the so-called "Tasmanian dodge." This fraudulent scheme is still tried occasionally in American elections, but it cannot work in elections in which stubs are used. The scheme involves the stealing of an official ballot before the polls open or the printing of a counterfeit one. The stolen or counterfeit ballot is marked for the candidates those working the scheme wish to see elected. It is then handed to a bribed voter who presents himself at the polls where he receives an official ballot. In the privacy of the polling booth he switches the ballots. The illegal ballot is dropped into the ballot box, and the official one is carried outside. The newly stolen ballot is marked as the first one, handed to another bribed voter, and cast in the same manner. The practice is carried on all day. Each bribed voter is paid only *after* he brings back a newly stolen ballot.

The Ballot. During most of our nation's early history voting was commonly by voice (*viva voce*). This encouraged vote-buying and intimidation and was gradually abandoned by the States for paper ballots.

The first paper ballots were unofficial ones prepared by the voters themselves. Then candidates and political machines began to print ballots and pay voters to cast them. Even after vote-buying was made a crime, the different parties printed their ballots on different colored paper. Thus, voting was just as public as by previous methods. A vote-buyer, friend, or employer could still know how a person voted from the color of the ballot used.

The Australian Ballot. The secret ballot was first devised in Australia. It found its way to the United States via Great Britain. The Kentucky legislature first adopted it in 1888 for use in municipal elections in Louisville, and in 1889 Massachusetts adopted it for all elections. It is used, in slightly varying form, in all States today.

The Australian ballot has three essential features: (1) It is printed at public expense.

(2) It contains the names of all the candidates in the election.   (3) It is voted in secret.   There are two basic types of the Australian ballot now in use: (1) the "office-group" ballot and (2) the "party-column" ballot.

The Office-Group Ballot.   The office-group ballot is also known as the Massachusetts ballot because of its early use in that State.   It is the original form of the Australian ballot and is now used in nearly half of the States.   This type of ballot is arranged so that the names of all candidates for a particular office are grouped together.   Originally the names of the various candidates for an office were printed in alphabetical order.   Most States now rotate the names because there is a psychological advantage in having one's name at the top of the list.

The Party-Column Ballot. The party-column ballot is also known as the Indiana ballot because it was first used in that State.   Today a little over half of the States use it.   On this type of ballot the names of each party's candidates for all offices are arranged in a vertical column under the party's name.   Usually there is a circle at the top of each party's column where, by marking an "X" in the circle, a voter may vote for all of the candidates of that party.   Because the party-column ballot makes "bullet" or "straight-ticket" voting much easier, most authorities favor the use of the office-group ballot.

Sample Ballots.   Sample ballots, clearly marked as such, are commonly available in most States.   In some States they are mailed to all voters before an election or are printed in the newspapers.   Of course, these cannot be used for voting, but they do help voters to prepare intelligently for an election.[16]

---

[16] First in Oregon, and now in about half of the States, an official *Voter's Pamphlet* is mailed to all voters before an election. This pamphlet lists all candidates and measures which will appear on the ballot.   In several States each candidate is allowed space to present his qualifications, and the proponents and opponents of each measure are allowed space to present their arguments.

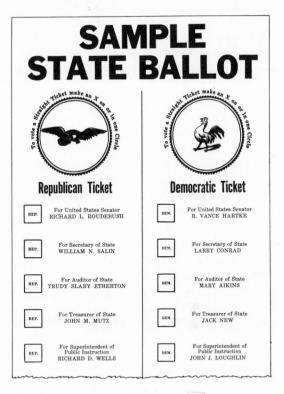

The party-column ballot (above) differs from the office-group ballot (shown on page 170) in that it lists each party's candidates in a column under their respective party's name. This type of ballot was first used in Indiana.

The Long Ballot. Ballots are often so long, contain so many names and measures, that even the most conscientious and well-informed voters have difficulty with them.   Obviously, the longer the ballot is, the greater the likelihood of blind or ignorant voting;   and the greater possibility, too, of nonvoting or corruption.

Ballots could be made much shorter if a number of elective officers were to be made appointive instead.   For example, there is little reason to elect such local officers as county surveyor, coroner, or chief of police.   These officials, and many others commonly elected today, do not *make* policy; they simply *administer* policies made by others.   For good government the rule should be: *Elect* policy-making officers and allow them to *appoint* those who only administer the policies they make.

Voting Machines. Thomas Edison secured the first American patent for a voting machine, and his invention was first used in an election in Lockport, Pennsylvania, in 1892. Since then, the use of voting machines has spread to approximately three-fourths of the States.

As voting machine laws are usually permissive, the devices are often used in some precincts or counties but not in others within the same State. Only a few States—New York and Rhode Island, for example—*require* their use in densely populated areas. All told, however, at least a third of the votes in national elections today are cast on them.

The typical voting machine serves as its own booth. The voter pulls a lever which closes the curtain and simultaneously unlocks the machine. He then pulls down a small lever over the name of each candidate he favors; or,

in most States using the party-column ballot, he may use a master lever to vote for all the candidates of one party.

Space is provided for measures as well as candidates, with *yes* and *no* levers for each. The voting machine is so constructed that the voter cannot pull more than one lever for each office or measure. Once all the levers are in the position the voter wants, he opens the curtain. This action records his vote and also clears the machine for use by the next voter.

The use of voting machines makes the prevention of election frauds much easier than is the case with paper ballots. Voting machines also make it impossible for the voter to spoil his ballot by mismarking it. Their automatic counters provide quick, accurate returns and thus eliminate the need for time-consuming, expensive, and not always accurate counting boards. Voting machines handle voters so conveniently that precincts can be consolidated and fewer election officials are needed.

The voting machine makes it impossible for the voter to "scratch" (spoil, improperly mark, or damage) his ballot. A vote on a voting machine is recorded mechanically by the voter himself as he leaves the machine. Thus, the vote is accurate and not subject to human errors. Note how the ballot is arranged on this model. (Talbot Lovering)

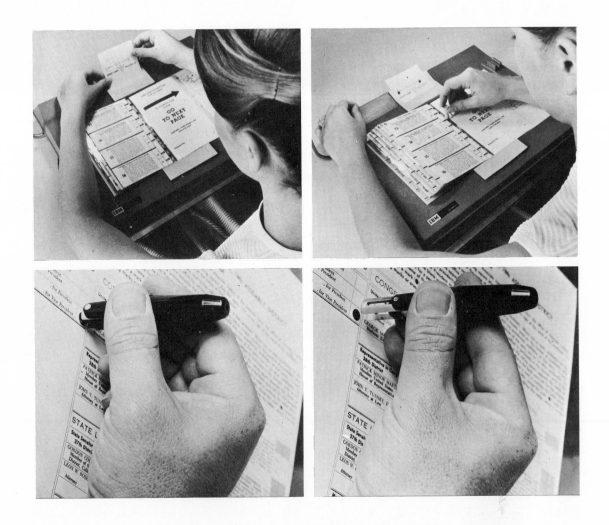

These voting systems are designed to speed up and reduce the costs of the election process. Punch card ballots (upper), on which the voter uses a stylus to punch holes opposite the choice of candidates, are quickly tabulated by a computer when the polls close. Paper ballots (lower) are marked with a special self-inking marking device. Electronic scanners "read" the black dots inside the voting squares and tabulate the results. (Upper, International Business Machines; lower, Cubic Corporation)

The voting machines in common use today are rather expensive, costing about $1800 apiece. Although they pay for themselves in time by reducing election costs, the initial expense often discourages their purchase. Then, too, they are quite bulky and present storage, moving, and maintenance problems. Some voters, especially older people and residents of rural areas, also complain that voting machines are too complicated and confusing. Clearly, voting machines are most useful in heavily populated areas where great numbers of voters must be handled at each polling place.

Electronic data processing techniques have been applied to the voting process in recent years—first in California and Oregon and now in several other States. To date, EDP applications have followed two general lines: (1) use of electronic scanners to "read" paper ballots marked with sensitized pencils, and (2) use of ballot cards punched by voters and then tabulated by high-speed computers (see illustration, page 173).

Proportional Representation. *Proportional representation,* often called PR, is a system of voting which attempts to give parties or groups of voters representation in a legislative body according to their actual voting strength. Several different types of PR are used in different countries of the world. One form, the Hare system, has been used in a few American cities — including New York (from 1937 to 1947) and Cincinnati (from 1924 to 1957) — but is now found only in Cambridge, Massachusetts.

Under the Hare system several representatives are elected from a single district. The voter marks his ballot by indicating his choices among the candidates. He makes as many rankings as there are representatives to be chosen. For example, if there are nine seats on the city council to be filled, the voter indicates his first through ninth choices among the candidates on the ballot.

The counting process is complicated, difficult, and not easily understood by the average voter. First, an "election quota" must be established; that is, the smallest number of votes a candidate needs in order to be elected. The quota is established by dividing the number of ballots cast by the number of candidates to be elected plus one. For example, take a PR election in which there are nine city council seats to be filled and there are 100,000 votes cast. The quota would be 10,001. The quota of 10,001 would be reached this way:

$$9 \text{ seats} + 1 = 10 \overline{)100,000 \text{ votes}} \quad \frac{10,000 + 1 = 10,001 \text{ quota}}{}$$

The ballots are then sorted according to first choices. All candidates having 10,001 or more first-choice votes are declared elected. Whatever votes these candidates have beyond 10,001 are credited to the second choices indicated on each of the ballots involved. This process of transferring votes is carried on until all nine seats are filled. If necessary, the candidates with the fewest number of first-choice votes are eliminated and their ballots distributed according to second choices.

Three major advantages are claimed for PR: (1) It guarantees minority representation. (2) It means that every ballot cast goes to elect someone and is not "wasted." (3) It cuts down the power of small but highly organized political machines. PR is most often criticized for it: (1) increases the number of groups or parties in a legislative body and thus promotes instability in government and (2) is too complicated.

The Recall. A *recall* is an election through which the voters may remove a public official before the end of his elected term. It originated in Switzerland in the nineteenth century and was first adopted in the United States in Los Angeles in 1903. The first State to apply it to all offices was Oregon in 1908. Today it is available Statewide in thirteen States.[17] Some 2000 cities and counties in over three-fourths of the States also have the recall.

A recall election is brought about through the circulation of petitions. A certain number of registered voters must sign the recall petitions. The required number varies from State to State, but it is usually twenty-five per cent of the votes cast at the last general election in the district served by the officer involved.

In some parts of the country recalls are not uncommon at the city and county level. They are rare at the State level, however. The only governor ever to be recalled was Governor Lynn Frazier of North Dakota, who was recalled in 1921. The very next year he was elected to the United States Senate!

---

[17] Alaska, Arizona, California, Colorado, Idaho, Kansas, Louisiana, Michigan, Nevada, North Dakota, Oregon, Washington, and Wisconsin.

Key Concepts

Both the nomination and the election process are fundamental to democracy.

Five different methods of nomination have been and are used in the United States: (1) *self-announcement,* the earliest method used and still common at the local level in many parts of the country; (2) the *caucus,* developed in colonial times, widely used in the early years of our national history, and used at the local level today in some parts of the country; (3) the *delegate convention,* which supplanted the caucus during the 1830's in national politics and is still used to select presidential and vice presidential candidates and for some offices in a few States; (4) the *direct primary,* which developed at the turn of the century as a substitute for the ills of the convention system and is the most widely used method today; and (5) *nomination by petition,* which is used in many local areas and by independent and minor party candidates at the State level.

There are two forms of the direct primary: (1) the *closed primary,* in which only party members may participate, and (2) the *open primary,* in which any qualified voter may participate. *Nonpartisan primaries* are used to nominate candidates for nonpartisan offices. *Run-off primaries* are commonly used in Southern States where a nominee must have a majority of votes for party nomination.

Some form of the *presidential primary* is now used in nineteen States and the District of Columbia; in most of those States a party's voters elect some or all of the national convention delegates, and in twelve they may also indicate the aspirant they favor for the party's presidential nomination.

The National Government has only limited control over the election process; it is mostly regulated by State law.

National elections are held on the first Tuesday following the first Monday in November in even-numbered years in every State. Most State elections are held at the same time. Local elections are commonly held in the spring.

Elections are conducted in precincts, each polling place being supervised by election judges. "Watchers" from each party are usually permitted in the polling place along with the judges, their clerks, and the voters.

In all States today the voter casts the Australian ballot, which is of either the *office-group* or the *party-column* type. Voting machines are now used in more populous areas of nearly all States.

Most ballots used in American elections are much too long; long ballots tend to confuse the voter and lead to blind voting.

Proportional representation (PR) is a complicated system of voting intended to guarantee minority representation in a legislative body. It has been used in local elections in a few places in this country.

A *recall* election is one at which a public official may be removed from office before his term has expired. It is provided for Statewide in thirteen States and in some 2000 cities and counties in the nation.

Important Terms

Australian ballot
"blanket" primary
caucus
challenge system
closed primary
cross-filing

delegate convention
direct primary
election
nomination
office-group ballot

open primary
party-column ballot
presidential primary
presidential preference
   primary

proportional representa-
   tion
recall
run-off primary
Tasmanian dodge
write-in candidate

Questions for Inquiry and Review

1. Why is the nominating stage so crucial an aspect of the election process?

2. What is the oldest method for the making of nominations in American politics?

3. What nominating method is employed whenever a write-in candidate appears?

4. What aspect of the nominating caucus made it subject to heavy criticism?

5. Why may it be said that in theory the convention system seems ideally suited to a representative system of government?

6. What is the most commonly used nominating method in American politics today?

7. What is the chief distinction between the open and the closed primaries?

8. What deficiency in the open primary led to developing the closed primary?

9. What is the essential purpose of the presidential primary? The presidential preference primary?

10. Why is the large bulk of electoral law in the nation State law rather than federal law?

11. When are most national and State elections held?

12. Why do many favor separate dates for national and for State and local elections?

13. How do most States prevent the use of the Tasmanian dodge today?

14. What are the three essential features of the Australian ballot?

15. How do the office-group ballot and the party-column ballot differ?

16. Why do most students of government favor the office-group ballot over the party-column ballot?

17. Why is the use of some type of voting machine usually held to be much better than the use of paper ballots in larger communities?

18. What dangers does the long ballot produce?

19. How might ballots be shortened?

20. What is the purpose of proportional representation?

21. What are the major advantages claimed for PR? What are the criticisms?

22. What is the purpose of a recall election?

For Further Inquiry

1. What did the Nazi political scientist Ernst Huber mean when he wrote that "it is not decisive for the character of an elected representative body who possesses the suffrage, but, to a much higher degree, who determines the candidates put up before the electorate"?

2. "We cannot make the voters all go into politics, but by a drastic reduction in the number of elective offices we can make politics come to the voters." What do you think is meant by this statement?

3. What offices are elective in your State, county, and city? Do you think any of them should be made appointive instead? If so, why?

4. H. G. Wells once wrote: "Until a man has an education, a vote is a useless and dangerous thing for him to possess." Does the fact that

one has a formal education necessarily mean that he will vote intelligently? Is the vote actually a "useless thing" in the hands of the uneducated?

5. Which in reality is the more important in our two-party system, the nominating of candidates or the electing of candidates? Why?

6. Why do party professionals usually favor the use of the party-column rather than the office-group form of the ballot?

7. Why does the fact that we have a federal system of government in the United States mean that our election system is a very complex one?

8. What arguments can you present in opposition to the author's contention (on pages 171–172) that: "For good government the rule should be: *Elect* policy-making officers and allow them to *appoint* those who only administer the policies they make"?

Suggested Activities

1. Stage a debate or class forum on one of the following: (a) *Resolved,* That this State should adopt the open (or closed) primary; (b) *Resolved,* That since PR is an unfair, unrealistic system of electing members to a legislative body, it has no place in American politics.

2. Prepare a bulletin board display of sample ballots from elections held in your State. (Contact local election officials or the office of the Secretary of State.)

3. Invite an election official to speak to the class on the conduct of elections in your locale.

4. From your State's election code, draw a flow chart of the steps involved in the casting and counting of ballots in elections in your State.

5. Write a report on one of the following topics: (a) a recent State nominating convention, (b) the history of the caucus, (c) historical highlights of national conventions.

6. Invite a recent candidate (either a successful or an unsuccessful one) to describe his campaign experiences to the class.

7. Stage a class forum or debate on one or more of the following topics: (a) *Resolved,* That this State should (adopt or abandon) the direct primary as its basic nominating device; (b) *Resolved,* That this State should (provide for or abandon) the recall of public officers; (c) *Resolved,* That this State should adopt the (office-group or party-column) ballot for use in all partisan elections.

Suggested Reading

COTTER, CORNELIUS P. (ed.), *Practical Politics in the United States.* Allyn and Bacon, 1969.

JAMES, JUDSON L., *American Political Parties.* Pegasus, 1969.

LEUTHOLD, DAVID A., *Electioneering in a Democracy: Campaigns for Congress,* Wiley, 1968.

McGOVERN, SENATOR GEORGE P., "Politics and the Presidency," *Harper's,* January, 1970.

NICHOLS, LOUIS, "The Battle Against Vote Frauds," *Reader's Digest,* July, 1969.

POWLEDGE, FRED, "The Flight From City Hall," *Harper's,* November, 1969.

"Republican Strategy for '70 Election," *U.S. News,* November 24, 1969.

RIBICOFF, ABRAHAM and NEWMAN, JON O., *Politics: The American Way.* Allyn and Bacon, 1969.

WHITE, THEODORE H., "The Making of the President 1968," *Life,* July 11 and 18, 1969.

WICKER, TOM, "The Place Where America Was Radicalized," *New York Times Magazine,* August 24, 1969.

10
PUBLIC OPINION AND PRESSURE GROUPS

✦✦✦ In a democracy are there any "right" answers to public policy questions?

✦✦✦ Do public opinion polls contribute to or do they threaten the effectiveness of representative government?

✦✦✦ Are pressure groups indispensable to democratic government?

Public opinion sets bounds to every government, and is the real sovereign in every free one.

JAMES MADISON

The concept of popular sovereignty is basic to the entire fabric of American government. In this country we believe that the people *should* and *do* rule — that the people are the only source for any and all governmental power and that the primary task of government is that of translating the public will into public policy. Of vital concern to the people in a government such as ours, is *how* its elected leaders respond to the public will. Government in the United States is, as Lord Bryce once observed, "government by public opinion."

Because we believe that government should be responsive to and controlled by the people, the process by which the public will is expressed, and by which it is translated into public policy, lies at the very heart of the governmental system. In a sense, this entire book concerns itself with that process. In this chapter, we are directly concerned with two particular aspects of it: the nature and role of public opinion and the nature and tactics of pressure groups.

PUBLIC OPINION

Nature of Public Opinion. What is *public opinion?* At first glance this question may seem an easy one — for, after all, few terms are more widely used in American politics. Public, officials, candidates, and lobbyists are especially fond of the phrase and tend to use it often. Editorial writers; press, radio, and television commentators; and even the fabled "man in the street" use it frequently, too.

Few who use the phrase ever pause to define it, however. Those people who do quickly discover that it is not readily definable. Even such authorities on the subject as public opinion pollsters and political scientists find it to be a vague and somewhat ambiguous thing, hard to pin down in terms of precise meaning.

"Public." To illustrate how vague and difficult the term is to define, consider this question: *Who* is to be included within the "public" which has an "opinion" upon which public policy is to be based?

Clearly, the "public" here does *not* include *all* of the people. A great many people have *no* opinion on a great many issues, either because they have no direct interest or know nothing about those issues. Does the "public" include all voters, then? Again, many who vote have no opinion on a great many issues, including issues involved in elections in which they vote; and, recall, more than one-third of the electorate does not vote. Then, too, government does many things (and there are many issues) upon which the voters never express an opinion.

Does the "public" include, then, only those persons who hold opinions which arise out of a direct interest they have in a particular issue? Surely this cannot be so—for there are a great many people who are directly *affected* by a given issue but who are never *aware* of that fact. Indeed, it is probably true that on most issues there are more who do *not* realize that they are affected by the matter than there are those who *do*. To eliminate from the "public"—upon whose opinion public policy is supposed to be based—those who do not perceive the ways in which they are affected by an issue would be to contradict the whole notion of democracy and to substitute for it rule by the minority.

Then, *who does* comprise the "public" upon whose opinion public policy is to be based? The most realistic answer is *different groups issue to issue*. That is to say, there is no *one* public which holds an opinion in our society; instead, there are *many* "publics." Each "public" consists of those persons who hold the same view on some particular issue of public policy.

"TEMPORARILY SAFE?" Public opinion against increased taxation is likely to exert greatest influence on legislators in an election year. (Shoemaker, Chicago American)

Each of these groups is a "public" with regard to that issue, and the view the group shares distinguishes it from all other "publics." For example, all persons who believe that capital punishment ought to be abolished belong to the "public" which holds that view; all persons who believe that the voting age should be lowered to eighteen belong to the "public" which shares that view. But note, there are many persons who belong to *one* of these "publics" but *not* to the other.[1]

---

[1] Notice, too, that because there is never unanimous agreement on any issue, there is always *more than one* "public" on a given issue. In fact, there are regularly *several* "publics" on a single issue. For example, on the question of capital punishment one "public" holds the view that the death penalty ought not be be imposed for *any* crime; another "public" takes the position that it should be imposed for *several* crimes, including murder, criminal assault, kidnapping, and treason; yet another "public" shares the view that it ought to be imposed only for a *few specific* crimes, such as murder committed by one serving a life sentence for a previous murder or for the killing of a policeman.

"Opinion." Just as we must analyze "public," so we must define "opinion" in order to understand the term *public opinion.* As used here, the word "opinion" refers to a judgment made and expressed with regard to a public issue. Thus, it involves three elements.

First, it is something more than a guess, a hunch, a mere impression; it is a consciously reached conclusion, a *judgment.* To serve as a sound basis for public policy an opinion *should* be the result of a judgment made after a careful examination of all relevant facts; unfortunately, many judgments are not made in such fashion.

Second, an opinion must be *expressed* in some way. A view which is *not* expressed cannot be called an "opinion" in the *public* sense. If it is not expressed, it cannot be known by others; and if it cannot be known by others, it cannot be identified with any public.

Third, an opinion which forms a part of a public opinion must deal with a *public issue,* not a private matter. A woman may be unhappy with the color of her hair or a man may be disturbed by his increasing weight, but the attitudes they have in these instances are ones they hold on *private* matters. An opinion is a *public* one only when the matter on which it is held is a subject of general concern, one of interest to a significant portion of the population.

Of course, *many* matters are of general interest to the public. For example, the antics of various movie stars attract public attention; so do the World Series, the Rose Bowl, and other athletic events. On each of these matters public opinions exist. Thus, the activities of a movie actress may be admired by many while condemned by others, or the New York Yankees may be favored over the Los Angeles Dodgers and vice versa in a given World Series. But our concern here is with public opinion *as it relates to public issues* — that is, with *political* matters, matters of *public policy.*

Definition. With what has been said, then, *public opinion* is used here to refer to a view pertaining to a matter of public policy which is held (shared) by a significant portion of the population. Public opinion is a compound of the points of view of many individuals; it consists of expressed group attitudes on questions of public policy.

Formation of Public Opinion. Social scientists have given a vast amount of study to public opinion in recent years. As a result, we know far more about the subject today than ever before. Still, we have much to learn, and there are many questions about it which can be answered only in relatively broad terms. Not the least of these are such questions as: How is public opinion formed? What are its roots? What factors shape and influence it?

In broad terms, public opinion is formed out of *all* of the factors that influence human thought and action. That is, the making of opinions is an extraordinarily complex process, and the factors influencing their formation are practically without number. Obviously, no one factor by itself determines a person's opinion in any matter; but, of course, some factors are more significant than others. For example, a person's family and the way in which he makes his living each play a greater role in the shaping of his opinions than does the climate in which he lives. But all aspects of his life — the totality of the circumstances in which he exists — contribute in some manner to opinion formation.

To illustrate the point, let's examine the following question: Should the State legislature enact a daylight saving time law? A great many factors will enter into the shaping of a person's opinion on the issue. But, for now, look only at the three just mentioned: family, occupation, and climate. The experiences he and his family have or have not had with the matter, what he has heard about it during family discussions, and whether the family includes small children (who usually awake in the early morning) will influence his judgment. Does his job require that he be at work early in the day? If so, daylight saving may mean that he must get up and go to work in the dark. On the other hand, if he must work late in the day, passage of the law may mean more daylight time available to him after work. Climate plays an obvious role here, too: How much and what kind of daylight would be "saved" by daylight saving time? If it is often chilly or windy in the late afternoons in the spring or summer, a person may take a different view of the matter than he might if the weather is usually balmy at that time of day.

Many of the innumerable factors which affect the content of a person's opinion *interact* upon one another; that is, some factors complement or supplement one another, while other factors tend to have a contradictory or weakening effect. For example, add another element to the daylight saving time illustration: recreational interests. A family with small children may go to drive-in movies as its chief recreation; thus, the time change would produce an obvious inconvenience for them. But perhaps the family often participates in outdoor activities after the father comes home from work; for them the time change would be beneficial. Or suppose the family's major leisure interests center around such things as reading or watching television; then, the time change may have no affect on their recreational interests.

The most important factors influencing opinion formulation appear to be the family, school, church, political party, labor union or business association, and other organized groups to which an individual belongs and from which he draws ideas. His age, sex, race, vocation, and social contacts contribute strongly, too. So do newspapers, books, magazines, radio and television, motion pictures, advertising, and all of the other means by which ideas and information on public affairs are disseminated.

The views expressed by opinion leaders also bear heavily upon the opinions held by most persons. An *opinion leader* is any person who, for any reason, has a more than usual influence over the opinions of others. Such persons are a distinct minority in the total population, of course; but they appear at every level in society, and they follow many different vocations. They include, for example, high-ranking public officials; political party, pressure group, business, and labor union leaders; newspaper editors and radio and television commentators; and the members of certain professions — especially those such as teachers, ministers, doctors, and lawyers who deal closely with the public. Whomever they may be — the President of the United States, a prominent businessman, an active clubwoman, or the neighborhood barber — opinion leaders are persons to whom others listen and from whom others draw their ideas and convictions. Whatever their political, economic, or social standing or outlook may be, they play a very significant role in opinion formulation.

Measurement of Public Opinion. If public policy is to be based on the dictates of public opinion, there must be ways in which it is possible to discover the answers to these questions: What is the *content* of public opinion on a particular public issue? Approximately *how many persons* share a given opinion in the matter? *How firmly* do those who express an opinion actually hold it? This is to say, it must be possible to "measure" public opinion.

Means of Expression. The *general* content of public opinion — what various groups of people say they want — may be determined in a very obvious way: by consulting the means by which public opinions are expressed in our society. These means are both many and varied. Those most commonly used include voting, lobbying,[2] books, pamphlets, magazine and newspaper articles, paid advertisements, editorial comments in the press and by radio and television, public speeches, petitions, demonstrations, letters to editors, legislators, and other public officials, and direct personal contacts with public agencies. These and other means of expression are the devices through which the content of public opinion becomes known. But most of the *means* tell little — and often nothing reli-

[2] See pages 192–194.

able—about the *size* of the group holding a particular opinion or the depth of *conviction* with which that opinion is held.

Measurement through Elections. In a democracy the voice of the people is supposed to be heard through the ballot box. Election results are regularly taken as indicators of public opinion. The votes cast for rival candidates are regarded as evidences of the peoples' approval or rejection of the stands taken by the candidates and of the platforms offered by the parties which nominated them. A victorious candidate and his party frequently claim to have been given a mandate to carry out their campaign promises.[3]

In actual practice, election results provide an *accurate* measure of public opinion only in rare instances, however. Voters make the choices they do in elections for any of several reasons, as we have already seen (pages 156–158). Some of the votes a candidate receives are votes which were cast *for him,* while others are votes which were cast *against his opponent;* and some of his votes were actually cast *for his party,* or *against the other party,* rather than for him. A candidate often disagrees with some, and occasionally even with many, of the planks of his party's platform. The stands a candidate and his party take in a campaign are frequently and purposely vague and general (see page 126); thus a vote cast for him may express little more than a vague and general approval of his campaign image or his party's traditional record. Then, too, voters often vote a "split ticket"; that is, they vote for the Democratic candidates for some offices and Republican candidates for other offices *at the same election.* Thus, those who do support one party and its candidates at a given election include a bewildering variety of interests which agree with one another on some issues and disagree, sometimes sharply, on others.

All of this suggests that to call a typical election a "mandate" for much of anything in terms of public policy is to be on very shaky ground. Elections are, at best, *useful indicators* of public opinion. Votes cast for a candidate cannot be interpreted accurately as votes cast for all of his views.[4]

Measurement through Pressure Groups. A *pressure group* is an organization composed of persons who share certain views and objectives and which actively seeks to influence the making and content of public policy. We shall consider them at some length in a moment (pages 185–195). But, for now, notice that, though they vary considerably in their size, power, and objectives, all pressure groups seek to influence public policy—and, in the process, they serve as a chief means by which public opinion is made known. They convey information and the views of their members through the efforts of their lobbyists, by letter and telegram campaigns, through electioneering, and by a variety of other methods. But, in dealings with pressure groups, public officials often find it very difficult to determine how many people each group actually speaks for, as well as how intensely those people hold the views which are attributed to them.

Measurement through the Press, Radio, and Television. The press, radio, and television

---

[3] The term *mandate* comes from the Latin *mandare*—literally, to place in one's hand or to commit to one's charge. In American politics the term refers to the instructions or commands a constituency gives to its elected officials.

[4] Elections at which voters approve or reject measures—State constitutional amendments, statutes, local ordinances, or such other proposals as bond issues— *are* elections in which public opinion is registered directly upon a public policy question. The accuracy of such an election as a reflection of public opinion depends in large part upon the proportion of the electorate participating in it, of course. See the discussion of the initiative and referendum, page 631–633.

are often described as "mirrors" as well as "molders" of public opinion. The peculiar importance of these media is reflected by these impressive statistics: More than 8000 newspapers, including nearly 1800 dailies, are published in this country; they have a combined circulation in excess of 140,000,000 copies per issue. More than 6000 commercial radio and nearly 700 commercial television stations are on the air. Their programs can be received by well over 100,000,000 radio sets and the more than 70,000,000 television sets in the United States. There is at least one radio and one television set in over nine out of every ten American households—and there are two or more of each in several million homes.

Editorial pages and news commentators are commonly believed to be fairly good indicators of majority opinion on public questions. Whether they are or not is in fact unknown. That they may not be as reliable as many think seems to be indicated by this fact: The overwhelming majority of newspapers have supported the Republican candidate for the Presidency in every election except one since 1932; most newspapers did not support Senator Barry Goldwater in 1964. Yet, over that period the Democrats won the Presidency seven times and lost it only three times; the Republicans won only with General Eisenhower as their candidate in 1952 and 1956 and Richard Nixon in 1968. The truth of the matter appears to be this: Newspapers are far more influential in terms of public attitudes on issue questions than they are on candidates—and far more influential in terms of State and local candidates as opposed to national candidates.

Measurement through Personal Contact. Public officials regularly attempt to sound out and assess public opinion on the basis of direct contacts with the people. These contacts are of many varied types. Thus, the President—or more often a Cabinet member or other major figure in his administration—will make a speaking tour of the country, discussing various aspects of the administration's program while at the same time attempting to gauge public sentiment. Congressmen return home to talk to the voters between sessions and frequently during a session, too; and they receive huge quantities of mail from their constituents and many visitors from home, as well. Governors, State legislators, and other public policymakers utilize the same techniques, of course. The success of these attempts to measure public opinion depends in good part upon the shrewdness with which a public official interprets what he sees and hears. The possibility that he will glean only what he *wants* to find—only that which supports the positions he favors—is an ever-present trap for the unwary.

Measurement through Public Opinion Polls. Public opinion polls have been used "to take the public pulse" in this country for more than a century. They are widely used today to discover sentiment on public questions and to forecast election results.

Most early polling attempts were of the "straw vote" variety; that is, they were polls in which accuracy was sought simply by asking a certain question of the largest possible number of persons. Straw votes are still fairly common today. Local newspapers occasionally run "ballots" for their readers to "clip out and mail in," and radio stations pose questions to which listeners may respond by post card. But this polling method is notoriously unreliable. It rests on the fallacious assumption that a relatively large response will tend to produce a fairly accurate picture of the public view on a given question. Nothing in the process insures that those who do respond—no matter how numerous—in fact represent an accurate sample (cross-section) of the population. The emphasis is upon *quantity* rather than upon the *quality* of the sample to which the question is posed.

Even an extraordinarily large sample can produce a highly inaccurate result if the sample itself is faulty. The most spectacular failure of a straw vote poll occurred in connection with the presidential election of 1936. During that

DON'T LAUGH, I'M SERIOUS!

POLITICAL POLLSTER

MAPS

Polling techniques are more scientific and sophisticated than the cartoon indicates, and have become increasingly more reliable. Former President Truman chuckled over his victory that upset the pollsters in 1948. (Photo by Wide World Photos; cartoon by James Dobbins, Boston Herald-Traveler)

campaign the *Literary Digest* mailed ballots to several million persons whose names had been drawn from telephone directories and automobile registration lists. Each person who received a ballot was asked to indicate his preference between the Republican candidate, Governor Alfred Landon of Kansas, and the Democratic candidate, President Franklin Roosevelt. More than 2,000,000 ballots were returned, and on the basis of them, the *Literary Digest* predicted an overwhelming victory for Governor Landon. But in the election itself, President Roosevelt won in a landslide; he carried every State except Maine and Vermont and received 27,751,597 popular votes to Governor Landon's 16,597,583. The magazine had managed to forecast the winners in the presidential elections of the 1920's; but its failure in 1936 was so colossal that it ceased publication almost immediately thereafter.

Since the 1930's, serious public opinion polling has been based on the concept of "scientific sampling." That is, it has been based on efforts to reach a carefully drawn sample of the population. Most responsible pollsters now attempt to tap an accurate cross-section of the population to be surveyed either by:

(1) drawing a "quota sample," in which several characteristics of the population—such as age, sex, place of residence, occupation, and income level—are represented in the sample in the same proportion as they exist in the total population. Thus, if 51.3 per cent of the population is female, females will make up 51.3 per cent of the sample, and so on.

Or, *(2)* drawing a "random sample" (also known as a "probability sample"), in which a limited number of clusters of people—in blocks, precincts, or other small districts—is selected with infinite care. Most major pollsters now use this method, choosing the particular areas for their interviews in mathematically random fashion.

Among the best-known polling organizations today are the American Institute of Public Opinion (Gallup Poll); the Survey Research Center, University of Michigan; and the National Opinion Research Center, University of Chicago. These and other groups using scientific polling techniques have not developed fool-proof methods for the measuring of public opinion. But—with the notable exception of the presidential election of 1948—they have produced generally useful and increasingly reliable results.

Still several problems plague public opinion pollsters. The drawing of accurate samples—an extraordinarily complex mathematical and sociological exercise—needs (and is receiving) constant refinement. Several factors affect the reliability of the responses to pollsters' questions, and many of those factors are difficult or even impossible to control. For example, an interviewer's physical appearance, his dress, or his accent or voice inflections may affect an answer. Then, too, there are unsolved problems in the wording of questions intended to tap opinions on issues. Clearly, questions must be very carefully phrased in order to avoid prejudicing the answers that will be given to them. For example, many persons will answer "yes" to a question put in these terms: Should taxes be reduced? But many of the same persons will also answer "yes" to such questions as: Should more money be spent to provide better schools? Do you think that Congress ought to appropriate larger funds for the armed forces in order to provide greater protection against any possible communist aggression?

One of the major weaknesses of scientific polls is that they do not accurately measure either the depth of knowledge or the strength of feeling behind the opinions they report. Answers given to pollsters' questions are sometimes nothing more than snap judgments. Others are ill-considered emotional reactions or answers of the sort the person interviewed thinks he "ought" to make. Some answers are those that the person thinks will please (or offend) the interviewer, rather than accurate

indications of opinion. Indecision and lack of interest or knowledge often warp responses.

Public opinion polls are sometimes accused of helping to shape the opinions they are *supposed* to measure. The charge is most often levied against polls which appear in syndicated columns in newspapers across the country.

Even with these problems, it is clear that scientific polls have proved of real benefit in the difficult task of measuring public opinion. They can be and are used much more frequently and conveniently than formal elections. Though they may not be *precisely* accurate, they do offer reasonably reliable guides to public thought. They tend to focus attention on public questions and to stimulate discussion of them. Their value is underscored by the widespread and growing use of them by candidates and public officials.

Constitutional Limitations on Majority Opinion. A final word is necessary before we turn to pressure groups. Public opinion is supposed to serve as the *principal guiding force* behind public policy in the United States. But its power is tempered. Our system of constitutional government is *not* designed to give free, unrestricted play to public opinion—and especially it is not designed to give such force to *majority* opinion. The doctrines of separation of powers and of checks and balances, and the constitutional guarantees of civil rights are intended to protect minority interests against the possible excesses of majority action.

PRESSURE GROUPS

Definition. A *pressure group* is an organization composed of persons who share one or more opinions or objectives and who seek to promote their common interests by influencing the making and the content of public policy.[5]

---

[5] Pressure groups are also known, less widely but somewhat more accurately, as *interest groups* or *special interest groups*.

In every society there are many persons with common aims and concerns in economic, religious, racial, sectional, and other social matters. It is only natural that they should join together to promote their interests. Whatever they may call the groups they form — clubs, associations, leagues, or unions, for example — these groups become pressure groups whenever they seek their ends by attempting to influence government.

Political Parties and Pressure Groups. Man learned long ago that there is strength in both numbers and unity. The existence of political parties and pressure groups are both reflections of that fact. While each of these types of organizations overlap in many ways, there are three vital differences between them.

Nominations. Parties nominate candidates for office; pressure groups do *not*. As we noted on page 125, the making of nominations is *the* principal function of a political party. If a pressure group were to nominate candidates, it would, in effect, become a political party.

Primary Interest. Parties are primarily interested in winning elections and maintaining control of government; pressure groups are especially concerned with controlling or influencing the policies of government. That is, parties are primarily interested in public offices, while pressure groups are primarily interested in public policies.

Scope of Interest. Parties are (and must be) concerned with the general range of public affairs; pressure groups are usually concerned only with those particular public questions that *directly* affect their members.

Scope of Pressure Groups. Pressure groups may have many thousands or even millions of members, or they may consist of only a handful of people. They may be rich and powerful or poor and weak. They may be long-established and permanent organizations or new and even temporary in character. But whatever the length of their membership rosters, the strength of their political muscle, and their age and life expectancy, they are found in virtually every field of human activity.

The largest number of pressure groups arises out of a common economic interest. Many exist on a variety of other bases, however. Thus, many are formed out of a particular geographic area, such as the South, the Columbia River Basin, or the State of Massachusetts. Others are based upon a common cause or idea, such as prohibition, governmental reform, or civil rights. Still others exist to promote the welfare of certain groups, such as veterans, the aged, racial minorities, or the disabled and the handicapped.

Most persons, even if they are not conscious of the fact, are members of several different pressure groups. A man who owns an automobile agency, for example, may belong to a car dealer association, a veterans organization, the local chamber of commerce, a particular church, a parent-teacher association, and several other local, regional, and national organizations. His wife may belong to some of these groups, as well, including the church and the parent-teacher association; and she may be a member of still others, including a local voters league and the auxiliary of her husband's veterans organization. All of these are, in one degree or another, pressure groups, even though the automobile dealer and his wife may never think of them in this light. For example, churches often express views on such public issues as the regulation of drinking, curfew ordinances, and Sunday store closures — and they often seek to influence public policy in these matters, too. When doing so, they are pressure groups.[6]

---

[6] Not *every* group to which individuals belong can be properly described as a pressure group. Thus, a garden club or a chamber music group may or may not be, depending on whether or not it attempts in some way to influence public policy. The most striking illustration of an unorganized interest in American politics is the consumer. All Americans are consumers, of course; but we have chosen to organize as *producers* rather than as consumers.

Groups Based on Economic Interests. Most pressure groups in the United States are formed on the basis of *economic interests* — that is, on the basis of the manner in which men make their living and the ways in which they acquire and use the property they hold. Among these groups the most active, and certainly the most effective, are those representing business, labor, and agriculture.

Business Groups. Business has long looked to government for the promotion and protection of its interests. Recall that merchants, creditors, and property owners were the groups most responsible for the calling of the Constitutional Convention of 1787. The concept of the protective tariff was fought for and won in the earliest years of the Republic, and business interests have worked to maintain it ever since. One of the oldest active pressure organizations today is the United States Brewers' Association, created when Congress levied a tax on beer in 1862. The association was established to insure "the brewing trade that its interests be vigorously and energetically prosecuted before the legislative and executive departments."

A vast number of business associations operate at the national, State, and local levels today. The National Association of Manufacturers (NAM) and the Chamber of Commerce of the United States are the most potent among them. Although both organizations speak for the interests of business in general, the NAM tends to represent the views of the larger industrial concerns, while the Chamber of Commerce tends to speak for the thousands of smaller businesses across the country and is organized into hundreds of local chambers.

Various segments of the business community also maintain their own specialized pressure groups, and their number is legion — for example, the American Trucking Association, Inc., the Southern States Industrial Council, the National Association of Electric Companies, the Association of American Railroads, and the National Association of Real Estate Boards.

Despite a common impression, groups based upon a particular economic interest do not always present a solid front in their attempts to influence public policy. In fact, the competition among them is often very intense. For example, the trucking industry regularly bends every effort to promote funds for federal aid for highway construction. But the railroads are less than happy with such "special favor" to their competition. At the same time, the railroads regard taxes on gasoline, oil, tires, and other "highway user levies" as valid and necessary sources of national revenue, while the truckers take quite another view.

Labor Groups. The interests of organized labor are also promoted by a host of pressure groups. The most potent of them is, of course, the AFL-CIO (the combined American Federation of Labor — Congress of Industrial Organizations). Its approximately 15,000,000 members belong to some 130 separate unions — such as the United Steel Workers, the United Shoe Workers, and the International Association of Machinists. Each of its constituent unions, like the AFL-CIO itself, is organized on a national, State, and local basis. There are also a number of powerful independent unions — that is, labor organizations not affiliated with the AFL-CIO — including, for example, the Brotherhood of Locomotive Engineers, the International Brotherhood of Teamsters, and the United Mine Workers.

We shall come back to the subject of the organization and functions of labor unions later (pages 474-479); but for now notice that organized labor is relatively united in promoting such positions as higher minimum wages, the closed shop, and increased unemployment compensation coverage and benefits and in opposing such matters as "right to work" laws. But, as with business and other groups, there are several areas in which labor opposes labor. For example, there are different points of view between "white collar" and "blue collar" workers and between skilled and unskilled union members. Sectional differences and interests arising out of the particular commod-

Lobbying

THROUGH PUBLIC OPINION

Influence of a Pressure Group

Directly

Radio and T.V. Advertising

Newspapers and Magazines

Books and Education

Indirectly

Work through Fronts and "Innocents"

By Use of Anonymous Propaganda

ON CONGRESS & GOVERNMENT AGENCIES

Directly

Influence on Party Platform

Influence on Legislative Committees

Election of Friendly Candidates

Influence on Administrative Agencies

Indirectly

By Use of Social Position to Influence Public Servants & Congressman

By Having Representatives in Key Administrative Positions

ities union members produce frequently split labor's forces, too. Thus, it is not uncommon to find labor groups opposing one another on such issue questions as higher or lower tariffs, public or private power developments, or subsidies for various transportation industries.

Agricultural Groups. Agriculture is served by a number of politically powerful associations, the most important being the National Grange, the American Farm Bureau Federation, and the Farmers' Union. The Grange was established in 1867 and is the oldest and most "conservative" of the three major national farm organizations. The Farm Bureau, which dates back to 1902 and has some 1,700,000 members, is the largest and generally the most effective of the three. It works closely with the so-called "farm bloc" in Congress, and it tends to favor governmental programs to promote agriculture more enthusiastically than does the Grange. The smaller Farmers' Union is more "liberal" than either of the older farm organizations and frequently disagrees with them. It generally

supports governmental programs designed to regulate the production and marketing of agricultural products.

A number of other agricultural groups — based upon the interests of the producers of such specific commodities as dairy products, grain, fruit, peanuts, livestock, cotton, wool, and corn — also operate as pressure groups; for example, the National Milk Producers Association, the National Association of Wheat Growers, the American Cattlemen's Association, and the Wool Growers League. As with business and labor groups, various farm organizations sometimes find themselves at odds with one another. Thus, dairymen and cotton, corn, and soybean growers often compete in their attempts to influence legislation relating to the regulation of oleomargarine, or cane sugar and beet sugar producers compete over the importation of sugar.

Professional Groups. The professions are generally organized for political purposes, too; but they generally are not nearly as influential

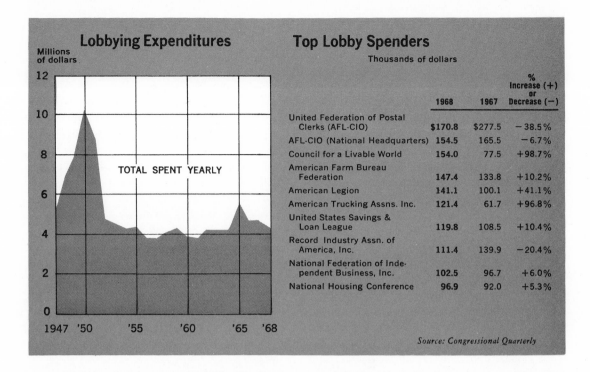

Lobbying Expenditures

Millions of dollars

TOTAL SPENT YEARLY

1947 '50 '55 '60 '65 '68

Top Lobby Spenders

Thousands of dollars

	1968	1967	% Increase (+) or Decrease (−)
United Federation of Postal Clerks (AFL-CIO)	$170.8	$277.5	−38.5%
AFL-CIO (National Headquarters)	154.5	165.5	−6.7%
Council for a Livable World	154.0	77.5	+98.7%
American Farm Bureau Federation	147.4	133.8	+10.2%
American Legion	141.1	100.1	+41.1%
American Trucking Assns. Inc.	121.4	61.7	+96.8%
United States Savings & Loan League	119.8	108.5	+10.4%
Record Industry Assn. of America, Inc.	111.4	139.9	−20.4%
National Federation of Independent Business, Inc.	102.5	96.7	+6.0%
National Housing Conference	96.9	92.0	+5.3%

Source: Congressional Quarterly

as the business, labor, and farm groups. Among the leading professional and most influential organizations are the American Medical Association, the National Education Association, and the American Bar Association. There are also dozens of less well-known and less politically active professional groups, such as the American Society of Civil Engineers, the American Dental Association, the American Library Association, and the American Chemical Society. Much of the effort of professional groups is directed to internal matters such as the standards of the profession, the holding of professional meetings, and the publication of scholarly journals and other papers. But each organization, in varying degrees, functions as a pressure group bent on promoting what it sees as the welfare of its members and their occupation.

Groups Based on Non-Economic Interests. There are many groups based upon the promotion of a particular cause or idea, the interests of a specific geographic region, and the welfare of such groups as veterans, the aged, racial minorities, and immigrants. Several of these organizations have a considerable amount of political muscle. Although they are essentially non-economic in character, they often become very actively involved in public issue questions which are *distinctly economic* in character. The number and range of such non-economic groups is so great that we can only hope to indicate their general nature here.

Among the many groups formed to promote a *cause* or an *idea* are such influential ones as: the Women's Christian Temperance Union, a vocal advocate of prohibition; the American Civil Liberties Union, interested in the promotion and safeguarding of political and civil rights; the Fair Campaign Practices Committee, concerned with the quality of electioneering in American politics; the League of Women Voters of the United States, dedicated to stimulating more active participation in and greater public knowledge about governmental affairs; and the National Reclamation Association, pledged to the cause of conservation. Of course, there are many other not-so-well-known but highly active "cause" groups.

Several pressure groups work to promote the *welfare* of certain elements within the population. Among the best organized and most powerful are the American Legion and the Veterans of Foreign Wars, both actively engaged in advancing the interests of the nation's veterans. Older Americans, Inc., is active in public policy areas related to the welfare of the aged, especially old-age pensions, medical care for the aged, and other retirement-related programs. Several organizations—for example, the National Association for the Advancement of Colored People, the Congress of Racial Equality, and the Urban League—are closely concerned with governmental policies of special interest to blacks.

A number of church-related organizations attempt to influence public policy from the standpoint of their separate religious positions. Thus, many individual Protestants and their local and national churches work through the National Council of Churches; Roman Catholics maintain the National Catholic Welfare Conference, and Jewish communicants have the American Jewish Congress and B'nai B'rith's Anti-Defamation League.

Pressure Group Tactics. Because pressure groups are vitally concerned with the shaping of public policy, they operate (exert their "pressures") wherever public policy is made or influenced. This means, of course, that they are to be found at *all* levels of government in the United States. Although Lord Bryce's classic comment may be somewhat indelicate, it is quite descriptive: "Where the body is, there will the vultures be gathered."

Propaganda and Public Opinion. As difficult as it may be to determine, public opinion is the most significant long-term force in American politics. That is, over the long run, no public policy can be followed successfully without the support of a considerable element within the population. Pressure groups are quite aware of this fact, of course. Because

they are, they frequently seek to create a favorable—or at least a neutral—reception for their positions in the general public.

Pressure groups attempt to create the public attitudes they want through the use of *propaganda.* Propaganda, much like public opinion, is a vague and somewhat inexact term. Its objective is to create a particular popular belief. That objective may be "good" or "bad," depending upon who assesses it. It may be factually true, false, or distorted. But as a *technique,* it is neither moral nor immoral; it is amoral. It does not employ objective logic; rather, it begins with a conclusion and proceeds to marshall the arguments that will support it. Propaganda and objective analysis sometimes arrive at the same conclusion, but their methods are vastly different. In short, the propagandist is not a teacher; he is an advertiser, a salesman.

Propaganda techniques have been developed to a high level in this country—especially in the field of commercial advertising. In large measure, they depend for their success upon appeals to emotions and to preconceived prejudices. The Institute of Propaganda Analysis has identified the propagandist's tools to include such devices as "name-calling," "the glittering generality," and "the testimonial." [7]

Seldom does the talented propagandist attack the logic of a policy he opposes. Rather, he employs name-calling—he labels it with some uncomplimentary term such as "communist," "fascist," "extremist," or "radical." He labels the policy he supports with some term designed to evoke a favorable response—a glittering generality, such as "American," "sound," "fair," or "just." He often uses symbols in an attempt to transfer to his policy the favorable reactions produced by his symbols; for example he uses

---

[7] The Institute's complete list of propaganda devices includes: (1) name-calling, (2) the glittering generality, (3) the transfer, (4) the testimonial, (5) the "plain folks" approach, (6) the bandwagon, and (7) card-stacking. Each of these labels is practically self-explanatory.

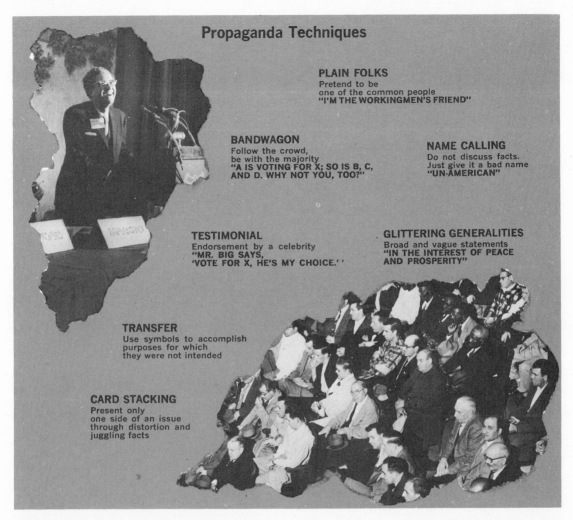

Propaganda Techniques

PLAIN FOLKS
Pretend to be
one of the common people
"I'M THE WORKINGMEN'S FRIEND"

BANDWAGON
Follow the crowd,
be with the majority
"A IS VOTING FOR X; SO IS B, C,
AND D. WHY NOT YOU, TOO?"

NAME CALLING
Do not discuss facts.
Just give it a bad name
"UN-AMERICAN"

TESTIMONIAL
Endorsement by a celebrity
"MR. BIG SAYS,
'VOTE FOR X, HE'S MY CHOICE.'"

GLITTERING GENERALITIES
Broad and vague statements
"IN THE INTEREST OF PEACE
AND PROSPERITY"

TRANSFER
Use symbols to accomplish
purposes for which
they were not intended

CARD STACKING
Present only
one side of an issue
through distortion and
juggling facts

such symbols as Uncle Sam and the flag to convey the idea his policy is patriotic. He may secure testimonials (supporting statements) from famed personalities such as movie stars, professional athletes, or military heroes to gain a favorable response, or he may identify his subject with "plain folks" through pictures and stories. Usually as a last resort, he may even employ "card-stacking" — that is, make something appear to be that which in fact it is not.

The means by which propaganda is broadcast include the press, radio, television, movies, billboards, books, magazines, pamphlets, and speeches — in fact, every device of mass communication. Pressure groups frequently use them all. The more controversial a particular position is, the more necessary the propaganda campaign becomes — for competing interests will likely be conducting one of their own.

Election Tactics. We know that pressure groups and political parties are significantly different creatures (page 186). This does not mean, however, that pressure groups are indifferent either to parties or to election results. Indeed, quite the opposite is true. Pressure groups are very much aware that it is through parties that those who make public policy are selected and through them that the policy-making machinery is organized. And they recognize the fact that if men favorable to their special interests are chosen to office their task is a much easier one than it would otherwise be. Thus, pressure groups often attempt to work within one or both of the major parties.

A few organizations are able to work actively to influence public policy and, at the same time, maintain a neutral position in relation to parties and their candidates. For example, the League of Women Voters has walked the tightrope of neutrality with outstanding success for half a century. But such feats are relatively rare today. Many pressure groups campaign actively for candidates partial to their views. Although most groups prefer to operate "behind the scenes," some openly identify themselves with and actively support one or the other of the major parties. Many contribute to the campaign funds of "good" candidates; and a few even contribute to the treasuries of both parties, just to play it safe. Occasionally, members of pressure groups work their way up

(Herblock in The Washington Post)

in party organizations in order to advance the aims of their group.

Of course, the election tactics a pressure group uses may involve some very delicate questions and finely-made decisions. For example, if a group supports a Democratic candidate for the United States Senate, it may not want to help him by attacking his Republican opponent. It may not because the Republican might stand a good chance of winning. Or the victorious Republican candidate for the House of Representatives, the governorship, or some other office may be offended by attacks upon his colleague even if sympathetic to the group's aims. The pressure group must always remember that its first concern is with the making of public policy; its interest in the election process is only secondary to that objective.

Lobbying Tactics. Lobbying is usually defined as the process by which group pressures are brought to bear upon the legislative process. Certainly it is this—but it is also much more. Realistically, *lobbying* is the process by which group pressures are applied to *all* aspects of the public policymaking process. Lobbying occurs in legislative bodies, of course; and it frequently has significant effects upon legislative action. But it also occurs in relation to administrative agencies, and on occasion even the courts.

What happens in a legislative body is often of vital concern to several interests. The provisions of a particular measure, not to mention whether it will be passed or not, can be critically important to them. For example, a bill to regulate the sale of firearms and require licenses for all who own them excites many persons and groups. Those firms which make firearms, those which sell them, and those which produce or sell such related items as ammunition, targets, and hunting apparel have a clear stake in the bill's contents and its fate. So, too, do law enforcement agencies and peace officers, hunters, wildlife conservationists, and the members of the National Rifle Association and various civil rights organizations.

Public policy is made by much more than the words contained in any statute, however. How a law's provisions are interpreted, how vigorously they are applied by the executive agency responsible for the law's enforcement, and what attitude the courts will take if the statute is challenged suggest the fact that pressure groups often have to extend their lobbying efforts beyond the legislature to the executive and the judicial branches.

Practically all of the more important organized interests in this country—business, labor, agriculture, the professions, veterans, the aged, churches, and a host of others—maintain *lobbyists* in Washington.[8]

Lobbyists themselves often prefer to be known by some other title—for example, legislative counsel or public representative. But, whatever a lobbyist calls himself, his major task is that of working for those matters of benefit to his clients and opposing those that will harm their interests. The competent lobbyist is thoroughly familiar with government and its ways, the facts of current political life, and the techniques of "polite" persuasion. Some lobbyists are former members of Congress (or of a State legislature); they know the "legislative ropes" and have many intimate contacts among present-day members. Others are frequently lawyers, former journalists and newspapermen, public relations experts, or specialists in some technical field.

The lobbyist at work employs any number of techniques. Often he attempts to persuade individual members to adopt his point of view. He sees that pamphlets, reports, and other information favorable to his cause are placed in

their hands. Regularly, he offers testimony before committees. When a committee is considering a bill on agriculture, for example, representatives of the Grange, the Farm Bureau, and other farm organizations are certain to be asked or to request permission to present their views. The information a lobbyist provides is "expert"; but, of course, it is couched in terms favorable to his client.

Frequently, a lobbyist brings pressure to bear through campaigns to create favorable public opinion. He may call upon the organization he represents to drum up opinion at the "grass-roots" level. He may urge that letters, cards, and telegrams be sent by the "folks back home." A Congressman's local newspaper may run an editorial urging him to support the lobbyist's position, and a delegation from his district may even call upon him in Washington. Favorable news stories, magazine articles, advertisements, endorsements by noted personalities, radio and television appeals, and other weapons of publicity are all within the arsenal of the competent lobbyist.

Today's lobbyist is a far cry from his early predecessors. The once common techniques of bribery and other corruption are virtually unknown. The lobbyist works in the open, and his major techniques come under the headings of friendliness, persuasion, and helpfulness. He is ready to buy lunches and dinners, to provide information, to write speeches, and to prepare bills in proper form. The information he gives is usually quite accurate, the speeches are forceful, and the bills are well drawn. He tries hard to influence debate and the final vote in the House or the Senate. If he fails in one house, he will carry his fight to the other. If he is beaten there, too, he turns his efforts to the executive branch in the hope of gaining some favorable action at that stage.[9]

---

[8] Of course, many lobbyists are also stationed in the various State capitals, particularly when the legislature is in session. The lobby is actually an anteroom or the main corridor or some other part of the capitol building to which the general public is admitted. The word has lent itself to the identification of those who attempt to influence the decisions of legislators and other policymakers, and to their activities.

---

[9] Notice that various governmental agencies often act much as pressure groups do in their relations with Congress—for example, when they press for appropriations or for or against a particular measure.

Regulation of Lobbying. Lobbying abuses do occur now and then, of course. False testimony, unethical pressures, and even bribery are not completely unknown. But instances of these and other shady lobbying tactics are quite rare today.

In order to keep lobbying within bounds, Congress enacted the Federal Regulation of Lobbying Act in 1946.[10] It requires lobbyists to register with the Clerk of the House of Representatives. They must list the names and addresses of their employers and give the amounts of salary and expense money they receive for their services. In addition, they must file quarterly reports showing all money they receive and the purposes for which it is spent. They also must list the names of all publications in which they have caused articles or editorials to be printed.

The law also requires that any organization which solicits or receives contributions to support its legislative goals must give an annual public accounting of these funds and of the expenditures made from them. Any failure to comply with the law may lead to a fine, imprisonment, or suspension of the organization's right to lobby.

The constitutionality of the law was attacked in the courts as a violation of the 1st Amendment's guarantees of freedom of speech, press, and petition. Although it was declared unconstitutional by a United States District Court, the Supreme Court upheld the law in 1954. In its opinion in the case (*Harris* v. *United States*) the Court declared:

> Congress has not sought to prohibit these pressures. It has merely provided for a modicum of information from those who for hire attempt to influence legislation or who collect or spend funds for that purpose.

---

[10] The statute was actually passed as part of the Legislative Reorganization (LaFollette-Monroney) Act of 1946; see page 235. About three-fourths of the States have enacted similar laws.

Since the registration requirement has been in effect, there have been more than 8000 registrations involving some 6000 different individuals and groups. Approximately 400 new registrations occur each year. The records of the Clerk of the House of Representatives also show that lobbyists now spend more than $4,000,000 a year on their activities.

Value of Pressure Groups. Lobbying and other pressure group activities involve the expression of the views of organized groups. As such, they are a part of the democratic process. But just how valuable a part they are has long been debated.

Pressure groups, especially through their lobbyists, perform a distinct and necessary service. They provide for representation on the basis of *functional* interests rather than geographic areas. That is, they provide for the representation of interests which arise out of occupational and other economic or social factors.

Representation in Congress (and the State legislatures) is based upon geography, of course. But the interests which unite many persons and groups today are at least as much related to how they make a living as they are to where they live. Thus, the interests of a labor union member in Chicago may be much more like those of a man who works at the same type of job in Seattle than those of a businessman in Chicago or a farmer in another part of Illinois. His Congressman and his Senators can represent the interests of his local *area;* but they may not be able or willing to represent the interests of his *economic* or *social* group. Pressure groups do provide this kind of representation—and this is especially why lobbyists are often referred to as members of "the third house of Congress."

The "third house" is certainly not a perfect mirror of the very many and diverse interests out of which our society is composed, however. The strength of a pressure group is not a valid indication of the number of people it speaks for or the degree of popular support it may, or may not, enjoy. Nor is it a valid indication of its relative importance to the nation's welfare.

Many of the most effective lobbies in Washington speak for only a small fraction of the American people. Nearly all segments of the business community are well represented. So, too, is organized labor. But the great mass of consumers is not. Thus, who speaks for those who travel on trains and in airplanes against those who own or those who work for the railroads and the airlines? Who represents the interests of those who use electricity against the interests of the owners of the utilities or those who work in the electric power industry? Public agencies — *e.g.,* the Interstate Commerce Commission, the Federal Aviation Administration, or the Federal Power Commission — do sometimes support the general consumer interest. But these agencies are themselves the targets of pressure group tactics, and sometimes they lose sight of the "public interest." The whole point here is that the representation of special interests is valuable; but so, too, is the representation of the general public interest, and sometimes the general public interest tends to get lost in the competition between and among the many special interests.

If there is a solution to the problem of representing the general public interest, it would seem to be with the voters at the ballot box. In the final analysis, public policies are made by the elected representatives of the people. If the voters perform their task as the democratic system intends that they should, the voice of the public interest will be heard with controlling force.

✳✳✳✳✳✳✳✳✳✳ CONCEPT BUILDING ✳✳✳✳✳✳✳✳✳✳

Key Concepts

In this country we believe that the primary task of government is that of translating the public will into public policy. Both public opinion and pressure groups are vital aspects of the process by which that is accomplished.

Public opinion is a vague and somewhat ambiguous term. As used here, it refers to a view pertaining to a matter of public policy held by a significant portion of the population. Many "publics" hold separate "opinions" on nearly all public issues. Public opinions arise out of all the factors which influence thought and action; but some factors have a more significant effect than others.

The general content of public opinion may be determined by consulting the many and varied means by which it is expressed. Determining the extent and intensity with which a given opinion is held is far more difficult; for this purpose we must rely upon such rough indicators as elections, the claims of pressure groups, the press, radio, and television, citizen contacts with public agencies and officials, and public opinion polls.

Pressure groups are organizations composed of persons who share one or more opinions or objectives and seek to promote their common interest by influencing the making and content of public policy. They overlap with parties in several ways, but they do not nominate candidates, are chiefly concerned with affecting policies rather than controlling offices, and are primarily concerned with only a small portion of the total range of public affairs.

Most pressure groups arise out of an economic interest; among them, the most potent are those representing business, labor, and agriculture. Pressure groups are also formed on several other bases, including sectionalism, racial and religious factors, a cause, and the welfare of a given group.

Pressure groups apply their pressures wherever public policy is made or influenced. They do so by attempting to influence public opinion (especially with propaganda), the use of electioneering techniques, and lobbying. They are a means for the expression of views in the democratic process and provide a means of functional representation; but all interests are not equally represented. The general public interest is, at best, insufficiently represented.

Important Terms

functional interests	opinion leaders	public policy
lobby	polls	quota sample
lobbyist	pressure group	random sample
mandate	propaganda	straw vote
opinion	public	the "third house"
	public opinion	

Questions for Inquiry and Review

1. What is the primary task of government in the United States?

2. Who comprises the "public" upon whose opinion public policy is to be based in this country?

3. What three elements are involved in "opinion" as that word occurs in the phrase "public opinion"?

4. As used in this book, what is "public opinion"?

5. Out of what factors is public opinion formulated?

6. In what ways do many of these factors interact upon one another?

7. Why are opinion leaders significant in opinion formation?

8. Why must public opinion be measured?

9. How may the general content of public opinion be determined?

10. Why do election results seldom provide an accurate measure of public opinion?

11. Through what other bases may opinion be measured?

12. What is the basic difficulty with the "straw-vote" as a reliable indicator of public opinion?

13. What is the basic concept in scientific sampling?

14. What is the basic reason for the existence of pressure groups?

15. What are some of the significant differences between political parties and pressure groups?

16. The largest number of pressure groups arise on the basis of what common interest?

17. Why do pressure groups attempt to influence public opinion?

18. What is propaganda?

19. Why do pressure groups participate in the election process?

20. Why is it erroneous to conceive of lobbying only in relation to the legislative branch?

For Further Inquiry

1. Alexander Hamilton once said: "All governments, even the most despotic, depend in a great degree, on public opinion." What did he mean? Do you agree?

2. In what respects might one argue that public opinion polls pose a threat to the continued success of representative democracy?

3. In what ways can the typical citizen best go about the attempt to inform himself as fully as possible in the realm of public affairs?

4. Why may political parties and pressure groups be described as "unofficial agencies of politics"? Are they more vital than such institutions as federalism, separation of powers, checks and balances, and judicial review?

5. How does the general structure of the American political system contribute to the strength of pressure groups in our politics?

6. Writing in the *North American Review* in 1878, Horatio Seymour observed: "It is necessary for those who have charge of public affairs to learn what men have in their minds, what views they hold, at what ends they aim.... The follies of fanatics frequently teach wisdom better than the words of the wise." How would you expand upon this comment?

7. Do you agree that pressure groups are inevitable in our political system? Why?

8. Can you cite an example of a government in the United States either *influencing* or *creating* public opinion (as opposed to *responding* to it)? Is this a proper function of government?

Suggested Activities

1. Invite a local newspaper editor to discuss with the class the role of his paper in relation to public opinion.

2. Invite a representative of one of the local pressure groups to describe to the class his organization and its aims and methods.

3. Conduct a sample poll on a local issue, using scientific sampling methods as best you can.

4. Write a report based on analyzing a newspaper editorial's use of propaganda techniques.

5. Hold a debate or class forum on the following question: *Resolved,* That Congress should enact a new federal lobbying practices act which would require that all professional lobbyists be licensed.

6. Invite a lobbyist, local legislator, or other person to discuss the subject of group pressures on the governmental process.

7. Attempt to list the number of ways in which your behavior is influenced by the propaganda efforts of both public and private agencies.

Suggested Reading

CROTTY, WILLIAM J. (ed.), *Public Opinion and Politics: A Reader.* Holt, Rinehart, and Winston, 1969.

DUNBAR, ERNEST, "Sex in School: The Birds, the Bees, and the Birchers," *Look,* September 9, 1969.

"Influence Peddling in Washington," *Time,* May 16, 1969.

KNOWLES, JOHN H., "The Man Whom the AMA Cut Down," *Life,* July 11, 1969.

NEWFIELD, JACK, "Nader's Raiders: The Lone Ranger Gets a Posse," *Life,* October 3, 1969.

PEKKANEN, JOHN, "The People Behind the Pollsters' Percentages," *Life,* July 19, 1968.

POLLAK, RICHARD, "Time: After Luce," *Harper's,* July, 1969.

"The Grapes of Wrath, 1969," *Time,* July 4, 1969; *Reader's Digest,* October, 1969.

"Whatever Happened to Charisma?" *Time,* October 17, 1969.

"Who Speaks for Negroes?" *U.S. News,* June 23, 1969.

"Who Speaks for the Cities?" *Newsweek,* April 7, 1969.

Part Two

NATIONAL

GOVERNMENT

The American system of government—the ways in which it is organized, the ways in which it is controlled by the people, and the ways in which it functions—is, as we said on the very first page, what this book is all about. To this point, through ten chapters and for nearly 200 pages, we have focused on that theme in a primary sense. That is, we have considered our governmental system in terms of its origins and development, the fundamental principles upon which it is based, and the basic means by which it is limited and by which it may be made to do the bidding of the American people.

Now we turn our attention to the National Government, to that vast and complex mechanism through which the governmental system operates at the national level. Over the course of the next twenty-four chapters and for some 400 pages, we shall examine the organization, powers, procedures, and functions of each of its three great branches. As we do so, you might weigh this description of the National Government made three decades ago by a panel of distinguished commentators, the President's Committee on Administrative Management:

The Government of the United States is the largest and most difficult task undertaken by the American people, and at the same time the most important and the noblest. Our Government does more for more men, women, and children than any other institution; it employs more persons in its work than any other employer. It covers a wider range of aims and activities than any other enterprise; it sustains the frame of our national and our community life, our economic system, our individual civil rights and liberties.... [Its] goal is the constant raising of the level of the happiness and dignity of human life, the steady sharing of the gains of our Nation, whether material or spiritual, among those who make the Nation what it is.

We begin our examination with the Congress — in part because it is the branch of the National Government for which the Constitution first provides. But we do so, too, because the Congress is, in James Madison's phrase, "the First Branch of Government" for other reasons as well. As the legislative body for the nation it is *the* central institution in our representative democracy. Its members are chosen *by* the people and they are chosen to *represent* the people; it is, both constitutionally and practically, the organ of government *closest* to the people. And it is also the body to which the Constitution gives the bulk of the powers held by the National Government. The executive and the judicial branches each play an important part in the making of the public policies of the United States; but it is to the Congress that the Constitution assigns major responsibility for the performance of that supremely important task.

Governments *may* operate without either legislatures or courts — but *no* government, whatever its form, can exist without some type of executive authority. Both the legislative and the judicial functions can be performed by the executive. Laws may be made by executive order, and public and private disputes can be settled and crimes can be punished in the same fashion. Obviously, a government with neither legislature nor courts could not be a democratic one — but it would be a government, nonetheless. Our governmental system, like any other, demands an executive authority.

In our consideration of the executive branch of the National Government we shall look first at the Presidency, of course — at the nature of the office of the President, at the manner in which its occupant is selected, and at the many and mighty powers he possesses. And then we shall survey the immense administrative apparatus under his direction and the multitude of functions which it performs.

Like the Congress and the Presidency, the federal judiciary occupies a vital place in the government of the nation. We have already taken note of the power of judicial review and the significant role of the federal courts in the interpretation and development of the Constitution (pages 52–53, 68–69). And we have also discussed their crucial role in the preservation of the concept of limited government (pages 98–99). Here we shall take a closer look at the structure, jurisdiction, and work of the judicial branch.

11
THE CONGRESS

❖❖❖Why is the legislative power so pivotally important in a democratic system?

❖❖❖Does the concept of representative government require that legislators be chosen by popular vote? Explain.

❖❖❖On which of these bases should a Member of Congress cast his vote: the views of a majority of his constituents or his own informed judgment? Why?

Anyone who is unfamiliar with what Congress actually does and how it does it, with all its duties and all its occupations, with all its devices of management and resources of power, is very far from a knowledge of the constitutional system under which we live.

WOODROW WILSON

Congress is the *legislative* (the lawmaking) branch of the National Government. Its basic function is to make law. That is to say, it exercises *the* basic function of government in a democratic system: that of translating the public will into public policy in the form of law.

How vitally important this function is, and how highly it was rated by the Founding Fathers, can be seen in the fact that the first and the lengthiest of the Articles in the Constitution is devoted to it. Section 1 of Article I reads:

> All legislative powers herein granted shall be vested in a Congress of the United States, which shall consist of a Senate and House of Representatives.

Bicameralism. Congress is *bicameral*—that is, composed of two houses—for a number of reasons. *Historically,* the British Parliament, with which the Founding Fathers and all other Americans were quite familiar, had consisted of two houses since the early years of the fourteenth century. Most of the colonial legislatures, and all but two of the State legislatures in 1787, were bicameral.[1] *Practically,* the compromise between the Virginia and the New Jersey Plans at the Constitutional Convention dictated a two-chambered Congress. *Theoretically,* the Founding Fathers favored a bicameral Congress in order that one house might act as a check on the actions of the other. The noted constitutional historian Max Farrand reports:

> Thomas Jefferson, who possessed great faith in "the voice of the people," was in France when the Constitution was framed. Upon his return, while taking breakfast with Washington, he opposed the two-body form of legislature, and was disposed to twit Washington

---

[1] Only Georgia and Pennsylvania had had wide experience with *unicameral* colonial and State legislatures. Georgia adopted bicameralism in 1789 and Pennsylvania in 1790. Among the fifty States today, only Nebraska (since 1937) has a unicameral legislature. See pages 615–616.

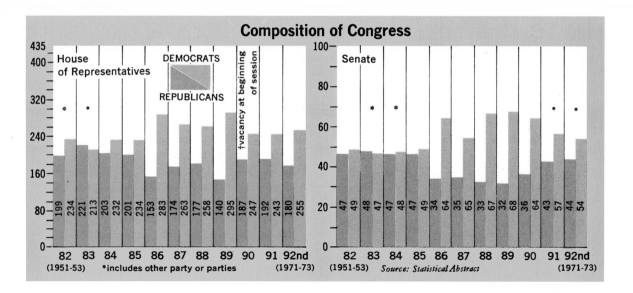

Composition of Congress

House of Representatives — DEMOCRATS / REPUBLICANS

†vacancy at beginning of session

435 400 320 240 160 80 0

199 234 221 213 203 232 201 234 153 283 174 263 177 258 140 295 187 247 192 243 180 255

82 (1951-53) 83 84 85 86 87 88 89 90 91 92nd (1971-73)

*includes other party or parties

Senate

100 80 60 40 20 0

47 49 48 47 47 48 47 49 34 64 35 65 33 67 32 68 36 64 43 57 44 54

82 (1951-53) 83 84 85 86 87 88 89 90 91 92nd (1971-73)

Source: Statistical Abstract

about it. At this time Jefferson poured his coffee from his cup into his saucer. Washington asked him why he did so. "To cool it," he replied. "So," said Washington, "we will pour legislation into the Senatorial saucer to cool it." [2]

A bicameral Congress has worked quite well over the years for several reasons. (1) A bill passed in the heat of the moment by one house can be submitted to the other, where perhaps cooler judgment will be exercised. (2) The more populous urban, industrial North and East control the House of Representatives while the less densely populated rural, agricultural South and West control the Senate. (3) One large house, elected for a short term, can express the wishes of the people rather promptly while the other smaller house, elected for a long term, can weigh and consider their merits. (4) The press, radio and television, groups especially affected, and the general public have a better opportunity to examine a bill and affect its fate when two houses, rather than one, must act on it.

It has been argued that the equal representation of the States in the Senate should be scrapped as undemocratic.[3] Some argue it is unfair, for example, that Alaska, the State with the least population (some 300,000), should have as many Senators as California, the largest (some 20,000,000). Those who argue against equal representation ignore the fact that Senators were never intended to represent people as such. The Senate represents the States as co-equal members and partners in the Federal Union. Besides, had not the States been equally represented in the Senate, there might never have been a Constitution!

Terms of Congress. Each *term* of Congress lasts two years [4] and is numbered consecutively — from the first term which began on March 4, 1789. The date for the convening of each term

---

[2] Max Farrand, *The Framing of the Constitution,* Yale University Press, 1913, p. 74.

[3] The prospects for any such change are so slim as to be nonexistent. Article V of the Constitution provides, in part: "... that no State, without its consent, shall be deprived of its equal suffrage in the Senate." In the face of this, the impossibilities of securing a change are obvious.

[4] Article I, Section 2, Clause 1 dictates a two-year term for Congress by providing that Representatives shall be "chosen every second year."

was reset by the 20th Amendment in 1933 and is now "noon on the 3rd day of January" of every odd-numbered year. The term of the 92nd Congress began at noon on January 3, 1971, and will end at noon on January 3, 1973.

Sessions of Congress. There are two *regular sessions* to each term of Congress. Section 2 of the 20th Amendment provides that:

> The Congress shall assemble at least once in every year, and such meeting shall begin at noon on the 3rd day of January, unless they shall by law appoint a different day.[5]

Congress adjourns each regular session as it sees fit. Before World War II a typical session ran for perhaps four or five months. But the many and pressing issues since then have forced Congress to remain in session through most of each year. Constitutionally, neither house may adjourn *sine die*—that is, finally, ending a session—without the consent of the other. Article I, Section 5, Clause 4 provides that:

> Neither House ... shall, without the consent of the other, adjourn for more than three days, nor to any other place than that in which the two Houses shall be sitting.[6]

Special Sessions. Only the President may call special sessions of Congress.[7] Only twenty-six such sessions have been held thus far. President Truman called the most recent one in 1948, to consider various anti-inflation and welfare proposals.

THE HOUSE OF REPRESENTATIVES

Size. The House of Representatives is the larger of the two chambers of Congress. Its exact size—today, 435 members—is not fixed by the Constitution. Rather, the Constitution provides that the total number of seats, however many that may be, shall be *apportioned* among the States on the basis of population.[8] Each State is entitled to at least one seat, whatever its population. Today (1971), five States—Alaska, Delaware, Nevada, Vermont, and Wyoming—each have only one Representative. New York has forty-one and California thirty-eight; see the map on page 203.

---

[5] Originally, the Constitution (Article I, Section 4, Clause 2) directed Congress to "assemble at least once in every year, ... on the first Monday in December, unless they shall by law appoint a different day." The outgoing Congress under the Articles of Confederation provided for the convening of the 1st Congress on March 4, 1789. Through 1820 Congress did "appoint a different day" eighteen times. But, from 1821 until 1933 and the 20th Amendment, it assembled regularly each year on the December date.

[6] Article II, Section 3 empowers the President to adjourn a session, but *only* when the two houses cannot agree upon a date for adjournment. No President has ever been called upon to exercise this power. The Legislative Reorganization Act of 1946 (see page 235) requires each regular session to adjourn no later than July 31—unless Congress should decide otherwise or a national emergency exists; but Congress has met this deadline only twice, in 1952 and 1956. Both Houses recess for brief periods during a session. The "spring recess" of about ten days in April has been a regular occurrence for several years; a two-week "Labor Day recess," first taken in 1969, will likely become a permanent annual feature, too.

[7] Article II, Section 3 provides that he may "convene both Houses or either of them" in a special session. The Senate has been called into special session alone on forty-seven occasions, to consider treaties and appointments; the House has never been called alone.

[8] Article I, Section 2, Clause 3.

Congressional Apportionment

GAINED REPRESENTATION
LOST REPRESENTATION
NO CHANGE

This map shows the changes in State representation due to the reapportionment of the House of Representatives on the basis of the 1970 Census. The new apportionment will become effective with the 1972 elections.

Large numbers indicate representation in the House. Small numbers indicate seats gained or lost.

The District of Columbia is represented in the House by a Delegate and Puerto Rico by a Resident Commissioner. Although neither is a *member* of the House, each is accorded the salary and privileges of one — but does not have the right to vote.

Reapportionment. The Constitution directs Congress to reapportion the seats in the House after each decennial census.[9] Initially, the Constitution set the size of the House in the 1st Congress (1789–1790) at sixty-five seats. The Census of 1790 showed a national population of 3,929,214 persons, and Congress then increased the House to 106 seats.

As the nation's population grew, and as the number of States increased, so did the size of the House: to 142 seats after the Census of 1800, to 186 after the Census of 1810, and so on.[10] By 1912 — following the Census of 1910 and the admissions of Arizona and New Mexico — the House had grown to 435 seats.

With the Census of 1920, Congress found itself faced with a major problem. The House had long since grown too large for effective floor action. To increase its size still further would only compound the difficulty. Yet, if the House were to be reapportioned without such an increase, some States would have to lose seats if each State were to be represented

---

[9] Article I, Section 2, Clause 3.

[10] Except after the Census of 1840 when it was decreased from 242 to 232 seats.

CASE STUDY

Quite regularly, the party in power—that is, the party which holds the Presidency—loses seats in Congress as a result of the off-year congressional elections. The elections of 1970 followed the general pattern, as the table below indicates. It details the seat gain (+) or loss (−) for the President's party in the eighteen off-year congressional elections held in this century.

Year	Party in Power	House	Senate	Year	Party in Power	House	Senate
1902	R	+9	+2	1938	D	−71	−6
1906	R	−28	+3	1942	D	−45	−10
1910	R	−57	−10	1946	D	−55	−12
1914	D	−59	+5	1950	D	−29	−6
1918	D	−19	−6	1954	R	−18	−1
1922	R	−75	−8	1958	R	−47	−13
1926	R	−10	−6	1962	D	−4	+4
1930	R	−49	−8	1966	D	−47	−3
1934	D	+9	+10	1970	R	−9	+1

Why do you think that this general pattern of presidential party loss is repeated election after election through the off-years? How important a phenomenon is this in our national politics? Does it lend support to those who argue that we should supplant the presidential system with a parliamentary government? Would the historic pattern continue if the Constitution were amended to provide that all members of the Senate and House be elected for four-year terms and at the same election at which the presidential electors are chosen?

on the basis of its population. But Congress was unable to find a satisfactory solution to the problem. So, despite the Constitution's command, nothing was done. There was *no* reapportionment on the basis of the Census of 1920.

The Reapportionment Act of 1929. With the approach of the Census of 1930 Congress moved to avoid a repetition of its earlier lapse. It did so with the passage of the Reapportionment Act of 1929, which provides for what may be called an "automatic reapportionment." The law, with the few amendments made to it since 1929, now provides that:

(1) The "permanent" size of the House of Representatives shall be 435 members. Of course, that figure is "permanent" only so long as Congress decides not to change it. (When Alaska and Hawaii were admitted to the Union in 1959, each was given one seat in the House

—thus, membership rose to 437. But the increase was only temporary. In admitting the two States Congress declared that the size should revert to 435 after the Census of 1960 —that is, with the elections of 1962.)

(2) Following each census, the Census Bureau is to determine the number of seats to which each State is entitled according to its population.

(3) When the Census Bureau's plan is available, the President is to send it to Congress via a special message.

(4) If, within sixty days of its receipt from the President, neither house rejects the plan, it becomes effective.

Today (1971) each seat in the House of Representatives represents an average of some 471,000 persons.

Election. The Constitution provides a two-year term for Representatives, and it decrees that all persons a State permits to vote for members of the "most numerous branch" of its legislature are qualified to vote in congressional elections.[11] It also declares that:

The times, places, and manner of holding [congressional] elections ..., shall be prescribed in each State by the legislature thereof: but the Congress may at any time, by law, make or alter such regulations....[12]

In 1872 Congress declared that congressional elections should be held on the same day in each State — the Tuesday following the first Monday in November of every even-numbered year.[13] The same law decreed that Representatives be chosen by written or printed ballots; voting machines were sanctioned in 1899.

According to the Constitution, a vacancy in the House of Representatives is filled by a special election called by the governor of the State involved.[14]

Districts. For more than half a century Congress left to each State the question of whether its Representatives should be chosen from districts within the State or by the general ticket system. Most of the States established congressional districts, with the voters in each electing one of the State's Congressmen. Several of the States, however, employed the general ticket system; that is, they provided that all of the State's Representatives were to be chosen *at-large* (from the whole State).

The general ticket system was grossly unfair: under it, a party with a plurality in the State, no matter how slight, could elect all of the State's Representatives in Congress. Congress finally eliminated the general ticket arrangement in 1842. It did so by providing that thereafter all seats in the House of Representatives were to be filled from districts within each State.[15] At the same time it made each State legislature responsible for the drawing of the congressional districts within its own State.

The 1842 law required that each district be composed of "contiguous territory." In 1872 Congress added the command that the districts contain "as nearly as practicable an equal number of inhabitants." And in 1901 it directed that the districts be of "compact territory."

These requirements of contiguity, population equality, and compactness were often disregarded by the States, and Congress made no serious effort to enforce them. They were omitted from the Reapportionment Act of 1929; and in 1932 the Supreme Court held that they had thus been repealed. Historically, then — and notably since 1929 — many districts

---

[11] Article I, Section 2, Clause 1; see page 144.

[12] Article I, Section 4, Clause 1; see pages 168–169.

[13] Congress has made an exception for Alaska, which may, if it chooses, hold its elections in October. To date, however, Alaskans have gone to the polls on the same November date as voters in each of the other forty-nine States. Through 1958 Congress permitted Maine to hold its congressional elections in September, but an amendment to the Maine constitution now provides that the State's congressional and other elections are to be held on the regular November date.

[14] Article I, Section 2, Clause 4.

[15] Except, of course, in States with but one Representative; in those States the one seat is filled at-large. Under the Reapportionment Act of 1929, whenever a State *gains* one or more seats and the legislature does not redistrict to account for the additional representation, the new seat or seats *must* be filled at-large until such time as the legislature performs its duty; whenever a State *loses* one or more seats after a census, *all* the remaining seats must be filled at-large if the legislature fails to redistrict.

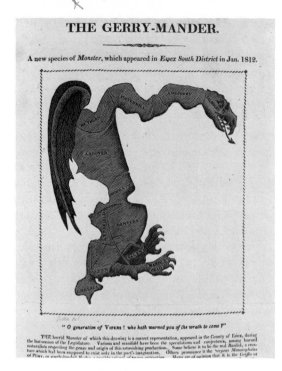

THE GERRY-MANDER.

A new species of *Monster*, which appeared in *Essex South District* in Jan. 1812.

" O generation of VIPERS *! who hath warned you of the wrath to come ?"*

THE horrid Monster of which this drawing is a correct representation, appeared in the County of Essex, during the last session of the Legislature. Various and manifold have been the speculations and conjectures, among learned naturalists respecting the genus and origin of this astonishing production. Some believe it to be the real *Basilisk*, a creature which had been supposed to exist only in the poet's imagination. Others pronounce it the *Serpent Monocephalus* of Pliny, or single-headed *Hydra*, a terrible animal of terror extinction. Many are of opinion that it is the *Griffin* or

This drawing of the gerrymandered Massachusetts district is discussed in the footnote on this page. (Mass. Historical Society)

have been of very peculiar geographic shapes; and in many of the States they have also been of widely varying populations.

Gerrymandering. Districts which on a map appear much like a shoestring, a dumbbell, or the letter Y—or take some other odd form— have been *gerrymandered;* [16] that is, they have been drawn to the advantage of the party or faction in power. Gerrymandering can be, and often is, accomplished in several ways—for example, by collecting as many of the minority party's voters as possible in one district, thus leaving the other districts comfortably safe for

the ruling party; or by drawing the districts to spread the minority party's voters as thinly as possible through all of the districts.

Population Variations. Through much of our history, congressional districts in most States have varied widely in terms of population. For example, the 1960 Census showed Michigan's 12th District (the Western Peninsula) to be the least populous in the nation, with only 177,431 residents. Yet, the districts in and around Detroit were among the nation's largest (the 16th had 802,994 residents, the 18th had 690,259, and the 7th had 664,556). In Texas, at the same time, the 5th District (Dallas) included 951,527 persons, but the neighboring 4th District had only 216,371 residents.

Obviously, the State legislatures were most responsible for this condition. In several States they purposefully gerrymandered the districts on a strictly partisan basis—and, in the process, produced such wide variations in population. In most States, however, the legislature performed in support of the State's *rural* interests. (As we shall see in Chapter 36, the typical State legislature has—until quite recently— been controlled by the less populous, over-represented rural areas of the State.)

Wesberry v. *Sanders,* 1964. Suddenly, and quite rapidly, the traditional pattern is now changing. In State after State congressional district lines have been—or are being—re-drawn to provide districts containing approximately equal numbers of persons.

This abrupt change has come as the result of a decision rendered by the Supreme Court in 1964. In *Wesberry* v. *Sanders* the Court found, by a 6–3 majority, that the variations among Georgia's congressional districts were so great as to violate the Constitution.

---

[16] The practice takes its name from Elbridge Gerry (1744–1814). In 1812, while Gerry was governor of Massachusetts, his supporters in the legislature re-drew the State's legislative districts to favor the Democratic-Republicans. It is said that a noted artist added a head, wings, and claws to Essex County on a district map which hung over the desk of a Federalist editor. "That will do for a sala-mander!" he said. "Better say Gerrymander," the editor growled.

In reaching its historic decision, the Court noted that Article I, Section 2 declares that Representatives shall be chosen "by the people of the several States" and shall be "apportioned among the several States. . . according to their respective numbers." These words the Court held, especially when viewed in the light of what the Founding Fathers intended, mean that:

> . . . as nearly as practicable one man's vote in a congressional election is to be worth as much as another's.

And, the Court added:

> While it may not be possible to draw congressional districts with mathematical precision, that is no excuse for ignoring our Constitution's plain objective of making equal representation for equal numbers of people the fundamental goal for the House of Representatives. That is the high standard of justice and common sense which the Founders set for us.

The results of the Court's decision were immediate and dramatic. In State after State legislatures drew new districts to meet the new "one-man, one-vote" stricture. Indeed, over half of the States had taken some action in the matter before the elections of 1966 were held. The Court has sharpened its original decision in several later cases. Thus, in *Kirkpatrick* v. *Preisler,* 1969, it rejected a plan drawn by the Missouri legislature in which no district varied from the average population of all districts by more than 3.1%. It held that *any* variation in population, however slight, must be justified, that a State must "make a good faith effort to achieve precise mathematical equality" — and that Missouri had not. Apparently the Court will not accept such traditional reasons for variation as geographic features, political boundaries, or population forecasts.

The consequences, in terms of the nature of the House and for American politics are hard to overstate. The nation's cities and their suburbs are now beginning to speak with a much stronger voice in Congress than they have to this point.

Qualifications. According to the Constitution, a Representative must be at least twenty-five years of age, have been a citizen of the United States for at least seven years, and an inhabitant of the State from which chosen.[17]

Political custom dictates that a Representative also reside in his district. The district custom dates from colonial times and is based on the feeling that a Representative should be thoroughly familiar with the locale and its problems. It often means, notice, that a Congressman is regarded by many of his constituents as an "errand boy"; see page 210. Some people claim that the district custom also means that the voters cannot always select the best possible man for the job. Whatever the merits of the custom, it is only very rarely that one who does not live in a district is chosen to represent it.

The Constitution makes the House "the judge of the elections, returns, and qualifications of its own members."[18] Thus, when the right of a member-elect to be seated is occasionally challenged, the House itself has the power to decide the matter. Challenges are only very rarely upheld.

The House may refuse to seat (exclude) a member-elect by majority vote. It may also "punish its own members for disorderly behavior" by majority vote, and "with the concurrence of two-thirds, expel a member."[19]

Historically, the House has viewed its power to judge the qualifications of any member-elect as the power to impose *informal* qualifications — beyond those of age, citizenship, and residence set out in the Constitution. But in 1969, in *Powell* v. *McCormack,* the Supreme Court held that the House can not constitutionally do so.[20]

---

[17] Article I, Section 2, Clause 2.

[18] Article I, Section 5, Clause 1.

[19] Article I, Section 5, Clause 2.

[20] Thus, in 1901 the House refused to seat Brigham H. Roberts of Utah, a polygamist. In

THE SENATE

Size. The Senate, a much smaller body than the House, is composed of two members from each of the States. As there are now fifty States, there are, of course, 100 Senators.

Senatorial Terms. Senators serve a six-year term,[21] a period three times as long as that for which Representatives are chosen. The shorter term tends to make Representatives more sensitive to the pressures of public opinion and of interest groups than are their colleagues in the Senate. The Constitution so staggers senatorial terms that only one third (thirty-three or thirty-four) of them end every two years.[22]

Election. Until the adoption of the 17th Amendment in 1913, Senators were chosen by the State legislatures. Now they are elected by the people in November of the even-numbered years and are sworn into office

---

1919 and again in 1920 it excluded Victor L. Berger of Wisconsin on grounds of sedition and "un-Americanism" during World War I. Berger was later cleared of the sedition charge and, after being elected for the third time, was finally seated in 1921. Adam Clayton Powell of New York, re-elected to a twelfth term in 1966, was barred in 1967. A special committee had recommended that Powell be seated but then be censured for "gross misconduct." It found that he had misused public funds, had defied the courts of his State, and was "contemptuous" in refusing to cooperate with the committee's investigation of him. The House voted instead to exclude him. The Court held, 7–1, that, as Powell had been "duly elected by the voters of the 18th Congressional District of New York and was not ineligible to serve under any provision of the Constitution, the House was without power to exclude him from its membership." Mr. Powell was chosen to fill his own vacancy in a special election in 1967 but did not attempt to claim the seat; he was re-elected to a full term in 1968 and was seated by the House in 1969. Mr. Powell was defeated for renomination in 1970 and is no longer a member of the House.

[21] Article I, Section 3, Clause 1.
[22] Article I, Section 3, Clause 2.

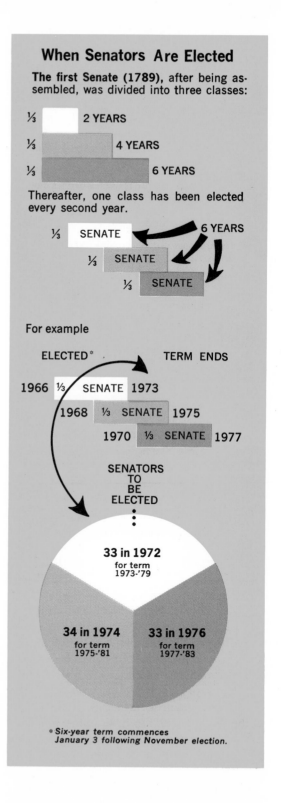

When Senators Are Elected

The first Senate (1789), after being assembled, was divided into three classes:

⅓   2 YEARS
⅓   4 YEARS
⅓   6 YEARS

Thereafter, one class has been elected every second year.

⅓ SENATE   6 YEARS
⅓ SENATE
⅓ SENATE

For example

ELECTED*   TERM ENDS

1966 ⅓ SENATE 1973
1968 ⅓ SENATE 1975
1970 ⅓ SENATE 1977

SENATORS TO BE ELECTED

33 in 1972
for term 1973-'79

34 in 1974
for term 1975-'81

33 in 1976
for term 1977-'83

*Six-year term commences January 3 following November election.

when the new Congress assembles the following January.[23] Each Senator is chosen from the State at-large, and all persons qualified to vote for members of the House of Representatives in their own State may also vote for members of the United States Senate.

Qualifications. A Senator must meet a higher set of qualifications than those the Constitution sets for a Representative. He or she must be at least thirty years of age, must have been a citizen of the United States for at least nine years, and must be an inhabitant of the State from which elected.[24]

The Senate, like the House of Representatives, is the sole judge of the qualifications of its members and may exclude a member-elect by a majority vote.[25] The Senate, too, may expel a member by a two-thirds vote.[26]

THE CONGRESSMAN AND HIS JOB

Who are the members of Congress? What are they like? What is their job? How well do they do it? These and dozens of other such questions should be asked, and the answers should be known by every informed citizen. After all, it is the members of Congress who decide such vital matters as how large our armed forces should be, at what age a young man may be drafted, how heavy federal taxes will be, how much foreign aid should be given, how labor-management relations should be regulated. These and the hundreds of other questions regularly decided by Congress affect all our lives intimately every day.

The Background of the Members. Representatives average fifty-two years of age and

[23] Article I, Section 3, Clause 1; 17th Amendment. Only one Senator is elected from a State at any one election, except when the other Senate seat has been vacated by death, resignation, or expulsion. The 17th Amendment provides that a vacancy may be filled by a special election called by the governor, or that the State legislature may authorize the governor to make a temporary appointment until the voters fill the vacancy at the next general election. Most States follow the latter practice. Because of vacancies caused by death and resignation, 35 Senate seats from 34 States were filled in the 1964 elections, 35 seats from 33 States in 1966, and 34 seats from 34 States in 1968; 35 Senators were elected from as many States in 1970.

[24] Article I, Section 3, Clause 3. Under the inhabitant qualification, a Senator need *not* have resided in the State for any prescribed period. Typically, of course, a Senator-elect has been a long-time resident of his State; the only contrary case in modern times is that of the late Senator Robert F. Kennedy, elected from New York in 1964. Note, too, that neither Senators nor Representatives may hold any other federal office while serving in Congress (Article I, Section 6, Clause 2).

[25] Article I, Section 5, Clause 1. As has the House of Representatives, the Senate has occasionally refused to seat a member-elect. For example, Frank Smith of Illinois was excluded in 1929 because $123,000 of his campaign expenses had been paid by officials of corporations regulated by the Illinois Commerce Commission of which Smith had been a member. In 1947 Theodore Bilbo of Mississippi was temporarily denied his seat while the Senate considered several charges against him, including one that he had "used his high office. . .for personal gain in dealings with war contractors" and another that, in his re-election campaign in 1946, he had urged "any means" to prevent Negroes from voting. His death in mid-1947 precluded final Senate action in the matter.

[26] Either house may also censure a member for his conduct. Cases have been rare; the most recent ones occurred in 1954, when the Senate disciplined the late Joseph McCarthy of Wisconsin, and in 1967, when the upper chamber censured Thomas J. Dodd of Connecticut.

Senators fifty-eight. Over half of the members of Congress are lawyers; after the law, the other major occupational fields represented are business and banking, teaching, agriculture, and journalism. Over three-fourths of the members have college degrees. Most of them were born in the States they represent, and only a bare handful were born outside the United States. Among the 535 members of Congress, there are a few millionaires.

Nearly all Congressmen are married, few are divorced, and they have, on the average, two children. Only a very few claim no church affiliation.

Most Congressmen have had some political experience. Nearly half of the Senators were once members of the House of Representatives and over a sixth of them governors of their home States. Some Senators have been members of a President's Cabinet or held other high national or State offices. The House of Representatives includes many former State legislators, prosecutors, and the like.

In short, Congress is largely composed of upper-middle-class Americans who, on the whole, are able and hardworking people.

The Job of a Congressman. The *primary* job of a Congressman is to make law. That is not the entire picture, however. A former Representative, Luther Patrick of Alabama, once described the job this way:

> A Congressman has become an expanded messenger boy, an employment agency, getter-outer of the Navy, Army, Marines, ward heeler, wound healer, trouble shooter, law explainer, bill finder, issue translator, resolution interpreter, controversy oil pourer, glad-hand extender, business promoter, convention goer, civil ills skirmisher, veterans' affairs adjuster, ex-service-man's champion, watchdog for the underdog, sympathizer with the upper dog, namer and kisser of babies, recoverer of lost luggage, soberer of delegates, adjuster for traffic violators, voters straying into Washington and into toils of the law, binder up of broken hearts, financial wet nurse, good samaritan, contributor to good causes—there

are so many good causes—cornerstone layer, public building and bridge dedicator, ship christener—to be sure he does get in a little flag waving—and a little constitutional hoisting and spread-eagle work, but it is getting harder every day to find time to properly study legislation—the very business we are primarily here to discharge, and that must be done above all things.

Congressman Wendell Wyatt of Oregon outlines a "typical" day this way: [27]

6–8 A.M. Arise, drive to Capitol, scan morning papers, dictate, plan day's schedule.

8–8:30 Breakfast with colleagues, discuss pending legislative business.

8:30–9:45 Read portion of morning mail, dictate, confer with staff.

9:45–12 Interior Committee hearings.

12–1 P.M. House convenes, check floor schedule for afternoon.

1–1:30 Lunch with constituents.

1:30–2 Staff conference, urban problems.

2–3:30 House floor, debate on bill to increase Civil Service retirement pay.

3:30–4 Visit with constituents off floor.

4–4:30 Greet Miss Oregon and her entourage.

4:30–5:15 Return to office, read more mail.

5:15–6:30 Return to floor, continued debate on Civil Service bill.

6:30–7:15 Back to office, read and sign outgoing mail.

7:15–9 Reception and dinner, Federal Deposit Insurance Corporation group.

9–10 Return to office, more dictation.

10–10:30 Drive home.

10:30–12 Read evening papers, study reports for committee and House sessions next day.

12 A.M. Try to sleep.

The "Errand-Boy" Concept. As we know, members of Congress represent the people. Some of the people, however, take this to mean that a Congressman is in Washington especially to do personal favors. The average member is

---

[27] Congressman Wendell Wyatt was first elected to Congress in November 1964.

plagued with many requests—as Mr. Patrick points out—from the time he enters until he leaves office. The requests may be for help in securing government contracts, appointments to West Point, free sight-seeing tours in Washington, help in marital disputes, or even personal loans. The Congressman knows that to refuse most of these requests would mean to lose votes.

Congressmen have a tremendous responsibility for the welfare of the United States, though many of them are criticized for the positions they take. It is in some ways a wonder that we are able to find so many men of ability willing to take the job.

Compensation. Members of Congress, unlike the other officials and employees of the Federal Government, fix their own salaries and other compensation. The only limits in the matter are the President's veto and voter reaction. The Constitution provides that:

> The Senators and Representatives shall receive a compensation for their services to be ascertained by law and paid out of the Treasury of the United States . . .[28]

Today (1971) each member receives:

(1) a salary of $42,500 per year; [29]

(2) various travel allowances, including expenses for several round trips a year between his home and the capital;

(3) publication and free distribution of speeches and other materials; [30]

(4) free postage for official business (the "franking privilege");

(5) an office in Washington (plus one at home for a Senator or two in his district for a Representative);

(6) an allowance for stationery, long-distance telephone calls and telegrams;

(7) an allowance for hiring an administrative assistant and other office help;

(8) a pension (to which members contribute) based on length of service which can run as high as $34,000 a year; and

(9) a $3000 tax exemption because of the need to maintain a place in Washington as well as one at home.

Then, too, there are additional items that cannot be measured in monetary terms. One is the matter of the prestige that one has as a member of Congress. Another is the opportunity to make democracy work through the most direct way in which any citizen can participate in the governing process. Also, a member of Congress is able to do many things that private citizens cannot ordinarily do—for example, travel about the country and to many parts of the world at public expense as a part of his official duties.

With a $42,500 salary and the various allowances, the typical member's annual compensation comes to about $70,000. Even at this attractive figure, however, it does not seem reasonable to argue that Congressmen are overpaid. Their responsibilities are so immense as to defy any attempt to determine an "ade-

---

[28] Article I, Section 6, Clause 1; from 1789 to 1795 members of each house were paid $6 per day In 1795 Senators received $7 per day and Representatives $6. From 1796 to 1816 the salary for both was again $6 per day. In 1816 it was raised to $15 per day, but it reverted to $6 in 1817. From 1818 to 1856, $8 per day; 1856 to 1866, $3000 per year; 1866 to 1873, $5000; 1873, $7500; 1874 to 1907, $5000; 1907 to 1925, $7500; 1925 to 1933, $10,000; 1933 to 1936, $8663; 1936 to 1946, $10,000; 1946 to 1955, $12,500 plus $2500 "expense account"; 1955 to 1965, $22,500; 1965 to 1969, $30,000.

[29] The Speaker of the House receives a higher salary (equal to that of the Vice-President), $62,500; the Senate President pro tem and the majority and minority floor leaders of both houses also receive a higher salary, $49,500.

[30] Many speeches which are not actually delivered on the floor of Congress are published in the *Congressional Record,* of which each Congressman receives sixty copies free. He may obtain any number of reprints of his speech by paying the Government Printing Office the actual cost of reprinting.

quate" salary. Then, too, the day-to-day expenses they must bear are unusually high. Many find that those "day-do-day expenses" regularly exceed the allowances provided—for such things as trips to their home State, monthly newsletters to their constituents, and the like. Senator Robert Packwood of Oregon estimates that just these two items—trips and newsletters—push his expenses approximately $40,000 above his allowances each year.

Add such items as the costs involved in election campaigns, in meeting the unusually high cost of living in or around Washington, in maintaining two homes, and in coping with the many other "extra" expenses imposed by the office, and it is not very difficult to appreciate the point.

Historically, Congress has been quite reluctant to raise the salary figure. The major reason for this timidity is fairly obvious: many members fear that the voters back home will misunderstand and that an opponent in the next election will use the action as effective campaign ammunition. They have much preferred to provide themselves instead with such "fringe benefits" as a special tax deduction and a generous pension program—items much less apparent to the voters than a pay increase would be.

Many persons who might serve with real distinction in Congress refuse to seek a seat for financial reasons. They feel that they cannot afford the sacrifices involved. It is obvious that a high salary, of itself, will not attract the best people to public office; but, certainly, it makes public service much more appealing to such persons.

Privileges of Congressmen. The Constitution commands that both Senators and Representatives

> shall, in all cases, except treason, felony, and breach of the peace, be privileged from arrest during their attendance at the session of their respective Houses, and in going to and returning from the same. . . .[31]

The provision dates from the practice of colonial days when the king's officers often arrested legislators on petty grounds in order to keep them from their official duties. It has been of little real importance in our national history—although it does save a Congressman from a minor traffic ticket now and then.

Another and much more important privilege is also established in the same provision in the Constitution:

Women as well as men serve in our Congress. Representative Patsy Mink of Hawaii, the first woman of Japanese descent to serve in the Congress, is shown here with former Vice President Humphrey. (Wide World Photos)

---

[31] Article I, Section 6, Clause 1.

... and for any speech or debate in either House, they shall not be questioned in any other place.

This protection against being "questioned in any other place" — that is, in the courts — is intended to throw what is often called a "cloak of legislative immunity" about members of Congress, to protect them against suits for libel or slander which might arise out of their official conduct.

The Supreme Court has held, in *Kilbourn* v. *Thompson*, 1881, that the immunity provided here applies "to things generally done in a session of the House [and Senate] by one of its members in relation to the business before it." The protection extends, then, beyond floor debate, to include reports, resolutions, committee proceedings, and the like.

But a member of Congress is not free to defame another person in a newspaper or magazine article, a public speech, a conversation, or otherwise. The very important and necessary object of the provision is to encourage and preserve freedom of legislative debate.

THE NONLEGISLATIVE POWERS OF CONGRESS

Although the basic function of Congress is to make law, the Constitution also vests it with certain nonlegislative powers.

Electoral. On rare occasion, the House of Representatives may be called upon to elect a President. If no candidate receives a majority of the electoral votes for President, the House, voting by States, must choose one from among the three highest candidates. Similarly, the Senate may be called upon to choose a Vice President when no candidate for that office receives an electoral college majority.[32]

The House of Representatives elected

Thomas Jefferson in 1801 and John Quincy Adams in 1825. The Senate chose Richard M. Johnson as Vice President in 1837.

Recall, too, that both houses may one day be called upon to fill a vacancy in the Vice Presidency. The 25th Amendment provides that, in the event of a vacancy in the Vice Presidency, the President should nominate a successor subject to a majority vote of both houses of Congress. See page 287.

Constituent. As we have seen, Congress may propose amendments to the Constitution by a two-thirds vote in each house. And it may call a national convention to propose amendments if such action is requested by two-thirds of the State legislatures.[33]

Judicial. The Constitution provides that the President, the Vice President, and all civil officers of the United States may be removed from office "on impeachment for, and conviction of, treason, bribery, or other high crimes and misdemeanors."[34] The House of Representatives *impeaches* (brings charges), and the Senate sits as a court to try the case.

A two-thirds vote of the Senators present is necessary for conviction, and the Chief Justice of the United States presides when a President is being tried. The penalty for conviction is removal from office, and if it desires, the Senate may add a provision against the holding of any future federal office. After removal, criminal charges may be brought in the regular courts.

To date there have been but twelve impeachments and four convictions. On several other occasions officers have resigned under the

---

[32] 12th Amendment; see pages 291–292, 299–301.

[33] Article V; see pages 54–55.

[34] Article II, Section 4. Military officers are not "civil officers" and are removed by court-martial. Nor are members of Congress. When the House impeached Senator William Blount of Tennessee in 1798, the Senate refused to try the case on grounds that it had the power to expel one of its own members if it saw fit. Blount was later expelled, and the precedent thus set has been followed ever since.

threat of impeachment.[35] When the House of Representatives impeached President Andrew Johnson in 1868, the Senate failed by only one vote to convict him.

Executive. The Constitution grants two "executive powers" to the Senate, one relating to appointments and the other to treaties made by the President.[36]

Approval by a majority vote of the Senate is necessary to all major appointments made by the President. Each such nomination is referred to the appropriate standing committee by the Vice President, unless the Senate orders otherwise. The committee's report may be considered by the Senate in secret ("executive") session.

The appointments of Cabinet officers and other top officials in the President's "official family" are seldom rejected by the Senate.[37] But the unwritten rule of "senatorial courtesy" enters the picture in the appointments of federal officers who serve in the various States.

This custom provides that the Senate will not approve an appointment if a majority party Senator from the State involved objects to the person named by the President. In practice, this means that the majority party Senators often dictate many appointments.[38]

Treaties are made by the President "by and with the advice and consent of the Senate. . . provided two-thirds of the Senators present concur." For a while after the adoption of the Constitution the advice of the Senate was asked before the President prepared a treaty, but now he merely consults with the Senate Foreign Relations Committee and with influential members of both parties. The Senate may reject a treaty in full or may suggest amendments, reservations, and understandings to it. Treaties may be considered in executive (secret) session.[39] Because the House of Representatives has a hold on the governmental purse strings, influential House members are frequently consulted, too.

---

[35] The four persons removed were all judges. One other judge resigned after the House impeached him but just before the Senate began his trial, and the case was dropped. Four other judges were acquitted. Aside from Senator Blount and President Johnson, W. W. Belknap, who was President Grant's Secretary of War, was impeached and acquitted in 1876 on the ground that the Senate no longer had jurisdiction because Belknap had resigned.

[36] Article II, Section 2, Clause 2; see pages 312–316

[37] All told, only nine of the more than 450 Cabinet appointments have been rejected by the Senate. The first was Roger B. Taney, Andrew Jackson's choice for Secretary of the Treasury in 1834; two years later President Jackson appointed Taney Chief Justice, the Senate confirmed him, and he served in that position until his death in 1863. The Senate rejected four of President Tyler's Cabinet appointees in 1843 and 1844, two by President Johnson in 1868 and 1869, and one by President Coolidge in 1925. The most recent rejection came in 1959 when the Senate refused to approve President Eisenhower's appointment of Lewis L. Strauss as Secretary of Commerce.

[38] See pages 59, 313. Those who criticize the practice often overlook the fact that a Senator is much more likely to be better informed about affairs in his own State than is the President.

[39] It is often said, erroneously, that the Senate "ratifies" a treaty. It does not. According to the Constitution, Article II, Section 2, Clause 2, the Senate must give its "advice and consent" to a treaty made by the President. After having secured senatorial approval, the President ratifies a treaty by exchanging the "instruments of ratification" with the other party or parties to the agreement.

Investigative. Congress, through its committees, has the power to investigate matters for three purposes: (1) to gather information that may be of use to Congress in the making of law, (2) to see how laws already enacted are working out and whether they need changing, and (3) to determine whether or not programs are actually being administered in the way that Congress intended they should be. See pages 225–226.

See pages 225–226.

❖❖❖❖❖❖❖❖❖❖❖❖ CONCEPT BUILDING ❖❖❖❖❖❖❖❖❖❖❖❖

Key Concepts

Congress is the *legislative* (lawmaking) branch of the National Government. It is composed of two houses—the House of Representatives and the Senate.

Congress is *bicameral* for several reasons: because of the familiarity of the Founding Fathers with the bicameral British Parliament, that all but two of the State legislatures in 1787 were bicameral, the Connecticut Compromise, and the feeling that one house could check the other.

A *term* of Congress lasts two years. There are two *regular sessions* to each term, one a year. *Special sessions* may be called by the President.

Members of the House of Representatives serve a two-year term and are popularly elected. The Congress reapportions the seats in the House among the States on the basis of population after every ten-year census, but each State is guaranteed at least one Representative. The House now consists of 435 members chosen from districts drawn by the legislature in each State. The districts must contain approximately equal populations *(Wesberry* v. *Sanders,* 1964), and may be *gerrymandered.*

A Representative must be at least twenty-five years old, seven years a citizen of the United States, and a resident of the State from which chosen. Political custom has added that he or she must also live in the district from which chosen. The Senate and House each have the power to decide contests over the seating of members-elect. Each house may refuse to seat a member-elect or may censure or expel a member; but in 1969 the Supreme Court held that the House could not properly exclude a member-elect who met the age, citizenship, and residence qualifications set by the Constitution.

Each State has two seats in the Senate. Senators serve a six-year term. One-third of the Senate terms regularly end every two years. Since 1913 (the 17th Amendment), Senators have been popularly elected. They must be at least thirty years old, nine years a citizen of the United States, and inhabitants of the State from which chosen.

Members of Congress fix their own salaries by law. Today they receive $42,500 a year along with various other compensations. They enjoy freedom from arrest for petty offenses while going to, attending, and returning from sessions of Congress, and immunity in debate and their official remarks.

Congress performs several nonlegislative functions—electoral, constituent, judicial, executive, and investigative.

Important Terms

adjourn	district	legislative	session
apportion	franking privilege	nonlegislative powers	*sine die*
bicameral	gerrymandering	reapportionment	special session
Congressman-at-large	impeachment	redistricting	term
decennial census			*Wesberry* v. *Sanders*

Questions for Inquiry and Review

1. Which Article in the Constitution deals especially with Congress? Is there significance to this?

2. What does each house of Congress represent?

3. Why has bicameralism tended to work so well in Congress? *one check up another.*

4. How long is a term of Congress? *2 years*

5. How often are regular sessions of Congress held? *2 regular sessions*

6. Who may call special sessions of Congress? *President*

7. How is the size of the House of Representatives fixed? Of how many members does it now consist? *41,000=1 435*

8. The constitutional duty of reapportioning the House of Representatives is vested where? *Since division.*

9. Do any States have more seats in the Senate than in the House of Representatives? If so, why? *2 seats*

10. By whom are congressional districts drawn? *state.*

11. What did the Supreme Court hold in *Wesberry* v. *Sanders*? *one men one vote. equal vote*

12. What is gerrymandering?

13. When are Representatives elected? Senators? How long is it after the election until they take their seats? What are their terms of office?

14. What are the qualifications for membership in the House of Representatives? In the Senate?

15. Of how many members does the Senate consist? How is its size determined?

16. What salary do Congressmen receive? What further compensation?

17. What is a Congressman's primary job?

18. What special privileges has a Congressman? *be*

19. What are the nonlegislative functions of Congress?

For Further Inquiry

1. It may seem at times that popularity is the only requisite for Congressmen aside from age, citizenship, and residence in the State. What additional qualifications for this important office could be listed?

2. Many times a Congressman finds himself faced with a conflict between his own thinking on a particular piece of legislation and that of his constituents, upon whom he must depend for re-election. Do you think that a Congressman should respond to public opinion or should he investigate, debate, and decide according to his convictions? Consider the words of the British statesmen, Edmund Burke, uttered in 1774:

> . . . Parliament is not a congress of ambassadors from different and hostile interests; which interests each must maintain, as an agent and advocate, against other agents and advocates; Parliament is a deliberative assembly of one nation, with one interest, that of the whole; where not local purpose, not local prejudices ought to guide, but the general good. You choose a member indeed.

But when you have chosen him, he is not a member of Bristol, but he is a member of Parliament.

3. In order to do what the people want them to do, Congressmen must know what it is the people want. How can private citizens inform their Congressmen?

4. Would you favor or oppose a constitutional amendment to lengthen (or shorten) the elected terms of Senators? Why?

5. Should gerrymandering be outlawed by law? How might this political practice be prevented otherwise?

6. In his State of the Union Message in 1966, President Johnson urged that Congress propose a constitutional amendment to increase the terms of Representatives to four years. Why would you favor or oppose such an amendment? Bearing in mind the fact that Senators serve *six*-year terms, why was the proposal greeted with much less enthusiasm by a number of Senators than it was by most members of the House?

Suggested Activities

1. Invite your Representative or Senator to address the class or entire student body on his duties as a member of Congress.

2. Write a report on the background of your Congressman. (Consult such sources as *Who's Who* and *The Congressional Directory*).

3. Stage a debate or class forum on the questions: (a) *Resolved,* That former Presidents should automatically become lifetime members of the Senate; (b) *Resolved,* That Senators should receive a higher salary than Representatives; (c) *Resolved,* That no member of either house be permitted to serve more than three consecutive terms.

Suggested Reading

ADRIAN, CHARLES P. and PRESS, CHARLES, *The American Political Process.* McGraw-Hill, 1969. Chapters 13, 14.

BROWNMILLER, SUSAN, "The First Black Woman Congressman," *New York Times Magazine,* April 13, 1969.

BURNS, JAMES M. and PELTASON, J. W., *Government By the People.* Prentice-Hall, 1969. Chapters 16, 17.

Congressional Directory, 91st Congress, 2nd Session. Government Printing Office, 1970.

DAVIDSON, ROGER H., *The Role of the Congressman.* Pegasus, 1969.

DYE, THOMAS R., *et al., American Government: Theory, Structure, and Process.* Wadsworth, 1969. Chapter 9

KEEFE, WILLIAM J. and OGUL, MORRIS S., *American Legislative Process.* Prentice-Hall, 1968.

LEUTHOLD, DAVID A., *Electioneering in a Democracy: Campaigns for Congress.* Wiley, 1968.

MAGRATH, C. PETER, *et al., The American Democracy.* Macmillan, 1969. Chapter 9.

METHVIN, EUGENE H., "Is Congress Destroying Itself?" *Reader's Digest,* April, 1969.

ODEGARD, PETER H. *et al., The American Republic.* Harper & Row, 1969. Chapter 12.

PRITCHETT, C. HERMAN, *The American Constitution.* McGraw-Hill, 1968. Chapter 10.

REDFORD, EMMETTE S., *et al., Government and Politics in the United States.* Harcourt, Brace and World, 1968. Chapter 12.

"Scandals in Congress: The Record," *U.S. News,* November 10, 1969.

SCOTT, ANDREW M. and WALLACE, EARLE (eds.) *Politics, U.S.A.: Cases on the American Democratic Process.* Macmillan, 1969. Chapter 8.

SHERRILL, ROBERT, "Wright Patman: The Last of the Great Populists," *New York Times Magazine,* March 16, 1969.

VINYARD, DALE, *Congress.* Scribner's 1968.

12
CONGRESS IN ACTION

✦✦✦ Do the details of legislative organization and procedure bear any significant relationship to the overall character of a governmental system? Explain.

✦✦✦ Which of the two houses of Congress is (or should be) the more important in the lawmaking process?

✦✦✦ How can such practices as the seniority rule and the filibuster be fitted into the rationale of representative democracy?

For this reason the laws are made: that the stronger may not have the power to do all that they please.

OVID

Many of the thousands of Americans who visit the House and Senate galleries each year leave with the feeling that all is not quite as it should be. They go fully expecting to see a most impressive scene, steeped in tradition, dignified, and dramatic. Occasionally, that is exactly what they do see. But a typical moment on the floor finds perhaps a dozen or so Senators or perhaps thirty-five or forty Representatives present. The visitors often wonder where all of the other members are and why they aren't "tending to business." From the galleries, much of what is done on the floor seems to be done amidst utter confusion or to be as dull and boring as can be. It is not at all unusual for a Senator or Representative to be speaking while his few colleagues present are chattering and moving about, reading newspapers, working in their seats, or otherwise not paying much attention to what is being said.

Is this Congress in action? Hardly. The view from the galleries is quite incomplete. If those who visit the Capitol could follow a mem-

ber of Congress through the full range of his work—for example, see him in committee sessions, working in his office, meeting with interest groups, contacting administrative agencies on behalf of a constituent, poring over his "home work" late at night—a much different, and a much clearer, view of Congress at work would emerge.

Woodrow Wilson once observed that "the making of laws is a very practical matter." It is also a very complicated, and a very important, matter.

THE CONVENING OF A NEW CONGRESS

Opening Day in the House. When the 435 men and women who have been chosen in their States as Representatives assemble at the Capitol on January 3, they are, in effect, just so many Representatives-elect. Because all its seats are refilled every two years, the House of Representatives has no sworn members, no rules, no organization until the opening-day ceremonies are held.

The Clerk of the preceding House of Representatives presides at the beginning of the first day's session. He calls the roll of members-elect as furnished by the several States.

The members-elect then choose a Speaker, the permanent presiding officer. The new Speaker is always a member of the majority party, and his election on the floor is a mere formality. The majority party *caucus* (conference of party members) has in fact chosen him beforehand.

The new Speaker is then sworn in by the "Father of the House," the member-elect with the longest record of service in the House of Representatives.[1] Once he has taken the oath, the Speaker proceeds to swear in the rest of the members as a body. The Democrats take their seats to the right of the center aisle and the Republicans take their seats to the left of the center aisle.

Then the House members elect the chamber's Clerk, Chaplain, Sergeant-at-Arms, Doorkeeper, and Postmaster. As with the Speaker, their elections are little more than a formality. The majority party caucus has already decided whom they shall be. Unlike the Speaker, these other officers of the House of Representatives are never members of that body.

Having selected the House officers the members then adopt the House rules. The rules, which have developed over a period of more than 180 years, are in fact those of the preceding House of Representatives and are usually approved with little or no change. Finally, the members of the various standing committees of the House are appointed by a vote of the chamber, and the House of Representatives is fully organized.

---

[1] The "Father of the House" today (1971) is Emanuel Celler of New York who has been a member of the House of Representatives since March 4, 1923.

Opening Day in the Senate. The Senate is a continuous body; that is, it has been continuously organized since its first session in 1789. As we have seen, only one-third of its seats are normally up for election every two years. Term to term there is a regular carryover of two-thirds of its membership.

The Senate thus does not have the problems the House of Representatives faces on opening day. Unless the most recent elections produced a change in party control, its proceedings are usually quite brief and a largely routine formality. The newly elected and re-elected members must be sworn in, vacancies in its organization and on committees must be filled, and a few other details attended to. Then the Senate is ready to deal with those matters which will come before it.

The President's State of the Union Message. When the Senate is notified that the House of Representatives is organized, a joint committee of the two houses informs the President that the Congress of the United States is organized and prepared to receive any communication from him. Within a few days the President delivers his annual State of the Union Message to Congress. The members of the two houses, together with members of the Cabinet, the Justices of the Supreme Court, members of the foreign diplomatic corps, and many other dignitaries, assemble in the House chamber to receive him. In his speech the President presents his observations on the state of the nation in all its concerns, foreign and domestic; and he makes many specific legislative recommendations.

These messages are usually delivered by the President in person and to a joint session of the two houses. Each of them is followed closely both at home and abroad—for in them the President indicates the administration's policies and the course he has charted for the nation. At the conclusion of the President's speech the joint session is adjourned, and each house then turns to the first order of business to come before it.

At this joint session of Congress, Senator Richard Russell, the President <u>pro tem</u> of the Senate, announced that Congress had formally certified the electoral college victory of Richard M. Nixon. (UPI Photo)

THE ORGANIZATION OF CONGRESS

The national legislature is a much larger operation than is generally realized. It now costs some $300,000,000 annually to run.

Only $22,792,500 of this is spent to pay the salaries of the 535 members of the two houses. More than $65,000,000 goes to hire office assistants for members, and the annual stationery bill runs to well over $1,500,000.

There are some 12,000 congressional employees. We have already mentioned a few of them, the Clerk of the House of Representatives, for example. There are hundreds of committee assistants, office clerks, research experts, guards, maintenance men, shorthand reporters, page boys, and groundkeepers. Each of these, in his or her own way, is important to the successful working of Congress.

The Presiding Officers. The *Speaker of the House* is by far the most important and the most powerful member of the House of Representatives. His post is provided in the Constitution and, as the Constitution commands, he is formally elected to office by a vote of the full membership of the House.[2] As a matter of *practical* fact, however, he is the leader of the majority party in the House and is actually chosen by the members of that party in caucus.

Although neither the Constitution nor its own rules require it, the House has invariably selected the Speaker from among its own members. Typically, he has been a long-time member who has risen in stature and influence through his years of service. Speaker John W. McCormack (D., Mass.), who has retired, first entered the House in 1928 and served as Speaker from 1962 to 1971.[3]

At base, the immense power wielded by the Speaker arises out of this fact: He is, at one and the same time, the elected presiding

[2] Article I, Section 2, Clause 5.

[3] The late Sam Rayburn of Texas served as Speaker for a record 17 years, 62 days. Except for two terms in which the Republicans controlled the House of Representatives (1947–1948, 1953–1954), he held the post from September 16, 1940 until his death November 16, 1961. "Mr. Sam," first elected in 1912, also set a record for service in the House: 48 years, 258 days; but this was surpassed on July 16, 1963, by Carl Vinson of Georgia, who served in the House from November 3, 1914, until he retired January 3, 1965, a total of 50 years, 61 days.

officer of the House *and* the acknowledged leader of its majority party. He is expected to preside in a fair and judicial manner, and he regularly does so. But he is also expected to aid the fortunes of his own party and its legislative goals—and he regularly does that, too.

Nearly all of his specific powers revolve about two duties: to preside and to maintain order. He presides over all sessions of the House, or appoints those who take his place when he cannot be present. No member may speak unless and until he is "recognized" by the Speaker. He interprets and applies the rules, refers bills to the standing committees, decides points of order (questions of procedure raised by members), puts questions to a vote, and determines the outcome of most of the votes taken.[4]

The Speaker also appoints the members of all special and conference committees and must sign all bills and resolutions passed by the House. He may order the galleries cleared if he feels that action is necessary. If a member is speaking and strays from the subject at hand the Speaker may rule him out of order and thus force him to relinquish the floor.

Whenever the House is in session, the *mace* (the symbol of the Speaker's authority), rests in a stand to his right. If the Speaker cannot maintain order, he may direct the Sergeant-at-Arms to approach an unruly member with the mace to demand it; if necessary, he may even order the arrest of a defiant member.

As a member, the Speaker may debate and vote on any matter before the House; but when he does engage in debate he must appoint a temporary presiding officer and vacate the chair. Although he may vote on *any* question, he is *required* to vote only to break a tie. (In the House a tie vote results in the defeat of a question. On occasion, then, the Speaker of the House can *cause* a tie and so defeat a measure.)

After the Vice President, the Speaker is next in the line of succession to the Presidency—a considerable testimony to the power and the importance of the office and of its occupant. See page 287.

The *President of the Senate,* who is also the Vice President of the United States, is a much less significant presiding officer than the Speaker of the House. He did not reach his post by dint of long service in the Senate; rather, he came to it out of a strikingly different process, as we shall see in Chapter 16. In fact, he may even be—as he is today (1971)—a member of the party with a minority of the seats in the Senate.

As the regular President of the Senate, the Vice President does have the usual powers of a presiding officer. He recognizes members, puts questions to a vote, and generally acts as an impartial chairman. Since he is not a member of the Senate, he cannot take the floor to argue for his party's program. As President of the Senate, he may, but is not required to, vote *only* to break a tie.

Whatever influence he may have in the Senate comes largely out of his personal qualifications and ability to command that influence. Each of the most recent Vice Presidents—Harry Truman, Alben Barkley, Richard Nixon, Lyndon Johnson, and Hubert Humphrey—had previously served in the Senate and so enhanced the importance of their post.

The Senate does have another presiding officer, the *President pro tempore,* who presides in the absence of the Vice President. He is elected by the Senate itself; hence, he is always a leading member of the majority party and a potent figure in his own right. The Senate's President *pro tem* today (1970) is Senator Richard B. Russell (D., Georgia); he has been in the Senate since 1933 and became President *pro tem* in 1969.

---

[4] On most matters the House takes a *voice vote:* The Speaker puts the question, those in favor respond (shout) "Aye," then those opposed respond "No," and the Speaker decides and declares the result; see page 231.

President Nixon and Vice President Agnew, Republicans, must work with a Congress that is organized under the leadership of the majority party, the Democrats. (UPI Photo)

The Vice President is occasionally absent from the Senate because of his other duties — a more frequent occurrence in late years because recent Presidents have made increasing use of their Vice Presidents. And eight times, thus far, fate has suddenly made the Vice President the President of the United States. See pages 286–288.

Various other members of the Senate also preside over the chamber on a day-to-day basis; a freshman Senator is regularly accorded this "honor" early in his term.

Committee Chairman. Next to the presiding officers in each house, the most important congressional officers are the chairmen of the *standing* (regular, permanent) committees. A large bulk of the actual work of Congress, especially in the House of Representatives, is done in committee. The chairman of each committee is chosen by the majority party caucus, and he is always a ranking member of the majority party.

The chairman usually has the power to decide when his committee will meet, which bills it will consider, if public hearings are to be held, and what witnesses should be called. When a bill has been reported, he manages the debate and attempts to steer it to final passage.

In a moment we shall see how the committees operate in the legislative process, thus returning to the chairman's role; but first we should examine the *seniority rule.*

The seniority rule is an *unwritten custom* closely followed in each house. Under it, the most important posts in the formal and in the party organization of each house usually go to the members who have served the longest in Congress. The rule is applied most strictly in the case of committee chairmen. The chairmanship of each committee always goes to the majority party member who has the longest service on the particular committee.

Those people who attack the rule have a strong case. They claim that it ignores ability, puts a premium on mere length of service, and discourages younger members. They also note that the rule means that a committee chairman almost always comes from a "safe" constituency — that is, a State or district where, election after election, he and his party have no effective opposition. They argue that because the play of fresh and contending forces is almost nil, committee chairmen are often out of touch with current public opinion.

Those people who defend the rule argue that it means that a powerful and experienced member will head each committee. They also cite the fact that the rule is easy to apply, and it practically eliminates intraparty feuds.

Although the weight of the argument is against the rule, there is little prospect for change in the near future. Those who have the power to alter it are the very ones who benefit most from its operation.

Party Organization. The *majority* and *minority floor leaders* are the managers of their party's program on the floor in each house. They are not *official* officers of the House of

Representatives or the Senate; rather, they are *party* officers chosen by the party caucus. Though their positions are unofficial, each is given a huge desk on his own side of the center aisle.

Each of these "quarterbacks" watches over and attempts to control floor action to the benefit of his party. He must try to persuade the members to vote in accord with the wishes of the party leadership—and this is often a difficult task. The majority leader is more important than the minority leader for the simple reason that his party has the most seats (votes) in the house.

Each of the floor leaders is assisted by a *party whip*—who is, in effect, his party's assistant floor leader. He is chosen by his party's caucus, usually upon the recommendation of the floor leader. The whip canvasses the sentiments of party members on legislative questions and advises the floor leader of the number of votes that can be counted upon in any particular matter. Each whip also attempts to see that the members vote with the party's leadership and that they are present when an important vote is to be taken. If a member is away from Washington, the whip sees that he is "paired" with a member of the other party who is also absent or who agrees not to vote on certain measures.

The *party caucus* is a closed meeting of the members of each party in each house. It meets just before Congress convenes in January, and occasionally during a session. In recent years the Republicans have referred to their caucus in each house as the *party conference;* the Democrats have adopted the newer term only in the Senate.

The party caucus decides such questions as the candidate for Speaker and who the floor leaders shall be, and it attempts to secure united party action on certain measures. Often the work of the party caucus is to determine the attitude of the members on pending legislation. Neither party imposes an ironclad acceptance of party caucus decisions on its members—nor

can it. The *Policy Committee,*[5] composed of the party's principal leadership, acts as an "executive committee" for the party caucus.

THE COMMITTEE SYSTEM

Both the House of Representatives and the Senate are so large and their business so great that each has divided itself into several standing committees and many temporary ones.

Standing Committees. In 1789 the House of Representatives and the Senate adopted the practice of appointing a special committee to handle each bill as it was introduced. The situation soon got out of hand, however. By 1794 there were more than 300 committees in each chamber. Each house then began to create permanent groups—standing committees—to which all similar bills could be referred.

The number of standing committees has varied over the years. By 1946 there were forty-eight in the House of Representatives and thirty-three in the Senate. Many members were forced to spend practically all of their time in committee work. On the average, each Representative was serving on two committees and each Senator on five. Several members held even more assignments, and some were serving on two or more of the most important (and work-laden) groups. So, by the Legislative Reorganization Act of 1946, in which many procedures were streamlined, the number of committees was sharply reduced.

Today (1971) there are twenty-one standing committees in the House of Representatives and sixteen in the Senate. The size of each committee now varies from nine to fifty-one members in the House and from seven to twenty-four in the Senate. The rules of the

---

[5] Until recent years both parties in each house referred to this group as the Steering Committee; the older title is still used by the Democrats in the House of Representatives.

STANDING COMMITTEES OF CONGRESS

House Committees

Agriculture	Government Operations	Post Office and Civil Service
Appropriations	House Administration	Public Works
Armed Services	Interior and Insular Affairs	Rules
Banking and Currency	Internal Security	Science and Astronautics
District of Columbia	Interstate and Foreign Commerce	Standards of Official Conduct
Education and Labor	Judiciary	Veterans' Affairs
Foreign Affairs	Merchant Marine and Fisheries	Ways and Means

Senate Committees

Aeronautical and Space Sciences	Commerce	Interior and Insular Affairs
Agriculture and Forestry	District of Columbia	Judiciary
Appropriations	Finance	Labor and Public Welfare
Armed Services	Foreign Relations	Post Office and Civil Service
Banking and Currency	Government Operations	Public Works
		Rules and Administration

lower house limit Representatives to service on only one major committee, and Senate rules allow members to serve on two.

The Speaker and the President of the Senate refer bills to the appropriate standing committee. For instance, the Speaker refers tax bills to the House Ways and Means Committee, and the President of the Senate refers them to the Senate Finance Committee. A bill to amend the Selective Service Act goes to the Armed Services Committee in either chamber.

We have already seen how the committee chairmen are selected according to the seniority rule. Each house also formally elects the other members of its committees.[6]

The majority party controls each committee,[7]

but the minority party also has a substantial representation on each. In fact, party membership on the committees is proportionate to party strength in the entire house. Thus, if the Republicans have 220 seats in the House of Representatives and the Democrats 215, the party split in committee seats is also very close; on a 25-member committee the division would be 13 Republicans and 12 Democrats.

Except for the House Committee on Rules and the Senate Committee on Rules and Administration, each of the standing committees is a "subject-matter" group. That is, each deals with bills relating to particular subjects — for example, the Senate Public Works Committee or the House Committee on the Judiciary.

[6] Though the committee members are *formally* elected by each house, they are *actually* chosen in a much different manner. In the House of Representatives, the Democratic caucus first selects its members for the Ways and Means Committee and these members then act as a "committee on committees" to fill the seats on the rest of the standing committees. The Republicans in their House caucus select a Committee on Committees consisting of one member from each State with Republican representation. Each member of this group has as many votes as there are Republican Representatives from his State. This body fills *all* the Republican committee seats. Each party in the Senate has a Committee on Committees chosen by the party caucus.

[7] The newest House committee, the Committee on Standards of Official Conduct created in 1967, is the only exception here; it is a bipartisan twelve-member body.

We shall discuss the standing committees again when we trace a bill from its introduction to final enactment. But for now, special note should be made of one of them.

The House Committee on Rules. Until 1880, the House Rules Committee was a *special* (temporary) committee set up at the beginning of each term of Congress. Its function was to propose the adoption of the rules of the preceding House and to offer whatever changes, if any, the committee might think necessary. Since it was made a standing committee in 1880, however, the House Rules Committee has grown in power to the place where today it has life-and-death say over most bills.

So many measures are introduced in the House each term—an average of some 20,000 now—that some sort of screening process is obviously necessary. Most bills die in the committees to which they are referred. But many more than the House can possibly handle are reported out by the committees. Hence, before most bills can reach the floor, they must first clear the Rules Committee.

This potent fifteen-member committee has the power to bring in a *special rule* to consider a bill out of its regular order, to limit the length of debate on a bill, or to allow the amendment of no (or only some) sections of a bill on the floor. Thus, it has the power to hasten, delay, or prevent action on a bill. When a special rule is granted, the minority often cries "gag rule!" But each party and faction in the House of Representatives tries to use the device to its own advantage.

In theory, the committee works closely with the House leadership. In fact, however, it has been dominated since the late 1930's by a Republican-Southern Democratic coalition which has often successfully blocked or delayed the consideration of "liberal" legislation.

In the smaller Senate, with its much less strict rules, the Committee on Rules and Administration is only a shadow of its counterpart in the lower house.

Special Committees. From time to time each house creates special committees. These special committees, also known as *select committees,* are temporary and exist only until they accomplish a particular purpose. The members are appointed by the Speaker or by the President of the Senate. The best-known special committee in recent years has been the Senate Select Committee on Improper Activities in the Labor or Management Field, popularly known as the McClellan or Senate Rackets Committee.

Joint Committees. A joint committee is a committee composed of members of both houses of Congress. The Senators and Representatives are appointed to the committee by the presiding officer in their own house and act together in this single body. To date, except for the Joint Committee on Atomic Energy, the Congress has used joint committees most often only for routine and minor matters—for example, the Joint Committee on Printing and the Joint Committee on the Library of Congress. Because the standing committees in each house often duplicate the work of one another, a much wider use of joint committees has long been urged by many authorities on the legislative process.

Conference Committees. Before a bill may be sent to the President for his action, it must be passed in identical form by each house. When the two houses pass differing versions of the same bill, and the first house will not agree to the changes the other house has made, a temporary "conference committee" is appointed.

A conference committee is composed of a varying number of members of each house appointed by the respective presiding officers. Its members attempt to iron out the differences in the House and Senate versions of a bill, aiming at a compromise that will be acceptable to both houses.

Investigating Committees. The power of Congress to investigate is *essential* to the exercise of its law-making function. It must inform itself on matters before it. It must investigate to determine the need for legislation in a given field, the adequacy of legislation previously enacted, and whether the executive branch is functioning effectively and in accord with policies set by law. Investigations are often conducted, as well, to inform the public and arouse its interest in various matters.

Investigations are usually conducted by standing committees, or by their subcommittees. Special committees are sometimes appointed for this purpose; only rarely is an investigation handled by a joint committee. The most widely known investigating committees today are those working in the field of subversive activities, most notably the House Committee on Internal Security and the Internal Security Subcommittee of the Senate Judiciary Committee.

Congressional investigations cover a wide variety of subjects. In recent years some of the major investigations have included one which exposed racketeers in the Teamsters' Union, another which dramatized the need for

and resulted in tighter legal control of prescription drugs, and a third which laid bare the long-secret details of the organization and operations of "Cosa Nostra," the vicious national crime syndicate.

Most congressional investigations, those of which the public seldom is aware, are less spectacular. Examples of these would include instances when the House Committee on Agriculture looks into the question of providing price supports for a particular farm commodity or when the Senate Interior and Insular Affairs Committee tries to determine the need for national forest access roads.

HOW A BILL BECOMES A LAW

Some 20,000 bills are now introduced in each term of Congress. Less than ten per cent ever become law. Where do these bills originate? Why do so few become law? What steps are involved in the making of law?

An important part of the work of Congress is done in committees. Congressional committees, as the Senate Committee on Foreign Relations shown here, hold hearings on affairs that affect the country and its government. (Dennis Brack, Black Star)

Both Houses of Congress must approve a bill in the same form before it is submitted to the President for his signature. This bill to extend programs of assistance for education was referred to a committee in each House after the first reading. Would you judge that this bill made its way through <u>both</u> Houses quickly?

To answer these questions, we shall first trace a bill through the House of Representatives. Then, because the process in the two houses is in many respects quite similar, we shall note the major differences found in the procedures followed in the Senate.

Authorship and Introduction. Very few of the bills introduced in either house are actually written by Congressmen themselves. Many of the most important measures are prepared in the executive departments and handed to a member to introduce. Business, labor, agriculture, education and other pressure groups often draft bills. Some come from private citizens, and many are drafted by the standing committees of the House of Representatives and the Senate.

The Constitution provides that all bills for the raising of revenue must originate (be first introduced) in the House of Representatives.[8] But once a revenue bill passes the House and

is sent to the Senate, the upper house may amend it just as it may amend any other bill.

Only a member may introduce a bill in the House of Representatives. He does so by dropping his bill in the "hopper."[9] As many as 2500 bills have been introduced in the House on opening day.

Types of Bills and Resolutions. Some measures take the form of bills, while others are called resolutions.

Public Bills are measures of general application, such as the Selective Service Act.

Private bills are those that apply to specific persons or places. For example, Congress recently passed an act to pay a man $1229.52, the amount he would have made on a govern-

---

[8] Article I, Section 7, Clause 1.

---

[9] The hopper is a large box hanging at the edge of the Clerk's desk. Only a Senator may introduce a bill in the upper chamber; he does so by addressing the chair.

The Resident Commissioner from Puerto Rico, although not a member, may introduce bills in the House of Representatives.

ment contract if a Wyoming post office had handled his mail promptly.

Joint resolutions differ little from bills and when enacted have the force of law. They usually deal with routine matters but are also used to propose constitutional amendments. A typical use would be one citing a certain week as Boy Scout Week.

Concurrent resolutions deal with matters in which joint action of the House of Representatives and the Senate is necessary but for which a law is not needed. The setting up of a joint committee is usually handled by this device.

Resolutions deal with matters concerning either house alone and are passed only by it; for example, creating a special committee.

A bill usually relates to only one subject, but sometimes a rider dealing with an entirely different matter is included. A *rider*[10] is a provision which rides through a legislative body attached to an important bill certain to pass. Thus, some years ago all barrooms in the Capitol were abolished by a short sentence in an annual appropriations bill.

Reference to Committee. The Clerk of the House of Representatives gives each bill a short *title* (summary of its principal contents) and assigns it a number; H.R. 3410 would be the 3410th bill introduced during the term.[11]

Following its titling the bill gets what is known as its "first reading." Each bill that finally passes in either house is read three times along the legislative route. In the House of Representatives the second reading comes during debate, if the bill gets that far; and the third reading occurs just before the final vote.[12] Each of these readings is usually by title only — "A bill to . . ." — except for important or controversial measures. These are usually read in full, line-by-line, at the second reading.

The Speaker then refers the bill to the appropriate standing committee. The bill is also recorded in the House *Journal* and in the *Congressional Record*[13] for the day.

The Committee Stage. The standing committees have been described as "sieves," sifting out most bills and considering and reporting only the more important or worthwhile ones. Woodrow Wilson once wrote that "Congress in its committee rooms is Congress at work."

Most bills die in committee. They are *pigeonholed*[14] and never see the light of day. Many

---

[10] The term "rider" probably comes from the field of music. A musical string vibrates in sections. If you pinch a strip of paper and hang it over the string at an interval where the string vibrates least, the paper will *ride* the string; if you hang the paper at the wrong interval, it will bounce off.

[11] Bills originating in the Senate receive the prefix "S." — as S. 210.

[12] All bills introduced are immediately printed and distributed to the members. The three readings, really unnecessary now, were quite important in the days when some members could not read.

[13] The *Journal* contains the minutes of the daily proceedings; and these are read at the opening of each day's session, unless dispensed with. The *Congressional Record* is a word-for-word record of the debates, motions, votes, and disposition of bills in each house. Each morning each Congressman has a temporary copy of the previous day's proceedings on his desk. The official reporters often correct the grammar in speeches and give them a more elegant finish without changing the meaning. A Congressman may also "dress up" his remarks before permanent copies are printed.

[14] The term comes from the old-fashioned roll-top desks with pigeonholes into which papers were often put and promptly forgotten. A great number of "by request" bills are regularly killed in each committee. These are bills that Congressmen introduce only because some person or group at home has asked them to do so.

of the bills killed in committee deserve their fate. Occasionally, however, for political or personal reasons, a committee majority will pigeonhole a measure that the majority of the House of Representatives wishes to consider. The bill may be "blasted" out of committee under the *discharge rule*,[15] but this is seldom done successfully.

The bills that a committee, or at least the chairman, does wish to consider are discussed and considered at times indicated by the chairman. Most committees work through *subcommittees,* which are actually "committees within committees." When more important measures come up, committees may decide to hold public hearings on them. Interested persons, private organizations and pressure groups, and government officials are invited to give testimony at these hearings.[16]

Occasionally, subcommittees make *junkets* (trips) to particular areas affected by a measure. Thus, some members of the House Agriculture Committee may journey to the Southwest to look into drought conditions, or members of the Senate Interior and Insular Affairs Committee may visit the Pacific Northwest to gather information on a public power bill.

These junkets are made at public expense, and Congressmen are sometimes criticized for

[15] Under the rule, after a bill has been in committee at least thirty days (seven days in the Rules Committee) a petition signed by a majority (218) of the House membership can force a floor vote on the question of discharging the bill—that is, bringing it to the floor for action. Once the required signatures have been obtained, a seven-day delay occurs. If the committee does not report the bill during that period, any member who signed the petition may (on the second or fourth Monday of the month) move that the committee be discharged. Debate on a discharge motion is limited to twenty minutes. If the motion carries, the House turns to floor consideration of the discharged bill immediately.

[16] If necessary, a committee has the power to *subpoena* a witness. A subpoena is an order compelling one to appear or produce evidence under penalty of contempt for failure to comply.

taking them. But an on-the-spot investigation often proves to be the best way a committee may inform itself.

After examining a bill, the full committee may do one of several things. It may:

(1) Report the bill favorably, with a "do pass" recommendation. It is then the chairman's job to steer the bill through debate.

(2) Refuse to report the bill—pigeonhole it. On occasion some committee chairmen refuse to report a bill they oppose even though a majority of committee members may favor it. The Legislative Reorganization Act (page 235) requires a chairman to report a bill "promptly" after committee approval, but the practice continues.

(3) Report the bill in amended form. Many bills are changed in committee, and several bills on the same subject may be combined before they are reported out.

(4) Report the bill with an unfavorable recommendation. This does not often happen, but sometimes a committee feels that the full body should have a chance to consider a bill or that it does not want to take the responsibility for killing it.

(5) Report a "committee bill." In effect, this is an entirely new bill which the committee has substituted for one or more referred to it. The chairman reports this new bill, and it goes on from there.

The Rules Committee and the Calendars. Before it goes to the floor for consideration, a bill reported by a standing committee is placed on one of several calendars. A *calendar* is a schedule of the order in which bills will be considered on the floor. There are five of these calendars in the House of Representatives:

(1) *The Calendar of the Committee of the Whole House on the State of the Union,* commonly known as the *Union Calendar*—for all bills relating to revenues, appropriations, or government property.

(2) The *House Calendar*—for all other public bills.

IT HAPPENS EVERY YEAR. The mounting press of legislative business, struggles over important measures, archaic procedures, and other causes result in a "logjam" as Congress nears the end of each session. (White, Akron Beacon Journal)

(3) *The Calendar of the Committee of the Whole House,* commonly called the *Private Calendar*—for all private bills.

(4) *The Consent Calendar*—for all bills from the Union or House Calendar which are taken up out of order by unanimous consent of the House of Representatives   These are usually minor bills to which there is no opposition.

(5) *The Discharge Calendar*—for petitions to discharge bills from committee.

Theoretically, bills are taken from the calendars on a first-come-first-served basis. As we have seen, however, the Rules Committee has the power to bring in a special rule to consider a bill out of its regular order, and this is often done. The Rules Committee also can prevent a bill from getting to the floor by failing to bring in a special rule. It is no wonder that the Rules Committee is sometimes known as the "traffic cop of the House."

The Rules Committee is often criticized, and it is true that some members use it for personal or political advantage. But it must be remembered that despite the number of bills that die in committee, many more than the House of Representatives can consider are reported.

For certain bills, definite days are assigned. Bills from the Consent Calendar are considered on the first and third Mondays of each month, District of Columbia measures on the second and fourth Mondays, and private bills each Friday. On "Calendar Wednesdays" the various committee chairmen may call up any bills their committees have acted on.

None of these arrangements is followed too closely, however. What generally happens is rather complicated. Some bills are "privileged." That is, they may be called up at almost any time, interrupting other business less privileged. Privileged bills include general revenue and appropriations measures, reports of conference committees, and special rules. On some days, often the first and third Mondays, a two-thirds vote of the House of Representatives may suspend all rules. When this happens, the House departs so far from its established rules that a major bill can go through all the necessary steps for enactment in a single day.

The House calendars and the complicated order of business developed over the years for several reasons, especially because of: the large size of the House of Representatives, the number and variety of bills introduced, and the fact that no one member could hope to know the contents, to say nothing of the merits, of each bill to be considered. As we have seen, custom, too, has played a large part in the development of the procedures as they exist today.

Consideration on the Floor. When a bill finally manages to reach the floor it receives its "second reading." It is this part of House procedure that is usually seen by the visitors in the galleries.

Many of the bills that the House of Representatives passes are minor ones to which there is little or no opposition. Bills of this kind are usually called from the Consent Calendar, get their second reading by title only, and are quickly disposed of. Nearly all of the more important measures are dealt with in a much different manner, however. They are considered in *Committee of the Whole,* an old parliamentary device for speeding business.

The Committee of the Whole [17] is the House of Representatives sitting not as itself but as one large committee of itself. Its rules are much less strict, and debate is freer. A *quorum* (a majority of the full membership, 218) must be present to permit the House of Representatives to do business, but in Committee of the Whole only 100 members are needed.

When the House of Representatives resolves itself into Committee of the Whole, the Speaker steps down, and the mace is removed; for the House is not legally in session. Another member takes the chair and presides.

General debate is held, and then the bill receives its second reading, section-by-section. As each section of the bill is read, amendments may be offered. Under the "five-minute rule," the supporters and opponents of each amendment have just five minutes to present their case. Votes are taken on each section and its amendments as the reading proceeds.

When the entire bill has been gone through, and some run to many pages, the Committee of the Whole has completed its work. It adjourns, the House of Representatives is back

---

[17] Technically, there are two committees of the whole: the Committee of the Whole House, which considers private bills, and the Committee of the Whole House on the State of the Union, which considers public bills; but both are simply the House of Representatives sitting as a committee of itself. The device has not been used in the Senate, except to consider treaties, since 1930. Because of the Senate's smaller size, many types of committees are somewhat less necessary than in the House of Representatives.

in session, and the committee's work is formally adopted.

Debate. Because of the large size of the House of Representatives, debate must be severely limited A rule adopted in 1841 limits each member to no more than one hour on any point unless he has unanimous consent to speak for a longer time. Since 1880 the rules have provided that if a member strays from the subject the Speaker may force him to sit down.

The majority and minority floor leaders usually decide in advance how much time will be spent on a bill. At any time, however, a member may "move the previous question." That is, he may call for a vote. If the motion is adopted, the Speaker may then allow each side another twenty minutes of debate. After the forty minutes a vote must be taken. The "previous question" is the only motion used in the House of Representatives to *close* (end) debate, but it is a very effective device.

Methods of Voting. Four methods of voting are used in the House of Representatives: (1) *Voice votes* are the most common, with the members shouting "Yea" or "Nay." (2) If any member thinks the Speaker has erred in judging which side has the most voice votes, he may call for a *standing vote,* technically known as a "division of the House." All in favor, and then all opposed, stand and are counted by the Clerk of the House. (3) One-fifth of the members present may demand a *teller vote.* Each of the members voting passes between two tellers, one from each party, and is counted for or against. (4) Finally, a *roll-call* (or *record*) *vote* may be demanded by one-fifth of the members present.[18] On a roll-call vote the Clerk of the House reads the roll and the members are recorded for, against, present but not voting, or absent.

Roll-call votes take from twenty-five to forty-five minutes and are sometimes called for by

---

[18] The Constitution (Article I, Section 7, Clause 2) requires a record vote on the question of overriding a presidential veto.

those who want to delay matters while gathering their strength. Throughout a session all of the roll-call votes taken total about *three months* of working time in the House! If the House of Representatives had an electrical voting system, as half the State legislatures do, much time could be saved.

Voting procedures in the Senate are quite similar, except that the teller vote is not used. Only six or seven minutes are required for taking a roll-call vote in the Senate.

Final Steps in the House. Once a bill is approved at second reading, it is *engrossed,* printed in its final form with all changes made. Then it is read a third time, by title, and the final vote is taken. If the bill is defeated, it must begin all over again if it is ever to pass the House of Representatives. If it is approved, as most bills which reach this stage are, it is signed by the Speaker and taken to the Senate by a page boy who lays it on the Vice President's desk.

THE BILL IN THE SENATE

As the steps in the legislative process are quite similar in each house, we need not trace a bill in the Senate as we did in the House of Representatives. Bills are introduced by Senators, read twice, given a number and short title, and referred to standing committees. In committee they are dealt with much as they are in the House.

The Senate has only one calendar for all bills and they are called up at the discretion of the majority floor leader. Proceedings are less formal, and the rules are less strict than in the much larger House of Representatives.

The Filibuster. The chief difference in Senate and House procedure comes in debate. It is strictly limited in the House of Representatives, but it is almost unfettered in the Senate —and most Senators are intensely proud of belonging to "the greatest deliberative body in the world."

Free debate in the Senate is sometimes abused, however, by a *filibuster,* the practice of "talking a bill to death." Under Senate rules, once a Senator gets the floor he may hold it for as long as he chooses. One or more Senators filibuster by monopolizing the floor, talking on and on, in an attempt to force the Senate to drop the bill involved or change it in some manner.

No Senate rule requires a member to speak only on the subject at hand, so filibusterers usually supply themselves with several documents, books, dictionaries, and the like. In 1935 Senator Huey Long of Louisiana spoke for fifteen and a half hours; he stalled along by reading from the Washington telephone directory and a mail-order catalog, and regaled his colleagues with recipes for "pot-likker," corn bread, and turnip greens. In 1947 Glen Taylor of Idaho spent eight and a half hours talking on his children, Wall Street, baptism, and fishing.

The current filibuster record was set by J. Strom Thurmond of South Carolina; he held the floor for twenty-four hours and eighteen minutes in an unsuccessful effort against the Civil Rights Bill in 1957. Mrs. Maurine Neuberger of Oregon became the Senate's first woman filibusterer when she spoke for four and a half hours against the Communications Satellite Bill in 1962.

While talk is the filibusterer's major weapon, time-consuming motions, repeated quorum calls, roll-call votes, and points of order are often used, too. Anything to obstruct action is grist for the minority as it attempts to thwart the majority in the dispute.

Over the past century, some 200 measures, most of them appropriations bills, have been killed by filibusters; and the *threat* of a filibuster has resulted in the failure to consider or the amending of many more. Most, but by no means all, filibusters in recent years have been staged by Southern Senators.

The Senate often tries to beat a filibuster with lengthy, even day-and-night, sessions to

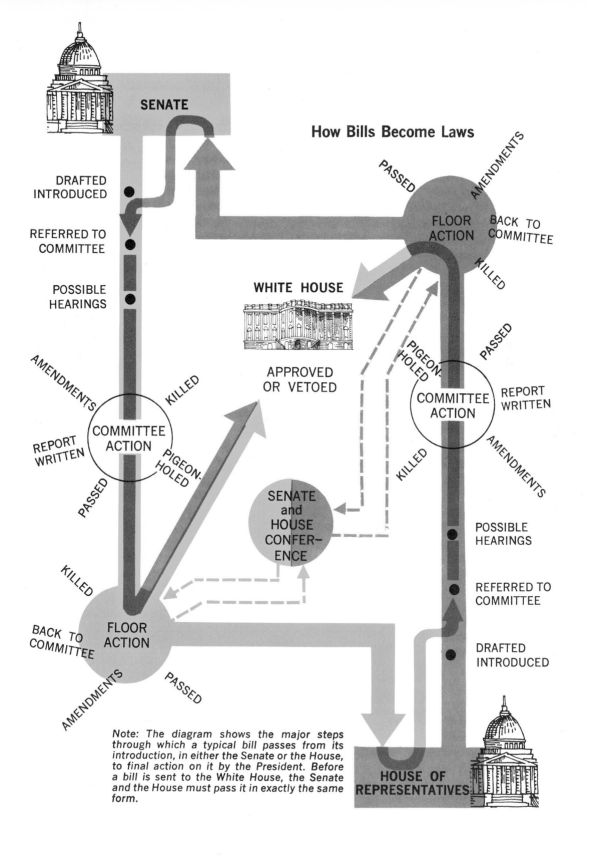

How Bills Become Laws

SENATE

DRAFTED
INTRODUCED

REFERRED TO
COMMITTEE

POSSIBLE
HEARINGS

AMENDMENTS

KILLED

REPORT
WRITTEN

PASSED

COMMITTEE
ACTION

PIGEON-
HOLED

KILLED

BACK TO
COMMITTEE

AMENDMENTS

FLOOR
ACTION

PASSED

WHITE HOUSE

APPROVED
OR VETOED

SENATE
and
HOUSE
CONFER-
ENCE

FLOOR
ACTION

PASSED

AMENDMENTS

BACK TO
COMMITTEE

KILLED

PIGEON-
HOLED

KILLED

COMMITTEE
ACTION

REPORT
WRITTEN

AMENDMENTS

POSSIBLE
HEARINGS

REFERRED TO
COMMITTEE

DRAFTED
INTRODUCED

HOUSE OF
REPRESENTATIVES

Note: The diagram shows the major steps through which a typical bill passes from its introduction, in either the Senate or the House, to final action on it by the President. Before a bill is sent to the White House, the Senate and the House must pass it in exactly the same form.

wear down the participants. At times some little-observed Senate rules are strictly enforced — for example, the requirement that a member stand, not sit or lean on his desk or walk about as he speaks; or that he not use "unparliamentary language." But these techniques seldom work.

The Cloture Rule. The Senate's ultimate antifilibuster weapon is the Cloture Rule. It was first adopted in 1917, but it does not regularly apply and is difficult to bring into play As the rule now stands, a vote to invoke *cloture* (limit debate) must be taken two days after a petition calling for it has been submitted by at least sixteen Senators. A two-thirds majority of the members *present and voting* is needed for approval. Thereafter, each member has *one hour* in which to discuss the bill; then a final vote *must* be taken.

All told, from 1917 to 1971, forty-seven attempts to invoke cloture have occurred. Of these, only eight succeeded — and thus closed debate on: the Versailles Treaty in 1919, joining the World Court in 1926, a banking bill in 1927, a prohibition bill in 1927, the Communications Satellite Act in 1962, the Civil Rights Act of 1964, the Voting Rights Act of 1965, and the Civil Rights (Open Housing) Act of 1968.

THE FINAL STAGES

The Conference Committee. Before a bill may be sent to the White House, each house must have passed it in exactly the same form Most routine bills go through both houses in identical form, but the two chambers often disagree on various sections in more important pieces of legislation.

When the two houses do pass differing versions of the same bill, and the first house will not agree to the changes the other has made, a *conference committee* — a temporary joint committee — is appointed. It seeks to "iron out" the differences and produce a compromise bill which will be acceptable to both houses.

Each conference committee is composed of a varying number of Representatives and Senators appointed by the respective presiding officers. Almost invariably the conferees ("managers") from each house are leading members of the standing committee which originally handled the disputed measure. In fact, the chairman and the ranking minority member of that committee are usually appointed, along with others who were conspicuous on each side in the consideration of the bill. The majority position in each house is always represented by a majority of the conferees from that chamber; but the minority is always represented, too.

The rules of each house restrict a conference committee to the consideration of those points in a bill upon which the two houses have disagreed. The rules also prohibit the inclusion of new material in a compromise version. In practice, however, the conferees possess a large amount of discretion. They meet in secret, almost never hold public hearings or invite outside testimony, and keep no record of their proceedings; and very often their product contains provisions not previously considered in either house.

A conference committee's report — the compromise bill it has hammered out — must be considered as a whole in each house. It cannot be amended on the floor. It must be accepted or rejected as it comes from the committee. Given the potent membership of the typical conference committee, and, too, the fact that its report is usually made toward the end of a congressional session, it is small wonder that neither house very often rejects a conference committee's work.

In short, the conference committee stage is an extraordinarily strategic step in the legislative process — a point at which many important legislative decisions may be, and in fact often are, made. Indeed, the late Senator George Norris of Nebraska once aptly described the hard-working conference committees as "the third house of Congress."

The President's Action. After passing both the House of Representatives and the Senate in the same form, a bill is sent to the President. He has ten days, not counting Sundays, in which to act. If he signs it, it becomes the law of the land. If he does not act within the ten-day period, it becomes law without his signature. Should Congress adjourn within the ten days and the President has not signed it, the bill dies — the "pocket veto" has been applied.

If the President does not approve of a bill, he may veto it. In this case, he must send it back to the house in which it was first introduced, together with his objections to it. Congress seldom passes a bill over the President's veto, but it may by a two-thirds vote in each house. See pages 317–318.

CONGRESSIONAL REFORMS

Much of the internal organization and rules of procedure in Congress are strongly in need of streamlining. Congress itself has recognized the problem. The Legislative Reorganization Act of 1946 was passed to bring about some much needed reform. That act reduced the number of standing committees in each house, furnished committees with expert professional staffs, and expanded the Legislative Reference Service to aid Congressmen. It further provided for the registration of lobbyists, attempted to reduce the number of private bills, and relieved Congress of many petty tasks.

Indeed, many Congressmen were surprised that so much was accomplished in 1946. But much still remains to be done. Petty politics and vested interests have several times blocked further improvement.

The seniority rule for committee chairmanships still vexes both houses. At the end of each session a logjam of unpassed bills always piles up. Many of these are then passed with inadequate consideration, while other more worthy bills are lost in the shuffle. Filibustering in the Senate is still a matter for debate.

Many Congressmen have long complained of the need for closer contact with the executive branch of the National Government. Several members think that this can be accomplished by allowing members of the President's Cabinet and other officials to appear on the floor of each house at regularly scheduled times for questioning and debate.

The investigative power, a very valuable legislative tool, has occasionally been abused. Witnesses before certain committees have at times been denied their rights, and some have suffered unjustified damage to their reputations. Some, but by no means most, who have refused to answer committee questions and have been cited for contempt of Congress have later been found by the courts to have been justified in their refusals. A few ambitious Congressmen have used investigations for publicity purposes to attract attention to themselves, especially when they were planning to seek re-election or another office.

Many constituents make unreasonable demands on their Congressman, who feels obligated to meet these demands if he is to keep good will at home (in his district). Some Congressmen spend more time with their private affairs than with the nation's business.

Reforms and improvements in these and similar matters are not easy to achieve. It is up to Congress, supported by public opinion, to meet and solve these problems.

THE LIBRARY OF CONGRESS

The Library of Congress is the largest library in the world and is one of the oldest agencies of the National Government. It was established in 1800 when Congress appropriated $5000 to purchase "such books as may be necessary for the use of Congress."

The Library of Congress is administered by the Librarian of Congress who is appointed by the President and confirmed by the Senate. It now occupies two huge buildings near the

Capitol, and will soon need a third. Its thirty-five acres of floorspace and shelving house more than 55,000,000 items including 14,000,000 books and pamphlets and 28,500,000 manuscripts. The number of photographs, maps, and musical manuscripts total more than 3,000,000 each. There are over 220,000 recordings and 200,000 fine prints, as well as a gigantic number of newspapers, magazines, posters, motion pictures, microfilms, and other published materials in the Library's collections. The holdings grow steadily, even though millions of pieces not worth saving are discarded each year.

First priority in the Library's work goes to its original purpose: serving Congress. The Library's Legislative Reference Service is almost exclusively concerned with making studies and compiling information to aid the committees and individual members of Congress.

While the Library of Congress fits its title and is *the* Library *of* Congress, it performs other services, too. In more than a century and a half its range of services has come to include the entire National Government and the general public.

The Library of Congress is open to all adults who wish to use its unmatched research facilities. It has 200 research rooms, many of them air-conditioned. It will photo-duplicate materials at a reasonable cost for those unable to visit the Library in person. If other business permits, it will provide some reference services by correspondence. It loans many of its books on an interlibrary loan basis and has developed a card catalog system now in use in most of the libraries throughout the nation. As a special service, it provides books in Braille and recordings for the blind. The Copyright Office is also within the Library of Congress.[19]

---

[19] The Register of Copyrights is appointed by and subordinate to the Librarian of Congress. His office is located in the annex of the Library. When a book or other piece is published and is to be protected by copyright, it must be registered. Promptly upon publication two of the best copies of an edition of a book must be sent, together with a $6 fee and a copyright application form, to the Register of Copyrights. For a work of art, a photograph may be sent. Lectures, dramas, and music, published or not, may also be copyrighted for a fee of $6. The fee is also $6 for any print or label used for an article of merchandise.

❖❖❖❖❖❖❖❖❖❖❖ CONCEPT BUILDING ❖❖❖❖❖❖❖❖❖❖❖

Key Concepts

Opening day in the House of Representatives is filled with ceremony. A Speaker must be chosen, the members sworn in, employees selected, the rules adopted, and committee posts filled. The Senate's first day is much more simple because it is a continuous body and does not require such wide reorganization.

After organizing, the two houses await the President's State of the Union Message. In this speech the Chief Executive reports on the condition of the country and makes many specific legislative recommendations.

The Speaker is the most important member of the House of Representatives. His chief duties are to preside and to maintain order. He uses his powers in a partisan way. The Vice President (or the President *pro tem*) presides over the Senate.

Committee chairmen, chosen under the controversial seniority rule, have almost life-and-death power over bills in their committees. Much of the actual work of Congress is done in committees.

The majority and minority floor leaders manage their parties' programs on the floor, assisted by the party whips. The party caucus consists of all the party's members in either house and has an "executive committee" known as the Policy or Steering Committee.

Congress does a great deal of its work in committees, especially in the House of Representatives. Standing committees are permanent, and bills introduced are referred to them for consideration. One, the House Rules Committee, is "the traffic cop of the legislative process." Special committees are temporary. Joint committees, consisting of members of each house, are generally permanent. Conference committees "iron out" differences in bills passed by both houses. Investigating committees provide information to Congress.

Bills may be introduced only by Senators or Representatives, though they usually originate with another source, the executive branch, for example. After introduction they are referred to committee, where most of them die. Bills reported out go on one of five calendars in the House of Representatives to be called up through the Rules Committee. There is only one calendar for bills in the Senate, and they are called up by the majority floor leader. The House Rules Committee, through its power to bring in special rules, is very powerful.

Bills are debated in the House of Representatives at the second of the three readings. The House, but not the Senate, considers most important bills in Committee of the Whole.

Debate is sharply limited in the House of Representatives but not in the Senate. Filibustering, talking a bill to death, may be prevented in the Senate, but seldom has been.

Bills passed in different form by the two houses go to a conference committee. Then the bill goes to the President who may sign it, allow it to become law without his signature, veto it, or pocket veto it. Congress may override a veto by a two-thirds vote in each house.

Congress is in need of many reforms, but political considerations many times block much needed changes.

The Library of Congress, the largest library in the world, is intended especially for the use of members of Congress, but it does much for the general public, too.

Questions for Inquiry and Review

1. Why is the opening day of a term a much simpler matter in the Senate than the House of Representatives?

2. Who presides over the House of Representatives? How is he chosen?

3. Who presides over the Senate? How is he chosen?

4. Why does the Senate have an alternate presiding officer?

5. On what basis are committee chairmen selected? By whom are they chosen? Why are they so powerful?

6. Who selects the floor leaders? The whips? What are their major jobs?

7. May the party caucus bind its members to follow its decisions?

8. How many standing committees are there in the House of Representatives? The Senate?

9. What role does the Rules Committee play in the House of Representatives?

10. Why is it essential that Congress have the power to investigate?

11. Who may introduce bills in each house? About what proportion of those introduced actually become law? Where are many of the most important actually prepared?

12 Who refers bills to committee in the House of Representatives? The Senate?

13. What is the function of the various calendars in the House of Representatives?

14. Why is the Committee of the Whole a much more important and widely used device in the House of Representatives than in the Senate?

15. Why is debate more drastically limited in the House of Representatives than in the Senate?

16. What four methods of voting are used in the House of Representatives? Which is used most often? Which is not used in the Senate?

17. How may a filibuster be ended?

18. What four actions may the President take when he receives a bill from Congress?

19. By what vote may a presidential veto be overridden?

20. What seem to be the major obstacles to needed reforms in congressional organization and procedures?

21 What is the primary function of the Library of Congress?

For Further Inquiry

1. Many Congressmen are reluctant to vote on certain roll calls Why? Would you favor or oppose an electrical voting system which would provide a record of voting by each Congressman for the information of his constituents?

2. One of the most famous filibusters in Senate history occurred in March, 1917. President Wilson had asked Congress to enact a law authorizing him to arm merchant vessels for protection against German submarine attacks. The bill passed the House of Representatives by a vote of 403 to 13. Nearly all members of the Senate favored it. But a small handful managed to kill it by filibustering. The public was outraged, and President Wilson wrote: "A little group of willful men, representing no opinion but their own, have rendered the great Government of the United States helpless and contemptible." As a result of this episode, the Senate passed the Cloture Rule. The rule is a weak one, however. What is your own attitude toward filibusters? Should they be prohibited? Allowed?

3. Such surveys as the Gallup Poll, the Roper Poll, and those conducted by various newspapers and magazines indicate public opinion. Should a Congressman vote in accordance with the results of these polls even when he personally disagrees with the majority opinion? Should he vote for the national good even when this conflicts with what might be best for his own district or State? Explain.

4. Do you think, as many do, that sessions of Congress should be broadcast and televised? Why?

5. Many political scientists strongly urge congressional reform. What do you consider the most needed congressional reform? Why?

6. Explain the meaning of this comment: "Ideally, a member of Congress should be both *responsive* and *responsible.*" Which of these characteristics do you consider to be the more significant to democratic government?

7. Why do conference committees meet in executive session? What would likely be the effect of open sessions on their work?

8. Why do you think the Founding Fathers provided that: (a) "All bills for raising revenue shall originate in the House of Representatives" (Article I, Section 7, Clause 1); and (b) ". . . but no appropriation of money to that use [to raise and support Armies] shall be for a longer term than two years" (Article I, Section 8, Clause 12)?

Important Terms

calendar
caucus
cloture rule
committee of the
  whole
conference committee
Congressional Record
discharge rule
filibuster
joint committee
junket
majority floor leader
minority floor leader
party whip
pigeonhole
President pro tem
private — public bill
resolution
rider
roll-call vote
rule of seniority
Speaker of the House
special committee
standing committee
standing vote
teller vote
veto
voice vote

Suggested Activities

1. Stage a class forum or debate on one of the following questions: (a) *Resolved,* That the seniority rule should be abolished in both houses of Congress; (b) *Resolved,* That filibusters should be prohibited in the Senate; (c) *Resolved,* That congressional committees should be denied the power to make investigations; (d) *Resolved,* That Republican and Democratic Party members in each house should be required to vote in accord with the decisions of their respective party caucuses.

2. Trace a current bill in Congress as it goes through the legislative mill. Write to your Congressman and Senators to learn their positions on it. Ask them if they would kindly forward to you the committee reports relating to the measure. Then, give an oral report to the class.

3. Write a report on one of the following topics: (a) the work of the House Rules Committee, (b) the office of Speaker, (c) the seniority rule, (d) congressional reform, or (e) the Library of Congress.

4. Make a bulletin board display depicting the course of a bill in becoming a law.

Suggested Reading

"A Raise for Members of Congress — And That's Not All," *U.S. News,* February 17, 1969.

"Breakdown Near In Congress?" *U.S. News,* October 6, 1969.

Congressional Directory, 91st Congress, 2nd Session. Government Printing Office, 1970.

DAVIDSON, ROGER H., *The Role of the Congressman.* Pegasus, 1969.

FINNEY, JOHN W., "The Long Trial of John Paton Davies," *New York Times Magazine,* August 31, 1969.

"Influence Peddling in Washington," *Time,* May 16, 1969.

KING, LARRY L., "Inside Capitol Hill: How the House Really Works," *Harper's,* October 1968.

METHVIN, EUGENE H., "Is Congress Destroying Itself?" *Reader's Digest,* April, 1969.

MORROW, WILLIAM L., *Congressional Committees.* Scribner's, 1969.

PETTIT, LAWRENCE K. and KEYNES, EDWARD, *Legislative Process in the U.S. Senate.* Rand, McNally, 1968.

RIPLEY, RANDALL B., *Majority Party Leadership in Congress.* Little, Brown, 1969.

"Scandals in Congress: The Record," *U.S. News,* November 10, 1969.

13
THE POWERS
OF CONGRESS

***Why has Congress <u>only</u> those powers delegated to it by the Constitution?

***Are there any powers which, in your view, Congress should possess but does not? If so, which ones?

***Is the concept of implied powers a corruption of the concept of federalism? Why or why not?

All legislative powers herein granted shall be vested in a Congress of the United States....

ARTICLE I, SECTION I
CONSTITUTION OF THE UNITED STATES

As the opening words of Article I of the Constitution indicate, and as we have seen, the basic function of the Congress is to legislate, to make law. In this and the next two chapters we shall be concerned with the legislative powers of Congress—that is, with those constitutional powers upon the basis of which Congress can and does make law.[1]

The Scope of Congressional Powers. At this point it would be wise to recall the discussion of the division of powers in the American Federal System (pages 63–67). Neither Congress nor the National Government as a whole is all-powerful. The Constitution imposes a number of restrictions and prohibitions. Large areas of power are denied—in so many words by the Constitution, because of that document's silence on many subjects, or because of the very nature of the Federal System itself.

In short, Congress possesses *only* those powers delegated to it by the Constitution. It cannot do a great variety of things. For example, it cannot create a national public school system, require that all eligible voters cast ballots on election day, nor insist that all persons attend church. It cannot enact a uniform marriage and divorce law, regulate city transit systems, nor prohibit trial by jury. These and many other things it cannot do because it has not been granted power to do so.

Recall, too, that Congress *is* granted the power to do many things. The Constitution delegates specific powers to Congress in three distinct ways: (1) expressly, in so many words (the *expressed powers*), (2) by implication, by reasonable deduction from the expressed powers (the *implied powers*), and (3) by virtue of the fact that it creates a *national* government for the United States (the *inherent powers*).

Strict Versus Liberal Construction. Hardly had the Constitution come into force when a dispute arose as to just how broad the

---

[1] The *non-legislative* powers of Congress are treated in Chapter 11, pages 213–215.

powers it granted to Congress actually were. The *strict-constructionists,* led by Thomas Jefferson, favored retaining as much power as possible in the States. They agreed with Jefferson that "that government is best which governs least." In essence, they wanted to restrict Congress to those powers actually stated in the Constitution. The *liberal-constructionists,* led by Alexander Hamilton, favored a strong National Government and, therefore, a liberal or broad interpretation of the Constitution in order to widen the powers of Congress.

As we shall see, those who favored a liberal interpretation prevailed. They established a general pattern which has been followed through our history to the present day. They set a precedent from which, over the years, national power has increased markedly.

Several factors have been responsible for this growth in national power. Wars, economic crises, and other national emergencies have been very important causes. The demands of the people themselves for more and more governmental services have also played a significant part, as have the tremendous industrial and technological advances the nation has made.

These, and perhaps other similar factors, have led Congress to view its powers in broad terms. In the same sense, most Presidents have regarded and exercised their powers in this fashion. The Supreme Court in deciding cases involving the powers of the National Government has generally adopted a like position. And, significantly, the American people have been in general agreement on a liberal rather than a strict interpretation of the Constitution.

THE EXPRESSED POWERS

Most, but not all, of the expressed powers are found in Article I, Section 8, Clauses 1 through 17 of the Constitution. The grants of power are very brief. What these grants permit Congress to do—and what they do not permit—often cannot be discovered by reading the few words involved. Rather, their meanings are to be found in the ways in which Congress has in fact exercised its powers since 1789 and in scores of Supreme Court decisions in cases involving these powers.

To illustrate, the Constitution (Article I, Section 8, Clause 3) gives to Congress the power "to regulate commerce with foreign nations, and among the several States, and with the Indian tribes." This wording of the Commerce Clause is both brief and general. Congress and the Supreme Court have had to answer numerous questions in defining the meaning of the Commerce Clause. For example, what does "commerce" include? Does it include persons? Radio and television broadcasts? Air transportation? Business and labor organization? What is *interstate commerce?*

In answering these and numerous other questions about this one brief provision Congress and the Supreme Court have spelled out, and are still spelling out, the meaning of the Commerce Power. So it is with each of the other provisions of Article I, Section 8 and of other portions of the Constitution which vest power in Congress.

The Taxing Power and the Commerce Power. The two most important legislative powers of Congress are those to *tax* and to *regulate foreign and interstate commerce.* In fact, they are of such significance that we shall consider them separately in Chapters 14 and 15.

Power to Make Money. Congress has the power "to coin money [and] regulate the value thereof." [2] The States are forbidden to do so. [3]

---

[2] Article I, Section 8, Clause 5.

[3] Article I, Section 10, Clause 1 forbids the States to coin money, emit *bills of credit* (paper money), or make anything but gold and silver coin a tender in the payment of debts Congress can make coins or paper money legal tender. (*Legal tender* is any kind of money a creditor is required by law to accept in payment of a monetary debt.)

Only the National Government has the power to print United States currency. Paper money is carefully examined for flaws before it is issued. (Bureau of Engraving and Printing, United States Treasury Department)

Before the Revolutionary War the English shilling was the recognized unit of value, and the restraining hand of the mother country kept issues of depreciated paper money within bounds. With the coming of independence, however, the legislatures of several States printed the States' names on paper and called it money. As always happens, bad money drove good money from circulation. With each State's money unstable and declining in value, local business was at best uncertain, and interstate trade was quite intolerable.

The Founding Fathers gave Congress the power to *coin* money. But the Constitution says nothing of paper money, except to forbid to the States the power to issue it.

From the beginning, the United States has issued coins—in gold (until 1933), silver, and other metals. Congress chartered the First Bank of the United States in 1791, but the *notes* (paper money) it issued were not made legal tender. Congress did not create a national paper currency as legal tender until 1863.[4]

At first the new national notes ("greenbacks") could not be redeemed for coin at the Treasury and their worth fell to less than half their face value on the open market. In 1870 the Supreme Court held the issuance of the notes to be unconstitutional. Said the Court, "to coin" meant to stamp metal and this could not be held to include paper money.

The Supreme Court soon reversed itself, however. In 1871 and 1884 it upheld the issuing of paper money as legal tender as a proper exercise of the power to coin money and regulate its value, as well as a proper exercise of the power to borrow and the war-making powers.

The Borrowing Power. The Constitution gives Congress the power to "borrow money on the credit of the United States."[5] When there are unusual undertakings—such as the construction of the Panama Canal, wars, relief for large numbers of unemployed, or as today extraordinary costs of the war in Viet Nam —the national revenue often is not adequate to cover the costs involved. Congress borrows to meet the deficit. There is no constitutional limit on the amount which may be borrowed, but Congress has placed a ceiling on the public debt—one which it raises or lowers as conditions demand. At the start of fiscal year 1971 the nation's outstanding public debt totalled more than $370,918,000,000.

---

[4] Although they could not issue paper currency, the States chartered private banks whose notes did circulate as money. As these notes interfered with the new national currency, Congress imposed a 10% tax on their issuance in 1865, and they soon disappeared. The tax was upheld as constitutional in 1869. See page 261.

[5] Article I, Section 8, Clause 2; see pages 371–377.

The most common method of governmental borrowing is through the sale of bonds. Bonds used by governments or corporations when they borrow money are like *promissory notes* ("I.O.U.'s") given by individuals when they borrow—a promise to pay a certain sum at a specified time.

These government bonds are purchased as investments by individuals, business concerns, and especially insurance companies and banks. The National Government could borrow all the money it needs from banks, or it could simply print all the money it wants. But to do either of these things would mean placing more money in circulation, thus contributing to inflation.

The constitutional right to borrow makes borrowing a national function; hence federal bonds cannot be taxed by the States. The right to borrow also implies the right to establish national banks to assist the National Government in securing loans. It would have been very difficult to finance World War II had not the nation's banks bought most of the bonds.

Bankruptcy. Congress has power to pass "uniform laws on the subject of bankruptcies throughout the United States" [6] *Bankruptcy* is a legal proceeding for the distribution of a debtor's assets among his creditors when he is unable to pay his bills in full. When a person has been declared a bankrupt, he is no longer legally responsible for any debts made before his bankruptcy.

The National Government and the States both have power in the field of bankruptcy It is, then, a concurrent power. Except for three brief periods, Congress left the matter entirely under State control for more than 100 years In 1898, however, Congress passed a general bankruptcy law, and today the law is so all-inclusive that it practically excludes the States from the field.

Bankruptcy proceedings are usually handled by the United States District Court in the dis-

[6] Article I, Section 8, Clause 4

The Government borrows money through the sale of bonds. On the $1000 bond (above) the Government will pay interest semi-annually for five years. Savings Bonds (below), in $25 to $10,000 denominations, mature in seven years.

trict in which the bankrupt lives. The court generally appoints an officer (referee) to handle the details of the case. The referee investigates and advises the judge. After a hearing, the judge either declares the person a bankrupt or dismisses the case.

Today, any individual or corporation, except railroads, banks, building and loan associations, insurance companies, and cities, may voluntarily begin bankruptcy proceedings. Creditors may begin proceedings against any individual or corporation, except those just listed and wage earners.

Depending on State law, a bankrupt is allowed to keep certain kinds of property, such as tools or land, so that he can support himself and his family. In some instances, it is possible for one to be declared a "debtor" and have his debts adjusted downward without actually becoming a bankrupt.

Naturalization. Naturalization is the process by which citizens of one country become citizens of another. Congress has the power "to establish a uniform rule of naturalization." [7] As we have seen, Congress has provided that certain classes of persons may not become naturalized citizens.

The Postal Power. Congress has the power "to establish post offices and post roads." [8] Post roads are all letter carrier routes, including railroads and the waters of the United States during the time that mail is carried thereon.

The United States Postal Service, created by Congress in the Postal Reorganization Act of 1970, operates the mail system as a public monopoly. There are presently some 32,000 post offices, most of them in buildings leased from private owners, which do nearly $7,000,000,000 in business annually. The more than 720,000 postal workers now handle over some 85,000,000,000 pieces of mail a year.

Under its power to establish post roads, Congress has made it a federal crime to obstruct the passage of the mails "knowingly and willfully." Thus, if someone purposely wrecked a train carrying mail, he would be committing a federal as well as a State offense.

States cannot interfere unreasonably with the mails. For example, they cannot require trains carrying mail to make an unreasonable number of stops, require a license for cars owned by the United States, nor tax gas used in mail trucks. The States, however, can tax those who carry mail on contract.

No person can use the mails to commit a federal or State crime. Articles which are banned by a State's laws, such as whiskey or firecrackers, cannot be sent into a State through the mails. A great many other items — including such things as poisons, obscene literature, and lottery tickets — cannot be mailed.

Copyrights and Patents. Congress is given the power "to promote the progress of science and useful arts, by securing, for limited times, to authors and inventors, the exclusive right to their respective writings and discoveries." [9]

A *copyright* is the exclusive right of an author or his assignee to print and publish his literary or artistic work. The copyright laws, administered by the Copyright Office in the Library of Congress, guarantee an author or an artist the exclusive right to publish, sell, or reproduce his work for a twenty-eight-year period. This protection is renewable for an additional twenty-eight years. A copyright covers all products of literary and artistic efforts — books, magazine articles, musical compositions, photographs, paintings, maps, cartoons, and motion pictures.

If an author's copyright is infringed upon by another person, he may sue for damages in the federal courts (see page 578). We have treaties with several foreign nations which extend the protection of our copyright laws to their citizens and which, in turn, afford similar protection to American citizens. Unfortunately, we do not have such treaties with all countries. The "pirating" of works by American authors, composers, and artists has become a fairly common and quite serious problem in such countries as the Soviet Union, Communist China, and Nationalist China in recent years.

A *patent* is a grant of the exclusive right to manufacture, use, or sell "any new and useful art, machine, manufacture, or composition of matter, or any new and useful improvement thereof." A patent is good for a varying period of years — seventeen on a patent of invention. The term of a patent may be extended only by a special act of Congress. The patent laws are enforced by the Patent Office in the Department of Commerce.

Weights and Measures. Congress possesses the power to "fix the standard of weights and

---

[7] Article I, Section 8, Clause 4; see Chapter 5.
[8] Article I, Section 8, Clause 7; see Chapter 22.

[9] Article I, Section 8, Clause 8; see pages 235, 458–460.

measures."[10] In 1838 Congress followed the English system establishing the pound, ounce, mile, foot, gallon, quart, and so on as the standards of weights and measures for the United States. In 1866 it also legalized the use of the French metric system. The original standards by which all other measures in the United States are tested and corrected are maintained by the National Bureau of Standards in the Department of Commerce.

The National Bureau of Standards was created in 1901, especially to test and set specifications for items purchased by the National Government. Today it is a great scientific and technological research agency constantly engaged in a wide variety of projects. Its activities range from the promotion of standardization of such things as nuts and bolts to highly advanced research in physics, chemistry, and mathematics. It determines the measures for our groceries, the specifications of a doctor's thermometer, and the strength of concrete and steel. It can accurately weigh the penciled crossing of a "t" on a sheet of paper. It has developed a clock verified by observations of the stars and an atomic clock which would vary no more than one second in 300 years.

Power over Territories and Other Areas. Congress has power to acquire, govern, and dispose of various federal areas.[11] The importance of this power can be seen in the fact that it relates to much more than the District of Columbia and such possessions as the Virgin Islands, Puerto Rico, the Canal Zone, and Guam. It also involves the hundreds of military and naval stations, forts, arsenals, dockyards, post offices, parks and forest preserves, prisons, and other holdings throughout the country.

The National Government may acquire

UNITED STATES PATENT OFFICE.

THOMAS A. EDISON, OF BOSTON, MASSACHUSETTS, ASSIGNOR TO HIMSELF AND DEWITT C. ROBERTS, OF SAME PLACE.

IMPROVEMENT IN ELECTROGRAPHIC VOTE-RECORDER.

Specification forming part of Letters Patent No. 90,646, dated June 1, 1869.

To all whom it may concern:

Be it known that I, THOMAS A. EDISON, of Boston, in the county of Suffolk and State of Massachusetts, have invented a new and useful apparatus named "Electrographic Vote Recorder and Register," of which the following is a full, clear, and exact description, reference being had to the accompanying drawing, which represents a plan view of the apparatus, and to the letters of reference thereon.

The object of my invention is to produce an apparatus which records and registers in an instant, and with great accuracy, the votes of legislative bodies, thus avoiding loss of valuable time consumed in counting and registering the votes and names, as done in the usual manner; and my invention consists in applying an electrographic apparatus in such a manner that each member, by moving a switch to either of two points, representing an affirmative and opposing vote, has his name imprinted, by means of electricity, under the desired head, on a previously-prepared paper, and at the same time the number of votes is indicated on a dial-plate by the operation.

Referring to the drawings, in the central portion of the plate a a is secured a block, k, upon which are set, in metallic types, two columns of names, n n', the one being headed by | upon the types, and is, furthermore, in communication with battery b by means of conducting-wire r r, or in any other suitable manner.

The rollers q q' communicate with the two magnets v v' by the wires s s, and through them operate the armatures v' v'', the escapements w w' and the pointers x x', which latter show the numbers of votes on the dial-plates marked with as many figures as there are voters.

The battery b, with the two poles c and d, is connected with and operates the apparatus in the following manner: The pole c is in constant communication with the metallic types l m, representing, respectively, "no" and "yes," by means of the conducting-wires y z; but the pole c is connected by the wires c' c' c'', with as many switches e e' as there are voters.

From the points f f' g g' the conducting-wires i i' h h' pass to the metallic strips o o o', and from thence to the nearest metallic type, or they may pass first to the types and then branch back to the respective strips, as seen in the column to the left.

From the pole d of battery b communication is established with the cylinder p by the wire r r, and from the same pole by the wire u u t to the two magnets, where the aforesaid con-

The Constitution places all patent control in Congress. Among the many inventions patented since the first patent laws were enacted in 1790 was an electric vote-recorder invented by Thomas A. Edison. (U.S. Patent Office)

---

property by exercising its power of *eminent domain*—the inherent power to take private property for public use. Whenever it does so, however, the owner must receive a fair price for his property; otherwise the power would amount to that of sheer confiscation.[12] Territory may also be acquired from a foreign state as a result of the power to admit new States, the war powers, and the President's treaty-making power.[13] Under international law,

---

[10] Article I, Section 8, Clause 5; see pages 457–458.

[11] Article I, Section 8, Clause 17; Article IV, Section 3, Clause 2; see Chapter 34.

[12] The 5th Amendment restricts the National Government's exercise of the power with the words, "nor shall private property be taken for public use, without just compensation." Each of the State constitutions contains a similar provision. Private property may be taken by eminent domain only: (1) for a public use, (2) with proper notice to the owner, and (3) for a fair price. What in fact constitutes a public use, proper notice, or a fair price often becomes a matter for judicial determination.

[13] Article IV, Section 3, Clause 1, see page 75; Article I, Section 8, Clauses 11–16; Article II, Section 2, Clauses 1 and 2.

any sovereign state may acquire unclaimed territory by discovery.

Judicial Powers. Congress has the power to create all federal courts below the Supreme Court; to provide for the organization and composition of the federal judiciary; [14] to define and provide for the punishment of federal crimes; [15] and to impeach and remove any civil officer of the United States.[16]

Powers over Foreign Relations. The National Government has greater power in the field of foreign relations than it has in any other. This, Congress shares with the President, who is primarily responsible for the conduct of our relations with other states. The States in the Union are not sovereign and are, hence, unrecognized in international law. The Constitution forbids them to participate in foreign relations.[17]

Authority for the power over foreign relations arises from two sources. *First,* from several of the delegated powers, including the powers to make treaties, to regulate foreign commerce, to send and receive diplomatic representatives, and to define and punish piracy and other crimes committed on the high seas and offenses against the law of nations. The war powers and the power to acquire and govern territories are also the basis for action in the field of international relations. *Second,* power to act in this field arises from the fact that the United States is a sovereign member of the world community. As such, it has the inherent power to deal with matters which affect the interests and security of the United States.

War Powers. Several of the powers provided for in Article I, Section 8 deal exclusively with war and national defense. Although the President is Commander in Chief of the Armed Forces, Congress has power to declare war, to grant letters of marque and reprisal,[18] to make rules concerning captures on land and water, to raise and support armies, to provide and maintain a navy, to make rules governing the land and naval forces, to provide for calling out the militia and for the organizing, arming, and disciplining of it.[19]

Congress cannot appropriate money for "armies" for longer than a two-year period.[20] This restriction does not apply to the Navy, but is intended to insure that the Army will always be subordinate to civil authorities.

THE IMPLIED POWERS

The Necessary and Proper Clause. Thus far we have considered the expressed powers of Congress, most of which are found in Article I, Section 8, Clauses 1–17. Clause 18 of Article I, Section 8 is the so-called "Necessary and Proper" or "Elastic" Clause:

> The Congress shall have power: ... To make all laws which shall be necessary and proper for carrying into execution the foregoing powers, and all other powers vested by this Constitution in the Government of the United States, or in any department or officer thereof.

Much of the amazing vitality and adaptability of the Constitution can be traced directly to this clause, and to the manner in which both Congress and the Supreme Court have interpreted and applied it over the years.

Liberal Versus Strict Construction. As

---

[14] Article I, Section 8, Clause 9; Article III, Section 1; see Chapter 33.

[15] Article I, Section 8, Clauses 6 and 10.

[16] Article I, Section 2, Clause 5; Article I, Section 3, Clauses 6 and 7.

[17] Article I, Section 10, Clauses 1 and 3.

[18] *Letters of marque and reprisal* are commissions authorizing private persons to fit out vessels to capture or destroy in time of war. They are forbidden in international law by the Declaration of Paris, 1856, to the principles of which the United States subscribes.

[19] Article I, Section 8, Clauses 11–16.

[20] Article I, Section 8, Clause 12.

Congress alone has the power to declare war. It took such action in December 1941, against Japan, Germany, and Italy, at the request of President Franklin D. Roosevelt following the attack on Pearl Harbor. (Wide World Photos)

was previously noted, the Constitution had barely come into force when the meaning of Article I, Section 8, Clause 18 became the subject of one of the most famous and important disputes in American political history. Was the Constitution to be so construed that Congress could exercise only those powers *expressly* stated in so many words in that document, or could Congress exercise additional powers which could be reasonably *implied* as necessary and proper?

The dispute came to a head almost immediately. In 1790 Alexander Hamilton, as Secretary of the Treasury, proposed that Congress create a Bank of the United States. Thomas Jefferson led the opposition to the plan, saying that the Constitution gave Congress no power which would allow the creation of such a bank. Hamilton replied that such a step was necessary and proper to the execution of such powers as those to borrow, to coin money and regulate its value, and to tax. This Jefferson rebutted by claiming that such reasoning would give the National Government almost unlimited powers and practically destroy the reserved powers of the States.[21]

Logic and practical necessity won the dispute for Hamilton and the liberal-constructionists. In 1791 Congress chartered the First Bank of the United States. The bank's charter expired

---

[21] When, in 1800, a bill was introduced in Congress to incorporate a company to mine copper, Jefferson, as Vice President, ridiculed the proposal with this sarcastic comment: "Congress is authorized to defend the nation. Ships are necessary for defense; copper is necessary for ships; mines necessary for copper; a company necessary to work the mines; and who can doubt this reasoning who has ever played at 'This Is the House That Jack Built'?" While Jefferson himself was President (1801–1809), he and his party were many times forced to reverse their earlier position. For example, it was only on the basis of the implied powers doctrine that the Louisiana Purchase in 1803 and the embargo on foreign trade in 1807 could be justified.

in 1811 with the bank's constitutionality, and the basis upon which it was created (the implied powers doctrine) unchallenged in the courts.

McCulloch v. *Maryland,* 1819. In 1816 Congress issued a charter to the Second Bank of the United States. This action was taken only after another struggle over the extent of the powers of Congress.

Several States attempted to limit the new bank's authority in various ways. In 1818 Maryland imposed a tax upon all notes issued by any bank doing business in that State which was not chartered by the State legislature. This tax was aimed directly at the Second Bank's branch in Baltimore. McCulloch, the bank's cashier, purposely issued notes on which no tax had been paid in order to challenge the Maryland law. Maryland brought suit to collect the tax, and the United States, in McCulloch's behalf, then carried the case to the Supreme Court in 1819.

Maryland based its case on the argument that Congress had no constitutional authority to incorporate a bank. The United States, represented by such able men as Daniel Webster and William Pinkney, defended the doctrine of implied powers and further argued that Maryland had no right to tax an instrumentality of the United States.

Chief Justice John Marshall delivered one of the Supreme Court's most important and far-reaching decisions in this case. Here, for the first time, the Court was squarely faced with the thirty-year-old question of the constitutionality of the implied powers doctrine. It upheld the constitutionality of the Second Bank as a necessary and proper step in the execution of such expressed powers as to borrow, to coin and regulate the value of money, and to tax. But, far more important, the Supreme Court thereby upheld the doctrine of implied powers. The decision is so important that we quote its central passage:

> We admit, as all must admit, that the powers of the government are limited, and that its limits are not to be transcended. But we think

the sound construction of the Constitution must allow to the national legislature that discretion, with respect to the means by which the powers it confers are to be carried into execution, which will enable that body to perform the high duties assigned to it, in the manner most beneficial to the people. Let the end be legitimate, let it be within the scope of the Constitution, and all means which are appropriate, which are plainly adapted to that end, which are not prohibited, but consist with the letter and spirit of the Constitution, are constitutional.[22]

This broad interpretation of the powers granted to Congress has become firmly fixed in our constitutional system. Indeed, it is impossible to see how our nation could have developed as it has under the Constitution without it.

Examples of Implied Powers. There are literally thousands of examples of the application of the doctrine of implied powers. Decisions of the Supreme Court and the manner in which Congress has regarded and used its powers have made Article I, Section 8, Clause 18 truly the Elastic Clause. Today the words "necessary and proper" really read "convenient and useful," especially when applied to the power to regulate commerce and to tax.

The original Constitution gave the National Government the express power to punish only four specific crimes—counterfeiting, felonies committed on the high seas, offenses against the law of nations, and treason.[23] But many other laws Congress has the expressed power to enact—for example, tax laws—would be worthless if they could not be enforced. Congress has the *implied* right to define and provide

---

[22] The decision also invalidated the Maryland tax. Because "the power to tax involves the power to destroy," said the Supreme Court, Maryland could not be permitted to tax the United States or any of its instrumentalities. See pages 65, 260.

[23] Article I, Section 8, Clauses 6 and 10; Article III, Section 3.

the punishment for all offenses against the United States. The Constitution does not expressly provide for river and harbor improvements, but the power is *implied* from the expressed powers to regulate commerce and maintain a navy. The words *Air Force* do not appear in the Constitution; but should anyone ever question its constitutionality, the courts could imply it from the war powers.

A listing of examples of the use of implied powers could go on and on; there are many throughout this book. *But, remember,* the basis for *any* implied power must *always* be found among the expressed powers.

THE POWERS VESTED IN CONGRESS BY ARTICLE I, SECTION 8 OF THE CONSTITUTION

Expressed Powers

I. **Peace Powers**
  1. To lay taxes.
     a. Direct (not used since the War Between the States, except income tax).
     b. Indirect.
           customs = tariffs.
           excises = internal revenue.
  2. To borrow money.
  3. To regulate foreign and interstate commerce.
  4. To establish naturalization and bankruptcy laws.
  5. To coin money and regulate its value; to regulate weights and measures.
  6. To punish counterfeiters of federal money and securities.
  7. To establish post offices and post roads.
  8. To grant patents and copyrights.
  9. To create courts inferior to the Supreme Court.
  10. To define and punish piracies and felonies on the high seas; to define and punish offenses against the law of nations.
  17. To exercise exclusive jurisdiction over the District of Columbia; to exercise exclusive jurisdiction over forts, dockyards, national parks, federal buildings, and the like.

II. **War Powers**
  11. To declare war; to grant letters of marque and reprisal; to make rules concerning captures on land and water.
  12. To raise and support armies.
  13. To provide and maintain a navy.
  14. To make laws governing land and naval forces.
  15. To provide for calling forth the militia to execute federal laws, suppress insurrections, and repel invasions.
  16. To provide for organizing, arming, and disciplining the militia, and for its governing when in the service of the Union.

Implied Powers

  18. To make all laws necessary and proper for carrying into execution the foregoing powers.
      For example—to punish the breaking of federal law.
                  to establish national banks.
                  to improve rivers, harbors, and canals.
                  to condemn property by eminent domain.

✳✳✳✳✳✳✳✳✳✳ CONCEPT BUILDING ✳✳✳✳✳✳✳✳✳✳

Key Concepts

Congress may exercise only those powers (1) *expressly* granted to it in the Constitution, (2) those that may be reasonably *implied* from the expressed powers, and (3) those that are *inherent* in the existence of the National Government.

Early in our history the question of whether the powers granted to the National Government were to be strictly or liberally interpreted became an issue. It was finally resolved by the Supreme Court decision in *McCulloch* v. *Maryland* (1819). The Supreme Court ruled that the powers were to be liberally construed, thus upholding the doctrine of implied powers. It is difficult to see how the nation could have developed as it has under the Constitution without the idea of implied powers.

Important Terms

bankruptcy	legal tender	*McCulloch* v. *Maryland*	post roads
copyright	letters of marque	Necessary and Proper	promissory note
counterfeit	and reprisal	Clause	strict construction
eminent domain	liberal construction	patent	war powers

Questions for Inquiry and Review

1. Where in the Constitution are most of the *expressed powers* to be found?

2. Upon what clause is the theory of *implied powers* based?

3. What are the *inherent powers?*

4. What was the nature of the dispute between the liberal-constructionists and the strict-constructionists?

5. What are the two most important expressed powers of Congress?

6. Why was Congress given the exclusive power to coin money?

7. How did Congress get its right to issue paper money?

8. Why is the congressional power over bankruptcy classed as a *concurrent power?*

9. Is the postal power a *concurrent* or an *exclusive power?*

10. What is the chief distinction between a *copyright* and a *patent?*

11. Why may it be said that the National Government has greater power in the field of foreign relations than any other? With whom does Congress share authority in the field of foreign relations?

12. What are the *war powers?* With whom does Congress share authority in this field?

13. What are the implied powers?

14. Why is the Supreme Court's decision in *McCulloch* v. *Maryland* of such outstanding importance in the development of our governmental system?

For Further Inquiry

1. Great Britain has no written constitution, and Parliament may enact any law it believes is necessary. Why has Congress only the expressed, implied, and inherent powers?

2. In his decision in *McCulloch* v. *Maryland* Chief Justice Marshall wrote that "the power to tax involves the power to destroy." What did he mean by this?

3. Woodrow Wilson in *Congressional Government* published in 1885 wrote:

> The Constitution itself is not a complete system; it takes none but the first steps in organization. It does little more than lay a foundation of principles ... The growth of the nation and the consequent development of the governmental system would snap asunder a constitution which could not adapt itself to the new conditions of an advancing society ... There can be no question that our Constitution has proved lasting because of its simplicity.

What examples can be cited to illustrate Wilson's thought?

4. Would commercial progress in the United States be promoted if each of the States had its own monetary system? Weights and measures? Explain.

5. Why must the source for each and every exercise of an implied power be found in an expressed power?

Suggested Activities

1. Write a report explaining why Congress was given each of the expressed powers it possesses.

2. Trace the legislation which has been enacted or is under consideration in the present session of Congress. In a report indicate those bills which are based on the expressed powers and those which are applications of the doctrine of implied powers.

3. Stage a debate or class forum on one of the following questions: (a) *Resolved,* That the National Government should be permitted to do only those things expressly provided for in the Constitution; (b) *Resolved,* That the federal monopoly over the postal system ought to be abolished; (c) *Resolved,* That the metric system should be the sole standard of weights and measures in the United States.

4. Prepare a bulletin display on patents and copyrights.

Suggested Reading

BUNZEL, JOHN H., *Issues of American Public Policy.* Prentice-Hall, 1968.

CORWIN, EDWIN S. and PELTASON, J. W., *Understanding the Constitution.* Holt, Rinehart and Winston, 1967.

KUTLER, STANLEY L., *The Supreme Court and the Constitution: Readings in American Constitutional History.* Houghton Mifflin, 1969.

LAHR, RAYMOND M. and THEIS, J. WILLIAM, *Congress: Power and Purpose on Capitol Hill.* Allyn and Bacon, 1969.

PELTASON, J. W. and BURNS, JAMES M., *Functions and Policies of American Government.* Prentice-Hall, 1967.

PRITCHETT, C. HERMAN, *The American Constitution.* McGraw-Hill, 1968. Chapter 11.

14
THE TAXING POWER

Why is the power to tax classed as a legislative power?

Is it proper that the power to tax is sometimes used for regulatory purposes? If so, when?

How can (or might) a government ever justify spending more than it takes in?

*Taxes are what we pay
for civilized society.*

JUSTICE OLIVER WENDELL HOLMES

The power to tax is absolutely necessary to the existence of a government. A government must have the power in order to raise the revenues with which to support its functions. The Supreme Court once made the point in these words:

> The power to tax is the one great power upon which the whole national fabric is based. It is as necessary to the existence and prosperity of a nation as is the air he breathes to a natural man.

We have already seen that the lack of an adequate taxing power was one of the fatal weaknesses of the Articles of Confederation. Some idea of the relative importance of the power can be seen in the fact that it heads the list of the powers granted to Congress in the Constitution. Article I, Section 8, Clause 1 provides:

> The Congress shall have power: To lay and collect taxes, duties, imposts, and excises, to pay the debts, and provide for the common

defense and general welfare, of the United States; but all duties, imposts, and excises shall be uniform throughout the United States.

SCOPE OF THE TAXING POWER

The *basic* purpose of the exercise of the power to tax is, of course, to raise the revenues necessary to finance the operations of government. The dictionary definition of "a tax" is "a charge laid by government upon persons or property to meet the public needs." Clearly, the definition is a correct one. Taxes *are* most often imposed in order to raise revenue—that is, in order to "meet the public needs." In this chapter we are especially concerned with the use of the taxing power in just this sense. But, before we continue, notice that the definition above is also an *incomplete* one. Taxes may be imposed for purposes *other* than the raising of revenue—and they often are.

Illustrations of the use of the power to tax

252

LITTLE HIM

MIDWINTER NIGHT'S DREAM

Tax collecting is one of the oldest of governmental functions. Who can disagree with Benjamin Franklin's observation that "in this world nothing is certain but death and taxes"? (Pletcher, The Sioux City Journal; James Dobbins, Boston Herald-Traveler)

for non-financial purposes are many. The *protective tariff* is probably the oldest example one may cite. Although a protective tariff does bring in some revenue, its primary object is that of "protecting" domestic industry against foreign competition. On page 242 we noted the fact that in 1865 Congress imposed a ten per cent tax on all notes issued by State-chartered banks. It did so *not* to raise funds for the National Treasury but, rather, to protect the new national currency by destroying the State banknotes. A tax may be levied in order to protect the public health and safety; for example, the bulk of federal regulation of the use of narcotics is carried on through taxation —in this instance, licensing for legitimate dealing in narcotics.

We shall come back to this matter of the "other uses" of the taxing power later in this chapter. But, for now, as we deal with the Constitution's grant of the power to Congress, bear in mind the point that the taxing power is *not only* a revenue-raising power.

LIMITATION ON THE TAXING POWER

The power to tax, and the manner in which Congress has used it, has been a key factor in the growth of the powers of the National Government over the past 180 years. Congress has leaned most often upon it, and the commerce power, as the constitutional basis for its major actions in domestic affairs.

The power to tax is not an unlimited one, however. As with all of the other powers of the National Government, it must be exercised with due regard to all of the other provisions of the Constitution. For example, Congress could not lay a tax upon the conduct of religious services. Obviously, such a tax would be a gross violation of the 1st Amendment's guarantee of religious freedom. Nor could it impose a tax upon a person in order to punish him for some action; such a tax would amount to a bill of attainder and is prohibited by Article I, Section 9.

The Average Taxpayer's Burden

Based on a man (with wife and 2 children) who had income of $11,000 in 1970.

Federal Income Tax	$1,525
Social Security Tax	$ 374
State Income Tax	$ 209
Local Property Tax on Home (this includes School Taxes of $643)	$1,351
State and Local Sales Taxes	$ 390
TOTAL BASE TAXES	**$3,849**

In addition some or all of these approximate taxes will be paid

On a new car	$200
On cigarettes at 15¢ a pack, a pack a day	$ 54.75
On gasoline at 12¢ a gallon, 15 gallons a week	$ 93.60
A substantial tax on all spirits (including wine and beer)	

Plus varying rates per dollar on toll telephone calls, air-travel, fishing equipment, and other items.

SO

MORE THAN 34 CENTS OF EACH DOLLAR IS TAKEN BY FEDERAL, STATE AND LOCAL TAXES

Source: Tax Foundation, Inc.

More specifically, the Constitution imposes four *expressed* and one *implied* limitation on the taxing power. These limitations are summarized in the chart on page 262.

Taxes for Public Purposes Only. Article I, Section 8, Clause 1 provides that taxes may be levied only to "pay the debts, and provide for the common defense and general welfare, of the United States." That is, Congress may tax only for *public* purposes, not for private benefit. Thus, in 1936 the Supreme Court invalidated the Agricultural Adjustment Act of 1933. That law provided a broad program for the control of agricultural production. Among other things, it levied a tax on the processors of farm commodities, and the proceeds of the tax were used to pay subsidies to farmers who had agreed to reduce their production. This, said the Supreme Court, amounted to the taxing of one private group (the processors) for the benefit of another (the farmers) and was prohibited by the Constitution.[1]

Notice that Congress is given the power to tax to "provide for the . . . general welfare." But it does not have the power to *legislate* for the general welfare. That is to say, the power to tax — and to spend the proceeds — is a broader power than the others granted to Congress in Article I, Section 8. To illustrate the point: Congress does not have the power to establish a national system of public schools; but it does have the power to tax and then *spend* the receipts to aid the States to support *their* school systems.

Export Taxes Prohibited. Article I, Section 9, Clause 5 provides:

> No tax or duty shall be laid on articles exported from any State.

---

[1] The Supreme Court also struck down the law on another and broader basis. It held the control of agricultural production to be a matter within the reserved powers of the States and thus beyond the reach of Congress. The Court soon reversed itself on this point, however; see pages 447–451.

Thus, *customs duties* (tariffs) may be applied only to imports; Congress may not levy duties on exports. The restriction was written into the Constitution because Southerners were fearful that Congress, controlled by the Northern States, would attempt to choke off their profitable cotton trade with Great Britain, diverting it to the new mills in the New England States.

Equal Apportionment of Direct Taxes. A *direct tax* is one which is in fact borne by the person upon whom it is imposed; for example, a tax on land or buildings or a *capitation* (head or poll) tax. A direct tax cannot be shifted to another for payment.

Article I, Section 9, Clause 4 provides:

> No capitation, or other direct tax, shall be laid, unless in proportion to the census or enumeration hereinbefore directed to be taken.

This provision means that any direct tax levied by Congress must be apportioned among the States according to the population of each, with the share to be collected in each being derived from its percentage of the total national population. Thus, a direct tax which raised $1,000,000,000, for example, would have to produce nearly $100,000,000 from California and approximately $10,000,000 from Oregon —because California has nearly ten per cent of the nation's population and Oregon approximately one per cent.

Since wealth is not evenly distributed among the States, a direct tax levied in proportion to population would be unjust to the people in certain States. Except for an income tax, Congress has not levied a direct tax outside the District of Columbia in more than a century —since 1861.

The Federal Income Tax. An income tax is a direct tax. But Congress is permitted to levy it without regard to population because of the 16th Amendment:

> The Congress shall have power to lay and collect taxes on incomes, from whatever source derived, without apportionment among the several States, and without regard to any census or enumeration.

Congress first levied an income tax from 1862 to 1872, and the Supreme Court found it to be constitutional as an excise tax (that is, an indirect rather than a direct tax). But a later income tax law, enacted in 1894, suffered a different fate; it was declared unconstitutional in 1895. The Supreme Court held that taxes levied on incomes derived from land or other property were direct taxes, and that the tax law was invalid because it did levy taxes on such incomes but did not apportion them among the States as the Constitution required. The obvious impossibility of taxing incomes fairly in accord with any plan of apportionment led, finally, to the adoption of the 16th Amendment in 1913.

The income tax is the largest single source of federal revenue today. It became the major source during the war years of 1917 and 1918. Except for a few years during the Great Depression of the 1930's, it has remained so for more than a half century.

Several factors suit the income tax to its role as the major source. It is flexible: its rates can be readily adjusted to meet the current needs of the National Government. It is also easily adapted to the principle of ability to pay; the rates have always been *progressive* (that is, the higher the income the higher the rate). Then, too, because the tax falls directly upon the one who must pay it, it tends to make the taxpayer aware of the costs of the many governmental services he receives.

Ever since 1913 the tax has been levied on both the income of individuals and corporations.

The Individual Income Tax. The tax on individual incomes regularly produces the larger amount. The first year's returns under the 16th Amendment (fiscal year 1914) came to only $28,000,000. For the year ending June 30, 1970 (fiscal year 1970), the tax is expected to produce at least $90,000,000,000.

The tax rates applied to income earned in 1970 vary from a low of fourteen per cent on the first $500 of taxable income for a single person (or $1000 for a married couple) to a high of seventy per cent on all such income over $100,000 ($200,000 for a married couple)—plus a surcharge of ten per cent,[2] added by Congress in 1968. The rates are applied to *taxable income* (one's total income minus exemptions and deductions).

A tax exemption of $600 is allowed for each dependent, including the taxpayer himself. Thus, a man with a wife and two children has dependency exemptions totaling $2400. An exemption can be taken for any person who lives with the taxpayer and receives at least half of his support from him. An additional $600 is allowed for each person sixty-five or older or blind. Deductions are permitted for many things—for example, business expenses; interest on debts; most State and local taxes; certain medical, dental, drug, and hospital expenses; and charitable contributions up to thirty per cent of one's income.

By April 15 all persons under age sixty-five who earned $600 or more in the previous year must file a tax return. Those over sixty-five must file a return if their income was $1200 or more. Husbands and wives may file a joint return, even if one of them had no income at all. The returns, filed either on Form 1040A or Form 1040, are sent to the nearest Director of Internal Revenue.

Form 1040A is a small card about the size of a bank check. It may be used by anyone with less than $10,000 income from wages or salary and no other income over $200. On it, the taxpayer enters his full income and depend-

ency exemptions, plus any tax already "withheld." High-speed machines process the return, allowing a standard deduction of ten per cent for such things as State taxes, interest, and charitable contributions. If a person with over $5000 income uses this return, he must pay any tax due when he files the card; if his income is less than that, however, his tax will be automatically figured for him and he will be sent a bill for any amount due. If a person using this form (or Form 1040) has made an overpayment—that is, if his withholdings are greater than the tax he owes—he will receive whichever he prefers: a refund or a credit against his next year's tax bill.

Form 1040, known popularly as the "long form," is more complicated. It *must* be used by anyone with over $10,000 income or over $200 income from any source other than wages or salary. It may also be used by any person with less than $10,000 who wishes to itemize his deductions. On this form the taxpayer figures his own tax. He lists his income, subtracts his dependents and deductions, and finds the tax due in a table which appears in the booklet of instructions accompanying the form. If he chooses, he can take a standard deduction of ten per cent of his income up to $1000 or he can itemize his deductions.

Under the "pay-as-you-go" plan (payroll withholdings), the law requires each employer to withhold a certain amount from each employee's paycheck. The employer sends this withholding tax to the Treasury where it is credited to the taxpayer's account. Because most people receive their income from salaries or wages, this arrangement softens the tax blow; the total tax is not due in one large payment, but is paid in several smaller ones.

A single person with an income over $5000 (or a married couple with over $10,000) must make an annual estimate of income for the coming year and pay the tax in *advance,* in quarterly installments beginning April 15.[3] A

---

[2] *I.e.,* an additional 10% of the tax due (a *surcharge,* a tax on the tax) is now added to most income tax bills. The first $1000 of a single person's and the first $2000 of a married couple's taxable income is exempted from the surcharge. The surcharge was slated to expire June 30, 1969, but was extended by Congress to at least December 31, 1969.

---

[3] Unless the tax is paid through withholdings.

Form 1040 US Department of the Treasury / Internal Revenue Service **Individual Income Tax Return** **1970**

For the year January 1–December 31, 1970, or other taxable year beginning ...., 1970, ending ...., 19.......

First name and initial (If joint return, use first names and middle initials of both) | Last name | Your social security number

Please attach Copy B of Form type

Income

12 Wages, salaries, tips, etc. (Attach Forms W–2 to back. If unavailable, attach explanation) .` | 12 |

13a Dividends (see pages 5 and 9 of instr.) $.......................... 13b Less exclusion $.......................... Balance . ▶ | 13c |
(Also list in Part I of Schedule B, if gross dividends and other distributions are over $100)

14 Interest. Enter total here (also list in Part II of Schedule B, if total is over $100) . . . | 14 |

15 Income other than wages, dividends, and interest (from line 40) . . . . | 15 |

16 Total (add lines 12, 13c, 14 and 15) . . . . | 16 |

17 Adjustments to income (such as "sick pay," moving expense, etc. from line 45) . . . | 17 |

18 Adjusted gross income (subtract line 17 from line 16) . . . . | 18 |

The old "short form" which was used by taxpayers who had incomes of less than $10,000 annually has been done away with. All taxpayers now file their reports on this new United States Individual Income Tax Return.

special allowance is made for farmers. They are allowed to file an estimate and pay their taxes after the year is over, after having had time to harvest and market their crops.

Income Tax on Corporations. All of a corporation's earned income above the expenses of the business is taxable. On this income the tax now runs as high as forty-eight per cent on all earnings over $25,000—plus, today, a five per cent surcharge.

Nonprofit organizations, such as churches, colleges, fraternal lodges, co-operatives, and labor unions, are exempted from the income tax. The corporation income tax is expected to produce about $38,000,000,000 in 1970.

Enforcement of the Tax Laws. The overwhelming number of taxpayers are honest, of course. Some people quite honestly underfigure their taxes; others often over-figure. The Treasury has a "conscience fund" into which goes all the money—several thousands a year—that people send to ease their consciences over past "mistakes." Not long ago a retired businessman sent in $5000 *just in case* he had made any mistakes through the years. After checking his returns the Internal Revenue Service not only returned the $5000 but an

additional $17,000 for overpayments he had made in the past.

There are always a few cheaters, however, and the law provides for them. Those who intentionally fail to report part or all of their taxable income may be fined up to $10,000, imprisoned for as long as five years, charged a penalty of fifty per cent of the amount not reported, or all three. Honest mistakes are excused if not found within three years, but the Internal Revenue Service has six years in which to discover and bring criminal charges (tax-evasion) against those who make false returns or none at all.[4] Tax evasion charges have sent many known criminals to federal prison when State and local police have been unable to gather enough evidence to convict them of their other crimes.

The files of the Internal Revenue Service are filled with cases of tax evasion. A woman in Alabama claimed her mule "William" as a

---

[4] There is *no* statute of limitations concerning civil prosecutions. Thus, although after six years one may not be charged with a *crime* for falsifying his tax return, the Government may take steps to recover the taxes due plus interest.

dependent for three years before agents caught her. A man in California claimed nine children on five annual returns when he actually had none. An Internal Revenue Service agent heard a man voicing some especially low opinions of income tax laws and, on a hunch, decided to check the man's returns. He had never filed any. In the end the complainer paid $76,000 in penalty and interest.

Indirect Taxes Must Be Uniform throughout the United States. It is very difficult to draw a precise distinction between direct and indirect taxes. In the final analysis the question of whether a particular tax is direct or indirect rests with Congress and the Supreme Court. As a general rule, however, indirect taxes are those that, although they are paid by one person, are actually passed on to another and are therefore *indirectly* paid by the second person. For example, the excise tax on cigarettes is paid by the producer; he passes it on to the wholesaler and distributor who, in turn, pass it on to the retailer. The retailer includes it in the price he charges for the cigarettes, so the consumer actually pays the tax. Customs duties are another good example. They are paid by the importer but ultimately are passed on to the purchaser.

Article I, Section 8, Clause 1 provides that:

> . . . all duties, imposts, and excises shall be uniform throughout the United States.

That is, all indirect taxes must be levied at the same rate in all parts of the country. Thus, the federal excise tax on the manufacture of tobacco, automobiles, or alcoholic beverages must be the same in New York as it is in New Mexico; the import duty on cut diamonds must be the same at the port of New York as it is at the port of New Orleans.

Excise Taxes. *Excises* are taxes which are levied on the manufacture or the sale of goods and the performance of services. They rank as the third largest source of federal revenue and are expected to produce approximately $16,000,000,000 in fiscal year 1970.

Excise taxes are levied now (1970) on a great many items, including gasoline, oil, tires, tubes, automobiles, trucks, buses, cigarettes, cigars, pipe tobacco, liquor, wine, beer, airline tickets, and firearms.[5] Those levied on the *production* of various items (automobiles, for example) are regularly figured into the price a producer charges for his product and are often called "hidden taxes." Those levied on the sale of various items or services (airline tickets, for example) are, in effect, selective sales taxes. Because they are often levied on goods not usually considered necessities (liquor, for example), they are often called "luxury taxes."

Customs Duties. *Customs duties* (tariffs) are taxes on commodities imported from foreign countries. The most recent tariff act is that of 1930, but it has been amended frequently. The rates vary on different articles, now being as high as 80 per cent on some. Articles entering the United States without tariff are said to be on the "free list"—for example, Bibles, raw silk, coffee, bananas, and agricultural implements. All articles imported solely for display at the international trade fairs held periodically in various parts of the United States are permitted to enter the country duty free. Articles taxed at a low rate are said to

---

[5] Congress repealed a host of other excises in the Excise Tax Reduction Act of 1965, including those on luggage, toilet articles, jewelry, furs, business machines, musical instruments, photographic equipment, phonographs and records, radios and television sets, freezers, refrigerators, air conditioners, pens, lighters, matches, and playing cards. The act, as modified by Congress in 1966 and in 1968, also provided for the reduction of several excises—for example, the present ten per cent tax on local and long-distance telephone service and the seven per cent tax on new automobiles are to be reduced January 1, 1970, and again on the same date in 1971 and 1972—and to be eliminated on January 1, 1973.

Most noncompeting imports are either on the "free list" or are taxed for revenue only. Bananas are not grown in the United States and are allowed to be shipped into the country duty free. (The Port of New York Authority)

be taxed "for revenue only"—for example, diamonds, chamois skins, and raw hair. Articles taxed at a high rate are said to be taxed "for protection"—for example, sugar at $\frac{1}{2}$¢ a pound, tomatoes at $1\frac{1}{2}$¢ a pound, beef at 3¢ a pound, eggs at $3\frac{1}{2}$¢ a dozen, wool at from 11 to 28¢ a pound, wheat at 21¢ a bushel, shoes at 20 per cent *ad valorem* (of their value), silk products at 25 per cent, articles of knit rayon at 25¢ per pound plus 65 per cent of their value. See page 366.

The tax is often so high that certain articles are not shipped into this country at all. Then, of course, no revenue is collected; but the manufacturer of the articles in this country can charge more for these articles than otherwise, since foreign competition is removed. The tax is "for protection" to home industry.[6]

Foreign Trade Zones may be established by cities, where importers can hold imports for reshipment to foreign countries without the payment of a tariff. See page 461.

A United States resident returning from a brief trip abroad may bring in, once in any thirty-one day period, merchandise worth a maximum of $100 retail duty free (but including not more than one quart of alcoholic beverages and 100 cigars).[7] Members of a family may pool their exemptions if they live and have been traveling together.

Tariffs were the major source of federal revenue for more than a century. Now they produce only a small fraction of the total —an estimated $2,300,000,000 in 1970.

---

[6] The particular extent to which domestic industry is affected by tariffs, and by imports generally, is the subject of continuing study by the United States Tariff Commission. The Commission, created as an independent agency in 1916, reports its findings to both Congress and the President. Its six members are appointed for six-year terms by the President subject to Senate confirmation; not more than three of the commissioners may be drawn from the ranks of the same political party.

[7] The liquor allowance applies only to residents who are at least twenty-one.

Estate Tax. The *estate tax* [8] varies from three per cent on a net estate not exceeding $5000 to 77 per cent on that portion of a net estate in excess of $10,000,000. "Net estate" means what remains after the payment of debts, bequests to governmental, religious, charitable, and educational institutions, the cost of settling the estate, and an exemption of $60,000. The exemption does not apply if the deceased was not a resident or a citizen of the United States at death.[9]

If a husband leaves an estate to his wife, or a wife to her husband, the tax is levied on only half of the estate's net value. When the survivor dies, however, the tax applies to all of the original estate left by the deceased.

An estate or inheritance tax (or both) is usually paid to a State. A partial credit for this is allowed on the federal estate tax. The Supreme Court has ruled the estate tax to be an indirect tax, holding it to be a tax on the *privilege* of bequesting.

Gift Tax. A *gift tax,* with a rate only about three-fourths as high as the estate tax, is also collected. It prevents a person from evading the estate tax by making gifts before death. Gifts to governmental, religious, charitable, and educational institutions are not taxed. Gifts within the year to any one individual amounting to not more than $3000 and gifts to all individuals taken together of not more than $30,000 are exempt.

When a husband or wife makes a gift to the other, the gift tax applies to only one-half of the value of the gift, because only one-half is considered as coming from the giver. The other half is considered as already belonging to the spouse.

Social Security Taxes. *Social security taxes,* collected under the Social Security system, now provide more than $45,000,000,000 a year in federal revenue. Old-age, survivors, and disability insurance and health care for the elderly are financed by a 4.8 per cent tax on the first $7800 of an employee's wages and an identical tax on the employer's payroll. The employer deducts the tax from the employee's wages and sends the combined 9.6 per cent to the Treasury. Self-employed persons pay a 6.9 per cent tax on the first $7800 of their income; this tax is paid by those liable for it in quarterly installments. State unemployment compensation programs are financed in large part by federal grants, the funds for which come from a 3.1 per cent tax on the payrolls of businesses with four or more employees. These payroll taxes are all credited to trust accounts maintained by the Treasury, and Congress appropriates the funds as they are needed. See pages 472, 486.

Taxation of State and Local Governments. As we have noted before,[10] the National Government may *not* tax the States or their local units in the exercise of their governmental functions. As the Supreme Court declared in *McCulloch* v. *Maryland,* "the power to tax involves the power to destroy." If Congress could levy taxes on the governmental functions of the States and their local governments, it could conceivably destroy them. This, of course, the logic of our constitutional system clearly prohibits.

The National Government, however, *may* tax State and local activities which are of a *nongovernmental* (or *corporate*) character—that is, activities which are not necessarily or ordinarily engaged in by the States and their local subdivisions. For example, in 1893 South Carolina created a State-owned monopoly to sell liquor at government dispensaries and claimed exemption from the federal saloon

---

[8] The tax upon the estate of one who dies might be levied upon the entire net estate before it is divided, thus being an "estate tax"; or the tax might be levied upon the portion inherited by each heir, thus being an "inheritance tax." The present federal tax is an *estate tax.* Most States have *inheritance taxes.* Some States have both taxes.

[9] If a nonresident alien dies owning property in the United States, the exemption is only $2000.

---

[10] See pages 65, 248.

Taxes stir deep emotions, produce many conflicting opinions, and generate a vast amount of political heat. Most Americans seem to accept their tax burdens rather resignedly, even fatalistically. They recognize and accept the fact that a large share of the money raised goes for national defense purposes; and, although they obviously favor the lowest practicable level of taxation, they tend to agree with Justice Holmes that with taxes we "buy civilization." But there are also many Americans who regard taxes as, at best, onerous deprivations of personal property and freedom. In this context, Senator Barry Goldwater has written:

> We have been led to look upon taxation as merely a problem of public financing: How much money does the government need? We have been led to discount, and often to forget altogether, the bearing of taxation on the problem of individual freedom. . . . One of the foremost precepts of natural law is man's right to the possession and use of his property. And a man's earnings are his property as much as his land and the house in which he lives. Indeed, in the industrial age, earnings are probably the most prevalent form of property. . . . How can a man be truly free if he is denied the means to exercise freedom? How can he be free if the fruits of his labor are not his to dispose of, but are treated, instead, as part of a common pool of public wealth? Property and freedom are inseparable: the extent government takes the one in the form of taxes, it intrudes on the other. *The Conscience of a Conservative,* 1960.

Which of these two general attitudes toward taxation do you tend to accept? Why? Do you think that a taxing system ought to be based upon the concept of ability to pay or, instead, upon the concept of benefits received?

---

license tax. The Supreme Court, however, required the State to pay the tax for each dispensary because the sale of liquor is not a necessary or usual governmental activity. Similarly, the Court held in 1946 that spring water bottled and sold by the State of New York at Saratoga Springs is subject to federal taxation. The employees of State and local governments must pay federal income taxes on their salaries the same as other citizens.

TAXATION FOR NON-REVENUE PURPOSES

As we noted on page 253, the power to tax may be, and often is, used for purposes other than the raising of revenue. The most common non-revenue use is for the purpose of regulation. We have already cited several such uses: for example, the taxation of notes issued by State-chartered banks and the requirement of

a license for legitimate dealing in narcotics.

In upholding the tax on State banknotes in 1869, the Supreme Court declared:

> Having, in the exercise of undisputed constitutional powers, undertaken to provide a currency for the whole country, it cannot be questioned that Congress may, constitutionally, secure the benefits of it to the people by appropriate legislation.

Thus assured of the constitutionality of the technique, Congress has used the taxing power as a regulatory weapon frequently. For example, in 1912 it imposed a tax of 2¢ a hundred on matches made of white or yellow phosphorous, since phosphorous is very poisonous and was highly injurious to workers in match factories where it was being used. The effect of the tax was to make the phosphorous matches prohibitively expensive, and that segment of the match industry was destroyed.

But Congress may not use its power to tax

in order to regulate in whatever manner it chooses. Here, as in all other matters, it is bound by the provisions of the Constitution.

Three 1968 decisions of the Supreme Court illustrate the point:

In one case the Supreme Court overturned the conviction of a man prosecuted under the National Firearms Act of 1934. In that statute Congress had required the registration and payment of a $200 tax on the ownership of such weapons as sawed-off shotguns and submachineguns. The man had been convicted for knowing possession of an unregistered (and thus untaxed) sawed-off shotgun. The Court held that to require one to register and pay the tax on an *unlawfully* possessed weapon would be to open that person to immediate prosecution *because* of that possession. This, said the Court, would amount to forcing the shotgun owner to testify against himself—

in violation of the 5th Amendment's ban on self-incrimination.

The Court also upset the convictions of two professional gamblers. They had been tried under a 1951 law requiring the registration of professional gamblers, imposing a $50 tax on each such person, and levying additional taxes on their activities. The Court held that to require a person to register and pay taxes as a gambler would be to automatically lay him open to State and local prosecution for gambling—again in violation of the 5th Amendment's ban on self-incrimination. (Note that in these cases the Court did *not* rule that Congress may not tax such matters as the ownership of firearms or gambling. Rather, it held that Congress had here chosen unconstitutional means to enforce such taxation.)

Taxation may be used to accomplish any number of other ends, too. For example, a tax may be levied on chain stores in order to

THE TAXING POWER OF THE NATIONAL GOVERNMENT

Congress may "lay and collect duties, taxes, imposts, and excises" subject to:

Expressed Limitations

1. Taxes must be levied "to pay the debts, and provide for the common defense and general welfare, of the United States." Article I, Section 8, Clause 1.
2. No export tax may be laid. Article I, Section 9, Clause 5.
3. Direct taxes must be apportioned among the States on the basis of population. Article I, Section 9, Clause 4.
4. Indirect taxes must be levied at a uniform rate throughout the United States. Article I, Section 8, Clause 1.

Implied Limitation

1. Congress may not tax the basic governmental functions of the States or their local governments. (Implied from the nature of the federal system.)

Beyond the four expressed limitations on the taxing power, Congress cannot use that power in any way to violate any other provision of the Constitution; for example, it cannot tax in such a manner as to deprive one of his right to freedom of religion or speech or press (1st Amendment) or to deprive him of his property without due process of law (5th Amendment).

The 16th Amendment gives Congress the power to impose an income tax as an exception to the requirement that direct taxes be apportioned among the States on the basis of population.

improve the competitive position of independent retail outlets.[11]   Or, the power may be used to influence consumer buying habits. Congress repealed federal excise taxes on a long list of items—ranging from jewelry and furs through radio and television sets to lighters, matches, and playing cards—in 1965. Congress took such action in order to encourage their purchase and, in turn, stimulate the national economy.

Among many other illustrations of the point: the relatively heavy taxation of large incomes tends to equalize the distribution of income among the population.   The heavy taxation of an article may discourage many from buying it.   Higher taxes on personal and corporate income in times of rising prices may reduce purchasing power and thus help to keep a lid on inflation.

---

[11] Several States levy such taxes; see Chapter 40, Financing State and Local Government.

✳✳✳✳✳✳✳✳✳✳✳ CONCEPT BUILDING ✳✳✳✳✳✳✳✳✳✳✳

Key Concepts

The power to tax is absolutely necessary to the existence of a government. The lack of an adequate taxing power was one of the chief weaknesses of the Articles of Confederation.

Article I, Section 8, Clause 1 of the Constitution gives Congress the power to tax, subject to four expressed and one implied limitations.

The four expressed limitations are: (1) Taxes must be levied for a public purpose, not for private benefit. (2) Congress cannot levy export taxes. (3) Direct taxes, except the income tax, must be apportioned among the States on the basis of population. (4) Indirect taxes must be uniform throughout the United States.

A direct tax is one that is borne directly by the person upon whom it is imposed, as a head tax.   An indirect tax is one that may be shifted to another person.

The income tax is a direct tax provided by the 16th Amendment and need not be levied in proportion to population.   It is a progressive tax which on personal income today nets some $90,000,000,000 annually.   The tax is laid on total income minus certain deductions and exemptions.   The corporation income tax, levied on corporations organized for profit, now produces some $38,000,000,000 annually. Most taxpayers are honest, but the penalties for dishonesty are stiff.

Excises are taxes imposed on goods produced or sold or on services performed in the United States.   Customs duties are taxes levied on imported goods. An estate tax is levied on the estate of the deceased and a gift tax is levied on expensive gifts made.   Social security taxes are levied on employers, employees, and the self-employed.

The implied limitation is: Congress may not tax the *governmental* functions of State and local governments.   It may tax the *nongovernmental* (businesslike) functions, however.

Of course, Congress cannot use its taxing power to violate *any* provision of the Constitution. But it may and does tax for purposes of regulation and for other non-revenue purposes.

Important Terms

ad valorem	excises	indirect tax	tariffs
customs duties	gift tax	internal revenue	taxable income
direct tax	income tax	payroll taxes	withholding tax
estate tax	inheritance tax	16th Amendment	

Questions for Inquiry and Review

1. What expressed restrictions does the Constitution of the United States place upon the taxing power?

2. Why is the power to tax a broader power than the others granted to Congress in the Constitution?

3. Why did the Founding Fathers write a ban on export duties into the Constitution?

4. Why has Congress not levied a direct tax, other than the income tax, outside of the District of Columbia in more than a century?

5. Why is the income tax, a direct tax, constitutional even though it is not apportioned among the States on the basis of population?

6. What is the primary distinction between a direct tax and an indirect tax?

7. Which federal tax produces the largest amount of revenue each year?

8. Why is an excise tax sometimes referred to as a "hidden tax"? A "luxury tax"?

9. Does Congress levy an inheritance tax or an estate tax? What is the distinction between the two? On what ground is the one levied by Congress regarded as an indirect tax?

10. What is the particular purpose of the federal gift tax?

11. What type of State and local governmental functions may Congress tax? What type may it not tax?

12. In what ways has Congress exercised its power to tax for other than revenue-raising purposes?

For Further Inquiry

1. Commenting on the high level of taxation during World War II, the late Congressman Robert L. Doughton of North Carolina, observed: "You can shear a sheep once a year; you can skin him only once." How would you explain what Mr. Doughton meant?

2. Even at today's high rate of taxation, the National Government does not always live within its income. Why? How does the National Government secure the additional money necessary to finance its operations? Suggest various ways in which federal expenditures might be reduced, discussing and evaluating each.

3. Do you think it fair to require employers, acting at their own expense, to collect (*i.e.,* withhold) federal income and social security taxes from their employees' paychecks?

4. What arguments can you advance in favor of and against the use by Congress of its power to tax as a regulatory device?

5. On what grounds do you think you might build an argument against the Supreme Court's decisions in the firearms and wagering tax cases cited on page 262?

6. The power to tax is a concurrent one enjoyed by both the National Government and the States. Many items, such as individual and corporation incomes, gasoline, liquor, and tobacco are taxed by the United States and by all, or most of, the States, too. A steadily increasing number of local governments also tax these items. Approximately 90 per cent of all federal and State tax collections come from the same sources. Why have authorities in the field of public finance repeatedly urged the

development of a coordinated tax policy for the nation? What particular problem does the high rate of federal taxation create for the States?

7. Some authorities propose a "tax-sharing plan" under which the National Government would be given the exclusive power to levy certain taxes—for example, on income or gasoline; the National Government would than share the revenue from these taxes with the States. In most such proposals the National Government would "rebate" to each State an amount based upon that State's population and the State would then be free to spend the money it received in whatever manner it thought proper. What arguments can you advance for and against this idea?

8. The University of Georgia and Georgia Institute of Technology claimed that taxing admissions to their football games was in fact taxing the State and hence unconstitutional. In 1938 the Supreme Court decided that the taxes could be collected. Why?

9. Are direct taxes or indirect taxes more just? Which are easier to collect?

10. What do you think of the description of taxes by Mr. Justice Holmes on page 252?

11. Because the income from them is exempt from federal taxation, the bonds issued by States and their local units frequently provide a "tax haven" for persons with large incomes. How? Do you think this proper?

12. Do you think that the National Government should be forbidden the power to spend in any year a greater amount than it receives in taxes during that period? Should a similar restriction be applied to State and local governments?

Suggested Activities

1. Secure copies of the latest income tax returns and make them out as though they were actually to be filed. The Internal Revenue Service will supply forms and instruction booklets.

2. If your State has an income tax, compare it with the federal income tax.

3. Invite a representative of the Internal Revenue Service to speak to the class on the work of the agency.

4. Write a report on one of the following topics: (a) excise taxes, (b) tax evasion, (c) the history of the protective tariff.

5. Stage a debate or class forum on one or more of the following: (a) *Resolved,* That the Congress should enact a general sales tax; (b) *Resolved,* That the National Government should conduct a regularly scheduled lottery to help finance its operations; (c) *Resolved,* That since a person is taxed on his earned income in the year in which he receives it, it is unjust to tax that portion of his estate upon his death.

Suggested Reading

GREENE, LEE S. and PARTHEMOS, GEORGE S., *American Government: Policies and Functions.* Scribner's, 1967. Chapter 4.

INTERNAL REVENUE SERVICE, *Your Federal Income Tax.* Government Printing Office, 1970.

PELTASON, J. W. and BURNS, JAMES M., *Functions and Policies of American Government.* Prentice-Hall, 1967. Chapter 2.

PRITCHETT, C. HERMAN, *The American Constitution.* McGraw-Hill, 1968. Chapter 13.

SHARKANSKY, IRA, *The Politics of Taxing and Spending.* Bobbs, Merrill, 1969.

"Should Churches Pay Taxes?" *U.S. News,* June 16, 1969.

STERN PHILIP M., "How 381 Super-Rich Americans Managed Not to Pay a Cent in Taxes Last Year," *New York Times Magazine,* April 13, 1969.

"Why Tax Reform Is So Urgent," *Time,* April 4, 1969.

15
THE COMMERCE POWER

✦✦✦What might the United States be like today had the Commerce Clause <u>not</u> been written into the Constitution?

✦✦✦Why and in what ways does the Commerce Clause provide for these roles: Government as Regulator, Government as Promoter, Government as Manager?

✦✦✦Should government, in fact, perform any of these roles in the nation's economy? Why or why not?

The prosperity of commerce is now perceived and acknowledged by all enlightened statesmen to be the most useful as well as the most productive source of national wealth, and has accordingly become a primary object of their political cares.

ALEXANDER HAMILTON

We saw in Chapter 2 that the weak Congress under the Articles of Confederation had no power to regulate commerce among the States and that it had very little authority over foreign commerce. The Critical Period of the 1780's was marked by intense commercial rivalries and jealousies among the newly independent States. High trade barriers and spiteful State laws created confusion and chaos in both interstate and foreign commerce. Indeed, the situation was so grave that George Washington was moved to remark: "We are one nation today and thirteen tomorrow. Who will treat with us on such terms?"

Because of these conditions, no group was more responsible for the calling of the Constitutional Convention than the merchants and creditors. They had an obvious interest in

orderly commerce and a stabilized economy, and they favored the creation of a government with the power necessary to regularize the economic life of the Republic.

The Founding Fathers were generally agreed on the need for national regulation of commerce, and they spent little time discussing the point. Some particular problems, especially the slave trade and export duties, did provoke extended debate, however. Once compromises had been reached on these matters, the Founding Fathers unanimously agreed that Congress should have the power:

To regulate commerce with foreign nations, and among the several States, and with the Indian tribes.[1]

This Commerce Clause has done more to

---

[1] Article I, Section 8, Clause 3. The Founding Fathers viewed the Indian tribes very much as they did foreign nations, and so they gave Congress the power to regulate trade with them. They also realized the importance of keeping "firearms" and "firewater" from them. Later, when the transcontinental railroads were built, Congress had the power to grant rights of way through Indian lands for railroads.

"The Congress shall have power ... to regulate commerce with foreign nations, and among the several States, and with the Indian Tribes."

Article I,
Section 8,
Clause 3

BUT Congress is forbidden to:

1. Regulate the slave trade prior to 1808. *Article I, Section 9, Clause 1* (obsolete)
2. Levy duties or taxes on articles exported from any State. *Article I, Section 9, Clause 5*
3. Give preference to ports of one State over those of another. *Article I, Section 9, Clause 6*
4. Require vessels bound to or from ports of one State to enter, clear, or pay duties in another. *Article I, Section 9, Clause 6*
5. Deprive any person (including artificial persons: corporations) of life, liberty, or property without due process of law. *5th Amendment*

AND the States are forbidden to:

1. Lay imposts or duties on imports or exports. *Article I, Section 10, Clause 2*
2. Lay any duty on tonnage. *Article I, Section 10, Clause 3*

} Except with the consent of Congress [a]

3. Place an unreasonable burden upon interstate or foreign commerce — by virtue of the Constitution's grant to Congress of the expressed power to regulate commerce. *Article I, Section 8, Clause 3*

[a] *Article I, Section 10, Clause 2* permits a State to levy "imposts or duties on imports or exports [if] absolutely necessary for executing its inspection laws" but "the net produce of all [such charges] shall be for the use of the Treasury of the United States; and such laws [levying these charges] shall be subject to the revision and control of the Congress."

develop a loose confederation into a strong Union than has any other part of the Constitution. It has permitted the development in the United States of the greatest unrestricted market in the world. Along with the power to tax, it has contributed most to the vast growth of the National Government's power.

SCOPE OF THE COMMERCE POWER

The Meaning of "Commerce." As it is used in the Constitution, the word "commerce" cannot be precisely defined. Rather, what it includes and what it does not include are continuously being determined by: (1) Congress as it exercises its commerce power and (2) the

Supreme Court as it decides cases involving the exercise of that power.

An Ever-Broadening Interpretation. The chief and perhaps the only purpose in the minds of those who wrote the Commerce Clause was to prevent the States from interfering with the free flow of goods among themselves. To the Founding Fathers, the word "commerce" meant the exchange of goods by purchase and sale — the *articles* to be traded, not the *means by which* they are traded.

Like so many other parts of the Constitution, however, the meaning of the Commerce Clause has changed and expanded over the years. This has been especially true because of: (1) the spectacular improvements that have been made in transportation and communication in this

Scope of the Commerce Power

Congress shall have power . . . to regulate commerce with foreign nations, and among the several States, and with the Indian tribes. Article I, Section 8, Clause 3.

Under the Commerce Power Congress Regulates:

TRANSPORTATION

Railroads—freight, passenger, and express
Trucks and buses as contract or common carriers
Water transportation by contract or common carriers
Pipelines (except water and natural gas)

By the Interstate Commerce Commission

Aircraft

By the Civil Aeronautics Board and the Federal Aviation Administration

Natural gas and
electric power transmission

By the Federal Power Commission

INDUSTRIAL ACTIVITY

Labor—collective bargaining, minimum wages, maximum hours, working conditions, etc.

By the National Labor Relations Board, the Department of Labor, and other agencies

Combinations in restraint of trade

By the Federal Trade Commission, the Department of Justice, and other agencies

Products injurious to health

By the Food and Drug Administration and other agencies

Unfair trade practices

By the Federal Trade Commission

FINANCIAL ACTIVITY

Stock exchanges and their operations
Issuance of securities
Holding companies

By Securities and Exchange Commission

Credit and loans

By the Federal Housing Administration, the Export-Import Bank, the Commodity Credit Corporation, the Small Business Administration, and other agencies

AGRICULTURE

Production and marketing quotas
Stockyards
Commodities exchanges

By the Department of Agriculture

COMMUNICATIONS

Wire transmission—telephone, telegraph, and cable
Wireless transmission—radio and television

By the Federal Communications Commission

CRIME

Involving interstate or foreign commerce—
e.g., auto theft, kidnapping, white slavery, flight to avoid prosecution, etc.

By the Department of Justice and other agencies

The States may also regulate interstate commerce but ONLY if such regulations do not unduly burden that commerce. ANY State regulation in conflict with national regulation is invalid.

country since 1789, and (2) the revolutionary change in our economy from one based on simple local agriculture in 1789 to one geared to the industrialism and technology of today. Remember, the horse and the sailing ship were the principal means of both transportation and communication when the Constitution was written.

To appreciate the vast change that has taken place in the meaning of "commerce," one need glance at a list of only *some* of the things Congress has done under its commerce power. It has enacted literally thousands of statutes dealing with such subjects as radio and television broadcasting, the telephone and telegraph, railroads, steamships and nuclear-powered vessels, aircraft, automobiles, trucks, buses, bridges, ferries, rivers, harbors, canals, and pipelines. It has provided for the regulation of the transmission of electric energy, the building of dams, and the setting of freight and passenger rates. It has regulated the transporting of firearms, firecrackers, alcoholic beverages, stolen goods of various kinds, kidnaped persons, foods, drugs, cosmetics, agricultural sprays, and an almost endless list of other items.

Furthermore, it has restricted or forbidden the importing and exporting of many articles; provided for minimum wages, maximum hours, and safety conditions in many industries; guaranteed the rights of employees to join unions and bargain collectively; regulated monopolistic business practices; provided subsidies for farmers; built highways and aided the States to build others; and done a veritable host of other things.

Gibbons v. *Ogden,* 1824. The very first case to reach the Supreme Court involving the Commerce Clause set the stage for the vast expansion the clause has undergone. In 1807 Robert Fulton's steamboat, the *Clermont,* made its first successful run from New York to Albany; and the New York legislature gave Fulton and his partner, Robert Livingston, an exclusive long-term grant to navigate the waters of the State by steamboat. From this monopoly, Aaron Ogden secured a permit for steam navigation between New York City and the New Jersey shore.

Thomas Gibbons, operating under a coasting license granted by the United States Government, began a competing line. Upon Ogden's petition, the New York courts ordered Gibbons to discontinue his business. Gibbons appealed to the Supreme Court. He claimed that the New York grant conflicted with the congressional power to regulate commerce.

The decision in this case was bound to have far-reaching effects. It was the first case involving the Commerce Clause to come before the Supreme Court. Even Congress itself had not been able to agree upon the extent of its powers over commerce.

The Supreme Court ruled unanimously in favor of Gibbons. It held the New York law in violation of the Constitution's grant of the commerce power to Congress. In reply to Ogden's argument that "commerce" should be narrowly defined as "traffic" or the mere buying and selling of goods, Chief Justice Marshall wrote:

> Commerce, undoubtedly, is traffic, but it is something more — it is intercourse. It describes the commercial intercourse between nations, and parts of nations, in all its branches, and is regulated by prescribing rules for carrying on that intercourse.

The Supreme Court's decision was immensely popular because it dealt a death blow to the steamboat monopolies. But it had a much broader significance, which became apparent only with the passage of time. The Court in giving a sweeping definition of commerce had greatly increased the powers of Congress to regulate it. Freed from restrictive State regulation, steam navigation increased at an amazing rate on all the country's waterways. And in a few years, the railroads, similarly freed, revolutionized the nation's domestic transportation.

The Meaning of "Regulate." Just as the meaning of the word "commerce" has undergone a great transformation, so has the constitutional meaning of "regulate." Originally, to regulate meant *to restrict, to restrain, to prohibit.* In the years since then it also has come to mean *to protect, to promote, to encourage.* For example, in regulating commerce Congress has protected the people against misbranded foods and from such crimes as auto theft and kidnaping. It has promoted commerce by aiding railroads, trucking and bus companies, airlines, and steamship companies. It has encouraged agriculture by aiding farmers.

FOREIGN COMMERCE

The Commerce Clause gives to Congress the power "to regulate commerce with foreign nations"—that is, *foreign commerce.* The foreign commerce of the United States includes any American trade which begins, passes through, or ends in any foreign country. The States have no power whatever in this field; hence, the congressional power to regulate foreign commerce is even broader than is its power over interstate commerce.

Exclusion of Imports. Congress has prohibited the importation of many items. Here are only a few of them: diseased animals and plants, opium except for medical purposes, obscene literature, literature advocating the forceful resistance to any law of the United States, lottery tickets, adulterated and misbranded foods, and articles having names or emblems simulating domestic trademarks.

Embargo on Exports. Congress also has power under the Commerce Clause to forbid the export of commodities. Thus, since the end of World War II, the exportation of war materials and certain heavy machinery has been controlled by a strict licensing system. We do not want to help build the war machines of the Soviet Union, Communist China, or other countries behind the Iron Curtain.

Protection against State Interference. In *Brown* v. *Maryland,* 1827, the Supreme Court first announced the *Original Package Doctrine,* which is generally followed to this day. This rule forbids a State to tax or exercise its police powers [2] over imports until the original package has "come to rest"—that is, has reached the importer in this country and is broken open, sold, or used by him. Thus, a State cannot interfere with the sale of shoes from Italy until the retailer opens the shipping packages or sells them. If a State could interfere with commodities in their original packages, a coastal State could erect various barriers to prevent imports from reaching inland States.

Regulation of Navigation. Congress has the power to regulate all aspects of navigation. For example, it sets the conditions under which a vessel may fly the American flag, including such factors as registration of vessels, seaworthiness, wireless and lifesaving equipment, minimum pay for crewmen, passenger and cargo limits, and the qualifications to be met by officers and crews. It provides for various navigational aids such as channel markers, lighthouses and lightships, and weather services. It prescribes the manner in which ships may enter and leave our ports and, for health purposes and as a protection against smuggling or espionage, has provided for the inspection of vessels entering American waters.

Regulation of Foreign Communication. The courts have interpreted "commerce" to include the communication of ideas as well as the exchange or transportation of commodities. Congress regulates cables, telegraph, and telephone wires extending to foreign countries, radio and television broadcasts beamed from the United States, and all incoming wire, wireless, and printed communications.

Regulation of Immigration. The Consti-

---

[2] The *police power* of a State is its power to act to protect, promote, and regulate for the public health, safety, morals, or welfare of its citizens. See page 104.

A nation's place in international commerce is related to its merchant fleet. The nation's first nuclear-powered merchant vessel, the <u>N.S. Savannah</u>, is helping the United States to maintain its position as one of the world's leading maritime powers. (Maritime Administration, U. S. Department of Commerce)

tution does not in so many words give Congress the power to regulate immigration. But, as we have seen, the power is an inherent one; and, too, the courts consider the movement of people to be commerce. Acting, then, on the basis of both inherent and implied powers, Congress has provided for the exclusion of certain classes of aliens altogether, has prescribed the conditions under which others may enter permanently or temporarily, and has also provided for the deportation of undesirable aliens.[3]

INTERSTATE COMMERCE

The Commerce Clause grants to Congress the power "to regulate commerce ... among the several States"—that is, *interstate commerce.* Interstate commerce includes any and all trade

---

[3] See Chapter 5, pages 82–88.

between and among the States and the means by which it is conducted. Trade which is carried on wholly *within* one State is known as *intrastate commerce* and is subject to State regulation.

What commerce is interstate in character and thus subject to congressional control? What is only intrastate and thus beyond the power of Congress? These seemingly simple questions are indeed quite complicated.

Although there is no simple test for distinguishing interstate and intrastate commerce, this much can be said: Any transaction or movement that crosses a State line is interstate in character; so, too, is any transaction or movement that is *a part of* such an action. More and more as the country has grown, commerce once regarded as only intrastate has come to be viewed as interstate by both Congress and the courts.

Whenever State regulation of intrastate commerce conflicts with federal regulation of interstate commerce, the State regulation must yield. The *Shreveport Case (The Houston, East and West Texas Railway Company* v. *United States),* decided by the Supreme Court in 1914, illustrates this point.

Shreveport, Louisiana, is located near the Texas border. Shreveport merchants and those in Dallas, Texas, competed for the trade of the Texas towns between them. The freight rates from Dallas to these towns had been fixed by the Texas Railway Commission. They were much lower per mile than the rates from Shreveport, set by the Interstate Commerce Commission. The Shreveport merchants complained that they were being discriminated against because they happened to be located across a State line. The ICC held that the intrastate rates from Dallas were too low; thus, it ordered those rates raised to a par with the interstate rates from Shreveport.

The case was taken to the Supreme Court. The Court held that the ICC's order was valid, *that the authority to regulate interstate commerce carries with it the right to regulate intrastate commerce when that is necessary to the protection of interstate commerce.*

When Does Commerce Become Interstate? At what point does the shipment of goods from one State to another actually enter the stream of interstate commerce? The answer to this question is vital: *Before* the goods reach that point they are subject only to *State* regulation; *after* they reach it they pass under federal control. The Supreme Court has regularly held that when goods are *started on a continuous journey* that will take them across a State line, or when they are delivered to a carrier for such a journey, they become interstate commerce, no longer subject to local control.

A case *(Coe* v. *Errol,* 1886) decided by the Supreme Court more than eighty years ago demonstrates the point very well, and it also shows how important the point can be even in the most routine of situations. A New Hampshire lumberman, Coe, had refused to pay the property taxes the town of Errol had

imposed on a large quantity of logs he had dragged to the river bank. The logs had remained on the bank for several weeks while Coe waited for the river ice to melt so that he could float them to a sawmill in Maine. They were still there on the annual property tax assessment day. Coe claimed that they could not be taxed by the town because they were in interstate commerce. The Supreme Court held that he was liable for the tax, however. It ruled that the interstate journey did not begin until the logs were actually rolled into the river; hauling them to the river was merely a preparation for the journey, not actually a part of it.

When Does Interstate Commerce End? Determining the point at which goods *leave* interstate commerce and again become subject to State control is equally important. As we noted on page 270, the point at which goods leave *foreign* commerce is determined by the Original Package Doctrine. In general, the same rule applies to interstate commerce; but in some cases the courts have held that the States may tax and otherwise regulate goods shipped in interstate commerce once they have reached the *consignee* (the party to whom they are shipped). But a State cannot regulate goods simply because they happen to have come from outside the State.

Commerce Includes Navigation. As we know, the Supreme Court held commerce to include navigation in *Gibbons* v. *Ogden.* Thus, Congress has the power to regulate vessels in interstate trade and also the use of the waters in which these vessels navigate. Congress requires that the vessels be inspected as to seaworthiness and that they carry life preservers and other safety devices. It sets the number of passengers that a ship may carry and the minimum working conditions for a ship's crew.

Congress appropriates money for dredging rivers and harbors, constructing canals, marking channels, and operating lighthouses. It forbids obstructions in navigable streams; and a bridge, causeway, or dam cannot be built across navigable streams without the consent of the Secretary of the Army.

Without the express permission of Congress, foreign vessels cannot carry freight or passengers from one port in the United States to another. In this way Congress protects Americans engaged in interstate shipping against the competition of foreign vessels.

The regulatory power of Congress extends to all navigable waters which are used or are susceptible of being used for interstate commerce. Congress has authority over navigable streams running through two or more States and over those located wholly within one State which connect with other navigable waters so as to form a continuous channel of communication with other States.[4]

The authority of Congress also extends to navigable waters that are wholly within one State and connect with no exterior water if these waters are actually navigated by vessels which connect with other interstate carriers —for example, a ferry plying a lake and connecting two rail lines which extend to another State.

Commerce Includes Transportation by Land and Air. The first rail lines were built in this country in the early 1830's. Over the next generation their development was generally encouraged by both the States and the

To aid shipping Congress appropriates funds for the International Ice Patrol. Coast Guard cutters and planes track stray icebergs in the North Atlantic shipping lanes and warn vessels in the area of the danger. (U.S. Coast Guard)

National Government. In the 1870's and 1880's, however, several States began to impose drastic regulations, especially under the Granger Movement in the Middle West. The Supreme Court checked this interference with

[4] Only those streams "navigable in their natural condition" were originally considered to be within the power of Congress. This interpretation has been greatly modified by a series of congressional actions and court decisions over the past century, however. In the *Daniel Ball Case* in 1871 the Supreme Court upheld the requirement of a federal license for a vessel operating only on the Grand River between Grand Rapids and Grand Haven, wholly within the State of Michigan, since the steamer carried goods on a part of its journey in interstate commerce. The Court held that "those rivers must be regarded as public navigable rivers in law which are navigable in fact. And they are navigable in fact when they are used, *or are susceptible of being used,* in their ordinary condition, as highways for commerce." In 1940 the Supreme Court, in *United States* v. *Appalachian Electric Power Co.,* upheld the requirement of a Federal Power Commission license for a dam on the New River, flowing through Virginia and West Virginia. The Court ruled that the river, although not *navigable in fact,* is *navigable in law* and thus subject to federal regulation because it is "capable of being made navigable" and because it flows into and affects another river which is navigable in both fact and law.

A common sight on the highways of the nation is the huge trailer trucks that carry freight and property interstate. The activities of these motor carriers are regulated by the Interstate Commerce Commission. (Talbot Lovering)

Commerce Includes the Communication of Ideas. The first telegraph line was built in 1842, and the first telephone was exhibited at the Centennial Exposition in 1876. Both means of communication are regulated under the commerce power. So, too, are radio and television broadcasting. The Federal Communications Commission, created by Congress in 1934, regulates all interstate wire and wireless communications today.[6]

Commerce Includes the Movement of Persons. The movement of persons across a State line, whether for business or pleasure, is included within the scope of the commerce power. Even persons walking across a State line are involved in interstate commerce.

During the Great Depression of the 1930's several States passed "anti-Okie" laws. These were statutes prohibiting any nonresident *indigent* (poor person) from entering the State. In 1941 the Supreme Court struck down these laws when it held California's version to be invalid on the ground that it imposed an unconstitutional barrier to interstate commerce.

Under the Mann Act of 1910 (White Slave Act) Congress made it a federal crime for any person to transport a woman across a State line for an immoral purpose. Some years ago a movie actor was tried for paying the fare of and accompanying a single woman from Hollywood to New York. In Washington, D.C., a taxi driver was convicted for knowingly transporting a woman four blocks to a hotel for an immoral appointment. And a Mormon was found guilty for taking his plural wife across a State line.

Congress has made many other actions involving interstate travel federal crimes. Thus, it is unlawful to transport a kidnap victim or a stolen automobile or other goods from one State to another, or to obstruct interstate commerce by the threat or use of violence. And it is unlawful to flee to another State to avoid arrest, imprisonment, or testifying

interstate commerce in 1886, and Congress created the Interstate Commerce Commission in 1887. As other forms of interstate transportation—including motor vehicles, aircraft, power lines, and pipelines—developed, they were also brought under federal control.

Today, acting for Congress, the ICC regulates the railroads, interstate motor carriers, most ships plying between coastal ports and on the nation's lakes and rivers, and all interstate pipelines except those carrying water or natural gas. The Civil Aeronautics Board and the Federal Aviation Administration regulate private and commercial air transportation. The Federal Power Commission regulates the transmission of electricity and natural gas from one State to another.[5]

---

[5] See pages 522, 531–535, 538, 540.

[6] See pages 536–538.

in a felony case. The Civil Rights Act of 1964 makes it a federal crime to flee from a State after bombing a church, school, or other structure.

A major portion of the Civil Rights Act of 1964 is based upon the commerce power. Title II of the act (Public Accommodations) provides that no person may be denied access to or service in various public establishments on grounds of race, color, religion, or national origin. Places covered by the law are those in which lodgings are provided to transient guests or in which interstate travelers are served, and those in which a substantial portion of the goods sold or the entertainment presented moves in interstate commerce. Such public accommodations include: restaurants, cafeterias, lunch counters, and other eating places; movie theaters, concert halls, and other auditoriums; gasoline stations; sports arenas and stadiums; and hotels, motels, and rooming houses (except owner-occupied units with less than six rooms for rent). The law also covers any public establishment *within* or which *contains* such an accommodation—for example, a barber shop in a hotel or a store with a soda fountain. Private clubs are specifically exempted from the provisions of the law—except in those cases where they offer their facilities to the patrons of some covered establishment, as in a hotel.[7]

The Civil Rights Act of 1968 makes it a federal crime for any person to travel in or use such facilities of interstate commerce as the telephone, telegraph, radio, or television with intent to incite, organize, or take part in a riot, or assist others to do so.

---

[7] The Supreme Court upheld the constitutionality of Title II and the use of the Commerce Clause as a basis for civil rights legislation—at least in the area of access to public accommodations—in 1964. In reaching its unanimous decision, in *Heart of Atlanta Motel, Inc.* v. *United States,* the Court noted that there was "overwhelming evidence of the disruptive effect [of] racial discrimination . . . on commercial intercourse."

Commerce Includes Securities. Corporations are financed in large part through the sale of their securities to the public, usually through security exchanges, or "stock markets." Millions of Americans own stock in most of the nation's larger and many of its smaller business concerns; and millions have also lent vast sums to business enterprises by purchasing their bonds and other securities. Indeed, it is impossible to see how our huge private enterprise system could have been financed in any other way.

Without effective governmental regulation, investors may be misled, even by reliable brokers. Fraud is more than a mere possibility. Ill-advised, widespread speculation can have disastrous economic consequences—for individuals and for the nation itself.

The States first began to regulate the traffic in securities more than a half century ago; Kansas and then Rhode Island passed the first "blue sky laws" in 1911.[8] By 1933 every State except Nevada had enacted such statutes. The stock market crash of 1929, which marked the beginning of the Great Depression, proved State regulation to be inadequate, however. Indeed, it demonstrated the fact that the interstate character of corporate financing makes effective State control a practical impossibility. The losses suffered by often gullible investors from the purchases of highly speculative and frequently fraudulent stocks and bonds amounted to an estimated $25,000,000,000 as the country moved from the boom of the 1920's to the depression of the 1930's.

The onslaught of the Great Depression brought an overwhelming public demand for effective national regulation of securities and of the exchanges through which they are sold. In response, Congress passed the Securities Act of 1933, created the Securities and Exchange Commission (SEC) in 1934, and has

---

[8] The term originated with the remark of a Kansas legislator who claimed that dishonest promoters would sell "the bright blue sky above" if they could.

Government inspectors examine shrimp being cleaned. Food products must be clean and wholesome before they can be packaged and shipped interstate. (Food and Drug Administration)

By the turn of this century it had become difficult for many honest vendors to sell their goods because some of their competitors indulged in a variety of dishonest practices—from misrepresenting the quantity in a package to selling fraudulent medicinal remedies. The homely squash when doctored, flavored, colored, and attractively packed became "canned peaches"; the apple with a little seed added became "preserved strawberries"; oleomargarine dyed yellow took the name of "butter"; veal became "potted chicken"; and even mineral earths mixed with cheap meals became "flour." Congress first reacted to these outrages with the Pure Food and Drug Act of 1906 and later with other statutes which prohibit the circulation in interstate commerce of foods, beverages, drugs, cosmetics, and goods that are misbranded as to quantity, quality, or place of production or are injurious to health.[10]

Protection against Unreasonable State Interference. A package in interstate commerce retains federal protection against State taxation until it is delivered to its consignee or comes to rest. Moreover, it retains federal protection against other State regulations until the original package is once sold, broken open, or used. Thus, a State cannot tax cigarettes as they cross the State border but must wait until they are delivered or come to rest. Moreover, a State must wait until the package is once sold, broken open, or used before regulating the sale of the cigarettes.[11]

since enacted several statutes designed to protect the nation's investors.[9]

Articles Prohibited from Interstate Commerce. Congress has forbidden the shipment of many items across State lines. Among the many things excluded from interstate shipping are lottery tickets, dangerous explosives, firearms shipped by unlicensed persons, switchblade knives, disease-infected goods, gambling devices, and impure or misbranded foods and drugs.

---

[9] See pages 551–554. The Supreme Court first upheld the constitutionality of national regulation, as a valid exercise of both the commerce and the postal powers, in *Electric Bond & Share Company* v. *Securities and Exchange Commission* in 1938.

[10] See pages 535–536.

[11] The original package which has federal protection is one which the trade ordinarily uses for transportation. Thus, a ten-pound package of oleomargarine was held to be an original package; but paper cartons containing a pound of oleomargarine are not original packages. Goods brought into a State by peddlers and sold in the original package cease to have the federal protection given to consigned commodities Note, however, that peddlers goods are subject to State taxation and regulation as soon as they are brought into the State because the retail transactions begin at once.

If the States could tax or otherwise interfere unreasonably with goods being shipped in interstate commerce, the whole value of the Commerce Clause would be lost. We would, in effect, find ourselves living under the same conditions which plagued the original States before the adoption of the Constitution.

States may, however, under their police powers require interstate commerce to comply with *reasonable* State regulations pertaining to health, morals, safety, and general welfare. For example, States may require proper heating of passenger trains as well as the supplying of sanitary drinking cups. They may forbid gambling on all trains, require crews of sufficient size to protect the public against accident, require all trains to slow down when going through cities, and require them to make a reasonable number of stops in a State.

Notice, too, that the 21st Amendment, adopted in 1933, gives to each State an *unrestricted* right to regulate alcoholic beverages without regard to the question of interstate commerce. Section 2 provides:

> The transportation or importation into any State, Territory, or possession of the United States for delivery or use therein of intoxicating liquors, in violation of the laws thereof, is hereby prohibited.

Protection against Monopolies. By 1890 most of the major industries in the country were dominated by such combinations as the Sugar Trust, the Beef Trust, the Whiskey Trust, and the Standard Oil Trust.[12] Many supposedly competing companies made agreements with one another to limit production or fix prices. Sometimes they agreed not to compete in certain sections of the country assigned to one or another of them. Often the same persons sat on the boards of directors of competing companies (*interlocking directorates*) and could thus control competition.

The Sherman Antitrust Act of 1890. State regulation proved largely ineffective against these powerful interstate combinations; thus federal regulation became necessary. Acting under the commerce power, Congress passed the famous Sherman Antitrust Act of 1890. This act remains the basic law against monopolies today. It prohibits "every contract, combination in the form of a trust or otherwise, or conspiracy in restraint of trade or commerce among the several States, or with foreign nations." It also provides penalties for violations.

Because of the general wording and inadequate enforcement of the law, little was accomplished until 1911. In that year the Supreme Court decided two cases involving monopoly prosecutions of the American Tobacco Company and the Standard Oil Company of New Jersey. In forcing the dissolution of the two monopolies, the Supreme Court announced the "rule of reason." Although the Sherman Antitrust Act prohibits *every* agreement in restraint of trade, the Court interpreted this to mean *every unreasonable* agreement.

In 1914 Congress passed the *Clayton Antitrust Act,* making four specific practices illegal: (1) the purchase by one corporation of the

---

[12] The *trust* was originally a device by which several corporations engaged in the same line of business would combine to eliminate competition and regulate prices. This was done by creating a central board composed of the presidents or general managers of the different corporations and transferring to them a majority of stock from each of the corporations to be held "in trust" for the stockholders who thus assigned their stock. The stockholders received in return "trust certificates" showing that they were entitled to receive dividends on their assigned stock, though the voting power of it had been passed to the trustees. This enabled the trustees to elect all the directors of all the corporations and thus prevent competition and insure better prices.

"WE ALWAYS INSISTED ON A SALUTE TO THE FLAG" (from Straight Herblock, Simon & Schuster, 1964)

stock of a competitor, (2) interlocking directorates among competitors, (3) "exclusive agreements" requiring a dealer to sell the products of only the one company, and (4) price discriminations in the sale of the same product to different purchasers (expanded by the *Robinson-Patman Act,* 1936).

Several economic groups have been specifically exempted by Congress from the provisions of the Sherman and Clayton Antitrust Acts. For example, under the *Transportation Act of 1920* railroads are allowed to agree to the division of traffic or earnings with the approval of the Interstate Commerce Commission. Labor unions are exempt on the grounds that "labor is not a commodity of commerce." Some utilities, farmer and dairy co-operatives, and exporters are exempted. The Supreme Court has held that the antitrust laws do not apply to professional baseball but that they do apply to professional football and boxing.

The biggest case in the history of the nation's antitrust laws was decided in a United States District Court in Philadelphia in 1961. The defendants were twenty-nine electrical equipment concerns — including the largest, General Electric and Westinghouse — and forty-five of their executives. All were convicted of a huge price-fixing and market-dividing scheme to monopolize the sale of heavy electrical equipment in the United States. Officers of the firms involved met secretly to agree on prices and to rig the supposedly competitive bids that they would then submit on contracts to supply their products. The companies took turns in submitting the low bids in order that each of them would win a previously-agreed-to share of the multi-billion dollar business.

The "Fair Trade" Controversy. Many manufacturers of nationally advertised brand-name products attempt to set the price at which retailers may sell their products. Commonly, they require a dealer to sign a contract binding him to sell at the "fair trade" price the manufacturer sets and making him liable for damages if he does not abide by the terms of the agreement.

Signing all dealers who handle a particular product is a cumbersome, costly procedure, of course; and many dealers refuse to sign such agreements. Because of this, and as an attempt to prevent price wars, business groups began to persuade State legislatures during the 1930's to enact "fair trade laws." [13]

These laws legalize "fair trade pricing" by manufacturers. Most of them also provide that when one or a few dealers in the State have signed "fair trade" contracts, the contracts become binding on *all* dealers selling the particular item in the State whether or not they themselves have signed such contracts.

---

[13] By 1950 forty-five of the then forty-eight States had enacted fair trade laws. Only Missouri, Texas, and Vermont had not.

Of course, these State laws by themselves cannot bind those retailers who deal in *interstate* commerce—only those who deal in intrastate commerce. In 1937, however, Congress passed the *Miller-Tydings Amendment* to the Sherman Antitrust Act. This amendment provides that "interstate price-fixing" is legal in any State whose laws permit such a practice in intrastate commerce—that is, in any State in which a fair trade law is in force. The Miller-Tydings Amendment did not, however, contain any mention of the binding of nonsigners.

The question of the legality of the nonsigner provisions of State laws insofar as interstate commerce is concerned reached the Supreme Court in 1951. The Calvert Corporation, a liquor concern, had signed several "fair trade" contracts with dealers in Louisiana. That State's law bound both signers and nonsigners. Schwegmann Brothers Giant Supermarkets, Inc., of New Orleans had not signed a contract and was selling Calvert's liquors at cutrate prices. Calvert sued, but the Supreme Court held that in the Miller-Tydings Amendment Congress had *not* intended to bind nonsigners.

In order to bind nonsigners, business groups persuaded Congress to amend the Sherman Antitrust Act to that effect. The *McGuire Act*, passed in 1952, provides that if a State's laws decree that both signers *and* nonsigners are bound in intrastate commerce, they are also bound in interstate commerce.

With manufacturers now attempting to force nonsigners to comply as provided in the McGuire Act, dozens of court cases were instituted across the country. One of the principal cases again involved Schwegmann Brothers, this time against Eli Lilly & Co. The Lilly Company obtained an injunction against Schwegmann Brothers in the United States District Court in Louisiana, ordering Schwegmann Brothers to halt the sale of its drug products below the "fair trade" price. In 1953 the Court of Appeals upheld the injunction and thus upheld the McGuire Act. The Supreme Court refused to review the case.

Fair trade acts have now been tested in most State supreme courts. The acts, or at least the nonsigner provisos, have been thrown out by several. As a result, "fair trade" backers are

"Fair trade" laws have had little success in preventing gasoline price wars. Areas where a variety of service stations are competing with each other will often see prices cut to beat or meet the competition. (National Petroleum News, © 1960 McGraw-Hill Publishing Company)

now lobbying for a federal fair trade act. Many observers expect a fair trade bill—now often termed a "resale price maintenance" or "quality stabilization" bill—to reach the floor of Congress sometime soon. To date (1971), however, no such measure has gone beyond committee in either house.

The Pro Argument. "Brand name" manufacturers, thousands of small independent merchants, the drug trade, and some department stores support "fair trade" laws. They argue that such laws prevent big department and chain stores from offering "fair traded" items at cutrate prices the small merchants cannot meet. They also contend that the larger stores use the reduced price on brand-name goods, employing them as "loss leaders" to lure customers into the store.

Manufacturers supporting "fair trade" laws claim that they protect their products and good name from being "cheapened and debased" by retail price-cutting. They also feel that the manufacturer should be allowed to set the price to be charged for his product, adding that if the price is too high, the customer is likely to turn to a competitor.

The Con Argument. The opponents of "fair trade" laws argue that they violate the basic principles of free enterprise. The large retailers believe that they are in a much better position than the manufacturer to determine what the fair retail price of any item that they sell ought to be.

Macy's of New York, the world's largest department store, claims that "fair trade" is a "misleading title—the real title is 'price-fixing.' The simple truth is that no group fights for price-fixing privileges except to make prices higher than they would be under free and open competition."

❖❖❖❖❖❖❖❖❖❖ CONCEPT BUILDING ❖❖❖❖❖❖❖❖❖❖

Key Concepts

In order to establish an orderly commerce and a stabilized economy the Framers of the Constitution vested the power to regulate foreign and interstate commerce in Congress. The Commerce Clause has done more to create a strong Union of States than has any other provision in the Constitution. With the taxing power, it has been the basis for most of the growth in the powers of the National Government.

No precise definition of "commerce" is possible. It is being continually defined and enlarged by Congress and the Supreme Court. Both Congress and the Court have given it a very broad interpretation.

In its first case on the subject (*Gibbons* v. *Ogden,* 1824), the Supreme Court held commerce to be more than mere traffic in goods; the Court held it to be "intercourse . . . in all its branches."

Foreign commerce includes any American trade which begins, passes through, or ends in a foreign country. In regulating it, Congress has excluded many things from importation. It has regulated shipping, provided for protection from State interference, and regulated immigration and foreign communications.

Interstate commerce includes any and all trade between and among the States and the means by which it is conducted. In controlling it, Congress regulates most aspects of navigation, transportation on land and in the air, communications, the movement of persons across State lines, securities, and insurance.

Congress may and does protect interstate commerce, and it prohibits the shipping of certain articles. Unreasonable State interference is prohibited. Monopolies in restraint of trade are prevented under the commerce power.

"Fair trade acts" allowing a manufacturer to set the retail price of his product have produced an interesting and complicated controversy in interstate commerce.

Important Terms

"anti-Okie" laws	"fair trade" acts	monopoly	regulate
commerce	foreign commerce	navigable waters	Sherman Antitrust Act
Commerce Clause	*Gibbons* v. *Ogden*	Original Package	*Shreveport Case*
consignee	interstate commerce	Doctrine	trust
embargo	intrastate commerce	police powers	

Questions for Inquiry and Review

1. Why was the Commerce Clause written into the Constitution? Where is it found? What does it provide?

2. Why is a precise definition of "commerce" impossible? By whom is it being constantly defined?

3. What was the significance of the Supreme Court's decision in *Gibbons* v. *Ogden?*

4. Why is the power to regulate foreign commerce a broader one than the power to regulate interstate commerce?

5. What trade is included within the foreign commerce of the United States? By whom is it regulated?

6. What trade is interstate in character? By whom is it regulated?

7. What trade is intrastate in character? By whom is it regulated?

8. At what point does commerce become interstate in character?

9. At what point does interstate commerce end?

10. May Congress exercise its commerce power so as to reach the transportation of goods by a carrier operating wholly within a single State? Why?

11. Why are the States prohibited from impeding unreasonably the flow of foreign and interstate commerce?

12. Under the exercise of what power may the States require interstate commerce to comply with reasonable State regulation?

13. What special area of State regulation is marked out by the 21st Amendment?

14. What is the "rule of reason" with regard to the enforcement of the Sherman Antitrust Act and other such statutes?

15. What are "fair trade" laws? What are the major arguments made in behalf of them? The major arguments advanced against them?

For Further Inquiry

1. The Fair Labor Standards Act of 1938 provides a minimum wage and maximum hours for workers engaged in interstate commerce, in producing goods for interstate commerce, and in work essential to that production (see page 468). The Supreme Court has upheld the application of the act to the caretakers of a twenty-two-story building in New York City

because heat was essential to warm the fingers of seamstresses working in the building for a manufacturer of clothing to be shipped in interstate commerce. It has also upheld the coverage of the employees of a window-washing company who worked on the windows of plants producing goods for interstate commerce and the elevator operators in the Chicago office building of a corporation engaged in interstate commerce. Do you agree or disagree with these interpretations of the commerce power?

2. Under the Federal Kidnaping Law (the Lindbergh Act) it is a federal crime to carry a kidnaped victim across a State line. If the victim is not found within twenty-four hours after the crime has been committed, the law provides that it is to be assumed that he has been carried across a State line. But, in fact, in most kidnap cases it is later found that interstate commerce was in no way involved. In view of this, why do you think Congress wrote the twenty-four-hour provision into the law?

3. In enacting the Civil Rights Act of 1964 (see page 275), Congress declared Title II of the statute, dealing with public accommodations, to be based upon the Commerce Clause. Why did it not choose to rely instead upon the Due Process and Equal Protection Clauses of the 14th Amendment?

4. A corporation is owned by its stockholders. As a rule, however, the stockholders have little real control over the management and policies of the corporation. Effective control is actually held by a board of directors or some other small group. To what extent, if any, do you think that separation between ownership and the actual control of the modern corporation undermines the principle of individual initiative as the basis for our economic system?

Suggested Activities

1. Draw up a listing of the activities of the National Government which are based upon the commerce power.

2. Prepare and present to the class a report on economic and commercial conditions in the United States during the Critical Period.

3. Stage a debate or class forum on one of the following questions: (a) *Resolved,* That this State should (enact a / repeal its) "fair trade" law. (b) *Resolved,* That since professional football and boxing are subject to the antitrust laws, professional baseball should be brought under these laws, too.

4. Write a report on one of the following significant cases, tracing its background, the issues involved, and the court rulings: (a) *Gibbons* v. *Ogden,* (b) *Brown* v. *Maryland,* (c) *The Shreveport Case,* (d) *Coe* v. *Errol,* (e) The *Daniel Ball Case.*

5. Prepare a bulletin board display chart to illustrate in graphic form the scope and importance of the commerce power.

Suggested Reading

CORWIN, EDWIN S. and PELTASON, J. W., *Understanding the Constitution.* Holt, Rinehart and Winston, 1967.

GREENE, LEE S. and PARTHEMOS, GEORGE S. *American Government: Policies and Functions.* Scribner's, 1967. Chapters 4–6, 10.

PELTASON, J. W. and BURNS, JAMES M., *Functions and Policies of American Government.* Prentice-Hall, 1967. Chapters 5–7.

SLESINGER, REUBEN E. and ISAACS, ASHER, *Business, Government, and Public Policy.* Van Nostrand, 1968.

Special Issue, "American Business Abroad: The New Industrial Revolution," *Saturday Review,* November 22, 1969.

STANS, SECRETARY MAURICE H., "Is U.S. Being Squeezed Out of World Markets?" *U.S. News,* September 8, 1969.

The Presidency is more than executive responsibility. It is the inspiring symbol of all that is highest in America's purposes and ideals ... No one could think of it except in terms of solemn consecration.

HERBERT HOOVER

✦✦✦Why does the Constitution provide that "the executive power shall be vested in" one man, the "President of the United States of America"?

✦✦✦What might the American political system be like today had the Framers not abandoned their early decision that the President be chosen by Congress?

✦✦✦Why have nearly all the men who have served as President been experienced professional politicians?

On April 30, 1789, George Washington placed his left hand on the Bible, raised his right hand, and swore that he would "preserve, protect, and defend the Constitution of the United States." As he did so, at New York which was then the temporary capital, he became the first President of the United States. Since then, and for more than 175 years, each of his successors has repeated that ceremony and recited the words of the constitutional oath. Most of them have done so in Washington, as Thomas Jefferson did for the first time in 1801; and most of them have done so on the steps of the Capitol, as James Monroe did for the first time in 1817.

Richard Milhous Nixon recited the constitutional pledge in the wintry chill of the nation's capital on January 20, 1969. As he did so, he became the thirty-seventh President of the United States.

As the nation's Chief Executive, Mr. Nixon occupies the most important and the most powerful office known to the history of man.

His powers are vast, his responsibilities are well-nigh immeasurable, and his functions are many.

As President, he is the chief of state, the ceremonial head of the Government of the United States. He is a symbol of the people and of the nation as a whole. He is, in former President Taft's words, "the personal embodiment and representative of their dignity and majesty."

In many countries the chief of state reigns but does not rule. This is certainly true of the Queens of England and the Netherlands, the Kings of Norway, Sweden, Denmark, and Belgium, the President of Italy, and the Emperor of Japan, for example. It is just as certainly not true of the President of the United States. He both reigns *and* rules.

He is the chief architect of the nation's public policy. As President, he is the one who proposes, requests, supports, demands, and insists that Congress enact most of the major legislation that it does. He is also the head of one of the largest governmental machines ever created, directing an administration which includes some 2,900,000 civilian employees and now spends more than $180,000,000,000 annually. Then, too, he is the leader of a major political party and its ardent supporters.

As President, he is the chief formulator of American foreign policy and the nation's spokesman to the rest of the world. His words and actions are of the utmost importance, and they are closely watched everywhere. He is the Commander in Chief of the armed forces of the United States, with more than 3,000,000 men equipped with the latest weapons of war subject to his immediate control. In addition to each of his many other roles, he is also the leader of the free world in its struggle against the forces and designs of international communism.

The many problems the President faces are as complex and as difficult as his powers are extensive. The burdens of his office are monumental. Every day he must make decisions — many of them minor and somewhat routine, but others of earth-shaking importance. For all of them, and for their consequences, he is responsible.

When he announced that he was a candidate for the presidential nomination in 1900, Admiral George Dewey opined: "The office of President is not such a difficult one to fill, his duties being mainly to execute the laws of Congress." Let us see why this statement must rank as one of the most ridiculous ever made in American public life.

QUALIFICATIONS, TERM, COMPENSATION

Constitutional Qualifications. Whatever else he must be to gain this highest of offices, the Constitution requires that the President must: (1) be a natural-born citizen, (2) be at least thirty-five years of age, and (3) have resided in the United States for at least fourteen years.[1]

Term of Office. The Framers of the Constitution considered several possibilities for the length of the presidential term. Most of their debate on the question centered around a four-year term with the incumbent eligible for re-election versus a six- or seven-year term without re-eligibility. They finally settled upon the four-year term [2] — feeling, as Hamilton explained, that this was a sufficient period of time for a President to demonstrate his abilities, gain the value of experience, and institute stable policies.

Until 1951 the Constitution placed no limit upon the number of terms a President might serve. Several Presidents, beginning with George Washington, refused to seek more than two terms, however. Soon, the "no-third-term tradition" became an unwritten rule of presidential politics. The move to nominate Ulysses S. Grant for a third term in 1876 brought a storm of public reaction; and Theodore Roosevelt, who succeeded to the Presidency in 1901 and was elected to a full term in 1904, was sharply criticized by many when he ran again in 1912.

---

[1] Article II, Section 1, Clause 5. Under the doctrine of *jus sanguinis* (page 88) it is possible that a person born abroad might someday become President. Martin Van Buren, who was born on December 5, 1782 was the first President actually born in the United States; each of his seven predecessors was born prior to the Declaration of Independence. The late President Kennedy was at forty-three, the youngest ever elected to the office; Theodore Roosevelt reached it by succession at age forty-two. Only five others (Polk Pierce, Grant, Garfield and Cleveland) have become President at less than age fifty. By custom, the fourteen years involved include *any* fourteen years in a person's life.

[2] Article II, Section 1, Clause 1.

PRESIDENTS OF THE UNITED STATES

Name	Party	State *	Born	Died	Entered Office	Age on Taking Office	Vice Presidents
George Washington	Federalist	Virginia	1732	1799	1789	57	John Adams
John Adams	Federalist	Massachusetts	1735	1826	1797	61	Thomas Jefferson
Thomas Jefferson	Dem.-Rep.**	Virginia	1743	1826	1801	57	Aaron Burr George Clinton
James Madison	Dem.-Rep.	Virginia	1751	1836	1809	57	George Clinton Elbridge Gerry
James Monroe	Dem.-Rep.	Virginia	1758	1831	1817	58	Daniel D. Tompkins
John Q. Adams	Dem.-Rep.	Massachusetts	1767	1848	1825	57	John C. Calhoun
Andrew Jackson	Democrat	Tenn. (S.C.)	1767	1845	1829	61	John C. Calhoun Martin Van Buren
Martin Van Buren	Democrat	New York	1782	1862	1837	54	Richard M. Johnson
William H. Harrison	Whig	Ohio (Va.)	1773	1841	1841	68	John Tyler
John Tyler	Democrat	Virginia	1790	1862	1841	51	......
James K. Polk	Democrat	Tenn. (N.C.)	1795	1849	1845	49	George M. Dallas
Zachary Taylor	Whig	La. (Va.)	1784	1850	1849	64	Millard Fillmore
Millard Fillmore	Whig	New York	1800	1874	1850	50	......
Franklin Pierce	Democrat	New Hampshire	1804	1869	1853	48	William R. King
James Buchanan	Democrat	Pennsylvania	1791	1868	1857	65	John C. Breckinridge
Abraham Lincoln	Republican	Illinois (Ky.)	1809	1865	1861	52	Hannibal Hamlin Andrew Johnson
Andrew Johnson	Democrat***	Tenn. (N.C.)	1808	1875	1865	56	......
Ulysses S. Grant	Republican	Illinois (Ohio)	1822	1885	1869	46	Schuyler Colfax Henry Wilson
Rutherford B. Hayes	Republican	Ohio	1822	1893	1877	54	William A. Wheeler
James A. Garfield	Republican	Ohio	1831	1881	1881	49	Chester A. Arthur
Chester A. Arthur	Republican	N.Y. (Vt.)	1830	1886	1881	50	......
Grover Cleveland	Democrat	N.Y. (N.J.)	1837	1908	1885	47	Thomas A. Hendricks
Benjamin Harrison	Republican	Ohio	1833	1901	1889	55	Levi P. Morton
Grover Cleveland	Democrat	N.Y. (N.J.)	1837	1908	1893	55	Adlai E. Stevenson
William McKinley	Republican	Ohio	1843	1901	1897	54	Garret A. Hobart Theodore Roosevelt
Theodore Roosevelt	Republican	New York	1858	1919	1901	42	...... Charles W. Fairbanks
William H. Taft	Republican	Ohio	1857	1930	1909	51	James S. Sherman
Woodrow Wilson	Democrat	N.J. (Va.)	1856	1924	1913	56	Thomas R. Marshall
Warren G. Harding	Republican	Ohio	1865	1923	1921	55	Calvin Coolidge
Calvin Coolidge	Republican	Mass. (Vt.)	1872	1933	1923	51	...... Charles G. Dawes
Herbert Hoover	Republican	Calif. (Iowa)	1874	1964	1929	54	Charles Curtis
Franklin D. Roosevelt	Democrat	New York	1882	1945	1933	51	John N. Garner Henry A. Wallace Harry S Truman
Harry S Truman	Democrat	Missouri	1884		1945	60	...... Alben W. Barkley
Dwight D. Eisenhower	Republican	N.Y.-Pa. (Tex.)	1890	1969	1953	62	Richard M. Nixon
John F. Kennedy	Democrat	Massachusetts	1917	1963	1961	43	Lyndon B. Johnson
Lyndon B. Johnson	Democrat	Texas	1908		1963	55	...... Hubert H. Humphrey
Richard M. Nixon	Republican	N.Y. (Calif.)	1913		1969	55	Spiro T. Agnew

* State of residence when elected; if born in another State that State is shown in parentheses.
** Democratic-Republican. *** Andrew Johnson, a War Democrat, had sought and won the Vice Presidency as Abraham Lincoln's running mate on the ticket of the coalition Union Party in 1864.

After Franklin D. Roosevelt broke the tradition by winning a third and then a fourth term in 1940 and 1944, the unwritten custom became a part of the written Constitution. The 22nd Amendment, adopted in 1951, reads in part:

> No person shall be elected to the office of the President more than twice, and no person who has held the office of President, or acted as President, for more than two years of a term to which some other person was elected President shall be elected to the office of the President more than once.

As a general rule, then, each President is now restricted to a maximum of two full terms — eight years — in office. *But* a President, who has *succeeded* to the office *beyond the midpoint* in a term to which another was originally elected, may serve for more than eight years — but, at the very outside, *not more than ten years.* Mr. Johnson may be used to illustrate the point: he was constitutionally eligible to seek a second four-year term in 1968. Had he done so and won, he would have served nine years, one month, and twenty-nine days at the end of that term on January 20, 1973.

Compensation. The President's salary is fixed by Congress, and it can neither be increased nor decreased during his term of office.[3] The salary was originally set at $25,000 a year in 1789. It was raised to $50,000 in 1873, to $75,000 in 1909, and to $100,000 in 1949. Congress increased the figure to its present level — $200,000 a year — in 1969. Since 1949 each President has also received a $50,000 a year expense account (which is taxable and is, in effect, really a part of the President's pay).

---

[3] Article II, Section 1, Clause 7. At the Constitutional Convention, Benjamin Franklin argued that, since money *and* power might corrupt a man, the President ought to receive nothing beyond his expenses. Franklin's suggestion was never put to a vote.

The Constitution forbids the President "any other emolument from the United States, or any of them." But this does not prevent him from being provided with the White House, a magnificent and priceless 132-room mansion set on an 18.3 acre estate in the heart of the nation's Capital; a sizable suite of offices and and a large official staff; a 92-foot yacht and a 60-foot cruiser; a fleet of automobiles, including the famous bubble-top Lincoln; three lavishly fitted Boeing 707 jets and several other planes and helicopters; Camp David, the resort hideaway in the Catoctin Mountains in Maryland; medical and dental care for himself and his family; liberal travel and entertainment funds; and a great many other perquisites.

Many of the services and facilities made available to the President cannot be measured in dollars and cents, of course. Who, for example, could possibly put a price-tag on the White House? Just to *operate* the mansion now requires more than $3,500,000 a year. But, to live as the President does, to have available all of the material benefits provided to the Chief Executive, it has been estimated that a private citizen would need an annual after-taxes income in excess of $10,000,000. And to generate that amount of "take-home pay" he would have to have a gross income of about $35,000,000 a year.

Since 1958 each former President has received a lifetime pension of $25,000 a year and an office, staff, and free mailing privileges. Each widow of a former President is entitled to a pension of $10,000 annually.

PRESIDENTIAL SUCCESSION

Section 1 of the 25th Amendment provides that:

> In case of the removal of the President from office or his death or resignation, the Vice President shall become President.

Strictly speaking, before the adoption of the 25th Amendment in 1967, the Constitution did *not* provide that in such situations the Vice President should succeed to the Presidency. Rather, it declared that the *powers and duties* of the office (*not* the office itself) were to "devolve on the Vice President." [4] But tradition—begun by John Tyler—has always dictated that should the office become vacant the Vice President succeeds to it. The effect of the ratification of the 25th Amendment was to make what had been one of the many *informal amendments* of the Constitution a formal part of the written document.

Congress fixes the order of succession following the Vice President.[5] The present law on the point is the Presidential Succession Act of 1947. Under its terms, the Speaker of the House and then the President *pro tem* of the Senate are next in line. They are followed, in turn, by the Secretary of State and eight of the other eleven heads of Cabinet departments in order of precedence.[6]

---

[4] Article II, Section 1, Clause 6. On removal of the President by impeachment, see Article I, Section 2, Clause 5; Article I, Section 3, Clauses 6 and 7; Article II, Section 4; and page 213.

[5] Article II, Section 1, Clause 6.

[6] That is, in the order in which their departments were created; see page 308. A Cabinet member is to serve only until a Speaker or President *pro tem* is available and qualified to supersede him. The heads of the most recently created departments—Health, Education, and Welfare (1953), Housing and Urban Development (1965), and Transportation (1966)—are not included; when they were created the 1947 law was not amended to accommodate their Secretaries. But should the nation ever find itself that far down the list of presidential successors, the question of who should be President would probably be among the least of our concerns.

Note the effect here of Section 2 of the 25th Amendment, quoted on page 289. It guarantees that any future vacancy in the Vice Presidency will be a brief one. Hence, the question of succession after the Vice President is a far less important matter than it was prior to 1967.

Presidential Disability. Until the recent adoption of the 25th Amendment serious gaps existed in the succession arrangements under the Constitution. Neither that document nor the Congress made any provision for determining *when* a President was so disabled that he could not perform his duties—nor was there any provision to indicate *by whom* such a determination was to be made.

For nearly 180 years, then, the nation played with fate. President Dwight D. Eisenhower suffered two temporarily disabling illnesses—a heart attack and ileitis—during his tenure. Two earlier Presidents were incapacitated for much longer periods of time. James Garfield lingered between life and death for eighty days before finally succumbing to the assassin's bullet in 1881. During that period he was able to perform only one official act: to sign an extradition warrant. Woodrow Wilson suffered a paralytic stroke in 1919 and was largely incapacitated for the remainder of his term. He did not attend a meeting of his Cabinet until seven months after the attack. His Vice President, Thomas R. Marshall, humbly refused to assume any of the presidential duties.

Sections 3 and 4 of the 25th Amendment fill the constitutional gap in detail. They provide that the Vice President shall become Acting President (1) if the President informs Congress in writing that he is unable to perform his duties or (2) if the Vice President and a majority of the Cabinet (or another body authorized by law) inform Congress in writing that the President is incapacitated. In either case, the President may resume the powers and duties of his office by notifying Congress that no inability exists. Should the Vice President and a majority of the Cabinet (or other body authorized by law) dispute the President's ability to resume his office, Congress is given twenty-one days in which to resolve the matter. If two-thirds of both houses decides the President's incapacity still exists, the Vice President shall continue as Acting President.

Vice President Spiro T. Agnew performs many important duties. He presides over the Senate when it is in session and, sometimes, he is called on to carry out special assignments for the President. (UPI Photo)

THE VICE PRESIDENT

Through much of our history the Vice Presidency has been treated as of little consequence, a "fifth wheel on the coach of state." John Adams, the first to hold the office, called it "the most insignificant office that ever the invention of man contrived or his imagination conceived." While he was President, Theodore Roosevelt, who had also been Vice President,

was annoyed by the tinkling of a chandelier in his study. He ordered it removed and said, "Take it to the office of the Vice President. He doesn't have anything to do. It will keep him awake." And John Nance Garner once described the office as "not worth a bucket of spit."

Despite the jokes about the importance of the office, the Vice Presidency is significant — if for no other reason than the fact that the occupant is "only a heartbeat away from being President." So far in our history eight of the thirty-six men who have held the Presidency have died in office.[7]

Too often when the national conventions are selecting the vice presidential candidates they ignore this vital fact. A candidate is usually nominated to "balance the ticket" — that is, with an eye to what he might add to the prospects of success for the presidential nominee. Typically, he is chosen to help carry a doubtful State, to appease a disappointed faction in the party, to replenish the party treasury, to appeal to a particular section of the country, to reward a faithful party work horse, or for some similar political reason.

The qualifications for the Vice President are the same as those for the President whom he might have to replace. His only constitutional duty, unless he succeeds to the Presidency, is to preside over the Senate. Most of our Vice Presidents have been men with years of legislative experience. Because of this, they have often proved valuable links between the White House and the Capitol.

On sixteen separate occasions in our history, the Vice Presidency has become vacant — once by resignation, seven times by death, and eight

---

[7] William Henry Harrison contracted pneumonia during his inauguration and died one month later (April 4, 1841); Zachary Taylor succumbed to typhus (July 9, 1850); Abraham Lincoln (April 15, 1865), James Garfield (September 19, 1881), and William McKinley (September 14, 1901) were assassinated; Warren Harding died of a sudden and undisclosed illness (August 2, 1923); Franklin D. Roosevelt suffered a fatal cerebral hemorrhage (April 12, 1945); and John F. Kennedy was assassinated (November 22, 1963).

times because of succession to the Presidency.[8] Yet, not until the 25th Amendment did the Constitution treat the problem. Section 2 provides that:

> Whenever there is a vacancy in the office of the Vice President, the President shall nominate a Vice President who shall take office upon confirmation by a majority vote of both houses of Congress.

The Vice President's salary is fixed by Congress and is now (1971) $62,500 a year. Many have suggested that he be given more responsibility in the executive branch. In this manner he would be more aware of the problems of the office should the President die. Then, too, he could be used to relieve the President of some of his tremendous burdens of office.

Recent Presidents, notably Eisenhower, Kennedy, Johnson, and Nixon, have made very considerable use of their Vice Presidents. Today he attends Cabinet meetings, chairs the National Aeronautics and Space Council, is a member of the National Security Council, and performs social, diplomatic, and some routine administrative chores for the President. But no Chief Executive has been tempted to "upgrade" the Vice President to the point where he would become an "Assistant President." The reason for this is simple: of all of the members of the President's official family, the Vice President is the *only* one who does not owe his office to the President. Like the President, the Vice President is chosen by the electoral college for a fixed four-year term.

PRESIDENTIAL NOMINATION AND ELECTION

In strictly formal terms, the President is chosen in accord with the provisions of the Constitution—that is, through the electoral college system.[9] In actual practice, however, he is elected through an altogether extraordinary process. As that process has developed over the span of forty-six presidential elections, it is a composite of constitutional provisions, a few State and federal laws, and—in largest measure—a number of practices born of and applied by the nation's political parties. No other election—here or abroad—can match its color, drama, or suspense, the tremendous popular interest and participation it attracts, the high level of party activity it involves, or the huge amounts of time, effort, and money it consumes.

Original Constitutional Provisions. The Constitutional Convention devoted more of its time to the method for choosing the President than to any other matter. It was, said James Wilson of Pennsylvania, "the most difficult of all on which we have had to decide." The matter was a difficult one largely because most of the Founding Fathers were opposed to selecting the President by either of the obvious alternatives: direct election by the people or election by Congress.

Nearly all of the Founding Fathers opposed the popular election of the President because they feared that it would produce, in Alexander Hamilton's words, "tumult and disorder" and "mob rule." Many of them also felt that the

---

[8] John C. Calhoun resigned to become a Senator from his native State, South Carolina, in 1832. The seven Vice Presidents who died in office were George Clinton (1812), Elbridge Gerry (1814), William R. King (1853), Henry Wilson (1875), Thomas H. Hendricks (1885), Garret A. Hobart (1899), and James S. Sherman (1912). The eight who succeeded to the Presidency on the death of a President were John Tyler (1841), Millard Fillmore (1850), Andrew Johnson (1865), Chester A. Arthur (1881), Theodore Roosevelt (1901), Calvin Coolidge (1923), Harry S Truman (1945), and Lyndon B. Johnson (1963).

[9] Article II, Section 1, Clauses 2 and 4; 12th, 20th, and 23rd Amendments.

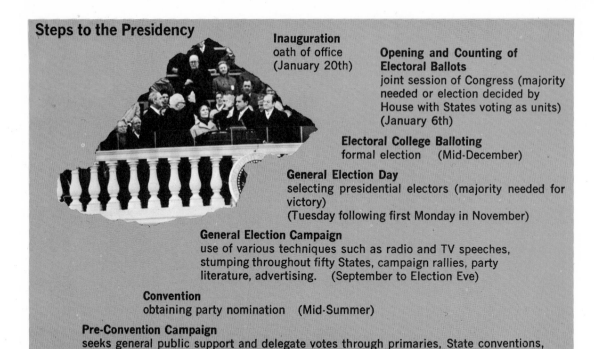

Steps to the Presidency

Inauguration
oath of office
(January 20th)

Opening and Counting of Electoral Ballots
joint session of Congress (majority needed or election decided by House with States voting as units) (January 6th)

Electoral College Balloting
formal election   (Mid-December)

General Election Day
selecting presidential electors (majority needed for victory)
(Tuesday following first Monday in November)

General Election Campaign
use of various techniques such as radio and TV speeches, stumping throughout fifty States, campaign rallies, party literature, advertising.   (September to Election Eve)

Convention
obtaining party nomination   (Mid-Summer)

Pre-Convention Campaign
seeks general public support and delegate votes through primaries, State conventions, and influence of powerful State leaders and factions   (February through July)

Decision to Seek Nomination
self-announcement or draft by influential group   (Pre-Election Year)

people, scattered over so vast an area, could not possibly know enough about the available candidates to make a wise and informed choice. George Mason of Virginia spoke for most of his colleagues when he said on the floor of the Constitutional Convention:

> The extent of the country renders it impossible that the people can have the requisite capacity to judge of the respective pretensions of the candidates.

Early in the convention most of the delegates favored selection by Congress. Nearly all of them later abandoned that position, however. They came to the view that it would destroy the system of separation of powers by placing the President "too much under the legislative thumb."

After weeks of debate and thirty separate votes, the Founding Fathers finally adopted a plan first suggested by Hamilton. Under it the President would be chosen by a special body of electors. Briefly, the plan provided that: (1) each State would have as many presidential electors as it had Senators and Representatives in Congress; (2) these electors would be chosen in each State in whatever manner the State legislature directed; (3) the electors, meeting in their own States, would each cast two ballots—each for a different person; (4) the electoral votes from the several States would be opened and counted before a joint session of Congress; (5) the person receiving the largest number of electoral votes, provided his total was a majority of all the electors, would be President, and the person with the next largest number, if his total were also a majority, would become Vice President. If a tie occurred, or if no candidate received the votes of a majority of the electors, the President would be chosen by the House of Representatives, voting by States. If a tie or lack of majority occurred for the Vice Presidency, that office would be filled by the Senate.[10]

The Founding Fathers thought and spoke of the electors as "free agents" who would "deliberate freely" as they sought the men best qualified to fill the nation's two highest offices. In the struggle for ratification, the electoral college system proved to be one of the few major features of the new Constitution to escape widespread criticism.

Impact of the Rise of Parties. The system worked as the Founding Fathers intended for only as long as George Washington held the Presidency. In 1789 and again in 1792 each of the electors cast one of his two ballots for the great Virginian. Flaws began to appear in the system in 1796. Political parties had begun to form. John Adams, a Federalist, was elected President and Thomas Jefferson, an archrival and Democratic-Republican, became his Vice President.

The system collapsed in the election of 1800. By then, two well-defined parties had emerged —the Federalists under Adams and Hamilton and the Democratic-Republicans (later renamed the Democrats) led by Jefferson. Each of the parties nominated presidential and vice presidential candidates. Each also nominated elector candidates in the various States, with the understanding that the electors who were chosen would vote for their party's nominees.

Each of the seventy-three Democratic-Republicans who became electors voted for that party's nominees: Thomas Jefferson and Aaron Burr. Of course, the result was a tie between the two men for the Presidency. The Constitution gave each elector two votes, each to be cast for a different person but each to be cast for someone *as President.* Although popular opinion clearly favored Jefferson for the Presidency, and the party had intended Burr for the Vice Presidency, the House of Representatives had to take thirty-six ballots in 1801 before it could name Thomas Jefferson the third President of the United States.

The spectacular election of 1800 left a lasting imprint on the presidential election process. It marked the introduction into that process of: (1) party nominations for the Presidency and Vice Presidency, (2) the nomination of candidates for presidential electors who were pledged to vote for their party's presidential ticket, and (3) the automatic casting of the electoral votes in line with those pledges. Gone forever was the notion that the electors would be chosen as "free agents" to "deliberate" over the selection of a President.

The 12th Amendment. The election of 1800 also produced another notable result. The 12th Amendment was added to the Constitution to prevent a repetition of the fiasco of 1800. Although the amendment is a lengthy one, it provided for only one major change in the original electoral college system. It provided that the electors shall cast two ballots but also that "they shall name in their ballots the person voted for as President, and in distinct ballots the person voted for as Vice-President." [11]

With the emergence of political parties, the election of 1800, and the adoption of the 12th

---

[10] Article II, Section 1, Clauses 2, 3, and 4. Several of the Framers expected that each State's electors would vote for a man from their State and so throw the election into the House of Representatives regularly. George Mason predicted that this would happen "nineteen times in twenty."

[11] Not only does the amendment preclude a repetition of the circumstances that produced the tie of 1800; it almost certainly guarantees that the President and Vice President will always be elected from the same political party. With the adoption of the amendment the character of the Vice Presidency underwent an unintended change: ever since, the two major parties have nominated their vice presidential candidates with little regard for the question of their capacity for the Presidency. See page 288.

Amendment, the constitutional setting was laid for the development of the presidential election system as we know it today—a far cry from that the Founding Fathers designed at Philadelphia in 1787.

National Conventions. The Constitution made—and still makes—no provision for the nomination of candidates for the Presidency. As the Founding Fathers designed the system, the electors would, out of their own knowledge, select the "wisest and best man" as President. Nominations, therefore, were unnecessary. But, as we have seen, the rise of parties altered the system drastically. It brought with it the need for nominations.

The first method the parties developed to nominate presidential candidates was the congressional caucus—which, as we noted on page 162, was regularly used in the elections of 1800 to 1824. But, as we know, the closed and unrepresentative nature of the caucus brought its downfall in 1824. For the election of 1832 both major parties adopted the national convention as their nominating device. It has continued to serve the two major parties ever since.

Extent of Control by Law. The convention process—through which the choice for the Presidency is, for all practical purposes, narrowed to one of two persons—is a process almost entirely controlled by the parties. There is virtually no legal control of the process. We have already noted that the Constitution is completely silent on the subject of presidential nominations. There is, as well, almost no statutory law on the matter. No federal laws exist, and only a very small body of State law deals with a few aspects of convention organization and procedure—for example, the method for selecting delegates and the manner in which they may cast their votes is prescribed by law in some States. But, in very large part, the convention is a creature and a responsibility of the parties themselves.

Convention Arrangements. In both parties the national committee is charged with making the plans and arrangements for the quadrennial conclave (see page 135). As much as a year before it is held the committee meets (usually in Washington, D.C.) to set the time and the place for the extravaganza. July is the typically favored month, but each party's convention has been held as early as mid-June and as late as the latter part of August.

Where the national convention is held is a matter of prime importance. For the party, there are two major considerations. First, the site must satisfy certain physical requirements—for example, there must be an adequate convention hall, sufficient hotel accommodations, plentiful entertainment outlets, and convenient transportation facilities. Political considerations are also brought to bear; thus, for example, a city in a doubtful State—one which might be expected to go either way in the election—is usually chosen, in the obvious hope of influencing the election outcome, of course.

Many of the nation's larger cities bid for the "honor"—and the financial return to local business—of hosting a national convention; and business groups in a city which is chosen regularly contribute a considerable sum to the party's treasury. The Republicans selected Miami Beach for 1968 and scheduled their convention to begin there on August 5th. Miami Beach officials pledged $650,000 in cash and another $150,000 in goods and services to attract the party. The Democrats picked Chicago and set August 26th as the opening date. Chicago offered them a record $750,000 in cash plus $150,000 in goods and services.

Both of the major parties have met in Chicago more often than in any other city—a fact which reflects that city's central location and other physical attractions, as well as points up the significance of Illinois as a doubtful or "pivotal" State. The Democrats held each of their first six conventions—from 1832 through 1852—in Baltimore. Since 1856—when the Republicans held their first convention in Philadelphia—the two parties have met:

City	Republicans	Democrats
Atlantic City		1964
Baltimore	1864	1860, 1872, 1912
Chicago	1860, 1868, 1880, 1884, 1888, 1904, 1908, 1912, 1916, 1920, 1932, 1944, 1952, 1960	1864, 1884, 1892, 1896, 1932, 1940, 1944, 1952, 1956, 1968
Cincinnati	1876	1856, 1880
Cleveland	1924, 1936	
Denver		1908
Houston		1928
Kansas City, Mo.	1928	1900
Los Angeles		1960
Miami Beach	1968	
Minneapolis	1892	
New York		1868, 1924
Philadelphia	1856, 1872, 1900, 1940, 1948	1936, 1948
St. Louis	1896	1876, 1888, 1904, 1916
San Francisco	1956, 1964	1920

Apportionment of Votes. Once the date and the location have been set, the national committee issues a "call" to each of the State party organizations. The call names the time and place and also indicates the number of convention votes to which each State is entitled.[12] Traditionally, both parties have allotted to each State a quota of convention votes roughly equal to twice the number of seats it has in Congress. Over the past several conventions, however, both parties have concocted rather complicated apportionment formulas to give additional delegates to those States which have supported the party's candidates in recent elections.

For 1968 the Republicans apportioned 1333 votes (each to be cast by one delegate) among its State organizations. The Democrats distributed 2622 votes (which were cast by a total of 2989 delegates).[13] Each party also provides for alternate delegates; in 1968 the Republicans had 1333 alternates and the Democrats 2512. Clearly, neither party's convention could be described as "a deliberative body" in terms of its size.

[12] The Republican call for 1968 was issued in September 1967; the Democrats issued theirs somewhat later than usual, in January 1968. The number of *votes* per State is a more realistic indication of the size of a State's convention delegation than the number of *delegates* per State, at least insofar as the Democrats are concerned. In several States the Democrats select more delegates than their quota of convention votes; in such instances, some or all of the delegates cast a fraction of a vote. The practice is sometimes carried to the absurd; for example, fifty-four delegates selected in one Mississippi congressional district cast *two* votes at the Democratic convention in 1940 — that is, each had 1/27th of a vote! The Republicans do not permit fractional voting; each delegate has one full vote.

[13] For 1968 the *Republicans* gave a basic allotment of four votes to each State, *plus:* six additional votes if the State went for the Republican presidential nominee in 1964 or elected a Republican Senator or governor in 1964 or 1966, another vote for each congressional district in which the 1964 presidential nominee or the 1966 candidate for the House received at least 2000 votes, and yet another for each congressional district in which the presidential nominee or House candidate received at least 10,000 votes in the preceding election. For 1968 the *Democrats* assigned to each State three votes for each electoral vote, an additional vote for each 100,000 popular votes cast for the party's presidential candidate in 1964, ten additional votes to each State that gave its electoral vote to the Democrats in 1964, and one vote each for a State's national committeeman and committeewoman. Each party also assigned votes (and delegates) to the District of Columbia, Puerto Rico, and the Virgin Islands; and the Democrats to the Canal Zone and Guam, as well.

Selection of Delegates. State law usually determines how delegates are to be selected, but in some States the matter is left to the parties themselves. Some, and usually all, of the delegates are now chosen in presidential primaries in seventeen of the States and in the District of Columbia.[14] In the other States they are selected by State or district conventions or by party committees. In a number of States—including several of the larger ones—the delegates are or may be "instructed" by the convention or primary to support ·a certain aspirant for the presidential nomination. See pages 166–168.

The Convention at Work. Each party's national convention meets in a huge auditorium lavishly bedecked with flags, pennants, and various party symbols, including portraits of the great figures of the party's past. The front of the hall is dominated by a platform and speaker's rostrum from which the proceedings are managed. The floor itself is jammed with rows of hundreds of chairs, and standards and placards mark the sections reserved for the several State delegations. Loudspeakers and microphones, including one for the chairman of each delegation, are spotted at strategic points. Extensive facilities are provided for the veritable army of press, radio, and television reporters, cameramen, and technicians. The galleries surrounding the floor seat the spectators who come from all over the nation to see "the greatest political show on earth."

Amidst all of this—and the turbulence and confusion that accompanies nearly all that it does—the convention meets to accomplish two principal ends: the adoption of the party's platform and the nomination of its presidential and vice presidential candidates.

---

[14] Alabama, California, Florida, Illinois, Maryland, Massachusetts, Nebraska, New Hampshire, New Jersey, New York, Ohio, Oregon, Pennsylvania, Rhode Island, South Dakota, West Virginia, Wisconsin. Indiana and New Mexico hold only preference primaries; the delegates are chosen by party conventions.

The Opening Session. The order of business is much the same in both major party's national conventions. The opening session is called to order by the chairman of the national committee. The official call is read, prayer is offered, the temporary roll of delegates is called, and welcoming speeches are made by the national chairman and one or two local dignitaries.

The national chairman then sets the stage for the high point of the first day's session. He announces the slate of temporary officers, including the temporary chairman of the convention, nominated by the national committee. These officers are promptly elected by the delegates and the temporary chairman takes the rostrum to deliver the *keynote address*—a lengthy speech in which he assails the opposition, eulogizes his own party, pleads for harmony, and predicts victory in November.

Following the keynoter's oratorical efforts, the delegates routinely elect the convention's standing committees. There are four major committees in every national convention: the committees on rules and order of business, permanent organization, credentials, and platform and resolutions. Each State delegation is now entitled to two members (a man and a woman) on each of these standing committees. With their selection the first session generally ends.

The Second and Third Days. The next two or three, and sometimes four, sessions of the national convention—usually consuming the second and third days—are devoted to speeches by leading party figures and the receiving of committee reports. Typically, the committee on rules and order of business reports first. It regularly recommends the adoption of the rules of the preceding convention with, perhaps, a few changes.[15] Its report, which also includes an agenda for the remainder of the

---

[15] In both parties the convention rules are based largely upon the rules of the House of Representatives.

The national conventions are responsible for the nomination of candidates and the drafting of platforms. The pageantry and excitement of the event serve as the initial campaign thrust toward election victory. (Wide World Photos)

CASE STUDY
Speaking at a dinner held to honor his seventieth birthday, May 8, 1954, former President Harry S. Truman observed:

> When the Founding Fathers outlined the presidency in Article II of the Constitution, they left a great many details out and vague. I think they relied on the experience of the nation to fill in the outlines. The office of chief executive has grown with the progress of this great republic. It has responded to the many demands that our complex society has made upon the Government. It has given our nation a means of meeting our great emergencies.... Justice Holmes' epigram proved true. He said a page of history is worth a volume of logic. And as the pages of history were written they unfolded powers in the presidency not explicitly found in Article II....

Do you think the view of the Presidency and its powers Mr. Truman expresses here is a *correct* one? Is it a proper one? Do you agree with Mr. Truman and Justice Holmes that "a page of history is worth a volume of logic"? Why?

convention, is usually adopted with little or no dissent.

The credentials committee prepares the permanent role of delegates entitled to seats and votes in the convention. Occasionally, contests develop in which competing sets of delegates claim a State's seats. When this happens, it usually involves a State in which the party is faction-ridden and in which the delegates are chosen in local conventions. The credentials committee must decide such disputes. Although its decisions may be appealed to the floor, the committee's report is customarily upheld.

The committee on permanent organization nominates the permanent convention officers who succeed their temporary counterparts and serve for the remainder of the convention's sessions. The committee's principal job is that of selecting the permanent chairman.[16] His selection is frequently a test of the strength of rival contenders for the presidential nomination. After his election he delivers a lengthy speech in which he, too, follows the usual pattern of convention speeches: he attacks the opposition party, praises his own, pleads for harmony, and foresees a smashing victory at the polls in November.

The report of the platform and resolutions committee—in the form of a proposed platform—usually reaches the floor on the third day. The committee frequently holds informal sessions before the convention assembles, and spokesmen for various pressure groups appear to urge their views on the platform-makers. Much of the platform emerges from a preliminary draft drawn up by party leaders or, for the party in power, by the President and his advisors. A struggle may develop within the committee, and the fight occasionally spills over to the floor. Platform-writing is a fine art; the document is intended to win as many votes as

possible, while alienating none. As a result, both parties tend to produce vague, generalized comments on the hard issues of the day. The platforms may reflect the compromise nature of our politics and of the two major parties, but their value is open to serious question.

Nominating the Candidates. The national convention turns to its real reason for being by the fourth day. The secretary reads the role of the States alphabetically, beginning with Alabama. As it is called, each State may place a name before the convention, second a nomination already made, yield to another State further down the list, or simply pass.[17] Nominating speeches are now limited to fifteen minutes in the Republican convention (with no more than four seconding speeches, held to five minutes each); the Democrats allow only fifteen minutes for both nominating and seconding speeches for each candidate.

The nominating speeches are lavish and flowery hymns of praise to "The man who...." Although the name of the person to be nominated is well-known before the nominator begins his speech, tradition dictates that the name not be mentioned until the very end of the speech—when its bombastic announcement triggers a lengthy, wild, noisy demonstration on the floor. These "spontaneous" demonstrations—designed to show widespread support for the aspirant, whether he has it or not—are carefully planned and organized, of course.

When all of the States have been called for nominations the balloting itself begins. The secretary again reads the roll alphabetically

---

[16] Except for the temporary and permanent chairmen, the convention's officers are regularly members of the national committee.

[17] Occasionally a State will nominate a "favorite son," who has no real chance to become a party's presidential candidate but whom the delegates wish to honor. The State usually votes for its favorite son on the first ballot, especially when a close contest seems to be developing between the leading contenders. The tactic permits a State to judge the relative strength of the leading contenders and puts it in a good position to "jump on the bandwagon" of the apparent winner at the opportune point.

and, as each State is called, the chairman announces the vote of his delegation. Each complete roll call is known as a "ballot." A majority of all votes cast is necessary to select the presidential candidate in both parties, and succeeding ballots are taken until one nominee receives the requisite number. Most often, the first ballot produces a choice. In the eighteen conventions each party has held in this century (1900–1968), the Republicans have made their choice on the first ballot fourteen times and the Democrats thirteen.[18]

Once the presidential nomination has been made, the choice of his vice presidential running mate comes as an anti-climax. He is almost always the presidential candidate's hand-picked choice. See page 288.

Having nominated its candidates, the convention authorizes the chairman to appoint two special committees, each composed of several delegates, to notify formally the candidates of their nomination—something which, of course, they knew the instant it happened. The committees used to meet the candidates at their homes, or where large audiences could gather, and each nominee would then deliver his "acceptance speech." Franklin D. Roosevelt broke this tradition in 1932 by flying to Chicago to deliver his acceptance speech to the convention itself. Each candidate since then has followed this practice. In fact, today each of the party's hopefuls is near at hand throughout the convention.

The Presidential Campaign. For a brief period after the conventions the opposing candidates rest and map campaign strategies. Then the presidential campaign—the gruelling effort to win voter support—begins in earnest. Every means to put the candidates and their ideas before the voters, and in the most favorable light, is used. Radio and television speeches, "whistle-stop" tours, press conferences, press releases, public rallies, party dinners, newspaper, radio, and television advertisements, campaign stickers and buttons, placards and pamphlets, billboards and matchcovers—all bombard the voters in behalf of each party's nominees. The candidates pose for hundreds of photographs, shake thousands of hands, and strive to convince the electorate that a victory for the opposition would mean hard times for the country. Whether the campaign changes a significant number of votes or not—and the point is debatable—the massive efforts continue right up to election eve.

The Electoral College System Today. The presidential campaign ends with election day. The voters go to the polls in the fifty States and the District of Columbia to make their choice. Technically, of course, the voters do not vote on the presidential candidates directly. Rather, they vote to elect the members of the electoral college. As noted on page 291, the Framers of the Constitution intended that the presidential electors would exercise their own judgment in the selection of a President. But since the early 1800's the parties have nominated their slates of electors who are, in effect, rubber stamps. They go through the form prescribed by the Constitu-

---

[18] From 1832 until 1936 the Democrats required a two-thirds vote for nomination. The practice often produced deadlocks in the convention and the nomination of "dark-horse" candidates—one who did not appear a likely prospect before the convention. The most spectacular deadlock occurred in the Democratic convention of 1924, when nine days and 103 separate ballots were needed to nominate John W. Davis. The Republicans have required a simple majority for nomination from their first convention in 1856. Until 1968 the Democrats permitted any State delegation to follow the "unit rule" under which all members of the delegation had to cast their votes for the aspirant favored by a majority of them. The Republicans have never had a unit rule.

OFFICIAL
PRESIDENTIAL BALLOT

Make a cross (X) or other mark in the square opposite the names of the candidates for whose electors you desire to vote. Vote in ONE square only.

RICHARD M. NIXON ---------------President
SPIRO T. AGNEW --------------Vice President   } Republican ☐

HUBERT H. HUMPHREY -------------President
EDMUND S. MUSKIE ------------Vice President   } Democratic ☐

HENNING A. BLOMEN ---------------President
(Socialist Labor Party)
GEORGE S. TAYLOR ----------Vice President   } Independent ☐
(Socialist Labor Party)

FREDERICK W. HALSTEAD ----------President
(Socialist Workers Party)
PAUL B. BOUTELLE ------------Vice President   } Independent ☐
(Socialist Workers Party)

GEORGE C. WALLACE ---------------President
S. MARVIN GRIFFIN ------------Vice President   } Independent ☐

Voters in Wisconsin used this ballot to choose electors for their candidates in the presidential election of 1968.

The presidential electors are chosen by popular vote on the same day—the Tuesday following the first Monday in November of every fourth year—in every State. In 1968 the presidential election fell on November 5th; in 1972 it will occur on November 7th.

The electors are chosen at large—from the entire State—in every State except, now, Maine.[20] There is, then, a "winner-take-all" system: the presidential candidate (technically, the slate of elector candidates) receiving the largest popular vote in a State wins *all* of that State's electoral vote. The names of the elector-candidates now appear on the ballot in less than one-fourth of the States. In most States only the names of the presidential and vice presidential candidates are listed—they stand as "shorthand" for the elector slates.

Let us now illustrate the process. If a Republican in Wisconsin votes for the twelve Republican elector-candidates, he does so by marking an X after the names of the Republican presidential and vice presidential candidate on the official ballot. (Or he accomplishes the same thing by pulling the appropriate lever on a voting machine.) If, after the State elec-

tion in order to meet the letter of the Constitution's requirements.[19]

---

[19] In practice, the electors are expected to vote for the presidential candidate who carries their State and, as loyal party members, they almost always do. They are *legally* bound to do so by only about a third of the States, however. To date, electors have voted for someone other than their own party's nominee on only seven occasions: in 1796, 1824, 1912, 1948, 1956, 1960, and 1968. In the most recent instance, one North Carolina elector voted for George C. Wallace although the Republicans won his State and the other twelve electors cast their ballots for that party's nominee, Richard M. Nixon. The Supreme Court has held—in a case from Alabama, *Ray* v. *Blair,* 1952—that a State law permitting the State party organization to require their elector-candidates to pledge that, if elected, they will support the national party's nominees does not violate the Constitution.

[20] The Constitution (Article II, Section 1, Clause 2) provides that the electors are to be chosen in each State "in such manner as the legislature thereof may direct." In 1969 the Maine legislature provided that, henceforth, two of the State's four electors will be chosen at-large while the other two will be picked from each of the State's congressional districts. (By the election of 1832 all of the States had provided for the popular election of electors, except South Carolina where the legislature continued to appoint them until 1860. Electors were chosen by the legislature in Florida in 1868 and in Colorado in 1876; otherwise, the rule has been popular election in every State for over a century.)

tion board has received all of the returns from all of the local election boards in the State, it is found that the Republican slate has received more votes than any other set of elector-candidates, it is officially declared to be elected. The Republican electors then assemble at the capitol in Madison on the date set by Congress — the Monday following the second Wednesday in December [21] — and cast their ballots which are then signed by the electors, sealed, and sent by registered mail to the President of the Senate in Washington.[22]

Which party has won a majority of the votes in the electoral college and who will then be the next President of the United States are usually known by midnight of election day. But the *formal* election of the President and of the Vice President take place on January 6. On that date the President of the Senate opens the returns from each State, and the electoral votes are then counted in the presence of both houses of Congress.[23] The candidate who receives a majority of the votes for President is declared elected — as, too, is the one with a majority of the votes for Vice President.

If no one has a majority for President (at least 270 of the 538 electoral votes in 1972), the election is thrown into the House of Repre-sentatives. This happened as we saw, in 1800, and again in 1824. The House chooses a President from among the top three candidates in the electoral college. Each State delegation has one vote, and it takes a majority (twenty-six) to elect. If the House fails to choose a President by January 20th, the 20th Amendment provides that the newly elected Vice President shall act as President until it does.

If no man receives a majority for Vice President, the Senate decides between the top two candidates. It takes a majority of the whole Senate to elect. The Senate has had to choose a Vice President only once. It elected Richard M. Johnson in 1837.

Defects in the Electoral College System. Criticisms of the electoral college system have been heard almost from the beginning. Perhaps the most serious shortcoming of the system is that in *any* presidential election it is possible for a candidate to win fewer *popular* votes than his opponent but to receive a majority of the *electoral* votes and thus win the Presidency. The "winner-take-all" method of choosing the electors in each State is the major reason for this possibility, of course.

Two Presidents — Rutherford B. Hayes and Benjamin Harrison — were in fact elected under

---

[21] Article II, Section 1, Clause 4 provides that the date Congress sets "shall be the same throughout the United States." The 12th Amendment provides that the electors "shall meet in their respective States." Congress has directed that they meet "at such place in each State as the legislature of such State shall direct." Each of the legislatures has designated the State capital.

[22] Two copies of the ballots are also sent to the Archivist of the United States in the General Services Administration, two to the State's secretary of state, and one to the local federal district court. If neither the President of the Senate nor the Archivist receive a State's votes by the fourth Wednesday in December, and they cannot be obtained from the secretary of state by that date, the President of the Senate sends a special messenger for the votes filed with the federal court.

[23] The 12th Amendment commands the President of the Senate to open the returns. Hence, on January 6, 1961, Vice President Richard Nixon presided over the joint session of Congress at which his opponent, John F. Kennedy, was formally declared the winner of the 1960 presidential election. But on January 6, 1969, Vice President Hubert Humphrey absented himself; the joint session that found Richard Nixon the winner of the 1968 election was chaired by the Senate's President *pro tempore,* Senator Richard Russell of Georgia.

these circumstances. In the election of 1876, Hayes, the Republican candidate, received 4,033,950 popular votes, while his Democratic opponent, Samuel J. Tilden, garnered 4,284,757. Although Tilden had a popular plurality of 250,807 votes and received 184 electoral votes, Hayes received 185 electoral votes and thus became President. In 1888 incumbent President Grover Cleveland received 5,540,050 popular votes—95,713 more than his Republican opponent, Harrison. But the latter won 233 electoral votes to Cleveland's 168—thus Harrison succeeded Cleveland as President.

Although the system has not "misfired" to produce the same distorted result since 1888, it *could* have happened on *several* occasions. Take the extremely close election of 1960 as an illustration of the point. John F. Kennedy won a popular plurality of only 119,450 votes over his Republican opponent, Richard M.

Nixon—*less than two-tenths of one per cent* of the total of 68,836,385 votes cast:

	Popular Vote	%	Electoral Vote	%
Kennedy	34,227,096	49.7	303	56.4
Nixon	34,107,646	49.6	219	40.8
Byrd	—	—	15	2.8
Others	501,643	.7	—	—

If only a small handful of voters in a few States had voted for Nixon instead of Kennedy, Nixon would have had a majority of the electoral votes and been elected President. Combinations involving as many as nine States can be used to play this game, but the simplest one involves Illinois and Texas. If only 4429 of the 2,377,846 Kennedy votes in Illinois (with twenty-seven electoral votes in 1960) and 46,233 of the 1,167,932 in Texas (twenty-four electoral votes) had gone for Nixon instead,

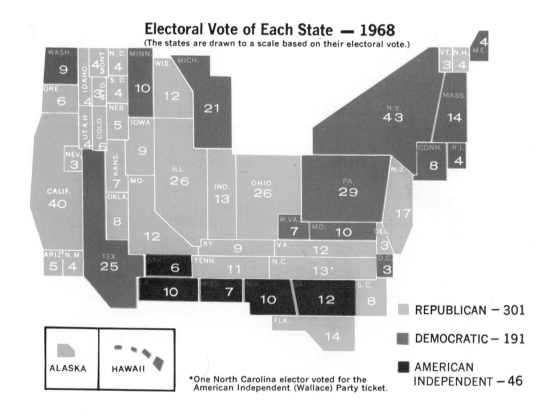

Electoral Vote of Each State — 1968
(The states are drawn to a scale based on their electoral vote.)

REPUBLICAN — 301

DEMOCRATIC — 191

AMERICAN INDEPENDENT — 46

*One North Carolina elector voted for the American Independent (Wallace) Party ticket.

Nixon, not Kennedy, would then have won the Presidency—and he still would not have had a plurality of the popular votes.[24]

In short, the record shows that the electoral vote bears only a very indirect relationship to the people's choice as shown by the popular vote. Even the one-sided results of the 1964 contest illustrate this fact:

	Popular Vote	%	Electoral Vote	%
Johnson	43,128,956	61.0	486	90.3
Goldwater	27,177,873	38.5	52	9.7
Others	336,697	.5	—	—

And the same conclusion can be drawn from the results in 1968:

	Popular Vote	%	Electoral Vote	%
Nixon	31,785,480	43.4	301	55.9
Humphrey	31,275,165	42.7	191	35.5
Wallace	9,906,473	13.5	46	8.6
Others	244,444	.4	—	—

The two other major weaknesses in the electoral college system—both of which threaten the democratic character of the presidential election process—have already been mentioned. The first of these is the fact that there is no provision in the Constitution, or in any federal statute, requiring the electors to vote for the candidate favored by the popular vote in their States. As noted on page 298, electors have "broken their pledges" on now seven different occasions to date.

The other major weakness is in the fact that in *any* presidential election it is possible that the contest will be decided in the House of Representatives. As we know, this has happened only twice—and not since the election of 1824. But in several elections, a strong third-party bid has threatened to win enough electoral votes to make it impossible for either major party to win a majority of the electoral votes—in 1912, 1924, 1948, and 1968.[25]

Three serious objections can be raised concerning a presidential election being thrown into the House of Representatives: (1) Recall that the voting in the House in such a case is *by States,* not by individual members. Thus, a small State like Alaska or Nevada will have as much weight as even the largest States, California and New York. (2) If the Representatives from a State were so divided over the question that no candidate is favored by a majority of them, the State would lose its vote. (3) The Constitution requires a majority of the States for election in the House—today, of course, twenty-six. If a strong third party candidate were involved, it might prove impossible for the House to make a decision.[26]

[24] Although only two Presidents (Rutherford B. Hayes and Benjamin Harrison) have won a majority of the electoral vote while losing the popular vote contest, eleven others were elected with only a plurality, not a majority, of the popular vote. These "minority Presidents": John Q. Adams (1824), James K. Polk (1844), Zachary Taylor (1848), James Buchanan (1856), Abraham Lincoln (1860), James A. Garfield (1880), Grover Cleveland (1884 and 1892), Woodrow Wilson (1912 and 1916), Harry S Truman (1948), John F. Kennedy (1960), Richard M. Nixon (1968).

[25] In 1968 George Wallace, the American Independent Party candidate, received more popular votes than had any previous third-party presidential candidate; but Theodore Roosevelt in 1912 and Robert M. LaFollette in 1924 each received a larger share of the popular vote, 27.4% and 16.6%, respectively; and Roosevelt also received a larger number of electoral votes (88) in 1912.

[26] It is even mathematically possible for the minority party in the House to have control of a majority of the individual State delegations. That part could then elect its candidate even though he may have run second in both the popular and the electoral votes.

Proposed Reforms. As with the criticisms of it, proposals to remedy the defects of the electoral college system have been heard almost from the beginning, too. Constitutional amendments proposing electoral college reform have been introduced in every term of Congress since 1789.

The proposal most often made has been, of course, the obvious one: to abolish the present system and provide instead for the direct popular election of the President. Few would deny the merits of this proposal, and opinion polls have long indicated overwhelming public support for it.

Acting at long last, the House did approve a direct popular vote amendment by an overwhelming vote in 1969. But that measure was killed by a Senate filibuster in 1970.

The chance that any such proposal will be adopted in the near future seems slight. The major obstacle lies in the fact that the smaller States—such as Alaska, Delaware, Nevada, Vermont, and Wyoming [27]—hold a relative advantage over the larger States which they would not enjoy under a system of popular choice. Their advantage—a weighted strength in the electoral college—arises out of the fact that each State, regardless of size, has two electoral votes on the basis of its Senate seats. The extreme example illustrates the point: Alaska, with a 1970 population of less than 300,000, has three electoral votes. California, on the other hand, with a 1970 population of nearly 20,000,000, has forty-five electoral votes. Thus, on the basis of their respective populations (and potential electorates), Alaska outweighs California by almost five to one in the electoral college.

In short, it is doubtful that enough States would approve a popular vote amendment to bring about its ratification. Several other "practical" obstacles support that conclusion — especially the contentions that: (1) The States, as *States,* would lose their role in the choice of a President, and (2) Because *every* vote cast in *each* State would figure in the *national* total of votes cast, parties and their candidates would have to campaign strenuously in *every* State [28] — with very significant consequences in terms of campaign time, effort and, especially, financing.

Two other proposals for change have attracted substantial support in recent years. One would retain the electors and the present method of distributing electoral votes among the States; but it would provide that only two of the electors be chosen at large in each State and that the others be chosen in the various congressional districts. This arrangement would eliminate the "winner-take-all" feature of the present system, but it would not destroy the distorting effect of the fact that each State has two electoral votes on the basis of its Senate seats. See page 298.

The other proposal would eliminate the electors as such, but it would retain the electoral votes and the present method of distribution. Each State's electoral vote would be

---

[27] Each of these States now has the minimum number of electoral votes to which any State is entitled—three, one for each of its two seats in the Senate and one for its single seat in the House.

[28] Under the existing "winner-take-all" system, the candidates naturally focus their campaigns on the larger States—those with the largest blocs of electoral votes. In fact, it is possible for a candidate to win the Presidency if he carries only the eleven largest States—because they have a total of 272 electoral votes, 2 more than the minimum of 270 to win. The eleven States (and their electoral votes) are: California (45), New York (41), Pennsylvania (27), Texas (26), Illinois (26), Ohio (25), Michigan (21), New Jersey (17), Florida (17), Massachusetts (14), and Indiana (13).

apportioned among the candidates on the basis of the popular vote each received in the State, with a plurality of at least forty per cent of all the electoral votes needed for election. This proposal would remove the possibility that electors will refuse to cast their ballots in accord with the popular vote; and, of course, it would also destroy the "winner-take-all" system. But, like the other plan, it would not reach the difficulty caused by the Senate-based electoral votes.

All in all, given the objections to each of these proposals, there seems (at least to this point, early 1971) little real chance of significant reform in the electoral college system within the near future.

✳✳✳✳✳✳✳✳✳✳✳ CONCEPT BUILDING ✳✳✳✳✳✳✳✳✳✳✳

Key Concepts

The Presidency is the most important and the most powerful office known to the history of man. The President's many roles include those of chief of state, chief architect of the nation's public policy, chief administrator, leader of his party, chief formulator of American foreign policy, Commander in Chief of the Armed Forces, and leader of the free nations of the world. The problems he faces are as difficult as his powers are vast.

The Constitution provides that the President must be a natural-born citizen, at least thirty-five years of age, and must have resided in this country for at least fourteen years. He is chosen to a four-year term and is limited to serving two full terms or not more than ten years in office. His salary is $200,000 a year and he receives much else in compensation.

A vacancy in the Presidency is filled by the Vice President who succeeds to the office. The line of succession passes to the Speaker of the House, the President *pro tem* of the Senate, and nine of the eleven Cabinet Department heads. The problems of presidential disability are, at long last, treated by the 25th Amendment.

The Vice President, until recently regarded as a "fifth wheel," occupies a most significant office, particularly because of the possibility of succession. His one constitutional duty is to preside over the Senate. Recent Presidents have "upgraded" the office. The 25th Amendment provides for filling a vacancy in the Vice Presidency.

In strictly formal terms, the President is elected in accord with the Constitution's provisions for the electoral college system. In actual practice, he is chosen through a largely extralegal process which is chiefly the product of party practices. Presidential candidates are nominated by the parties in huge, boisterous, and complex national conventions. Technically, the President is elected by the presidential electors chosen by the voters in each State; but the electors have long since become rubber stamps for their parties, reflecting the popular election results in their States.

The electoral college system suffers several shortcomings. The most serious are that: it can produce a President who has won a majority of the electoral votes even though he lost the popular vote contest, the electors can break their pledges, and a presidential contest can be decided in the House of Representatives. No proposal for reform of the system, including direct election, is likely to be approved in the near future.

Important Terms

committee on credentials
committee on permanent organization
committee on platform and resolutions

committee on rules and order of business
dark-horse candidate
delegates
electoral college

electoral votes
favorite son candidate
inauguration
keynoter
pivotal State
permanent chairman

platform
presidential disability
presidential electors
presidential succession
temporary chairman

Questions for Inquiry and Review

1. What are the formal constitutional qualifications for the Presidency?

2. For what term is a President elected?

3. To how many terms may a President be elected?

4. What is the maximum length of time any person may serve as President?

5. Who fixes the President's salary, and how much is it now?

6. By virtue of what does the Vice President succeed to the Presidency?

7. If the President is unable to do so, who then determines the question of presidential disability?

8. Why are the formal qualifications for the Vice Presidency identical with those for the Presidency?

9. Why has no President of the United States made his Vice President a true "Assistant President"?

10. What three events combined to lay the constitutional setting for the present-day presidential election system?

11. What body handles arrangements for a party's national convention?

12. Why have the two parties developed complicated formulas for the apportionment of convention delegates?

13. Who delivers a keynote address?

14. Around what four committees is much of a national convention organized?

15. Why are party platforms usually written in vague, general terms?

16. What is *the* major purpose of a national convention?

17. Why may the selection of presidential electors be described as a "winner-take-all" system?

18. A minimum of how many electoral votes will be necessary to win the Presidency in 1972?

19. What are the three most serious weaknesses of the present electoral college system?

20. What is the major obstacle to the adoption of a direct popular vote system for electing the President?

For Further Inquiry

1. Beyond the formal constitutional qualifications, what characteristics do you think a President ought to possess?

2. What arguments can be made *for* and *against* limiting a President to two terms in office?

3. What would the Presidency be like today if the Constitutional Convention had maintained its early position in favor of selection by Congress?

4. In 1969 the Maine legislature provided for the election of two of the State's four presidential electors from the State at-large and of the other two in the State's two congressional districts. Would you favor the adoption of a similar arrangement in your State?

5. A noted French observer once characterized the national convention system as "a colossal travesty of popular institutions." Do you agree with this assessment? On what grounds can you defend the continued use of the national convention as the device for presidential nominations?

6. Why is it well that the 25th Amendment has finally added a procedure for filling a vacancy in the Vice Presidency?

Suggested Activities

1. Construct a diagram or poster to illustrate (perhaps with newspaper clippings and photographs) the various roles of the President noted on pages 283–284.

2. Stage a debate or class forum on one of the following questions: (a) *Resolved,* That the 22nd Amendment should be repealed. (b) *Resolved,* That the President ought to be elected by a direct popular vote.

3. Invite a recent delegate to a national convention of either major party or a presidential elector to speak to the class on his role in the nominating or electing of a President.

4. Prepare a report on one of the following topics: (a) the "stolen election" of 1876, (b) reform of the electoral college, (c) the presidential campaign and election of 1968, and (d) the adoption of the 25th Amendment.

Suggested Reading

ADRIAN, CHARLES P. and PRESS, CHARLES, *The American Political Process.* McGraw-Hill, 1969. Chapter 15.

"Agnew: Nixon's Other Voice," *Newsweek,* November 14, 1969.

"American Roulette: The Electoral College," *Time,* September 22, 1968.

BURNS, JAMES M. and PELTASON, J. W., *Government By the People.* Prentice-Hall, 1969. Chapters 14, 15.

CHESTER, LEWIS, *et al., An American Melodrama: The Presidential Campaign of 1968.* Viking, 1969.

"Eisenhower: Soldier of Peace," *Time,* April 4, 1969.

FRADY, MARSHALL, "Cooling Off with LBJ," *Harper's,* June, 1969.

JAMES, DOROTHY B., *The Contemporary Presidency.* Pegasus, 1969.

KOENIG, LOUIS W., *The Chief Executive.* Harcourt, Brace and World, 1968.

LARNER, JEREMY, "Inside the McCarthy Campaign," *Harper's,* April and May, 1969.

MCGOVERN, SENATOR GEORGE P., "Politics and the Presidency," *Harper's,* January, 1970.

MICHENER, JAMES A., "Our Reckless Presidential Lottery," *Reader's Digest,* May, 1969.

——————, *Presidential Lottery: The Reckless Gamble in Our Electoral System.* Random House, 1969.

"Planes, Boats, Expenses . . . President's Pay Is Many Things," *U.S. News,* January 27, 1969.

SIDNEY, HUGH, "White House West," *Life,* September 5, 1969.

WEINBAUM, MARVIN G. and GOLD, LOUIS H., *Presidential Election: A Simulation with Readings.* Holt, Rinehart, and Winston, 1969.

WHITE, THEODORE H., "The Making of the President 1968," *Life,* July 11 and 18, 1969.

WICKER, TOM, "Number 37 Is Ready," *New York Times Magazine,* January 19, 1969.

17
THE PRESIDENCY IN ACTION

✦✦✦Why might some people be concerned that the Presidency has become too powerful an office?

✦✦✦Why do many people seem to fear the growth of presidential power in the abstract, but yet urge the President to take vigorous action in specific situations?

✦✦✦Why has each recent President been described as the nation's chief legislator as well as its chief executive?

When I ran for the Presidency . . ., I knew that this country faced serious challenges; but I could not realize — nor could any man who does not bear the burdens of this office — how heavy and constant would be those burdens

JOHN F KENNEDY

Article II of the Constitution begins with the words:

> The executive power shall be vested in a President of the United States.

With these thirteen words the Founding Fathers established the Presidency and laid the basis for the well-nigh immeasurable powers its occupant possesses today. The Constitution contains several specific grants of presidential power — for example, to command the armed forces, make treaties, approve or veto acts of Congress, make appointments to office, send and receive diplomatic representatives, grant reprieves and pardons, and "take care that the laws be faithfully executed."[1]

Notice that the Constitution sets out the powers of the Presidency in only sketchy fashion. Article II provides only a general outline of them. Over the course of eighteen decades much has been added to that outline. Thus, the manner in which the stronger Presidents — such as Washington, Jackson, Cleveland, and the two Roosevelts — used their powers has done much to shape the office and its prerogatives. A large number of acts of Congress and court decisions have also made a considerable contribution to extending the powers of the President. Then, too, much of the real nature of the office and its powers is overlooked by those who forget that the President is the leader of his political party.

In the latter half of this chapter and in several to follow we shall take a closer look at the powers of the Presidency and at the manner in which and the many agencies through which they are exercised. But, first, we shall turn to a brief consideration of the top layer of assistance provided for the President — his "official family."

---

[1] Most of the specific constitutional grants of presidential power are found in Article II, Sections 2 and 3. A few are found elsewhere; for example, the veto power in Article I, Section 7, Clause 2.

THE EXECUTIVE OFFICE OF THE PRESIDENT

Every officer, employee, and agency in the sprawling executive branch is legally subordinate to the President and aids him in the performance of his duties. But his chief right arm is the Executive Office of the President—a complex of twelve separate agencies staffed by most of his closest advisers and assistants.

The White House Office. This Office is the "nerve center" of the entire executive establishment. It houses the President's key personal and political staff, including a score of senior advisors and other top aides as well as several hundred research and clerical people. Foremost among them are the Counsellor to the President and a number of Assistants and Consultants who advise and otherwise serve him in such fields as foreign policy, congressional relations, personnel matters, and relations with the press, other information media, and the general public. There are several others, too, including the President's physician, his military aide, and his personal and social secretaries, as well as a secretary to his wife.

The National Security Council. This Council has been called "America's cold-war general staff." It advises the President on all matters—domestic, foreign, and military—relating to the nation's security. The Council is composed of the President, the Vice President, the Secretaries of State, Defense, and the Director of the Office of Emergency Preparedness, and it is served by a highly competent professional staff. The super-secret Central Intelligence Agency operates under the Council—gathering and evaluating information bearing on the nation's security, making reports and recommendations to the Council, and performing whatever other tasks that body assigns to it.

The Office of Emergency Preparedness. The OEP advises the President in all phases—military, industrial, and civilian—of the national preparedness activities of the Government. Most of its work is directly related to defense preparedness, but it also prepares plans and supervises programs in somewhat less critical fields. Thus, it coordinates the aid given to States and locales hit by such natural disasters as floods and hurricanes. The OEP also advises the President in civil defense matters and manages the stockpiling of strategic materials.

The Council of Economic Advisers. This Council is composed of three expert economists appointed by the President to advise him in all matters pertaining to the nation's economy. It studies and analyzes the economy and its various segments on a continual basis, keeps the President constantly informed of the state of the nation's economic health, and assists him in the preparation of the economic reports he submits to Congress.

The Bureau of the Budget. The Bureau, headed by a Director appointed by the President, is a sort of "handy man" agency to the Chief Executive. Its major job is that of directing the preparation of the annual budget which the President submits to Congress, and it oversees the expenditure of the funds Congress provides. But it also has a number of other important functions. It conducts continuing studies of all of the elements of the executive branch, keeps the President informed of the work of all of the many agencies under him, and coordinates the many legislative proposals those agencies support. It assists the President in the preparation of executive orders and veto messages, aids other federal agencies with their fiscal and organizational problems, and strives to promote closer working relationships between those agencies and the States and their local governments.

The National Aeronautics and Space Council. This Council advises the President on all aspects of policies, plans, and progress in the Federal Government's far-ranging aeronautical and space activities. It is chaired by the Vice President, and its other members include the Secretaries of State and Defense, the

Administrator of the National Aeronautics and Space Administration, and the Chairman of the Atomic Energy Commission. See pages 400–401.

The Office of Science and Technology. This Office serves as the President's "right hand" in all scientific matters. Its Director and his staff assist the President in development of policies and programs to insure the most effective use of our scientific and technical resources for the nation's security and welfare.

The Office of Special Representative for Trade Negotiations. This Office advises the President on the administration of the nation's foreign trade agreements. Its head, the Special Representative, represents the President in trade negotiations with other countries. He and his top aide, the Deputy Special Representative, each carry the rank of ambassador.

The Office of Economic Opportunity. This Office was created by Congress in the Economic Opportunity Act of 1964. The OEO, headed by a Director, is responsible for the administration of a number of economic assistance programs. Its work is discussed in detail on pages 514–516.

The National Council on Marine Resources and Engineering Development. This Council is chaired by the Vice President; its other members include the Secretaries of State, Navy, Interior, Commerce, Health, Education and Welfare, and Transportation, and the Chairman of the Atomic Energy Commission and Director of the National Science Foundation. Its basic function is that of advising the President and supervising and coordinating the work of all federal agencies in the broad and fast-developing field of marine science (oceanography).

The Council for Urban Affairs. This agency was created by President Nixon in 1969 and has a most impressive membership. It is chaired by the President himself and includes the Vice President, the Attorney General, the Secretaries of Agriculture, Commerce, Labor, HEW, HUD, and Transportation, and the Director of the OEO. It is charged with aiding the President in the development of a national urban policy, promoting the coordination of federal programs in urban areas, and encouraging cooperation among federal, State, and city governments in all matters affecting the nation's urban areas and population. The Council's staff is headed by an Executive Director appointed by the President.

The Office of Intergovernmental Relations. This Office, also created in 1969, is under the immediate supervision of the Vice President. Its general mission is that of strengthening the relationships between the Federal Government and the nation's more than 80,000 State and local governmental units. Essentially, the Office acts as a clearinghouse for the handling and solution of those federal-State-local problems brought to the notice of the President or the Vice President by executive and legislative officers of the States and their local governments.

THE CABINET

The Cabinet is an informal and extralegal advisory body assembled by the President to serve his needs. The Constitution makes no specific reference to it,[2] nor did Congress create it. Rather, it is a product of custom and usage developed over the years since George Washington's first administration.

The first session of the 1st Congress created the posts of Secretary of State, Secretary of the Treasury, Secretary of War, and Attorney General in 1789. By his second term, President

---

[2] The closest approach in the Constitution is found in Article II, Section 2, Clause 1, in which the President is authorized to "require the opinion, in writing, of the principal officer in each of the executive departments upon any subject relating to the duties of their respective offices."

Washington was regularly seeking the counsel of the men whom he had selected for the key executive positions: Thomas Jefferson in the Department of State, Alexander Hamilton who was guiding the Treasury Department, Henry Knox in the War Department, and Edmund Randolph, the Attorney General. Thus, the Cabinet was born.

Today, the Cabinet consists of the heads of the twelve executive departments and, as well, the United States Representative to the United Nations. The latter post was raised to Cabinet rank by President Kennedy. The various Cabinet posts and when each was created are:

Secretary of State	1789
Secretary of the Treasury	1789
Secretary of Defense [3]	1947
Attorney General	1789
Postmaster General	1792
Secretary of the Interior	1849
Secretary of Agriculture	1889
Secretary of Commerce	1903
Secretary of Labor	1913
Secretary of Health, Education, and Welfare	1953
United States Representative to the United Nations	1961
Secretary of Housing and Urban Development	1965
Secretary of Transportation	1967

The Vice President regularly participates in all Cabinet meetings and other officials are invited from time to time for the discussion of particular subjects. One of the President's Special Assistants serves as Cabinet Secretary to provide for the orderly handling and follow up of matters brought before the group.

Each of the members of the Cabinet is appointed by the President, subject to confirmation by the Senate. Although the Senate must confirm Cabinet members, rejections are exceedingly rare. Of the more than 450 appointments the various Presidents have made thus far (1970), only nine have ever been rejected.[4]

With the single exception of the Postmaster General, who is appointed for a definite term, Cabinet members serve at the President's pleasure — that is, indefinitely.[5] When a new President assumes office, all of the members of his predecessor's Cabinet tender their resignations.

Innumerable factors influence the President in his choice of Cabinet members. Party considerations are always paramount. There are party stalwarts to be rewarded; for example, the Postmaster General is very frequently the man who served as the party's national chairman in the successful presidential campaign. Of course, professional qualifications are taken into account, especially

---

[3] Congress created the Department of Defense in 1947, including within it the old War Department (1789), the old Navy Department (1789), and a new Air Force Department. The Secretaries of the Army, Navy, and Air Force do not hold Cabinet rank.

[4] The most recent rejection occurred in 1959 when the Senate refused by a narrow vote (49 to 46) to approve President Eisenhowers selection of Lewis Strauss as Secretary of Commerce. The Senate also refused to confirm Andrew Jackson's appointment of Roger B. Taney as Secretary of the Treasury in 1834; John Tyler's appointments of Caleb Cushing and James Green as Secretary of the Treasury in 1843 and 1844 respectively, David Henshaw as Secretary of the Navy in 1844, and James M. Porter as Secretary of War in 1844; Andrew Johnson's appointments of Henry Stanberry as Attorney General in 1868 and Alexander Stewart as Secretary of the Treasury in 1869; and Calvin Coolidge's appointment of Charles B. Warren (rejected twice) as Attorney General in 1925.

[5] Congress has provided that the Postmaster General's term "shall be for and during the term of the President by whom he is appointed, and for one month thereafter, unless sooner removed."

in the selections of the Secretary of State and the Attorney General. Geography plays its part, too; thus, the Secretary of the Interior often comes from the West, where most of his department's work is carried out.

Various social and economic groups are particularly interested in certain departments and have an influence in some of the choices. Thus, the Secretary of Agriculture is usually a farmer or has a background closely related to agriculture. The Secretary of the Treasury always comes from the financial world and the Secretary of Commerce from the ranks of business. The Secretary of Labor must be a person acceptable to the major labor organizations. The steady growth in the place and power of both women and Negroes in politics now effects Cabinet selections, and the appointment of women and Negroes can be expected to become increasingly important in the years to come.[6]

The factors a President must weigh, and the influences operating upon him, in making Cabinet appointments — as well as the hundreds of others he makes — are so many and varied that they really defy cataloging.

The Cabinet meets at the President's call, usually about once a week in a room in the executive offices which adjoins the White House. Proposals and reports are made, and advice is offered to the Chief Executive. He need not take the advice he receives, of course. Lincoln once laid a proposition he favored before his Cabinet. Each member opposed it. Lincoln then declared: "Seven nays, one aye; the ayes have it."

---

[6] Franklin Roosevelt named the first woman to the Cabinet when he nominated Frances Perkins who served as Secretary of Labor from 1933 to 1945. Oveta Culp Hobby was the first Secretary of Health, Education, and Welfare, serving in the Eisenhower Cabinet from 1953 to 1955. Lyndon Johnson appointed the first Negro to the Cabinet when he selected Robert C. Weaver as the first Secretary of Housing and Urban Development in 1966

Cabinet sessions are usually held in private but other officials are often invited to attend. For example, as Vice President, Richard Nixon regularly attended and took part in meetings of the Eisenhower Cabinet — as did Lyndon Johnson under President Kennedy, and Hubert Humphrey under President Johnson. Today Spiro Agnew plays a leading role in the meetings of the Nixon Cabinet.

Several Presidents have had unofficial advisory groups in addition to the Cabinet. Andrew Jackson formed the first such group. It often met in the kitchen of the White House and, of course, came to be known as the "Kitchen Cabinet." The other most notable illustration was Franklin Roosevelt's "Brain Trust" of the early 1930's. Each of these groups had more influence with the President than did his regular Cabinet.

THE PRESIDENT'S POWERS

As we examine the powers held and exercised by the President, it is well to keep this point constantly in mind: What the Presidency *is* depends not only upon its legal framework but also, to a very large extent, upon the manner in which each of the Presidents — and especially the one in office at any given time — has viewed and exercised the office. As we have already suggested, much of the shape of the office and its powers has come from the stronger of its occupants.

Over the course of our history two general and contrasting views of the Presidency have been voiced by the men who have held the office. The stronger, and the more effective and successful of them, have taken a broad view of the scope of their powers. Theodore Roosevelt expounded their position in what he called the "stewardship theory":

I declined to adopt the view that what was imperatively necessary for the nation could not be done by the President unless he could find some specific authorization to do it.

My belief was that it was not only his right but his duty to do anything that the needs of the nation demanded unless such action was forbidden by the Constitution or by the laws.... I did not usurp power, but I did greatly broaden the use of executive power.[7]

Ironically, the most cogent presidential statement of the opposing view was made by Roosevelt's handpicked successor, William Howard Taft:

My judgment is that the view of Mr. Roosevelt, ascribing an undefined residuum of power to the President, is an unsafe doctrine.... The true view of the executive function is, as I conceive it, that the President can exercise no power which cannot be fairly and reasonably traced to some specific grant of power or justly implied and included within such express grant.... Such specific grant must be either in the Federal Constitution or in an act of Congress passed in pursuance thereof. There is no undefined residuum of power which he can exercise because it seems to him to be in the public interest.[8]

Executive Powers. The opening words of Article II lodge *the* executive power of the United States in the President. The specific powers included within that broad grant are many and potent.

Law Execution and Enforcement. The President's primary duty is to execute and enforce federal law. His power to do so rests upon two brief constitutional provisions. The first is the oath of office which he must take:

I do solemnly swear (or affirm) that I will faithfully execute the office of President of the United States, and will, to the best of my ability, preserve, protect, and defend the Constitution of the United States.[9]

The other is in the Constitution's command that he "shall take care that the laws be faithfully executed." [10]

The power to execute and enforce the laws is often thought of in terms of *criminal* law enforcement—and, of course, the power does include such matters as those involved in the activities of the various federal police agencies such as the FBI and the Secret Service. But it includes much more than this. It involves the application and administration of *all* federal laws, including those on such diverse subjects as flood control, social security, customs duties, selective service, labor-management relations, foreign aid, agricultural research, postal service, highway construction, conservation, and housing, and scores of others.

As with the Congress and the courts, the President and his subordinates have much to say about the meaning of the law. That is, in executing and enforcing law, the executive branch also *interprets* it. The Constitution requires the President to administer *all* laws, regardless of his own views of any of them. But he has a wide range of discretion concerning how *vigorously* and in what particular manner any given law will be applied.

To examine the point more closely: most of the statutes enacted by Congress are written in broad terms. In them Congress sets out the basic policies and standards to be followed and usually leaves the details necessary to the actual administration of the law to the President and his subordinates. The immigration and naturalization laws (pages 84–86) provide among other things that all immigrants seeking admission to this country must be literate enough to "read and understand some dialect or language." But what does this mean in actual practice? What words must be known, and how many of them? How well must the alien be able to read? What kind of test should

---

[7] *Theodore Roosevelt: An Autobiography.* New York: Charles Scribner's Sons, 1920, page 357.

[8] *Our Chief Magistrate and His Powers.* New York: Columbia University Press, 1916, pages 139–140, 144.

[9] Article II, Section 1, Clause 8.

---

[10] Article II, Section 3; the provision gives to the President what is sometimes called the "take-care power."

be applied to determine these things? The law does not say. Rather, the answers to these and many similar questions are made by the executive branch—specifically in this case, by the Immigration and Naturalization Service in the Department of Justice.

Direction of Administration. From what has just been said, it is clear that the President may be called the Chief Administrator as well as the Chief Executive. The actual day-to-day job of administering and applying most federal law is done through the many departments, bureaus, boards, administrations, councils, offices, and commissions that make up the mammoth executive branch. All of the some 3,000,000 men and women who staff these agencies are subordinate to the President. They work under his control and direction, no matter what their specific jobs may be. Properly, they may be regarded as extensions of the President himself.

The Ordinance Power. As the size and complexity of governmental problems have grown, it has become more and more necessary for Congress to give wider discretion to the President in the administration of the laws that it passes. Congressmen are not, and cannot be expected to be, experts in all of the fields with which they must deal.

The details of congressional statutes are spelled out by the President, and his subordinates acting for him, in the form of *executive ordinances* (or orders). These ordinances are a valid form of federal law, although they must not violate an act of Congress or the Constitution.

The ordinance power is not mentioned in the Constitution. Rather, it rests on grants of power made by Congress to the President and others in his administration. For example, Congress has provided for the payment of price supports on twelve specified farm products (discussed fully in Chapter 24); it also has given the Secretary of Agriculture the power to add other commodities to that list. He does so by executive orders.

Power of Appointment. No President can hope to succeed unless his subordinates are loyal to his policies and support his administration. No matter how able he may be or how wise his policies, he cannot succeed without this loyalty and support.

The Constitution provides that the President:

> by and with the advice and consent of the Senate, shall appoint ambassadors, other public ministers, and consuls, judges of the Supreme Court, and all other officers of the United States whose appointments are not otherwise herein provided for, but the Congress may by law vest the appointment of such inferior officers, as they think proper, in the President alone, in the courts of law, or in the heads of departments.[11]

The *President alone* appoints only a relative handful of the some 3,000,000 federal civilian employees. Most of those he does are members of his personal staff in the White House Office.

With the *consent of the Senate* he appoints the most important officers of the National Government. These include ambassadors and other diplomats, Cabinet members and their chief assistants, federal judges, officers of the Armed Forces, the heads of such agencies as the Interstate Commerce Commission, United States attorneys and marshals, and most postmasters.

When the President makes one of these appointments, he sends his "nomination" to the Senate. There it is referred to the appropriate standing committee. For example, the appointment of a federal judge is sent to the Judiciary Committee, an officer in the Armed Forces to the Armed Services Committee, and a Secretary of Agriculture to the Agriculture Committee. If a majority of the committee

---

[11] Article II, Section 2, Clause 2. Those whose appointments are "otherwise provided for" are the Vice President, Senators, Representatives, presidential electors, and congressional employees.

favors the appointment, it reports that fact to the Senate. The Senate then votes. A majority of the Senators present is necessary to confirm a presidential nominee.

The unwritten rule of *senatorial courtesy* plays an important part in the appointing process. It applies to the approval of those federal appointees who will serve within one of the States —for example, a judge or a postmaster. Under the rule the Senate will approve only those appointees who are acceptable to the majority party Senator or Senators from the State involved. The practical effect of this custom is, in many instances, to place the *actual* appointment in the hands of one or two Senators. See pages 59, 214.

Approximately one-half of all federal civilian employees are selected on the basis of competitive civil service examinations. The *United States Civil Service Commission* examines applicants for more than 2,000,000 positions, such as postal clerks and letter carriers, internal revenue agents, agricultural extension agents, patent examiners, stenographers, and the like. See Chapter 32.

Removal Power. Except for the cumbersome impeachment process, the Constitution is silent on the power to remove appointive officers. But the 1st Congress gave the President the power to remove any officer he appoints, except judges. Without such a power, he could be saddled with political opponents and other misfits in his administration.

In its Reconstruction fight with President Andrew Johnson Congress passed the Tenure of Office Act of 1867. It prohibited the President from removing certain officers without Senate consent. Though Johnson and his supporters charged that the law was unconstitutional, it was never challenged in the courts. It was finally repealed in 1887.

The question of the President's removal power did not reach the Supreme Court until *Myers* v. *United States* in 1926. In 1876 Congress had passed a law requiring Senate consent before the President could remove any first-,

After confirmation by the Senate, presidential appointees are sworn into office. Here, President Nixon witnesses the swearing in of Elliot L. Richardson to the cabinet post of Secretary of Health, Education and Welfare. Chief Justice Warren Burger administers the oath. (AP Wirephoto)

second-, or third-class postmaster. In 1920, without consulting the Senate, President Wilson removed Frank S. Myers as postmaster at Portland, Oregon. Myers sued for the salary he claimed was due him for the remaining portion of his four-year term, basing his claim on the fact that he had been removed in violation of the 1876 law. The Supreme Court held the act of 1876 unconstitutional. Chief Justice William Howard Taft, himself a former President, delivered the Court's opinion, declaring that the removal power was essential to the carrying out of the President's constitutional duty to "take care that the laws be faithfully executed."

The Supreme Court limited the President's removal power somewhat in 1935 in *Humphrey's Executor* v. *United States.* President Herbert Hoover had appointed William Humphrey to a seven-year term on the Federal Trade Commission in 1931. When President Franklin D. Roosevelt entered office in 1933, he found Humphrey in sharp disagreement with many of his policies. He asked Humphrey to resign, saying that the purposes of his administration could be better realized with someone else on the FTC. Humphrey refused, and Roosevelt then removed him. Humphrey challenged the legality of the President's action but died before a case could be brought. His heirs then filed a suit for back salary. The Supreme Court upheld their claim. It based its decision on the act creating the FTC. The law provided that a member of the Commission may be removed only for "inefficiency, neglect of duty, or malfeasance in office." President Roosevelt had cited none of these reasons. He had dismissed Humphrey simply because of political disagreements. The Court also held that Congress had a right to set the conditions under which a member of the FTC and similar agencies might be removed because these agencies are not purely executive ones. The agencies are, instead, *quasi-legislative* and *quasi-judicial* in character.[12]

As a general rule, however, the President may remove those whom he appoints. Those employees who are appointed under the Civil Service system may be removed for any cause deemed to be "for the good of the service."

Diplomatic Powers. The Constitution makes the President the nation's chief diplomat. It gives him the power to make treaties (with the consent of two-thirds of the Senate), to appoint diplomatic and consular officers (subject to Senate confirmation), and to receive foreign diplomatic representatives (that is, *recognize* foreign governments).[13]

The Treaty Power. Whenever the United States wishes to enter into commercial compacts, establish defensive alliances, define its boundaries, make peace, or conclude any other agreements with foreign states, it may do so by treaties. The President, with the assistance of the State Department, negotiates these international agreements. The Constitution requires Senate approval by a two-thirds vote of the members present before a treaty may become effective.[14]

The small original Senate of twenty-six members was considered a suitable council to advise the President in foreign affairs. Secrecy in debating the subject was considered necessary, and it was thought that secrecy could not be maintained in a body as large as the House of Representatives. The two-thirds requirement helped to compensate the House for its exclusion from the treaty process.

Turn the two-thirds rule around, and it becomes a one-third rule. In other words, one third of the members plus one is all that is necessary to defeat a treaty—no matter how vital it might be or popular with the people generally. Because of this, many have criticized the rule and suggested a change to a simple majority requirement.

After World War I the Treaty of Versailles, which included the creation of the League of Nations, was rejected by the Senate even though 49 Senators voted for it and only 35 against it. This was 7 votes short of the necessary two-thirds. More than once a President

---

[12] That is, their duties are partly legislative and partly judicial; they *make rules* and *decide controversies.* See page 531.

[13] Article II, Section 2, Clause 2; and Section 3.

[14] The Senate does *not* "ratify" treaties. The Constitution requires Senate "advice and consent" to a treaty made by the President. *After* senatorial approval, the President ratifies a treaty. Treaties have the same legal standing as acts of Congress. Congress may repeal (*abrogate*) a treaty by passing a law contrary to its provisions, or an existing law may be repealed by the terms of a treaty. When a treaty and an act of Congress conflict, the courts consider the latest enacted to be the law. The terms of a treaty cannot conflict with the Constitution; but the courts have not yet found a treaty to be unconstitutional. Money cannot be appropriated by a treaty, but in practice, whenever the Senate has approved a treaty requiring an expenditure, the House has agreed to a bill appropriating the necessary funds.

has been forced to bow to a small minority in the Senate in order to secure passage of a treaty — even when this involved concessions opposed by the majority.

On other occasions Presidents have had to resort to roundabout methods. When a Senate minority rejected a treaty to annex Texas, President Tyler accomplished annexation in 1845 by a *joint resolution* of both houses — a move which required only a majority in each house. Hawaii was also annexed by a joint resolution in 1898 after a treaty had failed.

Executive Agreements. Agreements entered into with a foreign state do not always take the form of treaties. More and more, our international agreements, especially routine ones, are made as *executive agreements.* These agreements are concluded between the President and the chief executive of the foreign state or states involved — but they do not require senatorial approval. Such agreements are sometimes submitted, however, for approval (by simple majority) by *both houses* of Congress. Although this is not common, it is usually done when appropriations are needed to implement the agreement.

The Supreme Court has held executive agreements to be as legally binding as treaties and a part of the supreme law of the land. Indeed, some argue that executive agreements can be used instead of treaties in any and all cases.

One of the most notable executive agreements came in 1940. President Roosevelt gave 50 overage destroyers to Great Britain in exchange for 99-year leases to several island bases extending from Newfoundland to South America. Hundreds of executive agreements are made each year.

Power of Recognition. When the President receives the diplomatic representatives sent to the United States by another sovereign state, he exercises the very important power of recognition. That is, the President, acting for the United States, acknowledges the legal existence of that country and its government.

He signifies that the United States accepts that country as an equal in the family of nations and is prepared to conduct relations with it.[15]

Recognition does not necessarily indicate that one government approves of the character and conduct of another. The United States recognizes several governments about which we have serious misgivings, most notably that of the Soviet Union. The facts of life in world politics make it necessary for us to maintain relations with these regimes.

Recognition is often used as a weapon in foreign relations, too. Prompt recognition of a new state or government may do much to guarantee its life. By the same token, the withholding of recognition may have a serious effect on its continued existence. President Theodore Roosevelt's quick recognition of the Republic of Panama in 1903 provides one of the classic examples of American use of the power as a diplomatic weapon. He recognized the new state less than three days after the Panamanians had begun a revolt against Colombia. His action guaranteed the revolt's success. See page 592.

The United States has consistently refused to recognize the Communist regime in Peking as the lawful government of China. Its character and conduct have never been acceptable to the United States, and we have refused to permit it to "shoot its way" into the family of nations. Instead, we recognize the Nationalist Government of Chiang Kai-shek on the Island of Taiwan (Formosa).

The President may indicate American displeasure with the conduct of a foreign diplomat or his government by requesting the recall of that official (declaring him to be *persona non*

---

[15] Sovereign states normally recognize one another through the exchange of diplomatic representatives. Recognition may be accomplished in any of several other ways, however; for example, by proposing to negotiate a treaty, since under international law only sovereign states are capable of making such agreements.

grata). The withdrawal of recognition is the sharpest diplomatic rebuke one government may give another and is often a step to war.

Military Powers. The Constitution makes the President the Commander in Chief of the nation's Armed Forces.[16] Congress also possesses certain war powers—especially, the power to declare war, to provide for the raising of the Armed Forces, to make the rules by which they are governed, and to appropriate the funds necessary to the nation's defense.[17]

Even though the President shares his military powers with the Congress, his position is as dominant in military policy as it is in the field of foreign affairs. He may literally force Congress to act; and, in effect, he may use the Armed Forces much as he pleases. For example, in 1907 Theodore Roosevelt sent the Great White Fleet around the world. He did so partly as a training exercise for the Navy, but especially to impress other nations with America's naval strength. Several Congressmen objected to the cost and threatened to withhold the necessary appropriation—to which TR replied: "Very well, the existing appropriation will carry the Navy half way around the world and if Congress chooses to leave it on the other side, all right."

Almost from the beginning, Presidents have used the Armed Forces abroad—and often in combat—without a declaration of war by Congress. John Adams was the first to do so; in 1798 he ordered American warships into action against French naval vessels harassing American merchant ships. Since then, various Presidents have followed his precedent on no fewer than 150 separate occasions. Jefferson did so against the Barbary Coast pirates in 1801. Polk brought on the Mexican War by ordering troops across the Nueces River in 1846, and Buchanan sent troops across the border to punish Mexican bandits in 1859. More recently, President Truman sent the Armed Forces into action in Korea in 1950, as did Eisenhower in Lebanon in 1958 and Johnson in the Dominican Republic in 1965. And, of course, the war in Viet Nam is being fought in the absence of a declaration of war by Congress.

The President's military powers are far greater in war than in peacetime, of course. During a war Congress grants him vast powers in addition to the authority given him by the Constitution. In this day and age his wartime authority extends far beyond the traditional military field. In World War II, for example, the President was given the power to do such things as ration food, control wages and prices, and seize industries vital to the war effort.

The President may use his military powers to preserve domestic peace, as we saw in Chapter 4.[18] He also has the power to call a State's militia into federal service when necessary,[19] and he may use the Armed Forces to enforce federal law anywhere in the United States.

Legislative Powers. As part of the system of checks and balances, the Constitution grants certain legislative powers to the President. With these—and the skill with which he fills his role as party leader—the President is usually able to exert considerable influence over the actions of Congress.

Power to Recommend Legislation. The Constitution requires that the President:

> shall, from time to time, give to the Congress information of the state of the Union, and recommend to their consideration such measures as he shall judge necessary and expedient.[20]

Shortly after the beginning of each congressional session, the President delivers his State of the Union Message to Congress. This is quickly followed by the proposed budget and

[16] Article II, Section 2, Clause 1; see also page 384.

[17] Article I, Section 8, Clauses 11–17; see also pages 246 and 384.

[18] See page 70 and Article IV, Section 4.

[19] Article I, Section 8, Clause 15; Article II, Section 2, Clause 1.

[20] Article II, Section 3; see also page 219.

The signing of an important piece of legislation has become a ceremonial affair in which the President uses several pens and distributes them as souvenirs to those who played an important role in the act's passage. (Wide World Photos)

an economic report. He also submits occasional special messages on particular subjects. In all of these messages he recommends laws that he considers necessary.

In a real sense, the President has become the leader in lawmaking. In fact, Congress spends a good share of its time considering the measures that he has requested.

There are several ways in which the President may influence Congress in behalf of his legislative program. He has considerable influence as the leader of his party. Most Presidents have tried to ease the way for their programs by maintaining rather intimate friendships with congressional leaders.

One of the most useful devices is the "patronage" power, the practice of doing or refusing to do favors for individual Congressmen. Abraham Lincoln once allowed a Congressman to name the appointee to a $20,000 position in the Custom House in New York. The Congressman's vote was needed to admit Nevada to the Union, and Nevada was needed to ratify the 13th Amendment. Appointments or other administrative actions are often withheld from Congressmen who want some favorable action on a matter in the executive branch until they support and pass the bill in which the administration is interested.

The press, radio, and television follow everything the President does very closely. His press conferences, official statements, and public speeches affect public opinion—which is keenly felt by many Congressmen, especially in an election year.

The Veto Power. The Constitution requires that every bill or joint resolution [21] passed by Congress must be sent to the President for his action. If he signs it, it becomes law. If he vetoes it, he must send it back to the house in

---

[21] Except those proposing amendments to the Constitution which, by custom, are not sent to the White House.

which it originated, with his reasons for the veto.[22]

The veto power enables the President, who is the only representative of *all* of the people, to act as a check on Congress. Many times the mere threat of a veto is enough to defeat a bill or bring about its modification before passage.

Bills must be vetoed in their entirety. The President does not have the power to veto certain items in a bill; that is, he does not possess the "item veto," as do most State governors. If he had the item veto, needless or wasteful projects might be eliminated from appropriations bills, or he might delete an objectionable provision in a bill which he otherwise would prefer to see become law. On the other hand, if he had the item veto, he might use it as a weapon with which to punish or pressure an opponent in Congress. Every President from Woodrow Wilson to Richard Nixon has favored a constitutional amendment to equip the Chief Executive with the item veto power.

Other Legislative Powers. The President has the power to call special sessions of Congress. He may also adjourn a session of Congress whenever the two houses are unable themselves to agree upon an adjournment date — though no President has ever done so.[23]

Judicial Powers. The Constitution declares that the President:

shall have the power to grant reprieves and pardons for offenses against the United States, except in cases of impeachment.[24]

A *reprieve* is the postponement of the execution of a sentence. A *pardon* is legal (though not moral) forgiveness of a crime.

The President's power to grant reprieves and pardons is absolute, except in cases of impeachment where they may never be granted. Of course, these judicial powers may only be exercised in federal criminal cases and have no application to State offenses.

Presidential pardons are usually granted to persons accused of federal crimes *after* they have been convicted in court. The President may pardon a federal offender even before he is tried, however. Thus, in 1889 President Benjamin Harrison issued a proclamation of *amnesty* (group pardon) pardoning all Mormons who had violated the antipolygamy laws in the federal territories.

The President's pardoning power includes the power to issue a *conditional pardon,* provided the condition be reasonable. It also includes the power to *commute* a sentence — that is, to reduce the time to be served or the fine to be paid. The Pardon Attorney in the Department of Justice advises the President on all matters relating to the exercise of executive clemency. The Board of Parole, also in the Justice Department, has the sole power to grant, modify, or revoke paroles of federal prisoners. See page 409.

REORGANIZATION OF THE EXECUTIVE BRANCH

In the early part of this chapter we began an examination of the organization of the huge, sprawling executive branch — and we shall continue that examination through the next several chapters. As we do so, bear this thought in mind: the organization is dynamic, not static; that is, it is a continually growing, changing thing. The march of time, fresh circumstances, adoption of new policies and programs, and expansion — or, occasionally, de-emphasis or even abandonment — of existing ones all call

---

[22] Article I, Section 7, Clause 2. Recall that the President has ten days (excluding Sundays) in which to act on a bill. If he does not sign or veto it within ten days of its presentation by Congress, it becomes law without his signature unless Congress adjourns during that ten-day period. If Congress does adjourn and the President does not sign the bill, the measure dies — the "pocket veto" has been applied. See pages 51, 235.

[23] Article II, Section 3; see also page 202.

[24] Article II, Section 2, Clause 1.

for the creation, reshuffling, and elimination of agencies. In short, the story of the organization of the executive branch can be told in good part as a tale of organization and *reorganization*.

Basic responsibility for the structure of the executive branch rests with Congress. It has created nearly all of the complex of agencies beneath the President.[25] But Congress has been traditionally slow to react to the continuing need for organizational change. Because of this, and beginning with President Taft in 1911, every Chief Executive has asked Congress to grant him authority to reorganize the executive branch. Since the depression years of the 1930's, Congress has responded with several statutes. The earlier ones usually provided for the creation of a commission to study the problems involved and make recommendations for their solutions. The most notable of such groups were the President's Committee on Administrative Management, which reported in 1937, and the Commission on Organization of the Executive Branch, the "Hoover Commission," which reported in

1949. As a result of the work of these groups, several changes and improvements have occurred over the past few decades.

The Reorganization Act of 1949. As we have already indicated, the problems of governmental organization demand *continuing* oversight and analysis. Recognizing this, the Hoover Commission strongly urged that Congress grant the President the power to create, reshape, and abolish executive agencies — which Congress then did in the Reorganization Act of 1949.[26]

Under that statute the President is authorized to issue reorganization plans covering any segment of the executive branch. If neither house of Congress rejects a reorganization plan within sixty days, it takes effect.[27] Each of the most recent Presidents has used the law quite extensively, and much of the executive branch has been reorganized. But, once again, the task is a never-ending one.

---

[25] Except for those it has in specific statutes authorized the President to create and those created, as we shall note in a moment, in presidential reorganization plans.

[26] The act, adopted unanimously by both houses, was originally scheduled to expire in 1953; its life has been extended periodically by Congress ever since — most recently to 1971.

[27] The act sets only two major restrictions on the scope of such plans; reorganization cannot provide for the abolition of any Cabinet department, nor can it extend the life of any agency created by Congress to exist only for a specified period of time.

❖❖❖❖❖❖❖❖❖❖❖❖ CONCEPT BUILDING ❖❖❖❖❖❖❖❖❖❖❖❖

Key Concepts

Every officer, employee, and agency of the executive branch is subordinate to the President and aids him in the performance of his duties. His chief right arm is the Executive Office of the President — a complex of twelve agencies staffed by his key advisers and assistants. The Cabinet, composed of the heads of the twelve executive departments and the United States Representative to the United Nations, is also a major source of advice to him.

The President's powers arise from the Constitution, acts of Congress, usage, and his position as party leader. The nature of his powers has been most tellingly shaped by the manner in which the stronger Presidents have used their powers.

The President's powers include:

    (1) Executive powers: to execute and enforce the law, to direct administration, to issue executive orders, and to appoint and remove major officers.

    (2) Diplomatic powers: to make treaties, to make executive agreements, and to send and receive diplomatic representatives.

    (3) Military powers: to act as Commander in Chief and to preserve domestic peace.

    (4) Legislative powers: to recommend legislation, to approve or veto acts of Congress, to call special sessions of Congress, and to adjourn Congress when the two houses cannot agree on an adjournment date.

    (5) Judicial powers: to exercise executive clemency (pardons, reprieves, amnesties, commutations).

    The organization and reorganization of the executive branch demands constant attention. In the Reorganization Act of 1949 Congress granted to the President substantial authority to reorganize the agencies subordinate to him.

Important Terms

amnesty	executive agreements	patronage	reprieve
Cabinet	Executive Office of the	*persona non grata*	senatorial courtesy
Commander in Chief	President	recognition	treaties
commute	executive ordinances	Reorganization Act of	veto
	pardon	1949	

Questions for Inquiry and Review

1. In whom does the Constitution vest *the* executive power?

2. From what sources has the sketchy outline of the President's powers in Article II been filled out?

3. Why may the Executive Office of the President be called the Chief Executive's "right arm"?

4. What agencies compose the Executive Office of the President?

5. The occupants of what posts are today members of the Cabinet?

6. For what term and by whom are Cabinet members appointed?

7. What two general and contrasting views of the Presidency have been taken by its various occupants?

8. Why is it true that in executing and enforcing the law the President also has much to say about its meaning?

9. Why may the President be called the Chief Administrator as well as the Chief Executive?

10. Why is the President's power of appointment so critically related to the success of his administration?

11. What is the general rule regarding the President's removal power?

12. By whom are treaties made?

13. By whom are treaties ratified?

14. How does the President ordinarily exercise the power of recognition?

15. What is the President's major military power?

16. Why does the Constitution vest certain legislative powers in the President?

17. For what crimes may a President grant pardons?

18. Why is the problem of reorganization of the executive branch a constant one?

For Further Inquiry

1. What do you think President Eisenhower meant by the following observation? "The duties of the President are essentially endless. No daily schedule of appointments can give a full time table—or even a faint indication of the President's responsibilities.... In Washington, on a week end absence, indeed even at a ceremonial dinner, the old saying is true: 'A President never escapes from his office.'"

2. On what basis do you think the line should be drawn between those appointments made by the President that require senatorial confirmation and those made by the President that do not?

3. Which of the contrasting views of the nature of the Presidency do you favor? Explain your answer.

4. While he was President, Mr. Truman had on his desk a small sign which read: "The buck stops here." Can you explain the meaning of this small sign?

5. Each of the President's powers is limited in one or more important ways by the Constitution, the Congress, or the courts. Why?

Suggested Activities

1. Prepare a bulletin board display illustrating the various powers exercised by the President.

2. Stage a debate or class forum on one of the following questions: (a) *Resolved,* That the President should be granted the item veto. (b) *Resolved,* That the President as Commander in Chief should not have the power to use the armed forces in combat without a declaration of war by Congress. (c) *Resolved,* That all presidential appointments to office be made for a fixed term.

3. Prepare a report on the manner in which one (or more) of the Presidents viewed his office and exercised his powers.

4. Give a talk to the class explaining why a President of your choice was the strongest in our history.

Suggested Reading

BELL, JACK, *The Presidency: Office of Power.* Allyn and Bacon, 1969.

BURNS, JAMES M. and PELTASON, J. W., *Government by the People.* Prentice-Hall, 1969. Chapter 15.

EISENHOWER, DWIGHT D., "Some Thoughts on the Presidency," *Reader's Digest,* November 1968.

FURLOW, BARBARA, "Portrait of Two Presidents: Nixon and Johnson," *U.S. News,* July 28, 1969.

"How Mr. Nixon Made His Choice," *U.S. News,* June 2, 1969.

"Key Men At the White House Now," *U.S. News,* November 17, 1969.

KOENING, LOUIS W., *The Chief Executive.* Harcourt, Brace and World, 1968.

"Power of a President—Too Much, Too Little," *U.S. News,* November 11, 1968.

PRITCHETT, C. HERMAN, *The American Constitution.* McGraw-Hill, 1968. Chapters 17–19.

SCOTT, ANDREW M. and WALLACE, EARLE (eds.), *Politics, U.S.A.: Cases on the American Democratic Process.* Macmillan, 1969. Chapters 7, 9.

WICKER, TOM, "The Presidency Under Scrutiny," *Harper's,* October, 1969.

WILDAVSKY, AARON (ed.), *The Presidency.* Little, Brown, 1969.

18
THE DEPARTMENT OF STATE

✤✤✤ Why do the President and Congress share power in the field of foreign affairs? Which should be pre-eminent?

✤✤✤ Is the congressional role in foreign affairs better described as that of policy formulator or policy critic? Why?

✤✤✤ Should public opinion play a dominant role in the making and/or the execution of foreign policy? Why?

✤✤✤ Why do most Americans regularly display relatively little interest in the knowledge of foreign affairs?

Observe good faith and justice toward all nations. Cultivate peace and harmony with all.

GEORGE WASHINGTON

It would be impossible to overstate the importance of our foreign relations and of the manner in which they are conducted. The United States is the most powerful nation on earth and the leader of the free world in the struggle against communist tyranny. The ways in which the might and influence of the United States are used — the ways in which our relations with other nations are conducted — affect the fate of all mankind.

The ways in which other nations conduct themselves today is of vital concern to us, too. For more than 150 years American foreign policy was characterized by a refusal generally to become involved in the affairs of the rest of the world. Our policy of *isolationism* demanded that we steer clear of "entangling alliances" and similar international commitments. The years since 1945 have seen a profound change in American policy, however. Two world wars, followed by two decades of cold war, have taught us that we cannot live in isolation in the modern world — that, in many

ways and whether we like it or not, we live in "one world."

The inescapable fact that this is "one world" — that our own peace and security are intimately bound up with that of the rest of the world — can be seen in many ways. It can be seen, for example, in the fact that man's inventive genius has produced an age of ultra-rapid travel and communication and thus made the world almost a neighborhood. It took *The Mayflower* sixty perilous days to cross the Atlantic in 1620; today that trip can be made in a few safe, comfortable hours by air.

Wars and political upheavals anywhere on the globe vitally affect the interests of the United States. Four times in this century we have become involved in wars thousands of miles from home. Numerous other times our security has been threatened by lesser events thousands of miles away — by a flareup in the Formosa Strait, an outbreak in the Middle East, an incident in Berlin, a revolution in Latin America, and strife in Africa.

Economic conditions abroad make themselves felt quite directly in the United States, too. Cheaper labor costs in Europe's steel mills and Japanese factories, a coffee shortage in Brazil, a shutdown in the oil fields of Iran all are reflected in our domestic markets.

In these and many other ways, then, we live in "one world." In some ways, however, we do not. The communist world, especially the Soviet Union and Communist China, and the free world, led by the United States, confront one another on many issues and in many places. Most of the newer nations of Africa and Asia compose yet another grouping, a "non-aligned" or neutralist bloc of growing importance in world politics. In this divided world of the second half of the twentieth century, World War III remains a dreaded possibility.

As we noted in Chapter 17, the President is the nation's chief diplomat. Congress shares power with him in the field of foreign affairs, but the President is primarily responsible for the formulation and the conduct of American foreign policy. Obviously, he cannot perform his role singlehandedly; the Department of State is his firm "right hand."

ORGANIZATION AND FUNCTIONS

The Secretary of State. The Secretary of State is appointed by the President with the consent of the Senate and is the President's chief aide in the field of foreign relations. He ranks first in the order of precedence among the Cabinet officers, in part because of the importance of his function but especially because the Department of State was the first

In 1968, at Paris, special negotiators representing the United States began to meet with the delegation from North Viet Nam in an effort to end the war in Viet Nam. (UPI Photo)

executive department created by Congress in 1789.[1]

Many distinguished Americans have held the post. The entire list reads like a roll call of the nation's great and include such men as Thomas Jefferson, John Marshall, James Madison, James Monroe, John Quincy Adams, Henry Clay, Martin Van Buren, Daniel Webster, John C. Calhoun, William Seward, James G. Blaine, John Hay, Elihu Root, William Jennings Bryan, Charles Evans Hughes, and Cordell Hull. The most recent Secretaries of State

---

[1] Under the Continental Congress foreign affairs were conducted by its Committee of Secret Correspondence (1775–1777) and Committee for Foreign Affairs (1777–1781); under the Articles of Confederation by the Department of Foreign Affairs. The latter was reconstituted, following the adoption of the Constitution, by an act of Congress approved on July 27, 1789; its name became the Department of State by virtue of a statute approved on September 15, 1789.

have been George C. Marshall (1947–1949), Dean Acheson (1949–1953), John Foster Dulles (1953–1959), Christian Herter (1959–1961), and Dean Rusk (1961–1969), and William P. Rogers (1969–   ).

Some Presidents have entrusted foreign affairs largely to the Secretary of State, while others have held the reins in their own hands. But, in either case, the Secretary of State has been an important officer. His duties are partly concerned with domestic matters, but to a much greater extent with foreign affairs.

Domestic Duties. The Secretary of State attends to all official correspondence between the President and the governors of the several States. Thus, if the President calls a State's National Guard into federal service, or if a governor requests the extradition [2] of a criminal who has fled to another country, the process takes place through the Secretary of State. The Secretary of State also has custody of the Great Seal of the United States; but many of his former domestic functions, such as the safekeeping of the statutes enacted by Congress, have now been transferred to others in the executive branch.

Foreign Duties. Under the President the Secretary of State has primary responsibility for the framing and implementing of the foreign policies of the United States, and he is the "caretaker" of American interests abroad. Merely to mention such matters as Cuba, Berlin and West Germany, the United Nations, South Viet Nam, NATO, the Congo, Korea, threats of international aggression, the seething and oil-rich Middle East, foreign economic and military aid, international control of atomic energy, nationalism in Southeast Asia, hemispheric solidarity and the Good Neighbor Policy, the protection of American citizens and property abroad, aid and advice to American importers and exporters, passports, visas, and tariffs is to suggest the wide and vital range of the activities of the Department of State and its more than 25,000 employees.

Organization. The Secretary of State directs the Department's farflung work through his chief aide, the Under Secretary of State, and his other top lieutenants, including the Under Secretary for Political Affairs, the Deputy Under Secretary for Economic Affairs, and several special assistants. The Deputy Under Secretary for Administration oversees the internal management of the Department and its posts abroad. The Counselor is a close consultant and adviser to the Secretary and also undertakes special projects at the Secretary's direction.

There are now (1971) ten Assistant Secretaries of State, for: Public Affairs, Congressional Relations, Inter-American Affairs, European Affairs, East Asian and Pacific Affairs, Near Eastern-South Asian Affairs, African Affairs, International Organization Affairs, Economic Affairs, and Educational and Cultural Affairs. The Legal Adviser, the Director of International Scientific and Technological Affairs, the Director of Intelligence and Research, the Administrator of the Agency for International Development, the Administrator of Security and Consular Affairs, the Inspector General of Foreign Assistance, the Chief of

---

[2] Extradition means the handing over by one state to another of fugitives from justice. The United States has extradition treaties with most of the nations of the world. When a person accused of crimes flees from an American State to a foreign country, the governor of the State applies to the Secretary of State for the return of the fugitive, furnishing evidence of probable guilt. The governor also names a person who will go for the fugitive. The proper papers are sent to our diplomatic representative, and he is instructed to request the extradition of the fugitive. The "President's warrant" is given the agent whom the governor has designated to bring back the accused.

Protocol, the Director of Planning and Co-ordination, the Director of Politico-Military Affairs, and the Director of the Peace Corps each also rank at the Assistant Secretary level.

The various Assistant Secretaries head "bureaus"—for example, the Bureau of Economic Affairs and the Bureau of African Affairs. Each bureau is, in turn, organized in "offices"—for example, the Office of German Affairs in the Bureau of European Affairs, and the Passport Office in the Bureau of Security and Consular Affairs.

The Department of State is organized along *geographic* and *functional* lines. Some of its agencies deal with a particular country or region in the world. Others are concerned with particular subjects such as legislation and congressional relations, planning and research, or relations with international organizations. Because it is so organized, the Department of State is able to keep abreast of developments in many areas simultaneously; and it can move quickly whenever new problems arise, whether in some particular country or involving some functional question.

The Foreign Service. The Foreign Service represents this nation abroad. Its ranks include positions ranging from that of ambassador down to the lowliest alien clerk or employee in some distant outpost.

Under international law [3] every nation has the *right of legation*—to send and receive diplomatic representatives; the severing of diplomatic relations between states has usually been a step toward war. We maintain representatives in nearly all of the states of the world, and most states are also represented in Washington. The practice of exchanging diplomatic representatives is ancient; history indicates that the Egyptians followed it more than 6000

Peace Corps volunteers, as this one helping to build a school in Somalia, serve two-year terms teaching and working in underdeveloped countries. (Peace Corps Photo by Charles Overholt)

years ago. Benjamin Franklin became the first American foreign service officer when he was elected by the Continental Congress to serve as our minister to France in 1778.

Today the United States is represented by an ambassador stationed in the capital of each of the states with which we maintain diplomatic relations—that is, *recognize*.[4] By 1971, American embassies were operating at the seats of government in 117 different countries throughout the world.

---

[3] *International law* consists of those rules and principles followed by states in their dealings with one another. Its sources include treaties, decisions of international courts, reason, and custom, with treaties the most important source today.

---

[4] See page 315. An ambassador's official title is that of *Ambassador Extraordinary and Plenipotentiary.* When there is a vacancy in the office, or when the ambassador is absent, the post is usually filled by a lesser-ranking Foreign Service officer. That officer, temporarily in charge of his country's affairs, is known as the *chargé d'affaires.*

Ambassadors. Ambassadors are appointed by the President with the consent of the Senate and serve at his pleasure. There is no prescribed term of office, and there are numerous changes whenever there is a change of party in power.

An ambassadorship is a much-to-be-desired political plum. Too often mere amateurs have been appointed because of their social position or party service. Fortunately, an increasing number are now being named from the ranks of our career diplomats in the Foreign Service. Mr. Truman appointed our first woman ambassador to Denmark in 1949, and several women have since been appointed to high diplomatic posts. Mr. Johnson appointed our first Negro ambassador — also a woman — to Luxembourg in 1965.

The President may refuse to receive an ambassador from another state if he is for any reason objectionable to the United States. In

The U. S. Ambassador to Greece makes his home at the American Embassy in Athens. It, like our other embassies throughout the world, serves as headquarters for the State Department delegation in that country. (Department of State)

such circumstances, the diplomat is declared *persona non grata.* In order to avoid having this happen to our own appointees, the State Department inquires beforehand about the acceptability of the person we propose to send. Any country may demand the recall of any diplomatic official it finds undersirable.

Under international law ambassadors and ministers and their staffs enjoy the special privileges of diplomatic immunity. They cannot be taxed, nor may they be arrested. When a war breaks out between two countries, they are given safe conduct home. Mail and other communications are sent and received in a diplomatic pouch safe from any inspection. Important messages are usually sent in code, and the code is changed frequently to preserve secrecy. Embassies and legations are not subject to the jurisdiction of the state in which they are located.

The duties of an ambassador include: (1) transmitting official communications; (2) giving information to foreigners concerning American institutions, laws, and customs; (3) keeping the government advised of the progress of events in the country where he is stationed; (4) protecting American citizens; (5) negotiating treaties and other agreements if requested to do so by the President; and (6) promoting American interests in every way.

To perform these duties efficiently an ambassador must be on terms of friendly intimacy with the leading men in the country to which he is sent. A knowledge of the language, history, customs, and culture also helps, of course.

The following extracts from a letter written by Walter Hines Page, when he was our Ambassador to Great Britain, give a close-up view of an ambassador's day-to-day job:

> If you think it's all play, you fool yourself;
> I mean this job. There's no end of the work.
> It consists of these parts: Receiving people
> for two hours every day, some on some sort
> of business, some merely to "pay respects";
> attending to a large (and exceedingly miscellaneous) mail; going to the Foreign Office on

all sorts of errands; looking up the oddest sort of information that you ever heard of; making reports to Washington on all sorts of things; then the so-called social duties — giving dinners, receptions, etc., and attending them. I hear the most important news I get at so-called social functions. Then the court functions; and the meetings and speeches! The American Ambassador must go all over England and explain every American thing. You'd never recover from the shock if you could hear me speaking about Education, Agriculture, the observance of Christmas, the Suffrage, Medicine, Law, Radio-Activity, Flying, the Supreme Court, the President as a Man of Letters, the Hookworm, the Negro — just get down the Encyclopaedia and continue the list!

I forgot, there are a dozen other kinds of activities, such as American marriages, which they always want the Ambassador to attend; getting them out of jail when they are jugged (I have an American woman on my hands now, whose children come to see me every day); looking after the American insane; helping Americans move the bones of their ancestors; interpreting the income-tax law; receiving medals for Americans; hearing American fiddlers, pianists, players; sitting for American sculptors and photographers; sending telegrams for property owners in Mexico; reading letters from thousands of people who have shares in estates here; writing letters of introduction; getting tickets to the House Gallery; getting seats in the Abbey; going with people to this, that and t'other; getting tickets to the races, the art-galleries, the House of Lords; answering fool questions about the United States put by Englishmen. With a military attache, a naval attache, three secretaries, a private secretary, two automobiles, Alice's private secretary, a veterinarian, an immigration agent, consuls everywhere, a despatch agent, lawyers, doctors; messengers — they keep us all busy. A woman turned up dying the other day. I sent for a big doctor. She got well. As if that wasn't enough, both the woman and the doctor had to come and thank me (fifteen minutes each). Then each wrote a letter!

Then there are ... Rhodes Scholars from Oxford ... women who wish to go to court ... Negroes from Liberia ... passports, passports to sign ... opera singers going to the United States; artists who have painted some American portraits — don't you see?

Special Diplomats. In addition to the ambassadors regularly stationed in foreign capitals, those who hold certain other diplomatic posts are also given the rank of ambassador — for example, the American member of the North Atlantic Treaty (NATO) Council, the United States Representative to the UN in New York, and the Chief of the United States Mission to the International Atomic Energy Agency in Vienna. On various occasions, individuals are appointed to the *personal* rank of ambassador to undertake special assignments from the President.

Ministers. Historically, ministers have been sent to represent the United States in countries of lesser importance; but in recent years this country has raised each of its ministerial posts to the status of ambassadorial assignments as a gesture of international goodwill. Ministers, who are also appointed by the President and confirmed by the Senate, are officially outranked by ambassadors; their official residences are known as legations rather than embassies.

Until recently, *Chiefs of Missions* (ambassadors or ministers) received salaries much smaller than those paid by other great nations. Even today it is impossible for one without personal wealth to represent us at a major post, for example in London. The salaries paid today range from $36,000 to $42,500 plus various expense allowances.

Assistants. At each embassy a *counselor* advises the ambassador on matters of internal law and diplomatic practice and one or more *diplomatic secretaries* assist him in his duties. His staff also consists of several technical experts, clerks, interpreters, and others. The more responsible of these aides are drawn from the Foreign Service, but some are alien employees recruited on the scene. Most American embassies have one or more military attaches assigned from the Army and Air Force Departments. In those nations which are naval powers there are also naval attaches assigned from the Navy Department. These attaches and those from other departments, Labor, for example, are subject to the orders of their own departments.

Let us take a military attache to illustrate the duties performed by a departmental attache. He is military adviser to the ambassador or minister; he collects information on the military situation in the country to which he is accredited; he is constantly on the alert for new ideas which can be applied to our own army; and he makes confidential reports, through the diplomatic pouch, to the Army Department where information digests of world conditions are kept.

While ambassadors and ministers are sometimes political appointees of the President, more than 10,000 highly trained career men assist these diplomats and man the consulates. It is from this group of Foreign Service officers that the candidates for the top positions are increasingly being drawn. Many are now serving as ambassadors and ministers. Entrance examinations for the Foreign Service are difficult, but promotion comes on merit. The salaries today (1971) range from $7639 for new Foreign Service officers to as high as $33,495, plus allowances, leaves, and a retirement and disability program.

Consular Service. The Consular Service is a part of the Foreign Service. Its agents are appointed by the President with the consent of the Senate from those who have passed civil service examinations. They are commercial agents, "America's lookouts on the watchtowers of international trade." The United States maintains some 160 consular offices in major cities around the world.

Consuls perform a great variety of duties, primarily commercial in nature. Their chief task lies in the promotion of American trade and commerce abroad by discovering new promised lands of commercial opportunity. They answer inquiries addressed to them by American exporters and importers and send reports regarding foreign markets for American products to the State Department. This information includes the special demands of local markets due to prevailing customs or prejudices or to unusual shortage of crops; changes in foreign laws bearing on commerce, such as customs regulations, patent laws, and food laws; and foreign business methods.

Consuls also enforce customs regulations of the United States, assist in excluding prohibited classes of immigrants, and aid stranded or wrecked vessels and shipwrecked American seamen. They *visa* (approve) passports for aliens coming to the United States, and some may issue passports to Americans abroad. They assist American citizens in legal transactions of all sorts, taking oaths and depositions and even acting as witnesses to marriages. The consul has some jurisdiction over whatever relates to the internal economy of American vessels. He settles disputes among masters, officers, and men.

Consular officials are not entitled to diplomatic immunity, but treaties usually exempt them from arrest in civil cases and also guarantee the protection of their archives. An American consulate in an unstable state is usually a fairly safe place in times of disturbances.

The Foreign Service Institute. Each new Foreign Service officer is first assigned to three months of study at the Foreign Service Institute in Washington, D.C. Run by experienced "FSO's," the Foreign Service Institute has a full-time faculty and draws visiting lecturers from government, business, and the academic world. In addition to a course in diplomatic and consular practice for all new officers, it offers advanced and specialized training for all FSO's throughout their careers—including work in several languages and special seminars in such topics as communist strategy and the peaceful uses of the atom.

Passports. The Passport Office regulates the issuing of passports. A passport is a certificate used to identify a citizen of one country when he is traveling or living in another country. It permits him to enjoy all the privileges that international law, treaties, and the prestige of his native country can insure.

An American citizen who wants to obtain a passport may apply to the Passport Office in Washington, D.C., at one of the passport agencies maintained in a few principal cities, or to a clerk of a United States District Court or any State court of record. The application must be accompanied by a certificate from a reliable witness, two photos, and a $10 fee.

Within the United States passports are granted by the Passport Office, in the territories by the governor, and abroad by the higher ranking consuls. Passports are valid for three years and may be renewed by an American consul for two more years.

A *visa* should not be confused with a passport. A visa is a permit to enter another country and must be obtained from the country a person wants to enter.

THE NATURE OF FOREIGN POLICY

A nation's foreign policy is actually many different policies on many different topics. It is made up of all the stands that a nation takes on a wide variety of problems arising out of a large number of situations. Insofar as the United States is concerned, the term *foreign policy* refers to the official American positions on such matters as international trade, disarmament, nuclear weapons testing, control of the Suez Canal, freedom of the seas, military aid, fishing rights in the North Atlantic, aid to underdeveloped countries, colonialism, nationalism, the United Nations, collective security

Safeguarding passports and acquiring visas are responsibilities of the traveler. The bearer of an American passport can be a "good-will ambassador" for our country. Poland issued the visa (right) for a person to visit there. (Wes Kemp)

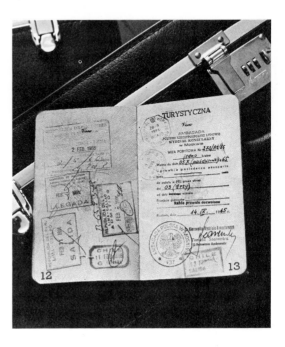

agreements, cultural exchanges, immigration, and many others.

Obviously, some of our policies remain fixed (largely unchanged) year in and year out. For example, an insistence on freedom of the seas has marked American foreign policy from our very beginning. Other policies are flexible, subject to change as the circumstances involved change. Thus, thirty years ago opposition to the German and Japanese dictatorships was a basic aspect of American foreign policy; but today West Germany and Japan are among our staunchest allies in the struggle against world communism.

Foreign policy is not made in a vacuum. It would be ideal if the President and his advisers were able to sit down, free from all outside pressures and influences, to map out our foreign policies. Unfortunately, many factors over which the United States has little or no control play a large part in the shaping of policies and cannot be ignored. For example, the Soviet Union's military strength and that of Communist China, and the nature of the relations between those two powers, are matters which bear heavily on our policies but over which we have practically no control.

Sometimes we are able to take the initiative in international relations. We are able to introduce new policies and programs that win friends for the United States and heighten American prestige abroad. Thus, the decision to help rebuild the war-torn countries of Europe and restore their shattered economies after World War II (the Marshall Plan) was a bold, effective action which did much to foster among the western democracies trust and confidence in the United States.

At other times our foreign policy must be defensive in nature. It must be adjusted to meet a change in the policy of some other country. Thus, our decision to "contain" the spread of communism, initiated by the Truman Doctrine, came in reaction to the Soviet Union's aggressive policy of expansion after World War II.

SOURCES OF FOREIGN POLICY

Although the President and the Secretary of State are the principal figures in the making of foreign policy, it would be naive to think that they are the only sources for policy. They have the legal responsibility for the making and conduct of policy, but major contributions come from many sources.

The people themselves exert powerful, if indirect, influences. Policies contrary to widely held popular opinion would undoubtedly work to the disadvantage of the President who pursued them. For example, no President could pursue policies sympathetic to the aims of Communist China today — even if one could imagine a President who would be so inclined. To foster policies so sharply contrary to public opinion would, at the very least, bring overwhelming defeat to the President and his party at the next election — though in all likelihood he would be impeached before then.

Congress exercises important controls over the making and conduct of foreign policy. Through its powers in foreign affairs, through its power of the purse, and through investigations by its committees, Congress influences almost every facet of our foreign relations.

Then, too, our foreign policy is profoundly affected by the actions of other governments. As we have already noted, foreign policy is often defensive in nature. We must always bear in mind the effects our policies have on our allies as well as on our opponents.

The State Department is, of course, *the agency* primarily responsible for the making and conduct of foreign policy, but many other agencies also participate. The Department of Defense, for example, is directly concerned with foreign policy. It is charged with protecting national security. Foreign policy and national defense are but two sides of the same coin. (See Chapter 21.) The National Security Council, his many special assistants, and members of the Cabinet all advise the President in foreign policy.

A large number of other agencies participate in our foreign relations, too. For example: the Immigration and Naturalization Service in the Department of Justice deals with citizens of other countries; the Bureau of Customs in the Treasury Department deals with imports from other nations and maintains agents abroad to detect smuggling; the Coast Guard, in the Department of Transportation in peacetime, maintains an iceberg patrol in the North Atlantic to protect the shipping of all nations; the Public Health Service in the Department of Health, Education, and Welfare works with other governments and international organizations on world health problems; and the Bureau of International Commerce in the Commerce Department promotes American trade abroad.

As a matter of fact, it is not stretching matters *too* much to say that *all* our governmental agencies are in some way involved in foreign relations. This is so because today it is increasingly more difficult to draw a clear and distinct line between *foreign* and *domestic* affairs.

Take the Interstate Commerce Commission as a simple example. Its major function is to regulate freight rates in interstate commerce. The cost for shipping a carload of cashmere sweaters made in Portland, Oregon, to a department store in Dallas, Texas, enters into the price the store charges for each sweater. The price charged for each domestically produced cashmere sweater has a direct bearing on the sales of cashmere sweaters imported from Scotland or other foreign nations.

Special note should be made of three agencies directly and immediately concerned with foreign affairs: the super-secret Central Intelligence Agency, the United States Information Agency, and the United States Arms Control and Disarmament Agency.

The Central Intelligence Agency. The *CIA,* our chief "cloak-and-dagger" agency, functions under the National Security Council (page 307). It collects and evaluates the information which is so vital to the making of foreign policy decisions. Its data is gathered by its own secret agents and from all other federal agencies, our allies, refugees, foreign journals, and every other possible source. The nature of its methods and the contents of its reports are such closely-kept secrets that even Congress shies away from a close look at its activities. CIA officials occasionally brief key members of Congress on foreign policy developments, but these sessions are always held behind closed doors.

The United States Information Agency. The *USIA,* with over 200 field offices around the globe, operates the "Voice of America" and conducts other programs to combat the

USIA Information Centers, in nearly 100 countries overseas, help to develop understanding of the United States and our foreign policies. In reading rooms, such as this one in Malaya, visitors come to learn more about our country.

huge communist campaign of propaganda against the United States. In cooperation with the State Department it broadcasts the official views of our Government, presents news and feature programs on the American way of life, and attempts to promote our friendship with other peoples. Its shortwave broadcasts go out from New York in some forty languages through transmitters in the United States and relay stations in Manila, Honolulu, and Munich. It also operates a floating transmitter to help broadcast behind the Iron Curtain.

Motion pictures, libraries, and the exchange of persons also are used to promote international understanding and good will. For example, we are engaged in a vast international student exchange program. Thousands of foreign students are now studying in American colleges and observing various phases of our national life. At the same time, thousands of Americans are studying abroad. This exchange program is intended to spread understanding between the United States and our world neighbors.

The United States Arms Control and Disarmament Agency. The *USACDA* functions in a very critical segment of the foreign policy field. It is responsible for the preparation and management of American participation in international disarmament negotiations. Its Director also serves as the President's principal adviser in all matters relating to the subject.

A major share of the Agency's work thus far has centered on nuclear test ban and disarmament meetings, held at Geneva intermittently since 1958. The late President Kennedy dramatized the crucial importance of the Agency's field when he observed: "Mankind will put an end to war — or war will put an end to mankind."

CONCEPT BUILDING

Key Concepts

The importance of our foreign relations and of the manner in which they are conducted cannot be overstated. The ways in which the might and influence of the United States are used in today's "one world" affect the fate of all mankind.

The President is the nation's chief diplomat; the Secretary of State and the Department of State are his "right hand" in the formulation and conduct of foreign policy. Under the Secretary of State the State Department is organized on a geographic and functional basis. Our diplomatic agents abroad look to the Secretary of State and his staff in Washington for information and instructions. The Foreign Service, from ambassadors, ministers, and consular officers down to the lowliest clerks, represent the goals and serve the interests of the United States in other countries.

A nation's foreign policy is composed of many different policies on many separate subjects; it is made up of each of the positions a nation takes on a wide variety of problems arising out of a large number of situations. Some policies are relatively permanent in nature, while others change as the circumstances with which they are involved change. No policy is made in a vacuum; rather, each is influenced by innumerable factors. Some policies represent the taking of the initiative in international affairs, while others must be defensive in nature.

Although the President and the Secretary of State are the principal figures in the making of foreign policy, Congress, public opinion, and the actions of other governments have a significant influence on policy content, too. No sharp and definitive line can be drawn between foreign and domestic matters today. Although the State Department is the agency with primary responsibility in the field, many governmental agencies participate in the conduct of our foreign relations. In fact, it is not too much to say that *all* governmental agencies are in some way involved in the field.

Important Terms

ambassador	diplomatic immunity	international law	passport
attache	embassy	legation	*persona non grata*
charge d'affaires	foreign policy	minister	right of legation
consul	Foreign Service	non-aligned nations	visa

Questions for Inquiry and Review

1. In what ways may it be said that today we live in "one world"?

2. In what ways may it be said, on the other hand, that we do not?

3. Why does the Secretary of State rank first among Cabinet members?

4. What is the Secretary of State's primary responsibility?

5. Why is the State Department organized along geographic and functional lines?

6. What are the principal duties of an ambassador?

7. Why does the United States maintain no legations abroad today?

8. Most of the duties performed by consular officers are primarily of what nature?

9. How does a passport differ from a visa?

10. Of what in overall terms is a nation's foreign policy composed?

11. Why is it an error to conceive of the formulation and execution of foreign policy only in terms of the President and the State Department?

12. Why may it be said that *all* governmental agencies are, in one way or another, involved in the conduct of the nation's foreign relations?

For Further Inquiry

1. The Constitution grants exclusive power to the National Government in the field of foreign affairs. Do you think that it was wise of the Founding Fathers to exclude the States from any role whatever in the field?

2. It has often been noted that the only checks upon the exercise of power by the National Government in the field of foreign affairs are political, not legal, in character. Do you think that this is either wise or proper in a nation with a governmental system founded

upon the principles of popular sovereignty and limited government?

3. In a leading case involving the extent of the National Government's power in the field of foreign affairs (*United States* v. *Curtiss-Wright Export Corporation,* 1936) the Supreme Court declared:

> The powers to declare and wage war, to make treaties, to maintain diplomatic relations with other sovereignties, if they had never been mentioned in the Constitution,

would have been vested in the Federal Government as necessary concomitants of nationality.

Why would this have been so?

4. Constitutionally, the executive and legislative branches share power in the field of foreign affairs. What factors have led, in fact, to presidential supremacy in the field?

5. Do you agree with some columnists and some other commentators who argue that the influence of public opinion on the making of foreign policy is a source of great potential danger to us? Is it wise for Americans to look at foreign policy largely in terms of principles and ideals?

Suggested Activities

1. Stage a debate or class forum on one of the following questions: (a) *Resolved,* That the Secretary of State should be chosen by direct popular vote. (b) *Resolved,* That all ambassadors should be drawn from the ranks of the Foreign Service rather than be the subjects of presidential patronage. (c) *Resolved,* That the consent of the House of Representatives as well as that of the Senate should be required for the approval of treaties made by the President.

2. Write a report on our foreign relations during the term of a particular Secretary of State.

3. Give a biographical talk on one of the following Secretaries of State: James Monroe, John Quincy Adams, Daniel Webster, William Seward, John Hay, Elihu Root, Cordell Hull.

4. Invite a person in the Foreign Service or a former Foreign Service officer to speak to the class on career opportunities in the Foreign Service. (Descriptive material, including sample questions from the Foreign Service entrance examination, can be obtained from the Director, Office of Public Services, Bureau of Public Affairs, Department of State, Washington, D.C., 20520.)

5. Obtain information on the work of and opportunities for service in the Peace Corps from the Director, Office of Public Information Peace Corps, Washington, D.C., 20525.

6. Draw up a list of as many examples as you can of the ways in which the content and conduct of the nation's foreign policies are reflected in the everyday life of your community.

Suggested Reading

ACHESON, DEAN, "Memories of Joe McCarthy," *Harper's,* October, 1969.

APPLETON, SHELDON, *United States Foreign Policy.* Little, Brown, 1968.

ASTOR, GERALD, "Henry Kissinger: Strategist in the White House Basement," *Look,* August 12, 1969.

CLARK, BLAKE, "U.S. Diplomat No. 1," *Reader's Digest,* December, 1969.

DULLES, ELEANOR L., *American Foreign Policy in the Making.* Harper & Row, 1968.

HARR, JOHN E., *The Professional Diplomat.* Princeton, 1969.

MANCHESTER, WILLIAM, "The U.S. Embassy: Our Man in Paris," *Holiday,* March, 1969.

NEVIN, DAVID, "Autocrat in the Action Area," *Life,* September 5, 1969.

ORGANSKI, A. F., *World Politics.* Knopf, 1968.

RADWAY, LAURENCE I., *Foreign Policy and National Defense.* Scott, Foresman, 1969.

ROSS, IRWIN, "America's 'Mr. Catastrophe,'" *Reader's Digest,* October 1968.

SPANNER, JOHN W., *American Foreign Policy Since World War II.* Praeger, 1968.

"Who's Making Foreign Policy?" *U.S. News,* April 7, 1969.

AMERICAN FOREIGN POLICY

Today we are faced with the pre-eminent fact that, if civilization is to survive, we must cultivate the science of human relationships—the ability of all peoples, of all kinds, to live together and work together, in the same world, at peace.

Franklin D. Roosevelt

❊❊❊ How can the United States best provide for and maintain its own security?

❊❊❊ If the United States and the Soviet Union shared the same political and economic ideologies would the conflict between them be largely eliminated? Why or why not?

❊❊❊ Why have the extraordinary advances man has made in transportation and communication over the past century failed to produce "one world"?

Today—as, indeed, through all of our history—the foreign policy of this country is directed toward one constant and overriding end: the maintenance of the security of the United States. At the opening of Chapter 18 we emphasized the obvious but vitally significant fact: In this day and age no matter is—or possibly can be—of greater or more critical importance to the American people than the nature and conduct of American foreign policy. In this chapter we shall turn first to a brief account of the historical development of that policy and then to a survey of its present-day content.

HISTORICAL DEVELOPMENT

The Early Years. From its beginnings and for a period of 150 years this nation's posture in international affairs was characterized by a policy of *isolationism*—that is, by a refusal to become generally involved in the affairs of the rest of the world. Isolationism was born in the earliest years of our history. President George Washington, in his Farewell Address in 1796, reminded his countrymen that:

> Europe has a set of primary interests, which to us have none, or a very remote relation. Hence she must be engaged in frequent controversies, the causes of which are essentially foreign to our concerns. Hence, therefore, it must be unwise in us to implicate ourselves, by artificial ties, in the ordinary vicissitudes of her politics, or the ordinary combinations or collisions of her friendships or enmities.

He advised the young republic to have "as little political connection as possible" with foreign nations—"to steer clear of permanent alliances with any portion of the foreign world." In 1801 Thomas Jefferson added his warning against "entangling alliances."

At the time, and for decades to come, isolation seemed a wise policy: the United States was a new and a relatively weak nation, with

MONROE DOCTRINE REJECTS—1962. President Kennedy invoked the Monroe Doctrine against the Soviet Union during the Cuban missile crisis (see page 342) and forced them to withdraw their offensive weapons. (James Dobbins, Boston Herald-Traveler)

at a stroke doubled the size of the country. With the Florida Purchase of 1819 we completed our continental expansion to the south.

The *Monroe Doctrine,* proclaimed by James Monroe in a message to Congress in 1823, gave new expression to the policy of isolationism. A wave of revolutions had swept Latin America, destroying the old Spanish and Portuguese empires. The prospect that other European powers would seek to aid those nations to recover their lost possessions posed a threat to our own security and a challenge to our economic interests. In his message President Monroe declared it to be our intention to remain out of the affairs of Europe; but he warned the nations of Europe, including Russia which then controlled Alaska, that the United States would regard:

> any attempt on their part to extend their system to any portion of this hemisphere as dangerous to our peace and safety. With the existing colonies and dependencies of any European power we have not interfered and shall not interfere. But with the governments who have declared their independence and maintained it, and whose independence we have, on great consideration and on just principles, acknowledged, we could not view any interposition for the purpose of oppressing them, or controlling in any other manner their destiny, by any European power in any other light than as the manifestation of an unfriendly disposition toward the United States.

problems of its own, a continent to settle, and the Atlantic and Pacific Oceans to separate it from the rest of the world. The policy did not demand a *complete* insulation, however. From the first, the United States accepted the fact of its existence as a member of the family of nations—exchanging diplomatic representatives, making treaties, building an extensive foreign commerce, and otherwise participating in world affairs as and when it seemed in its interests to do so.

We began our westward expansion, and at the same time the elimination of European influence from this continent, almost at once. The Louisiana Purchase in 1803 embraced all of the vast area drained by the Mississippi and

The Monroe Doctrine is not law; rather, it is a self-defense policy—a policy of "America for the Americans" that opposes any non-American encroachment on the independence of any country in the Western Hemisphere. It has been supported by each Congress and every President for nearly a century and a half. At first, most Latin Americans paid little attention to the Monroe Doctrine. They knew that it was the Royal Navy and Great Britain's interest in their trade rather than the influence of the United States and Monroe's paper pronouncement that protected them. Later, as the United States became more powerful, Latin Americans came to regard it as a selfish policy. They felt that we were more concerned with our own security and commercial fortune than with their independence. Happily, matters have taken a brighter turn in recent decades, as we shall see.

Continued Expansion. While the United States remained aloof from the affairs of Europe, we continued to fill out the continent. Texas was annexed in 1845. We obtained the Oregon Country by treaty with Great Britain in 1846. Mexico ceded California and the land between after its defeat in the Mexican War of 1846–1848. The southwestern limits of the United States were rounded out by the Gadsden Purchase in 1853. In that year we bought from Mexico a strip of territory in what is now the southern part of Arizona and New Mexico as the best rail route to the Pacific.

In 1867 we purchased Alaska from Russia to become a colonial power. In that same year the Monroe Doctrine got its first real test. While we were beset with conflict at home, Napoleon III had enthroned Prince Maximilian of Austria as Emperor of Mexico. We backed the Mexicans in forcing the withdrawal of France and the downfall of the Maximilian regime.

The United States a World Power. The United States emerged as a first-class world power just before the end of the nineteenth century. American feeling against Spain's mistreatment of its colonial possessions in the Caribbean had produced an explosive situation. When the *U.S.S. Maine* was mysteriously sunk in Havana Harbor on February 15, 1898, the United States and Spain went to war. The actual fighting of the Spanish-American War lasted only four months. With Spain decisively defeated, we gained the Philippines and Guam in the Pacific and Puerto Rico in the Caribbean. Cuba became independent, under American protection, in 1899. At the same time, we annexed the Hawaiian Islands.

HANDS OFF! Theodore Roosevelt's "big stick" policy put stronger teeth in the Monroe Doctrine and prevented European intervention in the Caribbean in 1904. (The Bettmann Archive)

By 1900, then, the United States had become a colonial power with interests extending 3000 miles across the continent, to Alaska and the Arctic, to the tip of Latin America, and clear across the Pacific to the Philippines.

The Good Neighbor Policy. Our relations with Latin America have ebbed and flowed. The Monroe Doctrine has always served two purposes: (1) it has guaranteed the independence of Latin America, and (2) it has protected our position in the New World.

The threat of European intervention, which gave rise to the doctrine, declined in the last half of the nineteenth century. It was replaced by problems within the hemisphere. Political instability, revolutions, unpaid debts to foreign countries, and injuries to citizens and property of the United States and other countries plagued Latin America.

Under the Roosevelt Corollary of 1904 the United States began to police the Western Hemisphere. For example, in 1902 British and German ships blockaded the Venezuelan coast to force that country to pay debts it owed. The United States stepped in and forced a settlement. Carrying a "big stick," the United States used marines to police customhouses and trouble spots throughout Central America. We stabilized political and financial conditions, settled boundary disputes, protected foreign lives and property, paid off foreign debts through customs collection, and generally maintained order. In 1903 Panama revolted and became independent of Colombia, with our blessings. In the same year we gained the right to construct a canal across the Panamanian Isthmus, which opened in 1914. In 1917 we purchased the Virgin Islands from Denmark to help guard the Panama Canal. Latin Americans were resentful and suspicious of our actions, even though they benefited greatly. They complained about what they called "Yankee imperialism" and "dollar diplomacy."

In the late 1920's and early 1930's our Latin-American policies took a decisive turn. We began a conscious effort to "win friends and influence people" to the south. The Roosevelt Corollary was abandoned, and what Franklin D. Roosevelt termed the Good Neighbor Policy was begun. New life was breathed into the Pan American Union, first founded in 1890 and now known as the Organization of American States (OAS).

Today we and most of our Latin-American neighbors are partners in "hemispheric solidarity." The central proviso in the Monroe Doctrine—the warning against foreign encroachments in this hemisphere—is now enshrined in the Rio Treaty and is enforced by both the United States *and* the OAS. That the principle remains a vital part of American foreign policy was made abundantly clear to the Soviet Union during the Cuban missile crisis in 1962.

The Open Door in China. While American foreign policy interests were directed primarily toward Europe and Latin America in the first century of the nation's history, we were also concerned in the Far East. Forty-five years before the United States acquired territory in the far Pacific, Admiral Matthew C. Perry had opened Japan to American trade (1854). In 1899 we found our commercial interests in the Orient seriously threatened. Great Britain, France, Germany, and Japan were on the verge of grabbing slices of the coast of China as their own private trading preserves. Secretary of State John Hay announced American insistence on an "open door" to all nations trading with China and our insistence on the preservation of China's independence and sovereignty over its own territory.

The other powers came to accept the American position, although our relations with Japan worsened from then until the climax at Pearl Harbor in 1941. The Chinese remained grateful to us, and World War I and World War II strengthened the open door concept. But, since the Communists took over in China in 1949, our relations there have sunk to the lowest depths. We do not recognize the Chinese Communists as constituting the lawful government of China. We recognize and continue to support the Nationalist Government of Chiang Kai-shek on the Island of Taiwan (Formosa).

World War I and the Return to Isolationism. Germany's submarine campaign against American shipping forced the United States out of its isolationist cocoon in 1917. We entered World War I to "make the world safe for democracy."

After the defeat of Germany and the Central Powers, however, we retreated from the involvements brought on by the war. We refused to join the League of Nations, conceived by President Woodrow Wilson. Europe's problems and those of the rest of the world, so many Americans thought, should be no concern of ours.

Americans and Russians were allied against the Axis during World War II. Since then the United States has met the aggressive Soviet threat with a foreign policy to contain Communist expansion. (Wide World Photos)

The rise of Mussolini in Italy, of Hitler in Germany, and of the militarists in Japan cast a dark cloud on the horizon. But for twenty years following World War I we continued to "wrap our two oceans around us."

World War II. It took the coming of World War II to awaken us finally and fully to the fallacies of isolationism in the modern world. Most Americans were pro-Ally at the start of the war in 1939, but our policy was to stay out of the war if at all possible. While the official position of the United States was one of neutrality, large scale aid was nonetheless provided to the Allies through such devices as the Lend-Lease Act. Under that 1941 law the President was authorized to "sell, transfer title to, exchange, lease, lend, or otherwise dispose of defense articles" to any countries judged vital to our own security.

With the sudden Japanese attack on Pearl Harbor, December 7, 1941, all thoughts of neutrality vanished. From then until the war ended in 1945, we fought side by side with our allies in Europe and the Pacific. Our forces fought and defeated the Axis Powers (Germany, Italy, and Japan) on battlefields around the world. During the war we were the "arsenal of democracy." Through Lend-Lease our allies received nearly $50,000,000,000 in food, munitions, medicines, clothing, and other supplies.

AMERICAN FOREIGN POLICY TODAY

The years since 1945 have been marked by a fundamental change in the role of the United States in world affairs, and with this shift has come a transformation in American foreign policy. Within the span of a very few years, this nation grew from a position as *one* of the world's major powers to its present role as *the* responsible leader of the world's free nations. We know now that, even if we wanted to, we cannot shut ourselves away from the rest of the world. From the isolationism of former years, our policy has become one of *global,* full-scale participation in international affairs.

Yet, while specific American foreign policies reflect this great change, the continuing, overall goal of our foreign policy remains as it has throughout our history: the maintenance of our national security. We hope, pray, and work for peace. But we recognize the inescapable fact that there can be no lasting peace for us unless and until there is a just and lasting peace between all nations and for all mankind.

While we strive for peace, we also recognize another inescapable fact. The years since World War II have taught us that we can remain free and we can work for a just and lasting peace only so long as we remain strong. The various aspects of our foreign policy now to be outlined are each aimed at achieving the overall goal of that policy.

The Policy of Deterrence. One of the basic planks in current American foreign policy is that of *deterrence*—that is, the policy of making ourselves and our allies so strong that our very strength will deter aggression. We hope that our military and economic might will make the Soviet Union, Communist China, or any other potential aggressor realize that to attack the United States would be suicidal. In President Nixon's words:

> We cannot expect to make everyone our friend but we can try to make no one our enemy. But...let us leave no doubt that we will be as strong as we need to be for as long as we need to be.

In effect, we have taken a page from our own revolutionary history: "Put your trust in God, my boys, but keep your powder dry."

Peace through Collective Security and the United Nations. We live in "one world" in the sense that no nation can live in peace and prosperity while others are at war or in want. Hence, *collective security*—the preserving of international order through the united efforts of free nations—has become a corner-

stone in our foreign policy. Therefore, in 1945 we were determined not to repeat the basic error of 1919–1920 when we refused to join the League of Nations. We took the lead in creating the United Nations, dedicated "to save succeeding generations from the scourge of war...and to maintain international peace and security."

Through the UN, other international organizations, direct negotiations with the Soviet Union—in short, through every available means, we have sought and seek ways to lessen international tensions and to bring the world closer to peace. Thus, we have proposed steps to strengthen the UN. We have made continuing efforts to achieve an effective disarmament agreement, one which contains effective provisions for inspection and control to insure that it will be observed by all nations. We have given wholehearted support to the improvement of international law. We have promoted cultural exchange programs with the Soviet Union and other nations. We have pioneered the development and sharing of the peaceful uses of the atom. In these and many other ways we seek to promote peace.

In our search for collective security we have also made a number of *regional alliances* (mutual defense pacts) with several friendly nations around the world. See the map on page 347.

Resisting Communist Aggression. Another pillar of our policy is that of resistance to communist aggression. As President, General Eisenhower stated the root of our policy in these terms:

> The threat to our safety, and to the hope of a peaceful world, can be simply stated It is communist imperialism.

We had hoped to work with the Russians through the UN to build the peace after World War II. It was soon clear, however, that the Communists had not abandoned their plans of world domination. At the Big Three conferences at Yalta and Potsdam in 1945, Stalin had guaranteed free elections in occupied East

Germany and the nations of Eastern Europe. Instead, puppet communist regimes were quickly established, and an "iron curtain" was clamped tight around an empire of Soviet-dominated satellites By 1949, when the Chinese Communists succeeded in overrunning the mainland of China, postwar communist aggression had brought over 700,000,000 people and 7,500,000 square miles of territory under its control.

The Truman Doctrine. The critical turning point in American policy toward the designs of the Soviet Union came in the early months of 1947. Greece and Turkey were in desperate straits; without immediate and substantial aid from the United States, they were certain to fall under Soviet control. The response was immediate. At President Truman's request Congress quickly provided for economic and military aid to both nations. In his message to Congress, President Truman declared that it was:

> the policy of the United States to support free peoples who are resisting attempted subjugation by armed minorities or outside pressures.

This statement and the actions which followed it came to be known as the *Truman Doctrine.* It is clear now that its enunciation, March 12, 1947, marked the beginning of the policy followed ever since in combating communist aggression around the world.

The Truman Doctrine has been applied many times and in many places over the years since 1947. Our military effort and other aid in support of South Viet Nam is the leading illustration of the point today, of course. But there are many others; for example: the Navy's Seventh Fleet has patrolled the Formosa Strait continuously since 1950, to forestall a Red Chinese invasion of the Nationalist held island of Formosa; similarly, Army and Air Force units have shielded isolated West Berlin against a Soviet-East German threat since the blockade of 1948.

In 1948–1949, the United States "airlift" carried tons of needed supplies to West Berlin and broke the Soviet blockade of that isolated city. (U.S. Air Force)

Communist Aggression. Each of the major clashes of the Cold War thus far—in Korea, Cuba, and Viet Nam—furnish prime examples of collective security and resistance to communist aggression.

Korea. The Korean War began on June 25, 1950, when Communist North Korea attacked the UN-sponsored Republic of South Korea. The UN immediately called upon its members to aid in repelling the invaders, and American forces went into action at once. The war pitted the UN Command (largely American and South Korean forces, but with contingents from fifteen other nations [1]) against Soviet-trained

---

[1] Australia, Belgium, Canada, Colombia, Ethiopia, France, Great Britain, Greece, Luxembourg, the Netherlands, New Zealand, the Philippine Republic, Thailand, Turkey, and the Union of South Africa.

and -equipped North Korean and Communist Chinese forces. The fighting ended with an armistice signed on July 27, 1953. Final peace terms have not yet been agreed to, however; and American and South Korean troops still stand guard against any renewed aggression.

The bitter Korean conflict did not end in a clear-cut UN victory in the sense that the enemy was beaten to his knees. The war cost the United States 157,530 casualties, including 33,629 combat deaths, and over $20,000,000,-000. South Korea suffered many hundreds of thousands of casualties, and nearly all of Korea was laid to waste.

Still, much was accomplished. The enemy was repulsed, and with far heavier losses. *For the first time in history* armed forces fought under an international flag to resist aggression. In the hope of preventing World War III, communist encroachment had to be stopped somewhere, and soon; there is no telling how far it might have gone had South Korea not been defended. Only history can judge how effective the war was in preventing another global conflict. But the Korean War did furnish the spark which finally aroused and united the free world.

Cuba. The United States has challenged the USSR often, and at many places, in the Cold War. Nowhere has it done so more forcefully than in the Cuban missile crisis in the fall of 1962.

Cuba slipped into the Soviet orbit not long after the Castro dictatorship gained power in 1959. The United States severed diplomatic relations with that regime in early 1961. The action came after a series of provocations, including the seizure of American properties, mass executions of anti-Castro Cubans, and vicious propaganda attacks on this country. The island was drawn even deeper into the Soviet sphere after an abortive invasion attempt by American-trained Cuban exiles in April 1961. The invaders, lacking air support, were quickly crushed by Soviet-equipped Castro forces.

By mid-1962 huge quantities of Soviet arms and thousands of Soviet "technicians" were being sent to Cuba. The Soviet Union insisted that the military buildup was purely defensive, intended to protect Cuba from a supposed threat of American invasion.

Suddenly, in October, the already massive buildup became unmistakably offensive in character. Despite repeated Soviet assurances to the contrary, aerial photographs revealed missile installations capable of launching nuclear strikes against this country and much of Latin America.

With this development, President Kennedy moved quickly. On October 22 he declared that the United States would not "tolerate deliberate deception and offensive threats by any nation, large or small." He ordered a quarantine to prevent further deliveries of offensive weapons to Cuba, demanded the withdrawal of those already there, and directed that a close aerial inspection of the island be continued.

For several days the world seemed perilously close to all-out war. On October 28, however, with UN prompting, but especially through an exchange of letters between President Kennedy and Premier Khrushchev, the Soviet Union began to back down. Rather than risk all, so far from home, the missile installations were dismantled, and the weapons were returned to the USSR.

The United States is now officially committed to the elimination of communist influence in Cuba. Still, despite the success of our firm stand in 1962, a communist-dominated Cuba under Fidel Castro, bolstered by Soviet military and economic aid, remains as a continuing threat to our peace and security—and, literally, on our doorstep.

South Viet Nam. Our commitment to the policy of blocking communist aggression is most clearly demonstrated today in South Viet Nam. There—for the second time since the end of World War II—the Armed Forces of the United States are involved in a direct military confrontation with a communist enemy. Our now massive participation in the Vietnamese war began in the early 1950's. American involvement rose sharply in the early 1960's, and especially in the period 1964 to 1968.

The United States is involved in South Viet Nam for several reasons. We are there to resist aggression—because, as President Johnson declared:

> We have learned that to yield to aggression brings only greater threats and more destructive war. To stand firm is the only guarantee of lasting peace.

We are there because South Viet Nam is crucial to the security of all Southeast Asia. Were it to fall to the Communists, that whole region of the world could become prey to Red Chinese domination and subjugation. The Southeast Asia Treaty (page 348) protects South Viet Nam, Cambodia, and Laos as well as the members of SEATO.

Our presence is also based upon our insistence upon the rule of law in world affairs. The long record of communist aggression in Viet Nam is in patent violation of international law. Specifically, it violates the ban of the use of force in the UN Charter and in the Geneva Accords of 1954. It was in the latter agreement that the Republic of Viet Nam (South Viet Nam), the Democratic Republic of Viet Nam (North Viet Nam), and the neighboring states of Laos and Cambodia were created out of that region which had been French Indo-China.

Then, too, the United States is in South Viet Nam at the request of South Viet Nam itself. President Eisenhower first responded to that request in 1954 when he pledged the United States:

> to assist the Government of Viet Nam in developing and maintaining a strong, viable state, capable of resisting attempted subversion or aggression through military means.

At the President's direction, American military advisers and aid were sent to bolster the South Vietnamese armed forces in their fight with the Viet Cong—the communist guerrilla elements in South Viet Nam which are trained, supplied, and directed from North Viet Nam with the support of the Communist Chinese regime.

The Viet Cong effort had become a full-scale guerrilla war by 1961, replete with bombings, kidnappings, torture, assassinations, and other terroristic activities. The Communists label the struggle a "war of national liberation"—in their idiom the term for any war which furthers the communist design for world conquest.

President Kennedy reaffirmed the pledge to preserve the security of South Viet Nam in 1961. The military aid and adviser programs were expanded, American advisers began to accompany South Vietnamese troops in combat, and Air Force helicopters were directed to fly South Vietnamese units into battle.

President Johnson ratified the policy of his predecessors immediately after taking office in late 1963. But, despite the expansion of American support in the early 1960's, the communist forces continued to make substantial gains into 1964.

Several events brought a change in the course of the war beginning in 1964—and with them came a radical alteration in the nature of the United States' role in it. A series of governmental crises had weakened South Viet Nam's ability to carry the war to the enemy. North Viet Nam had stepped up its infiltration of men and supplies to aid the Viet Cong in the south. Direct attacks on American forces and installations began to occur. As a result, American combat units were ordered to South Viet Nam in growing numbers in 1965. Almost immediately, Army and Marine Corps forces began operations against the Viet Cong, and against North Vietnamese units in the south, too. Air Force and carrier-based Navy planes began to fly missions in support of ground troops in the south and against strategic targets in North Viet Nam.

The United States soon took over from the

South Vietnamese primary responsibility for the prosecution of the war, and fierce fighting punctuated the next several years. By 1968 more than 500,000 American troops were involved.

Throughout our involvement in Viet Nam, from the early 1950's, our purpose there has remained constant. First expressed by President Eisenhower, then by Presidents Kennedy and Johnson, and now by President Nixon, it has been and is to resist aggression, to avoid a wider conflict, and to bring about a peaceful solution. Even as the pace of the war was accelerated, the United States continued its efforts to prompt a settlement of the conflict. These efforts have been two-pronged: by *diplomatic* means to *persuade* the Hanoi regime to a peaceful settlement and by *military* means to *force* them to one.

President Johnson made a dramatic bid to prompt the North Vietnamese to negotiate in early 1968—by ordering a drastic reduction in the air attacks on factories, bridges, and other strategic targets in the North. (The bombing of North Viet Nam was halted altogether in late 1968.)

Hanoi then did agree to peace talks. Negotiations—involving the United States, South Viet Nam, North Viet Nam, and the NLF (Viet Cong)—began in Paris in May of 1968. They have continued, inconclusively, ever since.

As President Nixon has reported:

Hanoi has refused to discuss our proposals. They demand our unconditional acceptance of their terms, which are that we withdraw all American forces immediately and unconditionally and that we overthrow the Government of South Viet Nam as we leave.

The Nixon Administration has adopted a policy of "Vietnamization" of the war—a policy Mr. Nixon has thus described:

The primary mission of our troops is to enable the South Vietnamese forces to assume the full responsibility for the security of South Viet Nam. . . . We have adopted a plan in cooperation with the South Vietnamese for the complete withdrawal of all U.S. combat ground forces, and their replacement by South Vietnamese forces on an orderly scheduled timetable. This withdrawal will be made from strength and not from weakness. As South Vietnamese forces become stronger, the rate of American withdrawal can become greater.

Whatever the future may hold, this much can be said: As 1971 opened, the Viet Nam conflict remained at the difficult and delicate "talk-fight" level.

In South Viet Nam—as in Korea, Cuba, Berlin, the Formosa Strait, and elsewhere—the United States has demonstrated in clear and unmistakable terms that it is ready and will fight to preserve freedom wherever and whenever it becomes necessary.

Foreign Aid. The granting of aid to other nations has been a basic feature of American foreign policy for over twenty years now. It began with a number of emergency programs at the end of World War II. Thus, we lent $3,750,000,000 to Great Britain in 1946, and the next year we began the program of aid to Greece and Turkey.

Foreign aid became a permanent part of our foreign policy with the launching of the Marshall Plan in 1948. Through it, we played a major role in the recovery of war-ravaged Western Europe. Since World War II, we have provided more than $135,000,000,000 in aid to other nations.

Our aid policy has undergone many changes over the years. In the early years the bulk of the aid we gave was economic in form, in the 1950's much of it was military, and today we provide roughly equal measures of each form. Until the mid-1950's Western Europe received the lion's share of our help; in recent years the largest amount has gone to Asia and Latin America.

From the beginning our aid policy has sought to advance our interests by winning friends and influencing peoples—in both military and

CASE STUDY

For twenty-five years now the United States has been caught up in the Cold War with the Soviet Union, and over that period of time much of this nation's foreign policy has been a direct reflection of that fact. Some students of world politics now argue that that struggle, as it developed in the late 1940's and as it was waged through the 1950's and the 1960's, is all but over; therefore, they insist, the basic features of American foreign policy must be radically altered in order to accommodate new circumstances. But many other authorities believe that the Cold War will go on for many years, and perhaps even for generations (although Red China may someday replace the Soviet Union as the major protagonist); hence they argue that our current foreign policy stances ought to be reinforced, not abandoned.

Which of these contrasting viewpoints do you think is more likely to prove to be the correct one? What consequences might there be for the United States, internally as well as externally, in the event either of these alternatives becomes fact? Or, is it possible that within the foreseeable future some new matter for concern — such as the population explosion — will replace Russia and/or China as our major concern in world affairs? In this vein, note that the world's population in 1960 was just over 3,000,000,000; it is expected to *double* before the year 2000 — and most of the increase will occur in the hungry nations of the world.

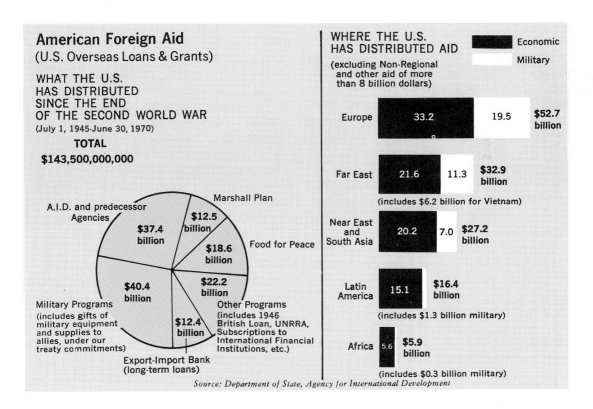

Source: Department of State, Agency for International Development

humanitarian terms. President Eisenhower put the case for the policy on a practical level:

> We need allies, and these allies must be bound to us in terms of their own enlightened self-interest, just as in like terms we are bound to them.

A new and immediately successful aid program was launched in 1961: the Peace Corps, a group of carefully selected and trained volunteers with special skills in such fields as engineering, teaching, and agriculture. These volunteers work with and help better the lot of underdeveloped peoples. The Peace Corps undertook its first mission, a road project, in Tanganyika in late 1961. Today its volunteers are at work in some sixty countries.

Regional Security Treaties. Security treaties help to spell out collective security and our resistance to communism. They are based on the realization that distance and oceans are no longer guarantees against foreign attack. Nuclear weapons, missiles, and other modern devices of mass destruction have pushed our defensive frontiers to the far corners of the earth. Because of this the United States now has eight separate "regional security" treaties with forty-two nations. Each of these agreements is defensive in nature. They pledge the parties to aid one another in case of an attack on either. The objective of each treaty is clear — security for us and for the rest of the free world. Each regional security treaty bolsters and implements the UN Charter and the principle of collective security.

The North Atlantic Treaty. Signed in 1949, the North Atlantic Treaty set up an alliance which now includes the United States, Canada, Great Britain, France, Italy, Portugal, Belgium, the Netherlands, Luxembourg, Denmark, Norway, Iceland, Greece, Turkey, and West Germany. The member nations have agreed that "an armed attack against one or more of them in Europe or North America shall be considered an attack against them all." The

pact's object is mutual defense — particularly against the USSR, of course. We have given billions of dollars in aid to our allies in the North Atlantic Treaty Organization and powerful American units are part of an integrated NATO command. France, long an uneasy partner, cracked NATO's solidarity in 1966; General De Gaulle ordered the withdrawal of French forces from the NATO command and the removal of all NATO units from French soil. Still, France remains a member of the alliance. The United States also has an agreement with Spain giving us air bases in that country in return for economic and military aid.

The Rio Pact. Signed in 1947, the Inter-American Treaty of Reciprocal Assistance (the Rio Pact) binds the United States and twenty Latin American nations to aid one another in case of an attack in this hemisphere. Our neighbors to the south are essential to our own defense; they are, in effect, our own backyard. We cannot afford to have enemies, or even unfriendly states, so close at hand. When President Kennedy moved against the Soviet missile buildup in Cuba in 1962, he did so under the terms of the Rio Pact; and each of the other American republics immediately supported the position taken by the United States.

President Johnson's use of American troops to effect a cease-fire between the rebel and government forces in the strife-torn Dominican Republic in 1965 also came as a move to preserve the security of this hemisphere. The first contingents were air-lifted to Santo Domingo on April 28. Their mission was that of protecting the lives of foreign nationals in that beleaguered city. They had been sent only after Dominican authorities had indicated that they could no longer guarantee the safety of American citizens and requested military help for that purpose.

On the following day, additional units were dispatched to the Dominican capital, and the original mission was expanded. By then it had become plain that the rebel movement was about to be taken over by the Communists.

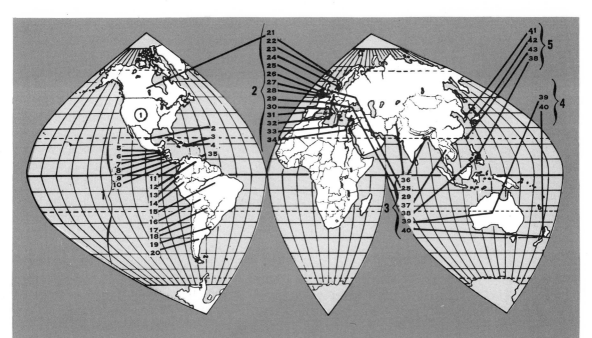

The United States and Its Collective Defense Arrangements

1 Rio Pact (21 Nations)

① United States	6 Honduras	11 Colombia	16 Bolivia
2 Mexico	7 El Salvador	12 Venezuela	17 Paraguay
3 Haiti	8 Nicaragua	13 Ecuador	18 Chile
4 Dominican Republic	9 Costa Rica	14 Peru	19 Uruguay
5 Guatemala	10 Panama	15 Brazil	20 Argentina
	35 Trinidad and Tobago		

2 North Atlantic Treaty (15 nations)

① United States	24 Denmark	28 Luxembourg	32 Federal Republic of Germany
21 Canada	25 United Kingdom	29 France	
22 Iceland	26 Netherlands	30 Italy	33 Greece
23 Norway	27 Belgium	31 Portugal	34 Turkey

3 Southeast Asia Treaty (8 nations)

① United States	25 United Kingdom	37 Thailand	39 Australia
36 Pakistan	29 France	38 Philippines	40 New Zealand

4 Anzus Pact (3 nations)

① United States	39 Australia	40 New Zealand

5 Individually Allied with U.S.

38 Philippines	41 Republic of Korea	42 Japan	43 Republic of China (Formosa)

We acted, said President Johnson, "in keeping with the great principles of the inter-American system" — "to help prevent another communist state in this hemisphere" and to guarantee the creation of "a government freely chosen by the will of all the people."

On May 19, acting on the basis of a proposal made by the United States, the OAS created an inter-American force to help restore order in the Dominican Republic. Most of the American force was then withdrawn; but some units remained, together with troops from other member-countries, under an OAS command until the fall of 1966.

The Anzus Pact. Signed in 1951, the Anzus Pact unites Australia, New Zealand, and the United States in a defensive alliance. If any of the three nations or their territories is attacked in the Pacific area, the other two agree to come to its aid.

The Japanese Pact. First signed in 1951, the Japanese Pact was revised and extended between Japan and the United States in 1960. After six years of military occupation we and our World War II allies (not the Soviet Union, however) concluded a peace treaty with Japan. At the same time we also signed a mutual defense pact with the Japanese. In return for American protection, we are permitted to maintain land, sea, and air forces in and about Japan We have added to our own security by converting a former foe into a friend.

The Philippines Pact. Signed in 1951, the Philippines Pact serves notice on any potential aggressor that the United States and the Philippines will stand together in the Pacific area.

The Korean Pact. Signed in 1953, the Korean Pact pledges the United States to come to the aid of South Korea should it be attacked again. (In addition to this pact, the sixteen UN members whose troops fought in Korea have promised prompt action should the Communists renew the war.)

The Southeast Asia Treaty. Signed in 1954, the SEATO pact is patterned after the NATO pact. It pledges eight nations — the United States, Great Britain, France, Australia, New Zealand, the Philippines, Pakistan, and Thailand — to guarantee the security of one another (and of South Viet Nam, Laos, and Cambodia) in Southeast Asia.

The Formosa Pact. Signed in 1954, the Formosa Pact pledges the United States and Nationalist China to come to the aid of the other in the event either is attacked in the Formosa area. The United States does not recognize the Chinese Communist government at Peking, and we oppose the admission of the Chinese Communists to the UN. We are committed to the defense of the Nationalist stronghold on the island of Formosa, and the United States Seventh Fleet guards the Formosa Strait between it and the mainland.

An Overview. *Our most important ally* is Great Britain. Our two nations are closely tied by history, tradition, and a common stake in freedom. The resources and strategic locations of the far-flung parts of the British Empire are key factors in the East-West struggle. Without Great Britain we would find our task of world leadership much more difficult.

Our most powerful foe is the Soviet Union. Through the years of the Cold War we have waged a continuing struggle against the threat of international communism. Our chief antagonist in this fight to preserve and, eventually, extend the limits of the free world has been — and today remains — the Soviet Union. The emergence of Communist China as yet another potent foe *may* prove to be more helpful than dangerous to us in the long run: the frictions between the two major communist powers have grown to severe — and perhaps unbridgeable — proportions over the past few years.

Every nation in the world is important to us. *Germany,* for example, is the key to the future of much of Europe. Thus, we are working for a strong, peaceable, and united Germany. So long as the Soviet Union prevents this by keeping East Germany in bondage as a satellite and refusing to permit free, all-German elections, we are pledged to support the free, democratic government of the Federal Republic of (West) Germany.

India, with its resources and teeming millions, is the key to the future of much of Asia. Thus, we are attempting to work with it for the peaceful, noncommunist development of that whole vast region.

The Middle East is the land bridge connecting Europe, Africa, and Asia and is immensely rich in oil. These two factors — its strategic location and its vast oil resources — make the region a rich prize. Many other factors — especially the nationalistic jealousies and factionalism among the several Arab states and the bitter Arab-Israeli enmity — also make the region an extremely volatile one. We seek to prevent the extension of Soviet influence in the Middle East. Under the *Eisenhower Doctrine* of 1957 we have pledged support to any Middle Eastern state threatened by internal subversion or external aggression. Acting under the doctrine, American forces were sent to Lebanon, at its request, to protect that nation from revolt in 1958.

Most of the *newly-independent states in Africa* are underdeveloped and in desperate need of economic assistance. In deadly competition with the Soviet Union and Communist China we are striving to bring these new nations, like the Congo, to the side of the free world.

As a nation, we lead the free world in the search for a just and lasting peace. The search thus far has not been an easy one, nor does it promise to be in the future. Still, we know we must carry it forward. To shirk our duty now would be to doom the world as we know it and as we would like it to be.

THE UNITED NATIONS

The decisive change in the basic pattern of American foreign policy in the years since World War II — the shift from isolationism to full participation in international affairs — is

The headquarters of the United Nations, the Secretariat, Conference, and General Assembly buildings, are situated on the East River in New York. (United Nations)

strikingly illustrated by our membership in and support of the United Nations.

Birth of the UN. On January 1, 1942, less than one month after the United States entered World War II, twenty-six nations [2] then at war with the Axis Powers met at Washington, D.C., to sign and proclaim the Declaration of the United Nations. In that document each of the signatories committed itself to an all-out effort to win the war and pledged that it would not seek a separate peace with the enemy. The declaration — signed by an additional twenty-

[2] The United States, Australia, Belgium, Canada, China, Costa Rica, Cuba, Czechoslovakia, Dominican Republic, El Salvador, Great Britain, Greece, Guatemala, Haiti, Honduras, India, Luxembourg, the Netherlands, New Zealand, Nicaragua, Norway, Panama, Poland, the Soviet Union, Union of South Africa, and Yugoslavia.

three states later in the war [3] — marked the first official use of the term "United Nations."

In 1943 both houses of Congress gave overwhelming approval to resolutions urging the creation of an organization to preserve peace in the postwar world. Later that same year at Moscow, Secretary of State Cordell Hull pledged American cooperation in establishing "at the earliest practicable date a general international organization for the maintenance of international peace and security." In 1944 representatives of the United States, Great Britain, China, and the Soviet Union met at Dumbarton Oaks, an estate just outside Washington, D.C., to compose a general plan for such an organization. Then, in February, 1945, President Roosevelt, Prime Minister Churchill, and Premier Stalin, meeting at Yalta in the Crimea, called for a United Nations Conference on International Organization to be convened at San Francisco on April 25, 1945.

The San Francisco Conference. Delegates from fifty nations gathered at San Francisco to draft a charter for the United Nations. Although much preliminary work had been done, the conference faced a number of serious problems — for example, the ways in which economic pressures and military force might be used to preserve peace, the voting strength of the large and small powers in the new organization, and the administration of former enemy territories. On these and several other issues the United States and Great Britain stood on one side and the Soviet Union on the other. Despite difficulties, however, the delegates of the assembled nations were able to forge the charter and gave it their unanimous approval on June 26, 1945.

The United States became the first nation to ratify the UN Charter. The Senate agreed to

---

[3] Argentina, Bolivia, Brazil, Chile, Colombia, Denmark, Ecuador, Egypt, Ethiopia, France, Iran, Iraq, Lebanon, Liberia, Mexico, Paraguay, Peru, San Marino, Saudi Arabia, Syria, Turkey, Uruguay, and Venezuela.

it by the overwhelming vote of 89–2 on July 28, 1945. It was then ratified in quick order by Great Britain, France, China, the Soviet Union, and twenty-four other states and went into formal effect on October 24, 1945. Within a very short time, all of the states which had participated in the San Francisco Conference had approved the charter, and the organization's first meeting, a session of the General Assembly, opened at London on January 10, 1946.

The UN Charter. The UN Charter opens with an eloquent preamble which declares that the UN exists in order "to save succeeding generations from the scourge of war." The body of the document begins in Article I with a statement of the organization's purposes, proclaiming them to be: the maintenance of international peace and security, the development of friendly relations among all nations, and the promotion of justice and cooperation in the solution of international problems.

Membership. The United Nations is composed of its fifty-one original members (those which drafted and first ratified the charter) plus the many other states admitted by the organization since its creation. According to the UN Charter, membership is open to those "peace-loving states" which accept the obligations of the charter and which will, in the UN's judgment, carry out those obligations. New members may be admitted by a two-thirds vote of the General Assembly on the recommendation of the Security Council. As the map on page 351 indicates, there are now (1971) 127 members of the world organization. The General Assembly is empowered to suspend or expel any member whenever the Security Council recommends such action; to date this has not occurred.

Basic Organization. Six "principal organs" are provided for in the UN Charter: the General Assembly, the Security Council, the Economic and Social Council, the Trusteeship Council, the International Court of Justice, and the Secretariat. We shall examine each of them briefly in a moment.

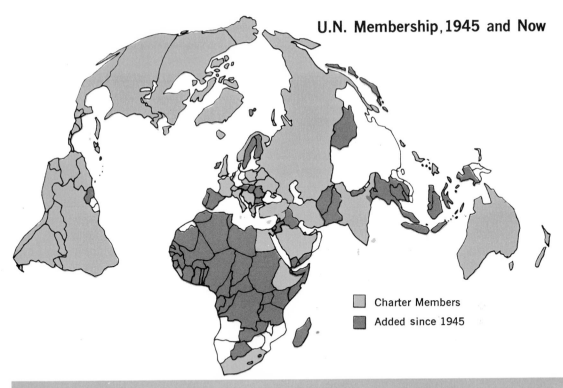

U.N. Membership, 1945 and Now

☐ Charter Members

■ Added since 1945

51 Charter Members (in alphabetical order)

Argentina	Cuba	Honduras	Norway	Union of Soviet
Australia	Czechoslovakia	India	Panama	Socialist Republics
Belgium	Denmark	Iran	Paraguay	United Arab
Bolivia	Dominican Republic	Iraq	Peru	Republic
Brazil	Ecuador	Lebanon	Philippines	United Kingdom
Byelorussian S.S.R.	El Salvador	Liberia	Poland	United States
Canada	Ethiopia	Luxembourg	Saudi Arabia	Uruguay
Chile	France	Mexico	South Africa	Venezuela
China (Formosa)	Greece	Netherlands	Syrian Arab Republic	Yugoslavia
Colombia	Guatemala	New Zealand	Turkey	
Costa Rica	Haiti	Nicaragua	Ukrainian S.S.R.	

Admitted Since 1945

Afghanistan	Congo (Brazzaville)	Israel	Mali	Somalia
Albania	Congo (Kinshasa)	Italy	Malta	Southern Yemen
Algeria	Cyprus	Ivory Coast	Mauritania	Spain
Austria	Dahomey	Jamaica	Mauritius	Sudan
Barbados	Equatorial Guinea	Japan	Mongolia	Swaziland
Botswana	Finland	Jordan	Morocco	Sweden
Bulgaria	Gabon	Kenya	Nepal	Tanzania
Burma	Gambia	Kuwait	Niger	Thailand
Burundi	Ghana	Laos	Nigeria	Togo
Cambodia	Guinea	Lesotho	Pakistan	Trinidad and Tobago
Cameroon	Guyana	Libya	Portugal	Tunisia
Central African	Hungary	Malagasy Republic	Rumania	Uganda
Republic	Iceland	Malawi	Rwanda	Upper Volta
Ceylon	Indonesia	Malaysia	Senegal	Yemen
Chad	Ireland	Maldive Islands	Sierra Leone	Zambia
			Singapore	

Other Major Features. The "sovereign equality" of each member-state is recognized by the UN Charter, and the UN is expressly forbidden "to intervene in matters which are essentially within the domestic jurisdiction of any state." Each member is obligated to accept and fulfill the principles and purposes of the charter, and the document declares that the UN will also ensure that *nonmembers* act in accord with the charter, as well—at least insofar as is "necessary for the maintenance of international peace and security."

Several of the charter's provisions relate to methods for the peaceful settlement of disputes between nations and to the use of force to halt armed conflicts or deal with other threats to peace. Each member of the UN is guaranteed the "right of individual and collective self-defense" in the event of attack upon it. Thus, the UN Charter recognizes such regional defense alliances as the North Atlantic Treaty and the Organization of American States.

Amendments to the charter may be proposed by a two-thirds vote of the General Assembly. To become effective they must be ratified by two-thirds of the members of the organization, each acting in accord with its own constitutional processes. The ratifying states, however, *must* include the Big Five members—the United States, Great Britain, the Soviet Union, France, and China. Because the UN Charter is a treaty, the United States Senate must agree to any amendment to it. A general conference to revise the charter may be called by a two-thirds vote of the General Assembly and the votes of any nine members of the Security Council.

Only two amendments have thus far been added to the original UN Charter. Both were proposed in 1963, ratified in 1965, and became effective in 1966. One increased the size of the Security Council from eleven to fifteen members and raised from seven to nine the number of affirmative votes needed for Security Council decisions. The other enlarged the membership of the Economic and Social Council from eighteen to twenty-seven.

The General Assembly. Each member of the UN is represented in the General Assembly. Thus today the General Assembly consists of 127 members.

Sessions and Voting. The General Assembly meets in regular session once each year, normally in September. Although the General Assembly may meet in other places, most of its sessions are held at the site of the UN's permanent headquarters in New York. Special sessions may be called by the Secretary-General at the request of a majority of the UN membership or at the request of the Security Council.

The General Assembly is organized on the basis of the equality of all of its members. Each nation has one vote in its proceedings, regardless of size. On important issues, such as those involving elections or finances, the UN Charter requires that decisions be made by a two-thirds vote; on lesser matters, a simple majority is sufficient.

Powers and Functions. The General Assembly has often been called the "town meeting of the world," and its powers and functions are many. It may consider any matter within the scope of the UN Charter,[4] and may make such recommendations as it deems appropriate to the Security Council, the other UN organs, and the member-states. Its recommendations to member-states are not legally binding, but they do carry substantial weight since they have been made with the approval of a significant number of the governments of the world. Just how potent its recommendations can be may be seen from the fact that the prosecution of the Korean War rested on such a basis.

The General Assembly elects the ten non-permanent members of the Security Council, the members of the Economic and Social Council, and some of the members of the

---

[4] Except matters currently under consideration by the Security Council. This restriction is intended to prevent the confusion that might result from the simultaneous consideration of matters by the UN's two major agencies.

Trusteeship Council. With the Security Council, it also selects the Secretary-General and the judges of the International Court. And, as we have seen, it shares with the Security Council the power to admit, suspend, or expel members. It alone may propose amendments to the UN Charter.

Much of the work of the other UN organs is supervised by the General Assembly. It provides for the staffing of the Secretariat, requires both annual and special reports from the other organs, and creates the relationships with the UN's Specialized Agencies.

The General Assembly also controls the world organization's finances. It prepares the annual budget and sets the portion of it that each member is obligated to provide. For 1969, the budget amounted to approximately $154,000,000. Of that sum, over $27,000,000 came from such sources as the sale of United Nations postage stamps—which are coveted by collectors all over the world—and of guided tours of the UN's headquarters building. Of the remainder, the United States paid nearly one-third, the Soviet Union one-seventh, Great Britain one-fourteenth, and China one-twentieth. The minimum annual share for any member, paid by many of the smaller states, is set at four-hundredths of one per cent—only some $57,000 currently.

The costs of maintaining UN troops on the Israeli-Egyptian border (UNEF) from 1956 to 1967 and in the Congo (UNOC) from 1960 to 1964 were not included in the regular annual budgets. Rather, they were covered by special assessments based on each member's share of the regular budget. Because several members — including the Soviet Union and France — have thus far (1970) refused to pay some or all of their special assessments, the UN has been plagued by stubborn financial problems for the past several years.[5]

The Security Council. The Security Council is composed of fifteen members. Five of them—the United States, Great Britain, the Soviet Union, France, and China—are *permanent members* of the Security Council. The ten *nonpermanent members* are chosen by the General Assembly, with five being elected each year. The Security Council is in continuous session, and the UN Charter requires that its members be represented at the UN seat at all times.

Voting and the Veto. On *procedural* questions —that is, routine or relatively unimportant matters—decisions of the Security Council may be made by an affirmative vote of any nine members. On more important matters—*substantive* questions—nine affirmative votes are also required; *but* in such cases the nine *must* include the votes of each of the permanent members. Thus, on substantive questions, each of the permanent members has a *veto* it can use to prevent Security Council action.

Because of the veto power, the Security Council can function effectively only when the Big Five cooperate. Thus far (1971), the Soviet Union has used its veto more than a hundred times; France has invoked it four times, Great Britain twice, and Nationalist China once. The United States did not find an occasion to use it until 1970.

[5] The UN Charter (Article 19) provides that any member failing to meet its financial obligation in an amount equal to two years' assessments may be denied its vote in the General Assembly. In 1962 the International Court of Justice ruled that this penalty may be applied to the special as well as the regular budget assessments. To date, however, the penalty has not been invoked against any member. The UNEF operation cost the UN nearly $200,000,000 and UNOC some $393,000,000. Their liquidations have eased the organization's financial problems considerably. Unlike UNEF and UNOC, the peace-keeping force stationed on Cyprus since 1963 (UNFICYP) is financed voluntarily by those nations providing troops, other UN members, and Cyprus itself.

Powers. The Security Council is the UN organ especially responsible for maintaining international peace and dealing with threats to or breaches of that peace. Many of its powers concern the pacific settlement of disputes. It may call on disputing parties to settle their difficulties by peaceful means. If it chooses to, it may investigate a dispute and recommend terms for its settlement. Whenever the Security Council finds that a threat to or breach of the peace exists or that an act of aggression has been committed, it may call upon the nations involved to take certain steps to ease the tensions or halt the spread of hostilities.

In order to make its decisions and recommendations effective, the Security Council may call on all members to sever economic and diplomatic relations with an offending state. If these measures prove inadequate, it may call on all members to take military action against the offender, as was done when the North Koreans invaded South Korea.[6]

The UN Charter provides for a Military Staff Committee to be composed of the chiefs of staff of the armed forces of the Big Five. The committee would advise the Security Council on disarmament matters and on the use of military force. Each UN member is also required to make certain units of its armed forces available for use by the Security Council. These provisions have never become effective, however, because of disagreements between the Soviet Union and the other members of the Big Five.

Actions against an Aggressor. Those who framed the UN Charter clearly intended the Security Council as the organ to take action against an aggressor whenever such action became necessary. But, as we have seen, the

Security Council may be paralyzed by a veto cast by any one of the Big Five; it can act only when one of them does not object.

Because of this (and because of the Soviet Union's frequent use of the veto), the United States proposed and the General Assembly adopted the "Uniting for Peace" Resolution in late 1950. Under its terms, whenever the Security Council cannot act in a case in which there "appears to be a threat to the peace, breach of the peace, or act of aggression," the matter may be considered by the General Assembly immediately. The General Assembly may *recommend* that the members take steps, including military action, to preserve or restore peace. This measure, in effect, revised the original scheme of the UN. It gave to the General Assembly, as well as the Security Council, the power to act to maintain international order. Remember, *there is no veto power in the General Assembly.*

The "Uniting for Peace" Resolution has been the basis for several peace-keeping actions in the years since its adoption. For example, it provided the basis for UN action in the Suez Crisis of 1956. When the Israeli-Egyptian war broke out anew in the fall of that year, Great Britain and France invaded Egypt. They seized the Suez Canal in order to keep that vital lifeline open to shipping. The Security Council was powerless to act in the matter in the face of British and French vetoes. The General Assembly, acting under the 1950 resolution, took over the matter and soon secured a cease-fire. It then created the United Nations Emergency Force, an international police unit, to maintain the truce. The withdrawal of UNEF in 1967 was followed almost immediately by a renewal of the Arab-Israeli conflict; this time the Security Council was able to obtain only a very uneasy truce.

The Economic and Social Council. Each member of the UN has pledged itself to cooperate with other nations to achieve several broad social objectives. These objectives aim at the fostering of friendlier relations among

---

[6] When, on June 25, 1950, the Security Council called upon all UN members to aid South Korea to repel the North Korean aggressor, the Soviet delegate was boycotting sessions of the Security Council; hence, he was not present to veto the action.

The United Nations

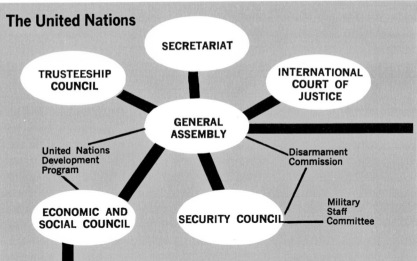

SECRETARIAT

TRUSTEESHIP COUNCIL

INTERNATIONAL COURT OF JUSTICE

GENERAL ASSEMBLY

United Nations Development Program

Disarmament Commission

ECONOMIC AND SOCIAL COUNCIL

SECURITY COUNCIL

Military Staff Committee

International Atomic Energy Agency
·
UN Conference on Trade & Development
·
UN Special Fund
·
UN Children's Fund (UNICEF)
·
UN High Commission for Refugees
·
UN Relief and Works Agency
·
International Law Commission
·
UN Organization for Industrial Development (UNIDO)
·
Other Subsidiary Organizations

The Commissions

Regional Economic Commissions for:		Statistical	Social
Europe	Latin America	Human Rights	Population
Asia & Far East	Africa	Status of Women	Narcotic Drugs

Specialized Agencies

Educational, Scientific & Cultural Qrganization	International Labor Organization
International Telecommunication Union	Food & Agriculture Organization
International Bank	World Health Organization
International Development Association	International Monetary Fund
International Finance Corporation	Universal Postal Union
World Meteorological Organization	Intergovernmental Maritime Consultive Organization
International Civil Aviation Organization	

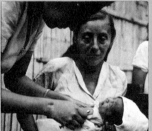

Some ways in which U.N. agencies help people all over the world.

all nations and the producing of a more stable international community. According to the UN Charter, these objectives include the promotion of: (1) higher standards of living, full employment, and other conditions for social and economic progress; (2) the solutions of economic, social, and health problems; (3) international, cultural, and educational cooperation; and (4) universal respect for human rights and fundamental freedoms for all men.

Acting under the direction of the General Assembly, the Economic and Social Council is the organ especially responsible for implementing these goals. ECOSOC is now a twenty-seven-member body. Its members are elected by the General Assembly for three-year terms, nine members being chosen each year.

ECOSOC does its work chiefly through conferences, studies, and recommendations in the economic, social, cultural, educational, scientific, and health fields. It maintains several commissions which operate in specific problem or regional areas, as the organizational chart on page 355 indicates.

The Specialized Agencies. One of ECOSOC's most important functions is that of coordinating the work of the UN's Specialized Agencies. These are independent international bodies which, by special agreement, function under the world organization's general supervision. Much of the UN's efforts to eliminate the causes of war by raising the level of world economic and social conditions is actually done by these agencies.

There are now thirteen Specialized Agencies. The *International Labor Organization* (ILO) was first established under the League of Nations in 1919 and was the only major body of the League of Nations to which the United States belonged. ILO works to promote the health and welfare of workers everywhere. The *World Health Organization* (WHO) seeks to improve health conditions throughout the world. The *Food and Agriculture Organization*

(FAO) conducts projects to improve and increase world food production. The *United Nations Educational, Scientific, and Cultural Organization* (UNESCO) is the agency through which members exchange ideas and information; it works to raise the level of international understanding. The *International Civil Aviation Organization* (ICAO) promotes international cooperation in the interests of expanded commercial air traffic. The *Universal Postal Union* (UPU) is the oldest of the Specialized Agencies; it was first established in 1875 and has long been successful in facilitating international communications by mail. The *International Telecommunications Union* (ITU) promotes international communication by wire, radio, and similar means. The *World Meteorological Organization* (WMO) seeks to improve meteorological activities around the globe. The *Intergovernmental Maritime Consultative Organization* (IMCO) attempts to promote safety at sea and the expansion of the world's maritime trade.

The *International Monetary Fund* (IMF) encourages trade and prosperity by stabilizing the value of the currencies of member-states. The *International Bank for Reconstruction and Development* (World Bank) makes or insures loans for the development of the productive facilities of its members. The *International Finance Corporation* (IFC) and the *International Development Association* (IDA) are affiliates of the World Bank and assist it in the performance of its lending function.

The Trusteeship Council. The UN Charter requires each member to promote the interests and well-being of the people of all "non-self-governing territories" as a "sacred trust." It sets out general policies for the governing of all dependent areas and establishes rules for the governing of all territories placed under the UN trusteeship system.

The Trusteeship Council is composed of all UN members administering trust territories, those Big Five members which do not, and enough other members (elected by the General

Assembly) to provide an equal balance of members which administer trust territories and members which do not. The trust territories include: (1) colonies which were originally mandates under the League of Nations, (2) colonies taken from the enemy in World War II, and (3) other colonies voluntarily placed under the trusteeship system by colonial powers.[7] The Trusteeship Council receives reports from all nations possessing non-self-governing territories, oversees the administration of the trust territories, and generally seeks to improve the lot of the people and to encourage self-government for all of the world's dependent areas and people.

The International Court of Justice. The ICJ is the judicial arm of the United Nations. It is dealt with only briefly in the UN Charter but is the subject of a lengthy and detailed Statute appended to that document. The ICJ is composed of fifteen judges chosen for nine-year terms by the General Assembly and the Security Council. No two judges may come from the same country. It holds regular sessions at The Hague in the Netherlands. Only states (both members and nonmembers of the UN, but not individuals) may be parties in cases before the court. It deals with cases involving the interpretation of treaties, questions in international law, and any other legal matters brought before it. Decisions of the International Court of Justice are made by a majority vote.

The ICJ cannot hear a case unless both parties to a dispute agree to accept its jurisdiction. A nation may agree to the court's jurisdiction over a specific case, or it can agree in advance to ICJ jurisdiction over a general class of cases in which it might become involved. For example, in their regional security treaties of 1951 and 1960 the United States and Japan

have agreed to ICJ jurisdiction over any dispute involving the meaning or application of those treaties.

Under the forementioned Statute, any nation may sign that document's "optional clause." By so doing, it agrees to the ICJ's jurisdiction in any legal dispute it may have with any other nation which has also signed the clause. About one-half of the UN's members have signed the optional clause. Several of these acceptances, however, have been accompanied by reservations. For example, the United States made several reservations to its acceptance in 1946. One declares that the ICJ shall not have the right to hear and decide "disputes which are essentially within the jurisdiction of the United States as determined by the United States." Such reservations have severely limited the ICJ's usefulness.

The ICJ may give an advisory opinion on any legal question when requested by the General Assembly, the Security Council, or other UN organs, with the consent of the General Assembly.

Thus far the ICJ has played only a minor role in settling international disputes. The problem has not been a lack of international law that might be applied in specific cases. Instead, it has been that most of the serious disputes have been treated as "political" rather than "judicial" questions, and the nations involved have not been willing to submit those disputes to the Court for settlement.

The Secretariat. The Secretariat is the civil service branch of the UN. It is headed by the Secretary-General who is chosen by the General Assembly upon the recommendation of the Security Council. Its 9000-odd employees come from most of the member-states.

The Secretary-General has a wide variety of functions. He is responsible for the administrative work of the principal organs of the UN, except for the International Court of Justice, and he prepares annual reports to the General Assembly on the workings of the UN. The UN Charter gives him the power to bring to

---

[7] By 1968 there were only two trust territories, administered by two nations: *New Guinea* (by Australia); and the *Trust Territory of the Pacific Islands* (by the United States; see page 590).

In the Security Council, representatives of nations big and small attempt to resolve differences among nations. (United Nations)

the attention of the Security Council any matter which, in his opinion, constitutes a threat to international peace and security.

The Secretary-General was originally looked upon as little more than the UN's chief clerk. The late Secretary-General Dag Hammarskjöld made far more of the office, however. Relying largely on his own persuasive diplomatic talents, he established the office as an important channel for the negotiated settlement of international disputes. He also made the office a chief trouble-shooting agency, heading off several world crises by bringing them to the prompt attention of the Security Council. The effectiveness with which the UN met the Congo crisis in 1960 and 1961 was due very largely to the skill and dispatch with which Mr. Hammarskjöld reacted to the situation. His successor, U Thant, has sought to follow the pattern he set.

As a part of its routine administrative duties, the Secretariat provides secretarial and translation services, keeps records, makes studies of the functioning of the UN, publishes reports, provides press, radio, and television facilities, sees that visitors are received courteously and efficiently, and handles official communications between the world organization and member-states.

The UN Charter requires that all treaties made between member-nations be recorded with and published by the Secretariat; unrecorded treaties cannot be invoked in any matter before any organ of the UN.

The UN and Disarmament. For the more than twenty years of Cold War the world has lived with the threat of World War III — the threat of a nuclear holocaust in which man could, quite literally, wipe himself off the face of the earth. As never before, these years have given new and compelling urgency to the ancient hope for the day when, in Isaiah's words, men:

> shall beat their swords into plowshares, and their spears into pruning-hooks;

and the day when:

> nation shall not lift up sword against nation, neither shall they learn war any more.

Should that day ever come, the incredible amount of effort and expense the world now pours into its warmaking machines could be spent for incomparably more constructive purposes. The costs of the Cold War are staggering—indeed, they are well-nigh incalculable. Just in monetary terms, the United States has spent over $1,000,000,000,000 on its Armed Forces since the *end* of World War II. President Eisenhower pointed up the costs of the Cold War in terms of human value when he described the present era in these words:

> Under the cloud of threatening war, it is humanity hanging from a cross of iron.... Every gun that is made, every warship launched, every rocket fired signifies—in the final sense—a *theft* from those who hunger and are not fed, those who are cold and are not clothed. The world in arms is not spending money alone. It is spending the sweat of its laborers, the genius of its scientists, the hopes of its children.

Certainly, one of the surest ways to end this tragic waste and to prevent another global war would be a general international disarmament plan, agreed to and honored by all nations. Just as certainly, any such plan would have to provide the most stringent controls over the use of atomic energy.

The United States unleashed the horror of atomic weapons in 1945. The war against Japan was ended in August of that year with two awesomely destructive atomic bombs. The first one was dropped on Hiroshima on August 6th. The second one fell on Nagasaki three days later. The Hiroshima bomb produced an explosion equivalent to that of 20,000 tons of TNT. The blast, flash burns, fires, and falling debris from that one explosion killed more than 78,000 people; injured more than 37,000 others, many of whom later died of radiation sickness; and left another 13,000 missing. At least 170,000 more people were reported ill, homeless, hungry, or indigent after the attack. That one bomb leveled some five square miles of Hiroshima. The bomb that hit Nagasaki was equally devastating.

Since 1945, the United States has been producing and stockpiling atomic and hydrogen bombs and other nuclear weapons, all with incredible destructive power. Today our supply of them exceeds by many times the explosive equivalent of *all* bombs and *all* shells that came from *every* plane and *every* gun in *every* theater of war through *all* the years of World War II.

The Soviet Union exploded its first atomic device in 1949; and it, too, has been stockpiling nuclear weapons ever since. Two other nations are also nuclear powers today: Great Britain made its first tests in 1952, and France joined the "nuclear club" in 1960. With all that it could portend, Communist China may acquire a nuclear capability within the next few years; it exploded its first atomic device in 1964 and is steadily building its nuclear muscle.

Each of the factors mentioned here—(1) the dreaded prospects of a nuclear war, (2) the tragic waste of arms costs, (3) the dangers inherent in the growth of nuclear powers—underscore the vital importance of the international control of arms today. So does yet another: the harmful physical and biological effects that can be produced by radioactive fallout from nuclear testing.

The UN Disarmament Commission. The UN Charter empowers the General Assembly to recommend general principles for disarmament to the Security Council. The Security Council is charged with formulating a specific disarmament plan for all nations. Most of the postwar efforts to achieve arms control and disarmament have therefore centered in the UN.

Early in 1946 the UN created an Atomic Energy Commission, and the next year it created a Commission on Conventional Armaments. In 1952 both commissions were combined into the Disarmament Commission, now composed of all members of the UN. From the beginning disarmament efforts have aimed at one overall goal—an agreement outlawing the production or use of weapons of mass destruction and providing for the reduction of armaments and of armed forces to the minimum levels necessary for domestic policing and for the maintenance of peace through the UN.

The Disarmament Stalemate. Almost immediately in 1946 the United States presented a plan for international control of atomic power. The American proposal (the Baruch Plan) called for the creation of an International Atomic Development Authority with broad powers to own and control all atomic production and materials. Although the Baruch Plan was favored by a majority of the UN's members, the Soviet Union refused to accept its strict international inspection and enforcement provisions. They argued instead for only very limited inspection and supervision.

Despite a long series of disarmament conferences since 1946, the East-West deadlock — in both atomic and conventional weapons — had not been resolved by 1971. The chief stumbling block continues to be an inspection system acceptable to both sides.

A few bright spots have appeared on this depressing record, however. One of them came with the implementation of a proposal first made by President Eisenhower in 1953: the creation, at Vienna in 1957, of the *International Atomic Energy Agency.* The more than 100 nations which now belong to IAEA have pledged to "seek to accelerate and enlarge the contribution of atomic energy to peace, health, and prosperity throughout the world."

In yet another attempt to reach agreement, a general disarmament conference was begun in Geneva in 1958 and has met periodically since. The conference achieved a limited success when, in late 1958, the United States, Great Britain, and the Soviet Union informally agreed to a temporary suspension of nuclear testing. The voluntary test ban was ended suddenly when, without warning, the Soviet Union resumed its program in mid-1961. Both sides then conducted extensive tests until mid-1963. The Geneva talks continued, however.

Thus far, the UN's continuing disarmament efforts have produced three significant international agreements:

The Limited Test Ban Treaty, 1963. In 1963 the United States, the Soviet Union, and Great Britain agreed to a partial ban on nuclear testing. Their accord, in the form of a treaty, was registered with the UN and, immediately, the General Assembly called upon all states to ratify it. Under its terms, each signatory nation agrees not to conduct nuclear test explosions in the atmosphere, underwater, or in outer space. Underground tests, which are extremely difficult to detect, are permitted — but only so long as they do not spread radioactive debris beyond the territory of the nation conducting such a test. By 1970 over 120 states had signed the agreement — but France and Red China are not among the signatories.

The Outer Space Treaty, 1967. In 1967 the United States, the Soviet Union, and Great Britain signed an agreement to promote the peaceful exploration and use of outer space. The treaty outlaws in outer space and on all celestial bodies: all claims of national sovereignty, the stationing or orbiting of nuclear or other weapons of mass destruction, military bases or maneuvers, and all weapons testing. It calls for international cooperation in space activities and the reporting of their results, guarantees to all states unrestricted access to all celestial bodies, and requires prompt aid for astronauts who accidentally land in another state or on the high seas. The treaty also requires all countries to avoid all space activities that might cause contamination in outer space or harm the earth's environment.

The Nuclear Nonproliferation Treaty, 1968. In 1968 the United States, the Soviet Union, Great Britain, and sixty other nations signed an agreement to prevent the spread of nuclear weapons and explosives to those nations not already possessing them. By 1970 more than 100 states — but, again, not including France or Red China — had approved the treaty.

Evaluating the UN. The UN seems fairly well designed to accomplish the social, economic, and other humanitarian goals set by its Charter. It has served as the meeting place for airing international grievances and moulding world wide public opinion. It has been able to settle or bring about the settlement of several disputes between smaller nations.

The UN has been much less successful in controlling the conduct of the major powers and in settling disputes in which they are involved, however. Unless the Big Five members cooperate, the organization is virtually paralyzed in such cases—as the situation in Viet Nam so amply demonstrates. Unfortunate though it may be, it remains true that in international politics the power of might is as important a factor as the power of right.

Because the UN has not brought an end to world tensions and the threat of a third world war, some say that it is a failure. But those who do overlook a most important fact: the UN is *not* a world government. Like water which can rise no higher than its source, the UN can be no more effective than its members, especially the larger ones, are willing to make it.

Then, too, one should not overlook the UN's many accomplishments. Among other things, it prevented the Soviet Union from seizing the oil fields of northern Iran in 1946. It halted the Arab-Israeli war of 1948 which erupted when Israel gained its independence. It helped to settle the Berlin Blockade dispute in 1948–1949. It arranged a truce between India and Pakistan in their dispute over Kashmir in 1949 and again in 1965.

When, in June, 1950, the Security Council called upon "all members to render every assistance" in meeting the North Korean attack upon South Korea, sixteen nations responded (see page 341). *For the first time in history an international organization met aggression with armed force.*

The UN brought an end to the fighting in Egypt in late 1956 and forced the withdrawal of the Israeli and Anglo-French forces from Egyptian soil. The General Assembly created the United Nations Emergency Force, *the first international police force in history,* to guard the truce. Although UNEF's withdrawal in 1967 was followed by yet another Arab-Israeli war, the Security Council was soon able to obtain another cease-fire supervised by UN observers. The Security Council created another UN police force (UNOC) to meet the crisis in the Congo in 1960; UNOC restored order when internal strife threatened to destroy the new nation after it became independent, and remained on duty until mid-1964. It has been widely proposed that a permanent police force be available for the UN's use whenever trouble flares anywhere.

A few international disputes have been settled by the ICJ. For example, when a British ship was sunk by an Albanian mine in the Adriatic Sea, the two states went before the court; the British won damages, and a dangerous incident was closed.

Much has been done by the Specialized Agencies, whose work may seem unspectacular yet is very important. International peace can hardly become a lasting reality when millions of the world's people are hungry, lack shelter, suffer from disease, and live in ignorance. WHO stopped a cholera plague in Egypt, is spearheading a worldwide drive against malaria which has reduced the incidence of the disease by more than fifty per cent in Central America, and is conducting massive attacks on disease through spraying, vaccination, and other programs. FAO has defeated a chestnut tree blight in Italy, found vast reservoirs of underground water in parched Saudi Arabia, and has sent agricultural experts, seeds, and machinery to aid millions in the world's underdeveloped areas. UNESCO is fighting illiteracy all over the world, helping to establish public school systems and build more and better schools in backward areas. ICAO has organized a network of weather stations across the North Atlantic to provide for greater air safety and has brought a relaxation of various travel restrictions throughout Latin America.

In these and numerous other ways the United Nations has served the interests of world peace. The organization is far from perfect but, at the very least, much of its work is quite helpful.

✳✳✳✳✳✳✳✳✳ CONCEPT BUILDING ✳✳✳✳✳✳✳✳✳

Key Concepts

American foreign policy has always been directed toward one overriding end: the maintenance of the security of the United States. We began our history with a policy of isolationism dictated by our relative weakness, internal problems, and geographic position. From the beginning we also pursued a policy of continental expansion and warned Europe through the Monroe Doctrine not to interfere in Western Hemisphere affairs. As we expanded, we grew more powerful and became a first-class power in the world with the Spanish-American War. By 1900 our interests extended throughout this hemisphere and across the Pacific.

World War I brought the United States out of its isolationism for a brief period, but we returned to it until the coming of World War II. That conflict convinced us of the fallacy of isolationism in the modern world and wrought a basic transformation in American foreign policy. Today—through our own might, collective security agreements, support of and participation in the United Nations, and aid to the free world—we oppose communist aggression, work to prevent World War III, and seek a just and lasting peace for all mankind.

The UN dramatically illustrates the postwar transformation of American foreign policy. Formed at San Francisco in 1945, it is intended "to save succeeding generations from the scourge of war." Under its charter, it functions through six principal organs: the General Assembly, in which all of its 127 members are represented; the Security Council, composed of the Big Five and ten nonpermanent members, which is intended as the organization's major peace-keeping arm but is sometimes crippled by the veto power, the Economic and Social Council, with twenty-seven members, which is designed to attack the world's economic and social problems; the Trusteeship Council, which oversees the trust territories and promotes the well-being of the world's dependent peoples; the International Court of Justice, composed of fifteen judges, which is the UN's judicial arm; and the Secretariat, headed by the Secretary-General, which is the UN's civil service.

On balance, the UN is far from perfect but, at least, has been more than helpful in advancing the cause of world peace. It has had several notable successes in promoting the humanitarian goals set by the UN Charter and in resolving disputes among the smaller nations. It has been much less successful in regulating the conduct of the Big Five powers.

Questions for Inquiry and Review

1. What has been and is the constant aim of American foreign policy?

2. Why did isolationism seem a wise policy in our early years?

3. With what major event did the United States become a first-class power in the world?

4. What basic transformation did the coming of World War II bring in American foreign policy?

5. What is the policy of deterrence?

362   CHAPTER 19

6. How do the UN and our regional security treaties illustrate the concept of "collective security"?

7. The enunciation of what doctrine inaugurated the policy of resistance to communist aggression?

8. What have, at least thus far, proved to be the major clashes of the Cold War?

9. The United States has given how much in economic and military aid to other nations since the end of World War II?

10. When and where was the UN Charter drafted?

11. What, according to the UN Charter, are the UN's basic purposes?

12. How many nations now belong to the UN?

13. What are the major functions and powers of the UN's six principal organs?

14. In which of the UN's organs are all of the organization's members equally represented?

15. What is the veto power?

16. What are the Specialized Agencies?

17. Of what member-states is the Trusteeship Council composed?

18. Who may be parties to cases before the International Court of Justice?

19. Who heads the Secretariat?

20. Is the UN a failure? Why?

For Further Inquiry

1. Some critics have argued that the history of the United States demonstrates that we are not a "peace-loving people." How would you answer such critics?

2. The United States refused to join the League of Nations after World War I but took a leading role in the formation of the United Nations at the end of World War II. How do you explain this sharp reversal of policy?

3. According to former Secretary of State Christian Herter: "Eighty-five cents out of every dollar spent by the Federal Government since the beginning of this Republic has been spent on wars, preparation for wars, or repairing the damages caused by wars." Thus far (over the period from 1789 to date) the Federal Government has spent more than $2,000,000,000,-000 altogether. Accepting Mr. Herter's formula, approximately how much have the American people spent on past, present, and future wars? Why have we born this stupendous burden? Why do we continue to do so? Might this burden be lightened in the foreseeable future? If so, how?

4. The United States insisted upon the veto power when the UN was founded and does not favor its abolition today. Why might the United States take this position?

5. Articles 9 and 18 of the UN Charter provide that all member-states shall be represented equally in the General Assembly and that each shall have one vote in that body. Thus, the United States and the organization's smallest member (today the Maldive Islands) each casts one vote in the General Assembly. Do you think this is either fair or realistic? Why does the United States not press for a change in this arrangement?

Important Terms

Big Five
collective security
deterrence
Good Neighbor Policy
isolationism

Monroe Doctrine
Open Door Policy
optional clause
procedural questions

regional security
  treaties
Specialized Agencies
substantive questions

Truman Doctrine
trust territories
"Uniting for Peace"
  Resolution
veto power

Suggested Activities

1. Stage a debate or class forum on the following question: *Resolved,* That the United States should withdraw immediately from the United Nations and all other "entangling alliances."

2 Present a brief report to the class on a problem in our current foreign relations—for example, our policy toward Communist China or the proliferation of nuclear weapons.

3. Write an essay on the necessity of preventing World War III.

4. Secure a copy of the United Nations Charter and prepare a brief outline of its major provisions.

Suggested Reading

BUNKER, AMBASSADOR ELLSWORTH, "A Close Look at Progress Inside Viet Nam," *U.S. News,* November 17, 1969.

BURKE, ADMIRAL ARLEIGH A., "The Hazards of Negotiating with the Communists," *Reader's Digest,* October 1968.

COLLINS, EDWARD, *International Law in a Changing World.* Random House, 1970.

DULLES, ELEANOR L., *American Foreign Policy in the Making.* Harper & Row, 1968.

FULBRIGHT, SENATOR J. WILLIAM, "The Wars in Your Future," *Look,* December 2, 1969.

GIBNEY, FRANK, "Japan: New Face of World Power," *Look,* October 21, 1969.

HAMILTON, ANDREW, "The Arms Race: Too Much of a Bad Thing," *New York Times Magazine,* October 6, 1968.

HOFSTADTER, RICHARD, "Uncle Sam Has Cried Uncle Before," *New York Times Magazine,* May 19, 1968.

HOUGHTON, NEAL D. (ed.), *Struggle Against History: U.S. Foreign Policy in an Age of Revolution.* Simon & Schuster, 1968.

HUIZINGA, J. H., "America's Lost Innocence," *New York Times Magazine,* January 26, 1969.

"NATO: After 20 Years a Renewed U.S. Pledge," *U.S. News,* April 21, 1969.

LAPP, RALPH E., "China's Mushroom Cloud Casts a Long Shadow," *New York Times Magazine,* July 14, 1968.

McNAMARA, ROBERT S., "Under the Shadow of the Bomb," *Life,* September 3, 1968.

"Pitfalls for U.S. in Arms Talks," *U.S. News,* November 10, 1969.

"President Nixon's Address to the U.N.," *U.S. News,* September 29, 1969.

RADWAY, LAURENCE I., *Foreign Policy and National Defense.* Scott, Foresman, 1969.

"Remember Korean Negotiations?" *U.S. News,* January 22, 1968.

"Rethinking U.S. China Policy," *Time,* June 6, 1969.

SAPIN, BURTON M., *Contemporary American Foreign and Military Policy.* Scott, Foresman, 1969.

SPANNER, JOHN W., *American Foreign Policy Since World War II.* Praeger, 1968.

STOESSINGER, JOHN G., *The Might of Nations World Politics in Our Time.* Random House, 1969.

————, *The United Nations and the Superpowers.* Random House, 1969.

"The Changing Geopolitics of World Oil," *U.S. News,* April 14, 1969.

"The Cuban Missile Crisis: As Told by Robert Kennedy," *U.S. News,* October 28, 1968.

TREVOR-ROPER, H. R., "The Dilemma of Munich Is Still with Us," *New York Times Magazine,* September 15, 1968.

"U.S., Japan on a Collision Course?" *U.S. News,* November 24, 1969.

VELIE, LESTER, "The Week the Hot Line Burned," *Reader's Digest,* August 1968.

WHITNEY, ALLEN S., "How We Almost Went to War With China," *Look,* April 29, 1969.

YOST, CHARLES, *The Insecurity of Nations: International Relations in the Twentieth Century.* Praeger, 1969.

THE DEPARTMENT OF THE TREASURY

Money is, with propriety, considered as the vital principle of the body politic; as that which sustains its life and motion, and enables it to perform its most essential functions.

ALEXANDER HAMILTON

❖❖❖ What should be the objectives of the nation's tax policies?

❖❖❖ Should (or should not) the National Government be constitutionally prohibited the power to spend more than it receives in any fiscal year? Why?

❖❖❖ Of what significance is the relationship between the size of the national debt and the gross national product?

The National Government will collect some $200,000,000,000 from all sources in fiscal year 1971, and it will spend very nearly that same amount in the same period. To put that stupendous figure in more manageable terms: on the average, it costs every man, woman, and child in the country more than $975 each year to support the functions and services of the National Government. Each year the National Government accounts for about twenty cents of every dollar of our total national income.

DEPARTMENTAL ORGANIZATION

The Treasury Department was created by Congress during its first session in 1789 to "supervise and manage the national finances." Over the years, a variety of other functions has been added to the Department's work, as we shall see. In addition to its domestic duties, it is responsible for many of our policies and programs in the field of international finance. Thus, the State and Treasury Departments work closely together in these matters; for example, in the granting of loans to foreign governments, the reduction of tariff rates, or the protection of the soundness of the dollar in world trade.

The Treasury Department is headed by the *Secretary of the Treasury* who, like all other Cabinet officers, is appointed by the President with the consent of the Senate. His principal aides include two Under Secretaries, the General Counsel, the Fiscal Assistant Secretary, the Assistant Secretary for Administration, and four other Assistant Secretaries.

The six major agencies within the Department, employing most of its over 90,000-man working force today, are the:

Bureau of Customs
Internal Revenue Service
Fiscal Service
Office of the Comptroller of the Currency
Bureau of Engraving and Printing
United States Secret Service

REVENUE COLLECTION

The Constitution gives to Congress the expressed power "to lay and collect taxes, duties, imposts, and excises."[1] The actual collection of most of the levies Congress has provided for is made through the Bureau of Customs and the Internal Revenue Service. The large bulk of all federal revenues is funneled through these two agencies. Lesser amounts, mostly in the form of nontax revenues, reach the Treasury through other channels.

Some impression of the amounts and the job involved in the collection of federal revenues can be seen in this striking comparison:

If on the day that Christ was born, a machine had been invented that ground out a one-dollar bill every second of every hour of every day of every year since then, it would not yet have produced *half as much* as the National Government now collects in revenue *each year!*

Bureau of Customs. A Commissioner of Customs appointed by the President with Senate consent heads the Bureau of Customs. Under him, the nation and its possessions are divided into nine Customs Regions, each headed by a Regional Commissioner. These areas are further divided into forty-one Districts, each headed by a District Director. Through this geographic complex, encompassing the nation's 290 ports of entry, the Bureau must assess and collect import duties, guard against smuggling, and arrest violators of the customs laws.

Customs duties were the major source of federal revenue for more than a century. Today they produce only a minor fraction of the total, however—for fiscal year 1971, an estimated $2,260,000,000.

All articles brought into the country must enter at specified points, *ports of entry*. The ports of entry are located along the Atlantic, Pacific, and Gulf Coasts and include several inland cities, such as St. Louis and Chicago. More than half of all customs are collected at the Port of New York.

Customs on about 2000 taxable articles are of three kinds—*specific, ad valorem,* and *mixed*. *Specific* means so much per unit, a $\frac{1}{2}$¢ a pound on sugar or $3\frac{1}{2}$¢ per dozen on eggs. *Ad valorem* means "in proportion to value," as 55% on mesh bags valued at less than $5 per dozen and 35% if valued at more. *Mixed* means that both a *specific* duty and an *ad valorem* duty are imposed upon the same article.

As the determination of values is very difficult, persons exporting to the United States articles valued at over $100 are required to have invoices certified by an American consul. When articles are valued at $100 or less, an oral statement is accepted. If the consul is not certain of the value, he may demand three samples: one for himself, one for the United States Customs Court, and one for the appraiser at the port to which the merchandise is sent.

To prevent fraud when merchandise is received at a port, ten per cent of the packages, selected at random, are opened and examined. All personal baggage is also subject to examination. Special agents here and abroad and the Coast Guard keep watch against smugglers. Recently, one smuggler was arrested as he stepped off a ship from Europe; he had nearly $50,000 in uncut diamonds hidden in his socks and in a money belt he was wearing under a surgical belt.

Any person, except an officer of the United States, who gives original information leading to conviction of smugglers may be rewarded by the Commissioner of Customs. Not long ago, an employee of the Cunard Steamship Company received a reward of $17,119. His tip to a customs agent led to the discovery of $171,197.60 in gold bullion concealed in a car and about to be smuggled out of the country aboard the *Queen Elizabeth*.

The Internal Revenue Service. The overall operations of the Internal Revenue Service

---

[1] Article I, Section 8, Clause 1; see Chapter 14.

are directed by the Commissioner of Internal Revenue, who is appointed by the President and confirmed by the Senate. Under him, the IRS is organized on a geographic basis. There are now seven Internal Revenue Regions, each headed by a Regional Commissioner. These areas are further divided into Internal Revenue Districts, fifty-eight in all, each headed by a Director. The Regional Commissioners and the Directors are appointed under civil service. The IRS collects billions of dollars each year and guards against tax evasion.

The income tax on individuals and corporations produces more than eighty per cent of all federal revenues (see pages 255–257). *Other internal revenue* is derived from taxes levied on bequests and inheritances, liquor, wine, beer, cigarettes and other tobacco products, gasoline, diesel fuels, automobiles, airline tickets, and many other items.

The National Government has various methods of checking upon the honesty of those who should pay income taxes. It requires the keeping of records of business; it requires employers to withhold and turn in the tax due from employees; it requires corporations to report dividends and interest, and those paying royalties on patents and copyrights to report the sums of money paid; it exchanges information with State income tax collectors; it compels witnesses to testify; and it employs special agents. The National Government can inspect bank accounts, records, and, to some extent, safe deposit boxes. It even has international treaties granting inspection privileges in other countries.

Those who fail to report all of their taxable income may be imprisoned, may be fined, and may have a penalty added equal to 50 per cent of the amount not reported. For example, it was discovered that a movie star had short-changed the Government $118,364. For this fraud he was required to pay the $118,364, plus a penalty of 50 per cent of it, plus a $3000 fine —or a total of $180,546. Evasions may be detected even after death.

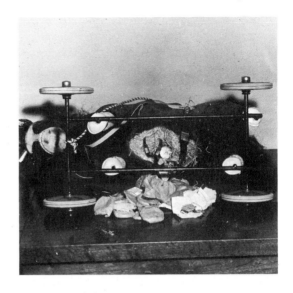

Experienced Customs inspectors know that even toys are worth more than a superficial examination. Hidden in this toy pony, by an importer determined to bypass customs duty (tax), were a number of undeclared watch movements. (Bureau of Customs, U.S. Treasury Department)

Information on tax evasion comes from all kinds of sources. In one interesting case, a man told his fiancee how he had cleverly cheated the tax collector. When he later jilted her, she reported him out of spite. So years after he thought he had gotten by, he paid the price of dishonesty.

Most taxpayers are honest, but there are enough who attempt to cheat the government to keep the agents of the IRS active. "T-Men" rival FBI agents in excellence and work with various other federal and State agencies to enforce the tax laws.

Nontax Revenues. Some $3,000,000,000 in nontax receipts reach the Treasury each year. They come from a wide variety of sources including the fines imposed by courts; interest and principal on loans; canal tolls; fees for such items as passports, patents, and copyright; the sale or lease of public lands; and the sale of surplus property.

One of the many little-known sources for nontax revenues is *seigniorage,* the profit obtained from the minting of coins. This profit, of approximately $400,000,000 in fiscal year 1971, is the difference between the value of the metals used to produce coins and the face value of the minted coins. Another source is the sale of postage stamps to collectors. The Philatelic Sales Unit in the Post Office Department sells approximately $3,000,000 in mint stamps each year. Many times that amount are bought by collectors at local post offices, and few of these stamps are ever used on mail.

SAFEKEEPING AND DISBURSEMENT OF THE NATIONAL REVENUES

The Constitution provides that:

> No monies shall be drawn from the Treasury, but in consequence of appropriations made by law; and a regular statement and account of the receipts and expenditures of all public money shall be published from time to time.[2]

The Fiscal Service. The Fiscal Service, the National Government's general bookkeeping office, houses three agencies:

The Bureau of Accounts is the central accounting and financial reporting agency for all federal activities. Pursuant to the constitutional requirement, it publishes a daily, monthly, and annual *Statement of the Receipts and Expenditures of the United States Government.* The data in the table on page 369 is drawn from the annual *Statement* for fiscal year 1970.

The Bureau of the Public Debt has general supervision of the public debt transactions of the nation. We shall turn to that subject in a moment.

The Treasurer of the United States, who heads the Office of the Treasurer, is *the* officer responsible for every cent of the billions of dollars involved in our national financing. By custom, the President usually appoints a woman to the post. By law, she is charged with the responsibility for the receipt, custody, and disbursement of the public monies and the keeping of records of the sources, present locations, and disposition of these funds. Funds are paid out by the Treasurer upon the presentation of a *warrant* (an order to pay, as a check) drawn by the Secretary of the Treasury and approved by the Comptroller-General.

Some 50,000 banks, other organizations, and individuals bring batches of burned or mutilated currency to the Treasury for replacement each year. The "money surgeons" in the Currency Redemption Division of the Office of the Treasurer examine it and redeem as much as possible. A few years ago, a man brought in a large stack of bills that had rotted underground. Experts were able to redeem $53,000, but $48,000 had to go to the tax collector; the man was a professional gambler who had never reported his winnings.

A man in North Carolina put $600 in an electric heater for "safekeeping." He forgot about the money, and months later the Currency Redemption Division was able to identify $570 from his handful of ashes. The experts were also able to save $8500 out of a $9000 lump of black char belonging to a South Dakota farmer who didn't trust banks.

General Accounting Office. The *Comptroller-General,* who heads the General Accounting Office (GAO), is often called the "Watchdog of the Treasury." The GAO is charged with the responsibility of seeing that all expenditures are made as and for the purpose Congress intended.[3]

---

[2] Article I, Section 9, Clause 7.

[3] The Comptroller-General may prevent the expenditure of funds whenever, in his opinion, such spending would not be in complete accord with congressional appropriation acts. His rulings may be appealed to the courts, but they seldom are. Notice, however, that his power is over the *legality,* not the *wisdom,* of expenditures.

RECEIPTS AND EXPENDITURES OF THE UNITED STATES GOVERNMENT

Note: Figures are rounded in millions of dollars and may not add to totals shown.	Fiscal 1969	Fiscal 1970
Receipts by Source		
Individual Income Taxes	$ 87,249	$ 90,371
Corporation Income Taxes	36,678	32,829
Excise Taxes	15,222	15,711
Estate and Gift Taxes	3,491	3,620
Customs	2,319	2,430
Employment Taxes (Social Security, Railroad Retirement, Federal Unemployment Taxes)	39,917	45,296
All Other (interest on loans, sales on property, leases, tolls, fines, seigniorage, etc.)	2,916	3,587
Total Receipts	$187,792	$193,844
Outlays by Major Agency		
The Legislative and Judicial Branches	$ 386	$ 468
The President, Executive Office	31	36
Office of Economic Opportunity	1,813	1,801
Foreign Aid, Military	789	731
Foreign Aid, Economic	1,781	1,606
Other	585	639
Dept. of Defense	79,145	78,310
Dept. of State	437	447
Atomic Energy Commission	2,450	2,453
National Aeronautics and Space Administration	4,247	3,749
Veterans Administration	7,669	8,653
Dept. of the Treasury, Interest on Public Debt	16,588	19,257
Other	336	234
Dept. of Health, Education, and Welfare	46,594	52,350
Dept. of Transportation	5,970	6,418
Dept. of Housing and Urban Development	1,529	2,603
Dept. of Commerce	854	1,027
Dept. of Labor	3,475	4,358
Dept. of Agriculture	8,330	7,548
Dept. of the Interior	837	1,119
Dept. of Justice	515	637
Post Office Dept.	920	1,514
Civil Service Commission	1,682	2,647
All Other Agencies	2,713	3,546
Deduct: Interest to Trust Funds	− 3,099	− 3,934
Contributions to Federal Employee Retirement	− 2,018	− 2,443
Total Outlays	$184,556	$196,752
Budget Surplus (+) or Deficit (−)	+ $3,236	− $2,908

Actually, the GAO is not located within the Treasury Department. It was set up in 1921 in order that Congress might have a check on the spending of funds it appropriates and is independent of the executive branch. The Comptroller-General is appointed by the President and is confirmed by the Senate. He serves for a fifteen-year term and may be removed only by Congress.

In 1934, when it seemed that the prairie States were becoming a dustbowl, President Roosevelt ordered that $15,000,000 of the $525,000,000 drought relief fund authorized by Congress be used for planting strips of trees to stop soil erosion (see page 444). The Comptroller-General ruled that the drought relief fund was intended for *direct* and *immediate* relief, not for projects whose results lay so far in the future; thus, he allowed only $1,000,000 to get the program started.

The General Accounting Office also superintends the recovery of debts owed to the United States. For example, a military officer received an extra allowance for his dependent mother. When it was found that his mother was worth $42,500, the GAO took steps to recover the excess payment.

The Comptroller of the Currency exercises general supervision over the operations of national banks. His office was created in the National Banking Act of 1863. See pages 545–546.

THE PUBLIC DEBT

The cost of government has mounted rapidly and to well-nigh astronomical heights in the past few decades. In 1900 the National Government spent less than $500,000,000. By 1940, it was spending nearly twenty times as much — or just over $9,000,000,000. The heavy expenditures required by World War II and in the peril-fraught years since have pushed the annual rate to more than *350 times* the 1900 figure. The National Government now spends more *each year* than it did during all of the first 150 years of our history!

When governmental spending exceeds its income, it must borrow and thus go into debt. The Framers of the Constitution recognized the necessity for — and the inevitability of — a public debt and so gave to Congress the expressed power "to borrow money on the credit of the United States." [4]

Today (1971) the public debt stands above $370,000,000,000 — or just about $1750 for every person in the country. This huge sum is primarily the result of World War I, the Great Depression of the 1930's, World War II, and the present defense program. Interest on the debt now comes to some $20,000,000,000 annually, a rate of more than 5 per cent.

Over the period since 1930, the Government's expenditures have exceeded its receipts in all but six fiscal years. Only in fiscal years 1947, 1948, 1951, 1956, 1957, and 1969 did the Government report receiving more than it spent.

For selected, significant fiscal years, the gross public debt has been:

1916, pre-World War I	
	$ 1,225,000,000
1919, post-World War I	
	$ 25,482,000,000
1930, start of Great Depression	
	$ 16,185,000,000
1940, after decade of Great Depression	
	$ 42,968,000,000 '
1941, pre-World War II	
	$ 48,961,000,000
1946, post-World War II	
	$269,422,000,000
1950, pre-Korean War	
	$257,357,000,000
1953, post-Korean War	
	$266,071,000,000
1964, prior to massive Viet Nam commitment	
	$311,713,000,000
1970, latest fiscal year	
	$370,918,706,849

[4] Article I, Section 8, Clause 2.

How the United States Borrows Money.
The Government borrows on both a "short-term" and a "long-term" basis. For short-term borrowing, *notes, bills,* and *certificates of indebtedness* are issued; they run anywhere from thirty days to seven years. *Bonds* are issued for long-term borrowing purposes, and they usually mature in ten or, more often, twenty or thirty years. The short-term interest rate now (1971) ranges as high as 7 per cent. A ceiling of 4.25 per cent on the interest payable on long-term bonds was imposed by Congress from 1918 to 1970. Even with a higher ceiling (now 5 per cent) the Treasury has for several years found it difficult to market any of its long-term issues.

The National Government issues both bearer bonds and registered bonds. Bearer bonds may be passed around like money, and the interest is collected every six months by clipping and cashing at any bank the coupons attached to the bottom of each bond. Registered bonds are registered at the Treasury in the name of the owner. They can be circulated only by transferring ownership to another party. The interest is paid by checks from the Treasury.

Series E Savings Bonds are the most popular bonds issued by the Treasury. The E or Savings Bonds bought today mature in seven years and they pay a handsome 5.5 per cent interest, compounded semi-annually, when held to maturity. These bonds were originally offered at 2.9 per cent to mature in ten years. The terms have been liberalized five times in recent years to make them more attractive to the small investor. The bonds may be registered in the name of one person, two persons as co-owners, or one as owner and another as beneficiary. If lost or stolen, the Treasury will replace them. They may be cashed at a bank any time after sixty days from date of issue. They are issued in $25 to $10,000 denominations, but no one may purchase over $10,000 in these attractive government savings bonds in any one year.

Debt Ceiling. The Constitution places no ceiling on the amount of the national debt, but Congress has legislated one. As of January, 1971, the limit was $395,000,000,000 —but Congress may and does vary the figure.

THE NATIONAL CURRENCY SYSTEM

The Currency Power. The Articles of Confederation had given to Congress the power to coin money and regulate its value, but the States were not prohibited from doing so, as well. As we have seen, the lack of a stable and uniform currency was one of the prime economic difficulties of the 1780's.[5]

The Founding Fathers were nearly all agreed upon the need for a "hard" currency for the nation. The Constitution gives to Congress the power "to coin money [and] regulate the value thereof."[6] It also forbids the States the power to coin money, issue paper money, or make anything but gold or silver legal tender.[7] In effect, then, Congress is given the power to establish a national system of currency.

Development of the Currency System.
Congress first provided for a national currency system in the Mint Act of 1792. Both gold and silver were selected as the base for the nation's money, with coins minted of each metal to circulate side by side. The content of the silver dollar was fixed at 371.25 grains and that of the gold dollar at 24.75 grains.

The ratio between the two, 15 to 1, reflected the market price of the two metals at the time. But the fact that the law said that one ounce of gold was worth fifteen ounces of silver had

---

[5] See the Articles of Confederation (Article IX) page 753 and pages 37, 242.

[6] Article I, Section 8, Clause 5; see pages 63, 242.

[7] Article I, Section 10, Clause 1; see pages 65, 241. *Legal tender* is any kind of money a creditor is required by law to accept when offered in payment of a monetary debt.

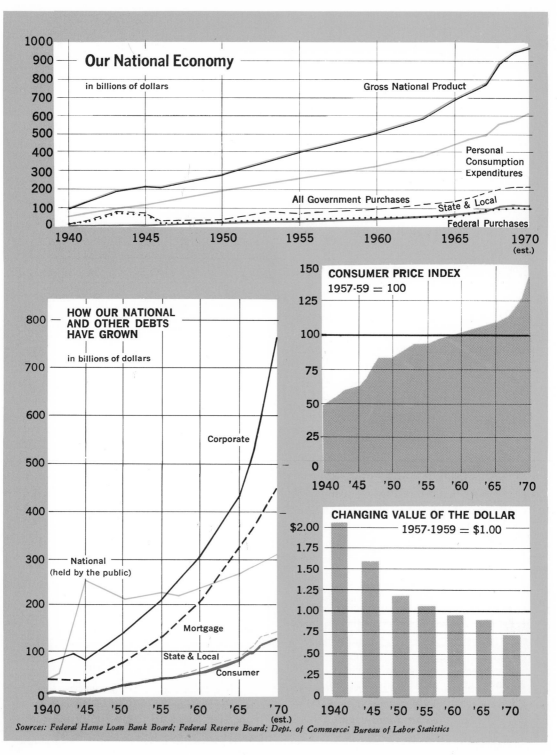

Our National Economy

in billions of dollars

Gross National Product

Personal Consumption Expenditures

All Government Purchases

State & Local

Federal Purchases

1940   1945   1950   1955   1960   1965   1970 (est.)

HOW OUR NATIONAL AND OTHER DEBTS HAVE GROWN

in billions of dollars

Corporate

National (held by the public)

Mortgage

State & Local

Consumer

1940   '45   '50   '55   '60   '65   '70 (est.)

CONSUMER PRICE INDEX
1957-59 = 100

1940   '45   '50   '55   '60   '65   '70

CHANGING VALUE OF THE DOLLAR
1957-1959 = $1.00

$2.00
1.75
1.50
1.25
1.00
.75
.50
.25
0

1940   '45   '50   '55   '60   '65   '70

Sources: Federal Home Loan Bank Board; Federal Reserve Board; Dept. of Commerce; Bureau of Labor Statistics

The Federal Budget

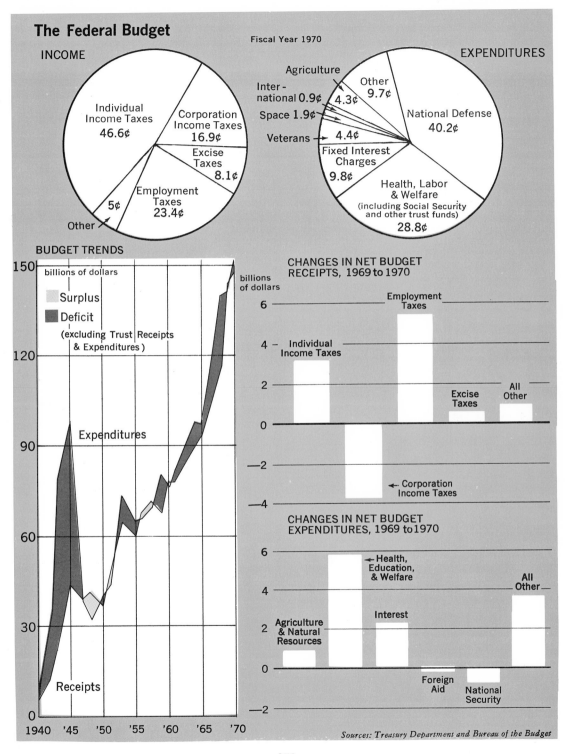

Fiscal Year 1970

INCOME

Individual Income Taxes 46.6¢

Corporation Income Taxes 16.9¢

Excise Taxes 8.1¢

Employment Taxes 23.4¢

Other 5¢

EXPENDITURES

Agriculture

Inter-national 0.9¢

Space 1.9¢

Veterans

Other 9.7¢

4.3¢

4.4¢

National Defense 40.2¢

Fixed Interest Charges 9.8¢

Health, Labor & Welfare (including Social Security and other trust funds) 28.8¢

BUDGET TRENDS

billions of dollars

150
120
90
60
30
0

Surplus
Deficit
(excluding Trust Receipts & Expenditures)

Expenditures

Receipts

1940 '45 '50 '55 '60 '65 '70

CHANGES IN NET BUDGET RECEIPTS, 1969 to 1970

billions of dollars

6
4
2
0
—2
—4

Employment Taxes

Individual Income Taxes

Excise Taxes

All Other

Corporation Income Taxes

CHANGES IN NET BUDGET EXPENDITURES, 1969 to 1970

6
4
2
0
—2

Health, Education, & Welfare

Interest

Agriculture & Natural Resources

Foreign Aid

National Security

All Other

Sources: Treasury Department and Bureau of the Budget

little or no effect upon their actual market prices, and they fluctuated constantly. Attempts to adjust the ratio between the two metals — in terms of the gold and silver content of the nation's dollars — was the source of violent political controversy throughout the nineteenth century.

As silver declined in value, silver dollars became "cheaper" than gold dollars, and the latter were hoarded by many people. To counteract this, Congress reduced the gold content of the dollar in 1834, establishing the ratio at 16 to 1. Of course, this made gold dollars worth more than they had been. Silver dollars were virtually driven out of circulation because those with debts to pay or who bought almost anything quite naturally preferred gold to silver money.

When Congress suspended the coinage of silver dollars altogether in 1873, it stirred one of the sharpest fights in all of American political history. Opponents, especially in the agricultural Middle West and the mining areas of the West, battled tooth and nail for the "free coinage of silver" — that is, for the resumption of the minting of silver at 16 to 1. The issue dominated the nation's politics for the next quarter of a century, with the Democrats generally supporting silver and the Republicans gold. The presidential election of 1896 was waged on this one question to the exclusion of nearly all else.

The Republican victory in 1896 led to the enactment of the Gold Standard Act of 1900. Congress made the gold dollar, pegged at 23.22 grains, *the* monetary standard and required that all other money (silver and paper currency) be kept at a parity with gold. That is, it provided in law what had been true in fact for years: the nation was declared to be on the gold standard. The bimetallic base (gold and silver) established in 1792 was abolished. Henceforth, all currency was to be backed by gold, and all silver and paper money could be redeemed at the Treasury for its face value in gold. The law also required the Treasury and

national banks to maintain reserves of gold sufficient to back all other money in circulation.

The gold standard was abandoned in 1933–1934, however.[8] The Great Depression which began in 1929 brought severe business and financial crises. The public lost confidence in the security of bank deposits and the value of paper money. Hundreds of financial institutions failed, and millions of people suffered heavy personal losses. Gold began to disappear from circulation as millions of dollars worth were hoarded and millions more were shipped abroad.

President Roosevelt moved to maintain the nation's gold reserves soon after taking office in 1933. He ordered the Treasury to halt its gold payments (the redemption of silver and paper currency in gold). Congress voided the "gold clauses" in all long-term bonds and contracts — provisions requiring the payment of both principal and interest in gold dollars.

Congress also authorized the President to reduce the gold content of the dollar — which he promptly did: from 23.22 grains to 13.7 grains. The action was especially intended to give a boost to the depressed economy. It had the effect of making gold dollars worth more than before and thus meant that there was now more money in circulation.[9]

In the Gold Reserve Act of 1934 and a number of other statutes Congress made several other significant changes in the currency system. Gold coinage was suspended, and it has not been resumed. All holders of gold coin and of gold certificates (paper money redeemable in gold) were required to turn them in to

---

[8] That is to say it was abolished because gold coins no longer circulate. The nation's money is now backed by the gold bullion held by the National Government. In effect, a *gold bullion* standard replaced the former gold standard.

[9] The legal price of gold was thus raised from the $20.67 per ounce fixed by the Gold Standard Act of 1900 to $35 per ounce, which remains the price today.

the Treasury in exchange for paper money. In effect, gold was nationalized; the National Government became the sole owner of all gold bullion in the country. All private transactions in gold were prohibited; mere possession was made subject to heavy penalty.[10]

The Nation's Gold Supply. When gold was withdrawn from circulation in 1934, Congress directed the Treasury to accumulate a gold stock sufficient to support a hugely expanded paper currency. This reserve stood at about $22,000,000,000 until 1958; but an "outflow of gold," especially over the next five years, reduced the amount to its present (1971) level of about $12,000,000,000. The outflow was due largely to the fact that we lend and spend more abroad than we earn there. Our commercial exports regularly exceed imports each year. But economic and military aid to our allies, maintaining our armed forces abroad, and tourist spending make up the difference and produce an unfavorable balance. Although the rate of outflow has been reduced in recent years, it does continue. Even so, with the nation's gold reserves at about the $12,000,000,000 mark, the United States holds approximately one-third of all of the world's supply of monetary gold.

Present Forms of Currency. In the exercise of its currency power, Congress has provided for its issuance in two forms: metallic and paper.

Metallic Currency. All United States coins are stamped by the Bureau of the Mint at the United States Mints in Philadelphia and Denver.[11] The Bureau also maintains Assay Offices in New York and San Francisco and operates a Bullion Depository for gold at Fort Knox and for silver at West Point.

Our Gold Reserves

$25 billion — $20 billion — $15 billion — $10 billion — $5 billion — 0

1935 '40 '45 '50 '55 '60 '65 '70

Source: Federal Reserve System

---

[10] Except for such strictly limited purposes as jewelry or industrial use or in coin collections.

[11] The old San Francisco Mint was converted from coin production to a storage facility in 1955 but minting was resumed there on a temporary basis in 1965–1966.

The coins of the United States in circulation today include pennies, nickels, dimes, quarters, half-dollars, and dollars. The metals used to make them are purchased from the lowest bidders at the Philadelphia and Denver Mints, under the supervision of the Director of the Mint.

The one-cent piece is minted of bronze (nineteen parts copper and one part tin or zinc). The five-cent piece is minted of three parts copper and one part nickel.

The ten and twenty-five cent pieces, *first put into circulation in late 1965,* are faced with a copper-nickel alloy (3 parts copper, one part nickel) which is bonded to a core of pure copper. These newer dimes and quarters, then, resemble the nickel in outward appearance — except, of course, in size and design and the fact that their copper core gives them a copper edge.

Older dimes and quarters,[12] which circulate side by side with the newer ones, are silver coins. They contain ninety per cent silver (a silver content of .72 per ounce).

The fifty-cent pieces, *first put into circulation in 1966,* are also silver coins. They contain forty per cent silver. They are faced with an alloy of four parts silver and one part copper bonded to a core of 21 parts silver and 79 parts copper. They are very nearly indistinguishable from the older half-dollars which, like the other older coins, contain ninety per cent silver.

The dollar-pieces are silver coins, too, containing more than ninety-six per cent silver (a silver content of .77 per ounce). None has been minted since 1935.

The recent coinage changes resulted from two factors: (1) a marked increase in the use of coins over the past several years and (2) a steadily rising demand for silver for coinage and for industrial and other uses.

The nation's need for coins has reached such proportions that coin shortages have occurred in most sections of the country in recent years. A number of factors produced this situation, notably our population growth, a continuing prosperity, and a steadily expanding economy. Several other and more specific factors also combined to cause coin shortages. For the past several years the demand for silver, for coinage and industrial uses, has increased at a faster rate than the supply. The spectacular rise in the use of vending machines — to dispense a wide variety of goods and services — added to the problem. So, too, did coin collectors, and speculators hoarding against a sharp hike in the market price of silver.

Several recent actions have helped to relieve the situation — especially the passage of the *Coinage Act of 1965* which brought about a sharp reduction in the amount of silver used to produce our coins. In fact, coinage now takes only about ten per cent of the silver that was required for the purpose before the legislation was enacted.

For decades the Treasury maintained a huge reserve of silver; as recently as early 1967 it held more than 500,000,000 ounces of the metal. Only a small portion of the stockpile was used to mint new coins. Most of it was held in order to control the world market price for silver — to keep it below the point (approximately $1.40 an ounce) at which it would be profitable to melt down our coins to recover their silver content. Had the price not been thus artificially controlled, the bulk of the nation's coinage would have disappeared — and with disastrous consequences.

The stockpiling policy was finally abandoned in mid-1967, however; the Treasury withdrew from the silver market, thus "freeing" the price of the metal. This became possible because, through a massive effort, the mints had turned out enough of the new silverless "clad" coins to meet the nation's needs.[13]

Paper Currency. Most of the money we see and use today is paper money. The government's gold supplies stand as security for it.

Recall that the Constitution gives to Congress the power to *coin* money; but it says nothing about *paper* money — except to prohibit the States from issuing it.[14] As we noted on page 242, however, the Supreme Court upheld the right of Congress to authorize the issuance of paper currency and to make it legal tender in 1871. All paper currency issued by the United States is today legal tender — that is, it must be accepted by a creditor when tendered in payment for a monetary debt (see pages 241-242).

---

[12] These coins (and the older half-dollars) were minted until 1965.

[13] Although the price of silver immediately rose substantially above the $1.40 level, the threat to our older coins is minimized by the fact that it is unlawful to melt down or otherwise deface any of the nation's currency; also the Treasury has been withdrawing the older coins from circulation since 1968.

[14] Article I, Section 8, Clause 5 and Section 10, Clause 1; see pages 241-242.

The United States Mint at Denver, Colorado, is one of two which produce our coins. This coin press places blanks in position to be stamped, pushes the stamped coins off the dies, and the feeder fingers return for more blanks. The Director of the Mint, upon the approval of the Secretary of the Treasury, selects the design for our coins. (Bureau of the Mint, U.S. Treasury Department)

Better than ninety-five per cent of all the paper currency in circulation today (or about $50,000,000,000 is in the form of *federal reserve notes*. These notes are issued by each of the twelve Federal Reserve Banks (see pages 547-549) in denominations from $1 up to $10,000. They are direct obligations on the United States Government. In effect they are "warehouse receipts" against the National Government's gold reserves—but, recall, they cannot be redeemed in gold. The power of the Federal Reserve Board to increase or decrease the amount of federal reserve notes in circulation has a fundamental effect upon the nation's economy—as we shall see later, on pages 548-549.

Several other forms of paper currency are in circulation, but only in limited and steadily decreasing amounts. The once very common *silver certificates,* issued by the Treasury until 1964, and mostly in the form of $1 bills, are being replaced by federal reserve notes. They were backed by silver bullion held by the Treasury, but they were discontinued in order to free the silver for coinage and other uses. National bank notes, Treasury notes of 1890, and a few other forms of paper money are also retired from circulation whenever they are deposited in banks.

All federal paper currency—that is, today, all federal reserve notes—are designed, engraved, and printed by the Bureau of Engraving and Printing in the Treasury Department. The Bureau also produces all of the Treasury's bonds, notes, bills, and certificates of indebtedness (see page 371); and all postage, revenue, customs, and savings stamps, and food coupons. It also prints military and civilian award certificates, commissions of office, many types of permits, and a wide variety of other items for several other federal agencies.

THE UNITED STATES SECRET SERVICE

The United States Secret Service was created by Congress in 1865 and is today the oldest of the various federal police agencies. It was originally established to suppress the counterfeiting of United States currency. Over the years a number of additional functions have been added to that original assignment—most notably, of course, the protection of the person of the President.

The Service is headed by a Director who is appointed by the President and Senate. His agency was extensively reorganized in the aftermath of the assassination of President Kennedy in 1963. The agents under his command now operate out of the Secret Service Headquarters in Washington and from seventy district offices located throughout the country, and from an office in San Juan, Puerto Rico, and another in the American Embassy in Paris. Although they are not nearly so well-known to the general public, the agents of the Secret Service today rival the "G-men" of the FBI in their training, competence, and effectiveness.

Counterfeiters are still the special prey of the Secret Service. Most of those tracked down and arrested by the T-men have forged or otherwise trafficked illegally with the monies of the United States. The Service also enforces the statutes which prohibit the counterfeiting of foreign monies in this country and, as well, the forging of any of the obligations or securities of the United States. It brings to justice those who forge such other public financial documents as government travel authorizations, those who make false claims to federal lending agencies or embezzle the funds of those agencies, and those who commit similar federal offenses. All told, Secret Service agents handle some 5000 forgery cases each month and destroy an average of more than $500,000 in bogus bills and coins each year. A widely distributed Service booklet, *Know Your Money,* is a handy guide for the detection of counterfeit money and offers several useful suggestions for the outwitting or thwarting of forgers and counterfeiters.

By any reckoning, the most important of the tasks assigned to the Secret Service is that of protecting the President of the United States—an assignment first given to it by Congress after the assassination of President William McKinley in 1901. No matter where he goes or what he does, the President is under the 'round-the-clock surveillance of the unobtrusive agents of the White House detail. Even the food that he eats is prepared and served under their supervision.

All of the members of the President's immediate family, no matter where they may live or travel, are kept under the same watchful eye. That protective shield is also cast about the person of the Vice President (or the officer next in the line of succession if the Vice Presidency is vacant) and his family, and about the President-elect and his family the moment it becomes known that he has won election to the office.

The Secret Service also protects a former President and his wife during his lifetime, and the widow and minor children of a former President for a period of four years after he leaves (or dies in) office—unless that protection is declined.

Congress added yet another dimension to the role of the Secret Service in this area in 1968—the protection of presidential and vice presidential candidates every four years. The move was largely prompted by two events in that year: the assassination of Senator Robert F. Kennedy in Los Angeles as he campaigned for the Democratic Party's presidential nomination and the violent disturbances at the Democratic National Convention in Chicago.

During the 1968 presidential campaign, then, Secret Service agents guarded the Republican candidates (Richard Nixon and then-Governor Spiro Agnew), the Democratic candidates (Hubert Humphrey—who was also protected as the Vice President at the time—and Senator

Edmund S. Muskie), and the American Independent Party candidates (George C. Wallace and General Curtis LeMay). The same mantle will, of course, be cast about the major party nominees—and any significant minor party ones, as well—during the 1972 campaign.

At present (1970), the Secret Service is charged with the protection of the President and the Vice President and their families and, as well, the safety of former President and Mrs. Harry S Truman and former President and Mrs. Lyndon B. Johnson. In addition, the children of former President John F. Kennedy—Caroline and John Jr.,—are now, and will be, protected by the Secret Service until they reach their majority or decline such protection.

Much of the work of the Secret Service is handled by its plainclothes agents in Washington and elsewhere. It does maintain two uniformed police units, however. One, the Executive Protective Service, protects the White House and the executive offices and grounds. The other, the Treasury Guard Force, is responsible for the safety of the Treasury Building and the billions of dollars in currency, bonds, and other securities in its vaults.

Two major agencies, long located in the Treasury Department, have been transferred to other Cabinet Departments in the past few years. The Coast Guard was shifted to the Department of Transportation in 1967 and the Bureau of Narcotics, now the Bureau of Narcotics and Dangerous Drugs, was moved to the Department of Justice in 1968. We shall deal with them later when we turn to those Departments, in Chapters 22 and 29.

Most counterfeit money is a poor reproduction of genuine money. Counterfeiters rely on people's lack of observation to pass bad bills. Note some of the differences between good and bad money. (Secret Service, U.S. Treasury Department)

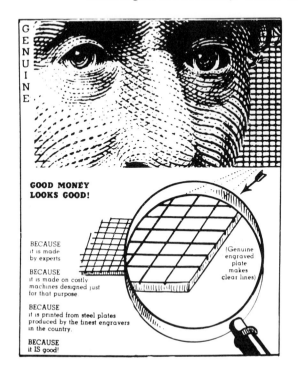

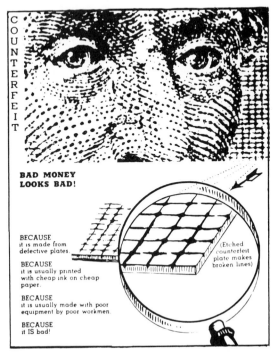

✶✶✶✶✶✶✶✶✶✶✶✶ CONCEPT BUILDING ✶✶✶✶✶✶✶✶✶✶✶✶

Key Concepts

The National Government will collect some $200,000,000,000 from all sources in fiscal year 1971, and will spend very nearly that same amount during the same period. The Treasury Department, headed by the Secretary of the Treasury, is charged with the major responsibility for the collection, safekeeping, and disbursement of the tremendous sums involved in national finance.

The Internal Revenue Service and the Bureau of Customs collect most of the federal revenue. The income tax levied on persons and on corporations produces approximately eighty per cent of all federal tax receipts. Other internal revenue comes from such sources as taxes on liquor, gasoline and other fuels, and cigarettes and other tobacco products. Customs duties (tariffs) are of three kinds: *specific, ad valorem,* and *mixed.* Nontax receipts, from a miscellany of sources, are also funneled through the Treasury Department.

The Fiscal Service is the central accounting agency for all federal activities and houses the Bureau of Accounts, the Bureau of the Public Debt, and the Office of the Treasurer of the United States. The Comptroller-General and his General Accounting Office are independent of the Treasury and of the executive branch, acting as a watchdog for Congress. The Comptroller of the Currency supervises the operations of national banks.

The nation's public debt now stands at more than $370,000,000,000. It is very largely the result of World War I, the Great Depression of the 1930's, World War II, and the defense programs of the postwar period. Deficit financing is accommodated through both long-term and short-term borrowing, and for these purposes the Treasury issues short-term notes, bills, and certificates of indebtedness and long-term bearer and registered bonds (including the Series E Savings Bonds). Although the Constitution places no ceiling on the size of the public debt, Congress may (and does) legislate one. The current (but frequently changed) ceiling is fixed (as of January 1971) at the astronomically high sum of $395,000,000,000.

Congress has created a currency system for the nation which is now based on the gold bullion standard. Currency circulates today in two forms, metallic and paper. The metallic currency—all of the nation's coinage—is produced by the Bureau of the Mint; the paper currency—almost wholly in the form of federal reserve notes today—is produced by the Bureau of Engraving and Printing.

The United States Secret Service was created by Congress in 1865 and is the oldest of the National Government's various police agencies. It was originally directed to combat the counterfeiting of United States monies but has acquired a number of additional responsibilities over the years—the most important one that of protecting the person of the President of the United States.

Important Terms

bullion	deficit	gold bullion standard	nontax revenue
currency	disbursement	gold standard	paper currency
currency power	federal reserve notes	legal tender	public debt
customs	fiscal year	metallic currency	redemption
debt ceiling			seigniorage

Questions for Inquiry and Review

1. Approximately how much are the net annual revenues and expenditures of the National Government today? What proportion is this of the total national income?

2. Who heads the Treasury Department? How is he selected?

3. Most of the taxes Congress has levied are collected by what two agencies?

4. What are nontax revenues? About how much do they amount to each year?

5. In what particular way is the independence of the Comptroller-General guaranteed?

6. What is the major task of the General Accounting Office?

7. To what particular causes is the nation's public debt largely due? Approximately how much is it today?

8. Why did the Founding Fathers give Congress the power to provide for a national currency system?

9. How is the national currency system protected against the competition of State currency?

10. Why was the fact that Congress originally selected both gold and silver as the bases for the national currency system an unfortunate one?

11. Why did Congress abandon the gold standard? What replaced it?

12. Why does the Treasury maintain a huge gold reserve?

13. What various pieces of metallic currency now circulate?

14. Why did Congress recently revamp some of our coinage?

15. What were the major underlying causes for the recent coin shortages? The more specific causes?

16. What is the meaning of the term *legal tender?*

17. The largest proportion of paper currency in circulation today is in what form? Is this form legal tender? Are coins legal tender?

18. What resource of the National Government serves as the security for the nation's paper money?

19. What is the oldest of the various federal police agencies? When and why was it created?

20. What other most significant task does that agency now perform?

For Further Inquiry

1. Some people, especially big-time gamblers and racketeers, operate on a strictly cash basis. They keep no records and do not deposit their profits in regular bank accounts. Thus, it is very difficult for the Internal Revenue Service to check on possible tax evasions. Former Congressman Sutton of Tennessee proposed that the United States change the color of its paper money and require that all "greenbacks" be exchanged for the newly colored currency within a specified time or become worthless. How would this uncover tax evaders who might not otherwise be caught?

2. Some people propose that the Constitution be amended to limit federal income taxes to a maximum 25 per cent, except in wartime emergencies. Assuming a continued high rate of federal expenditures (which seems certain),

what changes would be necessary in the National Government's tax program if such an amendment were adopted? Would you favor or oppose such an amendment to the Constitution? Why?

3. Justice Oliver Wendell Holmes once remarked that he liked to pay taxes, saying: "Taxes are what we pay for civilized society."

What do you think of this somewhat unusual view? How would you enlarge upon it?

4. On what basis would you criticize or defend the view that a consistent balancing of the National Government's budget is not necessary and that it may in fact be unwise from the standpoint of the health of the nation's economy?

Suggested Activities

1. Prepare an editorial on the temptations and the morality of tax evasion.

2. Stage a debate or class forum on the question: *"Resolved,* That the National Government should adopt a general sales tax."

3. Invite a local banker or an officer of some other financial institution to speak to the class on the subject of the nation's currency system.

4. Invite an agent of the Secret Service (or a representative of another Treasury agency) to speak to the class on his agency, its history, and its functions.

5. Write a report on one of the following topics: (a) narcotics and the teenager, (b) counterfeiting, (c) the ice patrol.

Suggested Reading

BUNZEL, JOHN H., *Issues of American Public Policy.* Prentice-Hall, 1968. Chapter 4.

DALE, EDWIN L., "After Peace Breaks Out, What Will We Do With All That Extra Money?" *New York Times Magazine,* February 16, 1969.

"How Negative Income Tax Works," *U.S. News,* May 27, 1968.

"Inflation: A Tax Everyone Pays," *U.S. News,* June 17, 1968.

Internal Revenue Service, *Your Federal Income Tax.* Government Printing Office, 1970.

PRITCHETT, C. HERMAN, *The American Constitution.* McGraw-Hill, 1968. Chapter 13.

"Prospects for Inflation and Recession," *Time,* November 14, 1969.

SHARKANSKY, IRA, *The Politics of Taxing and Spending.* Bobbs, Merrill, 1969.

SHERRILL, ROBERT, "Wright Patman: The Last of the Great Populists," *New York Times Magazine,* March 16, 1969.

"Should Churches Pay Taxes?" *U.S. News,* June 16, 1969.

SLESINGER, REUBEN E. and ISAACS, ASHER, *Business, Government, and Public Policy.* Van Nostrand, 1968.

STERN, PHILIP M., "How 381 Super-Rich Americans Managed Not to Pay a Cent in Taxes Last Year," *New York Times Magazine,* April 13, 1969.

"The National Debt—Getting Out of Hand?" *U.S. News,* November 3, 1969.

"When the U.S. Did Devalue the Dollar," *U.S. News,* February 19, 1968.

"Why Tax Reform Is So Urgent," *Time,* April 4, 1969.

Various publications, including: *Facts About United States Money, Know Your Money, Treasury Bulletin,* and *The United States Treasury,* are available from the Information Service, Treasury Department, Washington, D.C., 20220.

God granted liberty only to those who love it, and are always ready to guard and defend it.

DANIEL WEBSTER

***Does the fact that the United States possesses such tremendous military power pose any serious threat to the nation's democratic political system? Why or why not?

***Should (or should not) the Constitution be amended to require that before the United States can make war such action must be approved in a national referendum? Why?

***In your view, is a "preventive war" ever justifiable? If so, how? If not, why?

Above all else, the American people desire to live in peace and freedom. In today's world, however, we recognize that the achievement of that desire is complicated by two inescapable facts. The first of these is that there can be no just and lasting peace for the United States until there is a just and lasting peace among all nations and for all mankind. The second and equally important fact is that, as a people and as a nation, we can remain free and work for peace only so long as we remain strong.

Just as the foreign policy of the United States is designed to preserve the nation's security, so, too, is its defense policy. Indeed, the nation's foreign policy and its defense policy are but two sides of the same coin, each one inseparably linked with the other.

The Founding Fathers stressed the importance of national defense by including it among the Preamble's listing of the purposes for which the Constitution was written. They also emphasized its significance by mentioning it more often in the body of the Constitution than any other governmental function. Its continuing importance is testified to by the fact that, year after year, the largest single segment of the nation's budget is devoted to items directly involved with or arising out of our concern for national security. We spend astronomical sums each year — today more than $75,000,000,-000 — to maintain huge and powerful defense forces. We do so in order to achieve the basic objectives of our defense policy: (1) to defend the nation against foreign attack and (2) to deter any such attack by making it clear to any potential aggressor that to attack the United States would be to commit suicide.

THE WAR POWERS

Defense a National Function. The Constitution makes defense a *national* function. The States are expressly forbidden to "engage in war, unless actually invaded, or in such imminent danger as will not admit of delay." Nor may they "keep troops, or ships of war" without the consent of Congress.[1]

Each State may and does have a *militia* which it may use to keep the peace within its own borders. The militia of each State is legally a separate entity from that in each of the other States, but all are collectively the "militia of the United States" and subject to national control. Congress has the power to "provide for calling forth the militia to execute the laws of the Union, suppress insurrections, and repel invasions" and to provide for organizing, arming, and disciplining it.[2]

Congress first delegated to the President the power to call the militia into federal service in 1795. The regulation and control of the militia, however, was left largely to the individual States until the enactment of the National Defense Act of 1916. In that statute, Congress defined the militia of the United States to consist of all able-bodied males between the ages of seventeen and forty-five years of age. It declared the *organized* portion of that militia to be the *National Guard,* which is financed largely by federal funds appropriated by Congress and supervised by the Department of the Army.

Constitutional Provisions. As the National Government is charged with the responsibility for the nation's defense, the Constitution grants to it broad authority to perform that function. The powers it possesses to carry out the function — the *war powers* — are not contained in any one clause or section of the Constitution. Instead, they are to be found in several of its provisions. Among the most important of the war powers granted to Congress are the power to "declare war . . . and make rules concerning captures on land and water,"[3] to "raise and support armies,"[4] to

"provide and maintain a navy,"[5] and to "make rules for the government and regulation of the land and naval forces."[6] As we have previously noted, the President is made "Commander in Chief of the army and navy of the United States, and of the militia of the several States, when called into the actual service of the United States."[7]

Civil Control of the Military. While the Framers of the Constitution recognized the necessity and made provision for the nation's defense, they also appreciated the dangers inherent in military power. Hence, they built into the Constitution a firm guarantee of civilian control of the Armed Forces. Thus, they gave extensive war power to Congress and made the President the Commander in Chief of the Armed Forces. By vesting the "power of the purse" in Congress, they reinforced the principle of civilian control; its use determines such basic military matters as the size of the Armed Forces and the funds available to them.[8]

We have followed the principle of civilian control throughout our history. It has been a dominant consideration in the formation of defense policy and, as well, in the establishment and staffing of the agencies directly responsible for the execution of that policy. Nowhere is this more clearly illustrated than in the statutory requirement that the Secretary of Defense cannot have served on active duty in any of the Armed Forces for a period of at least ten years before taking office.

DEFENSE ORGANIZATION

The Department of Defense was established by Congress in 1947. It replaced the War

---

[1] Article I, Section 10, Clause 3. Note that the first clause of this section also forbids the States to enter into treaties, alliances, or confederations.

[2] Article I, Section 8, Clauses 15 and 16.

[3] Article I, Section 8, Clause 11.

[4] Article I, Section 8, Clause 12.

[5] Article I, Section 8, Clause 13.

[6] Article I, Section 8, Clause 14.

[7] Article II, Section 2, Clause 1.

[8] Congress is forbidden to appropriate funds for the Army for a longer period than two years at one time. Article I, Section 8, Clause 12.

Department, created by Congress in 1789, and the Navy Department, created in 1798. Within it today are the three non-Cabinet Departments of the Army, the Navy, and the Air Force.

The Secretary of Defense. The vast Department of Defense is headed by the Secretary of Defense. He is appointed from civilian life by the President, with the advice and consent of the Senate. Acting under the Commander in Chief, he is principally involved in the formulation of defense policy and the direction of the Department of Defense and of the three service departments within it. By virtue of his office he is a member of several defense policy groups outside the Department of Defense, however, including the National Security Council (page 307), the North Atlantic Treaty Council (page 345), and the National Aeronautics and Space Council (page 307).

Chief Civilian Aides. The Secretary of Defense's principal civilian assistant is the Deputy Secretary, who directs the day-to-day administration of the Department and becomes Acting Secretary in his absence. His other top aides include several Assistant Secretaries; a General Counsel; the Secretaries of the Army, Navy, and Air Force; and the Director of Defense Research and Engineering, who is the Secretary of Defense's scientific adviser and directs all space and other scientific research conducted by the Armed Forces.

Chief Military Aides. The Secretary of Defense's principal military advisers are the top-ranking officers in the armed services—the members of the Joint Chiefs of Staff. This group is composed of the Chairman of the Joint Chiefs, the Army Chief of Staff, the Chief of Naval Operations, and the Air Force Chief of Staff. The Marine Corps Commandant attends all meetings of the Joint Chiefs and serves as a member of the group whenever Marine Corps matters are considered.

The Armed Forces Policy Council. All of the Secretary of Defense's topmost advisers—the Deputy Secretary, the Secretaries of the Army, the Navy, and the Air Force, the Director of Defense Research and Engineering, and the members of the Joint Chiefs of Staff—form the Armed Forces Policy Council. As a group, the Council advises the Secretary of Defense on matters of broad policy relating to the Armed Forces and considers and reports on such other matters as he directs.

THE DEPARTMENT OF THE ARMY

Functions of the Army. Among the three major services, the United States Army has primary responsibility for all military operations on land. Its major duties are to defend the United States against attack, defeat enemy land forces, seize and occupy enemy territory, train and equip its forces, and perform what-

Four Firstclassmen (seniors) at the United States Military Academy at West Point enjoy lunch at Cadet Mess. Upon graduation, they will become commissioned officers. (U.S. Army Photo)

ever other missions are assigned to it by the Commander in Chief.

In addition to its purely military operations, the Army also performs several civil functions. Most notably, these include the operation and maintenance of the Panama Canal (page 593), river and harbor improvements (page 426), and flood control work (page 426).[9] Like the other armed services, the Army is often called upon to aid civil authorities—for example, in such disasters as floods, fires, hurricanes, and earthquakes.

Departmental Organization. The Department of the Army is headed by the *Secretary of the Army.* He is subject to the direction and control of the President and the Secretary of Defense, is appointed by the President with Senate consent, and must be a civilian. The Under Secretary and four Assistant Secretaries of the Army serve as his principal civilian aides. His key military adviser is the *Chief of Staff,* who commands the Army Staff and is directly responsible for the planning and execution of all Army operations.

The Army. The Army of the United States is composed of the Regular Army (including the Women's Army Corps—WAC), the Army National Guard, the Organized Reserves, and the Reserve Officers Training Corps (ROTC).

The Regular Army is the nation's standing army and the heart of the land forces. Today, its strength is approximately 1,300,000 officers and enlisted personnel—professional soldiers, volunteers, and Wacs, supplemented by draftees.[10] The Regular Army is organized around a series of major commands, each of which involves either a broadly defined general function or a geographic area of operations: the Continental Army Command; Army Air Defense Command; United States Army, Europe; United States Army, Pacific; United States Army Forces, Southern Command; United States Army, Alaska; United States Army Forces, Strike Command; the Materiel Command; Combat Developments Command; Strategic Communications Command; Intelligence Command; United States Army Security Agency; and Military Traffic Management and Terminal Service.

The Army National Guard consists of two elements. One is the National Guard for the District of Columbia and the territories; it functions under the direct control of the Regular Army. The other is the organized part of the militia, in each of the fifty States (page 384). When these National Guard units are not in federal service, they are under the command of the various State governors. When the President calls them up, however, they become a part of the Regular Army. The Organized Reserves are federal reserve forces entirely separate from the National Guard. All organized reservists must serve at least some period on active duty with the Army.[11] They

---

[9] Congress has provided that bridges, power and irrigation developments, and other works may be constructed on the navigable waters of the United States only with the consent of the Secretary of the Army. See page 273.

[10] During the first 150 years of the nation's history we maintained only a small professional army to keep the peace at home and to train and lead a larger force whenever the nation became involved in war. Thus, when World War II began in Europe in 1939, the Army had less than 190,000 officers and men; by the end of that war (1945) it had grown to more than 8,265,000. The nature of modern war and of world politics since 1945 has caused the abandonment of the traditional policy of a small standing army, however.

[11] Under the Reserve Forces Acts of 1952 and 1955 all persons entering the Armed Forces are currently obligated to a total of six years of military service. That portion of the obligation that remains when one is released from *active* duty must be met by service in an organized reserve unit.

form a reservoir of trained manpower that may be called into service quickly in the event of emergency.

The ROTC program is administered by the Regular Army and provides military training for young men in many of the nation's colleges and universities and in several high schools. When a college or university student completes the advanced ROTC course, he is commissioned as a reserve officer (2nd Lieutenant) and may be called to active duty when needed. Today the ROTC program is the major source for junior officers for the Army.

Enlistments, for periods ranging up to six years, and *selective service* (the draft) provide manpower for the Army. Any physically and mentally qualified young man of at least eighteen years of age (seventeen with his parents' consent), may enlist in the Regular Army or the National Guard. When the voluntary enlistment rate does not keep pace with the Army's needs, draftees fill the gap. Qualified young women may enlist in the WAC at age eighteen.

The GI, whether he enlists or is drafted, is presented with a wide range of educational opportunities. He may equip himself for one or more of many civilian occupations while on active service. The Army maintains several technical schools, and regular high school and college courses are offered through the Armed Forces Institute.

Commissioned officers, all of whom are appointed by the President, come from the United States Military Academy at West Point, the National Guard, officers candidate schools within the Army, the advanced ROTC program, and occasionally by direct appointment.

Units of the Army. The infantry, artillery, and armored cavalry are the combat units of the land forces. The infantry's foot soldiers engage the enemy in direct small arms combat and hold conquered ground. The artillery supports the infantry, smashes enemy concentrations with its heavier guns, and provides antiaircraft cover. The armored cavalry also supports the infantry, employing its tanks, other armored vehicles, and helicopters to spearhead assaults and breakthroughs and to oppose enemy counteroffensives.

Other units provide the services and supplies essential to the combat units. The infantry, artillery, and armored cavalry forces could not fight without the support of the signal, ordnance, chemical, quartermaster, engineer, intelligence, transportation, military police, and medical corps. Modern combat conditions often require that the men in these units fight at a moment's notice alongside the regular combat troops. As in each of the other services, a Chaplains' Corps ministers to the spiritual needs of the Army.

By the close of World War II the United States Army had become the most powerful fighting force in the history of ground warfare. Today's Army—even though it is much smaller than it was in 1945—is incomparably more powerful. The nuclear age has wrought vast changes, especially in firepower. Short- and long-range missiles, rockets with nuclear warheads, portable radar for battlefield use, helicopters for reconnaissance, attack, and transport purposes, and many other ultramodern weapons make land war a task for specialists.

Still, the age of "push-button warfare" has not arrived. Though one of the Army's greatest needs is for even more research and scientific development, troops remain the bedrock of its strength. We have always needed the Army to keep the peace at home and to defend the nation against foreign attack. Today the Army also mans our overseas defense posts, occupies former enemy territory, guards against the threat of renewed aggression in Korea, and helps to train the fighting forces of many of our allies—especially in South Viet Nam where much of the training is provided under combat battle conditions against the Viet Cong and the North Vietnamese. It stands ready to fight either an all-out war or smaller "brush-fire wars" anywhere on the face of the globe.

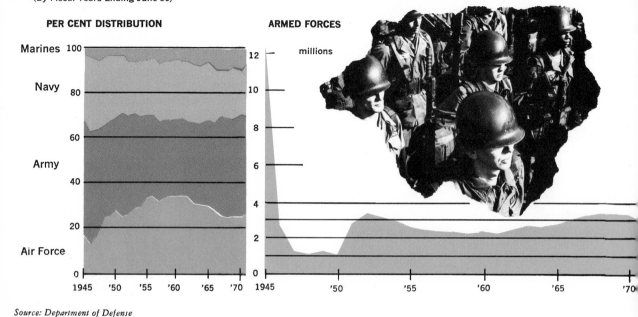

Military Manpower (1971 est.)
(By Fiscal Years Ending June 30)

PER CENT DISTRIBUTION

Marines — 100
Navy — 80
— 60
Army — 40
— 20
Air Force — 0

1945 '50 '55 '60 '65 '70

ARMED FORCES

12 — millions
10
8
6
4
2
0

1945 '50 '55 '60 '65 '70

Source: Department of Defense

THE DEPARTMENT OF THE NAVY

Functions of the Navy. The United States Navy has primary responsibility for sea warfare and defense. Its major duties are to defend the nation through prompt and sustained combat at sea, defeat enemy naval forces, train and equip its own forces, furnish support for the operations of the other services, and perform whatever other missions may be assigned to it.

Departmental Organization. The Department of the Navy is headed by the *Secretary of the Navy.* Like his Army and Air Force counterparts, he operates under the President and the Secretary of Defense, is appointed by the President with Senate consent, and must be a civilian. His chief civilian aides are the Under Secretary and four Assistant Secretaries.

The *Chief of Naval Operations* is the Secretary of the Navy's top naval adviser. He is the Navy's highest ranking officer and is re-

sponsible for its use in war and its preparations and readiness for war. He has direct command of both the seagoing forces and the related shore units and facilities. The only operating naval unit not under his direct command is the Marine Corps.

The Navy. The United States Navy is composed of the Regular Navy (including the WAVES), the Marine Corps, the Naval Reserve, the Naval Air Reserve, the Marine Corps Reserve, and the Naval Reserve Officers Training Corps (NROTC). The Coast Guard, although at all times a part of the Armed Forces, operates within the Department of Transportation. For administrative purposes, the Navy has divided the nation and its possessions into fifteen naval districts.

The Army's basic fighting unit is the soldier, trained as an efficient fighter. The Navy's basic fighting unit is not the sailor but the warship. The sailor seldom fights hand to hand; his

Federal Government Military Expenditures
(By Fiscal Years Ending June 30)

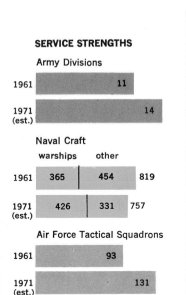

SERVICE STRENGTHS

Army Divisions

1961 — 11

1971 (est.) — 14

Naval Craft

	warships	other	
1961	365	454	819
1971 (est.)	426	331	757

Air Force Tactical Squadrons

1961 — 93

1971 (est.) — 131

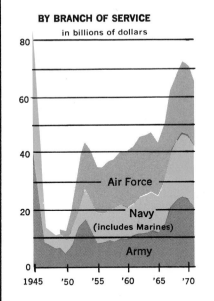

BY BRANCH OF SERVICE

in billions of dollars

Air Force

Navy (includes Marines)

Army

1945 '50 '55 '60 '65 '70

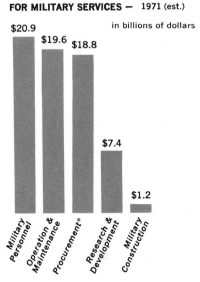

FOR MILITARY SERVICES — 1971 (est.)

in billions of dollars

$20.9 — Military Personnel

$19.6 — Operation & Maintenance

$18.8 — Procurement*

$7.4 — Research & Development

$1.2 — Military Construction

*(including aircraft, ships, missiles, guns, vehicles, electronic equipment, etc.)

---

major task is to make the ship an effective fighting machine.

The Navy depends upon enlistments—and only rarely the draft—for its manpower. The minimum enlistment age is seventeen, and a single enlistment may run for as long as six years. A sailor, like any soldier or airman, may re-enlist, of course. The real backbone of each of our armed services is found in the "career men"—those who spend their lives in the service of their country.[12]

A young man who wants to enlist in the Navy must first satisfy its physical, mental, and moral requirements. Once enlisted, he undergoes an intensive eight weeks of training in "boot camp." Then he may be trained in any one of a large number of special schools, such as those for submarine personnel, electronics

[12] Women as well as men now serve in the Regular Navy.

specialists, hospital corpsmen, torpedomen, pharmacist mates, deep-sea divers, photographers, fire controlmen, yeomen, electricians, radiomen, meteorologists, and navigators. Each of these schools provides the Navy with the trained specialists it needs; each also provides sailors with special skills they can put to use later in civilian life.

Commissioned officers come from the United States Naval Academy at Annapolis, the Reserves, the NROTC, and the ranks. There are now some 675,000 officers and men in the Navy.

Ships of the Fleet. The naval might of the United States today—above and beneath as well as on the high seas—is greater than any other the world has ever seen. The Navy's battleships are heavily armored and carry huge guns mounted in turrets. Their principal mission is to inflict long-range damage on enemy ships and shore installations. Heavy and light

Annapolis midshipmen here, training to be officers in the U.S. Navy, work on an assignment in a communications laboratory. In addition to their challenging academic program, midshipmen receive training in seamanship and navigation. (Official U.S. Navy Photo)

patrol craft, minelayers, minesweepers, and subchasers. A host of noncombat vessels — tankers, ammunition and supply ships, transports, hospital ships, and tenders — support the frontline ships of the fleet. The President has the authority to order the arming of any or all American merchant vessels in time of emergency.

At the end of World War II the Navy had about 1000 ships not needed for peacetime naval operations. Rather than destroy them, as we did surplus warships after World War I, they were "mothballed" — stripped and sealed against the effects of weather and time. The interiors of these vessels are kept so dry that a little moisture must be added occasionally to prevent dry rust. The "mothball fleet" gives us a reserve that can be made ready for active service on very short notice, as many were during the Korean War and have been again for service in Viet Nam.

The age of nuclear warfare has brought many changes to the Navy, just as it has to the other services. Today, the Navy places its greatest reliance on aircraft carriers and submarines. As a matter of fact, none of its battleships is now in active service. All combat vessels built in recent years have been armed with guided missiles, and most carry nuclear weapons. Aircraft carriers are equipped with atomic bombs and the long-range aircraft to deliver them.

Navy submarines range the seven seas, patrolling even the remotest areas of the globe, alert to threats to our national security. Many of them can surface, launch an atomic missile in a matter of minutes, and quickly submerge — while the deadly missile speeds to its target hundreds of miles away. Our newest submarines are capable of launching their missiles while submerged. The exploits of our fast-growing fleet of atomic-powered submarines have made even the wildest of Jules Verne's dreams seem commonplace. Nuclear subs have sailed around the world, completely submerged; have cruised across the top of the world under the Arctic ice pack and have

cruisers are more lightly armed and armored than battleships; they are designed for greater speed and maneuverability. Aircraft carriers are often as large or larger than battleships. These floating airbases can carry 100 planes or more. Their use against the Japanese in World War II and later against the Communists in Korea and Viet Nam proved their value in modern sea warfare. Destroyers are very lightly armored and armed. They are specially designed to operate at high speed for convoy and anti-submarine duty. Submarines operate mostly beneath the sea on long and dangerous patrols. Originally, subs were most useful against enemy shipping, but the modern missile-firing nuclear submarines are rapidly becoming the Navy's major offensive weapon.

Other combat vessels include such ships as

punched up through the ice to surface at the North Pole itself several times; and have found and sailed the fabled Northwest Passage. Even on routine patrols our nuclear subs are capable of staying submerged for months at a time.

The Marine Corps. The United States Marine Corps is a part of the Navy but does not operate under the command of the Chief of Naval Operations. Rather, it serves under the Commandant of the Marine Corps who is directly responsible to the Secretary of the Navy for the efficiency, readiness, and performance of the Corps and its reserve.

The 300,000 Marines act as a land force for the Navy, secure and fortify land bases from which the fleet and the Navy and Marine air arms can operate, and provide detachments for service on armed naval vessels. While the Marine Corps is organized much like the Army, it is almost entirely a combat force. For example, it does not have its own medical units; the doctors and medical corpsmen who serve with the Marines are naval personnel assigned to that duty.

None of the armed services is more intensely proud of its own history and traditions than the Marines. Their watchword is "First to Fight." Even the famous Marine Hymn claims that "if the Army or the Navy ever gaze on Heaven's scenes, they will find the streets are guarded by the United States Marines."

The Marines have provided several demonstrations of the many ways in which the Armed Forces often come to the aid of the civilian population. For example, two convicted murderers had escaped from a Southern penitentiary and taken refuge in a farmhouse. The local sheriff and his men were unable to go in after them because the convicts were holding the farmer and his family as hostages. A helicopter from a nearby Marine Corps base was sent to the scene. It hovered directly over the house, hidden from the fugitives inside. A marine was lowered to the roof. He climbed in an attic window, surprised and captured the escapees, and freed the hostages unharmed.

THE DEPARTMENT OF THE AIR FORCE

Functions of the Air Force. The United States Air Force has primary responsibility for military air operations. Its major duties are to defend the United States against air attack, defeat enemy air forces, strike military and related targets deep within enemy territory, provide combat and transport support for land and naval operations, train and equip its forces, and perform any other missions assigned to it by the President.

Departmental Organization. The Department of the Air Force is headed by the *Secretary of the Air Force*. He serves under the President and the Secretary of Defense, is appointed by the President with Senate consent, and must be a civilian. His top civilian aides are the

"Man's flight through life is sustained by the power of his knowledge." Thus reads the inscription on the Eagle statue overlooking the Cadet area at the United States Air Force Academy. (U.S. Air Force Academy)

Where U.S. Servicemen Are Stationed Abroad

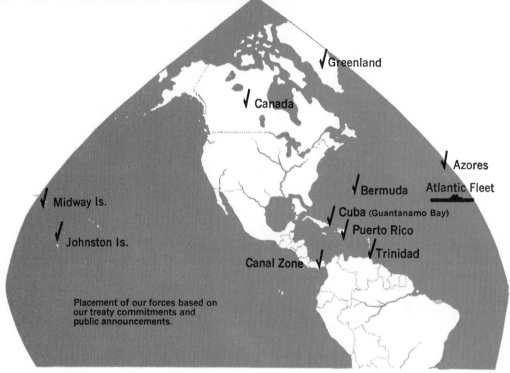

Greenland

Canada

Azores

Bermuda

Atlantic Fleet

Midway Is.

Cuba (Guantanamo Bay)

Johnston Is.

Puerto Rico

Trinidad

Canal Zone

Placement of our forces based on
our treaty commitments and
public announcements.

Under Secretary and, as in the other service departments, four Assistant Secretaries.

The Air Force *Chief of Staff* is the Secretary of the Air Force's chief military adviser. He commands the Air Staff and is directly responsible for the planning and execution of all Air Force operations.

The Air Force. The United States Air Force includes all military aviation not assigned to the other services. It is composed of the Regular Air Force (including the WAF), the Air Force Reserve, the Air Force ROTC, and the Air National Guard. The USAF performs its duties through fifteen operational commands in this country and elsewhere across the globe: the Aerospace Defense Command, Air Force Logistics Command, Air Force Systems Command, Air Training Command, Air University, Continental Air Command, Headquarters Command, Military Airlift Command,

Air Force Communications Service, Strategic Command, Tactical Air Command, Security Service, United States Air Forces in Europe, Pacific Air Forces, Alaskan Air Command, and Southern Command. Its aircraft include heavy, light, dive, and attack bombers; conventional and jet fighters and interceptors; and transport, hospital, weather, and reconnaissance planes.

The Regular Air Force has a strength of over 800,000 today, including some 12,000 Wafs. Enlistments are accepted on the same basis as in the other services, but airmen must pass stiffer physical examinations than those who enlist in the other services. Like the Navy, the Air Force has seldom had to turn to selective service for any of its personnel. Its commissioned officers come from the Air Force Academy at Colorado Springs, the Reserve, the AFROTC, and the ranks.

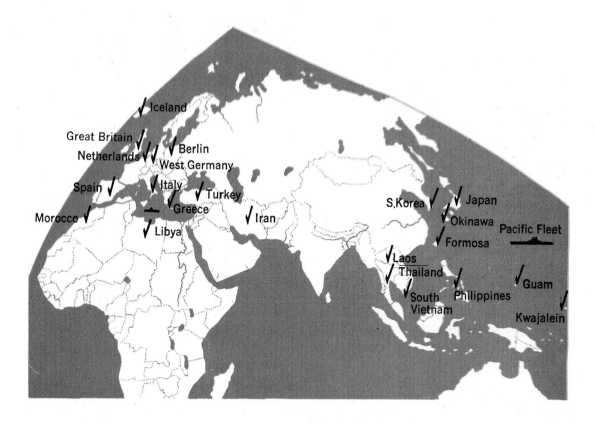

The USAF Today. The nation's overall defense strategy places its major emphasis on air power. This is not to say that the Army and the Navy are relegated to minor roles — far from it. But it is the Air Force we look to as the first line of defense against sudden enemy attack. No matter where the attack may occur, the Air Force will almost certainly strike the first counter blows against the aggressor and his home bases.

The striking power of the Air Force today is truly awesome, and it is being added to and improved upon constantly. Very few of its combat planes currently on the line were in use as recently as the Korean War. The mammoth, eight-engined B–52's are the backbone of its strategic — long-range — bomber fleet today. Just *one* of these planes carries a nuclear bomb load with more destructive power than that packed by *all* the bombs that

were dropped by both sides throughout all of World War II. The immense, incalculable striking power of these planes is spread across the globe in a state of constant combat readiness.

All American fighter and interceptor aircraft are now armed with air-to-air missiles for use against enemy planes and missiles. All tactical (short-range attack and dive) bombers also carry missiles for use against enemy ground targets.

Like the other services, the Air Force has several types of surface-launched missiles. It has the major responsibility for developing and firing military missiles, especially the long-range intercontinental (ICBM) and intermediate-range (IRBM) ballistic missiles. Many of its newest missiles are able to seek out and destroy fast flying targets even hundreds of miles away. Thus, the days of manned combat aircraft now seem numbered.

SELECTIVE SERVICE AND
UNIVERSAL MILITARY TRAINING

Throughout most of our history the Armed Forces have relied on volunteers to fill their ranks. Both the North and the South did use a limited conscription system during the Civil War.[13] It was not until 1917, however, that a true national compulsory military service system was used in this country, even in wartime. More that 2,800,000 of the 4,700,000 men who served in the Armed Forces of the United States in World War I were drafted under the Selective Service Act of 1917.

The first peacetime draft in American history was provided by the Selective Service Act of 1940, enacted as World War II raged in Europe. Voluntary enlistments were accepted after the United States entered the war, but most of the 16,353,000 who served entered the Armed Forces through selective service. The World War II draft was terminated in 1947.

The Draft Today. The crises of the post-war period persuaded Congress to enact a new conscription law, the Selective Service Act of 1948. Its limited provisions were replaced during the Korean War when Congress passed the Universal Military Training and Service Act of 1951. The present draft operates under a recent revision of the latter statute, the Military Selective Service Act of 1967.

The draft is administered by the Selective Service System, an independent executive agency under the President. It is headed by the Director of Selective Service who is appointed by the President with Senate consent. Most of the agency's functions are carried out through a selective service headquarters in each of the fifty States. The director of each State headquarters is appointed by the President on recommendation of the governor. He is responsible for the administration of the draft in his State. The actual selection of draftees is made through local selective service boards which exist on a county by county basis throughout the nation. Each of these boards consists of at least three local civilians chosen by the President upon recommendation by the governor; they serve without compensation.

The Secretary of Defense determines the number of draftees needed by the Armed Forces month by month and allots quotas among the States. The State directors apportion each month's quota among their local boards on the basis of the number of potential draftees available to each board.

Liability for Service. A military service obligation is imposed upon all males in the United States between the ages of eighteen-and-one-half and twenty-six. All young men must register with their local draft boards at age eighteen, however.[14] Conscientious objectors who are *sincerely* opposed to *any* service in the Armed Forces are required to perform essential civilian work. Some persons who are deferred from the draft remain liable until age twenty-eight

---

[13] Both the Union and the Confederacy began a draft in 1862. Each permitted a man to hire someone to serve in his place, however; and the North also allowed one to escape conscription by paying a $300 fee. Neither army contained many draftees: less than 50,000 of the 2,200,000 who served in the Union Army were drafted; some 200,000 others either paid the fee or hired substitutes.

[14] Registration must occur promptly after one's eighteenth birthday. Male aliens admitted for permanent residence (immigrants) must register for selective service within six months; they are then obligated for military service on the same basis as male citizens. Aliens not admitted for permanent residence may not be drafted until after a year's residence in the United States; they may refuse to be drafted, but if they do so, they are forever ineligible for American citizenship.

and others until age thirty-five.[15] Draftees must serve on active duty for two years and for an additional period (now up to four years) in the reserves.

Draft Classifications. Every draft registrant is classified by his local board in one of eighteen different classifications:

I–A: Registrant available for military service.

I–A–O: Conscientious objector available for noncombat military service only.

I–C: Member of the armed forces.

I–D: Member of the reserves or student taking military training.

I–O: Conscientious objector available for civilian work only.

I–S: Student deferred by law.

I–W: Conscientious objector already performing acceptable civilian work.

I–Y: Registrant available for military service only in wartime or emergency.

II–A: Registrant deferred because of civilian occupation.

II–C: Registrant deferred because of agricultural occupation.

II–S: Registrant deferred because of research and study activity.

III–A: Registrant with child or children or deferred by reason of extreme hardship to dependents.

IV–A: Registrant who has completed service, or is sole surviving son of parents who have had children killed in service.

IV–B: Public official deferred by law.

IV–C: Alien.

IV–D: Minister or divinity student.

IV–F: Registrant physically, mentally, or morally unfit.

V–A: Registrant over age of liability for military service.

Only those who are classified I–A or I–A–O are subject to call, but those in other classifications may be reclassified and then drafted. Decisions of local draft boards may be appealed

---

[15] Because of the critical need for their services, doctors, dentists, veterinarians, and related specialists remain liable until age fifty.

to a regional appeals board and to a National Selective Service Appeal Board.

The Draft, Pro and Con. Conscription for military service has been the subject of controversy through much of our history.

As early as 1790 George Washington recommended a program of compulsory military training for *all* of the nation's able-bodied young men. Similar proposals for a system of *universal*—rather than *selective*—training and service have been heard and debated ever since. Woodrow Wilson offered such a plan at the end of World War I, and there have been many proposals and much support for the idea (UMT) since the end of World War II.

UMT proposals continue to attract support, and opposition, from many quarters today. But the main focus of controversy has shifted to another aspect of the subject in the past few years. Most of the current debate swirls about the draft itself: Should it be retained in its present form, severely modified, or abolished altogether?

Most who support the draft concede that *no* system of *selective* service can be entirely fair. In fact, many of them favor extensive revision—such as that accomplished in 1970 by the substitution of a national lottery for the former local-board selection process. In general, though, they argue that the present draft is neither basically nor purposefully unfair and that it is an effective device for meeting the needs of the Armed Forces. Many proponents also insist that the draft promotes patriotism, builds physical and moral stamina, provides career training, and, by demonstrating the nation's will to fight, helps to deter potential enemies.

The draft's opponents claim that it violates basic American traditions, tends to promote militarism, usurps the historic training prerogatives of the home, the school, and the church, and interferes with the individual's right to plan his own life. Most critics also insist the draft is unfair because of its many deferments and wasteful because relatively few of the millions registered are ever in fact called. Many of them also claim that volunteers make better soldiers than do draftees and could be recruited in sufficient numbers if higher pay and other attractive incentives were offered.

In 1970, President Nixon pledged an end to use of the draft by 1973, "subject to over-riding considerations of national security."

THE VETERANS ADMINISTRATION

More than 28,000,000 persons — over one-eighth of our population today—are veterans of the nation's Armed Forces. In gratitude for their service, Congress now appropriates more than $8,500,000,000 annually for a vast array of veterans benefit programs.

A generous concern for the welfare of veterans has long been an established part of the nation's public policy. From its first session in 1789 Congress has enacted literally thousands of statutes reflecting that concern. In fact, the history of veterans benefits dates back well before the American Revolution to earliest colonial days. In 1636, the Pilgrim Fathers decreed that:

> If any man shalbee sent forth as a souldier and shall return maimed, hee shalbee maintained completely by the Collonie during his life.

The colonies and later the States provided pensions to their disabled militiamen, and most of them also made grants of land to those who had served in the Armed Forces. The Second Continental Congress and the Congress of the Confederation each enacted several pieces of legislation to provide benefits to veterans of the Revolutionary War.

The VA. By 1819 the scope of federal veterans benefits had reached such proportions that Congress found it necessary to create an agency—the Pension Bureau—to administer them. That agency has been continued in some form ever since. Its present-day descendant is the Veterans Administration.

The VA is an independent agency under the President. It is headed by the Administrator of Veterans Affairs who is appointed by the President subject to Senate confirmation. Under his direction, the VA furnishes a large number of services to millions of veterans and their dependents and the dependents of deceased veterans. It performs its functions through a working force of some 170,000 doctors, dentists, nurses, other medical personnel, accountants, lawyers, and clerks.

Medical Care. The VA provides medical and dental care at government expense to needy veterans and to those with service-connected disabilities. In doing so, it operates the largest chain of hospitals in the world. It maintains more than 150 hospitals throughout the country and also provides care through a nationwide system of domiciliaries and clinics.[16] Where necessary, the VA also authorizes medical care in non-VA hospitals and from private doctors and domiciliary care in rest homes operated by State and local governments.

Compensations and Pensions. The VA pays out well over one-half of its annual budget —over $6,000,000,000 a year—in compensations and pensions of several kinds. *Compensations* are monetary benefits awarded to veterans on the basis of service-incurred disabilities and to the dependents of deceased veterans in those instances in which the cause of the veteran's death was related to his service in the armed forces. *Pensions,* on the other hand, are payments made to meet needs *not* arising as a

---

[16] Services to veterans abroad are administered by the United States Foreign Service (page 325) except in the Philippines, where the VA maintains a regional office at Manila. Because of the large number of veterans now living in Mexico, the Foreign Service has stationed an attaché for veterans affairs at the American embassy in Mexico City. The VA also maintains an office in Rome to provide advice and assistance to veterans living in Europe.

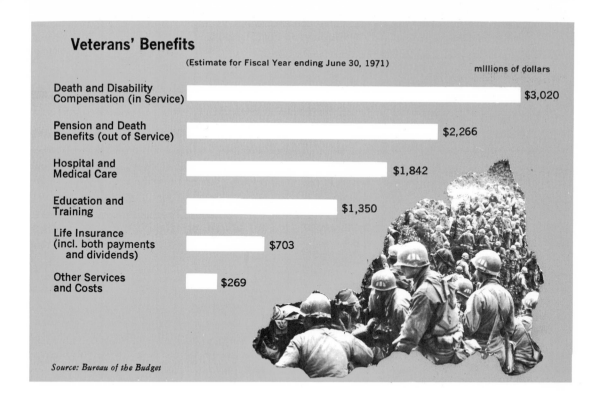

Veterans' Benefits

(Estimate for Fiscal Year ending June 30, 1971)

millions of dollars

Death and Disability Compensation (in Service)	$3,020
Pension and Death Benefits (out of Service)	$2,266
Hospital and Medical Care	$1,842
Education and Training	$1,350
Life Insurance (incl. both payments and dividends)	$703
Other Services and Costs	$269

Source: Bureau of the Budget

direct result of military service. Most of the pensions paid today go to aged and needy veterans and to the needy survivors of veterans who died of non-service-connected causes.

Life Insurance. The VA operates the nation's largest life insurance business. During both World Wars I and II and the Korean War Congress made low-cost life insurance policies available to members of the Armed Forces. Today those policies are still held by more than 200,000 World War I veterans, 5,000,000 World War II veterans, and 800,000 Korean War veterans. Although the premiums charged for these policies are much lower than the rates available from private insurance companies, the entire veterans insurance program is self-supporting. The total value of the policies still in force exceeds $38,000,000,000.

Readjustment Benefits. World War II brought an enormous expansion of federal veterans benefit programs, of course. In part, the ex-

pansion came because so many persons served in the Armed Forces during that conflict — some 16,353,000, more than in all other of the nation's wars combined. Another factor contributed to the expansion, as well. Throughout most of our history, veterans benefits had centered around compensations, pensions, and medical, hospital, and domiciliary care. To these traditional benefits, Congress added a series of new ones — "readjustment benefits" — during World War II. The purpose of these new aids was to help *all* veterans, including those who were neither disabled nor destitute, to make a smooth and successful transition back to civilian life. They were also intended to make up for the educational, business, and other opportunities that veterans had missed because of their service.

These new readjustment benefits were provided in a number of different statutes. The first of them was contained in the Selective

Service Act of 1940, which guaranteed that draftees would be able to return to their former civilian jobs once they were discharged from the Armed Forces. By far the most important of these statutes was the Servicemen's Readjustment Act of 1944, popularly known as the GI Bill of Rights. The GI Bill provided four new major benefits for World War II veterans: (1) the right to special assistance in seeking a job in civilian life, (2) the right to a maximum of thirty-six months of college or other educational or vocational training at government expense, including the payment of a cash allowance during that period, (3) the right to a maximum of twelve months unemployment compensation, and (4) the right to obtain VA-guaranteed loans for the buying of a home, farm, or business.

Similar readjustment benefits were later provided for veterans of the Korean War under the terms of the Korean GI Bill in 1952. In 1966 Congress also enacted the Cold War GI Bill, extending such assistance to all persons who have served in the Armed Forces for more than 180 days at any time since January 31, 1955.

THE ATOMIC ENERGY COMMISSION

When World War II ended in 1945, the United States was in sole possession of the knowledge necessary to produce and control atomic energy. That knowledge, and the techniques with which to apply it, had been gained as the result of a highly secret $2,000,000,000 crash program conducted during the war. Known by its code name, the *Manhattan Project,* the program was begun as the first battles were being fought in Europe. It progressed steadily to July 16, 1945, when a successful test explosion at Alamogordo, New Mexico, ushered in the atomic age.

In military terms, the success of the wartime program was demonstrated in the sharpest of terms in August, 1945. The two atomic bombs which were dropped on Japan—at Hiroshima on August 6th and at Nagasaki three days later—virtually obliterated their targets. Their awesome destructiveness brought an almost immediate surrender by the Japanese.

The harnessing of this vast new power heralded a new age in warfare. It also marked the beginning of a new age in man's peaceful pursuits. Man now has the power to destroy himself and every other living thing on the face of the globe. If he uses it properly, he also has the power to provide a far richer life for all of the peoples of the earth. (Recall that we considered the international use and control of atomic energy in Chapter 19; see pages 358–360.)

The AEC. Congress transferred control of the nation's atomic energy program from the Army to a civilian body, the Atomic Energy Commission, in 1946. The AEC is an independent executive agency under the President. Its five members are named by the President subject to Senate confirmation. The commissioners, each of whom must be a civilian, are chosen for overlapping five-year terms; one is named by the President to be Chairman.

The work of the Commission falls into two broad categories: (1) research, manufacturing and promotional activities and (2) licensing and regulatory functions. The former are under the administrative control of a General Manager who is selected by the Commission to act as its chief executive officer. The licensing and regulatory functions involve such work as the licensing of reactors, the handling and distribution of fissionable materials, and the prescribing of safety standards for their use. The performance of these functions is supervised by a Director of Regulation who is also chosen by and is directly subordinate to the Commission.

Four permanent committees function very closely with the AEC: (1) the General Advisory Committee, composed of nine civilians appointed by the President to advise the AEC on scientific and technical matters; (2) the

Advisory Committee on Reactor Safeguards, with up to fifteen members selected by the AEC to advise it on the hazards of reactor facilities; (3) the Military Liaison Committee, representing the Defense Department to advise the AEC on matters relating to the military uses of atomic energy; and (4) the Congressional Joint Committee on Atomic Energy, composed of nine Senators and nine Representatives as Congress' watchdogs over the AEC's operations.

The AEC's control over atomic energy and its use in this country is extremely broad. The Atomic Energy Act of 1946 declared the production of fissionable materials to be a government monopoly. It is unlawful to produce, possess, or transfer these materials without AEC consent. Anyone who violates the law with intent to injure the United States may be sentenced to death. Uranium ore produced in this country must be sold to the Commission, and none can be exported except under AEC license.

Much of the Commission's work is carried on under contracts which have been made with several universities and private industries. Most major production and research work is done by these contractors in facilities owned by the AEC. Its major production facilities are located at Oak Ridge, Tennessee; Richland, Washington; and at sites near Paducah, Kentucky; Aiken, South Carolina; and Portsmouth, Ohio. It maintains several major research centers, including the Atomic Energy Laboratory at Ames, Iowa; the Argonne National Laboratory at Chicago; the Brookhaven National Laboratory at Upton, New York; the Knolls Atomic Power Laboratory at Schenectady, New York; the Los Alamos Scientific Laboratory in New Mexico; the Lawrence Radiation Laboratory at Berkeley and Livermore, California; and the National Reactor Testing Station near Idaho Falls, Idaho.

Although a large share of the AEC's work remains military in character, more than half of its annual budget of some $2,500,000,000

is now devoted to developing more humane uses for the atom. Thus, the use of radioactive materials in medicine has received much attention. Small quantities of these materials are readily available to doctors and hospitals and have proved especially important in cancer research and treatment.

Private industry is now being permitted to take over and develop some of the peaceful aspects of atomic energy. Most of the private work done thus far has been concentrated in the search for and application of commercially feasible methods of using atomic energy to produce electric power.

THE NATIONAL AERONAUTICS AND SPACE ADMINISTRATION

Since the days of ancient Greece men have dreamed of conquering outer space. Now, at long last, those dreams are approaching reality. The developments which have occurred in space exploration in little more than a decade have been nothing less than astounding—in their scope, in the speed with which accomplishments have piled on top of accomplishments, and in their promise of things to come.

The Soviet Union opened the space age when it launched the first man-made satellite, Sputnik I, on October 4, 1957, and followed it a month later with Sputnik II. The Soviet feat provided a rude shock for the American people. Most Americans had been only vaguely, if at all, aware of the fact that we and the Russians had been engaged in a space race since the end of World War II. Our complacent attitude toward the progress of our own scientific research and development, especially in the military field, was shattered. Public attention was focused on our space programs, and they were expanded and intensified. The Army put America's first satellite, Explorer I, into orbit on January 31, 1958.

Since then, many satellites that circle the earth and others orbiting the sun have been thrust into space by the United States. Probes of outer space are now almost routine. Instrumented capsules have been recovered from outer space. A solar satellite has transmitted data from an incredible distance, more than 22,500,000 miles from the earth. A vast amount of information on solar-flare effects, cosmic radiation, magnetic phenomena, and other data on interplanetary space has been gathered. Thousands of pictures of the earth's cloud cover have been received, opening the way to a better understanding of weather formations and a revolution in weather forecasting. Television and telephone transmissions between ground stations have been sent via satellites. The list of our space accomplishments, already long and fantastic, continues to grow.

On July 21, 1969, the United States succeeded in landing the first men on the moon. As the Apollo 11, piloted by Astronaut Michael Collins, orbited the moon, Astronauts Edwin E. Aldrin, Jr., and Neil Armstrong descended in the Lunar Module to the surface of the moon. This photo of Aldrin and the Lunar Module was taken by Commander Armstrong. (NASA)

Man finally pushed himself into outer space in 1961 — when first the Soviet Union and then the United States accomplished the feat. In the years since, both nations have launched several manned spacecraft, and the exploits of American astronauts and of the Russian cosmonauts have surpassed the wildest imaginings of even a few short years ago.

And, of course, the absolutely incredible was accomplished on July 20, 1969, when two Americans — Neil A. Armstrong and Colonel Edwin E. Aldrin — became the first human beings to land and walk on the surface of the moon.

The military importance of space vehicles and missiles can hardly be exaggerated. But military advantage is only one reason for our space activities. They have many other practical uses — many of which will become evident only as the space age continues. We have already suggested the possibilities in communications and weather forecasting. Beyond these, there are many more; for example, the effects of cosmic and solar rays on the human body will expand medical knowledge; the mental stresses occasioned by a totally new environment will broaden understanding of the nature and working of the human mind; and accurate mapping of the earth's land surfaces and charting of the oceans and tides will be greatly enhanced.

NASA. Congress enacted the National Aeronautics and Space Act of 1958 as part of this nation's response to the challenge of the Soviet sputniks. The law declares that all of our research and exploration activities in outer space are "devoted to peaceful purposes for the benefit of all mankind."

The National Aeronautics and Space Administration was created to implement this policy. It is an independent executive agency directly responsible to the President and is headed by an Administrator appointed by him with Senate consent.

The act also created the *National Aeronautics and Space Council* in the Executive Office of the

President (page 307). The Council advises the President on all matters relating to aeronautical and space research and exploration. It is composed of the Vice President (as chairman), the Secretaries of State and Defense, the Chairman of the AEC, and the Administrator of NASA. The 1958 law named the President as the Council's chairman, but Congress elevated the Vice President to that post in 1961.

Functioning under the President and the Council, NASA is responsible for most of the Federal Government's aeronautical and space work that is not "primarily military" in character. More specifically, NASA is charged with: seeking solutions to problems of flight within and beyond the earth's atmosphere; the development, construction, testing, and operation of space vehicles; the exploration of space; and the promotion of the peaceful international use of space knowledge. It is often difficult to draw the line between those projects to be conducted by the military and those that should be handled by NASA; Congress has provided that in such cases the responsible agency is to be designated by the President and the National Aeronautics and Space Council.

NASA is engaged in a wide range of programs at its several research centers and laboratories throughout the country. For example, the training of astronauts and the development, testing, and flight operation of such manned spacecraft as those in the Gemini and Apollo series are directed from the Manned Spacecraft Center located in Houston. Propulsion and power plant research is concentrated at the Lewis Research Center in Cleveland. Most of the work on the guidance and control of space vehicles is conducted at the Ames Research Center at Moffett Field, near San Francisco. Flight evaluation tests of such research aircraft as the X–15 are carried on at the Flight Research Center located at Edwards, California. The development of launch vehicles, the missiles necessary to thrust payloads into space, is conducted at the George C. Marshall Space Flight Center at Huntsville, Alabama. Most of NASA's missile and satellite launchings occur at Cape Kennedy in Florida, although some also occur at Vandenberg Air Force Base in California and the Wallops Station on Wallops Island, a rocket and missile testing site off the coast of Virginia.

********** CONCEPT BUILDING **********

Key Concepts

Today we maintain huge and powerful defense forces both at home and abroad in order to: (1) defend the nation against foreign attack and (2) deter aggression. The Constitution makes defense a national function and excludes the States from the field, except to the extent of maintaining militia. Civilian control of the military is maintained through Congress, with its several war powers, and the President, who is Commander in Chief of the Armed Forces.

The Department of Defense is headed by the Secretary of Defense. He is assisted by a number of civilian aides, including the Secretaries of the Army, the Navy, and the Air Force, and by the Joint Chiefs of Staff and the Armed Forces Policy Council. Included within the Department of Defense are the three non-Cabinet Departments of the Army, the Navy, and the Air Force. The Army has primary responsibility for all military operations on land, the Navy (including the Marine Corps) on the sea, and the Air Force in the air.

Traditionally, the Armed Forces have relied on volunteers to fill their ranks; but during and since World War II, voluntary enlistments have been supplemented by the draft. The retention, extensive revision, or outright abolition of the draft is the subject of much controversy.

The nation has long displayed a generous concern for the veterans of its Armed Forces. The present array of veterans benefit programs is administered by the Veterans Administration. The Atomic Energy Commission is responsible for the control and development of atomic energy in the United States. The National Aeronautics and Space Administration, operating under the direction of the President and the National Aeronautics and Space Council, directs most of the Federal Government's nonmilitary aeronautical and space research and exploration.

Important Terms

aeronautics and space	deter	militia	reserves
atomic energy	draft	mothball fleet	ROTC
Commander in Chief	fissionable materials	National Guard	selective service
compensation	GI Bill	pensions	UMT
conscription	Joint Chiefs of Staff	readjustment benefits	war powers

Questions for Inquiry and Review

1. For what two basic purposes does the United States maintain its defense forces?

2. Why did the Framers of the Constitution insist on civilian control of the military?

3. How did the Framers attempt to guarantee civilian control of the military?

4. Who is directly responsible under the President for the formulation and execution of the nation's defense policies?

5. What are the major functions of each of the subordinate departments within the Defense Department?

6. Who is the top-ranking military officer in each of the armed services and what role does he play?

7. Traditionally, the Armed Forces have met their manpower needs from what source?

8. From what additional source are those needs met today?

9. What are the basic arguments advanced in defense of and in opposition to the present draft system?

10. What has been and is the general character of the nation's concern for the welfare of its veterans?

11. What two factors produced an enormous expansion in veterans benefit programs during and immediately after World War II?

12. Why, especially, did the United States embark on the quest for control of the atom?

13. What is the relationship between the National Aeronautics and Space Council and NASA?

14. What is NASA's primary function?

For Further Inquiry

1. It is often argued that the only way to win World War III is to prevent its ever occurring. What is the essence of the thought behind this view?

2. While he was President, Dwight D. Eisenhower remarked: "Americans, indeed all free men, remember that in the final choice a soldier's pack is not so heavy a burden as a

prisoner's chains." How would you explain his comment?

3. Why may it be argued that the draft often serves as a "shotgun behind the door" to stimulate enlistments in the Armed Forces?

4. Occasionally, judges offer persons convicted of minor crimes in their courts the choice of either going to jail or enlisting in one of the armed services. Do you think this is a wise policy?

5. It has been estimated that the NASA program that resulted in the moon landings of 1969 cost the nation at least $25,000,000,000. Do you think that that huge sum should in fact have been spent for such a purpose? Should it have been spent for some other purpose?

6. Do you think that the Veterans Administration should make pension payments to veterans who suffer from non-service-connected disabilities?

Suggested Activities

1. Invite a qualified veteran or present member of the United States Armed Forces to speak to the class on the general subject of military service.

2. Write an essay on one of the following themes: military service as an obligation of citizenship, the significance of civilian control of the military in a democracy, or the assets and liabilities of interservice rivalries.

3. Stage a debate or class forum on one of the following questions: (1) *Resolved,* That the Congress should repeal the present selective service system. (2) *Resolved,* That Congress should provide for universal military training.

Suggested Reading

"American Militarism," *Look,* August 12, 1969.

BURNS, JAMES M. and PELTASON, J. W., *Government By the People.* Prentice-Hall, 1969. Chapter 23.

CLARK, BLAIR, "What Kind of Army?" *Harper's,* September, 1969.

"Gas and Germ Weapons — A Look Inside the Arsenal," *U.S. News,* August 18, 1969.

HARTLEY, ANTHONY, "Anti-Militarism: Can Too Much Be Made of a Good Thing?" *New York Times Magazine,* October 19, 1969.

"How Useful Is the Moon?" *U.S. News,* July 28, 1969.

KAUFMAN, RICHARD F., "Eisenhower: 'We Must Guard Against Unwarranted Influence By the Military-Industrial Complex,'" *New York Times Magazine,* June 22, 1969.

"Man on the Moon," *Time,* July 25, 1969.

"Men on the Moon," *Life,* August 8, 1969.

"One Small Step — One Giant Leap," *Reader's Digest,* October, 1969.

RADWAY, LAURENCE I., *Foreign Policy and National Defense.* Scott, Foresman, 1969.

"ROTC: Case Study at One Big University," *U.S. News,* November 3, 1969.

SAPIN, BURTON M., *Contemporary American Foreign and Military Policy.* Scott, Foresman, 1969.

SCOTT, ANDREW M. and WALLACE, EARLE (eds.), *Politics, U.S.A.: Cases on the American Democratic Process.* Macmillan, 1969. Chapter 14.

"Space Patrol — How U.S. Watches Russians," *U.S. News,* November 24, 1969.

"The Case for a Volunteer Army," *Time,* January 10, 1969; *Reader's Digest,* April, 1969.

"The Dilemma of Chemical Warfare," *Time,* June 27, 1969.

"The Military-Industrial Complex," *Newsweek,* June 9, 1969.

TODD, RICHARD, "A Private's Communique on the Army Reserve — Life With the Conscientious Acceptors," *New York Times Magazine,* October 12, 1969.

22

THE JUSTICE AND
POST OFFICE DEPARTMENTS

✳✳✳ Why does government have a responsibility "to establish justice"?

✳✳✳ Are "law and order" and "justice" synonymous or compatible concepts? Explain.

✳✳✳ Is the postal system in fact a socialistic operation? Explain.

By its very nature, democratic government must insist upon justice for all its citizens. That is, it must insist that all men live in fairness and in equality with one another. As a people, we believe that government has no more important function in this country than that of insuring justice for all. The Founding Fathers emphasized the importance of this function by including it in the Preamble of the Constitution as one of the basic purposes for which that document was written.

Justice may be viewed from two basic standpoints—that of *social justice* and that of *legal justice*. Social justice is concerned with the material and spiritual well-being of men, with the ways in which they share in the advantages their society has to offer. Public health services, old-age assistance, public education, unemployment and workmen's compensation, public housing, and many other similar programs now conducted by National, State, and local governments are all indications of our increased concern for this aspect of justice.

Legal justice is the narrower concept. It involves the settlement of conflicts among men and the administration of justice under law by the courts. The history of governmental concern for legal justice is much older than its concern for social justice, but each is quite dependent upon the other.

In the first section of this chapter we turn our attention to the major executive department in the National Government responsible for promoting and maintaining legal justice. In the second section of this chapter we turn to the Post Office Department—an agency which, as we shall see, is far more involved with the concept of social justice than is commonly realized.

THE JUSTICE DEPARTMENT

The Attorney General. The Justice Department is headed by the Attorney General who is selected by the President and confirmed by the Senate. The Justice Department itself was not created until 1870, but the post of Attorney General was established by the First Congress in 1789. The nation's first Attorney General, Edmund Randolph, was a member of President Washington's Cabinet, and most of his successors have followed him in the role of an intimate adviser to the Presidents they have served.

Prior to 1870 the Attorney General's only formal functions were those of providing legal advice to the President and his aides and of representing the United States in court. Over the years since the creation of the Justice Department, however, he has been assigned a number of additional duties. Under his direction today, the Justice Department supervises the work of the United States attorneys and marshals, operates the federal prison system, investigates a large number of federal crimes and arrests violators, represents the United States in court, furnishes legal advice to the President and to the heads of the other executive departments, and administers the nation's immigration and naturalization and narcotics laws. The Attorney General's top aide is the Deputy Attorney General who assists him in the conduct of the department and its operations.

The Solicitor General. While the Attorney General heads the Justice Department and is almost always a well-known national figure, the principal officer in the department's work in the courts is one of his lesser-known lieutenants, the Solicitor General. He is chosen by the President and confirmed by the Senate and deserves the title "the Government's chief lawyer."

The Solicitor General represents the United States in all cases in which it is a party before

The Antitrust Library in the Department of Justice houses a vast collection of books and documents on law and related subjects. (Wide World Photos)

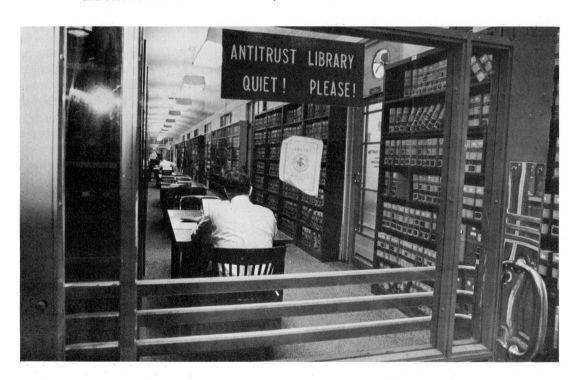

the Supreme Court,[1] and he may appear in the Government's behalf in any federal or State court. Many of the nation's great judicial figures have held the post. Mr. Justice Thurgood Marshall, appointed to the Supreme Court by President Johnson in 1967, is but the latest of many Solicitors General to have been elevated to the nation's highest bench.

The Solicitor General directs the National Government's court work from the ordinary run of cases prosecuted every day in the lower federal courts to the great constitutional cases which are carried to the Supreme Court. He decides which cases will, or will not, be appealed from decisions in the lower courts;[2] thus, he plays a vital role in the development of American constitutional law.

The Assistant Attorneys General. Much of the workload of the Justice Department is carried by the nine Assistant Attorneys General. Like their counterparts in the other Cabinet departments, the Assistant Secretaries, they, too, are appointed by the President and confirmed by the Senate.

One of the Assistant Attorneys General heads the Department's *Office of Legal Counsel.* He assists the Attorney General in the preparation of the formal opinions and advice requested by the President and carries out whatever special assignments the Attorney General may give him. Another, the Assistant Attorney General for Administration, supervises the Department's internal affairs and is responsible for the business management of the Department.

Each of the other Assistant Attorneys General heads a division within the Department:

---

[1] The Attorney General may argue the National Government's position in any case before the Supreme Court if he chooses; he does so only in rare instances, however.

[2] Of course, he can make such decisions only with regard to the civil or constitutional cases lost by the National Government in the lower courts; it is the other party's right to decide whether or not to appeal a case the National Government has won.

The Antitrust Division. This division investigates complaints charging violation of the Sherman, Clayton, and other antitrust statutes. Whenever it finds enough evidence to justify a prosecution, the division's lawyers (the "trustbusters") handle the case in court. It also enforces a number of related laws. For example, it represents the United States in cases which arise under various statutes administered by such independent regulatory agencies as the Interstate Commerce Commission (pages 530–531) and by the Secretary of the Treasury and the Atomic Energy Commission (pages 398–399).

The Tax Division. This division handles all cases involving the internal revenue laws, except for proceedings before the Tax Court.[3] Its chief function is to act as counsel for the Internal Revenue Service; and a great many of its cases are those which are brought against individuals and firms for tax evasion, failure to file returns, or the filing of false returns.

The Civil Division. This division is responsible for representing the United States in all civil (that is, non-criminal) cases to which the National Government is a party—except for those assigned to another division within the Department (for example, to the Antitrust or Tax Divisions). It defends the Government in all cases brought against it in the Customs Court and most such cases in the Court of Claims.[4] It also handles all of the civil cases to which the National Government is a party involving admiralty or maritime law;[5] damages arising out of fraud or misrepresentation; patent, copyright, and trademark laws; and veterans' benefit matters. And it manages the properties once owned by enemy aliens but seized by the United States during World War II. All profits from the administration and sale of these holdings are used to pay the

---

[3] See page 579; the Tax Division does handle appeals taken from decisions of the Tax Court.

[4] See pages 577, 578.

[5] See page 571, footnote 2.

claims of American citizens who suffered property losses because of enemy action.

The Land and Natural Resources Division. This division has charge of all non-criminal cases relating to the public lands or other real property owned by the United States. Its case load includes such varied matters as the title to or acquisition, sale, or condemnations of lands, boundary disputes, water rights, oil reserves, and mineral leases. It also represents the National Government's interests in all civil cases involving Indians and Indian affairs.

The Criminal Division. This division prosecutes most of those cases in which persons have been accused of committing federal crimes. The many federal crimes—those activities Congress has outlawed and provided punishment for—fill more than 160 pages in the *United States Code.* These crimes range from arson, assault, bank robbery, and counterfeiting through kidnaping, narcotics, and perjury to trespassing, vote fraud, and white slavery.

The Internal Security Division. This division is responsible for all cases involving such subversive activities as espionage, sabotage, treason, and violations of such statutes as the Alien Registration (Smith) Act, the Internal Security (McCarran) Act (pages 111–112), and the Atomic Energy Act (page 398). It also makes the National Government's presentations before the Subversive Activities Control Board (page 111).

The Civil Rights Division. This division is responsible for all cases arising out of constitutional and statutory guarantees of civil and political rights. Thus, it handles such cases as those involving the denial of the right to vote, racial segregation or other forms of discrimination, election frauds, slavery, the conduct of unlawful searches and seizures, the treatment of prisoners, and all other situations in which it appears that federal, State, or local authorities have misused their authority deliberately to deprive a citizen of his constitutional rights. The Civil Rights Division also handles all legal matters relating to the sentencing, custody, or escape of federal prisoners.

United States Attorneys. There is one United States attorney for each of the ninety judicial districts into which the nation is divided (see page 580). Under the direction of the Attorney General, and in close concert with the divisions we have just discussed, each of the United States attorneys represents the United States in the federal District Court of his particular district. Each has as many assistants as the Attorney General thinks necessary and the department's budget will allow. Of course, all of the facilities of the Justice Department are available to any and all of these officers.

The post of United States attorney has long been regarded as a patronage plum. The Attorney General regularly consults with the party's leaders in the district before recommending to the President the appointment of a particular person to the office.[6] The President's appointees must be confirmed by the Senate and usually serve four-year terms.

United States Marshals. There is also one United States marshal for each of the judicial districts. They, too, are chosen by the President, confirmed by the Senate, serve four-year terms, and are picked with an eye to politics.

A marshal's principal duties are to arrest those who violate federal laws, take charge of federal prisoners, and execute the orders of federal courts. Each marshal has several deputies and, in emergencies, may deputize as many citizens as are needed to enforce the law.

---

[6] The fact that partisan politics plays a large role in the selection of United States attorneys does *not* mean that those who are appointed are not competent lawyers; most are highly qualified. Most appointments to public office—national, State, and local—are made on the basis of politics. Recall, as we pointed out in Chapter 7 and elsewhere, politics is the very stuff of which government is made, and necessarily so.

The Immigration and Naturalization Service. The immigration and nationality laws of the United States are administered by the Immigration and Naturalization Service in the Department of Justice. It is headed by a Commissioner appointed by the President and confirmed by the Senate. The Immigration and Naturalization Service and the statutes it enforces are treated at length in Chapter 5, pages 84–87.

The Bureau of Prisons. The Director of, the Bureau of Prisons is also appointed by the President and confirmed by the Senate. Under his direction, the Bureau of Prisons supervises the six penitentiaries and twenty-nine other correctional institutions maintained by the National Government. The penitentiaries are located at Atlanta, Georgia; Marion, Illinois;

Terre Haute, Indiana; Leavenworth, Kansas; Lewisburg, Pennsylvania; and McNeil Island, Washington. Famed Alcatraz—"the Rock"—in San Francisco Bay was closed in 1963.

There are three reformatories for male first offenders over age seventeen and one for females guilty of committing federal crimes. Nine correctional institutions are provided for prisoners serving short-term sentences. Short-term male offenders may also be sent to one of three work camps where they are used in road-building or other useful outdoor work. Prisoners soon eligible for release are often transferred to these minimum-security camps.

Juveniles guilty of federal crimes are sent to a Federal Youth Center. Three such institutions are now operating: at Ashland, Kentucky, Morgantown, West Virginia, and Englewood,

Federal Penal Institutions

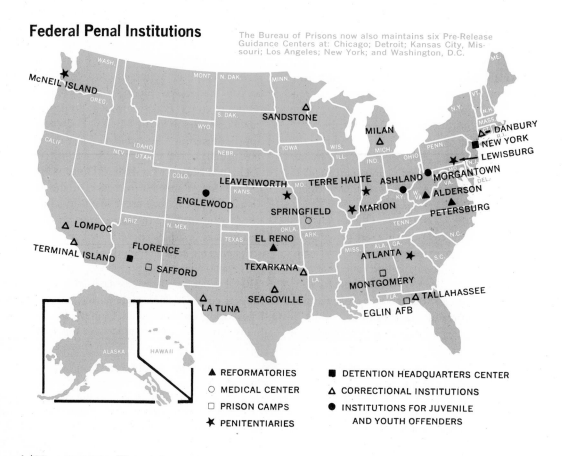

The Bureau of Prisons now also maintains six Pre-Release Guidance Centers at: Chicago; Detroit; Kansas City, Missouri; Los Angeles; New York; and Washington, D.C.

▲ REFORMATORIES

○ MEDICAL CENTER

□ PRISON CAMPS

★ PENITENTIARIES

■ DETENTION HEADQUARTERS CENTER

△ CORRECTIONAL INSTITUTIONS

● INSTITUTIONS FOR JUVENILE AND YOUTH OFFENDERS

Colorado. A prison medical center is maintained at Springfield, Missouri, to care for federal prisoners who are insane, tubercular, or otherwise chronically ill. Federal prisoners awaiting trial or serving only very short terms are often "boarded" in State and local jails.

The Director of the Bureau of Prisons is responsible for the Federal Prison Industries, Incorporated—the agency which manages all industrial enterprises and sponsors vocational training programs in the penitentiaries and correctional institutions. Its policies, however, are controlled by a board of six directors chosen by the President.

The Board of Parole. Sole authority to grant, modify, or revoke paroles for all federal prisoners is vested in the Board of Parole. Its eight members are appointed by the President and confirmed by the Senate.

The Board of Parole has supervision over all federal parolees and over those prisoners who are released "with time off for good behavior." In imposing sentences on those convicted of federal crimes, judges of the District Courts oftentimes specify that the date upon which a prisoner shall become eligible for parole is to be determined by the Board of Parole.

Under the Labor-Management Reporting and Disclosures (Landrum-Griffin) Act of 1959 (pages 476–479) the Board of Parole is also responsible for deciding whether a union official who has a criminal record is fit to hold office.

The Pardon Attorney. The Constitution gives to the President the power to grant pardons, reprieves, and amnesties.[7] The Pardon Attorney investigates each application for executive clemency and then recommends appropriate action to the President.

The Federal Bureau of Investigation. There is *no* single national police force. Rather, several agencies investigate violations of federal law and make the appropriate arrests. Among the more important and better-known of the

---

[7] Article II, Section 2, Clause 1; see page 318.

federal law enforcement agencies today are the Bureau of Customs, the Internal Revenue Service, and the United States Secret Service, all located in the Treasury Department; the Bureau of the Chief Postal Inspector in the Post Office Department; the Food and Drug Administration and the Public Health Service in the Department of Health, Education, and Welfare; The Provost Marshal General's Office in the Department of the Army within the Defense Department; and the Immigration and Naturalization Service in the Justice Department. There are many others. But the best known of all—and, indeed, the most famous and efficient law enforcement agency in the world—is the Federal Bureau of Investigation (FBI).

The FBI was first established in 1908. Its spectacular crime-busting history dates from 1934, however. During the early years of the Great Depression a wave of kidnapings, bank robberies, and other violent crimes swept the country. To meet it, the FBI was reorganized under its Director, J. Edgar Hoover. Moving swiftly and with almost frightening efficiency, Mr. Hoover and his agents stamped out the racketeering and lawlessness of the 1930's.

Mr. Hoover is still the Director of the FBI. He was originally appointed by President Coolidge in 1924 and has been reappointed by each Chief Executive since then.

Today the FBI has charge of investigating all violations of federal laws except those assigned to another federal law enforcement agency. Altogether the FBI has jurisdiction over some 170 investigative matters. Simply to list the more important of them is to dramatize the huge scope of its authority: espionage, sabotage, treason, and all other subversive activities; kidnaping, extortion, bank robbery, burglary, and larceny; crimes committed on government and Indian reservations; thefts of government property; interstate flight to avoid arrest or imprisonment; the interstate transportation of stolen automobiles, aircraft, cattle, or other property; the interstate transmission of gambling information or gambling devices; fraud against the National Government; election law violations; civil rights matters; and the assaulting or killing of a federal officer. In fact, the only major federal criminal matters beyond the FBI's jurisdiction are counterfeiting; postal, customs, and internal revenue violations; and illegal traffic in narcotic drugs.

FBI agents are carefully selected and highly trained. They must be American citizens, at least twenty-five years old and five feet seven inches in height, and in good physical condition. They use almost every device known to modern science in their crime-detection work. They work very closely with State and local police forces, maintain a National Police Academy to give them advanced training, and make the bureau's laboratory and extensive fingerprint files readily available to all law enforcement agencies.

The FBI is essentially a fact-finding agency. It develops the facts in a matter and then leaves to others, especially the courts, the conclusions to be drawn from that information.

The Community Relations Service. The Community Relations Service was created by Congress in the Civil Rights Act of 1964 (see page 120). It is headed by a Director appointed by the President and the Senate. He and his staff are charged with an extraordinarily sensitive and extremely important job: that of assisting local communities to resolve disputes and other difficulties arising out of discrimination based upon race, color, or national origin.

The Service may offer its help to any community in which peaceful relationships among its residents are threatened or have been disrupted; and it may do so at the request of local officials or other interested persons or upon its own motion. Once it has become involved in a local situation, it seeks the cooperation of any and all appropriate groups — local, State, or national and public or private. And, where it becomes involved, it also works to develop programs aimed at

preventing the outbreak of similar difficulties in the future.

The Bureau of Narcotics and Dangerous Drugs. The illegal use of narcotics and of other dangerous drugs may well be the most serious of all law enforcement problems in this country today.

An alarming share of all criminal activity can be traced directly to the problem. Many acts of violence are committed by persons under the influence of such illicit narcotics as opium, heroin, cocaine, or their many derivatives. Addicts often commit crimes in order to get the money with which to feed their cravings. And marijuana, LSD or other hallucinogenic drugs, or depressants or stimulants of uncountable variety are frequently present in criminal or otherwise irresponsible actions. The vicious parasites, the suppliers and peddlers who prey on addicts and other users, are often a part of organized operations also involved in such other nefarious activities as gambling, prostitution, and smuggling.

The regulation of narcotics and of other dangerous drugs is universally recognized as a proper and essential governmental function. Our law holds that the *only* legitimate uses for such drugs are in medicine and other scientific work, and that their sale and use should be limited to those purposes.

Each of the fifty States has strict narcotics control laws. But purely local control is virtually impossible. Control is inadequate even at the national level because the major sources of supply are abroad, especially in India, Communist China, Kuwait, and Mexico. The United States has joined with most other nations by treaty and through the United Nations to meet the problem.

The Bureau of Narcotics and Dangerous Drugs administers and enforces the federal narcotics laws and our international obligations. It is headed by a Director appointed by the President and Senate.

Working with the Public Health Service, the Bureau sets the amount of narcotics that may be brought into the country legally each year. Only those who have a valid federal license may lawfully deal in narcotics, and the penalties for violation are severe.

Most illegal drugs are smuggled into the country by ship or plane. Highly trained narcotics agents are stationed along the traditional routes of the illicit traffic, both in this country and abroad. The Bureau works in close harmony with the FBI, the Coast Guard, the Customs Bureau, other federal agencies, and with State and local police. In one recent case, agents broke up a ring so highly organized that it had its own fleet of planes to supply peddlers and addicts in various parts of the country.

Of all persons now sentenced to federal prisons each year for offenses of *all* types, approximately one in every eight is a narcotics violator. Despite the unrelenting efforts of various federal agencies, however, illegal drugs remain a big business. There are now more than 60,000 known adult drug addicts in the country. The most alarming aspect of the problem today involves the increased use of drugs among the youth.

THE POST OFFICE DEPARTMENT

The federal agency with which most Americans come into contact most often is the Post Office Department. By its own claim, it is the largest single business in the world and is a public monopoly.

Origins. The Post Office Department traces its ancestry to the early colonial period.[8] The first post office in America was established in Boston in 1639 by the General Court of the Massachusetts Bay Colony. The first successful postal system in the colonies, the Penn Post, was begun by William Penn in 1683. He established a post office at Philadelphia and provided regular weekly service from there to New Castle, Delaware.

William and Mary created a general postal system for the colonies in 1692. They granted a *patent* (monopoly) to Thomas Neale who began operating the Internal Colonial Postal Union the following year. Even though several of the colonial assemblies aided it financially, Neale's venture proved unprofitable, and the British Crown was forced to take over the mail service in 1707.

Under the British Post Office Act of 1710, all colonial postal matters were placed under the control of a Deputy Postmaster General of the British Colonies in North America, with headquarters in New York. For nearly half a century, however, this official system was marked by high rates and poor service; most colonists used it only when they could find no better way to send their messages.

It was not until Benjamin Franklin was appointed Co-Deputy Postmaster General in 1753 that the public postal system began to improve and flourish. Franklin had been postmaster at Philadelphia since 1737, and now the many improvements he had made there were extended throughout the colonies. Under him, the colonial post began to provide a faster, more reliable service than could any of the competing private carriers.

Franklin is generally recognized as the "Father of the United States Post Office." The British removed him from office in 1774 because of his political activities. In 1775, however, by unanimous choice of the Second Continental Congress, he became the first Postmaster General of the United States.

Under the Articles of Confederation Congress was given "the sole and exclusive right and power of. . .establishing and regulating post-offices. . .throughout all the United States."[9] With this authority, Congress created the United States Postal Service in 1782.

---

[8] The origins of postal service are lost in antiquity. The first mails were probably carried by the Egyptians before 4000 B.C.

[9] Article IX; see page 753.

History of the Post Office

1790

1792 Office permanently organized by Congress

1800

1810

1820

1829 Postmaster General became cabinet member

1830

1847 Postage stamps first introduced

1840

1855 Registry Service established

1858 Street letter boxes introduced

1863 Free city delivery and uniformed letter rate established

1850

1864 Railway Post Office Service and Money Order System established

1860

1867 Foreign Money Order System established

1870

1873 Postal Cards introduced

1874 Universal Postal Union formed

1880

1885 Special Delivery Service established

1890

1896 Rural Free Delivery Service established

1900

1910 Postal Savings System established

1910

1913 Parcel Post, Postal Insurance, and C.O.D. introduced

1920

1918 Air Mail Service established

1930

1941 Highway Post Office Service introduced

1940

1943 Postal Delivery Zone System introduced

1947 Helicopter Shuttle Service to speed delivery started

1950

1955 Certified Service established

1960 Intensified automation

1960

1963 Zip Code introduced

1965 Optical Scanner introduced

1970

1966 Postal Savings System discontinued

1968 Postal Service Institute training begun

1970 Postal Reorganization Act becomes law

How Zip Code Works

ZIP Code is a five-digit distribution code. It is designed to cut down the number of mail handling steps needed to move mail from the sender to the one addressed. It will also fit into the pattern of the steady increase in the use of electronic processing and sorting devices that businesses, and the Post Office Department, are installing.

The first number indicates to what section of the country the mail is to go. (See the map on the facing page.)

The second number identifies the state and possibly what part of the state.

10014

The third number identifies the particular town or city post office.

The last two numbers tell the station from which the mail is delivered.

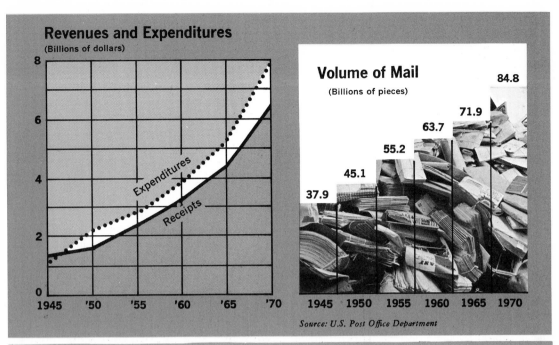

Revenues and Expenditures
(Billions of dollars)

Expenditures

Receipts

1945 '50 '55 '60 '65 '70

Volume of Mail
(Billions of pieces)

37.9 45.1 55.2 63.7 71.9 84.8

1945 1950 1955 1960 1965 1970

Source: U.S. Post Office Department

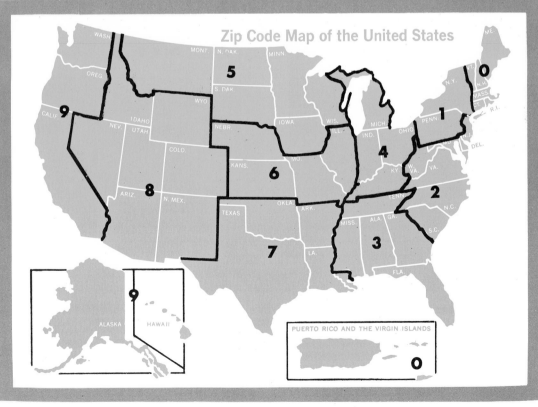

Zip Code Map of the United States

PUERTO RICO AND THE VIRGIN ISLANDS

The Constitution also vests the postal power in Congress, giving it the power "to establish post offices and post roads."[10] The First Congress made temporary provision for the postal system in 1789. It continued the Postal Service, making it an agency within the new Treasury Department, and President Washington appointed Samuel Osgood as Postmaster General. The Post Office Department was finally created as a separate agency in 1792.

Despite the pioneering work of Franklin and his successors, the new Post Office Department was a relatively crude operation. By 1789 there were only seventy-five post offices in all of the United States, and they were linked by no more than 1875 miles of mail routes. The vast system of today has grown from these rough beginnings.

Department Organization. As head of the Post Office Department, the Postmaster General is chosen by the President and confirmed by the Senate. Although Congress did not raise the Post Office to the rank of "executive department" until 1872, the Postmaster General has been a member of the Cabinet since Andrew Jackson's administration in 1829. He is the only Cabinet officer who is appointed for a definite term.[11]

The day-to-day work of the Post Office Department is directed by the Deputy Postmaster General through six major bureaus, each one headed by an Assistant Postmaster General: Operations, Personnel, Facilities, Finance and Administration, Planning and Marketing, and Research and Engineering. A Chief Postal Inspector and his agents keep tabs on the condition of the postal system and enforce the postal laws and regulations. Field operations are conducted through fifteen regional offices around the country, each of which is headed by a Regional Director.

Post Offices. There are approximately 32,000 post offices today (1971).[12] Each of them is graded into one of four classes, depending upon its annual receipts.

Postmasters in charge of offices of the first three classes are appointed by the President and confirmed by the Senate, and they serve indefinite terms. A postmastership is usually regarded as a "political plum." The Civil Service Commission examines applicants for these jobs, and the President must make his selection from among the three highest names on the Commission's roster. Even so, the posts usually go to faithful party supporters as a "reward" for past services; the President usually takes the advice of his party's organization in the locale involved. Many have long advocated "taking the Post Office out of politics."

Approximately one-fourth of all postmasters head fourth-class offices. Along with letter carriers, clerks, and all other postal employees, they are appointed by the Postmaster General under civil service regulations and enjoy permanent tenure.

A Huge Business. Some indication of the immense size of the Post Office Department's operations can be seen in these facts:

Its 720,000 employees now handle over 80,000,000,000 pieces of main annually—more mail than is handled by all of the other postal systems in the world combined. Postal receipts now amount to well over $6,000,000,000 a year.

Mail routes cover some 2,250,000 miles— or ninety times the distance around the earth at the Equator. Approximately 180,000 post-

---

[10] Article I, Section 8, Clause 7.

[11] The law provides that his "term...shall be for and during the term of the President by whom he is appointed, and for one month thereafter, unless sooner removed." Traditionally, but not always, the President appoints his party's National Chairman of the successful presidential campaign.

[12] The total number of local offices is being reduced steadily, as many of the smaller offices are consolidated with larger offices. There were 44,024 post offices in 1940, 41,464 in 1950, and 35,238 in 1960.

men deliver the mail on foot or from more than 50,000 government-owned or -rented vehicles.[13] The nation is crisscrossed by more than 120,000 miles of rail and air mail routes.

The 32,000 post offices sell some 25,000,-000,000 stamps annually and handle approximately 1,000,000,000 "special service" transactions—such as registering and insuring mail.

The Department's original and most important function is that of transmitting and delivering the mails. Congress has given it a number of additional tasks over the years, however, including: the issuing of postal money orders in 1864; special delivery in 1885; parcel post, including insurance and COD service, in 1913; and certified mail in 1955; in 1966 Congress directed that a postal savings system begun in 1910 be closed out by mid-1967.

Through the Philatelic Sales Unit, the Post Office Department sells about $3,000,000 in stamps each year to collectors. No one knows how many of the nation's 12,000,000 collectors buy stamps for their albums through local post offices, but their purchases run into the millions. Since most of these stamps are never used on mail, the Post Office realizes a tidy little eighty-five per cent profit on them.

Then, too, the Post Office performs many other "odd jobs." For example, it sells savings bonds and stamps, internal revenue stamps to indicate the payment of taxes on property transfers, and migratory bird stamps that must be attached to hunting licenses; it manufactures and repairs its own locks and mailbags; and it distributes the flags used to drape the coffins of deceased veterans.

Postal Rates. Congress sets the rates for the carrying of the various kinds of mail. A little over a century ago, when the letter rate was based on the number of pages and the distance involved, it cost a dollar to send a four-page letter from Boston to Charleston, South Carolina. Today, a six-cent stamp will carry a letter anywhere in the United States or the territories or to Canada or Mexico; a thirteen-cent stamp will carry a letter anywhere in the world.

First-class (surface) and air mail provide the fastest service. First-class rates are set a little above actual cost. Air mail has always been carried at less than cost; subsidies are paid to private airlines to carry it and account for a significant portion of their income. The United States was the first nation to provide air mail

First-day issues of commemorative postage stamps are highly valued by collectors. This issue commemorates the landing of the Pilgrims at Plymouth, Massachusetts. (Division of Philately, Post Office Department)

---

[13] Letters are still carried by dogsled on one route on a small island in Alaska's Bering Strait and by packhorse on another in the Grand Canyon in Arizona.

service. The first letters were carried by air between Washington and New York in 1918, and the first transcontinental service was begun in 1924. The mails were an important factor in the early development of aviation in this country.

Second-class mail—newspapers, magazines, and other periodicals—is carried below cost. The low rates encourage the dissemination of knowledge and information. They are also a subsidy to publishers; several periodicals would be beyond the reach of many of the nation's subscribers were it not for the low mail rates.

Third-class mail—mostly advertising matter —is also carried below cost. The rates are a boon to business, especially to mail-order houses. Some regard third-class mail as a boon to consumers, too, while others complain that most of it is "junk mail."

Fourth-class mail—most of it parcel post— includes merchandise, catalogs, and all other mailable matter not included in the other classes. It also includes a "special-rate" category—such educational matter as books, films, tapes, and recordings. Congress has given the Postmaster General authority to set parcel post rates. Most fourth-class mail is carried at or slightly below cost. Educational matter is carried at reduced rates.

Several million pieces of mail are carried free—including Braille books and recordings for the blind, mail sent by former Presidents or their widows, and the bulletins issued by agricultural colleges and experiment stations. Mail from Congressmen is carried "free" under the "franking privilege"; so, too, is that from all federal agencies. Congress appropriates an annual sum to the Post Office each year to cover the cost of most of this service. Newspapers are distributed free at any post office which does not have letter carrier service, but only within the county in which the newspaper is published.

The Postal Deficit. Until the middle of the last century, the Post Office was expected to make ends meet or even show a profit. Since 1852, however, service rather than profit has dominated our postal policy.

The rates for all classes of mail were raised most recently in 1968. Still, the Post Office operates at a loss year after year—the postal deficit now runs well above $1,000,000,000 each year.

The main cause for this deficit is the large volume of mail carried free or at reduced rates. Many argue that the Post Office should pay for itself and that the taxpayers should not be forced to subsidize some mail users. But those who benefit most directly from free or reduced postage and those who feel the postal system should be operated as a service and not for profit oppose additional rate increases.

Prohibited Articles. In addition to the minimum and maximum size and weight limits imposed on mailable matter, Congress has excluded several articles from the mails—for example, poisons, explosives, intoxicating liquors, live animals, and other articles dangerous to the mails or to postal employees; concealable firearms, except to dealers and peace officers; libelous, treasonable, or obscene matter; lottery tickets or other prize schemes dependent upon chance; and all fraudulent matters.

Whenever any person or firm attempts to procure money or property through the mails by fraud or a scheme of chance, the privilege of the mails is withdrawn. The Postmaster General issues a "fraud order" against the offender, and the local postmaster stamps the word "fraudulent" on any mail addressed to him and returns it to the sender.

The fraud and other postal laws and regulations are enforced by the Chief Postal Inspector and his agents. Violators are subject to heavy fine and imprisonment. In one recent case three livestock dealers in Iowa were convicted of "kiting" checks and defrauding two banks of $265,000. In another case a Chicago tire dealer was sentenced to two years in prison and placed on probation for another five for substituting junk tires for the new ones he had advertised; he had made $700,000 before inspectors caught up with him. Three Tennessee promoters were found guilty of obtaining $4,600,000 in a scheme the judge described as "the fraud of the century"; they sold fictitious warehouse receipts for nonexistent soybeans.

The most vicious illegal use of the mails today includes fraudulent "work-at-home" plans, various "cures" for diseases, and pornographic literature and pictures. Altogether, the Post Office Department estimates the potential loss to the public through such schemes to be at least $100,000,000 annually.

❋❋❋❋❋❋❋❋❋❋❋❋ CONCEPT BUILDING ❋❋❋❋❋❋❋❋❋❋❋❋

Key Concepts

Insuring justice to all its citizens is a primary function of democratic government. *The Justice Department* is the principal executive agency in the National Government responsible for promoting legal justice. It is headed by the Attorney General.

In addition to giving legal advice to the President and representing the United States in court, the Justice Department and its agencies operate the federal penal system, investigate many types of crimes and arrest violators, and administer the nation's immigration and naturalization policies.

The Solicitor General appears for the United States in the Supreme Court and is the National Government's chief lawyer. The several divisions in the Justice Department and the United States attorneys argue federal cases in the lower courts. United States marshals arrest criminals, handle prisoners, and execute court orders.

The Justice Department also includes the Immigration and Naturalization Service, the Bureau of Prisons which supervises the federal prison system, the Board of Parole, the Pardon Attorney, the Federal Bureau of Investigation, the Community Relations Service, and the Bureau of Narcotics and Dangerous Drugs.

The Post Office Department traces its ancestry to the creation of the first public post office in America in Boston in 1639. Benjamin Franklin, the "Father of the United States Post Office," was appointed the first Postmaster General of the United States by the Second Continental Congress in 1775.

Today the Post Office, headed by the Postmaster General, is the world's largest business enterprise and is a public monopoly. Its some 720,000 employees and some 32,000 post offices perform several "odd jobs" in addition to the primary one of carrying the mails.

Postal rates are set by Congress and vary according to the class of mail. Most mail is carried at a loss, producing an annual postal deficit. The dispute over the deficit centers around the question of whether the Post Office should be operated for service or for profit. Many matters are excluded from the mails, and the postal laws are enforced by postal inspectors who guard against illegal use of the mails.

Important Terms

amnesty	fraud order	pardon	prosecute
executive clemency	justice	parole	reprieve
franking privilege	legal justice	postal deficit	social justice

Questions for Inquiry and Review

1. From what two basic standpoints may justice be viewed? To what does each relate?

2. When was the post of Attorney General created? The Justice Department? Who selects the Attorney General?

3. What are the principal functions of the Justice Department today?

4. Why does the Solicitor General deserve the title "the Government's chief lawyer"?

5. What are the seven divisions within the Justice Department and their chief areas of work?

6. How many United States attorneys are there? What is their main function?

7. How many United States marshals are there? What are their main functions?

8. What does the Bureau of Prisons do? The Board of Parole? The Pardon Attorney?

9. When was the FBI originally created? When and why was it reorganized?

10. Who is the Director of the FBI? How long has he held that post?

11. What is the principal function of the Community Relations Service?

12. When and where was the first post office in America established? By whom?

13. Who is generally recognized as the "Father of the United States Post Office"?

14. In what body does the Constitution vest the postal power?

15. What officer heads the Post Office Department? How is he selected?

16. Approximately how many pieces of mail does the Post Office now handle annually?

17. Approximately how many local post offices are there?

18. Who sets the postal rates?

19. What is the approximate size of the annual postal deficit? What is the main cause of the postal deficit?

For Further Inquiry

1. Why are social justice and legal justice so dependent upon one another for their existence? Why is each so essential to democracy?

2. Do you agree with Benjamin Disraeli's observation: "Justice is truth in action." Why?

3. These words of a former Solicitor General are inscribed at the door to the office of the Attorney General of the United States: "The United States wins its point whenever justice is done to its citizens in its courts." How would you expand upon the philosophy underlying these words?

4. In most States public prosecutors (district attorneys) and sheriffs are popularly elected. Do you think their federal counterparts, the United States attorneys and marshals, should be chosen by the voters, too?

5. The Post Office is a huge business enterprise owned and operated by the National Government. Do you think this proper, or should the postal system be operated under private competition?

6. Should the Post Office perform the many "odd jobs" it does, besides transmitting and delivering the mails? Why?

Suggested Activities

1. Invite a local attorney or judge to speak to the class on the nature of justice and its role in a democracy.

2. Ask an FBI or other federal law enforcement agent to speak to the class about the nature of his work.

3. Write a brief editorial on the subject of the postal deficit.

4. Stage a debate or class forum on the question: *Resolved,* That Congress should establish a single national police force to replace the various federal agencies responsible for federal law enforcement.

5. Write a report on one of the following topics: (a) the federal parole system, (b) FBI training, (c) the colonial postal system.

6. In 1968 a presidential study commission recommended that Congress reorganize the Post Office Department as a nonprofit government corporation. Prepare a report setting forth the reasons for, details, pros and cons, and prospects for adoption of the proposal.

Suggested Reading

"A Corporation to Carry the Mails?" *U.S. News,* July 29, 1968.

"A New Postal System for U.S.," *U.S. News,* June 9, 1969.

"Attorney General Mitchell: Mr. Law-and-Order," *Newsweek,* September 8, 1969.

Cook, Fred J., "There's Always a Crime Wave —How Bad Is This One?" *New York Times Magazine,* October 6, 1968.

"Cosa Nostra—The Poison in Our Society," *Time,* August 22, 1969; *Reader's Digest,* December, 1969.

"Crimes While on Bail—The Hunt for a Remedy," *U.S. News,* February 17, 1969.

"FBI's Computer War Against Crime," *U.S. News,* October 20, 1969.

Hoover, J. Edgar, "The Story of Crime in the U.S.," *U.S. News,* October 7, 1968.

"Last Chance to Save the Post Office," *Life,* September 13, 1968.

Miller, James N., "Awful Truth About the U.S. Post Office," *Reader's Digest,* November 1968.

Mitchell, Attorney General John N., "Fighting Crime in America," *U.S. News,* August 18, 1969.

"Pro and Con: The Question of Bail Reform," *Congressional Digest,* April, 1969.

"Pro and Con: The Question of a Federal Postal Corporation," *Congressional Digest,* November, 1969.

Surface, Bill, "Will *Your* Car Be Stolen Next?" *Reader's Digest,* December, 1969.

"The Drug Question: Growing Younger," *Newsweek,* April 21, 1969.

"The U.S. Mail Mess," *Life,* November 28, 1969.

23
THE DEPARTMENT
OF THE INTERIOR

✳✳✳ Should self-sufficiency be a major goal of the nation's natural resources programs? Why?

✳✳✳ Do you perceive any conflicts between the goals of preservation and conservation, on the one hand, and those of economic security and development on the other?

✳✳✳ Is there, in this day and age, any justification for governmental policies which treat some persons as "wards" of the government? How might (or might not) these policies be justified?

Conservation means the wise use of the earth and its resources ... for the greatest good of the greatest number for the longest time.

GIFFORD PINCHOT

Nowhere on earth has nature been more generous than in the United States. The early settlers, and the millions who followed them, found a land of almost unbelievable natural wealth. They found an entire continent of vast forests, of mighty rivers and bountiful lakes, of grassy plains extending far beyond the distant horizons. Beneath the rich soil they found seemingly inexhaustible deposits of coal, iron, oil, copper, gold, and other minerals.

For nearly 300 years this great wealth was used with little or no thought for the future. There was a nation to be built, and nature's larder seemed boundless. Whole forests disappeared, grasslands were put to the plow, mineral deposits were overworked. The few who warned against exploitation and waste, who pleaded for conservation and wiser use, were seldom heard. Not until the turn of the twentieth century did Americans begin to

realize that the land's great natural wealth might not be inexhaustible after all.

The modern conservation movement was begun during the Presidency of Theodore Roosevelt (1901–1909). With the zeal of crusaders, the President and his Chief Forester, Gifford Pinchot, set out to make the nation "conservation conscious." Their battle has not been entirely won, even today. Some exploiters are still with us. On the whole, however, most citizens have come to realize the absolute necessity for conservation—for the wise use and restoration of our natural resources.

DEPARTMENTAL ORGANIZATION

Most of the National Government's activities in the field of conservation today are conducted by agencies within the Department of the Interior.[1] The Department was created by Con-

---

[1] The two major conservation agencies outside the Department are the Forest Service (pages 441–442) and the Soil Conservation Service (pages 442–444), both within the Department of Agriculture.

gress in 1849. Originally, it contained the General Land Office, the Office of Indian Affairs, the Pension Office, and the Patent Office. It also had supervision of public buildings, the census, the District of Columbia's penitentiary, and United States marshals, and it enforced federal mining laws. Over the years other functions were added to the Department's work, including activities in such fields as education, health, commerce, and labor.

As new departments and independent agencies were established, many of Interior's early functions were transferred to them. Gradually, the Department's role changed from that of general housekeeper for the National Government to its present one of general custodian of the nation's natural resources. Its principal work today is concerned with the management, conservation, and development of the public lands, water and power resources, oil, gas, and mineral resources, certain forest holdings, fish and wildlife, and the national park system.

The Department's jurisdiction extends over some 750,000,000 acres of land in the fifty States, to islands in the Caribbean and the South Pacific, and to lands in the Arctic Circle. It is responsible for mine safety, the protection of fish and wildlife, the preservation of scenic and historic areas, the reclamation of arid lands in the West, the management of hydroelectric power systems, and the welfare of over 200,000 persons in our territorial possessions and some 400,000 Indians residing on or near reservations.

The Secretary of the Interior. The Department is headed by the Secretary of the Interior. He is appointed by the President with the consent of the Senate and, as a rule, comes from the West—the region in which the bulk of his Department's work is located. The Under Secretary serves as his chief deputy and exercises general supervision over the several agencies which compose the Department. The top echelon of departmental command is filled out by six Assistant Secretaries—for: Public Land Management; Water and Power Develop-

ment; Fish and Wildlife, Parks, and Marine Resources; Mineral Resources; Water Quality and Research; and Administration.

Principal Agencies. Today the several major agencies within the Department include the:

> Bureau of Land Management
> Bureau of Reclamation
> Bonneville Power Administration
> National Park Service
> Geological Survey
> Bureau of Mines
> Fish and Wildlife Service
> Bureau of Indian Affairs

THE BUREAU OF LAND MANAGEMENT

The Bureau of Land Management has charge of the management, survey, and disposition of large areas of United States public lands, and of the minerals these lands contain. Most of the area under its supervision consists of grazing and mineral lands.

Federal Land Policy. The total area of the United States today is estimated to be 2,271,-343,000 acres. Approximately one third of this huge domain—some 760,000,000 acres—is now owned by the National Government.

The building of the *public domain* (lands owned by the United States) was begun in the years 1781–1802, as the original States ceded their western land claims to the National Government. Other public lands were acquired by conquest and purchase as the nation expanded—as the table on page 585 shows. At one time or another since 1781, over eighty per cent of all of the land within the nation—some 1,837,-762,560 acres—has been held by the National Government, including practically all of the area west of the original thirteen States except Texas.

Over sixty per cent of all of the land which at some time or another has been within the public domain—approximately 1,140,000,000 acres, amounting to just over half of the total area of the United States—has been disposed of over the years. To gain revenue, and more importantly, to encourage western settlement, a vast amount of public land was given away or sold at very low prices. Much of it went to homesteaders in 160-acre lots. The attraction of free or very inexpensive land in the West was a major factor in the building of the nation. Large tracts were given to the railroads to encourage the building of lines across the country. The States were granted huge areas for the support of public education and of various institutions, for the construction of canals and roads, for river improvements and reclamation, and for many other purposes. Other grants were made to veterans, and much land was sold at very cheap prices to foster the reclaiming of desert lands.

Nearly all of the public land best suited for agriculture has long since been disposed of. Only within the past thirty years or so has Congress provided for the planned management and development of the remaining public lands—much of which no one wanted.

Today, the BLM controls about 453,000,000 acres, most of it in the West. Indeed, the large bulk of federally held lands of all types is located in twelve western States: [2]

FEDERAL LANDS

State	Acres	% of State
Alaska	348,468,000	95.3
Nevada	60,725,000	86.4
Utah	35,061,000	66.5
Idaho	33,849,000	63.9
Oregon	32,182,000	52.2
Wyoming	30,060,000	48.2
Arizona	32,432,000	44.6
California	44,394,000	44.3
Colorado	24,152,000	36.3
New Mexico	26,375,000	33.9
Montana	27,654,000	29.6
Washington	12,570,000	29.4
All others	47,423,000	6.3

BLM practices "multiple use management" on the lands it administers. That is, it promotes the widest and wisest possible uses of those lands and of the resources they contain. In doing so, it engages in many varied and related activities.

It sells public lands and also grants leases or permits for mining and other types of mineral extraction and for livestock grazing. It works to conserve and develop the water, soil, and wildlife resources on its holdings and to provide for the sustained yield of its timber lands. It promotes the recreational use of public lands and also sells or leases to the States for that purpose. The land records it keeps are often vital in deciding disputes over property ownership in those States where there are large public land holdings.

Congress enacted two extraordinarily important public lands laws—the most significant in years—in 1964.

The Land and Water Conservation Act was passed with an eye to the nation's future outdoor recreation needs. It created a Land and Water Conservation Fund designed to promote federal and State action to plan for and meet those needs.

The Fund provides money from which the Secretary of the Interior may purchase lands and from which the States may receive grants-in-aid for the purchase and development of lands and other recreational facilities. It makes these actions possible *now*—before many desirable areas become too costly or are taken for other uses.

---

[2] The other major landholders among federal agencies today are: Agriculture Department (chiefly the Forest Service), 187,300,000 acres; other Interior Department agencies (chiefly Reclamation, Indian Affairs, National Parks), 80,000,000 acres; Army, 11,500,000 acres; Corps of Engineers (civil functions), 7,100,000 acres; Air Force, 8,600,000 acres; Navy, 3,650,000 acres; Atomic Energy Commission, 2,200,000 acres; Tennessee Valley Authority, 805,000 acres.

It is estimated that the Fund will have received as much as $1,500,000,000 by the end of its first decade, 1975. Its monies come from four sources: the admission and user fees charged in various federal recreation areas, the sale of surplus federal lands, the 2¢ federal tax on motorboat fuels, and congressional appropriations (which are to be repaid beginning in 1975).

The Wilderness Act was passed to provide future generations of Americans with "the benefits of an enduring resource of wilderness." It created a National Wilderness Preservation System of federal lands which are to be managed so that they will remain forever as primitive, wilderness areas. Congress placed some 9,100,000 acres in the System and directed the Secretaries of Interior and Agriculture to review another 52,000,000 acres of park, forest, and other federal lands for possible inclusion within the System's protective cover by 1975.

Congress added another set of significant statutes in 1968, creating:

(1) *The National Scenic Rivers System* — to preserve stretches of wild and scenic rivers in their natural state. It placed segments of these rivers in the System: the Salmon and Clearwater Rivers in Idaho; the Rogue River, Oregon; the Feather River, California; the Eleven Point River, Missouri; the Rio Grande and four miles of the Red River in New Mexico; the Saint Croix River in Minnesota and Wisconsin; and the Wolf River, Wisconsin. It also ordered the Secretaries of Interior and Agriculture to study several other rivers for later inclusion. Those within the System are to be preserved from incompatible uses, pollution, and commercialization.

(2) *The National Trails System* — to preserve scenic and recreational trails in various parts of the country for hiking and similar uses. Congress designated the 2000-mile Appalachian Trail and the 2350-mile Pacific Crest Trail as the first two in the System. It directed the Secretaries of Interior and Agriculture to study several more for later inclusion. Attention is to be given first to routes near cities, with second priority to go to trails in remote areas.

The Tidelands Controversy. There has been considerable legal and political controversy in the past several years over the ownership of the "tidelands." Should they be controlled by the National Government or by the particular coastal States?

Actually, the *tidelands* (those covered by the ebb and flow of the tides) have never been in dispute. All agree that these lands have always belonged to the States. The dispute really involves the *offshore submerged* lands (those reaching out under the sea from low tide to the territorial limit of the United States). The importance of these lands is in the resources they contain, especially the immense oil deposits off the Florida, Alabama, Louisiana, Texas, and California coasts.

In 1947 the Supreme Court held that the marginal sea lands were controlled by the National Government, not the States. Some became alarmed that Congress might now claim federal control over the other submerged lands, such as river and lake beds. Many in the coastal States saw a fabulous revenue source if the States controlled the offshore lands.

Following the Court's decision, Congress debated proposals to give the disputed lands to the coastal States. Many urged, instead, that the lands be leased out by the Federal Government, with the revenue to be used to aid the nation's schools. Congress finally passed a quitclaim bill — vesting title in the States — in 1952; but President Truman vetoed that measure. President Eisenhower signed a similar bill the following year, however.

The *Submerged Lands Act of 1953* gives each coastal State control over the lands out to its "historic boundaries" — that is, out to the seaward limits as they existed when the State involved was admitted to the Union. In no case, however, can these limits extend more than three miles into the Atlantic or Pacific Ocean or three marine leagues (ten and one-half miles) into the Gulf of Mexico.[3]

In 1953 Congress also passed the *Outer Continental Shelf Lands Act.* This statute provides for federal control over all resources in the submerged lands on the Continental Shelf beyond the State limits.[4] The Shelf involves those lands beneath shallow water—usually less than 600 feet—out well beyond the territorial limits. In the Atlantic the Shelf extends as far out as 250 miles in some places; in the Gulf it runs as far as 140 miles. The Interior Department has leased many sites on the Shelf to private oil concerns in the past several years.

THE BUREAU OF RECLAMATION

In large parts of the West successful farming and ranching is all but impossible without a water supply to supplement the limited rainfall.

More than a century ago, Brigham Young and his followers began a startling demonstration of what irrigation can accomplish. Young, traveling with his Mormon caravan to Utah in 1847, told his Indian scout that he intended to plant a farming community beyond the mountains. The scout laughed and offered a thousand dollars for the first ear of corn grown.

On July 24, 1847, the Mormons came from Immigration Canyon into the parched Salt Lake Valley. They unhitched their teams along the little stream now known as City Creek. The same afternoon they unloaded their plows and began breaking the dry desert land. The next day the stream was diverted, the plowed land irrigated, and potatoes planted—and thus began modern irrigation in the West. Today some 400,000 people live in the Salt Lake Valley in the State of Utah.

The Reclamation Act of 1902. Largely at the urging of Theodore Roosevelt, Congress directed the Secretary of the Interior in 1902 to "locate, construct, operate, and maintain works for the storage, diversion, and development of waters for the reclamation of arid and semiarid lands" in the Western States. The Reclamation Service was established to carry out the purposes of the new law. The 1902 and later acts set aside money from the sale of public lands in a "revolving fund" to finance reclamation projects. Reclaimed lands are usually sold to farmers in small tracts on easy terms, with the proceeds going to the revolving fund.

The Bureau contracts with water users' associations and individual farmers to provide their lands with continuing irrigation service. It now furnishes water to more than 7,000,000 acres of farm land, nearly a fourth of all the irrigated land in the country. The crops now being produced on those acres have a market value in excess of $1,100,000,000 a year.

The Bureau also works closely with the States and with the Agency for International Development to promote the effective use of water resources both at home and abroad.

---

[3] In 1960 the Supreme Court held that the Submerged Lands Act sets the Texas and Florida boundaries at 10.5 miles while those of Alabama, Louisiana, and Mississippi reach out only 3 miles. The latter three States have since been seeking changes in the 1953 law to give them the maximum limits, too.

[4] International law generally recognizes the three-mile limit for territorial waters; historically, the United States has supported the three-mile rule. The assertion of federal control over the Shelf lands beyond that point raises questions that may ultimately lead to international complications. The United States has been careful *not* to claim that its boundaries extend to the limits of the Shelf, but only that its jurisdiction over the resources existing there does. In recent years both Russian and Japanese fishing fleets have regularly worked the waters immediately off our Pacific Coast. As a result, Congress extended the area of exclusive American fishing rights in 1966, from the previous three-mile limit out to twelve miles.

Multipurpose Dams. Originally, most of the Bureau's projects were relatively small ones. Since the 1930's, however, Congress has provided for very extensive reclamation work along with several huge multipurpose dams—"multipurpose" because they provide for many things at once: including hydroelectric power, flood control, recreation, and improved navigation, as well as irrigation.

The first of them, Hoover Dam, was authorized in 1928. Today, other federal agencies, notably the Army's Corps of Engineers, are also involved in dam building. At times, this overlapping has led to political wrangling.

Let us take a brief look at a few of the Bureau's major projects.

The Boulder Canyon Project and Hoover Dam. The hot semitropical Imperial Valley at its lowest point is 279 feet below sea level. It was originally part of the Gulf of California. But the Colorado River brought down enough mud every year to cover 100,000 acres a foot deep. When in flood the river was too thick to drink and too thin to plow. So in time it filled the Gulf of California and built up a deltaic ridge, which is now over 100 feet above sea level at the international boundary.

This ridge forms the southern rim of the Imperial Valley. The Colorado River, flowing along it until it turns south to the Gulf of California, was kept out of the low valley by a levee seventy miles long; but as the river became higher each year, there was danger of a break in the levee and of flooding the homes of a hundred thousand people.

The mighty Hoover Dam, completed in 1936, created the 115-mile long Lake Mead which now catches the silt that had been raising the level of the river downstream at the levees.

The dam rises 726 feet above the river and is the highest concrete dam in the nation. Its mammoth U-shaped bulk is 1244 feet long at the top and contains 4,400,000 cubic yards of concrete. Its power plant holds seventeen main generators with a total capacity of 1,344,800 kilowatts of power.

Lake Mead is capable of holding some 31,250,000 acre feet of water. That is, it can store more than enough to cover an area larger than the entire State of New York with a foot of water. It is the principal storage unit for flood control on the lower reaches of the Colorado River.

The dam and its mighty power plant cost $160,000,000—all of which is being repaid to the Treasury. Most of the total cost ($135,000,000) is being repaid at three per cent interest out of the revenue from power and water uses. The balance, which is credited to flood control work, is being returned without interest.

Hoover Dam is the principal unit of the Boulder Canyon Project which includes other dams downstream, like the Davis, Parker, and Imperial Dams. Together these multipurpose units irrigate large parts of Arizona, New Mexico, and southern California. They also provide water for the whole Los Angeles area, 265 miles from Hoover Dam.

The giant Hoover Dam, brilliantly lit at night, presents a spectacular view to visitors. (Bureau of Reclamation, U.S. Department of the Interior)

Grand Coulee Dam. The Columbia River rises in British Columbia, flows through eastern Washington, then turns west to the Pacific to form the Oregon-Washington border. It holds approximately one-third of all of the potential water power in the United States. Grand Coulee, the nation's largest concrete structure, is located on the Columbia in eastern Washington, 240 miles east of Seattle. It was completed by the Bureau in 1942.

The dam is 550 feet high and is 4173 feet long. It contains over 10,585,000 cubic yards of concrete, more than twice the volume in Hoover Dam. Nearly half of its huge bulk lies below the surface of the river. Its eighteen generators can produce 1,974,000 kilowatts, making its power plant the mightiest ever built. The dam's central spillway is over a quarter of

a mile wide and the waterfall it creates is half as wide and twice as high as Niagara Falls.

Grand Coulee is the major water control unit for the vast Columbia River Basin Project, encompassing large portions of Washington, Oregon, Idaho, and Montana. Its reservoir, Lake Roosevelt, holds 9,400,000 acre feet of water—enough to flood all of Connecticut to a depth of three feet; and its storage will eventually irrigate more than 1,200,000 acres of once valueless wasteland.

Several other giant multipurpose dams have been and are being built on the Columbia and its tributaries, including Bonneville, Chief Joseph, The Dalles, McNary, and John Day. Some of these involve the Bureau and others the Army Engineers. Together, they provide irrigation, flood control, navigation aids, and

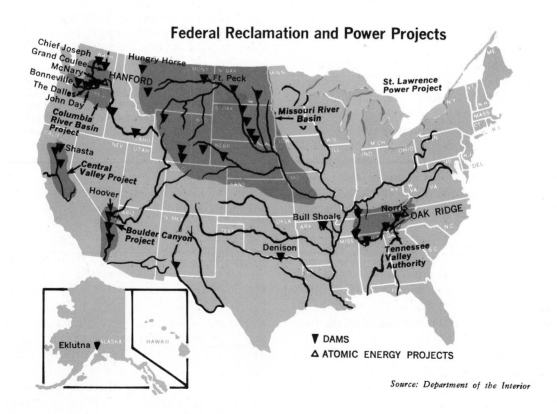

Federal Reclamation and Power Projects

▼ DAMS
△ ATOMIC ENERGY PROJECTS

Source: Department of the Interior

recreation facilities, as well as power for the rapidly expanding Pacific Northwest.

The total cost of the Basin Project thus far is estimated at $1,700,000,000. Almost all of it will be returned to the Treasury out of water user payments and power sales. The costs allocated to power are being repaid at three per cent and those chargeable to irrigation without interest. The other features, such as flood control, are classed as "nonreimbursable" expenses.

THE POWER ADMINISTRATIONS

There are four Power Administrations within the Department, three of which market the hydroelectric power produced at various federal projects: the Bonneville Power Administration, the Southeastern and Southwestern Power Administrations, the Defense Electric Power Administration, and the Alaska Power Administration.

The Bonneville Power Administration. By far the largest of the four agencies is the Bonneville Power Administration (BPA). It was originally created in 1937 to market the power obtained from Bonneville Dam on the Columbia River. The dam itself, completed in 1936, was built and is maintained by the Corps of Army Engineers.

A unique system of "fish ladders" was built along with the dam in order to insure that the multimillion-dollar Columbia River salmon industry would not be destroyed. Salmon swimming upstream to spawn enter a fishway which winds around a hill imitating a real creek. Two fish locks float the fish over the dam, and the salmon then "climb" three fish ladders to get beyond the dam. Variations of the fish-ladder system are now common at many of the newer dams on the Columbia and elsewhere.

BPA also markets the power produced at all federal projects on the Columbia River and in other parts of Oregon, Washington, northern Idaho, and western Montana. The projects themselves have been built and are operated

"Fish ladders," such as this one at the Bonneville Dam on the Columbia River, have been built to help the salmon get around the dams and to the spawning grounds upstream. (U.S. Department of the Interior, Fish and Wildlife Service)

either by the Bureau of Reclamation or the Corps of Army Engineers. BPA constructs and operates the transmission systems. It sells the power at wholesale to public power groups, such as those financed by the Rural Electrification Administration (REA), and to private power companies which then resell it. BPA also sells power direct to large users such as industrial plants. Altogether BPA operates more than 8000 miles of high voltage transmission lines and some 200 substations in the Northwest.

The Southeastern and the Southwestern Power Administrations. These agencies market the surplus power generated at various Army Engineers and Bureau of Reclamation

National Parks and Seashores

projects in their respective regions. In effect, they act as business offices for those projects outside the areas in which the major works of the Bureau of Reclamation and BPA are concentrated.[5]

The Defense Electric Power Administration. The DEPA is essentially a civil defense agency. It is responsible for the preparation of the detailed plans for the operation of the nation's public and private power facilities in the event of a war or other national emergency situation. It also serves the Government's several other civil defense

agencies as their link with all of the nation's public and private power producers in preparedness matters.

The DEPA's Administrator and his staff are advised by eighteen area directors; these men, who serve the Government without compensation, hold high posts in public and private power utilities across the country.

The Alaska Power Administration. As we noted on page 422, nearly all of the land within the State of Alaska—95.3 per cent of it—is owned by the Federal Government. The Alaska Power Administration is the agency through which the Interior Department promotes the development and utilization of the water, power, and related resources in this huge domain.

---

[5] The huge Tennessee Valley Authority is an independent federal agency which markets the power it generates; see pages 433–435.

The Administration also operates the Eklutna Project, a hydroelectric power complex north of Anchorage, at the head of Cook Inlet. The Project supplies electricity to Anchorage, the State's largest city, and to the Matanuska Valley and several Army and Air Force installations.

THE NATIONAL PARK SERVICE

The National Park Service was created in 1916 to promote and regulate the use of national parks and monuments in order to "conserve the scenery and the natural and historic objects and the wildlife therein and to provide for the enjoyment of the same in such manner and by such means as will leave them unimpaired for the enjoyment of future generations." The various programs carried on by the Service stem primarily from this responsibility to provide areas for public recreation and to give the fullest possible protection to the nation's natural and historic resources.

The National Park System now contains some 270 parks, historic sites, memorials, monuments, recreation areas, and other properties of historic and archaeological significance. The Service oversees an estimated half-a-billion dollars worth of real estate embracing some of the most breathtaking scenic beauty in the world.

Its 28,000,000-acre domain stretches from the gleaming beaches and undersea splendors of the Virgin Islands to flamethrowing volcanoes in Hawaii. It soars as high as Alaska's 20,320-foot Mt. McKinley and drops as low as Oregon's 1966-foot-deep Crater Lake. It includes many other towering peaks, massive glaciers, lakes, sand dunes, seashores, and deserts, giant sequoias over 3500 years old, cascading waterfalls and geysers, and caves and petrified forests.

These natural splendors are like magnets pulling Americans and foreign visitors. Each year now tourists, campers, hikers, skiers, fishermen, naturalists, and many others pay more than 170,000,000 visits to the national playgrounds maintained for their use and pleasure by the Park Service.

THE GEOLOGICAL SURVEY

In 1879 Congress created a still little-known agency, the Geological Survey. It develops and publishes geographic and geologic facts for public use. It has made topographic and geologic maps which now cover nearly half of the country. Their worth cannot be estimated. Because of them, we know the heights of mountains, the volume of water which flows in streams, the areas where valuable minerals are most likely to be found beneath the surface, and other vital and useful facts.

The varied work of the Survey can best be illustrated by a few examples. A number of years ago the Lackawanna Railroad relocated thirty-four miles of its main line. The chief construction engineer was able to sit in the comfort of his office and run all of the preliminary surveys, and even make the final location for the $21,000,000 improvement from the Survey's topographic sheets.

A Survey research project found usable quantities of uranium in phosphate rock in Florida. From maps developed by the Survey, a mining company discovered zinc deposits worth $100,000,000 in Tennessee. From its glacial maps, building contractors are able to find great stores of excellent sands and gravels, and well drillers are able to locate waters trapped in glacial rubble.

Late in World War II the Japanese launched some 9000 balloons intended to drift to our Pacific coast to start forest fires. Less than 300 of them reached this country. By examining only four cupfuls of sand from the ballast, the Survey was able to pinpoint the tiny strip of beach southeast of Tokyo where the balloons were being launched; the Air Force then bombed the launching sites.

Over and over again, the Survey's work has led to rich oil discoveries and other important finds. No wonder its scientists are called "Uncle Sam's treasure hunters."

THE BUREAU OF MINES

The Bureau of Mines was created in 1910. Its major concerns are with the conservation and development of our mineral and fuel resources and the improvement of health and safety conditions in the mining industry.

The Bureau has examined thousands of mineral deposits in the United States and the territories. Through its work, domestic supplies of such strategic minerals as bauxite (essential to aluminum production) and manganese (essential to steel production) have been made available.

The Bureau and several of the major oil companies have long worked together to unlock the nation's vast oil-shale deposits. If an economically practical way to extract the rockbound oil in volume can be found, the United States could become wholly independent of foreign oil and our own oil reserves could be prolonged indefinitely.

Much of the Bureau's research is helpful to private industry and to the States and their local governments. Explosion hazards from dusts, fumes, and gases are under constant study, and the results are especially valuable to the mining industry. Cities have benefited from the Bureau's work on such problems as the explosion hazards of sewer gases, the dangers involved in storing and handling gasoline, firefighting techniques, smoke abatement, and tunnel ventilation.

THE FISH AND WILDLIFE SERVICE

The Fish and Wildlife Service is the direct descendant of the oldest of all federal conservation agencies. It traces its ancestry back to the Bureau of Fisheries, created by Congress in 1871 to preserve the fishing banks of the Great Lakes.

Today the Service consists of two subagencies: The Bureau of Sport Fisheries and Wildlife and the Bureau of Commercial Fisheries. Through these two agencies, the Service is charged with the task of conserving and restoring fish and wildlife resources and promoting their more effective use. It works closely with other federal and similar State agencies and with private organizations in the forestry, agriculture, and recreation fields.

The range of the Service's activities are quite broad. It maintains more than 100 fish hatcheries on the coastal and inland waters, plants millions of eggs and fingerlings each year, and enforces federal commercial fishing laws. The great seal herds in the Pribilof Islands of Alaska, once near extinction, are under its protection. Its professional hunters and trappers work constantly to destroy such natural predators as wolves, coyotes, and mountain lions; the Service has found that in many areas its marksmen can hunt much more effectively from planes than on the ground. It maintains more than 300 wildlife refuges covering some 30,000 square miles. Its research findings on the lives and habits of all manner of fish and game have proved very valuable to conservationists and commercial concerns alike. The United States now has a number of treaties with Canada and Mexico for the protection of migratory birds; the Fish and Wildlife Service carries out our obligations under these treaties.

Many species of wildlife have become extinct in the United States. The passenger pigeon and the heath hen, once nesting here by the millions, proved too attractive on the dinner table and are now completely gone. Many other fish and game have come close to extinction, including the American buffalo, the snowy egret, and the whooping crane. They have been saved only by the intervention of Congress and the work of the Fish and Wildlife Service.

The fight to save the whooping crane is still a critical one. Only about forty of the birds are known to exist. They migrate from their breeding grounds far to the north in west central Canada to winter on the Gulf of Mexico in southeastern Texas. Each year their number is closely checked, and all persons who live along their migratory route are warned to protect them. Indeed millions follow their progress, and newspapers, radio, and TV report their condition every fall.

THE BUREAU OF INDIAN AFFAIRS

The Bureau of Indian Affairs was first established in 1824 as a part of the old War Department and was shifted to the Department of the Interior when that Department was created in 1849.

Our Indian policy has developed by fits and starts, and many of its earlier pages are none too glorious. At first, the National Government treated the Indian tribes much as foreign nations and attempted to deal with them by treaty. As the nation moved westward and the Indians were pushed from their ancestral homes, lands were set aside as "reservations" where the Indians might live by themselves. Many of the treaties were violated by the thoughtlessness and greed of white men. Even the Congress, and at times the Indians, broke the agreements.

By 1871 Congress stopped making treaties with the various tribes, and our policy soon became one of attempting to school the red man to take a full and complete place in the general population. But sad experience proved this to be the wrong approach. For example, lands were allotted to individual Indians as private holdings. Most of these grants were soon squandered or lost to unscrupulous whites. In general, the Indians proved ill-suited to our way of life.

Our Indian policy changed abruptly in 1933. Instead of trying to break down the tribal relationships and wipe out the distinctions between Indians and other people, the policy became one of developing the Indians within the framework of their own particular cultures and their own distinctive way of life.

Many Indians have bridged the gap between their own culture and that of our society as a whole. Most Indians still live in tribal communities on government reservations under the general supervision of the Bureau, however.

Contrary to the trend of earlier years, our Indian population is growing rapidly today. There are now approximately 540,000 Indians in the United States.[6] Of these, some 400,000 receive special services from the Government, and about 285,000 of them live on some 250 reservations, mostly in the Western States.

The Bureau has two major responsibilities in its work with the Indians: (1) assisting and encouraging the Indians in the wise and efficient use of their lands and resources, and (2) providing public services in education, public health, and welfare.

In 1953 Congress declared that the Bureau should seek to end the Indians' status as wards of the government as rapidly as possible. Even with inadequate funds, much progress by the Bureau has been made in that direction. Significant work has been done in the field of education, particularly. Thus, just since the early 1950's the number of Indians between ages six and eighteen attending school has jumped from seventy-five to ninety-five per cent. Dormitories have been built or leased in communities near reservations to house Indian children so that they might attend the local public schools with other children. Federal funds have been granted to local school districts to defray the costs of educating them.

---

[6] The Bureau estimates that approximately 1,000,000 Indians lived in what is now the United States when Columbus discovered America in 1492. By the mid-1800's their number had dwindled to less than 250,000.

Federal and State Indian Reservations

Source: Bureau of Indian Affairs

A Yakima Indian at work in an industrial plant in Oregon.

A Lumni Indian (Washington) presents a totem he carved to former Secretary of the Interior Udall.

Suitable buildings have been converted into schools. Even trailer schools have been provided in areas too sparsely populated to justify regular schools. Some tribes have established scholarship programs to aid Indians who want to go on to college. An adult education program concentrating on English and basic arithmetic has been started, so has a vocational education program.

The Bureau works for the Indian in many other ways. For example, it is encouraging industries to locate near reservations, and it shares the costs of training unskilled Indians. It also helps Indians to find employment away from the reservations.

Still, with all of its efforts, the Indians' lot remains a far from happy one. After an exhaustive survey of the Bureau's work in 1966, the Senate Interior Committee declared that "Indians remain at the bottom of the economic ladder, have the highest rate of unemployment, and suffer chronic poverty." It directed the Bureau to redouble its efforts in order that Indians may soon "take their long-awaited, rightful place in our national life."

OTHER INTERIOR AGENCIES

The Office of Territories promotes the development of those territories Congress has placed under the Interior's jurisdiction and provides aid to the others. See Chapter 34.

The Bureau of Outdoor Recreation works closely with the National Park Service and the several States to promote the development and increase the use of the nation's outdoor recreation facilities.

The Office of Minerals Exploration aids private firms and individuals seeking to discover new domestic minerals reserves.

The Office of Minerals and Solid Fuels works with the Office of Emergency Planning (page 307) to stockpile scarce and strategic minerals, metals, and solid fuels in the event of a national emergency. *The Office of Oil and Gas* performs the same role with regard to the nation's oil and gas supplies.

The Oil Import Administration administers the program under which the importation of crude oil and petroleum products is restricted in the interests of national security and the domestic oil industry.

The Office of Coal Research works with the Bureau of Mines to find new and more efficient ways of mining and using coal.

The Office of Saline Water is seeking a practical method for converting salt water to usable fresh water. If and when one is found, the benefits to be realized for all of mankind defy the imagination.

The Federal Water Pollution Control Administration conducts research and administers grants and other assistance to the States. Its creation in 1966 evidences the fast-growing and now widespread concern for the quality and quantity of the nation's water resources. The Administration will likely become one of the major agencies within the Department of the Interior over the next few years.

THE TENNESSEE VALLEY AUTHORITY

The Tennessee Valley Authority, created by Congress in 1933, is an independent agency within the executive branch. It grew out of a World War I project—for the production of nitrogen for explosives—located at Muscle Shoals on the Tennessee River in Alabama. By the end of the war the Government owned a project which consisted of some 2300 acres, two nitrate plants, a powerhouse, and Wilson Dam.

Throughout the 1920's a controversy raged as to what should be done with this rather sizable investment. There were many who proposed that it be sold to private interests, and at one point it nearly was to Henry Ford. Others, led by Senator George W. Norris of Nebraska, urged that the project be expanded to become a huge federal multipurpose program for the entire region of the Tennessee River Valley. Bills which would have begun such a plan were vetoed by both Presidents Coolidge and Hoover.

Finally, in 1933 the first session of the Congress under the Roosevelt New Deal passed the Tennessee Valley Authority Act. The broad purposes and functions of TVA are stated in the law:

> To improve the navigability and to provide for the flood control of the Tennessee River; to provide for reforestation and the proper use of marginal lands in the Tennessee Valley; to provide for the agricultural and industrial development of said valley; to provide for the national defense by the creation of a corporation for the operation of the Government properties at and near Muscle Shoals in the State of Alabama, and for other purposes.

Thus, Congress provided for the "orderly and proper physical, economic, and social development" of an entire region. This region, the Tennessee River Valley, embraces some 41,000 square miles and parts of seven States —Tennessee, Kentucky, Virginia, North Carolina, Georgia, Alabama, and Mississippi.

TVA is headed by a three-man Board of Directors appointed by the President with the consent of the Senate for nine-year terms. Its operations are under the supervision of a General Manager responsible to the Board. Its program includes power development, flood control, and navigation work. Its activities also involve reforestation, soil conservation, fer-

tilizer production, agricultural experimentation, the development of recreational facilities, and the encouragement of private industrial growth in the Valley.

TVA has had a tremendous effect upon the Valley and upon its nearly 4,000,000 residents. There is now a nine-foot channel which makes the Tennessee River navigable from its mouth, where it empties into the Ohio River at Paducah, Kentucky, upstream 650 miles to Knoxville, Tennessee. There are nine enormous dams on the main stem of the Tennessee River and a series of power and storage dams has been built on its tributaries and the nearby Cumberland River.

The Tennessee River development under the Tennessee Valley Authority exemplifies multi-purpose planning. Among its many activities are improving navigation and flood control work in the Tennessee River Basin and the production of electric power for the region. (Tennessee Valley Authority)

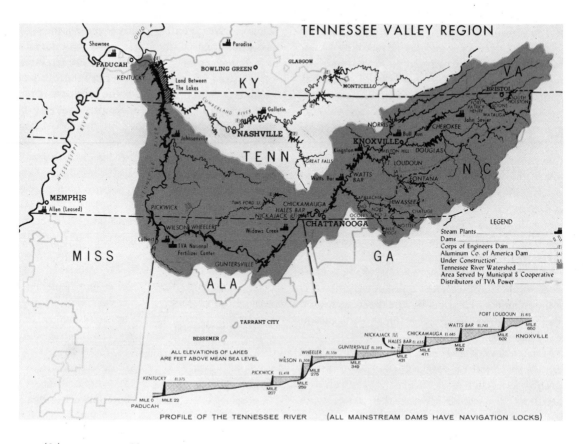

There have been no floods in the Valley since the completion of the storage system, and the flood pressures on the Ohio and Mississippi Rivers have been reduced. The per capita income of the residents of the region has risen sharply since the advent of scientific farming and plentiful electric power. Approximately ninety per cent of the Valley's farms now have electricity, compared to less than four per cent before 1933. A great deal of new industry has been attracted, and wide areas, once denuded, have now been reforested. The food-freezing industry owes much of its rapid growth to experimental work done by TVA.

TVA has been the subject of bitter argument from its beginning. Measured by any standards, it is one of the major illustrations of government participation in business. The Supreme Court found the whole TVA program constitutional in 1936. It held the original Muscle Shoals project valid under the war powers. The later projects were ruled constitutional as a proper exercise of the power to regulate interstate commerce. The sale of surplus electric power in competition with private industry—a major sore point today—was upheld under Congress' power to dispose of federal property.

Little criticism is directed against the quality of TVA's administration. No one disputes its tremendous accomplishments. The attacks have centered especially upon wholesale government participation in what are traditionally private fields. Many people, including Presidents Roosevelt and Truman, have proposed similar arrangements for the Columbia and Missouri River valleys. On the other hand, a number of people have urged the sale of TVA and all its facilities, which they condemn as "creeping socialism," to private interests.

TVA is financed through appropriations by Congress. Some additional funds come from the sale of power and fertilizers and from the Authority's limited power to issue bonds. A number of critics contend that it is unjust to spend tax money from the entire nation for the benefit of one particular region. TVA's supporters reply that actually the program is of benefit to the entire country, not just the Tennessee Valley. They cite as one example of this the providing of the large quantities of power consumed by the atomic energy works at Oak Ridge, Tennessee.

CONCEPT BUILDING

Key Concepts

For more than 300 years the vast natural wealth of America was used with little or no thought for the future. Today, however, the nation realizes the absolute necessity for conservation and wise use of its natural resources.

Most of the federal conservation agencies are within the Interior Department. Headed by the Secretary of the Interior, the Department was created in 1849. The Department has evolved from its original role as general housekeeper for the National Government to that of custodian of the nation's natural resources.

The Bureau of Land Management supervises much of the public domain and its mineral resources. Historic public lands action came with the passage of the Land and Water Conservation Act and the Wilderness Act in 1964, and creation of the National Scenic Rivers and National Trails Systems in 1968. The control of the offshore lands, especially those rich in oil, remains a problem.

The Bureau of Reclamation is responsible for the reclaiming of arid lands, irrigation, and many of the huge multipurpose dam projects in the United States. The Bonneville Power Administration markets the power produced by Bureau and Army Engineer projects in the Northwest. The Southeastern and Southwestern Power Administrations market the power from various federal projects in their regions. The Defense Electric Power Administration is a standby agency. The Alaska Power Administration oversees the development of water, power, and related resources in Alaska.

The National Park Service has charge of the national parks and monuments and of other sites of national and historical interest. The Geological Survey develops and publishes facts about the geographic and geologic nature of the United States. The Bureau of Mines is concerned with the conservation and use of our mineral and fuel resources and with mine safety.

The Fish and Wildlife Service works to conserve, restore, and promote the more efficient use of those resources. The Bureau of Indian Affairs has primary responsibility for the welfare of Indians still living on reservations. A number of lesser agencies in the Department perform a wide range of tasks. The huge Tennessee Valley Authority, an independent agency, is responsible for the development of the physical, economic, and social resources of the Tennessee River Valley.

Important Terms

conservation	Indian reservations	public domain	revolving fund
Continental Shelf	multiple use management	public lands	submerged lands
fish ladders	multipurpose dam	reclamation	tidelands

Questions for Inquiry and Review

1. What is meant by "conservation"?

2. Under which President did the modern conservation movement begin? Who was Gifford Pinchot?

3. When was the Department of the Interior created? What was the general nature of its original role?

4. What is the general nature of the Interior Department's role today?

5. From what part of the nation is the Secretary of the Interior usually appointed? Why?

6. For what major purposes was a huge portion of the public domain disposed of?

7. Where are most of the nation's public lands now located?

8. Under what basic standard does BLM manage most of the lands under its control?

9. Why is the "tidelands controversy" misnamed? Why is ownership and control of the lands involved of such importance?

10. What is a "multipurpose" dam?

11. What is the basic function of the National Park Service?

12. What is the basic function of the Geological Survey?

13. With what matters is the work of the Bureau of Mines principally concerned?

14. What was the nature of the abrupt change in the nation's Indian policy in 1933?

15. From what original project did TVA develop? What are its broad purposes and functions?

16. Why has TVA been a center of controversy from its beginnings?

For Further Inquiry

1. How would you expand on this statement: "Conservation is the wise use of our natural resources, not the refusal to use them."

2. Does the reclamation of arid lands increase or decrease the value of other arid lands not irrigated? Why is the reclamation of land becoming increasingly important today?

3. America was generously blessed with a vast supply of many minerals. World War II gave dramatic proof, however, that our supplies are not unlimited. Japanese conquests in Southeast Asia cut off our major sources of tin and rubber. We have about one-third of the world's known copper reserves but are using them at a rapid rate. We have huge reserves of many other underground resources, but some are in short supply and others may be in the near future. Our supply of high-grade iron ore is no longer an abundant one. We have little or no chromium, manganese, or nickel. Bauxite, from which aluminum comes, is relatively scarce. Our zinc supply is diminishing steadily. Lead is still relatively plentiful, but it, too, is being used rapidly. In what ways could we conserve our supplies of these important minerals and other resources?

Suggested Activities

1. Ask a representative of one or more of the agencies discussed in this chapter to speak to the class on the nature of the work of his agency.

2. Prepare as extensive a list as you can of illustrations of the work of agencies of the Department of the Interior in your locale.

3. Write a brief essay or editorial on the relationship between conservation and the nation's security.

4. Stage a debate or class forum on the topic: *Resolved*, That the National Government should sell its hydroelectric power projects to private interests; or: *Resolved*, That the National Government should sell or otherwise transfer its hydroelectric power projects to the States.

Suggested Reading

CAPRON, LOUIS, "Florida's Emerging Seminoles," *National Geographic*, November, 1969.

FRIGGENS, PAUL, "The Great Alaska Oil Rush," *Reader's Digest*, July, 1969.

FROME, MICHAEL, "Must Our Campgrounds Be Outdoor Slums?" *Reader's Digest*, September, 1969.

GOODMAN, GEORGE, "The Tragic Misuse of a Majestic River," *Look*, August 26, 1969.

GORDON, ARTHUR, "Oregon—Unspoiled Splendor," *Reader's Digest*, May, 1969.

HICKEL, SECRETARY WALTER J., "'America the Beautiful' Doomed?" *U.S. News*, November 10, 1969.

MACDONALD, ROSS and EASTON, ROBERT, "Santa Barbara: 'Thou Shalt Not Abuse the Earth,'" *New York Times Magazine*, October 12, 1969.

"Not Enough Electric Power—What to Do About It," *U.S. News*, September 22, 1969.

PERLMAN, DAVID, "America the Beautiful?" *Look*, November 4, 1969.

"Pesticides: Pro and Con," *U.S. News*, October 20, 1969.

PETERSON, ROGER T., "Mystery of the Vanishing Osprey," *National Geographic*, July, 1969.

SNELL, DAVID, "Death from the Sea," *Life*, June 13, 1969.

"The Great Oil Hunt," *Newsweek*, September 22, 1969.

U.S. Department of the Interior, *Conservation Yearbook*. Government Printing Office. Annual.

24
THE DEPARTMENT
OF AGRICULTURE

✦✦✦Is the basic function of the Department of Agriculture <u>regulatory</u> or <u>promotional</u>? Explain.

✦✦✦To whom are the programs administered by the USDA most beneficial?

✦✦✦Is it logical or wise for the government to operate programs to encourage greater agricultural production while at the same time it maintains programs to restrict the flow of farm goods to the market? Why?

When tillage begins, other arts follow. The farmers therefore are the founders of human civilization.

DANIEL WEBSTER

Agriculture is one of the nation's basic industries. Indeed, in many ways it is *the* basic industry in the United States. The nearly 10,000,000 Americans who live on our 2,900,-000 farms produce the food upon which our entire population depends. They also produce food vital to millions elsewhere in the world and a goodly share of the raw materials essential to our nation's manufacturing industries.

We began our history as an agricultural people. For 300 years, from the very first settlements along the Atlantic seaboard until the dawn of the present century, *the* dominant theme in American history was westward agricultural expansion. The First Census in 1790 reflected the fact that ninety-five per cent of the 3,929,214 persons then residing in the United States lived in rural areas. Nearly all of them lived on farms. In fact, until about 1910 agriculture was the way of life for the majority of Americans.

Considering the size and the importance of agriculture throughout our history, it is not at

all strange that the National Government has been so directly concerned with it. Nor is it strange that agriculture has played such a prominent role in American politics. As Woodrow Wilson once observed, without the farmer "every street would be silent, every office deserted, every factory fallen into disrepair."

DEPARTMENTAL ORGANIZATION

Origins. The history of governmental activity in American agriculture dates back to the early colonial period. In 1622 James I promoted—though an unsuccessful venture—the growing of mulberry trees and the breeding of silkworms in the colonies. Parliament and the colonial legislatures also subsidized other farm products on various occasions. As early as 1776, the Second Continental Congress considered measures to aid agriculture. In his last annual message to Congress in 1796 President Washington urged the creation of boards of agriculture to provide information for farmers.

It was not until 1839, however, that Congress began to develop the present Department of Agriculture. In that year it appropriated $1000 to be used "to distribute seeds, conduct agricultural investigations, and collect agricultural statistics." A single clerk in the Patent Office administered the program. Then, in the period of a few short months in 1862, Congress passed three acts of lasting importance to farmers: (1) the act creating a Department of Agriculture (though not of Cabinet rank), (2) the Homestead Act, which made grants of 160-acre plots to people who would settle on and develop such plots, and (3) the Morrill Act which made grants of land to the States to establish colleges of agriculture and mechanical arts.

From 1862 to 1889 the Department of Agriculture was administered by a Commissioner of Agriculture. Then in 1889 Congress enlarged the powers and duties of the Department. It was raised to Cabinet rank, and the Commissioner became the Secretary of Agriculture.

The Secretary of Agriculture. The Secretary, like the heads of each of the other executive departments, is appointed by the President and confirmed by the Senate. His department is often cited as a model of administrative organization and efficiency. Sir Horace Plunkett, a noted authority on public administration, once described it as "perhaps the most popular and respected of the world's great administrative institutions." The USDA is constantly examining and evaluating itself in order to improve its operations. Nearly all of the agencies within it have been reformed in recent years.

The Under Secretary is the Secretary of Agriculture's chief aide in directing the work of the more than 100,000 persons who now staff the various agencies of the Department. The top echelon of departmental management now includes a Director of Agricultural Eco-

At the Institute of Forest Genetics in California, researchers squirt pollen from young, vigorous trees onto pine conelets. The resulting seeds then produce fast-growing seedlings. (The Forest Service, U. S. Department of Agriculture)

nomics, a Director of Science and Education, and four Assistant Secretaries—for administration, rural development and conservation, international affairs and commodity programs, and marketing and consumer services.

The major functions of the USDA may be grouped under four broad headings: (1) research and education, (2) conservation and rural development, (3) marketing, and (4) crop stabilization and credit.

RESEARCH AND EDUCATION ACTIVITIES

None of the Cabinet departments makes greater use of science than does the Department of Agriculture. Its thousands of scientists conduct studies and experiments in a wide range of agricultural fields in order to benefit farming in the United States.

The Agricultural Research Service. Most of the physical, biological, chemical, and engineering research work of the USDA is carried out by the Agricultural Research Service. The scope of its work is very broad, indeed. The ARS carries on both basic and applied research relating to the production, marketing, and use of agricultural products; enforces plant and animal inspection, quarantine laws, and pesticide control regulations; and administers programs to control and eradicate the pests and diseases of plants and animals.

Much of the Service's scientific research is conducted at the 11,000-acre Agricultural Research Center at Beltsville, Maryland. Much work is also done at laboratories and experiment stations throughout the country, in the territories, and abroad. The States, private companies, and public and private colleges also work on projects in conjunction with the Service.

As an outgrowth of research in water-vapor movement through dry soil, the USDA developed this pocket-model "solar still." Within hours after it is set up in the desert, enough water for emergency survival will be available. (Agricultural Research Service, U. S. Department of Agriculture)

The Service's many accomplishments can be illustrated by these few examples: Many different pests menace crops, animals, and even humans. One method used to fight those brought here from abroad is to seek out their native homes and natural enemies. Thus, ladybugs were imported from Australia when white scale threatened California's multi-million dollar citrus industry. A spray program is now being waged against the gypsy moth in the Northeast; a successful campaign was recently fought against the Mediterranean fruit fly in Florida; and an attempt is now underway to stamp out the dangerous screwworm in the Southwest by releasing millions of male screwworm flies which have been made sterile by exposure to radioactive cobalt.

More than 100,000 kinds of plants and seeds have been brought here from abroad, and many have become quite important in our agriculture. The long-fiber Pima cotton was brought from Egypt and is a basis of prosperity for the Salt River Valley in Arizona. The navel orange was brought from Brazil and is now one of California's principal crops.

Better ways of storing food and cooking it; improvements of such farm machinery as harvesters, hay driers, and flax machines; meat inspection; new and better dairy processing methods; and the fight against the hoof-and-mouth disease are a few more of the hundreds of examples that could be listed. These illustrations, however, should be sufficient to indicate how valuable the Agricultural Research Service is to the farmer—and, in turn, how valuable it is to all of the rest of us in the United States.

The National Agricultural Library. The USDA's National Agricultural Library is the largest storehouse of knowledge of its kind in the world. Its more than 1,300,000 volumes cover the field of agriculture in the broadest sense, ranging over such areas as botany, chemistry, entomology, forestry, plant pathology, veterinary medicine, and zoology as well as thoroughly blanketing general agriculture.

The Library's huge resources are made available to literally anyone, both here and abroad. Through such techniques as loans, photocopies, bibliographical lists, translations, and the furnishing of specific data, it provides its services to educational institutions, research organizations, other governmental agencies, farm groups, industry, individual farmers and scientists, and the general public.

The Cooperative State Research Service. This service dates back to 1888 when Congress established an agricultural experiment station at each of the nation's land-grant colleges.[1] Today these stations are located in each of the fifty States and Puerto Rico and conduct thousands of experiments each year in agriculture, farm marketing, and problems of rural life. The results of the stations' projects are made available to farmers through bulletins which are carried free by the Post Office.

Congress now appropriates about one-fourth of the approximately $280,000,000 these stations spend each year; the balance of the funds come from State and private sources. The USDA works in close harmony with the stations through the Cooperative State Research Service which administers the federal funds involved in their undertakings.

The Farmer Cooperative Service. The four out of every five farmers in the country who belong to farm cooperatives are provided with research and educational assistance by the Farmer Cooperative Service. The Service aids these farmers with such important matters as the organization, financing, membership, and improvement of their farm cooperatives.

The Federal Extension Service. Created in 1914, the Federal Extension Service, together with the States and nearly every county, provides "beyond-the-classroom" education in the rural areas of the nation. The Extension Service works through hundreds of specialists stationed at State land-grant colleges and thousands of county agents, home demonstration agents, and 4-H Club agents to lend assistance and know-how to the farmer and to the farm community.

CONSERVATION AND RURAL DEVELOPMENT ACTIVITIES

As noted in Chapter 23, the Department of the Interior is primarily responsible for the conservation of the nation's natural resources. By improving farm products, promoting better farming methods, and in its other related work, the USDA also helps to conserve those resources. Two of the Department's major agencies—the Forest Service and the Soil Conservation Service—are directly engaged in the traditional field of conservation. The forest, water, range, and soil resources of the United States are foundation blocks in the nation's economic structure. From them come our food, the bulk of our municipal, industrial, and agricultural water supplies, most of our clothing, paper, and other fibers, much of our shelter, and a large part of the public's opportunities for outdoor recreation. How well these resources are protected and improved has a direct bearing on the income and the standard of living enjoyed by all Americans —and a direct bearing, as well, on the beauty of the environment in which we live.

The Forest Service. No one need be told of the importance of the forests and of wood products to our way of living. Our forests

---

[1] The land-grant colleges are those State colleges and universities established as a result of the Morrill Act of 1862. This and later acts of Congress provided for the granting of land (altogether nearly 11,000,000 acres, much of it very valuable) to the States for the establishing and maintaining of colleges to teach "without excluding other scientific and classical studies and including military tactics ... such branches of learning as are related to agriculture and the mechanical arts."

Forest fires burn more than 3,500,000 acres of forest lands annually. "Smokejumpers" of the U.S. Forest Service, skilled fire-fighters, move into action quickly. (U.S. Forest Service)

Beginning in 1891, and especially under the leadership of Theodore Roosevelt and Gifford Pinchot in the early years of this century, the Congress authorized the setting aside of certain timberlands as national forests. The Forest Service administers the 154 national forests which now cover more than 186,000,000 acres in thirty-nine States and Puerto Rico.[2] Its forest rangers are charged with promoting the conservation and best use of our forest lands.

The Forest Service provides fire protection, disease control, and recreational facilities in our public timberlands. Its "smokejumpers" and ground fire crews would be able to provide even better protection if it weren't for the fact that approximately ninety per cent of all forest fires are caused by man's carelessness—which *each year* destroys enough timber to replace every home in Lansing, Michigan; Atlantic City, New Jersey; and Salem, Oregon!

The forests are under careful management for the permanent production and use of their timber, water, forage, wildlife, and recreational resources. The Forest Service scientifically regulates livestock grazing on its lands, and it also controls the exploitation of minerals the lands may contain. New trees are constantly planted. Selective logging is practiced to clear out mature trees which would otherwise decay and to promote the growth of younger trees. Several experiment stations and laboratories maintained by the Service conduct continuing studies of all phases of forestry.

The Soil Conservation Service. Wasteful and mistaken land-use practices have caused erosion which has ruined some 300,000,000 acres of land in the United States, or an area twice the size of the State of Texas. In earlier

provide natural cover for wildlife. They act as great natural reservoirs to collect rainfall and, by releasing it gradually, help to prevent floods and droughts. They also help to hold the soil against erosion.

Over forty per cent of what is now the United States was once covered by forests. Much of this natural wealth, however, has disappeared through the clearing of farmlands and the cutting of timber for fuel and construction. Much of it has also been destroyed through outright carelessness.

---

[2] All except Connecticut, Delaware, Hawaii, Kansas, Maryland, Massachusetts, New Jersey, New York, North Dakota, Rhode Island, and South Dakota. About 40,000,000 acres of other forest lands are under the jurisdiction of other federal agencies—especially the Bureau of Land Management, the Bureau of Indian Affairs, and the National Park Service within the Interior Department. State and local governments hold some 28,000,000 acres, and about 365,000,000 acres are privately owned.

days farmlands in many parts of the East were "mined out." So long as new, fertile lands could be had to the west, no one seemed to be concerned about "overcropping" and erosion. Once the good lands in the West had been taken up, however, the problems of proper soil care could no longer be ignored.

For many years the Department of Agriculture has attempted to promote soil conservation by educating the farmer in soil-saving practices. In 1935 the Soil Conservation Service was created to assist farmers and ranchers in soil conservation. Its principal duty is to assist farmers in locally organized and locally directed soil conservation districts. There are now some 3000 districts in the fifty States, Puerto Rico, and the Virgin Islands. They include 96 per cent of the nation's farms and over 93 per cent of its farmlands.

The SCS also administers the paying of subsidies to farmers and ranchers who will undertake supervised soil conservation projects under a broad federal-State program. Soil conservation scientists have helped nearly 2,000,000 farmers and ranchers, with holdings totalling some 700,000,000 acres, plan and put into operation their own projects.

Soil abuse today is due mostly to old-fashioned methods of "square farming." Plowing in straight rows uphill and downhill has produced *sheet erosion*, in which the top layer of soil is skimmed off the land and *gullies* are formed that eat away the earth in big chunks, leaving worthless subsoil. Other abuses include one-crop farming which exhausts and ruins the soil, *overgrazing* which destroys the grass and causes erosion, and the *wasteful use* of forests and woodlands.

The Soil Conservation Service attempts to persuade the nation's farmers to do such things as to:

Contour plow — "on-the-level-plowing" which follows a contour line around a sloping hill. The level furrows hold the rainfall.

Strip farm — the growing of different kinds of crops in alternate strips. This blankets the soil better than large fields of a single crop, such as corn. It checks the rush of water and breaks up air currents.

Terrace — the use of broad-based ridges thrown up across a sloping hill and following the contour of the slope. This slows down erosion by even heavy rains.

Set up gully controls — the planting of trees, shrubs, and grass and the building of dams.

Set up windbreaks — planting trees to break the force of wind and cut down wind erosion.

Air-Conditioning the Dust Bowl. In the drought-ridden year of 1934, President Franklin D. Roosevelt promoted a program to plant some 300,000,000 trees from the Canadian border to Texas to salvage the Dust Bowl area of the country. Some 40,000 windbreaks, each with about twenty rows of trees, some of them as high as a house, now cover

The Soil Conservation Service works diligently educating farmers on how to prevent the kind of erosion shown below. (Soil Conservation Service, U.S. Department of Agriculture)

this area. The original plantings were made by the Forest Service, but they are now managed by local farmers in soil conservation districts. The stately string of trees stands as a growing monument to an idea which was once a target of a barrage of doubts and jokes.

These windbreaks help to "condition" the air by slowing down the winds which blew thousands of tons of topsoil halfway across the continent in the early 1930's. Valuable topsoil and moisture are now held in place, the danger of uncontrollable prairie fires is lessened, and insect-eating birds like pheasant and quail are again plentiful. The planting continues, and the trees are cheap, coming very largely as a gift from the National Government and the States.

The Rural Electrification Administration. When the REA was created in 1935, only ten per cent of all farms in the United States were receiving electricity. Today, ninety-eight per cent of the nation's farms are electrified. Private power companies have expanded their service in rural areas, of course; but more than half of the farms which now have electricity have it because of the REA.

The REA administers loan programs for two general purposes: rural electrification and rural telephone service. Electrification loans are made to provide electric distribution, transmission, and generation facilities in order to bring or improve service in rural areas. Some short-term loans are also made to finance wiring and the purchase of electrical and plumbing appliances in order to bring some of the taken-for-granted comforts of city living to our rural population.

More than 1100 REA-financed power systems, with some 1,650,000 miles of line serving 6,250,000 rural customers, are now in operation. By 1970 Congress had authorized the lending of some $7,000,000,000 for the rural electrification program; and it has provided that, in the making of loans under the program, preference must be given to public bodies and cooperatives.

REA loans to finance rural telephone service are made to telephone organizations, with preference going to existing companies and cooperatives. Unlike the electrification program, telephone borrowers are required to provide a portion of the investment themselves. By 1970 REA had made more than $1,650,000,000 in telephone loans and thus helped to bring new or better service to some 2,400,000 rural subscribers. Thousands more are being added each month.

A flat two per cent interest rate is charged on all REA loans, and the loans may be paid in installments over a period extending up to thirty-five years. The agency and its work stand as one of the many examples of how government can help people to help themselves.

Farmers Home Administration. By the mid-depression year 1935 forty-two per cent of the nation's farmers had slipped from farm ownership to farm tenancy. Today fewer than one-fifth of our farmers are tenants. The Farmers Home Administration helps to keep the independent farmer solvent and assists tenants to buy farms by extending credit to those farmers who cannot obtain loans at reasonable rates elsewhere. All of its loans are made through the agency's 1680 local offices, generally located at county seats. A local committee of three persons, at least two of whom must be farmers, decides whether or not a loan should be granted.

Farm ownership loans are made for the purchase of a family-type farm, to improve or enlarge a farm in order to make it an efficient family-type unit, or for such other purposes as the construction or repair of buildings; land improvement; water, forestry, and fish resources development; and the refinancing of debts. These loans are made in amounts up to $60,000 and for as long as forty years at five per cent interest. The payments may be arranged so that advance installments are paid in good years, thus protecting the farmer against falling behind in lean years.

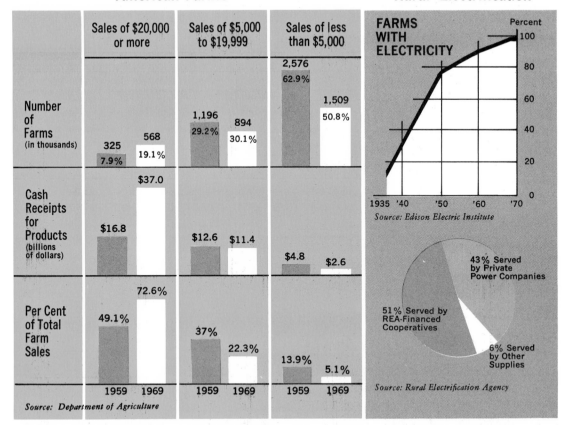

American Farms

	Sales of $20,000 or more		Sales of $5,000 to $19,999		Sales of less than $5,000	
Number of Farms (in thousands)	325 7.9%	568 19.1%	1,196 29.2%	894 30.1%	2,576 62.9%	1,509 50.8%
Cash Receipts for Products (billions of dollars)	$16.8	$37.0	$12.6	$11.4	$4.8	$2.6
Per Cent of Total Farm Sales	49.1%	72.6%	37%	22.3%	13.9%	5.1%
	1959	1969	1959	1969	1959	1969

Source: Department of Agriculture

Rural Electrification

FARMS WITH ELECTRICITY

Source: Edison Electric Institute

43% Served by Private Power Companies

51% Served by REA-Financed Cooperatives

6% Served by Other Supplies

Source: Rural Electrification Agency

Operating loans are made for the purchase of such things as livestock, seed, feed, equipment, and fertilizer. Not more than $35,000 will be lent to any one person. The interest rate is now (1970) 5.5 per cent; the repayment period can run as long as seven years.

Other loans are made to construct modest homes (especially for the elderly), to provide water facilities such as wells and pumps, and for such other purposes as disaster relief.[3] Practically all of the loans made by the agency are made with funds advanced by private lenders on an insured basis and from funds collected on loans previously made.

---

[3] Another major farm loan agency, the Farm Credit Administration, operates independently of the USDA; see page 550.

MARKETING ACTIVITIES

Farming is at best a risky business. One thing that makes it so is the weather—which is often the farmer's friend, but which can be his mortal enemy, too. Too much sun, not enough sun, too much rain, not enough rain, too much wind—any of these and the other quirks of nature are natural hazards over which he has no control. Another factor that makes farming a gamble is the market in which the farmer must deal—something, too, over which he has little control.

As farming methods have improved, the annual output of farm products has naturally increased. When the supply of farm products exceeds the demand for them, the farmer suffers unless government steps in to take care of the surplus. As we shall see shortly, the National Government does step in to take care of a substantial amount of the annual farm surplus. It also provides aid to help the farmer plan and market his crops to avoid surpluses.

The Consumer and Marketing Service. The Consumer and Marketing Service aids the farmer in the orderly marketing and effective distribution of his products. The Service collects marketing information and releases regular up-to-the-minute reports on crop conditions, prices, and prospects at home and abroad. These releases are made available to the farmer in the press, by radio and television, and bulletins sent to him through the mail. Through such releases the farmer is able to learn the best marketing times and methods. He is also able to plan ahead in selecting the best crops to plant. In addition to providing market news, the Service also provides uniform standards for commodities and containers and inspects and certifies farm products to guarantee quality.

The Federal Government also buys and stores surplus farm products to protect the farmer's market, as we shall see in a moment. The financing of surplus disposal through such devices as the school lunch program, the food stamp program for needy families, and grants to public institutions and welfare agencies is handled by the Service.

The Commodity Exchange Authority. Food brokers often buy and sell agricultural commodities (trade in futures) long before those commodities reach the market. The brokers serve a useful purpose by establishing

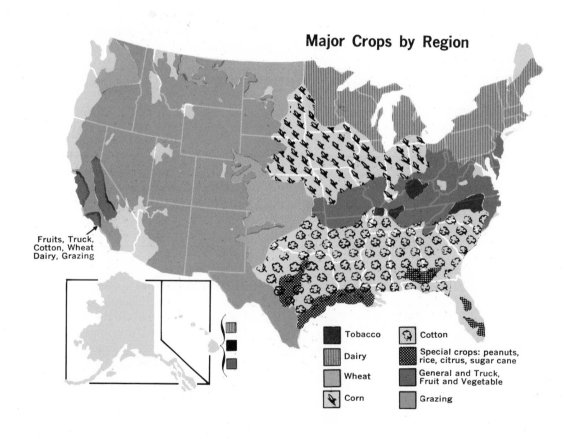

Major Crops by Region

Fruits, Truck, Cotton, Wheat Dairy, Grazing

Tobacco

Dairy

Wheat

Corn

Cotton

Special crops: peanuts, rice, citrus, sugar cane

General and Truck, Fruit and Vegetable

Grazing

a known price for a crop well before the delivery and thus give some stability to the market. But, of course, dishonest traders could do serious harm to farmers, retailers, and consumers. To prevent this, Congress created the Commodity Exchange Authority in 1922.

The Commodity Exchange Authority attempts to prevent price manipulations, cornering of the market in a particular crop, dissemination of false or misleading crop and market information, and similar fraudulent practices. It has the power to designate those exchanges which may engage in futures trading, to license brokers, and to limit the size of transactions which can be made, as well as to prevent dishonest schemes. The CEA now regulates these major commodity exchanges: the Chicago Board of Trade, the Chicago Mercantile Exchange, the Minneapolis Grain Exchange, the Kansas City Board of Trade, the New York Produce Exchange, the New York Mercantile Exchange, and the New York Cotton Exchange, and several smaller ones.[4]

The Federal Crop Insurance Corporation. Some of the risks of farming are also reduced by the Federal Crop Insurance Corporation. The FCIC will insure farmers who raise several different crops [5] against losses from such causes as weather, insects, and diseases; but it will not protect a farmer against the results of his own negligence or poor farming practices. Thus far FCIC policies are available in just over one-half of the nation's agricultural counties, and the program is gradually being extended throughout the country. The costs

[4] Currently (1970), the CEA supervises trading in these commodities: wheat, corn, oats, butter, rye, flaxseed, soybeans, cotton, wool, wool tops, eggs, potatoes, cottonseed oil, soybean oil, soybean meal, grain sorghums, frozen pork bellies, live hogs and cattle, hides, and frozen orange concentrates.

[5] Currently (1970), wheat, cotton, tobacco, corn, flax, dry beans, soybeans, barley, grain sorghums, oats, peanuts, peas, potatoes, raisins, apples, sugarcane, grapes, rice, citrus fruit, peaches, tomatoes, sugar beets, and tung nuts.

of the indemnities paid out by the program are borne by the premiums paid by those who hold policies.

The Foreign Agricultural Service. The Foreign Agricultural Service is constantly seeking new markets for our farm products abroad. With so much of the world hungry and in want, and with our current farm surpluses, the work of the Service can be of untold value in promoting friendships abroad and the cause of world peace; see page 451.

STABILIZING FARM PRICES

Following World War I there was a gradual decline in the general price level throughout the nation's economy. The decline in farm prices was much sharper than that in other fields. Wheat dropped from the wartime price of $2 a bushel to less than 40¢. Cotton skidded from 29¢ a pound in 1923 to less than 6¢ in 1933. The farmer found that his income was far below that of his city friends.

The First AAA, 1933. After trying several plans to rescue the farmer in the late 1920's, Congress passed the first Agricultural Adjustment Act in 1933. The act encouraged farmers to reduce production in order to force prices up. Those who did so were paid a subsidy out of funds collected by a processing tax levied on the commodities which were produced. Thus, a tax was levied on each bushel of wheat a miller processed. The proceeds went into a fund to pay farmers a subsidy for the wheat they did not grow.

The law met with considerable public opposition, but it did raise farm prices an average of more than 60 per cent in three years. In 1936 the Supreme Court held the processing tax unconstitutional. It described the tax as "the expropriation of money from one group for the benefit of another" in order to control agricultural production which, added the Court, was a matter properly within the reserved powers of the States. See page 254.

The Second AAA, 1938. After attempting for two years to accomplish crop reduction through payments under the soil conservation program, Congress enacted the second Agricultural Adjustment Act in 1938. Essentially, the new law provided what the first one had but without the processing tax.

It also provided for the "ever-normal granary." As Joseph in ancient Egypt stored up grain in years of plenty to use in years of famine, so the new law provided for storing surpluses against future shortages. The second AAA directed the *Commodity Credit Corporation* (CCC) to make loans to farmers to help them carry over their surpluses in government warehouses and elevators for sale in the short years.

War and the Farm Problem. World War II brought a sudden change in the nature of the farm problem. Instead of the need to *limit* farm production, it became necessary to expand it rapidly. Everything possible was done to increase the output of food products. The heavy demands of the Armed Forces and the needs of millions abroad gave vital meaning to the wartime slogan "Food Is Ammunition."

A major shift in the price support program was made in 1942. To stimulate wartime production, Congress provided that farmers were to be guaranteed a minimum price for certain crops; that is, Congress inaugurated a program of *rigid price supports.* A floor was placed under the prices for certain crops; the farmer was to be guaranteed a minimum price for these crops no matter what the condition of the market might be. The Secretary of Agriculture was authorized to add crops to the list of supported commodities as the war effort demanded it.[6] The new support program was to continue for two years beyond the end of the war. Most

---

[6] By the end of the war (1945), 165 different crops were on the support list. The minimum price was set at ninety per cent of parity. (*Parity* refers to a ratio between prices farmers receive for their products and prices they must pay for nonfarm items they purchase.)

farm prices stayed generally above the support level during the war, but the mere existence of supports encouraged expanded production. The farmer knew that no matter how much he produced he could sell his production, either on the open market or to the Federal Government.

Postwar Developments. With the expiration of the 1942 program, Congress provided for a system of *flexible price supports* in 1948. The Secretary of Agriculture was authorized to support basic crops at sixty, seventy-five, or ninety per cent of parity, depending upon whether in a particular year the supply of a crop was unusually large, normal, or below normal. But the 1948 law proved immediately unpopular, especially among farmers. The presidential and congressional election of that year gave ample indication of the dissatisfaction. Congress then returned to the rigid price support program in 1949 with a statute setting the price support figure for most crops covered at a flat ninety per cent of parity.

A flexible support policy was reintroduced in 1954 and has remained in effect since. Under the present law various crops are supported at from sixty-five to ninety per cent of parity. The law provides that certain crops (the "basic crops") *must* be supported: corn, wheat, rice, barley, oats, rye, grain sorghums, tobacco, wool, cotton, peanuts, tung nuts, mohair, honey, milk, and butterfat. Other items may be supported at the discretion of the Secretary of Agriculture, who also sets the actual support figure for each crop each year.

A steady decline in farm prices convinced Congress to return once more to rigid supports in 1956, but President Eisenhower vetoed the bill. At his urging, Congress then established the *Soil Bank program.* Under it farmers are paid for planting trees and grasses to halt erosion and build up the soil rather than for producing certain crops. No new lands have been added to the Soil Bank since mid-1960.

Parity. The support price guaranteed on a crop is figured in terms of *parity.* Parity means *equality*—and refers here to an equality between the purchasing power of farmers and that of city dwellers. Or, put another way, parity refers to a *ratio* between the prices a farmer *receives* when he *sells* agricultural products and the prices he must *pay* when he *buys* nonagricultural items. Under the parity arrangement an attempt is made to ensure that the farmer's purchasing power today will be roughly comparable to the purchasing power of his urban cousin.

The parity price on a particular commodity is figured on the basis of some earlier period in which farmers enjoyed a favorable purchasing power. To illustrate, if during the earlier period the price of four bushels of wheat would buy a pair of shoes, then the parity price of wheat would be approximately the cost of the same pair of shoes on today's market. Until 1948 parity was figured on the base period

1909–1914, a period in which the farmer did hold a favorable position in purchasing power. In 1948 Congress provided that parity could be figured for each crop either on the "old" base period or on a "new" one: the ten years immediately preceding the year in which the parity figure was being set. Since 1957, Congress has required the exclusive use of the "new" base period.

Acreage Allotments. In order to prevent the depression of the prices of those crops under price support, the Federal Government also operates an acreage allotment program. It is administered by the *Agricultural Stabilization and Conservation Service.*

Each year the Service estimates the probable market demand for each supported crop. The number of acres necessary to produce that amount is also determined. This total acreage is then distributed among (*allotted to*) farmers.

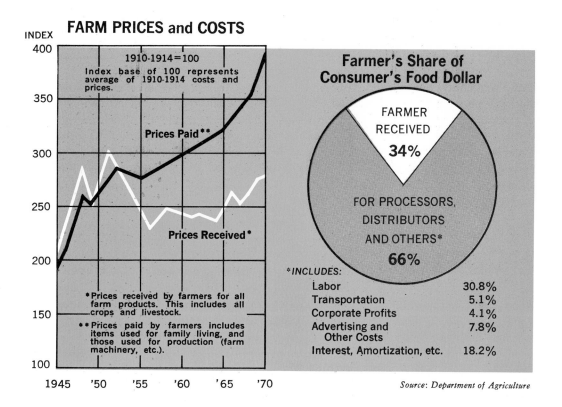

FARM PRICES and COSTS

INDEX

1910-1914=100
Index base of 100 represents average of 1910-1914 costs and prices.

Prices Paid**

Prices Received*

*Prices received by farmers for all farm products. This includes all crops and livestock.

**Prices paid by farmers includes items used for family living, and those used for production (farm machinery, etc.).

1945 '50 '55 '60 '65 '70

Farmer's Share of Consumer's Food Dollar

FARMER RECEIVED
34%

FOR PROCESSORS, DISTRIBUTORS AND OTHERS*
66%

*INCLUDES:

Labor	30.8%
Transportation	5.1%
Corporate Profits	4.1%
Advertising and Other Costs	7.8%
Interest, Amortization, etc.	18.2%

Source: Department of Agriculture

Agricultural Production – 1968

(This graph compares production in 1968 with that of 1955)

1955 = 100%

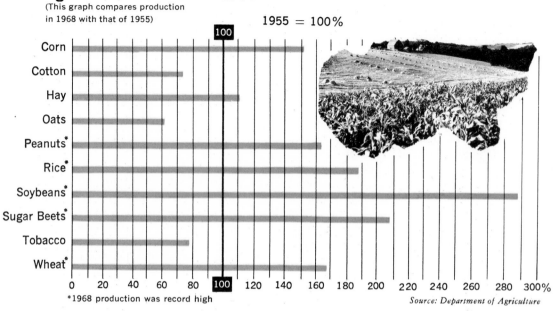

Crop	
Corn	
Cotton	
Hay	
Oats	
Peanuts*	
Rice*	
Soybeans*	
Sugar Beets*	
Tobacco	
Wheat*	

0   20   40   60   80   100   120   140   160   180   200   220   240   260   280   300%

*1968 production was record high

Source: Department of Agriculture

The actual allotment is done by a series of State and county farmer committees elected by the farmers themselves. Farmers are not *required* to observe their individual allotments, but those farmers who ignore their allotments can receive no support payments.

Market Quotas. If at harvest time it becomes clear that a surplus of a supported crop will occur despite acreage allotments, the Agricultural Stabilization and Conservation Service may take a further step. It may establish a *market quota* for that crop—that is, limit the amount of the crop that may be sold.

In order to go into effect, a market quota must be accepted in a national referendum among the farmers producing the crop involved. The vote required for approval is two-thirds. Quotas are usually accepted by a safe margin. If a quota is rejected, no price supports are paid for that crop for that year.

If a quota is accepted, any farmer who violates his individual quota is subject to a fine.

Crop Loans. If market conditions are such that a farmer is unable to sell his allotted share of a particular crop at or above the parity price level, the Federal Government takes further action. The Commodity Credit Corporation will lend him whatever the support price is on his crop, and the CCC holds the crop as security for the loan.[7] If the market price later rises above the amount of the loan (that is, above the parity price support level), the farmer may sell his crop on the open market, repay the loan, and pocket the difference as his profit. If the market price does not climb to the support level, he lets the CCC have his crop.

---

[7] The CCC actually performs most of its functions through the staff and facilities of the Agricultural Stabilization and Conservation Service.

The price support program has piled up huge surpluses in government-owned and -leased warehouses and other storage facilities. Despite acreage allotments, market quotas, the Soil Bank, surplus disposal programs, and other efforts, the CCC now holds some $1,000,000,-000 in stored farm commodities. The problem is not so severe today as that huge figure may suggest, however; as recently as 1960 the CCC held surplus stocks valued at more than six times that amount. (Sorghum grains are now the major crop in surplus.)

Surplus Disposal. Disposing of the farm surpluses now on hand poses tremendously difficult problems. If they were to be sold here at home, our domestic markets would become flooded, and farm prices would be forced down. This would mean that the Federal Government would have to step in and maintain prices through the support program and thus build the surpluses right back up again. Selling the surpluses abroad could undermine world markets and hurt those friendly nations which produce and export the same commodities.

Even so, a substantial portion of the surplus is regularly used up. In fact, the surplus now on hand stands at less than two-thirds of what it was as recently as 1960. Much of it is taken by the school lunch program, aid to the needy, assistance to such public and private institutions as mental hospitals and juvenile homes, and disaster relief. Billions of dollars worth have gone abroad under the "Food for Peace" program which, since 1954, has channeled surplus commodities abroad in direct sales, barter deals, famine relief, and other foreign assistance.

The CCC's holdings of wheat and feed grains (corn, oats, and sorghum)—crops that for years piled up in huge amounts—are now (1970) down to about the minimum levels the USDA has set as necessary to combat the shortages another war could bring. Our domestic needs, combined with the importance of food as a weapon for peace in a hungry world, may soon mean that the "surplus problem" of the 1950's and early 1960's will be replaced by the pressing need to *increase* the production of several crops.

✳✳✳✳✳✳✳✳✳✳ CONCEPT BUILDING ✳✳✳✳✳✳✳✳✳✳

Key Concepts

Agriculture is a, and perhaps *the,* basic industry in the United States. We began our history as an agricultural people, and agriculture has played a primary role throughout the nation's development. Although the Department of Agriculture did not achieve Cabinet status until 1889, governmental concern for agriculture dates back to the early colonial period.

The USDA's functions may be grouped under four broad headings: (1) research and education, conducted mainly through the Agricultural Research Service and the Cooperative State Research Service; (2) conservation and rural development activities, conducted through the Forest Service, the Soil Conservation Service, the Rural Electrification Administration, and the Farmers Home Administration; (3) marketing activities, conducted mostly through the Consumer and Marketing Service and the Commodity Exchange Authority; and (4) crop stabilization and credit, conducted chiefly through the Agricultural Stabilization and Conservation Service and the Commodity Credit Corporation.

Since the 1920's the Federal Government has made determined efforts to raise the agricultural price level and to stabilize it at a relatively high point. Today those efforts center on parity price supports, acreage allotments, market quotas, and crop loans. These policies have produced a huge surplus of several commodities, but the "surplus problem" may soon be replaced by the need to increase the production of several crops.

Important Terms

acreage allotments	Food for Peace program	market quotas	Soil Bank program
basic crops	futures trading	parity	subsidy
flexible price supports	land-grant colleges	rigid price supports	support level

Questions for Inquiry and Review

1. Why may agriculture by called *the* basic industry in the United States?

2. What was the dominant theme of American history from the earliest colonial period to the dawn of this century?

3. Why was the year 1862 of such particular significance to American agriculture?

4. Who heads the Department of Agriculture, and how is he selected?

5. Under what four broad headings may the activities of the USDA be grouped?

6. Which agency carries out most of the physical, biological, chemical, and engineering research work of the USDA?

7. Why might the USDA be described as a conservation agency?

8. What factor is responsible for approximately ninety per cent of all forest fires?

9. The REA administers loan programs for what two general purposes?

10. What two factors are largely responsible for making farming a risky business?

11. In what ways does the government aid the farmer in the marketing of his products?

12. Why was it necessary for Congress to enact a *second* Agricultural Adjustment Act in 1938?

13. How did the coming of World War II affect the "farm problem"?

14. What prompted Congress to abandon almost immediately the flexible price support program it provided for in 1948?

15. Is the present policy built upon *rigid* or *flexible* price supports?

16. Who determines what crops are to be supported under the price support program?

17. What particular fact prompts most affected farmers to observe their acreage allotments?

18. What particular fact usually prompts most affected farmers to vote for market quotas?

19. Why would it be unwise to solve the surplus problem simply by selling the surplus commodities on the open market here and abroad?

20. Why might it be true that the surplus problem is nearly a thing of the past?

For Further Inquiry

1. Is it wise that on the one hand the USDA aids farmers to produce bigger and better crops while at the same time helps farmers restrict the volume of farm goods flowing to the market?

2. Generally speaking, Republican Congressmen have favored a policy of flexible price supports and Democrats one of rigid price supports. Which — if either one — do you think is preferable? Why?

3. Erosion removes approximately 500,000,-000 tons of topsoil in the United States each year. Why should this fact be a cause of grave concern to all of our people rather than to the farmer alone?

4. Does the money spent on agricultural research benefit farmers more than it does the nonfarm consumers of agricultural production?

5. Labor unions have been far more effective in seeking and winning higher wages and better working conditions for their members than farm organizations have been in securing higher incomes for farmers. Why do you think this has been so?

6. Figured on the basis of sales, less than one-half of all of the farm production in the United States is covered by price supports, and most farmers do *not* receive price support subsidies. The price support program tends to help the larger producers and does little for the small and the poorer farmers. Do these facts suggest to you that the price support program ought to be abolished?

Suggested Activities

1. Stage a debate or class forum on the question: *Resolved,* That the Federal Government should abandon, as rapidly as possible, its various programs designed to subsidize American agriculture.

2. Invite your local county agent to describe his work in your community to the class.

3. If there is an REA, Soil Conservation Service, Agricultural Stabilization and Conservation Service, or other USDA agency in your locale, make a study of its operations and prepare a report on it.

4. Invite a member or representative of a national farm organization (such as the Farm Bureau or the Grange) or a representative of a local farm-related business to speak to the class on the general subject of federal agricultural policy.

Suggested Reading

BLACKMORE, CHARLES P. and YESELSON, ABRAHAM (eds.), *The Fabric of American Democracy.* Van Nostrand, 1969. Chapter 12.

BUNZEL, JOHN H., *Issues of American Public Policy.* Prentice-Hall, 1968. Chapter 7.

BURNS, JAMES M. and PELTASON, J. W., *Government By the People.* Prentice-Hall, 1969. Chapter 25.

FERGUSON, JOHN H. and MCHENRY, DEAN E., *The American System of Government.* McGraw-Hill, 1968. Chapter 25.

GALTON, LAURANCE, "Agriculture Is More than a Dream," *New York Times Magazine,* June 18, 1967.

HIGDON, HAL, "Obituary for DDT (in Michigan)," *New York Times Magazine,* July 6, 1969.

KOTZ, NICK, "Hunger in America: Let Them Eat Words," *Look,* December 2, 1969.

"One War U.S. Is Winning—Bigger Crops for Hungry World," *U.S. News,* June 10, 1968.

"Pesticides: Pro and Con," *U.S. News,* October 20, 1969.

Soil Conservation Service, *Our American Land: Use the Land, Save the Soil.* Government Printing Office, 1968.

TALBOT, ROSS B. and HADWIGER, DON F., *The Policy Process in American Agriculture.* Chandler, 1968.

"The Grapes of Wrath, 1969" *Time,* July 4, 1969; *Reader's Digest,* October, 1969.

"Truth About Hunger in America," *U.S. News,* April 28, 1969.

U.S. Department of Agriculture, *Yearbook of Agriculture.* Government Printing Office. Annual.

WARSHOFSKY, FRED, "Most Destructive Creature on Earth," *Reader's Digest,* Sept. 1967.

25
THE DEPARTMENT OF COMMERCE

❖❖❖ Should the basic function of the Commerce Department be promotional or regulatory in character? Why?

❖❖❖ To whom are the programs administered by the Commerce Department most beneficial?

❖❖❖ Does the National Government possess the power to limit the growth of the national population? Should it have such power?

❖❖❖ Is it, in your view, proper for government to subsidize business in the United States?

I go for all sharing the privileges of government who assist in bearing its burden.

ABRAHAM LINCOLN

The concept that government exists *only* to satisfy the needs and wishes of the people lies at the very heart of our political creed. This conviction—that government is the servant and never the master—stands in sharp contrast to the concept basic to dictatorial systems: that government exists as an end in itself and to serve the interests of the few who control the power of the state.

This basic concept is nowhere better illustrated in our governmental system than in the area of government's economic activities. Government at all levels in the United States—national, State, and local—is deeply involved in the economic life of the nation, and virtually everything that government does affects that life.

A great many pages of this text illustrate the importance of government in and to the economy. Each page of this chapter is devoted to numerous examples of this importance, for here we are concerned with the Department of Commerce and its role in promoting the nation's economic well-being.

DEPARTMENTAL ORGANIZATION

The Department of Commerce was originally created in 1903 as the Department of Commerce and Labor. Congress established a separate Department of Labor in 1913 and the original agency became the Department of Commerce. It describes its basic mission today as that of "promoting healthy growth of the American economy through programs of assistance to business and commerce, the community, and the general public." To this end, thousands of men and women work in the several agencies of the Department.

The Secretary of Commerce. The Department is headed by the Secretary of Commerce. He usually comes from the ranks of successful businessmen and, like each of his colleagues in the Cabinet, is appointed by the President with the consent of the Senate. He is a major adviser to the President on all matters relating to the commercial and industrial segments of

454

the nation's economy and is responsible for making the services of his Department available to the business community and to the public.

The Under Secretary serves as the Secretary's chief deputy and exercises general supervision over the several agencies and the more than 35,000 men and women who work in the Department. The balance of his top-level staff consists of five Assistant Secretaries— for Economic Affairs, for Domestic and International Business, for Science and Technology, for Economic Development and for Administration.

Principal Agencies. Today the several major agencies within the Department include the:

Bureau of the Census
National Bureau of Standards
Patent Office
Bureau of International Commerce
Environmental Science Services Administration
Maritime Administration

THE CENSUS BUREAU

The Constitution requires that an "enumeration" of the nation's population be made every ten years.[1] It does so, as we noted on page 203, in order that the seats in the House of Representatives and direct taxes may be apportioned among the States on the basis of their respective populations.

The First Census was taken in 1790 and the Nineteenth Census began on April 1, 1970. From the Census of 1790 to that of 1960, the nation's population grew from 3,929,214 to 179,323,175; see the tables on pages 82, 617, and 719. The population climbed past 200,-000,000 in mid-November, 1967, and it is estimated that the 1970 Census will show a population of very nearly 206,000,000.

---

[1] Article I, Section 2, Clause 3.

Census Bureau population projections are shown on this Census Clock in the lobby of the Commerce Building in Washington, D.C. Clock-like dials indicate a birth every 8½ seconds, a death every 16½ seconds, an immigrant arriving every 71 seconds, and an emigrant leaving every 23 minutes. (Bureau of the Census)

The earliest censuses were merely head countings. Little use was made of them beyond the reapportioning of the House. Beginning in 1810, however, the questions asked by the census takers were broadened, and now they produce a great variety of detailed information about our people. Through the Twelfth Census in 1900 each of the decennial head counts was made by a temporary agency created for the purpose. Congress finally established the Census Bureau as a permanent agency in 1902.

This nation would be in dire straits without a mass of reliable statistical data on the population today. The Bureau's reports have an almost unlimited number of uses. They show our military leaders how many males are of military age now or will be at some future date; educators, the educational attainments of our population; school boards, how many children will soon be of school age; employers and social workers, how many are unemployed; and advertisers and the Federal Communications Commission, how many radios and TV's are in each locality.

The census volumes on manufactures and agriculture are especially valuable to those who are involved in these industries. For instance, if a manufacturer of corn cutters, milk cans, or poultry food wants to know where there is a demand for his products, he can learn how much corn is produced and about how many cows and chickens there are in each county

in the United States. From the population figures a razor manufacturer can readily discover those communities where there are more men than women; a cosmetics dealer can find the areas in which there are more women than men; or a baby products manufacturer can locate those places where the birth rate is highest.

Millions were born in the country before birth records were universally kept. Being able to prove one's age or show the location of one's birth is often important in such matters as getting a job, registering to vote, draft registration, obtaining insurance, establishing citizenship, securing a passport, and applying for social security benefits. Thus far, more than 3,500,000 persons have secured tran-

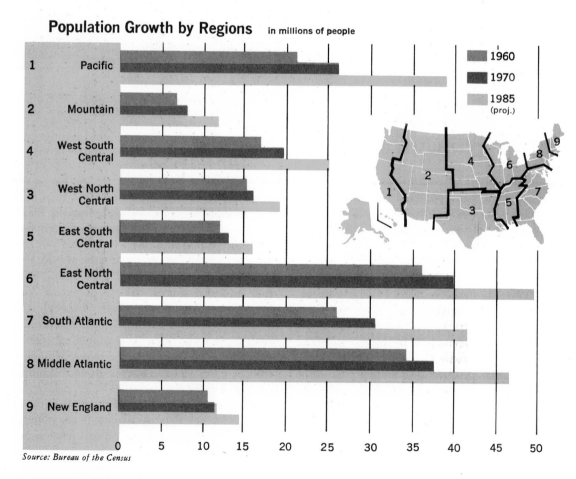

Population Growth by Regions in millions of people

Legend:
1960
1970
1985 (proj.)

1 Pacific
2 Mountain
4 West South Central
3 West North Central
5 East South Central
6 East North Central
7 South Atlantic
8 Middle Atlantic
9 New England

0 5 10 15 20 25 30 35 40 45 50

Source: Bureau of the Census

scripts of information they or their parents once gave a census taker.

The population census is taken every tenth year, but many other periodic and special censuses are taken as well—for example, on housing, manufactures, agriculture, mineral industries, governmental units, and transportation. In 1970, in addition to the regular decennial census, the Bureau plans to survey the nation's housing facilities, collecting such information as the number of rooms in dwellings, value, state of repairs, cooking and plumbing facilities, and the like. Special population surveys are often conducted for local governments. These studies are important because many States make grants to their local governments from the funds collected from such taxes as those on liquor, cigarettes, and gasoline, and these grants are usually based on population.

The old-fashioned census-taker will be replaced by a count-by-mail and computer system in most of the nation for the 1970 Census. About sixty per cent of the population will count itself by mailed questionnaires. The rest of the people—chiefly those who live in rural and slum areas—will be visited by the traditional enumerators. The Census of 1790 was simply a head count and cost slightly more than $44,000 to take; the more complex 1970 count will cost more than $200,000,000.

The individual census report forms and the personal information they contain are kept in the strictest confidence. One cannot even see the report forms pertaining to himself, even though he may have supplied the information involved. The Bureau will provide a summary (a transcript) of the data it has about the person who requests it or about the person's children or deceased parents. But it will not supply the information to anyone else. The enumerators must take an oath of secrecy. If they reveal any of the personal facts they have gathered, they may be fined as much as $1000 and imprisoned for a period up to two years. Not even the FBI or the Internal Revenue Service has access to the Bureau's massive files.

This proving ring is being calibrated in a new 1,000,000-lb capacity deadweight machine which reduces the time required to calibrate large force-measuring standards by almost half. (National Bureau of Standards)

THE NATIONAL BUREAU OF STANDARDS

Because of the absolute need for standardized weights and measures, Article I, Section 8, Clause 5 of the Constitution gives Congress the power to "fix the standard of weights and measures." Acting under this power, Congress established in 1838 the English system (pound, ounce, mile, foot, gallon, quart, and so on) as the legal standards of weights and measures in the United States. In 1866 it also legalized the use of the French metric system now so widely used in technical and scientific work.

In 1901 Congress created the National Bureau of Standards which it made responsible for the custody, maintenance, and development of the national standards of physical measurement. The originals, by which all other standards in the United States are tested and corrected, are kept in the Bureau's extensive laboratories in Washington, D.C.

The Bureau was also created as a scientific research and testing center for the National Government, and as an aid to American science and industry. Over the years it has become one of the world's truly great scientific institutions.

Much of the Bureau's activities are now centered in its huge laboratory facilities at Gaithersburg, Maryland and Boulder, Colorado; but it also maintains field stations elsewhere in this country and abroad. The scope, the complexity, and the importance of its activities defy the imagination.

Its several thousand highly skilled scientists and technicians perform a wide range of experimental and testing tasks — for example, the analysis of all manner of materials, the development of new and improved machines and measuring devices, and the determining of the resistance of products and substances to fire, cold, stress, and strain. The Bureau also renders invaluable aid to other federal agencies in the testing of materials and in setting specifications for governmental supply purchases.

The largest part of the Bureau's work today involves research and development in the physical sciences, especially in physics, chemistry, and mathematics. The primary goal of this work is the improvement of the national standards of measurement for such physical quantities as length, mass, time, volume, temperature, light, sound, X-ray intensity, electrical energy, radioactivity, and viscosity.

Simply to list the Bureau's many significant accomplishments would more than fill this book. They range all the way from the standardization of clothing sizes to research on the very frontiers of nuclear physics. When one realizes how vital and how indispensable the standardization of measurements, of tools, and of parts is in our highly technical mass-production economy, he has barely begun to appreciate the importance of the work of the Bureau of Standards.

As but one illustration, the Bureau is now able to make measurements to the nearest *ten* *millionth* of an inch. But industry is now beginning to demand even *more* exact measurements, and the Bureau is hard at work on a system of atomic standards to produce measuring devices that will be accurate to at least *one billionth* of an inch.

THE PATENT OFFICE

The Constitution grants to Congress the power:

> to promote the progress of science and useful arts, by securing, for limited times, to authors and inventors, the exclusive right to their respective writings and discoveries.[2]

The copyright laws enacted by Congress under the terms of this provision are administered by the Copyright Office in the Library of Congress (page 236). The patent laws enacted under this authority are administered by the Patent Office in the Department of Commerce.

A *patent* is an exclusive grant made by the Government which extends to an individual or a corporation "the right to exclude others from making, using, or selling" the object of the patent "throughout the United States" for a certain period of time. Two major types of patents are now issued: *patents of invention* and *patents of design*.[3]

Patents of invention are the more common of the two types. They are grants of an exclusive right to make, use, and sell any new and useful process, machine, manufacture, or composition of matter, or any new and useful improvements thereto, for a limited period — now 17 years. This type of patent cannot be renewed except by special act of Congress — something quite rare.

---

[2] Article I, Section 8, Clause 8.

[3] Patents are also issued to protect those who originate and develop new varieties of certain living plants.

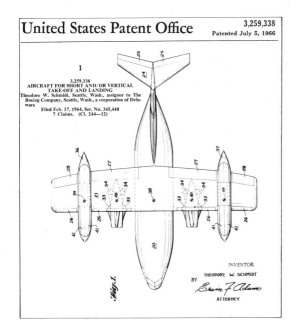

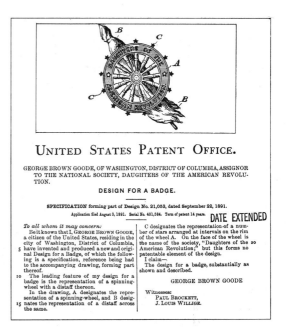

Of the approximately 90,000 patent applications filed with the Patent Office each
year, about 60 per cent are granted. The badge of the Daughters of the American
Revolution (above) is a patent of design. (U.S. Patent Office)

Patents of design are grants of an exclusive right to make, use, and sell any new, original, and ornamental designed article of manufacture — good for a period of $3\frac{1}{2}$, 7, or 14 years, as the applicant elects.[4] Patents of design are issued to cover such things as automobile bodies, fraternity insignia, wallpapers, and lighting fixtures; unlike patents of invention, their life is sometimes extended by Congress. The badge of the Daughters of the American Revolution, originally patented in 1891, has been renewed by an act of Congress at the end of each 14-year period.

Any person may file an application for a patent. A $65 fee must accompany an application and an additional $100 fee must be paid if the patent is granted. The applicant must declare to the Commissioner of Patents that he believes himself to be the original inventor or designer. He must submit with his application a full description of the object, a drawing in cases that can be illustrated, and a model if the Commissioner requests it.

The issuing (registering) of a patent does *not* mean that the Government will act to protect the rights of the holder. The patentee does have a "right," but, if it is ignored, infringed upon, or challenged by others, he must act to protect it. His usual recourse is to the federal courts. The federal District Courts have jurisdiction over cases involving the pirating or infringement of patents.

Appeals from actions of the Patent Office — for example, the refusal to issue a patent — may be taken first to the Board of Appeals within the Office itself and, from there, to the Court of Customs and Patent Appeals (page 578).[5]

---

[4] A patent right may be assigned (sold or given) to another person by its holder and it may be inherited as other property.

[5] Treaties with other nations protect American patents throughout much of the rest of the world.

More than 3,500,000 patents have been issued thus far. Among the earliest ones were those for Eli Whitney's cotton gin (1793) and Robert Fulton's steamboat (1809). When the Wright brothers invented the biplane, they specified every phase of the invention to be protected by the patent. Thomas Edison is credited with more than 1000 patents, including those for the incandescent light bulb, the phonograph, the carbon transmitter which made the telephone commercially feasible, the motion picture camera, and the sound motion picture.

Today some 75,000 patents are issued annually. Among the most recent important ones is a patent for a computer designed to aid in the diagnosis of disease. There are over 10,000 known diseases, and some have as many as 600 separate symptoms. The computer stores data on the principal diseases and their symptoms in a memory device. When a patient's symptoms are fed into the computer, it attempts to match them with those for a particular malady.

The Patent Office also issues (registers) *trademarks*. A trademark is a distinctive word, emblem, symbol, or other device used on goods actually sold in commerce to identify the manufacturer or seller. Any individual or firm providing service but not manufacturing or selling goods may also register a certain mark to identify its particular service. Trademarks are registered for 20 years and may be renewed any number of times. There would be little point in a firm's spending huge sums in advertising and using a distinctive trademark if others were allowed to imitate it. A trademark is often worth a very substantial sum to its owner. Some trademarks have national reputations and serve to guarantee the quality of a product.

The power to provide for the protection of trademarks is derived by Congress from its power to regulate interstate and foreign commerce—and only those marks on articles associated with such commerce may be registered with the Patent Office.

THE BUREAU OF INTERNATIONAL COMMERCE

The Bureau of International Commerce is the federal agency primarily responsible for promoting the foreign trade of the United States and assisting American business in its operations abroad. It does so in a variety of ways and in all of its activities works in close harmony with the State Department and the United States Information Agency.

The Bureau maintains detailed files on thousands of foreign firms engaged in international trade. These records, compiled with the aid of the Foreign Service, are readily available to American firms. Its weekly magazine, *International Commerce,* reports on business conditions and trade and investment prospects around the world. With local chambers of commerce, it holds "trade clinics" to acquaint businessmen with the opportunities for marketing their products in other countries.

The Bureau sends trade missions abroad to make contacts for American firms, and conducts international trade fairs and maintains permanent trade centers in other countries to display American goods to potential foreign customers. It is also responsible for the enforcement of the Export Control Act of 1949 —the statute designed to prevent the export of strategic materials, equipment, and data to countries within the Soviet and Red Chinese spheres. As we noted on page 270, the United States has no desire to contribute to the war-making capacity of any potential enemy nation.

The Bureau also provides the working personnel necessary to carry out the functions of the *Foreign Trade Zones Board.* The latter is an independent agency composed of the Secretaries of Commerce, Treasury, and the Army. At the direction of Congress, it establishes "foreign trade zones" at selected American ports of entry. These zones are small enclosed areas where foreign goods intended for transshipment to other countries may be stored and processed free of customs duties. Storage and processing facilities are also available for domestic goods intended for export. Trade zones are now (1970) maintained at seven ports of entry: New York, San Francisco, Seattle, Toledo, New Orleans, Honolulu, and Mayaguez near San Juan, Puerto Rico.

THE ENVIRONMENTAL SCIENCE SERVICES ADMINISTRATION

Two long-established and highly important federal agencies—the Weather Bureau, created in 1890, and the Coast and Geodetic Survey, dating from 1807—were combined to form the Environmental Science Services Administration (ESSA) in 1965. Later that year, the Central Radio Propagation Laboratory with its research facilities at Boulder, Colorado, was transferred to ESSA from the National Bureau of Standards. The new agency carries on the functions of its much-praised predecessors; it is charged by law to "describe, understand, and predict the state of the oceans, the state of the lower and upper atmosphere, and the size and shape of the earth."

Weather observations made at thousands of places across the nation, from ships and aircraft, and from satellites orbiting the earth are of incalculable value. The Administration receives countless daily reports of heat, cold, clouds, rain, snow, wind direction and velocity, and similar conditions. From this data weather conditions can be forecast with remarkable accuracy.

The benefits all of us realize from the forecasts can hardly be exaggerated. To cite only a comparatively few examples of their myriad applications: Frost warnings allow fruit growers to protect their orchards; daily storm warnings aid pilots and fishermen; flood warnings, often more than a week in advance, allow cities some time in which to prepare for the high water and enable farmers to save livestock and other property that might otherwise be lost. The spotting and tracking of hurricanes saves untold numbers of lives; freezing forecasts permit railroads to save perishables in transit and warn motorists to add antifreeze to automobile cooling systems; rain forecasts govern planting and harvesting and are watched very closely by building contractors.

While the Administration's work in the fields of weather and atmospheric conditions—the work of the Weather Bureau—is well-known, its survey work—that of the Coast and Geodetic Survey—is not. Even so, its maps, charts, and other reports are indispensable in such fields as navigation, radio, engineering, construction, and aviation. As but one example, its seismological research is critical in the reduction of earthquake damage. Thus, many of the larger buildings and dams in the United States were designed and built on the basis of the Coast and Geodetic Survey's data on the nature and incidence of earthquakes.

In an effort to help man cope with the forces of nature, the U.S. Weather Bureau provides advisory information and extended forecasts of weather conditions to all parts of the country. (U.S. Weather Bureau)

Today the Administration carries on its survey work with several oceanographic research vessels, mobile field parties and aircraft; and it maintains field offices, laboratories, and observatories at several points across the continent, in Hawaii, Alaska, and Puerto Rico, and at three locations in Antarctica—including a magnetic and seismological observatory at the South Pole itself.

THE MARITIME ADMINISTRATION

The Maritime Administration is responsible for the implementation of the nation's historic maritime policy. That policy, pursued from the earliest days of the Republic, has been the development and operation of a strong merchant marine—one adequate to carry the nation's waterborne domestic trade and the bulk of its foreign commerce, and capable as well of serving as a naval auxiliary in time of war.

The Administration is the present-day descendant of a long line of federal maritime agencies dating back more than half a century. A steady decline in the nation's merchant marine—caused in large part by the lower construction and operating costs enjoyed by foreign shipping concerns—prompted Congress to create the United States Shipping Board in 1916. That agency and its several successors were given powers with which to promote and regulate the nation's shipping efforts.

Many aids are provided to American shipping. Congress has long granted subsidies to shipbuilders, owners, and operators to help them meet overseas competition. Today the subsidy program is conducted by the Maritime Administration through its Maritime Subsidy Board. The Administration also guarantees loans to shipbuilders and pays the costs of defense features—such as troop-carrying facilities—built into vessels that are certified by the Navy as necessary for national defense. It conducts an extensive research and development program aimed at improving the quality

and efficiency of the merchant marine. Thus it studies such problems as ship design, safety, propulsion, cargo handling, and ship management. The world's first nuclear-powered merchant vessel, the NS *Savannah,* was built and is operated and maintained by the Maritime Administration.

In both World Wars the Government became directly involved in shipbuilding. Thousands of Liberty, Victory, and other ships were built in Government shipyards. This program has been continued in recent years. The Maritime Administration keeps over a thousand of these vessels in a national defense reserve fleet for emergency use. Many of the ships are used by the Navy and other agencies, and the rest have either been chartered or sold to private operators. A fully-equipped shipyard is also maintained on a stand-by basis at Richmond, California.

The Maritime Administration operates the United States Merchant Marine Academy at Kings Point, New York, to train officers for the merchant marine. Its graduates are licensed as ship's officers by the Coast Guard and are also qualified for commissions as ensigns in the Naval Reserve. The Administration also administers a grant-in-aid program in support of the maritime academies operated by the States of California, Maine, Massachusetts, New York, and Texas.

The Federal Maritime Commission. Over the years Congress has given the several maritime agencies extensive power to regulate the rates, services, and labor practices of American vessels engaged in foreign and offshore water commerce. Today, that power is exercised by an independent regulatory agency, the Federal Maritime Commission.[6] The Commission is composed of five members appointed by the

---

[6] Vessels operating on the inland waters of the United States are subject to regulation by the Interstate Commerce Commission, pages 531–535. On the general nature of independent regulatory commissions, see pages 530–531.

President and Senate for four-year terms. One of its members is designated by the President to serve as its chairman and he is the Commission's chief administrative officer. He and the other commissioners work in close cooperation with the Maritime Administration.

OTHER AGENCIES

The *Office of Business Economics* is the Government's major economic research unit. It maintains a close, continuous, and studious eye on the structure, condition and prospects of the nation's economy. For example, it gauges and makes continuing reports on the gross national product—GNP, the total national output of goods and services. The information it provides indicates growth and recession trends in all segments of the economy. This, and the Office's other statistical data and analyses are of incalculable value to other executive agencies, to Congress, and to the business community in charting the nation's economic course. Public, private, and academic economists find its monthly journal, *Survey of Current Business,* an indispensable tool.

The *Business and Defense Services Administration* collects and analyzes data on the nation's commercial and industrial growth. It does so to provide information and advice to the business community and to other federal agencies. It works closely with the Office of Emergency Preparedness in the planning for industrial mobilization and the control of production in the event of a national emergency, and on the stockpiling program. See page 307.

The *Economic Development Administration* identifies those locales which are economically distressed and so eligible for aid under the Public Works and Economic Development Act of 1965. EDA's primary function is that of promoting the long-range development of such areas. In carrying out this task, it makes loans and grants and furnishes planning advice and other assistance, as provided in the 1965 law. It also coordinates the efforts of other federal agencies concerned with combatting heavy and chronic unemployment in depressed communities (see pages 472–473), and provides help to State and local agencies engaged in economic development activities.

The *Office of Field Services* performs various staff services to other agencies within the Department. It does so through forty-two offices scattered in major cities across the country—that is, "in the field." For example, its field offices serve as collection stations for much of the data vital to the work of the office of Business Economics. Its field offices also are the major outlets for the reports and other materials published by the other departmental agencies for the use of the business community, State and local governments, and the general public.

The *Office of State Technical Services* is charged with providing support for State programs designed to place commercially useful scientific findings in the hands of American business. It makes grants-in-aid to State agencies—usually to State universities or colleges—for this purpose.

The *United States Travel Service* is a sort of super tourist agency. Its particular function is to attract tourists and other foreign visitors to this country—for study, business, recreation, and the like. Its work is really quite broadranging. Thus, within the United States, it prompts the development of such things as low-cost travel tours and tourist facilities, conducts an extensive advertising program to encourage Americans to welcome foreign visitors, and seeks to overcome various inconveniences involved in international travel. Most of its effort is spent abroad, though. Across much of the world the United States Travel Service conducts a vast promotional campaign—in newspapers and magazines, by radio and television, with pamphlets, brochures, posters, slides, films, and many other devices—to attract visitors to this country.

Key Concepts

The Department of Commerce, originally created in 1903, is charged with the promotion of the health of the nation's economy through providing aids to business and commerce, communities, and the public. The principal agencies within it today are the Census Bureau, the National Bureau of Standards, the Patent Office, the Bureau of International Commerce, the Environmental Science Services Administration, and the Maritime Administration.

The Census Bureau conducts the decennial enumeration required by the Constitution. The National Bureau of Standards has custody of the national standards of weights and measures and conducts much vital research. The Patent Office administers the patent and trademark laws. The Bureau of International Commerce promotes our trade abroad. The Environmental Science Services Administration consolidated the Weather Bureau and the Cost and Geodetic Survey in 1965 and now directs their functions. The Maritime Administration fosters the nation's merchant marine and works closely with the Federal Maritime Commission, an independent regulatory agency. Several other departmental units also work to promote the economy—and, especially, American business: the Office of Business Economics, the Business and Defense Services Administration, the Economic Development Administration, the Office of Field Services, the Office of State Technical Services, and the United States Travel Service.

Important Terms

decennial census	GNP	metric system	standards of weights
foreign trade zone	maritime	patent of design	and measures
	merchant marine	patent of invention	trademark

Questions for Inquiry and Review

1. When and out of what was the Department of Commerce created?

2. What is the Commerce Department's basic function?

3. For what two specific purposes does the Constitution require a decennial census?

4. Why does the Constitution grant to Congress the power to "fix the standard of weights and measures"?

5. What two principal types of patents does the Patent Office issue?

6. On the basis of what constitutional power does Congress possess the authority to provide for trademarks?

7. In what federal court would one initiate a case involving patent infringement? A suit challenging a decision made in the Patent Office?

8. What is the primary task of the Bureau of International Commerce?

9. What older agencies were combined or consolidated to form the Environmental Science Services Administration? When was ESSA created?

10. What is the basic mission of ESSA?

11. What is the historic maritime policy of the United States? What agency is responsible for implementing it?

12. What is the nature and function of the Federal Maritime Commission?

13. What is the particular function of the United States Travel Service?

For Further Inquiry

1. The pages of this chapter are devoted to a large number of services which the National Government provides to business and the general public. Do you feel that such services *should* be furnished by the Government? Would you eliminate any of them? Why?

2. None of the nineteen censuses to date has ever included a question asking one's religious preferences. Many church groups would welcome the information that such a question would provide, but many others oppose it. Why do some favor and some oppose this?

3. What would likely result if Congress were to repeal the existing statutes relating to patents and trademarks?

4. Do you think it is fair that the National Government should provide subsidies to such special groups as shipowners when these aids are financed by taxes levied upon the entire population?

Suggested Activities

1. Make a list of as many examples as you can of the ways in which economic activities in your area are regulated by the National, State, and local governments.

2. Make a similar list of the ways in which these three levels of government aid the economy of your community. Make a list of as many publicly conducted business enterprises as you can in your community.

3. If possible, ask a local businessman to explain the ways in which government regulates and aids his particular business.

4. Prepare a list of as many illustrations as you can of the ways in which your locale might cooperate with the Commerce Department's efforts to attract foreign visitors to the U.S.

5. Most libraries and many local government offices have Census Bureau Reports on file. Prepare a report on the character of the population in your area based on the Census Reports.

Suggested Reading

BLACKMORE, CHARLES P. and YESELSON, ABRAHAM (eds.), *The Fabric of American Democracy.* Van Nostrand, 1969. Chapter 11.

BUNZEL, JOHN H., *Issues of American Public Policy.* Prentice-Hall, 1968. Chapter 7.

BURNS, JAMES M. and PELTASON, J. W., *Government By the People.* Prentice-Hall, 1969. Chapter 25.

FERGUSON, JOHN H. and McHENRY, DEAN E., *The American System of Government.* McGraw-Hill, 1968. Chapter 22.

PELTASON, J. W. and BURNS, JAMES M., *Functions and Policies of American Government.* Prentice-Hall, 1967. Chapter 7.

SIMPSON, ROBERT H., "Curbing Hurricanes — the Chances," *U.S. News,* September 1, 1969.

Special Issue: "American Business Abroad; The New Industrial Revolution," *Saturday Review,* November 22, 1969.

STANS, SECRETARY MAURICE H., "Is U.S. Being Squeezed Out of World Markets?" *U.S. News,* September 8, 1969.

"What the 1970 Census Will Show," *U.S. News,* June 2, 1969.

"Where the People Will Be: U.S. in the '70's and '80's," *U.S. News,* January 29, 1968.

WHITE, PETER T., "Satellites Gave Warning of Midwest Floods," *National Geographic,* October, 1969.

26
THE DEPARTMENT OF LABOR

❖❖❖Should the basic function of the Labor Department be regulatory or promotional? Why?

❖❖❖To whom are the programs administered by the Labor Department most beneficial?

❖❖❖Why is the concept of free contract labor so vital to our economic and political system?

❖❖❖What is government's proper role in the labor-management relationship?

❖❖❖Should (or should not) public employees possess the right to strike? Why?

Labor is prior to, and independent of capital. Capital is only the fruit of labor, and could never have existed if labor had not first existed. Labor is the superior of capital, and deserves much the higher consideration.

ABRAHAM LINCOLN

Some type of labor system — that is, some basic pattern of labor-management relationship — exists within every society. Whatever form that system takes — whether slavery, serfdom, forced state labor, free contract labor, or some other — it determines the relationship between the worker and his work and the worker and those who direct his work. Clearly, no aspect of the organization of a society can be more important to the nature of that society than its labor system.

In this country, both by tradition and by law, the system is that of free contract labor. No person in the United States is born to a master, to a job, or to a piece of land which he cannot leave. Nor — except for military purposes or as punishment for crime — can any person be forced to work against his will. For us, each person is free to contract as he will for the use of his services. We are firmly committed to the concept of the laborer's freedom of contract. We are also firmly committed to the concept that it is the duty of government to protect that freedom and, in protecting it, to regulate its use.

DEPARTMENTAL ORGANIZATION

As we noted at the beginning of the preceding chapter, the Department of Labor was created as a separate Cabinet department in 1913. Congress had first established a Bureau of Labor in the Department of the Interior in 1884. That agency was later made an independent department, but without Cabinet status. An increasing concern for the problems of labor in our growing industrial economy led to the establishment of the Department of Commerce and Labor in 1903. A separate Department of Labor was created in 1913.

In the statute creating the Department, Congress directed it to:

advance the public interest by promoting the welfare of the wage earners of the United

States, improving their working conditions, and advancing their opportunities for profitable employment.

The Secretary of Labor. The Secretary of Labor is appointed by the President with the consent of the Senate. He is responsible for the management of the Department and all of its activities and also serves as the President's chief advisor in all labor matters. The Under Secretary serves as his chief aide. The day-to-day operations of the Department are managed by a Deputy Under Secretary for International Labor Affairs and five Assistant Secretaries.

The Assistant Secretary for Policy Development and Research coordinates and has overall responsibility for the development of departmental policies and programs. The Assistant Secretary for Administration is the Department's budget officer and general "housekeeper."

The other Assistant Secretaries — for Wage and Labor Standards, Manpower, and Labor-Management Relations — and the Commissioner of Labor Statistics run the Department's major agencies — to which we shall turn in a moment.

Labor employs only some 10,000 persons and is the smallest of the twelve Cabinet-level departments. Its work is essentially *promotional* in character. It is primarily concerned with bringing about improvements in the labor field, *not* with the settlement of disputes between labor and management. Although it lends a helping hand at times, the settling of disputes is a function of other agencies that have no formal ties to the Department of Labor — agencies such as the National Labor Relations Board and the Federal Mediation and Conciliation Service. (See pages 477–479.)

THE BUREAU OF INTERNATIONAL LABOR AFFAIRS

The Bureau of International Labor Affairs is headed by an Administrator responsible to the Under Secretary for International Labor Affairs. His agency directs and coordinates all of the Department's activities in the international labor field. Thus, it furnishes advice and information to the State Department, other federal agencies, and to foreign governments. It supervises the work of the labor attachés who are assigned to most of our embassies abroad and is responsible for United States participation in the International Labor Organization.

The Bureau's major purpose is that of fostering cooperation and the exchange of technical know-how in the international labor field. It supplies consultants for foreign assignments, provides technical materials for use abroad, and conducts training programs for labor leaders and officials from other countries. It also sponsors an exchange program under which American labor officials go abroad and foreign union representatives visit the United States.

The Bureau conducts extensive and continuing studies of labor developments abroad in order to perform its role as a source for advice on the ways in which the interests of the United States may be promoted in the foreign labor field. Similarly, it must remain thoroughly familiar with the conditions and problems of labor in the United States in order to judge their effects upon our relations with other countries.

THE BUREAU OF LABOR STATISTICS

The Bureau of Labor Statistics was first established as the Bureau of Labor in the Department of the Interior in 1884 and is the agency out of which the present-day Department of Labor grew. Today it is the Government's principal fact-finding and reporting agency in the field of labor economics. It collects, analyzes, and publishes data on a wide range of topics — most notably employment and unemployment, wages, hours of work, productivity, industrial accidents, labor-management relations, prices, and costs and standards of living.

The Bureau is headed by a Commissioner of Labor Statistics appointed by the President and Senate. He and his agency have no enforcement or other administrative functions. Practically all of the basic data the Bureau of Labor Statistics gathers is supplied voluntarily by labor and business groups and by other governmental agencies. The information it collects and the research it conducts are reported in special bulletins and in its official publication, the *Monthly Labor Review*.

The work of the Bureau gives real meaning to the phrase "cost of living." It makes continuing studies of the current wholesale and retail prices of thousands of commodities and reports its findings in daily, weekly, and monthly "price indexes." These indexes provide a measure of the purchasing power of the dollar and are, in effect, a barometer of the nation's economic health.

The Bureau of Labor Statistics keeps a file of current labor-management contracts and union constitutions—and these frequently serve as valuable background data in the settlement of disputes and the writing of new working agreements. To the same end, it analyzes various topics—for example, health insurance and pension plans—which are often at the heart of labor-management negotiations.

The Bureau's surveys of employment trends can be of special interest and use to young people. All significant trends in employment and job opportunities are continually analyzed to determine which types of jobs are and will be most in demand. The results of these studies are published in a series of "occupational outlook" pamphlets.

THE WAGE AND LABOR STANDARDS ADMINISTRATION

The Wage and Labor Standards Administration is headed by an Administrator who is also the Assistant Secretary for Wage and Labor Standards. He is responsible for all of the Department's wage and labor standards programs and supervises the work of a number of agencies.

The Wage and Hour and Public Contracts Divisions. The WHPC is, despite its plural title, a single agency headed by an Administrator appointed by the President and the Senate.

Its *Wage and Hour Division* administers the oft-amended Fair Labor Standards Act of 1938 which placed a floor under wages and a ceiling over hours. That is, the statute sets a minimum wage and a maximum work week for those who hold jobs covered by its provisions.

The Act covers the employees of most firms engaged in or producing goods or services for interstate or foreign trade. More than 42,000,000 workers are now (1970) covered by its provisions. Several categories of workers are specifically exempted from its terms, however—for example, domestic servants and taxi drivers.

Congress first set the minimum wage at 25¢ an hour. After several increases, it is now (1970) pegged at $1.60 an hour. The statute provides that those it covers must be paid at least that much [1]—and that they must also be paid at least one-and-a-half times that rate ("time-and-a-half") for any work beyond eight hours a day or forty hours in any week.

The law also prohibits the use of *child labor* by most firms engaged in or producing goods or services for interstate or foreign commerce. Such concerns are prohibited from hiring anyone under age sixteen for most jobs and anyone under eighteen for those jobs classed as hazardous. Several types of employment are exempted from the child labor prohibition, however—notably agricultural work, newspaper delivery, acting, and most jobs in which children work for their parents.[2]

The Division also enforces the Equal Pay Act of 1963. Under its terms, some 7,000,000 women—all who are covered by the Fair Labor

Standards Act—must be paid the same amount as that paid to men who do comparable work.

The *Public Contracts Division* enforces the Public Contracts (Walsh-Healey) Act of 1936. That statute requires that all employees working for firms with government contracts be paid the minimum wage and "time-and-a-half" for overtime, and that they be afforded certain welfare benefits and safety protections.

The Bureau of Labor Standards. The Bureau of Labor Standards, administered by a Director appointed by the President and Senate, is essentially a service agency. Like the Bureau of Labor Statistics, it has no enforcement functions. Rather, it acts as a clearinghouse for information and provides technical advice on labor standards to Congress, other federal agencies, the States, employer and labor groups, and civic organizations. It also coordinates the work of all federal and State agencies concerned with the enforcement of wage, hour, child labor, and industrial health and safety laws. It has aided many of the States in the writing or improvement of their industrial safety codes.

The Women's Bureau. Women now (1970) constitute a third of the nation's total labor force. The welfare of these nearly 30,000,000 women is the special concern of the Women's Bureau. It is a research and advisory agency studying such matters as the wages, hours, and working conditions of women; family and property law; and the care of working mothers' children. As the

---

[1] Congress has raised the minimum wage several times since 1938: to 40¢ in 1945, 75¢ in 1949, $1 in 1955, $1.15 (until September 1963) and $1.25 (thereafter) in 1961. When Congress fixed the present rate in 1966 it also brought some 8,000,000 additional workers under the law—most notably those employed on larger farms and most hotel, motel, restaurant, laundry, and hospital employees. For the newly covered workers the wage floor was set at $1 from February 1, 1967 to February 1, 1968 and at $1.15 from then until February 1, 1969; on the latter date it rose automatically to $1.30 and, for all but farm workers, increased to $1.45 on February 1, 1970; it will go to $1.60 on February 1, 1971.

[2] The Supreme Court held federal child labor laws unconstitutional in the *Child Labor Cases* of 1918 and 1922. In *Hammer* v. *Dagenhart,* 1918, the Court voided a 1916 statute in which Congress had prohibited the shipment in interstate commerce of the products of any factory or cannery employing children under age fourteen and of any mine employing those under age sixteen. The Court said: "That there should be limitations upon the right to employ children in mines and factories in the interest of their own and the public welfare, all will admit;" but it held that the control of child labor involved the regulation of *production* rather than commerce and thus rested with the States rather than Congress. Congress then attempted to tax child labor out of existence; in 1918 it imposed a tax of ten per cent on the net profits of any manufacturing concern that employed children under fourteen or, in the case of mining concerns, under sixteen. The Court invalidated the levy as an unconstitutional use of the taxing power in *Bailey* v. *Drexel Furniture Company,* 1922; it described the law providing for the tax as "not a revenue measure; it is an attempt to do by the taxing power that which it [Congress] cannot do directly."

The child labor provisions of the Fair Labor Standards Act were upheld by the Supreme Court in *United States* v. *Darby Lumber Company,* 1941. By then the Court had come to the position that production is an integral part of commerce and cannot be realistically separated from it. Said the Court in the 1941 case: "*Hammer* v. *Dagenhart* . . . should be and now is overruled."

Bureau has described its work, it is concerned "with all women at work, or seeking work, and with their training and skills; with women in all fields of employment; with the student selecting her career; with the girl on her first job and the older woman worker; and with women who are both homemakers and wage earners." It furnishes its reports and advice to Congress, other federal and State agencies, private groups and foreign governments.

The Bureau of Employees' Compensation. The statutes which provide injury and accident benefits for federal employees — similar to State workmen's compensation laws — are administered by the Bureau of Employees' Compensation. The Bureau decides whether federal workers who are injured or disabled are entitled to benefits and, if so, how much their compensation should be. Decisions made by the Bureau may be appealed to the Employees' Compensation Appeals Board, also within the Department.

THE MANPOWER ADMINISTRATION

The Manpower Administration is responsible for all of the Labor Department's programs involving the use of the nation's manpower resources. It is headed by the Manpower Administrator who also holds the post of Assistant Secretary of Labor for Manpower. Two important sub-agencies form the major elements of the Manpower Administration: the United States Training and Employment Service and the Bureau of Apprenticeship and Training.

The United States Training and Employment Service. The USTES is only little known but its work is vitally important to the nation's well-being. It assists the States in the operation of their employment services and the conduct of their unemployment compensation programs. It also administers federal programs designed to relieve the effects of unemployment and to promote effective use of the nation's manpower resources. In this

This graph shows the growth of the labor force and the percentage of unemployed in the United States since 1920. Note that unemployment was at its highest during the decade of the Great Depression.

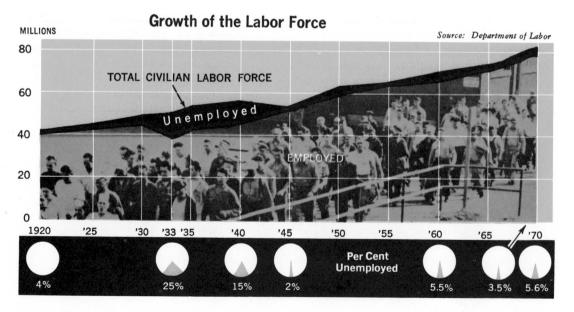

Growth of the Labor Force

MILLINS

Source: *Department of Labor*

latter function it works closely with several other agencies, especially with the Economic Development Administration in the Department of Commerce (page 463). The United States Training and Employment Service deals with one of our most serious and pressing domestic problems — that of unemployment.

The problem of unemployment is most critical and widespread during periods of recession and depression, of course. A certain amount of unemployment always exists, even in "normal" times, however. For the idled worker and his family the problem is immediate and serious no matter when it arises. An employee can be laid off as the result of any of a number of causes: new inventions, automation, bad weather, a shift in buying habits, seasonal demands, moving of a plant, depletion of natural resources, aging, and many more.

The mass unemployment of the Great Depression of the 1930's brought the plight of the unemployed into sharp national focus. The number out of work had leaped from less than 2,000,000 in 1929 to more than 13,000,000 by 1933. The crisis prompted national action on a number of fronts. One of the most significant and far-reaching of the many steps taken was the enactment of the Social Security Act of 1935 (see page 484). Along with the several other relief and welfare programs provided in that omnibus act was an unemployment compensation program.

Unemployment Compensation. Strictly speaking, there is no *national* unemployment compensation program. Rather, there exists a system of federal-State cooperation in which each State administers its own program under standards set by Congress and supervised by the USTES.

The heart of the unemployment compensation system is in its complex financing. Federal law imposes a payroll tax on most employers with four or more workers.[3] The tax, 3.1 percent in 1970, is laid on the first $3000 of annual wages paid to employees.[4] The proceeds from the payroll tax are credited to each State's account in the Unemployment Compensation Trust Fund maintained in the United States Treasury. Actual unemployment payments are made by the States from this fund and from whatever additional funds they themselves make available for the purpose. The benefits and the number of weeks that unemployed workers will be paid vary widely among the States; the average now is about $45 a week for twenty-six weeks.

If a State's program meets the minimum federal standards, the National Government grants to the State the money necessary to pay the administrative costs of running its program. If a State's program fails to meet the minimum federal standards, it not only is denied the administrative grant but it cannot draw from the Trust Fund, either. Among the standards that must be met are the requirements that States

---

[3] Every State's law exempts some employers and their employees from coverage. Agricultural workers, domestic servants, and public employees are commonly excluded. In 1938 Congress established a separate program of unemployment compensation, health insurance, and retirement benefits for railroad workers. It is financed by a payroll tax and is administered by the independent Railroad Retirement Board. Congress enacted an unemployment compensation law for federal workers in 1954.

[4] No State *must* maintain an unemployment compensation program. However, the 1935 law provided that any State tax an employer must pay to support such a program may be deducted from his federal tax — up to a maximum today of 2.7 points of the present 3.1 per cent federal levy; hence an employer's federal tax may be reduced to as low as .4 per cent, depending on how much his State levies. This offset feature prompted each State to set up its own program.

During the Great Depression when very few jobs were available, some of the unemployed turned to selling apples on street corners to support themselves and their families. (Wide World Photos)

make benefit payments promptly, that all payments be made through a public employment service which has been approved by the Secretary of Labor, that workers have the right to an impartial hearing if their benefit applications are denied, and that no worker loses his benefits for refusing to take another but unsuitable job.

State Employment Services. In 1935 Congress provided for grants-in-aid to any State which would establish an employment service, match the federal funds with money of its own, and operate the service in accord with the minimum federal standards. Each State promptly did so.

These employment services provide help to both employers and workers. Offices are maintained in the large and middle-sized communities in each State, and employment agents visit the smaller towns regularly. In addition to bringing jobs and job-seekers together, the employment offices also function as a part of each State's unemployment compensation program. All benefit applications and payments are made through them.

Unemployment compensation is *not* designed to take care of the sick, the disabled, or the aged. It is intended for those who are willing and able to work but who are involuntarily unemployed. An idle worker who refuses to take a suitable job when it is offered through a State employment office may lose his right to further compensation.

Manpower Programs. Through nearly all of our history we have enjoyed a general and steadily rising level of prosperity. Those relatively brief times in which this happy condition has not been fact have been few and far between; and the most recent and serious of these periods of economic hardship, the Depression of the 1930's, is now more than a quarter of a century behind us.

But, despite this general well-being, there are disturbing and continuing pockets of economic distress. Prosperity has not been spread evenly across the country or among all of our people. There are many communities and regions in which heavy and persistent unemployment is well known. For example, the migration of New England textile mills to the South has left behind a labor force which has not been absorbed by other local industries, and the lag in coal mining in various sections of West Virginia, Kentucky, and Pennsylvania has thrown thousands of men out of work.

The Kennedy and Johnson Administrations pushed for a broad attack on unemployment in these and other areas. Congress responded with the passage of four major statutes: the Area Redevelopment Act of 1961, the Manpower Development and Training Act of 1962, the Public Works and Economic Development Act of 1965, and the Economic Opportunity (Anti-Poverty) Act of 1964.

The Economic Development Administration (page 463) and the United States Training and Employment Service play the major roles under the first three of these laws. On the basis of data from the USTES, the EDA designates those areas in which heavy, chronic unemployment exists as "redevelopment areas" eligible for aid.

The aid provided takes two chief forms: (1) *loans,* made to State and local agencies and private firms, especially to encourage industries to open new job-producing facilities, and (2) *grants* to States to finance basic education programs for jobless illiterates and retraining programs for other unemployed workers, and to provide them with allowances (instead of unemployment compensation) while they are in training.

The Economic Opportunity Act is administered in large part by the Office of Economic Opportunity. See pages 308, 514–516.

The USTES also administers a number of programs specially aimed at providing youths and adults with work-experience, training, and income. Its most notable effort is the Neighborhood Youth Corps — an attempt to help young people from low-income families to remain in school, and "drop-outs" to return, by providing them with income through on-the-job training. Most NYC jobs are in such fields as public health, food service, and recreation. Another of its programs, Operation Mainstream, seeks permanent jobs at decent wages for adults with a history of chronic unemployment; it seeks these jobs in such community betterment fields as wildlife protection and park improvement.

The Bureau of Apprenticeship and Training. The Manpower Administration is also charged with promoting standards of apprenticeship in the training of skilled workers. Through its Bureau of Apprenticeship and Training it works with State labor agencies and vocational education groups to bring labor and management together in the acceptance of apprenticeship standards for a variety of trades.

THE LABOR–MANAGEMENT SERVICES ADMINISTRATION

The Assistant Secretary for Labor-Management is charged with responsibility for the Department's labor-management relations activities. He performs his duties in this area as the Administrator of the Labor-Management Services Administration.

The Labor-Management Services Administration. Several offices, each headed by a Director, constitute the Labor-Management Services Administration.

The Office of Labor-Management and Welfare Pension Reports. The Welfare and Pension Plans Disclosure Act of 1958 requires full public access to the terms and functioning of the many "fringe benefits" funds maintained under various labor-management contracts. The Act also directs the Secretary of Labor to police the administration of these funds. He does so through this Office, which also administers the provisions of the Labor-Management Reporting and Disclosure (Landrum-Griffin) Act of 1959. See page 479.

The Office of Labor-Management Relations Services. This Office is essentially an advisory and clearinghouse agency to aid employers and unions to meet the many-faceted problems involved in labor-management relations.

The Office of Labor-Management Policy Development. This Office serves as the Labor-Management Services Administration's chief research arm in the broad field of labor-management relations.

The Office of Veterans Reemployment Rights. Several statutes, dating back to the Selective Service Act of 1940, guarantee that draftees and others entering the Armed Forces have a later right to return to the jobs they held before entering the service. These statutes are administered by the Office of Veterans Reemployment Rights in close cooperation with the Defense Department, the Veterans Administration, and, when necessary, the Department of Justice.

LABOR–MANAGEMENT RELATIONS

The Development of Labor Unions. In our early history the nation's economy was a relatively simple one in which most persons worked for themselves. Those who did work for others usually bargained with their employers on an individual basis. That is, the details of the labor contract—wages, hours, and working conditions—were settled by an employer and an employee as a personal, face-to-face matter between two persons well known to one another.

The coming of the industrial revolution, with the factory system and mass production, wrought a drastic change in the employer-employee relationship. Especially in the years following the Civil War, the small shop gave way to the huge corporation. Where the demand had once been for the services of "Tom Smith, skilled mechanic" it became a demand for "fifty precision machinists." To meet the growing power of corporate industry labor began to develop organizations of its own to protect the workingman.

The history of union organization goes back almost to the days of the Revolution. Before 1800 mechanics and artisans in a few of the larger cities had joined together to form unions. The industrialization of the 1830's spurred local union growth, but unionization gained real momentum only in the latter three decades of the 19th century.

The Knights of Labor. A number of attempts were made to combine various local unions into national groups in the 1850's and 1860's. The Knights of Labor, formed in 1869, was the most successful of the early national unions. The Knights sought to organize men and women of every craft, creed, and color, and it included both skilled and unskilled workers. By 1886 the organization reached a peak of some 700,000 members. It advocated such policies as the prohibition of child labor, progressive income and inheritance taxes, and equal pay for men and women.

The Knights began to fade in 1886 for a number of reasons. Several disastrous and unsuccessful strikes discouraged many members. The union contained locals and individual members with widely differing views and was often torn by internal strife. The bloody Haymarket Riot in Chicago in 1886 produced splits within the union that threatened to destroy it completely. Several large unions, especially the Railroad Brotherhoods, refused to join the Knights of Labor. By 1917 the union had dissolved.

The American Federation of Labor. In 1881 a group of union officials, socialists, and dissatisfied members of the Knights of Labor formed the Federation of Organized Trades and Labor Unions. It was organized as a union of skilled workers in particular crafts. The Federation and the Knights became intense rivals, and in 1886 the Federation called upon all unions not members of the Knights of Labor to join together for protection against the Knights. Thus, in 1886, the American Federation of Labor (AFL) was born out of the Federation of Organized Trades and Labor Unions. This new organization soon led the field.

The AFL was formed as a federation of *craft unions.* A craft union is one which is composed only of those workers who possess the *same* craft or skill—for example, a plumbers union, a carpenters union, or an electricians union.

The Congress of Industrial Organizations. The development of mass production industries in the United States created a large class of industrial workers not skilled in any particular craft. Many of these workers are organized into *industrial unions.* An industrial union is one which includes *all* workers, skilled or unskilled, in a single major industry—for example, the United Auto Workers and the United Steel Workers.

The AFL, with its traditional craft-union organization, found it difficult to organize workers in the new mass-production industries. A majority of the craft unions opposed the admission of unions composed of unskilled workers into the AFL. Finally, after a long and bitter fight over craft versus industrial unionism, a group led by John L. Lewis was expelled from the AFL. In 1938 Lewis and his followers established the Congress of Industrial Organizations – the CIO.

The Merger of the AFL and the CIO. After nearly two decades of existence as separate and rival national unions, the AFL and the CIO combined into one huge labor organization in 1955. The huge new group took the name *American Federation of Labor and Congress of Industrial Organizations* – and is commonly referred to as the AFL–CIO. It chose as its first president George Meany, the former head of the AFL, and he remains in that post today (1970).

The AFL–CIO holds a national convention to shape its policies every two years. It is governed in the period between conventions by an executive council composed of nineteen leaders from the former AFL unions and ten from the old CIO. The combined organization is now (1970) made up of 122 different affiliated unions.

Union Membership Today. The Labor Department reports that some 19,100,000 workers now belong to American labor unions.[5] The AFL–CIO has a membership of about 13,600,000. Several million other workers belong to various independent unions – that is, to unions not affiliated with the AFL–CIO.

The largest of the independents are the International Brotherhood of Teamsters (expelled by the AFL–CIO in 1957), 1,800,000 members; the United Auto Workers (who withdrew from the AFL–CIO in 1968), 1,600,000 members; the United Mine Workers, 450,000 members; and the United Electrical, Radio, and Machine Workers, 165,000 members. By 1970 there were more than 80,000,000 employable persons in the United States. Thus,

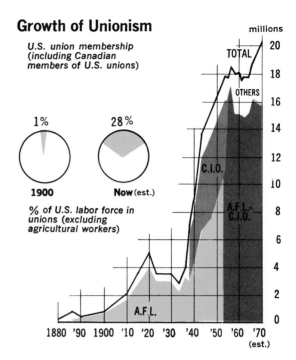

Growth of Unionism

U.S. union membership (including Canadian members of U.S. unions)

1900 Now (est.)

% of U.S. labor force in unions (excluding agricultural workers)

Source: Department of Labor

---

[5] Including more than 1,000,000 who work outside the United States, most of them in Canada.

only about one fourth of our total national labor force is actually unionized today.

Government Regulation of Labor-Management Relations. Government has an obvious interest and obligation in the maintaining of industrial peace. A dispute between a small employer and one or two of his employees over wages, hours, and other conditions of employment is quite important to the parties directly involved. The results of such a dispute may have widespread consequences, but they seldom do; still, the rights of each party must be protected. A labor dispute which involves a large employer and hundreds or thousands of employees can and frequently does have a tremendous effect upon the health or the safety of the entire nation.

Collective Bargaining. Collective bargaining is the process of negotiation between an employer and his organized employees (that is, employees as a group rather than individually) to determine the terms of a labor contract. It is the cornerstone upon which the present-day system of labor-management relations in the United States is laid. It takes place when representatives of management and labor sit down to work out an agreement which sets forth the wages, hours, and other conditions under which workers are to be employed.

Collective bargaining is a two-way street. Management makes its proposals for a contract to govern employment. Labor makes its proposals, too. The two sides then bargain (discuss and compromise) with one another in order to reach an agreement satisfactory to each side.

Early Governmental Regulation. The right of workers to organize and bargain collectively is now recognized by all States and the National Government. In their early days, however, unions were commonly regarded with suspicion and disfavor. The common law, inherited from England, held combinations of workers to be criminal conspiracies. Unions were never declared to be illegal as such, but organized efforts to gain higher wages or better working conditions were often prosecuted as conspiracies.

The Supreme Court of Massachusetts pioneered the change in governmental attitude in 1842 when it expressly recognized the legality of unions and upheld their right to strike. Through the latter part of the nineteenth century and into the early decades of this one, government tolerated rather than encouraged and protected union organization. Being legal, unions were permitted to pursue their objectives, but only through what were then regarded as "lawful" means.

An employer was generally free to oppose unions, and the law paid little attention to his methods. "Yellow-dog" contracts were common. These were contracts in which, as a condition of his employment, a worker agreed not to join a union. Company police and labor spies were used, and many workers who favored unions were "black-listed." As a last resort, company unions were formed to stall the growth of legitimate labor unions. Injunc-

tions [6] were used frequently to break strikes, and in the early years of this century courts often held union attempts to enforce labor contracts to be violations of the Sherman Anti-Trust Act (page 277).

Unions continued to grow despite the many obstacles raised against them. As they grew in number so did their political power through the votes of their members. By 1900 labor's political strength had become a force to be reckoned with in the halls of Congress. In the Clayton Act (page 278) of 1914 unions were specifically exempted from the provisions of antitrust laws. Other legislation designed to protect the workingman and promote his interests in such matters as wages, hours, and working conditions began to appear on federal and State statute books.

The depression which began in 1929 brought widespread unemployment and other hardship. It also produced a wave of new legislation favorable to labor, especially after the inauguration of the New Deal in 1933. Three statutes enacted by Congress in the 1930's—the Norris-LaGuardia (Anti-Injunction) Act of 1932, the Wagner (National Labor Relations) Act of 1935, and the Fair Labor Standards Act of 1938—are often referred to as "labor's bill of rights." These laws made collective bargaining a standard feature of labor-management relations, placed a number of restrictions on management, and otherwise strengthened the hand of organized labor.

The Taft-Hartley (Labor-Management Relations) Act of 1947 was passed by Congress later to provide a fairer balance between labor and management in the bargaining relationship.

Four particular statutes form the base of national regulation of labor-management relations today: the Norris-LaGuardia Act of 1932, the Wagner Act of 1935, the Taft-Hartley Act

---

[6] An *injunction* is a court order that prevents (enjoins) one from performing some act which would injure the personal or property rights of another.

of 1947, and the Landrum-Griffin (Labor-Management Reporting and Disclosure) Act of 1959.

The Norris-LaGuardia Act of 1932. The Norris-LaGuardia Act severely restricts the power of federal courts to issue injunctions in labor disputes. Before an injunction may be issued it must be shown that every reasonable effort has been made to settle the dispute peacefully, that specific unlawful actions have been threatened, and that local police officers have not furnished needed protection. The Act also provides that no one may be prevented from joining a union, striking or urging others to strike, or engaging in other normal union activities.

The Wagner Act of 1935. The Wagner Act expressly recognizes the right of workers to organize and to bargain collectively. Employers in any industry engaged in interstate commerce are required to bargain with those unions favored by a majority of their employees. Such employers are also prohibited from committing certain "unfair labor practices."

The Act created the *National Labor Relations Board* (NLRB) to administer its provisions.[7] The NLRB was given two broad functions: (1) to conduct elections among employees to determine which, if any, union they favored as their bargaining agent, and (2) to enforce the unfair labor practices provisions of the law.

The unfair labor practices listed in the Wagner Act are quite broad. Employers are especially forbidden: (1) to refuse to bargain collectively with recognized unions, (2) to interfere in union organization, (3) to exert undue influence or pressure on any employee with regard to union membership or activity, and (4) to discharge or otherwise punish an employee for union membership or activity. The

---

[7] The NLRB is an independent regulatory commission (see pages 530–531). It is composed of five members appointed by the President and Senate for five-year terms.

Act contained no similar list of restrictions on workers or unions.

The Wagner Act was the subject of intense criticism from the moment of its passage. Most of its critics accepted the law's insistence upon the principle of collective bargaining; but they criticized it on grounds that unions and union leaders were granted great power without being made responsible for the manner of its exercise. Put another way, critics objected to the fact that the law contained no list of unfair labor practices unions could not commit. As specific examples, they objected to the law's failure to prohibit unions from preventing the use of labor-saving machines or from insisting upon "featherbedding." Featherbedding —which is still fairly widespread—is the practice of forcing an employer to hire a worker he does not in fact need.

The Taft-Hartley Act of 1947. The Taft-Hartley Act was passed by Congress to meet the criticisms of the Wagner Act—or, as its proponents described it, to "redress the balance between labor and management." Its provisions are in the form of a series of amendments to the Wagner Act.

The Taft-Hartley Act increased the size of the original NLRB from three to five members and added to it a general counsel—an officer whose function it is to prosecute cases involving alleged unfair labor practices before the Board. The unfair labor practices listed in the Wagner Act were expanded to include restrictions on the activities of labor unions. Like employers, unions may not refuse to bargain collectively, and they are forbidden to coerce an employee or force an employer to coerce an employee to support union policies or activities.

Unions may not charge excessive or discriminatory fees or attempt to force an employer to accept featherbedding. "Secondary boycotts" are prohibited; that is, unions are forbidden to strike against one employer in order to force him not to do business with another employer who is involved in a labor dispute. Also, unions may not strike to force an em-

"THE KICKING MACHINE" Oftentimes when labor and management quarrel and a strike results, the general public suffers the most. The public is always a "silent party" at the labor-management bargaining table. (Cartoon by Hesse, St. Louis Globe-Democrat; photo by Leo Choplin, Black Star)

ployer to deal with one union when the NLRB has certified another as the employees' bargaining agent. Strikes against the National Government are absolutely forbidden.

Unions and union leaders are legally responsible and may be sued for damages which result from unfair labor practices.

Union leaders must make periodic reports of union finances to the union members and to the Secretary of Labor. They must file sworn statements with the NLRB that they are not affiliated with the Communist Party or any other group that advocates the violent overthrow of government in the United States.

Failure to file either the financial reports or the noncommunist affidavits bars a union from using the NLRB to advance its interests or protect its rights under the law.

The Act outlaws the *closed shop* in any industry in interstate commerce. It permits a *union shop* in such industries only: (1) where a majority of the workers agree to its establishment and (2) in those States where State law does not forbid it.[8] No union may refuse to admit a worker to membership nor may it expel a member except for nonpayment of union dues.

The Taft-Hartley Act also created the *Federal Mediation and Conciliation Service,* an indepen-

---

[8] A *closed shop* is one in which, as a condition of the labor contract, union membership is a prerequisite to employment—one in which, then, only union members may be hired. A *union shop* is one in which employees must join the union within a short time after being hired. Several of the States now have so-called "right-to-work" laws which ban *both* the closed and the union shops; they provide only for the *open shop*—in which a worker may join a union or not, as he sees fit.

dent executive agency which works to promote labor-management agreement. In effect, it seeks to prevent strikes or, when they occur, to facilitate settlements. When a labor contract expires, or when a union wishes to change the terms of an existing one, the law prohibits the calling of a strike except with sixty days' notice. This "cooling-off period" is designed to allow time for continued bargaining. If a strike which endangers the national health or safety is called, the President, acting through the Attorney General, may seek an eighty-day injunction to halt the walkout. This additional "cooling-off period" allows time for further negotiation — and for congressional action if that becomes necessary in some critical situation.

No union may contribute funds to *any* campaign for *any federal* office. Of course, any individual union member may make a political contribution if he chooses to do so and unions may — and do — maintain political action groups to support candidates sympathetic to the views of organized labor. Among such groups, the most potent today is the AFL–CIO's Committee on Political Education (COPE). See page 138.

The Landrum-Griffin Act of 1959. The Landrum-Griffin Act was passed following a three-year investigation by a special Senate Rackets Committee. Its investigation disclosed a shocking record of corruption on the part of a few union leaders — including the misuse (even theft) of union funds, associations with known racketeers, fraud in union elections, perjury, bribery, extortion, falsification of union and tax records, and the use of threats and violence to silence members who dared to challenge the actions of union officials.

The Act was passed to protect union members and the general public against such abuses. It is lengthy and quite detailed but its formal title — the Labor-Management Reporting and Disclosure Act — indicates its chief purpose: to make union records and proceedings public.

The statute strengthens many sections of the Taft-Hartley Act. For example, it broadens the definition and coverage of the ban on secondary boycotts. It forbids "hot-cargo contracts," in which an employer agrees that he will not do business with a firm labeled as unfair by a union.

Anyone convicted of a felony is banned from holding a union office for at least five years after his conviction or imprisonment. Misuse of union funds and similar practices are federal crimes, and stiff penalties are provided for violations. Detailed annual reports of union finances and other activities and copies of all labor-management contracts must be filed with the Secretary of Labor (page 473).

This labor reform law also contains a "bill of rights" for union members. These provisions guarantee to members the right: to participate freely and to ballot secretly in union meetings; to nominate and vote for union officials; and to have access to all financial and other union records and contracts. Union members also may sue their union officers to prevent a violation of members' rights, a misuse of union funds, or a refusal of access by the members to union records.

✶✶✶✶✶✶✶✶✶✶✶✶ CONCEPT BUILDING *✶✶✶✶✶✶✶✶✶✶✶✶*

Key Concepts

The Department of Labor was created as a separate Cabinet department in 1913. It is charged with the responsibility of promoting the welfare, working conditions, and employment opportunities of the nation's wage earners. The principal agencies within it today are the Bureau of International Labor Affairs, the Bureau of Labor Statistics, the Wage and Labor Standards Administration, the Manpower Administration, and the Labor-Management Services Administration.

The Bureau of International Labor Affairs is concerned with the international aspects of labor problems. The Bureau of Labor Statistics is one of the Government's principal fact-finding and reporting agencies and is a veritable mine of information on the economy. The Wage and Labor Standards Administration's principal work involves enforcement of the minimum-wage, maximum-hours laws. The Manpower Administration and its sub-agencies aid the States with their unemployment compensation programs and employment services. The Labor-Management Services Administration has charge of the Department's activities in the broad field of labor-management relations.

Labor unions existed in the United States before 1800, but their real growth began with the industrial revolution. About 19,100,000 workers today belong to organized labor unions. The combined AFL–CIO has about 13,600,000 members while several million belong to independent unions. Thus, only about one-fourth of the more than 80,000,000 employable persons belong to unions today.

Despite early opposition, unions grew, and as they did they gained political power through the votes of their members. Four particular acts form the base of federal regulation of labor-management relations today: the Norris-LaGuardia (Anti-Injunction) Act of 1932, the Wagner (National Labor Relations) Act of 1935, the Taft-Hartley (Labor-Management Relations) Act of 1947, and the Landrum-Griffin (Labor-Management Reporting and Disclosure) Act of 1959 which was passed to combat abuses by some labor leaders.

Important Terms

closed shop	featherbedding	open shop	unemployment com-
collective bargaining	industrial union	price index	pensation
craft union	injunction	"right-to-work" laws	union shop
	minimum wage	"time-and-a-half"	

Questions for Inquiry and Review

1. When was the Department of Labor established?

2. What is its basic function?

3. What agency is especially concerned with labor matters as they affect our foreign relations?

4. What is the basic nature or function of the Bureau of Labor Statistics?

5. What was the basic purpose of the Fair Labor Standards Act of 1938? What agency is primarily responsible for its enforcement?

6. What is the minimum wage now provided by federal law?

7. What is the principal work of the Bureau of Labor Standards?

8. What is misleading about the phrase, "a national unemployment compensation program"?

9. What effect did the coming of the industrial revolution have upon the nature of labor-management relations?

10. Which labor organization was the most

successful of the early attempts to form a national labor union?

11. What is the major national labor union in the country today?

12. Approximately how many workers belong to labor unions in the United States today?

Approximately what proportion of the national labor force belongs to unions today?

13. What is an independent union?

14. What federal laws form the base of regulation of labor-management relations today?

For Further Inquiry

1. The American labor system is often described as a "free contract labor system." How would you define this phrase? What practical examples of its operation can you provide?

2. Would you favor or oppose eliminating the present federal-State unemployment compensation program and its replacement with a purely federal arrangement? Why?

3. How would you express in your own words the following comment by Abraham Lincoln? Do you agree with all that it says? "Property is the fruit of labor; property is desirable, is a positive good in the world.

That some should be rich shows that others may become rich, and hence is just encouragement to industry and enterprise. Let not him who is houseless pull down the house of another, but let him work diligently and build one for himself, thus, by example assuring that his own house shall be safe from violence when built."

4. What are the constitutional bases for federal action in the field of labor-management relations? Do you think that this is a proper and legitimate area of concern for the National Government?

Suggested Activities

1. Prepare as extensive a list as you can of examples of the activities of the various agencies of the Department of Labor in your locale.

2. Invite a local labor union officer to address the class on the subject of his union, its membership, organization, history, and policies.

3. Invite a State or federal labor official to address the class on the work of his bureau or agency.

4. Stage a debate or class forum on the question: *Resolved,* That this State should adopt a (or repeal its) "right-to-work" law.

Suggested Reading

BUNZEL, JOHN H., *Issues of American Public Policy.* Prentice-Hall, 1968. Chapter 7.

BURNS, JAMES M. and PELTASON, J. W., *Government By the People.* Prentice-Hall, 1969. Chapter 24.

PELTASON, J. W. and BURNS, JAMES M., *Functions and Policies of American Government.* Prentice-Hall, 1967. Chapter 8.

"Pro & Con: Should the Federal Government Guarantee a Minimum Annual Income to all Citizens?" *Congressional Digest,* October 1967.

RASKIN, A. H., "A Kind of Economic Holy War," *New York Times Magazine,* February 18, 1968.

SANDERS, MARION K., "James Houghton Wants 500,000 More Jobs," *New York Times Magazine,* September 14, 1969.

SCHULTZ, SECRETARY GEORGE P., "Wages . . . Prices . . . Strikes — A New Approach," *U.S. News,* June 2, 1969.

"Some Plain Talk from George Meany," *U.S. News,* September 8, 1969.

"Working Wives: Revolution in American Family Life," *U.S. News,* November 17, 1969.

27
THE DEPARTMENT OF HEALTH, EDUCATION, AND WELFARE

✦✦✦ Why do we recognize a public responsibility for social welfare?

✦✦✦ To whom are the programs administered by HEW most beneficial?

✦✦✦ Should the conduct and finance of social welfare programs be a primary responsibility of the States or of the National Government?

✦✦✦ Which is the more important goal for public policy: a sound economy or a decent standard of living for all persons?

The productivity of our heads, our hands, and our hearts is the source of all the strength we can command.

DWIGHT D. EISENHOWER

Most Americans today would agree to this definition of a nearly perfect society: one in which all persons were properly fed, adequately clothed, and comfortably sheltered, in which the health and the safety of all were properly protected, and in which all were afforded the opportunity for a good education, the chance to earn a decent living, and reasonable prospects for security in old age. There is not now, nor has there ever existed, such a society. But we in the United States have come closer to the goal of creating such an environment than have any other people on earth.

Today nearly all Americans would also agree to this proposition: that it is a proper function of government to help in the march toward the goal of such a society. Through the years we have come to accept both the need for and the desirability of governmental responsibility for social welfare.

In earlier days, the States and especially their local governments—and even before them, the colonies—did make some provision

for the unfortunates in society. The "relief" they provided was quite limited, however; mostly, it came in such forms as county poor farms, almshouses, and orphanages.

By and large, the problems of the poor, the sick, and the aged, of the blind, the crippled, and the feebleminded were looked upon as private matters—as essentially the responsibility of the family and the church. Sanitation, disease prevention, education, and similar problems were viewed in much the same light.

Of course, the picture is a radically different one today. Now the States and the National Government spend literally billions of dollars each year on a wide range of social welfare programs. Over the past three decades or so— since the Depression of the 1930's—what amounts, in effect, to a "national welfare system" has been created. Because it has been built into the federal system—that is, it is based upon a complex mixture of national, State, and local governmental activity—it may also be said that the field of social welfare has become the common responsibility of all levels of government in the United States.[1] But it seems most accurate to emphasize its *national* character. It is conducted largely under the leadership of the National Government, in accord with standards set at the national level, and, in large part, at national expense.

DEPARTMENTAL ORGANIZATION

The Department of Health, Education, and Welfare (HEW) was created by Congress in 1953. Today it administers most of the major social welfare programs conducted by the National Government.

The Department is headed by the *Secretary of Health, Education, and Welfare.* Like each of his fellow Cabinet members, he is appointed by the President and must be confirmed by the Senate. With the assistance of his chief aide, the Under Secretary, he supervises the many and wide-ranging activities of HEW and its more than 100,000 employees. His top-level staff today also includes seven Assistant Secretaries — for Community and Field Services, Education, Health and Scientific Affairs, Legislation, Planning and Evaluation, and Administration — and a Comptroller who assists the Secretary in all fiscal matters.

Principal Agencies. The major agencies around which the Department is built today are the:

> Social Security Administration
> Social and Rehabilitation Service
> Public Health Service
> Office of Education

In addition to these and a few other agencies

Recognizing the fact that tomorrow's leadership is the youth of today, the Federal Government has increased its participation in education through more extensive grant-in-aid programs. (Learning Through Seeing, Inc.)

we shall consider, three private corporations are supported in part by federal funds and supervised to a limited extent by the Secretary of Health, Education, and Welfare:

Howard University, in Washington, D.C., was established in 1867 as an institution of higher education for Negroes. Today it offers a full-fledged university program for students without regard to race, color, creed, or national origin; but, as its president puts it, it still "discharges a special responsibility for the admission and training of Negro students." It is supported by congressional appropriations and also by the funds it receives from private persons and foundations.

Gallaudet College, also in the nation's capital, was first established in 1857. It remains today the world's only institution offering higher education for the deaf. Its declared purpose would do credit to any of the nation's institutions of higher education: "To produce men and women who have the power of sound judg-

---

[1] The point here — the existence today of a *federalized* welfare system — is demonstrated several times in this chapter, but we have encountered it before; see, for example the discussion of grants-in-aid on pages 71-72 and unemployment compensation on pages 471-473.

ment, and who are well informed about the world around them, about their civilization and its achievements, and about themselves as human beings."

The American Printing House for the Blind in Louisville, Kentucky, distributes Braille books, talking books, and other devices without cost to public institutions for the education of the blind pursuant to a federal act of 1879.

THE SOCIAL SECURITY ADMINISTRATION

The passage of the Social Security Act of 1935 highlighted the massive entry of the National Government into the welfare field in the 1930's. The Depression threw millions of persons out of work and millions more were impoverished. In 1929 there were some

Blind persons read books printed in Braille by passing their fingers over a series of raised dots on the pages. (American Printing House for the Blind)

2,000,000 unemployed workers in this country. By 1933 the figure had leaped to 13,500,000. In 1935 there were 18,000,000 persons, including children and aged, who were wholly dependent upon emergency public relief programs; some 10,000,000 workers had no employment other than on relief projects.

Only a handful of States had made any provision to meet such a crisis, and even these were utterly swamped. Poverty and need had become nationwide problems overnight.

The inauguration of Franklin D. Roosevelt as President in 1933 began the New Deal era. Almost at once Congress established temporary programs and appropriated billions of dollars for direct relief and for public works projects intended to stimulate employment. These early steps to combat the nation's ills were stopgap in nature, however; they were designed to meet the immediate situation. What was clearly needed was a permanent, long-range program to help the country to right itself and help prevent such disasters in the future.

The Social Security Act was among the most important of the steps taken in that direction. The Act, which has been amended scores of times since 1935, created a number of different welfare programs, including the unemployment compensation system (pages 471–473) and aid for the needy aged and several other groups (to which we shall turn next.) At its heart, however, the law created the Old-Age and Survivors Insurance plan (OASI) – or, as it has been popularly known since its beginnings, "social security."

The original OASI program has since been expanded several times. Today, it is the Old-Age, Survivors, and Disability Insurance program (OASDI) – and, since 1966, a health care insurance program ("medicare"), as well.

Both the OASDI and medicare programs are administered by the Social Security Administration. It is headed by a Commissioner appointed by the President with the approval of the Senate. The bulk of the Administration's large force of examiners, actuarial experts, economists, lawyers, and clerical and other personnel work in the agency's huge headquarters in Baltimore; but several thousand are stationed at its more than 600 offices scattered throughout the country.

OASDI. OASDI is a long-range, contributory insurance plan to provide a minimum income to those persons who are covered by the program when they (1) retire or (2) become permanently disabled. It also provides benefits for the dependents of a retired or disabled worker and for the dependents (survivors) of a worker who dies before or after reaching retirement. In short, it is a program under which individuals contribute during their working years to create a fund for their own protection and for that of their families and their survivors.

Coverage. All employed persons in the United States, except those few whom the law specifically exempts, are covered by the program.[2] Today (1970) over 78,000,000 persons made OASDI contributions, and benefits are paid to more than 25,000,000 others (including over 20,000,000 retired or disabled workers and their dependents and some 5,000,000 survivors.)

Financing. OASDI is financed by taxes levied on employers, employees, and the self-employed. A major portion of the medicare program (the basic plan) is paid for in the same manner.

To finance *both* programs, employees now (1970) pay a tax of 4.8 per cent on the first $7800 of their annual salary or wages (or a maximum tax of $374.40 a year). Employers pay a like tax—that is, an amount equal to that paid by each of their employees. The taxes levied on both employees and employers are "payroll taxes" and are actually collected from the employers. Self-employed persons now pay a 6.9 per cent tax on all of their income

up to $7800 a year (or a maximum annual tax of $538.20).[3]

The OASDI-medicare tax on employees and employers is scheduled to increase to 5.2 per cent in 1971, 5.65 per cent in 1973, and eventually reach 5.9 per cent in 1987; the self-employed tax is slated to rise concurrently, to 7.9 per cent in 1987.

The Treasury Department collects all social security taxes. The tax monies actually go into the general treasury, and Congress appropriates annual sums to the Old-Age and Survivors and Disability Insurance Trust Funds to cover the collections. All benefits are paid out of the money in these Funds—now more than $34,-000,000,000 that may be invested but only in interest-bearing bonds issued or guaranteed by the Government.

Benefits. Monthly OASDI benefits are paid to those insured under the system who reach retirement age, to those who are permanently disabled before retirement, to their spouses, and to the survivors (widows or widowers, minor children, and dependent parents) of those insured persons who die.

The *usual* retirement age is sixty-five. An insured person *may* retire as early as age sixty-two if he or she chooses, but then his or her monthly benefits are less than if retirement had come at age sixty-five. Of course, no one is *forced* to retire at *any* age. A person may work beyond sixty-five if he cares to; and he may retire when he wants to. If he does continue to work after sixty-five, however, his OASDI benefits are reduced in any year in which he earns more than $1680—but this restriction (reduction in benefits) does not apply to anyone over age seventy-two.

---

[2] Federal civilian employees covered by the civil service retirement system (page 564) are the only sizable group of workers now (1970) exempted.

[3] The employee-employer tax for OASDI (excluding the medicare levy) is 4.3 per cent of the first $7800 of an employee's salary or wages; the OASDI tax on the self-employed is 6.4 per cent of the first $7800. This distinction between the OASDI and the medicare tax rates is hardly meaningful, however; those liable for the one must also pay the other.

A very complicated formula, based upon one's average monthly earnings in covered employment, is used to determine his retirement benefits—and the benefits due to his dependents or his survivors. The monthly benefit paid to the wife or husband of a retired person equals one-half of the amount paid to that retired person; but the spouse must also have reached retirement age before he or she may receive it.

The following table may make this a bit clearer; it illustrates the benefits paid (as of January 1, 1970) to retired persons and to their eligible spouses:

	Monthly Benefits Paid at Age 65 to Retired Persons	
Average Monthly Earnings	Without Eligible Spouse	With Eligible Spouse
$ 67	$ 55.00	$ 82.50
150	88.40	132.60
250	115.00	172.50
350	140.40	210.60
450	165.00	247.50
550	189.90	284.90
650 or more	218.00	323.00

The widow of an insured person is paid a survivor's benefit, which now may run as high as $179.90 a month, beginning at age sixty-two. If she is left with one or more children under age eighteen, however, she may receive a pension of as much as $434.40 a month—paid without regard to her age. Smaller survivor benefits are also paid to the dependent parent or parents of a deceased person.

If an insured person becomes so disabled that he cannot work, he receives a monthly benefit equal to the amount that would have been due had he retired at sixty-five.

Medicare. What role should the National Government play in meeting the people's need for and the costs of adequate medical care? The question is one of grave and of continuing national concern. It is also a sharply controversial one, and has been for many years.

Adequate medical care is both necessary *and* expensive. The need is widespread. Nine out of every ten (more than 40,000,000) of the nation's families require some kind of medical care each year. One out of every eight persons in the country (or some 25,-000,000) becomes a patient in a general hospital during the same period.

The nation's total private medical bill—for physicians, dentists, hospitalization, medicines, and other medical goods and services—now amounts to nearly $40,000,000,000 a year. The average annual family medical bill is in excess of $300; at least 5,000,000 families face medical bills of more than $500 each year.

Concern prompted by these needs and costs —and by the state of the nation's health in general—has mounted steadily in recent years. Many—including individual doctors, medical societies, public agencies and officials, and other interested persons and groups—have worked to find means by which adequate medical care could be provided to all Americans on the basis of need. One of the major results of this concern has been the extensive growth of various *private* health insurance programs— that is, of programs for the voluntary pre-payment of at least a portion of the subscribers' medical bills. Some 165,000,000 persons in this country are now covered by such arrangements.[4]

---

[4] Among the many such programs, the *Blue Cross Hospital Plan* is by far the most popular. Under it, a subscriber pays a monthly fee. In return, the Blue Cross Hospital Service pays a member hospital a flat fee (the amount of which depends upon the subscriber's policy) toward the costs of hospitalization for him or a dependent for a certain number of days. Such special services as anesthetic and operating room fees are covered on a similar basis. Under the related *Blue Shield Plan,* Blue Cross members are usually able to cover a significant portion of their doctors' bills, as well.

Many people have long advocated the establishment of a national — that is, *public* — system of health insurance. Most who have urged such an arrangement have called for a *compulsory* pre-paid program tied into the existing social security system. President Truman offered such a plan to Congress as early as 1949. He proposed a program of hospitalization and medical care benefits to cover nearly all of the population; it would have been financed by a payroll tax much like that imposed to support OASDI.

Congress rejected the Truman proposal by a decisive margin in 1950. But, over the next several years, a continuing campaign was waged in behalf of a restricted version of it: a federal program of hospitalization and medical benefits for the elderly (those over age sixty-five) financed by increasing the existing OASDI taxes. This latter proposal — which came to be popularly known as "Medicare" — drew its chief support from organized labor and, in later years, from the Kennedy and then the Johnson Administrations. It was one of the chief issues in the presidential elections of 1960 and 1964.

Those in favor of some form of national health insurance have long argued that such a program is necessary to overcome the fact that many millions cannot afford adequate medical care today. They contend that a national program would reduce the per person cost of medical care and would also encourage the upgrading of existing care and medical facilities. They insist that the proposals for such a medical insurance program are not "radical" but simply an extension of the present and generally favored social security system.

The opposition to such proposals has been led especially by the American Medical Association. The AMA and other opponents have branded them as "socialized medicine" and have urged instead the expansion of such *private, voluntary* programs as Blue Cross. They claim that a federal program is unnecessary because the nation's health is generally good

and is improving steadily. They also argue that such a national health insurance program would require a huge and wasteful agency to administer it, would destroy the traditional and confidential doctor-patient relationship, and would lower the present high standards of medical care.

Congress capped years of debate by enacting the Medicare proposal as a part of a general expansion of the social security system in 1965. As it now operates, Medicare involves two broad programs of health care for most persons age sixty-five and older.

The Basic Plan. One of these programs — called the *basic plan* — provides for the coverage of at least the major portion of the costs of hospital, nursing home, and similar care for the nation's more than 19,000,000 elderly. It is financed by an increase in the compulsory taxes levied to support OASDI (page 485).

The details of the coverage afforded by the basic plan are quite complicated. In general outline, the plan covers: (1) up to sixty days of hospital care (for which the patient must pay the first $40 of costs involved), plus the costs above $10 per day for up to thirty additional days; a patient must have been out of the hospital for at least thirty days to be eligible for another period of this coverage, but he does have a "lifetime reserve" of ninety days of coverage that may be used in emergency situations; (2) twenty days of skilled nursing home or other convalescent unit care after a hospital stay of three days or longer; an additional eighty days are available if the patient will pay the first $5 for each additional day; and (3) the costs of up to 100 home visits by a nurse or therapist for the year after a hospital stay of at least three days.

The Supplementary Plan. The other program is a *voluntary* one. Those over 65 who wish to participate pay a flat monthly fee which is then matched by the Government. The fee was originally set at $3 a month but costs in the program forced the fee to $4 in 1968. Over 18,500,000 elderly persons are now covered.

Under the plan, the patient must pay the first $50 of his doctors' bills in a calendar year. Eighty per cent of nearly all of the additional bills are then paid by the program. The medical costs covered include: (1) treatments by physicians and surgeons, except for routine physical checkups; (2) up to 100 home health-care visits by nurses or therapists even if there was no prior hospitalization and (3) other services such as X-rays, surgical dressings, casts, and artificial limbs, regardless of whether they are rendered in a hospital, a doctor's office, at home, or elsewhere.

President Johnson hailed the passage of the Medicare program as a "landmark ... in the historic evolution of our social security system." Clearly, it ranks as one of the most comprehensive pieces of social legislation ever enacted by Congress. Note, however, that its terms apply to less than ten per cent of the nation's population. The evidence of the need for more and, especially, for easier-to-afford medical care for the rest of the population seems overwhelming. How to meet *this* need will almost certainly be one of the most hotly contested of public issue questions in the years ahead. No matter what solution is eventually reached, all sides to the controversy are agreed that individual initiative within the medical profession is vital and *must* be preserved.

THE SOCIAL AND REHABILITATION SERVICE

The Social and Rehabilitation Service was established in 1967 as the successor to several older federal welfare agencies. It is headed by an Administrator appointed by the President and Senate and administers most of HEW's programs designed to aid needy persons and families. Nearly all of these welfare programs involve grants-in-aid to the States—with the States receiving federal monies to finance substantial portions of programs which they oper-

ate in accord with federal standards. Thus, the Social and Rehabilitation Service's primary role is that of promoting and supervising activities which the States themselves have established and which they conduct. It performs this role through five sub-agencies:

The Assistance Payments Administration. The Assistance Payments Administration administers several grant-in-aid programs under the Social Security Act to help the State provide assistance to: the needy aged, the blind, families with dependent children, and the permanently and totally disabled.

The various groups of needy involved in these programs are not covered under the OASDI arrangement. For example, there are today some 2,000,000 needy aged who during their working years never qualified for OASDI benefits. For them, the Assistance Payments Administration directs the Old-Age Assistance program—under which the States receive grants to help these indigent persons.[5]

Under the involved formula by which the States receive grants to aid each of these needy groups, the more of its own funds a State uses for them the greater will be the amount of the federal contribution to the State's effort.

The Medical Services Administration. When Congress amended the Social Security

---

[5] Note here the contrast with the OASDI program—in which retired persons receive benefits based upon the contributions they made during their working years. In 1966 Congress attempted to insure that at least most of the elderly not eligible for OASDI benefits would receive at least some public assistance. It provided for direct monthly payments to such persons age seventy-two or older. Such single persons receive $35 a month and married couples one-and-a-half times that sum, or $52.50; but the amount of any such payment is reduced by whatever amount a person receives under any other federal pension program—for example, a veteran's or civil service pension.

Act to provide for Medicare in 1965, it also established another health care program— *Medicaid,* which is now administered by the Medical Services Administration.

Medicaid is a program under which federal grants go to the States to help them help to pay the medical costs of two general groups: (1) Those disadvantaged persons just noted— the needy aged, families with dependent children, the blind, and the permanently and totally disabled, and (2) Persons whom the law calls "medically indigent"—those able to feed, clothe, and house themselves and their families but unable to meet even routine medical bills, let alone the costs of a major illness.

Medicaid grew out of a limited program begun by the Kerr-Mills Act of 1960—in which Congress made grants available to the States to encourage them to help their needy aged to meet their medical costs. The broadening of the Kerr-Mills program in 1965 produced Medicaid, and now (1970) more than 10,000,-000 persons are benefiting from it.[6]

The Children's Bureau. The Children's Bureau was originally established within the old Department of Commerce and Labor in 1912. It manages nearly all of the federal programs especially related to the health and well-being of children. To this end, it cooperates with other federal agencies—for example, the Bureau of Indian Affairs in the Interior Department and the Wage and Hour and Public Contracts Divisions in the Labor Department—and with many State and local agencies and private groups.

The Bureau is a clearinghouse for research and information on child life. Its booklet *Infant Care* has long been the bestseller at the Government Printing Office. It administers grants to the States for a large number of maternity and infant care programs—for example, for maternity and pediatric clinics, well child clinics, and school health programs. And it also makes grants to support such other State programs as those providing special care for crippled children and the mentally retarded, mental health facilities, immunization against preventable diseases, and day-care centers.

The Rehabilitation Services Administration. For almost fifty years the States have been receiving federal aid for their efforts in the field of vocational rehabilitation—that is for their efforts to help the physically and mentally handicapped to overcome or adjust to their disabilities, perform useful work, and thus lead richer, more normal lives.

Congress first authorized such grants in the Vocational Rehabilitation Act of 1920. Since then, a wide range of rehabilitation programs has been developed. Today these aid programs, directed by the Rehabilitation Services Administration, include support for such many and varied things as: medical diagnosis to determine the extent of a handicapped person's disability and the possibilities of improvement, necessary medical and hospital care, artificial limbs, hearing aids, and braces, counselling, job training, special tools, job placement, workshops and treatment facilities, training of qualified personnel to work with the handicapped, and research to advance knowledge of the ways in which handicapping conditions may be overcome.

The Administration on Aging. The Administration on Aging was created in the Older Americans Act of 1965. It is a clearinghouse for information on the problems of the elderly. It also administers grants to the States and to local and private agencies for studies of the aged and for the development of programs especially designed for them.

Praising the work of the agency in 1967,

---

[6] The Kerr-Mills Act was passed in 1960 as a first and limited response to the growing demands that finally culminated in the enactment of the Medicare program in 1965.

OUR SOCIAL INSURANCE STRUCTURE

Source of Funds ▶

STATE AND FEDERAL TAXES (general revenue)	PAYROLL TAXES (paid by employers and employed workers)	PAYROLL TAXES (paid by employers)

Coverage ▶

FEDERAL-STATE PUBLIC ASSISTANCE	MEDICARE	OASDI	UNEMPLOYMENT INSURANCE

For the Needy:
Blind
Dependent
Children
Aged
Disabled
Child Welfare
Services

Medical Insurance for the Aged

Retirement Income
Income to Family
of Worker Who Dies
Disability Income

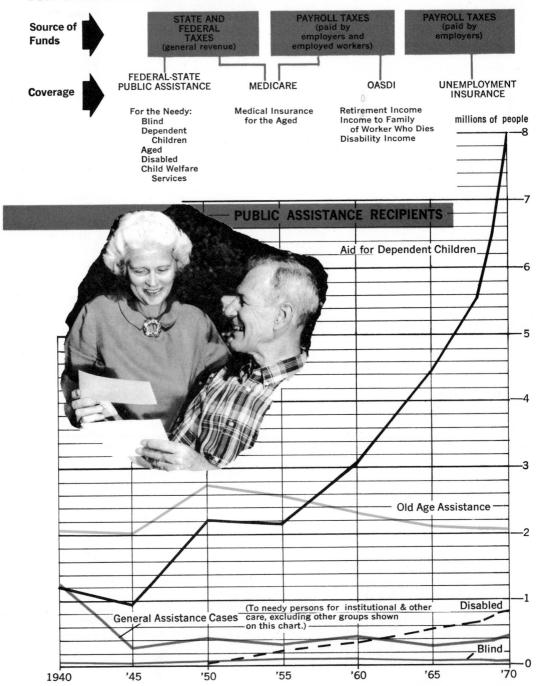

PUBLIC ASSISTANCE RECIPIENTS

millions of people

Aid for Dependent Children

Old Age Assistance

Disabled

General Assistance Cases (To needy persons for institutional & other care, excluding other groups shown on this chart.)

Blind

1940   '45   '50   '55   '60   '65   '70

Source: Department of Health, Education and Welfare

490

PATIENTS IN MENTAL HOSPITALS
thousands

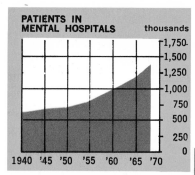

1,750	
1,500	
1,250	
1,000	
750	
500	
250	
0	

1940 '45 '50 '55 '60 '65 '70

PRIVATE HEALTH AND MEDICAL CARE EXPENDITURES
(by category)

in billions of dollars

COST OF MEDICAL CARE INDEX

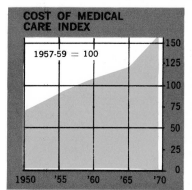

1957-59 = 100

150	
125	
100	
75	
50	
25	

1950 '55 '60 '65 '70

TOTAL PRIVATE HEALTH EXPENDITURES
in billions of

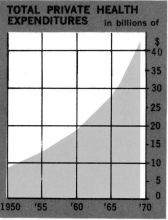

$40	
35	
30	
25	
20	
15	
10	
5	
0	

1950 '55 '60 '65 '70

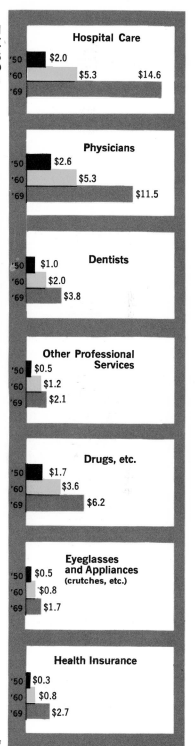

Hospital Care
'50 $2.0
'60 $5.3 $14.6
'69

Physicians
'50 $2.6
'60 $5.3
'69 $11.5

Dentists
'50 $1.0
'60 $2.0
'69 $3.8

Other Professional Services
'50 $0.5
'60 $1.2
'69 $2.1

Drugs, etc.
'50 $1.7
'60 $3.6
'69 $6.2

Eyeglasses and Appliances (crutches, etc.)
'50 $0.5
'60 $0.8
'69 $1.7

Health Insurance
'50 $0.3
'60 $0.8
'69 $2.7

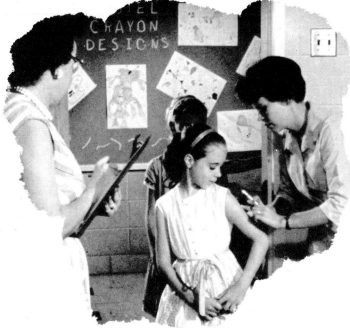

Sources:
Dept. of Health, Education, and Welfare, Social Security
Administration, Public Health Service.; Department of Commerce ; Bureau of the Census

President Johnson also in effect described its mission:

> These programs have ignited a sure sense of usefulness in lives once lost to loneliness and boredom. Thousands of older people have found friendship, education, and recreation. Thousands more have volunteered their still valuable services to their communities.

Other Programs. A number of other significant welfare programs are also administered by the Social and Rehabilitation Service. Two of them are especially significant today:

A juvenile delinquency grant program — in which support is given for research into and projects for the control and prevention of juvenile delinquency, and for the training of personnel to work in that field.

A Cuban refugee aid program — in which the Service directs a wide-ranging program of aid for those who have fled Castro-dominated Cuba (see page 85.). By 1970 approximately 500,000 refugees had come to this country from Cuba since the communist takeover there in 1959.

Since early 1961 HEW has operated a relief program to meet the exiles' needs and, as well, the problems their arrival has brought. Most of this work is carried on through the Cuban Refugee Emergency Center in Miami, with the help of other federal and many State, local, and private agencies. The Center's emergency efforts include such immediate aid as food, clothing, health care, and assistance in the moving of many of the refugees from Florida to homes and jobs elsewhere across the country. It also provides financial aid to the schools of Dade County (Miami), Florida, to defray at least some of the costs of schooling the exiles' children. The Center itself operates schools to teach Cubans new skills and the English language.

How long the flow of refugees will continue seems to be anyone's guess. For almost a decade now they have arrived by boat and by plane at an average rate of 1000 a week.

THE PUBLIC HEALTH SERVICE

The general health of the American people is quite good — and it has improved steadily over the years. Where male children born in 1900 could expect to live, on the average, forty-eight years, those born today have a life expectancy of at least seventy years. The infant death rate now stands at an all-time low in the United States. A generation ago (1935) there were fifty-six deaths under one year for every 1000 live births; today (1970) there are only about twenty.

The generally high level and continuing improvement in the nation's health can be seen in a raft of other statistics. For example, in 1900 there were some 3,000,000 persons — only 4.1 per cent of the total population — over age sixty-five. By 1970, over 19,000,000 persons — nearly ten per cent of the population — were over sixty-five.

Tremendous strides have been and continue to be made in medical and scientific research. New "wonder drugs" and methods of treating and preventing diseases have done much to protect and improve health. Such once-dreaded killers as typhoid fever, smallpox, diphtheria, scarlet fever, and cholera have now been all but eradicated. The fact that scientists can in some cases even replace vital organs in the human body is but one of the evidences of the amazing advances being made constantly in medical research.

But, while the nation's health is improving steadily, it is quite obvious that much remains to be done. During World War II some 5,000,000 men were rejected by the draft for physical or mental defects — and more than one of every three examined are rejected today.

Approximately 1,900,000 persons now die in this country each year.[7] According to federal

---

[7] More than 4,000,000 live births were registered in the United States in each of the years 1954-1964; the birth rate has declined since 1964, to an estimated 3,400,000 live births in 1969.

health authorities, a fifth of these deaths could be prevented each year through the medical skill and knowledge we now possess. Sickness and accidents take a serious economic toll. It has been estimated that the nation loses 4,300,000,000 man-years of work each year because of ill-health and at least $27,000,000,000 in national wealth annually due to sickness and partial or total disability.

Medical science has long since taught us the value and wisdom of programs designed to prevent diseases and to eradicate their causes. Both public health agencies and private medicine are deeply concerned with and involved in the prevention and eradication — as well as the treatment and cure — of diseases, of course. Generally, however, public health agencies are primarily concerned with prevention and eradication while treatment and cure lie chiefly within the province of private medicine.

The history of the Public Health Service (PHS) is nearly as long as that of the Government itself. It dates from an Act of 1798 in which Congress established the Marine Hospital Service to provide care for merchant seamen.[8] From this beginning, it has grown to the point where it now administers most of the public health activities of the National Government.

Today the Service describes its wide-ranging mission in these terms:

> The Public Health Service is the federal agency specifically charged with promoting and assuring the highest level of health attainable for every person, in an environment which contributes positively to healthful individual and family living.

The PHS has been extensively reorganized in the past few years. It now consists of three major operating agencies: the Consumer Pro-

---

[8] The origins of the public health function are lost in antiquity. At least as early as the 3rd Century, B.C., the Greeks realized the value of and practiced quarantine to control the spread of disease.

tection and Environmental Health Service, the Health Services and Mental Health Administration, and the National Institutes of Health. The unified direction of these agencies is the responsibility of the Assistant Secretary for Health and Scientific Affairs; his chief deputy is the Surgeon General of the United States.

The Consumer Protection and Environmental Health Service. The Consumer Protection and Environmental Health Service (CPE) houses three important sub-agencies: the Food and Drug Administration, the Environmental Control Administration, and the National Air Pollution Control Administration. According to the Administrator of the CPE, their collective purpose is "to assure effective protection for every American against hazards to health in his environment and in the products and services which enter his life."

The Food and Drug Administration. When foods and drugs are mass-produced, as are most of ours today, the consumer has little or no chance to check for himself the quality and purity of what he buys and uses — except perhaps through its effect on his health, and that may come a bit late.

Toward the turn of the century, a number of shocking abuses in the food and drug industries were brought to light. Many foods were adulterated and made attractive by the use of poisonous dyes. Misbranding became common; for example, canned veal was often sold as chicken. Unsanitary practices were widespread in packinghouses and canning plants, away from the eyes of the consumer. Cures for every ache and pain flooded the market, and many unsuspecting sufferers put their faith and their money into useless and often harmful concoctions.

To counteract these conditions, Congress passed the Pure Food and Drug Act of 1906, from which the present Food and Drug Administration has descended. The FDA is headed by a Commissioner appointed by the President and Senate. Today his agency is charged with the protection of the nation's public health against hazards that may be involved in foods, drugs, cosmetics, therapeutic devices, such household substances as soap and other cleaning preparations, poisons, pesticides, food additives, flammable fabrics, and a wide variety of other consumer products.

The FDA works closely with such other federal agencies as the Federal Trade Commission and the Agricultural Research Service, as well as other segments of the PHS and State and local health authorities. It performs much of its scientific, investigative, and research work from its Washington headquarters. To provide nationwide coverage, it also operates through a series of regional offices and laboratories — each manned by chemists, investigators, and other personnel, and several local inspection stations. Much of its scientific work is also done by contract with several universities and various other public and private clinical research groups.

FDA agents regularly check factories to guard against unsanitary conditions, inspect the raw materials used, and examine the controls exercised in the compounding, processing, packaging, and labeling of products destined for interstate commerce. Retail drug stores are kept under surveillance to prevent the dispensing of dangerous drugs without prescription. In cooperation with the Customs Bureau, regular inspections are also made at the nation's ports of entry.

The FDA conducts continuing campaigns of public education — in the schools, through newspapers, magazines, radio, and television, and by other means — to warn consumers against harmful products. It also seeks — and often secures — the voluntary compliance of manufacturers in the observance of the federal pure food, drugs, and related laws. Violations of these statutes are reported to the Justice Department — along with the FDA's recommendations for seizure of offensive articles, criminal prosecution, or other actions in the federal courts.

Thousands of samples are tested in the FDA's laboratories each year. Those products it finds adulterated, misrepresented, or otherwise dangerous are banned from interstate shipment. Labels must accurately list the ingredients and quantity in any package. Narcotic drugs must be labeled: "Warning — May Be Habit-Forming." Poisonous drugs and other preparations must be plainly tagged; instructions must be given for their use and antidotes for their misuse. Applications for the distribution of new drugs, accompanied by the results of careful tests by the manufacturers, must be approved by the Food and Drug Administration before each new drug may be placed on the market.

The work of such agencies as the FDA has, over the years, saved the lives of thousands upon thousands of Americans and has protected the health and well-being of millions more. Yet, too often the dedicated public servants who staff these agencies have gone largely unnoticed and unsung.

The sedative, thalidomide, and the integrity of Dr. Frances O. Kelsey of the FDA brought them to public notice quite dramatically a few years ago, however. Thalidomide had been developed by German scientists, and after exhaustive tests, had been used widely in Europe for several years. Administered as a tablet, the drug was widely accepted in medical circles as one of the safest and most effective tranquilizers yet devised.

An American concern had applied for an FDA license and was anxious to manufacture and distribute it in this country. For more than a year, and in the face of strong pressure from the company, Dr. Kelsey refused to approve the application. Alerted by an obscure note in a British medical journal, she was skeptical of some of the claims made for the drug and suspected that it could produce unintended and harmful side-effects.

By mid-1962 thalidomide had indeed been identified as highly dangerous when prescribed in certain types of cases. Especially, the drug was found to cause horrible deformities in the children born to women who had taken it in the early stages of pregnancy.

Because she was skeptical, and because she had refused to bow to the demands of the company or of her other work, Dr. Kelsey kept thalidomide off the American market—and the United States was spared the tragedy repeated in countless thousands of births in Europe for several years.

A federal court case of a few years ago provides another good illustration of the work and value of the FDA. Forseveral years, a man had sold a device he called the "Spectro-Chrome." He claimed that it could cure practically any ailment. His device was, in reality, nothing more than a box containing a strong light bulb and several different colored panes of glass. But he sold more than 9000 of them at $90 apiece.

He claimed that when the light was passed through one of the panes and then onto the "patient" it would cure cancer; when passed through another it would cure ulcers, and so on. At his trial, a defense witness testified that the machine made calving easier for cows when they were faced to the north during treatment. Another claimed that the machine had cured a dachshund of constipation.

But Government witnesses told of many persons suffering from serious illnesses who had died while being "treated." One defense witness who claimed that the Spectro-Chrome had cured him of epilepsy suffered an epileptic attack in the courtroom. He might have strangled to death had not a doctor, a witness for the prosecution, treated him. The defendant was convicted and sentenced to a long term in a federal penitentiary.

Because the Food and Drug Administration is understaffed and because of public indifference, it is estimated that for every criminal convicted of fraud of this kind two others are at large and preying on the public. Most of them are petty crooks, selling fakes in a bottle for a dollar or two—but some of them are extraordinarily dangerous.

The Environmental Control Administration. The very title of the Environmental Control Administration reflects the nation's increasing concern with all aspects of man's physical environment. It also indicates the agency's primary mission—which it defines in these terms: "to reduce the levels of exposure of people to the hazards of improper housing and use of space, noise, rodent and insect vectors, occupational and community accidents, waterborne diseases, and waste accumulation."

It administers several federal laws aimed at preventing the transmission of communicable diseases across State lines, works to prevent accidents and disease and promote health and safety in the working population, and conducts programs to reduce radiation from TV sets and other electronic products.

The ECA carries on most of the Government's work in water hygiene. Thus it sets standards for and polices the potable water used by such carriers as the railroads and the airlines. It also furnishes grants-in-aid, research help, and other assistance to State and local water pollution agencies and to local public water supply and sewage systems.

The ECA is also concerned with solid waste disposal—with what has been called "the ugly die of plenty," the nation's mounting garbage crisis.

Until quite recently, few worried about the problem. Most garbage was burned at home or in dumps, thrown into a handy body of water, fed to pigs, or similarly disposed of. But population growth and urban sprawl have far outstripped such traditional, haphazard, and never satisfactory methods.

Solid waste and what to do with it have now become a major national health problem. It is estimated that for every man, woman, and child in this country collectors haul away *five pounds* of food, paper, plastics, metal, glass, and other waste *each day*—an *estimated 183,000,000 tons a year.* Factories and other producing sources contribute another *170,000,000 tons* a year. And the total may reach a *half billion tons* by 1980. The cost of disposing of the nation's solid waste is mounting even faster than the tide of the garbage itself. Our annual garbage bill now runs to approximately $4,-500,000,000. Clearly, something must be done to meet this enormous, odorous, and constantly growing problem.

The ECA is working to find new and improved means of storage, collection, and disposal of solid wastes. For example, it is seeking ways to reduce the amount of waste that will ultimately need to be disposed of—through such approaches as reuse, recycling, and source reduction.

The National Air Pollution Control Administration. Much the same pattern is evident in the field of air pollution as that to be seen in such related environmental areas as water quality, noise, and waste disposal: an alarming increase in the nature and scope of the problem and a recent and rising public and governmental concern with it.

The National Air Pollution Control Administration is now the major federal agency at work to combat air pollution. It conducts extensive research programs aimed at the identification and control of such stationary sources as factories, garbage dumps, heating systems, and the like, and such other sources as motor vehicles.

The Administration works closely with the Weather Bureau and State and local authorities on a surveillance and reporting program and provides grants and other aid to State and local pollution control agencies. It also administers a national motor vehicle pollution control program specifically aimed at countering the massive air pollution caused by the approximately 110,000,000 automobiles, trucks, and buses operating in this country.

The Health Services and Mental Health Administration. Many of the functions historically associated with the Public Health Service are now the responsibility of its Health Services and Mental Health Administration (HSM).

Much of HSM's work centers around the development and improvement of the health care given the American people. Its medical and other personnel—and that of each of the other Public Health Service agencies—strive to prevent health disasters. When emergencies do occur—whether in the form of epidemics, in the aftermath of floods, fires, or other natural disasters, or from any cause—they rush to the aid of the stricken area.

HSM operates the National Communicable Disease Center at Atlanta. The Center conducts research and action programs to prevent and control disease throughout the country. It also enforces quarantine regulations in foreign and interstate commerce and inspects and licenses clinical laboratories operating in interstate commerce. Because disease respects no boundaries, the Center cooperates with foreign governments and such international organizations as the Food and Agriculture Organization and the World Health Organization to promote the use of both older and newly gained knowledge for the prevention and control of disease.

HSM also operates several hospitals and outpatient clinics to provide care for certain classes of patients. It maintains two hospitals for drug addicts, a turberculosis hospital, and a leprosarium. Freedman's Hospital in the District of Columbia is a general hospital for the treatment of acute medical and surgical cases, with an extensive system of outpatient clinics; the hospital also provides internship and clinical experience for graduates of Howard University's College of Medicine. A number of hospitals are maintained in various parts of the country to care for merchant seamen, personnel of the Coast Guard, the Coast and Geodetic Survey, and the Public Health Service, and their dependents, and Indians and Alaskan Aleuts. The HSM also directs the medical care of federal prisoners and furnishes psychiatric service in federal courts.

A severe hospital shortage exists in nearly every part of the country. This serious condition is reflected by this disturbing fact: there are no hospital facilities of any kind in approximately a third of the nation's counties. Many of the existing general, mental, tuberculosis, and other hospitals are badly overcrowded or otherwise fail to meet approved standards. Congress passed the Hospital Survey and Construction (Hill-Burton) Act of 1946 to help meet the problem. Under its terms, grants are made for the construction and expansion of hospitals and other public health facilities. Since the law was enacted, more than $3,000,-000,000 in federal funds has gone to the States. Usually, one dollar of federal money is put up for every two dollars from the State—and in many communities the necessary State money has been raised through local fund drives.

The National Institute of Mental Health, a sub-agency within HSM, conducts research and related work in the specialized field of mental health and administers grants to the States to promote their work in the field.

The National Institutes of Health. The National Institutes of Health (NIH) constitute the major research arm of the Public Health Service. There are now ten separate NIH research Institutes, for: General Medical Sciences, Environmental Health Sciences, Neurological Diseases and Stroke, Dental Research, Child Health and Human Development, Arthritis and Metabolic Diseases, Heart, Eye, Cancer, and Allergy and Infectious Diseases.

The Clinical Center of the National Institutes is a huge medical research center near Bethesda, Maryland.

NIH administers several grant and loan programs to help overcome a serious national shortage of doctors, nurses, dentists, and other trained health personnel. Several factors account for that shortage. Among them are our increasing population (especially the elderly), the demands of the Armed Forces and other public agencies, increasing specialization among doctors, and the growing number of

persons able to afford at least some health care. The problem is further complicated by the fact that doctors and other medical personnel are not distributed across the country on a population basis. Rather naturally, they prefer to live in the wealthier and more comfortable locales—and, as a result, the shortage is most severe in the nation's poorer and rural areas. Moreover, two factors tend particularly to hold down the number of persons who enter medical fields: (1) the high cost of a medical education (as much as $20,000 today) and (2) the lack of a sufficient number of medical schools to meet the need.

To help meet the problem, NIH administers grants for the construction and rehabilitation of medical, dental, nursing, and related professional schools. It also provides loans and scholarships to students and makes awards to educational institutions to encourage the training of persons who will enter the public health field. NIH also maintains a post-graduate fellowship program for promising research scientists, both in this country and from abroad.

Through its Division of Biologics Standards, NIH must evaluate and approve most biological products—vaccines, serums, antitoxins, and the like—before they may be shipped in interstate commerce.

THE OFFICE OF EDUCATION

The providing of public education is one of the major powers reserved to the States in the American federal system—and in most of the States it is essentially a local responsibility. Still, the National Government does enter the field—typically through the grant-in-aid route. Indeed, although its participation is largely indirect it has been quite extensive through most of our history; and it has grown considerably in recent years, as we shall see.

Measured by any standards, public education is a huge enterprise today. It is the largest single object of State and local governmental

The Office of Education headquarters in Washington, D.C., houses the Office of the Commissioner, the National Center for Educational Statistics, the Bureau of Elementary and Secondary Education, the Bureau of Research, and other agencies charged with promoting the cause of education. (U.S. Office of Education)

activity. In terms of expenditures, it ranks second only to national defense in the list of *all* governmental activities. The States and their local governments today (1970) spend nearly $65,000,000,000 a year in the field of public education.

Today over *one-fourth* of all our people attend school. There are now over 58,000,000 students enrolled in the nation's public and private schools and colleges. More than eighty per cent of that huge number, about 50,000,000 attend publicly financed institutions. Nearly 37,000,000 are enrolled in elementary schools (through the 8th grade), some 14,600,000 now attend high schools, and more than 7,100,000 now go to college.

The school population has increased by leaps and bounds in recent years. In 1950 there were only some 31,000,000 students in the population. Today, over 3,500,000 children

reach school age *each year,* and it is expected that enrollments in the elementary, high school, and college levels will exceed 65,000,000 by 1975.[9]

The Office of Education. From the earliest years of our history, the National Government has played a role in the field of education. Even before the adoption of the Constitution, in the Ordinance of 1785, Congress required that one section of land in each township in the territories be set aside for the support of public schools. In the Morrill Act of 1862 it authorized grants of land to the States for the development of colleges of agricultural and mechanical arts. The National Government

---

[9] All but two States (Mississippi and South Carolina) have compulsory school attendance laws. These statutes usually require attendance by all persons between ages seven and sixteen.

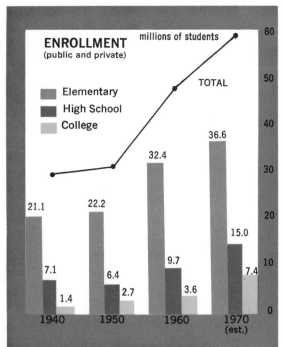

ENROLLMENT
(public and private)

millions of students

- Elementary
- High School
- College

TOTAL

60
50
40
30
20
10
0

36.6
32.4
22.2
21.1

15.0
9.7
7.1
7.4
6.4
3.6
2.7
1.4

1940   1950   1960   1970
                              (est.)

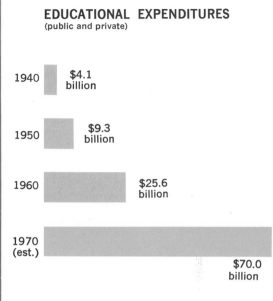

EDUCATIONAL EXPENDITURES
(public and private)

1940 $4.1 billion

1950 $9.3 billion

1960 $25.6 billion

1970 (est.) $70.0 billion

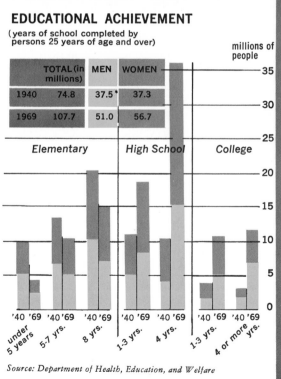

EDUCATIONAL ACHIEVEMENT

(years of school completed by
persons 25 years of age and over)

millions of people

	TOTAL (in millions)	MEN	WOMEN
1940	74.8	37.5	37.3
1969	107.7	51.0	56.7

Elementary   High School   College

35
30
25
20
15
10
5
0

'40 '69   '40 '69   '40 '69   '40 '69   '40 '69   '40 '69   '40 '69
under   5-7 yrs.   8 yrs.   1-3 yrs.   4 yrs.   1-3 yrs.   4 or more
5 years   yrs.

Source: Department of Health, Education, and Welfare

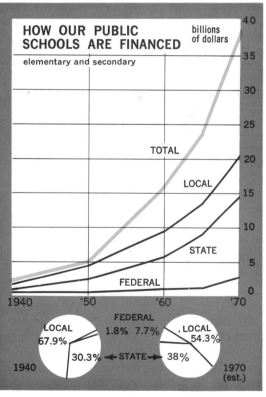

HOW OUR PUBLIC SCHOOLS ARE FINANCED

billions of dollars

elementary and secondary

40
35
30
25
20
15
10
5
0

TOTAL
LOCAL
STATE
FEDERAL

1940   '50   '60   '70

FEDERAL
LOCAL 67.9%   1.8% 7.7%   LOCAL 54.3%

30.3% ◄ STATE ► 38%

1940   1970 (est.)

499

has long provided schools for various groups, including members of the Armed Forces and their dependents, Indians, and residents of the District of Columbia and the territories.

Hundreds of millions of dollars in federal funds have been, and are being, spent for a host of educational matters, including: the support of land-grant colleges, scientific, agricultural, and military research, vocational education, veterans' benefits, school lunch programs, aid to school districts with populations swollen by military or other heavy federal activity, laboratory equipment, language laboratories, audio-visual equipment, student loans and fellowships, and many others.

Much, but by no means all, of this massive federal participation is channeled through the Office of Education. The Office is headed by a Commissioner of Education, usually a distinguished educator, appointed by the President and Senate. Congress created the agency in 1867:

> ...for the purpose of collecting such statistics and facts as shall show the condition and progress of education in the several States and Territories, and of diffusing such information respecting the organization and management of schools and school systems, and methods of teaching, as shall aid the people of the United States in the establishment and maintenance of efficient school systems, and otherwise promote the cause of education....

Today the Office carries out that directive in many ways—especially through research, the providing of advice and information, and through the administration of several grant-in-aid programs.

Its studies cover the full gamut of education; for example, from the schooling of the gifted and the retarded to the graduate training of teachers. Its findings and recommendations go to Congress, other federal agencies, the States, and private groups.

It administers the funds that Congress provides for the land-grant colleges and for voca-

tional education in the public schools. It handles the grants made to those local school systems where enrollments have been swollen by federal activities in their areas. It also administers the grants, loans, and fellowships that Congress has provided for in the several far-reaching pieces of aid-to-education legislation it has enacted in recent years.

Among its numerous other activities, the Office distributes funds for the extension of library services in rural areas, promotes the international exchange of students and teachers, cooperates with the Commerce and Labor Departments in redevelopment and retraining programs, provides captioned films for the education of the deaf, and subsidizes work in the field of educational television and adult education.

Federal Aid to Education. Surveys of the public school systems in the fifty States indicate quite clearly that, despite their general caliber, there are a number of areas in this country in which the educational opportunities and the facilities available are far from what they should be. This variation in quality occurs both within each and among the various States.

In large part it is caused by the uneven geographic distribution of wealth—some areas are wealthier and some are poorer than the national average. Obviously, the wealthier an area is the more it has available to spend on its schools. A number of recent studies show that the income of the total population in relation to the total school enrollment (that is, the income per pupil) in some States is as much as four to five times as high as it is in some other States.

This uneven distribution of wealth, together with the current shortages in teachers and classrooms, plus the rapid rise in school enrollments, has in recent years led Congress to enact a vastly expanded program of federal aid to education.

The extent to which the National Government *should* provide such aid has been vigorously debated through much of our history.

The extent to which it actually *does* provide it has grown considerably in recent years.[10]

The major extensions of federal aid over the past twenty-five years have included:

1944 — The Servicemen's Readjustment Act (the GI Bill of Rights), providing a huge program of educational benefits for veterans of World War II; the program was later extended to cover Korean and Cold War veterans as well (see page 398).

1946 — The National School Lunch Act, authorizing aid in the form of funds and surplus foodstuffs for the serving of hot lunches to students in public and nonprofit private schools (see page 451).

1950 — The Impacted Areas Program, making federal grants to help meet the school costs in those districts which are either overcrowded ("impacted") because of federal activities in or nearby them or which are deprived of local revenues because of the tax-exempt status of federal lands located in the district. In the same year, Congress also provided a long-term, low-interest loan program for the construction of dormitories at both public and private colleges and universities.

1955 — The White House Conference on Education, staged after a series of State conferences financed with federal funds. The Conference report called for expanded federal aid to the nation's schools.

1958 — The National Defense Education Act, providing for more than $1,000,000,000 in grants and loans to upgrade the teaching of science, mathematics, and foreign languages at all school levels, to aid teacher-training work in counseling and guidance, to provide long-term, low-interest loans to bright but needy college students studying to become scientists, teachers, or linguists, and for such other purposes as developing scientific teaching aids and research on visual aids. NDEA came very largely as a result of the nation's reaction to the launching of the first Russian space satellites.[11]

1963 — The Health Professions Educational Assistance Act, providing for a three-year $175,000,000 program of grants to match the funds of public and non-profit private agencies for the construction and rehabilitation of medical and dental schools, and for student loans.

1963 — The Higher Education Facilities Act, creating a five-year $1,195,000,000 program of grants and loans to public and private institutions for libraries, classrooms, and engineering, mathematics, science, and foreign language facilities.

1963 — The Vocational Education Act, providing $731,000,000 over five years for expanding existing vocational education aid. Most of the new funds are committed to helping workers, the youthful unemployed, and school dropouts learn new industrial and technical skills. The former emphasis in vocational education aid has thus been shifted from farm-

---

[10] We have noted several times that in the American federal system public education is one of primary concern to the States and their local governments. We have also noted the National Government does play a key role in the field through a variety of programs, some dating back for a century and more. In the light of this federal participation, it is quite unrealistic to discuss, as some do, the recent *expansion* of federal aid as though it involved a new and radical departure from existing practice.

[11] In 1962 Congress repealed the controversial "non-disloyalty oath" requirement in the law. Originally, any person receiving a grant or loan under the law had to swear that he was *not disloyal* to the United States and that he did not believe in, belong to, or support any organization that teaches or advocates the violent overthrow of government in this country. He still must pledge his *loyalty* to the United States, however.

"HI MA'AM! I'M THE FUTURE YOU'RE SUP-POSED TO SHAPE." The increasing school population and the critical shortage of teachers have combined to cause one of the serious problems facing cities and towns in many parts of the country. (Sanders, Kansas City Star)

ing and home economics to the newer areas. The Act also provided additional funds for most NDEA programs.

1964 — The National Defense Education Act Amendments, providing a much greater expansion of NDEA than had been accomplished in 1963. Most significantly, the amendments broadened the academic fields covered under the Act to include history, civics, geography, English, and reading.

1964 — The Economic Opportunity Act, inaugurating President Johnson's many faceted "war on poverty," contained several aid-to-education features (see pages 514–516).

1965 — The Elementary-Secondary Educa-tion Act, providing over $1,250,000,000 in grants to the nation's elementary and secondary schools. The major sections of the law au-thorize: a $1,000,000,000 three-year program of aid to school districts with large numbers of low-income families or families on relief; a $100,000,000 five-year program for the pur-chase of library books and materials and text-books; a $100,000,000 five-year program to improve educational research and to train re-search personnel; and a $25,000,000 five-year program to strengthen State departments of education. The Act also provided for a Na-tional Teacher Corps — an organization to aid the States in the recruiting and training of teachers for schools in such depressed areas as city slums and impoverished rural sections.[12] Beyond these features, the Act is quite signifi-cant because in it, and *for the first time,* Con-gress provided for the support of the functions of the public schools *generally.* Notice that the several earlier programs provided for *selective* aid to the schools and were restricted to the support of *specific* school functions.[13]

1965 — The Higher Education Act, providing for an $800,000,000-a-year, three-year program

---

[12] Congress did not implement this program with the necessary funds in 1965 but did so — on a token basis only — in 1966 and 1967; it received a sub-stantial appropriation in both 1968 and 1969, how-ever, and its future now seems secure.

[13] The 1965 law is also highly significant because in passing it Congress managed to overcome an obstacle on which many similar bills had foundered: the question of whether federal aid should (and, in the case of parochial schools, constitutionally could) be given to private schools as well as public ones. The problem was met through the concept of "shared time" — under which grants for various purposes such as laboratory equipment, remedial courses, teach-ing machines, and guidance and counseling are made to public school agencies and then made available to (shared with) students in church and other pri-vate nonprofit schools. On the general subject of education, religion, and the Constitution, see pages 106–109.

of aid to the nation's public and private non-profit colleges and universities. It authorizes grants to enable those institutions to improve their library resources and facilities and to upgrade classroom instruction with the purchase of such new or additional devices as laboratory and closed-circuit television equipment. It also establishes special grants to aid the growth of newer and smaller institutions, and expands and liberalizes many of the programs created by the earlier National Defense Education Act and the Higher Education Facilities Act.

The major thrust of congressional action on aid-to-education legislation in the years 1966 through 1969 has been that of review and revision — and, in most instances, the expansion — of the several and far-reaching measures enacted in recent years.

Even with the recent expansions, the whole subject of federal aid to education remains a very controversial one. The major opposition to both new and expanded programs comes from those persons and groups who fear that federal aid will inevitably mean federal control over the educational systems of the States, and especially over the content of the subject matter to be taught. Some also argue that further aid is in fact unnecessary because, they say, the States can well afford to do the job themselves without it.

Two conflicts, both of them among the supporters of federal aid, long stood as effective barriers to the passage of new aid legislation. Both now appear to have been settled. One — over the questions of whether aid ought to be given to both public *and* private (particularly parochial) schools — seems to have been resolved in the Elementary-Secondary Education Act of 1965. The other — over the question of aid to school systems in those States where racially segregated schools still exist — was resolved in the Civil Rights Act of 1964. That statute prohibits such aid by the National Government unless a State in which racially segregated schools exist has formulated plans in good faith for the prompt end to segregation in its schools. See pages 119–120.

SAINT ELIZABETHS HOSPITAL

Saint Elizabeths Hospital was originally established by Congress in 1855 as the Government Hospital for the Insane. It acquired its present name in 1916.

Congress has charged the Hospital to provide "the most humane care and enlightened curative treatment" for the mentally ill. It serves as the mental institution for the District of Columbia. Its more than 7000 patients include residents of the District, patients referred to it by both the Public Health Service and the Veterans Administration, and mentally ill persons who are charged with or convicted of crimes in the federal courts.

The Hospital also conducts training programs in the mental health field and research projects concerned with the causes, treatment, and prevention of mental disorders.

❊❊❊❊❊❊❊❊❊❊ CONCEPT BUILDING ❊❊❊❊❊❊❊❊❊❊

Key Concepts

Over the years, Americans have come to accept both the need for and the desirability of governmental responsibility in the field of social welfare. Although the States and their local units have long been involved in the field, large-scale federal participation in social welfare dates from the Depression of the 1930's.

Most of the social welfare activities of the National Government are administered through the Department of Health, Education, and Welfare. HEW's principal agencies are the: Social Security Administration, Social and Rehabilitation Service, Public Health Service, Food and Drug Administration, and Office of Education.

The Social Security Administration manages the Old-Age, Survivors, and Disability Insurance program (OASDI)—a contributory insurance program financed by taxes levied on employees, employers, and the self-employed—and Medicare, a program of hospitalization and other health care for the aged financed in part by increased OASDI taxation and by monthly fees.

The Social and Rehabilitation Service supervises grants to the States for old-age assistance, aid to the blind, dependent children, the permanently and totally disabled, Medicaid, and similar welfare programs.

The Public Health Service directs most of the public health activities of the National Government. It provides hospital, medical, and other health care for various classes of patients, conducts extensive research and action programs in the very broadly defined field of environmental health, administers several grant-in-aid programs, and enforces the federal statutes which ban impure foods, drugs, and similar items from interstate and foreign commerce.

The Office of Education is the major artery through which federal aid—vastly expanded in recent years—is granted to the States for the support of public education.

Important Terms

grants-in-aid	Medicaid	payroll taxes	social security
HEW	Medicare	public health	social welfare
	OASDI	shared time	

Questions for Inquiry and Review

1. What major occurrence in our history brought the beginning massive federal participation in the social welfare field?

2. Which of the Cabinet Departments administers most of the federal social welfare programs today?

3. List the four major agencies within it.

4. The passage of what statute highlighted federal entry into the social welfare field?

5. What is the Old-Age, Survivors, and Disability Insurance program?

6. How is OASDI financed? Approximately how many persons make OASDI contributions? Approximately how many receive benefits?

7. What is Medicare? How is the "basic plan" financed? How is the "supplementary plan" financed? Which of these two plans is a voluntary one?

8. Through what particular method does the Social and Rehabilitation Service conduct most of its functions?

9. When was the Public Health Service first established? What is the general nature of its work?

10. When and why was the Food and Drug Administration created? What particular provision in the Constitution supports the existence of the FDA?

For Further Inquiry

1. Do you think it necessary or unnecessary for government to maintain social welfare programs?

2. If you feel that social welfare is a proper governmental function, do you feel that it should be handled by local governments, by the States, or by the National Government, or by government at all three levels? Why?

3. What potential dangers, if any, do you see in too-generous or too-inclusive welfare programs? How might such dangers be avoided?

4. Why may public education be described as "the bulwark of democracy"?

5. Do you think it fair that, under OASDI, a person between ages sixty-five and seventy-two who earns more than $1680 in a year receives a reduced social security benefit?

Suggested Activities

1. Prepare an essay or stage a class discussion based upon one or more of the following quotations. *Henry Adams:* "They know enough who know how to learn." *John Milton:* "As good almost kill a man as kill a good book: who kills a man kills a reasonable creature, God's image; but he who destroys a good book kills reason itself." *Euclid:* "There is no royal road to geometry." (Often misquoted: "There is no royal road to learning.")

2. Invite county, city, or other local welfare officers to describe their work to the class.

3. Prepare a list of as many different illustrations of the work of the agencies mentioned in this chapter as you can identify in your own locale.

4. Stage a debate or class forum on the question: "*Resolved,* That the Congress should henceforth refuse to appropriate funds to aid the States in the support of public education."

Suggested Reading

ALLEN, COMMISSIONER JAMES E., "Crisis in City Schools," *U.S. News,* June 30, 1969.

BALL, COMMISSIONER ROBERT W., "Is Medicare Worth the Price?" *U.S. News,* July 21, 1969.

BRANDT, NAT and YANNA, "They Turn Welfare Recipients into Taxpayers," *Reader's Digest,* September 1968.

COOPER, JOHN A. D., "Growing Crisis in Health Care," *U.S. News,* November 3, 1969.

"Desegregate Now—But How to Do It?" *U.S. News,* November 10, 1969.

GREER, COLIN, "Public Schools: The Myth of the Melting Pot," *Saturday Review,* November 15, 1969.

JENCKS, C., "A Reappraisal of the Most Controversial Education Document of Our Time," *New York Times Magazine,* August 10, 1969.

MAISEL, ALBERT Q., "Profiteers Are Wrecking Medicaid," *Reader's Digest,* October, 1969.

"Noise—More than a Nuisance," *U.S. News,* November 10, 1969.

"Pesticides: Pro and Con," *U.S. News,* October 20, 1969.

"Poverty in America," *Time,* May 17, 1968.

"Public Welfare Revision: Pro and Con," *Congressional Digest,* June–July, 1968.

Social Security Administration, *Your Social Security.* Government Printing Office, 1970.

TRIPPETT, FRANK, "The Epic of Garbage," *Look,* November 4, 1969.

"U.S. in Danger of Being Engulfed By Trash," *U.S. News,* September 8, 1969.

"What's Wrong With U.S. Medicine," *Time,* February 21, 1969; *Reader's Digest,* May, 1969.

28
THE DEPARTMENT OF HOUSING AND URBAN DEVELOPMENT

✱✱✱Why is the fact that we are now an <u>urban</u> people so extraordinarily significant?

✱✱✱Should the Federal Government attempt to retard or reverse the trend to urbanization in the United States? Why?

✱✱✱Has the rapid pace of urbanization in this country rendered federalism obsolete?

✱✱✱What should be the proper role of government in the field of housing?

Within the borders of our urban centers can be found the most impressive achievements of man's skill and the highest expressions of man's spirit, as well as the worst examples of degradation and cruelty and misery to be found in modern America.

LYNDON B. JOHNSON

Congress created the eleventh of the Cabinet departments, the Department of Housing and Urban Development, in 1965. Its creation and its very existence highlight one of the most significant of the facts of life in the United States today: We have become—rather suddenly and very largely—an *urban* people.

Nearly three-fourths of the nation's population, some 150,000,000, now live in urban areas—in cities and in their surrounding suburbs. Indeed, we have become so distinctly an urbanized people that ninety per cent of our urban population is now clustered in and around cities of 50,000 people or more. Fully one-third of all of our people today reside in the nation's two dozen largest metropolitan areas—and fully a fourth are concentrated in our ten largest metropolitan centers.

The pace of our urban growth has quickened in the past few decades—as the table on page 719 indicates. As it has, our older cities have tended to combine into huge clusters. The strip of land running from southern New Hampshire to northern Virginia now contains more than twenty per cent of the nation's population—and in less than two per cent of the nation's total area. On the West Coast, around the Great Lakes, and along the Gulf of Mexico other urban giants are growing, sprawling, merging, and growing ever larger.

This rapid pace of urban growth shows every sign of continuing—and, in fact, of accelerating—in the years to come. The Census Bureau estimates that between 1970 and 1980 some 20,000,000 people will be added to our urban population—a total equivalent to the *combined* present day populations of the cities of Los Angeles, Chicago, Philadelphia, and Baltimore. In each year of the decade of the 1970's, then, the nation's urban population will grow by the equivalent of ten cities with 200,000 population each.

As ever larger numbers of people have poured into our urban centers—and continue to do so—old problems have been aggravated and new ones have arisen. Increases in the densities of population have brought with them a compounding of the problems associated with such matters as adequate housing, health facilities, transportation systems, sewage disposal, water and power supplies, and a host of other concerns. These problems produce serious consequences for the millions of persons immediately involved with them, of course — and failure to meet them involves consequences of even more far-reaching significance, as the late President Kennedy observed:

> A nation that is partly ill-housed is not as strong as a nation with adequate homes for every family. A nation with ugly, crime-infested cities and haphazard suburbs does not present the same image to the world as a nation characterized by bright and orderly urban development.

A Changing Federal Role. In the American federal system, primary responsibility for meeting the problems of urban areas rests with the States and with their local governments — a matter to which we shall return in Chapters 42 and 43.

Traditionally, the National Government has played only a limited and indirect role in the field. That is, at least until quite recently, federal efforts have been largely confined to programs of aid and encouragement to action by the States, by local governments, and by private enterprise. Some federal programs have involved quite direct federal action, of course — for example, in combatting unemployment during the depression of the 1930's. But, by and large, the traditional federal role has been a limited one of helper and promoter rather than direct participant.

Now, however, the National Government's involvement in urban affairs appears to be undergoing a marked change. As urban problems have multiplied, as they have become more apparent and more critical, the National Government has become increasingly involved. Today — especially with the creation of the Department of Housing and Urban Development — we appear to be embarked upon an era of much greater and much more direct federal action in the field.

DEPARTMENTAL ORGANIZATION

Various federal agencies conduct programs related to the development of the nation's cities and metropolitan areas — including several in the Departments of Labor and Health, Education, and Welfare, as we have seen. In the Housing and Urban Development Act of 1965, however, Congress placed the major responsibility for the "administration of the principal programs of the Federal Government which provide assistance for housing and for the development of the nation's communities" in the Department of Housing and Urban Development (HUD).

The Department is headed by the *Secretary of Housing and Urban Development* who, like each of the other members of the Cabinet, is appointed by the President with the consent of the Senate. The first person selected to head the Department was Robert C. Weaver. Among his many other distinctions, Mr. Weaver, thus, became the first black appointed to a Cabinet office.[1] Among his responsibilities, the Secretary advises the President with respect to federal programs and activities relating to housing and urban development and recommends policies for fostering the orderly growth and development of the nation's urban areas. Congress has also directed him to coordinate all federal activities affecting housing and urban development, provide information and technical assistance to local governments, conduct continuing studies of urban needs, and en-

---

[1] Mr. Weaver formerly served for several years as the Administrator of the Housing and Home Finance Agency — the independent executive agency out of which Congress created the new Department in 1965.

Robert C. Weaver was the first Negro to have been appointed to a Cabinet Office, the Secretary of HUD. He is shown here at the dedication of a housing development for the elderly, in Washington, D.C., in which the Federal Housing Administration participated. (Department of Housing and Urban Development)

courage the cooperation of private enterprise in meeting the needs of urban areas.

The Secretary's chief aide in the management of the 14,000-man Department is the Under Secretary. His other major aides include seven Assistant Secretaries. One of them, the Assistant Secretary for Mortgage Credit, is also the Federal Housing Commissioner; the others are for Research and Technology, Model Cities and Governmental Relations, Renewal and Housing Assistance, Metropolitan Development, Equal Opportunity, and Administration. In addition to this top-echelon staff in Washington, HUD also maintains seven regional offices — in New York, Philadelphia, Atlanta, Chicago, Fort Worth, San Francisco, and San Juan, Puerto Rico. Each is headed by a Regional Administrator responsible for executing Departmental programs in his region.

Principal Agencies. Thus far in its development, HUD's major programs involve housing, slum clearance, and public works planning and construction programs. Hence, its major operating agencies today are the:

Federal Housing Administration
Federal National Mortgage Association
Housing Assistance Administration
Renewal Assistance Administration
Model Cities Administration
Community Resources Development Administration

Some of the Department's other agencies, to which we shall turn briefly, will almost certainly join this list in the near future — most notably the Urban Transportation Administration.

HOUSING PROGRAMS

The "housing problem" is as old as man himself. From the dawn of history, shelter (that is, some form of *housing*) has been recognized as one of the basic necessities of human existence. Most of the world's peoples have not yet reached the point where *adequate* shelter is regarded as one of man's prime needs; and we in this country have reached that point — recognition of the need for *decent* housing for all our people — only in recent years.

The task of providing housing for the American people is and always has been primarily the responsibility of private enterprise. It is a responsibility which it seeks to meet with a massive amount of public help today, however.

The Growth of Federal Involvement. The Federal Government did not enter the housing field until the nation plunged into the economic slough of the 1930's.[2] From the early years of the Depression on, however, it has been deeply involved. Its first efforts came as part of the larger attempt to restore the nation's economic stability and were prompted by catastrophic conditions throughout the country. New home construction had virtually ceased. Millions of homeowners could not meet their mortgage payments and many were losing their homes through foreclosures.

Congress began to respond to the crisis in 1932. It created a series of regional home loan banks (under the Federal Home Loan Bank System, page 549) to provide credit for banks and other local lending institutions engaged in home-financing — thus, in effect, expanding their capacity to make home loans. In one of the first major moves of the New Deal era, it also created the Home Owners' Loan Corporation in 1933. The HOLC was given the authority to make long-term, low-interest mortgage loans to persons who were in urgent need

of funds to protect or recover their homes from foreclosure and could not secure financing through normal lending channels.[3]

Almost immediately, another major step was taken to help shore up home ownership. The National Housing Act of 1934 established the Federal Housing Administration to insure local lending institutions against the losses they might suffer in the making of home construction, purchase, or improvement loans. We shall return to the FHA in a moment.

These early measures were designed especially to help people save their homes and to aid the depressed economy by stimulating employment in the housing field. Federal efforts were given a new emphasis — a more distinctly social, as well as economic, bent — in 1937. In the United States Housing Act of that year Congress moved to meet the housing needs of low-income families. It launched a program of long-term loans and grants to State and local housing agencies for the construction of housing projects and slum clearance work. In the statute's words, the federal funds were to be used "for the elimination of unsafe and unsanitary housing conditions [and] for the provision of decent, safe, and sanitary dwellings for families of low income." [4]

World War II aggravated the nation's housing problems. Federal programs begun in the 1930's came to an almost complete halt. The Government did finance and build housing projects for war workers in many parts of the country — and, of course, huge military installations. But with the nation's manpower, money,

---

[2] With the exception of a limited program of emergency housing for some shipyard and other war workers during World War I.

[3] The HOLC loaned some $3,500,000,000 and saved the homes of more than 1,000,000 families in the years 1933–1936. Its loan-making authority expired in 1936; from then until it was finally abolished in 1954, it was in the process of liquidation, collecting the loans it had made.

[4] The law created the United States Housing Authority to administer its terms. The USHA became the Federal Public Housing Authority in 1942 and then the Public Housing Authority in 1947; the latter agency was absorbed by HUD in 1965.

and other resources dedicated to the war effort, practically no civilian home construction occurred during the period. The pent-up demands of years of war on top of years of depression produced a severe housing shortage in the immediate postwar years. Postwar prosperity brought still more demand, and the nation's appetite for new and decent housing has not yet been filled.

The programs of the 1930's were revived following the war and, in 1947, Congress established the Housing and Home Finance Agency to manage and coordinate them. The latter 1940's saw lengthy and bitter debate, both in and out of Congress, over the whole concept of public housing. As a consequence, no significant new housing legislation was passed for several years. Finally, the earlier federal programs were generally expanded with the enactment of the Housing Act of 1949—in which Congress declared that:

> . . . the general welfare and security of the nation and the health and living standards of its people require housing production and related community development sufficient to remedy the serious housing shortage, the elimination of sub-standard and other inadequate housing through the clearance of slums and other blighted areas, and the realization as soon as feasible of the goal of a decent home and suitable living environment for every American family. . . .

Today, the National Government's housing activities—now centered in HUD—rest very largely upon that statute and subsequent expansions of it, most notably in the Housing Acts of 1954 and 1961 and the Housing and Urban Development Acts of 1965 and 1968.

The Federal Housing Administration. The Federal Housing Administration is easily the best known of HUD's agencies. The FHA itself does not build homes nor does it make housing loans, but it does operate a number of insurance programs for those who do. It guarantees banks and other lenders against loss on the loans they make for such purposes as home improvements, rental housing, trailer courts, low-income housing, housing for military, NASA, and AEC personnel, and nursing homes. But its *major* function is that of insuring mortgages on one- to four-family homes.

Congress sets the formulae under which the FHA may guarantee various loans; and it varies them from time to time depending on housing demands and the condition of the nation's economy. Today (1970) the FHA will insure ninety-seven per cent of the first $15,000 of a mortgage on a single- or up to a four-family dwelling, ninety per cent of the next $5000, and eighty per cent of the remainder of the mortgage, with the maximum to be insured on any such loan set at $30,000.

The maximum interest rate on FHA-covered mortgages for either new or existing homes is now (1970) set at 8.5 per cent—plus a one-half per cent premium to insure that the loan will be repaid. Fire insurance must be carried on all homes built or bought with FHA help and a home must meet the standards set by the agency in order to qualify for its aid. FHA-insured loans must be repaid in monthly installments; but the repayment period may run for as long as thirty years on existing homes and thirty-five years on newly built ones (and even forty years in certain "hardship" cases).

Let us illustrate how one of your local banks may lend money at low interest for home purchases because such loans are insured by the FHA. Any person of good reputation and sufficient income to justify buying, let us say, a new home worth $14,500, including the lot, may borrow ninety-seven per cent of the cost from the bank. In other words, he could get a mortgage to cover $14,065 of the total-price; he would have to make a downpayment of $435. He would then retire the mortgage with monthly payments to the bank over a period of as much as thirty-five years. A home valued at $20,000 would require a downpayment of $950, and one worth $30,000 would mean a downpayment of $2950.

The FHA's operations are not financed by

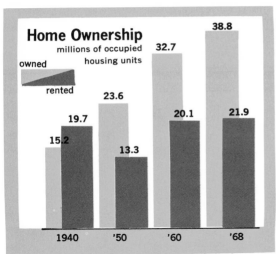

Home Ownership

millions of occupied housing units

owned

rented

1940: owned 15.2, rented 19.7
'50: owned 23.6, rented 13.3
'60: owned 32.7, rented 20.1
'68: owned 38.8, rented 21.9

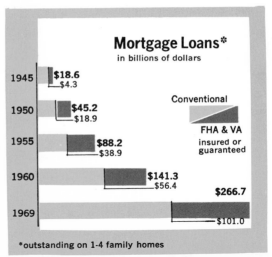

Mortgage Loans*

in billions of dollars

Conventional

FHA & VA
insured or
guaranteed

1945	$18.6	$4.3
1950	$45.2	$18.9
1955	$88.2	$38.9
1960	$141.3	$56.4
1969	$266.7	$101.0

*outstanding on 1-4 family homes

Housing Starts
(non-farm)

thousands of units

2,000 · 1,800 · 1,600 · 1,400 · 1,200 · 1,000 · 800 · 600 · 400 · 200 · 0

1945 · 1950 · 1955 · 1960 · 1965 · 1970 (est.)

Home Owners' Reasons for Owning a Home

(Percentage Distribution)

You can build an equity in a house.	22%
Children should have a real home to grow up in.	14%
When you rent you have nothing but receipts to show for the money.	10%
There is more room in a house than in an apartment.	9%
When you own your home you are free to do what you want with it.	9%
A man should provide a home for his family.	7%
Buying is cheaper than renting.	6%
A home gives greater privacy from neighbors.	5%
Owning a home gives you roots in the community.	4%
Buying a home is the normal thing for a family man to do.	4%
My wife wanted a house.	3%
You can live in a nicer neighborhood when you own a home.	3%
Children need space for playing.	2%
I wanted a yard.	1%
No response.	3%
TOTAL†	100%

† Total actually is greater than 100% because of multiple responses.

Sources: U.S. Savings and Loan League; Savings & Loan Foundation

511

Among the many programs directed by the Housing Assistance Administration are loans to build new low-rent housing—housing which the less fortunate in our communities can afford. (Department of Housing and Urban Development)

congressional appropriations. Rather, it pays all of its expenses and has built up an insurance reserve from its own income—mostly from the $\frac{1}{2}$ per cent premium we noted above. It has insured more than $100,000,000,000 in loans since its creation in 1934; currently it is insuring loans totaling about half of that amount.

The work of the FHA in encouraging home building and ownership is supplemented by that of the Federal Home Loan Banks which make credit available to local home-financing institutions (page 549). The Veterans Administration conducts a similar home loan program for veterans of World War II, the Korean War, and the Cold War (page 398).

The Federal National Mortgage Association. The Federal National Mortgage Association is often abbreviated FNMA, and is quite often called "Fanny May." It operates in the secondary mortgage market. Banks, building and loan associations, insurance companies, and other private lenders finance (hold mortgages on) most of the home building and buying that occurs in this country. Often they sell mortgages they hold in order to obtain cash with which to make better investments and for other purposes. "Fanny May" aids these private investors and the housing market by purchasing these "second mortgages," including many insured by the FHA and VA; it later resells them, as it can, to other private lenders. The FNMA has an operating capital of approximately $6,000,000,000 and has bought and sold billions of dollars worth of mortgages since its creation in 1938.

The Housing Assistance Administration. The Housing Assistance Administration conducts the federal low-rent public housing program first authorized by Congress in the United States Housing Act of 1937. It makes long-term, low interest loans to local housing authorities to help finance construction of low-rent housing projects. These loans cover as much as ninety per cent of the projects' costs. The Administration also grants subsidies to the local agencies so that they may set their rental rates at levels the low-income tenants can reasonably afford. Nearly 1,000,000 of the nation's approximately 60,000,000 families live in public housing units today.[5]

Among its other functions, the Housing Assistance Administration supervises a college housing loan program to assist institutions of higher education finance dormitories and other student and faculty housing and another loan program to aid elderly and handicapped persons obtain adequate housing. It also conducts a grant-in-aid program to help local communities buy "open-space" land in built-up urban areas for the development of parks and similar purposes.

---

[5] Approximately sixty-two per cent of the nation's families own the homes they occupy; the remainder rent from private individuals or agencies.

HAA also administers the *rent supplements* program—a new, much-disputed approach to subsidized housing for low-income groups. Under this program, HAA pays, directly to a landlord, the difference between the fair-market rent on a housing unit and one-fourth of a tenant's income. To illustrate the arrangement, take these facts: an apartment on which the fair rent is $80 a month and a renter with an income of only $225 a month. The Housing Assistance Administration would pay the landlord a subsidy of $23.75 a month—that is, the difference between the rent and one-fourth of the tenant's income ($80 minus $56.25). The tenant would then pay the balance of the rent due the landlord—$56.25.

Congress established the *rent supplements* program in 1965 and added a quite similar *mortgage supplements* program for low-income families in 1968. Both programs are today financed at the "pilot project" level. Those who favor them insist that they are much less costly approaches to subsidized housing than the traditional slum clearance-housing project method, and that they will take low-income families out of hard-core slums, distributing them among middle-income neighborhoods. In the main, opponents of the programs argue that potential costs are huge and that the programs amount to "forced integration."

The Renewal Assistance Administration. The existence of slums and other "blighted" and deteriorating areas pose very real and very serious problems in many of the nation's cities, large and small. The fact that most of the "civil rights riots" in northern cities in the past few years have erupted in just such areas points up how real and how serious those problems can be—to say nothing of health, morals, crime, and similar matters.

The Renewal Assistance Administration manages the slum clearance and urban renewal programs which date from the Housing Acts of 1949 and 1954. Its principal work is that of providing aid for the reclaiming of local residential and business areas. It makes grants and loans and gives advice to cities and other local governments for the planning and execution of "urban renewal" projects—local efforts aimed at preventing or eliminating and rehabilitating slum neighborhoods and other blighted sections. It also helps to meet a wide range of related redevelopment problems; for example, the relocation of families and businesses uprooted by slum clearance work and the reclamation of the blighted surroundings of such public institutions as hospitals and universities.

The Model Cities Administration. In 1966 Congress authorized a new and concerted attack on urban blight. It did so with the *Model Cities Program*—a projected $900,000,000 assault on city decay and the conditions out of which such blight breeds. It was funded with an initial appropriation of $312,000,000 in 1967, but Congress has since upped the program to the $1,000,000,000-a-year level.

Under the program, selected cities are to receive federal grants channeled through the Model Cities Administration. These funds will cover up to eighty per cent of the costs of reclaiming specific neighborhoods.

On the basis of preliminary plans submitted by nearly 200 cities, sixty-three were given one-year planning grants in late 1967. Those which successfully complete their planning projects will receive multi-million dollar grants for the execution of their models.

The model now (1970) being developed by Portland, Oregon, typifies the projects on which the selected communities are at work. Portland's plan calls for the use of all means, public and private, to remake a blighted section of the city. It encompasses five square miles bounded by two interstate freeways, another major arterial, and the Columbia River. Some 41,000 persons reside in the area and it includes the district in which most of the city's Negroes live. A new $14,000,000 community college campus is a central feature of the plan. So, too, are new and improved streets, parks, and schools as well as rehabilitated housing and business structures.

The Community Resources Development Administration. The Community Resources Development Administration is less directly concerned with the housing field than are the other of HUD's principal agencies. Its major function dates from the Housing Act of 1954; the making of loans to States, cities, and other public units for the construction of such "needed public works" as water, gas, and sewage facilities. Under the Housing and Urban Development Act of 1965 it also administers grants for park improvements, landscaping, and other "beautification" projects in cities and their surrounding locale. It is also responsible for cleaning up what still remains of the work of the once-huge Reconstruction Finance Corporation; that is, it supervises the collection of the few still-outstanding loans made by that Corporation (page 551).

OTHER HUD PROGRAMS

HUD was born out of the former Housing and Home Finance Agency in 1965, as we have noted. Thus far, it has played much the same role as did its predecessor: that of managing and coordinating the principal federal housing programs. But, recall, its basic mission extends beyond the field of housing. Congress has vested in it major responsibility for the "administration of the principal programs of the Federal Government which provide assistance for housing *and* for the development of the nation's communities."

At least to 1970, however, HUD's efforts in this other and broader realm — that of urban development — have not begun to match the magnitude of its housing work.

Among the Department's other agencies are:

The Office of Interstate Land Sales Registration which administers the Interstate Land Sales Full Disclosure Act of 1968. That law is designed to choke off a growing racket and, at the same time, protect legitimate land developers and the general public. It requires any developer who, by mail or any means in interstate commerce, offers to sell or lease a lot in any subdivision containing fifty or more lots to file the full details of his project with HUD.

The Urban Management Assistance Administration which administers grants to aid cities and other local governments in the planning of various projects which will later come under the wing of other HUD agencies; for example, the planning of an extension of a city's sewer system to be financed in part with funds from the Community Resources Development Administration.

The Office of Equal Housing Opportunity which enforces the "fair housing" provisions of the Civil Rights Act of 1968. That act makes it unlawful, in nearly all situations, for anyone to refuse to sell or rent a dwelling to any person on grounds of race, color, religion, or national origin.

The law became effective with regard to most multiple-unit housing on January 1, 1969, and was extended to almost all other housing — including privately owned, single-family dwellings — on January 1, 1970. It is estimated that approximately 80 per cent of all housing in the United States is now within the law's coverage.

The major exceptions the law allows to its coverage involve situations in which: (1) a private individual who owns not more than three houses, sells or rents without the services of a real estate agent or broker and does not indicate any preference or discrimination in advertising a house for sale or rent; (2) a dwelling contains not more than four living units and in which the owner has his own residence; and (3) a religious organization or private club provides housing for its own members on a non-commercial basis.

THE WAR ON POVERTY

In his State of the Union Message in 1964 President Johnson called upon the nation to declare "unconditional war on poverty in America." He noted that:

We are citizens of the richest and most fortunate nation in history.

But, he added:

There are millions of Americans—one fifth of our people—who have not shared in the abundance which has been granted to most of us.

And he proposed a massive program to "pursue poverty wherever it exists"—a program

designed to help each and every American citizen to fulfill his basic hopes: his hopes for a fair chance to make good; his hopes for fair play from the law; his hopes for a full-time job on full-time pay; his hopes for a decent home for his family in a decent community; his hopes for a good school for his children with good teachers; and his hopes for security when faced with sickness, unemployment, or old age.

Congress responded to the President's call with the passage of the Economic Opportunity Act of 1964; it appropriated more than $750,000,000 to begin the "war on poverty" in 1965, and has provided more than double that amount to carry it on in each of the years since then.

The Office of Economic Opportunity. Most of the welfare programs created in the 1964 Act are administered by the Office of Economic Opportunity. OEO is not located within any of the Cabinet departments; rather, it functions directly under the Chief Executive as a part of the Executive Office of the President (page 308).

OEO is headed by a Director who is also responsible for coordinating its work with that of other federal agencies which administer related anti-poverty programs. Thus, for example, OEO works closely with such other agencies as the Manpower Administration in the Department of Labor (page 470) and the

Office of Education in the Department of Health, Education, and Welfare (page 497).

The key programs established in the Economic Opportunity Act include:

The Job Corps, designed to furnish basic education, vocational training, and useful work experience to young men and women between ages sixteen and twenty-two. It is aimed specifically at those young people who come from such impoverished areas as city slums and backwoods hill sections who have not completed high school ("dropouts"), have not been able to find satisfactory jobs, and lack reading and arithmetic skills.

Some Job Corps centers are located on public lands supervised by such federal conservation agencies as the Forest Service and the National Park Service. Others are located in or near major cities. In the rural camps the enrollees perform conservation work under the direction of experienced personnel of the Forest Service, National Park Service, Bureau of Indian Affairs, Bureau of Reclamation, and similar agencies. The urban centers, usually operated under contracts with colleges or universities, are housed in unused military or other public facilities. They offer more intensive and specialized vocational training—for such occupations as office machine operator, shipping, accounting, or file clerk, sales clerk, waiter, cook, meat cutter, hospital orderly, appliance or automobile repairman, and many others. Young women are also trained to meet family responsibilities; among other things, they are taught how to care for a home, manage money, buy food and clothing, and are given guidance on how to rear physically and emotionally healthy children.

Members of the Job Corps are paid a "terminal allowance" of $50 for every month they have spent in the Corps, payable after they have left it. They also receive "pocket money" of $30 a month plus room, food, clothing, and medical and dental care.

The Work-Training Program, to give underprivileged youths a chance to find work or job-training in their own communities. The program is conducted through grants made to local communities to assist them to pay trainees for work which is beneficial to them and to the community—as in a hospital, a mental health clinic, or a city recreation department.

The Work-Study Program, to make part-time work available to students from low-income families so that they might continue their education. The program is run via grants made to institutions of higher education, including junior colleges and technical institutes.

Any resident of the United States who is 18 years of age or older is eligible to apply as a volunteer in VISTA's fight against poverty. Volunteers help communities to help themselves by working and living with the people they seek to serve. This VISTA volunteer is working among the Indians in the Gila River Indian Community in Arizona. (James Foote, VISTA)

Community Action Programs, to provide grants to States and their local governments and to private non-profit groups conducting their own antipoverty programs. The aid goes for such efforts as those seeking to create new job opportunities, to improve public school or health facilities, or to provide job-training or vocational rehabilitation.

The Work-Experience Program, to furnish additional assistance, especially that of job-training, to unemployed heads of families already receiving some form of public assistance, such as aid to dependent children.

The Adult Basic Education Program, to provide grants to the States for the creation of local school programs of basic education for illiterate adults.

VISTA, the *Volunteers in Service to America,* a corps of several thousand volunteers trained by the OEO as the domestic counterpart to the Peace Corps. Many of its members are assigned to work with State and local agencies in such major fields as job counseling, welfare, and mental health. Other members work on Indian reservations, among migratory workers, and in the territories.

The Economic Opportunity Act also created a small-loan program for low-income farm families, a loan program to help small businesses hire handicapped workers and others chronically jobless, and a program to aid public and private agencies which seek to upgrade health, housing, and schooling conditions among migratory farm workers.

Obviously, these programs overlap one another considerably; and they overlap many other and older welfare programs, as well. Realizing this, Congress gave the Director of the Office of Economic Opportunity broad authority to mesh the various federal welfare programs.

Obviously, too, these programs, in themselves, will not eradicate poverty. But they do mark, as the President has said, "a commitment to pursue victory over the most ancient of mankind's enemies."

Key Concepts

The establishment by Congress of the Cabinet-level Department of Housing and Urban Development in 1965 reflects the highly significant fact that we are, and have rather suddenly become, an urban people. Nearly three of every four Americans today live in the nation's urban areas.

Primary responsibility for meeting the problems of urban areas rests with the States and their local governments. As these problems have multiplied, however, the extent of federal involvement has grown, as well.

Major responsibility for the principal federal programs in the fields of housing and community development are vested in the Department of Housing and Urban Development. The best-known of HUD's several agencies is the Federal Housing Administration which conducts various mortgage-guarantee programs. Among its other agencies, the Federal National Mortgage Association aids private lenders by buying and selling second mortgages; the Housing Assistance Administration conducts federal public housing programs; the Renewal Assistance Administration is responsible for aiding local urban renewal projects; the Model Cities Administration runs the model cities program; and the Community Resources Development Administration aids local communities with various public works projects.

The Office of Economic Opportunity, created in the Economic Opportunity Act of 1964, has the major responsibility for prosecuting the "war on poverty." Located in the Executive Office of the President, it administers a number of welfare programs designed to alleviate poverty throughout the country.

Important Terms

HUD	mortgage	second mortgage	urban renewal
Job Corps	public housing	slum clearance	VISTA
Model Cities Program	rent supplements	urban areas	"war on poverty"

Questions for Inquiry and Review

1. What very significant fact about the American people was highlighted by the creation of the Department of Housing and Urban Development?

2. Approximately what proportion of our population now lives in urban areas?

3. Where does the federal system assign the primary responsibility for meeting the problems of urban areas?

4. What federal agency has major responsibility for federal programs in the urban field? When was it created?

5. Who was appointed as the first Secretary of Housing and Urban Development? What unique factor was involved in his selection?

6. In what period did the National Government begin to become increasingly involved in the housing field?

7. What were the two primary purposes of the early federal housing legislation? What new emphasis was added in 1937?

8. Which is the best known of HUD's several agencies? In what particular way does it promote the building and buying of homes?

9. What is "Fanny May"? How does this association aid private lenders and the housing industry?

10. What is the basic function of the Housing Assistance Administration? The Renewal Assistance Administration? The Model Cities Administration? The Community Resources Development Administration?

11. With which of its basic responsibilities have HUD's agencies been most involved?

12. What is the "war on poverty"? By whom was it proposed? When?

13. What agency is chiefly responsible for its conduct? Where is that agency located?

14. At what particular group is the Job Corps program aimed? What is VISTA?

For Further Inquiry

1. What has been the record of population growth in your locale in recent decades? What factors have been largely responsible for that record? What would you identify as the three most important problems resulting from it?

2. If your community has a housing shortage, what factors do you think are responsible for it? What is being done to meet the situation, if one exists?

3. In enacting the Housing and Urban Development Act of 1965, Congress declared that

"the general welfare and security of the nation and the health and living standards of our people require, as a matter of national purpose, sound development of the nation's communities and metropolitan areas." With what specific illustrations can you amplify that declaration?

4. As a general matter, in which place would you rather live: a large metropolitan area, a small town, or a rural section? Why?

Suggested Activities

1. Prepare as extensive a list as you can of examples in your locale of the work of the various federal agencies discussed in this chapter.

2. Invite an officer of a local bank, a representative of another home-financing agency, or a homebuilder to speak to the class on housing conditions and related matters in your community.

3. Invite a representative of one of HUD's agencies or the Office of Economic Opportunity to discuss the work of his agency in your locale.

4. Stage a debate or class forum on the question: *Resolved,* That the present extent of federal activities in the fields of housing and urban development is inconsistent with the concepts of federalism and private enterprise.

Suggested Reading

BLACKMORE, CHARLES P. and YESELSON, ABRAHAM (eds.), *The Fabric of American Democracy. Van Nostrand, 1969. Chapter 13.*

"Department of Housing and Urban Development," *HUD Programs.* Government Printing Office, 1970.

GOLDFARB, ROBERT W., "Why Whitey Is Failing in the Cities," *Reader's Digest,* October, 1969.

LANGEWIESCHE, WOLFGANG, "The Suburbs Are Changing," *Reader's Digest,* Nov. 1969.

McQUADE, WALTER, "An Answer to the Housing Crisis?" *Fortune,* May 2, 1969; *Reader's Digest,* September, 1969.

MILLER, JAMES N., "Slum Swindlers Must Go!" *Reader's Digest,* November, 1969.

ROMNEY, GEORGE, "The Breakdown in Our Cities," *U.S. News,* July 28, 1969.

THE DEPARTMENT
OF TRANSPORTATION

In a nation that spans a continent, transportation is the web of union.

LYNDON B. JOHNSON

❖❖❖ Is it proper, in your view, for government to subsidize various forms of transportation in this country?

❖❖❖ To whom are the programs administered by DOT most beneficial?

❖❖❖ Should the basic function of DOT be promotional or regulatory in character? Why?

❖❖❖ Should the nation's rail transport system be nationalized? The air transport system? Why?

The Department of Transportation (DOT) is the newest of the twelve Cabinet departments. It was formally established on April 1, 1967, the date upon which the Department of Transportation Act of 1966 became effective.

Government's Involvement. The tender age of the new Department does not reflect a sudden or new-found governmental concern for the nation's transportation system. In fact, quite the opposite is true. From its beginnings, the Federal Government has been closely concerned with all forms of transportation. Several major reasons produced this long and continuing involvement. The nation's transportation facilities provided the physical basis for the creation of a politically united country. They also provided the means by which the huge expanse and vast resources of the country could be developed.

The intimate relationships between an adequate system of transportation on the one hand

and agricultural and industrial growth and prosperity on the other are obvious. The significance of the relationship between transportation and national defense is just as obvious. And other needs of government—especially in the enforcement of law, the collection of taxes, and the administration of public policies—provide other reasons for this interest.

Those forces and events that produced the Constitution clearly demonstrated the inevitability of a heavy federal involvement in transportation. As we have noted several times, the Founding Fathers were generally agreed upon the need for national regulation of commerce. And the Constitution's Commerce Clause was more responsible for the transforming of a loose confederation of States into a strong Union than any other provision in the document.[1]

Indeed, the nation's history may be told in good part in terms of the development of its transportation system. Our territorial expan-

---

[1] Article I, Section 8, Clause 3; see particularly pages 36–38 and 266–270.

sion, growth in population, and vast accumulation of wealth and power have gone hand-in-hand with the development of the means by which we move goods and persons—from the days of the horse and rider, the stagecoach, the sailing ship, and the covered wagon through the development of the steamboat, the railroad, the automobile, and the airplane to the age of jet propulsion, automation, and nuclear power.

A Private-Public Partnership. As we turn to the Department of Transportation and its many agencies and functions, bear these points in mind: The United States is the only major nation in the world that relies primarily upon *privately* owned and operated transportation. As a people, we are generally agreed that private enterprise has served us well and that its predominant role must be continued. But, at the same time, remember that private ownership has succeeded as it has only through the use of *publicly* granted authority and an immense investment of *public* resources. For example, notice how indispensable to our transportation system have been and are such governmental contributions as the construction of channels, locks, and dams on our rivers and inland waterways, the development of ports and harbors, the construction and operation of airports and airways, the development of a vast network of highways, grants of public land, and the use of the power of eminent domain.

In short, remember that government has been a most useful and willing partner with private enterprise in providing for the nation's transportation needs.

DEPARTMENTAL ORGANIZATION

In authorizing the establishment of the Department (DOT), Congress declared that:

... the establishment of the Department of Transportation is necessary in the public interest and to assure the coordinated, effective administration of the transportation programs of the Federal Government; to facilitate the development and improvement of coordinated transportation service, to be provided by private enterprise to the maximum extent feasible; to encourage cooperation of federal, State, and local carriers, labor, and other interested parties toward the achievement of national transportation objectives; to stimulate technological advances in transportation; to provide general leadership in the identification and solution of transportation problems; and to develop and recommend to the President and the Congress for approval national transportation policies and programs to accomplish these objectives with full and appropriate consideration of the needs of the public, users, carriers, industry, labor, and the national defense.

Succinctly, DOT's basic mission is that of administering the Federal Government's major promotional and safety programs in the field of transportation. Despite the broad sweep of the congressional statement, four major federal transportation agencies are not included within the Department. One of them is distinctly promotional in character: the Maritime Administration, within the Department of Commerce and with which we dealt in Chapter 25.[2] The other three are: the Federal Maritime Commission (see pages 462–463), and the Interstate Commerce Commission and the Civil Aeronautics Board, to which we shall turn in the next chapter. These latter three agencies are concerned with the *economic regulation* of transportation and continue to operate as independent regulatory commissions.

The Secretary of Transportation. DOT is headed by the Secretary of Transportation.

---

[2] See pages 462–463. The Johnson Administration had urged the transfer of the Maritime Administration to the new department. Strong pressures from the shipping industry and maritime unions persuaded Congress to leave the agency undisturbed, however.

Like each of his colleagues in the Cabinet, he is appointed by the President subject to Senate confirmation. An Under Secretary functions as his second-in-command and the top echelon of departmental staff is filled out by five Assistant Secretaries—for Policy and International Affairs, Public Affairs, Urban Systems and Environment, Research and Technology, and Administration.

Despite its youth, DOT ranks as the fourth largest of the Cabinet departments. More than 90,000 men and women now work within its various agencies. Its size is hardly surprising when one recalls such impressive facts as these: Our transportation system now accounts for approximately $1 in every $5 in the American economy, or some $130,000,000,000 annually; and well over 2,500,000 persons now earn their livelihoods by moving goods and persons in this country.

Principal Agencies. The creation of DOT brought together more than thirty agencies and functions that were formerly scattered throughout the Government.[3] The major units now within the Department are the:

National Transportation Safety Board
Federal Aviation Administration
Federal Highway Administration
Federal Railroad Administration
United States Coast Guard
St. Lawrence Seaway Development Corporation

THE NATIONAL TRANSPORTATION SAFETY BOARD

The *National Transportation Safety Board* is unique among DOT's agencies. It is located within the Department for *administrative* purposes only; otherwise, it operates independently of the Secretary. Its five members are appointed by the President and Senate for five-year terms, and no more than three of them may be members of the same political party. The President designates one of the members to serve as the Board's chairman and he also functions as its chief executive and administrative officer.

The Board is responsible for investigating and determining the causes of all civilian aircraft accidents that occur within the United States. It also conducts investigations (or reviews the inquiries made by other departmental agencies) of rail, highway, marine, and pipeline accidents. On the basis of its findings, it recommends to the Secretary those steps that might be taken to prevent or reduce the possibility of similar occurrences in the future. Its reports and recommendations also go to other appropriate public agencies—for example, to the Federal Highway Administration.

The Board is also charged with hearing appeals taken from the licensing actions of other agencies within the Department—for example, an appeal of a denial, suspension, or revocation of a commercial pilot's license by the Federal Aviation Administration. The Secretary cannot in any way modify a decision rendered by the Board in a licensing case; such a decision may be appealed only to the federal courts.

The Board's work—and, indeed, each of the other safety functions vested in DOT—is of critical importance. Even a quick glance at these tragic statistics makes that fact all too clear: Approximately 55,000 Americans now die each year in transport accidents. The

---

[3] Among his many duties, the Secretary of Transportation is responsible for the fixing of the standard time zones throughout the United States—a task formerly assigned to the Interstate Commerce Commission. He also enforces the Uniform Time Act of 1966—in which Congress required that, from 1967 on, standard time be advanced one hour (*i.e.*, that daylight time be observed) in all time zones from 2 A.M. on the last Sunday in April through 2 A.M. on the last Sunday in October each year; a State may exempt itself from the law only if the State legislature votes to keep the entire State on standard time.

automobile is the major killer, of course; it now claims over 50,000 lives a year—to say nothing of the annual toll of *millions* who are injured in traffic accidents.[4] In addition, some 1000 persons are killed each year in all types of railroad accidents, 1500 in ship and boat accidents, and 2000 in private and commercial aviation accidents.

THE FEDERAL AVIATION ADMINISTRATION

Congress first began to provide for the regulation of civil air transportation with the passage of the Air Commerce Act of 1926 (see page 538). Over the past four decades that regulation has evolved to the point where today three agencies are closely involved in it. The National Transportation Safety Board is especially concerned with determining the causes of air accidents, as we have just noted. The Civil Aeronautics Board has as its primary function the *economic* regulation of air transport, as we shall see in Chapter 30.

The other and major agency in the field is the *Federal Aviation Administration.* The FAA was first established as an independent agency in the executive branch in 1958 and became a part of DOT in 1967. It is headed by an Administrator appointed by the President and Senate.

By law, the FAA is "empowered and directed to encourage and foster civil aeronautics and air commerce in the United States and abroad." It possesses very broad authority to discharge this mission, beginning at the drawing board-research level and extending throughout the realm of aviation. It licenses all civilian pilots and aircraft, both private and commercial. It makes and enforces safety rules for all air traffic and regulates the use of all navigable air space within the United States—for both civilian *and* military purposes. Any conflict between the FAA and the Armed Forces over the regulation of air space must be resolved by the President himself.

Some notion of the scope of this portion of the Administration's work can be seen in the fact that there are now approximately 125,000 private and commercial planes in this country. Two decades ago there were less than 40,000. The present total is expected to double before 1975. And, by then, today's 2600 commercial airliners will number about 3500, and will include 1800-mile-an-hour supersonic transports and 450-passenger "jumbo jets." Twenty years ago the commercial airlines flew slightly more than 200,000,000 miles a year. Today they fly more than 2,000,000,000 miles annually, and passenger-freight mileage rises year to year.

The FAA is also responsible for the installation, maintenance, and operation of such air navigation devices as beacons, wind and directional signals, radar, and other and more sophisticated electronic aids to flight. It operates a nationwide air traffic communications system and equips and mans air traffic control towers and centers at hundreds of local airports. It fosters aviation research, maintains emergency landing fields, and administers a program of grants-in-aid for the construction and improvement of airports. No federal funds may be spent on *any* civilian airport, nor may the military build or alter any airport or missile site, without the FAA's approval.

As part of its extensive research program, the FAA is now using one of NASA's satellites in a series of experiments relating to the communications and navigation requirements of aircraft flying at high speeds and altitudes. The agency expects to launch its own satellite sometime in the near future.

---

[4] More than 1,500,000 persons have died in motor vehicle accidents in the United States in this century—*more than twice* the number of Americans killed in all of the wars this nation has fought.

THE FEDERAL HIGHWAY ADMINISTRATION

The United States is literally a nation on wheels. Among our 200,000,000 people today there are approximately 100,000,000 drivers who operate some 85,000,000 cars and 15,000,000 trucks and buses on 3,700,000 miles of roads and streets, traveling more than 900,000,000 miles a year. We have nearly one motor vehicle for every two persons, nearly thirty vehicles for every mile of road, and a mile of road for each square mile in the country. Four out of every five persons old enough to drive have driver's licenses. The figures grow larger every year. It is estimated that by 1975 more than 116,000,000 motor vehicles will travel more than 1,000,000,000,000 miles a year in the United States.

The first federal roadbuilding law was passed by Congress at least as early as 1806. Until the Age of the Automobile was well underway, however, the responsibility for road construction and maintenance was borne almost exclusively by the States and their local governments. They still bear the primary burden in this field. After education, roads are the most costly item in current State and local spending.

It was not until the "horseless carriage" had become a familiar part of the American scene that the National Government began to move into the highway picture in a significant way. The present hefty federal highway programs trace their direct ancestry back only to the modest Federal Aid Road Act of 1916. That statute set the basic pattern for highway legislation that Congress has followed ever since. It provided for yearly grants of $15,000,000 to the States, and required each of them to match its portion of that total on a dollar-for-dollar basis.

Grants-in-aid remain a basic feature of the federal highway programs. But the total amounts now involved have, by comparison with 1916, grown to astronomical heights.

The *Federal Highway Administration* is the principal federal roadbuilding agency today.

It is headed by an Administrator appointed by the President and Senate. It came into being with DOT in 1967 and is, in large part, the successor to the Bureau of Public Roads, formerly located in the Commerce Department.

The Administration conducts a number of different programs. It cooperates with the Forest Service, the National Park Service, and several other agencies in the construction and maintenance of roads on federal lands. It determines the reasonableness of tolls charged on bridges over the navigable waters of the United States, is responsible for the Inter-American Highway in Central America, and does extensive planning and research work in all phases of highway construction and maintenance. Through the State Department it provides as-

Overlooking Salt Lake City, the radar tower on Francis Peak is one of the many long range radars operated by the FAA. Its powerful antenna spots aircraft within a radius of 200 miles and up to 60,000 feet. (Federal Aviation Administration)

sistance to foreign governments in the fields of highway engineering and administration.

The Administration also now has a considerable role in the fast-developing area of federal concern for highway safety,[5] and administers a grant program to encourage the States in "highway beautification." But, with all of its other functions, its major task is the administration of the huge federal-aid highway program.

The Federal Aid Highway Act of 1956 is the basic federal road-construction law today. Its passage inaugurated the largest public works program in history—the construction of the 42,500-mile National System of Interstate Highways. The States now receive grants totaling over $4,000,000,000 a year for the building and improving of the system. By 1974 this herculean effort is expected to provide a coast-to-coast network of limited access, four-to-eight lane superhighways serving all of the nation's larger cities and thousands of smaller ones as well. When completed, the system will have cost over $52,000,000,000—with the

---

[5] Particularly it enforces the National Traffic Safety Act and the Highway Safety Act. Both were passed by Congress in 1966 to launch a far-reaching federal attack on the mounting number of highway deaths and injuries. The first statute gives the Administration the authority to set minimum safety standards that must be met by all new motor vehicles intended for use on public roads. It is designed to prevent accidents caused by mechanical defects and failures and deaths and injuries resulting from "second collisions"—that occur when an occupant collides with the internal features of a vehicle or is thrown from it. The Highway Safety Act provides grant-in-aid support for safety programs. To receive federal funds, State and local governments must meet minimum standards set by the Administration in such areas as driver education, licensing, accident investigation and records, traffic control, vehicle registration and inspection, and the construction and maintenance of highway safety devices. The States must match the federal grants on a dollar-for-dollar basis; those which do not comply with the program may suffer a ten per cent cut in federal-aid highway funds.

Federal Government paying nine-tenths of that cost. (See map, page 738.)

Under the law, the States also receive grants for the improvement of the additional 860,000 miles in the federal-aid network of *primary* (main), *secondary* (feeder, farm-to-market, and the like), and *urban* roads. These grants, which were begun under the 1916 law, have now reached the $1,000,000,000-a-year level. The States must match these federal-aid funds with equal amounts of their own money.

THE FEDERAL RAILROAD ADMINISTRATION

The *Federal Railroad Administration* (FRA) was born with the Department of Transportation in 1967. It is now the major federal promotional and safety agency in the field of rail transportation. It thus operates in the same general field as the Interstate Commerce Commission—and, in fact, acquired many of its functions by transfer from the ICC. The ICC continues to play its principal and historic role as *economic regulator* of the nation's rail, motor carrier, and domestic water-borne commerce, as we shall see in Chapter 30.

The FRA is headed by an Administrator appointed by the President and Senate. In addition to its general railroad functions, it also has responsibilities in two other related areas: It administers the Government-owned Alaska Railroad and includes the Office of High Speed Ground Transportation.

Through its Bureau of Railroad Safety, the FRA now administers the safety provisions of the Interstate Commerce Act of 1887 and a host of other statutes enacted over the years since. It issues and enforces safety regulations governing the operations of railroads, express and sleeping car companies, and those ships, barges, and other water carriers that operate in connection with rail lines. It also has safety jurisdiction over oil pipelines and the carrying of explosives or dangerous articles by rail.

The Alaska Railroad is an entirely federally-owned rail system. Congress authorized its construction in the then Territory of Alaska in 1914. It functioned under the direction of the Secretary of the Interior until 1967 and is now a sub-agency within the Federal Railroad Administration. Its basic objective has from its beginnings been that of encouraging settlement and the agricultural and industrial development of Alaska.

The Railroad operates 470.3 miles of main line from its southern terminus at Seward through Anchorage and on to Fairbanks in the interior of the 49th State. It also runs a number of shorter lines and a tug and barge service on the Tanana and Yukon Rivers. The ICC regulates its freight and passenger rates.

The Office of High Speed Ground Transportation is essentially a research and demonstration agency. Its chief concern is with the development of ultra-fast means for the carrying of goods and persons by land — especially between major metropolitan centers. In concert with private industry, it is now at work on such new transportation concepts as air-cushion vehicles, monorails, and gravity vacuum tubes. Currently, the Office is testing highspeed trains which have been designed largely on the basis of flight technology, with streamlined aerodynamic shapes and interiors much like those of jet airliners. These trains, capable of hitting speeds up to 160 miles an hour, are now being developed for use on Boston-to-New York and Washington-to-New York runs and along the east coast to Jacksonville, Florida.

THE UNITED STATES COAST GUARD

The *United States Coast Guard* is a military service and operates, at all times, as a branch of the nation's Armed Forces. It is now a unit within DOT; but in time of war, or at the President's direction, it becomes a part of the Navy.

The Coast Guard was formally established in 1915 as an agency within the Treasury Department and was transferred to DOT in 1967. It traces its history back to 1790, however; it is the present-day descendant of the old Revenue Cutter Service, the Lifesaving Service, the Lighthouse Service, and the Bureau of Marine Inspection and Navigation. It is directed by a Commandant chosen by the President and confirmed by the Senate. The 37,000 officers and men under his command are organized and function much like the Navy.

The Coast Guard is especially responsible for the enforcement of the laws of the United States relating to the high seas and to waters under the jurisdiction of the United States. Its specific duties are numerous. It maintains a system of inshore and offshore ships, aircraft, lifeboat stations, and radio facilities to carry out search and rescue operations. It mans six ocean stations on a continuous basis — four in the North Atlantic and two in the Pacific. While on station, its vessels conduct search and rescue missions, collect oceanographic data, provide meteorological information to the Weather Bureau, and furnish navigation and other aid to air and marine traffic.

It also enforces fishing and sealing laws in Alaskan waters; maintains lighthouses, radio beacons, fog signals, and buoys; clears ice-clogged channels; inspects all classes of vessels for seaworthiness and safety; and ferries ill seamen and passengers to shore hospitals. Coast Guard officers, detailed as Captains of the Port, are responsible for matters of port security and for the regulation of the anchorage and movement of vessels in American territorial waters.

The Coast Guard patrols the more than 12,000 miles of our coastline to prevent piracy, the operation of gambling ships, and the smuggling of dutiable goods, narcotics, liquor, and undesirable persons. In wartime it escorts convoys, operates landing craft in amphibious invasions, and guards against enemy landings along our shores. A number of its officers and men are now serving in Viet Nam. The Coast Guard Academy, at New London, Connecticut, trains new officers for the service.

THE SAINT LAWRENCE SEAWAY DEVELOPMENT CORPORATION

The *Saint Lawrence Seaway Development Corporation* was established by act of Congress in 1954. Since then, the Saint Lawrence Seaway and the related power development of the Saint Lawrence River—a dream for decades—have become firmly accomplished facts. The inland ports of the Great Lakes are now linked to the Atlantic Ocean, and the power of the river has been harnessed by a project that produces more energy than that generated at Hoover Dam and nearly that which comes from the mighty Grand Coulee.

Since the beginning of this century Congress had considered various proposals for joint United States-Canadian development of the St. Lawrence. It had been urged by every President from Woodrow Wilson on. The Senate rejected an international canal treaty in 1934 and both houses disapproved an executive agreement to the same end in 1941. Finally, in 1953, with strong backing from President Eisenhower, Congress gave to New York State the right to build the power project in cooperation with the Province of Ontario, and in 1954 it authorized the joint United States-Canadian construction of the Seaway itself.

The Corporation was established as the federal agency to construct, and then to maintain and operate, the new waterway in concert with the Canadian Saint Lawrence Seaway Authority. The Corporation, headed by an Administrator appointed by the President and Senate, was transferred from the Department of Commerce to the Transportation Department in 1967.

Work on the Seaway was begun in the spring of 1955 and it was opened to its first deep-sea traffic in 1959. The Seaway has given us a vast new 8000-mile seacoast and made seaports of such inland cities as Buffalo, Chicago, Cleveland, Detroit, Milwaukee, and Toledo. By 1970 the Seaway is expected to carry more than 50,000,000 tons of cargo a year. Iron ore from Labrador and South America constitute a major part of the inbound cargo.

Seventeen locks are required to overcome the 600-foot drop in the water level between Lake Superior and the Atlantic. Before the Seaway's completion, ocean-going vessels could navigate the 1000 miles up the St. Lawrence to Montreal, and similar ships plied the Great Lakes from Duluth, Minnesota, to Ogdensburg, New York. Thus the only *major* construction required was in the 120-mile stretch of the river between Montreal and Ogdensburg.

The power project involved the construction of dams and a hydroelectric power installation at the International Rapids, between Massena, New York, and Cornwall, Ontario. The New York State Power Authority was the official agent of the United States in the construction of the power project with the Ontario Hydro-Electric Power Commission. The project produces more than 12,000,000,000 kilowatt-hours of energy a year. Its product is divided between New York and Ontario, and New York must make a "fair share" of its power available to those neighboring States within economic transmission distance. New York's half of the power produced has added about ten per cent to that available to practically all of New England and the eastern two-thirds of New York.

The total cost of the Seaway was approximately $471,000,000. Of that amount, the United States share was some $131,000,000. Tolls on the American portion of the Seaway are rising each year and now (1970) amount to some $7,300,000 annually. They should soon produce enough to meet all operating expenses and eventually pay off the United States share, as well. The total cost of the completed power project is approximately $600,000,000; New York's share is being met from the sale of power produced by the project.

Key Concepts

The Department of Transportation (DOT) became the twelfth Cabinet department in 1967. Its creation reflects a close and long-standing federal involvement with all forms of transportation. Although the United States is the only major nation that relies primarily on privately owned and operated transportation, government has been a most willing and active partner in the development of the nation's transportation system.

DOT's basic mission is that of administering the Federal Government's many *promotional* and *safety* programs in the field of transportation. The bulk of *economic regulation* in the field is the prime responsibility of several independent regulatory commissions.

The Creation of the Department, headed by the Secretary of Transportation, brought together more than thirty transportation agencies and functions formerly scattered throughout the Government. The principal departmental agencies today are: The National Transportation Safety Board, which functions independently of the Secretary and is primarily concerned with the investigation of causes and the prevention of transportation accidents; the Federal Aviation Administration, which in concert with the Civil Aeronautics Board regulates and promotes nearly all aspects of civil aviation in the United States; the Federal Highway Administration, which has major responsibility for the administration of the huge federal-aid highway programs; the Federal Railroad Administration, which in concert with the Interstate Commerce Commission regulates and promotes the nation's rail transportation and also operates the Alaska Railroad and includes the Office of High Speed Ground Transportation; the United States Coast Guard, a branch of the Armed Forces with a multitude of duties centering on search and rescue operations, aids to navigation, and the enforcement of the nation's maritime laws; and the Saint Lawrence Seaway Development Corporation, which operates and maintains the Saint Lawrence Seaway.

Important Terms

air cushion vehicles	civil aviation	monorail	navigation
Alaska Railroad	DOT	National System of	Saint Lawrence Seaway
Captain of the Port	federal-aid highways	Interstate Highways	transportation system

Questions for Inquiry and Review

1. When was the Department of Transportation formally established?

2. Why has the nation's transportation system been a matter of long, close, and continuing governmental concern?

3. Why can the nation's transportation system be properly described as a "private-public partnership"?

4. What is DOT's basic mission?

5. Which major *promotional* transportation agency is not within DOT?

6. What makes the National Transportation

Safety Board unique among DOT agencies? What is its major function?

7. With what independent regulatory commission does the FAA share authority in the field of air transportation? What is the FAA's basic mission?

8. What is the National System of Interstate Highways? With which DOT agency is it most closely associated?

9. With what independent regulatory commission does the Federal Railroad Administration share authority in the field of rail transportation? The FRA exercises responsibilities in what three major areas?

10. What is the basic mission of the Coast Guard? When does it operate as a part of another of the Armed Forces? Which of them?

11. By whom was the Saint Lawrence Seaway built? It is operated and maintained by which DOT agency?

For Further Inquiry

1. The first Secretary of Transportation, Alan S. Boyd, has said: "One of the major thrusts of this new department will be an energetic effort to account for the social as well as the economic costs of transportation." What are some "social costs" of transportation?

2. Is it proper for the Government to promote the nation's air, rail, highway, and other transportation systems with aids financed by taxes levied on the entire population?

3. Secretary Boyd has said that the fact that the Maritime Administration was not included within DOT was "an error" and he is "confident that the maritime interests eventually will see that it is to their own best interest" to become a part of the Department. Why was the Maritime Administration left in the Commerce Department? Do you agree with Mr. Boyd's statement?

Suggested Activities

1. Stage a debate or class forum on one of the following questions: (1) *Resolved,* That the nation's rail transportation system be nationalized. (2) *Resolved,* That the nation's air transportation system be nationalized.

2. Prepare as extensive a list as you can of DOT agency functions now being performed in your locale.

3. Prepare as extensive a list as you can of functions now being performed in your locale by *State and local* agencies in cooperation with or akin to those performed by DOT agencies.

4. Invite a representative of the railroad, motor carrier, or aviation industry to discuss the operation of his business and the extent to which it is influenced by government.

Suggested Reading

BURNS, JAMES M. and PELTASON, J. W., *Government By the People.* Prentice-Hall, 1969. Chapter 24.

"Is There Any Answer to Plane Hijackers?" *U.S. News,* October 20, 1969.

LINDSEY, ROBERT, "The Air Traffic Cop—On the Hottest Spot in Aviation," *New York Times Magazine,* September 14, 1969.

"Northeast Meets Northwest," *Newsweek,* November 24, 1969.

"On Flying More and Enjoying It Less," *Time,* April 18, 1969.

"Pro and Con: Controversy Over Federal Financing of Urban Mass Transit," *Congressional Digest,* December, 1969.

"Trouble for Freeways," *U.S. News,* August 11, 1969.

VOLPE, SECRETARY JOHN, "How to Cure Traffic Jams," *U.S. News,* June 9, 1969.

Nothing is so galling to a people, not broken in from the birth, as a paternal or, in other words, a meddling government.

THOMAS B. MACAULAY

❖❖❖ Should such regulatory agencies as the ICC and the FCC be as independent of presidential control as they are? Why?

❖❖❖ Should any and all forms of monopoly be prohibited by law? Why?

❖❖❖ Why are not newspapers and motion pictures as closely regulated by government as are radio and television?

The Constitution makes only the barest mention of the organization of the executive branch of the National Government. It does provide for the offices of President and Vice President, of course; but beyond that the document is almost wholly silent on the matter.[1] The Founding Fathers obviously expected that a number of administrative agencies would be created, however. They realized that such agencies would be absolutely necessary in order that the President might carry out his constitutional duty to "take care that the laws be faithfully executed."[2]

Congress has created a great many administrative bodies over the years. The first session of the First Congress established three executive departments — the Departments of State, Treasury, and War — and also provided for the offices of Attorney General and Postmaster General. Since then, the number of Cabinet departments has grown to twelve, as we have seen.

Not all of the administrative activities of the National Government have been assigned to the various Cabinet departments, however. Several other agencies — the *independent agencies* — located outside of any of the departments, have also been established. Today they number more than fifty, and their functions range from the fields of transportation and communications through finance and labor-management relations to veterans affairs and atomic energy.

The reasons for the separate establishment of these agencies are nearly as numerous as the agencies themselves — but five major reasons may be cited. Some agencies have been set

---

[1] The Necessary and Proper Clause (Article I, Section 8, Clause 18) refers to "any department or officer" of the National Government. Incidental references are also made to "the principal officer in each of the executive departments" and to "the heads of departments" in Article II, Section 2, Clauses 1 and 2. Except for these provisions, the Constitution is completely silent. [2] Article II, Section 3.

529

up outside of the regular departmental structure because their work is of such nature that they do not fit readily within any of the existing departments. For example, the Civil Service Commission, to be discussed in detail in Chapter 32, is the personnel agency for nearly all other federal agencies. The General Services Administration provides another illustration of the point. It was created in 1949 as the general "housekeeping" agency for the entire executive branch. Its major responsibilities include the management of buildings, the furnishing of supplies and other equipment, the storage and preservation of records, and the providing of similar services for all of the executive departments and agencies.

In some instances agencies have been given an independent status in order to protect them, at least insofar as possible, from the play of partisan politics. Again, the Civil Service Commission affords a good example, as do the Civil Rights Commission (page 120) and the Tariff Commission (page 259). But in some cases, on the other hand, special interest groups have persuaded Congress to place an agency outside of a department and the protections it might provide against group pressures. Thus, the Veterans Administration (pages 396–398) quite logically might be lodged within either the Departments of Defense or of Health, Education, and Welfare. Various veterans organizations, notably the American Legion, were responsible for the separate indentity of the VA, however—and they have fought to preserve that condition over the years.

Then, too, some independent agencies have been established as such largely as the result of "accident." That is, they were created to meet a specific need with no particular thought given at the time to the administrative hodge-podge that has inevitably resulted—for example, the Office of Economic Opportunity (page 308).

Finally, some agencies are independent because of the functions they perform. This is especially true of the *independent regulatory commissions*—the agencies to which most of this chapter is devoted. The more important of the other independent agencies are dealt with at appropriate places elsewhere in the text.[3]

The Independent Regulatory Commissions. These commissions are agencies which Congress has created especially to regulate certain segments of the nation's economy. They include the Interstate Commerce Commission, the Federal Trade Commission, the Federal Power Commission, the Federal Communications Commission, and the Civil Aeronautics Board—all of which are dealt with in this chapter, the Federal Reserve Board and the Securities and Exchange Commission which are discussed in the next chapter, and the National Labor Relations Board which is treated on page 477.

Like the other independent agencies, the regulatory commissions are not housed within any of the Cabinet departments. Unlike the others, however, they are largely independent of the President, too. Each is headed by a board or commission composed of from five to eleven members—not more than a bare majority of whom may be drawn from the same political party. Their members are appointed by the President with Senate consent. They are appointed, however, for terms of such length—as long as fourteen years in the case of the Federal Reserve Board—that the President cannot gain control over any of these agencies through his appointing power during a single term in the White House. Furthermore, the terms of commission members are staggered so that the term of only one member on each

---

[3] For example, in addition to those cited in the preceding paragraphs, the independent agencies especially concerned with finance are considered in the next chapter; the United States Information Agency on pages 331–332; the Atomic Energy Commission, pages 398–399; the National Aeronautics and Space Administration, pages 399–401; and the Tennessee Valley Authority, pages 433–435.

commission expires in any one year. Their independence of presidential control is also heightened by the fact that they are subject to removal by the President *only* for those causes specified by Congress, not at his pleasure.[4]

As with the other independent agencies, the regulatory commissions possess administrative powers to carry out the functions Congress has assigned to them. But, unlike the other independent agencies, they also exercise what are known as *quasi-legislative* and *quasi-judicial* powers.[5]

The regulatory commissions exercise their quasi-legislative powers when they issue rules and regulations—which have the force of law —to implement (spell out the details of) those statutes Congress has entrusted to their enforcement. For example, Congress has provided that railroad rates must be "just and reasonable." The Interstate Commerce Commission exercises control over the *actual* rates charged in particular situations and establishes them by issuing appropriate regulations.

The regulatory commissions exercise their quasi-judicial powers when they conduct hearings and decide disputes in those fields in which Congress has given them regulatory authority. For example, if a railroad requests ICC permission to raise its rates for carrying goods between two points, that request may be opposed by shippers. The ICC would then conduct hearings to determine the merits of the matter and render a decision, much as a court would. Appeals from decisions made by the regulatory commissions may be taken to the United States Courts of Appeals (see page 572).[6]

In effect, Congress has created the regulatory commissions to act in its stead. Congress could, if it chose, hold hearings and set freight rates, license hydroelectric power projects and radio and TV stations, check trade practices, and perform the many other tasks it has assigned to the regulatory commissions. But these are complex and time consuming matters which demand constant and expert attention. If Congress itself were to do these things, it would have no time for the other important legislative business to which it must attend.

THE INTERSTATE COMMERCE COMMISSION

Creation. The Interstate Commerce Commission, created by Congress in 1887 to regulate the nation's railroads, was the first independent regulatory commission to be established. A number of factors—notably the growth of the interstate character of railroads, shortsighted and undesirable business practices, and a key Supreme Court decision—prompted its creation.

In the early days of railroading in this country —from the 1830's to the 1860's—the operations of the various lines were generally simple and sufficiently local to permit adequate regulation of them by the States. As early as the late 1830's, however, the railroads began to extend their lines through several States; by the time

---

[4] See page 313. The members of the Federal Communications Commission and the Securities and Exchange Commission are exceptions here. Congress has provided that they may be removed at the President's discretion.

[5] The prefix *quasi* is from the Latin, meaning "in a certain sense, resembling, seemingly."

[6] Because the regulatory commissions exercise all three basic functions of government—executive, legislative, and judicial—they provide an exception to the application of the principle of separation of powers. Several authorities, including the Hoover Commission, have long proposed that at least their administrative functions be assigned to regular Cabinet agencies.

Freight carried on trains is considered a part of interstate commerce, and is thus regulated and protected by federal law until it is delivered. (Association of American Railroads)

similar practices—brought a sharp reversal of that attitude by the 1870's. A number of State legislatures, especially in the Middle West, responded to the complaints of farmers and other shippers by enacting the so-called "Granger Laws"—statutes imposing strict regulations upon the railroads.

Attempts at State regulation received a severe setback from the Supreme Court in 1886, however. In a case from Illinois, the Court held that State regulation of interstate railroad rates was an unconstitutional infringement upon the power of Congress to regulate interstate commerce.[7]

The Court's decision finally prompted action by Congress. In 1887 it passed the Act to Regulate Commerce—now known as the Interstate Commerce Act of 1887—forbidding excessive or discriminatory rates and other unfair practices by railroads and creating the Interstate Commerce Commission to administer the law.[8]

Today the ICC's authority covers not only railroads but interstate motor carriers, most carriers operating by water between coastal points and on the nation's lakes and rivers, interstate carriers using routes which are partly water and partly land, interstate pipelines (except those carrying water and gas), sleeping-car companies, and freight forwarders, as well. Air transportation is not regulated by the ICC but by the Civil Aeronautics Board and, as we have seen, the Federal Aviation Administration.

Organization. The ICC is composed of eleven members appointed by the President and confirmed by the Senate. The members

the first transcontinental line was completed in 1869, some three-fourths of all rail traffic in the United States was interstate in character.

The early public attitude toward the railroads was distinctly a promotional one. Congress and several of the State legislatures made large grants of land and of funds to them to encourage their growth. But selfish exploitation of their favored position—reflected in the growth of monopolies, financial manipulations, the corruption of public officials, rate gouging, and

---

[7] The Supreme Court decided the case, *Wabash, St. Louis & Pacific Railway Co.* v. *Illinois,* as it did despite the fact that to that point Congress had enacted no legislation on the subject.

[8] Today the functions of the ICC are based upon a number of additional statutes enacted by Congress to meet other problems raised by rail transportation and by other and newer forms of transportation—especially the Hepburn Act of 1906, the Transportation Act of 1920, the Motor Carrier Act of 1935, the Transportation Act of 1940, the Interstate Commerce Act of 1942, and the Transportation Act of 1958. But the 1887 law remains as the core of the agency's authority.

are chosen for seven-year terms, and not more than six may be of the same political party. The President selects the chairman. He and the other commission members usually conduct their routine work in three-member panels, and are assisted by a staff of more than 1700 economists, attorneys, investigators, examiners, and other personnel.

Powers. Its powers to regulate rail, land, and domestic water carriers [9] are so broad that the ICC is sometimes described as "the nation's transportation czar." Space limits us to touch upon only the major areas of the ICC's many activities—rate-setting, service, and securities. But an indication of the broad scope of its authority may be seen from the fact that it ranges from requiring all utilities it regulates to keep uniform accounts and render periodic reports to the fixing of reasonable rates for mail transportation by railway carriers.

Rate-Setting. The setting of rates is one of the most difficult and important of the ICC's many duties. If the rates carriers may charge are set too low, the carriers will lose money or, at the least, their owners will not realize a fair return on their investment. If the rates are too high, shippers and, in turn, the consuming public will suffer. Carriers are forbidden to charge unjust rates, and they must publish their rate schedules for public inspection. Normally, they may not charge more for a short than a longer haul over the same line; but in some special circumstances the ICC may permit them to do so. Thus, rail rates from New York to the Rocky Mountain States are sometimes higher than those to the Pacific Coast. If the Pacific Coast rates were not lower, much more freight would be carried by water through the Panama Canal, and the railroads would lose

business that their expensive road beds can carry at little additional cost.

Carriers may not give rebates to individual shippers or otherwise discriminate unreasonably against particular shippers or localities. The rates charged between two points within the same State cannot be set so low as to put points outside the State at an unfair advantage (see page 272). "Passes" or free transportation can be given only to a very restricted group of persons—for example, present or retired employees.

The ICC is sometimes criticized because it often fixes bus and truck rates higher than necessary in order to help the rail lines compete with the motor carriers for freight and passenger traffic. Those who defend this policy argue that the railroads are essential to the nation's well-being, especially in wartime, and must be kept in a healthy condition.

Service. Common carriers are required to furnish "reasonable service" to the public. Before a carrier may begin operations or extend an existing route, a *certificate of convenience and necessity* must be secured from the ICC. Thus, uneconomic duplications of lines and services may be prevented and, in the case of motor carriers, some highway congestion may be avoided.

The ICC may require a common carrier to extend its routes to serve shippers where it seems necessary and reasonable, and the ICC's consent must be obtained before a carrier may abandon any established route or eliminate a scheduled stop along a route. Carriers may also be obligated to cooperate with one another in the interests of shippers. For example, the ICC may order the transfer of rail cars from one line to another to meet such emergency situations as those involving perishable commodities. It may also route rail traffic over another company's lines if the original one is unable to handle the load. And it may, and often does, require the joint use of stations and other terminal facilities for the convenience of shippers and passengers.

---

[9] The carriers—such as trains, ships, trucks, busses, and pipelines, and the companies operating them—regulated by the ICC fall into two general classes: (1) *common carriers,* those which offer their services to the public generally, and (2) *contract carriers,* those which carry only certain goods or persons.

Securities. Until Congress moved to combat the practice, railroads frequently "watered" their stock. That is, they issued stock in an amount far in excess of the value of the company. Thus, they could reduce the apparent profit made by the road's operations. For example, a company earning a twelve per cent profit might, by doubling its stock issue, appear to have earned only six per cent. While the practice may have benefited some stockholders, it served as the basis for unreasonably high rates and posed a serious threat to the financial stability of many companies.

Today carriers must have ICC approval before issuing stocks or bonds or borrowing by other means, except for certain short-term purposes. Congress has required that in approving or rejecting the borrowing plans of carriers the ICC must be guided by the "public interest."

We shall turn in a moment to a quick consideration of some of the problems that confront the nation's railroads today. But, for now, note that some of them have recently attempted to meet their difficulties through mergers. That is, they have done so by joining with one or more other lines to form a single company. Any consolidation or merger of railroad properties — or of express companies or motor or water carriers — must, to become effective, also have ICC approval.

Financial Plight of the Railroads. Many of the nation's more than 400 railroads are in serious financial straits today, and their difficulties have been mounting over the past several years. Considering the importance of the rails to the national well-being, in peace and war, this fact is one of grave concern.

The major cause for the rail lines' troubles lies in the steady, drastic decline in their intercity passenger traffic, especially since the end of World War II. The railroads once carried almost everyone almost everywhere. Today, however, they transport less than two per cent of all the intercity passenger traffic. Private automobiles now carry nearly ninety per cent of all such traffic. The airlines, busses, and waterways carry the balance.

With their huge investments in rolling stock and other equipment and property, and with high labor costs, most rail lines have found it impossible to make any profit on their passenger operations. Indeed, most lines lose vast sums of money on that part of their business each year. Over forty per cent of the net revenues from rail freight is now being used to cover the losses from passenger traffic.

Although the rail freight business still operates in the black, the roads' share of all freight shipments has dropped from over seventy-five per cent of the total in 1930 to under forty-five per cent today. Trucks and pipelines each now carry over twenty per cent of all freight. Water and air carriers account for the rest. In the face of this, several rail lines have merged in recent years.

Nothing the railroads have tried has helped to overcome the passenger problem. Some lines have tried light, fast trains of ultra-modern design. Low-cost sleeper service, "family-fare" plans, and similar schemes have been tried, too. Still, the problem persists.

An ICC study in 1958 predicted that all Pullman and parlor car service would disappear by 1965 (except for charters and other special situations, it very nearly had). It also forecast the end of all coach service by 1970. After that, said the report, only commuter trains will share the rails with freight cars — and the commuter trains will likely have to be subsidized heavily with public funds. A 1969 report predicted that, except for commuter trains and runs in such high-density corridors as New York to Washington, rail passenger service "will not survive the next few years."

While the railroads have been fighting their losing battle, billions of dollars in public funds have been spent on highways. Millions have gone into air and water travel facilities — incidentally aggravating the rail problem. (Of course, the railroads received huge subsidies, especially land grants, in the early years.)

Congress provided some aid to the railroads in their present distress in the Transportation Act of 1958. It authorized the ICC to guarantee up to $500,000,000 in loans to the roads. The act also gave the ICC full power to adjust *intrastate* rates where they give an undue advantage to other carriers and increased its authority to permit lines to discontinue unprofitable trains, even those operating wholly within one State.

THE FEDERAL TRADE COMMISSION

Creation. Congress attempted to destroy the growth of monoplies and monopolistic practices with the passage of the Sherman Antitrust Act of 1890. The statute outlawed "every contract, combination in the form of a trust or otherwise, or conspiracy in restraint of trade or commerce among the several States, or with foreign nations." Monopolistic growth continued despite the law, however—a fact which led Congress to refine the general terms of the Sherman Antitrust Act with the more detailed Clayton Antitrust Act of 1914. Several specific business practices were made illegal in the newer statute, as we noted on page 277. At the same time Congress also adopted a new approach to the monopoly problem. It created an independent regulatory body—the Federal Trade Commission—to enforce various provisions of the Sherman and Clayton Antitrust Acts and directed it to prevent persons, partnerships, and corporations from using "unfair methods of competition" or other "deceptive acts or practices" in interstate and foreign commerce.

Organization. The Federal Trade Commission is composed of five members appointed by the President with Senate consent. The commissioners serve staggered seven-year terms, and not more than three of them may be members of the same political party. The President designates the chairman who is responsible for the administrative management

At a Federal Trade Commission laboratory cigarettes are tested for tar and nicotine content. The reports of these tests are helpful in the study of the possible effects of cigarette smoking on the health of the smoker. (Federal Trade Commission)

of the agency. An executive director, chosen by the chairman with the approval of the other commissioners, supervises the work of the Commission's staff of more than 1100 economists, lawyers, investigators, statisticians, and others.

Duties. Congress has expanded the powers of the FTC several times over the years since its creation. Today the agency itself describes its role in these terms:

The basic objective of the Commission is the maintenance of free competitive enterprise as the keystone of the American economic system. Although the duties of the Commission are many and varied under the statutes, the foundation of public policy underlying all of these duties is essentially the same: to prevent the free enterprise system from being stifled or fettered by monopoly or corrupted by unfair or deceptive trade practices.[10]

The FTC works in close concert with the Antitrust Division in the Department of Justice (page 406). But, unlike the "trustbusters," it is much more concerned with securing compliance with the law than it is with the prosecution of violators; it need not wait for clear-cut violations of the law to occur before it may act. Thus, two areas of its activities—investigations and consultations—form the major part of its work.

Investigations. The FTC undertakes investigations of business practices at the direction of Congress or the President or on its own initiative. Often, too, it conducts an investigation as a result of a complaint filed by a business firm against a competitor and occasionally on the basis of a complaint made by a consumer.

When an investigation has been concluded, the FTC may issue a *cease-and-desist order,* propose a *stipulation* or, of course, simply drop the matter. A cease-and-desist order commands an accused party to halt the practice that produced the order. Any party against whom a cease-and-desist order has been issued may challenge its validity in the United States Court of Appeals; on the other hand, the FTC may seek enforcement by the courts if its issuance does not bring a prompt compliance. In many cases, the FTC finds the less harsh stipulation to be an appropriate remedy. Under a stipulation the FTC offers the accused a chance to reform—to agree to discontinue the objectionable practice. Where a stipulation is used the accused is not formally charged with wrongdoing, but his failure to mend his ways invariably leads to the issuance of a cease-and-desist order.

Consultations. In addition to its case actions, the FTC attempts to prevent unfair trade practices by promoting self-regulation in the business community. From time to time, and often at an industry's request, the Commission holds trade practice conferences—meetings at which representatives of an industry and commission specialists consider and draft codes of fair practice for that segment of the business community. About a dozen of these codes are promulgated each year, and nearly 200 of them are now in force. They have the advantage of defining violations in advance and, thus, of promoting higher standards of commercial behavior.

Perhaps the real nature of the FTC's work can best be illustrated with an example. For years fur dealers in this country attempted to enhance their sales by giving imaginative and glamorous—but fictitious—names to common furs. Rabbit fur was sold under at least thirty different commercial aliases, including "French Chinchilla," "Electric Beaver," and "Baltic Fox." A trade practice conference proved unsuccessful and so, at the FTC's urging, Congress enacted the Fur Products Labeling Act. The law requires that all furs be sold under their actual common names and authorizes the FTC to issue regulations for its enforcement. Today rabbit must be called rabbit fur; a coat made of ordinary cat's fur must be labeled "domestic cat"; and a coat sold as "Persian lamb" must, in fact, have been produced from fur imported from the Middle East.

THE FEDERAL COMMUNICATIONS COMMISSION

Creation. In most foreign countries such means of communications as the telephone, telegraph, cable services, radio, and television are largely government-owned and -operated. In this country, however, these systems of communication have been developed and are gen-

---

[10] For accuracy's sake, it must be noted that the FTC is charged with preventing monopolies and unfair trade practices in those areas of interstate and foreign commerce not assigned by law to other regulatory bodies—such as the Interstate Commerce Commission, the Federal Reserve Board, and the Securities and Exchange Commission.

erally owned and operated privately. The National Government does maintain extensive communications facilities, especially in the Armed Forces. State and local governments do, too, especially for police purposes. Then, too, several States own and operate educational radio and television stations. But, by and large, the field is dominated by private ownership and operation – with, however, a considerable amount of federal regulation and control.

There was comparatively little governmental activity before 1934. The responsibility for that which did occur was shared by the ICC, the Post Office Department, and the Federal Radio Commission which had been created in 1927. In the Communications Act of 1934, however, Congress broadened and consolidated federal regulation in the hands of a single agency, the Federal Communications Commission.

Organization. The FCC is composed of seven members appointed by the President and Senate for staggered seven-year terms. Not more than four of the commissioners may come from the same party, and the President designates the agency's chairman. The chairman is the FCC's chief executive officer and manages its operations through an executive director he selects with the consent of the other commissioners.

Duties. Under the Communication Act of 1934, the Federal Communications Commission is charged with:

> ... regulating interstate and foreign commerce in communications by wire and radio [and television] so as to make available, so far as possible, to all people of the United States, a rapid, efficient, nationwide and worldwide wire and radio [and television] communication service with adequate facilities at reasonable charges ...

The FCC's regulation of telephone, telegraph, and cable services is much like that of the ICC's over interstate land and water transportation. The lines or wires are "common carriers." The services provided must be adequate, and the rates charged must be fair and reasonable. Interstate rates can be changed only with Commission approval and must be published for the information of clients. *Certificates of convenience and necessity* must be secured before new interstate lines may be built or existing ones extended, and an existing service may not be abandoned without FCC approval.

The FCC does not have as broad authority over telephone, telegraph, and cable facilities as the ICC has over interstate transportation, however. It has no regulatory power over securities issued by the companies operating them, for example. It has very broad authority to regulate radio and television communications, however. These fields present special problems in contrast to the others. Not all telephone and telegraph service is interstate

The FCC licenses commercial broadcast stations to use the nation's airwaves in the public interest and to serve the programming needs of their communities. (NBC)

in character. Much of it is purely local, in fact, and thus subject only to State regulation. But radio and television broadcasts are no respecters of State lines; their waves range far and wide. The FCC regulates both interstate and foreign broadcasting but, of course, control over foreign broadcasting can extend only to outgoing communications. If objectionable matter is broadcast into the United States — from Mexico, for example — the problem must be met through diplomatic channels.

The Communications Act of 1934 specifically declares that radio and television stations are *not* common carriers. Hence, the FCC has no direct authority to regulate such matters as the rates that are charged to advertisers. But all radio and television operators and stations — commercial, amateur, and governmental — must be licensed by the FCC in order to go on the air. Operators are licensed on the basis of FCC examinations, and stations only after investigations and public hearings.

When licensed, stations are assigned particular frequencies and frequently have other limits imposed, too — for example, broadcasting power and the hours of use. The licenses are issued for periods of three years and may be renewed at the FCC's discretion. The Commission assigns licenses, wave lengths, periods of operation, and station power among the States and their local communities in a manner intended to provide, as the law directs, "a fair, efficient, and equitable distribution of service to each."

All stations and operators are regulated under a strict set of rules closely policed by the FCC. For example, when paid matter is broadcast, the name of the sponsor must be announced; the broadcast of obscene or pornographic matter is prohibited; and if a station permits a broadcast by or in behalf of a candidate for public office, it must offer opposing candidates equal time at the same rates. Failure to observe any of the Commission's rules can lead to the suspension, revocation, or refusal to renew a license.

THE CIVIL AERONAUTICS BOARD

Congress first provided for the regulation of the fast-growing field of aviation in the Air Commerce Act of 1926. That statute applied to all interstate flying but, of course, left the regulation of local flights and facilities to the individual States. It created a Bureau of Air Commerce (later renamed the Civil Aeronautics Administration) in the Department of Commerce to test and license pilots, fix safety standards, and provide for the regulation of the increasing volume of air traffic. As the whole field of aviation continued to develop in spectacular fashion, Congress broadened federal authority over it in the Civil Aeronautics Act of 1938. That statute, as amended especially by the Federal Aviation Act of 1958, forms the basis of present-day federal authority. Today two major agencies operate in the field: the Civil Aeronautics Board, with which we shall deal here, and the Federal Aviation Administration, which we treated in Chapter 29.[11]

The Civil Aeronautics Board. The CAB was originally established in 1938 to promote and regulate the major aspects of civilian air transportation in the United States. It is composed of five members appointed by the President with Senate consent for staggered six-year terms. As with the other independent regulatory bodies, no more than a bare majority of its members may come from the same political party. Each year the President designates its chairman who directs the work of its staff of more than 600 economists, accountants, lawyers, and other personnel.

---

[11] As we noted in the preceding chapter, the general regulation and promotion of air commerce is the responsibility of the Federal Aviation Administration; the task of investigating and reporting on civilian aircraft accidents and other air safety matters was a CAB function until 1967 but is now assigned to the National Transportation Safety Board.

Today the CAB is primarily responsible for the assigning of routes to and supervising the rates and service of the nation's airlines and other commercial air carriers. Thus, passengers and freight may be carried only along those air lanes and at those times and prices by those carriers approved by the Commission.

The CAB also sets the sums to be paid for the carrying of mail by air and administers the subsidies paid to certain air carriers where such payments are "required by the public convenience and necessity." Foreign air carriers may operate within and from the United States only with CAB sanction.

THE FEDERAL POWER COMMISSION

Creation. Until the 1930's the development of the nation's hydroelectric power resources was largely in private hands, and much of that development was grossly shortsighted in both economic and conservation terms. Such federal regulation as did exist was scattered and duplicated among several agencies. For example, the consent of the War Department was necessary to the erection of a dam or other structure which might impair river navigation, and the Interior Department held the power to approve or reject the construction of projects on most public lands—except in the national forests where the Department of Agriculture's consent was required.

To bring order out of the confusion, and to provide for the wise and orderly development of the nation's water power resources, Congress enacted the Federal Water Power Act of 1920. That law established the Water Power Commission—an agency composed of the Secretaries of War, Interior, and Agriculture. Despite good intentions, however, the Water Power Commission proved to be an inadequate vehicle for the task assigned to it. It failed to achieve its purpose in large part because Congress failed to provide it with an adequate

Subject to the jurisdiction of the FPC, transmission pipelines have been laid to carry natural gas from the producing areas of the Southwest to every metropolitan area in the United States. (Federal Power Commission)

staff and because its members were burdened and naturally pre-occupied with the affairs of their respective departments. Finally, at President Hoover's urging, Congress replaced the Water Power Commission with a full-time independent regulatory agency, the Federal Power Commission, in 1930.

Organization. The FPC is composed of five commissioners appointed by the President with Senate consent for five-year terms. The members serve staggered terms, and no more than three may be members of the same political party. The President designates the chairman who serves as the agency's principal executive officer, directing the work of a staff of more than 1000 engineers, lawyers, economists, and other personnel.

Duties. The FPC's powers arise chiefly from three statutes—the Federal Water Power

Act of 1920, the Federal Power Act of 1935, and the Natural Gas Act of 1938. In broad terms these laws give the FPC the authority to license power projects, regulate interstate electric utilities, and set reasonable rates for the interstate sale of natural gas.

The production of hydroelectric power and of natural gas service divides rather naturally into three basic steps: (1) its manufacture, (2) its transmission to the locality in which it will be used, and (3) its distribution to consumers.[12] It is with the second of these steps

---

[12] Practically all of the electricity and gas produced *from fuels* are produced in the localities where they are used; thus, their production, transmission, and sale seldom involve interstate commerce and federal regulation.

—transmission—that federal regulation and the FPC are primarily concerned. This is rather obviously so because the transporting of electricity and natural gas almost always involves interstate commerce. The manufacturing (production) and the distributing (sale) steps are usually local in character and are, therefore, largely controlled by State and local agencies.

Notice that while the FPC must approve (license) the construction of any hydroelectric power project on the nation's navigable waters or public lands (see page 273), it does *not* build dams or other projects. These federal activities are performed largely by the Bureau of Reclamation, the Army's Corps of Engineers, and the Tennessee Valley Authority, as we saw in Chapter 23, in our discussion of the Department of the Interior.

✳✳✳✳✳✳✳✳✳✳ CONCEPT BUILDING ✳✳✳✳✳✳✳✳✳✳

Key Concepts

The Constitution is notably silent on the matter of administrative organization. In addition to the twelve Cabinet departments, Congress has, for a variety of reasons, created a great many independent agencies. These agencies are located outside any of the Cabinet departments. Among these is a special group, the "independent regulatory commissions." They are *not only* independent of any Cabinet department but are largely independent of the President as well. These commissions have been created especially to regulate certain aspects of the American economy. In addition to administrative powers, they possess quasi-legislative and quasi-judicial powers.

The Interstate Commerce Commission, created in 1887 to regulate interstate railroad transportation, now also regulates interstate motor carriers, water transportation, pipelines (except those carrying water and gas), sleeping-car companies, and those interstate carriers using routes which are partly water and partly land.

The Federal Trade Commission was created in 1914 to combat monopolistic and other unfair trade practices in interstate and foreign commerce.

The Federal Communications Commission was created in 1934 to regulate interstate telephone, telegraph, and cable communications, radio, and television.

The Civil Aeronautics Board, created in 1938, is primarily responsible for the assigning of routes and supervision of the rates and service of the nation's airlines and other commercial air carriers.

The Federal Power Commission, originally created in 1920, regulates the building of hydroelectric power projects on the nation's navigable waters and public lands and the interstate transmission of electrical energy and natural gas.

Important Terms

cease-and-desist orders
certificate of convenience
   and necessity
common carriers
contract carriers

Granger Laws
independent agencies
independent regulatory
   commissions
monopoly

quasi-judicial powers
quasi-legislative powers
stipulations
trade practice conferences
watered stock

Questions for Inquiry and Review

1. Why did the Founding Fathers expect that Congress would create a number of administrative agencies under the President?

2. Why have some of these agencies been established independently of any of the Cabinet departments?

3. For what general purpose has Congress created some of these independent agencies as regulatory commissions?

4. In what particular ways have the independent regulatory commissions been made largely independent of the President?

5. How do these commissions exercise their quasi-legislative and quasi-judicial powers?

6. When and why was the Interstate Commerce Commission created?

7. What aspects of interstate transportation are within the Interstate Commerce Commission's authority today?

8. Why is rate-setting one of the ICC's most difficult and important duties?

9. When and why was the Federal Trade Commission created?

10. How does the FTC's general approach to its functions differ from that of the Antitrust Division in the Justice Department?

11. When and why was the Federal Communications Commission created?

12. In what general sense does the regulation of radio and television broadcasting pose a different order of problems than those involved in the regulation of telephone and telegraph communications?

13. When and why was the Civil Aeronautics Board created?

14. What is the CAB's primary responsibility today?

15. When and why was the Federal Power Commission created?

16. With which of the three basic steps in the production of electric power and natural gas is the FPC most concerned?

For Further Inquiry

1. Television quiz programs of a type immensely popular only a few years ago have now all but disappeared. They were programs in which the viewing public was led to believe that contestants vied for large sums of money strictly on the basis of their own intellectual abilities. But many of the programs were rigged, certain contestants were carefully rehearsed and often given answers to the questions they were to be asked. Some have defended such shows as "pretense justified in the name of entertainment." Others contend that they were "deceitful" because they involved "intentional and dishonest duping of the public." With which position do you agree? Why do you think the networks abolished the programs?

2. Why are such utilities as telephone, power

and light, and natural gas companies almost always operated as publicly-sanctioned monopolies? Does the fact that they are increase or decrease the need for their regulation by government?

3. Both radio and television are extraordinarily useful and important political campaign tools. They are also very expensive: a single half hour on the three major television networks can cost as much as $500,000. The Communication Act of 1934 provides that when a political broadcast is made by or in behalf of a candidate, those stations which carry it must offer any opposing candidate equal time at the same rates. Congress suspended the equal time provision for the presidential contest in 1960. Why did it do so for the presidential race but not for others in 1960? Why wasn't there a similar suspension in 1964 or 1968? Why do some suggest that, as a condition for licensing, all stations should be required to provide free time to at least the two major parties and their candidates in election campaigns?

Suggested Activities

1. Write a report on the work of the ICC, the FTC, the FCC, the CAB, or the FPC in your community.

2. Prepare a talk on the work of *State and local* regulatory agencies in your community.

3. Stage a debate or class forum on one of the following questions: (1) *Resolved,* That the nation's railroad industry be nationalized. (2) *Resolved,* That in the interest of freedom of expression all governmental regulation of commercial radio and television be abolished.

(3) *Resolved,* That our present system of commercial broadcasting be abolished in favor of government-operated radio and television systems.

4. Invite a local manufacturer, shipper, or radio or television station manager involved with the functions of one of the independent regulatory commissions to speak to the class about the nature of his work and relationships with the federal agency.

Suggested Reading

BLACKMORE, CHARLES P. and YESELSON, ABRAHAM (eds.), *The Fabric of American Democracy.* Van Nostrand, 1969. Chapter 10.

BURNS, JAMES M. and PELTASON, J. W., *Government By the People.* Prentice-Hall, 1969. Chapters 15, 24.

"Does TV Tell It Straight?" *Newsweek,* November 24, 1969.

ECK, ROBERT, "The Real Masters of Television," *Harper's,* March 1967; *Reader's Digest,* May 1967.

FISCHER, JOHN, "What Happened on the Night of November 5?" *Harper's,* November 1967.

LINDSEY, ROBERT, "The Air Traffic Cop—On the Hottest Spot in Aviation," *New York Times Magazine,* September 14, 1969.

"New Lift from an Old Fuel," *U.S. News,* October 23, 1967.

"Not Enough Electric Power—What to Do About It," *U. S. News,* September 22, 1969.

"On Flying More and Enjoying It Less," *Time,* April 18, 1969.

"Pro and Con: Controversy Over Cigarette Advertising on Television," *Congressional Digest,* June–July, 1969.

"When Pay TV Arrives—," *U.S. News,* November 3, 1969.

YOUNG, WARREN R., "An Answer at Last to Collisions in the Sky?" *Reader's Digest,* July, 1969.

31
THE INDEPENDENT
FINANCIAL AGENCIES

*Finance is not mere arithmetic....
Without sound finance no sound government is possible; without sound government no sound finance is possible.*

WOODROW WILSON

***Why is the condition of the nation's financial system so critical to the nation's security and overall well-being?

***Should the National Government be prohibited from operating any program in competition with private lending agencies? Why?

***To whom are the functions performed by the various federal lending agencies most beneficial?

***Should the country's banking system be nationalized? Why?

In Chapters 18 through 29 we focused attention upon the organization and functions of the Cabinet departments. In the preceding chapter, Chapter 30, we considered several of the Government's independent agencies —especially the independent regulatory commissions. In this chapter we are concerned with still more of these non-Cabinet agencies —those especially concerned with the nation's financial system.

Certainly few persons would consider the financial agencies to be as interesting or as glamorous a subject as the Armed Forces, the Foreign Service, or the FBI. Their work is of incalculable importance, nonetheless. The condition of the nation's financial system is as critical for the nation's security and well-being as are its defenses, the conduct of its foreign relations, and the enforcement of its criminal laws.

THE BANKING SYSTEM OF THE UNITED STATES

Early National Regulation. The economic ills of the 1780's had been one of the chief causes for the drafting and adoption of the Constitution. Two years after the Constitution went into force, Congress created the Bank of the United States. It did so largely at the urging of Alexander Hamilton who, as the first Secretary of the Treasury, had proposed the bank as a major step toward righting the financial chaos of the Critical Period (see pages 36–38).

As we saw earlier, Hamilton's proposal touched off one of the most momentous debates in all of our constitutional history. Hamilton and his supporters (the liberal constructionists) were pitted against Thomas Jefferson and his followers (the strict constructionists) over the extent of the powers of the new National Government.

The First Bank of the United States. Logic and practical necessity convinced Congress of the need for a centralized national banking system, and the Bank of the United States was created in 1791. The bank was granted a twenty-year charter. The National Government held twenty per cent of its capital stock of $10,000,000; the other eighty per cent was subscribed by private individuals. The bank issued notes which circulated as paper money.

With its eight branches located in principal cities, the bank proved of great value to both business and the National Government. It aided in the collection of revenue, made loans to the National Government, and served as a depository for public funds. Although many continued to oppose the bank after its creation, its constitutionality was not challenged in the courts. When its charter expired in 1811, the Congress simply did not renew it.

The Second Bank of the United States. The financial crisis brought on by the War of 1812 led Congress to re-charter the Bank of the United States in 1816. It was quite similar to the first bank but was established on a much larger scale. Its capital stock was $35,000,000; the division of stock between private holders and the National Government, however, remained the same.

The Second Bank had a much more stormy career than its predecessor. The constitutionality of its charter was attacked, but it was upheld by the Supreme Court in 1819 in the landmark case of *McCulloch* v. *Maryland*.[1] The Second Bank was not as well managed as its predecessor, and it was opposed by State-chartered banks which resented its competition. The bank became an issue in the presidential election of 1828 when Andrew Jackson and his supporters charged that it was being used to support the re-election of President John Quincy Adams. With Jackson's victory,

the fate of the "monster," as he called it, was sealed. As President, Jackson vetoed a bill to extend the bank's charter in 1832 and crippled it by withdrawing all federal funds. The bank finally died when its charter expired in 1836.

Period of State Bank Monopoly. From 1836 to 1863 *State banks* (private banks chartered under State law) held a monopoly of the nation's banking business. State banking laws were generally lax.

The Constitution forbids the States to issue paper money,[2] but the Supreme Court had held that the States were *not* forbidden from authorizing private banks to do so. Some States permitted banks to issue only as much in notes as they could redeem in gold. Most States, however, allowed their banks to issue any amount that they pleased. Inevitably, the country was flooded with a bewildering variety of paper money. The value of the private bank notes varied from being "as good as gold" to being worth "next to nothing," depending upon the bank of issue. Two of the most spectacular banking crises in our history, those of 1837 and 1853, came during the period of "wildcat banking."

The National Banking System. The chaos brought on by the lack of a centralized banking system led many to argue for renewed federal control. The difficult problem of financing heavy wartime expenditures (those of the Civil War) finally forced Congress to act. A national banking system was created by the National Banking Acts of 1863 and 1864.

The new laws did not create another Bank of the United States; instead, they provided for the chartering of private banks by Congress. These *national banks* (private banks chartered under federal law) were each permitted to issue notes up to the amount of their capital stock, but these notes had to be secured by federal bonds owned by the bank and deposited with the United States Treasury. Each member bank had to agree to periodic inspection to

---

[1] The case is especially important, recall, because in it the Supreme Court for the first time upheld the doctrine of implied powers (see pages 247-249); the Court also ruled in the same case that the States could not tax the instrumentalities of the National Government (see pages 248, 684)

---

[2] Article I, Section 10, Clause 1.

insure its sound condition and to protect its depositors, and each was limited as to the amount of loans it might have outstanding at any one time. Any private bank could become a part of the national banking system by meeting these same conditions.

In 1865 Congress destroyed the power of the State banks to issue paper money by imposing a ten per cent tax on the notes issued by any bank that was not a part of the new national system. The Supreme Court upheld the move as a valid use of the taxing power in 1869, as we noted on page 262. The national banking system brought a marked improvement in the condition of the nation's banking and currency. The system remained largely unchanged for fifty years, until the creation of the Federal Reserve System in 1913.

Two Systems of Banks Today. There are two principal systems of banks in the United States today: *State* and *national.* State banks are chartered under State law and national banks under federal law. Both kinds of banks are subject to extensive regulation by the States in which they do business. Most are also subject to extensive federal regulation.[3]

Of course, State banking regulations vary from State to State. Nevertheless, State and federal authorities cooperate well in safeguarding the public interest without disrupting the American principle of private enterprise. In particular, the creation of the Federal Reserve System in 1913 and the Federal Deposit Insurance Corporation in 1933 has produced considerable uniformity in the regulation and supervision of banks in general to safeguard the funds of depositors.

All national banks and the majority of State banks do the general business of *commercial*

banks. That is, they receive deposits for safekeeping, accept saving accounts, perform trust functions, use their funds to make loans and investments, and render various other services to individuals and groups.

One group of State banks, the mutual savings banks, however, usually restrict their business exclusively to the receipt and investment of small savings deposits. Today there are approximately 500 mutual savings banks, located chiefly in New England and other Eastern States. Although they comprise only a small portion of the some 13,700 banks in the nation, they have impressive deposits that today total to well over $70,000,000,000.

With the passage of the National Banking Act of 1863, State banks all but disappeared. Most State banks at the time became national banks in order to be able to continue the issuing of notes. Then, as the use of checks increased, as mutual savings banks began to grow, and as trust companies began to do general banking business, the number of State banks began to increase again. Today there are more State banks (about 9000) than there are national banks (about 4700).

National banks came into being to provide a sound control of bank note currency. When the currency-issuing Federal Reserve Banks were set up in 1914, national banks lost the power to issue notes. National bank notes are now retired whenever deposited in banks, and there are few such notes in circulation today. National banks today are merely federally-controlled commercial banks much like the State-chartered commercial banks.

Organization and Functions of National Banks. With the approval of the Comptroller of the Currency,[4] any five or more persons may secure a charter of incorporation for a national bank. They must have a capital stock varying from $50,000 in places of less than 6000 inhabitants to $200,000 in cities of more than 50,000 inhabitants.

---

[3] A relatively small number of State banks are not members of the Federal Reserve System and are not as closely regulated by federal law as are other State and all national banks. A national bank must have the word "national" in its corporate title: for example, the First National Bank.

[4] Within the Treasury Department; see page 370.

The official Federal Deposit Insurance Corporation sign, indicating that deposits are insured up to $15,000 for each depositor, is required by law to be displayed by all insured banks at each teller station or window where insured deposits are normally received. (Talbot Lovering)

These banks receive deposits from individuals and corporations and lend money to individuals and corporations. They must be examined by federal examiners at least three times every two years. They must also make reports to the Comptroller of the Currency at least four times a year. Reports must be made *anytime* the Comptroller of the Currency requests a bank to do so.

Insurance of Deposits. All national banks, and State banks which are members of the Federal Reserve System, must insure their deposits up to $15,000. State banks not members of the Federal Reserve System may also qualify for this insurance, however.[5] Insured banks pay an annual premium in proportion to their average deposits. In return each bank depositor's account is insured up to $15,000.

The insurance program is administered by the *Federal Deposit Insurance Corporation,* created when the insurance program was set up by Congress in 1933. It is an independent agency composed of the Comptroller of the

Currency and two members appointed by the President with Senate consent for six-year terms.

Congress makes no appropriations to the FDIC. Its entire income consists of the premiums paid by insured banks and returns on investments. Its insurance fund now amounts to more than $3,800,000,000. The FDIC has the authority to borrow up to $3,000,000,000 from the United States Treasury in order to cover its insurance commitments. The nation's banks are in such sound condition and the Federal Reserve System and the insurance program have worked so well, however, that the FDIC has never had to call upon the Treasury.

When a national bank is closed, the FDIC is appointed receiver. A new bank is organized and assumes the liabilities of the closed bank. If stock in the new bank can be sold, the new bank will continue. If not, the assets may be sold to another bank. If neither of these arrangements is possible within two years, the bank will be liquidated (abolished).

Branch Banks. National banks may establish branch banks in their home cities if those cities have 25,000 or more inhabitants and also in

---

[5] Unsound practices cause a nonmember bank to lose its insurance privilege, a State bank to lose its membership, and a national bank to be closed.

foreign countries. Those with $500,000 or more capital may, with the consent of the Comptroller of the Currency, establish branches within the State to the extent that State banks are permitted to create branches.

Examinations. In general, national banks are subject to unannounced examinations by specially trained examiners. These examiners check to see that the banks are in sound condition and are being properly run.

THE FEDERAL RESERVE SYSTEM

The banking reforms of the 1860's did much to cure the abuses of the earlier "wildcat banking" period. Still, the system was far from perfect, and crises continued to occur. The

Panics of 1873 and 1893 were especially severe.

The chief defect of the banking system after 1863 lay in the fact that national banks were each separate institutions with no direct ties to one another. Financial reserves could not be shifted quickly from bank to bank to meet a credit emergency. Thus, in the Panic of 1907 several sound banks were forced to close their doors because they did not have the ready cash at hand to meet a "run" by their depositors.

The Federal Reserve Act. To remedy this weakness and to give national banks the strength of unity, Congress passed the Federal Reserve Act which established the Federal Reserve System in 1913. The Act has been amended several times since, most notably in 1933 and 1935.

The Federal Reserve System

— BOUNDARIES OF FEDERAL RESERVE DISTRICTS

— BOUNDARIES OF FEDERAL RESERVE BRANCH TERRITORIES

★ BOARD OF GOVERNORS OF THE FEDERAL RESERVE SYSTEM
• FEDERAL RESERVE BANK CITIES ○ FEDERAL RESERVE BRANCH CITIES

Organization. The United States is divided into twelve *Federal Reserve Districts*. A *Federal Reserve Bank* is located in a principal city in each of the districts.[6] Each of the twelve Federal Reserve Banks is supervised by a nine-member Board of Directors. Six of the nine members are chosen by the member banks: three must be bankers and three must represent industry, commerce, and agriculture in the district. The other three members are appointed by the *Board of Governors of the Federal Reserve System* and represent the public.

The Federal Reserve Banks do not carry on regular private banking operations. Instead, they perform central banking functions for their member banks.

Member Banks. Every national bank *is* a member of the Federal Reserve System. As such, it is required to purchase a share of the capital stock of the Federal Reserve Bank in its district. State banks and trust companies may also become member banks by meeting the same conditions imposed on national banks.

Board of Governors. The entire Federal Reserve System is supervised by a seven-member Board of Governors appointed by the President with Senate consent. No two members of the Board may come from the same district. Each member serves a single fourteen-year term, with one member retiring every second year. The President selects one of the Board's members to serve as its chairman for a four-year term.

Powers of the Board. The principal duties of the Board of Governors are to: (1) supervise the operations of the Federal Reserve Banks and member banks and (2) control the use and effect of credit in the nation's economy.

Supervision of Banks. The Board of Governors has general control over the operations of all banks within the system. In exercising this control, it decides whether or not a bank may become a member, may suspend a bank, or may even remove its officers if a situation warrants such action. It examines all member banks periodically and requires them to submit regular reports on their condition.

The Reserve Requirement. The Board of Governors sets the "reserve requirement" for the member banks. That is, it requires each member bank to deposit a certain percentage of its funds with its Federal Reserve Bank. By varying the reserve requirement, the Board can expand or contract the lending capacity of member banks. When there is a threat of inflation, the Board helps to check it by upping the reserve requirement to reduce risky or speculative borrowing and spending. By doing such, it creates what is known as a "tight money" condition. When, on the other hand, economic conditions seem to justify it, the Board can relax its reserve requirements and thus make more money available to stimulate business activity.

Rediscounting. The Board of Governors also controls the amount of credit in the economy by varying the "rediscount rate." When a member bank makes a loan, the borrower gives the bank his note. The bank may carry the loan itself, or it may "rediscount" the note. That is, it may borrow on it from the Federal Reserve Bank and thus receive additional funds with which to make still more loans. The interest that member banks pay on such loans (the rediscount rate) is set by the Board of Governors. The lower the rediscount rate the more member banks will be encouraged to make loans. The higher the rate the less anxious member banks will be to make loans.

"Open-Market" Operations. Still another important control over the amount of credit arises out of the functioning of the Federal Reserve System's Open Market Committee. The committee is composed of the seven members of the Board of Governors and five representatives of the Federal Reserve Banks. It controls the buying and selling of government securities by the Federal Reserve Banks. If

---

[6] In Boston, New York, Philadelphia, Cleveland, Richmond, Atlanta, Chicago, St. Louis, Minneapolis, Kansas City, Dallas, and San Francisco.

an expansion of credit is desired, the committee authorizes the Federal Reserve Banks to purchase government securities on the open market — thus, putting more money into business channels as well as helping to keep the price of government bonds up. If the committee wants to restrict credit, it may authorize the sale of a certain amount of government obligations held by the Federal Reserve Banks to drain money away from regular investment channels.

Federal Reserve Notes. Under the supervision of the Board of Governors any Federal Reserve Bank may issue paper currency — Federal Reserve Notes. These notes (bills) are legal tender, and they now account for over ninety-five per cent of all money in circulation in the United States. The Board's power to increase or decrease the amount of notes in circulation also has a vital effect on the economy, of course. See page 376.

Interest Rates on Deposits. The Board of Governors limits the rates of interest that member banks may pay on their time and savings deposits. Thus, it prevents banks from attempting to attract depositors by offering higher interest rates than they can safely pay.

The Government's Banker. By the principal functions just listed, it is easy to see that the Federal Reserve System acts, in effect, as a banker's bank. It also operates as the Federal Government's banker. It is through the Federal Reserve Banks that the Federal Government makes and receives many of its payments, sells a large portion of its "IOU's," and conducts many other financial transactions.

FEDERAL HOME LOAN BANK SYSTEM

The Federal Home Loan Bank System was created by Congress in 1932 to provide a credit reserve for local institutions involved in home financing. It is composed of several regional banks from which its member institutions may borrow to meet local home financing needs and withdrawal demands by their investors.

Organization. The system is managed by the *Federal Home Loan Bank Board,* an independent agency composed of three members appointed by the President with Senate consent for four-year terms. The Board supervises the operations of twelve regional *Federal Home Loan Banks* located in principal cities across the country.[7] Each of these banks is, in turn, managed by from twelve to fifteen directors — some appointed by the central board and some elected by its local member institutions. The directors of each bank elect a president and other officers subject to the approval of the Federal Home Loan Bank Board.

Functions of the Banks. The twelve regional Federal Home Loan Banks make loans to savings and loan, building and loan, and homestead associations, savings and cooperative banks, and insurance companies. These member institutions — of which there are now more than 5000 throughout the country — make direct loans to home builders; most of them are of the savings-and-loan type.

Federal savings and loan associations can be organized by any group of responsible persons who make application to their regional Federal Home Loan Bank. In these associations (local banks) individuals may earn interest on their savings; or, if they are good risks, they may borrow money for home financing purposes. Deposits in these local associations are insured up to $15,000 by the *Federal Savings and Loan Insurance Corporation* — a federal agency operating under the supervision of the Federal Home Loan Bank Board.[8] There are over

---

[7] In Boston, New York, Pittsburgh, Greensboro (North Carolina), Cincinnati, Indianapolis, Chicago, Des Moines, Little Rock, Topeka, San Francisco, and Spokane.

[8] Other federal agencies in the field of home financing, most of them within the Department of Housing and Urban Affairs, are discussed in Chapter 28.

6000 of these associations today, and they have assets totalling more than $130,000,000,000.

SYSTEM OF FARM CREDIT BANKS

The first piece of federal farm credit legislation was enacted by Congress more than a half century ago: the Federal Farm Loan Act of 1916. It came as a response to two basic — and continuing — facts of agricultural economics: (1) farming is usually, at best, a highly risky venture, and (2) farmers often need large amounts of credit, frequently on a long-term basis.

The Farm Credit System. Most federal agricultural loan programs today are supervised by the *Farm Credit Administration*.[9] It was created by Congress in 1933 to coordinate the various programs established since 1916.

The FCA's policies are made by a part-time, thirteen-member *Federal Farm Credit Board.* Twelve of its members are appointed by the President and the thirteenth by the Secretary of Agriculture. The Board selects a governor who directs the agency's work.

The FCA is *not* itself a lending agency. It supervises the operations of the *Federal Land Banks* and the other banks in the Farm Credit System.[10]

The Federal Land Banks were created in 1916 to give the farmer an opportunity to borrow money at low rates against a long-term mortgage on his land. There is a Federal Land Bank in a principal city in each of twelve farm credit districts.[11] The Federal Land Banks make loans to local *Federal Land Bank Associations* which, in turn, make loans to their farmer-members. As the stock of each of the approximately 700 associations is held by its members, and these groups hold the stock of the Federal Land Banks, the whole system is completely farmer-owned.

The Federal Land Banks raise money through the sale of bonds to the investing public. They use the notes and mortgages put up by their farmer-borrowers, together with their other assets, as collateral for the bonds.

The associations make long-term loans to farmers and ranchers for such purposes as the purchase or improvements of land, buildings, and equipment. The loans, made to a maximum of $200,000, may not exceed sixty-five per cent of the value of the land on which a mortgage is taken nor run beyond forty years. Repayments are usually made on an annual or semi-annual basis.

An indication of the size and importance of the operations of the Farm Credit Administration can be seen in this fact: Farmers and their cooperatives borrowed more than $9,400,-000 from the banks and associations under its supervision in 1968. The bulk of this huge sum was borrowed by many of the approximately 385,000 individual members of the local Federal Land Bank Associations.

---

[9] Several farm credit programs are administered through the Department of Agriculture; see Chapter 24.

[10] They are (1) *Federal Intermediate Credit Banks* which make credit available to Production Credit Associations which, in turn, make *short-term* loans to their farmer-members and to such other lending bodies as commercial banks and loan companies which also make loans to farmers; and (2) the *Central Bank for Cooperatives* and its twelve district banks which make loans to farm cooperatives in which farmers act together in marketing products, purchasing farm supplies, or furnishing farm business services.

[11] In Springfield (Massachusetts), Baltimore, Columbia, Louisville, New Orleans, St. Louis, St. Paul, Omaha, Wichita, Houston, Berkeley, and Spokane.

THE SMALL BUSINESS
ADMINISTRATION

Until World War I American business depended almost entirely on banks and other private lenders for needed credit. In 1918, however, Congress created the *War Finance Corporation* as the first major federal lending agency for business. The corporation made loans to industries vital to the war effort. Although the need for such business loans disappeared with the end of the war, the corporation did make loans again during the postwar farm depression in 1921. It was not until 1939 that all of its war and farm loan books were closed and the agency itself disappeared.

The Reconstruction Finance Corporation. The RFC was created during the Hoover Administration in 1932. It was born at a time when, because of economic conditions, *only* the National Government was able to provide the huge sums business required to meet the crisis of the Great Depression. Once the nation's largest lender, it was the subject of bitter controversy throughout its existence. Most of the criticism arose because the RFC was in direct competition with private lenders. It was finally abolished by Congress in 1954 after disclosures of corruption among a few of its employees.

Altogether, during its stormy life, the RFC chalked up an impressive record in lending operations. It lent vast sums to large and small commercial, industrial, and governmental borrowers. Without its help a number of railroads, banks, and other concerns would have failed during the 1930's. RFC loans also saved many local governments from bankruptcy and helped several hard-pressed States over the same period.

During World War II the RFC made loans to finance the expansion of war industries, as the War Finance Corporation had done during World War I. It also owned and operated a number of war-born industries, such as synthetic rubber. After the war it helped many concerns reconvert to civilian production and made large loans to such companies as Kaiser and Northwest Airlines. In addition to the businesses it saved and its valuable wartime work, the RFC also made a tidy profit of several millions of dollars in interest for the United States Treasury.

The Small Business Administration. The SBA was created as a "temporary" agency to replace the RFC in 1953. Congress made the agency a permanent one in 1958. It is headed by an Administrator appointed by the President with Senate consent.

The scope of the SBA's operations is much smaller than its predecessor, the RFC. The SBA is designed especially to help small businesses by rendering financial aid and advice and by helping them to secure government contracts in competition with larger concerns. It also makes loans to small businesses, nonprofit organizations, State and local govern-

Much of the advice offered by the Small Business Administration is readily available in a number of special pamphlets and brochures.

ments, and individuals for a variety of other purposes—for example, to help overcome the results of such natural disasters as storms, floods, forest fires, droughts, or epidemics; to assist those displaced by a federally-aided urban renewal or highway construction project or any other construction financed with federal funds; and to help firms adjust to changed economic conditions resulting from increased competition from articles imported from abroad.

Its business loans may be made only to those firms which, although good risks, are unable to secure adequate private financing on reasonable terms. It is often able to help these firms by locating private lenders who can meet their needs. Most SBA loans are relatively small, averaging less than $50,000 and with many under $1,000. The SBA, however, may lend as much as $350,000 to a single borrower.

THE EXPORT–IMPORT BANK

The Export-Import Bank was created in 1934 to help stimulate our foreign trade which had sagged during the worldwide depression. The bank was originally created by an executive order issued by President Roosevelt. Congress made it a permanent agency in 1935. It is headed by a five-man Board of Directors appointed by the President with Senate consent.

In carrying out its primary purpose of encouraging foreign trade, the Export-Import Bank performs two major functions: (1) it makes loans to American exporters and importers and (2) it makes loans to foreign governments to help them develop their natural, industrial, and commercial resources. Congress has directed the bank to supplement, not compete with, private capital and to make loans only where there are reasonable prospects for repayment.

Congress provided the Export-Import Bank with its original capital stock of $1,000,000,000 and has given it authority to borrow up to $6,000,000,000 from the United States Treasury. It may have as much as $13,500,000,000 in loans outstanding at any one time. Congress has made no appropriations to the bank since providing its original capital stock. The bank has operated quite successfully for more than a third of a century on the income from its loans.

Altogether, the Export-Import Bank has made more than 1700 loans totalling well over $13,000,000,000 and has fostered more than $1,000,000,000 in private American investments abroad. It also has paid more than $200,000,000 into the United States Treasury as dividends on its capital stock.

In the 1930's the Export-Import Bank made several loans to enable other countries to buy American goods. During World War II it made loans to China and several Latin American countries to help stabilize their economies. After the war it made a number of rehabilitation loans. For example, it lent millions to several Italian concerns to help them reestablish their war-destroyed businesses; the loans were guaranteed by the Italian Government, and the money loaned was then spent in the United States.

Among typical recent loans have been one to Israel for $25,000,000 to finance the purchase of heavy equipment from American concerns and another for $60,000,000 to the Bank of Tokyo for the purchase of raw cotton in the United States.

THE SECURITIES AND EXCHANGE COMMISSION

Millions of Americans own stock in the nation's large and small business concerns. Millions more have loaned vast sums to businesses by purchasing their bonds and other securities. As we suggested on page 16, it is impossible to see how our huge private enterprise system could possibly have been financed in any other way.

Among the many honest dealers in stocks

and bonds there are always a few dishonest ones willing to bilk unwary investors. Indeed, at one point in our history the sale of bogus mining stocks had become so common that Mark Twain defined a mine as "a hole in the ground owned by a liar." Fraud had become so widespread that the States began to regulate the traffic in securities in the early years of this century. By 1933 every State except Nevada had enacted "blue sky laws" designed to protect investors. But, as we noted earlier, the stock market crash of 1929 proved these State attempts to be largely ineffective. It has been estimated that investors in fraudulent stocks lost some $25,000,000,000 as the country passed from the boom of the 1920's into the Great Depression of the 1930's.

The SEC. The Great Depression led Congress to create an independent regulatory agency—the Securities and Exchange Commission—to police the securities field. Established in 1934, the SEC is composed of five members appointed by the President with Senate consent for five-year terms. Not more than three of the commissioners may come from the ranks of the same political party, and one member's term expires each year. The President designates the agency's chairman who directs the work of the SEC's more than 1300 economists, lawyers, accountants, and other employees.

The SEC's primary task is that of protecting the interests of investors and the general public against fraud and misrepresentation in the

Stock certificates, most commonly registered in 100 share blocks or a fraction thereof, are issued to all stock purchasers. Common stock usually carries voting privileges; preferred stock offers greater financial security, having a par value and dividend preferential. (American Telephone and Telegraph Co.)

securities field. To that end, the SEC administers several statutes.

The Securities Act of 1933. Sometimes known as the "Truth-in-Securities Act," the Securities Act of 1933 requires a full disclosure of all of the material facts with regard to the issuance of new securities. Thus, an investor may have sufficient and reliable information on which to make judgments involving the purchase of securities. The law makes it a crime to sell or offer to sell to the public, by mail or in interstate commerce, any security not properly registered with the Securities and Exchange Commission.

Under the Act, the Federal Government does *not* guarantee any security issue or purchase. In effect, however, the law adds to the ancient rule of *caveat emptor* ("let the buyer beware") the newer rule of *caveat vendor* ("let the seller beware").

The Securities Exchange Act of 1934. As a logical follow-up to the 1933 law, the Securities Exchange Act of 1934 lays down regulations concerning trading in securities *after* their issuance. All securities listed on the nation's securities exchanges, the best-known of which is the New York Stock Exchange, must be registered with the SEC. The SEC prepares elaborate forms with questions covering whatever it thinks will help the public to understand the real condition of a corporation.

The Securities Acts Amendments of 1964. Congress broadened the coverage of the Acts of 1933 and 1934 with the passage of the Securities Acts Amendments of 1964. Under the newer law those larger companies with stock issues which are *not* listed on the national exchanges but which *are* sold "over the counter" must also disclose the material facts about their securities. More specifically, the 1964 Act applies to any such firm which engages in or affects interstate commerce and has assets of more than $1,000,000 and at least 500 stockholders.

The Public Utility Holding Company Act of 1935. This law was brought about by the pub-

lic utility "holding companies." These were corporations chartered in one State and holding the controlling stock in operating companies scattered around the country. Because of their interstate character, they were able to evade State regulation.

The public utility holding company device came to be widely used by electric power and gas companies. Financiers who controlled holding companies claimed that their holding companies promoted large-scale production and greater efficiency. Opponents showed that their very complexity made it possible for shrewd financiers to conceal profits which should rightfully have been used to reduce the price of electricity and gas.

Therefore, in 1935 Congress directed the SEC to require full and fair disclosure of the corporate structure of holding company systems. The Commission was also directed to eliminate uneconomic holding company structures and to supervise security transactions and other operations of *electric* and *gas* holding companies.[12]

Other acts administered by the SEC include the *Investment Company Act of 1940,* which regulates the conduct of investment companies, and the *Investment Advisers Act of 1940,* which covers the operations of investment counselors and their relationships with clients. Trading operations on the nation's several agricultural commodity exchanges—in such farm items as wheat, corn, cotton, barley, eggs, and butter —are regulated by the Commodity Exchange Authority in the Agriculture Department (page 446).

United States District Courts often call upon the SEC for assistance in bankruptcy cases. This happens most often in those proceedings in which it has become necessary to reorganize a debtor corporation.

---

[12] The actual *operating* electric and gas companies, as distinguished from the *holding* companies, are regulated by the Federal Power Commission. See page 540.

Key Concepts

The Banks of the United States (1791 to 1811 and 1816 to 1836) were the forerunners of the system of national banks created by Congress in 1863. Today there are two principal systems of banks in the United States: State banks and national banks.

All national banks and most State banks do the general business of commercial banks. One group of State banks, mutual savings banks, restrict their business to the receipt and investment of small savings deposits. National banks are subject to both State and national regulation.

The Federal Deposit Insurance Corporation insures deposits up to $15,000 in banks eligible for its coverage.

The Federal Reserve System was created by Congress in 1913 to give the nation's banks the strength of unity.

The Federal Home Loan Bank System was created in 1932 to provide a credit reserve for savings and home financing institutions. These member institutions, now numbering more than 5000, make loans to home builders.

The system of Farm Credit Banks was created by Congress in 1933 to coordinate various lending programs intended to aid the farmers.

The Small Business Administration was set up in 1953 to replace the Reconstruction Finance Corporation. The SBA is designed to encourage small businesses by making financial help available and otherwise assisting them.

The Export-Import Bank, created in 1934, makes loans to encourage trade by other countries with the United States.

The Securities and Exchange Commission, also established in 1934 is the general policeman for the trading of securities in the United States.

Important Terms

"blue sky laws"	Federal Reserve System	"open market"	rediscount rate
caveat emptor	holding company	operations	reserve requirement
caveat vendor	mutual savings banks	public utility holding	State banks
commercial banks	national banks	company	"wildcat banking"

Questions for Inquiry and Review

1. What was the principal argument that arose over the proposed creation of the Bank of the United States?

2. Why is the case of *McCulloch* v. *Maryland* so important in our history?

3. What are the two principal systems of banks in the United States today?

4. Why did State banks all but disappear after the passage of the National Banking Act of 1863?

5. Are mutual savings banks national banks?

6. What is the basic function of the Federal Deposit Insurance Corporation?

7. What independent regulatory agency directs the operations of the Federal Reserve System?

8. What banks are members of the Federal Reserve System?

9. How many Federal Reserve Banks are there?

10. What are the two principal duties of the Board of Governors of the Federal Reserve?

11. What is a Federal Home Loan Bank?

12. What is a Federal Land Bank?

13. The Small Business Administration replaced what major federal lending agency?

14. What is the primary mission of the Small Business Administration?

15. The Export-Import Bank performs what two major functions?

16. What led the States to enact "blue sky laws"?

17. What led Congress to create the Securities and Exchange Commission?

18. What is the Securities and Exchange Commission's basic task?

For Further Inquiry

1. During hard times a merchant in a small city will quite likely borrow money from a national bank by giving his note. Why is he more liable to get his money now than before the creation of the Federal Reserve System?

2. The Panic of 1907 was caused largely by a hoarding of money. Why is such a situation almost impossible today?

3. For what reasons do you favor or oppose federal insurance of bank deposits up to $15,000?

4. In 1936 private bankers wanted five per cent interest for money to refinance Great Northern Railway bonds which were coming due. The Reconstruction Finance Corporation agreed to refinance the bonds at four per cent. With this encouragement, the railroad was able to sell its bonds at four per cent to its own stockholders and bondholders, thus saving $1,000,000 annually. Why do you favor or oppose such government competition with private banks?

Suggested Activities

1. Investigate the stormy life of the Second Bank of the United States and present your findings to the class.

2. Invite a local banker to address the class on commercial banking operations.

3. Invite an officer of a local savings and loan association or an investment counselor to speak to the class on the making of sound financial investments

4. Hold a debate or class forum on the following question: *Resolved,* That FDIC maximum protection should be raised to $20,000 on individual accounts and $40,000 on joint accounts.

5. Write a report on one of the following topics: a SEC investigation of security fraud, the history of a major RFC loan, or "wildcat banking" malpractices.

Suggested Reading

BURNS, JAMES M. and PELTASON, J. W., *Government By the People.* Prentice-Hall, 1969. Chapter 26.

DALE, EDWIN L., "After Peace Breaks Out, What Will We Do With All That Extra Money?" *New York Times Magazine,* February 16, 1969.

"Federal Reserve Head Talks on Inflation, Interest, Controls," *U.S. News,* Sept. 22, 1969.

NEWFIELD, JACK, "Nader's Raiders: The Lone Ranger Gets a Posse," *Life,* October 3, 1969.

"Prospects for Inflation and Recession, *Time,* November 14, 1969.

"The Dollar Squeeze," *Life,* August 15, 1969.

***Is patronage an unleavened evil? Why?

***Are there any circumstances under which public employees should have the right to strike?

***Are there any factors more critical than salary in the recruitment of qualified public servants?

***Can a valid distinction be drawn between the phrases "public employee" and "public servant"?

Government is a trust, and the officers of the government are trustees; and both the trust and the trustees are created for the benefit of the people.

HENRY CLAY

The National Government is the largest single employer in the United States today. It now employs some 3,000,000 persons—not counting those in uniform.[1] Of this huge number, only 537—the President, and Vice President, and the 535 members of Congress—are elected. All of the others are appointed.

It is upon the shoulders of these appointees, the federal "civil servants," that most of the burden of the day-to-day work of the National Government rests. The quality of these appointees determines in very large measure the quality of the National Government itself. No matter how wisely Congress and the President may formulate public policies, the people and the country cannot benefit unless those policies are properly and successfully executed. For, as Woodrow Wilson once observed, the administration of governmental policy is "government in action."

It is obvious, then, that the hiring of qualified men and women for the public service is among the most important problems government faces. In this chapter we are especially concerned with the civil service at the national level. But, obviously, capable and qualified public servants are equally vital to the successful administration of government at the State and local levels.

DEVELOPMENT OF CIVIL SERVICE

The Constitution says very little about governmental personnel. Indeed, the only directly pertinent provision is to be found in Article II. Section 2, Clause 2 provides that the President:

shall nominate, and, by and with the advice and consent of the Senate, shall appoint ambassadors, other public ministers, and consuls,

---

[1] There are some 13,000,000 civilian government employees all told, including approximately 2,500,000 now (1971) employed by the States and another 7,500,000 by their local governments.

judges of the Supreme Court, and all other officers of the United States whose appointments are not herein otherwise provided for; but the Congress may by law vest the appointment of such inferior officers, as they think proper, in the President alone, in the courts of law, or in the heads of departments.

A Good Beginning. As our first President, George Washington knew that the success or failure of the new government under the Constitution would hinge in large measure upon those whom he appointed to office. He declared his policy to be that of selecting "such persons alone . . . as shall be the best qualified." He demanded that his appointees be loyal to the Constitution; but he did not insist that they be loyal to him personally or to those who supported him politically.

As the party system developed, however, Washington's successors began to give weight to political considerations in the making of appointments. John Adams followed Washington's policy rather closely in that he insisted upon competence, but he was also careful to see that none of his political enemies gained appointive office.

When Thomas Jefferson entered the White House in 1801, he found that most of the positions in the National Government were held by men who were both politically and personally opposed to him. Although he agreed in principle with Washington's concept of "fitness for office," he combined it with "political acceptability," replacing many Federalists with his own Democratic-Republicans. Even so, not many offices were involved. When the national capital was moved to the new city of Washington in 1800, there were only about 1000 federal employees. The Treasury Department employed sixty-nine persons; War, eighteen; Navy, fifteen; and State and Post Office, nine each.

Jefferson's immediate successors—James Monroe, James Madison, and John Quincy Adams—found little occasion to remove any-

one for partisan reasons, though they did insist on party loyalty by their appointees.

Jackson and the Spoils System. By the latter 1820's the number of federal employees had risen well into the thousands. When Andrew Jackson came to the Presidency in 1829, he dismissed many officeholders and replaced them with his own supporters.

Jackson is often cited as the father of the *spoils system*—the practice of giving offices and other favors of government to those who have supported the party.[2] This is not altogether fair. Jefferson had laid its foundations in the National Government in 1801, and it was used among the States and their local governments long before Jackson became President.

Jackson looked upon his appointing policy more as a "democratic" one than as a system for rewarding friends and punishing enemies. In his first message to Congress he explained and defended his program on four grounds. He held that (1) since the duties of public office were essentially simple, any normally intelligent person was capable of holding office; (2) there should be a "rotation in office" in order that a wider number of persons might have the privilege of serving in the National Government; (3) long service by any person would promote tyranny and intolerance; and (4) the people were entitled to have the party which they placed in power control all of the offices of government from top to bottom.

Whatever Jackson's high purposes and "democratic" concepts may have been, there were others who saw the spoils system as a means for building and holding power. For the next half-century the spoils system held sway. Every change in administration brought a new round of rewards and punishments; and, as governmental activities and agencies increased, so did the spoils.

---

[2] The famous words "To the victors belong the spoils of the enemy" were first uttered by Senator William L. Marcy of New York on the floor of the United States Senate in 1832.

Competent persons were squeezed out of the public service or, more often, refused to "soil their hands" by entering it. Efficiency was mostly an idle dream of a few reformers. Huge profits were made on public contracts at the people's expense. Much of the nation's natural wealth was stolen. Political power was centered in the horde of officeholders and others who owed their livelihood to the party in power.

The Movement for Reform. Congress made feeble attempts to correct matters in 1851 and 1853. It required several thousand clerkships to be filled on the basis of examinations given by department heads. This minor reform produced no significant results. Nor did an 1871 law which established the first national civil service commission and introduced the idea of *competitive* examinations.

Able men pressed for major reform. Civil service reform was debated in every session of Congress after 1865. Men like William Cullen Bryant and Carl Schurz spoke out for it, and leading journals like *Harper's Weekly* and *The Nation* took up the cry. Groups like the National Civil Service Reform League,[3] which was founded in 1881, fought for it.

It finally took a tragedy to transform talk and hope into the reality of action. The assassination of President James A. Garfield by a disappointed officeseeker roused the nation. Garfield's successor, Chester A. Arthur, pushed vigorously for reform, and Congress passed the Civil Service Act of 1883.

The Pendleton Act. The Civil Service Act of 1883, better known as the Pendleton Act, established the basic pattern of the federal civil service system. Although it has been amended many times over the past eight decades and has been supplemented by other statutes, its major features remain in effect today. It created the *United States Civil Service Com-*

mission as an independent agency under the President. The Commission is composed of three members appointed by the President with Senate consent. They serve staggered six-year terms and not more than two of them may belong to the same political party.

The Pendleton Act divided the administrative employees of the Federal Government into two groups: (1) those in the *classified* and (2) those in the *unclassified* service. The power to determine under which of these services most agencies were to operate was given to the President.

Appointment to a position under the classified service was to be made on the basis of merit. Merit was to be determined on the basis of competitive and "practical" examinations given by the Civil Service Commission. The Commission was required to draw up lists (*registers*) on the basis of examination standings, and appointments were to be made from the registers. The Pendleton Act also directed that, insofar as possible, appointments to the classified service should be made on a geographic basis. The number of employees from a particular State was to correspond approximately to that State's proportion of the national population. After a six-months' probation an employee was to become a permanent member of the service and be removable only for cause ("the good of the service").

Under the Pendleton Act employees were forbidden to participate actively in politics, and Congressmen and others were forbidden to attempt to influence the Civil Service Commission in regard to the employment of any person. The act established a system of preference for any honorably discharged war veteran, and especially for disabled veterans and the widows of veterans. Finally, it specifically exempted from its operations any person appointed to office by the President and confirmed by the Senate.

Extension of the Classified Service. Originally the Pendleton Act applied to only some 14,000 of the then 131,000 federal employees.

---

[3] Renamed the National Civil Service League in 1945, this organization is one of the most influential groups promoting the merit system today.

The term *bureaucracy* is both much used and abused in American politics. In its "unloaded" sense, it is regularly used to identify the whole of the administrative structure—all of the agencies, personnel, and procedures—of a government. When the term is used in this sense, a bureaucracy is characterized by formal organization based upon a hierarchy, by a specialization in the assignments of its personnel, with known rules governing their actions, and vesting of legal authority in positions as distinguished from people.

But the term is also frequently used as one of derision. As such, it is usually applied to government agencies and their officials whom their critics think are too much involved in "red tape" and precedent, overly dedicated to routine and opposed to change, "empire builders," excessively powerful, and unresponsive to public opinion. To some critics the growth of bureaucracy is a symptom of the moral degradation of the American people of today in contrast to Americans of an earlier period. And some see the growth of bureaucracy as the result of an insidious plot to destory individual freedom, hatched by power-hungry politicians who think that they know what is best for everyone.

The governments of all modern-day nations have equipped themselves with extensive and complex administrative organizations—that is, with bureaucracies. It is one of the continuing imperatives of a democracy that it keeps its public servants responsive to the law and to the well-being of the people and their elected representatives.

Is the growth of bureaucracy an inevitable fact of life for modern-day government? What safeguards do we have in the United States—in the form of institutions, procedures, beliefs, and the like—to forestall irresponsible bureaucracy? Are they used effectively? Explain.

Gradually the various Presidents have extended the ranks of the classified service.[4]

There were many fits and starts, adding to and removing from the classified service, in the administrations of Presidents Cleveland, Harrison, and McKinley. Theodore Roosevelt, who had headed the Civil Service Commission under Presidents Harrison and Cleveland, was a firm believer in the merit system, however, and had the courage to carry out his conviction. He shifted more than 115,000 positions from the unclassified to the classified service. Later Presidents have followed his example. Today more than ninety per cent of all the employees working in the federal government are covered by the merit system.

Congress has had a major hand in extending civil service coverage in recent years, too. In 1939 it required all State and local governments to follow a merit system in all agencies receiving grants-in-aid under the social security system. Many federal grant-in-aid programs now carry this stipulation. Under the Ramspeck Act of 1940 the President was given the authority to place *all* federal civilian employees under the classified service except those in a few agencies such as the TVA and FBI which have their own merit systems.

THE CIVIL SERVICE SYSTEM TODAY

Because the Government of the United States is the largest single employer in the nation—and, in fact, in the world—the job

---

[4] The term *civil service* is often used quite loosely to refer to governmental employees in the *classified service* only. Correctly, the civil service includes *all* federal civilian employees except those who are elected to office, the other topmost policy-making officers such as Cabinet members, and judges.

and the problems of the federal civil service system are understandably immense. Abraham Lincoln once likened his task as personnel appointer to that of a landlord so busy showing prospective renters (officeseekers) around one wing of the building that he had little time to put out the raging fire (a war) in the other. Lincoln was speaking in a day when there were only some 50,000 government workers. Today, the *annual turnover* in federal jobs is ten times that number, or about 500,000. In other words, some 500,000 federal employees (approximately twenty per cent of the total) resign their positions or otherwise leave government service each year.

The Changed Emphasis in Civil Service. The primary goal of those who led the movement for civil service reform was the elimination of the spoils system in the selecting of government personnel. As this goal has come closer and closer to realization in fact, the em-

phasis in civil service has shifted. Today primary concern is not so much with eliminating politics and favoritism from the selection process (this has been largely accomplished), but with the task of securing the best available and most qualified persons and of improving in other ways the efficiency and standards of the civil service.

Position Classification. An effective government personnel program must be firmly based upon a logical system of *position classification*. That is, it must be based upon a breakdown of the service into related classes or groups of positions. Under this arrangement all positions with similar duties and responsibilities are grouped together into a single class. For example, all clerk-typists are put into a single class regardless of the agency in which a clerk-typist may work. The clerk-typist job is essentially the same in all government agencies.

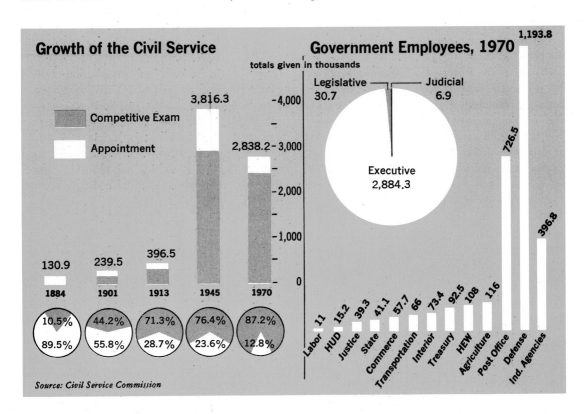

Source: Civil Service Commission

Position classification is necessary to the handling of the other basic problems of the personnel system, including recruitment, appointment, pay, promotions, retirement, and the like. For example, the exact nature of a particular job to be filled must be known in order that the best available person can be sought to fill that job.

Recruitment. The phrase "government worker" often conjures up an image of file clerks, mailmen, typists, messengers, telephone operators, janitors, and the like. Of course, the Federal Government employs thousands of people for these jobs — and their work is absolutely essential to its effectiveness. But the federal civil service also includes nearly all of the occupations to be found in private life, including doctors, dentists, lawyers, chemists, botanists, biologists, political scientists, social workers, teachers, skilled mechanics, carpenters, plumbers, electronics technicians, draftsmen, photographers, physicists, nurses, psychologists, and so on. Altogether more than 2000 different occupational specialties are included in the civil service.

How does the Federal Government go about the important task of attracting people to its ranks? Until the 1950's recruitment was carried on almost entirely by the Civil Service Commission, but today it is primarily the responsibility of the various operating agencies themselves. Job announcements are usually posted in public buildings, especially in post offices. Announcements are also placed in the classified advertisements sections of newspapers and sent to schools and radio and television stations. Until recently, however, most applicants for federal jobs learned of their opportunities more by chance than through any real effort on the part of the National Government. There has been improvement in recent years, but still more could be done to dramatize available job opportunities.

Application. When a person does learn of an opening which interests him, he must fill out an application form. Forms are available at nearly every post office in the country. The most common one is Form 170, an envelope-sized card containing fifteen questions and covering application for most federal jobs. It asks such information as one's name, address, sex, date of birth, educational record, and previous employment experience. It does *not* ask an applicant's race or religion; neither of these factors may be considered in the hiring of any federal employee.

Form 170 is actually a preliminary application. If an agency is attracted by the data supplied on it, it will then request that an applicant file a more detailed form. The higher and more skilled positions (for example, lawyer, accountant, nurse, doctor, chemist) regularly involve the filing of additional and more detailed forms.

Examination. If a person's application meets the requirements set for the job he is seeking, he is notified when and where to take an examination. The Civil Service Commission uses two general types of tests.

Assembled. The *assembled examination* is used for most federal positions. Its name comes from the fact that all of the candidates in a particular area are "assembled" in a given place at a given time for the examination. It is a practical test designed to discover a person's particular qualifications for a particular job. The written questions are usually objective ones: true-false, matching, and multiple-choice. If the job requires a special skill such as typing, this skill is also tested.

Non-Assembled. The *non-assembled examination* is commonly used for the higher positions. The applicant for one of these posts is seldom required to report at any special place. Indeed, he often doesn't really take an "examination" at all. Rather, he is ranked on the basis of his training, experience, and accomplishments. He may be asked to write a report or an essay on some topic, thus placing the emphasis on thought and originality.

Entry into the federal service today is regarded as more than the taking of a temporary job. It is looked upon as the beginning of a permanent career with promotion through the ranks to higher posts. In line with this, the whole federal civil service testing program now lays much stress on general all-round ability.

The Registers. All those applicants who pass the required examinations—a score of 70 is a passing grade on most—have their names placed on a *register*. A register is a list of persons eligible for appointment to a particular position or class of positions. Each applicant is ranked on an appropriate register according to his examination score. The registers are used by appointing officers among the various agencies; when one is exhausted or becomes obsolete, new examinations are held.

Appointment. The Civil Service Commission does *not* appoint anyone to a federal job—except the employees of the Commission itself. Appointments (other than presidential) are made by the agency in which there is a vacancy.

In the past the Civil Service Commission maintained centralized registers for the entire range of government positions covered by the merit system. This led to a good deal of confusion and delay, however. For example, the names of the top persons on a particular register might be under consideration in several agencies at once. Today separate registers are kept for many agencies. Only the more common positions, such as clerk and stenographer, are now kept on central registers. An appointment to a job must be made from among the top three persons on the appropriate register.

Veterans' Preference. Veterans' preference in civil service appointments antedates the original Pendleton Act. Today an automatic five extra points on an examination are given to any honorably discharged veteran. A total of ten points is added to the score of a disabled veteran, the wife of a disabled veteran unable to work, or the widow of a veteran who has not remarried. Some federal jobs, such as messengers and guards, are reserved especially for disabled veterans.

Nearly one-half of all federal jobs are now held by those with veterans' preference. Nearly all State and local civil service systems also give preference to veterans. The granting of this privilege to those who have served their country can be easily justified. Notice, however, that it is a departure from the principle of appointment on the basis of individual merit.

Geographical distribution in the making of appointments also complicates the process somewhat. Ever since the Pendleton Act, the number of persons in the civil service from any State is supposed to bear a close relation to that State's share of the total national population. Thus, if a State has six per cent of our total population, approximately six per cent of the total number of federal workers must come from

Examinations for many positions of employment with the Government are offered by the Civil Service Commission in hundreds of cities throughout the nation. (United States Civil Service Commission Photo)

that State. This geographic barrier often complicates the appointing process and hardly promotes the hiring of workers on the basis of merit alone.

Probation. After his appointment, the civil servant must serve a period of *probation* (trial period) up to six months. If by the end of this period the employee is found suitable, his appointment becomes permanent. If his superiors find him unsuitable, he may be dropped. *Temporary appointments* may be made without examination for the filling of short-term jobs. In periods of national emergency government employment usually rises quite rapidly, and temporary appointments are often made to meet the sudden demand for additional workers.

Compensation. Recruiting well-qualified public servants, and persuading them to remain in government service, is very obviously and importantly affected by the matter of compensation. As the matter now stands, the salaries paid by the National Government at the middle and lower levels of federal employment compare well with those available in similar private jobs. The same cannot be said at the higher levels, however.

Salaries. Salaries paid in the classified service are set by the *General Schedule*, a pay scale established by act of Congress. It provides for eighteen basic pay grades. The salaries now (1971) paid under it range from $3889 a year for those starting in the lowest grade (GS–1) to a top of $33,495 in GS–18. In every grade except GS–18 there is a series of raises ("step increases") which may be had on the basis of length of service and demonstrated ability.

An employee need not begin his government career at the very bottom of the General Schedule. Remember, in the position classification scheme each job is classed according to its nature, and suitable pay is one of the bases for classification. Thus, a job requiring some training and ability might be ranked GS–9. A person appointed to it would not start at $9320 a year.[5]

Government can never hope to compete with private industry on a dollar-for-dollar basis in the upper grades. For example, an agency head whose federal salary is $33,495 a year might command a significantly higher salary in a similar position outside the government. How government service can attract and keep better people for the higher jobs is a major headache in the civil service system.

Other Compensation. Several "fringe benefits" are provided to federal workers—but these generally lag behind those common in private industry. Most civil servants are covered by retirement, disability, and survivor insurance programs. As the civil service retirement system now operates, the employee's contributions are matched by the Federal Government and, at compound interest, produce a relatively generous retirement pension. The usual retirement age is sixty-two, but one may retire on the full annuity at fifty-five after thirty years of service. Some fringe benefits are also available during the working years: for example, overtime and sick pay, paid vacations, and group life, health, accident, and unemployment insurances.

Promotion. The question of promotion is an extremely important one to the civil service worker. If he knows that his chances for promotion are good, his morale and efficiency are likely to be much higher than if he knows that they are not.

---

[5] Congress sets the salaries of all federal employees, from the President on down. It has provided separate pay schedules for a few groups; for example, postal workers and Foreign Service personnel. It permits individual agencies to set the hourly wages paid to manual laborers. By law only some 2600 persons, or about one-tenth of one per cent of all federal civilian employees, may hold the "supergrade" positions (GS–16, GS–17, and GS–18).

As we know, there is an opportunity for promotion within each salary grade. These promotions are made largely on the basis of seniority (length of service), but every employee is also rated on the basis of efficiency by his superior. Merit does play a part in these promotions. Merit plays its biggest part in the promotion from one job to a higher one. When there is a vacancy in a higher position, it is supposed to (and usually does) go to the person who has best demonstrated his abilities. The ambitious, capable, and hard-working person who makes government his career can expect promotion because merit is basic to the classified service.

Restrictions on Political Activity. One of the basic purposes of the merit system has always been to protect federal workers from political pressures. Thus, ever since 1883, the Civil Service Act has prohibited the dismissal or the disciplining of a classified worker for his failure or refusal to make a campaign contribution.

At the same time, acts of Congress and Civil Service Commission regulations restrict the partisan political activity of federal workers. Federal employees may vote at elections, attend party meetings, voice their opinions in political matters, make voluntary contributions to a party treasury, and even hold office in a political organization. But they may not take an active part in any campaign for public office. They cannot do such things as serve as delegates to party conventions, distribute campaign literature, and collect funds for a party or a candidate. To do any of these things provides grounds for dismissal from employment with the federal government.

These restrictions apply to all federal workers covered under the classified service and, as well, to all but the top-most officials outside the merit system. The Hatch Acts of 1939 and 1940 extended these same curbs to all State and local government employees who work in programs financed, even in part, by federal funds.

GOVERNMENT EMPLOYEES AND UNIONS

As we saw in Chapter 26, private employers are required by law to allow their workers to join unions and to bargain collectively if their workers choose to do so. Logically, the National Government must grant the same rights to its own employees.

The first union of government employees, the National Association of Letter Carriers, was formed as early as 1889. Its activities, however, were severely restricted by executive order. In 1912 Congress specifically permitted unions of federal employees. Since then, many such groups have sprung up. The early government unions were *craft* unions. That is, they were organized on the basis of particular kinds of jobs; for example, the National Association of Letter Carriers or the Railway Mail Association. In addition to postal employees, most of the other craft workers—such as carpenters, electricians, and plumbers—in the National Government are also unionized today.

In the last several years a number of *industrial* unions (those of broader scope) have also developed. Today the National Federation of Federal Employees (an independent union), the American Federation of Government Employees, and the United Federal Workers (both AFL-CIO) each claim sizable membership. The several postal workers' unions still contain the largest number of organized federal workers, however.

These unions of federal workers exist for the same reasons unions exist in private industry. Their major purpose is to promote the interests of their members. They cannot bargain quite as effectively as private unions may, however, because wages, hours, and working conditions in the Federal Government are set by Congress. Thus, these unions must spend much of their time in lobbying activity in order to promote their interests.

The most important difference between the government employee unions and private unions arises in the right to strike. The Taft-Hartley Act of 1947 specifically prohibits strikes by government workers.[6] The national health and safety must be protected against sudden walkouts. Another important difference arises in the fact that no federal employee may be forced to join a union in order to get a job or to retain one. In other words, both the *closed shop* and the *union shop,* common in private industry, are prohibited in public service.

THE PROBLEM OF LOYALTY

Throughout our history the American people have had the right to expect and demand that every public employee be loyal to the United States. The threat we face from international communism has made the whole matter of loyalty more urgent over the past several years.

A "loyalty-review program" was begun under President Truman in 1947. It was drastically revised under President Eisenhower in 1953 and has since been a "security-risk system." No one may be employed by the National Government unless such employment is "clearly consistent with the interests of national security."

All employees or applicants for federal jobs are screened to prevent subversion and infiltration. When a sensitive position (one vital to the nation's security, as in the State Department) is involved, or when "derogatory information" is turned up, the FBI makes a thorough

---

[6] Before 1947 federal workers who went on strike could be prosecuted for such acts as obstructing the mails or conspiring against the National Government.

"field investigation" of the person concerned. Less elaborate investigations of prospective employees are made by the agency involved or by the Civil Service Commission.

A person may be judged a "security risk" on several grounds. Membership in or sympathy with the Communist party, communist front groups, or other totalitarian organizations makes one a "security risk" under the present loyalty program. So does close association with known or suspected Communists. Drunkards, sex deviates, anyone who is for any reason subject to blackmail or any other pressures, and a host of other persons with defects in their personal backgrounds cannot be hired or cannot remain in the government service.

Before an employee may be dismissed, the charges against him must be stated in writing. He may demand a hearing before a security board, but the witnesses against him need not appear at his hearing nor need they be available for cross-examination by the accused. Indeed, they may be wholly anonymous. In all cases the final decision is in the hands of the head of the agency involved.

The whole loyalty-security program has been the subject of intense controversy for several years. At one extreme are those who insist upon an exaggerated standard of loyalty, too often one in accord with their own peculiar definition. At the other extreme are those who insist that the danger we face has been grossly exaggerated for political reasons. In between are the great number of people who are genuinely concerned about the problem and seek an approach which will safeguard the nation's security and, at the same time, protect the civil rights of federal employees.

Key Concepts

The National Government, with now some 3,000,000 civilian employees, is the largest single employer in the nation — in fact, in the world. Nearly all of these employees are appointed, not elected, and the day-to-day operations of the National Government are largely in their hands.

George Washington inaugurated "fitness for office" as a qualification for federal employment, but in later administrations "political acceptability" became a qualification, too. Andrew Jackson brought the full-blown "spoils system" to the National Government. The spoils system reigned supreme until the passage of the Pendleton Act (1883).

The Pendleton Act created the United States Civil Service Commission and divided federal employees into two groups: the *classified* and the *unclassified* services. Over ninety per cent of all federal employees are within the classified service today.

Whereas the original emphasis in civil service reform was on eliminating the spoils system, today it is on the securing of the best possible employees. The federal civil service is based upon position classification. A civil service applicant takes either an *assembled* or a *non-assembled* examination given by the Civil Service Commission. If he passes, his name is placed on a register from which appointments are made. Veterans' preference and geographic distribution are required in appointments. Appointees serve a brief probationary period.

Compensation of those federal employees in the classified service is based on the General Schedule. Those with jobs in the middle and lower grades of this pay scale are relatively well-paid, but the Federal Government cannot hope to compete with private industry for the services of top administrators. Overtime, vacation, sick leave, retirement are also provided for. Promotion is based on seniority and merit. There are several government employee unions, but a federal worker may not strike nor be forced to join a union. The threat of international communism has made the whole matter of the loyalty of government employees more vital now than ever before in our history.

Important Terms

assembled examination	merit system	probation	seniority
civil service	non-assembled examination	recruitment	spoils system
classified service	Pendleton Act	register	unclassified service
General Schedule	position classification	security risk	veterans' preference

Questions for Inquiry and Review

1. Approximately how many civilians are currently employed by the National Government?

2. Why may it be said that the hiring of qualified persons is among the most important governmental problems?

3. What does the Constitution provide for a governmental personnel program?

4. How did George Washington lay an excellent basis for a civil service system?

5. How did Washington's immediate successors modify his standard?

6. On what bases did Andrew Jackson justify his version of the spoils system?

7. Why was the Pendleton Act passed?

8. What is the essential difference between the classified and the unclassified services?

9. Who determines which federal jobs are to be included within the classified service?

10. From what original goal to what present emphasis has concern for the quality of the civil service shifted over the years?

11. Why is position classification of central importance to an effective governmental personnel program?

12. For what two general types of positions does the Civil Service Commission utilize its two general types of examinations?

13. For what purposes are the registers used?

14. How do veterans' preference and the requirement of geographic distribution modify the concept of appointments based on merit?

15. What is the most significant difference between government employee unions and private workers unions?

16. What two conflicting goals make the problem of the loyalty of government employees a difficult and controversial matter?

For Further Inquiry

1. Do you think that federal workers should be hired because of particular practical skills they possess or because of their general background, education, and overall abilities?

2. How might a civil service career be made more attractive to young people?

3. Should civil servants whose work is not directly connected with the nation's health or defense be permitted to strike?

4. The restrictions placed on the political activities of federal employees are regarded as necessary by most of them. Some, however, argue that their rights as citizens are being violated and that the nation's political health suffers because of the "political sterilization" of those who work for the nation's largest employer. With which position do you agree?

5. Why do you think it is true that, with a few notable exceptions, civil service systems based upon merit have been much slower to develop at the State and local levels than in the National Government?

Suggested Activities

1. Prepare a report comparing the local governmental personnel system in your locale with the federal civil service system.

2. Stage a debate or class forum on the question: *Resolved,* That public employees should be guaranteed by law the right to strike.

Suggested Reading

"Another Hike in Federal Pay," *U.S. News,* June 30, 1969.

BURNS, JAMES M. and PELTASON, J. W., *Government By the People.* Prentice-Hall, 1969. Chapter 16.

DIMOCK, M. E. and GLADYS, *Public Administration.* Holt, Rinehart, and Winston, 1969.

MAGRATH, C. PETER, *et al., The American Democracy.* Macmillan, 1969. Chapter 11.

"Rules on Relatives — Who Can Be Hired for a U.S. Job?" *U.S. News,* April 21, 1969.

U.S. Civil Service Commission, *Working for the U.S.A.* Government Printing Office, 1970.

THE NATIONAL JUDICIARY

❖❖❖ Is the power of judicial review consistent with the basic principles of democracy?

❖❖❖ Should there be two separate court systems, federal and State, in the United States? Why?

❖❖❖ Should judges be elected or appointed to office? Why?

❖❖❖ Should federal judges be appointed for fixed terms of office? Why?

For man, when perfected, is the best of animals, but when separated from law and justice, he is the worst of all.

ARISTOTLE

The American system of government is built upon the rock of separation of powers. In our system, it is the duty of the legislative branch to make the laws, of the executive to administer and enforce those laws, and of the judiciary to interpret and apply them to cases as they arise.

The men who framed the Constitution were convinced that an independent judiciary—a national system of courts—was essential to the success of the government they created. The Articles of Confederation had made no provision for a national judiciary, and that fact proved a major weakness of the government established under that document.

Over the period the Articles of Confederation were in force (1781–1789), the laws of the United States were interpreted and applied among the States as each of them saw fit. Disputes between States [1] and between residents of different States were decided—if at all—by the courts of one of the States involved. More

often than not, decisions made by the courts of one State were not accepted or enforced by the other States.

Alexander Hamilton was speaking for all of the Founding Fathers in *The Federalist No. 78* when he called "the want of a national judiciary . . . a circumstance which crowns the defects of the Confederation." Arguing the need for a *national* system of courts, he added:

> Laws are a dead letter without courts to expound and define their true meaning and operation.

To meet the need, the Founding Fathers wrote Article III into the Constitution. Article III, Section 1 creates the national judiciary in one brief sentence:

> The judicial power of the United States shall be vested in one Supreme Court, and in such inferior courts as the Congress may from time to time ordain and establish.

---

[1] The Articles of Confederation (Article IX) did provide a complicated procedure for the settlement of such disputes by Congress, but it was rarely used.

And Congress is given the expressed power "to constitute tribunals inferior to the Supreme Court" in Article I, Section 8, Clause 9.

Types of Federal Courts. As we have just noted, the Constitution creates only the Supreme Court of the United States. It leaves to Congress the creation of the "inferior courts" — those beneath the Supreme Court. Exercising its power, Congress has created two distinct types of federal courts: (1) constitutional courts and (2) special courts.

The constitutional courts are those Congress has created under Article III to exercise "the judicial power of the United States." Together with the Supreme Court, these courts — the Courts of Appeals, the District Courts, the Court of Claims, the Customs Court, and the Court of Customs and Patent Appeals — comprise what is often called the "regular courts system."

The special courts do not exercise "the judicial power of the United States." Instead, they have been created by Congress to handle cases arising out of the exercise of particular congressional powers. Today these courts — often referred to as the "legislative courts" — include the territorial courts, the courts of the District of Columbia, and the Court of Military Appeals.

THE CONSTITUTIONAL COURTS

Jurisdiction. Jurisdiction may be defined as the right of a court to hear and determine (to *try* and *decide*) a case. Under Article III the federal courts have jurisdiction over a case either because of (1) the subject matter involved in the case or (2) the parties involved in the case.

Subject Matter. Two classes of cases may be

The United States Supreme Court Building was completed in 1935. The two statues flanking the steps reflect thought on the problems of justice and strong enforcement of the law. On the frieze of the white marble structure, the inscription "Equal Justice Under Law" proclaims to one and all a basic tenet of our democratic system.

brought into the federal courts because of the subject matter involved: (1) those arising under the Constitution, laws, or treaties of the United States, and (2) those in the field of admiralty or maritime law.[2]

Parties. Six classes of cases may be brought into the federal courts because of the parties involved: (1) cases affecting ambassadors, other public ministers, and foreign consuls, (2) cases to which the United States itself is a party, (3) cases between two or more States, (4) cases between citizens of different States (known as cases in *diverse citizenship),* (5) cases between citizens of the same State who claim land under grants from different States, and (6) cases between a State, or its citizens, and a foreign state, or its citizens.[3]

Exclusive and Concurrent Jurisdiction. In some of the cases we have just cited, the federal courts have *exclusive jurisdiction;* that is, the cases may be tried *only* in the federal courts. For example, cases involving ambassadors, other public ministers and consuls, or patents and copyrights are within the exclusive jurisdiction of the federal courts.

Some cases, particularly those involving residents of different States, may be tried *either* in a United States District Court *or* in a State court. In such instances, the federal and State courts have *concurrent jurisdiction;* that is, they share jurisdiction. Congress has provided that the District Courts may hear such a case *only*

if the amount involved exceeds $10,000. In such a case, the plaintiff [4] may bring the suit in the State or federal court, as he chooses. If he brings it in the State court, however, the defendant [5] may have the case transferred to the United States District Court.

Original and Appellate Jurisdiction. A court in which a case is first heard is said to have *original jurisdiction* over it. A court which hears cases on appeal from lower courts is said to have *appellate jurisdiction.* In the national court system, the District Courts have only original jurisdiction; the Courts of Appeals have only appellate jurisdiction; and the Supreme Court has both.

The District Courts. The federal trial courts, the District Courts, were established by the First Congress in 1789. There are ninety of these courts today. The fifty States are divided into eighty-eight judicial districts, with one court for each district. There is also one District Court for the District of Columbia and another for Puerto Rico.

Each State forms at least one district, but the larger States include two or more districts, as the map on page 572 indicates. Each district has at least one judge, but many have several. Thus, New York is divided into four districts, one with twenty-four judges. All told, there are now (1971) 333 district judges.

District Court cases are usually heard by a single judge. In a few cases three judges form

---

[2] *Admiralty law* relates to matters which arise on the high seas or the navigable waters of the United States. *Maritime law* relates to matters arising on land but directly related to the water—for example, a contract to deliver ship's supplies at dockside.

[3] Under the 11th Amendment a State *may not* be sued in the federal courts by a citizen of another State or a foreign state. A State *may* be sued without its own consent in the federal courts only by the United States, another State, or a foreign state. If a citizen of the State, another State, or a foreign state wishes to sue a State, he may do so only with that State's consent and only in its own courts. But a State may bring a suit against a citizen of another State, an alien, or a foreign state in the federal courts.

[4] A *plaintiff* is one who commences a suit in law against another.

[5] A *defendant* is a party accused and summoned into court to defend himself.

Federal Judicial Circuits and Districts

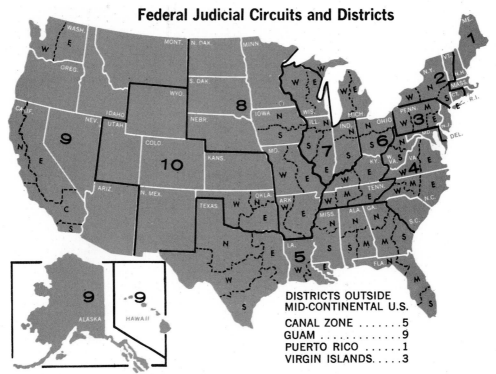

DISTRICTS OUTSIDE
MID-CONTINENTAL U.S.

CANAL ZONE 5
GUAM 9
PUERTO RICO 1
VIRGIN ISLANDS. 3

Letters indicate northern, southern, eastern, western, central and middle judicial districts. Numbers indicate judicial circut for each State.

the court. In these instances, it is said that the court sits *en banc*. They sit *en banc* when an effort is made to have the District Court *enjoin* (issue an *injunction* against) the enforcement of a State law or an order of a State or federal agency.

Jurisdiction. The District Courts have original jurisdiction over all federal cases except those within the original jurisdiction of the Supreme Court and those that are heard in the Court of Claims, in the Customs Court, in the Court of Customs and Patent Appeals, or in the special courts.[6]

Cases tried in a District Court may be appealed to the Court of Appeals. In a few cases, however, appeals may go directly to the Supreme Court: injunctions issued *en banc,* certain decisions holding acts of Congress unconstitutional, and certain decisions in criminal cases.

The Courts of Appeals. The Courts of Appeals were created by Congress in 1891 to

---

[6] The 6th Amendment provides that in a federal criminal prosecution the accused is entitled to a trial in "the State and district wherein the crime shall have been committed." This guarantee is designed to give the defendant the benefit of a court and jury familiar with the locale of the crime. But the defendant may ask for a "change of venue" — that is, a transfer of the trial to another locality — on grounds of local prejudice in his case. When such a request is made, the judge assigned to the case must determine whether a change of venue is warranted.

relieve the Supreme Court of the large number of cases appealed from the District Courts. The appeals had become so numerous that the Supreme Court was almost three years behind in its business.

There are eleven Courts of Appeals. The United States is divided into ten judicial circuits, and there is a Court of Appeals for each circuit. There is also one Court of Appeals in the District of Columbia. Each Court of Appeals has from three to fifteen judges (now ninety-seven in all), and one Justice of the Supreme Court is also assigned to each. For example, the Court of Appeals for the Fifth Circuit covers Texas, Louisiana, Mississippi, Alabama, Georgia, Florida, and the Panama Canal Zone. It now has fifteen judges plus Associate Justice Hugo Black of the Supreme Court. It sits at Fort Worth, New Orleans, Montgomery, Atlanta, and Jacksonville.

Jurisdiction. Congress has severely limited the types of cases that may go to the Supreme Court as a matter of right — that is, because of their nature. The highest court hears only the more important cases. Of course, this adds to the importance of the Courts of Appeals. They hear appeals from the District Courts and from such *quasi-judicial* agencies as the various independent regulatory commissions.

Cases brought before a Court of Appeals are usually heard by three of the judges, but the courts may, and occasionally do, sit *en banc.* (in which all the judges of that particular court hear the case). One or more District Court judges may be assigned to serve with the circuit judges when their case load becomes particularly heavy. In such instances, a district judge may not sit on cases which were before him on the lower bench.

The Supreme Court. The Supreme Court of the United States is the only court specifically created in the Constitution.[7] It is composed of the Chief Justice, whose office is also estab-

William Howard Taft has the distinction of being the only man who served as President of the United States and as Chief Justice of the United States. (Culver Pictures, Inc.)

lished in the Constitution,[8] and eight Associate Justices.[9]

It would be well-nigh impossible to overstate the significance of the role of the Supreme Court in the American system of government — in terms both of the historical development of the system and its present-day operations. The Framers of the Constitution purposely placed it on a co-equal plane with the President and Congress and designed it as the apex of

---

[7] Article III, Section 1.

[8] Article I, Section 3, Clause 6.

[9] Congress determines the size of the Supreme Court. The Judiciary Act of 1789 provided for a Court of six justices, the Chief Justice and five Associate Justices. Its size was reduced to five in 1801, increased to seven in 1807, to nine in 1837, and to ten in 1863; it was reduced to seven in 1866 and then raised to the present figure in 1869.

the nation's judicial system. As the highest court in the land, the Supreme Court stands as the court of last resort in *all* questions of federal law—that is, in *any* case involving *any* question arising under any provision in the Constitution, an Act of Congress, or a treaty of the United States.

As we have noted before, most courts in this country, both State and federal, exercise the power of judicial review—the power to determine the constitutionality of a governmental action, whether executive, legislative, or judicial.[10] The *ultimate* exercise of that power rests with the Supreme Court of the United States. It is the final authority on the meaning of the Constitution; it is, as Chief Justice Charles Evans Hughes once put it, "a continuous constitutional convention."

The dramatic and often far-reaching effects of the Supreme Court's exercise of the power of judicial review tends to overshadow other aspects of its work. Each year it hears dozens of cases in which questions of constitutionality are *not* raised but in which federal law is nevertheless interpreted and applied. Thus, many of the more important statutes enacted by Congress—for example, the Interstate Commerce Act, the Sherman Antitrust Act, the Social Security Act, the National Labor Relations (Wagner) Act, the Alien Registration (Smith) Act, the Labor-Management Relations (Taft-Hartley) Act, the Internal Security (McCarran) Act—and many of the lesser ones, as well, have been brought to the Supreme Court repeatedly for decision. In construing them and applying them to specific situations, the Supreme Court has had a considerable impact upon their meaning and effect.

As we have noted, the Supreme Court also serves as the arbiter or referee in the federal system.[11] It decides the legal disputes which arise between the National Government and the States and between or among the States.

Jurisdiction. The Supreme Court has both original and appellate jurisdiction. But it is primarily an appellate tribunal. Most of the cases it hears come to it on appeal from the lower federal and the State courts. Article III, Section 2 defines two classes of cases which may be heard by the Supreme Court under its *original* jurisdiction: (1) those in which a State is a party, and (2) those affecting ambassadors, other public ministers, and consuls.

Congress cannot enlarge upon this constitutional grant of original jurisdiction. Recall that this is what the Supreme Court ruled in holding a portion of the Judiciary Act of 1789 unconstitutional in *Marbury* v. *Madison.*[12] If Congress could do so, it would in effect be amending the Constitution. But Congress can *implement* the constitutional provision, and it has. It has provided that the Supreme Court shall exercise original *and exclusive* jurisdiction over: (1) all controversies between two or more States and (2) all cases *against* ambassadors or other public ministers (but not consuls). The Supreme Court may take original jurisdiction over the other cases covered by the broad wording of Article III; but these cases may also be, and usually are, tried in the lower courts.

How Cases Reach the Court. Some 2500 to 3000 cases are now appealed to the Supreme Court each year. Of these, only a few hundred are accepted for decision, however. In the large bulk of cases, then, the petitions for review are denied—usually because the Supreme Court is in agreement with the decision of the lower court or because it feels no significant point of law is involved.

More than half of the cases actually decided by the Court are disposed of in brief orders—for example, an order remanding (returning) a case to a lower court for reconsideration in the light of some other recent and related case decided by the Supreme Court. All told, the Court decides, after hearing arguments and

[10] See pages 52–53.
[11] See pages 68–69.

[12] See pages 68–69.

with full opinions, only about 100 to 120 cases each year.

Generally, cases come to the Supreme Court either by *certiorari* or on *appeal*. Most cases reach the Court by *writ of certiorari* — an order by the Court directing a lower court to send up the record in a given case because one of the parties alleges some error in the lower court's handling of that case. An *appeal* involves a petition by one of the parties to a case requesting the Court to review the lower court's decision in the case. A few cases do reach the Court in a third way, by *certificate*. The process is used when a lower court is unsure of the procedure or the rule of law that should apply in a particular case; it asks the Supreme Court to certify the answer to a specific question in the matter.

Most cases which reach the Court do so from the highest State courts and the federal Courts of Appeals. Some do come, however, from the federal District Courts, as we have seen, and from the Court of Claims, the Court of Customs and Patent Appeals, and the Court of Military Appeals, to which we shall turn shortly.

Speaking of the appellate role of the Supreme Court, the late Chief Justice Fred M. Vinson once told a meeting of the American Bar Association:

> The Supreme Court is not, and never has been, primarily concerned with the correction of errors in lower court decisions. In almost all cases within the Court's appellate jurisdiction, the petitioner has already received one appellate review of his case. The debates in the Constitutional Convention make clear that the purpose of one supreme national tribunal was, in the words of John Rutledge of South Carolina, "to secure the national rights & uniformity of Judgmts." The function of the Supreme Court is, therefore, to resolve conflicts of opinion on federal questions that have arisen among lower courts, to pass upon questions of wide import under the Constitution laws, and treaties of the United States, and to exercise supervisory power over lower fed-eral courts. If we took every case in which an interesting legal question is raised, or our *prima facie* impression is that the decision below is erroneous, we could not fulfill the Constitutional and statutory responsibilities placed upon the Court. To remain effective, the Supreme Court must continue to decide only those cases which present questions whose resolution will have immediate importance far beyond the particular facts and parties involved. Those of you whose petitions for certiorari are granted by the Supreme Court will know, therefore, that you are, in a sense, prosecuting or defending class actions; that you represent not only your clients, but tremendously important principles, upon which are based the plans, hopes, and aspirations of a great many people throughout the country.[13]

The Supreme Court at Work. The Supreme Court sits for a term of about eight months each year — from the first Monday in October until some time the following June. Customarily, the Justices hear arguments in the cases before them for two weeks, then they recess for two weeks to prepare their opinions. While arguments are being heard, the Supreme Court opens at 10 A.M. Monday through Thursday.

Monday is usually "decision day"; the decisions ready for release are announced at the beginning of that day's session.[14] Once the decisions have been announced, and the Justices have read their opinions which accompany them, the Supreme Court turns to the hearing of oral arguments in the next cases on the docket.

Each of the parties to a case (the *litigants*) is normally allowed one hour in which to present

---

[13] Chief Justice Fred M. Vinson, "The Work of the Supreme Court," *Supreme Court Reporter,* 1949.

[14] Since 1965, however, the Supreme Court has adopted the practice of releasing decisions on other days, as well.

oral arguments. The Justices often interrupt a presentation with questions. The litigants also submit written *briefs,* detailed and systematic arguments which often run to hundreds of pages. Regularly, the Justices rely very heavily upon these briefs submitted by the attorneys in reaching their decisions.

On Friday of most weeks of a term the Justices meet in conference to discuss the cases they have heard and to determine their disposition. These conferences are held in the closest secrecy, and no formal report of their conduct is ever made. Several years ago, the late Chief Justice Harlan Fiske Stone wrote one of the very few descriptions which exist:

> At Conference each case is presented for discussion by the Chief Justice, usually by a brief statement of the facts, the question of law involved, and with such suggestions for their disposition as he may think appropriate. No cases have been assigned to any particular judge in advance of the Conference. Each Justice is prepared to discuss the case at length and to give his views as to the proper solution of the questions presented. In Mr. Justice Holmes' pungent phrase, each must be able to "recite" on the case. Each Judge is requested by the Chief Justice, in the order of seniority, to give his views and the conclusions which he has reached. The discussion is of the freest character and at its end, after full opportunity for each member of the Court to be heard and for the asking and answering of questions, the vote is taken and recorded in the reverse order of the discussion, the youngest, in point of service, voting first.
>
> On the same evening, after the conclusion of the Conference, each member of the Court receives at his home a memorandum from the Chief Justice advising him of the assignment of cases for opinions. Opinions are written for the most part in recess, and as they are written, they are printed and circulated among the Justices, who make suggestions for their correction and revision. At the next succeeding Conference these suggestions are brought before the full Conference and accepted or

rejected as the case may be. On the following Monday [usually] the opinion is announced by the writer as the opinion of the Court.[15]

Six Justices constitute a quorum for the decision of a case, and at least four must agree before a case can be decided. If (as usually happens) all nine Justices participate, a case may be decided by a 9-0, 8-1, 7-2, 6-3, or 5-4 vote. Although many cases are decided unanimously, several find the Supreme Court split.

As Chief Justice Stone indicated, a *majority opinion* regularly accompanies the deciding of a case. A Justice who disagrees with the majority's decision often writes a *dissenting opinion.* Indeed, two, three, or even four dissents are occasionally presented. A Justice who agrees with the Court's decision, but not with the reasoning by which it was reached, often prepares a *concurring opinion* — and one or more of these are often presented, too.

The Supreme Court is sometimes criticized because many cases are not decided by unanimous vote, but rather by "split decisions." But the critics often overlook the fact that nearly all of the cases the Court hears involve very difficult and quite controversial issues. In many of them, too, there have been contradictory lower court decisions. The "easy" cases seldom reach the Supreme Court.

Neither the majority nor the concurring or dissenting opinions are actually necessary to the decision of a case. In fact, decisions are occasionally handed down without opinion. But the opinions do serve valuable purposes. The majority opinions stand as precedents to be followed in similar cases as they arise in the lower courts or reach the Supreme Court. The concurring opinions may prompt the Supreme Court to go beyond its present position in future cases. Chief Justice Hughes once described dissenting opinions as "an appeal

---

[15] Justice Harlan F. Stone, "Fifty Years of Work of the United States Supreme Court," *Report of the American Bar Association,* 1928.

CHIEF JUSTICES OF THE UNITED STATES

Name	State From Which Appointed	President By Whom Appointed	Years Of Service	Life Span	Age When Appointed
John Jay	New York	Washington	1789–1795	1745–1829	44
John Rutledge [a,b]	South Carolina	Washington	1795	1739–1800	55
Oliver Ellsworth	Connecticut	Washington	1796–1800	1745–1807	51
John Marshall	Virginia	John Adams	1801–1835	1755–1835	46
Robert B. Taney	Maryland	Jackson	1836–1864	1777–1864	59
Salmon P. Chase	Ohio	Lincoln	1864–1873	1808–1873	56
Morrison B. Waite	Ohio	Grant	1874–1888	1816–1888	58
Melville W. Fuller	Illinois	Cleveland	1888–1910	1833–1910	55
Edward D. White [b]	Louisiana	Taft	1910–1921	1845–1921	65
William Howard Taft	Ohio	Harding	1921–1930	1857–1930	64
Charles Evans Hughes [b]	New York	Hoover	1930–1941	1862–1948	68
Harlan F. Stone [b]	New York	F. Roosevelt	1941–1946	1872–1946	69
Fred M. Vinson	Kentucky	Truman	1946–1953	1890–1953	56
Earl Warren	California	Eisenhower	1953–1969	1891–	62
Warren E. Burger	Dist. of Columbia	Nixon	1969–	1907–	61

[a] Rutledge was appointed Chief Justice by President George Washington on July 1, 1795, while the Congress was not in session. He presided over the August 1795 term of the Supreme Court; but the Senate refused to confirm his appointment, rejecting it on December 15, 1795. Rutledge subsequently went insane.

[b] Four men served as Associate Justice before being appointed as Chief Justice: John Rutledge, from 1789 to 1791; White, 1894 to 1910; Hughes, 1910 to 1916; and Stone 1925 to 1941. Rutledge was appointed an Associate Justice when the Supreme Court was first organized in 1789; but he resigned a year and a half later, having attended no sessions of the Court. Hughes resigned as an Associate Justice in 1916 in order to seek the Presidency. White and Stone each were serving as Associate Justices when elevated to Chief Justice.

to the brooding spirit of the law, to the intelligence of a future day." The minority opinion of the Supreme Court today might become its majority opinion in a later case.

The Other Constitutional Courts. Three other constitutional courts — each originally created by Congress as special courts — exist today.

The Court of Claims. The United States may not be sued by one of the States or by an individual without its consent.[16] If this were not

the case, the courts would be flooded and hamstrung by all manner of unfounded claims.

Originally, any person having a claim against the United States could secure *redress* (satisfaction of the claim, payment) only by special act of Congress. In 1855, however, Congress, acting under its power to pay the debts of the United States,[17] created the Court of Claims as a special court. Congress established it as one of the constitutional courts in 1953.

The Court of Claims is composed of a chief judge and six associate judges who sit *en banc* in Washington, D.C. It hears claims arising

---

[16] This doctrine of non-suability comes from the ancient principle of English public law summed up by the phrase: "The king can do no wrong."

[17] Article I, Section 8, Clause 1.

out of acts of Congress, the actions of the various executive agencies, and contracts entered into by the United States.[18] Appeals from decisions of the Court of Claims may be carried to the Supreme Court.

Awards made by the Court of Claims cannot be paid unless and until Congress makes the necessary appropriations. The funds are provided almost as a matter of course, however. Occasionally, those who lose in the Court of Claims still manage to secure compensation. Some years ago, for example, a mink rancher lost a case in which he claimed that low-flying Navy planes had caused several of his female mink to become sterile. He asked $100 per mink, but the Government was able to show that any one of several factors—including diet, weather, and fights and jealousies in the group —could have caused the condition. Even so, his Congressman introduced a bill that eventually paid him $10 for each animal.

The Customs Court. The Customs Court was originally created in 1890 as the Board of United States General Appraisers. Congress renamed it in 1926 and made it one of the constitutional courts in 1956.

The Customs Court consists of nine judges, one of whom serves as chief judge. It hears disputes arising out of the administration of the tariff laws; most of its cases involve decisions made by customs officers in the Treasury Department. Its judges sit in divisions of three and hear cases at such principal ports of entry as New York, Boston, New Orleans, and San Francisco. Appeals from decisions of the Customs Court are taken to the Court of Customs and Patent Appeals and, in cases involving questions of constitutionality, directly to the Supreme Court.

---

[18] Under the Federal Tort Claims Act of 1946 the District Courts also have jurisdiction over many claims cases, but their jurisdiction is limited to those claims not exceeding $10,000. The Federal Tort Claims Act also gives executive agencies the authority to settle claims of $1000 or less.

The Court of Customs and Patent Appeals. The Court of Customs and Patent Appeals was established as a special court in 1909 and made a constitutional court in 1958. Its chief judge and four associate judges sit *en banc,* usually in Washington, D.C.

It reviews decisions of the Customs Court dealing with the classification and duties upon imported goods, decisions of the Patent Office relating to applications for and infringements on patents and trademarks, and the findings of the Tariff Commission concerning unfair practices in the nation's import trade. It often hears cases involving such questions as: Are golf socks subject to duty as "wool half hose" or at a lower rate as "athletic equipment"? Are jew's harps "musical instruments," or should they be dutied at a higher rate as "toys"? Appeals from the decisions of the Court of Customs and Patent Appeals may be taken to the Supreme Court.

THE SPECIAL COURTS

The special courts are those Congress has created to exercise jurisdiction only in certain cases—cases involving specific subjects within the expressed powers of Congress. These courts have no jurisdiction under Article III of the Constitution.

The Territorial Courts. Acting under its authority to provide for the governing of the territories,[19] Congress has created local courts for the Panama Canal Zone, the Virgin Islands, Puerto Rico, and Guam. These courts function in much the same manner as the local courts in the fifty States.

Courts of District of Columbia. Acting under its power to exercise exclusive authority over the District of Columbia,[20] Congress has provided a judicial system for the nation's capital. Congress restructured the system in

---

[19] Article IV, Section 3, Clause 2.
[20] Article I, Section 8, Clause 17.

1970. It is now built around a single trial court, the superior court, with jurisdiction blanketing the District and covering all local cases. The federal Court of Appeals for the District serves as an appellate court, hearing appeals from decisions rendered by the judges of the superior court.

The Court of Military Appeals. Acting under its power to make rules for the Armed Forces,[21] Congress created the Court of Military Appeals in 1950. It is composed of a chief judge and two associate judges. The Court is independent of the executive and legislative branches, as are *all* of the federal courts, but is attached to the Defense Department for administrative purposes. Sometimes called the "GI Supreme Court," the Court of Military Appeals reviews the more serious court-martial decisions (decisions in trials of members of the Armed Forces under an act of Congress, the Uniform Code of Military Justice).

The Tax Court. The Tax Court is *not* a part of the national judiciary. Rather, it is an independent agency within the executive branch. It was first created as the Board of Tax Appeals in 1924, and it became the Tax Court in 1942. The Tax Court is composed of sixteen judges appointed by the President, with Senate confirmation, for twelve-year terms. Every second year the judges select one of their number to serve a term as chief judge. The Tax Court hears appeals from the decisions of tax officers within the Treasury Department. Although their offices are in Washington, the judges hear cases throughout the country.

JUDGES

Appointment. The Constitution provides that the President shall appoint the Justices of the Supreme Court, subject to Senate confirmation.[22] Congress has provided for the same procedure for all other federal judges. The Constitution prescribes no qualifications for judges and Congress has not done so, either. Hence the President is free to appoint whomever the Senate will confirm.

Most of those who are appointed to federal judgeships are drawn from the ranks of leading attorneys, professors of law, former members of Congress, and from the State courts. As in other appointments, the President tends to favor members of his own political party in making judicial selections.

Term. All judges of the constitutional courts are appointed for a term of "good behavior." [23] That is, they are appointed in effect, until they resign, retire, or die. They may be removed only through the impeachment process. Only nine federal judges have ever been impeached, of whom only four were found guilty by the Senate.[24]

---

[21] Article I, Section 8, Clause 14.

[22] Article II, Section 2, Clause 2.
[23] Article III, Section 1.

[24] Judge John Pickering of the District Court for New Hampshire was removed for drunkenness in 1803; Judge West Humphreys of the District Court for Tennessee, for disloyalty in 1862; Judge Robert Archibald of the Commerce Court, for improper business relations with persons having cases in court in 1913; and Judge Halsted Ritter of the District Court for Southern Florida, for bringing his court into scandal and disrepute in 1936. Four other judges (Samuel Chase, James Peck, Charles Swayne, and Harold Louderback) have been impeached by the House of Representatives but acquitted by the Senate. The most famous of these was Associate Justice Chase of the Supreme Court who was accused in 1804 of "expressing himself too freely in regard to politics." A few District Court judges have resigned to avoid impeachment. One (George English) was impeached in 1926 but resigned before he could be tried. See pages 213–214.

The judges of the territorial courts and those of the District of Columbia are appointed for terms varying from four to eight years. The judges of the Court of Military Appeals serve fifteen-year terms.

Compensation. The Constitution provides that federal judges:

> ... shall, at stated times, receive for their services a compensation which shall not be diminished during their continuance in office.[25]

Congress sets the salary scale for all federal judges. Today (1971), judges of the District Courts and of the Customs Court receive $40,000 a year. Those of the Courts of Appeals, the Court of Claims, the Court of Customs and Patent Appeals, and the Court of Military Appeals are paid $42,500 a year. The Associate Justices of the Supreme Court receive $60,000 and the Chief Justice $62,500 a year.

Congress has provided a rather generous retirement arrangement for the judges of the constitutional courts. They may retire at age seventy and, if they have served for at least ten years, receive their full salary for the remainder of their lives; or they may retire on full salary at age sixty-five after at least fifteen years of service on the federal bench. The Chief Justice may call any retired judge back to active service in the lower federal courts at any time, however.

JUDICIAL ADMINISTRATION

Federal judges are today only very little involved in the day-to-day administrative operations of the courts over which they preside. Their primary mission is to hear and decide the cases which are brought before them. Other judicial personnel provide the support services necessary to the performance of that mission.

---

[25] Article III, Section 1.

Court Officers. Each federal court appoints a *Clerk* who has custody of the seal of the court and keeps a record of the court's proceedings. He is assisted by a number of deputy clerks, stenographers, bailiffs, and such other court attendants as may be needed.

Until now (1971), *United States Commissioners* have been appointed to four-year terms by each of the District Courts, in whatever number needed and congressional appropriations would allow. The Commissioners have performed such functions as the issuing of search and arrest warrants, the setting and taking of bail, and often the hearing of evidence to determine whether or not a person accused of a federal crime should in fact be held for action by the grand jury. Now, however, the Commissioners are being replaced in each judicial district by new officers, *United States Magistrates*—who, in addition to the powers of their predecessors, also have the authority to try some minor federal criminal cases.

The President appoints, subject to Senate confirmation, a *United States Attorney* for each federal judicial district. He and his assistant are responsible for the prosecution of all persons charged with the commission of federal crimes within the district, and they represent the United States in all civil action to which it may be a party within the district.

The President and Senate also appoint a *United States Marshal* to serve each District Court. Each federal marshal and his deputies perform duties much like those assigned to a county sheriff and his deputies. They make arrests in federal criminal cases, keep those accused in custody, secure jurors, serve legal papers, keep order in the courtroom, and execute the orders of the court.

United States Attorneys and Marshals are each appointed for four-year terms. Although they are officers of the court, they are also officers of the Department of Justice and serve under the direction of the Attorney General. See page 407.

Key Concepts

The lack of a national judiciary was one of the most serious weaknesses in the Articles of Confederation. The Founding Fathers corrected this in Article III of the Constitution. There the Supreme Court is provided for and Congress is given the power to create whatever lower courts may be needed.

Two types of federal courts have been created: the constitutional courts and the special courts. The constitutional courts are the District Courts, the Courts of Appeals, the Supreme Court, the Court of Claims, the Customs Court, and the Court of Customs and Patent Appeals. The special courts are the territorial courts, the courts of the District of Columbia, and the Court of Military Appeals.

The constitutional courts, which exercise the judicial power of the United States, have jurisdiction over a case either because of the subject matter or the parties involved. Some cases are within the exclusive jurisdiction of the federal courts, while in others concurrent jurisdiction exists with State courts. Cases first heard in a court are within its original jurisdiction; those heard on appeal are within its appellate jurisdiction.

The ninety District Courts hear the bulk of federal cases. The eleven Courts of Appeals hear appeals from the District Courts and the independent regulatory commissions. The Supreme Court is the highest court in the land. It generally chooses the cases it will hear from the lower federal courts and the highest State courts. It has original jurisdiction over cases against ambassadors, and other public ministers and over cases involving controversies between two or more States. The Court of Claims hears cases involving claims against the United States. The Customs Court hears disputes involving the administration of the tariff laws. The Court of Customs and Patent Appeals hears appeals from decisions of the Customs Court, from patent and trademark decisions of the Patent Office, and Tariff Commission findings of unfair practices in the import trade.

The special courts are those which Congress has created *not* under Article III. They do not exercise the judicial power of the United States but handle cases arising out of the exercise of particular congressional powers. The territorial courts and the District of Columbia courts are special courts. The Court of Military Appeals, also a special court, reviews serious court-martial decisions. The Tax Court is an independent agency in the executive branch, hearing appeals from decisions of tax officials in the Treasury Department.

Questions for Inquiry and Review

1. Which Article of the Constitution deals principally with the judiciary?

2. What is the chief distinction between the two types of federal courts that have been created: the constitutional courts and the special courts?

3. On what two general bases do the federal courts have jurisdiction of cases?

4. Why are there more District judges than District Courts in the national judiciary?

5. Do the District Courts exercise appellate jurisdiction?

6. Why were the Courts of Appeals created?

7. Do the Courts of Appeals exercise original jurisdiction?

8. Which is the only federal court specifically created in the Constitution?

9. How is the size of the Supreme Court determined? What is it now?

10. From what courts are cases appealed to the Supreme Court?

11. In what classes of cases does the Supreme Court have original jurisdiction? Exclusive jurisdiction?

12. How many men have thus far served as Chief Justice of the United States? Who holds this office today?

13. Why are many of the decisions of the Supreme Court split decisions?

14. Which of the constitutional courts were originally created as special courts?

15. Over what particular types of cases does the Court of Claims have jurisdiction? The Customs Court? The Court of Customs and Patent Appeals?

16. Which are the special courts in the national judiciary?

17. Over what particular types of cases do the territorial courts have jurisdiction? The courts of the District of Columbia? The Court of Military Appeals?

18. Who appoints all federal judges? For what terms?

19. How may judges be removed from office?

20. What restriction does the Constitution place on Congress' power to set judicial salaries?

21. What are the major functions of the clerks of the federal courts?

22. What are the major functions of the United States Magistrates?

For Further Inquiry

1. The Constitution prescribes no qualifications for judicial office beyond the provision that those whom the President appoints must be acceptable to the Senate. What qualifications do you think a President should set in making appointments to the federal bench? Would you favor the popular election of federal judges?

2. Do courts, as they decide cases, "make law" when they interpret and apply provisions in statutes or in the Constitution? Explain.

3. A few years ago a handful of States (including Alabama, Arkansas, Florida, and Wyoming) petitioned Congress to call a convention to propose a constitutional amendment to create a "Court of the Union." The Court, composed of the chief justices of the fifty States, would have the power to review any decision of the United States Supreme Court involving federal-State relations. Why would you favor or oppose such an amendment to the Constitution?

4. Do you agree or disagree with this observation: The principles of popular sovereignty and majority rule, on the one hand, and that of judicial review on the other are clearly contradictory and cannot logically exist together in a governmental system. Explain.

Suggested Activities

1. Write a short essay based on this comment by Chief Justice Hughes:

Democracy will survive only as long as the quick whims of the majority are held in check by the courts in favor of a dominant and lasting sense of justice. If democratic institutions are long to survive, it will not be simply by maintaining majority rule and by the swift adaptation to the demands of the moment, but by the dominance of a sense of justice which will not long survive if judicial processes do not conserve it.

2. If possible, attend a session of the nearest United States District Court and report your

observations of the proceedings to the class.

3. Invite a local judge or attorney to speak to the class on the nature of the law, the legal profession, and our court system.

4. Hold a debate or class forum on the question: *Resolved,* That since Justices of the Supreme Court serve as the final arbitrators regarding the constitutionality of legislative and executive action, they should be selected by means other than by presidential appointment, thus removing them from the sphere of politics.

Important Terms

appeal
appellate jurisdiction
concurrent jurisdiction
concurring opinion

constitutional courts
dissenting opinion
en banc
enjoin

exclusive jurisdiction
jurisdiction
litigants
majority opinion

original jurisdiction
special courts
split decisions
writ of *certiorari*

Suggested Reading

ABRAHAM, HENRY J., *The Judiciary: The Supreme Court in the Governmental Process.* Allyn and Bacon, 1969.

ADRIAN, CHARLES R. and PRESS, CHARLES, *The American Political Process.* McGraw-Hill, 1969. Chapter 17.

BECKER, THEODORE L. (ed.), *The Impact of Supreme Court Decisions.* Oxford, 1969.

BLACKMORE, CHARLES P. and YESELSON, ABRAHAM (eds.), *The Fabric of American Democracy.* Van Nostrand, 1969. Chapter 7.

BURNS, JAMES M. and PELTASON, J. W., *Government By the People.* Prentice-Hall, 1969. Chapter 19.

DYE, THOMAS R. *et al., American Government: Theory, Structure, and Process.* Wadsworth, 1969. Chapter 13.

KUTLER, STANLEY L., *The Supreme Court and the Constitution.* Houghton Mifflin, 1969.

LEWIS, ANTHONY, "A Talk With Warren," *New York Times Magazine,* October 19, 1969.

MAGRATH, C. PETER, *et al., The American Democracy.* Macmillan, 1969. Chapter 12.

MASON, ALPHEUS T., *The Supreme Court from Taft to Warren.* Louisiana State University Press, 1969.

"New Era for Supreme Court," *Newsweek,* June 2, 1969.

RODELL, FRED, "Can Nixon's Justices Reverse the Warren Court?" *Look,* December 2, 1969.

SCOTT, ANDREW M. and WALLACE EARLE (eds.), *Politics, U.S.A.: Cases on the American Democratic Process.* Macmillan, 1969. Chapter 10.

"The Legacy of the Warren Court," *Time,* July 4, 1969.

"The Supreme Court: Move Toward the Middle," *Time,* May 30, 1969.

"Why the Supreme Court May Be Different Now," *U.S. News,* September 1, 1969.

WILSON, JAMES Q. and VORENBERG, JAMES, "Is the Court Handcuffing the Cops?" *New York Times Magazine,* May 11, 1969.

WRIGHT, JUDGE J. SKELLY, "The Courts Have Failed the Poor," *New York Times Magazine,* March 9, 1969.

34
THE AMERICAN EMPIRE

✻✻✻ Should the United States grant political independence to all of its territorial possessions as rapidly as that goal can be accomplished? Why?

✻✻✻ Should international law prohibit any state from either acquiring or retaining territorial possessions? Why?

✻✻✻ Should the National Government work as diligently as possible to bring about Statehood for Puerto Rico? Why?

✻✻✻ Is the United States, in your view, an imperialistic nation? Why?

We seek not to extend the power of America but the progress of humanity. We seek not to dominate others but to strengthen the freedom of all peoples.

LYNDON B. JOHNSON

The original thirteen States emerged from the Revolutionary War as a loose Confederation spreading some 1300 miles along the Atlantic seaboard. By the Treaty of Paris, which officially ended the war in 1783, the new nation also held all the territory from the Great Lakes on the north to Spanish Florida on the south and west to the Mississippi.

At the end of the Revolutionary War, then, the United States held title to a vast domain — 888,811 square miles. Much of it was among the richest of lands on earth, an area nearly ten times as large as Great Britain.

This proved to be only the beginning, however. From it, the United States has grown to a Union of fifty States embracing more than four times its original area — 3,615,211 square miles. The Louisiana Purchase in 1803, the annexation of Florida in 1819, the annexation of Texas in 1845, the Oregon Treaty in 1846, the cessions from Mexico in 1848, the Gadsden Purchase in 1853, the Alaska Purchase in 1867, and the annexation of Hawaii in 1898 all added

to the territory that now forms the fifty States of the United States of America.

Today the American flag flies over other territory as well. It is with this far-flung insular empire that we are especially concerned — an "empire," if, indeed, it may be called that, unlike any other the world has ever known.

POWER OVER TERRITORIES

The Power to Acquire. No clause in the Constitution gives to the United States the *expressed* power to *acquire* (take possession of) new territory. Nonetheless, the power exists. And, as we know, it has been exercised several times in our history.

The Supreme Court has held on a number of occasions that, just as has any sovereign state in the world, the United States has the *inherent* right to acquire territory. For example, in 1856 Congress authorized the President to take jurisdiction over any guano islands discovered

ACQUISITION OF THE TERRITORY COMPRISING THE FIFTY STATES

Acquisition	Date Acquired	Area (Square Miles)	How Acquired
Original 13 States and the Western Lands	1775– 1783	888,811	Revolutionary War and Treaty with Great Britain
Louisiana Purchase	1803	827,192	Treaty with France
Florida	1819	72,003	Treaty with Spain
Texas	1845	390,144	Admission of an independent state
Oregon Country	1846	285,580	Treaty with Great Britain
Mexican Cession	1848	529,017	Conquest and Treaty with Mexico
Gadsden Purchase	1853	29,640	Treaty with Mexico
Alaska	1867	586,400	Treaty with Russia
Hawaii	1898	6,424	Annexation of an independent state

by American citizens. Upholding the act in 1890, the Supreme Court said:

> By the law of nations, recognized by all civilized states, dominion over new territory may be acquired by discovery and occupation, as well as by cession or conquest.

In addition to this basis in "the law of nations" —that is, international law—the power to acquire territory is clearly implied by three of the expressed powers contained in the Constitution. The *power to make treaties* [1] implies the power to gain territory by treaty. The *power to make war* [2] implies the right to make conquests. The *power to admit new States* [3] implies the power to obtain new territory from which new States might be made. The United States has relied, at one time or another, on each one of these implied powers in acquiring its territorial holdings.

Power to Govern. While the Constitution is silent on the power to acquire territories, it *does* give to the Congress the expressed power to provide for the governing of those territories

the United States holds. Article IV, Section 3, Clause 2 provides:

> The Congress shall have power to dispose of and make all needful rules and regulations respecting the territory or other property belonging to the United States.

In time of war the President, by virtue of his role as Commander in Chief,[4] has the power to govern any territory occupied by the Armed Forces.

Notice that Article IV provides for the *disposal* as well as for the governing of American territories. Acting under this power, the United States granted independence to the Philippines in 1946, and it has promised independence for Puerto Rico whenever the Puerto Ricans themselves feel ready to accept it.

Classification of Territories. Congress has divided our territorial possessions into two classes: the *incorporated territories* and the *unincorporated territories*.

The *incorporated territories* are those that Congress may declare to be *a part of* the United States. Until 1959 there were two incorporated territories, Hawaii and Alaska. Since

---

[1] Article II, Section 2, Clause 2.
[2] Article I, Section 8, Clause 11.
[3] Article IV, Section 3, Clause 1.

[4] Article II, Section 2, Clause 1.

both are now States, no incorporated territories exist today. But, while these two States were territories, all of the Constitution's provisions — except those that apply clearly and expressly only to the States — applied fully within each of them.

For example, the constitutional requirement that indirect taxes must be "uniform *throughout the United States*" [5] meant that all such federal taxes as those on gasoline, cigarettes, liquor, and cosmetics had to be levied at the same rates in Hawaii and Alaska as within the then forty-eight States.

An incorporated territory is one that is looked upon as capable of governing itself and as on the road to becoming one of the States in the Union.

The *unincorporated territories* include all our possessions which are not incorporated — in other words, all American possessions today. They *belong to* but are *not* legally *a part of* the United States. As we shall see, Congress has granted a considerable measure of self-government to some of these territories, especially Puerto Rico, Guam, and the Virgin Islands.

The District of Columbia is *not* a "possession" or "territory" in the sense that the other areas are. Rather, it is a federal district within the continental United States, set aside as the site for the nation's capital and specifically provided for in Article I, Section 8 of the Constitution.

In the case of our other territories — such as the Panama Canal Zone and the various island possessions in the Pacific — little, if any, self-government exists. They are held only for some special reason, usually for their strategic locations as defense bases.

The Office of Territories. Although Congress has the exclusive power to provide for the government of the territories, it has never enacted a uniform pattern of territorial government. Instead, governmental arrangements have varied as widely among the territories as do their sizes, locations, and importance.

_____
[5] Article I, Section 8, Clause 1.

In recent years, however, some measure of uniformity has been brought about through the work of the Office of Territories in the Department of the Interior. This agency, created by Congress in 1950, is charged with promoting the development of our overseas possessions — especially Guam, the Virgin Islands, American Samoa, and the Trust Territory of the Pacific Islands; but, notably, not that of the Panama Canal Zone which remains under the strict control of the Army.

The Office of Territories provides advice and assistance to the various territorial governments, and it is the major channel of communication between other federal agencies and those governments. It also administers Canton, Enderbury, Wake, Palmyra, Baker, Jarvis, and Howland Islands in the Western Pacific.

THE COMMONWEALTH OF PUERTO RICO

Puerto Rico was discovered by Christopher Columbus on November 19, 1493, on his second voyage to the New World. It was conquered for Spain by Ponce de Leon, who became its first governor-general, in 1509. The island remained under Spanish rule for nearly 400 years — until the Spanish-American War in 1898 when it was occupied by American troops under the command of General Nelson A. Miles. Spain ceded formal possession of Puerto Rico to the United States by the Treaty of Paris on December 10, 1898.

Puerto Rico lies southeast of the United States on the northeastern rim of the Caribbean Sea, some 1600 miles southeast of New York. It is almost rectangular in shape, 105 miles long and 35 miles wide. It has a total area of 3435 square miles. In 1950 the population was 2,210,703, and in 1960 it was 2,349,544. Three-fourths of the population is white, the rest predominantly Negro or Mulatto.

Government. Puerto Rico was governed by the Army for two years after its conquest from Spain. In 1900 Congress passed an Organic Act for the island. This statute, the *Foraker Act,* created a territorial government with a popularly elected legislature and a governor appointed by the President and confirmed by the Senate. In 1947 Congress amended the law to give Puerto Ricans the right to elect their own governor.

The Foraker Act served as the territorial "constitution" until the present Commonwealth was established in 1952. United States citizenship was granted to Puerto Ricans by act of Congress in 1917.

Throughout the years since 1898, various Puerto Rican groups agitated for a change in the island's relationship with the United States. Some favored outright independence, others Statehood, and still others the creation of an *Estado Libre Asociado* (an Associated Free State or Commonwealth). Finally, in 1948 Congress provided for an election at which the Puerto Ricans themselves were asked to help set the island's future. Only 10.2 per cent of the voters favored independence; 28.5 per cent cast ballots for Statehood; an overwhelming 61.2 per cent voted for a commonwealth. In a 1967 referendum, more than 700,000 of the island's 1,100,000 registered voters declared these preferences: for independence, less than 1 per cent; for Statehood, nearly 39 per cent; for a continuation of the present commonwealth arrangement: 60.5 per cent.

The Puerto Rican Constitution. In 1950 Congress passed an enabling act directing the calling of a convention to draft a constitution. The resulting document was submitted to the voters of Puerto Rico early in 1952 and approved by a vote of better than four to one. Congress then gave its approval. The Puerto Rican Constitution went into effect on July 25, 1952 — fifty-four years to the day after General Miles' troops had hauled down the Spanish flag and raised the Stars and Stripes above the island's capital, San Juan.

The Puerto Rican constitution declares Puerto Rico to be a "commonwealth . . . within our union with the United States of America." The basic relationship between Puerto Rico and the United States remains largely unchanged. Thus, Puerto Ricans are still American citizens. The island remains within the American tariff system and continues to enjoy free trade with the mainland. Its citizens are still subject to federal law, but they have control over their own internal affairs much as do the States of the Union. For example, Congress no longer has power to repeal laws enacted by the Puerto Rican legislature.

The governor is popularly elected for a term of four years. He must be at least thirty-five years of age, and he must have been, for at least five years preceding his election, a citizen of the United States and a *bona fide* resident of Puerto Rico. The governor is vested with those powers usually lodged with a chief executive under our form of government, including the veto power. He appoints, with Senate consent, the heads of departments in the executive

Both houses of Puerto Rico's bicameral legislature are elected by direct popular vote and meet in the capital, San Juan. (Puerto Rico News Service)

branch. Succession to the governorship falls to the secretary of state.

The *Legislative Assembly* consists of a Senate and a House of Representatives. The Senate has twenty-seven members, two from each of the eight senatorial districts plus eleven at large. The House of Representatives contains fifty-one members, one from each of forty districts and eleven at large. Under a novel scheme, whenever one party gains more than two-thirds of the seats in either house the number of seats in that house may be increased to broaden the representation of the minority party or parties.[6]

Members of both houses are popularly elected for a term of four years and must be citizens of the United States and of Puerto Rico. A governor's veto may be overridden by a two-thirds vote of the total membership of each house. Although Congress and the President no longer have the power to void laws passed by the Puerto Rican legislature, these laws must not be contrary to the Constitution, laws, or treaties of the United States.

The *judiciary* has long since been almost completely Americanized in form, law, and procedure. The supreme court is the Commonwealth's highest court. It consists of a chief justice and four associate justices who are appointed by the governor with consent of the Senate for life, subject to good behavior. The number of justices cannot be changed unless at the direct request of the supreme court itself. The lower courts are established by the Legislative Assembly. There is also a United States District Court.

A *Resident Commissioner,* elected by the voters every four years, represents Puerto Rico in Washington. Although he has no statute right to a seat in the House of Representatives, it is provided as a matter of courtesy. The House rules give him the privilege of debate. He also serves on committees, though he may not vote. He receives the same salary and allowances as a Congressman.

The *bill of rights* in the Commonwealth's constitution includes provisions similar to those in the Constitution of the United States and those of the States. In addition, it contains express provisions regarding public education, the conditions of labor, and the protection of private property.

Constitutional amendments may be proposed by two-thirds of the total membership of each house of the Legislative Assembly. They are ratified by a majority of the voters at a general or special election.

Finances. The finances of Puerto Rico are not handled in the same manner as are those of the other territories. Instead of paying the internal revenue taxes levied by Congress, the local legislature levies these taxes for Puerto Rico, including the income tax. Commodities between Puerto Rico and the United States do not pay tariff duty; but articles entering the United States from Puerto Rico must pay the United States internal revenue tax, and articles from the United States entering Puerto Rico must pay the Puerto Rican internal revenue tax. Articles entering Puerto Rico from countries other than the United States pay the same

---

[6] This provision amounts in effect to a modified form of proportional representation (see page 174). If one party gains more than two-thirds of the seats in either house, but does not gain more than two-thirds of the votes cast for governor, the number of seats at large is increased. This is done by declaring enough candidates of the minor party (or parties) elected to bring its total to nine in the Senate or seventeen in the House of Representatives, as the case may be. If the majority party obtains *more* than two-thirds of the votes for governor, enough additional minority candidates (but not exceeding nine in the Senate and seventeen in the House of Representatives) are declared elected to bring the representation of minority parties as close as possible to the proportion of votes cast for each party in the gubernatorial election.

tariff duties that they would pay if entering the United States. All these taxes go into the Island treasury.

Tax revenues and federal grants-in-aid come to over $1,000,000,000 annually. Included in this total are some $170,000,000 from excise taxes, $210,000,000 from local income and property taxes, a refund of about $75,000,000 in United States internal revenue taxes (most of that amount on rum), and now well over $120,000,000 in grants-in-aid.

Economic Conditions. Writing in 1897, a high official in Spanish Puerto Rico had this to say about the typical Puerto Rican laborer:

> With a pale face, bare feet, lean body, ragged clothes, and feverish look, he walks indifferently, with the shadows of ignorance in his eyes, dreaming of the cockfight, the shuffle of the cards, or the prize in the provincial lottery.

Although the masses continue to be very poor in Puerto Rico, a dramatic improvement has taken place, especially over the past two decades. Even so the annual income per person is now about $1200, just over one-third of that in the States. Some 2,800,000 people live on the Island, averaging 800 people to the square mile, compared with 56 people to the square mile in the United States. The total population is increasing at the rate of 70,000 each year. Only one-half of the land is arable, and there is little mineral wealth. The migration of thousands of Puerto Ricans to the United States and to neighboring Spanish-speaking countries in this hemisphere is a practical, though temporary, solution to the plight.[7]

---

[7] As Puerto Ricans are citizens of the United States they may come here without restriction. In recent years several thousands have come to New York by boat and plane each month. Most of them settle in already overcrowded areas and get jobs in the needle trades, restaurants, as janitors, or in helping crews clean ships.

Some of the facts just cited once led observers to call Puerto Rico "Uncle Sam's neglected stepchild." Today, the child is coming of age. The Puerto Rican government, with the backing of Washington, is bringing about a modern "industrial revolution," and a dynamic Commonwealth is in the making.

"Operation Bootstrap," as it is called, is a concerted effort to free Puerto Rico of its economic chains. American businesses are being encouraged to build new plants in Puerto Rico. As one way of attracting these businesses, the Puerto Rican government grants acceptable firms an almost complete exemption from Puerto Rican income and property taxes for a ten-year period. The large population provides a ready labor source, and the government is more than willing to cooperate in every way. A program of hydroelectric development is bringing in new industry.

While taxes in the States are going up and regulations are becoming more stringent on the mainland, Puerto Rico becomes all the more attractive to American investors. More than 1500 new factories have been opened by American and Puerto Rican capital since the program began. Under present plans it is hoped that 2500 will be operating by 1975.

This recent and rapid expansion has been accompanied by related governmental efforts in other fields, such as education and social welfare. As one observer puts it, the program "has been like a sack of feed set in front of a starving chick." Just over a decade ago, in 1955, the income received by all of the residents of the Commonwealth totaled $996,000,-000; by 1970 personal income had more than doubled, rising above $2,000,000,000. Employment has increased greatly. The sharp lines between the many poor and the few rich are being erased by a rising middle class.

Great strides have been made in public education in recent years; for example, the island's literacy rate, which stood at 68.5 per cent in 1940, is now nearly 90 per cent. A great many slum areas still exist, but a vigorous low-cost housing program is making inroads. Dairying and livestock have recently replaced sugar as the backbone of the island's agricultural economy. Tourism is an increasingly significant economic asset.

Puerto Rico still has a long way to go, but the future is bright. This proud island promises to become, as did the Philippine Islands, a model for other colonial domains throughout the free world.

GUAM

Guam lies in the Western Pacific some 5000 miles west of San Francisco and 1500 miles east of Manila. It is the largest and southernmost of the Marianas, an island group discovered by Magellan in 1521. It is volcanic and only about 209 square miles in area.

Because Guam lies just to the west of the International Date Line, its official slogan proclaims it to be the place "Where America's Day Begins." Approximately sixty per cent of the population (67,044 in 1960) is native Guamanian (Chamorro); the military accounts for most of the rest. Today (1970) the island has an estimated population of 100,000.

The United States acquired Guam by the Treaty of Paris in 1898. Except for the two years of Japanese occupation in World War II, it was governed by the Navy until 1950. In that year Congress passed the Organic Act for Guam, establishing a civil government and vesting responsibility for its administration in the Secretary of the Interior.

Although Guam remains an unincorporated territory, the 1950 law extended American citizenship to all Guamanians. In addition, it granted a bill of rights to the island's residents, provided for a governor appointed by the President and Senate for a four-year term, and established a popularly elected, twenty-one member, single-house legislature.

Congress has since enacted several laws intended to further self-government for Guam.

Most notably, in 1968 it provided for the popular election of the governor and of a newly-created lieutenant governor; and both were chosen by the island's voters for four-year terms for the first time in 1970.

A judge, who is appointed by the President and Senate for an eight-year term, presides over the territorial district court. His court and all other elements of the territorial government sit at the capital, Agana.

Guam's economic importance is practically nil. It exports virtually nothing, except for salvaged World War II scrap metal. The chief value of the island lies in its usefulness for air and naval purposes. It is the principal Pacific base for the Air Force's Strategic Air Command (SAC).

TRUST TERRITORY OF THE PACIFIC ISLANDS

The United States Trust Territory of the Pacific Islands consists of three island groups: the Marshalls, the Marianas (except Guam), and the Carolines. They lie east of the Philippines and include some 98 islands and island clusters. About 97,000 persons now live in the 8484 square-mile area.

The islands were held by Germany until the peace settlements of World War I when Japan received them as a mandate from the League of Nations. The United States conquered them in World War II, and in 1947 the islands became a trusteeship of the United States by unanimous vote of the UN Security Council. Only a few of these picturesque, volcanic islands are self-sustaining. The area is worthless to us except for defense purposes.

The Trust Territory is governed by a High Commissioner responsible to the Secretary of the Interior. He is appointed by the President with Senate consent.

Other Mid-Pacific Islands. Johnston and Sand Islands and Kingman Reef are administered by the Navy and Midway by the Fed-

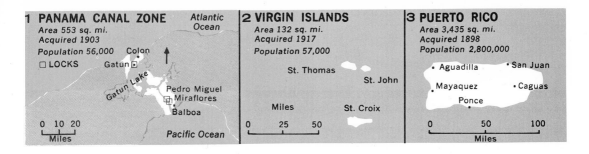

1 PANAMA CANAL ZONE
Area 553 sq. mi.
Acquired 1903
Population 56,000

Atlantic Ocean

☐ LOCKS   Colon

Gatun

Gatun Lake

Pedro Miguel
☐ Miraflores
Balboa

0 10 20
Miles

Pacific Ocean

2 VIRGIN ISLANDS
Area 132 sq. mi.
Acquired 1917
Population 57,000

St. Thomas

St. John

Miles

0   25   50

St. Croix

3 PUERTO RICO
Area 3,435 sq. mi.
Acquired 1898
Population 2,800,000

• Aguadilla   • San Juan

• Mayaquez   • Caguas

Ponce

0   50   100
Miles

Important American Territories

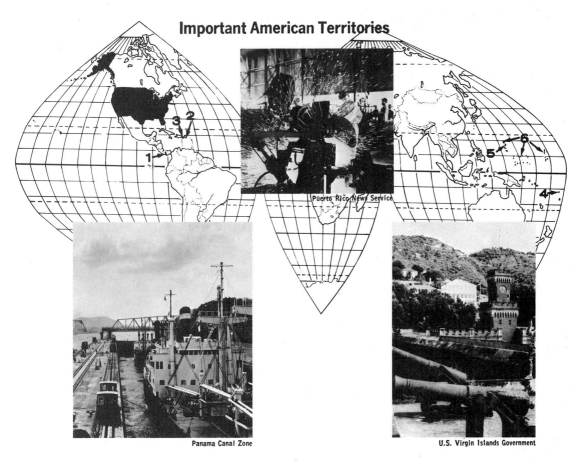

Puerto Rico News Service

Panama Canal Zone

U.S. Virgin Islands Government

4 AMERICAN SAMOA (Tutuila)
Area 76 sq. mi.
Acquired 1899
Population 31,000

• Pago Pago

0   10   20
Miles

5 GUAM
Area 209 sq. mi.
Acquired 1898
Population 100,000

Timoneng
Agana • Sinajana
Agat

0   10   20
Miles

6 TRUST TERRITORY
Area 8,484 sq. mi.
Acquired 1947
Population 97,000

Marianas

Carolines   Marshalls

0   1000   2000
Miles   *Source: Bureau of Census*

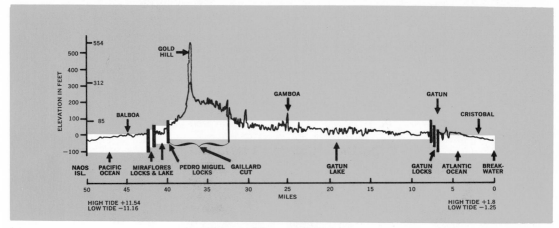

PROFILE OF THE PANAMA CANAL

eral Aviation Administration. The Interior Department administers Wake, Palmyra, Samoa, Baker, Howland, Jarvis, Canton and Enderbury Islands — the latter two jointly with the British. They are valuable for aeronautical, naval, meterological, and radio purposes.

The Ryukyus, a chain of sixty-four islands stretching southwest from Japan to Taiwan, were wrested from the Japanese in World War II. The United States continues to occupy and administer them under the terms of the Japanese peace treaty. The principal island, Okinawa, is a major American military base in the Far East.[8]

PANAMA CANAL ZONE

The history of the Panama Canal dates back nearly 400 years. In 1573 Philip II of Spain ordered a study of the feasibility of a waterway across the narrow strip of Central America. Actual construction of a canal did not begin until 1880, however. In 1878 New Granada

---

[8] The Bonin and Volcano island groups and Parece Vela, Rosario, and Marcus Islands in the Western Pacific, also captured in World War II, were returned to Japanese control in 1968.

(now Colombia) had granted a concession to a French syndicate to construct a canal across its territory on the Isthmus of Panama. The French Canal Company's project was headed by Ferdinand de Lesseps, the famed builder of the Suez Canal. The effort came to grief, however, and was abandoned in 1889. Another French attempt failed in 1899.

The United States bought the rights and properties of the second French Canal Company for $40,000,000 and negotiated a treaty with Colombia for the rights to a canal zone. The United States Senate approved the new treaty promptly, but Colombia rejected it on October 31, 1903. Three days later the Panamanians revolted, declaring their independence on November 4. American naval vessels prevented Colombia from landing troops, and on November 6th, less than three days after the revolt had begun, President Theodore Roosevelt granted American recognition to the infant Republic of Panama.

On November 18, 1903, the United States and Panama concluded the Hay-Bunau-Varilla Treaty granting to the United States the right to construct and maintain a canal and to "exercise all rights, power, and authority" in a zonal strip on either side of it "as if it were sovereign." The grants were made "in perpetuity" (forever). In return the United States paid Panama

$10,000,000, agreed to an annual rent of $250,000 beginning in 1912, and guaranteed Panamanian independence. The Senate approved the treaty on February 23, 1904. Years later, TR was to boast: "I *took* the Canal Zone."

A new treaty in 1936 raised the annual rental figure to $430,000; it also eliminated the American guarantee of Panamanian independence. A still later treaty, in 1955, set the annual rent at $1,930,000.

Although U.S.-Panamanian relations have been generally cordial since 1903, there have been frequent disagreements on the question of sovereignty over the Canal and the Zone. Recent years have seen increased Panamanian agitation for change. Some have even demanded complete American withdrawal. Violent riots erupted in 1959 and again in 1964—outbreaks sparked, at least in part, by Castro agents and other Communist sympathizers.

The 1964 riots prompted Panama to sever diplomatic relations with the United States for nearly three months. More than five years of negotiations have followed, aimed at a new set of agreements covering the matters of sovereignty over and administration of the Canal and the Zone, defense, and authority for this country to build a second canal across Panama should it choose to do so. American defense interests and the economic welfare of both nations suggest that the United States will *not* relinquish effective control over either the Canal or the Zone within the near future.

The Panama Canal. American construction of the Panama Canal was begun in 1904, and the first traffic passed through it on August 15, 1914. From deep water in the Atlantic to deep water in the Pacific, the Panama Canal is just over fifty miles in length. Its locks provide a water bridge between the two oceans. Gatun Locks on the Atlantic side and Pedro Miguel and Miraflores Locks on the Pacific side lift or lower ships between sea level and the level of Gatun Lake.

Average ship passage today requires about ten hours. To date, some 300,000 vessels have made the passage. Privately-owned ships are charged a toll of $1.20 per ton. Thus, a 10,000-ton ship pays $12,000 to go through the canal. The tolls that were collected in 1970 came to more than $90,000,000.

The construction of a second interoceanic canal somewhere on the Central American Isthmus will likely be undertaken within the next few years. Congress provided for a detailed feasibility study of the long-proposed project in 1964. The new canal, if there is to be one, will likely be located also within Panama, although other sites are under serious consideration. The construction of a new canal may well see the first large-scale use of nuclear explosions for man's benefit.

The Canal Zone is a strip of land ten miles wide. It extends for five miles on either side of the Panama Canal, running across the entire width of the Isthmus. The Canal Zone also includes a stretch of the Chagres River where dams have been built to store water in the rainy season to help operate the locks in the dry season, and it also includes all of the twenty-three-mile-long Gatun Lake.

The Canal Zone is under the very strict control of the Army. It is administered by a governor, who also serves as the president of the Panama Canal Company. The governor is appointed by the President with Senate consent for a four-year term and is usually an Army officer from the Corps of Engineers. He serves directly under the Secretary of the Army.

There is no local legislature for the Canal Zone. The laws which operate in the Canal Zone are either acts of Congress or presidential orders. Organized towns, with no elective officials, and a system of courts have been provided by Congress. There is a territorial court with several local magistrates' courts under it. Congress has provided for the extension of the guarantees of the Bill of Rights to the residents of the Canal Zone.

The population today includes some 56,000 persons, excluding the members of the Armed Forces stationed there. These residents are mainly canal employees, their families, and the dependents of military personnel.

THE VIRGIN ISLANDS

The Virgin Islands of the United States, made up of fifty-odd islands, are part of the West Indies archipelago that separates the Caribbean from the Atlantic Ocean. They lie east of Puerto Rico and some 1500 miles southeast of New York. Christopher Columbus discovered the island group in 1493 and named it for St. Ursula and her 11,000 virgins because the islands were too many to name individually.

The total area is only 132 square miles, and the 57,000 residents (1970) are concentrated on the principal islands of St. Thomas, St. Croix, and St. John. Approximately fifty per cent of the population is Negro in descent.

The United States purchased the Virgin Islands from Denmark for $25,000,000 in 1917. They are most valuable to us because of their strategic location and the fine harbor at the capital, Charlotte Amalie on St. Thomas.

Congress extended American citizenship to the residents in 1927 (see page 91). Congress first extended limited self-government to the islands in the Organic Act of 1936. A large degree of local autonomy was provided in the Revised Organic Act of 1954, and Congress strengthened territorial self-government by extensive amendment of the 1954 law in 1968.

A governor, appointed by the President and Senate, formerly served as the territorial chief executive. In 1968, however, Congress provided for the popular election of the governor and, at the same time, for the popular election of a lieutenant governor. Both were selected by the voters, for four-year terms, for the first time in 1970. The territorial legislature is a unicameral body composed of fifteen popularly elected members. A territorial district court, with a judge appointed by the President and Senate, and several local courts comprise the judiciary.

Congress has granted the islands a considerable tax benefit. Federal income taxes collected there are retained for territorial use, and a large share of the federal excise taxes on products from the Virgin Islands (mostly rum) are also returned for local use.

Other Caribbean Islands. Great Corn Island and Little Corn Island, total area four square miles, lie forty miles off the southeast coast of Nicaragua. They were leased from Nicaragua in 1914 for 99 years because of their strategic proximity to the Panama Canal.

The two Swan Islands lie 125 miles northeast of Honduras. The Weather Bureau maintains an observation station and the FAA operates a small navigation-communications station on Great Swan Island (one square mile); Little Swan is uninhabited. The United States first occupied the islands in 1863; Honduras also claims sovereignty over them.

THE DISTRICT OF COLUMBIA

The Framers of the Constitution were agreed that, as James Madison put it, there was an "indispensable necessity" that the National Government have "complete authority at the seat of government." Accordingly, Article I, Section 8, Clause 17 of the Constitution gives to the Congress the power:

> To exercise exclusive legislation in all cases whatsoever, over such District (not exceeding ten miles square) as may, by cession of particular States, and the acceptance of Congress, become the seat of the government of the United States. . . .

The Founding Fathers provided for the location of the nation's capital outside of any of the States in order to eliminate interstate jealousies and suspicions over its location and to guarantee against State interference with the activities of the National Government. The actual selection of the site for the District was the subject of stormy debate. Philadelphia, New York, Trenton, Baltimore, and other cities vied for the honor of being the official seat of government; but none of them was chosen. The decision to locate the capital along the Potomac was reached in July of 1790. President George Washington marked out the exact site for the ten-mile-square area. In 1791 Congress accepted grants of the land involved from Maryland and Virginia.

A city "of magnificent distances" was then laid out along the Maryland side of the Potomac (see page 732) The cornerstone of the north wing of the Capitol was laid by President Washington on September 18, 1793. President Adams and the Congress moved from Philadelphia, and Washington became the national capital in June, 1800.[9]

The original size of the District was the maximum set by the Constitution, 100 square miles. It included the towns of Georgetown in Maryland and Alexandria in Virginia. On the mistaken notion that it would never be needed, Congress returned Virginia's donation in 1846. Today, the District of Columbia consists of sixty-nine square miles on the Maryland side of the Potomac. Its suburbs, however, reach deep into west central Maryland and into northern Virginia.

In one sense, Washington is an "artificial" city. It was originally created as the site of the National Government, and government remains the District's only major industry. Forty-three per cent of its available land area is owned by the National Government. One-third of the total personal income of its 764,000 residents today comes from the salaries and wages paid by the National Government.

Government. Congress created the first government for the District of Columbia in 1802. It consisted of a mayor appointed by the President and a city council elected by the residents. The council was granted the right to choose the mayor in 1812, and in 1820 the mayor's office was made a popularly elected one. In 1871, however, Congress abolished the existing local structure in favor of a territorial government. The new government was intended to speed development of the national capital. But it was overly zealous and highhanded in its operations and piled up a huge debt.

In 1874 Congress placed the debt-ridden District in the hands of a sort of receivership under three commissioners. The arrangement was supposed to be only a temporary one, but Congress was unable to agree on a substitute for it. So, in 1878, Congress provided for a continuation of the commission plan—an arrangement that was to last for eighty–nine years.

From 1878 to 1967, the District was administered by a three-man Board of Commissioners. Two were local residents appointed for three-year terms by the President with Senate consent. The third commissioner was an officer detailed by the President from the Army's Corps of Engineers to serve an indefinite term. Operating under congressional direction, each of the commissioners was separately responsible for certain aspects of the city's administration and the three of them were jointly responsible for others. The system proved to be both clumsy and inefficient and was finally replaced by the present District government in 1967.

Today the District is administered by a single Commissioner and a nine-member Council. The Commissioner serves as the District's chief executive officer. He manages its government, administers its programs and functions, and prepares its annual budget. Both he and his chief aide, the Assistant to the Commissioner, are appointed by the President with Senate consent for four-year terms. At least one of them must have been a resident of the District for at least three years prior to his appointment.

---

[9] George Washington was inaugurated President, and the First Congress met, in Federal Hall in New York in 1789. The temporary national capital was moved to Philadelphia in 1790 and remained there until 1800.

The Council is also chosen by the President and Senate. Its nine members serve three-year terms, with three of the terms expiring each year. Each of the councilmen must also have resided in the District for at least three years. The Council is a quasi-legislative body. That is, it exercises its policy-making powers within the limits set by Congress—for example, the approval of urban renewal plans, the adoption of rules for the licensing of professions, and the setting of property tax rates for the District. It also reviews and may revise the Commissioner's budget before it is submitted to the President. The Commissioner may veto actions of the Council; but it may override him by a three-fourths majority.

Like the old Board of Commissioners, the new District government cannot be compared accurately with the typical city government to be found among the States. Rather, as the Constitution provides, Congress remains the principal governing body for the District. The Commissioner and the Council may act only within the limits set by acts of Congress.

All bills relating to the District of Columbia are considered by committees, usually by the Committees on the District of Columbia in the House of Representatives and the Senate, or by the Committees on Appropriations in either house. These committees have their hands full, and they often disagree with each other. Unfortunately, most of the other Congressmen tend to ignore the District's problems. In 1970 Congress did create the long-sought post of District Delegate; see page 203.

In addition to the Congress, the District government is subject to several other federal agencies. Thus, its budget goes to Congress through the Budget Bureau and its parks are administered by the National Park Service. Until 1969 the members of the District's Board of Education were all selected by the judges of the local U.S. District Court; but in 1968 Congress took another step toward self-government for the District by providing for a popularly elected, nonpartisan school board.

From 1878 to 1921 Congress provided half of the District's annual budget, but now it appropriates about one-eighth of the necessary total (for 1971, $108,938,000). This "federal payment" is made because the National Government owns so much otherwise taxable property, uses many services rendered by District agencies, and wants an especially fine city for its capital.

The Problem of Self-Government. Our whole philosophy of government is firmly based on the right of the people to govern themselves. Yet, paradoxical as it may be, this right is denied to the residents of the nation's capital.

The residents of the District of Columbia have not been permitted to elect the officers of their own local government since 1874. And, with a brief exception from 1871 to 1875, they were denied representation in Congress until the first occupant of the newly-created office of District Delegate was seated by the House of Representatives early in 1971.

Under the 23rd Amendment, District voters elected presidential electors for the first time in 1964. Only an act of Congress would be necessary to grant full home rule.

Various bills for municipal home rule have come close to final passage in recent years. The Senate has passed such legislation six times since 1948, and most recently in 1965; but the House of Representatives has balked each time thus far.

The new governmental arrangement for the District inaugurated in 1967 was established by a presidential reorganization plan (see page 319). Because neither house of Congress rejected the plan within the sixty days following its proposal, it became effective. In urging Congress to accept the new system, President Johnson described it as designed to bring "twentieth century government to the Capital." And he added:

> I remain convinced more strongly than ever that home rule is still the truest course. We must continue to work toward that day when

the citizens of the District will have the right to frame their own laws, manage their own affairs, and choose their own leaders. Only then can we redeem that historic pledge to give the District of Columbia full membership in the American Union.

The first commissioner for the District — in effect, its "mayor" — was named in 1967. He is Walter Washington, a Negro with a long and outstanding record in public administration at the urban level.

Although the Founding Fathers gave Congress exclusive powers over the District, they clearly assumed that local self-government would exist, too. James Madison wrote in *The Federalist Papers* that "a municipal legislature for local purposes, *derived from their own suffrages,* will of course be allowed" to the District's residents. The majority of the country favors home rule for the District of Columbia; it probably will become fact some time in the near future.

THE AMERICAN EMPIRE

Principal Territories	Date Acquired	Prior Status	How Acquired	Area (Square Miles)	Population (1960)
Guam	1898	Spanish possession	Conquest and Treaty, Spanish-American War	209	67,044
Puerto Rico	1898	Spanish possession	Conquest and Treaty, Spanish-American War	3,435	2,349,544
Panama Canal Zone	1904	Panamanian territory	Treaty with Panama, rented in perpetuity for $10,000,000 plus annual payment (now $1,930,000)	553	42,122
Virgin Islands	1917	Danish possession	Treaty with Denmark, purchased for $25,000,000	132	32,099
Trust Territory of the Pacific Islands	1947	Japanese mandate	Conquest in World War II and UN Trusteeship	8,484	84,777 (1963)
District of Columbia	1791	Portion of Maryland	Donated by Maryland, accepted by acts of Congress, 1790–91	69	763,956

❈❈❈❈❈❈❈❈❈❈❈ CONCEPT BUILDING ❈❈❈❈❈❈❈❈❈❈❈

Key Concepts

In addition to the continental United States, we hold a far-flung insular empire unique in the history of the world. Congress has the power to acquire territory because the United States is a sovereign nation and, by implication, because of the war and treaty powers and the power to admit new States. Congress has the expressed power to govern the territories.

Congress has divided the territories into two classes. (1) The incorporated territories (there are none today) are those Congress has declared to be *a part of* the United States; all applicable parts of the Constitution extend to them; (2) the unincorporated territories *belong to* but are not *a part of* the United States. These territories are: Puerto Rico, the Panama Canal Zone, the Virgin Islands, Guam, the Trust Territory of the Pacific, and several other mid-Pacific islands.

The District of Columbia is not actually a territory but a federal district provided for in the Constitution.

Important Terms

acquire	incorporated territory	"Operation Bootstrap"
cession	"in perpetuity"	Resident Commission
Commonwealth	interoceanic canal	trusteeship
home rule	mandate	unincorporated territory

Questions for Inquiry and Review

1. What are the constitutional bases for the power to *acquire* territory? To govern territory?

2. What is the chief distinction in the status of those territories Congress classes as *incorporated* and those territories it classes as *unincorporated?*

3. Which territories are incorporated today? Unincorporated?

4. What is the basic function of the Office of Territories?

5. How and when did we acquire Puerto Rico?

6. Are Puerto Ricans American citizens?

7. What title does its constitution give to Puerto Rico?

8. How is the governor of Puerto Rico chosen?

9. What is the purpose of the novel scheme of legislative representation provided in the Puerto Rican constitution?

10. By whom is Puerto Rico represented in Washington? How is he chosen?

11. What is "Operation Bootstrap"?

12. How and when did we acquire Guam?

13. Why is Guam important to us?

14. How and when did we acquire the Trust Territory of the Pacific?

15. Why is the Trust Territory of the Pacific important to us?

16. How and when did we acquire the Panama Canal Zone?

17. What official heads the Canal Zone government?

18. What official heads the Panama Canal Company?

19. What two factors strongly suggest that the United States will not relinquish its control over either the Panama Canal or the Canal Zone in the foreseeable future?

20. What are the general dimensions of the Canal Zone?

21. What recent indication is there that a second interoceanic canal will likely be built in the near future?

22. How and when did we acquire the Virgin Islands?

23. What is the chief importance of the Virgin Islands to us?

24. Why does the Constitution provide for the location of the national capital outside the jurisdiction of any State?

25. What does the 23rd Amendment provide?

26. What action is necessary to accord home rule to the residents of the nation's capital, the District of Columbia?

27. What general scheme of government has recently been provided for the District?

28. Which house of Congress is the more favorably disposed to home rule for the District of Columbia?

For Further Inquiry

1. If you and a foreign student were to discuss the colonial policies of the world's major powers, what would you say has been the overall pattern of American policy? Which present and former territorial possessions would you cite in making your case? Why would you cite each of these?

2. Do you agree with those who would internationalize the Panama Canal? Why?

3. Article 73 of the UN Charter provides in part that those nations with dependent people should guide the dependent people toward self-government. In what ways has the United States honored this provision with its territories?

4. Despite apparently favorable national opinion and, in recent years, strong pressures from the White House, a number of Congressmen continue to oppose home rule for the District of Columbia. What is the major basis for their position?

5. The title of this chapter is The American Empire. Is the title appropriate? In what ways does the American "empire" differ from the empires of the sixteenth, seventeenth, and eighteenth centuries?

Suggested Activities

1. Stage a debate or class forum on the question: *Resolved,* That Puerto Rico should be granted Statehood.

2. Write a report on the history, government, and people of one of our possessions.

3. Write to your Senators and Representative to learn how they stand on the question

of home rule for the District of Columbia. What reasons do they have for their positions?

4. Prepare a display map showing the growth of the United States to a Union of fifty States. Identify the territorial possessions and the manner in which they were acquired (see the table on page 597).

Suggested Reading

BOYER, DAVID S., "Micronesia—The Americanization of Eden," *National Geographic,* May 1967.

REED, DAVID, "Countdown on Okinawa," *Reader's Digest,* November, 1969.

"The 50th State, Still Growing, But . . .," *U.S. News,* November 10, 1969.

"The Uncertain Future of the Panama Canal," *U.S. News,* August 28, 1967.

"U.S., Japan on a Collision Course?" *U.S. News,* November 24, 1969.

"Washington: Tourists Come Back," *U.S. News,* April 21, 1969.

Part Three

STATE AND LOCAL

GOVERNMENTS

To this point in our study of the American system of government we have been very largely concerned with the constitutional basis of that system, the democratic processes by which it is controlled and operated, and the organization, powers, and functions of the National Government. Now we turn to an examination of the States and their local governments.

We live in an age in which most of the attention the American people pay to public affairs is focused on those affairs at the national level. This seems altogether natural—and a glance at the front page of nearly any daily newspaper is enough to show why. Most of the vital questions of public policy today, especially those relating to the nation's security and its foreign relations, involve the powers and functions of the National Government. Indeed, the word "government" itself is, in the mind of the average citizen, practically synonymous with the government centered in Washington, D.C.

To a much greater extent than most of us realize, however, it is the States and their local governments which most directly, intimately, and regularly affect our daily lives. Nearly every citizen of the United States is a resident of one of the fifty States. And most of us are also, at the same time, residents of a county within that State and of one of its villages, towns, townships, boroughs, or cities. Each of us usually resides within the boundaries of a number of other units (special districts) of local government, as well.

Practically everything that we do, at any time of the day or night, is influenced — and frequently in quite important ways — by the laws of the State in which we live and by the ordinances of its local governments. That this is so can be illustrated by an almost limitless number of examples drawn from a great many fields — including, especially, public education, roads and highways, law enforcement, and public health and sanitation. The fact that we are not constantly or often consciously aware of them does not diminish the degree of their importance to us.

As we examine the governments of the States and their local units, it will become clear that the governmental arrangements in each State are much like those to be found in all States. Thus, each of the States has a written constitution which serves as its fundamental law. Under it, the State is organized and the relationships of individuals with one another and with the State are regulated. In each State the powers of government are divided among three branches: executive, legislative, and judicial; and each branch possesses powers with which to check the other two to insure that no one of them will become all-powerful. And, similarly, the patterns of local government tend to resemble one another from State to State.

Variations do exist among the States, to be sure. As we shall see, for example, the legislature in Nebraska is unicameral while in each of the other States that body is bicameral. Only North Carolina does not give to its governor the power to veto acts of the legislature. Only Oregon does not permit its legislature to remove public officials by impeachment. County governments function in all of the States except Alaska, Connecticut, and Rhode Island. But these and the other modifications to be found are much more differences in degree than they are differences of kind. The American philosophy of government demands that government be conducted by and with the consent of the people. And, in essence, whatever the variations among them, American State and local governments are designed to that end.

Unfortunately, as we have noted before, and as you can discover with but little effort yourself, many Americans are not well informed and do not take an active part in public affairs. And this regrettable fact is most noticeably apparent in the arenas of State and local government. Over 130 years ago, Alexis de Tocqueville observed that:

> The federal system was created with the intention of combining the different advantages which result from the magnitude and the littleness of nations; and a glance at the United States of America discovers the advantage which they have derived from its adoption. . . . The Federal System rests upon a theory which is complicated, at the best, and which demands the daily exercise of a considerable share of discretion on the part of those it governs.

By "discretion" de Tocqueville meant *knowledge* and *informed judgment*. Clearly, our governmental system — at the *State and local* as well as at the National level — can be no better than the people are capable of and willing to make it. Indeed, as the American Assembly has put it, interest and participation in public affairs by *informed* citizens is "the only final assurance of effective and responsive government." Despite oft-heard clichés, participation by everyone, regardless of interest or knowledge, is *not* a source of strength for democratic institutions. The hope for the future of government at all levels in this country lies in the ability of informed citizens to separate the true from the false, the wise from the unwise, and to make their influence felt in the councils of the nation.

35
STATE CONSTITUTIONS

❈❈❈ Are the States now obsolete units in the federal system? Why?

❈❈❈ Are there any situations in which it should be possible for a provision in a State constitution to override a provision in the United States Constitution?

❈❈❈ As a general rule, should a State's constitution be relatively easy or relatively difficult to amend? Why?

He that goeth about to persuade a multitude, that they are not so well governed as they might be, shall never want attention and favorable hearers.

THOMAS HOOKER

A State constitution is the fundamental law under which the government of the State is organized and the relations of individuals with each other and with that government are regulated. It is the supreme law within the sphere of State powers in the American federal system. Its provisions may not conflict with those of the Constitution of the United States nor with any other form of federal law;[1] but they are superior to all other forms of State law—statutes, charters, and ordinances.

EARLY STATE CONSTITUTIONS

When the thirteen colonies threw off the yoke of British rule in 1776 and declared their independence, each faced the problem of estab-

lishing a new government. The Second Continental Congress, on May 15, 1776, before the declaration of independence, had advised each of the new States to adopt:

> ... such governments as shall, in the opinion of the representatives of the people, best conduce to the happiness and safety of their constituents in particular, and America in general

Colonial Origins. Even with their faults, most of the colonial charters served as models for the new State constitutions. Indeed, in Connecticut and Rhode Island the old charters seemed so well adapted to the needs of the day that they were carried over as constitutions almost without change. Connecticut did not adopt a new fundamental law until 1818, and Rhode Island not until 1842.

---

[1] Recall, Article VI, Section 2 of the Constitution of the United States provides: "This Constitution, and the laws of the United States which shall be made in pursuance thereof, and all treaties made, or which shall be made, under the authority of the United States, shall be the supreme law of the land; and the judges in every State shall be bound thereby, anything in the constitution or laws of any State to the contrary notwithstanding." See pages 67–68.

602

Adoption of the First Constitutions. The earliest of the State constitutions were adopted in a variety of ways. The people were given scant opportunity to approve or reject them anywhere. In Connecticut and Rhode Island the legislature made the minor changes in the old charters, and no special action by the people was involved in either State.

In 1776 the Revolutionary legislatures in six States (Maryland, New Jersey, North Carolina, Pennsylvania, South Carolina, and Virginia) drew up new constitutions and proclaimed them to be in force. These new constitutions were not submitted to the voters for ratification.

In Delaware (1776), New Hampshire (1776), Georgia (1777), and New York (1777) the constitutions were drafted by conventions called by the legislature; but none of these constitutions was submitted to the voters.

In 1780 a popularly elected convention drafted the Massachusetts constitution which was then submitted to the voters for ratification. Thus, Massachusetts set the pattern of popular participation that has been followed since.[2]

As new States have come into the Union, and as the constitutions of the older States have been revised, popular participation has been the rule. All of the State constitutions in existence today were drafted by assemblies representing the people, and most of them have been approved by a vote of the people.[3]

Congress has regularly required that territories desiring Statehood must hold a constitutional convention and then submit its

The Massachusetts constitution of 1780 was drafted by John Adams and was based on the doctrine of natural rights and on a faith in democracy. (Secretary of the Commonwealth)

product to a popular vote prior to admission. See pages 75–78.

Contents. While the details of the first State constitutions varied considerably, they shared many general features. In each of them the people were recognized as the sole source of the authority of government, and the powers vested in each of the new governments were severely limited. Seven of the documents began with a lengthy bill of rights, and all of them made it clear that the sovereign people had "unalienable rights" which must always be respected.

Separation of powers was followed in each State, and each branch was given powers with

---

[2] New Hampshire adopted its second and present constitution in 1784; in doing so, it followed the Massachusetts practice of a popularly elected convention and popular ratification of the convention's product. The Massachusetts constitution of 1780 and the New Hampshire constitution of 1784 are the oldest of the written constitutions in force anywhere in the world today.

[3] Of the State charters in effect today (1970), only those in Delaware (1897), Louisiana (1921), Mississippi (1890), South Carolina (1895), Vermont (1793), and Virginia (1902) became effective without first being submitted to the people.

which to check the others. In actual practice, however, the theory of separation of powers was weakened. With the memory of the hated royal governors still fresh, the legislatures were given most of the authority the States possessed.

In all States except Georgia (until 1789) and Pennsylvania (until 1790) the legislatures were *bicameral* (two-chambered).[4] At first, only Massachusetts and South Carolina gave the governor the power to veto acts passed by the legislature. The governor was generally limited to a one-year term, and he was chosen by the legislature in all States except Massachusetts and New York.

For their time, the first State constitutions were quite democratic. Each, however, contained several provisions (and some important omissions) which today would be considered quite undemocratic. For example, none provided for complete religious freedom, each set rigid qualifications for voting and officeholding, and all gave property owners a highly preferred status.

STATE CONSTITUTIONS TODAY

The fifty State constitutions today deal with a broad range of matters and contain many variations. Their major provisions, however, fall into general categories.

Basic Principles. There is a striking similarity amongst all of the present-day State constitutions in terms of the principles upon which they are based. Each is founded upon the concepts of *popular sovereignty* and *limited government*. That is, each recognizes that the people are the ultimate source of any and all governmental authority and that the powers vested in government are confined within often closely-detailed boundaries. In each State constitution the powers of government are distributed among the legislative, executive, and judicial branches, in accordance with the principles of *separation of powers* and *checks and balances*. And each of the documents provides, either explicitly or by implication, for *judicial review*.

Bill of Rights. Each State constitution includes a bill of rights listing the rights which individuals hold against the State. Most of the State constitutions contain most or all of the guarantees also found in the first ten amendments to the Constitution of the United States, and usually a number of others as well—for example, the right to self-government, to be secure from imprisonment for debt, to migrate from the State, and to join with others to bargain collectively.[5]

Structure of Government. Any constitution is, in major part, a statement of the framework of government; and each of the State documents provides for the organization of government at both the State and the local levels. The major variation among the State constitutions in this regard is in terms of the detail with which each treats the matter. A few State constitutions follow the national pattern by providing only a broad outline, but most of them treat State and local governmental organization in considerable and specific detail.

Governmental Powers and Processes. Every State constitution deals with the powers and processes of government at some length. The powers vested in the governor and the executive branch, the legislature, the courts, and counties, cities, and other units of local government occupy a large portion of each. The powers to tax, spend, borrow, and provide for public education are especially prominent in terms of space and detail. So, too, are provisions relating to such processes as elections,

---

[4] Vermont, which became the fourteenth State in 1791, had a unicameral legislature until 1836. Nebraska (since 1937) is the only State with a unicameral legislature today. See page 615.

[5] See pages 99–100.

The Common Parts of Most State Constitutions

Preamble States the general purposes for organizing government.

Bill of Rights Lists certain fundamental rights of all persons that government must respect.

Organizational Provisions for the Executive, Legislative, and Judicial Branches
Their qualifications, powers, and duties.

Special Provisions
Deals with suffrage, elections, revenues and expenditures, education, and the like.

Amendment Process
Provides for future change, including a schedule for putting new document into effect.

Provisions for Local Government
General outline of organization and powers.

legislation, and (in several States) the initiative, referendum, and recall and to the matter of intergovernmental relations.

Constitutional Change. Constitutions are, after all, man-made products. None are perfect. Sooner or later, changes become necessary or at least desirable. Recognizing this, each State constitution provides for the means by which it may be formally changed—and we shall turn to those means in a moment.

Miscellaneous Provisions. Every State document contains several sections of a miscellaneous character. Most begin with a Preamble which has no legal effect but serves as a statement of the intentions of the framers and of the people who adopted the constitution originally. Most also contain a *schedule*, provisions for putting a new document into effect and for avoiding conflicts with its predecessor. Finally, most contain a number of "dead letter" provisions—those with no current force and effect but which remain nonetheless a part of the constitution.

CONSTITUTIONAL CHANGE

Even the wisest of constitution-makers cannot build for all time. An essential part of any constitution, therefore, is the provision of methods by which the document may be altered. Some State constitutions have proved more durable than others, but among the fifty now in effect (1969), only one of them—the newest, Connecticut's constitution adopted in late 1965—has thus far had no amendments added to it.

Formal and Informal Amendment. As you recall from the discussion on pages 53–59, the Constitution of the United States has been changed over the years through both the *formal* and the *informal* amendment processes. State constitutions have been subjected to both processes, too. *But*—and this is an important *but*—the informal amendment process has *not* been nearly so significant at the State level as it has been nationally. For one thing, State constitutions have been and are much less *flexible* (are more rigid and detailed) than the national document. The structure, powers, and procedures of State government are usually treated at great length in State constitutions.

The State courts have often proved a block to the wide use of the informal amendment process. Unlike the federal courts, they have generally been quite strict in their roles as constitution-interpreters. Thus, the States have had to rely upon formal amendment as the chief method of constitutional change.

As we turn to the methods of formal change, the distinct meanings of two sets of terms—proposal-ratification and amendment-revision—must be borne in mind. First, the process of formal change involves two basic steps: *proposal* and *ratification*. Proposals for change may be made by a constitutional convention, by the legislature, or by initiative petition. Ratification comes through popular vote.[6] As to the second set of terms, note that *amendment* usually refers to a limited change, involving only one or a few provisions in a constitution. The term *revision* is usually used to refer to changes of a broader scope—for example, an entire new document. Amendments are most often proposed by the legislature or by initiative petition; revision is commonly undertaken by a constitutional convention.

Constitutional Conventions. The convention is the principal method by which new constitutions have been written and old ones revised in the United States.[7] Thus far, more than 200 have been held among the States and, except for Georgia's, each constitution now in effect is the product of such an assembly.

In every State the legislature has the power to call a convention.[8] Regularly, its call must be submitted to the people for their approval or rejection. In eleven of the States the constitution requires that the question of calling a convention *must* be presented to the voters at regular intervals.[9]

Three elections commonly accompany the work of a convention: (1) the vote at which the people authorize the calling of the convention, (2) the popular election of delegates, and (3) the submission of the convention's product to the people. On occasion, one or more of these votes may be dispensed with. Louisiana's constitution provides an example. The legislature's call for a convention was approved at the regular election in November 1920. The next month the voters elected delegates who then met in convention from March 1 to June 18, 1921. Then the convention itself, acting as "the people of the State of Louisiana in Constitutional Convention assembled," adopted the new constitution for the State.

The most recently adopted of the fifty State constitutions were each written by conventions. Alaska's constitution went into effect with Statehood in 1959; the present Michigan constitution went into force on January 1, 1964, and Connecticut's on December 30, 1965. The two newest documents, those of Florida and Hawaii, became effective on November 5, 1968.

---

[6] Except in Delaware; see page 610.

[7] Only Florida's new constitution expressly provides for one, but a *constitutional revision commission* is occasionally used instead. Such a body is usually created by the legislature with members appointed by the governor or the legislature to recommend revisions in the existing constitution or to frame a new one. It reports to the legislature which may then propose all or some of its recommendations to the voters. The Georgia constitution of 1945, produced by a commission, was presented to the voters in the form of a single amendment.

[8] The power is provided in the constitutions of forty States. In the other ten States (Arkansas, Indiana, Louisiana, Massachusetts, New Jersey, North Dakota, Pennsylvania, Rhode Island, Texas, and Vermont) it rests upon custom, statute, court decision, or the attorney general's opinion.

[9] Every ten years in Alaska and Iowa; every sixteen years in Michigan; every twenty years in Connecticut, Maryland, Missouri, New York, Ohio, and Oklahoma; at least once in any ten-year period in Hawaii and New Hampshire.

STATE CONSTITUTIONS

State	Present Constitution Became Effective in [a]	State Entered Union in	Number of Previous Constitutions	State	Present Constitution Became Effective in [a]	State Entered Union in	Number of Previous Constitutions
Alabama	1901	1819	5	Montana	1889	1889	0
Alaska	1959	1959	0	Nebraska	1875	1867	1
Arizona	1912	1912	0	Nevada	1864	1864	0
Arkansas	1874	1836	4	New Hampshire	1784	1788	1
California	1879 [b]	1850	1	New Jersey	1948	1788	2
Colorado	1876	1876	0	New Mexico	1912	1912	0
Connecticut	1965	1788	2	New York	1939 [d]	1788	4
Delaware	1897	1788	3	North Carolina	1876	1789	3
Florida	1968	1845	5	North Dakota	1889	1889	0
Georgia	1945	1788	7	Ohio	1851	1803	1
Hawaii	1968	1959	1	Oklahoma	1907	1907	0
Idaho	1890	1890	0	Oregon	1859	1859	0
Illinois	1870	1818	1	Pennsylvania	1874	1788	3
Indiana	1851	1816	1	Rhode Island	1843	1790	1
Iowa	1857	1846	1	South Carolina	1895	1788	6
Kansas	1861	1861	0	South Dakota	1889	1889	0
Kentucky	1891	1792	3	Tennessee	1870	1796	2
Louisiana	1921	1811	9	Texas	1876	1845	4
Maine	1820 [c]	1820	0	Utah	1896	1896	0
Maryland	1867	1788	3	Vermont	1793 [c]	1791	1
Massachusetts	1780	1788	0	Virginia	1902	1788	6
Michigan	1964	1837	3	Washington	1889	1889	0
Minnesota	1858	1858	0	West Virginia	1872	1863	1
Mississippi	1890	1817	3	Wisconsin	1848	1848	0
Missouri	1945	1821	3	Wyoming	1890	1890	0

[a] Fourteen of the present-day State constitutions were actually ratified a year or more before they became effective: Alaska (1956), Arizona (1911), Kansas (1859), Maine (1819), Michigan (1963), Minnesota (1857), New Jersey (1947), New Mexico (1911), New York (1938), Oregon (1857), Pennsylvania (1873), Rhode Island (1842), Utah (1895), Wyoming (1889).

[b] California's constitution became effective July 4, 1879, for purposes of the election of officers, the beginning of their terms of office, and the meeting of the legislature. It became effective for all other purposes January 1, 1880.

[c] The Maine constitution in 1876 and the Vermont constitution in 1913 were rearranged by incorporating the amendments into the text itself.

[d] The New York constitution of 1939 includes many articles unchanged from the 1895 constitution.

The Michigan Experience. Michigan was wracked by a series of financial crises and other difficulties through the 1950's. A major cause for the State's troubles lay in a continuing deadlock between the governor's office (controlled by the Democrats with the support of organized labor) and the legislature (controlled by the Republicans with heavy rural majorities).

The decision to revise the State's often amended constitution of 1908 was made by the voters at a special election held on April 1, 1961.[10] The legislature then provided for partisan primaries in August and the election of delegates in September.

The convention met at Lansing on October 3, 1961. Over the next seven months, and through several sharp partisan conflicts, the 144 delegates hammered out a new document. In doing so, they retained many of the provisions of the old constitution. But much of the new material they drafted was agreed to only after hard-fought compromises had been reached.

The key changes they accepted included provisions which strengthened the governor's position (for example, those increasing his term to four years, broadening his appointment power, reducing the number of other elected officers, and reorganizing the executive branch), required the apportionment of legislative seats more nearly in accord with the distribution of population in the State, reorganized the judiciary, prohibited a graduated income tax, and provided for county home rule.

The delegates recessed for three months and reconvened to approve their handiwork

---

[10] The old constitution required a vote every sixteen years on the question of a convention. Several groups, led by the League of Women Voters and the Junior Chamber of Commerce, waged a vigorous but unsuccessful campaign for a convention ("con-con") in 1958. Undaunted, they then sponsored an initiative amendment, calling for yet another "con-con" vote, which was approved by the voters in 1960.

on August 1, 1962. After an intense campaign — and only by a very narrow majority (50.7 per cent) — the State's new constitution was then adopted by the voters at a special election on April 1, 1963.

Amendment. Formal changes in State constitutions are most often made by amendment rather than revision. Among the States, amendments may be proposed by a convention, by the legislature, or by initiative petition.

Convention Proposal. Although the convention is most often used for the broader purposes of revision, in some States it can be and sometimes is used to propose amendments. Indeed, until 1965, the convention was the only method by which amendments could be proposed in New Hampshire. The Tennessee constitution of 1870 proved so difficult to amend by the regular method (that is, through legislative action) that no changes were made in it until 1953. In that year the people approved the calling of a convention which then proposed eight amendments; all eight were later ratified by the people at a special election.

In several other States the constitution provides that a convention might be used to propose amendments. For example, in Ohio conventions may be used to "revise, amend, or change" the constitution; in Oklahoma "alterations, revisions, or amendments" may be proposed by a convention; and in Oregon a convention has the power to "propose amendments or to propose a new constitution."

Again, although conventions *may* be used to propose amendments, the device is seldom used for that purpose. It is quite expensive and time-consuming and the other methods of amendment are usually much easier to use.

Legislative Proposal. Amendments are most often proposed by the legislature, which has the power to do so in every State. Details of the method vary widely. In some States the process is simple, in others quite difficult. Thus, to date (1970) the California constitution of 1879 had been amended more than 350 times and the Louisiana constitution of 1921 some 500 times. In both of these States the legislature may submit any number of amendments by a two-thirds vote in each house, and ratification is secured by a simple majority of those voting on each measure at the polls. The Tennessee constitution of 1870, by contrast, has been amended only eighteen times — all since 1953 and *none* by legislative proposal. There, the legislature may propose amendments only by a majority vote in each house at one session and a two-thirds vote at the next; a popular vote at least equal to a majority of the votes cast for governor at the same election is required for ratification.[11]

In thirty-eight States amendments may be proposed at a *single* session. Only simple majority approval is required in each house in nine of these States,[12] but nineteen others require two-thirds,[13] and another nine States demand three-fifths.[14] Only Connecticut requires a three-fourths majority.

Most of the thirteen States requiring proposal at *two successive* sessions require only a majority vote in each house at each session.[15]

A few States limit the number of amendments that may be submitted to the voters at any one election; for example, in Kansas no more than three and in Kentucky two. In Illinois no single legislature may propose amendments to more than three articles, in Colorado to more than six articles. Similar restrictions are found in a few other States.

Proposal by Initiative. Beginning with Oregon in 1902, fourteen States now provide for the proposal of constitutional amendments by the people themselves.[16] This procedure is known as the *initiative* because the amendments are initiated by the voters. Any individual or group may draft a proposal and then circulate *initiative petitions* to secure the signatures of a specified number of voters.

The number of signatures required varies considerably among these States. At least 20,000 qualified voters must sign the petitions in North Dakota. Nevada requires that they be signed by at least ten per cent of the qualified voters. In California the figure is at least 8% of the number of votes cast at the last election for governor; in Ohio and Michigan it is 10% of the votes cast at the last gubernatorial elec-

---

[11] Until 1953 Tennessee required that an amendment proposed by the legislature (none were) could be ratified only if approved by a vote at least equal to a majority of all votes cast for representatives at the last election.

[12] Arizona, Arkansas, Minnesota, Missouri, New Mexico, North Dakota, Oklahoma, Oregon, and South Dakota.

[13] Alaska, California, Colorado, Georgia, Hawaii, Idaho, Illinois, Kansas, Louisiana, Maine, Michigan, Mississippi, Montana, South Carolina, Texas, Utah, Washington, West Virginia, and Wyoming.

[14] Alabama, Florida, Kentucky, Maryland, Nebraska, New Hampshire, New Jersey, North Carolina, and Ohio.

[15] Indiana, Iowa, Massachusetts, Nevada, New York, Pennsylvania, Rhode Island, Virginia, and Wisconsin. For the votes required in the two successive sessions in Tennessee, see the text above. Delaware requires two-thirds in each house at each session. Vermont requires two-thirds of the Senate and a majority of the House at one session and a majority of both houses at the next. In Connecticut, Hawaii, and New Jersey a majority of both houses at two successive sessions is provided as an alternative to proposing amendments at a single session.

[16] Arizona, Arkansas, California, Colorado, Florida, Massachusetts, Michigan, Missouri, Nebraska, Nevada, North Dakota, Ohio, Oklahoma, and Oregon. The initiative may also be used to propose and enact *statutes* in these States (except Florida) and in six others (Alaska, Maine, Montana, South Dakota, Utah, and Washington; see page 631.)

tion. Some of these States require, as well, that the signatures be gathered from various parts of the State. For example, Arkansas demands that the signatures total at least 10% of the number of votes cast at the last gubernatorial election *and* that the petitions be signed in at least fifteen of the State's seventy-five counties.

Ratification of Amendments. In every one of the States except Delaware amendments must be ratified by popular vote before they may become effective.[17] In Delaware ratification is accomplished when two successive sessions of the legislature approve an amendment.

Generally, approval of a majority of those voting *on the amendment* makes it a part of the constitution. But again there are exceptions: For example, Rhode Island requires a three-fifths majority and New Hampshire two-thirds; Minnesota, Oklahoma, and Wyoming require a majority of all *voting in the election,* not just those who vote on the measure. Illinois requires a majority of all votes cast in the election *or* at least a two-to-one majority favoring the amendment. Tennessee, as we saw, requires a majority of all voting for governor at the most recent election. Many times amendments have been defeated in these States even though they actually received more *yes* than *no* votes because many voters fail to vote on the ballot measures.

GENERAL OBSERVATIONS

The Need for Reform. There are individuals and groups at work in nearly every State to reform the State's constitution. Most constitutional authorities agree that the need is urgent. Most of the documents are far too long, and many are sadly outdated.

The Problem of Length. The original State constitutions were quite brief. Their framers intended them as statements of basic principles and organization. They left to the legislature and to practice the task of providing the details as they became necessary. The longest of the original documents was the Massachusetts constitution of 1780; it contained some 12,000 words. The shortest was the New Jersey constitution, with only about 2500 words.

Through the years State constitutions have become longer and longer. Today the fifty State documents run to an average of more than 25,000 words. The shortest constitutions are those of Rhode Island and Connecticut, each with less than 8000 words. At the other extreme, Louisiana's constitution now contains over 250,000 words and Alabama's constitution more than 106,000.

Why are the documents becoming longer? The reasons are not difficult to find. The people generally tend to distrust the legislature and so write provisions into the fundamental law where they cannot be so easily changed. Pressure groups know that a provision that benefits them is safer in the constitution than in a mere statute. Liquor interests, for example, are often successful in this regard. The result is that State constitutions are cluttered with a great deal of material that could, and should, be handled by ordinary legislation.

Then, too, court decisions can be (and often are) effectively overridden by amendments. For example, the Wisconsin Supreme Court had held that the public financing of school bus transportation for parochial school students

---

[17] In South Carolina *final* ratification, after a favorable vote by the people, rests with the legislature. The Georgia constitution of 1945 provides that an amendment of local rather than Statewide application need be approved only by voters of the affected locale. Of the more than 550 amendments added to 1970, less than one-sixth are Statewide in nature. Counting all of the local amendments, the State's constitution contains more than *half a million* words.

was in violation of the State constitution; in 1967 the voters approved a constitutional amendment to permit such transportation.

Two additional reasons are important: (1) State and local functions have expanded greatly in recent years, and many new powers and agencies have been called for, and (2) the people have not been stingy in their use of the initiative in most of the States where it is now permitted.

In short, there is an unfortunate failure in nearly every State to distinguish between *fundamental law* (that which should be in the constitution) and *statutory law* (that which ought to be handled through ordinary legislation).

The Problem of Age. If you look again at the table on page 607, you will see that most of our State constitutions are comparatively ancient. Though most have been amended many times, these changes have, usually, compounded the clutter in the documents.

Using just one State as a *typical* example, the Oregon constitution was written more than a century ago, in 1857. It has been amended more than 130 times and now contains *two* Articles VII and *nine* Articles XI! Like most of the other State constitutions, it is full of statutory material and is in urgent need of updating. Among other things, its bill of rights guarantees to those of legal age the right to buy liquor by the glass across a bar! It also makes

dueling a disqualification for holding public office, devotes nearly 800 words of detail to providing farm and home loans to veterans, and prohibits the levy of any tax, the spending of any money, or the contracting of any debt for the construction of a capitol building prior to the year 1865.

The oldest documents in force today are those of Massachusetts (1780), New Hampshire (1784), and Vermont (1793). Using the table on page 607, note that nineteen of the States still retain their original constitutions. Sixteen States have documents that are at least 100 years old, and twenty-four others have constitutions which were written between 50 and 100 years ago. The average age of our State constitutions is over eighty years.

The Model State Constitution. The Model State Constitution was drafted by a group of distinguished political scientists and published by the National Municipal League in 1921. Since then, it has been revised and improved upon five times. It is intended to serve as a model and a stimulation for constitutional reform. Several of its provisions, for example, the legislative council idea, have had much influence in that direction.

If more citizens would study their State constitutions and learn that many improvements—resulting in better and more economical government—could be made, State government would be greatly improved.

❊❊❊❊❊❊❊❊❊❊❊ CONCEPT BUILDING ❊❊❊❊❊❊❊❊❊❊❊

Key Concepts

The State constitution is the fundamental law under which the government of the State is organized and the relations between individuals and with their government are regulated.

When independence came, eleven of the original States adopted their own constitutions. In Connecticut and Rhode Island the colonial charters continued to serve as constitutions. Generally, the people had little to do with the adoption of the new documents until 1780. In that year, Massachusetts adopted a constitution that was drafted by delegates elected by the voters and ratified by them. Popular participation is now the almost universal rule.

The first State constitutions varied widely in details but had many features in common: the principles of popular sovereignty, of limited government, and of separation of powers and checks and balances; a relatively strong legislature and weak governor; and high suffrage qualifications.

Present-day State constitutions also vary in many regards, but all contain major sections which make quite similar provision for certain basic principles, guarantees of civil liberties, the structure of State and local government, the powers and processes of government, and the methods of constitutional change. Each document also includes several provisions of a miscellaneous character, especially a preamble and a schedule.

The details vary from State to State, but changes in a constitution may be proposed in each State by a convention or the legislature—and by initiative petition also in fourteen States. The ratification of a new constitution or a revision of the existing one commonly must be by popular vote. Amendments must be ratified by popular vote in all States except Delaware.

Nearly every State constitution is in urgent need of reform. Most are much too long, generally outdated, and contain much material better handled by statute.

Important Terms

amendment	initiative	preamble	revision
convention	initiative petition	proposal	schedule
fundamental law	Model State Constitution	ratification	statutory law

Questions for Inquiry and Review

1. What is a State constitution?
2. What is the relationship of a State constitution to the supreme law of the land?
3. What is the relationship of a State constitution to other forms of State law?
4. Which State possesses the oldest constitution in force in the world today?
5. What pattern of constitution-making did Massachusetts set?
6. What was the general nature of the early State constitutions?
7. Were the early State constitutions democratic?
8. Upon what basic principles are each of the present-day State constitutions based?
9. Has the process of formal or of informal amendment been more significant in the development of State constitutions?
10. Why are provisions for formal change necessary in a constitution?
11. Which five States have the most recently written State constitutions?
12. What is the principal method used to write a new State constitution?
13. What is the usual method for the proposal of amendments to State constitutions?
14. By what process may amendments be proposed by the people of a State?
15. Formal constitutional changes are usually ratified in what way?
16. What is the approximate average age of the State constitutions today?

For Further Inquiry

1. The constitution of Hawaii requires a two-thirds vote in each house at one session or a majority vote in each house at two successive sessions for the proposal of amendments to that document. The Model State Constitution would require a simple majority vote of a unicameral legislature. Which system for the proposal of amendments to the constitution would you prefer? Why?

2. If State constitutions were abolished, would it make the governments more or less democratic?

3. By what method or methods may your State's constitution be amended? Do you believe that the process should be made an easier or a more difficult one, or do you think that the amendment procedures are satisfactory as they stand? Why?

4. Do you favor a State constitution being skeletal in nature, or should it be rigid and detailed? Why?

5. From an analysis of the provisions of your State's constitution, how well would you say that it meets this standard set by Alexander Hamilton in *The Federalist No. 57:*

> The aim of every political constitution is, or ought to be, first to obtain men who possess most wisdom to discern, and most virtue to pursue, the common good of the society; and in the next place, to take the most effectual precautions for keeping them virtuous whilst they continue to hold their public trust.

Suggested Activities

1. Secure a copy of your State constitution from the secretary of state. Study its contents, then in a brief report answer the following questions: (a) When was it adopted? (b) How many times has it been amended? (c) By what process may it be amended? (d) How long is it (in words)? (e) Does it deal largely with basic principles and with the framework (organization) of the State government, or does it contain much material that ought to be handled through ordinary legislation?

2. Draw up an outline of your State constitution. What, if any, changes would you recommend and why?

3. Hold a debate or class forum on the question: *Resolved,* That the constitution of this State be replaced with a new one.

4. Invite one of the State legislators and representatives of such major groups as agriculture, business, labor, and education to discuss your State constitution, its content, and the changes (if any) they would recommend.

Suggested Reading

ADRIAN, CHARLES R., *Governing Our Fifty States.* McGraw-Hill, 1967. Chapters 1, 2.

"Comeback of the States," *U.S. News,* October 27, 1969.

DYE, THOMAS R., *Politics in States and Communities.* Prentice-Hall, 1969. Chapter 1.

FESLER, JAMES W., *et al., The 50 States and Their Local Governments.* Knopf, 1967. Chapters 1, 2, 3.

JONAS, FRANK H. (ed.), *Politics in the American West.* University of Utah Press, 1969.

LOCKARD, DUANE, *The Politics of State and Local Government.* Macmillan, 1969. Chapters 4, 5.

ODEGARD, PETER H., *et al., The American Republic.* Harper & Row, 1969. Chapter 19.

"State Constitutions: It's Tough to Write a Good One," *Time,* October 20, 1967.

The Book of the States, 1970–1971. Council of State Governments, 1970.

Your State's Constitution—usually available from the Secretary of State.

36
STATE LEGISLATURES

✦✦✦ Is the trend away from part-time and toward full-time State legislators a healthy one? Why?

✦✦✦ What should a representative represent?

✦✦✦ Is there any basis or combination of bases of representation more democratic than that based upon population?

✦✦✦ What extra-constitutional qualifications should a governor possess?

The legislature . . . is so much the strongest force in the several States that we may almost call it the Government and ignore all other authorities.

JAMES BRYCE

The size of the legislature, the details of its organization and its procedures, the frequency and the length of its sessions, and even the official name given to it vary among the States. But the basic reason for its existence is everywhere the same: the legislature is the lawmaking branch of State government. It is charged with the high duty of translating the will of the people into the public policy of the State.

The legislature has been described as "the powerhouse of State government." Through the exercise of its vast lawmaking powers, it creates the energy necessary to keep the governmental machinery of the State and its local units operating.

THE OFFICIAL NAME

The "State legislature" is known *officially* by the title in only twenty-six States. In nineteen States it is the "General Assembly."[1] Three States—Montana, North Dakota, and Oregon—call it the "Legislative Assembly," and in Massachusetts and New Hampshire it is known as the "General Court."

Forty-nine of the fifty State legislatures are two-chambered. The upper house in each of them is called the "Senate."[2] The lower house is known by several names among the States, most commonly as the "House of Representatives." But in California, Nevada, New York, and Wisconsin it is called the "Assembly"; in New Jersey the "General Assembly"; and in the States of Maryland, Virginia, and West Virginia the "House of Delegates."

---

[1] Arkansas, Colorado, Connecticut, Delaware, Georgia, Illinois, Indiana, Iowa, Kentucky, Maryland, Missouri, North Carolina, Ohio, Pennsylvania, Rhode Island, South Carolina, Tennessee, Vermont, and Virginia.

[2] Nebraska applies that term to its single chamber.

BICAMERALISM

With the exception of Nebraska, all of the State legislatures are bicameral today.[3] Nebraska's voters approved the creation of a unicameral legislature in 1934, and the first session of that body was held in 1937.

Bicameralism has been the predominant pattern of legislative organization among the States for two major reasons: (1) the influence of both English and early colonial experience, and (2) the tendency amongst the newer States to follow the precedent set by both the original States and the National Government. The first colonial legislatures were typically unicameral; the elected representatives commonly sat with the governor and his council in the making of colonial laws. As the popularly chosen legislators gained political power in most of the colonies, the governor's council assumed the role of a second, or upper, chamber. Thus, well before the coming of independence, most of the colonies had created bicameral legislative bodies quite similar in their structure to the Parliament. After independence, those States which had not already done so soon established two-chambered legislatures—setting the pattern that was followed by virtually all of the States later admitted to the Union.

Unicameralism Versus Bicameralism. Unicameralism is widely recommended today as one of the most significant steps that could be taken to upgrade the quality of State legis-

The unicameral legislature of Nebraska consists of 49 members elected on a nonpartisan ballot for four-year terms. The legislators represent districts organized on the basis of population. Regular sessions begin on the first Tuesday in January of odd-numbered years.

latures, their procedures, and their product.[4] Those who support bicameralism have long argued that one house may act as a check on the other and thus prevent the enactment of unwise legislation. But the critics of bicameralism point to numerous examples to show that the

---

[3] Georgia until 1789, Pennsylvania until 1790, and Vermont until 1836 had unicameral bodies. In opposing the change to bicameralism in Pennsylvania, Benjamin Franklin quoted the fable of the snake with two heads and one body: "She was going to a brook to drink, and on her way was to pass through a hedge, a twig of which opposed her direct course; one head chose to go on the right side of the twig, and the other on the left; so that time was spent in the contest, and, before the decision was completed, the poor snake died with thirst."

[4] Contrary to the popular assumption, unicameral legislative bodies are far more numerous than bicameral ones in this country. Virtually all *local* legislative bodies (city, county, and special district) are composed of only one chamber; see Chapters 41, 42.

theory has not worked very well in practice. Although one house often fails to pass bills it receives from the other, the major reason for this is that many of those bills never receive consideration in the second house. Typically, bills that pass both houses are seldom changed in any way by the second house. Too, many routine, noncontroversial bills pass *both* houses with little or no attention paid to them in *either.* Most often, the governor's veto, the press, and public opinion have proved to be a much better check against harmful legislation than has bicameralism.

The fact that the bicameral system has worked well in Congress is often cited in support of the system for the State legislatures. But bicameralism in Congress reflects the *federal* character of the Union; the States are *not* federal, they are *unitary* in character. Recall, too, a bicameral Congress was the direct result of the Connecticut Compromise — without which there very well might not have been the Constitution.

Until quite recently, many supported bicameralism at the State level because they favored a "little federal plan" for their own State's legislature. That is — despite the non-federal character of the States — they favored two houses, with one based upon area and the other upon population. Otherwise, they insisted, the more populous cities would so thoroughly dominate the legislature that rural interests would be virtually unrepresented. As we shall note in a moment, however, the Supreme Court destroyed their position in 1964 — by holding that the 14th Amendment's Equal Protection Clause requires that *both* houses of a State's legislature must be apportioned on the basis of population.

The critics of bicameralism point to the fact that in the complicated structure and procedures of a two-house system special interests have many more opportunities to block popular legislation. Significantly, the need for conference committees is eliminated in a unicameral arrangement. See pages 234, 628.

The advocates of unicameralism also argue that with two chambers involved in the lawmaking process it is almost impossible to fix the responsibility for action, or inaction. They also note that with only one house it is much easier for the public to know what the legislature is doing and for the legislature to control lobbying activities.

The Nebraska experiment has not proved to be a cure-all for all the ills of legislatures, but it has worked quite well. Legislative costs have been reduced, greater efficiency in operation has resulted, the influence of lobbyists has been lessened, a generally higher caliber of legislator has been chosen, and the legislator usually has been more responsible to his constituents than under the previous two-house system. The early fears of "hasty and ill-considered legislation" have not been borne out. Even so, at least to 1971, unicameralism has made little headway in the other States. Both tradition and inertia stand on the side of bicameralism — so, too, do a lack of interest and knowledge on the part of the general public.[5]

SIZE AND APPORTIONMENT

Size. As the table on page 622 indicates, the fifty State legislatures vary widely in terms of size. None of them contains as many members as there are in Congress, but several do run to more than 200 members. Clearly, there is no precise figure to be cited as the *ideal* size for a legislative body, but two basic considerations are important. First, a legislature (and each of its houses) should not be so large that its very size poses difficulties for the orderly conduct of the public's business.

---

[5] An upswing of interest in and support for unicameralism may be in the offing, however. It may be argued that the requirement that *both* houses be based upon population means that one house is but a mirror of the other — and, hence, that *two* houses are unnecessary.

POPULATION OF THE UNITED STATES

Rank 1970 (Est.)	Rank 1960	State	Capital	Population 1970 (Est.)	Population 1960	Per Cent of Change
21	19	Alabama	Montgomery	3,373,006	3,266,740	3.3
50	51	Alaska	Juneau	294,607	226,167	30.3
33	35	Arizona	Phoenix	1,752,122	1,302,161	34.6
32	31	Arkansas	Little Rock	1,886,210	1,786,272	5.6
1	2	California	Sacramento	19,696,840	15,717,204	25.3
29	33	Colorado	Denver	2,195,887	1,753,947	25.2
24	25	Connecticut	Hartford	2,987,950	2,535,234	17.9
46	47	Delaware	Dover	542,979	446,292	21.7
—	40	District of Columbia		764,000	763,956	—
9	10	Florida	Tallahassee	6,671,162	4,951,560	39.7
15	16	Georgia	Atlanta	4,492,038	3,943,116	13.9
40	44	Hawaii	Honolulu	748,575	632,772	18.3
42	43	Idaho	Boise	698,275	667,191	4.6
5	4	Illinois	Springfield	10,973,986	10,081,158	8.9
11	11	Indiana	Indianapolis	5,143,422	4,662,498	10.3
25	24	Iowa	Des Moines	2,789,893	2,757,537	1.2
28	28	Kansas	Topeka	2,222,173	2,178,611	2.0
23	22	Kentucky	Frankfort	3,160,555	3,038,156	4.0
20	20	Louisiana	Baton Rouge	3,564,310	3,257,022	9.4
38	36	Maine	Augusta	977,260	969,265	0.8
17	21	Maryland	Annapolis	3,874,642	3,100,689	25.0
10	9	Massachusetts	Boston	5,630,224	5,148,578	9.4
7	7	Michigan	Lansing	8,776,873	7,823,194	12.2
19	18	Minnesota	St. Paul	3,767,975	3,413,864	10.4
30	29	Mississippi	Jackson	2,158,872	2,178,141	−0.9
13	13	Missouri	Jefferson City	4,636,247	4,319,813	7.3
41	42	Montana	Helena	682,133	674,767	1.1
35	34	Nebraska	Lincoln	1,468,101	1,411,330	4.0
47	50	Nevada	Carson City	481,893	285,278	68.9
41	46	New Hampshire	Concord	722,753	606,921	19.1
8	8	New Jersey	Trenton	7,091,995	6,066,782	16.9
36	37	New Mexico	Santa Fe	998,757	951,023	5.0
2	1	New York	Albany	17,979,712	16,782,304	7.1
12	12	North Carolina	Raleigh	4,961,832	4,556,155	8.9
45	45	North Dakota	Bismarck	610,648	632,446	−3.4
6	5	Ohio	Columbus	10,542,030	9,706,397	8.6
27	27	Oklahoma	Oklahoma City	2,498,378	2,328,284	7.3
31	32	Oregon	Salem	2,056,171	1,768,687	16.3
3	3	Pennsylvania	Harrisburg	11,663,301	11,319,366	3.0
39	39	Rhode Island	Providence	922,461	859,488	7.3
26	26	South Carolina	Columbia	2,522,881	2,382,594	5.9
44	41	South Dakota	Pierre	661,406	680,514	−2.8
18	17	Tennessee	Nashville	3,833,777	3,567,089	7.6
4	6	Texas	Austin	10,989,123	9,579,677	14.7
37	38	Utah	Salt Lake City	1,060,631	890,627	19.1
48	48	Vermont	Montpelier	437,744	389,881	12.3
14	14	Virginia	Richmond	4,543,249	3,966,949	14.5
22	23	Washington	Olympia	3,352,892	2,853,214	17.5
34	29	West Virginia	Charleston	1,701,913	1,860,421	−8.5
16	15	Wisconsin	Madison	4,366,766	3,951,777	10.5
49	49	Wyoming	Cheyenne	328,591	330,066	−0.4
		United States		204,800,000	179,323,175	14.8 %

Secondly, it should not be so small that the many shades of opinion within the State cannot receive adequate representation.

The upper house in most States consists of from thirty to fifty seats. But there are now (1971) only nineteen members in Delaware's Senate and twenty in Alaska's and Nevada's. Minnesota's upper house is the largest with sixty-seven members.

The lower house usually ranges between 100 and 150 members. However, there are only thirty-nine seats in Delaware's lower chamber and but forty in those of Alaska and Nevada. Massachusetts' lower house is composed of 240 seats and New Hampshire's 400.

Apportionment. On what particular basis should the seats in the legislature be distributed *(apportioned)* within the State? Should they be distributed among legislative districts of substantially equal populations? Or should the apportionment be on the basis of area, with districts drawn along economic and geographic lines? Or should some combination of both population and area be the basis of apportionment? Clearly, these are vital questions. The answers to them determine which groups and regions in a State control its legislative machinery and shape its public policies.

Each State's constitution makes some provision for apportionment. Although there are wide variations among them, most State constitutions follow the principle of "one man, one vote" and provide for population as either the only or the major basis for apportionment.

Reapportionment. Most State constitutions assign the task of *reapportionment* to the legislature itself. They direct the legislature to make periodic adjustments in the distribution of its seats to account for increases, decreases, and shifts of population within the State.

Usually, the constitution orders the legislature to reapportion after each federal census. But, short of constitutional amendment, or in some States the use of the initiative, there was —*until 1962*— no way to force a legislature to reapportion itself.

Rural Over-Representation. Although the pattern is now changing, most State legislatures have long been controlled by the rural, less-populated sections of the State. That is, in well over one-half the States, more lawmakers have been elected from the rural than from the more heavily populated urban areas.

This general pattern of *rural over-representation* and *urban under-representation* developed largely because of: (1) the failure of many State legislatures to reapportion, either fully or at all, despite constitutional provisions or population changes and (2) the use of area as well as population as a basis for apportionment.

Baker v. Carr, 1962. Now, suddenly, the long-standing pattern of rural control is ending in State after State. This marked shift in political power was prompted by a 1962 decision of the Supreme Court. In a case from Tennessee, the Court held, for the first time, that the federal courts could properly hear cases in which it is charged that the way in which a State legislature is apportioned violates the Equal Protection Clause of the 14th Amendment.[6]

---

[6] Until 1962 it was generally argued that reapportionment was a "political question" to be decided by the State legislature or the voters, not the courts; but in *Baker* v. *Carr* the Supreme Court held that earlier cases had *not* established a rule of judicial nonintervention.

Rural over-representation has been overcome in some States without resort to court action; for example, in Oregon, where reapportionment had not occurred in over forty years, the voters forced one by initiating and adopting a constitutional amendment in 1952.

In some States reapportionment is no longer a legislative function; thus, in Ohio it is done by the governor, auditor, secretary of state, and a representative of each major political party; in Arkansas by the governor, secretary of state, and attorney general. A few States provide that if the legislature fails to reapportion, or does so inadequately, it will be done otherwise; for example, in Maine by the State Supreme Judicial Court, and in Oregon by the secretary of state.

Almost at once, suits challenging existing apportionments were filed in over one-half of the States. Prodded by both State and federal court decisions, reapportionment had either been accomplished or was very nearly completed in all of the States by 1970. In fact, *some* form of reapportionment action has been necessary in every one of the fifty States since the *Baker* decision. Among the States, many lower court decisions were appealed to the Supreme Court, however; and many of the new apportionments were subjected to new court challenges, as well.

Reynolds v. Sims, 1964. In *Baker* v. *Carr* the Supreme Court decided only a *jurisdictional* question. It did *not* hold that a malapportionment does in fact violate the 14th Amendment. Rather, that direct question was left to future cases—and has been answered in several of them since. Regularly in those cases the Court *has* held that the 14th Amendment does require that *both houses* of a State's legislature *must be* apportioned in accord with the principle of "one-man, one-vote"—that is, on the basis of population. Said the Court in deciding the leading case (from Alabama), *Reynolds* v. *Sims:*

Legislators represent people, not trees or acres. Legislators are elected by voters, not farms, or cities, or economic interests. As long as ours is a representative form of government, and our legislatures are those instruments of government elected directly by and directly representative of the people, the right to elect legislators in a free and unimpaired fashion is a bedrock of our political system. . . . To the extent that a citizen's right to vote is debased he is that much less a citizen. The fact that an individual lives here or there is not a legitimate reason for overweighting or diluting the efficacy of his vote. The complexions of society and civilizations change, often with amazing rapidity. A nation once primarily rural in character becomes predominantly urban. Representation schemes once fair become archaic and outdated. But the basic principle of representative government

remains, and must remain, unchanged—the weight of a citizen's vote cannot be made to depend on where he lives. Population is, of necessity, the starting point and the controlling criterion for judgment in legislative apportionment controversies.

The significance of the ongoing "reapportionment revolution" cannot be overemphasized. Reapportionment solely on the basis of population means that the majority of seats in most State legislatures will be held by legislators chosen from urban areas. The days of rural domination through over-representation have, in effect, passed. The base of political power—and the emphasis in public policies—

Disagreement on reapportionment forced the 1964 Illinois election of State representatives to be conducted on an at-large basis. Voters were faced with a separate ballot, more than three feet long, listing 236 candidates for the 177 seats in the House. (Wide World Photos)

in most States is shifting (or has already shifted) to the cities.[7]

QUALIFICATIONS, PAY, ELECTIONS, TERMS

Qualifications. Each of the State constitutions sets forth qualifications for membership in the State legislature. These formal qualifications, based upon age, citizenship, and residence, are rather easy to meet. A representative must be at least twenty-one in every State except Hawaii, where the minimum age is twenty. Some States do set a higher minimum age for senators, however; thus, in Texas a State senator must be at least twenty-six.

Each State requires that its legislators be United States citizens, but only Maine (at least five years), Alabama and California (three years), and New Jersey (two years) specify any particular period. State legislators must also be residents of their State in every instance; and usually, either by law or custom, they must also reside in the districts they represent.

Practical politics regularly imposes additional, *informal* qualifications upon candidates seeking seats in the State legislature. These factors of *political availability* vary considerably from State to State—and often from district to district within a State. They relate to a candidate's vote-getting abilities and are based upon such characteristics as occupation, national origins, race, education, record of public service, party membership, and name familiarity. The "right" combination of these factors will help a candidate in seeking nomination and then election. On the other hand, any one "wrong" factor, or combination of them, will very likely doom a candidate's chances.

---

[7] As State legislatures draw the boundaries of congressional districts, which must also be laid out on the basis of "one-man, one vote," the effect upon Congress and upon national policies is also a fundamental one; see pages 206–207.

Compensation. How much legislators are paid is a very serious matter. Some people seem to feel that it is payment enough for one to have the honor of sitting in the State legislature, while a few feel that legislators are not really worth paying. But, in general, most people seem to be unaware of the problem.

The cold, hard facts are these: it costs money for legislators to live and to take time from their normal occupations to serve the State. Far too often, capable, hardworking men and women refuse to run for the legislature because they feel they cannot afford the financial sacrifices involved.

From the table on page 622 you can see the salaries paid in each State. Most States provide some sort of additional allowances. For example, in Alaska legislators receive $35 a day for subsistence during a session, in Maine $16 a day for a session, and in Michigan $3000 for each annual session. But in many States additional allowances are only for postage and mileage for a single round trip.

In most States the legislature sets its own pay. But most legislators hesitate to vote for adequate salaries for fear the move would be used against them at the next election.

Election. State legislators are elected by popular vote in every State. Typically, legislative elections are partisan in character, with the opposing candidates nominated in their respective party primaries. But in a few of the States —in Delaware, for example—nominations are made by conventions. In two States—Minnesota and Nebraska—legislators are chosen on a nonpartisan basis; that is, legislative candidates are nominated at nonpartisan primaries, and the opposing candidates are not identified by party label on the general election ballot.

In most States legislators are chosen at elections held in November of the even-numbered years, and they take their seats the following January. But in Kentucky, Mississippi, New Jersey, and Virginia the elections occur in November of the odd-numbered years, in the hope of separating the consideration of State candidates and issues from national politics.

Terms. As the table on page 622 indicates, State legislators serve for either two- or four-year terms. Senators are usually elected for a longer term than are their colleagues in the lower house. They are chosen for four-year terms in thirty-eight States (including Nebraska) and for two-year terms in the other twelve. Representatives serve two-year terms in forty-five States and four-year terms in only four — Alabama, Louisiana, Maryland, and Mississippi.[8]

The rate of turnover in legislative seats is fairly high, although it tends to vary from State to State and time to time. Typically, there are more new members ("freshman") in the lower house than in the senate in each State each term — because of the larger size of the house, the longer term served by senators, and the fact that members of the lower house seek "promotion" to the upper chamber far more often than the reverse. In any given year *nearly one-half* of all State legislators in the country are serving their first term in office. The major reasons for this high turnover seem to be low pay and political instability. The fact that legislators tend to remain in office for longer periods in those States paying the higher salaries and in which one party tends to dominate elections testifies to the importance of these reasons.

LEGISLATIVE SESSIONS

Annual Sessions. Thirty-one States now (1971) hold regular legislative sessions on an annual basis.[9] The trend among the States is toward annual sessions as, more and more, it is seen that the increasing workload of the legislature cannot be handled well on an every-other-year-for-a-few-months basis.

Biennial Sessions. Nineteen legislatures still meet in regular sessions only every other year. Only in Kentucky and Virginia now do the biennial sessions occur in even-numbered years; in the other States they are held in the odd-numbered years. The steadily increasing pressure of State business has meant that special sessions have become fairly common in most of these States; so, too, has the use of *interim committees* (those which function in the *interim,* between sessions).

Length of Sessions. As a general rule, both annual and biennial legislative sessions are becoming lengthier and still lengthier affairs. As the table on page 622 shows, some State constitutions limit the meeting of a regular session to a definite number of days, weeks, or months; others provide for an indirect limit by allowing legislators no compensation for their services beyond a certain period. But, again because of the growing volume of State business, these restrictions are gradually disappearing.

Budget Sessions. In three of the annual session States — Colorado, New Mexico, and West Virginia — the legislative sessions now (1971) held in the even-numbered years are "budget sessions," held especially to consider fiscal matters. In Louisiana the budget sessions are held in the odd years.

Special Sessions. In every State the governor has the power to call the State legislature into special session, and in sixteen States the legislature itself also possesses the power.[10] As the term suggests, special sessions are held to permit the legislature to consider matters that require its attention between the regular

---

[8] Recall, Nebraska has no lower house.

[9] Alaska, Arizona, California, Colorado, Delaware, Florida, Georgia, Hawaii, Idaho, Illinois, Iowa, Kansas, Louisiana, Maryland, Massachusetts, Michigan, Mississippi, New Jersey, New Mexico, New York, Ohio, Oklahoma, Pennsylvania, Rhode Island, South Carolina, South Dakota, Tennessee, Utah, Vermont, West Virginia, Wisconsin.

---

[10] Alaska, Arizona, Connecticut, Florida, Georgia, Hawaii, Louisiana, Massachusetts, Nebraska, New Hampshire, New Jersey, New Mexico, Pennsylvania, Tennessee, Virginia, West Virginia.

State	Year Held	Regular Sessions Limitations on Length	Regular Sessions Month Convenes	Upper House No. of Members	Upper House Term of Members	Lower House No. of Members	Lower House Term of Members	Salary of Members [d]
Alabama	odd	36 days	May	35	4	106	4	$300 per mo.
Alaska	annual	None	Jan	20	4	40	2	$9000 ann.
Arizona	annual	None	Jan	30	2	60	2	$6000 ann.
Arkansas	odd	60 days	Jan	35	4	100	2	$12,000 bien.
California	annual	None	Jan	40	4	80	2	$19,200 bien.
Colorado	annual [b]	None	Jan	35	4	65	2	$7600 ann.
Connecticut	odd	5 months [c]	Jan	36	2	177	2	$3250 bien.
Delaware	annual	6 months	Jan	19	4	39	2	$6000 ann.
Florida	annual	60 days	Apr	40	4	119	2	$12,000 ann.
Georgia	annual	45 days 40 days	Jan Jan	56	2	195	2	$4200 ann.
Hawaii	annual	60 days	Feb	25	4	51	2	$12,000 ann.
Idaho	annual	60 days [a]	Jan	35	2	70	2	$10 per day
Illinois	annual	6 months [c]	Jan	58	4	177	2	$12,000 ann.
Indiana	odd	61 days	Jan	50	4	100	2	$4000 ann.
Iowa	annual	None	Jan	50	4	100	2	$5500 ann.
Kansas	annual	90 days [a] 60 days	Jan Jan	40	4	125	2	$10 per day
Kentucky	even	60 days	Jan	38	4	100	2	$3000 session
Louisiana	annual [b]	60 days 30 days	May May	39	4	105	4	$9750 ann.
Maine	odd	None	Jan	32	2	151	2	$2500 session
Maryland	annual	70 days	Jan	43	4	142	4	$2400 ann.
Massachusetts	annual	None	Jan	40	2	240	2	$11,400 ann.
Michigan	annual	None	Jan	38	4	110	2	$15,000 ann.
Minnesota	odd	120 days	Jan	67	4	135	2	$4800 ann.
Mississippi	annual	90 days [e]	Jan	52	4	122	4	$5000 session
Missouri	odd	6 months [c]	Jan	34	4	163	2	$4800 ann.
Montana	odd	60 days	Jan	55	4	104	2	$20 per day
Nebraska	odd	None	Jan	49	4	—	—	$4800 bien.
Nevada	odd	60 days [a]	Jan	20	4	40	2	$40 per day
New Hampshire	odd	None	Jan	24	2	400	2	$200 bien.
New Jersey	annual	None	Jan	40	4	80	2	$10,000 ann.
New Mexico	annual [b]	60 days 30 days	Jan	42	4	70	2	$20 per day
New York	annual	None	Jan	57	2	150	2	$15,000 ann.
North Carolina	odd	120 days [a]	Feb	50	2	120	2	$2400 ann.
North Dakota	odd	60 days	Dec	49	4	98	2	$5 per day
Ohio	annual	None	Jan	33	4	99	2	$12,750 ann.
Oklahoma	annual	90 days	Jan	48	4	99	2	$8400 ann.
Oregon	odd	None	Jan	30	4	60	2	$3000 ann.
Pennsylvania	annual	None	Jan	50	4	203	2	$7200 ann.
Rhode Island	annual	60 days [a]	Jan	50	2	100	2	$5 per day
South Carolina	annual	None	Jan	46	4	124	2	$4000 ann.
South Dakota	annual	45 days 30 days	Jan Jan	35	2	75	2	$3000 bien.
Tennessee	annual	None	Jan	33	4	99	2	$3600 ann.
Texas	odd	120 days	Jan	31	4	150	2	$4800 ann.
Utah	annual	60 days 20 days [b]	Jan Jan	29	4	69	2	$25 per day
Vermont	annual	None	Jan	30	2	150	2	$4500 bien.
Virginia	even	60 days	Jan	40	4	100	2	$35 per day
Washington	odd	60 days	Jan	49	4	99	2	$3600 bien.
West Virginia	annual [b]	60 days 30 days	Jan Jan	34	4	100	2	$1500 ann.
Wisconsin	annual	None	Jan	33	4	100	2	$8900 ann.
Wyoming	odd	40 days	Jan	30	4	61	2	$15 per day

Sources: State constitutions and statutes and information furnished by appropriate State officials.

sessions (see page 644). California now provides for a five-day and Connecticut a two-day "veto session" to be held a month after the adjournment of each regular session — for the reconsideration of bills rejected by the governor following that adjournment.

POWERS OF THE LEGISLATURE

Of course, you recall the *division of powers* between the National Government and the States in the federal system. The National Government possesses those powers *delegated* to it and the States those powers *reserved* to them by the Constitution of the United States.[11] The 10th Amendment lays out the basic division quite clearly:

> The powers not delegated to the United States by the Constitution, nor prohibited by it to the States, are reserved to the States respectively, or to the people.

No State constitution contains a complete, detailed listing of the powers vested in the State legislature. Rather, it possesses all of those powers which the State constitution does not grant exclusively to the executive or judicial branches or to local governments and which neither it nor the National Constitution specifically deny to the State legislature.

To put it another way, the State legislature possesses all of those powers which are not granted elsewhere and which are not prohibited to it by some constitutional provision. This means, in effect, that *most* of the powers held by a State are vested in its legislature.

Legislative Powers. Because a State legislature may enact any law not in conflict with either federal law or the State constitution, it is impossible to provide an all-inclusive list of a State legislature's powers. Even so, such powers as those to tax, appropriate and borrow money, regulate commercial activities within the State, establish courts and fix their jurisdiction, define crimes and provide for their punishment, and create and maintain public schools are commonly mentioned in State constitutions.

Every State legislature's powers include the extremely important *police power* — that is, the legislature's power to act to protect and to promote the public health, safety, welfare, and morals (see pages 102–104). Although this broad power cannot be more precisely defined, it is the basis for literally thousands of State laws. Its vast scope can be illustrated by a few examples. Under it, laws may be (and are) enacted to require vaccinations, impose quarantines, provide for food inspections, forbid gambling, regulate the sale and consumption of alcohol, ban the manufacture and sale of fireworks, prohibit the ownership of dangerous weapons, set speed limits, bar immoral or indecent entertainments, compel school attend-

---

[11] See pages 63–67.

(Footnotes accompanying "THE STATE LEGISLATURES" table on page 622.)

---

[a] Indirect limit; legislators' pay ceases, but session may continue.

[b] Annual session every other year is budget session; budget session held in even-numbered years except in Louisiana.

[c] Approximate length. In Connecticut, session must adjourn by the Wednesday after first Monday in June; in Illinois, any legislation passed after July 1 not effective until following July 1, except bills containing an emergency clause; in Missouri, session must adjourn by July 15.

[d] Several States also provide expense allowances for legislators.

[e] Except 125 days every fourth year (the first year of a new gubernatorial term).

Restrictions On State Legislative Power

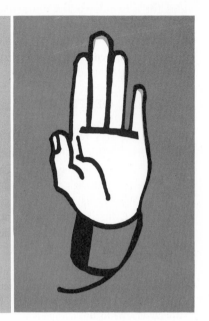

ance, prescribe safety devices in industrial plants, and control the use of child labor. Indeed, a list of this sort could be carried on for pages.

Nonlegislative Powers. Each State legislature possesses, in addition to its lawmaking powers, certain nonlegislative powers.

Executive Powers. Some of the powers vested in each legislature are *executive* in nature. For example, the governor's power to appoint high State officials is frequently made subject to the approval of the State legislature, or at least the upper house. In some States the legislature itself is authorized to appoint various high-ranking officers. For example, the State treasurer is selected by the legislature in Maine, Maryland, New Hampshire, and Tennessee, and the legislature also selects the attorney general in Maine.

Judicial Powers. Each State legislature also exercises certain *judicial* powers. The chief illustration, of course, is the power of impeachment. In every State except Oregon the legislature may impeach executive and judicial officers and, upon conviction, remove them from office.[12]

Each State legislature also possesses judicial powers with regard to its own members. Thus, disputes involving the election or the qualifications of a member-elect are regularly decided by the house involved in the matter. Then, too, because legislators themselves are not subject to impeachment, each legislative chamber has the power to discipline—and, in extreme cases, even expel—any of its own members.

Constituent Powers. As we saw in Chapter 35, each State legislature plays a significant role in both the constitution-making and constitutional amendment processes. When it pro-

---

[12] The Oregon constitution does not provide for impeachment. It does provide, however, for the *recall* of any elected official by the voters and also that "incompetency, corruption, malfeasance, or delinquency in office may be tried [in court] in the same manner as criminal offenses."

poses an amendment or issues a call for a constitutional convention, a State legislature does not make law; rather, it exercises a non-legislative power—its *constituent* power.

ORGANIZATION OF THE LEGISLATURE

In general terms, the legislature in each of the fifty States is organized in much the same manner as Congress. See Chapters 11 and 12.

Presiding Officers. The lower house in each one of the bicameral legislatures elects its own presiding officer, the *speaker*. The constitutions of thirty-eight States provide for a lieutenant governor, and he serves as *president of the senate* in each of those States except Hawaii and Massachusetts. In those two States

and in the eleven which have no lieutenant governor,[13] the senate chooses its own presiding officer. In those States where the lieutenant governor does preside, the senate also selects a *president pro tempore* to serve in his absence. In actual practice, the majority party caucus really chooses the presiding officers in each house—except for the lieutenant governors who are popularly elected in all States, of course.

The presiding officers—and especially the speaker—are powerful and influential figures in the legislature and in their own party. Their

---

[13] Alaska, Arizona, Maine, Maryland, New Hampshire, New Jersey, Oregon, Tennessee, Utah, West Virginia, and Wyoming. By law in Tennessee the presiding officer chosen by the senate is called the "lieutenant governor." See page 640.

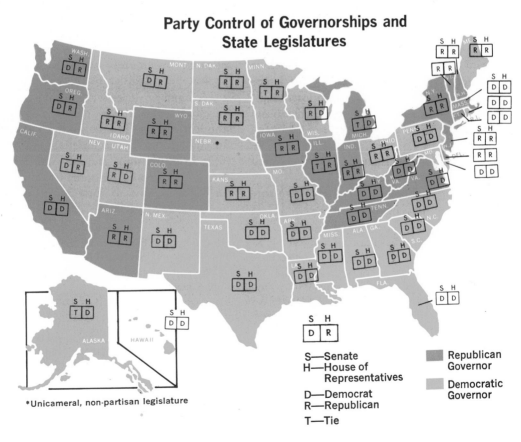

Party Control of Governorships and State Legislatures

S—Senate
H—House of Representatives

D—Democrat
R—Republican
T—Tie

Republican Governor

Democratic Governor

*Unicameral, non-partisan legislature

chief duties—which are also potent political weapons—include the power of recognition, the interpretation and application of the rules, and the reference of bills. Unlike the Speaker of the House in Congress, the speaker in every State except Alaska and Kentucky also has the power to appoint the chairmen and all other members of house committees.[14] The senate president or president *pro tem* has the same power in two-thirds of the States; in the others, the senate itself usually elects the chairmen and members of its own committees. Most presiding officers regularly use the power to reward friends, punish enemies, and otherwise work their influence in the legislature.

The clerks, secretaries, sergeants-at-arms, and other non-member employees are chosen by each house in most States. Almost always this means that their selections are made on a distinctly partisan basis by the majority party.

The Committee System. The number of measures introduced at each session of the various State legislatures runs from some 500 in many of the smaller States to as much as ten times that volume in some of the larger States. This veritable flood of proposed legislation makes the committee system as obviously necessary at the State level, as it is in Congress. Then, too, as in Congress, a major share of the work of the State legislatures is accomplished in its committee rooms.

Committees make their most important contributions to the lawmaking process: (1) as they sift out those measures which merit floor consideration, and (2) when they inform the full house upon those measures they have handled.

The standing committees in each house are usually organized on a subject-matter basis. That is, there are regularly such committees as those on taxation, appropriations, highways, education, health and welfare, elections, the judiciary, and local government. These committees occupy a very strategic spot in the legislative process. It is to them that all bills are referred, and it is in them that most bills are subjected to the closest attention the bills receive in the legislative process. In committee a bill may be entirely rewritten, amended in varying degree, or—as frequently happens—ignored altogether. Whether a bill is or is not to be considered on the floor of a legislative chamber usually depends upon the actions taken by the committee to which it has been referred.[15]

There are, on the average, fifteen to twenty standing committees in each house in the typical State legislature. But, of course, the exact number varies widely State-to-State. In recent sessions, the number of committees in the lower house has ranged from as few as six in Maine and Massachusetts to as many as fifty in Mississippi and fifty-one in Florida; and in the Senate from three in Maine and four in Massachusetts to forty-five in Florida and forty-six in Mississippi. Although there is no

---

[14] In Alaska in each house and in Kentucky in the lower house committee members are nominated by a Committee on Committees and are elected on the floor. Among the other States, only Oklahoma provides that the speaker's committee appointments must be approved by the House of Representatives.

[15] The "pigeonholing" of bills is as well-known in the States as it is in Congress (see page 228). In fact, in most States one of the standing committees in each house, nicknamed the "graveyard committee," regularly performs the bill-killing function. The judiciary committee, to which bills may be referred "on grounds of doubtful constitutionality," most often fills the role. A striking illustration of a "graveyard committee" existed for several years in Oklahoma: the House Committee on Deep Sea Navigation. Notice that the committee existed in a *landlocked* State; and recall that the Commerce Clause gives to Congress the exclusive power to deal with the subject of deep sea navigation.

formula by which the ideal number for a chamber may be determined, a relatively small number of committees, each with well-defined areas of jurisdiction, seems the arrangement best suited to accomplish a legislature's work. Strong support for this view can be found in this fact: In nearly all States most of the bills introduced during a session are referred to only a few of the more important standing committees.

The number of members per committee varies considerably among the States. Ten to twelve is a fairly common size, but in some States some committees in each house have as many as thirty or even forty or more members. Then, too, it is not uncommon for a legislator to serve on six or more committees. In short, in many States little or no attention is given to the obvious relationship between the number and size of committees, on the one hand, and the effectiveness with which the legislature functions, on the other.

Joint committees — permanent groups composed of members of both houses — can produce substantial savings in terms of legislative time and effort. They have been used extensively in a few States for several years — most notably in Connecticut, Maine, and Massachusetts. Their use is now spreading; one or more joint committees function in approximately one-half of the legislatures today. The use of *interim committees* — committees which meet between legislative sessions — is also increasing. These groups make detailed studies of particular problems and then report their findings and recommendations to the next session.

THE LEGISLATIVE PROCESS

The basic function of the State legislature is, of course, to make law. The major features of the legislative process as it operates in a typical State are shown in the diagram on page 628. Because they are shown there—

and because, in general terms, the legislative machinery in each State functions in much the same manner as it does in Congress (see pages 226–235) — we shall comment briefly here.

Source of Bills. Legally, only a member may introduce a bill in either house of any State legislature. So, in a legal sense, it may be said that legislators themselves are the source for the thousands of measures introduced each year. But, in a broader view, legislators are the actual source for only a relative handful of bills.

A large number of bills come from *public sources;* that is, they originate with various officers and agencies of the State and a State's many units of local government. The governor's office is generally the prime source for legislation. Every governor has a legislative program of one kind or another, and frequently the governor's desires are both ambitious and extensive. His proposals are usually expressed

Bill comes from the Latin word bulla, a seal that was used on documents during the Middle Ages. Gradually the word came to be used for the paper itself. In lawmaking, it refers to the written form of a proposed statute. After passage it is known as an act.

STATE OF MICHIGAN

75TH LEGISLATURE

REGULAR SESSION OF 1970

Introduced by Senators Stamm, DeGrow, Bouwsma, Zaagman, Kuhn, VanderLaan, Gray and Lodge

ENROLLED SENATE BILL No. 568

AN ACT to amend sections 791 and 792a of Act No. 116 of the Public Acts of 1954, entitled "An act to reorganize, consolidate and add to the election laws; to provide for election officials and prescribe their powers and duties; to provide for the nomination and election of candidates for public office; to provide for the resignation, removal and recall of certain public officers; to provide for the filling of vacancies in public office; to provide for and regulate primaries and elections; to provide for the purity of elections; to guard against the abuse of the elective franchise; to define violations of this act; to prescribe the penalties therefor; and to repeal certain acts and all other acts inconsistent herewith," as amended by Act No. 331 of the Public Acts of 1965, being sections 168.791 and 168.792a of the Compiled Laws of 1948.

The People of the State of Michigan enact:

Section 1. Sections 791 and 792a of Act No. 116 of the Public Acts of 1954, as amended by Act No. 331 of the Public Acts of 1965, being sections 168.791 and 168.792a of the Compiled Laws of 1948, are amended to read as follows:

Sec. 791. As soon as the polls of election are officially closed and the last voter has voted, the inspectors of election shall seal the operating lever of the machine, if any, against voting, with the numbered metal seal provided for that purpose and open the counter compartment in the presence of the challengers and all other persons lawfully within the polling place, giving full view of all the counter numbers. The chairman of the board shall then under the scrutiny of another member, in the order of the offices as their titles appear

The Course of a Bill

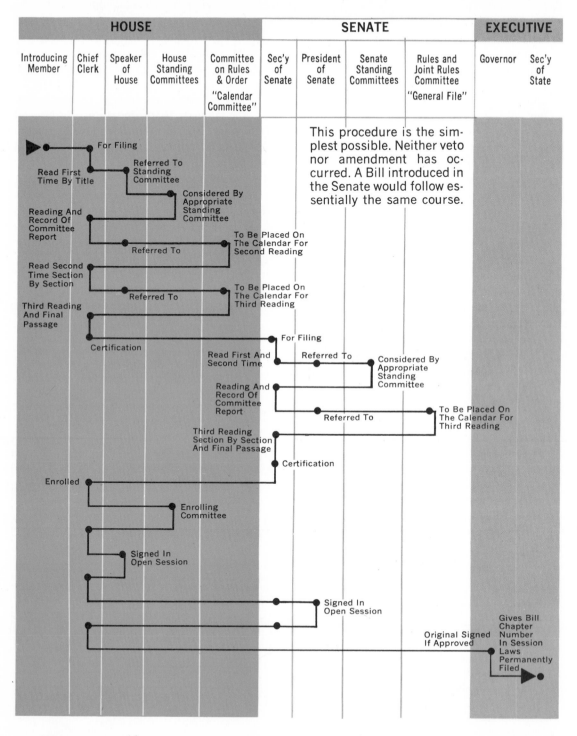

HOUSE					SENATE				EXECUTIVE	
Introducing Member	Chief Clerk	Speaker of House	House Standing Committees	Committee on Rules & Order "Calendar Committee"	Sec'y of Senate	President of Senate	Senate Standing Committees	Rules and Joint Rules Committee "General File"	Governor	Sec'y of State

For Filing

Read First Time By Title

Referred To Standing Committee

Considered By Appropriate Standing Committee

Reading And Record Of Committee Report

To Be Placed On The Calendar For Second Reading

Referred To

Read Second Time Section By Section

To Be Placed On The Calendar For Third Reading

Referred To

Third Reading And Final Passage

Certification

For Filing

Read First And Second Time

Referred To

Considered By Appropriate Standing Committee

Reading And Record Of Committee Report

To Be Placed On The Calendar For Third Reading

Referred To

Third Reading Section By Section And Final Passage

Certification

Enrolled

Enrolling Committee

Signed In Open Session

Signed In Open Session

Original Signed If Approved

Gives Bill Chapter Number In Session Laws Permanently Filed

This procedure is the simplest possible. Neither veto nor amendment has occurred. A Bill introduced in the Senate would follow essentially the same course.

in campaign speeches, inaugural addresses, messages to the legislature, and the budget he submits to each session. His desires are expressed in less formal terms, too, as he exerts his political influence on the legislative process.

Many bills also come from other public sources. For example, a measure authorizing the investment of surplus funds in short-term public securities may, in fact, have been drafted in the State treasurer's office; a proposed revision of the compulsory school attendance law may have been prompted by the superintendent of public instruction; an amendment to the rules of criminal procedure may have come from the supreme court or the attorney general; and a bill relating to the use of the receipts of the State's gasoline tax may have been born in a city council or a city manager's office. And the legislature itself, in its committees, often produces legislative proposals.

A substantial number of bills considered at each session arise from *private sources.* Indeed, the largest single source for proposed legislation in the States appears to be pressure groups. Recall that these groups, and the lobbyists who represent them, exist for one overriding purpose: to influence public policy to the benefit of their own particular interests (see pages 192–194). Of course, some bills also originate with private individuals — lawyers, businessmen, farmers, and other constituents who, for one reason or another, think that "there ought to be a law...."

Preparation of Bills. Although most legislators are of above average intelligence, few are trained to prepare bills in clear, unmistakable language or in such a way as to avoid conflict with federal law and the State constitution.[16]

Years ago lawyer-members or an experienced clerk did most of the bill-drafting in a legislative chamber. Lobbyists often did the job for members whose good will they valued. A few bills are still drafted by members, clerks, lobbyists, or someone else — for example, an officer in an executive agency. But today each State furnishes the legislature with a staff of trained aides who put into proper form the proposals legislators wish to see enacted into law. These bill-drafting experts are usually employed in an agency known as the legislative reference service or are on the attorney general's staff.

A *legislative reference service* is now maintained in nearly all States. It commonly functions as a division of the State library or as an adjunct of the legislature itself. Its specialists render a variety of services to the lawmakers, including especially the drafting of bills and the conduct of research and preparation of reports on legislative matters.

Voting. In most State legislatures votes on the floor may be taken in various ways.[17] The methods cited here are the principal ones.

Viva-Voce Vote. A voice vote, in which the presiding officer puts the question and then determines the outcome from the volume of the response from the members for and then those against the measure, is the method most often used in most States. Its major advantage lies in the speed with which it permits votes to be taken. But its use does allow the presiding officer some useful latitude in assessing the result.

Division of the House. This method is often called a "standing vote," because members voting for and then those voting against a motion rise and are counted by the presiding officer. It is regularly used when somewhat greater accuracy than that provided by a voice vote is desired.

[16] To illustrate what can happen when legislators are not careful: A few years ago the Oregon House of Representatives approved a bill to require the filling in of all abandoned wells; but the measure, as originally passed, was so worded as to require the filling of such wells *before* digging.

[17] But in some States the State constitution dictates the use of a particular method; for example, in Oregon all floor votes must be taken by roll call.

Teller Vote. Under a teller vote members are counted as they file past tellers. Usually two tellers, one for and one against, stand in the front of the chamber, counting their votes as the members file past. Its use provides for a more accurate count than does either the voice vote or division method; but, as with those methods, it does not produce a record of how individual members vote.

Record Vote. Commonly called a "roll call vote," a record vote is one in which the roll of the membership is called and each member is recorded in terms of "yea," "nay," "present but not voting," or "absent." Its use provides a permanent record of the way in which each legislator votes on those questions for which it is used. But the method is quite time-consuming, especially in larger chambers; and a demand for a record vote is often made as a delaying tactic.

The time a State legislature spends voting during a session totals up to a substantial bloc, especially when many roll calls are involved. In the latter days of a session time is often at a premium, and its loss can be serious. Thus, many States now use electrical voting devices to speed the process. The first of these devices was installed in the Wisconsin Assembly in 1917, and they are now found in at least one house in over one-half of the States. In Wisconsin's lower house, where formerly each roll call consumed ten minutes, votes are now recorded in less than one minute. Over the years electrical voting has saved approximately 125 hours of legislative time per session there.

LEGISLATIVE COUNCILS

Both the weight and the complexity of the workload facing each session of a State's legislature is immense—and becoming more so session-to-session. The workload has long since passed the point at which legislators can cope with it without special assistance. The need for wise pre-session planning and for reliable, detailed information is acute in every State. Most States now attempt to meet that need through a *legislative council.*

Kansas created the first legislative council in 1933 and similar agencies are now (1971) found in forty-three States.[18] Of course, the details of organization and the effectiveness of the legislative councils differ from State to State. In most States they are composed of ten to fifteen members of the two houses appointed by the presiding officers of each.

The legislative councils meet periodically between sessions and are, in effect, permanent joint interim committees. Their members consider the major problems that will likely face the next session of the legislature, make detailed studies of many of these problems, and often make recommendations in the form of draft legislation. In several States the councils suggest a lawmaking agenda for the entire session. The more effective councils are aided by a competent and permanent professional research staff.

IMPROVING STATE LEGISLATURES

The State legislatures are, of course, man-made creatures. Like their creators, each exhibits a number of weaknesses and shortcomings. Quite happily, recent years have seen a considerable growth of interest in and efforts toward their improvement. Several developments indicate that much-needed improvement is well underway in various States— for example, the trend toward annual sessions, the generally rising level of legislators' salaries, and the widespread adoption of the legislative council.

---

[18] In some States these agencies are known by another title: in Missouri, the Committee on Legislative Research and in Ohio, the Legislative Service Committee. Those States without such agencies are: California, Florida, Hawaii, Mississippi, New York, Oregon, and West Virginia.

Still, much remains to be done in many States. Some years ago the Council of State Governments (page 650) published a series of recommendations which—despite the encouraging signs of late—remain pertinent. In summary form, the Council of State Governments urged that:

(1) Restrictions on the length of regular sessions should be removed. Legislatures should be permitted to meet as often and as long as conditions require.

(2) Adequate salaries, sufficient to permit competent persons to serve in the legislature, should be provided. Salaries should be determined by statute rather than by constitutional provision.

(3) Legislative terms of office should be lengthened and staggered to provide continuity in membership.

(4) Skilled and essential full-time legislative employees should be appointed on the basis of merit and should retain their positions regardless of changes in party majorities.

(5) Committees should be reduced in number wherever practical; and they should be organized with regard to subject matter, equalization of work, and cooperation between the two houses. Permanent and public records of committee action should be kept.

(6) Committees should provide for public hearings on all major bills, with advance notice of time and place.

(7) Legislative councils or interim committees, with adequate clerical and research facilities, should be provided.

(8) Legislative reference services and similar organizations should be established and strengthened.

(9) Legislative rules should limit the time period during which new bills may be introduced in order to prevent congestion at the end of the session.

(10) Legislative rules should be revised wherever necessary to expedite procedure, although with regard for full deliberation and minorities.

(11) The legislature should make suitable provision, by means of a budget, for all of its own expenditures.

(12) Special legislation should be avoided. Claims against the State should be handled by judicial or administrative agencies. Municipal affairs should be regulated by general or optional legislation or by conferring home rule upon municipalities.

DIRECT LEGISLATION

Beginning with South Dakota in 1898, some States now permit the people to play a direct part in the making of State law—through the initiative and the referendum.

Initiative. In Chapter 35 we noted that the voters themselves may propose (initiate) constitutional amendments in thirteen States.[19] In twenty States they may initiate ordinary *statutes*.[20] The *initiative* is a device by which interested persons or groups may draft proposed laws or constitutional amendments and, by securing a certain number of signatures of qualified voters, place such proposal before the electorate for approval or rejection.

The number of voters who must sign the initiative petitions proposing a statute varies from State to State.[21] For example, 10,000 signatures are required to propose a law in North Dakota, ten per cent of the number of votes cast for governor at the last election in Arizona and Maine, and five per cent of the total number of qualified voters in South Dakota.

---

[19] Arizona, Arkansas, California, Colorado, Massachusetts, Michigan, Missouri, Nebraska, Nevada, North Dakota, Ohio, Oklahoma, and Oregon; see page 609.

[20] The thirteen noted in footnote 19 plus Alaska, Maine, Montana, South Dakota, Utah, Washington, and Wyoming. The initiative (and the referendum) is also available for use in local matters in hundreds of cities and counties. The Idaho constitution provides for the initiative (and the referendum), but legislation necessary to make the initiative effective has never been enacted.

[21] We considered the initiation of constitutional amendments on page 609.

Popular Participation in Lawmaking

INITIATIVE

1. DIRECT (Constitutional amendments and statutory laws)

   Referred directly to the voters without being submitted to the legislature

2. INDIRECT (Statutory laws only)

   Referred to the legislature; if not enacted, the measure is submitted to the people

REFERENDUM

1. MANDATORY (State constitution requires referral to voters)

   Examples: State constitutional amendments, bond issues

2. OPTIONAL (Legislature may refer to voters)

   Submitted for Ratification

   Example: The legislature submits a measure it has passed to the voters for ratification

   Submitted for Advice

   Example: The legislature submits a proposed law to the voters for their recommendation before taking legislative action

3. POPULAR (People may veto acts of the legislature)

   Example: The voters may petition that a measure passed by the legislature be referred to them for final approval or rejection

---

When enough valid signatures have been collected, a proposed measure goes either directly on the ballot *or* to the State legislature — depending upon whether the State provides for the *direct* or the *indirect initiative.*[22]

The *direct initiative* is the most common form. Under it the proposed law goes *directly* on the ballot to be voted on at the next election. Under the *indirect* initiative procedure the proposed law goes *first* to the State legislature; if the legislature does not then enact the measure, it goes to the voters.

Here are some recent examples of the use of the initiative:

Alaska (1968) approved a measure requiring registration as a qualification for voting in the State.

Nebraska (1968) defeated a measure which would have forbidden to the State the power to levy an income tax.

Nevada (1968) defeated a measure providing for a State lottery.

Oregon (1968) defeated a measure setting a drastic limitation on the property-taxing power of local governments.

[22] Twelve States provide for the *direct initiative.* Five provide for only the *indirect:* Maine, Massachusetts, Michigan, Nevada, and South Dakota. Ohio, Utah, and Washington have both forms.

Referendum. There are three distinct forms of the referendum used in the various States—the *mandatory,* the *optional,* and the *popular.*

Mandatory Referendum. In every State except Delaware, the mandatory referendum is provided for proposed constitutional amendments. A mandatory referendum *must* be *referred* to the voters and be approved by them if it is to become effective (see page 609).[23] In 1965, for example, New York voters approved an amendment requiring the governor to submit his annual budget message to the legislature at an earlier date than that formerly required, defeated an amendment that would have simplified the State's constitutional amending process, and approved a measure calling for a constitutional convention to meet in 1967. In 1967, Wisconsin voters adopted an amendment providing four-year terms for the governor, lieutenant governor, attorney general, treasurer, and secretary of state, beginning with the elections of 1970.

Optional Referendum. If a measure is not required to be but is *voluntarily* referred to the voters by the State legislature, it is said to be an *optional* (or legislative) referendum. Such referenda are relatively rare, but a State legislature is sometimes willing to refer a measure to the people when it is itself unwilling to assume responsibility for its passage. In 1960, for example, Oregon voters rejected a measure that would have provided for daylight saving time, long a controversial issue in that State; but two years later the legislature resubmitted the proposal, and it was approved by a comfortable margin.

Popular Referendum. The popular referendum is the device most often associated with "direct legislation." It is now found in twenty-four States—the twenty which have the statutory initiative (page 631) plus Idaho, Maryland, New Mexico, and Kentucky (where it may be used *only* to refer tax measures).

Under this form of referendum the people may demand that a measure passed by the legislature be referred to them for final approval or rejection.[24] That is, they may veto acts of the legislature. The demand must be made by petitions signed by a certain number of qualified voters—for example, five per cent of the vote cast for governor at the last election in Arizona, California, Michigan, and Oregon; and 7000 voters in North Dakota. Here are two examples of the use of the popular referendum:

Oregon (1956) defeated a measure providing for a three-cent sales tax on cigarettes but not on other tobacco products (cigars, pipe tobacco, and the like).

Oregon (1963) defeated a measure to revise the State's income tax law to raise an additional $48,000,000 in the 1963–1965 biennium.

---

[23] In several States, some other measures must also be referred to the voters; the calling of a constitutional convention and bond issues are common examples.

[24] Typically, a measure enacted by the State legislature does not become effective immediately; rather, it does so at some prescribed time thereafter—usually sixty or ninety days after the legislature has adjourned. In the twenty-two States using the popular referendum, then, this delay permits time (and a deadline) for the circulation of a referendum petition. Some measures, however, need to become effective at once. To these "emergency measures" the State legislature may attach an "emergency clause" to make them law upon their approval. To prevent the legislature from attaching an emergency clause to a measure in order to avoid its being referred, most States give the governor the power to veto an emergency clause; and one State, Oregon, forbids an emergency clause in *any* tax measure.

Key Concepts

The details of organization and procedure and even the official name of the legislature varies from State to State, but the legislature's basic function is everywhere the same—to make law.

The legislature is bicameral in every State except Nebraska today. Those who support bicameralism most often argue that it provides for a State legislature in which one house can act as a check on the other and in which a "little federal plan" can be maintained. Critics insist that one house seldom, in fact, checks the other and that the States are unitary rather than federal in form.

The size of the legislature varies considerably among the States, but in each the apportionment of seats is a critical matter. The longstanding pattern of rural over-representation is now disappearing, largely as a result of court action.

Each State constitution requires that legislators be qualified voters, and some States prescribe slightly higher qualifications. The informal qualifications imposed by practical politics are far more significant than those imposed by law. In many States legislators are seriously underpaid, with the result that many capable persons refuse to seek the office.

Legislators are elected by popular vote in every State. Senators are chosen for four-year terms in thirty-eight States and for two-year terms in the other twelve. Representatives serve two-year terms in forty-five States and four-year terms in four States.

The increasing pressures of State business have forced most legislatures to hold increasingly lengthier regular sessions and numerous special sessions in recent years. Thirty-one legislatures now meet in regular sessions annually, but the others continue to convene only biennially.

Each State legislature possesses all of those powers the State constitution does not grant exclusively to the executive or judicial branch or to local government and which neither it nor the National Constitution specifically deny to the legislature. Its extensive legislative powers include the police power, and it also exercises certain nonlegislative powers.

The organization and the procedures of the typical State legislature are generally similar to those of Congress. The presiding officers are generally powerful figures in the legislature and in their respective parties. As in Congress, a major share of the State legislature's work is done in committee. Bills originate with both public and private sources. Legislators today commonly have the bill-drafting, research, and other services of a legislative reference service available to them. Four principal methods of voting are used among the State legislatures: *viva voce*, division of the house, teller vote, and record vote.

Legislative councils now exist in forty-three States. They serve as planning and research agencies, often presenting the legislature with a lawmaking program for the session. Recent years have seen some encouraging signs of improvement in several State legislatures.

Through the various forms of direct legislation (the initiative and referendum), voters in several of the States may take a direct, active role in the lawmaking process.

Important Terms

apportionment
Baker v. *Carr*
bicameralism
division of the house
emergency clause
initiative

interim committee
joint committee
legislative council
legislative reference
   service

lieutenant governor
"one man, one vote"
police power
reapportionment
record vote

referendum
Reynolds v. *Sims*
roll call
teller vote
unicameralism
viva voce

Questions for Inquiry and Review

1. What is the basic function of the State legislature?

2. By what name is the legislature and each of its houses in your State known?

3. For what two major reasons has bicameralism predominated among the States?

4. How many members are there in each house of your State legislature?

5. Why is the basis upon which legislative seats are apportioned a significant matter?

6. What is the essential meaning of the phrase "one man, one vote"?

7. What provision in the Constitution has served as the basis for the reapportionment decisions rendered by the Supreme Court in recent years?

8. Why are the factors of political availability more important considerations in legislative elections than the formal qualifications prescribed by the State constitutions?

9. What salary is paid to the members of your State legislature?

10. In what way does the level of legislative pay exert an influence on the general caliber of the legislature itself?

11. How frequently are regular legislative sessions held in your State? Is the length of the session restricted?

12. Why are the States turning increasingly to the annual session?

13. What is the general scope of the powers possessed by each State legislature?

14. What is the *police power?*

15. What officer presides over the lower house in your State legislature?

16. What officer presides over the upper house in your State legislature?

17. Why must and do State legislatures rely so heavily upon their committees?

18. Why is the use of joint committees and interim committees increasing?

19. What appears to be the largest single source for legislative proposals in the States?

20. Why is voice voting *(viva voce)* the most commonly used voting method among State legislatures?

21. Why do legislative councils now exist in forty-three States?

22. What is the basic purpose of both the initiative and the referendum?

23. What is the essential difference between the initiative and the referendum?

For Further Inquiry

1. As the table on page 622 indicates, many State constitutions impose a limit on the length of the legislature's regular sessions. Why do most authorities and experts in this field recommend that such a restriction be eliminated?

2. The Supreme Court has held that both houses of a State legislature must be apportioned solely on the basis of population. In view of this, do you think there is any valid argument to be made for the continued existence of *two* houses?

3. What particular qualifications would you require all candidates seeking election to the State legislature meet?

4. On page 621 we noted that low pay and political instability appear to be the major reasons for the relatively high turnover in legislative seats in most States. What other reasons for this condition can you suggest?

5. In your judgment, are the members of your State legislature paid an adequate salary? On what factors do you base your judgment in this matter?

6. Can the voters in your State propose and adopt laws through the use of the initiative and the referendum? If so, on what bases might it be argued that the initiative (or referendum) ought to be eliminated in your State? If not, do you think your State constitution should be amended to permit the use of the initiative (and referendum)?

7. Lord Bryce's observation quoted at the beginning of this chapter (page 614) was made in 1888. How apt do you think his judgment is today?

Suggested Activities

1. When your State legislature is in session, arrange for the class to visit it.

2. Invite a member of the State legislature from your locale to speak to the class on the duties and responsibilities of a legislator.

3. Write a short biography on each of the legislators from your locale.

4. Stage a debate or class forum on the subject: *Resolved,* That the State legislature should be reorganized on a unicameral basis.

5. Hold a mock program on the steps involved in enacting a bill currently before your State legislature.

6. Based on the list of recommendations made by the Council of State Governments (page 631), write a report concerning those which you consider applicable to your State legislature.

7. Prepare a chart indicating the course of a bill through your State's legislature. The chart on page 628 might prove to be useful as a model.

Suggested Reading

ADRIAN, CHARLES R., *State and Local Governments.* McGraw-Hill, 1967. Chapter 14.

DYE, THOMAS R., *Politics in States and Communities.* Prentice-Hall, 1969. Chapter 5.

FESLER, JAMES W., *et al., The 50 States and Their Local Governments.* Knopf, 1967. Chapters 8, 9.

GRANT, DANIEL R. and NIXON, H. C., *State and Local Government in America.* Allyn and Bacon, 1968. Chapters 9, 10.

JEWELL, MALCOLM E., *The State Legislature: Politics and Practice.* Random House, 1969.

LOCKARD, DUANE, *The Politics of State and Local Government.* Macmillan, 1969. Ch. 10.

————, *Governing the States and Localities.* Macmillan, 1969. Chapter 4.

"New Shake-Up of Voting Districts?" *U.S. News,* April 21, 1969.

SAMUELS, GERTRUDE, "A New Lobby: Ex-Cons," *New York Times Magazine,* October 19, 1969.

ZIEGLER, HARMON and BAER, MICHAEL, *Lobbying: Interaction and Influence in American State Legislatures.* Wadsworth, 1969.

THE GOVERNORSHIP AND STATE ADMINISTRATION

Energy in the Executive is a leading character in the definition of good government.... A feeble Executive implies a feeble execution of the government. A feeble execution is but another phrase for a bad execution; and a government ill-executed, whatever it may be in theory, must be, in practice, a bad government.

ALEXANDER HAMILTON

❈❈❈ Is popular election the most satisfactory method for the selection of a governor? Why?

❈❈❈ Is the governor properly described as the one representative of <u>all</u> the people of his State?

❈❈❈ What extra-constitutional qualifications should a governor possess?

Historical Development. The governor is the principal executive officer in each of the fifty States. He occupies an office which is the direct descendant of the earliest executive office in America. The history of the post dates back to the first colonial governorship, established in Virginia (at Jamestown) in 1607.

Much of the resentment that finally brought on the Revolutionary War was directed at the royal governors. When the first State constitutions were written, most of the powers given to the original State governments were vested in the legislature. The governor had, for the most part, meager authority. In every State except Massachusetts and New York he was chosen by the legislature, and in most States for only a one-year term. Only in Massachusetts and South Carolina did the governor have the veto power.

The early State governors were often de-

scribed as "figureheads." Thus, addressing the Constitutional Convention in 1787, James Madison was able to say:

> The executives of the States are in general little more than ciphers; the legislatures are omnipotent.

Gradually, however, the people began to realize that the original separation of powers between the State legislature and the governor was an unsatisfactory one. The legislature often abused its powers, and the weak governor was unable to check it. So, as new State constitutions were written and the older ones amended, the legislature's powers were lessened and those of the governor generally increased.[1]

Through the early years of the nineteenth century the power to choose the governor was taken from the State legislature and given to the voters. The veto power was granted to

[1] The title of one of the better studies of the governorship illustrates the evolutionary process through which the position has passed: Leslie Lipson, *The American Governor: From Figurehead to Leader,* University of Chicago Press, 1939.

the governor, and his powers of appointment and administration were increased. But, at the same time, new, popularly elected officers, boards, and commissions were also provided for in several States. These executive officers, supposedly within the governor's administration, were actually independent of him. He could exercise no real control over them because they, like him, were elected by the people. Many States are still plagued by too many examples of this development.

The most striking developments in the character of the governorship have taken place only in the past four to five decades. Beginning with Illinois in 1917, most States have reorganized the executive branch to make the governor a chief executive in something more than name. Of course, some States have gone farther than others in the strengthening of the office. In all States, however, the governor is much more important and powerful now than in earlier days—and the trend to a stronger governor continues.

THE OFFICE

Selection. The governor is chosen by popular vote in every State.[2] In all but three States, he must receive a plurality (more votes than any other candidate) in order to be elected. In Georgia, Mississippi, and Vermont, however, the winning candidate must have a majority of all votes cast for the office.[3]

Qualifications. Every State's constitution sets out certain formal qualifications for the office of governor. Those in the Texas constitution are typical: No person may be chosen governor unless he or she (1) is an American citizen, (2) has lived in the State for at least five years, and (3) is at least thirty years of age. Texas and seven other States [4] also bar atheists from the governorship.

Of course these formal qualifications (citizenship, residence, age) are not difficult to satisfy and are, in fact, met by hundreds of thousands of persons in each State. Far more important are the *informal* qualifications imposed by State politics on a candidate for the office. He must usually live in a populous area; have an acceptable record of accomplishment in politics, business, or some other field; be acceptable to the various wings of his party or, at least, not have made too many enemies; and so on.

Term. Under the first State constitutions governors were commonly chosen to one-year terms; but, as a feature of the strengthening of

---

[2] In Mississippi each county or legislative district has as many "electoral votes" as it has members of the State house of representatives. The candidate receiving the most popular votes in a county receives all of that county's electoral votes. To win, a candidate must receive a majority of both the electoral and the popular votes in the State. If no candidate receives both, the choice of a governor falls to the house of representatives. In Colorado, Connecticut, Florida, Hawaii, Massachusetts, Michigan, New Mexico, Pennsylvania, and Wisconsin each party's candidates for governor and lieutenant governor, and in Alaska for governor and secretary of state, now run jointly, as a team; each voter casts one vote for the two offices.

[3] If no candidate receives a majority in Vermont, the governor is elected by a joint session of the State legislature; in Mississippi the lower house alone makes the choice; in Georgia a run-off election must now be held.

[4] Arkansas, Maryland, Mississippi, North Carolina, Pennsylvania, South Carolina, and Tennessee; but in 1961 the United States Supreme Court unanimously held Maryland's requirement of "a declaration of belief in the existence of God" to be an unconstitutional "invasion of freedom of belief and religion."

the office over the years, the term has been lengthened in every State. Now (1971) forty-one of the States provide for a four-year term and the other nine for a two-year term.[5]

Today one-half of the States still place some limit on the number of terms a governor may serve. In ten States[6] he cannot succeed himself in office; in fifteen others he cannot serve more than two consecutive terms.[7]

Removal. The governor may be removed from office by the impeachment process in every State except Oregon. Only four governors have been impeached and removed since Reconstruction days—William Salzer of New York in 1913; James E. Ferguson of Texas, 1917;[8] J. C. Walton of Oklahoma, 1923; and Henry S. Johnston of Oklahoma, 1929.

The governor may be recalled from office by the voters in thirteen States,[9] though only one has ever been so removed. Governor Lynn J. Frazier was recalled in North Dakota in 1921—but the very next year he was elected to the United States Senate!

---

[5] Two-year terms are now provided in Arkansas, Iowa, Kansas, New Hampshire, New Mexico, Rhode Island, South Dakota, Texas, and Vermont.

[6] Georgia, Indiana, Kentucky, Mississippi, Missouri, North Carolina, South Carolina, Tennessee, Virginia, West Virginia.

[7] Alabama, Alaska, Delaware, Florida, Louisiana, Maine, Maryland, Nebraska, New Jersey, New Mexico, Ohio, Oklahoma, Oregon, Pennsylvania, South Dakota.

[8] "Pa" Ferguson was later "pardoned" by the Texas legislature and immediately announced his candidacy for the governorship. But the State supreme court held the legislature's action unconstitutional in 1920. Article XV, Section 4 of the Texas constitution provides that any officer removed by impeachment is thereafter forever barred "from holding any office of honor, trust, or profit" in the State. Most State constitutions contain a similar clause.

[9] Alaska, Arizona, California, Colorado, Idaho, Kansas, Louisiana, Michigan, Nevada, North Dakota, Oregon, Washington, and Wisconsin. See page 174.

STATE GOVERNORS

State	Term in Years	Annual Salary
Alabama	4	$25,000 and residence
Alaska	4	$40,000 and residence
Arizona	4	$27,500
Arkansas	2	$10,000 and residence
California	4	$49,100 and residence
Colorado	4	$40,000 and residence
Connecticut	4	$35,000 and residence
Delaware	4	$35,000 and residence
Florida	4	$36,000 and residence
Georgia	4	$42,500 and residence
Hawaii	4	$42,000 and residence
Idaho	4	$17,500 and residence
Illinois	4	$45,000 and residence
Indiana	4	$25,000 and residence
Iowa	2	$30,000 and residence
Kansas	2	$20,000 and residence
Kentucky	4	$30,000 and residence
Louisiana	4	$20,000 and residence
Maine	4	$20,000 and residence
Maryland	4	$25,000 and residence
Massachusetts	4	$35,000
Michigan	4	$40,000 and residence
Minnesota	4	$27,500 and residence
Mississippi	4	$35,000 and residence
Missouri	4	$37,500 and residence
Montana	4	$23,250 and residence
Nebraska	4	$25,000 and residence
Nevada	4	$25,000 and residence
New Hampshire	2	$30,000
New Jersey	4	$50,000 and residence
New Mexico	2	$22,000 and residence
New York	4	$85,000 and residence
North Carolina	4	$35,000 and residence
North Dakota	4	$18,000 and residence
Ohio	4	$40,000 and residence
Oklahoma	4	$35,000 and residence
Oregon	4	$25,000
Pennsylvania	4	$45,000 and residence
Rhode Island	2	$30,000
South Carolina	4	$25,000 and residence
South Dakota	2	$18,000 and residence
Tennessee	4	$30,000 and residence
Texas	2	$40,000 and residence
Utah	4	$22,000 and residence
Vermont	2	$30,000
Virginia	4	$35,000 and residence
Washington	4	$32,500 and residence
West Virginia	4	$35,000 and residence
Wisconsin	4	$25,000 and residence
Wyoming	4	$25,000 and residence

Sources: State constitutions and statutes and information furnished by appropriate State officials.

In most States, the governor is provided with an official residence, usually called the Governor's Mansion. In Louisiana the Governor's Mansion is located in Baton Rouge, the capital city of that State. (Louisiana Tourist Development Commission Photograph by Dave Gleason)

Succession. Every State constitution provides for a successor should the governor die, resign, be removed from office, or be physically unable to carry out his duties. In thirty-nine States there is a lieutenant governor, and he is first in line to succeed. In seven other states [10] the president of the senate succeeds to the office, and in the remaining four States the secretary of state succeeds to the office.[11]

Most States also provide for a temporary successor or "acting governor" whenever the chief executive is out of the State. Oregon recently had seven "governors" within a period of five days. This happened because the governor was absent from the State for five days and, during that period, several other high officials found it necessary to travel elsewhere, too.

The importance of provisions for succession is tragically illustrated by an airplane crash in Oregon in 1947. The crash took the lives of three of the State's top officials: the governor, secretary of state, and president of the senate. The speaker of the house then became governor.[12]

Compensation. The governor today is treated much more generously in the matter of salary than are most other State officeholders. A glance at the table on page 639 will show that annual salaries now range from $10,000 in one State, Arkansas, up to $45,000 in Illinois and Pennsylvania and $85,000 in New York. Many States also provide the governor with an expense account and other perquisites. Thus in Iowa the governor's salary is $30,000 and, in addition, he receives a yearly expense account of $5000 and lives in a fine mansion furnished by the State.

To the governor's salary and other compensation must be added the honor and prestige that go with the governorship. It is this "prestige," as well as a sense of public service, that often leads many of our better citizens to seek the office. Many governors have later served in high national office. About one-third of the members of the United States Senate are former governors — and a number of Senators have later served as governors. Former Chief Justice Earl Warren went to the United States Supreme Court from the governor's chair in California. Several Presidents, including Woodrow Wilson and Franklin D. Roosevelt, were governors of their respective States before entering the White House.

---

[10] Maine, Maryland, New Hampshire, New Jersey, Oregon, West Virginia, and Tennessee (where by law the senate's presiding officer is called the "lieutenant governor").

[11] Alaska, Arizona, Utah, and Wyoming.

[12] The importance of a State's succession provisions is further underscored by this fact: The plane crash and several later events (including a resignation, a fatal heart attack, and three election defeats) gave Oregon *seven* governors in a *twelve-year* period (1947–1959) — even though its constitution provides for a four-year term.

THE GOVERNOR AT WORK

The powers and duties of the governor of each State may be classified under three major headings: (1) his executive powers, (2) his legislative powers, and (3) his judicial powers; a fourth and lesser category may be added: (4) his miscellaneous and ceremonial powers and duties. To appreciate the nature of the office it is of value to examine each of these categories. But, at the same time, it is imperative to remember that the office is in fact a single whole, and it is occupied at any given time by only one man.

All this is to say, then, that the governor of each State, like the President of the United States, is "many men." He is an executive, an administrator, a party leader, a legislator, and a ceremonial figure. What his office amounts to depends in no small part upon the way in which he plays each of his roles. The way in which he does depends, in turn, upon the strength of his personality, his political muscle, and his overall ability. Some, even many, of his formal powers may be hedged with various constitutional restrictions. But the powers he does possess, combined with the prestige of his office, make it quite possible for a capable, persuasive, dynamic incumbent to be a "strong" governor, accomplishing much for his State and the public good.

Executive Powers. Although the Presidency and the governorship can be likened in several ways, the comparison can be pushed too far. This is most strikingly true in the area of executive powers. The Constitution of the United States makes the President *the* executive in the National Government. State constitutions, on the other hand, regularly describe the governor as merely the *chief* or *supreme* executive in State government.

"This distinction," as one authority has put it, "is more than a matter of mere terminology." Most State constitutions distribute the executive power among several "executive officers," thus making the governor only "first among equals." For example, Article IV, Section 1 of the Texas constitution provides:

> The Executive Department of this State shall consist of a Governor, who shall be the Chief Executive Officer of the State, a Lieutenant Governor, Secretary of State, Comptroller of Public Accounts, Treasurer, Commissioner of the General Land Office, and Attorney General.

As we shall see, these other executive officers are usually popularly elected and thus beyond the governor's direct control. In most States the executive power is fragmented; that is, the governor may be described as the captain of a ship of state navigated by a crew which he does not select and over which he has only limited powers of command. Despite this, however, it is the governor who is commonly held responsible by the people for the conduct of State affairs.

The basic legal responsibility of the governor in every State is regularly contained in a constitutional provision directing him to "take care that the laws be faithfully executed." While the executive authority may be fragmented among several officers, the governor does possess several specific powers designed to enable him to perform this responsibility.

Appointment and Removal Powers. The governor can best perform his duty to execute — to enforce and to administer — the law with subordinates of his own choosing. Thus, his powers of appointment and removal are, or should be, among his most important.

A leading characteristic of any competent administrator is his ability to select loyal and able assistants. The governor has little, if any, formal control over the other elected executive officers created by the State constitution; the people choose them, and he may not remove them. The concept of civil service appointment on the basis of merit is making steady headway in most States; and this places a limit, although wholesome, on the scope of the governor's authority to appoint and remove

Powers and Duties of a State Governor

Supervises administration and enforcement of State laws

Appoints and removes certain officials

Draws up and submits State budget to legislature

Sends messages to State legislature suggesting needed laws

Holds power to veto bills

Calls special sessions of legislature

Has power to grant reprieves and pardons to persons convicted of crime

Performs miscellaneous functions—ceremonial, arbitration

subordinates. Still, he must fill many important posts within his administration. Recent reorganization efforts have usually stressed the consolidation of governmental functions in the hands of relatively few departments, headed by administrators selected by and responsible to the governor.

Most of the major appointments a governor makes must be confirmed by the State senate.[13] The legislature often attaches restrictions upon the appointment to offices it creates by statute. In vigorous two-party States, for example, the requirement that not more than a certain number of the members of each board

and commission be from the same party is quite common. The members of professional licensing boards must usually be licensed themselves in the particular field; for example, a State board of medical examiners may usually be composed only of doctors and a real estate board only of licensed realtors.

The appointing power may be, and frequently is, used to "reward friends and punish enemies." With it, a governor can gain support for his legislative program, reward campaign contributors, and pay off other political debts. It is often politically sound to appoint some members of racial, religious, and other minority groups to a few posts. Some positions are viewed as symbols of honor or achievement, such as the seats on advisory groups and the governing bodies of educational institutions. These posts regularly go to distinguished citizens of the State—and the identification of such persons with his administration seldom

---

[13] In Alaska all of the governor's major appointees, and in Virginia nearly all of them (including the secretary of state, treasurer, adjutant general, comptroller, and superintendent of public instruction) must be confirmed by *both* houses of the State legislature.

hurts either the governor or his party at the next election.[14]

The governor's removal power is severely limited in most States. Seldom can he remove an official at his pleasure, and in no State does he have the power to remove an elected official. In many States the senate must approve the removal of any appointee whose original selection it confirmed. In most States the governor must at least cite some specific "cause" for his action, such as incompetence, neglect of duty, or malfeasance in office.[15] Here, again, however, the trend is toward wider power for the governor. For example, the Missouri constitution of 1945 provides that "all appointive officers may be removed by the governor."

Supervision of Administration. In taking "care that the laws be faithfully executed," the governor must direct the day-to-day work of the several State administrative agencies. Many of these agencies are subject to his direct control, but many are not. As we previously noted, he is often hamstrung because some agencies are headed by popularly elected officers. Then, too, some of the agencies, along with their powers and duties, are established in the State constitution. Moreover, the legislature has the power to create various departments, boards, commissions, and other agencies and to define their functions.

The governor's ability to supervise State administration depends, then, in a large part on just how much the State constitution and the State legislature allow him to control the agencies within the executive branch. His ability to supervise the agencies also depends

upon the extent of his power to appoint and remove his principal subordinates. Quite often, when a governor has little formal power to control State administration, he is still able to do so because of his position as party leader and as a representative of all of the people of the State. Happily, the reorganization movement in several States is aiding the governor to gain more direct command of his administration and the personnel within it.

Law Enforcement. As a part of his executive duties, the governor is responsible for general law enforcement in the State. In its broadest sense, the job of law enforcement is done by all of the State's administrative agencies. For example, the State board of medical examiners is enforcing the law when it examines and licenses doctors who wish to practice in the State.

A Connecticut State Police officer provides road directions for an out-of-State driver. Too often we forget that officers of the law do much more than enforce restrictions. (Wes Kemp)

---

[14] As we have noted many times, the distinctly "political" use of the appointed power is an altogether natural—and usually wholesome—feature of our governmental system. Recall, as we pointed out in Chapter 7, politics is the stuff of which democracy is made.

[15] *Malfeasance in office* involves official misconduct through the performance of an act which an officer had no legal right to perform.

In its particular sense, the governor's overall responsibility for law enforcement involves the enforcing of criminal law. Once again the governor usually does not have the authority to match his responsibility. His chief legal officer, the attorney general, is popularly elected in forty-two States, chosen by the State legislature in Maine, and chosen by the State supreme court in Tennessee.[16] Many local law enforcement officers, such as sheriffs, constables, coroners, and district attorneys, are also elected.

Several years ago a governor of Pennsylvania sarcastically remarked that he was charged with maintaining peace and order throughout the State (45,333 square miles) with no one to assist him except his secretary and stenographer. Today every State has a State police force or highway patrol to aid the governor in law enforcement. In most States the main task of the State police is enforcement of the motor vehicle laws. In some States, however, the State police has become the major arm of law enforcement; and in most States it systematically enforces law in rural areas, supplementing the work of local sheriffs and constables.

Military Powers. Every State's constitution makes the governor commander in chief of the State militia. Defense is a function of the National Government, as we saw in Chapters 4 and 21. But each State has a militia to maintain peace within the State.

In 1916 Congress provided that each State's militia should consist of all able-bodied males between seventeen and forty-five years of age. The National Guard is the *organized* part of the militia. It is trained by the Regular Army and supported by federal grants-in-aid. In case of national emergency the President may call it into federal service.

---

[16] The attorney general is appointed by the governor in only six States: Alaska, Hawaii, New Hampshire, New Jersey, Pennsylvania, and Wyoming.

When the State's National Guard units are not in federal service, they are commanded by the governor. He is assisted by an adjutant general and commissions its officers. Many governors have used (called out) the National Guard to deal with emergencies such as prison riots and strike disturbances, to aid in evacuation and relief work, to prevent looting during and after floods, violent storms, and other natural disasters, and to augment the State police in campaigns to reduce holiday traffic mishaps.

Financial Powers. As a part of the reorganization of State administration in the past several years, the governor has been given increasing authority over finances. In most States he is now responsible for drawing up and submitting the budget to the State legislature. More and more he is being given control over spending by all State agencies once the legislature has appropriated the money. The control over spending has made it possible for many governors to achieve a higher degree of control over administrative agencies. See pages 692–693.

Legislative Powers. The governor is the State's chief *executive* officer; yet, he possesses three very important legislative powers: (1) to send messages to the State legislature, (2) to call special sessions of the State legislature, and (3) to veto bills passed by the State legislature.

The Message Power. The value of the governor's power to send messages—that is, to recommend legislation—depends largely on his personality, popularity, and party position. A strong governor is often able to accomplish a great deal with the message power and can sometimes enhance the power by addressing the State legislature in person. Such informal tactics as appeals to the people, close relationships with legislative leaders, and a judicious use of his appointing power frequently help a governor with his legislative program, too.

Special Sessions. Every State constitution gives the governor the power to call the State legislature into special session (see page 621).

In several States the constitution forbids the legislature to consider any subjects at a special session except those for which the governor called it into session. Governors have often found the power an important weapon. For example, governors have many times forced a reluctant legislature to pass a measure by threatening to call it back into a special session if it adjourns its regular session without having done so.

Special sessions are becoming more and more common among the States as both the volume and complexity of State business grows. This is especially true in those several States which still hold regular sessions on a biennial basis, and even more so in those States in which the biennial sessions are limited as to length.

Special sessions were called in several of the States in 1969. In Connecticut, for example, Governor John N. Dempsey called the lawmakers back after he had vetoed the major revenue-raising measure they had enacted at the regular session. That statute had hiked the State's sales tax from 3.5 to 6 per cent. The special session then approved a 5 per cent sales tax, raised the tax rates applied to a number of other items, and imposed new taxes on profits from the sale of stocks, bonds, and real estate, on medical and hospital insurance premiums, and on amusement admissions.

The Veto Power. With the single exception of North Carolina, the governor in every State has the power to veto bills passed by the legislature. This power, including the *threat* to use it, is often the most potent weapon he has in influencing the State legislature. When

National Guardsmen train regularly to build a strong defense force for their State and nation and are always ready to answer the governor's call in cases of emergency. To carry out their mission National Guardsmen take to the field each year for fifteen days of maneuvers. (Michigan National Guard)

a bill is sent to the governor, he has from three to fifteen days to act on it.[17]

In forty-two States[18] the governor's veto power includes the *item veto*. That is, it includes the power to veto a specific section or item in a bill without disapproving the entire measure.

The item veto is used many times to check extravagant appropriations. Sometimes, however, the fact that the governor has this power encourages the legislature to vote appropriations in excess of revenues and then "pass the buck" for balancing the State budget to the governor. Often, too, the governor finds that the item veto is a useful device with which he may persuade or punish lawmakers who do not favor his policies and proposals.

The governor does not have an absolute veto in any State; in each the State legislature may override him. The size of the vote necessary to override a governor's veto varies among the States, but two-thirds of the full membership in each house is the most common requirement.[19]

Judicial Powers. In every State the governor has some power of mercy toward persons accused or convicted of crime. It may be to remit fines, to shorten sentences, to pardon a prisoner conditionally or absolutely, to postpone the execution of a death sentence, or to change a death sentence to life imprisonment. That is, a governor may have some or all of these powers, but they are commonly shared with a board of pardons.

These powers exist in order that the ends of justice may best be served. They impose a heavy responsibility on the governor. In this connection former Governor Herbert Lehman of New York has written that this task:

> ... particularly weighed upon me; I felt it most keenly in the cases of men condemned to die. I established a rule that prison wardens must call me personally no more than fifteen minutes before an execution, to establish that no new late evidence had turned up. The knowledge that my word would mean life to a condemned man was deeply perturbing. I never learned to take it "in stride." [20]

---

[17] Three days in Indiana, Iowa, Kansas, New Mexico, North Dakota, South Carolina, South Dakota, and Wyoming; six days in Alabama, Maryland, Rhode Island, and Wisconsin; seven days in Florida; ten days in California, Colorado, Delaware, Hawaii, Illinois, Kentucky, Louisiana, Massachusetts, New Jersey, New York, Ohio, Pennsylvania, and Texas; fourteen days in Michigan and Minnesota; and fifteen days in Alaska and Missouri; five days in the other twenty States. The period allowed *after* adjournment is longer in some States. For example, it is twenty days in Alaska and Oregon and forty-five days in New Jersey and Hawaii. On the "veto session" in California and Connecticut, see page 623.

[18] All except Indiana, Maine, New Hampshire, Nevada, Rhode Island, Vermont, West Virginia, and, of course, North Carolina.

[19] A majority of the full membership of each house in Alabama, Arkansas, Indiana, Kentucky, Tennessee, and West Virginia; three-fifths of the members present in Rhode Island; three-fifths of the full membership in Delaware, Maryland, Nebraska, and Ohio; two-thirds of the members present in Florida, Idaho, Maine, Massachusetts, Montana, New Hampshire, New Mexico, Oregon, South Carolina, South Dakota, Texas, Vermont, Virginia, and Wisconsin; three-fourths of the full membership on revenue and appropriations bills and two-thirds on all other bills in Alaska; and two-thirds of the full membership in the remaining twenty-three States. (North Carolina, having no gubernatorial veto, is not involved, of course.)

[20] From "Albany and Washington—a Contrast," *New York Times Magazine*, September 4, 1950. By permission.

A good illustration of the wise use of the pardon occurred some years ago in New Jersey. A young boy found a rabbit destroying his garden and shot it. He was then arrested for shooting a rabbit out of season. Under the law the judge could do nothing but pronounce a jail sentence. The judge, however, immediately wired the governor requesting a pardon, and it was quickly granted.

There is always the danger that a governor will use the pardoning power too freely. Mrs. James A. ("Ma") Ferguson, Governor of Texas from 1925 to 1927, pardoned 3737 prisoners during her term. The pardons were issued so abundantly that several Texas newspapers published daily "pardon columns" and the late Will Rogers remarked that her successor would have to start his term by catching his own prisoners.

When he sends or receives extradition papers for the return of fugitives, the governor is also acting in a judicial capacity.

Miscellaneous Duties. Much of a governor's time is taken up by a great many other activities. In every State he serves as an *ex officio* (that is, by virtue of his office) member of several State boards—for example, a Board of State Institutions. He must receive official visitors and welcome distinguished people to the State, hear persisting job applicants, meet with party leaders, wade through stacks of documents, sign official papers, and speak to innumerable organizations and public gatherings. More and more today's governors are also being called upon to help settle labor disputes.

OTHER EXECUTIVE OFFICERS

In the early part of this chapter we mentioned the fact that in most States the governor must share the control of "his" administration with a number of other elected executive officers. The particular offices involved vary from State to State. The more important ones, and those most often found, were usually created in the original constitution in each State and still exist today. Many of the lesser offices were created by statute.

Some States have made good progress in reorganizing their executive branches. They have done so chiefly by making some or most (in New Jersey all) of these offices directly subordinate to the governor, giving him the power to appoint their heads. The details of the organization of State administrations vary so widely that it-would be impossible to present a complete treatment of them; the major facets are covered here.

Major Executive Officers. The major executive officers most often found in the various States include lieutenant governor, secretary of state, auditor, treasurer, attorney general, and superintendent of public instruction. As you will see, each of them is usually filled by popular election.

Governor Rockefeller of New York, as do the governors of other States, sometimes has to come before the legislature to urge the enactment of a vital program. (Wide World Photos)

Lieutenant Governor. Thirty-nine States [21] elect a lieutenant governor. He succeeds to the governorship whenever a vacancy occurs and becomes acting governor whenever the chief executive is out of the State. He presides over the senate of each of these States except in Hawaii, Florida, and Massachusetts. See page 625.

The eleven States without lieutenant governors seem to have done well without them. Many urge that the office be abolished, including former Governor Clyde Crosby of Nebraska who, as lieutenant governor, wrote a magazine article entitled: "Why I Want to Get Rid of My Job."

Secretary of State. There is a secretary of state in every State but Hawaii. He is elected by the voters in thirty-nine States; the governor appoints him in seven; [22] and the State legislature chooses him in the other three. [23]

He is the State's chief clerk and records the official acts of the governor and the legislature. He has charge of various official documents, usually administers the State election laws, and keeps the State seal. In several States he also handles automobile and driver licensing and other clerical functions.

Auditor and Comptroller. Every State forbids any money to be spent from the public treasury except as authorized by law. Some official must perform the *pre-audit* function — that is, must authorize the actual spending of public money *before* it is spent. He must issue a *warrant* (an order to pay, such as a check) on the State treasury. He will not issue the warrant

until he is assured that the expenditure is in all respects legal. Some official must also perform the *post-audit* — that is, must audit (examine and verify) the accounts of all officers and agencies handling public funds *after* expenditures are made to ensure that the funds have been legally spent.

Experts in public finance are agreed that the pre-audit should be performed by a comptroller appointed by the governor and that the post-audit should be performed by an auditor selected by the State legislature.

The actual organization for these purposes varies widely among the States. Only twelve States give the pre-audit function to a gubernatorial appointee and the post-audit task to a legislative appointee. [24] In the other thirty-eight States an elected official, usually known as the comptroller or the auditor, is involved in one or both functions. Many States have both an elected comptroller and an elected auditor; in Oregon pre- and post-audits both are made by the elected secretary of state. Altogether, only twenty States now give the all-important post-audit to an official or agency chosen by the State legislature. [25]

Treasurer. The voters in forty States elect a treasurer. In New Jersey and Virginia he is appointed by the governor. In Maine, Maryland, New Hampshire, and Tennessee he is appointed by the State legislature. [26] He receives the State's moneys for safekeeping. In many States the treasurer is also the chief

---

[21] All except Alaska, Arizona, Maine, Maryland, New Hampshire, New Jersey, Oregon, Tennessee, Utah, West Virginia, and Wyoming.

[22] Delaware, Maryland, New Jersey, New York, Pennsylvania, Texas, and Virginia. In Alaska a candidate for secretary of state must run on the same ticket (in tandem) with his party's candidate for governor, as his running mate; the voters cast one ballot for both officers.

[23] Maine, New Hampshire, and Tennessee.

---

[24] Alaska, Arizona, Colorado, Georgia, Hawaii, Maine, Michigan, New Hampshire, New Jersey, Rhode Island, Tennessee, and Virginia.

[25] The twelve States listed in footnote 24 plus Arkansas, California Connecticut, Louisiana, Nevada, South Dakota, Texas, and Wisconsin.

[26] The duties elsewhere handled by the treasurer are assigned to the Commissioner of Taxation and Finance in New York, Director of the Department of Administration in Alaska and Michigan, and Director of Finance in Hawaii. These officials are appointed by the governor in all four States.

tax collector. He is also usually the officer who makes payments out of the treasury on the basis of a warrant from the auditor or comptroller. In short, he is the State's banker.

Attorney General. The State's chief legal officer, the attorney general, is elected in forty-two States. The governor appoints him in Alaska, Hawaii, New Hampshire, New Jersey, Pennsylvania, and Wyoming. He is chosen by the State legislature in Maine and by the supreme court in Tennessee. The attorney general acts as legal adviser to the governor, other State officers, and the legislature; is the State's chief prosecutor; defends the State in actions brought against it; and institutes suits in the State's name. His office often provides bill-drafting services to the members of the legislature.

Superintendent of Public Instruction. Although he is known by various names among the States, a chief school administrator, commonly called the superintendent of public instruction, has general supervision of the State school system. He often shares his authority with a board of education. Twenty-one States elect him by popular vote, usually on a non-partisan ballot. In seven States [27] he is appointed by the governor, and in the other twenty-two he is appointed by the board. [28]

Lesser Executive Officers and Agencies. The executive offices we have just considered are the major ones found in all or most of the fifty States. There are, of course, many others. They vary in number, name, and function from State to State. Some have been created by State constitutions, others by statute. Some are headed by officers chosen by the voters and some by appointed officers.

In many States various functions are handled by boards or commissions rather than by agencies headed by single administrators. [29] For example, the supervision of charitable, correctional, mental, and educational institutions is usually in the hands of a board—for example, the State Board of Prisons and Parole or the State Board of Education. The administration of State laws relating to such matters as agriculture, health, highways, or conservation is usually the responsibility of such agencies as the State Board of Agriculture or Board of Health, the State Highway Commission, or the State Department of Conservation. Public utilities and other corporations are generally regulated by such agencies as the State Public Utilities (or Railroad) Commission, the Banking Commission, or the Commissioner of Insurance. There are a number of licensing and examining agencies in every State; for example, the State Board of Medical Examiners, the Department of Motor Vehicles, and the State Civil Service Commission.

Administrative Reorganization. As one function after another was added to the work of State governments, boards and commissions were established, often in a haphazard fashion. Usually these boards and commissions were made independent of one another, and often even of the governor. The inevitable result was confusion and, at times, chaos.

Overlapping, duplication, waste, lack of coordination—sometimes mingled with graft—resulted. Even today many governors find themselves saddled with the responsibility for the work of officials they cannot control.

A general reorganization movement began in several States about 1910. Illinois holds the honor of being the first State to effect a comprehensive reorganization of its State ad-

---

[27] Alaska, Iowa, New Jersey, Pennsylvania, Tennessee, Vermont, and Virginia.

[28] Arkansas, Colorado, Connecticut, Delaware, Hawaii, Kansas, Maine, Maryland, Massachusetts, Michigan, Minnesota, Missouri, Nebraska, Nevada, New Hampshire, New Mexico, New York, Ohio, Rhode Island, Texas, Utah, and West Virginia.

[29] These agencies vary so much from State to State that it would be fruitless to attempt to list them here. Nearly every State publishes a *Blue Book* or other directory listing and describing the organization and functions of State agencies.

ministration. It was able to do so in 1917 under the leadership of Governor Frank O. Lowden. At his urging, the State legislature abolished more than 100 offices, boards, and commissions. It replaced them with nine departments responsible to the governor: agriculture, finance, labor, mines and minerals, public health, public welfare, public works, registration, and trade and commerce. The Illinois reorganization went about as far as it could without amending the State constitution, a stumbling block to effective reorganization in most States.

Since 1917 most States have made at least some progress in reorganization. Among all the States today, the most efficiently organized administrations are those in Alaska, Hawaii, Michigan, Missouri, New Jersey, and New York. Much remains to be done in most States.

The basic principles of reorganization have been conveniently summarized by the Council of State Governments:

> (1) Consolidate all administrative agencies into a smaller number of departments (usually ten or twenty), organized by function.
> (2) Establish clear lines of authority running from the governor at the top of the hierarchy through the entire organization.
> (3) Establish appropriate staff (advisory, planning) agencies responsible to the governor.
> (4) So far as possible, eliminate the use of boards and commissions for administrative work.
> (5) Establish an independent auditor, with authority for post-audit only.

There is a growing and encouraging trend among the States to reorganize their administrations along departmental lines — that is, to place all similar and related activities under the control and direction of a single agency (a department). In the most thoroughgoing reorganizations, each of the departments is headed by an administrator appointed by and responsible to the governor. The departments most commonly found today are: administration,

agriculture, conservation, corrections, education, finance, health, highways, insurance, justice, labor, military, public works, and welfare.

If more citizens would take an active, informed interest in State governments and their problems, reorganization would be a relatively simple, and a highly profitable, task.

Interstate Agencies. There are numerous organizations which have been formed to promote interstate relationships, further uniform State action to meet common problems, and help the cause of better government.

The Council of State Governments. COSGO was founded in 1935 and is an organization to which all fifty States belong. In each State there is a Commission on Interstate Cooperation usually composed of five administrative officers and five members from each house of the State legislature.

The legislation creating these commissions in each State commonly provides that:

> The Council of State Governments is hereby declared to be a joint governmental agency of this State and of the other States which cooperate through it.

The commissions work with one another through COSGO. A central headquarters is located at Lexington, Kentucky; and offices are also maintained in New York, Chicago, Atlanta, San Francisco, and Washington, D.C.

COSGO is essentially a research organization, providing information to the States. It has furnished the States with much factual material and guidance in such matters as interstate compacts, crime control, social security, uniform taxation, milk control, flood control, interstate parks, liquor regulation, conservation, highway safety, sanitation, and the like. It publishes a quarterly journal, *State Government,* and a biennial summary of current material, *The Book of the States,* as well as its reports on the various matters it investigates.

Several other agencies for voluntary interstate cooperation exist. Examples are the

National Legislative Conference, the National Association of Secretaries of State, the National Association of Attorneys General, the National Association of State Budget Officers, the National Association of State Purchasing Officials, the National Conference of Court Administrative Officers, the Parole and Probation Compact Administrators Association, the Education Commission of the States, and the Conference of Chief Justices. COSGO is the secretariat and central clearing house for each of these organizations.

The Governors' Conference. In 1908 President Theodore Roosevelt called a Conference of Governors at the White House to consider problems regarding the conservation of the nation's natural resources. Since then, the various governors have held an annual conference. Meeting at various places around the country, they discuss common problems, promote interstate good will, and exchange experiences. Although few uniform laws have resulted from these gatherings, they have encouraged a useful exchange of ideas and brought about better interstate cooperation. In recent years, many regional conferences of governors in the West, Midwest, South, and New England have also been held.

✦✦✦✦✦✦✦✦✦✦✦ CONCEPT BUILDING ✦✦✦✦✦✦✦✦✦✦✦

Key Concepts

The governorship is the oldest executive office in America. The first State governors were given only very weak powers, as a reaction against the abuses of colonial governors. Most of the powers of the States were given to the State legislature. Gradually, this original separation of powers was changed as the legislatures tended to abuse their powers. The greatest reforms have come with the reorganization movements in the past five decades.

All States elect the governor by popular vote, although Mississippi combines the popular vote with a country electoral vote system. Each State constitution sets out certain formal qualifications for office, commonly citizenship, age, and residence. The informal political qualifications are important everywhere.

Governors now serve a two-year term in nine States and a four-year term in the rest. Today one-half of the States place a limit on the tenure of the chief executive.

The governor may be removed by impeachment in all States except Oregon and by recall in Oregon and twelve other States. Few have ever been removed from office. Succession to the office falls to the lieutenant governor in thirty-nine States, to the president of the senate in seven, and the secretary of state in four.

The governor's salary ranges from $10,000 a year in Arkansas to a high of $85,000 a year in New York. Most governors also have an expense allowance and an official residence provided by the State.

The powers of the governor are usually shared with several other elective officers over whom he has little real control. His executive powers include those of appointment and removal, supervision of administration, law enforcement, command of the militia and National Guard, and some control over State finance. His most important legislative powers are those to recommend legislation by messages to the State legislature, call special sessions, and (except in North Carolina) to veto bills or parts of them. The governor's judicial powers are those he has in regard to mercy toward prisoners—for example, the pardoning power.

The governor must also perform many miscellaneous duties, usually of a ceremonial nature. In most States his real power is dependent on his popularity, personality, and political position.

In nearly every State there are several other elected administrative officers, including a lieutenant governor, secretary of state, auditor, treasurer, attorney general, and superintendent of public instruction.

Recent years have seen a growing demand for and trend toward reorganization of State administrations. Several intergovernmental agencies, especially the Council of State Governments, exist to promote better cooperation among the States and better government.

Important Terms

administrative reorganization	*ex officio*	post-audit
chief executive	item veto	pre-audit
COSGO	law enforcement	recall
	malfeasance in office	warrant

Questions for Inquiry and Review

1. Why were the first State governors given little power by the first State constitutions?

2. To what extent have the powers of the office been increased in most States?

3. How is the governor chosen in every State?

4. For what term is he elected in your State?

5. How may the governor be removed from office in your State?

6. Who would then succeed him?

7. What salary does the governor in your State receive?

8. What is meant by the statement that the governor of each State is "many men"?

9. In what particular way is the executive power "fragmented" in most States?

10. What is the basic legal responsibility of the governor in every State?

11. Why are the governor's appointment and removal powers so significant?

12. What are the governor's major legislative powers?

13. Does the governor of your State possess the item veto?

14. What two objections may be raised to the possession of the item veto?

15. In what general area do the governors possess judicial powers?

16. What other major executive officers exist in your State?

17. How is each of these other officers chosen?

18. What are the basic principles of State reorganization that have been identified by COSGO?

19. Why have numerous interstate organizations been established and developed over the past generation?

20. What is the Council of State Governments?

For Further Inquiry

1. We noted on page 638 that in several of the States now each party's candidates for governor and lieutenant governor run "in tandem." What prompted the States to provide for such an arrangement? Would you favor it for your State?

2. In New Jersey the governor is the only executive officer elected by the voters, and he appoints all of the others and is responsible for their actions. Would you favor the amendment of your State's constitution to strengthen the governor to this extent in your State?

3. What particular characteristics do you think the governor of your State should possess?

4. For what constitutional term do you think a State governor should be elected? Should there be a limit to the number of terms?

5. Do you think that the salary now paid to the governor of your State is adequate?

6. Do you agree with this comment by Frank Bane, the long-time Executive Director of the Council of State Governments? "Today, as always, it remains true that people rather than systems are the foundations of good government—that no scheme of organization can create leadership, initiative, or performance. But a good system *can* create the framework in which all three may have maximum effectiveness."

Suggested Activities

1. Prepare a short biography of the governor of your State.

2. Prepare a table showing the successive governors of your State, the year in which each first took office, the manner in which each gained office (election or succession), the political party to which each belonged, and such other facts as the term served and the years of birth and death of each.

3. From the State Constitution and the State Blue Book prepare a list of the executive offices in the government of your State. Outline each office in terms of selection, term, powers and duties, and similar factors.

4. Invite a State official to visit the class to discuss his work.

5. Stage a debate or class forum on the following question or resolution: *Resolved,* That the governor of this State should be given the power to appoint all executive officers of this State, subject to their confirmation by the legislature.

Suggested Reading

ADRIAN, CHARLES R., *State and Local Governments.* McGraw-Hill, 1967. Chapters 13, 15.

BRODIE, FAWN M., "California's Unruh and Reagan: Big Daddy vs. Mr. Clean," *New York Times Magazine,* April 21, 1968.

DYE, THOMAS R., *Politics in States and Communities.* Prentice-Hall, 1969. Chapter 6.

FESLER, JAMES W., *et al., The 50 States and Their Local Governments.* Knopf, 1967. Chapters 8, 9, 10.

FRADY, MARSHALL, "California: The Rending of the Veil," *Harper's,* December, 1969.

GRANT, DANIEL R. and NIXON, H. C., *State and Local Government in America.* Allyn and Bacon, 1968. Chapters 11, 12, 13.

"Jay Rockefeller, Tall Democrat," *Look,* April 29, 1969.

LOCKARD, DUANE, *Governing the States and Localities.* Macmillan, 1969. Chapter 5.

_____, *The Politics of State and Local Government.* Macmillan, 1969. Chapters 12, 13.

"The President's Speech to the National Governors Conference," *U.S. News,* September 15, 1969.

38
STATE COURT SYSTEMS

✦✦✦By what method should judges be selected? Should judicial tenure be limited?

✦✦✦Who should decide disputes over the facts in a case—a jury of one's peers or the presiding judge? Why?

✦✦✦What extra-constitutional qualifications should judges possess? Jurors? Prosecutors?

If the lamp of justice goes out in darkness, how great is that darkness.

LORD BRYCE

Courts are tribunals established by the State for the administration of justice according to law. All of the courts of a State compose its "court system," or *judiciary*.

The basic function of the courts is to settle disputes between private persons, and between private persons and government. They protect the right of individuals as guaranteed by the Constitution of the United States and by the various State constitutions. They determine the innocence or guilt of persons accused of crime. They also act as a check on the conduct of the executive and legislative branches of government.[1]

Recall that in our federal system there are two separate and distinct court systems—or, perhaps more accurately, fifty-one of them: The national court system (see Chapter 33) and those of the fifty States. The federal courts have jurisdiction over certain classes of cases, as we saw on pages 570–571 All other cases heard in courts in the United States—and by far the overwhelming number—are heard in State courts.

ORGANIZATION OF STATE COURT SYSTEMS

The constitution in each State provides for the judicial branch. Typically, detailed organization of the court system is left to the legislature. Thus, the Constitution of Iowa provides:

> The judicial power shall be vested in a Supreme Court, District Courts, and such other Courts, inferior to the Supreme Court,

---

[1] In several States courts also perform a variety of *non*-judicial functions. In some States school boards are appointed by the judiciary, for example; and in Tennessee the Supreme Court appoints the Attorney General. In various States, courts also supervise elections, grant business licenses, administer estates, and manage the properties of bankrupts.

as the General Assembly may from time to time, establish.[2]

Justice of the Peace. Justices of the peace stand at the base of the State judicial ladder. They preside over what are commonly known as *justice courts.* Once found in every State, the "JP" is gradually disappearing from the American judicial scene. The office has been abolished in many States and shorn of many of its already limited powers in several others. Justice courts once functioned throughout each State; but today, they are usually found in smaller towns and the rural areas.

Justices of the peace are appointed by the governor in some States; in most States, however, they are popularly elected. As a general rule, justices of the peace are chosen on partisan ballots from a township or other district within a county for a short term—commonly two or four years.

The jurisdiction of a justice court usually extends throughout the county, but it is regularly confined to minor legal matters. In addition to such tasks as performing marriages and witnessing documents, most justices of the peace have jurisdiction of only misdemeanor[3] and minor civil cases.[4] To illustrate, a justice

of the peace often hears such misdemeanor cases as traffic violations, disregard of health ordinances, breaches of the peace, and charges of drunkenness and loitering. He often hears such civil cases as those involving money demands (seldom over $50 or $100), the ownership of personal property, and wrongs or injuries to property. He generally does not have jurisdiction in such civil cases as those involving title to real estate, titles to office, and torts to the person. A "JP" regularly has the power to issue warrants for the arrest of persons accused of even the most serious of crimes. He also has the authority to hold *preliminary hearings*—at which he decides whether the evidence against a person is sufficient to hold that person (bind him over) for action by the grand jury or the prosecutor.

Police or Magistrates' Courts. The lowest courts in urban areas, especially in small and medium-size towns and cities, are known as *police* or *magistrates' courts.* These courts are much like the justice courts, with practically the same jurisdiction. The judges are usually elected, and salaries are generally quite low. Like the justice courts, the police or magistrates' courts are often criticized because the judges are seldom trained in the law,[5] and corruption and political favoritism are not unknown.

Municipal Courts. Unhappy experience with police courts has led to the creation of *municipal courts* in many of our larger cities. The first was established for Chicago in 1906,

---

[2] Article V, Section 1   Considerable attention is paid to the court system in some constitutions, however. For example, Article VII of the Louisiana constitution contains nearly 100 sections dealing with the courts and related agencies.

[3] Crimes are of two kinds: felonies and misdemeanors. A *felony* is the greater crime and may be punished by a heavy fine, imprisonment, or death. A *misdemeanor* is the lesser crime involving a small fine or a short jail term.

[4] A *civil case* is a suit brought by one party against another for the enforcement or protection of a private right or the prevention or redress of a *tort* (a private wrong). It is distinguished from a *criminal case* which is brought by the State against one accused of committing a crime—a public wrong. The State is at times a party to a civil case, but it *always is* (as prosecutor) to a criminal case.

[5] Though a local lawyer presides over some of these courts, this is not common. A California study some years ago indicated that nonlawyer justices included carpenters, ministers, truck drivers, school teachers, real estate agents, contractors, bookkeepers, and druggists (not to mention a wife who held court when her husband went fishing). Several States, including California, have been attempting to remedy this situation. In Missouri and Nevada, for instance, JP's have now been replaced with magistrates' courts with judges selected from the legal profession.

and they are now found in such major cities as Atlanta, Buffalo, Cleveland, Detroit, New York, and Philadelphia. The jurisdiction of these courts is usually citywide, extending to all civil and criminal cases arising within the city.

Municipal courts are often organized into functional divisions. That is, they are frequently composed of divisions, each of which regularly handles cases of a given type. Thus, many of these courts now have such divisions as: civil, criminal, juvenile, domestic relations, misdemeanor, traffic, small claims, and probate.

Functional organization makes possible the creation of divisions especially well suited to hear the major types of cases regularly heard in municipal courts. Take small claims courts as an example. Many people cannot afford to pay the costs involved in suing for the collection of a small debt. A paper boy can hardly afford to hire an attorney and pay court costs in order to collect a month's subscription due from one of his customers, or a widow who runs a lodginghouse can hardly afford to sue for a month's rent. Many small tradespeople have been forced to forget such debts or sell them at about one-half to collection agencies.

Small claims courts have been created to cover just such situations as these. In them a person can bring his claim at an extremely low cost or at no cost at all. The proceedings are quite informal, the judge usually handling matters without attorneys for either side.

Juvenile courts, now found in most of the nation's larger and many of its smaller cities, regularly handle cases involving those under eighteen years of age. The first such court was created in Chicago in 1899. The notion of a separate system of justice for minors — in which a court could consider charges against them in informal, more compassionate, and less public proceedings — spread quickly to the other States.

Typically, juvenile courts have not been given the power to convict minors of criminal charges. Rather, they may adjudge them to be "delinquents." Depending upon the facts in a given case, a juvenile court judge may simply offer good advice, place a delinquent on probation, or, where it seems warranted, commit a minor to an institution for an indefinite period of rehabilitation.

Increasingly today, juvenile courts are presided over by judges especially trained in and concerned with the problems of youth. And more and more, they are being provided with competent assistants, many of them themselves trained in psychology.

Unfortunately, however, both experience and close study have shown that the laudable concept underlying the juvenile courts — the desire to cast a fatherly mantle of protection about minors — has often left much to be desired in practice. While most juvenile court judges are well-meaning and dedicated, some are neither well-trained nor -suited to their roles. Court dockets are frequently so overloaded with pending cases that it is physically impossible to provide the kind of approach assumed by the theory.

Most importantly, the informality of the procedures in juvenile courts have, in many instances, led to gross denials of justice. Hence, in 1967 the United States Supreme Court declared that "neither the 14th Amendment nor the Bill of Rights is for adults only." In an opinion documenting the shortcomings of the system, it ruled that juvenile courts must hereafter provide to minors at least four basic procedural safeguards: (1) timely notice of the charges against them, (2) the right to counsel, court-appointed if necessary, (3) the right to confront and cross-examine accusers and witnesses, and (4) the privilege against self-incrimination, including adequate indication of the right to remain silent.

As a consequence of the Court's decision, the juvenile courts in most of the States are now undergoing a considerable shake-up.

General Trial Courts. The *general trial courts* rank above all local tribunals in a State's court system. They are the courts in which

Addressing the Pennsylvania Bar Association in 1960, Supreme Court Justice William J. Brennan, Jr., who, prior to his appointment to the Court, had been an Associate Justice of the New Jersey State Supreme Court, observed:

> The work of the Supreme Court, especially significant, as, of course, it is, must not divert justice. Actually the composite work of the courts in the 50 States probably has greater significance in measuring how well America attains the ideal of equal justice for all. We emphasize this when we remind ourselves that the Supreme Court is intruded between the State courts and litigants in a very narrow class of litigation. That, of course, is the class of cases in which the State courts deal with federal questions. This intrusion is required because the Supreme Court has been assigned the unique responsibility for umpiring our federal system. That role has always been and remains the Court's most important function. . . .
>
> It is important, however, to stress how infinitesimally small is the class of cases as to which the State courts have to share judicial power with the Supreme Court because they raise federal questions. I suppose the State courts at all levels must decide annually literally millions of controversies which involve vital issues of life, liberty, and property of human beings of this Nation. Even the yearly total of decisions handed down by the highest courts of the 50 States must run into the tens of thousands. Yet only a dribble of this vast number raises any federal question. . . .

Do you think that Mr. Justice Brennan over-emphasized the importance of the State courts in this comment? For what reasons do you think it can be argued that "the composite work of the courts in the 50 States probably has greater significance [than do United States Supreme Court decisions] in measuring how well America attains the ideal of equal justice for all?"

all but the least important cases are regularly heard first.

These trial courts are variously known among the States as the circuit, district, county, common pleas, or superior courts. The judges of these courts are popularly elected in about three-fourths of the States and commonly serve four-, six-, or eight-year terms. Their jurisdiction is quite broad. The district (or circuit) each serves usually encompasses several counties. In the more populous counties, where the case load is especially heavy, each of these courts usually has several judges.

The trial courts exercise both original and appellate jurisdiction. When cases come to them on appeal from one of the lower courts (from a justice court, for example), they are usually heard *de novo* (as though they had not been heard before).

Cases in a trial court are most often heard by the judge and a *petit jury* (the trial jury which hears and decides the facts at issue in a case). Criminal cases are presented to a trial court either by a grand jury or on motion of the prosecuting attorney. See page 662.

The trial court is seldom limited as to the kinds of cases it may hear or the amount that may be in controversy in a civil case. Its decision is usually final insofar as the facts in a case are concerned, but disputed questions of law may be carried on appeal to a higher State court.

In some of the more heavily populated areas, such matters as the settlement of estates or the handling of the affairs of minors are handled by separate courts—often called surrogate, probate, or orphans' courts. In most districts, however, these matters are handled by the regular trial courts.

Intermediate Appellate Courts. In over

one-third of the States today there are courts of appeals between the trial courts and the State s highest court.[6] These *intermediate appellate courts* have been created in an attempt to ease the burden of the high court.

Like the trial courts, the intermediate appellate courts are known by a variety of names among the States.[7] The judges who sit on these tribunals are appointed by the governor in a few States—for example, in New Jersey and New York; most often, however, they are popularly elected on a Statewide basis. Their terms of office range from six up to twelve years.

Most of the work of these courts involves the reviewing of decisions made by lower courts. Their original jurisdiction is quite limited. In exercising the appellate function, the judges consider the arguments presented in written briefs, hear the oral arguments of attorneys, and confer among themselves. The appearance of witnesses, taking of evidence, and other procedures associated with the trial courts occur only when their limited original jurisdiction is invoked—for example, in the instance of a contested election.

State Supreme Court. The State's *supreme court* stands at the apex of its judicial system.[8] Its primary function is to review the decisions

of lower courts. It is the final interpreter of the State's constitution and laws.

The justices—ranging from three in one State, Delaware, to nine in Alabama, Iowa, Mississippi, Oklahoma, Texas, and Washington— are usually elected by the voters. In about one-third of the States the elections are nonpartisan, while in another third they are by party. In the remaining third the justices are selected by the governor or the legislature, or by a process involving both of these branches.

Review of a State supreme court decision may be considered by the United States Supreme Court, but *only* when a "federal question" is involved—that is, when the case hinges upon the meaning of a provision in the Constitution of the United States or a federal statute or treaty. Otherwise, review is not available, and the State supreme court stands as the "court of last resort." [9]

Unified Court Systems. Most State judiciaries are organized on a geographic basis. Each of the courts at each level in the system has the same jurisdiction within its prescribed territory as the others. For example, each general trial court has the same power as every other such court to hear and determine cases in its particular district.

In these geographically-oriented systems a judge must be prepared to render decisions in every area of the law included within the jurisdiction of his court. A backlog of cases may build up in some districts, while judges sit in comparative idleness in others. Uneven interpretations and applications of the law may occur from one part of the State to another.

To overcome these difficulties several States

---

[6] Alabama, Arizona, California, Colorado, Florida, Georgia, Illinois, Indiana, Louisiana, Maryland, Michigan, Missouri, New Jersey, New Mexico, New York, North Carolina, Ohio, Oregon, Pennsylvania, Tennessee, Texas, and Washington.

[7] In New York, for example, there is an Appellate Division of the Supreme Court. The highest court in the New York judicial system is known as the Court of Appeals.

[8] The court of last resort is known as the supreme court in forty-three States. But in Kentucky, Maryland, and New York it is styled the Court of Appeals, in Maine and Massachusetts the Supreme Judicial Court, and in Virginia and West Virginia the Supreme Court of Appeals. In Oklahoma and Texas there is a separate three-judge Court of Criminal Appeals as the court of last resort in criminal cases.

---

[9] In some minor cases lower courts are given final jurisdiction. That is, review by a higher court cannot be obtained. In these instances the lower court becomes the State court of last resort and the only review available is in the Supreme Court of the United States. Such reviews are rare; the most recent one occurred in 1959 when the Supreme Court reversed a decision by the police court of Louisville, Kentucky.

have abandoned the traditional pattern of geographic organization in recent years. They have turned, instead, to a *unified court system.*

In the ideal unified court system there is technically only one court for the entire State, presided over by a chief judge or judicial council. Within this single court are a number of levels including supreme, intermediate, appellate, and general trial sections, with divisions established for proceedings in equity, juvenile, family relations, small claims, and other functional areas that demand special attention. As an illustration, see the chart of the New Jersey court system on this page.

In a unified court a judge can be assigned to that section or division to which his talents and training best suit him. Because judges may be shifted from one section or division to another, the delays imposed by crowded dockets can be prevented. In short, the unified court system is a modern response to the old common law adage: "Justice delayed is justice denied."

Today (1970) the States of Alaska, Illinois, Michigan, New Jersey, and North Carolina have unified court systems. Major steps toward such a system have also been taken in such States as Colorado, Connecticut, Missouri, New Hampshire, and New York.

SELECTION OF JUDGES

Although there is much variation among the States, judges are commonly chosen in one of three ways: by (1) popular election, (2) appointment by the governor, and (3) appointment by the legislature.[10]

---

[10] In some States some judges are selected by other means. In Hawaii, for example, judges of the supreme court and the circuit courts are appointed by the governor with the consent of the Senate, but district court judges are appointed by the chief justice of the supreme court. In Arizona all judges are elected except for police magistrates appointed by the various city councils.

New Jersey Court System

SUPREME COURT

Chief Justice and six Associates. Jurisdiction — final appeals in selected cases defined by the Constitution. First term — seven years, tenure on reappointment, retirement at 70.

SUPERIOR COURT

Term, tenure, and retirement of judges same as Supreme Court. Court has State-wide jurisdiction and is divided into three divisions.

Law Division	Appellate Division	Chancery Division
	Decides appeals from Law and Chancery Divisions, County Courts, and others as may be provided by law.	

COUNTY COURT

Minimum of one judge in each county. Equity powers when complete determination of case so requires. Jurisdiction subject to change by law.

INFERIOR COURTS

Either created prior to and not abolished by the Constitution or created by law subsequent to the Constitution. All subject to abolition or change by law.

District Court	Municipal Court	Juvenile and Domestic Relations Court	Surrogate's Actions (Partially Judicial)

Most judges are appointed by the Governor with Senate approval. Municipal judges are appointed by governing body unless serving in two or more municipalities, then appointed by the Governor. Surrogates are elected.

Methods of Selection. In most States, only one or another of these methods is used. But in some a combination of them is found. In Kentucky, Michigan, Minnesota, Ohio, Texas, Wisconsin, and several other States, for example, all judges are popularly elected. In Massachusetts and New Hampshire all judges are appointed by the governor. In South Carolina, on the other hand, the judges of the supreme and circuit courts are chosen by the legislature, municipal judges and some county judges are appointed by the governor, and probate judges and the other county judges are elected by the voters.

Until the 1860's nearly all State judges were appointed, either by the governor or by the legislature. After the Civil War, however, most States, acting in the belief that it was more democratic, switched to popular election; and this remains the overwhelmingly predominant method for selecting State judges today.

Despite the fact that most State judges are elected today, experience has clearly demonstrated that the process is not altogether satisfactory. The mere fact that a man has the support of his political party, or that he is a good vote-getter, does not mean that he is qualified to be a judge. There *are* many judges who owe their offices to popular election and who possess those qualities most needed in a judge — absolutely honesty and personal integrity, a judicial temperament and independence, and the necessary legal ability. But the process has also produced an unfortunate number of very poorly qualified judges, too.

Most students of the problem are convinced that the best process of selection is appointment by the governor. They also feel that selection by the legislature is the worst.

Reforms. Many reforms have been proposed, and several have been tried in various States. Popular election is so widespread, however, and attempts to abandon it have been so stoutly resisted by party organizations, that most of these reforms continue to involve at least an element of popular election.

More than one-third of the States now try to overcome some of the disadvantages of popular election by requiring that most or all judges be chosen in nonpartisan elections. Unfortunately, these contests are often nonpartisan in name only. Some States also attempt to reduce partisanship by scheduling judicial elections at some time other than the general election.

The Missouri Plan. Since 1940 Missouri has used a scheme of selection that combines both election and appointment. This arrangement, known as the "Missouri Plan," has attracted the support of nearly all students of judicial administration and the influential House of Delegates of the American Bar Association.

Under the Missouri Plan the governor appoints the judges of the supreme court, the other appellate courts, the Court of Criminal Corrections in St. Louis, and the circuit and probate courts in St. Louis and in Jackson County (Kansas City).[11] The governor must make each appointment from a list of three names submitted to him by the nonpartisan Appellate Judicial Commission. The Commission is composed of the chief justice of the Missouri Supreme Court, three attorneys chosen by the State bar, and three laymen appointed by the governor. Each judge is appointed to serve until the first general election to occur after he has been in office for one year. His name appears on the ballot at that election, without opposition. If the voters approve him, he then serves a regular term — six years for the trial court judges and twelve years for judges of the higher courts. If the voters reject him, the governor makes a new appointment from a list drawn by the Commission.

Under the Missouri Plan a judge must "run on his record." The more desirable appointment process is used, but the voters still have

---

[11] The other lower court judges in the State are still chosen on a partisan ballot; but the plan may be adopted by the voters in any of the State's judicial districts.

a voice in the matter. The chance that a governor might make a purely political appointment is reduced, since the bar participates in the selection of judges and the people are also represented in the selection process.

In California a somewhat similar arrangement has been used since 1934. Variations of it are now found, for at least some judgeships, in ten other States: Alaska, Colorado, Illinois, Iowa, Kansas, Maryland, Nebraska, Oklahoma, Utah, and Vermont, but have been rejected by the legislature or at the polls in other States.

ADVISORY OPINIONS

In eleven of the States the highest courts are authorized to render what are known as *advisory opinions*. In each of these States these opinions are available to the governor and, in all except three, to the legislature, as well.[12]

An advisory opinion makes it possible for the legislature, when considering the passage of a bill, and the governor, before signing a bill, to secure the high court's opinion as to its constitutionality. These opinions are *advisory* only. If a bill on which such an opinion has been rendered is passed and later challenged, the court is free to rule on the matter as it will.[13] But at least some indication of the court's attitude may be had in advance.

DECLARATORY JUDGMENTS

In nearly all States the various courts are authorized to render *declaratory judgments*. These judgments are available *before* an actual

LET'S GET DOWN TO CASES—MY CASES! One of the major problems facing the courts today is overcrowded dockets. Civil suits, especially those concerned with auto accidents, often do not come to trial for a year or even longer after being filed. (James Dobbins, Boston Herald-Traveler)

case is instituted and are designed to determine the legal rights of the parties to a controversy. Any person whose legal rights are affected by a statute, a rule promulgated by an executive agency, or a private agreement such as a contract may petition a court for a declaration indicating his legal rights and obligations.

To illustrate, suppose that the owner of a sand and gravel company wants to add a new gravel crusher to his plant but an adjacent property owner objects. Rather than the plant owner expanding his operation and the neigh-

---

[12] To both the governor and the legislature in Alabama, Colorado, Maine, Massachusetts, Michigan, New Hampshire, North Carolina, and Rhode Island; to the governor only in Delaware, Florida, and South Dakota. In the other States the attorney general performs this task.

[13] Except that in Colorado those opinions that do not involve private rights are considered to be binding.

bor seeking damages in court, either or both parties may ask a court for a declaratory judgment setting forth the rights of each.

Declaratory judgments are often confused with advisory opinions. But note that, unlike declaratory judgments, advisory opinions are not given in disputes between private parties; instead, they are intended only as legal advice to the governor or the legislature. An advisory opinion is not binding—even upon the judges who render it. A declaratory judgment, on the other hand, determines the rights and obligations of, and is binding upon, all parties involved in a dispute.

THE JURY SYSTEM

A jury is a body of persons selected according to law and sworn to declare the truth on the evidence laid before it. In the American legal system there are two kinds of juries; (1) the grand jury and (2) the petit jury.

The Grand Jury. A *grand jury* is a body of persons summoned into a court to consider the evidence against persons accused of crimes and to determine whether the evidence is sufficient to justify a trial. Depending upon the State involved, a grand jury may consist of as many as twenty-three persons or as few as six. Where larger juries are used, at least twelve of the jurors must agree that an accused is probably guilty before a formal accusation can be made. Similarly, where smaller juries are employed, an extraordinary majority is required to *indict* (bring the formal charge). In a few States, for example, Michigan, a single individual—a "one-man grand jury"—may be appointed to investigate for the judge of a court.

When a grand jury is *impaneled* (selected), the judge instructs the jurors to find a *true bill of indictment* (charge) against all persons whom the prosecuting attorney brings to their attention and whom they think probably guilty. He further instructs them to bring a *present-*

ment (accusation) against any person whom they of their own knowledge believe to have violated the criminal laws of the State within their county. They swear or affirm that they will do so and retire to the jury room, where they deliberate in secret. Their chairman, appointed by the judge or chosen by them, is known as the *foreman*.

The prosecuting attorney for the county brings into the jury room witnesses to testify against the accused and usually questions them himself; but after he retires, the jurors may resummon the same witnesses and question them further or may have the court summon other witnesses to testify against the accused. Nobody is allowed in the room with the jurors except the witnesses, the prosecuting attorney, and, in some States, his stenographer. All are bound to secrecy.

After all witnesses have been summoned and questioned, the jurors are left entirely alone to deliberate. When they have completed their finding, they proceed to the courtroom, and their bill of indictment is read in their presence. The bill is recorded in the clerk's office, and the jury is dismissed if the term has expired. If the term has not expired, the jury is adjourned until the court needs to call it into session again.[14]

In peaceful rural communities one grand jury a year is usually all that is needed. In larger urban areas there must either be a number of grand juries or one must sit from time to time for several months—unless the prosecuting attorney may bring an accusation by the filing of an *information.*

---

[14] It is not uncommon for a State to impose upon the grand jury duties other than the consideration of evidence against accused persons. For example, grand juries may be required to approve the erection of public buildings and bridges in Pennsylvania, fix the tax rate in Georgia, investigate the sufficiency of the bonds of county officers in Alabama and Tennessee, arrest intoxicated persons or those selling liquor illegally in Vermont.

Accusation by Information. As a substitute for the grand jury, over half of the States now permit the use of the *information* as a means of bringing criminal charges. The information serves the same purpose as an indictment; it is a formal charge brought by the prosecuting attorney without grand jury action.

The use of the information has much to recommend it. It is far less costly and time-consuming than indictment by a grand jury. Then, too, since grand juries tend to follow the recommendations that prosecutors make to them, many proponents of the information argue that the grand jury is really unnecessary.

The chief objection to abandonment of the grand jury appears to be the fear that some prosecutors may be over-zealous, that they may abuse their powers and harass defendants. The information is not available in many States, and in some it may not be used to accuse a person of one of the more serious crimes.

The Petit Jury. A *petit* (trial) jury is a group of persons summoned into court to hear the evidence on both sides of a case and to decide the disputed points of fact, the judge in most States deciding the points of law. Unlike the grand jury which is used only in criminal cases, the petit jury is used in both civil and criminal cases.

The number of petit jurors is usually twelve, but in some States a lesser number is sufficient in civil cases and minor criminal cases. In justice courts six jurors or less is the rule, though in several States this court, too, may have twelve jurors.

In about one-third of the States verdicts in civil cases and in minor criminal cases need not be unanimous, but there extraordinary majorities of two-thirds, three-fourths, or five-sixths are required. In most of the States, however, verdicts must be unanimous in all cases.

This petit jury was the first all-Negro jury selected to sit in the history of Houston County, Alabama. It listened to the evidence presented and found the defendant in the case guilty of second-degree murder. (Wide World Photos)

The Grand and Petit Juries Compared.
The same courts that have *grand* juries to *accuse* have *petit* juries to *try* the accused. Some courts, however, which do not have grand juries do have petit juries. For example, in most States justice courts may use petit juries, though in no State do they have grand juries. Courts which have no criminal jurisdiction have no need of grand juries.

Appellate courts of last resort do not use either grand or petit juries because they are concerned primarily with points of law which have been appealed to them from the lower courts. A grand jury investigates all indictable offenses committed during its existence and usually hears only accusations.

Selection of Jurors. In scarcely any two States are jurors selected in exactly the same manner, but in all they are selected in a similar manner. Once a year, or oftener, some county official [15] or special jury commissioners, appointed or elected as the law prescribes, prepare a list of persons eligible for jury service.

In some States any qualified voter of the county in which the court is sitting is eligible for jury duty, while in others only taxpayers may serve. In the former States the names can be obtained from the poll books and in the latter from the tax assessors' books. Persons under twenty-one and those over seventy years of age, criminals, and illiterates are commonly ineligible. In most States other classes of persons, such as State and federal officials, professional men, police and firemen, and State militiamen, are not required to serve on juries.

The chosen names are written on slips of paper and placed in a locked jury box,[16] which is usually kept in the custody of the clerk of the court. When the court needs a jury, the names are drawn from the box by a designated official, and the sheriff is directed to summon such persons by a writ known as a *venire facias* (you must come). After eliminating the names of those who, for good reason, cannot serve, the judge makes a list of those who can (*panel of veniremen*).

Grand jurors are commonly selected in the same manner as petit jurors, but in some States a separate list of names is prepared.

Many otherwise intelligent people think it "smart" to avoid jury duty. It is one of the most serious mistakes a citizen can make. An accused person, who may be entirely innocent, can hardly expect justice from a jury chosen from among the least intelligent in the community. Nor can the law be enforced properly if the best people beg off.

Criticism and Proposed Reforms. No aspect of the administration of justice in the United States has come in for more criticism, by lawyers and laymen alike, than the operation of the jury system. These criticisms are not so much directed at the system itself as at the *operation* of that system. All of the criticisms made do not apply to all juries everywhere, of course. Many times critics are inclined to forget this vital fact: the jury system is intended *first* to protect the innocent and only *second* to convict the guilty.

The jury system developed in medieval England on the theory that a man accused of

---

[15] This official is usually the clerk of the court, the sheriff, the judge, or county board of commissioners. In the New England States and in Michigan names of jurors are selected by township (town) officers and sent to a county officer.

[16] In New Jersey the *chancellor* (highest judge) appoints for each county a jury commissioner of the party opposed to that of the county sheriff. These two are commissioners of juries and select names of eligible persons as in other States; but instead of being put into the jury box, the names are numbered consecutively and a piece of metal with a corresponding number is dropped into the box in place of the name.

crime, or involved in a dispute with his neighbor, could expect fairer treatment in his case if the facts were weighed and decided by a group of his neighbors. Thus, jurors were selected because of their firsthand knowledge of local persons and events.

Today, however, the situation is completely reversed. Those with firsthand knowledge are excluded from service. In effect, as one student of the jury system has put it, in the attempt to get impartiality "ignorance [of the facts] is made virtually a prerequisite for jury service."

Other weaknesses are also pointed out. The process of selecting jurymen is frequently long and tedious with the result that the judge falls far behind his docket of cases. Busy people engaged in important business or professional pursuits are often excused from service. Too often this may mean that better qualified jurors escape service while others less qualified do serve.

Another criticism stems from the fact that many jury verdicts are, in reality, compromises reached in the interest of a formal verdict. At times a jury's verdict seems to be the result of emotional appeal rather than of unrefuted evidence. Jury tampering has occasionally been known—but then, too, so has the bribing of judges.

These and similar charges against the system have led most authorities to recommend various reforms, and a few authorities would even do away with juries. One proposal, already adopted in several States, involves reducing the size of juries from the usual twelve to five or six. A lesser number can, presumably, more readily reach agreement without any greater likelihood of injustice being done.

Another proposal, already adopted in several States, too, involves relaxing the unanimity requirement for jury verdicts. If a substantial majority, say three-fourths, is required, "hung" juries are largely eliminated.

Going to the very heart of the weaknesses charged to the jury system is the suggestion that persons accused of crime, or involved in

An IBM machine is now used in a New York county juror selection room for the selection of prospective jurors for county court trials. It has replaced the old jury wheel (in the foreground) from which a sufficient number of names were drawn to make up the panel of jurors to sit for a given term of court. (Wide World Photos)

civil suits, be allowed to waive their right to trial by jury and have their case heard only by the judge. This is now fact in nearly every State in civil suits and misdemeanor cases. About one-third of the States also allow for waiver in felony cases.

A few critics propose complete elimination of the jury in all cases and the hearing of disputes by a single judge or a panel of three judges. This suggestion assumes, of course, the complete impartiality and absolute incorruptibility of the bench.

Key Concepts

A court is a tribunal established by the State to administer justice according to law. The State courts hear all cases not heard by the federal courts.

The justice of the peace presides over the justice court at the base of the State judicial system. Police or magistrates' courts correspond to the justice courts and are usually found in more populous areas.

Municipal courts with full jurisdiction over all civil and criminal cases arising in the municipality are found in the larger cities and towns. In the largest cities they are organized into divisions to handle cases of a particular kind (such as juvenile cases and domestic relations cases) or in a particular area of the city.

General trial courts, known by a variety of names, stand above the courts so far mentioned. They have original jurisdiction over cases within their district and also hear appeals from lower courts.

Intermediate appellate courts, found in over one-third of the States, hear appeals from the general trial courts.

The State supreme court is the apex of the State judicial system. Except for cases which may be appealed to the United States Supreme Court, it is usually the court of last resort and is the final interpreter of the State constitution.

Most State judges are elected by the voters, but this process of selecting judges has not proved completely satisfactory. Among various reforms, some version of the Missouri Plan, which combines both election and appointment, is the one most widely supported today.

Advisory opinions on the constitutionality of a proposed law are given by the highest courts in eleven States. Declaratory judgments, indicating in advance the rights of parties to a dispute, are given by most State courts.

There are two kinds of juries. The *grand jury* determines whether or not the evidence is sufficient to hold the accused for trial. The *petit jury* hears a case and decides questions of fact. An *information* may be filed by the prosecuting attorney, as an alternative to the grand jury, in over half of the States. Jurors are selected in a variety of ways among the States.

The jury system is often criticized because it sometimes seems to put a premium on ignorance, the selection process is often a long one, the better qualified people are often excused, verdicts are sometimes compromises in order that a formal verdict can be returned, and emotional appeals sometimes overcome reason and fact.

Several reforms have been proposed, and many have been adopted in various States. These reforms include reducing the size of the jury, relaxing the unanimity requirement, and providing the right to waive trial by jury. Some even propose eliminating the jury.

Important Terms

advisory opinion	declaratory judgment	information	petit jury
appellate	felony	jurisdiction	presentment
civil law	grand jury	misdemeanor	veniremen
criminal law	indictment	Missouri Plan	

Questions for Inquiry and Review

1. What is a court?

2. What are a court's functions?

3. What two separate judicial systems exist in the United States?

4. On what bases are cases heard in the federal courts? What cases are heard in State courts?

5. What distinguishes a *civil* from a *criminal* case?

6. What is the difference between a *felony* and a *misdemeanor?*

7. Which courts are commonly the lowest in a State's judicial system?

8. Many larger cities now have what courts in place of the lower courts commonly found elsewhere? Why are these courts often organized into functional divisions?

9. In what level (or type) of court are most of the more important cases first heard?

10. Why do intermediate appellate courts now exist in over one-third of the States of our nation?

11. What is the primary function of a State supreme court?

12. Appeals may be taken from a State supreme court to the United States Supreme Court only under what circumstances?

13. What is a unified court system? Why is it widely recommended?

14. What are the three principal methods used for the selection of State judges? Which is most commonly used?

15. What is the "Missouri Plan"? Why is it, or some similar procedure, favored by nearly all students of judicial administration?

16. Where available, by whom are advisory opinions rendered? To whom?

17. Why are advisory opinions valuable?

18. By whom are declaratory judgments rendered? To whom?

19. Why are declaratory judgments valuable?

20. What is the primary function of the grand jury?

21. What device may be substituted for the grand jury in more than half of the States?

22. What is the principal difference between a *presentment* and an *information?*

23. Why do many oppose the use of the information?

24. What major criticisms are often made of the jury system? What reforms are suggested?

For Further Inquiry

1. What is "lynch law"? Is its use ever justified?

2. How are judges selected in your State? Would you advocate any changes in the existing arrangement? If so, why? Who might be expected to oppose your suggestions? Why?

3. The United States Supreme Court has held several times that no State may exclude a person from jury service on the basis of race, color, or sex. On what provision of the Constitution has it based this ruling? Why do you support or oppose this ruling? Would you favor a law requiring that women accused of crime be tried only before all-female juries and that men be tried only before all-male juries? Why?

4. A New Yorker kept account of the forty-six times he put a penny in a subway vending machine without getting a penny chocolate in return; he sued the company owning the machine and recovered his 46¢ plus $1.25 court costs. In Chicago a newsboy won a 45¢ suit against a client who refused to pay his bill. Both of these cases were heard in small claims courts. Does, or would, the presence of such a court in your community help to increase respect for the law? Why?

5. The office of justice of the peace and justice courts have been abolished in several States and in sections of others in recent years. They have been replaced with local courts presided over by judges trained in the law. Do you think the trend should be accelerated? Why? In many States justices of the peace are still paid out of the fines they collect; the more fines they impose, the higher their income. Why is this "fee system" vigorously opposed by virtually all students of judicial administration?

6. If you had the power to appoint the judges of the courts in your State what qualifications would you seek in making your selections? Would those qualifications vary depending upon the court involved? Why?

Suggested Activities

1. Invite a judge, the local prosecuting attorney, or a lawyer to address the class on the topic, the Administration of Justice.

2. Attend a session of a court and write a report on what took place.

3. Construct a chart of the courts in your State's judicial system. Indicate the jurisdiction of the various types of courts and by whom and for how long judges are selected. (Consult the State constitution, State manual, and local judges and attorneys.)

4. If your State's court system is unified, attempt to discover when and why the reorganization occurred. Then, write a report on the unification, using the data you have obtained.

5. Stage a debate or class forum on the question: *Resolved,* That felony cases should be decided by a two-thirds majority verdict rather than the present unanimous verdict requirement.

Suggested Reading

DYE, THOMAS R., *Politics in States and Communities.* Prentice-Hall, 1969. Chapter 7.

FESLER, JAMES W., *et al., The 50 States and Their Local Government.* Knopf, 1967. Chapter 12.

HAMMER, RICHARD, "Role Playing: A Judge Is a Con, a Con Is a Judge," *New York Times Magazine,* September 14, 1969.

KING, LARRY L., "Warren Burnett: Texas Lawyer," *Harper's,* July, 1969.

LOCKARD, DUANE, *Governing the States and Localities.* Macmillan, 1969. Chapter 6.

————, *The Politics of State and Local Government.* Macmillan, 1969. Chapter 15.

MADDOX, RUSSELL W. (ed.), *Issues in State and Local Government.* Van Nostrand, 1966.

MAYER, MARTIN, "The Criminal and the Law," *Saturday Evening Post,* February 11, 1967.

MAYERS, LEWIS, *The American Legal System.* Harper & Row, 1966.

MITAU, G. THEODORE, *State and Local Government: Politics and Processes.* Scribner's, 1966. Chapter 7.

"Reforming Juvenile Justice," *Time,* May 26, 1967.

SAMUELS, GERTRUDE, "A Judge with a 'Disciplined Indignation,'" *New York Times Magazine,* January 15, 1967.

*** Are there any circumstances in which one should be excused for disobeying the law?

*** Which, in your view, is the more important: the individual's right to a fair trial or society's right to protect itself? Explain.

*** What distinctions might be drawn between the phrases "a law" and "the law"?

*** Should the provisions of the criminal law be uniform throughout all fifty States? Why?

The life of the law has not been logic: it has been experience.

OLIVER WENDELL HOLMES, JR.

The basic function of the courts is to hear and decide cases—to resolve legal controversies or, as the point was put on page 654, to administer justice according to law. Despite the many different types and levels of courts in this country, and the many differences among them, they all exist to perform that basic function.

KINDS OF LAW APPLIED BY STATE COURTS

In dealing with the cases that come before them, State courts apply several different forms of law. They apply the Constitution of the United States, the constitution of the State, and city and county charters (constitutional law); the legislative acts of Congress, the State legislature, city councils, and county boards (statutory law); and the orders, rules, and regulations issued by executive officers and agencies of the National, State, and local governments (administrative law). They also apply two other forms of law to the cases they hear: *common law* and *equity*.

Common Law. In the words of James Kent, an early nineteenth-century American legal scholar and jurist, the *common law* may be defined as:

> ...the body of those principles and rules of action, relating to the government and security of persons and property, which derive their authority solely from usages and customs of immemorial antiquity, or from the judgments and decrees of the courts recognizing, affirming, and enforcing such usages and customs.

In less technical language, the common law is a body of unwritten, judge-made law. It originated centuries ago in England out of decisions made on the basis of local customs. It developed as judges, encountering situations similar to those found in previous cases, applied and reapplied the rulings from those earlier cases. Thus, gradually, the law of those cases became *common* throughout the land—and, eventually, throughout the English-speaking world. That is to say, the common law developed as judges followed the rule of *stare decisis*—"let the decision stand."

Under the rule of *stare decisis,* a decision, once made, becomes a precedent or guide to be followed in all later, similar cases, unless compelling reasons call for the establishing of new precedents. The rule of *stare decisis* gives stability to the law and to the legal relationships between and among individuals.

The common law is *not* a permanently fixed body of rules controlled in every instance by a precedent which may be easily found and readily applied. Judges are frequently called upon to interpret and reinterpret existing rules in the light of new situations and changing circumstances.

The importance of the common law in the American legal system cannot be overstated. It forms the basis of legal procedures in every State except Louisiana.[1] *Statutory law*—that enacted by a legislative body—overrides common law; but many statutes are based upon the common law and are interpreted and applied by the courts according to common law tradition.[2]

Equity. *Equity*—also known as *chancery*—is a branch of the law which supplements the common law. It is designed to provide equity—"fairness, justice, and right"—when the remedies available under the common law fall short of that goal.

As the common law developed in England, judges grew conservative and ceased to create means of obtaining justice as new and changing conditions demanded. They used forms, called *writs,* upon which one had to state his case; else his case could not be heard. Those who were thus barred from the courts appealed directly to the King for justice.

The appeals to the King became so numerous that he began to refer most of them to a member of his council, the chancellor.[3] The continued increase in such pleas led, by the middle of the fourteenth century, to the creation of permanent courts of equity. The decisions of these courts eventually resulted in the system of rules known as equity.

Probably the most important difference to be noted between common law and equity is that the common law is primarily remedial while equity is essentially preventive. That is, the common law deals with matters *after* they have happened; equity seeks to prevent threatened wrongs from occurring. To illustrate, suppose your neighbor begins to add a room to his house, despite your protest that the addition will encroach upon your property and destroy a portion of your garden of rare plants. You can prevent him from continuing the addition by securing an injunction from a court of equity. The *injunction*—a court order prohibiting a specified action by a party named in the order—can be issued not only because of the immediacy of the threat but also because the law could provide no adequate remedy for the destruction of the garden. It is true that damages might be assessed under common law, but in a legal sense money could not restore the satisfaction and enjoyment you derived from the prize plants.

---

[1] Because of the early French influence, Louisiana's legal system is based primarily upon the Napoleonic Code. Gradually, however, common law has been working its way into Louisiana law.

[2] Because the National Government is a government of delegated powers, there is no federal common law. But in some cases federal judges do apply the common law of the State in which their court sits—especially those cases involving citizens of different States and for which there is no applicable federal statute.

---

[3] The chancellor was, until the Reformation, always a member of the clergy. As a result of his function of dispensing equity, he became known as the "Keeper of the King's Conscience." The term *chancery,* a synonym for equity, was derived from his title.

The English colonists brought equity as well as the common law to America. At first, the two forms of law were administered by different courts. Today, however, only four States — Arkansas, Delaware, Mississippi, and Tennessee — maintain separate equity courts. In the other States the same courts administer both forms and, in general, the procedural distinction between the two are disappearing.

RULES OF PROCEDURE

Everything that takes place in an American court of law is done in conformity with rules of procedure. These rules are rather complicated and, as a result, justice often seems to move at a snail's pace. However, this is true for a very good reason — our whole legal system is designed to one great end: the protection of the individual in the lawful exercise of his rights.

The rules of procedure vary from State to State as well as according to the type of court. But despite these differences, there is a wide similarity among the States. This is so because the rules in each State have been developed from a common source — the forms developed in the early common law and equity courts. Thus, the procedures followed in a midwestern State, for example, are quite similar to those found in States in other parts of the country.

Civil Procedure. A *civil suit* usually involves a dispute between private parties over their respective legal rights and duties. A governmental unit is sometimes involved as a party in a civil suit, as for example when a State sues a person for damage to public property. Usually, however, civil suits involve private persons.[4]

A civil suit may be distinguished from a *criminal case,* as we shall see shortly, by the

---

[4] One or both persons may be artificial — that is, a corporation.

BALANCED GOVERNMENT. Under our legal system the accused is presumed innocent until proven guilty. The burden of proof rests with the prosecution. Our courts guard against any abuse of the rights of the individual. (LePelley, The Christian Science Monitor)

fact that the State is *always* a party to a criminal case — as the plaintiff against a person charged with a public offense (a crime).

There are two types of civil procedure — *law* suits and *equity* suits. We shall discuss each of these in turn in a moment, but a few examples of the distinctions between them may help at this point. If another person owes you money and refuses to pay, or does injury to your person or property, or violates a contract between you, you can sue him *at law* for money damages. If, on the other hand, you want to prevent the other person from doing some wrong, compel him to live up to a contract rather than pay money damages, or force him to pay you the income from property he holds in trust for you, you can sue him *in equity*.

In cases at law the judge ordinarily has a jury to decide the facts, and the witnesses usually testify in court. But in equity cases the judge usually decides the facts himself without a jury; and, rather than having witnesses in court, he often appoints a *referee* to gather the evidence and report his findings in written form.

In the following discussion the two types of suits are illustrated as they would proceed in a *typical* State. Of course, there are slight variations from State to State.

Suits at Law. Suppose that Mr. A is injured in a railway accident and that he brings suit against the railroad for damages of $50,000. Mr. A, then, is the *plaintiff,* and the railroad the *defendant.* Mr. A's attorney files A's claim against the railroad with the clerk of the court in the county or other judicial district in which the accident occurred. The railroad, through its attorneys, then enters a plea denying Mr. A's claim.

The case of *Mr. A* v. *The B Railroad Company* is placed on the court's *docket* (the schedule of cases pending before the court). The court will turn to Mr. A's case when the cases ahead of it on the docket have been disposed of. A jury will be impaneled unless the opposing lawyers and the judge agree to dispense with it; that is, the judge must agree to decide the facts at issue as well as the law involved. If a jury is impaneled, it will decide all disputed facts. For example, the jury will decide whether Mr. A was *in fact* injured and, if so, to what extent. The judge will decide all points of law and instruct the jury as to the law covering the case.

After counsel for each side argues the facts in the case and the judge has issued his instructions as to the law, the jury retires to the jury room. There it deliberates in secret. It may ask the judge for further clarification of the law, to read a transcript of some testimony it has heard, or to see some item of evidence again.

If the jury agrees that Mr. A was (or was not) in fact injured and to what extent (if any) he should be compensated, it renders a *verdict* (decision). If the jurors cannot agree, the judge declares the case a *mistrial;* and the case may, but need not, be tried again.

The judge renders a *judgment* in accord with the jury's verdict. If the judgment is in favor of the plaintiff, the defendant may appeal the case to the State supreme court.[5] If the defendant accepts the verdict but then fails to make prompt payment of damages awarded, the court will issue an *execution,* an order to the sheriff directing him to levy an execution (sell property of the defendants) to satisfy the judgment.

Suit in Equity. Suppose that Mr. X, a farmer, waters his stock from a fresh stream running through his farm and by his house. Meanwhile, Y Company establishes a large creamery on the stream above Mr. X's farm and empties greasy water and acids into the stream to such an extent that it produces a stench at Mr X's home and his cattle won't drink the water.

Mr. X will have his attorney file suit with the clerk of the court to *enjoin* (forbid) Y Company from emptying the grease and acids into the water, and the clerk will have the sheriff notify Y Company that suit has been brought. A jury is not needed to decide the facts, and witnesses need not appear in court.[6] A master in chancery, notary public, or justice of the peace — *the referee* — brings counsel for each side together at some convenient time and place to take *depositions* (testimony), which a stenographer records word for word. These depositions are given to the judge. The counsel for the plaintiff and the counsel for the defendant argue the points of law and evidence before the judge in court or in *vacation* (between terms).

If the judge is not satisfied as to the facts, he may go to the scene, call witnesses before him, or order the master in chancery to make further investigation as to certain facts. With

---

[5] In civil cases the plaintiff may appeal to the higher court on questions of law affecting the verdict, if the verdict is against him.

[6] In some States the evidence would be taken in open court, with lawyers for each side and the judge asking questions of the witnesses.

A suspected criminal is booked, formally charged with the crime, at the police station. From there he will be brought before a court for a preliminary hearing to determine if there is sufficient evidence to bind him over for action by the grand jury. (Wide World Photos)

the facts and the law both presented, the judge is prepared to render a decision, called a *decree* in equity cases. If the judge decides that the injury to Mr. X is as claimed, he will decree that Y Company must cease emptying grease and acids into the stream.

The court costs of a civil suit such as witness fees, jury fees, and recording fees are usually placed by the court upon the party losing the case. Sometimes some costs are granted with which to pay lawyers, but each party usually has to pay its own counsel.

Criminal Procedure. A *crime* is any act which is considered so dangerous to the public peace and safety that it is prohibited by law. Each State's *criminal code*—the compendium of its laws dealing with crime—defines certain acts as crimes, details the procedures to be followed in all criminal matters, and sets out the punishments that may be inflicted upon those convicted of crimes.[7]

Many crimes are immoral in themselves—as, for example, murder, assault, or robbery. But others are criminal only because they are so defined by law—as, for example, exceeding a highway speed limit or failing to obey an ordinance regulating the burning of trash. Crimes range all the way from the major and more serious offenses—*felonies,* such as murder and robbery—to the minor and less serious ones—*misdemeanors,* such as traffic violations.

Felonies. Those crimes which are ranked as felonies vary so much from State to State that no universal definition of the term is possible. But, generally among the States, all crimes which are punishable by death or by confinement in a penitentiary for a year or more are defined as felonies. Murder, arson, burglary,

---

[7] The large bulk of criminal law in the United States is State law, but the list of federal crimes is growing steadily; see Chapter 22.

robbery, grand larceny, aggravated assault, bigamy, perjury, forgery, embezzlement, rape, and kidnapping are classified as felonies in every State.

Misdemeanors. Misdemeanors are crimes of a less serious character than felonies and, like felonies, cannot be covered by any general definition applicable to all States. In Virginia, for example, offenses which are punishable with death or confinement in the penitentiary are felonies; all other offenses are misdemeanors. In the same State the following crimes are misdemeanors and, in general, would be so classified in other States: violation of town or city ordinances, carrying concealed weapons, cruelty to animals, attempting to defraud a hotelkeeper, petty larceny, nonsupport of a

A policeman searches a suspected felon for concealed weapons. The arrest of any armed suspect requires the arresting officer to take added precaution. (UPI Photo)

wife and minor children, permitting a gambling house on one's premises, libel, assault, and battery. These misdemeanors are punishable by confinement in jail or by fine. Such misdemeanors as drunkenness without disorder or profanity are punishable by fine only.

Arrest of Felons. A private citizen may arrest a person to prevent the commission of a felony in his presence; may, without a warrant, arrest a person whom he has seen commit a felony; or may even arrest a person without a warrant on reasonable suspicion of that person having committed a felony, provided a felony has been committed.[8]

An *officer of the peace* (sheriff, constable, policeman) may do anything a private citizen may do. Furthermore, he should pursue a felon who is making an escape though he has not actually seen the crime committed. If the policeman, constable, or sheriff does not attempt to arrest a felon, the prosecuting attorney will usually take the initiative and have the suspected felon arrested.

An injured party, or anyone knowing of a crime, may go to a justice of the peace or some other magistrate who has power to issue a warrant and, by taking oath as to the crime, have a warrant issued for the arrest of some designated person, provided the magistrate is satisfied as to the truth of the complaint. The *warrant* is a written document describing the felon, setting forth the offense, and directing that he be brought before some specified magistrate, usually the one who has issued the warrant. A policeman, constable, sheriff, or any other peace officer may make the *arrest* ("serve the warrant") and bring the felon before the proper magistrate for trial. In making the arrest the officer may call upon any person to assist him, may break into a building, or may

---

[8] When a person makes (or contemplates making) a citizen's arrest, he should, of course, be as certain of his facts as possible. The victim of an improper citizen's arrest often has ground for damages which he may secure through a suit for false arrest.

kill the felon *if necessary* in self-defense or to prevent escape.

Arrest of Misdemeanants. A private citizen may arrest another person without a warrant to quell a breach of the peace in his presence; but usually he may not arrest a person to prevent any other misdemeanor, nor may he arrest one for any misdemeanor already committed. A peace officer may arrest without a warrant for any misdemeanor committed in his presence. If the misdemeanor was not committed in his presence, he usually can arrest only on a warrant. The same magistrates who issue warrants for felons may issue them for misdemeanants, and arrests are made by the same officers in the same manner.

The Commitment. After the accused is arrested, he is brought before the magistrate, usually a justice of the peace, except in cities where there is a special police justice or in towns in which the mayor has the powers of a justice of the peace. If the crime is a misdemeanor, the accused is probably tried at once. If the crime is a felony, the magistrate normally holds a *preliminary hearing.* When the evidence indicates a probability of guilt, the accused is held for the grand jury or brought to a trial by *information.* If the crime is murder, the accused is usually committed to jail; otherwise, he is released on bail,[9] unless his being at large is considered especially dangerous.

The Indictment. The *prosecuting attorney* — called the State's attorney or district attorney in some States — investigates the evidence against persons the committing magistrates have held for grand jury action, or against any other persons whose probable guilt has been brought to his attention. If he thinks there is sufficient evidence to convict, he draws up a *bill of indictment* and has witnesses summoned for the grand jury.

If a certain majority of the grand jury (the majority varies from State to State) thinks there is sufficient evidence to warrant a court trial, the foreman of the grand jury writes across the face of the indictment the words, "a true bill" of indictment. The indicted person must then stand trial in court. If the prescribed majority of the grand jury does not think that the evidence justifies a trial, the words "not a true bill" are written, and the charge is dropped.

The Trial. The justice court usually has original jurisdiction in misdemeanor cases. Here the trial is very informal because justices of the peace are not always lawyers and must depend upon what they can glean from a volume of laws compiled for their use. With few exceptions, an appeal may be taken to the general trial court in criminal cases.

In misdemeanor cases sent from the grand jury or appealed from a justice court, an accused person need not appear in person in the general trial court. He often prefers to leave his case to an attorney. In felony cases sent to the trial court by the grand jury, the defendant must appear; a felony case cannot proceed unless the accused person is present. In appearing, the defendant is in the custody of the sheriff, deputy sheriff, or some similar officer.

The defendant is charged with committing a crime against the State, and his prosecution is

---

[9] Furnishing bail (from the Old French *bail* — meaning to be guardian) is theoretically putting a man in charge of a private jailer and in effect is the guarantee that an accused person will appear for trial if allowed to go at large. It is usually a sum of money, depending upon the character of the charge, and is determined by a judge or special bail officer. The cash, or other security, may be furnished by a friend or by the accused himself if he possesses the amount required. Professional criminals often secure bail through one who makes a business of going bail for a fee. Too often, the criminal commits another crime while out on bail to secure the money with which to pay his bail fee.

The Growing Crime Rate — and Crimes Committed

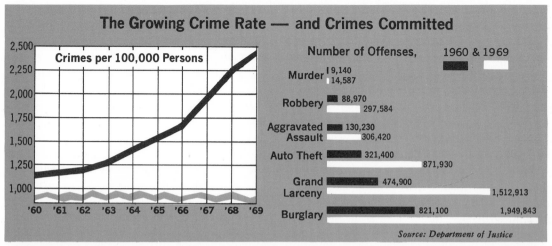

Crimes per 100,000 Persons

2,500 | 2,250 | 2,000 | 1,750 | 1,500 | 1,250 | 1,000

'60 '61 '62 '63 '64 '65 '66 '67 '68 '69

Number of Offenses, 1960 & 1969

Offense	1960	1969
Murder	9,140	14,587
Robbery	88,970	297,584
Aggravated Assault	130,230	306,420
Auto Theft	321,400	871,930
Grand Larceny	474,900	1,512,913
Burglary	821,100	1,949,843

Source: Department of Justice

The Prosecution of Felonies

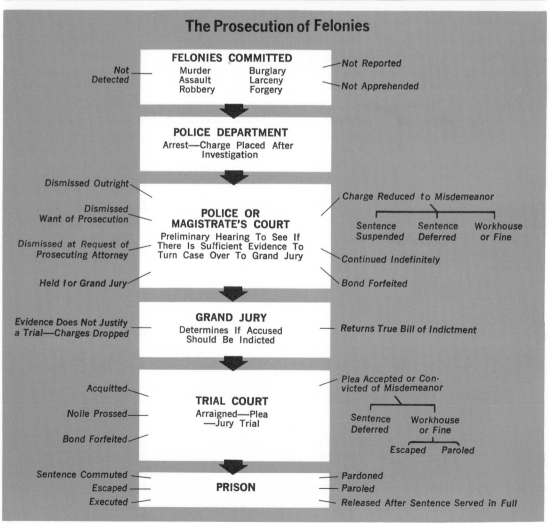

FELONIES COMMITTED
Murder   Burglary
Assault   Larceny
Robbery   Forgery

Not Detected — — Not Reported — Not Apprehended

POLICE DEPARTMENT
Arrest—Charge Placed After Investigation

Dismissed Outright — Charge Reduced to Misdemeanor
Dismissed Want of Prosecution
Dismissed at Request of Prosecuting Attorney

POLICE OR MAGISTRATE'S COURT
Preliminary Hearing To See If There Is Sufficient Evidence To Turn Case Over To Grand Jury

Sentence Suspended   Sentence Deferred   Workhouse or Fine
Continued Indefinitely
Held for Grand Jury — Bond Forfeited

GRAND JURY
Determines If Accused Should Be Indicted

Evidence Does Not Justify a Trial—Charges Dropped — Returns True Bill of Indictment

TRIAL COURT
Arraigned—Plea —Jury Trial

Acquitted — Plea Accepted or Convicted of Misdemeanor
Nolle Prossed
Bond Forfeited

Sentence Deferred   Workhouse or Fine
Escaped   Paroled

PRISON

Sentence Commuted — Pardoned
Escaped — Paroled
Executed — Released After Sentence Served in Full

conducted by the prosecuting attorney.[10] The clerk of the court reads the indictment or presentment to the defendant, who pleads "guilty" or "not guilty." If he pleads guilty and is of a sound mind, the judge usually pronounces sentence in accordance with the State law, and the case ends. But if he pleads not guilty, he is entitled to a trial by jury if he so desires. In most States a defendant may waive his right to trial by jury in at least some felony cases; in such instances, the judge hears and decides the case. If a defendant cannot afford an attorney, the judge appoints one to act as his counsel.

There are usually about twice as many persons summoned as are needed for the jury. When the court meets, however, the counsel for the accused and the prosecutor may challenge a certain number, which is limited by law, without giving any cause, and the judge will excuse such prospective jurors.[11] The counsel for the accused and the prosecutor may also challenge any prospective juror for cause; that is, for any reason which indicates the juror may not be impartial—for example, for holding a preconceived opinion as to the innocence or guilt of the accused or being related to the accused, the victim of the crime, or witnesses who are to give testimony. If so many prospective jurors are challenged that there are not a sufficient number to make up a jury, the judge may have the sheriff summon bystanders (*talesmen*) in some States. But in other States a new jury list must be prepared as the former was, and this procedure must continue until the prescribed number of suitable jurors is *impaneled;* that is, secured to serve.

After the jury is impaneled, the case is opened with the reading of the indictment, unless waived by the defense. The prosecutor, the State's attorney, then makes an opening statement setting forth the points that the State intends to prove. Following this, the counsel for the accused may make an opening statement or may wait until it is his turn to present the accused's defense. The prosecutor then presents the State's case by calling witnesses to give testimony. These witnesses are subject not only to examination by the prosecutor but to cross-examination by the defense counsel.

After the State has rested its case—called all of its witnesses—the bench will entertain motions. Usually the defense counsel will call for a *directed verdict;* that is, a dismissal of the charge on the ground that the prosecutor has failed to prove his case. If such a motion

---

[10] For a great many acts an accused person may be prosecuted criminally by the State because he has injured the community generally; he may also be sued in a civil action by another person because that person himself has been injured by the action which gave rise to the crime.

[11] Such challenges are known as peremptory challenges. In general, the procedures followed in impaneling a jury in a criminal case are also followed in the providing of a jury to hear a civil case; see page 662. In an important recent case (*Witherspoon* v. *Illinois,* 1968), the U.S. Supreme Court held that in capital cases the death sentence cannot be carried out if the jury which imposed or recommended it was chosen by excluding prospective jurors who voiced general objections to capital punishment or had religious or conscientious scruples against it. The defendant had been convicted of murdering a policeman and the jury had set the death penalty. A large number of prospective jurors had been successfully challenged because of their opposition to the death penalty. Said the Court: "Whatever else might be said of capital punishment, it is at least clear that its imposition by a hanging jury cannot be squared with the Constitution. The State of Illinois has stacked the deck against the petitioner. To execute this death sentence would be to deprive him of his life without due process of law."

is granted, the charge is dropped, and the accused is set free. Normally, however, the judge denies such a motion, and the defense counsel must then present the case for the accused. He calls witnesses to give testimony in behalf of the defendant. Like the witnesses for the State, they are subject to both examination and cross-examination. The defendant may, but is not compelled, to testify in his own behalf. After the defense has rested its case, first the prosecutor and then the defense counsel present their *summations* — their final arguments to the jury.

After final arguments, the judge instructs the jury as to the law relevant to the case. The jury then retires to consider the evidence in the case and arrive at a decision. If after reasonable deliberation the jury cannot agree, the foreman reports "no agreement." If the requisite number agree, usually all in a criminal case, he reports "guilty" or "not guilty." If guilty, the jury usually determines the punishment in its verdict,[12] which is read by the clerk of the court. The judge then pronounces the sentence.

If the penalty is merely a fine, this is paid to the clerk of the court. If the penalty is more than a fine, however, the sheriff takes charge of the defendant, who is taken to jail to serve his term, or until he can be transferred to the penitentiary for internment or execution in accordance with the sentence. If there has been a disagreement — a "hung jury" — the case is either set for a new trial or it is dismissed.

If the verdict has been "guilty," the defendant may petition for an appeal to a higher court on the grounds that the verdict is not according to the law, to the evidence, or that some error has been committed in the trial. If the appeal is granted and is sustained, the higher court will order the lower court to hold a new trial; if no error is found, the appeal is dismissed and the lower court order stands.

---

[12] In many States the judge determines the punishment after the jury has determined the guilt.

IMPROVING JUDICIAL PROCEDURES

Society has come a long way in the administration of justice from the "trial by ordeal" common in the Middle Ages. Then, a person accused of crime was subjected to various forms of physical torture. If he emerged uninjured, he was judged innocent of the crime with which he had been charged.

There are still many things about our judicial procedures that are in need of reform, however. For example, most State court systems lack any particular plan of organizational unity; that is, the structure is often "jerry-built" with much overlapping and lack of cooperation between the minor, general trial, and intermediate courts. When New Jersey rewrote its State constitution, the judiciary was completely reorganized to meet this criticism. That State now has only three levels of courts: the supreme court, superior courts, and county courts, all organized into a unified court system. See page 659.

Another criticism often heard centers around the delay and the cost in obtaining justice. As a common example of what this can mean, take the case of a man severely injured in an automobile accident. He is often forced to settle his claim against the other party out of court and at a much lower figure than he could win in a suit. Why? Because he must support his family and pay his bills like anyone else. He can't afford to wait for a year, eighteen months, or even longer until the case comes to trial to win a court award.

Court costs and attorneys' fees make the administration of justice expensive. Persons of moderate means often ˙cannot afford to appeal a case, even though they feel they have been denied justice in a lower court. Public defender offices and legal aid societies have been established in some States and in many larger cities and counties to provide counsel to those unable to afford it otherwise.

Courts *must* insist on precise and exact procedures in order to give the accused every benefit of a fair trial. Occasionally, however, this may be carried to ridiculous extreme. In a case in Texas, for example, a man admitted drowning his wife and son. But his conviction and death sentence were reversed on appeal because the indictment was faulty — it did not state that the drownings had taken place *in water!* He was retried three times and finally found guilty and sentenced to life. Similar instances can be cited in practically every State.

Achieving reform in judicial procedures is frequently an extremely difficult task. Often, the general public is unaware of or, at best, apathetic toward the need. In many States the detailed rules are provided by the State legislature in the form of statutes; thus, to secure reforms it is necessary to secure legislative action.

Fortunately, several of the States have recognized the need to adapt procedures to changing circumstances in recent years. Slightly over half of the States now vest at least some rule-making authority in the courts themselves; in a few States — Idaho, Illinois, and North Carolina, for example — the supreme court has been given virtually complete authority to provide rules of procedure for all courts in the State judicial system.

Judicial Councils are now found in about three-fourths of the States. Some are much more active than others. Among the most active are those in California, Connecticut, Kansas, Michigan, New York, and Texas They are usually composed of one or more supreme court justices, judges from the lower courts, the State's attorney general, legislators, and professors of law.

The Judicial Council usually gathers information, makes studies of particular judicial problems, and recommends needed legislation. In a few States, like California, it has wider powers — for example, to make rules of procedure, transfer judges to courts with crowded dockets, and coordinate the work of all the courts in the State judicial system.

✳✳✳✳✳✳✳✳✳✳✳ CONCEPT BUILDING ✳✳✳✳✳✳✳✳✳✳✳

Key Concepts

The basic function of courts is to hear and decide cases. They apply several forms of law: constitutional, statutory, administrative, equity, and common law.

Common law is judge-made law which has evolved over centuries from precedents built upon custom and usage. Equity developed alongside the common law to provide remedies not available under common law. Equity is preventive while common law is remedial, dealing with matters after they have happened.

Civil suits involve private parties (and occasionally governmental units) in disputes over their respective legal rights and duties. In criminal cases, the government is always involved as the prosecutor of one charged with a crime. There are two types of civil procedure — suits at law and suits in equity.

A crime is any act which is considered so dangerous to society that it is prohibited by law and punishment is provided for its commission. Crimes are of two classes: misdemeanors and felonies.

There is much room and need for improvement in our judicial procedures. Some of the most pressing problems revolve about delay, cost, complex organization, and overzealousness.

Important Terms

bail	deposition	Judicial Council	statutory law
chancery	directed verdict	misdemeanor	suit at law
civil suit	equity	opening statement	suit in equity
common law	felony	precedent	summation
crime	hung jury	preliminary	talesman
criminal code	injunction	public defender	verdict
decree	instructions	*stare decisis*	warrant

Questions for Inquiry and Review

1. What basic function do courts perform?

2. What various forms of law do State courts apply?

3. How did the common law originate? How did it develop? Why did it come to be known as the *common* law?

4. Which takes precedence in case of conflict: common law or statutory law?

5. What term is synonymous with the term equity?

6. Why did the system of equity develop?

7. What is probably the most important difference between common law and equity?

8. Is government ever involved as a party to a civil suit? A criminal case?

9. Would a case in which one person is attempting to prevent another from doing something be a suit at law or a suit in equity?

10. What particular fact determines whether or not a particular action is a crime?

11. Crimes are of what two degrees? Generally, what is the distinction between the two?

12. May a private person make a lawful arrest in any situation in which a peace officer is authorized to do so?

13. What is the chief purpose of a preliminary hearing in a felony case?

14. What is the purpose of bail?

15. Who draws up bills of indictment to present to the grand jury?

16. What is the major function of a grand jury?

17. What is the major function of a trial (or petit) jury?

18. By whom is the law governing a criminal case decided?

19. Why are reforms in judicial procedure often difficult to accomplish?

20. What are the usual functions of a Judicial Council?

For Further Inquiry

1. In 1970, the death penalty had been abolished altogether by nine States: Alaska, Hawaii, Iowa, Maine, Michigan, Minnesota, Oregon, West Virginia, and Wisconsin. In New York it may be imposed only for the killing of a peace officer or the slaying of a guard or another inmate by a prisoner attempting to escape; in North Dakota for murder committed by a life-term convict or for treason; in Rhode Island for murder committed by a life-term convict; and in Vermont for a second murder or slaying a peace officer. Why would you favor the abolition of capital punishment in all States? Would you favor abolition of the death penalty for some but not all crimes?

2. Are crimes more likely to be prevented by the severity of the punishments imposed or by the certainty of punishment?

3. Would you consider it extravagant for a State to spend $100,000 to apprehend a murderer and bring him to justice? A kidnapper? A petty thief? A reckless driver?

4. In a growing number of communities throughout the country high school students

are being given responsibility for setting the punishment of their fellow students who violate traffic laws. Phoenix, Arizona, has had such a program since 1958. Under the Phoenix plan, students charged with traffic violations have the choice of appearing before a jury of their fellow students or before regular juvenile court. The student juries are composed of fourteen jurors, two from each of the seven high schools in the Phoenix district. As many as 1000 students comprise the jury panel. The work of the student juries is supervised by the judge of the juvenile court who directs the entire program. The student juries have power to order suspension of a driver's license for as long as twenty-nine days, to refer the case to the State Department of Motor Vehicles for State suspension of a driver's license for as long as one year, and to order a student to attend a four-hour session of the teenage driver

correction clinic. If a violator refuses to accept the manner in which a student jury disposes of his case, the matter is automatically referred to the city's juvenile court. What do you think of the Phoenix program? Should such a program be adopted in your community?

5. Why may it be said with good reason that the prosecution and punishment of crime by government is a civilized substitute for personal vengeance?

6. In *Olmstead* v. *United States,* 1928, the Supreme Court, in a 5–4 decision, held that the 4th Amendment does not bar wiretapping or the use of evidence gained by the practice. Do you agree or disagree with the following sentiment expressed by Justice Oliver Wendell Holmes, Jr., in his dissenting opinion, ". . . for my part I think it a less evil that some criminals should escape than that the government should play an ignoble part"?

Suggested Activities

1. Attend a session of a local court and report to the class on the procedures employed.

2. Invite a judge, prosecuting attorney, or criminal lawyer to address the class on court procedures and their importance.

3. Hold a moot court session, re-enacting the actual steps of a real trial.

4. Write a report on a prominent court case being reported in the newspapers.

5. Stage a debate or class forum on the question: *Resolved,* That the State should provide the necessary funds to any person accused of a felony to insure that person's obtaining adequate defense.

Suggested Reading

ADRIAN, CHARLES R., *State and Local Governments.* McGraw-Hill, 1967. Chapter 17.

"Crimes While On Bail—The Hunt For a Remedy," *U.S. News,* February 17, 1969.

DYE, THOMAS R., *Politics in States and Communities.* Prentice-Hall, 1969. Chapter 7.

HAMMER, RICHARD, "The Case That Could End Capital Punishment," *New York Times Magazine,* October 12, 1969.

KING, LARRY L., "Warren Burnett: Texas Lawyer," *Harper's,* July, 1969.

LOCKARD, DUANE, *Governing the States and Localities.* Macmillan, 1969. Chapter 6.

"Prison System Breaking Down?" *U.S. News,* August 11, 1969.

"Pro and Con: The Question of Bail Reform," *Congressional Digest,* April, 1969.

SAMUELS, GERTRUDE, "A New Lobby: Ex-Cons," *New York Times Magazine,* October 19, 1969.

WILSON, JAMES Q. and VORENBERG, JAMES, "Is the Court Handcuffing the Cops?" *New York Times Magazine,* May 11, 1969.

WRIGHT, JUDGE J. SKELLY, "The Courts Have Failed the Poor," *New York Times Magazine,* March 9, 1969.

40
FINANCING STATE AND LOCAL GOVERNMENT

✳✳✳ Should local governments be prohibited from maintaining any program which competes with private enterprise? Why?

✳✳✳ Should the property owned by private religious, educational, or charitable organizations be exempt from State or local taxation? Why?

✳✳✳ Why may a governmental budget be properly described as a significant statement of public policy?

A government ought to contain in itself every power requisite to the full accomplishment of the objects committed to its care, and to the complete execution of its trusts, free from every other control but a regard to the public good and to the sense of the people.

ALEXANDER HAMILTON

Government costs money. Certainly no one in the United States should have to be reminded of that fact today. Nor should anyone need to be told that government consumes vast sums of money in this country every year. It is an essential ingredient in virtually everything government does. As we noted at the beginning of Chapter 14—and as is evident throughout the pages of this book—no government can exist without it.

The High Cost of State and Local Government Today. Just as the cost of government at the national level has risen to astronomical heights over the past several years, so has its cost at the State and local levels. Today, the fifty States and their thousands of local governmental units take in and spend over $130,000,000,000 a year.

The States and their local governments spent less than $1,000,000,000 a year for *all* purposes at the turn of the century; that figure has increased by *over ninety times* over the past six decades. Even as recently as 1946, State

and local spending came to only slightly more than $14,000,000,000; in the past two decades it has risen more than *six-fold*. Even excluding local expenditures, a fourth of the States now spend more each year than the National Government spent in any year prior to World War I; and one city—New York, with an annual budget of more than $7,000,000,000— now spends fourteen times as much.

The rapid and continuing rise in State and local spending can be traced to one overriding cause: As our population has increased—and especially as it has become more and more concentrated in urban and suburban areas—the people of each State have demanded more and still more services from government. See page 693.

STATE AND LOCAL REVENUES

State tax collections now total more than $40,000,000,000 a year. The various local governments now take in a sum only slightly

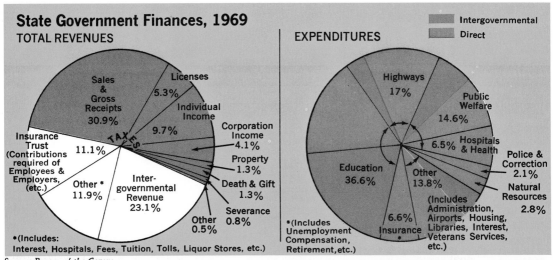

State Government Finances, 1969

TOTAL REVENUES

Sales & Gross Receipts 30.9%
Licenses 5.3%
Individual Income 9.7%
Corporation Income 4.1%
Property 1.3%
Death & Gift 1.3%
Severance 0.8%
Other 0.5%
Intergovernmental Revenue 23.1%
Other * 11.9%
Insurance Trust (Contributions required of Employees & Employers, etc.) 11.1%
TAXES

*(Includes: Interest, Hospitals, Fees, Tuition, Tolls, Liquor Stores, etc.)

EXPENDITURES

Intergovernmental
Direct

Highways 17%
Public Welfare 14.6%
Hospitals & Health 6.5%
Police & Correction 2.1%
Natural Resources 2.8%
Education 36.6%
Other 13.8% (Includes Administration, Airports, Housing, Libraries, Interest, Veterans Services, etc.)
Insurance * 6.6%

*(Includes Unemployment Compensation, Retirement, etc.)

Source: Bureau of the Census

State and Local Government Revenue and Expenditures

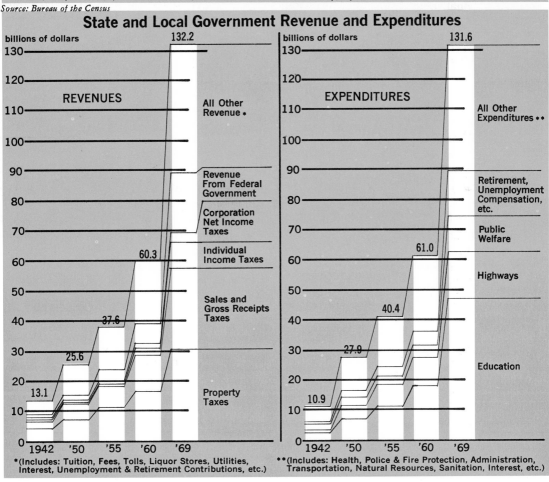

REVENUES

billions of dollars
132.2
130
120
110   All Other Revenue *
100
90   Revenue From Federal Government
80   Corporation Net Income Taxes
70   Individual Income Taxes
60.3
50   Sales and Gross Receipts Taxes
37.6
40
30
25.6
20
13.1   Property Taxes
10
0   1942 '50 '55 '60 '69

*(Includes: Tuition, Fees, Tolls, Liquor Stores, Utilities, Interest, Unemployment & Retirement Contributions, etc.)

EXPENDITURES

billions of dollars
131.6
130
120
110   All Other Expenditures **
100
90   Retirement, Unemployment Compensation, etc.
80
70   Public Welfare
61.0
60   Highways
50
40.4
40
30
27.9
20
10.9   Education
10
0   1942 '50 '55 '60 '69

**(Includes: Health, Police & Fire Protection, Administration, Transportation, Natural Resources, Sanitation, Interest, etc.)

under this amount annually. And the fifty States collect some $10,000,000,000 and their local units over $30,000,000,000 from various nontax sources each year, as well.

Taxes may be defined as charges imposed by a legislative body upon persons or property in order to raise money for public purposes. Taxes are the chief source for both State and local governmental income.

Limitations on State and Local Taxing Powers. A State's power to tax is an essential part of its reserved powers. It is, therefore, limited—at least in *legal* terms [1]—only by those restrictions contained in the National Constitution and its own State constitution. Local units acquire their taxing powers from their parent States—and are thus limited by State constitutional *and* statutory provisions as well as by the National Constitution.

Federal Limitations. Several important limitations on the taxing powers of State and local governments arise out of the Constitution of the United States.

(1) Interstate and Foreign Commerce. Article I, Section 10, Clause 2 of the Constitution provides that:

No State shall, without the consent of the Congress, lay any imposts or duties on imports or exports, except what may be absolutely necessary for executing its inspection laws; and the net produce of all duties and imposts, laid by any State on imports or exports, shall be for the use of the treasury of the United States; and all such laws shall be subject to the revision and control of the Congress.

And Clause 3 provides that:

No State shall, without the consent of Congress, lay any duty of tonnage, . . .[2]

In these two provisions the States are prohibited from taxing interstate and foreign commerce. And the Supreme Court has often held that, because the Constitution gives Congress the power to regulate interstate and foreign commerce, the States are generally prohibited from doing so. But they may and do impose taxes on property, even though it is used in commerce. For example, property taxes are often imposed upon railroad cars, steamships, airplanes, buses, taxicabs, and the like. See page 276.

(2) The National Government and Its Instrumentalities. As we have already seen, the States have been forbidden, ever since the Supreme Court's decision in *McCulloch* v. *Maryland,* 1819, to tax the National Government or any of its instrumentalities. As the eminent Chief Justice John Marshall said, "The power to tax involves the power to destroy."

The fact that the States and their local governments cannot tax federal property means that huge areas of land—for example, military reservations—cannot be taxed. The Congress, however, does appropriate money to be used to make "payments in lieu of taxes" ("lulu payments") to the States to make up for at least some of this. See pages 65, 72.

(3) The 14th Amendment. Two provisions in the 14th Amendment also limit the taxing powers of State and local governments. The Due Process Clause and the Equal Protection Clause read:

. . . nor shall any State deprive any person of life, liberty, or property, without due process of law, nor deny to any person within its jurisdiction the equal protection of the laws.

---

[1] The power may be, and regularly is, limited by a wide variety of "practical"—political and economic—considerations.

[2] *Tonnage* refers to a vessel's internal cubical capacity—how much it will hold—in tons of 100 cubic feet each. Tonnage duties are duties upon vessels in proportion to their capacity.

Essentially, the Due Process Clause requires that taxes: (1) be imposed and administered fairly, (2) not be so heavy as to actually confiscate (seize) property, and (3) be imposed only for a public purpose. As an illustration of a tax held to violate the Due Process Clause: Topeka, Kansas, once agreed to pay a sum of money to a manufacturer if he would locate his plant there. He did; but when the city levied a tax to pay the money promised, several taxpayers took the matter to court. The case eventually went to the Supreme Court of the United States which held the tax void, ruling that it had not been levied for a public purpose and was thus a denial of the taxpayers' property (their money) without due process of law.

The Equal Protection Clause forbids the making of *unreasonable* classifications for taxing purposes. Notice that most tax laws involve some form of classification; for example, an income tax is applied only to that class of persons who have income, a cigarette tax only to those who buy cigarettes, and a property tax only to those who own property. Of course, the Clause does not prevent these and similar classifications for they are reasonable ones. It does forbid tax classifications made on such bases as race, religion, nationality, political party membership, or similarly *unreasonable* factors, however. As an illustration, the Supreme Court once upheld as reasonable a Louisiana law which imposed a tax upon all manufacturers of sugar except those who refined the products of their own plantations. But a State could not thus tax Jews, Germans, Negroes, Republicans, or Catholics who manufacture sugar and exempt all others. Such classifications would be unreasonable ones.

The law in this area is extremely complicated, but the above illustrations should be enough to indicate the general nature of the 14th Amendment's limitations on the taxing powers of State and local governments.

State Constitutional Limitations. Beyond the limits imposed by the National Constitution, each State's own constitution limits the taxing powers of the State and its local governments in several ways. The limitations vary widely from State to State. Most State constitutions provide that taxes shall be uniform, that they be collected only within the geographic limits of the unit of government which levies the tax, and that there should be no arbitrary or unreasonable classifications.

Most State constitutions also exempt churches, schools, cemeteries, museums, and the like from taxation. Many fix a maximum property tax rate at so many mills [3] per dollar or at a certain percentage of market value. Some also prohibit the use of certain taxes—as, for example, a sales or an income tax.

As local units of government possess no independent powers, the only taxes they may impose are those the State permits them to levy. The States have been notoriously reluctant in the matter. Their constitutions and their legislatures have regularly restricted not only the kinds of taxes local units may impose but often the rates at which they may be levied, too. Even those units operating under home-rule charters [4] have been closely restricted in terms of their taxing powers. As metropolitan populations have continued to grow, so have their public service needs—and, thus, State limitations on local taxing powers pose a growing source of friction between cities and State legislatures throughout the country. [5] Of course, city and county charters commonly impose limitations on local taxing authority, too.

Principles of Sound Taxation. Practically any tax, taken by itself, can be shown to be an

---

[3] A *mill* is one-thousandth of a dollar, or one-tenth of a cent. Thus, for example, if the local property tax rate is fifty mills a man who owns property assessed at $1000 would pay a property tax of $50.

[4] On "home rule," see pages 722–723.

[5] Note that this is one of the many important areas in which the Supreme Court's "one-man, one-vote" decisions of recent years should have a telling impact; see pages 618–620.

TREADMILL. With the cost of governmental services rising sharply, the States are faced with the problem of raising new revenues. The most obvious source is new or increased taxes. (Ficklen, Dallas News)

unfair one. If all of the revenues of a government were to come from but one tax—such as a sales tax, an income tax, or a property tax—the tax system would be grossly unfair. It would hit some people much harder than others, and some not at all. Yet, each tax that is levied by a government should be defensible as *a part of* the *general* tax system, which aims at a fair taxation for all individuals.

Adam Smith's Canons. Nearly two hundred years ago, in his book *The Wealth of Nations,* the famous English economist Adam Smith laid down four principles of a sound tax system. Most tax experts today cite the same four:

1. The subjects of every state ought to contribute towards the support of the government, as nearly as possible, in proportion to their respective abilities; that is, in proportion to the revenue which they respectively enjoy under the protection of the state.

2. The tax which each individual is bound to pay ought to be certain and not arbitrary.

3. Every tax ought to be levied at the time, or in the manner, in which it is most likely to be convenient for the contributor to pay it.

4. Every tax ought to be so contrived as to take out and to keep out of the pockets of the people as little as possible over and above what it brings into the public treasury of the state.

Making any particular tax—let alone a tax system—fulfill these requirements of *equality, certainty, convenience,* and *economy* is an almost impossible task. But our problem at the State and the local level, and at the national level, is one of coming as close to these standards as possible in the interests of fairness to all.

Kinds of State and Local Taxes. Aside from the various limitations we have noted, each State may levy taxes as it sees fit. The State legislature determines what taxes the State will impose and their rates. It also determines what taxes the local governmental units—counties, cities, school districts, and the like—may levy.[6]

The General Property Tax. The general property tax is the chief source of income for local governments today. It now accounts for approximately eighty-five per cent of their tax revenues. Once the principal source of State income, it now brings in less than two per cent of all State tax revenues.

The general property tax is a direct tax levied on (1) *real property*—land, buildings, and improvements that go with the property if sold, or (2) *personal property*—either *tangible* or *intangible. Tangible personal property* includes all movable wealth which is visible and the value of which can be easily assessed—for example, farm implements, livestock, pianos, television sets, automobiles, and watches. Examples of *intangible personal property* include such things

---

[6] State constitutions sometimes grant certain taxing powers to local governments but, as we noted above, this is not common.

as stocks, bonds, mortgages, promissory notes, and bank accounts. Because intangibles can be hidden from the tax assessor more easily than tangibles, they are not taxed in some States, or they are taxed at a lower rate than real or tangible personal property.

The process of determining the value of the property to be taxed is known as *assessment*. The task is usually performed by a popularly elected county, township, or city assessor. Only in a handful of States must he be a trained specialist, and in those States he is usually appointed rather than elected. Most tax authorities believe that election is not likely to produce competent assessors; and elected assessors sometimes under-assess in order not to antagonize the voters upon whom they depend for their office.

Where personal property is taxed, the assessment is regularly made each year. Real property is usually assessed less often, commonly every second or fourth year. The assessor is expected to visit the property and examine it in order to determine its value. In practice the assessment is often made simply on the basis of the previous year's figures, which were arrived at the same way.

Property is usually assessed at less than its true market value. Most property owners seem better satisfied if the assessment is set at, say, one half of its real value. Thus, a house assessed at $10,000 may actually be worth $20,000. If the tax rate is set at forty mills (or four per cent) the tax will be $400. In reality, of course, this is the same thing as a twenty mills (or two per cent) tax on the $20,000 house.[7]

---

[7] Several reasons are advanced for assessing property at a fraction of its actual market value — none of them valid. Among them: the belief that full assessment means higher taxes; the wish to lessen the share of State or county taxes paid by an assessed area; political considerations, especially the desire of an assessor to be re-elected; the difficulty of making a fair full-value assessment.

If one person's property is assessed at a higher proportionate value than another's, there is usually some means by which the injustice may be corrected. Typically, complaints may be taken to a local board of equalization, to the county governing body (usually known as the county board of commissioners or supervisors), or to the courts. In many of the States the State tax commission or similar agency serves as a State board of equalization to see that assessments around the State are as fair and comparably equal as possible.

The property tax is usually collected by the same local officer who collects all other local taxes. In some States a tax bill is mailed to the property owner, but in others he must go to the tax collector's office to learn the amount of his tax. If the tax is not paid by a certain date, the owner is *delinquent*, and a small penalty is added to his tax. If the tax and penalty are not paid within a certain period, the property may be seized and sold for back taxes.

Three major arguments are commonly made in support of the use of a property tax: (1) because property is protected — and its value is often enhanced — by government it may logically be required to contribute to the support of government; (2) the rate at which the tax is levied may be readily adjusted to meet governmental needs; and (3) it is a dependable source of revenue.

Similarly, three major criticisms of the property tax are frequently heard: (1) the tax is not geared to ability to pay — where the amount of real property one owns may once have been a fair measure of one's wealth, it is not today; (2) it is all but impossible, even with the most competent of assessors, to assess all taxable property on a fair and equal basis; and (3) personal property, especially intangibles, is easily concealed from the assessor.

The Sales Tax. The sales tax ranks as the most important single source of State income. It now accounts for approximately sixty per cent of all State tax collections.

Amount of Sale	Tax	Amount of Sale	Tax	Amount of Sale	Tax
.19 thru .38	.01	18.19 " 18.38	.55	36.19 " 36.38	1.09
.39 " .78	.02	18.39 " 18.78	.56	36.39 " 36.78	1.10
.79 " 1.18	.03	18.79 " 19.18	.57	36.79 " 37.18	1.11
1.19 " 1.38	.04	19.19 " 19.38	.58	37.19 " 37.38	1.12
1.39 " 1.78	.05	19.39 " 19.78	.59	37.39 " 37.78	1.13
1.79 " 2.18	.06	19.79 " 20.18	.60	37.79 " 38.18	1.14
2.19 " 2.38	.07	20.19 " 20.38	.61	38.19 " 38.38	1.15
2.39 " 2.78	.08	20.39 " 20.78	.62	38.39 " 38.78	1.16
2.79 " 3.18	.09	20.79 " 21.18	.63	38.79 " 39.18	1.17
3.19 " 3.38	.10	21.19 " 21.38	.64	39.19 " 39.38	1.18
3.39 " 3.78	.11	21.39 " 21.78	.65	39.39 " 39.78	1.19
3.79 " 4.18	.12	21.79 " 22.18	.66	39.79 " 40.18	1.20
4.19 " 4.38	.13	22.19 " 22.38	.67	40.19 " 40.38	1.21
4.39 " 4.78	.14	22.39 " 22.78	.68	40.39 " 40.78	1.22
4.79 " 5.18	.15	22.79 " 23.18	.69	40.79 " 41.18	1.23
5.19 " 5.38	.16	23.19 " 23.38	.70	41.19 " 41.38	1.24
5.39 " 5.78	.17	23.39 " 23.78	.71	41.39 " 41.78	1.25
5.79 " 6.18	.18	23.79 " 24.18	.72	41.79 " 42.18	1.26
6.19 " 6.38	.19	24.19 " 24.38	.73	42.19 " 42.38	1.27
6.39 " 6.78	.20	24.39 " 24.78	.74	42.39 " 42.78	1.28
6.79 " 7.18	.21	24.79 " 25.18	.75	42.79 " 43.18	1.29
7.19 " 7.38	.22	25.19 " 25.38	.76	43.19 " 43.38	1.30
7.39 " 7.78	.23	25.39 " 25.78	.77	43.39 " 43.78	1.31
7.79 " 8.18	.24	25.79 " 26.18	.78	43.79 " 44.18	1.32
8.19 " 8.38	.25	26.19 " 26.38	.79	44.19 " 44.38	1.33
8.39 " 8.78	.26	26.39 " 26.78	.80	44.39 " 44.78	1.34
8.79 " 9.18	.27	26.79 " 27.18	.81	44.79 " 45.18	1.35
9.19 " 9.38	.28	27.19 " 27.38	.82	45.19 " 45.38	1.36
9.39 " 9.78	.29	27.39 " 27.78	.83	45.39 " 45.78	1.37
9.79 " 10.18	.30	27.79 " 28.18	.84	45.79 " 46.18	1.38
10.19 " 10.38	.31	28.19 " 28.38	.85	46.19 " 46.38	1.39
10.39 " 10.78	.32	28.39 " 28.78	.86	46.39 " 46.78	1.40
10.79 " 11.18	.33	28.79 " 29.18	.87	46.79 " 47.18	1.41
11.19 " 11.38	.34	29.19 " 29.38	.88	47.19 " 47.38	1.42
11.39 " 11.78	.35	29.39 " 29.78	.89	47.39 " 47.78	1.43
11.79 " 12.18	.36	29.79 " 30.18	.90	47.79 " 48.18	1.44

This tax chart is used by retailers in Massachusetts to help figure how much tax the consumer must pay on taxable items. The retailer collects the three per cent sales tax and turns the receipts over to the State.

A sales tax may be either general or selective in form. A *general sales tax* is one that is applied to the sale (and paid by the purchaser) of most commodities. A *selective sales tax* is one that is applied only to the sale (and paid by the purchaser) of certain commodities — such as tobacco, liquor, or gasoline.

Forty-five States [8] now impose a general sales tax, and the rates levied by them vary from two per cent to as high as six per cent of the sale price.

In some States the sales tax applies to *all* sales — wholesale as well as retail, but commonly it is applied only at the retail level.

---

[8] All except Alaska, Delaware, Montana, New Hampshire, and Oregon. Each of these States does impose various selective sales taxes, however.

Most of the sales tax States exempt certain items — such as bread or milk or all foods, produce sold directly by the farmer to the consumer, newspapers, or sales under a certain amount.

To prevent the evasion of the sales tax by residents who make purchases outside the State — that is, in a State without a sales tax — States using the sales tax commonly impose a *use tax* on articles bought elsewhere. Thus, Washington imposes a use tax on any newly-purchased article valued at $20 or more brought into the State by a resident; if a resident of Washington buys an automobile in Oregon, the State will not grant a license until the use tax is paid. Iowa holds mail-order houses outside the State, as well as those within, responsible for the collection of its sales tax on all goods sold to Iowa residents.

In most States the sales tax is collected by the retailer as he makes each taxable sale — that is, from his customers as they purchase taxable items from him. The retailer keeps a record of the amount he collects and turns the receipts over to the State at regular intervals. In some States — Illinois, for example — the retailer pays the tax periodically on his total (gross) sales; of course, in these States — where the sales tax is sometimes known as a *gross receipts tax* — the retailer figures the tax into the price he charges for his goods.

Each of the fifty States now (1970) levies a selective sales tax on gasoline and other motor fuels, alcoholic beverages, insurance policies, and cigarettes and other tobacco products. A number of other items are also very common targets for selectives sales taxes among the States today — for example, hotel and motel accommodations, restaurant meals, soft drinks, parimutuel betting, theater and other amusement tickets, and automobiles.

The sales tax is so widely used among the States especially because: (1) it is relatively easy for the States to collect and (2) it is a fairly dependable revenue producer. But, notice, it is a *regressive* tax — that is, it is not geared to ability to pay and falls most heavily upon those with lower incomes. A sales tax law, in effect, makes the merchant a tax collector for the State; some who oppose this form of taxation do so in part because of the inconvenience and added overhead that necessarily results from this fact.

Because the sales tax does provide a steady return, several larger cities, many smaller ones, and even some counties now also levy general or selective sales taxes.

The Income Tax. The income tax—levied on individuals and on corporations—yields over twenty per cent of State tax revenues today. Forty of the States now levy an individual income tax while forty-three employ a corporation income tax.[9]

The *individual income tax* rates are usually *progressive*—that is, the higher the income the higher the tax. The rates in most States vary from one or two per cent on the lower incomes to as much as nine or ten per cent. Various deductions are allowed in figuring taxable income; about half of the States now provide that one's taxable income for State purposes is that which he reports on his federal return.

The *corporation income tax* rates are uniform, a certain fixed percentage of income, in most of the States which have the tax. A few States fix their rates on the graduated (progressive) basis.

The progressive income tax is held by many to be the fairest possible form of taxation as it may be closely geared to the ability to pay. If the rates are too high, however, the tax discourages incentive, and incentive is essential to the success of our private enterprise system. The high federal income tax rates force the States to keep their rates relatively low.

Some cities also levy a small income tax. But city income taxes will never be significant revenue producers unless the federal and State rates are drastically lowered. The prospects for this are dim, indeed.

Inheritance or Estate Taxes. Every State except Nevada levies inheritance or estate taxes—so-called "death taxes." As we indicated on page 260, an *inheritance tax* is one levied on the beneficiary's share of an estate, and an *estate tax* is one levied directly on the full estate itself.

Whichever the State has, an inheritance or an estate tax, the rate is progressive—the larger the amount involved the higher the tax. The inheritance tax is also *collateral*—that is, the more distant the relationship between the deceased and the heir the higher the rate. Thus, a husband's or wife's share would be taxed at a much lower rate than, say, a cousin's share or the share of someone not related to the deceased. Several States also impose *gift taxes,* as does the Federal Government.

Business Taxes. A wide variety of business taxes, in addition to the corporation income tax, are imposed in all States and are an important source of revenue.

Capital Stock Taxes. Capital Stock taxes are taxes levied on the assessed valuation of the total shares of stock issued by a business concern. Once used by all States, such taxes have now been abandoned by most in favor of the corporation income tax. A few States still impose both taxes, however.

Severance Taxes. Twenty-nine States [10] today impose severance taxes—levies on the

---

[9] The States with *neither* type of income tax today (1970) are Florida, Nevada, Ohio, Texas, Washington, and Wyoming; the State of New Hampshire has *only* the individual income tax; Connecticut, Pennsylvania, Rhode Island, and South Dakota have *only* the corporation tax.

[10] Alabama, Alaska, Arkansas, California, Colorado, Florida, Idaho, Indiana, Kansas, Kentucky, Louisiana, Michigan, Minnesota, Mississippi, Missouri, Montana, Nebraska, Nevada, New Hampshire, New Mexico, North Dakota, Oklahoma, Oregon, South Dakota, Texas, Utah, Virginia, Wisconsin, Wyoming.

removal of such "natural products as timber, fish, oil, gas, and other minerals from the land or water."

License Taxes. All States require corporations to pay a license tax for the privilege of doing business in the State. Certain kinds of businesses, especially chain stores, amusement houses, bars and taverns, and transportation lines, must also have an additional license to operate. Then, too, individuals who wish to engage in certain occupations must have a license. Most or all of the States require licenses for doctors, lawyers, dentists, morticians, barbers, hairdressers, plumbers, engineers, chauffeurs, psychiatrists, and a host of others. More and more, local governments are requiring the payment of various business license taxes.

License taxes other than for business purposes are levied in all States today and are a very significant revenue source. The most important of these are the ones required for motor vehicles and motor vehicle operators. All States also issue hunting and fishing licenses, and most also require permits to sell alcoholic beverages.

Documentary and Stock Transfer Taxes. Twenty of the States [11] have levies known as documentary and stock transfer taxes. These are taxes imposed on the recording, registering, and transferring of such documents as mortgages, deeds, and securities.

Poll Taxes. Only five States [12] now levy a poll tax—a head or capitation tax; in effect, a tax on the privilege of living and breathing. As we noted on page 152, the poll tax was once widely employed as a suffrage qualification among the Southern States; it was finally abandoned by the last four of those States (Alabama, Mississippi, Texas, and Virginia) in 1966.

Other Taxes. A variety of other taxes are imposed among the States and by their local units. Thus, more than half of the States levy amusement taxes and several of them also allow their local governments to do so. Theater-admission taxes are widely found—but television has long since cut their production sharply. About half of the States tax admission to horse and dog races—but they derive a greater amount of revenue from taxes laid on the wagers made at such events.

Such privately-owned public utilities as telephone, electric light, and gas systems are widely taxed—and are an especially important source of city revenue.

Payroll taxes produce a huge sum—about $8,000,000,000—among the fifty States today. But these taxes produce revenue held in trust funds for such social welfare programs as unemployment compensation, accident, and retirement systems. See pages 260–261.

State-Local Tax Sharing. The fact that the various States tax so many different sources of revenue makes it impractical for their local governments to tap many of them. More and more, States are sharing with their local units portions of various taxes as they are collected or through appropriations by the legislatures. For example, most States do this with the revenues from gasoline taxes and motor vehicle licenses. Where this is done, the State has a good opportunity to apportion the money on condition that local governments use it for certain purposes—school systems, road building and maintenance, police protection, and the like—according to standards set by the States.

Nontax Revenues. The States and their local governments now collect over $40,000,000,000 a year from a wide range of nontax sources.

Federal Grants-in-Aid. Federal grants to both levels now account for more than $20,000,000,000 of these nontax funds. As

[11] Alabama, Delaware, Florida, Hawaii, Kentucky, Maryland, Massachusetts, Minnesota, Nebraska, New Hampshire, New York, Oklahoma, Pennsylvania, Rhode Island, South Carolina, Tennessee, Texas, Virginia, Washington, West Virginia.

[12] Alaska, Maine, New Hampshire, Virginia, West Virginia.

In many of our States toll roads bring in a substantial portion of State highway funds. Some of these highway funds, supplemented by federal grants, are used by the States to build and improve the Interstate Highway System, a vast network of limited access highways spanning the nation. (Photo on the left by Talbot Lovering; photo on the right, Bureau of Public Roads)

we noted on pages 71–72, these grants-in-aid are made for well over 100 different purposes—for everything from prenatal and maternity care to old-age assistance.

Government-operated Businesses. Each of the States and many of their local governments receive a handsome return from a large number of different publicly-operated business enterprises. Toll bridges and toll roads are found in many parts of the country. Several States—most notably Washington—are in the ferry business. North Dakota markets a flour sold under the brand-name "Dakota-Maid." Milwaukee produces and sells a plant fertilizer, "Milorganite." California operates a short railway line in San Francisco.

Eighteen States are in the liquor-dispensing business, selling it through State-operated stores.[13] For several years, Oregon and Washington jointly owned a distillery in the State of Kentucky and marketed its product in their stores.

Many cities own and operate their water, electric power, and bus transportation systems. Some cities operate farmer's markets and rent space in office buildings, warehouses, and housing projects, own and operate dams and wharves, and so on.

---

[13] Alabama, Idaho, Iowa, Maine, Michigan, Mississippi, Montana, New Hampshire, North Carolina, Ohio, Oregon, Pennsylvania, Utah, Vermont, Virginia, Washington, West Virginia, and Wyoming. North Carolina's stores are operated by the counties; Wyoming's liquor monopoly operates only at the wholesale level.

The profits from these businesses go toward the support of the governments which own them.

Other nontax sources include such things as court fines, the sale or leasing of public lands, the interest received on State investments, and similar items. In 1963, New Hampshire established the nation's first legal lottery since 1894, and New York followed suit in 1967.

Borrowing. Borrowing may be classed as a source of nontax revenue; but, as the loans must be repaid, this source is hardly in the same category with other nontax revenues.

States and their local governments often must borrow money for unusually large undertakings, such as public buildings, bridges and highways, or a veterans bonus, that cannot be paid for out of current revenues.

The borrowing is most often done through the issuing of bonds, as is federal borrowing. See page 371. Occasionally, States and local governments do receive direct loans from banks or other lenders, but this is not common.

State and local bonds are easy to market because the interest from them is not taxed. That is, they are easy to market if the credit rating of the particular government is good.

Many State and local governments have, in times past, borrowed so heavily that they had to default on their debts. Thus, most State constitutions very strictly limit the power to borrow. A ceiling is usually placed on the total governmental debt; the denominations in which bonds may be issued, repayment schedules, and interest rates are often prescribed; and other minute details of borrowing are spelled out in the constitution.

The total State debts now amount to more than $35,000,000,000 and all local governments now owe about $85,000,000,000.

STATE BUDGET SYSTEMS

Since California and Wisconsin led the way in 1911, every State has adopted some form of a budget system—some arrangement for the planned and effective control of the use of the State's money and property.

Before the adoption of budget systems, the appropriations made by a legislature and the expenditures made by the various State agencies were handled in a most haphazard manner. More often than not, the separate agencies would appear before the legislature's appropriations committees in a dog-eat-dog battle with one another.

No single official or agency in the executive branch was familiar with the entire business of the State. No official or agency reviewed the needs of the various departments of the government, cut them down where necessary, measured them against the funds on hand and the estimated revenues, and then presented a rounded and carefully prepared financial program to the legislature.

Proposals to spend money came forward every year by the thousands. Typically, their chances of adoption were not in proportion to their merit, but rather to the political influences behind them. When the legislature adjourned, no one had any real idea how much had been appropriated or for what. Local pressures, logrolling, and favoritism were all too common. Extravagance, graft, and debt were inevitable.

In several States, the governor was given the power to veto specific items in appropriations bills. All too often, however, this simply meant that the legislature appropriated millions more than there was either revenue or need for. Responsibility was passed to the governor, who then had to reduce appropriations or not, as he saw fit.

Budget Systems Today. Now every State has some sort of budget system. Of course, the systems vary widely from State to State, and some are much more effective than others. There are two fairly distinct types of systems in use today:

(1) Board or Commission Budget. The budget is prepared by a budget board or commission

in six States [14] today (1970). Typically, the agency is composed of the governor, one or two other executive officials, and a few key legislators. Thus, in South Carolina it is prepared by the Budget and Control Board which is made up of the Governor, the Treasurer, the Comptroller General, the Chairman of the Senate Finance Committee, and the Chairman of the House Ways and Means Committee.

(2) Executive Budget. The other forty-five States make the governor responsible for the overall preparation of the budget. In most of these States he is assisted by a budget director and the professional staff of a budget agency.

The budget, by whomever framed, is always drawn up to cover a particular period. In most States this means a fiscal period of two years. Most States' budgets are based on a fiscal biennium because most legislatures meet in regular sessions only every other year.

Steps in the Budget Process. Each of the following six steps is involved in the budget-making process. The more effectively each is followed, the better the budget system.

(1) The preparation of the estimates of probable revenues and the funds needed by each agency of the government.

(2) The review of each agency's estimates by a central budget office staffed by fiscal experts.

(3) The collecting of the revised estimates and all supporting information into a consolidated financial program (budget) for presentation (usually by the governor) to the legislative body.

(4) A thorough consideration of the budget and the appropriation of needed funds and enactment of necessary revenue measures by the legislature.

(5) Careful supervision of the actual execution of the budget as approved by the legislature.

(6) An independent check (post-audit) on the execution of the budget.

---

[14] Arkansas, Florida, Indiana, Mississippi, South Carolina, and Texas.

PATTERN OF EXPENDITURES

At the beginning of the chapter we commented on the high rate of State and local government spending today—of more than $120,000,000,000 a year. We also noted the sharp rise in the rate of spending in recent years —now more than six times what it was only twenty years ago.

Although there are several reasons for this spectacular increase, three must be singled out as the major ones; (1) the steady and rapid growth of our population; obviously, the more people government must serve the higher must be the cost; (2) the effects of inflation, which have been reflected in governmental finance just as they have in the cost of living for individuals; and (3) increased demands for governmental services. Of the three, the latter reason is by far the most important. The States and their local governments have been asked to do more in recent years than ever before. As the people have demanded more and more services, the inevitable result has been a sharp rise in the cost of government.

Expenditures by Purpose. State and local governments spend money for so many purposes that it would be next to impossible to list them all. Nationwide, four functions stand out as the most costly; education, highways, public welfare, and public health and hospital programs. They account for over three-fourths of all State and local spending, or about $90,000,000,000 today.

Of the four, education is by far the most costly. Each year the States now spend more than $24,000,000,000 and their local units spend some $30,000,000,000 on this one function alone. The States spend more than $12,000,000,000 and local governments some $5,000,000,000 for highways. Public welfare costs are now more than $8,000,000,000 at the State level and more than $5,000,000,000 at the local level annually. And each level of government now spends some $4,000,000,000 on public health and hospital programs.

The balance of State and local spending, something over $30,000,000,000 a year, goes for such items as the protection of persons and property, debt interest and repayment, the development and conservation of natural resources, recreational facilities, correctional institutions, public housing, and general government.

CONCEPT BUILDING

Key Concepts

Money is just as essential to the existence of government at the State and local levels as it is to the National Government; and, just as the cost of government at the national level has increased markedly in the past few decades, so has the cost of State and local government.

The States and their local units today collect and spend above $120,000,000,000 a year. State tax collections now total approximately $40,000,000,000 a year and those of their local governments reach close to that figure. Both State and local governments also receive some $40,000,000,000 from various nontax sources.

Taxes are charges imposed by a legislative body upon persons or property to raise money for public purposes. The canons of sound taxation center around the four concepts of equality, certainty, convenience, and economy.

The United States Constitution, each State constitution, State laws, and city and county charters impose a wide variety of limits on State and local taxing powers.

The principal State and local tax sources include the property tax, the general and selective sales tax, the individual and corporation income tax, the inheritance or estate tax, and various business taxes and license taxes.

Nontax revenues come especially from federal grants-in-aid, government-operated businesses, and such other sources as court fines and the sale or leasing of public lands.

Borrowing, which is subject to strict limitations in most States, is only in a sense a nontax source of revenue.

Each State now has a budget system for the planned and more or less effective control of State finances. There are two fairly distinct types of budget systems: board or commission budget and the executive budget. The budget-making process involves six steps: preparation of estimates, review of estimates, consolidation and presentation of the budget, consideration and adoption of the budget, execution of the budget, and a post audit.

Three factors are chiefly responsible for the spectacular increase in State and local expenditures: population increase, inflation, and (especially) the demand for more and more governmental services. Approximately three-fourths of all State and local spending today goes for: education, highways, public welfare, and public health and hospitals. Of these, education is by far the most costly.

Important Terms

Adam Smith's canons	equalization	nontax revenue	selective sales tax
assessment	general sales tax	personal property	severance tax
budget system	intangible property	property tax	tangible property
collateral tax	license taxes	real property	tonnage
confiscatory	mill	regressive tax	use tax

Questions for Inquiry and Review

1. Approximately how much do the States and their local governments take in and spend each year?

2. State tax collections now come to approximately how much annually? Local tax collections?

3. Approximately how much do State and local governments receive from nontax sources annually?

4. The United States Constitution places what four major restrictions upon the taxing powers of the States and their local units?

5. What is the essence of each of Adam Smith's four canons of sound taxation?

6. What tax is the chief source of income for local governments today?

7. What two classes of property are commonly subjected to property taxation?

8. By what process is property evaluated for tax purposes?

9. What arguments may be made for and against the property tax?

10. What tax is the chief source of tax revenue among the States today?

11. What is the difference between a general and a selective sales tax?

12. What arguments are commonly made for and against the sales tax?

13. What two types of income tax are levied by the States today?

14. Why is the income tax widely regarded as the fairest possible tax by most authorities in the field?

15. What is the difference between an inheritance and an estate tax?

16. Why do the States increasingly share their tax receipts with their local units?

17. What examples can you cite to illustrate the fact that the States and their local units receive huge sums of money from nontax sources?

18. Approximately how great is the total amount of State indebtedness today? Local government indebtedness?

19. Why is borrowing not a nontax source of revenue in the usual sense?

20. What is the purpose of a budget system?

21. What two fairly distinct types of State budget systems are in use today?

22. What are the six major steps in a State's budget-making process?

23. What are the three major causes for the increase in State and local spending in recent years? Which is *the* most significant?

24. What are the four most costly functions of State and local government?

For Further Inquiry

1. Until a gambling crackdown by State police, 95 slot machines in the town of Tallulah, Louisiana, provided the bulk of the revenues for the town and for Madison Parish (county). This income for the town and parish ran at about $150,000 a year. With this source Tallulah was able to levy property taxes as low as 70¢ for each $100 valuation (in contrast with a rate in New Orleans of about $10 per $100 for city and parish taxes).

With this revenue Tallulah (population 3000) was able to cover practically all of its operating expenses. The slot machines had also provided funds for nineteen new school buses, resurfacing of all Tallulah streets at a cost of $110,000, a $26,000 bridge, two football fields each costing about $50,000, a health building, several fire trucks, and a library.

Why would you favor or oppose permitting local governments to finance themselves in this manner?

2. Both the States and the National Government tax many of the same items: *e.g.,* income, gasoline, liquor, automobiles, cigarettes and other tobacco products, gambling, estates, and many others. What do you think of the proposal that the National Government alone collect these taxes and then refund an agreed portion to the States on the basis of population? If this were done, why would the rates on each item have to be the same throughout the country?

3. In fiscal 1968 the per capita State taxes collected (the average amount for every man, woman, and child in the State) ranged from $271 in Delaware and $312 in Hawaii down to $107 in New Hampshire. For all States and for the ten most populous, the per capita tax was:

All States	$183
California	243
New York	246
Pennsylvania	171
Illinois	158
Ohio	129
Texas	131
Michigan	216
New Jersey	135
Massachusetts	190
Florida	158

What explanations can you give for the great variations in per capita taxes State to State?

4. Why do you think that the quotation at the beginning of this Chapter was selected?

Suggested Activities

1. Invite your local tax officers to discuss their work with the class.

2. Stage a class debate or forum on the question: *Resolved,* That our State should abandon (or adopt) the sales tax.

3. Outline the provisions which are found in your State's constitution with regard to the regulation of both State and local finance.

4. Through the State Blue Book and by information obtained from State and local officers and others, discover the nature of your State and local taxing and budget systems. A series of class reports might be prepared here. From the same sources, discover how much your State and local governments spend each year and for what purposes. A series of charts might be made to illustrate the financial picture of your state and local government.

Suggested Reading

DYE, THOMAS R., *Politics in States and Communities.* Prentice-Hall, 1969. Chapter 17.

FESLER, JAMES W., *et al., The 50 States and Their Local Governments.* Knopf, 1967. Chapter 11.

"Growing Protest Against School Costs," *U.S. News,* October 20, 1969.

LOCKARD, DUANE, *Governing the States and Localities.* Macmillan, 1969. Chapter 1.

SHARKANSKY, IRA, *The Politics of Taxing and Spending.* Bobbs, Merrill, 1969.

"Should Churches Pay Taxes?" *U.S. News,* June 16, 1969.

U.S. Bureau of the Census, *Compendium of State Government Finances, 1969.* Government Printing Office, 1970.

"When A State Gets a 900-Million Dollar Windfall," *U.S. News,* September 22, 1969.

41

RURAL LOCAL GOVERNMENT

I believe that provincial institutions are useful to all nations, but nowhere do they appear to me to be more necessary than among a democratic people.... How can a populace unaccustomed to freedom in small concerns learn to use it temperately in great affairs?

ALEXIS DE TOCQUEVILLE

✳✳✳Why has governmental reform proceeded so slowly at the county level across the country?

✳✳✳Upon what factors should the geographic size of a local governmental unit depend?

✳✳✳Is the number of elected officials a useful measure of the democratic character of a particular governmental unit? Why?

✳✳✳Should the number of local governments in the United States be reduced? In your State?

We live in an age in which our people pay the closest attention to public affairs at the national level. A glance at the front page of any daily newspaper is enough to show why this is so: most of the vital and dramatic questions of the day, especially those relating to international peace and security, involve the powers and functions of the National Government. But the National Government is only one of the more than 80,000 units of government in this country. And, clearly, these other units deserve serious study, too.

While their concern might not encompass such matters of high policy as war and peace, these other governmental units do play very significant roles in the governmental system as well as in the everyday lives of all of us. In this and the next two chapters we shall consider those units of government often de-scribed as "closest to the people"—the tens of thousands of units at the local level. In Chapters 42 and 43 we shall turn to the more than 18,000 municipal governments across the country. In this chapter we focus on the more than 60,000 other local units: the 3040 counties, the 17,000-odd towns and townships, and the more than 42,000 special districts of local government.

COUNTIES

Nearly every part of the United States is located within some county. As the tables on pages 698 and 699 show, however, there are no organized counties in three States—Alaska, Connecticut, and Rhode Island—and some portions of other States which also lack organized county government.[1]

---

[1] Because these areas include several of the nation's major population centers—for example, Baltimore, New York, Philadelphia, and St. Louis—over eleven per cent of our population today is not served by any separately organized county government. In Louisiana the units that correspond to counties elsewhere are known as *parishes*.

UNITS OF GOVERNMENT IN THE UNITED STATES

Source: Census Bureau, *Census of Governments, 1967*

State	All Gov-ernmental Units [a]	Local Governments Except School Districts					School Districts
		Total	Counties	Munici-palities	Town-ships	Special Districts	
U.S., TOTAL	81,304	59,471	3,040	18,051	17,107 [b]	21,264	21,782
Alabama	797	677	67	359	—	251	119
Alaska	62	60	—	51	—	—	1
Arizona	395	152	14	62	—	76	242
Arkansas	1,253	850	75	423	—	352	402
California	3,865	2,625	57	400	—	2,168	1,239
Colorado	1,253	1,061	62	251	—	748	191
Connecticut	414	404	—	34	149	221	9
Delaware	171	120	3	52	—	65	50
District of Columbia	2	2	—	1	—	1	—
Florida	828	760	67	383	—	310	67
Georgia	1,204	1,009	159	512	—	338	194
Hawaii	20	19	3	1	—	15	—
Idaho	872	751	44	194	—	513	120
Illinois	6,454	5,103	102	1,256	1,432	2,313	1,350
Indiana	2,670	2,270	92	550	1,009	619	399
Iowa	1,803	1,324	99	945	—	280	478
Kansas	3,669	3,308	105	623	1,543	1,037	360
Kentucky	953	752	120	359	—	273	200
Louisiana	734	666	62	270	—	334	67
Maine	699	633	16	21	469	127	65
Maryland	362	361	23	151	—	187	—
Massachusetts	655	610	12	39	312	247	44
Michigan	2,905	1,969	83	522	1,254	110	935
Minnesota	4,185	2,902	87	850	1,817	148	1,282
Mississippi	784	622	82	268	—	272	161
Missouri	2,918	2,047	114	856	343	734	870
Montana	1,104	390	56	125	—	209	713
Nebraska	4,392	2.069	93	538	486	952	2,322
Nevada	147	129	17	17	—	95	17
New Hampshire	516	334	10	13	222	89	181
New Jersey	1,422	899	21	335	232	311	522
New Mexico	308	217	32	88	—	97	90
New York	3,486	2,569	57	616	931	965	916
North Carolina	753	752	100	437	—	215	—
North Dakota	2,758	2,219	53	357	1,378	431	538
Ohio	3,284	2,573	88	933	1,324	228	710
Oklahoma	1,774	813	77	522	—	214	960
Oregon	1,457	1,058	36	222	—	800	398
Pennsylvania	5,000	4,250	66	1,005	1,555	1,624	749
Rhode Island	110	106	—	8	31	67	3
South Carolina	562	453	46	259	—	148	108
South Dakota	3,511	1,526	64	306	1,050	106	1,984
Tennessee	792	777	94	297	—	386	14
Texas	3,448	2,139	254	884	—	1,001	1,308
Utah	446	405	29	213	—	163	40
Vermont	657	389	14	65	238	72	267
Virginia	376	375	96	231	—	48	—
Washington	1,653	1,306	39	267	63	937	346
West Virginia	456	400	55	225	—	120	55
Wisconsin	2,491	1,971	72	568	1,269	62	519
Wyoming	473	295	23	87	—	185	177

[a] Includes the National Government and the fifty States, not shown in distribution by type. [b] Includes "towns" in the six New England States, New York, and Wisconsin.

Counties serve almost entirely as judicial districts in the New England States, where *towns* perform most of the functions performed by counties elsewhere in the country. The functions of rural local government are shared by counties and *townships* in the States extending west from New York and New Jersey to the Dakotas, Nebraska, and Kansas. In the South and West, counties are the predominant units of local government in rural areas.

Chaotic Structure. County government in the United States has long been described as "the dark continent of American politics" — mainly because the average citizen knows little, and cares less, about the government of the county in which he lives despite its importance to him. It has often been said, also, that if county governments in the United States have any one principle of organization in common, it is that of confusion. In the typical county no one official can be identified as the chief administrator. Rather, governmental authority is scattered among a number of elected officials and boards, each largely independent of the others. Several of these officials and boards often have executive, legislative, and even judicial powers. As a result, it is seldom possible to fix the responsibility for lax or inefficient management or for inaction in county affairs.

In short, county government is in serious need of reform throughout the country. Fortunately, recent years have seen a slight trend in this direction. The reforms accomplished in a handful of counties in a few States — such as San Mateo, Santa Clara, and Sacramento in California; McMinn in Tennessee; Anne Arundel and Montgomery in Maryland; and Dade in Florida — offer hope for the future.

Number, Size, and Population of Counties. There are now (1970) 3040 counties in the nation. Among the States, they vary in number, from 0 in Alaska, Connecticut, and Rhode Island and 3 in Delaware to a high of 254 in Texas. San Bernardino County, California, is the largest, embracing 20,131 square miles. Arlington County, Virginia, is the smallest, embracing only 25 square miles. Counties also

---

AREAS LACKING COUNTY GOVERNMENT

Areas having certain types of county offices, but as part of another government (city, town, or State) —
Louisiana: Orleans Parish (New Orleans); East Baton Rouge Parish (Baton Rouge)
Massachusetts: Nantucket County (Town of Nantucket); Suffolk County (Boston)
New York: Bronx, Kings, New York, Queens, Richmond Counties (New York City)
Pennsylvania: Philadelphia County (Philadelphia)

Cities located outside of any county and administering functions elsewhere commonly performed by counties —
District of Columbia
Maryland: Baltimore (distinct from Baltimore County)
Missouri: St. Louis (distinct from St. Louis County)
Virginia: 35 cities independent of the State's 96 counties

Unorganized areas bearing county designations —
Connecticut: Fairfield, Hartford, Litchfield, Middlesex, New Haven, New London, Tolland, Windham
Rhode Island: Bristol, Kent, Newport, Providence, Washington
South Dakota: Shannon, Todd, Washabaugh (attached to other counties)

Other unorganized county-type areas: in *Alaska* (19 election districts); in *Idaho, Montana,* and *Wyoming* (areas within Yellowstone National Park, not organized for local government but administered by the National Government)

---

vary widely in terms of population. Hinsdale County, Colorado, with only 208 residents in 1960, has the least population, while approximately 7,000,000 people now live in Los Angeles County, California.

Legal Status of Counties. "While the county is an agency of the State, it is likewise a creature of the State." Thus, in 1924 the Supreme Court of Illinois stated a rule common throughout the nation. Counties are created by the State, are at all times subject to its control, and may be abolished by it.

In the early period of State history this absolute control was largely exercised by State legislatures, but abuses of legislative power have long since brought about many State constitutional provisions relating to counties. For example, many State constitutions now provide for definite county boundaries, fix the manner of selection, terms, and duties of county officials, and designate county seats. Then, too, as we shall note shortly (page 705), several State constitutions provide for county home rule.

Functions of Counties. Because counties are creatures of the State, they are responsible for administering State laws and such county laws *(ordinances)* as the State legislature and the State constitution permit them to enact.

The functions of counties vary considerably from State to State across the nation. The common ones are to preserve the peace; administer justice; maintain jails or workhouses; record deeds, wills, mortgages, marriage licenses, and other documents; assess property for taxation; collect taxes and expend county funds; issue licenses such as those for hunting, fishing, and marriage; maintain schools; build and repair roads, bridges, drains, and such other public works; administer elections; care for the poor; and protect the health of the inhabitants of the county.

In recent years some counties, especially the more populous ones, have also undertaken new functions. These counties now do such things as maintain parks, hospitals, and airports; operate water, sewage, and electricity systems; provide organized police and fire protection; and undertake other activities in such fields as recreation and conservation. Still, these counties are comparatively rare; the typical county continues to be primarily a unit of rural local government performing a limited number of traditional functions.

The ever-increasing demands for governmental services have brought a trend toward more and more State control over the performance of most county functions. Thus, today such traditional county activities as those involving schools, welfare, roads, and taxation are increasingly being directed by the State.

Organization of County Government. As we have already suggested, county governments are typically organized in complicated and chaotic fashion across the country. The point may be seen in the chart on page 701.

The County Board. Some kind of county governing body exists in every State except Alaska, Connecticut, and Rhode Island (where the counties serve only as judicial districts). It is commonly called the county board; but it is known by at least twenty other titles among the States—including county court, board of chosen freeholders, board of supervisors, board of commissioners, fiscal court, police jury, board of revenue, and quarter court.

In England counties were administered by the Quarter Sessions Court of the justice of the peace. Naturally this system was carried to America, and the county governing body of today has descended from it. In Kentucky, Tennessee, and Arkansas the local justices continue to administer most of the counties. Since they are elected for definite terms, however, the county system in those States is much like that elsewhere.

Members of the board, whatever its title, are almost everywhere popularly elected—for terms varying from one to eight years, but four-year terms are most common. They are usually chosen from districts within the county rather than on at-large basis.

Avery v. *Midland County, 1968.* In 1968, in a case from Texas, the United States Supreme Court held that the 14th Amendment's Equal Protection Clause "forbids the election of local officials from districts of disparate size." It thus extended the "one-man, one-vote" rule to the local level. See pages 618–619.

Generally speaking, county boards may be grouped into two distinct types—boards of commissioners and boards of supervisors. The details of size, terms of members, and the like for each type vary widely among the States— and often even within the same State.

Board of Commissioners. The board of commissioners is the smaller and more common type of county board. It is found practically everywhere in the South and West, but it is well known in other sections, too. It usually has three or five, but occasionally seven or more, members.

The Board of Supervisors. A board of supervisors is typically a much larger governing body—composed of an average of about fifteen members, but ranging in size to a hundred or more. Its members are often chosen by the voters from the various townships within the county—as in New York, Michigan, and Wisconsin. Each frequently has responsibilities as an officer of his own township, while all of the board members act together on country-wide matters.

In most States all counties use one or the other of these two general types of governing bodies; but in a few States—Illinois, for example—each county may use whichever it chooses.

Powers. The powers held by county governing bodies are prescribed—and often very narrowly defined—in State constitutional and statutory provisions. The governing bodies commonly possess both legislative and executive powers, despite the American tradition of separation of powers. Their most important legislative powers are often those relating to finance. For example, they may levy taxes, appropriate funds, and incur "limited" debts.

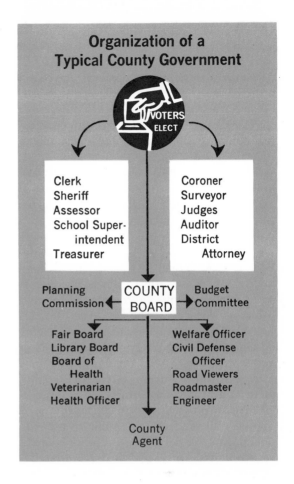

Organization of a Typical County Government

VOTERS ELECT

Clerk
Sheriff
Assessor
School Superintendent
Treasurer

Coroner
Surveyor
Judges
Auditor
District Attorney

Planning Commission ← COUNTY BOARD → Budget Committee

Fair Board
Library Board
Board of Health
Veterinarian
Health Officer

Welfare Officer
Civil Defense Officer
Road Viewers
Roadmaster
Engineer

County Agent

They also possess a number of lesser legislative powers, especially in the regulatory field—for example, to enact health and zoning ordinances and to control amusement places located outside of incorporated communities, particularly those where liquor is sold.

Subject to varying degrees of State control and supervision, most county boards perform a wide variety of administrative functions. They supervise the road program; manage county property; maintain jails, courthouses, poor farms, county hospitals, parks, and the like; and are often responsible for the supervision of poor relief and the conduct of elections. They also appoint certain county officers, deputies, and assistants of many kinds, as well as most other county employees, and regularly fix the salaries of most of those who work for the county.

In nearly every county, however, the county board shares its executive powers with such other elected officials as the sheriff, the county clerk, and the county treasurer—with the result that efficiency and economy are at best difficult to achieve and often, in fact, impossible.

Judicial Officers. The county is an important unit of government for judicial purposes in all parts of the country, including New England. But in less than one-half of the States there is a judge who presides over a court of general jurisdiction within each of the counties. Rather, as we noted in Chapter 38, a State's judicial system is usually organized into circuits or districts which often encompass two or more counties. Justices of the peace and probate, juvenile, and similar judicial officers frequently do hold court on a county or sub-county basis, however.

In nearly every county across the country there is a prosecuting attorney whose major job it is to prosecute cases which arise in his county. The exact title of his office varies considerably. If he serves two or more counties, he is often known as the district attorney. If he serves only one county, he is most frequently called the county attorney, State's attorney, or commonwealth attorney; and in some States he is known as the solicitor. In fact, he is sometimes known as the district attorney even though his district consists of only one county.

The Sheriff. In nearly all counties there is a sheriff who is almost everywhere popularly elected for a term of two or four years.[2] Traditionally, the sheriff's major function has been that of keeping the peace within the county —preventing crimes and arresting and jailing offenders. More and more, however, sheriffs now devote less and less time to that aspect of their work—as city and State police forces have assumed greater responsibility for law enforcement. Still, the county sheriff and his deputies are important agents of law enforcement in many of the nation's rural counties. In some of the most heavily urbanized counties—such as California's huge Los Angeles County—the sheriff's office is staffed with officers highly trained, organized, and effective in the work of criminal investigation and apprehension.[3]

The sheriff is an officer of the courts of record in his county. He or one of his deputies is required to attend court sessions and to perform such duties as serve warrants, summonses, and subpoenas. He also conducts foreclosures and confiscates illegal or abandoned property —which he usually then auctions off for the benefit of the county treasury. He is usually responsible for the keeping of the jail and its inmates and for transporting convicted criminals to those institutions to which they have been sentenced. In several States the sheriff is also required to perform some functions not directly related to law enforcement. For example, in the South and West the sheriff is usually the county's tax collector, and in many States he is responsible for issuing such licenses as those for hunting, fishing, and door-to-door peddling.

The Coroner. In nearly all States the coroner [4] is an officer of the county who holds inquests to determine the cause of deaths which occur

<hr/>

[2] The word "sheriff" evolved from *shire-reeve,* meaning "peace officer of the shire." The shire was the Anglo-Saxon term for what became the county (district of a count) following the Norman Conquest in 1066.

[3] In the performance of his criminal duties the sheriff may summon to his aid the posse—the *posse comitatus,* power of the county—which by law consists of all able-bodied male citizens within the county. In extreme cases he may request the governor to call out the State militia—the National Guard. See pages 384, 644.

[4] "Coroner" is the modern rendering of the old Anglo-Saxon word *crowner.* The crowner was appointed by the king to serve as one of his chief officers within the shire.

under violent or suspicious circumstances.[5] A growing number of States now require that coroners be licensed physicians, but in most States they continue to be local undertakers who are popularly elected and paid on the basis of the number of corpses they handle. The need for a knowledge of medicine and pathology in the office has also led some States to abolish the office altogether, replacing it with that of a county medical examiner. A study of coroner's verdicts some years ago suggests the wisdom of such a move; many reported death causes were almost meaningless and occasionally even illiterate—for example, "Found dead," "Diabetes, tuberculosis, or nervous indigestion," and "I lerned the man while under the Enfluence of Whiskey or white mule Just willfully drowned himself."

The County Clerk. The office of county clerk is now found in about one-half of the States. In those States the county clerk is usually popularly elected. His major functions usually include serving as the secretary to the county board and clerk of the local courts of record, preparing and keeping of public records, issuing of warrants against the county, and administering elections within the county. In his role as chief recordkeeper the county clerk through his office stores all books, records, and papers of the county and usually of the special districts within it, too. Deeds, mortgages, leases, plats, birth and marriage certificates, divorce records, adoption papers, and similar documents are regularly filed with him as well.[6] He may also handle applications for passports and naturalization papers in accord with federal law.

When the clerk issues *warrants* (orders to pay, such as a check) against the county treas-

ury, he acts as the county's *auditor*—though in about half of the States a separate officer with that title performs the function. The clerk—or the auditor—also checks the validity of the county's financial records and maintains and publishes them.

As the county's chief election officer, the county clerk performs many essential functions. He usually registers voters (when there is not a separate officer, the registrar of elections, to perform this important duty); prepares ballots; receives nominating petitions and, where the devices are available, initiative and referenda petitions; establishes precincts; canvasses the vote; and issues certificates of election to those who win local offices. In many counties the clerk also issues such licenses as those required for marriage, hunting, fishing, dog ownership, and the operation of certain types of businesses.

The county clerk is the custodian of the public records in the county. People in the county keep his office quite busy with their many requests for licenses, copies of legal documents, and a variety of other services. (Wes Kemp)

[5] In most States the coroner may empanel a coroner's jury, usually of six bystanders, to assist him in the determination of the probable cause of death.

[6] In several States a separate officer known as the *recorder* or the *register of deeds* has custody of those documents relating to property transactions.

The County Treasurer. In Connecticut and Rhode Island town officers have charge of local funds, and in several Southern States they are placed with the sheriff or a local bank. Elsewhere across the country the county treasurer receives, safeguards, and disburses county funds. He is usually popularly elected and almost invariably must be bonded to insure the State and the county against any losses from dishonesty, carelessness, or other misuse of public funds. Today most county treasurers are paid a definite salary; but in some places their compensation is still derived from the interest they are able to earn from the investment of public funds—a situation which in times past was an open invitation to corruption and which sometimes led to serious financial embarassment for some counties.

The County Assessor. As we noted in Chapter 40, the administration of the property tax depends upon a determination of the value of the properties against which the tax is levied. Throughout the country this task is performed by an officer known as the county (township or city) assessor. In most States the county assessor evaluates all taxable property within the county, and his assessments are then used by each of the governmental units within the county for property tax purposes. The critical importance of his function can be seen in the fact that some eighty-five per cent of all local governmental revenue today comes from the property tax. Typically, the assessor is popularly elected—a fact which often means that, if assessments are to be made properly, the assessor must rely upon competent assistants to perform the job for which he is elected and for which he is held responsible.

The Superintendent of Schools. There is an elected or appointed superintendent of schools in approximately three-fourths of the nation's counties. More often than not, he is elected by the voters of his county; but in several States he is chosen by a county school board, the State board of education, or the governor. In approximately one-third of the States the

schools are organized on a county-unit basis, and in them the county superintendent is responsible for the direction of most or all of the public elementary and secondary schools within his county. In the other States he serves primarily as an agent of the State department of education for the administration of the State's educational requirements. The superintendent's functions usually include responsibility for the improvement of curricula and methods of teaching, the encouragement of parental interest in the schools, the advising of school authorities, the enforcement of physical standards set for school buildings and equipment, the conduct of studies, the making of reports to appropriate State and federal agencies, and a host of other chores.

Other County Officers. Those county officers we have cited here by no means constitute a complete list—as a glance at the chart on page 701 will indicate. Among the many other county officers often found are a *surveyor,* who conducts land surveys and determines boundary lines; an *engineer* who supervises the construction of roads, bridges, drains, and other public improvements made by the county (in counties where there is no surveyor, he performs those duties); and *road viewers* who determine the routes for proposed roads.

THE REFORM OF COUNTY GOVERNMENT

Franklin D. Roosevelt once described county government as "no more fit for its purpose today than an ox-cart would be fit for the task of supplying modern transportation between New York and Chicago." Many students of local government join in that judgment. The county is the one unit of government which has been largely untouched by the reforms that have affected each of the other levels of American government during this century.

County government is too often lax and inefficient, and occasionally corrupt. The people themselves must take the major share of the blame for this condition because of general indifference to county government and its problems. But the chaotic structure of most county governments is also responsible.

The major weakness in county government is in its headlessness — the fact that it is almost impossible to locate responsibility among its many elected and independent officers. Another serious weakness is to be found in the large number of county officers — for example, the engineer or assessor — whose jobs require professional qualifications but who are chosen by the voters. Popular election is at best a poor way to guarantee the selection of a person with the technical abilities such posts demand. The larger the number of elected officials the less likely it is that the voters will be able to cast the informed votes upon which good government must depend. Still another difficulty with county government today arises out of the size and number of counties in most States. Nearly every one of the counties that now exists was laid out in the days of the horse and stage coach. As a general rule, these units are geographically ill-suited to present-day needs. And finally as one of the major criticisms of county government, we must mention the confusion that exists as to the proper functions of the county, its relation to the State, and its relation to the city or cities within it.

A number of reforms have been suggested for county government, and some have been implemented successfully in a few places in recent years.

The County Manager Plan. In order to eliminate waste, duplication and corruption, a few counties have adopted the county manager plan — quite similar to the council-manager plan to be discussed in Chapter 42 (pages 726–727). It is strongly favored by nearly all students of local government.

Under the county manager plan the voters of the county elect a county board. The county board, which usually consists of three or five members, serves as the policy-making body for the county. It selects a manager who is responsible to it and who administers its policies. The manager appoints his own assistants who work under him in such fields as finance, welfare, public works, recreation, and police. As an experienced administrator, appointed for a definite term and receiving an adequate salary, the manager is in a better position than the county board to remain above the play of local politics, to make wise appointments, and to conduct the county's business properly.

Much of the success of the county manager plan depends upon the caliber of the manager himself. He should be a highly-trained professional public administrator or someone equally well-qualified for the job. The manager system locates responsibility in a single person, the manager. When something goes wrong, he (either directly or through one of his subordinates) is responsible, and steps may be taken to correct the situation. With more

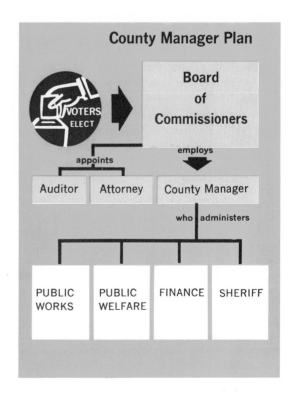

County Manager Plan

appointive and fewer elective officers, the county manager plan makes it possible for the county's voters to know more about the fewer candidates among whom they must choose.

Despite these impressive arguments, and the excellent results of the plan where it has been utilized, only some three dozen of the 3040 counties have county manager governments today.[7] The major obstacle to its widespread adoption seems to lie in the fact that the average person knows little and cares less about the government of his county. Where the system has been unsuccessfully proposed, the major opposition to its adoption has usually come from three principal sources: (1) local party organizations which depend on the multitude of offices and wealth of patronage for their existence, (2) the "courthouse gang," those currently in office who fear for their jobs, and (3) the traditionally conservative rural residents who tend to prefer the system their forefathers knew.

Two alternatives to the county manager system are found in some of the more populous counties across the country. One of these is the *chief administrative officer* arrangement in which that county officer is appointed by the county board and functions somewhat like a manager. However, he has much less authority than a manager, especially over appointments and budgetary matters; and a number of elective offices in addition to the county board usually continue to exist. Alameda, Contra Costa, Los Angeles, San Diego, and several other counties in California, such others as Cuyahoga in Ohio and Charleston in South Carolina, have had considerable success with this arrangement.

The second alternative is the *county president* (or *supervisor*) system under which one member of the county governing body is elected to function much like a mayor in the mayor-council form of city government (see pages 723–724). This arrangement is now found in several counties, including Cook County, Illinois; Jefferson Parish, Louisiana; Baltimore and Anne Arundel Counties, Maryland; St. Louis County, Missouri; Essex and Hudson Counties, New Jersey; and Milwaukee County, Wisconsin.

County Consolidation. Many students of local government advocate the refurbishing of counties through consolidation—that is, through the merger of existing counties into a smaller number. As we noted on page 705, most county lines were drawn in the days of the horse and stagecoach. That is, they were drawn in a time when it seemed wise to limit the size of counties in terms of the speed of horse travel to and from the county seat. Today, of course, one can drive by car through several counties in a matter of hours. It seems clear that if there were fewer counties the county would become a much more useful and satisfactory unit of government. Even so, practically no headway has been made with consolidation proposals in any State. Indeed, only two consolidations involving organized counties have occurred in this century.[8]

Replacing the County. Rather than attempting to reorganize county governments

---

[7] The first county manager government was established in Durham County, North Carolina, in 1930. At least nineteen States now allow for them: California, Florida, Georgia, Hawaii, Louisiana, Maryland, Missouri, Montana, Nevada, New York, North Carolina, North Dakota, Ohio, Oregon, Pennsylvania, Tennessee, Texas, Washington, and Virginia. The number of county manager systems is now increasing; as recently as 1961 there were only sixteen in operation. Very likely, this trend will continue as more counties are forced to face up to the ever-increasing pressures and problems caused by urban and suburban population growth.

---

[8] James County was joined to Hamilton County in Tennessee in 1919, and Campbell and Milton Counties were merged with Fulton County in Georgia in 1923. In 1957 the voters of Alabama approved a constitutional amendment giving the State legislature the power to abolish Macon County and distribute it among its neighboring counties; to date, the power has not been exercised.

or reduce the number of counties, some authorities propose that counties and their governments be done away with altogether. Most of those who favor such a drastic step would substitute a few *State administrative districts* for the present counties. These districts would be headed by State officials and would perform the functions now handled by the counties. The proponents of this plan argue that most of what the counties do today involves the execution of State law and that there is a growing need to care for such matters on a Statewide rather than a purely local basis.

Although there may be merit to the claim that such an arrangement would be more efficient than the present county system, there is little likelihood that any State will soon adopt it. Notice, though, that the trend toward greater State control over county functions is, in fact, a step in that direction.

County-City Consolidation or Separation. Another and quite different kind of proposal for the replacement of existing counties has been tried successfully in several places in the United States. In these places either a county and its major city have been merged into a single unit or a county and its major city have been made independent of one another.

Sixty years ago more than half the nation's population lived outside of any city or town. Today three-fourths of all Americans live in cities or towns or in the sprawling suburbs that surround them. This massive urbanization has created several problems — and duplication of functions and services by overlapping cities and counties is far from the least of them, as we shall see in Chapter 43.

To meet this situation, some cities and counties have been merged — most notably the cities and counties of Denver and San Francisco, and Davidson County and Nashville, Tennessee. The two units in each of these communities have identical boundaries, and the same governmental structure serves each. The boundaries of the city and county of Philadelphia are also identical, but a number of city and county offi-

cers remain independent of one another.[9] Elsewhere, some cities have been separated from the counties around them. St. Louis and Baltimore are the notable examples of such "independent cities" today. A special situation exists in Virginia where any city with 10,000 or more population is legally separate from the county in which it is located or, more precisely, by which it is surrounded (see page 699).

THE TOWNSHIP SYSTEM

Origin of Town Government in New England. The Pilgrims reached Plymouth Rock in 1620 as an organized congregation. They quickly established a compact and closely-knit community in which their church and their government were practically one. When they erected a meetinghouse on Burial Hill in 1622, they did so in order to have a place for common worship and for public meetings — a place for prayer and for the making of public policy. Sermons were preached on the inside to save souls from perdition, and a cannon was mounted outside to save bodies from the Indians.

As Puritan congregations settled in the region, they followed the Pilgrims' pattern. Their desire to be near their church, the Indian threat, the severe climate, and the fact that the country was unsuited to large plantations led them to form compact communities.

Town and Township. These communities soon came to be known as "towns," after the English practice.[10] As their number and pop-

---

[9] An unusual situation exists in Hawaii where the city-county of Honolulu includes all of the Island of Oahu, the principal island of the State.

[10] When a clan in Northern Europe or England fixed upon some spot for a permanent residence and built a wall around it, the wall was known as a *tun;* in time the space within the wall became known as a *tun* or *town.* The settlers were called by the clan name — for example, "the Boerings" or "the Cressings"; thus, the town came to be called *Barrington,* "town of the Boerings," or *Cressingham,* "home of the Cressings."

ulations grew, it was necessary to survey the boundaries between them, and the small irregular patches of land that resulted were called "townships" (townshapes).[11] Frontier communities are often not very discriminating in their use of terms, however, and "town" soon came to mean not only the cluster of buildings but the entire township, too. Thus, in New England today a "town" is a political subdivision of a county which in other parts of the nation is known as a "township."

Powers of the New England Towns. For much of the colonial period the New England towns were undisturbed by the King or Parliament, and they each exercised generally those powers now exercised by a State. They waged war against the Indians, established schools and roads, and as late as the Revolutionary War raised troops and appropriated money for war supplies. In fact, they created the States of which they are now parts.

Today the towns exercise only such powers as the States permit. They have control of most roads, bridges, schools, libraries, poor relief, and taxation for most local purposes. Some towns have charge of such public works and institutions as street pavements, sewers, waterworks, electric light plants, public baths, parks, and hospitals. They also have certain powers to enact police ordinances — for example, those setting speed limits.

Town Officers. Although there is considerable variation among the New England towns, the officers which are common to most towns include the board of selectmen, town clerk, moderator, town treasurer (or tax collector), board of assessors, overseers of the poor, justices of the peace, constables, commissioner of roads (under various titles), school committee (or board of education), planning board, and such lesser officials as park commissioners and trustees of the library.

In the smaller towns, those with less than

10,000 population, most of these officers are elected at the regular town meeting. In the larger towns, however, most town officers are elected at a general townwide election held a week or two before the regular annual town meeting. Terms of office vary not only among the various posts but also from town to town. Thus, a town clerk may be elected on an annual basis and the selectmen may be elected to terms that vary from one to three years. Then, too, assessors could be elected to terms of different length — that is, in one town to a one-year term and in the adjacent town to a three-year term.

Selectmen. The selectmen, of whom there may be three, five, seven, or nine (three or five being the more usual numbers), are the principal officers of the town. Commonly they are elected to three-year terms, with one or two being elected each year rather than the entire board.

The selectmen are charged with the overseeing of town administration. They issue warrants for holding regular or special town meetings, specifying generally the subjects which the citizens desire to have acted upon. They also grant licenses, arrange for elections, have charge of town property, appoint some of the minor officials, and perform those functions conferred upon them by the town meeting or the town's by-laws. It should be borne in mind, however, that they have no power to determine the tax rate (a function of the board of assessors) or appropriate money (a function of the town meeting).

Town Clerk. The town clerk is just as important as the board of selectmen and performs many duties which are imposed upon the county clerk outside of New England. He keeps the minutes of town meetings, of meetings of the selectmen, and other town records; records the votes for State and town officers; issues marriage licenses; registers qualified voters; and records births, marriages, and deaths. Generally, he is elected to a one-year term, but most town clerks are re-elected year after year.

---

[11] As used here, the suffix *ship* is from the Anglo-Saxon word *scip,* meaning shape.

Moderator. The moderator is the presiding officer of the town meeting. Normally he is elected to a term of one year; but since he usually is one of the town's most respected residents, he is re-elected year after year as a matter of course. Other than his major function of presiding over the town meeting, the moderator performs no other duties except to aid the selectmen in organizing those committees authorized by the town meeting.

The Town Meeting. Town laws have always been made in the town meeting. During the first few years the colonists attempted to hold monthly meetings; but this was found to be a cumbersome way to transact business and, as early as 1635, selectmen were chosen to administer the affairs of the town during the interval between the town meetings. Today the selectmen usually meet formally one evening a week throughout most of the year.

Regular town meetings today are usually held on an annual basis, but the selectmen may call special meetings whenever necessary. The meetings are normally held in the town hall or some other large public auditorium (usually the high school auditorium). March is the favorite time for the meetings—though some towns hold their meetings as early as February or as late as April, and many Connecticut towns prefer October. Generally the meetings are held in the evening and may run to many sessions, depending upon the number of articles to be acted upon.

Either the town clerk or the moderator calls the meeting to order. The general nature of the business to be transacted at the meeting must be previously announced in the *town warrant* which may be posted in various parts of the township, published in the local newspaper, or sent as a special printing to all of the town's registered voters. Once the meeting has been called to order and the invocation given, the moderator announces the rules under which the town meeting will operate—normally Robert's Rules of Parliamentary Procedure, with special time limits for individual debate.

The town meeting then begins in earnest. Each article of the town warrant is read and acted upon separately. Routine articles, such as the annual appropriation of funds for the July 4 town festivities, are approved quickly. But many articles, especially those dealing with changes in zoning ordinances and approval of land acquisitions, may be debated for hours. Considerable time is spent on the most important single article of any town warrant—the *town budget,* the appropriations for all town offices and departments—since the major function of the town meeting is to appropriate the funds necessary for conducting the town's business in the coming year.

A town warrant gives the time and place of the town meeting and the items of business to be considered. (Town of Randolph, Mass.)

1970 Town Meeting Warrant

1970 TOWN MEETING WARRANT

Commonwealth of Massachusetts   Norfolk, S.S.

To Any of the Constables of the Town of
Randolph in said

County.   Greetings:

In the name of the Commonwealth of Massachusetts, you are hereby directed to notify and warn the inhabitants of the Town of Randolph, qualified to vote in elections therein, to meet at the polling places in their respective precincts, to wit:

2 – MATURING DEBT & INTEREST – 2

ARTICLE 4

To see if the Town will vote to authorize the Treasurer, with the approval of the Selectmen, to borrow money from time to time in anticipation of the revenue for the financial years beginning January 1, 1970 and January 1, 1971 in accordance with the provisions of General Laws, Chapter 44, Section 4, to renew any note or notes as may be given for a period of less than one year, in accordance with the provisions of General Laws, Chapter 44, Section 17.

ARTICLE 5

To see if the Town will vote to raise and appropriate or transfer from available funds a sum of money or take any other action in connection therewith for the following purposes:

Purpose	Outstanding 12/31/69	1970 Principal Payment	1970 Interest	Total
Schools	$6,211,000.00	$655,000.00	$385,607.50	$1,040,607.50
Water	175,000.00	50,000.00	5,380.00	55,380.00
Sewer	2,729,000.00	305,000.00	99,433.50	404,433.50
Public Buildings	140,000.00	20,000.00	5,490.00	25,490.00
Anticipation of Revenue			40,000.00	40,000.00
	$9,255,000.00	$1,030,000.00	$535,911.00	$1,565,911.00

It is in regard to appropriations that the appointed *finance committee* (or advisory committee) plays a key role. Its recommendations regarding approval or rejection of the articles dealing with financial matters have significant effect on the voting outcome. The recommendations of the finance committee are arrived at only after months of investigation, in which the town's needs are carefully balanced against the effect specific appropriations have on the tax rate.

Representative Town Meeting. Population increases in recent years have left many New England towns with facilities too small to accommodate an open town meeting. To meet this problem, many towns now hold what is known as *representative town meeting* or limited town meeting—that is, a local representative assembly rather than a gathering of all registered voters of the town.

Brookline, Massachusetts, with a population of more than 50,000 today, became the first town to adopt representative town meeting. In 1915 the town meeting divided the town into nine precincts and provided for the election of twenty-seven town meeting members from each precinct.

Today, in towns which employ this arrangement, town meeting members are elected on a precinct basis. Their terms vary in length among the towns, with two- and three-year terms being the most common. In some towns all town meeting members are elected at one time, whereas in other towns they serve staggered terms. In towns having representative town meeting, only town meeting members and town officers are permitted to vote on the articles—even though town residents are permitted to attend the meetings and to participate in debate.

Difficulties of Town Government Today. Town government in New England has a long and noble heritage. But a number of factors have undermined its effectiveness over the years. The development of rapid means of transportation and communication have led to the centralizing of power over such matters as finance, roads, law enforcement, public health, and education in the State. Population growth resulting in representative town meetings has allowed factions in some towns to gain control of managing local affairs. Then, too, much debate in town meetings has been devoted to inconsequential matters; and, on occasion, important matters have been rushed through without adequate discussion. And finally, some attack town government today on the basis that much town business is conducted by the citizenry acting on a part-time basis rather than by a full-time professional staff.

THE COUNTY–TOWNSHIP SYSTEM

Extension of Township Government to the Middle West. Nowhere outside of New England is the township as important a basis for local government as in those six States. It is of considerable importance, however, in the tier of States extending from Ohio to Nebraska. In those States a mixed county-township system exists. That is, in those States some local governmental functions are assigned to the counties and others to the townships within them. This arrangement arose in good part out of the history of the original settlement of those States. Generally, their northern portions were settled by New Englanders accustomed to town government, whereas the other portions of those States were settled largely by people from New York, Pennsylvania, and the older States south of the Ohio River who were accustomed to the performance of local governmental functions by officers elected on a countywide basis.

Illinois presents a peculiar case study. When Illinois was admitted to the Union in 1818, the majority of its population had emigrated from the South and had settled in the southern part of the State. Under their influence Illinois was divided into counties, each

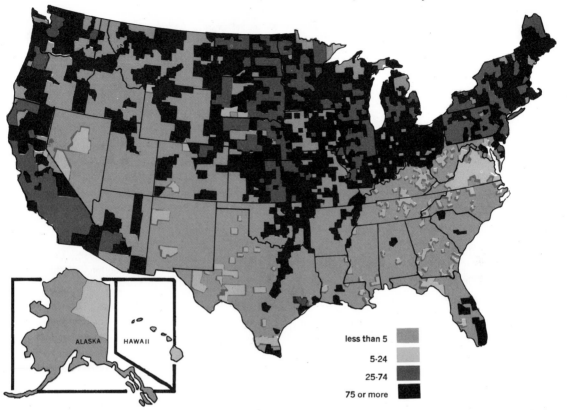

less than 5

5-24

25-74

75 or more

ALASKA   HAWAII

governed by a small board of commissioners elected at-large. By the time the State's second constitution was framed in 1848, however, New Englanders had settled in large numbers in the northern section of the State. Thus, from 1848 on, the Illinois constitution has contained a local option provision allowing the voters in each county to decide whether or not townships should exist. Today there are some 1400 townships in 85 of the State's 102 counties — but none in the other 17 counties.

Township Officers in the Central States. The New England title of *selectmen* is not found in the Central States. In Pennsylvania, Ohio, Iowa, Minnesota, and the Dakotas their place is taken by a *board of supervisors* or *trustees*. In other States there is a well-defined head officer who is assisted, and in some matters checked, by a township board. In New York, Michigan, and Illinois, where this officer is called a *supervisor,* he is also a member of the county board of supervisors. In Indiana, Missouri, Kansas, and Oklahoma he bears the title of *township trustee.* The other township officers usually found in these States include a clerk, assessor, treasurer, overseer of the poor, overseer of roads, and one or more justices of the peace and constables.

In these States the townships are regularly subject to more State and county control than is the case in New England. Then, too, villages

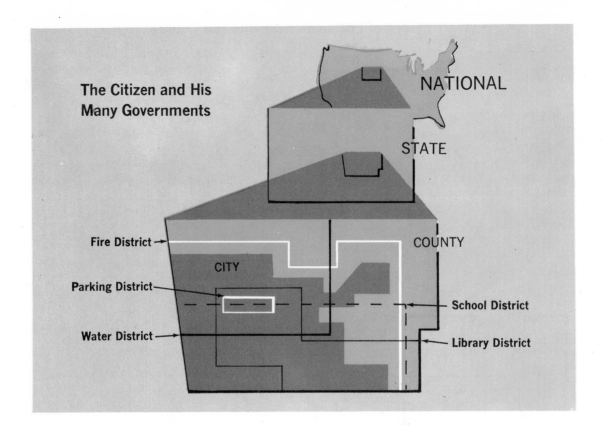

The Citizen and His Many Governments

NATIONAL

STATE

Fire District →

COUNTY

CITY

Parking District —

Water District →

School District

Library District

and towns are much more frequently chartered by the State with an existence and powers separate from those of the township and county in which they are located.

Absence of Township Government in the Southern and Western States. Although most of the counties in the States of the South and West are divided into subdistricts for one or several purposes, townships do not exist in them as in the New England and Central States. Rather, the districts which do exist have been created for the more convenient performance of such functions as the maintenance of schools and roads, the administration of justice, and the conduct of elections. Except for school districts, these units seldom have the power to tax or own property and usually do not have officers independent of those of the county. Then, too, given their purposes, they frequently overlap one another. The names assigned to the more important of these districts vary from State to State.[12]

---

[12] In North Carolina, South Carolina, Missouri, Arkansas, Montana, and Nevada these districts are (somewhat confusingly) known as *townships;* in California, *judicial townships;* in Virginia, West Virginia, and Kentucky, *magisterial districts;* in Tennessee, *civil districts;* in Mississippi, *supervisors' districts;* in Georgia, *militia districts;* in Texas, *commissioners' precincts;* in Delaware, *hundreds;* and in the remaining Southern and Western States, *election districts* or *precincts* — except in Louisiana, where the parishes (counties) are subdivided into *wards.*

SPECIAL DISTRICTS

In addition to the local governmental units and the municipal governments we shall turn to in Chapter 42, one other type of local unit must be considered: the *special district*.

The special district is a local unit created to perform a single or occasionally a few related functions. There are about 42,000 of them throughout the country today. By far the most common are the school districts. The first districts for school purposes were set up in New York in 1812. Of the 64,851 special districts reported by the Census Bureau in 1957, 50,446 were school districts. Continuing school district reorganization and consolidation in several States has reduced the number to about 21,000 today.

Most of the other special districts, which exist for a wide range of purposes, have been created since the Great Depression. They are found usually, but not always, in rural areas. Among the more important are those for the providing of water, sewage, or electrical service; for furnishing police, fire, or sanitary protection; for the construction and maintenance of highways, bridges, airports, swimming pools, parking lots, libraries, or parks; and for such other purposes as soil conservation, irrigation, housing, slum clearance, or reforestation.

The reasons for the creation of these special districts are many and varied. The principal one lies in the fact that most of the problems with which they deal cover much wider (or smaller) areas than a single county or township. For example, stream pollution might be a problem in each one of several counties through which a river flows. On the other hand, sewer and water service would ordinarily be confined to a rather small section. In other instances special districts have been formed because local governments could not or would not furnish the services desired—for example, police or fire protection in outlying regions. In some cases they also have been created in order to keep "politics" out of the matter.

An elected board is usually the governing body for the special district. It commonly has the power to tax and spend to perform the special function for which it was created.

CONCEPT BUILDING

Key Concepts

In addition to the National Government and the fifty State governments, there are more than 80,000 governmental units in the United States. Over 18,000 are municipalities. The rest include 3040 counties, some 17,000 townships, and about 42,000 special districts (approximately half of them school districts).

Counties exist in all but three States—Alaska, Connecticut, and Rhode Island. The county is mainly a judicial district in New England, shares the responsibilities for local rural government in the northeastern fourth of the country, and is the predominant local unit in the South and West. Only a very few points in the continental United States do not lie within some county.

Legally, counties are creatures of the State and have no existence apart from it. They administer State laws and such county ordinances as the State legislature and State constitution permit them to enact.

Counties vary considerably in size, population, and number among the States, and the organization of county governments varies almost as widely.

There is some kind of county governing body, whatever its name, in all States except Alaska, Connecticut, and Rhode Island. Generally there are two types, the smaller and more common board of commissioners and the larger board of supervisors. The county board exercises limited legislative and somewhat wider executive powers over county affairs.

The other major offices of county government commonly include the sheriff, coroner, county clerk, register of deeds, auditor, county treasurer, superintendent of schools, assessor, and surveyor or engineer. A judge and prosecuting attorney may serve several counties at once.

The major weaknesses of county government include its headlessness, the existence of too many elective offices, the outdated size, location and number of counties, and the confusion over its proper functions and its relation to the State and the city or cities within it.

The county manager plan is the reform proposal most strongly recommended by students of local government, but it and other reforms have made relatively little headway among the nation's counties.

The town or township is the more important local unit in New England. Township government is usually conducted through an annual town meeting and a small number of selectmen elected at the town meeting or at a townwide general election. The other township officers include a town clerk, assessor, justices of the peace, overseer of the poor, school committeemen, road commissioner, and so on.

Modern transportation and communications, industrialization, and population increase have all helped to make townships become outmoded in many areas. Townships are largely unknown in the South and West. A mixed county-township system exists in the tier of States from Ohio to Nebraska.

Special districts have been created in every State for the performance of one or occasionally several functions; of them, school districts are by far the most common.

Important Terms

assessor	clerk	selectmen	town meeting
auditor	coroner	sheriff	town warrant
board of commissioners	county manager plan	special district	township
board of supervisors	moderator	town	treasurer

Questions for Inquiry and Review

1. About how many different units of government are there in the United States?

2. Which States do *not* have counties?

3. Why is the governmental structure of the typical county said to be "chaotic"?

4. What is the essential legal status of the counties within each of the States?

5. From what legal sources do counties draw their authority to perform the various functions they do?

6. What are the two general types of county governing bodies found among the States?

7. Is the county sheriff's traditional role as a peace officer changing? Why?

8. What other principal officers are usually found in the typical county?

9. What is the major weakness in present-day county government?

10. What other significant weaknesses may be cited?

11. What have commonly proved to be the three principal sources of opposition to the county manager plan?

12. How successful have proposals for county consolidation (merger and reduction in number) been at least thus far?

13. What type of county reorganization is illustrated by the experiences of Denver and San Francisco? By the experiences of St. Louis and Baltimore?

14. What does "town" mean in New England? In the South and West?

15. Why did a mixed county-township system develop in the Central States?

16. What is the major function of the town meeting?

17. What is the most common type of special district found among the States?

For Further Inquiry

1. If you were called upon to recommend to your county board three particular matters which need urgent attention in your county, could you do so? If so, what matters would you list? Why?

2. We now have 3040 counties. Most of them were created before the development of present-day means of communication and transportation. Do you think that your State now has too many counties? Why?

3. St. Louis, Baltimore, all of Virginia's first-class cities, and a few others in various States have been made independent cities, outside of any county. Denver, San Francisco, and a few other cities have become city-counties. Which, if either, of these two methods of avoiding county-city duplication do you favor? Why?

4. Why would you favor or oppose the appointment of all officers in your county except the members of the county board?

Suggested Activities

1. Construct a chart of the organization of your county's government (see page 701).

2. Invite a member of the county governing board, the sheriff, and other county officers to speak to the class on their offices and functions and the government of your county in general.

3. Stage a debate or class forum on the question: *Resolved,* That this county should adopt the county manager system.

4. Visit the local county courthouse to observe the processes of county government and report to the class your observations.

Suggested Reading

"Big Changes in America's Small Towns," *U.S. News,* April 28, 1969.

FLINN, THOMAS A., *Local Government and Politics.* Scott, Foresman, 1969.

LANGEWIESCHE, WOLFGANG, "The Suburbs Are Changing," *Reader's Digest,* November, 1969.

LOCKARD, DUANE, *Governing the States and Localities.* Macmillan, 1969. Chapters 8, 11.

_____, *The Politics of State and Local Government.* Macmillan, 1969. Chapter 6.

MADDOX, RUSSELL W., and FUQUAY, ROBERT F., *State and Local Government.* Van Nostrand, 1966. Chapters 18, 20, 21, 22.

ORNSTEIN, FRANKLIN H., "Local Government Is a Farce," *Saturday Evening Post,* December 2, 1967.

42
MUNICIPAL GOVERNMENTS

✦✦✦ What factors should determine the geographic boundaries of a city?

✦✦✦ On what bases should the size of a city council be fixed?

✦✦✦ What extra-constitutional qualifications should a mayor possess? A city councilman? A city manager?

✦✦✦ Should city officials be elected on a partisan or a nonpartisan basis? Why?

A nation is known by the cities that it builds.

WILLIAM BENNETT MUNRO

We are fast becoming a nation of city dwellers. Where once our population was small, predominantly rural, and agricultural, it is now huge, largely urban, and industrial.

Urban Growth. The nation's cities have grown spectacularly in the past 100 years. Their growth, both in size and in importance, has had far-reaching effects on our way of life. When the First Census was taken in 1790, there were only 3,929,214 persons living in the United States. Of these, only 201,655 — or 5.1 per cent — lived in the nation's few cities. Philadelphia was then the largest city with a population of 42,000, New York had 33,000, and Boston 18,000.

Only nine years before the First Census, James Watt had taken out a patent for his double-acting steam engine and thus made large-scale manufacturing possible. Robert Fulton patented his steamboat in 1809 and George Stephenson his locomotive in 1829. These inventions made the transportation of raw materials to factories and the wide distribution of manufactured goods readily possible. Almost overnight the home-manufacturing system gave way to industrial factories, population began to concentrate in the budding industrial and transportation centers, and the nation's cities began to grow.

The invention of several mechanical farm implements reduced the labor required on the farms. More was produced by fewer people. The surplus farm population began to migrate to industrial areas to obtain work. By 1860 our urban population had grown thirty times larger than it had been in 1790 — 6,216,518 or 19.8 per cent of the population lived in cities. By the turn of the century nearly two-fifths of our population lived in cities, and by 1920 more than one-half was residing in urban areas.

With the Eighteenth Census in 1960 our urban population had grown to 125,268,750. Almost three-fourths of all our people live in cities and their surrounding suburbs today. The decade-by-decade increase in our urban population is shown in the table on page 719.

Again, the shift from a predominantly rural to a largely urban society in the United States is a fact of tremendous significance. Certainly, it makes a knowledge of municipal government essential to the informed, intelligent citizen. When large numbers of people live close to one another, the relationships among them are much more complex than are those among people who live in less settled areas. The rules governing their behavior become more numerous and detailed. Their local governments furnish them with a wide variety of services, including water, police and fire protection, streets, sewers, traffic regulation, transportation, public health, and recreation. The larger the population, the more extensive and expensive these services become.

The problems created by urbanization exist in rural areas only in small degree, if at all.[1] Some police and perhaps fire protection is found in rural areas, and there is a need to provide and maintain schools and such public works as roads and bridges. But even the smaller cities are faced with demands and problems far more complex and difficult than those common to the rural areas of the United States. We shall return to some of the problems of urban growth in Chapter 43.

VILLAGE GOVERNMENT

As people collect in a relatively small area — for example, at a crossroads or near a mill — they soon require such public improvements and services as fire protection, a public water supply, sidewalks, and street lights. Each State permits the people in such areas to form an organized community with a government dis-

tinct from that of the surrounding rural area — that is, then, separate from the town in New England, the county or township in the Middle West, and the county in the South and West.

These small organized centers of population are known by various names among the States. For example, they are commonly called "towns" in the South and West and "boroughs" in Pennsylvania, New Jersey, and Connecticut. But in most States they are generally known as "villages" and, for the sake of uniformity, we use that term here to include towns and boroughs.[2]

Incorporation. Each State prescribes, in its constitution or by statute, the conditions and manner in which a small community may be *incorporated* as a village.[3] In a few States — Alabama, for example — as few as 100 inhabitants are all that are necessary for incorporation, but a minimum of 200 to 300 is a much more common requirement. Several States also require that the necessary number of inhabitants reside within a limited area — one square mile in New York, for example.

In some States a community may be organized — become an incorporated village — by being granted a charter by the State legislature. But the usual process demands that a petition containing a prescribed number of signatures of the residents of a locale be presented to a designated public officer. When that officer (usually a judge) is satisfied that the legal requirements have been met, he will declare that

---

[1] As the nation's cities have grown, so have their surrounding suburbs, especially over the past three decades. In fact, in many cases a city's suburbs have grown much more rapidly than has the city itself in recent years — as we shall see when we consider the problems of "suburbanitis" in Chapter 43.

[2] Do not confuse the town (village) in the South and West with the New England town (township) nor the borough in Pennsylvania, New Jersey, and Connecticut with the borough in Alaska where it is a substitute for the county. See pages 697, 699. In the New England States villages have been created in only a very few instances, because the town is sufficiently organized to collect the necessary taxes and provide the services that villages provide elsewhere.

[3] *Incorporated* means created into a legal body, an artificial person. The term comes from the Latin *in* (into) and *corpus* (body).

The New England village of East Corinth, Vermont, like other small communities, offers a friendly atmosphere and attractive setting for people who prefer to live away from the hustle and bustle of the city. (A. Devaney, Inc.)

the people living within a defined area to be incorporated as the village of X, having such powers as the State grants to its villages. In most States he cannot declare a village to be incorporated until the residents of the area involved have voted for the action at a special election.

Powers of Villages. The few incorporated villages in New England continue as a part of the town (township) for many important purposes such as the providing of roads and schools. The New England villages may provide independently for such things as sidewalks, lights, water, sewers, and fire and police protection, however. In those States which adopted the New England township system, the villages remain a part of the township for certain purposes, but they are more independent than those in New England.

In certain other States—for example, in New Jersey, Pennsylvania, Wisconsin, and Minnesota—villages are entirely independent of the township. They perform within their limits the functions which the township performs out-

side as well as the usual village functions. In the South and West villages are usually included within the county; but as the county is relatively unimportant, the village has power to deal with practically all local problems.

Organization of Village Government. Typically, the pattern of village governmental organization across the country is a relatively simple one.

The Council. In every village there is a legislative body, commonly called the *council* or board of trustees. Its size varies from three to nine members who are seldom elected for longer than one- or two-year terms.

In every State the council has the power to determine the tax rate (within limits imposed by the State) and to appropriate money for the various needs of the village. Generally, the council can levy special assessments against adjacent properties for such improvements as the paving of streets or the laying of sidewalks. However, villages normally have only very limited power to borrow money and must submit the question of a bond issue to the voters.

The power to pass ordinances varies from State to State and from village to village within the State. Commonly the council may choose certain officers, such as a constable, fire warden, and clerk, and regulate their duties. It may pass certain health and police ordinances; determine the license taxes for movies, peddlers, public vehicles, and other businesses that are licensed; control streets, bridges, and parks; and administer such public services as the water system.

The Mayor. The principal executive officer in the village is the *mayor* or, as he is known in some States, the burgess, intendant, or warden. He is ordinarily elected for one or two years. He presides over council meetings and usually has the rights of a member — though in some villages he has the power to vote only to break a tie. Rarely does he have the power to veto council actions. His major job is that of enforcing village ordinances. In a number of States the mayor also serves as police justice.

Every village has a clerk or recorder, a treasurer or tax collector, and a police officer (constable, marshal, sergeant, or bailiff). Many villages also have a street commissioner, an assessor, and an attorney or solicitor. In the West these officers are often elected by the villagers. In the other sections of the country they are commonly appointed by the council or the mayor.

Some villages have a justice of the peace and, where the village forms a separate school district, there are school officers, too. Larger villages often have such other officers as health, fire, and cemetery commissioners.

CITY GOVERNMENT

A city is a governmental unit created by the State, with a greater population and wider powers than those possessed by a village or town. In each State the number of inhabitants necessary to constitute a city and the powers each may exercise is prescribed by the State constitution and statutes. In Georgia a community with as few as 200 inhabitants may become a city, but in Ohio at least 5000 residents are required. There are about as many States in the Union which create city governments with less than 2500 population, as there are those which require a greater population; but the Bureau of the Census classifies all incorporated places with at least 2500 inhabitants as cities.

Cities Subordinate to the State. Cities — like counties, villages, and other units of local government — are created by the State, are responsible to the State, and receive their powers from the State. State control over cities is exercised through the State constitution and through acts of the State legislature.

	URBAN POPULATION GROWTH		
Census	Total Population	Urban Population [a]	Per Cent Urban
1790	3,929,214	201,655	5.1
1800	5,308,483	322,371	6.1
1810	7,239,881	525,459	7.3
1820	9,638,453	693,255	7.2
1830	12,866,020	1,127,247	8.8
1840	17,069,453	1,845,055	10.8
1850	23,191,876	3,543,716	15.3
1860	31,443,321	6,216,518	19.8
1870	28,558,371	9,902,361	25.7
1880	50,155,783	14,129,735	28.2
1890	62,047,714	22,106,265	35.1
1900	75,994,575	30,159,921	39.7
1910	91,972,266	41,998,932	45.7
1920	105,710,620	54,157,973	51.2
1930	122,775,046	68,954,823	56.2
1940	131,669,275	74,423,702	56.5
1950	150,697,361	96,467,686	64.0
1960	179,323,175	125,268,750	69.9
1970 [b]	204,800,000	151,000,000	73.2

[a] These figures represent the number of persons residing in those places classified as "urbanized areas" by the Bureau of the Census — that is, those residing in incorporated places of at least 2500 population and those residing in the densely populated fringes of such places.

[b] Figures for 1970 estimates.

The endless lines of cars and trucks present a formidable obstacle on those daily trips into and out of our cities. (Talbot Lovering)

In our early history State constitutions contained few provisions directly relating to cities. Practically all State control was exercised through the State legislature. The degree of control the legislature possessed, and in many ways still possesses, over cities is well-illustrated by the following excerpt from an 1868 decision of the Iowa Supreme Court:

> Cities owe their origin to, and derive their powers and rights wholly from, the legislature. It breathes into them the breath of life, without which they cannot exist. As it creates, so it may destroy. If it may destroy, it may abridge and control. Unless there is constitutional limitation on the right, the legislature might, by a single act, if we can suppose it capable of so great a folly and so great a wrong, sweep from existence all the municipal corporations in the State, and the corporations could not prevent it.

As cities grew in population and multiplied in number, this complete legislative domination produced many difficult situations. Legislators were often unfamiliar with the problems of a city, and many of the laws they passed were grossly unfair or impractical. Some State legislatures, dominated by members from the rural sections of the State, were suspicious or jealous of cities and sought to restrict their growth by imposing unreasonable burdens upon them.

Today, in reaction against the legislature's misuse and abuse of its powers, most State constitutions contain a great many provisions concerning municipal government and its problems. These provisions generally relate to city charters, city officials, elections, council meetings and procedures, taxation and expenditures, and the classification of cities.

The City Charter. The charter is the city's fundamental law or constitution. Its contents vary somewhat from city to city; but commonly the charter contains the name of the city, a description of its boundaries, and declares it to be a *municipal corporation.*

As a municipal corporation, the city has certain rights similar to those of a private corporation. It becomes a legal (artificial) person, with the right to sue and to be sued in the courts, to have a corporate seal, to make contracts, and to acquire, own, and dispose of property. It also enjoys the "right of perpetual succession"; that is, a complete change in the city's population from generation to generation does not affect its status as a legal body.

The charter also regularly provides for other powers vested in the city, outlines its form of government, determines how and for what term its officers are to be chosen and their duties, and deals with finance and similar matters.

Broadly speaking, five fairly distinct types of city charters have been or are presently found among the States.

The Special Charter. In colonial days each city usually secured its charter from the governor. The State legislature assumed the charter-granting function after the Revolutionary

War. Even today, in a few States—Maine, for example—the legislature provides a special charter for each city in the State.

The General Charter. The general charter was developed to replace the special charter. Under the special charter arrangement the State legislature was able to treat cities much as it saw fit. Often those cities whose voters proved loyal to the majority party in the legislature received charters better suited to local needs than those granted to other cities. In some States all city charters were hopeless reflections of the ignorance, jealousies, and suspicions of rural legislators. By the middle of the nineteenth century several States began attempts to overcome the difficulties of the special charter process by providing a general charter—one for all cities in the State. But the newer arrangement soon proved to be as unfair. A charter that, was satisfactory for a small mining community was not at all adequate for a large seacoast city. None of the States today provides one general charter for all of its cities.

The Classified Charter. The defects of both the special and general charter systems led to the development of the classified charter system. Under this arrangement all cities within the State are classified (grouped) according to population, and a uniform charter is granted to all cities within the same class.

The classified charter system is much superior to either the special or general charter systems and is used in several of the States. Still, it leaves much to be desired. Even within the same population class there may be cities in the State which are vastly different from one another. The governmental problems which face an industrial community of 50,000 population, for example, are usually quite unlike those which face a community of the same size in a farming region.

Often a State will classify cities in such a way that only one city falls into a particular class. For example, there may be only one city in the State with more than 500,000 inhabitants, or

"A COUPLE HUNDRED BILLION WOULD HELP" More and more, cities are forced to turn to their State capitals and to Washington for help in confronting their many problems. (Hesse, St. Louis Globe-Democrat)

there may be only one city with a population between 200,000 and 500,000. Such classification can amount, in effect, to the old special charter system in disguise.

The Optional Charter. Over the past half century most States have turned to optional charters to meet the objections to the special, general, and classified charter systems. Ohio inaugurated the optional charter system when it offered to each of its cities a choice among three different charters. Several States soon followed Ohio's lead, and many of them continue to offer their cities a choice of charters today.[4] In Ohio today each city may choose

---

[4] Including the States of Iowa, Kansas, Massachusetts, Montana, Nebraska, New Jersey, North Carolina, North Dakota, Ohio, South Dakota, Virginia, and Wisconsin. Not all States use only one or another of the charter systems outlined above. Most use one system for *most* cities but another system for *some*.

from among three basic charters, with the final choice made by popular vote.

The optional charter system has much to recommend it. In large part it overcomes the major objections to the special, general, and classified arrangements. Still, it does not allow the fullest possible consideration of peculiar local circumstances, nor does it permit the broadest possible play of local desires in the framing of a city's charter.

The Home Rule Charter. The fact that none of the other charter systems has produced a satisfactory method for the providing of adequate charters to many cities spurred the development of municipal home rule. Two-thirds of the States now (1970) provide for municipal home rule. That is, they have provided—either by legislative enactment or by constitutional provision—that some or all of their cities may adopt and amend their own charters.

Statutory Home Rule. In most of these States municipal home rule has been established in constitutional provisions. In four States, however, it rests on the basis of legislative enactments alone.[5] That is, in those States the State legislature, exercising its powers over cities, has granted at least some degree of home rule to at least some of the cities within the State.

The providing of home rule by statute has proved generally unsatisfactory in those States where it has been attempted, however. In large part this has been due to the reluctance of the State legislature to relinquish a sufficient amount of its control over local matters, and to the additional fact that legislative grants are subject to modification and even outright repeal at any time. Florida stands as a notable exception to this observation, however; its legislature has given to cities quite broad powers with which to meet local problems.

Constitutional Home Rule. Beginning with Missouri in 1875, thirty-two States now provide for home rule in their constitutions.[6] In some of them *any* city may adopt a home rule charter—for example, in Minnesota, Oregon, Michigan, and Wisconsin. In most of these States *only certain* cities may have one. For example, home rule is available to cities of over 10,000 population in Missouri, of over 3500 population in California, of over 5000 population in Texas, and of over 2000 population in Colorado and Oklahoma.

Typically, constitutional home rule provisions grant cities the power to control "municipal affairs" or grant them "powers of local self-government." These generalized provisions leave the State legislature with at least some control over home rule cities, for there are many situations in which it is at least difficult to distinguish matters of purely *local* concern from those of *general State* concern—for example, the setting of a speed limit on city streets that are also State highways or the regulation of a city sewage system which empties into a river flowing through the State. The question of city versus State control in such borderline cases must be settled in the courts,

---

[5] Florida, New Hampshire, North Carolina, and South Carolina.

[6] Alaska (1959), Arizona (1912), California (1879), Colorado (1902), Connecticut (1965), Georgia (1950), Hawaii (1959), Iowa (1968), Kansas (1960), Louisiana (1946), Maryland (1915), Massachusetts (1966), Michigan (1908), Minnesota (1896), Missouri (1875), Nebraska (1912), Nevada (1924), New Mexico (1949), New York (1923), North Dakota (1966), Ohio (1912), Oklahoma (1908), Oregon (1906), Pennsylvania (1922), Rhode Island (1951), South Dakota (1962), Tennessee (1953), Texas (1912), Utah (1932), Washington (1889), West Virginia (1936), and Wisconsin (1924).

Home rule has been used most often by cities in California, Colorado, Michigan, Minnesota, Ohio, Oklahoma, Oregon, and Texas. In Nevada no city has as yet (1970) written its own charter.

but a few of the newer State constitutions attempt to solve the problem by listing the specific areas in which the cities have exclusive powers.

A home rule charter may be framed by the city council, by a group of interested citizens, or by a charter convention composed of elected delegates. Once drafted, the charter must be submitted to the city's voters for their approval. Amendments may be proposed by the council and in some cities by initiative petition; they must be ratified by the voters.

Altogether, well over 3000 American cities may, if they wish, make their own charters today. Nearly 1000 of them have done so. About two-thirds of our fifty largest cities are in home rule States. The major home rule cities include Baltimore, Cincinnati, Cleveland, Dayton, Detroit, Denver, Houston, Kansas City (Missouri), Los Angeles, Philadelphia, Portland (Oregon), and St. Louis.

Changing Municipal Boundaries. As a city's population grows, the areas surrounding it tend to grow, too. A city's fringe areas often create rather serious problems for the city itself. For example, shacks present fire hazards, septic tanks might pollute the city's water, or immoral roadhouses might complicate law enforcement.

Methods for the annexing (adding) of territory to the city are usually provided by the State constitution or by act of the State legislature. Compulsory annexation (that is, forcing an area into a city) is rare; usually a vote of the residents of the area to be annexed is required. In some States the voters in the city must also vote on the question.

Suburbs often tend to resist annexation. Thus, most States give their cities *extraterritorial powers* to regulate certain matters such as roadhouses, sanitation, or fire hazards in the thickly settled areas around the city. Cities sometimes induce suburbs to come into the city by agreeing not to raise taxes in the annexed area for a certain number of years, or to raise them only gradually.

FORMS OF CITY GOVERNMENT

Which is more important: a particular form of government or the men who operate it? Men have argued this question for centuries. In 1733 Alexander Pope penned this famous couplet:

> For forms of government let fools contest;
> Whate'er is best administer'd is best....

Certainly good men are essential to good government, and good men can make the best of even the worst of forms. But the form is important, too. The better the form of government, the more chance there is that capable people will be attracted to public service and that the public will receive the kind of service it wants.

There are three principal forms of city government in America: the mayor-council, commission, and council-manager forms. No two cities have *exactly* the same governmental arrangements, of course; specific details vary from city to city.

Mayor-Council Form. The mayor-council form of city government is the oldest and still the most widely used type. Its major features are a council to make the laws (*ordinances*) and a mayor to enforce them.

The council is almost always unicameral. In fact, only one of the nation's cities today (1970) has a bicameral council—Everett, Massachusetts. There are usually five, seven, or nine councilmen, but there are more in many larger cities. Chicago's council is the largest, with fifty members.

The councilmen (sometimes called aldermen) are nearly always elected by the city's voters for terms varying from one to four years. The councilmen usually are elected from *wards* (districts) within the city, but the trend today is toward election at-large (from the entire city). Partisan election is still the rule in most mayor-council cities, but an increasing number of cities in the nation are turning to the nonpartisan ballot.

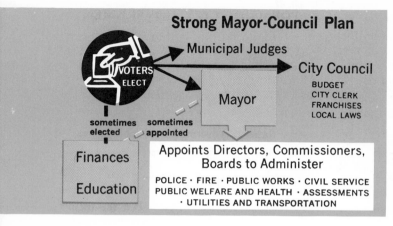

Strong Mayor-Council Plan

VOTERS ELECT → Municipal Judges

→ City Council
BUDGET
CITY CLERK
FRANCHISES
LOCAL LAWS

Mayor

sometimes elected — sometimes appointed

Finances

Education

Appoints Directors, Commissioners, Boards to Administer
POLICE · FIRE · PUBLIC WORKS · CIVIL SERVICE
PUBLIC WELFARE AND HEALTH · ASSESSMENTS
· UTILITIES AND TRANSPORTATION

Weak Mayor-Council Plan

Acts Must be Approved by Council

Mayor

VOTERS ELECT

City Council | Finance Officer | Other Elected Officials

Appointed Officials

The mayor is commonly elected by the voters, too—usually for the same term as the councilmen. He often is not a member of the council but presides over its meetings, votes in cases of tie, and may recommend and veto ordinances. The mayor's veto can in almost all cities be overridden by a two-thirds vote of the council.

Strong-Mayor and Weak-Mayor Plans. The mayor-council form is said to be of the *strong-mayor* or *weak-mayor* type, depending upon the powers of the mayor. In the strong-mayor type the mayor is placed at the head of the city administration, usually has the power to hire and fire city employees, prepares the budget, and otherwise has "strong" powers to conduct the city's business—subject to council control.

In the weak-mayor type the mayor has much less power. Sometimes he does not have the veto and cannot appoint or dismiss city officials. He is often simply the city's "major-domo" for ceremonial occasions.

Our larger mayor-council cities are almost all strong-mayor cities. Even so, Los Angeles has had a rather excellent city government for years with a weak-mayor arrangement.

Evaluation. The success of mayor-council government depends in large measure on the popularity and influence of the mayor. Especially in the weak-mayor cities, responsibility for government is hard to fix, as can be seen

from the diagram on this page. Leadership is almost wholly lacking.

The strong-mayor plan helps to solve the problem of leadership. Still, it is criticized by students of city government for three major reasons. First, whenever the mayor and the council become involved in a major dispute with one another, effective city government is liable to be stalemated. Secondly, the strong-mayor plan still relies for success upon the nature of the mayor himself. Thirdly, the mayor-council plan is complicated and often misunderstood by the average citizen. This sometimes makes it possible for a corrupt political machine to control the city. Corrupt machines are pretty much relics of the past, but they are not unknown today. Organizations of aroused citizens can and have defeated political bosses and their machines, as the Cincinnati Charter Committee did in the 1920's and as an organization of independents drawn from both major parties did in Philadelphia in 1951. Still, a less complicated form of city government stands as one of the major protections against corrupt or "invisible" rule.

Commission Form. Commission government was first tried with success in Galveston, Texas, in 1901. A tidal wave had swept over the island city in 1900 and left it in partial ruins. Nearly 7000 of Galveston's then 37,000 inhabitants were drowned, and property valued at

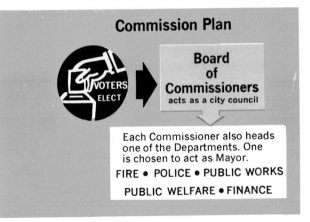

Commission Plan

VOTERS ELECT → **Board of Commissioners** acts as a city council

Each Commissioner also heads one of the Departments. One is chosen to act as Mayor.

FIRE • POLICE • PUBLIC WORKS

PUBLIC WELFARE • FINANCE

Council-Manager Plan

VOTERS ELECT → **Council** employs **Manager** who administers

FIRE • POLICE • PUBLIC WORKS

PUBLIC WELFARE • FINANCE

$20,000,000 was destroyed. The old mayor-council regime was too corrupt and too incompetent to meet the catastrophe.

The Texas legislature granted Galveston a new charter which provided for the governing of the city by five commissioners with power to make and enforce the laws. The plan was intended to be temporary, but it proved to be so efficient that it spread to other Texas cities and then to other parts of the country. In the past few decades, however, many cities have switched from the commission form to the newer council-manager system. In 1960 the voters of Galveston approved a new city charter establishing council-manager government for their city. Fewer than 10 per cent of the nation's cities of more than 5000 population now have commission government. The largest ones today are Portland (Oregon), St. Paul, and Tulsa.

The commission form of government is rather simple and uncomplicated. Three, five, or seven men are elected "commissioners" (usually there are five). Together the commissioners form the city council; individually they are the heads of the various departments of the city administration. In other words, both executive and legislative powers are centered in the one body.

In some cities the voters and in others the commissioners themselves designate one of the commissioners as mayor. Like the other commissioners, the mayor heads one of the departments; he also presides over council meetings and represents the city on ceremonial occasions. He seldom has any more authority than his fellow commissioners, and only rarely does he have the veto power.

The commissioners are usually elected for two- or four-year terms from the city at-large. Over three-fourths of the commission cities use the nonpartisan ballot, and the commissioners almost always serve as full-time officials.

The names of the various departments of city government may vary somewhat, but in general their work covers these activities: public affairs, finance, public safety, streets and public improvements, and parks and public property.

Various plans are used to determine which department each commissioner is to head. In most cities the commission itself assigns its members to particular posts. In some cities the voters elect commissioners to head specific departments. In a few cities the assignments are made by the mayor, who is almost always the commissioner of public safety.

In its early days the commission form was often criticized because it lacked a system of checks and balances and did nothing to eliminate the spoils system. In 1907 Des Moines,

Iowa, adopted a charter to help meet these criticisms. Des Moines added the initiative, referendum, and recall, the merit system, and nonpartisan election to the Galveston plan. These improvements stimulated the spread of the commission form.[7]

Evaluation. The advantages of the commission form of government are four: (1) The number of commissioners to elect is small. (2) They can act promptly. (3) They have full power to act and cannot shirk their responsibility by referring an aggrieved citizen to someone else. (4) They are easier to watch than if they were many.

The way to get good government is to give power to a few people and watch those few in order to hold them responsible. The commissioners meet in public, record their votes for the inspection of the public, publish their ordinances in the papers, and issue frequent financial reports.

If they refuse to enact an ordinance which the majority of voters desire, the voters themselves may initiate and pass it (the initiative). If the commission passes an ordinance which the voters do not want, they may have it referred to them and reject it (the referendum). If the commissioners are believed to be dishonest or are inefficient, a recall election may be called and one or all of the commissioners recalled by electing others to take their places (the recall). Thus, we get government for the people by a few who are responsible directly to the people.

In one sense, however, the commission form violates the principle that policy-makers should be elected by the people and that administrators should be appointed. In the commission form the people should and do elect their representatives as councilmen to make the city laws. These same councilmen also administer the laws. Efficient experts to enforce laws and administer a city, however, should not be subject

to those political influences and residential restrictions which control elective positions. Such experts are usually best secured through appointment.

The commission form, moreover, does not locate responsibility as well as the council-manager form. It often creates five little governments, since each commissioner often attempts to draw as much of the money and authority as he can to his own department.

Council-Manager Form. Council-manager government was born in Staunton, Virginia, in 1908. The Staunton city council, acting under a charter provision allowing it to appoint new officials as needed, created the post of "general manager" in that year. The general manager's chief duty was to shake up the inefficient and old-fashioned city administration in order to provide Staunton with an efficient city government. The council gave him full charge of the city departments and the power to hire and fire all employees.

The first city charter specifically providing for a council-manager government was granted by the South Carolina legislature to Sumter in 1912. Under its new charter Sumter elected three exceptionally capable men as its first three councilmen; one was a planter, another a banker, and the third a lawyer. They advertised for a manager and hired a man from another State.

The new manager brought efficiency and a number of economies to Sumter's government. For example, many of the fine old trees lining the city's streets were being choked out by mistletoe which hadn't been removed because of the great cost involved. The manager knew that mistletoe has a time and place value, however. He had it cut from the trees and sold it in the North at a price to cover the cost of the project.

Dayton, Ohio, was the first large city to adopt the council-manager plan. The residents of Dayton had long been disgusted with their inefficient city government. Just as a tidal wave in 1900 had brought commission government

---

[7] Galveston (since 1960) and Des Moines (since 1949) now have council-manager governments.

to Galveston, so a disastrous Miami River flood brought council-manager government to Dayton in 1913. Acting under Ohio's home rule amendment of 1912, the citizens of Dayton adopted a new charter in 1913 by an overwhelming vote.

The council-manager plan spread with the publicity Dayton gave it. Today (1970) it is found in over 2300 cities, including such large cities as Cincinnati, Dallas, Fort Worth, and Kansas City (Missouri).

Council-manager government is really a modification of the mayor-council form. Essentially, it consists of a strong council and a weak mayor with a manager appointed by the council. The manager has responsibility for city administration, is usually appointed for an indefinite term, and is held accountable by the council at all times. In effect, this form leaves the responsibility for policy-making where it belongs, in the hands of elected councilmen. It places the responsibility for administration in the hands of a nonpartisan expert.

Evaluation. The council-manager form has near-unanimous backing from students of government. It clearly locates responsibility; "if anything goes wrong, you know whom to blame." It makes possible the separation of politics and administration; and, because the more time-consuming and routine functions of administration are performed by the city manager, prominent and well-qualified residents are more likely to run for the *part-time* job of city councilman.

Council-manager government promotes efficiency. For example, the city manager of Saginaw, Michigan, reduced the number of full-time bridge tenders, who did nothing but raise and lower drawbridges an average of twice a week to allow barges to pass, from forty-two to seven by having police cars speed to bridges when they needed to be raised for an occassional barge.

The few criticisms sometimes advanced against the council-manager form are in almost every instance not criticisms of the system at all, but in reality are criticisms of the individuals involved in its operation.

Only a handful of cities which have once adopted the plan have later abandoned it, the chief ones being Cleveland and Houston. Today cities are switching to it in ever-increasing numbers.

LEGAL LIABILITIES OF CITIES

As we have said, cities are creatures of the State; they are a part of the State. As such, they usually enjoy the same immunity from suits that States do.

Generally speaking, a city may not be sued (is not liable) when it is engaged in a purely *governmental function* unless State law specifically permits a suit. Thus, a city is not usually liable for wrongs committed by such city employees as policemen, firemen, or public health officers. For example, if a fire truck crashes into a car on its way to a fire, the city cannot be held for damages. If a school child becomes infected because a city health officer used an unsterile needle in vaccinating him, the city is not liable. If a policeman is unnecessarily violent, the city cannot be sued. Of course, city employees may be sued as individuals. For example, a policeman who is negligent in operating his motorcycle and runs down a pedestrian may be held for damages by the injured party.

When a city is engaged in a *nongovernmental* or *corporate (business) function,* it may generally be sued. Activities which are commonly held to be nongovernmental include such functions as water, electricity, and gas supply, liquor stores, public markets, and transportation systems. Thus, we have the rather strange situation in which, for example, a pedestrian cannot sue the city if he is run down and injured by a city fire truck or police car but he can bring suit against the city if the vehicle which hits him happens to be from the water department!

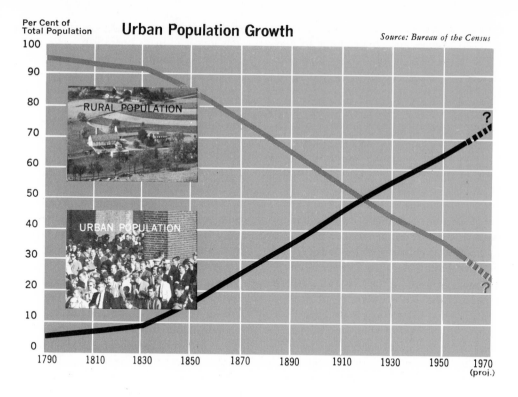

Per Cent of Total Population

Urban Population Growth

Source: Bureau of the Census

RURAL POPULATION

URBAN POPULATION

100
90
80
70
60
50
40
30
20
10
0

1790 1810 1830 1850 1870 1890 1910 1930 1950 1970 (proj.)

✳✳✳✳✳✳✳✳✳✳✳✳ CONCEPT BUILDING ✳✳✳✳✳✳✳✳✳✳✳✳

Key Concepts

America's cities have grown spectacularly in both size and importance, especially in the past 100 years. Where our population was originally and predominantly agricultural and rural, it is now largely industrial and urban. Nearly three-fourths of all our people now live in urban areas.

A village is an incorporated community in which the population is smaller and the government is simpler than that of cities in the same State. Villages exist to provide essential public services in areas where a relatively small population is concentrated. Village government consists almost wholly of a mayor and council, although their exact names vary somewhat from State to State.

A city is a governmental unit created by the State with more population and wider powers than a village. Cities are creatures of the State. In our early history most State control over cities was exercised through the State legislature, but legislative abuse has led to many constitutional protections for cities.

A city's charter is its fundamental law and is granted by the State, either through the State legislature or by constitutional home rule provisions. Broadly speaking, there are five types of charters: special, general, classified, and optional charters granted by the State legislature, and the home rule charter which is drafted by the city itself. Four States now provide for home rule by statute and thirty-two by constitutional provision.

City boundaries are extended by the annexation process, and cities are often given extraterritorial powers to deal with matters outside their boundaries.

The oldest and most widely used form of city government is the mayor-council form. It is of either the weak-mayor or strong-mayor type, depending upon the powers of the mayor. The weak-mayor type is especially criticized because responsibility is difficult to fix. The strong-mayor type is preferred over the weak-mayor plan, but still may be criticized because it tends to break down when the mayor and the council are at odds. Moreover, it places too much reliance upon the nature of the person who is mayor, and it is too complicated to be understood easily.

The commission form of city government originated in Galveston, Texas, in 1901 and spread across the country, though its use is declining today. It consists of elected commissioners who collectively form the city council and individually head the various departments of city administration. Commission government has much to recommend it although it still makes it difficult to locate responsibility and violates the principle of separation of powers.

The council-manager form of city government originated in Staunton, Virginia, in 1908 and was popularized by Dayton, Ohio, where it was adopted in 1913. It is now found in over 2300 cities, and more cities are adopting it each year. Essentially, council-manager government consists of an elected mayor and council to make policy and an appointed manager to administer that policy. It is backed by students of government as the best of the three major forms.

Generally, cities may not be sued when engaged in governmental functions but are liable to suit when engaged in nongovernmental functions.

Important Terms

annexation	council-manager form	incorporate	optional charter
borough	extraterritorial powers	mayor-council form	special charter
classified charter	general charter	municipal corporation	urbanization
commission form	home rule	nongovernmental functions	village

Questions for Inquiry and Review

1. What proportion of our population was urban in 1790? In 1970?
2. What were the chief causes of the rapid growth of cities?
3. What is a *village?*
4. What is a *town* in New England?
5. How does a city differ from a town?
6. What is a city charter?
7. What five general types of city charters have been or are used among the States?
8. What is the basic purpose of municipal home rule?
9. Does your State's constitution provide for home rule?
10. Why do many cities possess extraterritorial powers?
11. Why is the question of form important in terms of the quality of city government?
12. Which is the most common of the three major forms of city government?

13. What are the principal grounds upon which the strong-mayor and weak-mayor forms of mayor-council government are criticized?

14. Why have many cities abandoned the commission form?

15. Why is the council-manager form widely recommended by many students of city government?

16. May a city be sued for damages caused while performing one of its governmental functions? For damages caused by one of its non-governmental functions?

For Further Inquiry

1. Do you think that every city should be permitted to frame and adopt its own charter?

2. What sort of training do you think a city manager should have? If your city does not have council-manager government, do you think it should? What do you think of the old saying: "Experts should be on tap, not on top?"

3. Would a city be liable to suit in most States in the following situations?

(a) A policeman lost his temper when arresting a drunken driver and broke the latter's arm.

(b) The motorman of a city-owned and city-operated street railway started too soon and injury resulted to a boarding passenger.

(c) A city ambulance carrying a patient was driven at reckless speed and smashed into a legally parked private car.

(d) Typhoid fever was contracted from city water because of the carelessness of city employees at the city's reservoir.

4. Why are bicameral city councils almost wholly unknown among American cities?

5. In *Avery* v. *Midland County, Texas,* 1968, the Supreme Court held the "one-man, one-vote" rule to apply to all "units of local government having general governmental powers over the entire geographic area served by the body"—including, then, city councils. Has that decision had any effect on the composition of your city's governing body? If not, why?

Suggested Activities

1. Stage a debate or class forum on one of the following questions: (1) *Resolved,* That our city ought to adopt (or abandon) the council-manager form of government. (2) *Resolved,* That our city ought to be made legally responsible for any negligent act by one of its employees. (3) *Resolved,* That our city's chief of police ought to be elected by popular vote.

2. Obtain a copy of your city's charter and discover the exact nature of the organization of its government. What changes, if any, would you recommend be made in it?

3. Invite the mayor, a member of the city council, or the city manager (if there is one) to speak to the class on the city's government, its functions and problems, and his job.

4. If at all possible, attend a session of the city council.

Suggested Reading

BANFIELD, EDWARD C. (ed.), *Urban Government.* The Free Press, 1969.

"Cleveland's Carl Stokes: Making It," *Newsweek,* May 26, 1969.

FLAGLER, J. M., "Mayor in Motion," *Look,* June 24, 1969.

FLINN, THOMAS A., *Local Government and Politics.* Scott, Foresman, 1969.

JACOBS, JANE, *The Economy of Cities.* Random House, 1969.

POWELEDGE, FRED, "The Flight from City Hall," *Harper's,* November, 1969.

WINTER, WILLIAM O., *The Urban Polity.* Dodd, Mead, 1969.

WOLFF, ANTHONY, "All America Cities," *Look,* April 15, 1969.

Men come together in cities in order to live; they remain together in order to live the good life.

ARISTOTLE

*** What is the single most important problem confronting the nation's cities today?

*** Should a city's planning commission be composed of planning experts or of representatives of the people?

*** On balance, is the continuing national trend to suburbanization a good or a bad thing? Why?

A city exists in order to provide services to those who live within it. The range and the variety of those services, provided by cities day in and day out, are far broader and much more numerous than most of the residents ever realize. Much of what a city does seems so commonplace and familiar, is so taken for granted, that few ever pause to appreciate the real extent to which their city enters into their every waking and sleeping moment.

It would be impossible to compile a complete list of *all* of the functions cities perform. Consider, however, some of the many things that most or all of them do: provide police and fire protection; build and maintain streets, sidewalks, street lighting systems, parking lots, bridges, tunnels, parks and playgrounds, swimming pools, golf courses, libraries, hospitals, schools, correctional institutions, homes for the aged, airports, public markets, and auditoriums; furnish such health and sanitation services as disease prevention programs, sewers, and rubbish and garbage collection and disposal; operate water, light, gas, and transportation systems; and regulate traffic, building practices, and public utilities.

Then, too, many cities build and manage public housing projects, clear slums, conduct city "clean-up" campaigns, maintain youth camps, keep docks and wharves, and operate tourist attractions. Several cities, large and small, have built their own hydroelectric power dams. A growing number of them now operate profitable farms in connection with their sewage disposal plants.

The list of city functions is well-nigh endless. Today, nearly all of our large, and many of our smaller, cities issue an annual report—a summary of the city's condition and of the activities of its government over the past year. Many of these reports have become fair-sized books.

In carrying out their tasks, cities face many serious and difficult problems. In this chapter we point up some of the more important of them and indicate some of the ways in which various cities have attempted to meet them.

CITY PLANNING

Most American cities have, like Topsy, "just growed." With few exceptions, they have developed without plan, haphazardly and with no eye to the future. The narrow and crooked streets of the original city of Boston are said to have followed cow paths. The streets of most of our early cities were considered wide enough if one horse-and-wagon team could pass another.

The results of this shortsightedness have been unfortunate and are all too obvious. In many cities the busiest downtown streets are much too narrow. Main thoroughfares are often too close together and sometimes too far apart. Inadequate parking space is a constant and a growing problem. There are seldom enough parks and other recreational areas. Those that do exist are usually far too small. Such public buildings as schools, police and fire stations, and hospitals are often inconveniently located and sometimes quite difficult to find.

Planning Commissions. Fortunately, more and more of our cities have now recognized the need for city planning. That is, they have come to recognize the need to correct past mistakes in development and, as well, the values that can be realized from orderly growth in the future. The first permanent city planning commission was created at Hartford, Connecticut, in 1907; today, only a few cities of more than 10,000 population do not have one.

Washington, D.C., is one of the few cities in the nation that began as, and has remained, a planned city. The basic plan for the nation's capital was drawn up before a single building was erected. When Congress decided in 1790 to locate the city on the Potomac River, President Washington sent to France for Major Pierre-Charles L'Enfant. L'Enfant, an engineer, had served in the Continental Army during the Revolution and was now given the task of laying out the new city.

He laid it out on a grand scale with adequate parks and beautiful circles. Parallel streets, running in an east-west direction, were named according to the alphabet, and those running at right angles were numbered. Twenty-one avenues were provided to shorten distances by cutting diagonally through the city, and trees and shrubs were planted at the intersections. The streets were purposely made wide, and large areas were reserved for government buildings.

The National Capital Planning Commission guides the city's development today. In close cooperation with appropriate State and local planning agencies, it attempts to influence the growth of the surrounding areas in Maryland and Virginia.

Philadelphia also began as a planned city. It was first laid out by William Penn in 1682 much in the fashion of a checkerboard. Penn's simple scheme called for two main thoroughfares crossing one another at right angles, with an open place at the point of intersection; other lesser streets crisscrossed the pattern at regular intervals. In his plan, the City of Brotherly Love was to cover some two square miles.

Philadelphia has long since outgrown its founder's plan. It is now the fourth largest city in the United States and sprawls over some 130 square miles with a population of more than 2,000,000. Much of its growth has been haphazard and without plan, and, inevitably, has resulted in congestion. The city's problems were compounded by the fact that for seventy-five years, until the 1950's, it lay in the grip of a corrupt political machine.

For the past several years Philadelphia has been engaged in a vast and popular plan of self-improvement. Whole blocks of buildings have been torn down and replaced by beautiful parks, modern highways, and business and apartment buildings. The Pennsylvania Railroad's ancient Broad Street Station, in the heart of the city, was torn down. To celebrate the razing, the 103-piece Philadelphia Symphony Orchestra played a requiem in the train shed,

Typical of city planning for self-improvement is that which has gone on in Philadelphia. These before-and-after photos of the same district show quite clearly how the community benefits. (Philadelphia City Planning Commission)

and its conductor, Eugene Ormandy, led a large and enthusiastic crowd in the singing of *Auld Lang Syne.*

Many other large cities are gaining through wise city planning. Pittsburgh has accomplished a modern miracle by eliminating the industrial smog which only a few years ago blanketed its downtown area so completely that street lights often had to be turned on by 10 A.M. The heart of the city's business district, the Golden Triangle, has been rebuilt, and so have the areas around it, with modern skyscrapers and landscaped parks which include many levels of underground parking.

In Dallas, Houston, Seattle, Detroit, and elsewhere new expressways and one-way street systems have eased downtown traffic congestion. San Francisco, Los Angeles, Boston, and other cities have put in underground garages with beautifully planned and kept parks right on top of them in the middle of the busiest districts.

The accomplishments in these and other cities in recent years are largely the result of the efforts of public-spirited citizens, many of them prominent businessmen. A growing number of cities have been and are being helped by loans, grants, advice, and other aid from the

National Government.[1] Some of the major insurance companies have lent several cities a welcome hand, too, replacing slums with vast and modern housing projects—many of which are, in fact, "cities within cities."

Many smaller cities are now seeking solutions to their problems through intelligent, long-range planning. Of course, some cities—including some of our major ones—are still stuck in their own quagmires; but tremendous progress is being made in city after city across the country.

CITY ZONING

The practice of dividing a city into a number of districts (zones) and of regulating the kinds of property and the uses to which it may be put in each is known as *zoning*. Zoning is really a phase of the larger problem of city planning. Many cities, and especially the smaller ones, however, have enacted zoning ordinances and yet have no overall plan for city growth. Every city in the United States with more than 100,000 residents is zoned—except Houston, where zoning was rejected by popular vote.

It would be quite surprising to find a bathtub in the living room or a piano in the kitchen of a home. It seems equally absurd for cities to have allowed stores to crowd in at random among private homes, for factories and public garages to have elbowed in among neat retail stores and well-kept apartment houses, and for tall, bulky office buildings to have been jammed so closely together that their lower floors are almost dungeon-like.

---

[1] Most of this aid is now channeled through the Renewal Assistance Administration, the Community Resources Development Administration, and the Model Cities Administration in the Department of Housing and Urban Development (see pages 513–514); and, as we suggested in Chapter 28, it will probably be increased substantially in coming years.

At first, courts would not permit city councils to restrict an owner in the use of his property, except in the case of such well-recognized nuisances as pig pens, glue factories, tanneries, slaughterhouses, forges, gas works, oil tanks, powder magazines, and the like. The right to regulate the location of these nuisances had come down to us through the common law.

The developing science of sanitation taught us that there were many nuisances that had not been previously recognized. With the spread of education, ugliness began to hurt the eyes as noise had long offended the ears and odors the nose. The courts began to recognize new nuisances and gradually permitted more and more regulation of private property as a proper exercise of the police power. Boston, for example, was allowed to limit the height of buildings. Los Angeles excluded brickyards from residential districts, and Roanoke, Virginia, required that new buildings be erected at least a certain specified distance back from the street.

In laying out suburban plots, real estate dealers have long sold the lots subject to certain restrictions on their use. These restrictions are incorporated in each deed of conveyance. It was not until 1926, however, when the United States Supreme Court upheld the zoning ordinance enacted by the city council of Euclid, Ohio, that cities were assured of the legality of the zoning of an entire city with restrictions as to the height and size of buildings, the percentage of the lot that may be occupied, the size of yards and courts, the location and use of buildings, and the use of land for trade, industry, residence, and other purposes.

Usually, cities are divided into three basic zones: residential, commercial, and industrial or manufacturing. Each of these is commonly divided into subcategories; for example, the residential zones may be broken down into those areas reserved for one-family residences, those in which two-family dwellings are permitted, and those in which apartment buildings and other multi-family units are allowed.

The purposes of zoning are well stated in the following ten points set forth by the Boston City Planning Board:

1. Zoning divides the city into districts, according to the most suitable and valuable uses for each district, based on existing conditions and future needs, and regulates the location and use of new buildings.

2. Zoning makes provision for *general business districts* in suitable locations in which industrial plants may not impair the business environment.

3. Zoning chooses suitable land for *industrial districts* where the best of transportation facilities by rail, water, highway, and air may be secured and factories may easily expand without the tearing down of expensive buildings.

4. Zoning provides *unrestricted districts,* suitable places for those heavy industries such as stockyards, boiler works, coke manufacture, and other industries that would be objectionable elsewhere.

5. Zoning regulates the *height of buildings,* appropriate to their use, in order to provide an equitable distribution of light and air for all, minimizes overcrowding of people, and relieves traffic congestion.

6. Zoning provides *local business districts,* conveniently located near residential neighborhoods, where stores are concentrated rather than scattered.

7. Zoning protects the comfort, convenience, and quietness of *residential districts* by excluding stores, public garages, laundries, factories, and other business and industrial uses.

8. Zoning establishes *uniform building lines* in residential districts to assure an equal amount of light and air and access for all residences.

9. Zoning provides adequate light and air by *side and rear yards* around every building in the suburban residential districts and establishes the *percentage of area of a lot* that may be occupied by buildings.

10. Zoning preserves the home character of single- and two-family residence districts by segregating types of residences into appropriate districts.

Zoning Ordinances Must Be Reasonable. Recall that the 14th Amendment prohibits any State—including its cities, of course—from depriving any person of his life, liberty, or property without due process of law. Most of the State constitutions contain a similar provision.

Quite obviously, zoning *does* deprive a person of the right to use his property for certain purposes. Thus, if an area is zoned to permit only single-family residences, one may not build an apartment house or a service station on his property within that zone.[2] Notice, too, that zoning sometimes reduces the value of a particular piece of property; for example, a choice corner lot may be more valuable with a drive-in restaurant rather than a house on it.

But, although zoning may at times deprive one of his liberty or his property, the key question always is: Does it do so *without due process of law?* That is, does it do so *unreasonably?*

The question of reasonableness is one for the courts to decide. Thus, courts have held that zoning ordinances which require that buildings above a particular height must be torn down are unreasonable deprivations of property. So long as a city can show that its zoning ordinance is a reasonable exercise of its *police power,* however, the ordinance will be upheld.[3] For example, ordinances which require the removal of such nuisances as garbage dumps, slaughterhouses, stables, and wrecking yards have regularly been upheld as reasonable exercises of the police power.

A glance at the zoning map of almost any city will show many "spots" zoned differently

---

[2] However, nonconforming uses in existence *before* a zoning ordinance is enacted are almost invariably allowed to continue. Rarely are property owners required to abandon an established use of their property.

[3] The *police power* is the power of the State (and its local governments, including cities) to regulate in the interest of the public health, safety, morals, or welfare. See pages 104, 623.

from the larger areas in which they are located; for example, a single lot or a few lots will be zoned for commercial use in a residential area. Where these spots have been created *after* the area was zoned for other purposes, they are examples of what is known as *spot zoning*—and they are often the result of heavy pressures brought to bear on the city council. As a general rule, spot zoning should be discouraged.

SUBURBANITIS AND METROPOLITAN AREAS

Suburbanitis. Most of our larger cities are suffering from what has been called "suburbanitis." They are literally bursting at the seams, with their populations spilling over into their surrounding suburbs. Today more than 70,000,000 Americans—over a third of our total population and half of our urban population—are living in suburban areas.[4]

From 1950 to 1960 the nation's population grew by 18.5 per cent, or more than 28,000,000. Most of this huge increase came among the suburban population; it jumped some 19,000,000—about forty-seven per cent—over the decade. Many of the nation's larger cities actually *lost* population during the 1950's while their suburbs were growing by leaps and bounds. In fact, among our ten largest cities, only two—Houston and Los Angeles—actually gained in population between 1950 and 1960.

According to the Census Bureau, six major reasons have led people to move from the city to the near-by countryside: (1) fast and economical means of transportation, (2) noise and overcrowding in the cities, (3) the attractions of a home with a little ground and fresh air around it, (4) newer schools and safer playing conditions for children, (5) more and more

industrial and commercial building on the outer fringes of cities, and (6) increasing city taxes.

This shift to the suburbs has produced a great many problems for cities. Among the most important are: (1) the loss of many of the more able and civic-minded who might otherwise be helping the city to solve its problems, (2) the loss of tax revenues the city would otherwise collect from suburbanites who work within the city but live outside of it, (3) the loss of private capital, now used for suburban development, which might have been used for the making of downtown improvements, and (4) the dangers presented by the growth of illegal or other unsavory activities just beyond the city's boundaries.

Many of these suburban areas resist annexation. Most suburbanites moved out of the city purposely, and many are not anxious to rejoin it. In some cities, sales taxes have been imposed in an attempt to gain revenue from suburbanites who shop in the city; but in many instances this has only encouraged the growth of suburban shopping centers and the establishing of branches of downtown department stores. In some places, this spreading out has meant that neighboring cities have grown together like Siamese Twins.

Metropolitan Areas. While the growth and sprawl of suburbia has produced a number of difficult problems for cities, those who live in suburban areas face their share of problems, too. Water supply, sewage disposal, police and fire protection, transportation, traffic control, and planning for orderly development are only some of them. Duplication of functions by city and city, or city and county, is at best wasteful and at times even dangerous. More than one fire has burned on, for example, while neighboring fire departments quibbled over which, if either, of them was responsible for fighting it.

Attempts to meet the needs of metropolitan areas—that is, of the cities *and* their surrounding areas—have taken several forms. Historically, annexation has been the standard means;

---

[4] Recall that we have already noted the rapid growth of population in the nation's urban areas—that is, in cities and their surrounding suburbs; see pages 506–507, 719–720.

outlying areas have simply been brought within a city's boundaries. But, as we have already suggested, many suburbanites resist annexation; and cities, too, have often been reluctant to take on the burdens involved.

Another approach involves the creation of special districts, to which we referred on page 713. Although the best known and most common of these units are school districts, there are now more than 21,000 sanitary, water, fire protection, and other special districts across the country. Many of them have been established especially to meet the problems of heavily populated urban areas. Their boundaries frequently disregard county and city lines, and they are often called *metropolitan districts.*

These metropolitan districts are most often established for a single purpose; for example, park development in the Cleveland Metropolitan Park Development District and sewage in the Metropolitan Sanitary District of Greater Chicago. There is no reason why a district's authority cannot be expanded to include other functions, however. The Metropolitan District Commission, created by the Commonwealth of Massachusetts, controls sewage, water supply, and park development for the City of Boston and some neighboring communities, and it has duties connected with the planning of the development of the District as a whole. Boston itself accounts for only about a third of the District's total population and, altogether, some forty municipalities are now in it.

City-county consolidation and, on the other hand, city-county separation, have also been tried in a number of places—including San Francisco, Denver, St. Louis, Philadelphia, and Baltimore, as we noted in Chapter 41.

Yet another, and more recent, approach to meeting the problems of large and rapidly growing urban areas is that of increasing the authority of counties. Among existing local governments around the country, counties are generally the largest in area and are thus most likely to encompass those areas demanding new and increased services.

The functions of many urban counties have been increased in recent years, as we noted on page 700. Dade County (Miami), Florida, has undertaken the nation's most ambitious approach to metropolitan problems. In 1957 its voters approved the first home-rule charter to be specifically designed "to create a metropolitan government." Under it, a county-wide metropolitan government ("Metro") is responsible for such area-wide functions as fire and police protection; providing an integrated water, sewer, and drainage system; zoning; expressway construction; and the like. Miami and the other twenty-five cities within the county continue to perform the strictly local functions.

The Twelve Towns Relief Drains system in Oakland County, Michigan, is shown here under construction. Since its completion all odors originating from raw sewage that flowed through the exposed ditch have been eliminated. (Gargano Associates, Inc.)

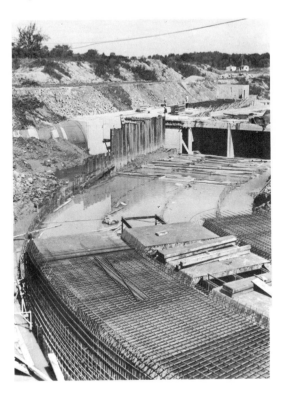

TRAFFIC CONGESTION

A few minutes on any street in the downtown area of any of our larger cities, and many of the smaller ones, are enough to convince anyone that traffic congestion is a major municipal problem today. The amount of time lost and the inconvenience caused by this congestion cannot be accurately measured. However, it is estimated that traffic congestion today costs the residents of New York City more than $1,250,000 a day and the residents of Philadelphia at least $400,000 a day.

Here are some of the things that have been done around the country to help meet the problem. Perhaps something quite similar is being done in your community.

Denver, Seattle, and several other cities have fixed traffic lights at many of the busiest intersections to flash red four ways at once. With traffic stopped in all directions, this "scramble" system permits pedestrians to cross the intersections every which way. This arrangement has speeded both street and sidewalk traffic.

Chicago has built its new rapid-transit lines between the lanes of its new freeways and has declared that no new freeways will be built within the city unless the same arrangements can be made in their construction.

Portland, Oregon, and many other cities now prohibit parking on certain downtown streets during all or the busiest parts of weekdays. One-way grid systems, with every other street one way in the same direction, are now commonly found in a large number of cities.

Cleveland, Chicago, and Boston have established huge parking lots well away from the downtown shopping and office areas with bus service to shuttle passengers downtown and back.

National System of Interstate Highways

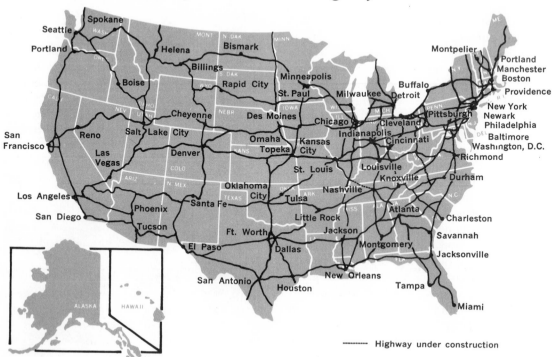

-------- Highway under construction

New York elevated the downtown continuation of Riverside Drive and also provided for fast traffic along the East River. It built the George Washington Bridge over the Hudson River, the Holland and Lincoln Tunnels under it, and the Battery Brooklyn Tunnel. It has also built a bus terminal to connect with the Lincoln Tunnel to handle New Jersey commuters and thus help relieve traffic jams in midtown New York City. Parking for 500 cars is provided on the terminal's roof. Private investors have built a garage to hold several thousand cars on the old Hippodrome site. The 1939 World's Fair parking field was reopened with space for another 3000 cars, and commuters ride to the city's center on fast trains or by subway.

Los Angeles now has more than 200 miles of freeways within the city, permitting cars to move free of cross streets and traffic lights. It has also built pedestrian tunnels under busy streets near its schools.

The Dallas Expressway makes it possible for a through traveler to go from one end of the city to the other in a matter of minutes.

San Francisco relieved congestion in front of the Municipal Ferry, where the electric cars from all sections of the city converge and circle, by digging a tunnel for the through traffic under the circle. Two enormous bridges span the harbor and the Golden Gate, and a third is in prospect. It also pioneered underground garages in the heart of a city with its garage beneath famous Union Square.

Pittsburgh's Mellon Square, in the Golden Triangle, conceals a layered parking garage for a thousand cars under an acre of trees, flowers, lawns, and fountains.

In Seattle, a two-level viaduct allows through traffic to skirt the downtown area. One-way traffic on each level moves at speeds up to 45 miles per hour and the downtown jam caused by through traffic has been reduced.

A huge expressway has also been built in Boston, and a spacious 2500-car garage has been opened beneath its historic Common.

Work is well underway on two of three expressways designed to encircle and bisect St. Louis.

When the old Erie Canal was abandoned, the city of Rochester turned the bed into a subway for passengers and freight and built an avenue over it. It has built a loop road to carry through traffic away from the downtown district, too. It also has built an unusual Midtown Plaza covering some nine acres in the heart of the city. Two existing department stores and a hotel have been joined by several new stores, restaurants, auditoriums, and an 18-story office building to create a downtown shopping center. The top four floors of the office building are occupied by a new hotel. A three-level garage with room for 2000 cars has been built under the Plaza. All the stores, the hotel, and the office building are linked by an air-conditioned and landscaped pedestrian mall two stories high. Escalators connect the mall and the underground parking levels.

A number of cities are turning parts of their core areas into park-like shopping malls. Minneapolis began such a project in 1966 and it promises to produce one of the most attractive in the country. Eight blocks of Nicollet Avenue in the heart of its cluttered downtown district are being remade. Water mains, power lines, and the complex of other services under the street are being modernized. The old street surface will be repaved with terrazzo, granite, and natural brick. A "transitway" for buses will curve through trees, fountains, and sculpture; all other vehicles except emergency ones will be barred and "the pedestrian will be king." Even street and direction signs, street and stop lights, and trash containers and flowerpots will be controlled to produce a pleasant environment.

These and similar projects in our major cities —and in several of the smaller ones, too—are helping to meet the problems of downtown congestion. But it is only too obvious that much remains to be done to handle the ever-increasing load of traffic.

PUBLIC UTILITIES

A *public utility* is an enterprise which, though privately owned, serves the public, makes use of public property, and is a natural monopoly. Electric power, gas, and water companies; telephone systems; and bus and street railway lines are good examples of public utilities now found within most cities.

It is almost always economically unsound for two concerns to compete in the business of providing these public services. For example, it would be well-nigh ridiculous to have two competing sets of telephone lines running down the same street. So these public utilities are made monopolies through State law and city ordinance.

Because public utilities are officially created monopolies, there must be some legal check to prevent them from abusing their privileges. A *public utilities commission* (sometimes called a *public services commission)* regulates such matters as rates and quality of service. The larger cities sometimes have commissions of their own. More often, State commissions regulate utilities within cities as well as those elsewhere in the State—because the utility often extends beyond the city's boundaries, the activities of the commission can be expensive, and a State-wide agency is less likely to be prejudiced in favor of a particular local utility.

Municipal Ownership. Public ownership of various utilities is increasing steadily in the United States, and we have come to accept this fact as a matter of course in most instances. Airports and water and sewage systems are good examples of city-owned utilities which are regularly taken for granted.

Several reasons account for the trend. Some services are so costly, or cover such broad areas and involve such overall planning, that they are frequently beyond the capacity of private concerns; for example, large scale slum clearance and housing projects. Some functions are so closely related to public health and welfare that it appears most desirable that they

be operated publicly; for example, water and sewage systems. Then, too, some activities necessary to the public have proved unprofitable for private business, and cities have had to assume their conduct; this process, sometimes known as "ashcan socialism," can be seen in many city-operated transit systems.

Municipal ownership and operation usually go hand in hand, though this is not always the case. Cincinnati owns a small railway and Philadelphia owns its local railway and subway system and a gas plant, but these are leased to private operators.

There are more than 2000 publicly owned power and light systems, most of them serving the smaller municipalities. More than two-thirds of our cities over 100,000 population own their own airports, including the new Greater Pittsburgh Airport which is larger than New York's La Guardia and Washington's National Airports combined.

While most city transportation systems are privately owned, outstanding cities like New York, Cleveland, Chicago, Detroit, San Francisco, and Seattle own their own. New York collects some 7,000,000 twenty-cent fares each day from subway passengers.

Those who favor public ownership claim that private ownership usually means poor service and often involves rate-gouging and graft. Opponents of public ownership claim that it results in poor service because of the lack of individual initiative and that it invites political corruption.

The truth of the matter seems to be that cities with capable, public-spirited citizens who are willing to donate their services usually make a good showing with public ownership where any profit is for public benefit. Where such capable people are lacking, however, private ownership, where the stockholders demand efficient management and public utilities commissions safeguard the people, is probably the best solution.

Water Systems. In 1907, when Los Angeles had a population of only 200,000, the city had sufficient vision to spend $25,000,000 on a water system. It brought water 250 miles — 54 miles through mountains and 150 miles across deserts. The gravity of the water supplied 120,000 horsepower of electrical energy through five power plants, and reclaimed 150 square miles of arid lands near the city. Each year this watered garden yielded products of a value equal to the cost of the entire water system. This water controlled by Los Angeles forced most of the surrounding suburbs to become a part of the city. The water has made possible the growth of the city from 200,000 to more than 2,500,000 population.

To keep the water supply ahead of the population, the city has built a series of dams at the mouths of the great canyon basins along the way. In these, water is stored during the wet season and allowed to pass through the power plants uniformly. If a break occurs along the pipe line, no waste results. The water is stored in the reservoir just above, and the lower reservoirs keep the power plants running and supply the city. One reservoir, completed in 1925, is about 300 feet in height, and another beautiful one completed the same year overhangs the very edge of Hollywood. There is a canyon full of water right at the edge of the city which will take care of any emergency.

As the rapid population growth of the Los Angeles area has continued, the city, other local governments, and the State have been forced to take several other steps to insure an adequate water supply. In recent years, covetous eyes have even been cast on the abundant waters of the Columbia River, nearly *a thousand miles* to the north.

Sewage Disposal. Most cities no longer contaminate streams by sewage. In Baltimore, for instance, sewage is siphoned from one tank to another, then flows through a revolving screen, is sprayed into the air by thousands of small fountains, and is filtered through stone and sand. The filtrate flows into Chesapeake Bay as pure as the water in the city reservoirs. As the water falls from the filtration beds into

"AH–H–H! WATER!" The increased dumping of wastes into our rivers and streams threatens to ruin the quality of our water resources. (© 1966 Chicago Sun Times; reproduced by courtesy of Bill Mauldin and WIL–JO ASSOCIATES, INC.)

the bay, it is used to generate electricity by which the disposal plant is operated. Pasadena uses the filtrate to water a city farm which produces oranges, walnuts, grain, and hay. Many other cities have similar systems.

Wharves. New Orleans owns nearly all of its waterfront, and the State of California has long been developing the San Francisco waterfront. New York City now owns nearly two-thirds of its 578 miles of waterfront.

Los Angeles, whose center is twenty-one miles from the coast, has a water frontage of forty miles, a large part of which is improved. The city also owns a forty-eight mile railway which prevents any railroad company from monopolizing the wharves.

The cities located on the Great Lakes, on the other hand, own very little of their wharfage. While the Army's Corps of Engineers has spent millions of dollars improving and maintaining a thirty-foot channel for the harbor of Galveston, the wharves are almost all privately owned.

Free foreign trade zones are areas where imports can be stored and reshipped to a foreign country without paying United States tariffs. Before the war there were forty-three of these zones, "free ports," in Europe.

Congress authorized such zones in 1934, and New York established a fenced-off, policed zone of ninety-two acres. Here importers can hold goods for seasonal demands, new markets, determining of import quotas, and other reasons. If goods are shipped out to United States consumers, all regular import requirements must be met. Goods may be processed if no basic changes are made. Swiss watch movements, for instance, are put into domestic cases and reshipped abroad. Other zones are now operating in New Orleans on the Gulf, San Francisco and Seattle on the Pacific Coast, Toledo on Lake Erie, in Honolulu, and in Mayaguez, Puerto Rico.

CIVIL DEFENSE

Through most of our history, this nation has been secure against foreign attack.[5] Atomic and hydrogen bombs, intercontinental missiles, and space technology have altered our traditional insulation radically, however. Our cities, and especially the major industrial centers, would be prime targets in any future war.

Defending the nation against foreign attack is primarily the function of the Armed Forces, of course. But, because modern war is total war, common sense dictates that all levels of government — national, State, and local — must cooperate to protect the nation.

Basic responsibility for preparing for any local emergency rests with the States and their local units. Few have done much to meet the need, however. Some States do provide some local aid, most of it in the form of advice. Federal civil defense officials have attempted to spark local action, but support in Congress has been only lukewarm at best. Even the Cuban crisis of 1962 failed to stir any sustained interest or action. Despite the frightening possibilities, Congress, most States, and millions of individual Americans have, so far at least, shown little real concern.

New York City is one of the few outstanding exceptions. It has made noteworthy strides in preparing for possible attack. Its Civilian Defense Commission estimates that a nuclear explosion a half-mile above Union Square

Some cities and towns take their Civil Defense preparations and tests seriously. In Peewaukee, Wisconsin, a mock disaster was staged to test all the agencies that would be involved in the event of a real disaster. (Wide World Photos)

---

[5] Except for an ineffectual shelling of the Oregon coast by a Japanese submarine and a few incendiary balloons blown across the Pacific to the forests of the Northwest from Japan in World War II, the United States itself has not been attacked by a foreign power since the War of 1812.

would lay waste to the city for two miles in every direction. The Empire State and Metropolitan Life Buildings, Peter Cooper Village and Stuyvesant Town, Rockefeller Center and Times Square, the Holland and Queens Tunnels, Pennsylvania and Grand Central Stations, the Metropolitan Opera House, and many schools, universities, and hospitals all would lie among the wreckage. Fire, explosions, flying debris, and broken gas and water mains and telephone and electric wires would add to the chaos and devastation.

City police and firemen, medical teams and rescue squads, and maintenance and evacuation crews are being trained and equipped for possible action. Mobile aid stations and kitchens, river fire pumps and heavy clearing equipment, shelter, and other facilities are also being readied.

But, again, while some cities have followed New York's lead, most have neglected the problem. It is doubtful much will be done unless and until public apathy is somehow overcome.

❈❈❈❈❈❈❈❈❈❈ CONCEPT BUILDING ❈❈❈❈❈❈❈❈❈❈

Key Concepts

Cities exist in order to provide services to their residents, and the range and variety of city activities are enormous. Most cities have developed haphazardly and with no eye to the future. More and more of them are recognizing the need for city planning, however. Zoning, which is a phase of city planning, is now a widespread practice. Many cities, without an overall plan for development, do utilize zoning. Zoning ordinances must be reasonable; they cannot deprive one of his liberty or property without due process of law.

"Suburbanitis" has created many problems for cities and for their outlying areas, too. A number of metropolitan districts, encompassing both cities and their suburbs, have been created, and the functions of some urban counties have been increased to meet the problems facing the growing municipalities.

Traffic congestion, a major city problem, is being met in a variety of ways by a number of cities. Public utilities are publicly-created monopolies regulated by State and sometimes city public utilities commissions. Municipal ownership of utilities is growing in the United States. Those who favor the trend claim that it prevents graft, rate-gouging, and poor service. Those who oppose municipal ownership of utilities claim that it fosters corruption and stifles individual initiative.

Despite its obvious importance to our cities and industrial centers, civilian defense suffers from serious neglect in most States and in their local communities.

Important Terms

annexation	metropolitan	"suburbanitis"
city planning	metropolitan districts	suburbs
foreign trade zones	public utilities	zoning

Questions for Inquiry and Review

1. Why, essentially, does a city exist?
2. List ten of the major functions all or most cities perform today.
3. What is meant by city planning? Why has it become so necessary in most cities?
4. Who laid out the original design for Washington, D.C.? What was his basic scheme?
5. What was William Penn's original plan for Philadelphia? What happened to it?
6. What is meant by *zoning?*
7. What provision in the United States Constitution restricts a city's authority to zone?
8. What are the three basic city zones?

9. What is meant by "suburbanitis"? What six causes for it are cited by the Census Bureau? Cite two major problems it has caused for cities.
10. Why, especially, has annexation proved a relatively unsatisfactory answer to meeting the needs of metropolitan areas?
11. What is a *metropolitan district?* What newer approach is being made in Dade County?
12. What is a *public utility?* Why are public utilities regulated by States and cities?
13. What is the process sometimes known as "ashcan socialism"?
14. Why is civil defense so important today?

For Further Inquiry

1. Do you agree with the observation by Aristotle which is quoted at the beginning of this chapter? If so, why? If not, why not?
2. When was your city established? What particular factors caused its creation? Has growth been generally orderly and well-planned? If so, why? If not, why not? What are

its most acute planning problems now?
3. If you were a member of your city's planning or zoning commission, where in your city would you permit residences only? Where would you locate new schools? Churches, hospitals, parks? Retail stores, filling stations? Light industry, heavy industry? stockyards?

Suggested Activities

1. From a week's issues of a local daily newspaper, identify as many of the functions performed by your city as possible. Reports on these functions could be prepared.
2. Invite a member of the city planning or

zoning commission to speak to the class on his work and the problems involved in it.
3. Stage a class forum or debate on the question: *Resolved,* That our city should acquire and operate (a particular utility.)

Suggested Reading

BARR, MAYOR JOSEPH M., "One Mayor's Story of the Mess in Cities," *U.S. News,* April 21, 1969.
"Big Changes in America's Small Towns," *U.S. News,* April 28, 1969.
LANGEWIESCHE, WOLFGANG, "The Suburbs Are Changing," *Reader's Digest,* November, 1969.

"New York's Master Plan," *Newsweek,* November 24, 1969.
ROMNEY, SECRETARY GEORGE, "The Breakdown in Our Cities," *U.S. News,* July 28, 1969.
"The Master Builder," *Newsweek,* Nov. 17, 1969.
VOLPE, SECRETARY JOHN, "How to Cure Traffic Jams," *U.S. News,* June 9, 1969.

STOP

THE

PRESSES

Bury me on my face: for in a little while everything will be turned upside down.

DIOGENES

On this and the following two pages you will find a number of last-minute additions, changes, and corrections which, for reasons of time, could not be included in the main body of the text itself.

❖❖❖ The figures reported for the 1970 Census indicate that five states will gain seats in the House of Representatives and that nine States will lose some seats. Altogether, eleven House seats appear to be involved.

California will probably gain five seats and Florida will pick up three; and three other States—Arizona, Colorado, and Texas—will each gain one seat.

New York and Pennsylvania seem certain to lose two seats each, while seven other States will each lose a seat: Alabama, Iowa, North Dakota, Ohio, Tennessee, West Virginia and Wisconsin.

Recall that the House will be reapportioned on the basis of the new Census in 1971, and the resulting redistribution of seats will become effective in elections of 1972. *And recall,* each State's electoral college vote is based upon the number of seats it has in Congress. *Pages 202–204, 289–290, 297–302, 455.*

❖❖❖ President Nixon made extensive use of his powers under the Reorganization Act in 1970. He created two new and vitally important units in the Executive Office of the President. One is an entirely new agency, the Domestic Council. It is designed to function in the domestic policy much as the National Security Council does in the realm of foreign policy—advising the President on the full range of the domestic policy matters and helping him to integrate its various aspects into a consistent whole. The Council is chaired by the President; its other members include the Vice President, the secretaries of the Treasury, Interior, Agriculture, Commerce, Labor, HEW, HUD, Transportation, and the Attorney General. The Council is supported by a staff under an Executive Director, who is also one of the President's Special Assistants.

The other new agency in the Executive Office, the Office of Management and Budget, replaces the old Bureau of the Budget. Like its predecessor, the OMB is the President's right hand in the preparation and execution of the Federal Budget. In addition, the newly shaped agency has been given a much larger role in upgrading the management function and procedures in the Executive Branch. *Pages 306–308, 318–319.*

Mr. Nixon also created the Environmental Protection Agency in late 1970. The EPA was also purposefully established as an independent agency and is designed to bring under one roof the major federal anti-pollution programs. *Pages 318–319, 433, 495–496, 529–530.*

The President created yet another major federal agency in 1970, the National Oceanic and Atmospheric Administration, in the Commerce Department. It absorbed the Environmental Science Services Administration (ESSA), including the Weather Bureau and Coast and Geodetic Survey; it also acquired the Bureau of Commercial Fisheries (BCF) from the Interior Department, along with some Oceanographic functions formerly housed in the Defense Department. *Pages 430–431, 461–462.*

✳✳✳ Congress enacted the long-sought Postal Reorganization Act in 1970. Under its terms, the Post Office Department will be phased out of existence. Its replacement, the United States Postal Service, will come into being some time in mid-1971.

The USPS will be an independent (non-Cabinet) federal agency fully authorized to operate the nation's mail system. It is to be headed by an eleven-member Board of Governors. Nine of the Board's members will be appointed by the President and Senate (with no more than five members of the same political party); a tenth member will be selected by the other nine and will serve as the Postmaster General; the eleventh member, the Deputy Postmaster General, will then be chosen by the other ten members.

The Postal Service is to be responsible for financing its own operations and capital needs from postal revenues and the issuing of securities; but Congress has also authorized some public subsidization of the effort. An independent Postal Rate Commission, with five members appointed by the President, will make recommendations as to rates, classifications of mail, and mail service to the Board. Each class of mail is expected to be self-supporting—except for those purposefully given free or reduced rates. *Pages 244, 308–310, 411–417.*

✳✳✳ Red China edged closer to a seat in the United Nations in 1970. Despite continuing American opposition, the General Assembly for the first time returned a majority vote on the perennial question of Red China's admission to the world body. The vote was: 51 member-nations for seating the Peking regime, 49 opposed, 25 abstaining, and 2 absent.

The State Department reacted to the vote with the observation that there is now a "new situation" with regard to the question of UN membership for Red China. The implication appears to be that the United States will re-examine its twenty-year policy of outright opposition and may embrace a "two-China concept," which provides seats for both the Red and the Nationalist Chinese governments. A two-China resolution supported by the United States would very likely win Assembly approval. *Pages 10, 330, 338, 348, 350.*

✳✳✳ In passing the Agricultural Act of 1970, Congress for the first time placed a ceiling on the amount of farm subsidy money any one farmer can receive. In the legislation, continuing the nation's basic agricultural policies for the next three years, Congress provided that no producer of wheat, cotton, corn, or other feed grains can be paid more than $55,000 in any year for holding land out of production. *Pages 447–451.*

❋❋❋ Late in 1970 the Supreme Court refused to hear a challenge, raised by the State of Massachusetts, to the constitutionality of United States involvement in the war in Viet Nam. Four justices must favor the hearing of a case in order for it to be docketed for argument; only Justices William O. Douglas, Potter Stewart, and John Marshall Harlan voted in favor of accepting the case.

Massachusetts sought to bring the suit in order to test a law passed by its legislature earlier in the year. That statute declared that no citizen of Massachusetts should, while serving in the armed forces of the United States, be sent into any hostile action not declared or ratified by Congress. *Pages 63–67, 316, 342–344, 382–384.*

THE DECLARATION OF INDEPENDENCE

In Congress, July 4, 1776

THE UNANIMOUS DECLARATION OF THE THIRTEEN UNITED STATES OF AMERICA

When in the Course of human events, it becomes necessary for one people to dissolve the political bands which have connected them with another, and to assume among the powers of the earth, the separate and equal station to which the Laws of Nature and of Nature's God entitle them, a decent respect to the opinions of mankind requires that they should declare the causes which impel them to the separation.

We hold these truths to be self-evident, that all men are created equal, that they are endowed by their Creator with certain unalienable Rights, that among these are Life, Liberty and the pursuit of Happiness. That to secure these rights, Governments are instituted among Men, deriving their just powers from the consent of the governed; That whenever any Form of Government becomes destructive of these ends it is the Right of the People to alter or to abolish it, and to institute new Government, laying its foundation on such principles and organizing its powers in such form, as to them shall seem most likely to effect their Safety and Happiness. Prudence, indeed, will dictate that Governments long established should not be changed for light and transient causes; and accordingly all experience hath shown, that mankind are more dis-posed to suffer, while evils are sufferable, than to right themselves by abolishing the forms to which they are accustomed. But when a long train of abuses and usurpations, pursuing invariably the same Objects evinces a design to reduce them under absolute Despotism, it is their right, it is their duty, to throw off such Government, and to provide new Guards for their future security. — Such has been the patient sufferance of these Colonies; and such is now the necessity which constrains them to alter their former Systems of Government. The history of the present King of Great Britain is a history of repeated injuries and usurpations, all having in direct object the establishment of an absolute Tyranny over these States. To prove this, let Facts be submitted to a candid world.

He has refused his Assent to Laws, the most wholesome and necessary for the public good.

He has forbidden his Governors to pass Laws of immediate and pressing importance, unless suspended in their operation till his Assent should be obtained; and when so suspended, he has utterly neglected to attend to them.

He has refused to pass other Laws for the accommodation of large districts of people, unless those people would relinquish the right of Representation in the Legislature, a right inestimable to them and formidable to tyrants only.

He has called together legislative bodies at places unusual, uncomfortable, and distant from the depository of their public records, for the sole purpose of fatiguing them into compliance with his measures.

He has dissolved Representative Houses repeatedly, for opposing with manly firmness his invasions on the rights of the people.

He has refused for a long time, after such dissolutions, to cause others to be elected; whereby the Legislative powers, incapable of Annihilation, have returned to the People at large for their exercise; the State remaining in the mean time exposed to all the dangers of invasions from without, and convulsions within.

He has endeavored to prevent the population of these States; for that purpose obstructing the Laws for Naturalization of Foreigners; refusing to pass others to encourage their migration hither, and raising the conditions of new Appropriations of Lands.

He has obstructed the Administration of Justice, by refusing his Assent to Laws for establishing Judiciary powers.

He has made Judges dependent on his Will alone for the tenure of their offices, and the amount and payment of their salaries.

He has erected a multitude of New Offices, and sent hither swarms of Officers to harass our people and eat out their substance.

He has kept among us in times of peace, Standing Armies, without the Consent of our legislatures.

He has affected to render the Military independent of, and superior to, the Civil power.

He has combined with others to subject us to a jurisdiction foreign to our constitutions, and unacknowledged by our laws; giving his Assent to their Acts of pretended Legislation:

For quartering large bodies of armed troops among us;

For protecting them, by a mock Trial, from punishment for any Murders which they should commit on the Inhabitants of these States;

For cutting off our Trade with all parts of the world;

For imposing Taxes on us without our Consent;

For depriving us, in many cases, of the benefits of Trial by Jury;

For transporting us beyond Seas, to be tried for pretended offenses;

For abolishing the free System of English Laws in a neighboring Province, establishing therein an Arbitrary government, and enlarging its Boundaries, so as to render it at once an example and fit instrument for introducing the same absolute rule into these Colonies;

For taking away our Charters, abolishing our most valuable Laws, and altering, fundamentally, the Forms of our Governments;

For suspending our own Legislatures, and declaring themselves invested with Power to legislate for us in all cases whatsoever.

He has abdicated Government here, by declaring us out of his Protection, and waging War against us.

He has plundered our seas, ravaged our Coasts, burned our towns, and destroyed the lives of our people.

He is at this time transporting large Armies of foreign Mercenaries to complete the works of death, desolation and tyranny, already begun with circumstances of Cruelty and perfidy scarcely paralleled in the most barbarous ages, and totally unworthy the Head of a civilized nation.

He has constrained our fellow Citizens taken Captive on the high Seas to bear Arms against their Country, to become the executioners of their friends and Brethren, or to fall themselves by their Hands.

He has excited domestic insurrections amongst us, and has endeavored to bring on the inhabitants of our frontiers the merciless Indian Savages whose known rule of warfare is an undistinguished destruction of all ages, sexes, and conditions.

In every stage of these Oppressions We have Petitioned for Redress in the most humble terms. Our repeated Petitions have been answered only by repeated injury. A Prince whose character is thus marked by every act which may define a Tyrant, is unfit to be the ruler of a free people.

Nor have We been wanting in attentions to our British brethren. We have warned them from time to time of attempts by their legislature to extend an unwarrantable jurisdiction over us. We have reminded them of the circumstances of our emigration and settlement here. We have appealed to their native justice and magnanimity, and we have conjured them by the ties of our common kindred to disavow these usurpations, which, would inevitably interrupt our connections and correspondence. They too have been deaf to the voice of justice and of consanguinity. We must, therefore, acquiesce in the necessity, which denounces our Separation, and hold them, as we hold the rest of mankind, Enemies in War, in Peace Friends. —

We, therefore, the Representatives of the United States of America, in General Congress, Assembled, appealing to the Supreme Judge of the world for the rectitude of our intentions, do, in the Name, and by the Authority of the good People of these Colonies, solemnly publish and declare, That these United Colonies are, and of right ought to be Free and Independent States; that they are Absolved from all Allegiance to the British Crown, and that all political connection between them and the State of Great Britain, is and ought to be totally dissolved, and that as Free and Independent States, they have full Power to levy War, conclude Peace, contract Alliances, establish Commerce, and to do all other Acts and Things which Independent States may of right do. And for the support of this Declaration, with a firm reliance on the protection of Divine Providence, we mutually pledge to each other our Lives, our Fortunes and our sacred Honor.

JOHN HANCOCK

New Hampshire

Josiah Bartlett
William Whipple
Matthew Thornton

Massachusetts Bay

Samuel Adams
John Adams
Robert Treat Paine
Elbridge Gerry

Rhode Island

Stephen Hopkins
William Ellery

Connecticut

Roger Sherman
Samuel Huntington
William Williams
Oliver Wolcott

New York

William Floyd
Philip Livingston
Francis Lewis
Lewis Morris

New Jersey

Richard Stockton
John Witherspoon
Francis Hopkinson
John Hart
Abraham Clark

Pennsylvania

Robert Morris
Benjamin Rush
Benjamin Franklin
John Morton
George Clymer
James Smith
George Taylor
James Wilson
George Ross

Delaware

Cæsar Rodney
George Read
Thomas M'Kean

Maryland

Samuel Chase
William Paca
Thomas Stone
Charles Carroll of Carrollton

Virginia

George Wythe
Richard Henry Lee
Thomas Jefferson
Benjamin Harrison
Thomas Nelson, Jr.
Francis Lightfoot Lee
Carter Braxton

North Carolina

William Hooper
Joseph Hewes
John Penn

South Carolina

Edward Rutledge
Thomas Heyward, Jr.
Thomas Lynch, Jr.
Arthur Middleton

Georgia

Button Gwinnett
Lyman Hall
George Walton

THE ARTICLES OF CONFEDERATION

*To all to whom these Presents shall come, we the under signed Delegates
of the States affixed to our Names, send greetings.*

Whereas the Delegates of the United States of America, in Congress assembled,
did, on the fifteenth day of November in the year of our Lord One thousand Seven
Hundred and Seventy seven, and in the Second Year of the Independence of America, agree to certain articles of Confederation and perpetual Union between the
States of Newhampshire, Massachusetts-bay, Rhodeisland and Providence Plantations, Connecticut, New York, New Jersey, Pennsylvania, Delaware, Maryland,
Virginia, North-Carolina, South-Carolina, and Georgia in the words following, viz.

*Articles of Confederation and perpetual Union between the States of Newhampshire,
Massachusetts-bay, Rhodeisland and Providence Plantations, Connecticut, New York,
New Jersey, Pennsylvania, Delaware, Maryland, Virginia, North-Carolina, South-
Carolina, and Georgia.*

ARTICLE I.—The Stile of this confederacy shall
be, "The United States of America."

ARTICLE II.—Each state retains its sovereignty,
freedom, and independence, and every Power,
Jurisdiction and right, which is not by this Confederation expressly delegated to the United States, in
Congress assembled.

ARTICLE III.—The said states hereby severally
enter into a firm league of friendship with each
other, for their common defence, the security of
their Liberties, and their mutual and general welfare,
binding themselves to assist each other, against all
force offered to, or attacks made upon them, or
any of them, on account of religion, sovereignty,
trade, or any other pretence whatever.

ARTICLE IV.—The better to secure and perpetu-
ate mutual friendship and intercourse among the
people of the different states in this union, the free
inhabitants of each of these states, paupers, vaga-
bonds and fugitives from justice excepted, shall be
entitled to all privileges and immunities of free
citizens in the several states; and the people of
each state shall have free ingress and egress to and
from any other state, and shall enjoy therein all the
privileges of trade and commerce, subject to the
same duties, impositions and restrictions as the inhabitants thereof respectively, provided that such
restrictions shall not extend so far as to prevent the
removal of property imported into any state, to any
other state, of which the Owner is an inhabitant;
provided also that no imposition, duties or restriction
shall be laid by any state on the property of the
united states, or either of them.

If any Person guilty of, or charged with treason,
felony, or other high misdemeanor in any state, shall
flee from Justice, and be found in any of the united
states, he shall, upon demand of the Governor or
executive power of the state from which he fled, be
delivered up and removed to the state having jurisdiction of his offence.

Full faith and credit shall be given in each of these
states to the records, acts and judicial proceedings of
the courts and magistrates of every other state.

ARTICLE V.—For the more convenient management of the general interest of the united states,
delegates shall be annually appointed in such manner
as the legislature of each state shall direct, to meet
in congress on the first Monday in November, in
every year, with a power reserved to each state, to
recall its delegates, or any of them, at any time within
the year, and to send others in their stead, for the
remainder of the Year.

No state shall be represented in congress by less
than two, nor by more than seven Members; and
no person shall be capable of being a delegate for
more than three years in any term of six years; nor
shall any person, being a delegate, be capable of
holding any office under the united states, for which
he, or another for his benefit receives any salary,
fees or emolument of any kind.

Each state shall maintain its own delegates in a meeting of the states, and while they act as members of the committee of the states.

In determining questions in the united states in congress assembled, each state shall have one vote.

Freedom of speech and debate in congress shall not be impeached or questioned in any court, or place out of congress, and the members of congress shall be protected in their persons from arrests and imprisonments, during the time of their going to and from, and attendance on congress, except for treason, felony, or breach of the peace.

ARTICLE VI. — No state, without the consent of the united states in congress assembled, shall send any embassy to, or receive any embassy from, or enter into any conference, agreement, alliance or treaty with any king, prince or state; nor shall any person holding any office of profit or trust under the united states, or any of them, accept of any present, emolument, office or title of any kind whatever from any king, prince or foreign state; nor shall the united states in congress assembled, or any of them, grant any title of nobility.

No two or more states shall enter into any treaty, confederation or alliance whatever between them, without the consent of the united states in congress assembled, specifying accurately the purposes for which the same is to be entered into, and how long it shall continue.

No state shall lay any imposts or duties, which may interfere with any stipulations in treaties, entered into by the united states in congress assembled, with any king, prince or state, in pursuance of any treaties already proposed by congress, to the courts of France and Spain.

No vessel of war shall be kept up in time of peace by any state, except such number only, as shall be deemed necessary by the united states in congress assembled, for the defence of such state or its trade; nor shall any body of forces be kept up by any state, in time of peace, except such number only, as in the judgment of the united states in congress assembled, shall be deemed requisite to garrison the forts necessary for the defence of such state; but every state shall always keep up a well regulated and disciplined militia, sufficiently armed and accoutred, and shall provide and constantly have ready for use, in public stores, a due number of field pieces and tents, and a proper quantity of arms, ammunition and camp equipage.

No state shall engage in any war without the consent of the united states in congress assembled, unless such state be actually invaded by enemies, or shall have received certain advice of a resolution being formed by some nation of Indians to invade such state, and the danger is so imminent as not to admit of delay till the united states in congress assembled can be consulted: nor shall any state grant commissions to any ships or vessels of war, nor letters of marque or reprisal, except it be after a declaration of war by the united states in congress assembled, and then only against the kingdom or state and the subjects thereof, against which war has been so declared, and under such regulations as shall be established by the united states in congress assembled, unless such state be infested by pirates, in which case vessels of war may be fitted out for that occasion, and kept so long as the danger shall continue, or until the united states in congress assembled, shall determine otherwise.

ARTICLE VII. — When land forces are raised by any state for the common defence, all officers of or under the rank of colonel, shall be appointed by the legislature of each state respectively, by whom such forces shall be raised, or in such manner as such state shall direct, and all vacancies shall be filled up by the state which first made the appointment.

ARTICLE VIII. — All charges of war, and all other expenses that shall be incurred for the common defence or general welfare, and allowed by the united states in congress assembled, shall be defrayed out of a common treasury, which shall be supplied by the several states in proportion to the value of all land within each state, granted to or surveyed for any person, as such land and the buildings and improvements thereon shall be estimated according to such mode as the united states in congress assembled, shall from time to time direct and appoint.

The taxes for paying that proportion shall be laid and levied by the authority and direction of the legislatures of the several states within the time agreed upon by the united states in congress assembled.

ARTICLE IX. — The united states in congress assembled, shall have the sole and exclusive right and power of determining on peace and war, except in the cases mentioned in the sixth article — of sending and receiving ambassadors — entering into treaties and alliances, provided that no treaty of commerce shall be made whereby the legislative power of the respective states shall be restrained from imposing such imposts and duties on foreigners as their own people are subjected to, or from prohibiting the exportation or importation of any species of goods or commodities, whatsoever — of establishing rules for deciding in all cases, what captures on land or water shall be legal, and in what manner prizes taken by land or naval forces in the service of the united states shall be divided or appropriated — of granting letters of marque and reprisal in times of peace — appointing courts for the trial of piracies and felonies committed on the high seas and establishing courts for receiving and determining finally appeals in all cases of captures, provided that no member of congress shall be appointed a judge of any of the said courts.

The united states in congress assembled shall also be the last resort on appeal in all disputes and differences now subsisting or that hereafter may arise between two or more states concerning boundary, jurisdiction or any other cause whatever; which authority shall always be exercised in the manner following. [In the original, a passage appears here as to the method of constituting commissioners to decide such contests.]

The united states in congress assembled shall also have the sole and exclusive right and power of regulating the alloy and value of coin struck by their own authority, or by that of the respective states — fixing the standard of weights and measures throughout the united states — regulating the trade and managing all affairs with the Indians, not members of any of the states, provided that the legislative right of any state within its own limits be not infringed or violated — establishing and regulating postoffices from one state to another, throughout all the united states, and exacting such postage on the papers passing thro' the same as may be requisite to defray the expenses of the said office — appointing all officers of the land forces, in the service of the united states, excepting regimental officers — appointing all the officers of the naval forces, and commissioning all officers whatever in the service of the united states — making rules for the government and regulation of the said land and naval forces, and directing their operations.

The united states in congress assembled shall have authority to appoint a committee, to sit in the recess of congress, to be denominated "A Committee of the States," and to consist of one delegate from each state; and to appoint such other committees and civil officers as may be necessary for managing the general affairs of the united states under their direction — to appoint one of their number to preside, provided that no person be allowed to serve in the office of president more than one year in any term of three years; to ascertain the necessary sums of money to be raised for the service of the united states, and to appropriate and apply the same for defraying the public expenses — to borrow money, or emit bills on the credit of the united states, transmitting every half year to the respective states an account of the sums of money so borrowed or emitted, — to build and equip a navy — to agree upon the number of land forces, and to make requisitions from each state for its quota, in proportion to the number of white inhabitants in such state; which requisition shall be binding, and thereupon the legislature of each state shall appoint the regimental officers, raise the men and cloath, arm and equip them in a soldier like manner, at the expence of the united states; and the officers and men so cloathed, armed and equipped shall march to the place appointed, and within the time agreed on by the united states in congress assembled: but if the united states in congress assembled shall, on consideration of circumstances judge proper that any state should not raise men, or should raise a smaller number than its quota, and that any other state should raise a greater number of men than the quota thereof, such extra number shall be raised, officered, cloathed, armed and equipped in the same manner as the quota of such state, unless the legislature of such state shall judge that such extra number cannot be safely spared out of the same, in which case they shall raise, officer, cloath, arm and equip as many of such extra number as they judge can be safely spared. And the officers and men so cloathed, armed and equipped shall march to the place appointed, and within the time agreed on by the united states in congress assembled.

The united states in congress assembled shall never engage in a war, nor grant letters of marque and reprisal in time of peace, nor enter into any treaties or alliances, nor coin money, nor regulate the value thereof, nor ascertain the sums and expences necessary for the defence and welfare of the united states, or any of them, nor emit bills, nor borrow money on the credit of the united states, nor appropriate money, nor agree upon the number of vessels of war to be built or purchased, or the number of land or sea forces to be raised, nor appoint a commander-in-chief of the army or navy, unless nine states assent to the same: nor shall a question on any other point, except for adjourning from day to day be determined, unless by the votes of a majority of the united states in congress assembled. [Passage follows, relating to adjournment stipulating publication of a journal of proceedings.]

ARTICLE X. — The committee of the states, or any nine of them, shall be authorized to execute, in the recess of congress, such of the powers of congress as the united states in congress assembled, by the consent of nine states, shall from time to time think expedient to vest them with; provided that no power be delegated to the said committee, for the exercise of which, by the articles of confederation, the voice of nine states in the congress of the united states assembled is requisite.

ARTICLE XI. — Canada acceding to this confederation, and joining in the measures of the united states, shall be admitted into, and entitled to all the advantages of this union: but no other colony shall be admitted into the same, unless such admission be agreed to by nine states.

ARTICLE XII. — All ... debts contracted by, or under the authority of congress, ... in pursuance of the present confederation, shall be deemed ... a charge against the united states, for payment ... whereof the said united states, and the public faith are hereby solemnly pledged.

ARTICLE XIII. — Every state shall abide by the determinations of the united states in congress assembled, on all questions which by this confederation are submitted to them. And the Articles of this confederation shall be inviolably observed by every state, and the union shall be perpetual; nor shall any alteration at any time hereafter be made in any of them; unless such alteration be agreed to in a congress of the united states, and be afterwards confirmed by the legislatures of every state.

And whereas it hath pleased the Great Governor of the World to incline the hearts of the legislatures we respectively represent in congress, to approve of, and to authorize us to ratify the said articles of confederation and perpetual union. Know Ye that we the undersigned delegates, by virtue of the power and authority to us given for that purpose, do by these presents, in the name and in behalf of our respective constituents, fully and entirely ratify and confirm each and every of the said articles of confederation and perpetual union, and all and singular the matters and things therein contained. And we do further solemnly plight and engage the faith of our respective constituents, that they shall abide by the determinations of the united states in congress assembled, on all questions, which by the said confederation are submitted to them. And that the articles thereof shall be inviolably observed by the states we respectively represent, and that the union shall be perpetual.

In witness whereof we have hereunto set our hands in Congress. Done at Philadelphia in the state of Pennsylvania the ninth day of July, in the year of our Lord one Thousand seven Hundred and Seventy-eight, and in the third year of the independence of America.

[THE SIGNATURES]

THE CONSTITUTION OF THE UNITED STATES OF AMERICA

Preamble

We, the People of the United States, in Order to form a more perfect Union, establish Justice, insure domestic Tranquility, provide for the common defence, promote the general Welfare, and secure the Blessings of Liberty to ourselves and our Posterity, do ordain and establish this Constitution for the United States of America.

Article I

LEGISLATIVE DEPARTMENT

SECTION 1. *Two Houses*

All legislative powers herein granted shall be vested in a Congress of the United States, which shall consist of a Senate and House of Representatives.

SECTION 2. *House of Representatives*

1. The House of Representatives shall be composed of members chosen every second year by the people of the several States, and the electors in each State shall have the qualifications requisite for electors of the most numerous branch of the State legislature.[1]

2. No person shall be a Representative who shall not have attained to the age of twenty-five years, and been seven years a citizen of the United States, and who shall not, when elected, be an inhabitant of that State in which he shall be chosen.[2]

3. Representatives and direct taxes[3] shall be apportioned among the several States which may be included within this Union, according to their respective numbers, [which shall be determined by adding to the whole number of free persons, including those bound to service for a term of years][4] and excluding Indians not taxed, [three-fifths of all other persons.][5] The actual enumeration shall be made within three years after the first meeting of the Congress of the United States, and within every subsequent term of ten years, in such manner as they shall by law direct. The number of Representatives shall not exceed one for every thirty thousand,[6] but each State shall have at least one Representative; [and, until such enumeration shall be made, the State of New Hampshire shall be entitled to choose three, Massachusetts eight, Rhode Island and Providence Plantations one, Connecticut five, New York six, New Jersey four, Pennsylvania eight, Delaware one, Maryland six, Virginia ten, North Carolina five, South Carolina five, and Georgia three.][7]

4. When vacancies happen in the representation from any State, the excutive authority thereof shall issue writs of election to fill such vacancies.

5. The House of Representatives shall choose

---

[1] "Electors" means voters. Each State must permit the same persons to vote for United States Representatives as it permits to vote for the members of the larger house of its own legislature. The 17th Amendment (1913) extended this requirement to the qualification of voters for United States Senators.

[2] In addition, political custom requires that a Representative also reside in the district in which he is elected. The first woman to serve in the House, Miss Jeannette Rankin, was elected from Montana in 1916.

[3] Modified by the 16th Amendment (1913) which provides for an income tax as an express exception to this restriction.

[4] Altered by the 14th Amendment (1868).

[5] The phrase refers to slaves and was rescinded by the 13th Amendment (1865) and the 14th Amendment (1868).

[6] The Constitution does not set a specific size for the House; rather, Congress does so when it reapportions the seats among the States after each census. It fixed the "permanent" size at 435 members in the Reapportionment Act of 1929; see pages 202–204. Today (1971) there is one House seat for approximately every 471,000 persons in the population.

[7] Temporary provision.

their Speaker [8] and other officers; and shall have the sole power of impeachment.[9]

SECTION 3. *Senate*

1. The Senate of the United States shall be composed of two Senators from each State [chosen by the legislature thereof] [10] for six years; and each Senator shall have one vote.

2. Immediately after they shall be assembled in consequence of the first election, they shall be divided, as equally as may be, into three classes. The seats of the Senators of the first class shall be vacated at the expiration of the second year; of the second class, at the expiration of the fourth year; and of the third class, at the expiration of the sixth year; so that one-third may be chosen every second year; [and if vacancies happen by resignation, or otherwise, during the recess of the legislature of any State, the executive thereof may make temporary appointments until the next meeting of the legislature, which shall then fill such vacancies.] [11]

3. No person shall be a Senator who shall not have attained to the age of thirty years, and been nine years a citizen of the United States, who shall not, when elected, be an inhabitant of that State for which he shall be chosen.

4. The Vice President of the United States shall be President of the Senate, but shall have no vote, unless they be equally divided.

5. The Senate shall choose their other officers, and also a President *pro tempore,* in the absence of the Vice President, or when he shall exercise the office of President of the United States.

6. The Senate shall have the sole power to try all impeachments. When sitting for that purpose, they shall be on oath or affirmation. When the President of the United States is tried, the Chief Justice shall preside; and no person shall be convicted without the concurrence of two-thirds of the members present.[12]

7. Judgment in cases of impeachment shall not extend further than to removal from office, and disqualification to hold and enjoy any office of honor, trust, or profit under the United States; but the party convicted shall, nevertheless, be liable and subject to indictment, trial, judgment, and punishment, according to law.

SECTION 4. *Elections and Meetings of Congress*

1. The times, places, and manner of holding elections for Senators and Representatives, shall be prescribed in each State by the legislature thereof: but the Congress may at any time, by law, make or alter such regulations, except as to the places of choosing Senators.[13]

2. The Congress shall assemble at least once in every year, [and such meeting shall be on the first Monday in December,] [14] unless they shall by law appoint a different day.

SECTION 5. *Powers and Duties of the Houses*

1. Each House shall be the judge of the elections, returns, and qualifications of its own members,[15] and a majority of each shall constitute a quorum to do business; but a smaller number may adjourn from day to day, and may be authorized to compel the attendance of absent members, in such manner, and under such penalties, as each House may provide.

---

[8] Although the Constitution does not require it, the House always chooses the Speaker from among its own members.

[9] Impeachment here means *accusation.* The House has the exclusive power to *impeach* (accuse) civil officers; the Senate (Article I, Section 3, Clause 6) has the exclusive power to *try* those impeached by the House.

[10] Modified by the 17th Amendment (1913), which provides for the popular election of Senators.

[11] Modified by the 17th Amendment (1913), which provides for the filling of vacancies by election and (if a State chooses) by a temporary gubernatorial appointment to fill the vacancy until the election.

[12] Those who object on religious grounds to the taking of an oath (for example, Quakers) are permitted to "affirm" rather than "swear."

The required "two-thirds of the members present" must be at least a quorum (Article I, Section 5, Clause 1.) A quorum (the number of members who must be present in order to conduct business) is 51 in the Senate and 218 in the House.

[13] In 1842 Congress required that Representatives be elected from districts within each State with more than one Representative. Alaska, Delaware, Nevada, Vermont, and Wyoming today (1971) have but one seat each. In 1872, Congress directed that Representatives and, in 1913, that Senators be chosen on the Tuesday after the first Monday in November of every even-numbered year. By special dispensation Maine was allowed to hold congressional elections in September but abandoned the practice beginning in 1960.

[14] Superseded by the 20th Amendment (1933), which fixes the date January 3rd.

[15] In 1969 the Supreme Court held that the House cannot exclude any member-elect who satisfies the qualifications set out in Article I, Section 2, Clause 2; see pages 207–208.

2. Each House may determine the rules of its proceedings, punish its members for disorderly behavior, and, with the concurrence of two-thirds, expel a member.

3. Each House shall keep a journal of its proceedings, and, from time to time, publish the same, excepting such parts as may, in their judgment, require secrecy; and the yeas and nays of the members of either House, on any question, shall, at the desire of one-fifth of those present, be entered on the journal.

4. Neither House, during the session of Congress, shall, without the consent of the other, adjourn for more than three days, nor to any other place than that in which the two Houses shall be sitting.

SECTION 6. *Privileges of and Prohibitions upon Members*

1. The Senators and Representatives shall receive a compensation for their services, to be ascertained by law, and paid out of the treasury of the United States. They shall, in all cases, except treason, felony, and breach of the peace,[16] be privileged from arrest during their attendance at the session of their respective Houses, and in going to, and returning from, the same; and for any speech or debate in either House, they shall not be questioned in any other place.[17]

2. No Senator or Representative shall, during the time for which he was elected, be appointed to any civil office under the authority of the United States, which shall have been created, or the emoluments whereof shall have been increased during such time;[18] and no person, holding any office under the United States, shall be a member of either House during his continuance in office.

---

[16] *Treason* is strictly defined in Article III, Section 3. A *felony* is any serious crime. A *breach of the peace* is any indictable offense less than treason or a felony; hence this exemption from arrest is of little real importance today.

[17] This "cloak of legislative immunity" extends to committee rooms and to the official publications of Congress, such as the *Congressional Record* and committee reports — but it does not extend to outside speech or publication.

[18] *Emolument* means compensation for service; salary or fees. After President Taft had appointed Philander C. Knox as Secretary of State in 1909, it was found that the salaries of Cabinet officers had been increased during Knox's service in the Senate. Congress solved the problem by reducing the Secretary of State's salary to its former figure.

SECTION 7. *Revenue Bills, President's Veto*

1. All bills for raising revenue shall originate in the House of Representatives; but the Senate may propose or concur with amendments as on other bills.

2. Every bill which shall have passed the House of Representatives and the Senate, shall, before it become a law, be presented to the President of the United States; if he approve, he shall sign it, but if not, he shall return it, with his objections, to that House in which it shall have originated, who shall enter the objections at large on their journal, and proceed to reconsider it.[19] If, after such reconsideration, two-thirds of that House shall agree to pass the bill, it shall be sent, together with the objections, to the other House, by which it shall likewise be reconsidered, and, if approved by two-thirds of that House, it shall become a law. But in all such cases the votes of both Houses shall be determined by yeas and nays, and the names of the persons voting for and against the bill shall be entered on the journal of each House respectively. If any bill shall not be returned by the President within ten days (Sundays excepted) after it shall have been presented to him, the same shall be a law, in like manner as if he had signed it, unless the Congress, by their adjournment, prevent its return, in which case it shall not be a law.

3. Every order, resolution,[20] or vote, to which the concurrence of the Senate and House of Representatives may be necessary (except on a question of adjournment), shall be presented to the President of the United States; and before the same shall take effect, shall be approved by him, or, being disapproved by him, shall be repassed by two-thirds of the Senate and House of Representatives, according to the rules and limitations prescribed in the case of a bill.

SECTION 8. *Legislative Powers of Congress*

1. To lay and collect taxes, duties, imposts, and excises, to pay the debts, and provide for the common defence and general welfare, of the United

---

[19] The President must veto a bill in its entirety; he does not possess an *item veto;* that is, the power to veto a specific section without disapproving the entire measure.

[20] *Concurrent resolutions* (which usually relate to the internal management of Congress — for example, creating a joint committee) do not have the force of law and so are not submitted to the President; neither are those joint resolutions which propose amendments to the Constitution.

States; but all duties, imposts, and excises, shall be uniform throughout the United States;

2. To borrow money on the credit of the United States;

3. To regulate commerce with foreign nations, and among the several States, and with the Indian tribes;

4. To establish a uniform rule of naturalization, and uniform laws on the subject of bankruptcies, throughout the United States;

5. To coin money, regulate the value thereof, and of foreign coin, and fix the standard of weights and measures;

6. To provide for the punishment of counterfeiting the securities and current coin of the United States;

7. To establish post offices and post roads;[21]

8. To promote the progress of science and useful arts, by securing, for limited times, to authors and inventors, the exclusive right to their respective writings and discoveries;

9. To constitute tribunals inferior to the Supreme Court;

10. To define and punish piracies and felonies, committed on the high seas, and offences against the law of nations;

11. To declare war, grant letters of marque and reprisal,[22] and make rules concerning captures on land and water;

12. To raise and support armies; but no appropriation of money to that use shall be for a longer term than two years;

13. To provide and maintain a navy;

14. To make rules for the government and regulation of the land and naval forces;

15. To provide for calling forth the militia to execute the laws of the Union, suppress insurrections, and repel invasions;

16. To provide for organizing, arming, and disciplining the militia, and for governing such part of them as may be employed in the service of the United States, reserving to the States respectively the appointment of the officers, and the authority of training the militia, according to the discipline prescribed by Congress;

17. To exercise exclusive legislation in all cases whatsoever, over such district (not exceeding ten miles square) as may, by cession of particular States, and the acceptance of Congress, become the seat of the Government of the United States, and to exercise like authority over all places, purchased by the consent of the legislature of the State in which the same shall be, for the erection of forts, magazines, arsenals, dockyards, and other needful buildings; — And

18. To make all laws which shall be necessary and proper for carrying into execution the foregoing powers, and all other powers vested by this Constitution in the Government of the United States, or in any department or officer thereof.[23]

SECTION 9. *Prohibitions upon the United States*
   [1. The migration or importation of such persons as any of the States now existing shall think proper to admit, shall not be prohibited by the Congress prior to the year one thousand eight hundred and eight; but a tax or duty may be imposed on such importation, not exceeding ten dollars for each person.] [24]

2. The privilege of the writ of *habeas corpus* [25] shall

---

[21] "Post" comes from the French *poste* meaning mail; "post roads" are those routes such as turnpikes, canals, rivers, streets, paths, and airways over which the mail is carried.
   This power, "to establish post offices," which was granted to Congress, continued the precedent that had been established under the Articles of Confederation.

[22] *Marque* is the French for "boundary"; the word "reprisal" comes from the French *représaille,* meaning retaliation. Hence, originally "letters of marque and reprisal" were licenses to cross the boundary into an enemy country to capture or destroy. As used here it means a commission authorizing private citizens to fit out vessels (privateers) to capture or destroy in time of war. They are forbidden in international law by the Declaration of Paris, 1856, to the principles of which the United States subscribes.

[23] This is the Necessary and Proper Clause — or, as it is also known, the Elastic Clause. *Necessary* here does not mean absolutely or indispensably necessary, but rather *appropriate.* The Clause has made it possible for Congress and the courts to extend the meanings of other provisions in the Constitution. The constitutional basis for the existence of the *implied powers,* those which are not specifically stated in the Constitution but which may be reasonably implied from the expressed powers, is found in this Clause.

[24] Temporary provision.

[25] A *writ of habeas corpus,* the "great writ of liberty," is a court order directing a sheriff, warden, or other public officer, or a private person, who is detaining another person to "produce the body" of the one being held in order that the legality of the detention may be determined by the court.

not be suspended, unless when, in cases of rebellion or invasion, the public safety may require it.

3. No bill of attainder or *ex post facto* law shall be passed.[26]

4. No capitation, or other direct tax, shall be laid, unless in proportion to the census or enumeration hereinbefore directed to be taken.[27]

5. No tax or duty shall be laid on articles exported from any State.

6. No preference shall be given by any regulation of commerce or revenue to the ports of one State over those of another; nor shall vessels bound to, or from, one State, be obliged to enter, clear, or pay duties, in another.

7. No money shall be drawn from the treasury, but in consequence of appropriations made by law; and a regular statement and account of the receipts and expenditures of all public money shall be published from time to time.

8. No title of nobility shall be granted by the United States; and no person holding any office or profit or trust under them shall, without the consent of the Congress, accept of any present, emolument, office, or title, of any kind whatever, from any king, prince, or foreign state.

SECTION 10. *Prohibitions upon the States*

1. No State shall enter into any treaty, alliance, or confederation; grant letters of marque and reprisal; coin money; emit bills of credit;[28] make anything but gold and silver coin a tender in payment of debts; pass any bill of attainder, *ex post facto* law, or law impairing the obligation of contracts, or grant any title of nobility.

2. No State shall, without the consent of the Congress, lay any imposts or duties on imports or exports, except what may be absolutely necessary for executing its inspection laws; and the net produce of all duties and imposts, laid by any State on imports or exports, shall be for the use of the treasury of the United States; and all such laws shall

be subject to the revision and control of the Congress.

3. No State shall, without the consent of Congress, lay any duty of tonnage,[29] keep troops, or ships of war, in time of peace, enter into any agreement or compact with another State, or with a foreign power, or engage in war, unless actually invaded, or in such imminent danger as will not admit of delay.

Article II

EXECUTIVE DEPARTMENT

SECTION 1. *Term, Election, Qualifications, Salary, Oath of Office*

1. The executive power shall be vested in a President of the United States of America. He shall hold his office during the term of four years,[30] and together with the Vice President, chosen for the same term, be elected as follows:

2. Each State shall appoint, in such manner as the legislature thereof may direct, a number of Electors, equal to the whole number of Senators and Representatives, to which the State may be entitled in the Congress; but no Senator or Representative, or person holding an office of trust or profit, under the United States, shall be appointed an Elector.

[3. The Electors shall meet in their respective States, and vote by ballot for two persons, of whom one, at least, shall not be an inhabitant of the same State with themselves. And they shall make a list of all the persons voted for, and of the number of votes for each; which list they shall sign and certify, and transmit, sealed, to the seat of the Government of the United States, directed to the President of the Senate. The President of the Senate shall, in the presence of the Senate and House of Representatives, open all the certificates, and the votes shall then be counted. The person having the greatest number of votes shall be the President, if

---

[26] A *bill of attainder* is a legislative act which inflicts punishment without a judicial trial. See Article I, Section 10, and Article III, Section 3, Clause 2. An *ex post facto* law is any criminal law which operates retroactively to the disadvantage of the accused. See Article I, Section 10. See also page 115.

[27] See note 3, page 755 and the 16th Amendment (1913) which permits the levying of an income tax without regard to this prohibition.

[28] "Bills of credit" means paper money.

---

[29] *Tonnage* is a vessel's internal cubical capacity in tons of one hundred cubic feet each. Tonnage duties are duties upon vessels in proportion to their capacity. These duties are paid as a ship enters a port.

[30] The Constitution did not originally set a limit to the number of times a person may be elected President. The 22nd Amendment (1951) now limits a President to two terms or not more than ten years in office.

such number be a majority of the whole number of Electors appointed; and if there be more than one, who have such majority, and have an equal number of votes, then, the House of Representatives shall immediately choose, by ballot, one of them for President; and if no person have a majority, then, from the five highest on the list, the said House shall, in like manner, choose the President. But in choosing the President, the votes shall be taken by States, the representation from each State having one vote; a quorum for this purpose shall consist of a member or members from two-thirds of the States, and a majority of all the States shall be necessary to a choice. In every case, after the choice of the President, the person having the greatest number of votes of the Electors shall be the Vice President. But if there should remain two or more who have equal votes, the Senate shall choose from them, by ballot, the Vice President.] [31]

4. The Congress may determine the time of choosing the Electors, and the day on which they shall give their votes; which day shall be the same throughout the United States. [32]

5. No person, except a natural-born citizen, or a citizen of the United States at the time of the adoption of this Constitution, shall be eligible to the office of President; neither shall any person be eligible to that office, who shall not have attained to the age of thirty-five years, and been fourteen years a resident within the United States.

6. In case of the removal of the President from office, or of his death, resignation, or inability to discharge the powers and duties of the said office, the same shall devolve on the Vice President, and the Congress may by law provide for the case of removal, death, resignation or inability, both of the President and Vice President, declaring what officer shall then act as President, and such officer shall act accordingly, until the disability be removed, or a President shall be elected. [33]

7. The President shall, at stated times, receive for his services a compensation, which shall neither be increased nor diminished during the period for which he shall have been elected, and he shall not receive, within that period, any other emolument from the United States, or any of them.

8. Before he enter on the execution of his office, he shall take the following oath or affirmation:

"I do solemnly swear (or affirm), that I will faithfully execute the office of President of the United States, and will, to the best of my ability, preserve, protect, and defend the Constitution of the United States."

SECTION 2. *President's Powers*

1. The President shall be Commander in Chief of the army and navy of the United States, and of the militia of the several States, when called into the actual service of the United States; he may require the opinion, in writing, of the principal officer in each of the executive departments upon any subject relating to the duties of their respective offices, [34] and he shall have power to grant reprieves and pardons [35] for offences against the United States, except in cases of impeachment.

2. He shall have power, by and with the advice and consent of the Senate, to make treaties, provided two-thirds of the Senators present concur; and he shall nominate, and, by and with the advice and consent of the Senate, shall appoint ambassadors, other public ministers, and consuls, judges of the Supreme Court, and all other officers of the United States whose appointments are not herein otherwise provided for, and which shall be established by law; but the Congress may by law vest the appointment of such inferior officers, as they think proper, in the President alone, in the courts of law, or in the heads of departments.

3. The President shall have power to fill up all vacancies that may happen during the recess of the Senate, by granting commissions which shall expire at the end of their next session.

---

[31] Superseded by the 12th Amendment (1804).

[32] Congress has set the date for the choosing of electors as the Tuesday after the first Monday in November every fourth year and for the casting of electoral votes as the Monday after the second Wednesday in December of that year.

[33] Modified by the 25th Amendment (1967), which provides expressly for the succession of the Vice President, for the filling of a vacancy in the Vice Presidency, and for the determination of presidential inability.

---

[34] The only authority in the Constitution for the President's Cabinet. There is no act of Congress which defines the membership of the Cabinet; rather, the matter is subject to the President's discretion.

[35] A *reprieve* is the postponing of the execution of a sentence; a *pardon* is legal (but not moral) forgiveness for an offense. The President may grant reprieves or pardons only in federal cases.

SECTION 3. *President's Duties*

He shall, from time to time, give to the Congress information of the state of the Union, and recommend to their consideration such measures as he shall judge necessary and expedient; he may, on extraordinary occasions, convene both Houses, or either of them, and in case of disagreement between them, with respect to the time of adjournment, he may adjourn them to such time as he shall think proper; he shall receive ambassadors and other public ministers; he shall take care that the laws be faithfully executed, and shall commission all the officers of the United States.

SECTION 4. *Impeachment*

The President, Vice President, and all civil officers [36] of the United States, shall be removed from office on impeachment for, and conviction of, treason, bribery, or other high crimes and misdemeanors.

Article III

JUDICIAL DEPARTMENT

SECTION 1. *Courts, Terms of Office*

The judicial power of the United States shall be vested in one Supreme Court, and in such inferior courts as the Congress may from time to time ordain and establish. The judges, both of the Supreme and inferior courts, shall hold their offices during good behavior, and shall, at stated times, receive for their services a compensation which shall not be diminished during their continuance in office.

SECTION 2. *Jurisdiction*

1. The judicial power shall extend to all cases, in law and equity, arising under this Constitution, the laws of the United States, and treaties made, or which shall be made, under their authority; to all cases affecting ambassadors, other public ministers, and consuls; to all cases of admiralty and maritime jurisdiction; to controversies to which the United States shall be a party; to controversies between two or more States, between a State and citizens of another State, between citizens of different States, between citizens of the same State claiming lands under grants of different States, and between a State, or the citizens thereof, and foreign states, citizens, or subjects. [37]

2. In all cases affecting ambassadors, other public ministers and consuls, and those in which a State shall be a party, the Supreme Court shall have original jurisdiction. In all the other cases before mentioned, the Supreme Court shall have appellate jurisdiction, both as to law and fact, with such exceptions and under such regulations as the Congress shall make.

3. The trial of all crimes, except in cases of impeachment, shall be by jury; and such trial shall be held in the State where the said crimes shall have been committed; but when not committed within any State the trial shall be at such place or places as the Congress may by law have directed. [38]

SECTION 3. *Treason*

1. Treason against the United States shall consist only in levying war against them, or in adhering to their enemies, giving them aid and comfort. No person shall be convicted of treason unless on the testimony of two witnesses to the same overt act, or on confession in open court.

2. The Congress shall have power to declare the punishment of treason, but no attainder of treason shall work corruption of blood, or forfeiture except during the life of the person attainted. [39]

---

[37] Restricted by the 11th Amendment (1795).

[38] Trial by jury is here guaranteed in federal courts only. The right to trial by jury in *serious* criminal cases in the *State* courts is guaranteed by the 6th and 14th Amendments (see note 49, page 764). Crimes committed on the high seas or in the air are tried in the United States District Court for the judicial district in which the prisoner is landed.

[39] These very specific provisions are intended to prevent indiscriminate use of the charge of treason. The law of treason covers all American citizens, at home or abroad, and all permanent resident aliens. The maximum penalty is death, but no person convicted of the crime has ever been executed by the United States. Note that treason may be committed only in wartime; but Congress has also made it a crime for any person (in either peace or wartime) to commit espionage or sabotage, to attempt to overthrow the government by force, or to conspire to overthrow the government by force, or to conspire to do any of these things.

---

[36] *Civil officers* subject to impeachment include all officers of the United States who hold their appointments from the National Government, high or low, and whose duties are executive or judicial. Officers in the armed forces are not civil officers; neither are Senators and Representatives so considered. Instead of the impeachment process, either house of Congress may expel one of its own members by a two-thirds vote (Article I, Section 5, Clause 2.)

Article IV

RELATIONS OF STATES

SECTION 1. *Full Faith and Credit*

Full faith and credit shall be given in each State to the public acts, records, and judicial proceedings of every other State. And the Congress may, by general laws, prescribe the manner in which such acts, records, and proceedings shall be proved, and the effect thereof.

SECTION 2. *Rights in One State of Citizens of Another*

1. The citizens of each State shall be entitled to all privileges and immunities of citizens in the several States.[40]

2. A person charged in any State with treason, felony, or other crime, who shall flee from justice, and be found in another State, shall, on demand of the executive authority of the State from which he fled, be delivered up, to be removed to the State having jurisdiction of the crime.[41]

3. No person held to service or labor in one State, under the laws thereof, escaping into another, shall, in consequence of any law or regulation therein, be discharged from such service or labor, but shall be delivered up on claim of the party to whom such service or labor may be due.[42]

SECTION 3. *New States, Territories*

1. New States may be admitted by the Congress into this Union; but no new State shall be formed or erected within the jurisdiction of any other State, nor any State be formed by the junction of two or more States, or parts of States, without the consent of the legislatures of the States concerned as well as of the Congress.

2. The Congress shall have power to dispose of and make all needful rules and regulations respecting the territory or other property belonging to the United States; and nothing in this Constitution shall be so construed as to prejudice any claims of the United States, or of any particular State.

SECTION 4. *Protection Afforded to States by the Nation*

The United States shall guarantee to every State in this Union a republican form of government, and shall protect each of them against invasion; and on application of the legislature, or of the executive (when the legislature cannot be convened), against domestic violence.

Article V

PROVISIONS FOR AMENDMENT

The Congress, whenever two-thirds of both Houses shall deem it necessary, shall propose amendments to this Constitution, or, on the application of the legislatures of two-thirds of the several States, shall call a convention for proposing amendments, which, in either case, shall be valid, to all intents and purposes, as part of this Constitution, when ratified by the legislatures of three-fourths of the several States, or by conventions in three-fourths thereof, as the one or the other mode of ratification may be proposed by the Congress; [provided that no amendment which may be made prior to the year one thousand eight hundred and eight shall in any manner affect the first and fourth clauses in the ninth section of the first Article;] [43] and that no State, without its consent, shall be deprived of its equal suffrage in the Senate.

Article VI

NATIONAL DEBTS, SUPREMACY OF NATIONAL LAW, OATH

SECTION 1. *Validity of Debts*

All debts contracted and engagements entered into, before the adoption of this Constitution, shall be as valid against the United States under this Constitution, as under the Confederation.[44]

SECTION 2. *Supremacy of National Law*

This Constitution, and the laws of the United States which shall be made in pursuance thereof, and

---

[40] The meaning is made more explicit by the 14th Amendment (1868).

[41] This section provides for what is known as *interstate rendition* or *extradition*. Although the Constitution here says the fugitive "shall . . . be delivered up" custom and court decisions have changed it to read *"may . . . be delivered up."* Governors sometimes refuse to return a fugitive.

[42] *Person held to service* refers to slaves and, since the 13th Amendment was adopted in 1865, the section has been of no importance.

[43] Temporary provision.

[44] Extended by 14th Amendment (1868).

all treaties made, or which shall be made, under the authority of the United States, shall be the supreme law of the land; and the judges in every State shall be bound thereby, anything in the constitution or laws of any State to the contrary notwithstanding.

SECTION 3. *Oaths of Office*

The Senators and Representatives before mentioned, and the members of the several State legislatures, and all executive and judicial officers, both of the United States and of the several States, shall be bound, by oath or affirmation, to support this Constitution; but no religious test shall ever be required as a qualification to any office or public trust under the United States.

Article VII

ESTABLISHMENT OF CONSTITUTION

The ratification of the conventions of nine States shall be sufficient for the establishment of this Constitution between the States so ratifying the same.*

Done in Convention, by the unanimous consent of the States present, the seventeenth day of September, in the year of our Lord one thousand seven hundred and eighty-seven, and of the Independence of the United States of America the twelfth. *In Witness* whereof, we have hereunto subscribed our names.

Attest: WILLIAM JACKSON, *Secretary*

GEORGE WASHINGTON
President and Deputy from Virginia

New Hampshire

JOHN LANGDON
NICHOLAS GILMAN

Massachusetts

NATHANIEL GORHAM
RUFUS KING

Connecticut

WILLIAM SAMUEL JOHNSON
ROGER SHERMAN

New York

ALEXANDER HAMILTON

New Jersey

WILLIAM LIVINGSTON
DAVID BREARLEY
WILLIAM PATERSON
JONATHAN DAYTON

Pennsylvania

BENJAMIN FRANKLIN
THOMAS MIFFLIN
ROBERT MORRIS
GEORGE CLYMER
THOMAS FITZSIMONS
JARED INGERSOLL
JAMES WILSON
GOUVERNEUR MORRIS

Delaware

GEORGE READ
GUNNING BEDFORD, JR.
JOHN DICKINSON
RICHARD BASSETT
JACOB BROOM

Maryland

JAMES MCHENRY
DAN OF ST. THOMAS JENNIFER
DANIEL CARROLL

Virginia

JOHN BLAIR
JAMES MADISON, JR.

North Carolina

WILLIAM BLOUNT
RICHARD DOBBS SPAIGHT
HUGH WILLIAMSON

South Carolina

JOHN RUTLEDGE
CHARLES COTESWORTH
PINCKNEY
CHARLES PINCKNEY
PIERCE BUTLER

Georgia

WILLIAM FEW
ABRAHAM BALDWIN

---

* Ratified by the ninth State on June 21, 1788, but not immediately effective; see pages 45–46.

Amendments

1ST AMENDMENT. *Freedom of Religion, Speech, Press, Assembly, and Petition* [45]

Congress shall make no law respecting an establishment of religion, or prohibiting the free exercise thereof; or abridging the freedom of speech, or of the press; or the right of the people peaceably to assemble, and to petition the government for a redress of grievances.

2ND AMENDMENT. *Right to Keep and Bear Arms*

A well-regulated militia being necessary to the security of a free state, the right of the people to keep and bear arms shall not be infringed.

3RD AMENDMENT. *Quartering of Troops*

No soldier shall, in time of peace, be quartered in any house, without the consent of the owner; nor, in time of war, but in a manner to be prescribed by law.

4TH AMENDMENT. *Searches and Seizures*

The right of the people to be secure in their persons, houses, papers, and effects, against unreasonable searches and seizures, shall not be violated; and no warrants shall issue, but upon probable cause, supported by oath or affirmation, and particularly describing the place to be searched and the persons or things to be seized. [46]

5TH AMENDMENT. *Criminal Proceedings, Eminent Domain*

No person shall be held to answer for a capital, or otherwise infamous, crime, unless on a presentment or indictment of a grand jury, except in cases arising in the land or naval forces, or in the militia, when in actual service, in time of war, or public danger; nor shall any person be subject, for the same offence, to be twice put in jeopardy of life or limb; nor shall be compelled, in any criminal case, to be a witness against himself; [47] nor be deprived of life, liberty, or property, without due process of law; nor shall

private property be taken for public use, without just compensation. [48]

6TH AMENDMENT. *Criminal Proceedings*

In all criminal prosecutions, the accused shall enjoy the right to a speedy and public trial, by an impartial jury of the state and district wherein the crime shall have been committed, which district shall have been previously ascertained by law; and to be informed of the nature and cause of the accusation; to be confronted with the witnesses against him; to have compulsory process for obtaining witnesses in his favor; and to have the assistance of counsel for his defence. [49]

7TH AMENDMENT. *Jury Trial in Civil Cases*

In suits at common law, where the value in controversy shall exceed twenty dollars, the right of trial by jury shall be preserved; and no fact, tried by a jury, shall be otherwise re-examined in any court of the United States than according to the rules of the common law.

8TH AMENDMENT. *Excessive Punishments*

Excessive bail shall not be required, nor excessive fines imposed, nor cruel and unusual punishment inflicted. [50]

9TH AMENDMENT. *Unenumerated Rights*

The enumeration in the Constitution of certain rights shall not be construed to deny or disparage others retained by the people.

10TH AMENDMENT. *Powers Reserved to the States*

The powers not delegated to the United States by the Constitution, nor prohibited by it to the States, are reserved to the States respectively, or to the people.

11TH AMENDMENT. *Suits against States* [51]

The judicial power of the United States shall not

---

[45] The first ten amendments, the Bill of Rights, were each proposed by Congress on September 25, 1789 and ratified by the necessary three-fourths of the States on December 15, 1791. They restrict only the National Government—*not* the States. But beginning in 1925 the Supreme Court has held some of their provisions applicable to the States through the Due Process Clause of the 14th Amendment; see pages 100–101.

[46] The 4th Amendment's provisions (including the Weeks Doctrine) apply against the States through the Due Process Clause of the 14th Amendment.

[47] The prohibition of double jeopardy and the guarantee against self-incrimination each apply against the States through the Due Process Clause of the 14th Amendment.

[48] Under the *power of eminent domain* government may take private property for public use.

[49] The rights to counsel, to speedy and public trial, to trial by jury (in *serious* criminal cases), of confrontation, and to compel witnesses apply against the States through the Due Process Clause of the 14th Amendment.

[50] The protection against cruel and unusual punishment applies against the States through the Due Process Clause of the 14th Amendment.

[51] Proposed by Congress September 5, 1794; ratified February 7, 1795 (but official announcement of the ratification was not made until January 8, 1798).

be construed to extend to any suit in law or equity, commenced or prosecuted against one of the United States by citizens of another State or by citizens or subjects of any foreign state.

12TH AMENDMENT. *Presidential, Vice Presidential Elections* [52]

The Electors shall meet in their respective States,[53] and vote by ballot for President and Vice President, one of whom, at least, shall not be an inhabitant of the same State with themselves; they shall name in their ballots the person voted for as President, and in distinct ballots the person voted for as Vice President; and they shall make distinct lists of all persons voted for as President, and of all persons voted for as Vice President, and of the number of votes for each, which lists they shall sign, and certify, and transmit, sealed, to the seat of the Government of the United States, directed to the President of the Senate; the President of the Senate shall, in the presence of the Senate and the House of Representatives, open all the certificates, and the votes shall then be counted; the person having the greatest number of votes for President shall be the President, if such number be a majority of the whole number of Electors appointed; and if no person have such a majority, then, from the persons having the highest numbers, not exceeding three, on the list of those voted for as President, the House of Representatives shall choose immediately, by ballot, the President.[54] But in choosing the President, the votes shall be taken by States, the representation from each State having one vote; a quorum for this purpose shall consist of a member or members from two-thirds of the States, and a majority of all the States shall be necessary to a choice. And if the House of Representatives shall not choose a President, whenever the right of choice shall devolve upon them, [before the fourth day of March next following,] [55] then the Vice President shall act as President, as in case of death, or other constitutional disability, of the President. The person having the greatest number of votes as Vice President, shall be the Vice President, if such number be a majority of the whole number of Electors appointed; and if no person have a majority, then, from the two highest numbers on the list, the Senate shall choose the Vice President; a quorum for the purpose shall consist of two-thirds of the whole number of Senators; a majority of the whole number shall be necessary to a choice. But no person constitutionally ineligible to the office of President shall be eligible to that of Vice President of the United States.

13TH AMENDMENT. *Slavery, Involuntary Servitude* [56]

Section 1. Neither slavery nor involuntary servitude, except as a punishment for crime, whereof the party shall have been duly convicted, shall exist within the United States, or any place subject to their jurisdiction.

Section 2. Congress shall have power to enforce this article by appropriate legislation.

14TH AMENDMENT. *Citizenship, Civil Rights, Apportionment, Political Disabilities, Debt* [57]

Section 1. All persons born or naturalized in the United States, and subject to the jurisdiction thereof, are citizens of the United States and of the State wherein they reside.[58] No State shall make or enforce any law which shall abridge the privileges or immunities of citizens of the United States; nor shall any State deprive any person of life, liberty, or property, without due process of law, nor deny to any person within its jurisdiction the equal protection of the laws.

Section 2. Representatives shall be apportioned among the several States according to their respective numbers, counting the whole number of persons in each State, excluding Indians not taxed. But when the right to vote at any election for the choice of electors for President and Vice President of the United States, Representatives in Congress, the executive and judicial officers of a State, or the

---

[52] Proposed by Congress December 12, 1803; ratified July 27, 1804.

[53] Modified by 23rd Amendment (1961), which provides presidential electors for the District of Columbia.

[54] Only two Presidents, Thomas Jefferson in 1801 and John Quincy Adams in 1825, have been chosen by the House of Representatives.

[55] Changed by the 20th Amendment (1933), which sets the presidential inauguration date as January 20th.

[56] Proposed by Congress February 1, 1865; ratified December 6, 1865.

[57] Proposed by Congress June 16, 1866; ratified July 9, 1868.

[58] This clause was primarily intended to make Negroes citizens, but it has much wider application. "And subject to the jurisdiction thereof" excludes children born to foreign diplomats in the United States or to alien enemies in hostile occupation.

members of the legislature thereof, is denied to any of the male inhabitants of such State, being twenty-one years of age, and citizens of the United States, or in any way abridged, except for participation in rebellion or other crime, the basis of representation therein shall be reduced in the proportion which the number of such male citizens shall bear to the whole number of male citizens twenty-one years of age in such State.[59]

Section 3.   No person shall be a Senator or Representative in Congress, or elector of President and Vice President, or hold any office, civil or military, under the United States, or under any State, who, having previously taken an oath, as a member of Congress, or as an officer of the United States, or as a member of any State legislature, or as an executive or judicial officer of any State, to support the Constitution of the United States, shall have engaged in insurrection or rebellion against the same, or given aid or comfort to the enemies thereof.   But Congress may, by a vote of two-thirds of each House, remove such disability.

Section 4.   The validity of the public debt of the United States, authorized by law, including debts incurred for payment of pensions and bounties for services in suppressing insurrection or rebellion, shall not be questioned.   But neither the United States nor any State shall assume or pay any debt or obligation incurred in aid of insurrection or rebellion against the United States, or any claim for the loss or emancipation of any slave; but all such debts, obligations, and claims shall be held illegal and void.

Section 5.   The Congress shall have power to enforce, by appropriate legislation, the provisions of this article.

15TH AMENDMENT.   *Right to Vote* [60]

Section 1.   The right of citizens of the United States to vote shall not be denied or abridged by the United States or by any State on account of race, color, or previous condition of servitude.

Section 2.   The Congress shall have power to enforce this article by appropriate legislation.

16TH AMENDMENT.   *Income Tax* [61]

The Congress shall have power to lay and collect taxes on incomes, from whatever source derived, without apportionment among the several States, and without regard to any census or enumeration.

17TH AMENDMENT.   *Election of Senators* [62]

The Senate of the United States shall be composed of two Senators from each State, elected by the people thereof, for six years; and each Senator shall have one vote.   The electors in each State shall have the qualifications requisite for electors of the most numerous branch of the State legislatures.

When vacancies happen in the representation of any State in the Senate, the executive authority of such State shall issue writs of election to fill such vacancies: Provided, That the legislature of any State may empower the executive thereof to make temporary appointment until the people fill the vacancies by election as the legislature may direct.

This amendment shall not be so construed as to affect the election or term of any Senator chosen before it becomes valid as part of the Constitution.

18TH AMENDMENT.   *Prohibition* [63]

Section 1.   After one year from the ratification of this article the manufacture, sale or transportation of intoxicating liquors within, the importation thereof into, or the exportation thereof from the United States and all territory subject to the jurisdiction thereof for beverage purposes is hereby prohibited.

Section 2.   The Congress and the several States shall have concurrent power to enforce this article by appropriate legislation.

Section 3.   This article shall be inoperative unless it shall have been ratified as an amendment to the Constitution by the legislatures of the several States, as provided in the Constitution, within seven years of the date of the submission hereof to the States by Congress.] [64]

---

[59] This section has never been enforced; some constitutional authorities argue that it was nullified by the 15th Amendment (1870).

[60] Proposed by Congress February 27, 1869; ratified February 3, 1870.   The amendment was intended to guarantee suffrage to newly-freed Negro slaves but is of much broader application today.

[61] Proposed by Congress July 12, 1909; ratified February 3, 1913.   The amendment modifies Article I, Section 9, Clause 4.

[62] Proposed by Congress May 13, 1912; ratified April 8, 1913.   The amendment modifies Article I, Section 3, Clauses 1 and 2.

[63] Proposed by Congress December 18, 1917; ratified January 16, 1919.

[64] The 18th Amendment was repealed in its entirety by the 21st Amendment (1933).

19TH AMENDMENT. *Woman Suffrage* [65]

The right of citizens of the United States to vote shall not be denied or abridged by the United States or by any State on account of sex.

Congress shall have power to enforce this article by appropriate legislation.

20TH AMENDMENT. *Presidential and Vice Presidential Terms, Interim Succession, Sessions of Congress* [66]

Section 1. The terms of the President and Vice President shall end at noon on the 20th day of January, and the terms of Senators and Representatives at noon on the 3d day of January, of the years in which such terms would have ended if this article had not been ratified; and the terms of their successors shall then begin.

Section 2. The Congress shall assemble at least once in every year, and such meeting shall begin at noon on the 3d day of January, unless they shall by law appoint a different day.

Section 3. If, at the time fixed for the beginning of the term of the President, the President-elect shall have died, the Vice President-elect shall become President. If a President shall not have been chosen before the time fixed for the beginning of his term, or if the President-elect shall have failed to qualify, then the Vice President-elect shall act as President until a President shall have qualified; and the Congress may by law provide for the case wherein neither a President-elect nor a Vice President-elect shall have qualified, declaring who shall then act as President, or the manner in which one who is to act shall be selected, and such person shall act accordingly until a President or Vice President shall have qualified.

Section 4. The Congress may by law provide for the case of the death of any of the persons from whom the House of Representatives may choose a President whenever the right of choice shall have devolved upon them, and for the case of the death of any of the persons from whom the Senate may choose a Vice President whenever the right of choice shall have devolved upon them.

Section 5. Sections 1 and 2 shall take effect on the 15th day of October following the ratification of this article.

Section 6. This article shall be inoperative unless it shall have been ratified as an amendment to the Constitution by the legislatures of three-fourths of the several States within seven years from the date of its submission.

21ST AMENDMENT. *Repeal of 18th Amendment* [67]

Section 1. The eighteenth article of amendment to the Constitution of the United States is hereby repealed.

Section 2. The transportation or importation into any State, Territory, or possession of the United States for delivery or use therein of intoxicating liquors, in violation of the laws thereof, is hereby prohibited.

Section 3. This article shall be inoperative unless it shall have been ratified as an amendment to the Constitution by conventions in the several States, as provided in the Constitution, within seven years from the date of the submission hereof to the States by the Congress.

22ND AMENDMENT. *Presidential Tenure* [68]

Section 1. No person shall be elected to the office of the President more than twice, and no person who has held the office of President, or acted as President, for more than two years of a term to which some other person was elected President shall be elected to the office of the President more than once. But this Article shall not apply to any person holding the office of President when this Article was proposed by the Congress, and shall not prevent any person who may be holding the office of President, or acting as President, during the term within which this Article becomes operative from holding the office of President or acting as President during the remainder of such term.

Section 2. This article shall be inoperative unless it shall have been ratified as an amendment to the Constitution by the legislatures of three-fourths of the several States within seven years from the date of its submission to the State by the Congress.

---

[65] Proposed by Congress June 4, 1919; ratified August 18, 1920.

[66] Proposed by Congress March 2, 1932; ratified January 23, 1933.

---

[67] Proposed by Congress February 20, 1933; ratified December 5, 1933. This amendment is the only one which has thus far been submitted to the States for ratification by the convention method set out in Article V. It is the only amendment that specifically voided a previous amendment.

· [68] Proposed by Congress March 21, 1947; ratified February 28, 1951.

23RD AMENDMENT. *Presidential Electors for the District of Columbia* [69]

Section 1. The District constituting the seat of Government of the United States shall appoint in such manner as the Congress may direct:

A number of electors of President and Vice President equal to the whole number of Senators and Representatives in Congress to which the District would be entitled if it were a State, but in no event more than the least populous State; they shall be in addition to those appointed by the States, but they shall be considered, for the purposes of the election of President and Vice President, to be electors appointed by a State; and they shall meet in the District and perform such duties as provided by the twelfth article of amendment.

Section 2. The Congress shall have power to enforce this article by appropriate legislation.

24TH AMENDMENT. *Right to Vote* [70]

Section 1. The right of citizens of the United States to vote in any primary or other election for President or Vice President, for electors for President or Vice President, or for Senator or Representative in Congress, shall not be denied or abridged by the United States or any State by reason of failure to pay any poll tax or other tax.

Section 2. The Congress shall have power to enforce this article by appropriate legislation.

25TH AMENDMENT. *Presidential Succession, Vice Presidential Vacancy, Presidential Inability* [71]

Section 1. In case of the removal of the President from office or of his death or resignation, the Vice President shall become President.

Section 2. Whenever there is a vacancy in the office of the Vice President, the President shall nominate a Vice President who shall take office upon confir-

mation by a majority vote of both Houses of Congress.

Section 3. Whenever the President transmits to the President *pro tempore* of the Senate and the Speaker of the House of Representatives his written declaration that he is unable to discharge the powers and duties of his office, and until he transmits to them a written declaration to the contrary, such powers and duties shall be discharged by the Vice President as Acting President.

Section 4. Whenever the Vice President and a majority of either the principal officers of the executive departments or of such other body as Congress may by law provide, transmit to the President *pro tempore* of the Senate and the Speaker of the House of Representatives their written declaration that the President is unable to discharge the powers and duties of his office, the Vice President shall immediately assume the powers and duties of the office as Acting President.

Thereafter, when the President transmits to the President *pro tempore* of the Senate and the Speaker of the House of Representatives his written declaration that no inability exists, he shall resume the powers and duties of his office unless the Vice President and a majority of either the principal officers of the executive departments or of such other body as Congress may by law provide, transmit within four days to the President *pro tempore* of the Senate and the Speaker of the House of Representatives their written declaration that the President is unable to discharge the powers and duties of his office. Thereupon Congress shall decide the issue, assembling within forty-eight hours for that purpose if not in session. If the Congress, within twenty-one days after receipt of the latter written declaration, or, if Congress is not in session, within twenty-one days after Congress is required to assemble, determines by two-thirds vote of both Houses that the President is unable to discharge the powers and duties of his office, the Vice President shall continue to discharge the same as Acting President; otherwise, the President shall resume the powers and duties of his office.

---

[69] Proposed by Congress June 17, 1960; ratified March 29, 1961.

[70] Proposed by Congress August 28, 1962; ratified January 23, 1964.

[71] Proposed by Congress July 6, 1965; ratified February 10, 1967.

INDEX

Council-manager plan: 705, 726–727
Council of State Governments (COSGO): 631, 650–651
Council for Urban Affairs: 308
Counterfeiters: 378, 379
County government: 638, 657, 697–707; abolishment of, 706–707; chaotic structure of, 699; consolidation in, 706–707; functions, 700; lacking, 699; legal status, 700; manager plan under, 705–706, 726–727; officers, 148, 171, 700–704; reform of, 704–705; statistics, 698–700
County-township system: 710–712
Court(s), federal: 57, 246; of Appeals, 112, 279, 531, 536, 570–573, 575, 578–580; of Claims, 406, 570, 572, 575, 577–578, 580; constitutional, 570–578; Customs, 406, 570, 572, 578, 580; of Customs and Patent Appeals, 459, 570, 572, 575, 578, 580; District, 90, 91, 104, 112, 153, 194, 243, 278, 299, 329, 459, 554, 570–573, 575, 578–580, 588, 596; of District of Columbia, 91, 570, 571, 573, 578–580; exclusive and concurrent jurisdiction of, 571, 574; judges, 579–580; legislative, 570; of Military Appeals, 570, 575, 579, 580; officers, 580; original and appellate, 571, 572, 574; special, 570, 572, 578–579; Tax, 406, 579; territorial, 570, 578, 580. *See also* Supreme Court
Court(s), State: advisory opinions, 661, 662; appellate (intermediate), 657–658, 664; civil procedure, 671–673; criminal procedure, 673–678; criticisms and reforms of, 660–661, 678–679; declaratory judgments, 661–662;

judges, 659–661; jury system, 116–117, 662–665; justice, 655; juvenile, 656; kinds of law applied by, 669–671; municipal, 52, 655–656; organization, 654–659; police (magistrates'), 655; of record, 52, 90–91; Supreme, 279, 476, 618, 658, 720; trial, 656–657; unified, 659. *See also* Law(s)
Crawford, William H.: 163
Crimes, criminal cases: 50, 72, 114–118, 246, 257, 572, 655, 657, 671, 673–678
Criminal Division: 407
Critical Period (1781–1787): 35–38, 266, 543
Cross-filing: 166
Cuba: 337, 349; Castro's, 118; missile crisis, 336, 338, 341, 342, 344, 742; refugees from, 85, 93, 492
Currency: Comptroller of the, 365, 370, 545–547; metallic, 374–376; paper, 374–377, 549; power, 371; system, 371–375
Currency Redemption Division: 368
Customs: 317; agents/officers, 105, 378, 578; Bureau, 331, 365, 366, 409; Court, 570, 572, 578, 580; duties, 258–259, 366, 367; kinds of, 366

Dams: 64, 73, 425–427
Daniel Ball Case: 273
Debt, Bureau of the Public: 368
Debts: 71, 370–371
Declaration of Independence: 118, 284, 748–750; complaint in, 81; forming, 7, 33–35, 39; quoted, 28, 34, 97
Declaration of Paris: 185, 246
Declaration of Rights: 32
Declaratory judgments: 661–662

Defendant, rights of, in court: 672, 677
Defense: civilian, 72, 742–743; national, 383–384; right to adequate, 117; State (militia) 384
Defense, Department of: 383–401, 409, 579; and foreign policy, 330; organization, 308, 384–385; Secretary of, 40, 307, 308, 384, 385, 388, 391, 394. *See also* Air Force, Army, *and* Navy
Defense Electric Power Administration (DEPA): 427, 428
De Gaulle, General Charles: 129, 346
Delaware: 30, 35, 38–40, 43, 119, 120, 164, 202, 302, 411, 442, 603, 606, 609, 610, 614, 618, 620, 621, 633, 639, 646, 648, 649, 658, 661, 671, 688, 690, 699, 712
Delegate, convention: 54, 163–164, 167, 293–297
Democracy: 55, 97; basic concepts of, 11–14, 570; defined, 10–11, 63
Democratic Party: 126, 129–132, 136, 163, 164; convention, 292, 293, 296–297
Democratic-Republican Party: 128, 129, 162, 206, 558
Demographic factors: 157–158
Denaturalization: 93, 94
Dennis v. *United States:* 111
Deportation: 87
Depression, Great: 130, 158, 255, 274, 275, 319, 471, 553; costs, 370, 551; results of, 82, 374, 409, 476, 482, 484, 509, 553, 713
"Des Moines Plan": 725–726
Dewey, George: 284
Dewey, Thomas E.: 130, 301
Dickinson, John: 39, 43
Dictatorships: communist, 24, 97–98; defined, 10, 52; election in, 129

Militia, State: *See* National Guard
Miller-Tydings Amendment: 279
Mines, Bureau of: 421, 430, 433
Ministers, foreign: 325, 327, 328
Minnesota: 145, 146, 165, 447, 526, 548, 550, 607, 609, 610, 620, 646, 649, 660, 689, 690, 711, 718, 722, 725, 739
Minority rights: 12, 13
Mint Act of 1792: 371
Mints, U.S.: 375, 377
Miranda v. *Arizona:* 117
Misdemeanors: 674–675; as cause for impeachment, 213; defined, 655
Missiles: 393. *See also* Cuba
Mississippi: 71, 120, 149, 152, 166, 168, 169, 209, 293, 298, 301, 424, 434, 498, 573, 584, 603, 609, 620, 621, 626, 630, 638, 639, 658, 671, 689, 693, 712
Missouri: 119, 120, 146, 148, 278, 366, 409, 548, 550, 606, 609, 614, 623, 630, 631, 639, 646, 649, 650, 655, 657, 659–661, 689, 697, 706, 707, 711, 712, 722, 723, 727, 737, 739
Missouri ex rel. Gaines v. *Canada:* 119
Missouri Plan: 660–661
Missouri River Valley: 435
"Mixed economy": 17
Model Cities Administration: 513
Moderator of town meeting: 709
Monaco: 6
Money: for armies, 246; power to borrow, 242–243; power to make, 241–242; State, 37; tight, 548. *See also* Currency *and* Paper
Monopolies: growth of, 535; protection against, 277–280, 536; State, 544
Monroe, James: 45, 283, 323, 336, 558
Monroe Doctrine: 336–337

Montana: 152, 165, 426, 427, 609, 614, 631, 646, 688, 689, 691, 706, 712, 721
Morrill Act of 1862: 439, 441, 498
Motor Carriers Act of 1935: 532
Mount Vernon, convention at: 38
Mugler case: 104
Multi-member districts: 128
Multi-party systems: 129
Munro, William Bennett: quoted, 716
Murray v. *Baltimore School Board:* 109
Muscle Shoals: 433, 435
Mussolini, Benito: 10, 24, 339
Mutual Film Corporation v. *Ohio:* 113
Mutual savings banks: 545
Myers v. *United States:* 313

Narcotics and Dangerous Drugs, Bureau of: 365, 379, 409
National Aeronautics and Space Act of 1958: 400
National Aeronautics and Space Administration (NASA): 308, 399–401, 510, 522, 530
National Aeronautics and Space Council: 222, 289, 307–308, 385; creation of, 400–401
National Agricultural Library: 440–441
National Air Pollution Control Administration: 493, 496
National Association of Letter Carriers: 565
National Association of Manufacturers (NAM): 187
National Banking Acts of 1863 and 1864: 370, 544, 545
National (private) banks: 544–547
National Bureau of Standards: 245, 455, 457–458, 461
National Civil Service (Reform) League: 559

National committee: 135; chairman, 135–136
National Communicable Disease Center: 496
National political convention: 58, 134, 292–297
National Council on Marine Resources and Engineering Development: 308
National Defense Act of 1916: 384
National Defense Education Act of 1958: 501; Amendments of 1964, 502, 503
National Education Association (NEA): 189
National Federation of Federal Employees: 565
National government: aids to the economy by, 64, 71–72; Bill of Rights' restriction on, 100–101; cooperation with State by, 71–72; decisions by, 70; economic regulation by, 17; geographic respect by, 71; obligations of, to States, 69–71; opposition to, 62; powers of, 50, 63–69. *See also* Congress, various Departments, Grants-in-aid, House of Representatives, President, Powers, *and* Senate
National Guard (Militia): Air, 392; Army, 72, 324, 384, 386, 387, 395, 644, 645, 702
National Housing Act of 1934: 509
National Institutes of Health: 493, 497
National Labor Relations (Wagner) Act: 476, 477, 574
National Labor Relations Board (NLRB): 476, 477–478; regulation by, 530
National Municipal League: 611
National Origins Act of 1929: 84
National Park Service: 421, 422, 429, 433, 442, 515, 522, 596

National Scenic Rivers System: 423

National School Lunch Act of 1946: 501

National Security Council: 289, 307, 330, 331, 385

National Security Training Corps: 395

National Teacher Corps: 502

National Trails System: 423

National Transportation Safety Board: 521–522

Natural Gas Act of 1938: 540

Naturalization: citizenship by, 90, 145; collective, 90; individual, 90–93; laws, 311–312; rules for, 88, 244

Navigation regulations: 269, 270, 272–273

Navy, U.S.: 384, 388–393; Academy, 389, 390; certification of vessels by, 462; Chief of Naval Operations, 385, 388; Coast Guard, 525; costs, 246, 316; departmental organization, 385, 388–391; functions, 328, 388, 590; as landholder, 422; Marine Corps, 385, 388, 391; NROTC, 388, 389; Regular, 388, 389; Reserves, 388, 389, 462; Secretary of, 308, 385, 388, 391; WAVES, 388

Nebraska: 145, 146, 166, 167, 200, 234, 294, 433, 550, 604, 609, 614–616, 620, 621, 631, 646, 648, 649, 661, 689, 699, 710, 721, 722, 725

Negroes: citizenship of, 88, 91, 153; and education, 483; on jury, 663; in public life, 310, 326, 507, 508; and voting, 144, 153, 157, 209

Nevada: 74, 152, 174, 202, 301, 302, 317, 609, 614, 618, 631, 632, 639, 646, 648, 649, 689

New Deal: 433, 476, 484, 509

New England: 31, 255, 247, 526, 651, 664; counties, 699, 702; towns, 707, 708, 710–712, 717, 718; villages, 717–719. *See also* Caucuses, County government, Towns, Townships, and six individual states

New Hampshire: 30, 32, 34, 35, 38, 45, 49, 149, 166–168, 294, 506, 579, 603, 606, 608, 609, 611, 614, 618, 621, 624, 625, 639, 640, 644–646, 648, 649, 659–661, 688–692, 722

New Jersey: 30, 37–41, 73, 108, 146, 166, 167, 169, 269, 292, 294, 302, 441, 594, 603, 606, 607, 609, 614, 620, 621, 625, 639, 640, 644, 646–650, 658, 659, 664, 678, 699, 706, 717

New Mexico: 120, 152, 203, 258, 337, 398, 399, 425, 607, 609, 621, 633, 638, 646, 649, 658, 689, 721, 722

New York: 30, 31, 36–40, 45, 73, 83, 100, 108, 146, 148, 149, 164, 166, 167, 172, 209, 219, 258, 261, 269, 274, 294, 301, 302, 399, 425, 442, 462, 526, 533, 558, 571, 603, 604, 606, 607, 609, 614, 621, 630, 637, 639, 640, 646, 648, 649, 650, 657–659, 679, 680, 689, 692

New York City: 32, 37, 38, 46, 169, 174, 207, 269, 280, 283, 317, 332, 349, 352, 360, 366, 404, 411, 416, 447, 461, 508, 548, 549, 578, 594, 650, 656

Nixon, Richard M.: 52, 130, 137, 146, 167, 169, 183, 221, 283, 285, 298–301, 310, 318

Nomination: by petition, 168; of political candidates, 125, 186, 296–297; process, 161–168; self-, 162

Nonimmigrants: 86

Norris, George W.: quoted, 433

Norris-La Guardia (Anti-Injunction) Act of 1932: 476, 477

North Atlantic Treaty Organization (NATO): 324, 327, 346, 347, 348, 352; Council, 346, 385

North Carolina: 30, 32, 35, 38, 74, 76, 120, 146, 149, 152, 166, 302, 368, 434, 549, 603, 609, 614, 638, 639, 645, 646, 658, 659, 661, 688, 691, 706, 712, 721, 722

North Dakota: 146, 148, 149, 165, 174, 442, 606, 609, 631, 632, 633, 639, 640, 646, 689, 691, 699, 706, 711, 721, 722

Nuclear test ban: 332, 360

Nuclear Nonproliferation Treaty, 1968: 360

Office of Economic Opportunity (OEO): 308, 529

Office of Emergency Planning: 307, 463

Office of Equal Housing Opportunity: 514

Office of Intergovernmental Relations: 308

Office of Interstate Land Sales Registration: 514

Office of Science and Technology: 308

Office of Special Representative for Trade Negotiations: 308

Ogden, Aaron: 269

Ohio: 55, 76, 106, 113, 146, 166, 167, 174, 294, 301, 302, 399, 401, 549, 606, 609, 614, 618, 630, 631, 632, 646, 649, 656, 658, 660, 689, 691, 706, 710, 711, 721–723, 726–727, 734, 737, 738, 740, 742

Oil: importation of, 433; tidelands, 423–424

Oklahoma: 76, 120, 146, 149, 166, 298, 606, 608–610, 621, 626, 631, 639, 658, 689, 711, 722

Old-Age Assistance: 491

Old-Age, Survivors, and Disability Insurance (OASDI): 484–486; Medicare, 486–489

Older Americans Act of 1965: 489

"One-man, one-vote" decision: 207

Standards, National Bureau of: 245, 455, 457–458, 461

Standing committees: 223–225, 312, 626–627

Stare decisis: 670

State, Department of: Assistant Secretary of, 324; in cooperation with other departments, 460, 467; and international agreements, 314; loyalty in, 566; organization, 308, 323–329; Secretary of, 124, 307, 308, 310, 323–324, 338, 350, 401

States(s), the: administration, 649–651; banks, 544–546; Bill of Rights, 604–605; cooperation with national government, 71–72; cooperation with other States, 73–75; costs, 682; defined, 6–7; employment services, 474; governor of, 637–647; interstate agencies among, 650–651; interstate commerce within, 271–280; lawsuits against, 571; legal separation of, 72; legislatures, 194, 604, 606, 614–633; local control by, 719–720; militia, 70, 324, 384, 644, 702; new, admission of, 75–78; officers, 299, 647–649; party organization within, 136; "police powers," 101, 270; powers denied to, 65, 70, 267, 270; powers reserved for, 65, 254. *See also* Constitutions, State; Courts, State; *and* names of various States

State of the Union Message: 219–220, 316, 514

Stevenson, Adlai: 129, 130

Stone, Harlan Fiske: 577; quoted, 576

Strategic Air Command (SAC): 590

Strauss, Lewis L.: 214, 309

Strict-constructionists: 240–241, 246–248

Submerged Lands Act: 423–424

Suburbs: 736

Subversive Activities Control Board (SACB): 111, 112, 407

Suez Canal: 329, 349, 354, 592

Suffrage: age requirements, 144–148; defined, 143–144; disqualifications, 152–154; literacy tests for, 149; Negro, 153; as a political right, 143–144; registration for, 148–149; residence requirements, 145–146; tax payment for, 152; citizenship for, 145; woman, 144. *See also* Vote/voting

Suits: in equity, 671–673; at law, 671–672; against State, 571

Superintendent of Public Instruction: 649

Supreme law of the land: 67, 68

Supreme Court, U.S.: 570, 573–577; as arbiter or referee in federal system, 574; at work, 575–577; cases tried before, 406; Clear and Present Danger Rule by, 111; Court of Appeals, representation in, 573; as final/ultimate authority, 58, 68–69; as guardian of civil rights, 98–102, 106, 109, 117; how cases reach, 574–575; judicial review power of, 69; jurisdiction of, 574; Justices, 406, 575; Justices, Associate, 573–580; Justices, Chief, 213, 573, 577, 580; liberal decisions by, 241; "one-man, one-vote" decisions of, 207, 685; powers, 569; salaries and terms of members, 580; size, 573. *See also* Supreme Court decisions (below); Courts, federal; *and* Judges, federal

Supreme Court decisions/opinions/rulings: 576–577; (on) agricultural production control, 254, 447; antitrust

laws, 278; appeals from lower courts, 658; appeals from Court of Claims, 578; appeals from Court of Customs and Patent Appeals, 578; bank charter, 544; certain criminal cases, 572; child labor, 469; citizenship loss for desertion, 93; city zoning, 734; Commerce Clause interpretation, 241, 269, 275; Commerce Power, 241; communism, 111, 112; conditions for admission of new states, 76; congressional acts which are held unconstitutional, 572; congressional consent for interstate compacts, 73; constitutionality of Customs Court decisions, 578; constitutionality of State statute, 100; on Constitution's meaning, 574; criticism of public officials, 110; denaturalization, 94; the draft, 105, 111; Due Process and Equal Protection Clauses, 616, 618, 684–685; Establishment Clause Interpretation, 108; executive agreements, 315; expatriation, 115; extradition, 75; "fair trade" laws, 279; grand jury accusation, 116; immigration, 81; implied powers, 246, 248, 544; imprisonment for a crime, 105; income tax, 68, 255; inherent right to acquire territory (by U.S.), 584, 585; injunctions issued *en banc*, 572; interstate divorces, 74; lobbying, 194; movie censorship, 113; navigable streams, 273; Necessary and Proper Clause, 246, 248; paper money as legal tender, 242; peaceful picketing, 112; poll tax, 144, 152; population equality, 207; prohibition, 104; punishment, 118; reapportionment, 205, 619; regulation of securities, 276; religious freedom, 638; sea lands, control of marginal, 423; sedition, 208; segregation, 119–120; State electors' vote, 298; State evidence illegally gained, 106; State reconsideration of Constitutional amendment, 54; State's form of government a political, not judicial, issue, 70; State's power to issue paper money, 545; State taxing the instrumentalities of National government, 544; tax law uniformity, 258; tax powers, 250, 252, 254; taxation on State-operated businesses, 261; Tennessee Valley Authority (TVA), 435; statutes enacted by Congress, 574; voting rights through ancestry, 149; writ of *habeas corpus*, 115. *See also* individual cases, italicized

Surgeon General: 493

Taft, William Howard: 76, 78, 83, 133, 283, 313, 319, 573; quoted, 311

Taft-Hartley (Labor-Management Relations) Act of 1947: 210, 476–479, 566, 574

Taney, Roger B.: 114, 214, 309

Tariff Commission: 259, 530, 578

Tariff duties: 253, 258, 259

Tasmanian dodge: 170

Taxation: defined, 252, 684; enforcement of, 257–258, 367; for other purposes, 261–263; protests against, 31, 32, 179; sound, 685–686

Tax Division, Department of Justice: 406

Taxes, federal: corporate, 257, 261, 367; customs, 258–259; direct, 68, 255–258; estate,

260; excise, 258; export, 254–255; gift, 260; income, 139, 255–258, 367; indirect, 258–261; power to levy, 58, 71, 241, 247, 252–263; regulatory, 261–263

Taxes, State and local: admission, 690; business, 689–690; business, government-operated, 691–692; capital stock, 689; collateral, 689; collection of, 649, 682, 719; documentary and stock transfer, 690; general property, 686–687; federal limitations on, 684–685; on federal property, 684; gift, 689; income, 689; inheritance or estate, 260, 689; license, 690; payroll, 471–472, 690; poll, 144, 152, 255, 690; property, 149, 152, 272, 685, 686, 704; regressive, 688–689; sales, 258, 687–689; severance, 689–690; sharing of, 690; State limitations on, 685; use, 688; from utilities, 690

Taylor, Zachary: 288, 301

Technical Services, Office of: 520

Tennessee: 76, 120, 146, 152, 166, 213, 399, 417, 429, 579, 608, 609, 614, 618, 624, 625, 638–640, 644, 646, 648, 649, 654, 658, 662, 671, 690, 699, 700, 706, 712, 722, 725

Tennessee Valley Authority (TVA): 422, 428, 433–435, 530, 540, 560; Act, 433

Tenure of Office Act: 313

Territories, U.S.: incorporated, 585–586; Office of, 433, 586; power over, 245–246, 584–585; unincorporated, 585, 586

Test Ban Treaty: 360

Texas: 62, 76, 91, 120, 145, 148, 152, 166, 206, 207, 220, 272, 278, 283, 300, 302, 315, 331, 337, 401, 421, 424, 431, 443,

462, 494, 508, 548, 550, 584, 606, 609, 620, 638, 639, 641, 646–649, 657, 658, 660, 679, 689, 690, 693, 699, 706, 712, 722–727, 733, 734, 736, 739

Texas* v. *White: 62

Thought, freedom of: 10, 14

Thurmond, J. Strom: 232, 301

Tidelands controversy: 423–424

Time zones: 521; Uniform Time Act of 1966, 521

"T-Men": 367, 378

Tocqueville, Alexis de: quoted, 697

Torcaso* v. *Watkins: 107

Totalitarianism: 55

Towns, townships: 699, 707–710, 718; county-, 710–712; meeting, 11, 709–710; officers, 708–709; outside New England, 710–712; powers in, 708

Trademarks: 406, 460

Traffic: 738–739

Transportation, Department of (DOT): 519–526; Coast Guard, 379, 525–526; Federal Aviation Administration, 522; Federal Highway Administration, 523–524; Federal Railroad Administration, 524–525; National Transportation Safety Board, 521–522; organization of, 520–521; Saint Lawrence Seaway Development Corporation, 526

Transportation Acts: of 1920, 278, 532; of 1940, 532; of 1958, 532, 535

Treason: 118, 213

Treasurer: county, 704; State, 648–649; U.S., 368

Treasury, Department of the: 257, 365–380, 529, 544; collections by, 472, 485, 552; Comptroller of the Currency within, 365, 370, 545–547;

currency in, 371–377; and government borrowing, 371, 552; interest gained by, 551; organization, 308, 365; and revenues, 366–370, 425, 427; Secretary of, 308–310, 365, 368, 377, 460, 543; "T-Men," 367; "Watchdog," 368. *See also* Customs Bureau, Internal Revenue Service, *and* Secret Service

Treaties: President's power to make, 214, 313–314; regional security, 346–348

Treaty of Paris: of 1783, 36, 584; of 1898, 586, 590

Treaty of Versailles: 234, 314

Treaty, Test Ban: 360

Trial: court, 116–117, 654–657, 675–678; by ordeal, 678; right to fair, 115–116, 143, 677. *See also* Jury

Truax v. *Raich:* 119

Truman, Harry S.: 57, 112, 130, 184, 202, 221, 289, 295, 301, 316, 326, 341, 423, 435, 487, 566; quoted 295

Truman Doctrine: 330, 341

Trusts: 277

Trust Territory of the Pacific Islands: 357, 586, 590–592

Twain, Mark: quoted, 553

Two-party system: 13, 126–129, 161

Tyler, John: 70, 214, 287, 289, 309, 315

Unemployment compensation: 471–472, 564; insurance, 71; taxes for, 471–472

Unemployment Compensation Trust Fund: 472

Unicameralism: 200, 604, 615–616

Union calendar: 229

Union shop: 478, 566

Unions: *See* Labor unions

Unitary government: 62; defined, 8, 53

United Auto Workers: 474, 475

United Electrical, Radio, and Machine Workers: 475

United Federal Workers: 565

United Mine Workers: 187, 475

United Nations: actions by, 340, 342, 354, 361, 378; Big Five, 353, 354, 356, 361; Big Three, 340–341; birth of, 349–350; Charter, 343, 346, 350–354, 356–360; Communist China nonmembership in, 348; in the Congo (UNOC), 353, 361; on Cyprus (UNFICYP), 353; and disarmament, 358–360; Economic and Social Council (ECOSOC), 350, 352, 354–356; Educational, Scientific and Cultural Organization (UNESCO), 356, 361; Emergency Force, 354, 361; evaluation of, 360–361; General Assembly, 349, 350, 352–354, 356, 357, 359, 361; headquarters, 349, 352, 353; Intergovernmental Maritime Consultative Organization (IMCO), 356; International Civil Aviation Organization (ICAO), 356, 361; International Court of Justice (ICJ), 350, 353, 357, 361; International Development Association (IDA), 356; International Finance Corporation (IFC), 356; International Monetary Fund (IMF), 356; International Telecommunications Union (ITU), 356; on the Israeli-Egyptian border (UNEF), 353, 354; and the Korean War, 341–342, 352, 354; Military Staff Committee, 354; organization, 340, 349–351, 355; right to make request of, 590; Secretariat, 349, 350, 357–358; Secretary-General, 352, 353, 357,

358; Security Council, 350, 352–354, 357–359, 361, 590; Trusteeship Council, 350, 353, 356–357; U.S. Ambassador/ Representative to, 309, 313, 327; "Uniting for Peace" Resolution, 354; Universal Postal Union (UPO), 356; veto power in, 353, 354; voting in, 350, 352, 353; World Bank, 356; World Health Organization (WHO), 356, 361, 495; World Meteorological Organization (WMO), 356

United Shoe Workers: 187

United States Arms Control and Disarmament Agency: 331, 332

United States Civil Service Commission: 153, 313

United States Code: 84, 407

United States Housing Act of 1937: 509

United States Information Agency (USIA): 331–332, 460, 530

United States Military Academy: 385, 387, 389

United States Naval Academy: 389, 390

United States Travel Service: 463

United States v. *Appalachian Electric Power Co.:* 273

United States v. *Communist Party:* 112

United States v. *Darby Lumber Company:* 469

United States v. *Wong Kim Ark:* 89

United Steel Workers: 187, 474

Universal military training (UMT): 394–396

Universal Military Training and Service Act of 1951: 394, 395

Universal Postal Union (UPU): 356

jure detela
moss & silver

Eastern European Poets Series #42

jure detela
moss & silver

TRANSLATED FROM THE SLOVENE BY
RAYMOND MILLER WITH TATJANA JAMNIK

WITH AN INTRODUCTION BY **IZTOK OSOJNIK**

UGLY DUCKLING PRESSE, 2018

Published with the kind permission of Andrej Detela and Martin Detela
Originally published as *Mah in srebro* by Založba Obzorja, Maribor, 1983

Eastern European Poets Series #42
Series Editors: Matvei Yankelevich & Rebekah Smith
Co-editor: Emily Wallis Hughes

ISBN 978-1-937027-94-0
First Edition, First Printing, 2018

Ugly Duckling Presse
The Old American Can Factory
232 Third Street #E-303
Brooklyn, NY 11215
www.uglyducklingpresse.org

Distributed in the USA by SPD/Small Press Distribution
Distributed in the UK by Inpress Books

Cover artwork by Mina Fina
Design and typesetting by Emily Wallis Hughes and Don't Look Now!
The type is Marion and Gill Sans

Books printed offset and bound at McNaughton & Gunn
Covers printed letterpress at Ugly Duckling Presse

This book was published with the support of the Trubar Foundation at the Slovene Writers' Association, Ljubljana, Slovenia. (Ta knjiga je bila objavljena s pomočjo Trubarjevega sklada pri Društvu slovenskih pisateljev, Ljubljana, Slovenija.) Additional support was provided by the National Endowment for the Arts and the New York State Council on the Arts.

table of contents

introduction

After all these years, it is difficult to remember which of Jure Detela's poems I read first. Or, rather, heard: Detela was an excellent performer of his own verse, and he loved to recite from early on.[1] It had to be some time in the early seventies, perhaps at an obscure public reading in an old prewar suburban theater; or in the privacy of his unforgettable room crammed with books, old cameras, and cigarette smoke; or maybe at one of the private parties of the older generation where we both for the first time met the Šalamun brothers and other luminaries of the day. In any event, my guess is that the first of his poems I heard was probably "Poem for the Harts." From its very first public presentation this work became legendary, and nothing better exemplified the principle that guided him as a thinker and as an artist: all living creatures have the right simply to live. Some time before, at the Lipizzaner stud farm in the village Lipica, not far from Trieste, I got the chance to get close to the stallions. I had known horses from before, but this was the first time I ever got to look a stallion in the eyes and touch his snout. How soft it was! And how innocent, clear, and trusting his gaze. When I heard "Poem for the Harts," I immediately recognized the same innocence, openness, and directness in the deer that Detela addresses.

In the seventies, there was a bar in Ljubljana, Šumi, where all the young artists and writers used to gather. Whoever wanted to join the club and meet interesting people went there, and that was how most of us then-anonymous future authors came

---

1 He performed his poetry from memory, and could also recite by heart the verses of many other poets, including the work of non-Slovene poets in their original languages. Sadly, only some of his legendary, hours-long literary performances were recorded (a few are available on Youtube), and in them we can still hear his powerful, melodious voice, which is unique even for Slovenian ears.

together. So I probably first met Jure Detela there. He was certainly easy to spot—slender, long hair, with dark, sparkling eyes and a memorably unique vocal style: melodious, elongated, longitudinal chords with a very particular accentuation that sounded like singing, if not the undulating of waves. There was, straight away, a unique chemistry between us and we immediately became friends, although we came from very different backgrounds: Jure was from the exceptionally well-educated urban elite, which could be considered an older-generation upper-middle class, while I belonged to a somewhat younger lower-class hippie group from the suburbs. (Actually, the two of us bridged the gap between the hippie and the upper-middle-class bourgeois worlds.) We engaged in endless discussions about philosophy and the arts, especially poetry, and it wasn't long before we started organizing now-legendary but then-scandalous cultural happenings.

Jure Detela was born in 1951, only six years after the end of World War II, in which Yugoslavia had suffered immensely. More than a sixth of its population had perished, most of the country was heavily damaged, and nearly all infrastructure was destroyed. After the split with the Soviet Bloc in 1948, Yugoslavia, although a country that had fought against the Axis Powers and won, was isolated from its former Western allies because of its new Communist rule under Josip Broz Tito, and from the Eastern Bloc because of Tito's split with Stalin. Life's necessities were sparse, and the regime was paranoid and cruel: right after the war, local troops that had collaborated with the Italian Fascist or Nazi occupiers were executed, and anybody considered to be a political threat to the existing system (much less part of a formal political opposition) was either sent to a political prison or executed. People were frightened, yet also proud and optimistic. On the one hand, they were persecuted by the workings of the secret police, yet on the other, they were still driven by a heroic spirit as victors over the Nazis, and buoyed by a Communist ideology that promised not only equality, friendship, and solidarity, but also explosive productivity and modernization.

The country rose out of the rubble and slowly stabilized itself. People found jobs, and while the standard of living was not high, there was no famine or shortage of basic needs. Many Slovenians saw their lives improving.

In the years before World War I, the Slovenian lands, as well as most of Croatia and Bosnia, belonged to the Austro-Hungarian Empire. Most of the rest of the country was ruled by the Ottomans. The differences in culture, standard of living, and economic development between these two "halves" was enormous, and between World War I and World War II the Kingdom of Yugoslavia could not bridge the gap. By the 1930s, there were no national republics, only administrative regions having nothing to do with the different ethnic populations living in different parts of the country. The contribution of the various ethnicities to the liberation of the country in World War II was recognized by the new regime after the war: the Partisans acknowledged the different cultures, languages, and traditional regions of the national groups, and reconfigured post-war Yugoslavia as a federation of six republics. Slovenia, with its own 1,400-year-long history, was one of them. After 1945, there arose a sharp disconnect with life before the war: the various national societies had to establish themselves anew not only materially, but also politically within a completely new system with entirely new values and new political and social conditions. Pre-war society had, in fact, completely disappeared, and along with it, most of its structure and political differentiation. There was now only one political view allowed— all other political parties had gone silent, and religions no longer played the important role they had before the war. Whoever did not support the new system was gone—suppressed, "reeducated," or simply eliminated.

Despite this new reality, all children were now being sent to school and, except for the oppressive political agenda, education was of high quality all the way to the universities, which were now available to all through a system of scholarships and other means of support. By the end of the 1960s, Yugoslavia had slowly opened its borders not only to foreign travelers but also to contemporary knowledge and international current events, as information became available through books, journals, magazines, radio, and TV. People could now obtain passports, travel abroad, and keep foreign currency accounts. It was no longer difficult to learn about the latest achievements of international science, art, philosophy, or technology.

Immediately after World War II, Tito's Communist regime insisted that artists and writers faithfully follow Soviet models, which in practice meant Socialist Realism: literature (and other art) reflecting proletarian values, featuring stories of working-class people, depicting their struggles, their suffering under unjust regimes, and their victorious, heroic fight for social justice. These works had to praise labor and communist ideology, and endings always had to be optimistic. There was no room for individual inner struggles, doubt, emotional wavering, spiritual quests, love, personal opinions, existential fear, and especially not for any avant-garde experimentation or contemporary Western art. Yet somehow, throughout the 1950s, alternative poetics and movements still managed to slowly find their way into the works of contemporary Slovenian artists. Edvard Kocbek, himself one of the leaders of the Partisan resistance movement, had already expressed his doubts about the heroic attitudes and optimistic enthusiasm of "socialist realist" literature during the war. His short stories expressed the inner fears and doubts of somebody who found himself in difficult or dangerous situations, exposed to mortal threats in combat and trying to survive under harsh conditions. The war poets were quick to abandon their revolutionary rhymes and started to write about private life and subjective experience. An anthology of four poets published in the 1950s—Ciril Zlobec, Janez Menart, Tone Pavček and Kajetan Kovič—heralded a new era. A number of other poets followed, among them Matej Bor, Ivan Minatti, Dane Zajc, Gregor Strniša, and Lojze Krakar. Modernist poetry flourished and opened the way for the neo-avant-garde and experimental poetry of the late 1960s. The publication in 1961 Srečko Kosovel's Constructivist poems of the 1920s detonated a poetic bomb: they were followed in the late 1960s by the work of Franci Zagoričnik, Iztok Geister, Aleš Kermauner, Tomaž Šalamun, Tomaž Hanžek, and other major avant-gardists. Around the same time, the international recognition of the Slovenian performance-art group OHO marked the opening of a dialogue with contemporary Western Conceptualists and other movements that quickly flooded Slovenian and Yugoslavian art and literary centers. This cultural scene marked the final liberalization of Yugoslavia, at least for a decade or so, and (with some effort, it is true) enabled an open intellectual, artistic, and even political dialogue with the rest of the world. Marxism was no longer the only possible philosophy: existentialism, structuralism, phenomenology (Heidegger), and psychoanalysis (both of Freud and, later, Lacan) rose to popularity and changed the theoretical discourse.

For young people in Yugoslavia, as for their counterparts throughout the world, this became a time of rebellion. They traveled abroad and brought back with them the new hippie and rock-and-roll counter-culture. Drugs penetrated the culture of the new urban tribes. Communes were established under the influence of Western youth. Rock music occupied the aural realm not only of exclusive social groups, but of the media in general; as in the West, young people worshiped The Beatles, The Rolling Stones, Bob Dylan, Jim Morrison and the Doors, and all the rest. The winds of 1970s-era New Age ideas and trends brought in the Western hippie obsession with Eastern religions, particularly Zen Buddhism and Hinduism into Yugoslavia's counter-culture. Long hair became a statement of resistance to any kind of establishment, a cry of freedom and independence.

In the 1970s, Detela and I instigated a number of cultural "happenings." The most notorious of these was the "Festival of Youth Culture" in the Ljubljana Opera House in 1978, and this is an event that encapsulates the cultural turmoil of the times. First, one has to understand that the Opera was a temple of elite classic cultural performance that would never willingly open its doors to any kind of subculture. Yet somehow we successfully persuaded its director that our intentions were noble. We even got the support of the political establishment (through another of our admirers, an ascending member of the Communist party), and in the end we convinced the director that we should present the work of the young generation with a decent, organized program that would respect the reputation of the Opera and attract many new younger visitors to future operatic events. We even promised there would be no political, religious, or social provocations. Of course, the actual happening could not have been further from our promises and their expectations. In a word, the event was the Opera board's worst nightmare. It seems impossible to describe the public sacrilege that challenged the active involvement of the audience and turned the event into chaos. Jure and I, along with two or three other friends, were the authors of this scandal, and with it we drove the last nail into the coffin of our long public excommunication by the cultural establishment. From that time on, we were inseparable: the radical activist post-romantic faun and the hippie-anarchist Buddhist Marxist. Along with a third member, proletarian intellectual Iztok Saksida, we started to execute our new activism against all formal, social, political, or artistic institutions. This culminated in the tricksterish "Subrealistic Movement," for which we even composed a "manifesto."

It goes without saying that we young rebels were not readily accepted in Yugoslav society. Most of our fellow citizens were like the Opera staff we had outraged—they looked upon us with suspicion and resentment. And our long hair became more than a positive declaration of independence: unfortunately, it was also a way for the system to identify its prey. One of its prime targets was Jure Detela. As Detela wrote in his famous book-length essay, *Under the Terrible Eyes of the Pontoon Bridge*, from 1974 through

1985 he was constantly harassed by the police: he was arrested frequently and subjected to endless interrogations without charges under various pretenses. The authorities attempted to turn him into an informer in order to learn more about the subculture they thought he was leading. He quickly realized this, never gave in to their pressure, and never disclosed even innocent information about his friends and fellow writers, or about any other intellectuals or artists. The whole affair turned into a personal trial, and for him it became an ethical test. It was not just that he never wanted to disclose the names of any of his friends; he was also concerned lest his interrogators compromise themselves ethically. Detela's stance recalled the Kierkegaardian dilemma of Jesus—who had always known that once he revealed himself publicly, he would force his enemies to commit the deadly sin of killing the Son of God. In Detela's case, it was not a matter of religious belief, but rather the expression of a fully realized personal illumination. In any case, this was the deep truth that Jure Detela revealed, fought for, and exercised again and again. He remained consistently true to his vision, whether it was a matter of rescuing an ant from a puddle or a spider from behind the door, saving pigeons that somebody was poisoning on the streets of Ljubljana. Whether it was commemorating the killing of Urlike Meinhof and her fellow Red Brigade prisoners by the German police with a candlelight vigil in a Ljubljana park, or declaring a hunger strike when towards the end of the eighties, just before the fall of Yugoslavia, the Serbian dictator Slobodan Milošević threatened the family of a friend because of the latter's critical newspaper commentaries. Due to his many public appearances and political protests, he was seen by some as a weirdo or a clown, or even a holy fool, but in fact, he was always deadly serious. He practiced what he preached: the fundamental right of any living creature to simply exist on its own terms. He dedicated the entirety of his work, including his writings, to all the different aspects of this living principle, regardless who or what was involved.

Jure Detela was a man of an unbounded integrity. He wrote again and again about the different aspects of his vision and the accompanying responsibilities in his exceptional essays, but we find its purest expression in his poems. Here his profound ethical insights attained the height of tragic poetic achievement. In his famous "Notebook of Reconciliation," Detela wrote down some basic rules for writing poetry (no doubt under the influence of Pound's *imaginisme*): no metaphors, be as simple and direct as possible without unnecessary stylistic adjectives, be truthful and ascetic in expression. Above all, a poem had to have a clear message without any allegoric meanings. As his leading principle he added the insistence on the right of all living creatures to live. More than once he claimed, "If all my poetry had to be forgotten forever in order to save a single sparrow or an ant, so be it." Thus, in his poetry, we see living experience through the eyes of the involved beings themselves, without any subjective or theoretical cant. Though his verses contain the true manifestation of a deeply-felt ethical position, it is their poetic power which makes him a leading figure of his times. He was far ahead of most of his contemporaries by declaring that the one true ecological issue was the inherent right of *all* planetary beings to exist. Aimé Césaire stood for the same cause: "Everything has a right to live," he wrote in *Poetry and Knowledge*. Detela deeply understood that standing up for that right not only requires fundamental changes in social, economic, and political systems, but also, even more crucially, demands new ways of symbolization and even using language. For him, human aggression did not begin and end with crimes against humanity; he tried to expose the much deeper nature of what he considered ritual murder. For him, the term "holocaust" should not be exclusively limited to human extermination: the mass killing of North American buffalo, the slaughterhouses of Chicago, whale hunts in the Atlantic, the extermination of African elephants, or even just the shooting of one innocent mountain goat or deer manifested the same ritual criminal deed. Detela saw no difference among those deadly acts. For him, the crime of killing a single innocent deer was enough to expose humankind's murderous nature.

Detela brought these ideas forward in two poetry collections, *Maps* (1978) and *Moss & Silver* (1983).[2] The structure of *Moss & Silver* is the more complex of the two. It includes at least three types of poems, actually three different expressions of the same "thing": I call them the darkness, the haiku, and the legacy. All of them reveal different perspectives on the same ethical stand that is at the foundation of Detela's art. "Ethical" does not mean moral or moralistic but an attitude beyond good or evil exposing some archaic right to live engagement. The first, "dark," type (e.g., "Antigone's poem" and "To a certain hermeticist...") addresses the ethical practice of the individual in the face of death. These poems deal with the deep personal abyss in which murderous, aggressive tendencies coexist with redemptive, salvatory traits and generate one's unique personal behavior and social action toward the other—human or animal—being, whether friend or foe or neither. One is responsible for the death as well as for the innocence of the other living creature, for its right to live. The atmosphere of those poems I would compare to that of a famous painting by the German Swiss painter Arnold Böcklin, "The Island of the Dead." As an art historian, Detela knew it well.[3] Written with a sharp awareness of death, these poems explore the dark symbolism and archetypal quasi-anthroposophical corridors of human awareness of primordial aggression, murder, and death. They all respond to Detela's unbending call for the right to live for all creatures, however small, soft-spoken, weak, or less noticeable (insects, for instance.) See, for example, poem

---

2   The other book published during his lifetime was the aforementioned essay, *Under the Terrible Eyes of the Pontoon Bridges*. Posthumously published books include a single volume containing the two previous poetry collections, and, after many years, a booklet of haiku, *Haiku=Haiku*, as well as three collections of his essays, art criticism, and other writings.

3   Detela was an art historian by profession, educated at the Faculty of Arts, University of Ljubljana; he was well read in an eclectic range of other subjects.

#8, "Bolt of white light: / insect nailed to cross," written on the death of an insect by the heat of a light bulb.

In contrast to the poems of the first type, the second, "haiku," type depicts the epiphanic beauty of nature and the innocence of the "unspoiled" life of animals beyond human horizons. Some of these are quite short, but so much the more powerful for that. They include some of his best poems, including "Poem for the Harts." They provide direct insight into the realm of animals. The third kind of poem I would call his legacy; these poems create an ethical testament both for his contemporaries and for future generations. They describe those who have freed or would like to free themselves from the dominant human matrix of aggressiveness, and by a firm ethical stand expand into "the fluid of universal growth unleashed." These include the poems dedicated to some of his poet friends: "In memory of a poem by Primož Piskernik" and "In memory of Vladimir Memon."

Thus, Detela was among the first ecological activists and may also be read as an early proponent of what we now call eco-poetics. His poetry, written with non-anthropocentric symbolization and with the express purpose of "standing up for life," puts forward the radical idea that every creature has the inalienable right not to be killed. Detela writes:

> Whoever sees death's pure colors
> though he still be ensnared
> in growth will never, till the day
> he dies, perceive another
> as himself. A cry is also
> the logic of the world.

In a way, this poetry belongs to the tradition of the English Lake Poets. In his ode *Intimations of Immortality* Wordsworth wrote: "Ye, blessed creatures, I have heard the call / Ye to each other make." Detela wrote about this line in his essay on Wordsworth. Though he did not say it directly, it is not hard to guess the identity of "the call" that reached him. In Wordsworth's ballad, "Hart-Leap Well," as he escapes the hunter in three giant leaps, the hart jumps from the top of the hill down to the spring at the foot of the hill; here he dies of exhaustion, yet since he never surrendered to the aggression of the hunter, he dies a free being:

> Three leaps have borne him from his lofty brow
> down to the very fountain where he lies.

It is my conviction that in answering the living tradition of the hart's call, Jure Detela's individual poetic talent shone through in all its ethical purity, and in this way he preserved and passed on the living tradition to future generations. In his death, he actually experienced the same fate: he died from the exhaustion of a persistent, sincere heart, one which refuses to surrender, even amid murderous circumstances.

What then is Detela's legacy for future readers and for humanity as a whole? No doubt his visionary realization of his ethical credo: the right of every living creature to live. Now, twenty-five years since his death, we see the prescience of his call to preserve the planet and the creatures who inhabit it. Today we talk about the sixth major geological extinction caused by humans: a number of animal species have recently disappeared from the planet, along with innumerable plant species. This trend is turning against the human race too—and not only in the developing world. Everywhere, human life too seems to have become a commodity. That is one facet of Detela's concern. Even more important, perhaps, is the idea of the poetic call. We do possess a "tool" that enables us to penetrate to the core of such issues, to reflect upon them, and to redirect the stream of murderous human endeavors toward the creative and sublime. Jure Detela offered us an answer to the question of this sublime quality by exposing the potential of poetic language as something living and visionary, something that offers us the alternative of survival. It is only now that younger generations are rediscovering Detela's poetry. Two years ago, a selection of his poems was published in

Poland, the only translation of him that has appeared so far. I sincerely hope that, through the translations in this book and elsewhere, Detela will become known throughout the world, for his message and his spiritual family are truly international.

— Iztok Osojnik, August 2017

moss & silver

I was left alone
Seeking the visible world, nor knowing why.

— William Wordsworth

1.

Ko slišim
spomin,
odmevajo
gongi
z roba
sveta.

1.

I hear a
memory
and gongs
resound from
the edge
of the world.

2.

Na levi je spanje,
slepota,
na desni me vleče
navzgor.

2.

On the left there is sleep,
there is blindness,
on the right it draws me
on high.

3.

S temnokarminskega
stožca v možganih,
ki sije
s svojo notranjo svetlobo,
padajo zvezde skoz prsi
in tonejo
v brezoblično,
mračno globino.

3.

From the dark scarlet cone
in the brain,
shining with an
inner light all its own,
stars fall
through the breast
sinking into murky depths
without faces.

4.

Poizkus dešifriranja pojava, ki ga imenujemo čarovnija

Čarovniki vejo o telesu tistega, ki
ga hočejo začarati, nekaj, česar
on sam ne ve. To misel investirajo
svoji žrtvi tako, da jo žrtev občuti
fizično, ne pa refleksivno. Ker je
najbolj pogostna reakcija na fizičen
občutek telesna, dobijo telo v oblast; in
ker je duša odvisna od tega, kar počne
telo, dobijo v oblast tudi dušo. Ta
reakcija je verižna. Čarovniki pogosto
čarajo zato, ker jim nekaj manjka
pri njihovem lastnem kontaktu med
dušo in telesom. Ta primanjkljaj
hočejo nadomestiti s tujim telesom, a
ker čarovniki nekaj vzamejo od kontakta
med dušo in telesom tistega, ki je
začaran, hoče tudi začarani postati
čarovnik. Tako nastajajo ogromni kompleksi
agresije, ki se velikokrat ne zaveda
zasužnjenosti svojega izvora. Ljudje, ki
sodelujejo v čarovniji, se nikoli
ne spominjajo intimnih vzrokov za
individualno dovzetnost do manipulacije
nad tujimi dušami in telesi. Imuniteta
pred čarovnijo raste iz spoznavanja teh
vzrokov in iz gnusa pred njimi, ne iz
sovraštva do čarovnikov in iz nasilja nad
njimi. Se spomniš verza: kar zgrabijo
čarovniki in peljejo v pošasti? Tudi
telesa so zmožna transformacij, ne samo
duše. Vsako utelešeno bitje neprenehoma

4.

An Attempt to Decipher the Phenomenon We Call Sorcery

Sorcerers know something about the body of
the one they want to bewitch that he
does not know himself. They instill this idea
in their victim in such a way that the victim
feels it physically, but not reflexively. Because
the most frequent reaction to a physical
sensation is a bodily one, they take control
of the body; and because the soul depends on what
the body does they take control of the soul, too. This
is a chain reaction. Sorcerers often cast spells
because something is missing in the connection between
their own soul and body. They want to make up this
deficiency with someone else's body, and
because sorcerers take something from the connection
between the soul and body of the one
bewitched, the bewitched one wants to become
a sorcerer, too. Thus arise huge complexes
of aggression, aggression that many times does
not realize its own origin is enslaved. People
who take part in sorcery never remember
the intimate reasons for their personal propensity
to manipulate other people's souls and
bodies. Immunity to sorcery comes from
recognizing these reasons and feeling disgust
before them, not from hating sorcerers and doing them
violence. Do you recall the verse: What sorcerers seize
and take to the monsters? Bodies are also
able to transform, not just souls. Every embodied being
constantly builds and changes the image
of its body. These changes lead either to fetters
or to freedom: there is no being that could not

gradi in spreminja podobo svojega
telesa. Te spremembe peljejo v vklenjenost
ali v svobodo: ni bitja, ki ne bi imelo
možnosti, da se odreši čarovnije. Noben
pekel ni večen.

have a chance to save itself from sorcery. No
hell is eternal.

5.

Prijatelj,
goriš mi v glavi
kakor kakšna
podoba.
Tvoja pesem
je črna luknja
vizije.
Če bi bil daleč,
bi pisal drugače.
V mislih sveta
si z vsem,
kar ljubiš
in česar ne ljubiš:
kako se giblješ,
kako prepevaš.
Kako se spomniš
na situacijo,
v kateri te drugi
naenkrat zagledajo.
Ko brez horizontov
in mask
izbruhnejo črni
transi čez nočno
ravnino.

5.

My friend,
you burn in my mind
as a kind of image.
Your poem
is the black hole
of a vision.
If you were far away,
you would write differently.
In the thoughts of the world
you are with all
that you love and all
that you don't love:
how you move,
how you sing.
How you recall
a situation
when others
suddenly notice you.
When without
horizons and masks
black trances erupt
across
the night plane.

6.

smreke
in kostanji
okoli lesene
kolibe

6.

spruces
and chestnut trees
around a wooden
shack

7.

Iz jeder cvetic
poganja sonce
prozorna krila
kristalnih živali
v jarke večerne
svetlobe.

7.

The sun drives
the transparent wings
of crystal animals
from the hearts of flowers
into trenches of
evening light.

8.

Udarec bele svetlobe:
žuželka pribita na križ.

8.

Bolt of white light:
insect nailed to cross.

9.

Hoelderlinovi Orli

Sinovi
višin
prebivajo
zgoraj,
le včasih
prihajajo
s tujo
vibracijo
po zemeljske
žrtve,
ki postanejo
v krempljih
enake
prozorni
modrini.

9.

Hoelderlin's Eagles

The sons of
the heights
dwell
above,
only coming
now and then
with an alien
vibration
for earthly
victims
who become
the same as
transparent
sky blue
in their talons.

10.

drvenje, drvenje, neskočno drvenje,
drvenje v popolni samoti

10.

rushing, rushing, infinite rushing
rushing in total aloneness

11.

Zimska noč v dolenjskem gozdu

Lepota me zmeraj nanovo določa
s celim vesoljem. Drhtenje
je večno, smrt pada skoz grlo: podobe
sproti pozabljam. Premiki

na nebu tonejo v led in gorenje,
zato sem telesno izbrisan.
Kličem priče? Sanje so neme
kot trupla. Povsod so prikazni,

ki družijo snov z govorico : tako
se praznijo brezna. Magija
oblakov krog lune je rojstvo simbolov.
Karma nesmrtnosti išče

morilca. Odprta usta otrpnejo
v snegu. Veter zapiha
v temno lobanjo. S transom norosti
ukaže sonce slepoto.

11.

Winter Night in a Lower Carniolan Forest

Beauty always defines me anew with the entire
        universe. The quivering
is eternal, death falls through the throat: I forget
        the images every time. Stirrings

in the sky sink into ice and burning,
        so that I am physically erased.
Do I call witnesses? Dreams are mute
        as corpses. Everywhere there are ghosts,

who unite matter with speech: in this way
        chasms are emptied. The magic
of clouds round the moon is the birth of symbols.
        The karma of immortality seeks

the murderer. The open mouth grows stiff
        in snow. The wind blows
through the dark skull. With a trance of madness
        the sun commands blindness.

12.

Nekemu hermetistu, za eksperiment z zajci

1.

Ni več skrivnosti v tvojem ošabnem
  eksperimentu, temni
čarovnik. Ker zdaj je dokončno vpisana
  v naše jezike izkušnja,

da energije, razdvojene na ženski
  in moški princip, prehajajo
v vsakem mikronskem segmentu prostora
  v zvezo, ki omogoča

utelešenim bitjem, da najdejo v sebi
  pretoke, ki z njimi čutenje
v selitvah skoz ogenj, zrak, zemljo in vodo
  prestopa meje vsakega

v en sam element zazrtega hipa. --
  Zdaj vidim tvojo magijo
kot mračno brezno sredi zelenih
  bavarskih gozdov. Za zajce

ni v njem nobene vode, le eros
  in smrt. Ker vodo in ogenj
si TI domislil; zakaj bi ju zajci
  za tabo? Si mislil, da raje

sledijo tebi kot svojim željam?
  V okultnih silah si zajcem
združil željo po seksu z željo
  po smrti. Ti si izključen

12.

To a Certain Hermeticist, for the Experiment with Rabbits

1.

There is no longer any mystery in your
        arrogant experiment, dark
sorcerer. For finally entered into our
        languages is the experience

that in every micronic segment of space,
energies divided into the male
and female principle cross into
        the connection that enables

embodied beings to find within themselves
        the channels through which the sensation
of migrations through fire, air, earth, and water
        crosses the boundaries of every

moment perceived in only one element.
        Now I see your magic as
a gloomy abyss in the middle of green
        Bavarian forests. For the rabbits

there is no water here, only eros
        and death. Because the water and
fire were YOUR bright idea; why should the
        rabbits follow your cue? Did you think

they would rather follow you than their own
        desires? In your occult powers
you joined the rabbits' desire for sex with
        a desire for death. You are

do takšne stopnje, da v tem karmatskem
trenutku še ni odrešena
tvoja magija. Preveč si vedel
in zajce zavestno prevaral.

2.

Računal si z nujnostjo pretoka
spolne energije
k prihodnjemu členu. Zakuril si ogenj
in v njem sežgal genitalije

umorjenega zajca. Pepel si stresel
v vodo, in vodo razlil
po gozdu. Z enim strašnim ognjem
si izrinil iz želje zajcev

vse ognje sveta. Tako si blokiral
spolno zvezo med vodo
in ognjem. Praznino so zajci izpolnili
s smrtjo. Odšli so v tolmun

in utonili. Prostost samomora ne odtehta
laži o ognju. Feedback
zajčjih smrti ostane. Toda
ne išči ga v elementih,

ne išči ga v tujosti seksa, niti
v naravi, ki vsako bitje
smrtno premaga. Tu si sklepal
pogodbe, ki jih sovražim.

excluded to such an extent that in this
    karmic moment your magic
still is unredeemed. You knew too much and
    willfully deceived the rabbits.

2.

You counted on the fact that sexual energy
    needs a channel to future
generations. You lit a fire, and in it
    burned the genitalia

of a murdered rabbit. You shook the ashes
    into water and watered
the forest with it. With one horrible fire
    you drove all the world's fires

out of the rabbits' desire. In this way you blocked
    the sexual connection between water
and fire. The rabbits filled this void with
    death. Off they went to a whirlpool

and drowned. The freedom of suicide does not
    outweigh the lie about fire. There is still
the fidbek from the rabbits' deaths. But do
    not look for it in the elements,

do not look for it in the alienness of sex, or
    in nature, which fatally
vanquishes every being. Here you have
    struck bargains which I hate.

3.

Ko sem napisal prva dva dela
  te pesmi, sem sanjal o zajcih,
čepečih v ozračju brez tal, presijanem
  s svetlobo deževnega jutra.

Videl sem tesno ob tilnike stisnjene
  uhlje, naježeno dlako
in skrčene šape. Vsi hkrati so zrli
  navzdol proti zemlji v daljavi.

Kako je vsak od teh zajcev pripadal
  le svoji samoti! Zemlje
si niso želeli, a niso mogli
  zreti drugam. Naenkrat

so izginili. Tuj in svetel glas
  je zadonel skozi mene:
«Nobenih pogodb za zajce.» Potem
  sem padel v molk in praznino.

3.

Having written the first two parts of this poem
      I dreamt of rabbits cowering
in an atmosphere with no ground, illuminated
      by the light of rainy mornings.

I saw long ears tucked tightly to the back of
      the neck, fur standing on end, and clenched
paws. At the same time they were all looking
      down at the earth in the distance.

How every one of those rabbits belonged
      only to its own seclusion! They
did not yearn for the earth, but they could not
      look anywhere else. Suddenly

they disappeared. A clear and alien voice
      thundered through me: "Strike no
bargains for the rabbits." And then I
      fell into silence and the void.

13.

Metulj

V deželi, kamor odleti vsak glas,
je bil metulj, totalno razpuščen,
v zamolklo ravnotežje potopljen
in vrnjen v cirkulirajoči čas,
ki je razkril drget srebrne kože
očem, ki jih metulj ni prepoznal,
ko je bil gledan iz svetlobe rože,
iz hrepenenja breztelesnih trav.

13.

Butterfly

In the land toward which all voices fly
was a butterfly, its pieces dispersed,
in hollow equilibrium immersed
and returned into circulating time
revealing the quiver of silvery skin
to eyes the butterfly did not know
as it was watched through the light of a rose,
through the longing of bodiless grasses.

14.

V tem, kar spomladi raste, noče sprave
oko, ki v soncu sebe prepozna.
Za Emily je zrak skrivnost menjave.
Za Isso so ravni pokrov pekla.

14.

The eye that sees itself in sunlight
seeks no placation in springtime's growth.
In air, for Emily, a mystery of exchanges.
Standards, for Issa, roof devils below.

15.

Mlečna cesta

Ti nisi moje ljudstvo, Kristus,
    neštetokrat sem rojen.
Še siješ od vzhoda do zahoda
    kot sonce. Tebi nihče

ne pogleda v obraz. Kot bager vzdiguješ
    s tilnikom zemljo. Zmeraj
je mavrična aura vsenaokoli
    ravnine križa. Tramova

sta v vetru in barvah lahkotni priči
    smrti, ki z umom pošasti
rjove iz davnine. Oko, ki sije
    skoz zvezdna vrata, počasi

ugaša. Nihče te ne čaka. Nihče
    me ne čaka. V samoti je zemlja
prozorna in pusta. Glavo sprejeti
    kot zarjo, in noge kot premog.

15.

Milky Way

You are not my people, Christ,
      countless times I've been born.
You still shine from the east to the west
      like the sun. Nobody

looks you in the face. Like a dredger you lift
      the earth with the nape of your neck. There
is an iridescent aura all around the flat
      surface of the cross. In the wind

and colors the two beams are gentle witnesses
      to death, which roars from antiquity
with the mind of a monster. The eye shining
      through the starry door slowly

goes out. Nobody waits for you. Nobody
      waits for me. In its solitude the earth
is transparent and empty. To accept the head
      as dawn, the feet as coal.

Antigonina pesem

Lepo je truplo, ki razpada,
    kakor trohni drevo.
Podoba drugih teles ni noben
    kriterij za mojo človeškost.
V zraku je kuga enaka vrtincu.
    Semena se krčijo v ognju.
Svizci si iščejo v gorah zavetje.
    Reke so razporejene.

Truplo je skrito mojim očem.
    Povsod je pokopano,
kjerkoli sem jaz. Vse sile, ki imajo
    moč, da ga dvignejo
nad zemljo, so razpršene po skalah.
    Kjer se zgoščujejo v forme,
je zmeraj dovolj že moja prisotnost,
    da jih nevtralizira.

Ko mislim na truplo, ki razpada,
    je moj obraz maska. Iz nje
se vsa potovanja stekajo v eno
    podobo: od zmeraj sem mrtva
in moje telo je vzorec vse zemlje,
    kamor so me rodile
molitve iz Hadesa. Gnitje trupel
    ne more vpiti k bogovom.

Ker vse, kar rečejo morilci,
    posrkajo živa telesa.

16.

Antigone's Poem

Beautiful is the corpse that decays
     in the way a tree rots.
The image of other bodies is no
     criterion for my humanity.
A plague in the air is like a whirlwind.
     The seeds shrivel in the fire.
Marmots seek shelter for themselves in the mountains.
     The rivers are well arranged.

To my eyes, the corpse has been hidden.
     It is buried everywhere,
wherever I am. All the forces that have the
     power to raise it above
the earth have been scattered about the cliffs.
     Wherever they congeal into shapes
my presence is always already enough
     to neutralize them all.

When I think of the corpse that decays,
     my face is a mask. From it
all journeys flow together into one
     image: I have been forever dead
and my body is the pattern of the whole earth,
     whereto prayers from Hades
have birthed me. The moldering of corpses
     cannot cry out to the gods.

Because everything murderers say
     is absorbed by living bodies.

Ker vsakogar, kdor je ubit, spoznajo
oči in roke. Moje
so izkopale grob. A v mrliškem mrmranju
sveta so še zmeraj prikazni,
ki gledanje stiskajo v trupla kot v ječo,
kjer tok vesolja otrpne.

Jaz sem za večno odrešena te
čarovnije. Nebeška bitja
poznajo prehode med živimi in mrtvimi.
Poznajo slo po neskončnih
spremembah. Poznajo svobodo, ki hoče,
da truplo trohni kot drevo:
grob je kot njihova ladja, kot vrata
za vse, ki živijo na zemlji.

Because eyes and hands recognize everyone
    who has been murdered. Mine
have dug a grave. But in the deathly muttering of
    the world there remain ghosts who squeeze
their gaze into corpses as into a jail where
    the current of the universe goes numb.

I am forever delivered from this
    sorcery. Heavenly beings
know of the passages between the living and the dead.
    They know of lust for infinite
changes. They know of the liberty that wants
    a corpse to rot like a tree:
the grave is like their ship, like a gateway
    for all those who dwell upon this earth.

17.

Pesem za jelene

Jeleni! Naj pride v mojo pesem
    zavest o nasilju? Kako
le zmorem zvestobo spominu na vas,
    ko se mi svet transformira

v sporočilo ubijanja? Za vas je drugače.
    Vi ste nedolžni. Vi ste
napadani. Zmeraj ste v smrtni nevarnosti.
    Vi ste totalno predani

bežečim čredam. Svoja telesa
    izpostavljate strelom, da ščitite
beg košut in mladičev. S prsmi,
    polnimi zraka, stojite

pred puškami. Takrat ste žalostni, sveti,
    ponosni. Vi gledate v lovce
s čistim pogledom. Vi sprejmete smrt
    brez vsake pogodbe. Ker vaše

želje so proste umorov. Že tu
    na zemlji je vaša hoja
totalno svobodna, čeprav vas lovci
    nenehno sledijo. Vsaka

pomlad vas odreši. Vsaka polna
    luna vas odreši. Vsaka
globel, ki skoznjo uidete lovcem,
    vas odreši. Vsaka zvezda

17.

Poem for the Harts

Harts! Harts! Should I let the consciousness of
      violence into my poem? How
can I remain faithful to your memory when
      the world is transformed for me

into a message of killing? For you it is different.
      You are innocent. You are
being attacked. You are always in mortal danger.
      You are totally committed

to the fleeing herds. You expose your
      bodies to the bullets so that you can protect
the flight of the hinds and the fawns. With chests
      full of air, you stand

before the rifles. When you do you are sad, holy,
      proud. You gaze into the hunters
with a pure gaze. You accept death without
      any formal agreement. Because your

desires are devoid of murders. Already
      here on earth your walking is
totally free, although the hunters ceaselessly
      follow you. Every single

springtime redeems you. Every single full moon
      redeems you. Every deep
hollow through which you can escape the hunters
      redeems you. Every star

vas odreši. Še zemlja, ki padete nanjo
    krvavi. s svincem v telesih,
vas odreši. Jeleni! S smrtnimi padci
    ne dajete lovcem odveze

za svoje življenje. Lovci prezirajo
    vašo nedolžnost. Zato
vas morijo z lahkoto. Jeleni! Jeleni!
    Kako bi mogel storiti,

da ne bi prišla ta krutost, navzoča
    po vaših gozdovih, v pesem
za vas? Jeleni! Jeleni! Jeleni!
    Kako je zemlja sproščena

pod vašimi parklji! Kako je presojna
    in zračna, sončna, zelena!
Kako jo vaša telesa družijo
    z nebom! Kako ste živi!

redeems you. The earth on which you fall down bloody,
　　with lead in your bodies, still
redeems you. O, harts, harts! When you fall down dead
　　you give the hunters no absolution

for your lives. O, don't the hunters despise your
　　innocence. That is why
they murder you with ease. O, harts, harts, harts!
　　How could I make it so

this cruelty present throughout your
　　forests not come into a poem
meant for you? O, harts! Harts! Harts! Harts!
　　How the earth is liberated

under your hooves! How translucent it is,
　　how airy and sunny and green!
And how well your bodies unite it with
　　the sky! O how alive you are!

18.

V tihi glasbi se sklanja vame
    speča glava in zbuja
trope zvezd, ki pršijo kot kaplje,
    ko steče konj čez potok.

18.

In quiet music a sleeping head
    leans into me and awakens
herds of stars that spray like droplets
    as a horse runs across a stream.

19.

V mojih mislih se vrte
doline, obtežene
s kamni, ki se kotalijo
z rekami navzdol
po strugah.

19.

Spinning in my thoughts
are valleys laden
with rocks rolling down
with rivers in
their beds.

20.

Neznanci

Popolnoma so brezbrižni do matric stvarjenja, s
    katerih drsijo.
S kromoksidnozeleno barvo v glavah zamaknjeno
    zrejo v zaprte horizonte.
Potem naenkrat zagledajo tisto svetlobo, ki je
    svetost življenja.
Potem zapustijo zemljo, tako da utonejo v svetlobo.
Nikoli več ne pridejo nazaj.

20.

Strangers

They are completely indifferent to the matrices of creation, off
      which they slide.
With a chromium oxide green in their heads, they look raptly
      into closed horizons.
Then all at once they discern the light that is the sanctity of life.
Then they desert the earth, so that they may sink into the light.
Never again do they come back.

21.

Pesem embria

Pred živim robom sveta je mama.
Nekje za robom sveta je smrt.

21.

Embryo's Poem

Before the living edge of the world is mama.
Somewhere beyond the edge of the world is death.

22.

Pesem otroka, ki naredi prvi korak

Gore, ki se gibljete
v toku, ki me nosi,
jaz vam hočem izkričati
svojo bolečino!
Ustavite se, gore!
Poslušajte moj krik!
S tokom, ki me nosi,
nočem več drveti!
Hočem izkričati
svojo bolečino!
Hočem vstati! Hočem biti
velik in svoboden!

22.

Poem of a Child Taking its First Step

You mountains who move in
the current that carries me,
how I want to cry out
all my anguish to you!
You stop now, you mountains!
You listen to my cry!
No more! I don't want to rush
with the current that carries me!
How I want to cry out
all of my anguish!
I want to stand! I want to be
big, I want to be free!

23.

Med divje
    brstečo
       ravnino
in majhnim
     presojnim
       oblakom
se v komaj
   zaznavnem
      premiku
obrača
  golobje
    pero.

23.

Between a
      wildly
           blossoming plain
and a tiny
      transparent
           cloudlet
a pigeon
      feather
      whirls
in barely
      perceptible
      motion.

24.

Na drobcih
peska,
pomešanih
s čiki,
papirčki
in suhimi
listi,
je vrabec,
ki zoblje
pohojeno
češnjo.

24.

On fragments
of sand,
mixed with
cigarette butts
wrappers
and dry leaves
a sparrow pecks
a trampled
cherry.

25.

Spomin na pesem Primoža Piskernika

Čutim,
da Primož,
ki je zdaj daleč
od mene,
vidi
to, kar je v meni
neuničljivo,
v prostranstvu
moje
ekstaze,
vzbujene
s krikom
galeba,
kričečega
v istem
prostranstvu
svoje
ekstaze,
ko leta
nad ladjo,
s katero se peljem.

25.

In Memory of a Poem by Primož Piskernik

I sense
that Primož,
who is now so far
away from me,
sees what
in me is
indestructible
in the vastness
of my
ecstasy
aroused by
the cry
of a gull
crying in
the same
vastness of
its own ecstasy
when it flies
over the ship
on which I travel.

26.

Vzlet

Z zamolklim brenčanjem
se težka žuželka
dviga
nad drobno rastlino,
ki v zmeraj krajših nihajih
ziblje
bleščeč, okrogel
cvet.

26.

Take-Off

With a hollow buzz
a heavy insect
lifts off
over a tiny plant
that in ever shorter oscillations
sways
a round, candescent
flower.

27.

gladka
stebla
mirno
ukrivljena
v enakomernem
vetru

27.

sleek
stalks
peacefully
bent
in a constant
wind

28.

Lačni glasovi, ki iz dlakastih grl
kličejo skozi zimske
gozdove pegam zelenja, naj vzniknejo
iz tal, se izlivajo v dušo,
ki mirno vibrira v ozračju in raste
k soncu čez trde vrhove.

28.

Let the hungry voices
calling from shaggy throats
across the winter forests
to spits of green rise up
from the ground. Let them
pour into the soul
that vibrates peacefully
in the atmosphere and grows toward
the sun across hard peaks.

29.

Mama, kako se osječaju mrtvaci?

Uvijek sam znao
   da suhi list
      na proljetnoj grani
        pati za sebe.
I u danima
   kad sam bio
      daleko od njega
ipak sam znao
  da suhi list
    na proljetnoj grani
      pati za sebe.

29.

Mama, How Do Dead People Feel?

I have always known
        the dry leaf
            on springtime branch
                suffers for itself.
And during the days
        when I have been
            far far away from it
I've known nevertheless
        that the dry leaf
            on springtime branch
                suffers for itself.

30.

Ion

Krog mene so ležali suhi listi,
ko sem ga prepoznal v svetlobi lune,
na tisti strani palic iz železa,
kjer mene ni bilo. Ker se je sprva
izmikal opredelitvam, sem začutil,
da nisem bil edini, ki je gledal vanj.
Ničesar nisem vedel o jetništvu,
poznal sem le prostore, kjer ni Iona.
Zapisal sem: samote ne poznam.
Poslušal sem Beethovna, ker je hotel
povsod svobodo, tudi za duhove
in za mrliče. Kajti zla ni v barvah
in ne v temi, temveč v koordinatah
in mrežah. Zgodovina vidi v Ionu
le ploskve, ki ločujejo prostore,
omejujoče živo ekspanzijo,
kot da nas družijo le dimenzije,
ne govorica. Mislil sem na tujost,
večjo od horizontov, in razkrinkal
sem zgodovinsko laž. Ker v vsakem klicu
se razodeva slutnja o neskončnih
daljavah. Brez ločitve od telesa,
sem zvedel iz vseh noči, v katerih sem
blodil v gozdovih. Rekel sem ljudem:
«Ion bi bil rad povsod, ne da bi hotel
postati vse.»

30.

Ion

Around me the dry leaves lay when
I recognized him by the light of the moon,
on that side of the rods of iron
where I was not. Because he at first
avoided definitions, I sensed that I
was not the only one who was looking at him.
I knew nothing of imprisonment,
I knew only the spaces where Ion was not.
I noted: I do not know solitude.
I listened to Beethoven, because he wanted
freedom everywhere, even for spirits
and for the dead. For there is no evil in colors,
nor in darkness, but in coordinates
and nets. Within Ion history sees
only the planes which separate the
spaces which limit living expansion,
as if only dimensions unite us,
not speech. I thought of an alienness
greater than horizons, and I revealed
the lie of history. Because every call
reveals a premonition of infinite
distances. Without leaving my body
I learned from all the nights I wandered
in the forests. I said to the people
"Ion would like to be everywhere,
without wanting to become everything."

31.

Epitaf

Distančni stimulus sveta
je kot ubiti cvet.
Kdor v čistih barvah vidi smrt,
kontrastno v rast zajet,
ne bo, dokler ne umre, nikdar
občutil drugega
tako kot sebe. Tudi krik
je logika sveta.

31.

Epitaph

The long-range stimulus of the world
is like a flower killed.
Whoever sees death's pure colors
though he still be ensnared
in growth will never, till the day
he dies, perceive another
as himself. A cry is also
the logic of the world.

32.

Kot se v spominu enotnega vesolja
samotna iskra, ki drsi v možganih,
razpre v upesnjen prostor: vodoraven,
kjer je lebdel nikoli ponovljen
galeb v amorfni zmesi mraka in zarje —
tako se le v ljubezni, Georg Trakl,
začarane poti sprostijo v sen.

32.

Just as in the memory of the uniform universe
the solitary spark that slides in the brain
opens into poeticized space: the horizontal
where once the never-to-be repeated gull
floated in an amorphous mixture of dusk and dawn—
so, too, only in love, Georg Trakl,
are enchanted paths unleashed into dream.

33.

Gozd šumi
na svetih ustih,
ko v njegovo
noč molčijo
žalostni
sinovi smrek

33.

The forest murmurs
on holy lips
when on its night
the melancholy sons
of pines
say nothing.

34.

Kakor z ostjo skozi grlo
se čutim
v spominu na jaso
nad strmim zalivom
Bohinjskega jezera:
ovce in praprot,
v sivini.

34.

As if a knifepoint through the throat
I sense
in my memory of the glade
above the steep bay
of Lake Bohinj:
sheep and ferns
in gray.

35.

Na robu gozda

Temna jadra. Kuna!

35.

On the Edge of the Forest

Dark sails. Marten!

36.

Spomin na Vladimirja Memona

Smrt se krči
iz groze pred znamenji
tujih zavesti
v kristalno gostoto
snovi;
prezgodaj umrli
pesnik, tvoja
nesmrtna samota
se širi iz neskončno
drobnega jedra
telesa v fluid
sproščene vesoljne
rasti.

36.

In Memory of Vladimir Memon

Out of horror
before signs of alien
consciousnesses
death contracts
into crystal
density of matter:
you, poet who has died
too soon, your
immortal solitude
expands from the body's
infinitely tiny core
into the fluid
of universal growth
unleashed.

37.

Z drobnimi kremplji
se čižek oklepa
gladke, iz grma
rastoče veje,
ki tik nad krajem,
kjer svetlo razpenjena
voda šumi
čez oblasto skalo,
ukrivljena niha
skozi prostrano
modrino.

37.

With tiny talons
the siskin clutches
a smooth branch
growing from a bush
right above the place where
brightly foaming water
roars over the rounded cliff—
a bent branch
swinging through vast
blue.

38.

oče
z dvignjeno roko
obrnjen nazaj
pred vrati ognja

38.

father
hand upraised
turned around
toward gates of fire

39.

razširjena zavest:
prijatelj na obzorju

39.

friend on the horizon—
consciousness expanded

40.

Pesem za Jureta Detelo

Morilec! suha trava jemlje
    iz tvojega zraka pesem,
ki snuje bodoče lesketanje
    v steptanih poljih, oblakih,

asfaltu in gozdu. V edini tišini,
    ki nima stika z jesensko
žejo, ni zate nobenih refleksnih
    gibov. Le veter vrtinči

žvenketajoče liste po strjeni
    hrapavi glini. Gamsi
s kompaktnimi, prožnimi trupi, pol metra
    nad parklji, so daleč. V tebi

se širi občutek rumene svetlobe,
    ki ga vzbuja ljubezen svetnikov
do morja, a ostro jih tolče vsaka
    krivica, ki stiska milijone

utelešenih bitij. V rahlih valovih
    polnijo zrak boleči
otroški kriki. Preveč je strahu,
    ki blokira ljubezen. Morilec,

v tisočih pesmih iščeš svetovno
    retrospektivo zločinov
in smrti. Vsi smo že zdavnaj umrli
    in nismo še našli nanovo

40.

A Poem for Jure Detela

Murderer! the dry grass takes a poem
    out of your air, takes a poem
that forges a brilliance in the
    trampled fields, in the clouds,

on asphalt and in forest. In the only silence
    that has no contact with autumnal
thirst, there are no reflexive movements left
    for you. Only the wind swirls

clattering leaves across the rough, hardened
    clay. And the chamois—their
firm, flexible trunks half a meter over their
    hooves—are far, far away. In you

the same sensation of yellow light expands
    that is aroused by the saints' love for
the sea, but they are hammered hard by every
    injustice that crushes millions

of embodied beings. In delicate waves
    the painful cries of children
fill the air. There is too much of
    this love-blocking fear. You murderer,

in thousands of poems you search for a universal
    reexamination of crimes
and deaths. We have already all died a long time
    ago and we haven't yet rediscovered

življenja. Kot da bi kvader železa
lebdel nad prahom, letijo
v cikcakastih črtah jate ptičev
v grmovje. Spomniš se davnega

roba doline: nad hosto ogromna
navpična skala, ki iz nje
priteče studenec. Drugje je lomastil
srnjak po goščavi. Kakšna

je žalost, ki z njo mineva tvoja
karma. Kopje švistne
skoz zrak in pribije grlo človeka
na desko. Skloniš glavo

misleč na resnico, ki nisi v njej hotel
nikogar ubiti. V glasovih
iščeš pomene sveta, a v njih
spoznavaš samoto groze

pred tujim trpljejem. Čez bore na rdeči
sipini je padla večerna
senca. Pozneje si videl črnega
konja na vlažnem zelenju.

our lives. Just as if a block of iron
     were floating over the dust, flocks
of birds fly in zigs and zags into
     the bushes. You recall the ancient

edge of the valley: above the scrub brush looms
     an immense cliff, from which
a spring flows. And somewhere else a roebuck
     trampled the thicket. What is this

sadness passing by with your
     karma. A spear whistles
through the air and nails a man's throat to
     a board. You lower your head,

while thinking of a truth in which you wanted
     to kill no one. You search for
the meanings of the world in voices, but there
     you recognize the solitude of

horror before another's suffering. The evening
     shade fell through the pines on the red
sand dune. Later you saw a black
     horse on the damp verdure.

41.

Ionova pesem

Ali čutite, da
ne bojo gore nikoli
kričale, in to zato, ker
je dejanje, ki ga ljubljeni
potrebujejo od mene, preveč
določljivo?

Ali čutite, da
se vsak moj premik zidarskega
orodja vmešča natančno na
prehod med indiferentnim šumom
vetra, vode in kamenja na
eni strani, in med kriki
ljudi in živali na drugi
strani, in da le s telesom, do
zadnje celice zvestim
misli: bitja izrekajo sebe, ne
mene, zmorem za svoja dejanja
vzdržati pozicijo brez
nasilja?

Nikoli si ne bom ostril
prstov kot svinčnike zato, da
bi z njimi razmajal zemeljske
sklade, ali da bi z njimi odkril
kako aherontsko špranjo—pa tudi
obli prsti, kot jih imam, bi zmogli
s tipanjem razločiti orožje, položeno
pred moja stopala.
Kar mi je za zmeraj
absolutno odveč.

41.

Ion's Poem

Do you sense
the mountains will never
cry out, precisely because
the act which my loved ones
demand of me is too
definite?

Do you sense
every move I make
with the mason's
tool goes directly upon
the passage between the indifferent noise
of wind, water, and stone
on one side, and between the cries
of people and animals on the other
side; and that I manage to hold
a position for my actions
without violence
only with a body
that is faithful, to its very
last cell, to the thought
that beings express
themselves, not me?

I will never sharpen my
fingers as pencils in order to
shake the earth's strata with them,
or to use them to discover
some Acheronian fissure—but also
round fingers, as I have, could
by touching discern the weapon placed

Tako na sredi velikega
mesta, med kanto za smeti in
cvetočim drevesom, ko vrabci
nad mano gradijo gnezda z ekstatično
željo po trajanju, brez vsake
pogodbe z destrukcijami in
s smrtjo, preberem pesem, v kateri
se je prijatelj, trenutno stoječ
zraven mene, ves koncentriral na
iskanje svoje definicije; zapomnim
si zlasti zaključne verze:
imenovana pika sem,
vzvratna pika sem,
resničen genij.

In pesnik mi reče:
«V sanjah sem spesnil
marsikaj, kar se je direktno
nanašalo nate, a kar si prebral, je
vse, kar mi je ostalo v spominu, ko
so se sanje končale.»

before my feet.
Which for me is forever
absolutely too much.

Thus, in the middle of a large
city, between garbage can
and blooming tree, when sparrows
build their nests above me with ecstatic
desire for continuity, without any
contract with destruction and
death, I read through a poem in which
a friend who is momentarily standing
next to me is completely focused on
searching for his definition; I remember
especially the concluding lines:
I am a point with a name,
I am a retroactive point,
a real genius.

And the poet tells me:
"I composed in a dream
many lines that directly
referred to you, and what you read
is everything that remained in my memory
when the dream ended."

42.

v dolgo vijugo
odpirajoča se ozka
dolina,
z gozdovi smrek
porasla
skoraj do dna,
do potoka

42.

opening into a long
winding curve a narrow
valley
grown over with
pine forests
nearly to the bottom
nearly to the stream

43.

V projekciji na plosko planjavo
povsod med razrito potjo
in sivorjavim obzorjem
zastrtim z meglo in mrakom:

in v sveti vertikali
globlje od podzemnih prepletov
klijočih skoz prazno ravnino
v drobne šope zelenja:

korenine
večnega
drevesa

za gnezda
prihodnjih
stoletij.

43.

In an image projected onto a flat
plain everywhere between the rutted
path and the gray-brown horizon
veiled by fog and by nightfall:

and in a holy vertical
deeper than underground interweavings
that sprout up through a flat, empty surface
into tiny tufts of greenery:

roots of an
eternal
tree

for the nests
of future
centuries.

44.

Za vso minulost
in vse, kar biva,
bojo telesa
sprejemala težo,
srca nemir,
in duše tesnobo
zaradi premajhne
moči spomina
v čuječi ljubezni
do tujih zavesti,
dokler ne pridejo
mravlje,
da raznesejo trupla
po zemlji.

44.

For all the past and
all that exists,
bodies will receive
gravity,
hearts unrest,
and souls anguish
because memory's
power is too slight within
the vigilant love for
alien consciousnesses,
until the ants
arrive to deliver
corpses
across the land.

I had never heard of Jure Detela before the summer of 2010, when my friend Tatjana Jamnik asked me to consider translating one of his collections into English. Few of my other Slovene friends seemed to know who he was, either. The name rang a faint bell associated with the roiling avant-garde scene that had transformed Slovene culture in the 1980s, which was, by then, a long time ago, before the wall came down, before the Balkan wars of the '90s, before Slovenia's emergence as an independent state and full-fledged member of post-Communist Europe. And, after all, Detela had died in 1992, leaving behind only two published collections of verse, an experimental novel/memoir, and a few essays. It was really no surprise, then, that no one seemed to know who he was.

However, as my work on *Moss & Silver* slowly progressed, I realized that this initial impression was, at best, misleading. First, I learned that virtually everyone who had lived in Ljubljana in the 1970s and '80s still remembered Jure Detela vividly. Indeed, he seemed to have been a person who made an indelible impression, a man exceptionally unconventional even by the rebellious standards of the time. One of his friends recalls Detela "swimming through the air, barely touching the ground on which he walked, head lifted ... his thoughts in dimensions unknown."[1] More significantly, however, I soon discovered that Detela was in fact remembered for much more than his eccentricities: this was a true Renaissance man—poet, activist, critic, philosopher—with a formidable intellect, deep erudition, and wide-ranging interests.

---

1   Metka Zupančič, "Jure Detela, the slender deer," in *Ecology through Poetry. The Right to Live*, ed. Jelka Kernev Strajn, Iztok Osojnik, Darja Pavlič (Calcutta: Sampark, 2013), back cover.

By the early 1980s, Slovene poets had accelerated "a free-wheeling rush toward innovation and exploration."[2] Tomaž Šalamun—probably the modern Slovene poet best known in the West—had essentially blown up traditional poetic conventions in the 1960s, and the following two decades "were the years when many 20-year-olds ... entered the space of poetry ... through the door opened for them by Šalamun, prodded by his radicalisms,"[3] much to the horror of the Slovene literary establishment. In fact, however, Detela stood somewhat aloof from these wars between the new avant-garde and the establishment: though he professed his allegiance to the new avant-garde aesthetic,[4] his background and erudition isolated him from the younger radicals, but at the same time he wanted nothing to do with the "defenders of Slovene beauty," as he called the establishment, whom he saw as being too invested in the privileges afforded them.[5] Meanwhile, Šalamun, who saw himself as a kind of mediator between the two camps, tried and failed to gain influence over him. "Jure and I tried to develop an alternative culture [of our own] on the margins," is Iztok Osojnik's rather dry comment on the matter.[6]

What was always important to Detela was poetry itself, and behind all these efforts to sway him in one direction or the other lies the fact that everyone recognized him as an exceptional poet. "In the context of what was happening in Slovene art at the

2   Henry R. Cooper, Jr., "Slovene Literature: A Brief Survey," in *A Bilingual Anthology of Slovene Literature*, ed. Henry R. Cooper, Jr. (Bloomington, IN: Slavica Publishers, 2003), 18.

3   Quoted in Vladimir Kopicil, "Writings of Death and Entertainment," in *Impossible Histories. Historical Avant-gardes, Neo-avant-gardes, and Post-avant-gardes in Yugoslavia, 1918-1991*, ed. Dubravka Djurić, Miško Šuvaković (Cambridge, MA and London: MIT Press, 2003), 109.

4   See Miklavž Komelj, "Za orfično levico," in *Orfični dokumenti: Teksti in fragmenti iz zapuščine* (Koper: Hyperion, 2011), 454.

5   Ibid., 454, footnote 8.

6   All quotes from Iztok Osojnik come from our conversation in Ljubljana on September 12, 2017.

time," writes poet and scholar Miklavž Komelj, "Detela's poetry stood out, was entirely singular, solitary."[7] This was a poet who tirelessly worked on his craft and studied it intensely: he was widely read, conversant with many different poetic traditions, and in constant, active dialogue with a wide variety of other poets. "In many ways, Detela was a classic Lake District poet," says Osojnik. "He didn't just read Wordsworth, he studied him: he understood him and what he was trying to do in the deepest sense, and he used what he learned to develop his own verse." Among the poets Detela directly addresses in his work are, besides Wordsworth, Emily Dickinson, Issa (and other Japanese haiku masters), Friedrich Hölderin, Percy Bysshe Shelley, and Georg Trakl. His oeuvre contains translations into Slovene of many of these writers,[8] and he enjoyed reciting their poems from memory in their original languages.

Detela based his poetic manifesto on principles layed out by Ezra Pound in "Hugh Selwyn Mauberley" and "Vorticism," in particular his call to "maintain the sublime in the old sense." The essence of Detela's espoused principles might be summarized as follows:

> (1) keep the poet's subjectivity out of the poem, from biographical data not otherwise specified in the text to figurative language that would mean something only to the poet;
> (2) use words and phrases strictly in their literal sense;
> (3) use poetic devices sparingly ("ascetically");
> (4) avoid symbolism and "metaphorical kitsch." [9]

Above all, for Detela, the poet is not an "individual," but the

---

7 Ibid., 455, footnote 9.

8 See the "Notes to the Poems" section below for details.

9 This list is adapted in English translation from Detela's comments in a 1987 interview that is included in a soon-to-be-released Slovene film, *Sočasje* (working English title, *Synchrony*) by Miha Vipotnik; I am currently in the process of translating the script for subtitles. In the film, Detela quotes Pound in English.

member of a linguistic collective, and thus should employ only those means that every other member has at their disposal: words used in their conventional meanings, grammatical rules, and tradition.

Detela's objection to subjective, formalistic artistry in poetry—in his own words, the "tyranny of aesthetics over reality"[10]—was more than just a matter of stylistic preference. For him, the message of the poems was of paramount importance, and this message was woven into the fabric of a sophisticated, holistic philosophy that was years ahead of its time: "the radical idea that every creature has the inalienable right not to be killed," to quote from Osojnik's introduction. For Detela, poetry was "an ethical practice that inspires critical reflection and the transformation of *everyday life*."[11] In his view, metaphor and symbolism are really acts of violence, for they exploit other beings (i.e., animals) as mere poetic material, "a means for projecting the emotions of the lyric speaker."[12] Metaphors, moreover, reduce complex beings to "one exclusive meaning ... in the process of which they have to chop the meaning off from the designated thing."[13] Detela rejected "cultivated poetic language ... [as] nothing more than a performance of (black) magic," and declared that he wished "to bring [his] poetry to the point of defining real relations in the material and inner worlds, without reducing the message to the mystique of the poet's subjectivity."[14]

* * *

---

10 Miklavž Komelj, "Uvodna pojasnila," in *Orfični dokumenti*, 10.

11 Alenka Jovanovski, "Violence, Animal Rights and Ecopoetry," (her emphasis), in *Ecology through Poetry. The Right to Live*, 94.

12 Ibid., 87.

13 Detela, "Ker nočem, da bi bralci mojih pesmi...," in *Orfični dokumenti*, 207.

14 Detela, "Želja po zvestobi dobesednemu pomenu...," ibid., 203.

Iztok Osojnik long recognized his friend Jure Detela, who had died an untimely death[15], as a poet whose work transcended Slovene literature and deserved wider recognition. In 2010, feeling responsible for the legacy of his friend, Osojnik approached Tatjana Jamnik, poet, translator, and director of the cultural organization Polica Dubova, about collaborating on the project of an English translation; she then approached me. It was Jamnik who chose *Moss & Silver [Mah in srebro]* as the book to work on.[16] For both Osojnik and Jamnik this was purely a matter of personal choice, as there is no qualitative difference among the poems in *Moss & Silver* and his other published collection *Maps [Zemljevidi]*, 1978.) As Osojnik related, "there is only one period in Jure's work: he didn't live long enough for more than that."

Our work began then and there in Ljubljana in June 2010. We completed a draft in 2013, and revisions have continued until the present—literary translations being eternal works in progress. Generally, the process involved me drafting a translation and running it by Jamnik for comment; fortunately, I was able to visit Slovenia once a year throughout this period, so that there was always the opportunity for face-to-face consultations. In particular, together we were able to work on the overall sound texture of the translations, reading original and translation aloud to one another; we considered this particularly crucial, given the fact that Detela was a dynamic reader of his own poetry and viewed this as a vital aspect of his art.

---

15 Detela passed away in 1992 due to complications from the hunger strike against the Milošević regime in Belgrade that Iztok Osojnik mentions in the introduction. Though specifics of the event remain controversial to this day (exactly what went wrong, what were Detela's own intentions, etc.), Osojnik insists that the death was a tragic accident.

16 Incidentally, Polica Dubova published a Polish translation (by Karolina Bucka Kustec) of *Mah in srebro* in 2014, which, until now, has been the only substantive translation of Detela's verse into another language.

Mah in srebro was Detela's second collection, published in 1983 by the liberal Maribor house Obzorja.[17] According to Komelj, at least 39 of the 44 poems printed in the volume had been completed by February 1981, the rest being written over the course of the next 22 months.[18] The poet's broad range of interests and ethical concerns are on display in *Moss & Silver*. There are poems to a number of animals, including several to insects (#7, #8, and #13, for example). Perhaps the best-known poem in the collection, "Poem to the Harts" (poem #17), wrestles with the ethics of hunting, a consciously provocative theme in a society that has a veritable cult of the hunter. The poems also name several different tree species and varieties of wild habitats (forests, groves, ravines, etc.). Detela's interest in Asian, particularly Japanese, culture is reflected in his use of the haiku form,[19] and in elliptical Zen-like images adapted therefrom, like the three-word poem:

Dark sails. Marten!

Meanwhile, he engages with English and German Romantics (the epigraph from William Wordsworth and poem #9) and the ancient Greeks (#16, #30, #41), and addresses Slovene poets in his circle (#25, #36), as well as other poets like Emily Dickinson and the Japanese haiku master Issa who appear in the final two lines of poem #14.

Although he openly and insistently rejected such traditional poetic tropes as metaphor and symbolism, Detela still crafted his poems meticulously[20] and employed sophisticated poetics that have been

---

17 Vladimir Kopicil writes that Obzorja's "unusually open publishing policy" had enabled many of the innovative young Slovene poets to appear in print; see "Writings of Death and Entertainment," 109.

18 Komelj, "Uvodna pojasnila," 10.

19 According to Osojnik, "Everybody then wanted to write haikus," and he attributes this trend to the influence of Iztok Geister (b. 1945), writer and ornithologist, co-founder of the conceptualist art group OHO (founded in 1966).

20 Komelj, "Uvodna pojasnila," 8.

called "original and astonishing."[21] A reader of Slovene might note that the sound texture of most of these poems is striking in some way, saturated with both alliteration and assonance. (Take for example, the six-line poem #7, with its preponderance of *rk/ kr*, *r*, *l*, *o*, and *a*.) Secondly, Detela has a strong sense of rhythm and employs a wide array of prosodic patterns, including traditional meters and syllabic and accentual verse. This rhythmic variety is enhanced by the multitude of stanzaic structures he uses, from traditional four- or eight-line stanzas, to poems of one or two lines, to examples of rhythmic prose. (For me personally, the epitome of this is #2, which is nothing less than a haiku written in amphibrachic meter!) Detela generally employs free verse, although two poems do rhyme (#13, #14), and there are many examples of partial rhymes within and between lines. Finally, it must be noted that several words are repeated throughout the collection, creating leitmotifs and echoes between poems.[22]

Detela thus presents an interesting challenge to the translator. The poet's insistence on strict literalness and eschewing figurative language makes the job that much easier, of course— when Detela, for instance, uses the word *žuželka*, you know he really *means* "insect" and nothing else; there is no deep symbolic baggage to unpack, no hidden subtext to uncover, before rendering the word into English. On the other hand, we had to replicate the rich poetics to some extent, the more so because they create such striking effect when the poems are read aloud. In the end, this is precisely what our goal became: to try to create

---

21 "Poetics. Jure Detela," *Literatur im Kontext*, accessed October 23, 2011, https:// lic.ned.univie.ac.at/en/node/24601. Ironically, the "defenders of Slovene beauty" welcomed Detela's dedication to poetic craft as a salvo against the new avant-garde aesthetic, much to his annoyance. See Komelj, "Za orfično levico," 454, footnote 8, and 455–56, footnote 9 for relevant excerpts from Detela's unfinished essay "The Legend of Slovene Beauty" ["Legenda o slovenski lepoti"]. Apparently, the establishment's praise was precisely for *Moss & Silver*, although in these quotes Detela does not mention any specific reviews.

22 See the "Notes to the Poems" for some specific comments on these points.

an aural effect in the translation roughly similar to the original while maintaining maximum clarity of the poet's message. And given Detela's passionately held tenets, the second half of the equation obviously had to take precedence over the first: poetics would have to be sacrificed when the necessary semantic choices demanded it.

Hearing the poems read aloud convinced me that it would be best to start with the rhythms, and so a rough-and-ready methodology gradually took shape: for each poem, I plotted the pattern of stresses on the number of syllables in each line and then attempted to adapt a rough, literal translation to this metric skeleton: i.e., can we at least express Detela's ideas in English in the same cadences? The short answer was, "Yes, and surprisingly well, too," although not without serious complications: stilted diction that the Slovene poet would have derided, anachronistic turns of phrase that go against his modernism, at times a flatness too flat even for this "strictly literal" poet. So the most difficult work went into hammering these rough "rhythmically correct" drafts into poems that we hope come closer to capturing the essence of Detela's art beyond the literal meaning of the words. Final refinements involved turning them more into modern English poems by loosening the rhythm and leaving behind some grammatical constuctions that were more Slavic than English.

Detela's technical choices are, in a few poems, so strongly marked, we had to assume they were fully intentional, even if his original motives were unclear. For example, poem #2 is structurally a 17-syllable haiku written in amphibrachs—i.e., a strict meter in three-syllable feet with the stress on the second syllable of each foot. Poem #13 is one of only two poems in *Moss & Silver* to rhyme, with the scheme of the first four lines (AbbA), unexpectedly differing from that of the second four (cDcD). The other rhyming poem is #14, in which Detela directly invokes Emily Dickinson and haiku master Kobayashi Issa, gesturing toward earlier poetic forms.

In the end, it was not hard to express the ideas in #2 in 17 syllables simply by staying close to the meaning of the Slovene, but the rhythm in English fell naturally into a mix of amphibrachs and anapests (three-syllable feet, stress on the third syllable)—in any case, there is a strong rhythm based on traditional three-foot meters. The trick for #13 was not so much creating rhyme as keeping the diction natural and the lexical material as neutral as in the original: as it turned out, the AbbA scheme of lines 1–4 fell together naturally. However, it proved impossible to recreate the cDcD of the second stanza—the only lexical choices available in English would not allow that last line to rhyme with any other. In the end, we distinguished the second half by using a scheme of CDDE, creating an aural surprise at the end reminiscent of other poems in the collection.[23] In looking for a solution to #14, I went as far as doubling the length of the poem with a second stanza in order to recreate the insistent meter and rhyme. This approach permitted some experimentation that led finally back to a four-line poem that reflects the speed, brevity, and enigmatic quality of the original. The diction is perhaps more stilted, but the imagery clashes with the traditional diction in such a way that Detela might have liked.

* * *

It is serendipitous that this translation of *Moss & Silver* is coming out precisely now, for it seems as though Jure Detela's name is suddenly everywhere in Ljubljana. The highly respected International Centre of Graphic Arts chose a poem from his first collection as the theme of its 32nd Biennial (June 16–October 29, 2017). Not only did the artists on exhibit have to wrestle directly with his ideas, but lines of his verse could be seen all

---

23   Often Detela makes the penultimate line of a poem different in length from the others, or else will include striking sound imagery.

over the city—on posters, billboards, even tote bags—and ancillary events throughout the summer and early fall focused on the poet. Meanwhile, September saw the premiere of the film *Sočasje* (*Synchrony*) by Miha Vipotnik, containing valuable footage from a 1987 interview in which Detela discusses his poetic credo and recites several poems from memory, including some from this volume; it is due to be released internationally in 2018. None of this could have been expected in 2010. It is exhilarating to think that this artist and thinker might finally be gaining the recognition he has always deserved, and that we have played our part in this process, if only by chance. Meanwhile, we have already begun work on a translation of that first collection, *Maps* [*Zemljevidi*]. We hope that, by the time it comes out, the name Jure Detela will have been etched in Slovenia's literary pantheon as more than just a curious echo from a bygone era.

* * *

The work that went into this volume was in large part made possible by the generous travel grants awarded by the Faculty Research Committee at Bowdoin College between 2010 and 2013: here I would like to thank all my Bowdoin colleagues, past and present, who offered me encouragement and advice and in the end recognized the importance of the Detela translation project. I am especially grateful, as well, to my friends Tatjana Jamnik and Iztok Osojnik, who entrusted me with a mission of such personal importance to them and were always there for guidance; whatever success has been attained here is as much theirs as mine, and it is hard to quantify how much I have learned from them. I would also like to thank other Slovene friends and colleagues who shared their insights on Jure Detela's poetry and person, as well as offered helpful suggestions and unwavering support: Darja Pavlič, Jelka Kernev Štrajn, Metka Zupančič, and everyone else involved with the

International Conference on Ecology Through Poetry (Škocjan na Krasu-Ljubljana, March 16–20 2012).

The two-volume collection of Detela's unpublished essays, *Orfični Dokumenti* (Koper: Hyperion, 2011), became for me a resource the value of which is impossible to overstate; I am grateful to its editor, Miklavž Komelj, for his own expressions of interest and support.

I would also like to thank the editors of the poetry journals *Idiot, Paperbag,* and *Poem,* where some of these translations have appeared.

Finally, many thanks to Matvei Yankelevich and Emily Wallis Hughes of Ugly Duckling Presse for their patience, their insight, and their encouragement. It was a pleasure working with them and everyone else on the staff who helped bring this project to fruition.

— Raymond Miller, October 2017

By far the best print reference for Jure Detela and his collection *Moss & Silver [Mah in srebro]* is the two-volume collection of previously unpublished texts, fragments, and letters from his literary estate: *Orfični dokumenti: Teksti in fragmenti iz zapuščine [Orphic Documents: Texts & Fragments from the Literary Estate]*, selected and edited by Miklavž Komelj, whose notes and commentary are indispensible. Most of our notes about individual poems (dates, historical background, Detela's own commentary) come from this collection. Useful sources in English include the essays in *Ecology through Poetry. The Right to Live* (Calcutta: Sampark, 2013; ed. Kernev Strajn, Osojnik, Pavlič), which also contains many references to the poems in *Moss & Silver*.

* * *

Author's Request

In the original 1983 edition, Detela included an author's request on the first page after the copyright information: "I want the poems in this book never to be printed in a publication bound in leather or using glue made from the carcasses of murdered animals." *["Želim, da pesmi iz te knjige ne bojo nikoli tiskane v publikaciji, vezani v usnje ali vezani z lepilom, narejenim iz trupel ubitih živali."]* We have heeded his request in the production of this edition.

Dedication & Epigraph

In the 1983 edition, on the same page as the epigraph, Detela placed a dedication which we have omitted in this edition. The dedication read: "With wishes for a safe delivery, this book is dedicated to all pregnant teenage girls and women." *["Z željo po srečnih porodih je knjiga posvečena vsem nosečim deklicam in ženam."]* Osojnik has suggested that it was for several women in Detela's circle who had just become pregnant at the time the book was going to print. Osojnik states, "We were young at the time, so this was something new, genuine, and important that we all wanted to celebrate." Detela may also have been responding to incidents of social conservatives harassing pregnant teenagers in 1980s Yugoslavia.

The epigraph is from William Wordsworth's "Prelude." Komelj writes that Detela "fell in love with Wordsworth already in high school, when he translated three of his poems."

2. "On the left there is sleep ..."

This poem is a haiku: 17 syllables and a juxtaposition of two ideas separated by a "cutting word" (Japanese: *kireji*), in this case, the natural opposition between left and right. Detela wrote a book of haikus and often referred to Japanese haiku masters in his criticism. (The haiku book was published posthumously, in 2004, by Društvo apokalipsa as *Haiku/haiku* alongside an edition with English translations titled *Haiku = Haiku*.)

4. An Attempt to Decipher the Phenomenon We Call Sorcery

Detela used the phrase "complexes of aggression" [*kompleksi agresije* or *nasilja*] generally to denote not only economic violence, but also "the way in which our senses and sensuality are manipulated by the capitalist perversion of desire." Here, "black magic" [*čarovnija*] refers to the use of traditional poetic language which is equated in Detela's thought with ritual dismemberment and ritual murder; hence, "sorcerers" [*čarovniki*] refer to the poets who use it, especially to further their own careers. The line "what do sorcerers seize / and take to the monsters" comes from a poem by Tomaž Šalamun; Komelj states further that in 1979 Detela "intended to use this line as the title of the book of poems that he later named *Moss & Silver*."

5. "My friend …"

It is not known to which friend Detela addressed this poem.

7. "The sun drives …"

Evidently from 1977.

8. "Bolt of white light …"

A poem about the violent death of an insect from the heat of a lamp.

9. Hölderin's Eagles

Friedrich Hölderin (1770–1843), German Romantic poet and philosopher. The eagles in question appear toward the beginning of Holderlin's 1802 poem "Patmos," in lines that Detela is clearly echoing here:

> Eagles live in the darkness,
> And the sons of the Alps
> Cross over the abyss without fear
> On lightly-built bridges.

Detela dedicated the original version of an earlier poem to Hölderin precisely for "Patmos": "Pentecost," eventually published in the 1978 collection *Maps [Zemljevidi]* as "Apostle's song at the coming of the Holy Ghost."

11. Winter Night in a Lower Carniolan Forest

Lower Carniola (Slo Dolenjsko) is the Slovenian province extending from just south of the capital Ljubljana to the Croatian border; according to Osojnik, this poem is about the poet France Balantič (1921–1943), who, with 31 other so-called right-wing nationalist Home Guardists, was burned to death during the shelling of the village of Grahovo in Lower Carniola by the communist Partisans.

12. To a Certain Hermeticist, for the Experiment with Rabbits

The experiment in question was allegedly performed by the Austrian philosopher and social reformer Rudolf Steiner in 1924 "to remove a plague of rabbits" from a Silesian estate. In notes to the poem, Detela writes that it "visualizes the principle of Satan"; in his commentary to this fragment, however, Komelj notes that Detela was obviously misinformed about Steiner and what he actually did, adding that "he was being unfair to Steiner, at least in part."

In the fourth stanza of the second part of this poem, Detela uses the word "feedback" in its English spelling and in its literal meaning; in our translation, we use the Slovene transliteration of this word ("fidbek") to create the same jarring effect for the reader.

13. Butterfly

One of only two poems to rhyme in *Moss & Silver*, with a rather unusual rhyme scheme that contrasts the first half with the second: AbbA versus cDcD.

14. "The eye that sees itself in sun ..."

"Emily" is of course Emily Dickinson (1830–1886). Detela often contemplated Dickinson's poetry, and even translated some of her poems into Slovene.

Kobayashi Issa (1763–1828) was a Japanese haiku master. Issa was one of many historical figures that were to appear in a "ritual drama" Detela was contemplating in 1979–80. Osojnik notes that Detela saw similarities between Dickinson's nature imagery and that found in traditional haiku. This is the second rhymed poem in the collection as well as the only one in iambic pentameter.

16. Antigone's Poem

In the most famous story in which she appears, Antigone disobeys the king's decree and performs a funeral rite over the corpse of her brother who was killed opposing the established power in Thebes; she dies, but Creon, the king, also loses his wife and son, who had supported Antigone in the name of the gods, to suicide. Komelj dates the writing of this poem to 1977.

17. Poem for the Harts

Komelj dates it to 1977. It is often cited as the poem that best captures the essence of Detela's philosophy. This poem has been translated under the title "A Poem for Deer," but it was inspired, in part, by Detela's reading of Wordsworth's "Hart Leap Well," a work he once called "one of the pinnacles of poetic concentration"; for this reason, Osojnik has argued that the Slovene word *jelen* should be rendered in English as "hart" (instead of "deer" or "stag"), which is what we have done here. Detela discussed the poem in an untitled article published originally in the journal *Mlade poti* in 1985: "In my ['Poem for the Harts'] I wished to articulate the feeling of helplessness in solving this [ecological] political problem"; and, from an earlier draft of the same piece: "in ['Poem for the Harts'] I did not wish to express my private feelings, but craft a message about violence, because of which deer really suffer."

20. Strangers

According to Osojnik, the "strangers" in this poem are "enlightened individuals," including Buddha.

21. Embryo's Poem
22. Poem of a Child Taking Its First Step

Komelj indicates that these two poems were originally intended to be part of a triptych with a poem called "Pesem umrlega" ["Poem of a Dead Person"].

24. "On fragments ..."

Dated by Komelj to 1978 or 1979.

25. In Memory of a Poem by Primož Piskernik

According to Komelj, Detela and Piskernik (b. 1956) had a particularly intense friendship in the late 1970s–early 1980s, and the poem Detela is referring to here is Piskernik's "The strangers have indeed come to you" [*"So ti tujci res prišli"*].

28. "Let the hungry voices ..."

Probably from 1979; the original title was "Poem for Orpheus." Komelj discusses the importance of the Orphic myths—and Orphism, the ancient mystery religion connected with Orpheus—extensively in *Orfični dokumenti*. He connects the poet's neo-Orphism with his stance on metaphor and poetic language, and especially with his anti-humanist philosophy: "Orphic is an attentive attempt to understand the traces left by beings from alien worlds [i.e. animals]—signs which by their presence demystify the human system of signs, that through which the human world is constituted." At the time he was writing the poems that went into *Moss & Silver*, Detela saw himself as a "poet who wishes to write Orphic hymns."

29. Mama, How Do Dead People Feel?

The original poem is written in Croatian, the only poem not in Slovene in *Moss & Silver*; it has the same title as a contemporary poem by Osojnik, and allegedly represents Detela's (incorrect) understanding of what Osojnik was trying to express.

30. Ion

In the play of the same name by Euripides, Ion is the son of Apollo and a mortal noblewoman, Creusa, whom he had raped in a cave. After being abandoned by his mother, Ion is saved by Apollo and raised at Delphi, where he serves as an attendant at the famous oracle. Creusa comes to the oracle to pray that she and her foreign-born husband Xuthus might have children. In the end, after much drama and tribulation, Ion and his mother discover his true origins, to much celebration; he eventually becomes the progenitor of the Ionians, one of Greece's primary tribes. Detela has a second poem about Ion in this collection (#41) and also wrote a poem called "Ion" for his first collection.

31. Epitaph

Komelj sees this as one of Detela's "Orphic hymns." "A cry is also / the logic of the world" apparently refers to the same cry that Detela connected with Orpheus as early as 1973: "Perhaps Orpheus's singing arises from the cry when you awake from a dream...": his singing modulates the cry, and this becomes the foundation of the world. Komelj connects this difficult image with important tenets in Detela's thought: the importance of understanding different creatures, not trying to identify with them, and acknowledging the infinite distance between us and them. Another phrase associated with these ideas is "the long-range stimulus of the world," which has been defined as "awareness of the radical otherness of other sentient beings."

32. "Just as in the memory of the uniform universe ..."

Georg Trakl (1887–1914) was an important Austrian Expressionist poet, highly regarded by Detela. The image of a bird ("the never-to-be-repeated gull") and the evocation of darkness ("dusk and dawn") are at least suggestive of common motives in Trakl's poetry.

34. "As if by a knifepoint through the throat ..."

Lake Bohinj is a glacial lake in northwestern Slovenia, the largest lake in the country and part of Triglav National Park.

36. In Memory of Vladimir Memon

Detela wrote this poem shortly after the untimely death of his friend Vladimir Memon (1953–1980).

37. "With tiny talons ..."

This poem was evidently written at the same time as #36.

38. "Father ..."

Detela's father was known to be abusive.

40. A Poem for Jure Detela

Written in 1980 or 1981, at the same time as #41, this poem clearly addresses Detela's "radical criticism of ideological mechanisms in the language of poetry," i.e. his connection of symbol and metaphor with ritual dismemberment and murder. See, for example, the sixth stanza, where he declares "in thousands of poems you search for a universal / reexamination of crimes / and deaths ...." It is characteristic, however, that in the very first word he calls himself "Murderer!" Detela never exonerated himself for such "crimes and deaths."

41. Ion's Poem

See the notes to poem #30 and #40 above.

43. "Opening into a long ..."

Written in 1981.

44. "For all the past and ..."

"Alien consiousnesses" *[tuje zavesti]* is a variation of the standard Detela formula "beings from alien worlds," by which he means non-human animals.

The Eastern European Poets Series from Ugly Duckling Presse